Kerrie Meyler
Byron Holt
Marcus Oh
Jason Sandys
Greg Ramsey

with Niall Brady
Samuel Erskine
Torsten Meringer
Stefan Schörling
Kenneth van Surksum
Steve Thompson

System Center 2012 Configuration Manager

UNLEASHED

SAMS | 800 East 96th Street, Indianapolis, Indiana 46240 USA

System Center 2012 Configuration Manager Unleashed

Copyright © 2013 by Pearson Education, Inc.

ISBN-13: 978-0-672-33437-5

ISBN-10: 0-672-33437-2

Library of Congress Cataloging-in-Publication Data:

System center 2012 configuration manager / Kerrie Meyler ... [et al.].
    p. cm.
  Includes index.
  ISBN 978-0-672-33437-5
  1. Microsoft System center configuration manager–Computer programs. 2. Computer networks–Management–Computer programs. 3. Software configuration management--Computer programs. I. Meyler, Kerrie.
  TK5105.5.M487 2013
  004.6'5–dc23

                              2012020282

Printed in the United States of America

First Printing: July 2012

Trademarks

Warning and Disclaimer

Bulk Sales

Pearson offers excellent discounts on this book when ordered in quantity for bulk purchases or special sales. For more information, please contact:

U.S. Corporate and Government Sales
1-800-382-3419
corpsales@pearsontechgroup.com

For sales outside of the U.S., please contact:

International Sales
+1-317-581-3793
international@pearsoned.com

Editor-in-Chief
Greg Wiegand

Executive Editor
Neil Rowe

Development Editor
Mark Renfrow

Managing Editor
Kristy Hart

Project Editor
Lori Lyons

Copy Editor
Apostrophe Editing Services

Indexer
Erika Millen

Proofreader
Sarah Kearns

Technical Editor
Steve Rachui

Editorial Assistant
Cindy Teeters

Interior Designer
Gary Adair

Cover Designer
Anne Jones

Compositor
Nonie Ratcliff

Contents at a Glance

Table of Contents

Part III   Configuration Manager Operations

About the Authors

Kerrie Meyler, System Center MVP, is the lead author of numerous System Center books in the Unleashed series, including *System Center Operations Manager 2007 Unleashed* (2008), *System Center Configuration Manager 2007 Unleashed* (2009), *System Center Operations Manager 2007 R2 Unleashed* (2010), *System Center Opalis Integration Server 6.3 Unleashed* (2011), and *System Center Service Manager 2010 Unleashed* (2011). She is an independent consultant and trainer with more than 15 years of Information Technology experience. Kerrie was responsible for evangelizing SMS while a Sr. Technology Specialist at Microsoft, and has presented on System Center technologies at TechEd and MMS.

Byron Holt, CISSP and an IT professional for more than 15 years, has been a lead SMS and Configuration Manager engineer for several Global 5000 corporations and was part of the Active Directory and Enterprise Manageability support teams while working at Microsoft. Byron's experience includes software development, security architecture, and systems management. He currently works for McAfee managing internal deployment and validation. Byron coauthored *System Center Configuration Manager 2007 Unleashed* (Sams, 2009).

Marcus Oh, System Center MVP, is IT Manager of Directory and Systems Management for a large telecommunications provider, running directory services and management infrastructure for ~30,000 systems. He has been a MVP since 2004 in System Center, specializing in Configuration Manager and Operations Manager. Marcus has written numerous articles for technology websites as well as his own blog. He coauthored *Professional SMS 2003, MOM 2005*, and *WSUS* (Wrox, 2006), and was a contributing author to *System Center Opalis Integration Server 6.3 Unleashed* (Sams, 2011). Marcus is also a coauthor to the upcoming *System Center 2012 Orchestrator Unleashed* (Sams).

Jason Sandys, ConfigMgr MVP, is currently the Director for Solutions Engineering for Adaptiva (Adaptive Protocols, Inc.) where he is responsible for delivery of ConfigMgr-centric solutions. Jason was formerly a managing consultant for Catapult Systems Inc. and has more than 15 years of experience in a wide range of technologies, environments, and industries with extensive experience implementing and supporting SMS and Configuration Manager beginning with SMS 2.0. Jason is also active in the online support community, was a contributing author to *System Center Configuration Manager 2007 Unleashed* (Sams, 2009), and is a frequent presenter at Microsoft TechEd and MMS.

Greg Ramsey, ConfigMgr MVP, has worked with SMS and desktop deployment since 1998. He currently works for Dell, Inc., as a ConfigMgr administrator, and previously was a sergeant in the United States Marine Corps. Greg is a columnist for myITforum.com, cofounder of the Ohio SMS User Group and Central Texas Systems Management User Group, and creator of SMS View. Greg previously coauthored *SMS 2003 Recipes: A Problem-Solution Approach* (Apress, 2006) and *System Center Configuration Manager 2007 Unleashed* (Sams, 2009).

About the Contributors

Niall Brady, ConfigMgr MVP, began working with SMS in 2003 and Forefront Endpoint Protection since it was first integrated with Configuration Manager 2007. Niall is a senior consultant at Enfo Zipper in Sweden and blogs extensively about using and configuring System Center 2012 Configuration Manager according to best practices on windows-noob.com.

Samuel Erskine, MCT, MCTS, is a senior IT consultant specializing in Configuration Manager and Service Manager. He holds an ITIL V3 foundation certification. Samuel has worked with the product since SMS 2003 and was an early tester for System Center 2012 Service Manager. With more than 15 years of IT experience, he focuses on providing training and consultancy services in the United Kingdom and other international locations.

Torsten Meringer, ConfigMgr MVP, is a self-employed senior consultant in Germany, starting his own business in 1999. His primary focus is to design, migrate, deploy, train, and troubleshoot Microsoft's deployment and management solutions, such as System Center Configuration Manager and Microsoft Deployment Toolkit, in small to large-scale companies of more than 200,000 clients. Torsten manages the German ConfigMgr blog http://www.mssccmfaq.de and holds various MCSA, MCSE, MCTS, and MCITP:EA certifications.

Stefan Schörling, ConfigMgr MVP, is a Swedish-based infrastructure consultant focusing on System Center and infrastructure management. With 13 years of experience, Stefan is an expert in system management, security, and IT operations. His primary focus lies in Microsoft technologies and technical security. Stefan has worked and presented at numerous conferences and events worldwide such as TechEd and MMS. Stefan is also the founder of System Center User Group Sweden.

Kenneth van Surksum, MCT and Setup & Deployment MVP, works as a trainer and System Center consultant at INOVATIV, a company based in the Netherlands, where he implements and advises customers about System Center and other Microsoft solutions. With more than 10 years of experience with IT, Kenneth has worked with SMS 1.2 and successive versions of the product since 1998, specializing in OS deployment. Kenneth coauthored *Mastering Windows 7 Deployment* (Sybex, 2011) and blogs at http://www.techlog.org.

Steve Thompson, ConfigMgr MVP, works for BT Global Services as a senior consultant specializing in all things System Center-related. He was first awarded MVP in Microsoft Access in 1995, was a SQL Server MVP for several years, and then joined the System Center team as a ConfigMgr MVP. Steve has presented at MMS on Configuration Manager, SQL Server, and reporting. You can follow his blog at http://myitforum.com/cs2/blogs/sthompson.

Dedication

To Wally and the ConfigMgr community.

Acknowledgments

Writing a book is an all-encompassing and time-consuming project, and this book certainly meets that description. Configuration Manager is a massive topic, and this book benefitted from the input of many individuals. The authors and contributors would like to offer their sincere appreciation to all those who helped with *System Center 2012 Configuration Manager Unleashed*. This includes John Joyner and Bob Longo of ClearPointe Technologies along with Joe Stocker and Greg Tate of Catapult Systems for dedicating lab resources, Wally Mead, Sherry Kissinger, Oskar Landman, Frank Rojas, Keith Thornley, Charles Applegrath of SoftMart, Cameron Fuller, Niall Brady, John Marcum, Roger Zander, and Jean-Sébastien Duchêne.

We would also like to thank our spouses and significant others for their patience and understanding during the many hours spent on this book.

Thanks also go to the staff at Pearson, in particular to Neil Rowe, who has worked with us since *Microsoft Operations Manager 2005 Unleashed* (Sams, 2006).

We Want to Hear from You!

As the reader of this book, *you* are our most important critic and commentator. We value your opinion and want to know what we're doing right, what we could do better, what areas you'd like to see us publish in, and any other words of wisdom you're willing to pass our way.

You can email or write me directly to let me know what you did or didn't like about this book—as well as what we can do to make our books stronger.

Please note that I cannot help you with technical problems related to the topic of this book, and that due to the high volume of mail I receive, I might not be able to reply to every message.

When you write, please be sure to include this book's title and author as well as your name and phone or email address. I will carefully review your comments and share them with the authors and editors who worked on the book.

Email: consumer@samspublishing.com

Mail: Sams Publishing
          ATTN: Reader Feedback
          800 East 96th Street
          Indianapolis, IN 46240 USA

Reader Services

Visit our website and register this book at informit.com/register for convenient access to any updates, downloads, or errata that might be available for this book.

Foreword

You are about to embark on a fantastic journey! System Center 2012 Configuration Manager is an exciting, new version of the Configuration Manager product line. While each release of Configuration Manager, or the predecessor product—Systems Management Server—has been a great improvement over the previous version, we believe that without a doubt this is the most feature-rich and revolutionary version of Configuration Manager that the product group has ever released. From the improved software distribution, focusing on user-centric delivery of applications, to the reduced infrastructure requirements, SQL Server-based replication and improved security, to the enhancements designed to make your lives easier as Configuration Manager administrators, this product is one that we're extremely confident you'll enjoy working with and find beneficial in your environments.

After years in development, this product has been thoroughly tested, not only within the Configuration Manager product group, within Microsoft IT, by numerous Technology Adoption Program (TAP) customers testing beta and release candidate releases in production, but also by thousands of open beta customers testing in lab environments. Through all this testing, we are confident that you can have a great experience with Configuration Manager 2012 in your production environments—and see great return on your investment.

To those of you who participated in the open beta, CEP, CEP for Production, OneTAP, and TAP programs: Thank you for your assistance in testing the pre-release versions of Configuration Manager 2012. Your feedback—whether suggestions for enhancements or requests for new features, as well as feedback that reported features not working as they should—certainly helped shape the product that you see today. I want to especially thank our TAP customers because you lived with us through production deployments of the beta 1 and beta 2 releases, which, for some of you, shall we say were somewhat challenging. Thanks for sticking with us and for helping us create a fantastic product, even though some of your experiences were not as smooth as you would have expected. It is through your efforts and dedication that the RTM version of the product is a great one that everyone can take pride in.

To those of you who are new to the Configuration Manager world: Welcome—we are glad to have you join us. To those of you who are migrating from previous releases: Thank you for your desire to venture into this brave new world from a previous version of the product that I am sure is providing great benefit to you. We appreciate your loyalty and trust in us as a product group and believe you can have a great experience with this new, groundbreaking release.

With my personal knowledge of a number of the authors and contributors for this book—and of their professionalism and knowledge—I am confident that this writing will be a great benefit to you for learning and experiencing System Center 2012 Configuration Manager. The best of luck to you all, and again, thanks for your loyalty and trust in us!

Wally Mead, Senior Program Manager
Configuration Manager Product Group
Microsoft Corporation

Introduction

Microsoft's most recent version of its systems management product can help you empower individuals to use the devices and applications they need while maintaining the corporate compliance and control your organization requires. By adding a layer of abstraction that delivers to the user rather than the device, System Center 2012 Configuration Manager (ConfigMgr) helps you enable users to be productive with a unified infrastructure that delivers and manages user experiences across corporate and consumer devices.

Seeing consumerization as a reality, ConfigMgr's infrastructure provides the means to deliver and manage user experiences based on identity, connectivity, and type of device—without giving up the control you need to protect corporate assets. Here are the benefits System Center 2012 Configuration Manager delivers:

▶ **Empowers users to be productive from anywhere on any device**

ConfigMgr manages a wide range of mobile devices using a single administration console for policies, asset management, and compliance reporting.

The product provides optimized and personalized application delivery, based on user identity, device type, and network capabilities.

ConfigMgr allows users to securely self-provision applications on demand using an easy-to-use web catalog.

▶ **Unifies the management infrastructure, integrating client management and protection against mobile, physical, and virtual environments**

ConfigMgr provides you with a single tool to manage all your client environments.

This version of ConfigMgr consolidates inventory management, software delivery, antimalware, vulnerability prevention and remediation, and compliance reporting, using a single infrastructure.

Integration with System Center 2012 Service Manager helps improve user satisfaction with integrated help desk capabilities.

▶ **Simplifies administration**

The new release of ConfigMgr uses the System Center-standard "Outlook" style user interface.

System Center 2012 Configuration Manager organizes administrative tasks by role, allows administrators to define an application once for delivery across multiple devices, and provides continuous settings enforcement to automatically identify and remediate noncompliant machines.

This release includes scalability enhancements, reduces data latency, and consolidates server roles to improve infrastructure efficiency.

In addition, System Center 2012 continues to become more integrated, including a common look and feel between the consoles of the various components, and with data integration between those components both operationally and in a consolidated data warehouse. This integration will continue to grow as System Center evolves and becomes more intertwined with cloud computing.

Part I: Configuration Management Overview and Concepts

System Center 2012 Configuration Manager Unleashed begins with an introduction to configuration management including initiatives and methodology. This includes Dynamic System Initiative (DSI), IT Infrastructure Library (ITIL), and Microsoft Operations Framework (MOF). Although some consider this to be more of an alphabet soup of frameworks than constructive information, these strategies and approaches give a structure to managing one's environment—from system configuration and inventory management to proactive management and infrastructure optimization. More important, implementing ConfigMgr is a project, and as such, it should include a structured approach with its own deployment. Chapter 1, "Configuration Management Basics," starts with the big picture and brings it down to the pain points that system administrators deal with on a daily basis, showing how System Center plans to address these challenges.

Chapter 2, "Configuration Manager Overview," shows how ConfigMgr has evolved from its first days in 1994 as Systems Management Server (SMS) 1.0, and introduces key concepts and feature dependencies. In Chapter 3, "Looking Inside Configuration Manager," the book begins to peel back the layers of the onion to discuss the design concepts behind System Center 2012 Configuration Manager, the major ConfigMgr components, its relationship with Windows Management Instrumentation (WMI), the ConfigMgr database, and more.

Part II: Planning, Design, and Installation

Before installing any software, you need to spend time planning and designing its architecture. ConfigMgr is no exception. Chapter 4, "Architecture Design Planning," begins this discussion with developing a solutions architecture and assessing your environment, and covers licensing, hierarchy and site planning, planning considerations for specific ConfigMgr services, and implementation considerations. Chapter 5, "Network Design," steps through the network concepts to consider when planning a ConfigMgr architecture and deployment.

When it is time to implement your design, Chapter 6, "Installing System Center 2012 Configuration Manager," steps through the installation process; and Chapter 7, "Migrating to System Center 2012 Configuration Manager," discusses how to move from a Configuration Manager 2007 to 2012 environment.

Part III: Configuration Manager Operations

The third part of this book focuses on ConfigMgr operations in your environment, which is where you will spend the bulk of your time. This includes navigating through the newly designed console discussed in Chapter 8, "The Configuration Manager Console." Using ConfigMgr requires an installed client on managed systems, as covered in depth in Chapter 9, "Configuration Manager Client Management."

Part IV: Software and Configuration Management

Compliance settings, discussed in Chapter 10, "Managing Compliance," provides a set of tools and resources to help assess, track, and remediate the configuration compliance of your client systems.

Configuration Manager's core capabilities have historically focused around software distribution, and System Center 2012 Configuration Manager adds new capabilities in this area. Software distribution is discussed in Chapter 11, "Packages and Programs," Chapter 12, "Creating and Managing Applications," and Chapter 13, "Distributing and Deploying Applications." Software and configuration management also includes activities such as patch management (Chapter 14, "Software Update Management"), managing mobile devices (Chapter 15, "Mobile Device Management"), endpoint management, previously known as Forefront Endpoint Protection (Chapter 16, "Endpoint Protection"), running queries (Chapter 17, "Configuration Manager Queries"), reporting (Chapter 18, "Reporting"), and operating system deployments (Chapter 19, "Operating System Deployment"). These chapters discuss those key functionalities and their use in System Center 2012 Configuration Manager.

Part V: Administering System Center 2012 Configuration Manager

This part of the book discusses administration of your ConfigMgr environment. This includes security requirements (Chapter 20, "Security and Delegation in Configuration Manager"), as well as backups and maintenance (Chapter 21, "Backup, Recovery, and Maintenance").

Part VI: Appendixes

By this time, you should have at your disposal all the tools necessary to become a Configuration Manager expert. The last part of the book includes four appendixes:

▶ Appendix A, "Configuration Manager Log Files," incorporates useful references you can access for further information.

▶ Appendix B, "Extending Hardware Inventory," takes a deep dive into how to extend hardware inventory.

▶ Appendix C, "Reference URLs," incorporates useful references you can access for further information about Configuration Manager and System Center, which is also included as live links available for download under the Downloads tab at Pearson's InformIT website, at www.informit.com/title/9780672334375.

▶ Appendix D, "Available Online," discusses value-added content also available at the InformIT page.

Throughout, this book provides in-depth reference and technical information about System Center 2012 Configuration Manager, as well as information about other products and technologies on which its features and components depend.

Disclaimers and Fine Print

There are several disclaimers. The information provided is probably outdated the moment the book goes to print. The authors began working on this book during the early beta releases of System Center 2012 Configuration Manager in an attempt to bring you this information as soon as possible after the release of System Center 2012. This means multiple chapters were written and then rewritten as the Configuration Manager product team continued to fine-tune the product's development. Screenshots were taken during late release candidate builds, and it is certainly possible Microsoft could slightly tweak the user interface in the production code release.

In addition, the moment Microsoft considers code development on any product complete, it begins working on a service pack or future release; as the authors continue to work with the product, it is likely yet another one or two wrinkles will be discovered! The authors and contributors of *System Center 2012 Configuration Manager Unleashed* have made every attempt to present information that is accurate and current as known at the time. Updates and corrections will be provided as errata on the InformIT website.

Thank you for purchasing *System Center 2012 Configuration Manager Unleashed*. The authors hope it is worth your while (and their effort). Enjoy the ride!

PART I

Configuration Management Overview and Concepts

IN THIS PART

CHAPTER 1

Configuration Management Basics

System Center 2012 Configuration Manager (ConfigMgr) represents a continuing maturation in Microsoft's systems management platform. ConfigMgr is an enterprise management tool that provides a total solution for Windows client and server management, including the capability to catalog hardware and software, deliver new software packages and updates, and deploy Windows operating systems with ease. In an increasingly compliance-driven world, ConfigMgr delivers the functionality to detect "shift and drift" in system configuration. ConfigMgr consolidates information about Windows clients and servers, hardware, and software into a single console for centralized management and control.

Configuration Manager gives you the resources you need to get and stay in control of your Windows environment and helps with managing, configuring, tuning, and securing Windows Server and Windows-based applications. For example, this version of Configuration Manager includes the following features:

▶ New look for the console, replacing the Microsoft Management Console (MMC) with the standard System Center Outlook-style interface

▶ Targeting management to the user, not the device; delivering the right application in the right way to the right user under the right condition

▶ Redesign of the software distribution process

▶ Architectural changes to simplify the site server hierarchy

This chapter serves as an introduction to System Center 2012 Configuration Manager. To avoid constantly repeating that long name, this book utilizes the Microsoft-approved abbreviation of the product name, Configuration Manager, or simply ConfigMgr. System Center 2012 Configuration Manager, the fifth edition of Microsoft's systems management platform, includes numerous additions in functionality as well as security and scalability improvements over its predecessors.

This chapter discusses the Microsoft approach to Information Technology (IT) operations and systems management. This discussion includes an explanation and comparison of the Microsoft Operations Framework (MOF), which incorporates and expands on the concepts contained in the Information Technology Infrastructure Library (ITIL) standard. It also examines the Microsoft Infrastructure Optimization Model (IO Model) used in the assessment of the maturity of organizations' IT operations. The IO Model is a component of Microsoft's Dynamic Systems Initiative (DSI), which aims at increasing the dynamic capabilities of organizations' IT operations.

These discussions have special relevance in that the objective of Microsoft System Center is the optimization, automation, and process agility and maturity in IT operations.

Ten Reasons to Use Configuration Manager

Why should you use Configuration Manager? How does this make your daily life as a systems administrator easier? Although this book covers the features and benefits of ConfigMgr in detail, it definitely helps to have some quick ideas to illustrate why ConfigMgr is worth a look!

Here is a list of 10 scenarios that illustrate why you might want to use ConfigMgr:

1. The bulk of your department's budget goes toward paying for teams of contractors to perform OS and software upgrades, rather than paying talented people like yourself the big bucks to implement the platforms and processes to automate and centralize management of company systems.

2. You realize systems management would be much easier if you had visibility and control of all your systems from a single management console.

3. The laptops used by the sales team have not been updated in more than two years because they never come to the home office.

4. You don't have enough internal manpower to apply updates to your systems manually every month.

5. Within days of updating system configurations to meet corporate security requirements, you find several have already mysteriously "drifted" out of compliance.

6. When you try to install Windows 7 for the accounting department, you discover it cannot run on half the computers because they have only 256MB of RAM. (It would have been nice to know that when submitting your budget requests!)

7. Demonstrating that your organization is compliant with regulations such as Sarbanes-Oxley (SOX), the Health Insurance Portability and Accountability Act (HIPAA), the Federal Information Security Management Act (FISMA), or *<insert your own favorite compliance acronym here>* has become your new full-time job.

8. You spent your last vacation on a trip from desktop to desktop installing Office 2010.

9. Your production environment is so diverse and distributed that you can no longer keep track of which software versions should be installed to which system.

10. By the time you update your system standards documentation, everything has changed, and you have to start over again!

While trying to bring some humor to the discussion, these topics represent real problems for many systems administrators. If you are one of those individuals, you owe to it yourself to explore how you might leverage ConfigMgr to solve many of these common issues. These pain points are common to most users to some degree (even those using Microsoft technologies!) and System Center Configuration Manager holds solutions for all of them.

However, perhaps the most important reason for using ConfigMgr is the peace of mind it brings you as an administrator, knowing that you have complete visibility and control of your IT systems. The stability and productivity this can bring to your organization is a great benefit as well.

The Evolution of Systems Management

Systems and configuration management has evolved significantly since Microsoft first released Systems Management Server (SMS), the name given to the predecessors Configuration Manager, and that landscape is experiencing great advancements still today. The proliferation of compliance-driven controls and virtualization (server, desktop, and application) has added significant complexity and exciting new functionality to the management picture.

System Center 2012 Configuration Manager is a software solution that delivers end-to-end management functionality for systems administrators, providing configuration management, patch management, software and operating system distribution, remote control, asset management, hardware and software inventory, and a robust reporting framework to make sense of the various available data for internal systems tracking and regulatory reporting requirements.

These capabilities are significant because today's IT systems are prone to a number of problems from the perspective of systems management, including the following:

▶ Configuration "shift and drift"

▶ Security and control

▶ Timeliness of asset data

▶ Automation and enforcement

▶ Proliferation of virtualization and cloud computing

▶ Process consistency

This list should not be surprising because these types of problems manifest themselves to varying degrees in IT shops of all sizes. Forrester Research estimates that 82% of larger IT organizations pursue service management, and 67% plan to increase Windows management. The next sections look at these issues from a systems management perspective.

Hurdles in the Distributed Enterprise

You may encounter a number of challenges when implementing systems management in a distributed enterprise. These include the following:

▶ **Increasing threats:** According to the SANS Institute, the threat landscape is increasingly dynamic, making efficient and proactive update management more important than ever (see http://www.sans.org/top20/).

▶ **Regulatory compliance:** Sarbanes-Oxley, HIPAA, and many other regulations have forced organizations to adopt and implement fairly sophisticated controls to demonstrate compliance.

▶ **OS and software provisioning:** Rolling out the operating system (OS) and software on new workstations and servers, especially in branch offices, can be both time-consuming and a logistical challenge.

▶ **Methodology:** With the bar for effective IT operations higher than ever, organizations are forced to adapt a more mature implementation of IT operational processes to deliver the necessary services to the organization's business units more efficiently.

With increasing operational requirements unaccompanied by linear growth in IT staffing levels, organizations must find ways to streamline administration through tools and automation.

The IT Automation Challenge

As functionality in client and server systems has increased, so too has complexity. Both desktop and server deployment can be time-consuming when performed manually. With the number and variety of security threats increasing every year, timely application of security updates is of paramount importance. Regulatory compliance issues add a new burden, requiring IT to demonstrate that system configurations meet regulatory requirements.

These problems have a common element—all beg for some measure of automation to ensure IT can meet expectations in these areas at the expected level of accuracy and efficiency. To get IT operational requirements in hand, organizations must implement tools and processes that make OS and software deployment, update management, and configuration management more efficient and effective.

Configuration "Shift and Drift"

Even in IT organizations with well-defined and documented change management, procedures can fall short of perfection. Unplanned and unwanted changes frequently find their way into the environment, sometimes as an unintended side effect of an approved, scheduled change.

You may be familiar with an old philosophical saying: *If a tree falls in a forest and no one is around to hear it, does it make a sound?*

Here's the configuration management equivalent: *If a change is made on a system and no one knows, does identifying it make a difference?*

The answer to this question is absolutely "yes." Every change to a system has some potential to affect the functionality or security of a system, or that system's adherence to corporate or regulatory standards.

For example, adding a feature to a web application component may affect the application binaries, potentially overwriting files or settings replaced by a critical security patch. Alternatively, perhaps the engineer implementing the change sees a setting he thinks is misconfigured and decides to just "fix" it while working on the system. In an e-commerce scenario with sensitive customer data involved, this could have potentially devastating consequences.

At the end of the day, your selected systems management platform must bring a strong element of baseline configuration monitoring to ensure configuration standards are implemented and maintained with the required consistency.

Lack of Security and Control

Managing systems becomes much more challenging when moving outside the realm of the traditional LAN-connected desktop or server computer. Traveling users that rarely connect to the trusted network (other than to periodically change their password) can make this seem an impossible task.

Just keeping these systems up to date on security patches can easily become a full-time job. Maintaining patch levels and system configurations to corporate standards when your roaming users connect only via the Internet can make this activity exceedingly painful. In reality, remote sales and support staff make this an everyday problem. To add to the quandary, these users are frequently among those installing unapproved applications from unknown sources, subsequently putting the organization at greater risk when they finally do connect to the network.

Point-of-sale (POS) devices running embedded operating systems pose challenges of their own, with specialized operating systems that can be difficult to administer—and for many systems management solutions, are completely unmanageable. Frequently these systems perform critical functions within the business (such as cash registers, automated teller machines, and so on), making the need for visibility and control from configuration and security perspectives an absolute necessity.

Mobile devices have moved from a role of high-dollar phone to a mini-computer used for everything: Internet access, global positioning system (GPS) navigation, and storage for all manner of potentially sensitive business data. From the chief information officer's perspective, ensuring that these devices are securely maintained (and appropriately password protected) is somewhat like gravity. It's more than a good idea—it's the law!

But seriously, as computing continues to evolve, and more devices release users from the structures of office life, the problem gets larger.

Timeliness of Asset Data

Maintaining a current picture of what is deployed and in use in your environment is a constant challenge due to the ever-increasing pace of change. However, failing to maintain an accurate snapshot of current conditions comes at a cost. In many organizations, this is a manual process involving Excel spreadsheets and custom scripting, and asset data is often obsolete by the time a single pass at the infrastructure is complete.

Without this data, organizations can over-purchase (or worse yet, under-purchase) software licensing. Having accurate asset information can help you get a better handle on your licensing costs. Likewise, without current configuration data, areas including Incident and Problem Management may suffer, as troubleshooting incidents will be more error prone and time-consuming.

Lack of Automation and Enforcement

With the perpetually increasing and evolving technology needs of the business, the need to automate resource provisioning, standardize, and enforce standard configurations becomes increasingly important.

Resource provisioning of new workstations or servers can be a labor-intensive exercise. Installing a client OS and required applications may take a day or longer if performed manually. Ad-hoc scripting to automate these tasks can be a complex endeavor. When deployed, ensuring the client and server configuration is consistent can seem an insurmountable task. With customer privacy and regulatory compliance at stake, consequences can be severe if this challenge is not met head on.

Proliferation of Virtualization and Cloud Computing

There's an old saying: *If you fail to plan, you plan to fail*. In no area of IT operations is this truer than when considering virtualization technologies.

When dealing with systems management, you must consider many different functions, such as software and patch deployment, resource provisioning, and configuration management. Managing server and application configuration in an increasingly "virtual" world, in which boundaries between systems and applications are not always clear, will require considering new elements of management not present in a purely physical environment.

Virtualization as a concept is exciting to IT operations. Whether talking about virtualization of servers or applications, the potential for dramatic increases in process automation and efficiency and reduction in deployment costs is very real. With virtualization, you can provision new servers and applications in a matter of minutes. However, with this newfound agility comes a potential downside, which is the reality that virtualization can increase the velocity of change in your environment. The tools you use to manage and track changes to a server often fail to address new dynamics that come when virtualization is introduced into a computing environment.

Many organizations make the mistake of taking on new tools and technologies in an ad-hoc fashion, without first reviewing them in the context of the process controls used to manage the introduction of change into the environment. These big gains in efficiency can lead to a completely new problem—inconsistencies in processes not designed to address the new dynamics that come with the virtual territory.

Lack of Process Consistency

For identifying and resolving problems, many IT organizations still "fly by the seat of their pants." Using standard procedures and a methodology can help minimize risk and solve issues faster.

A *methodology* is a framework of processes and procedures used by those who work in a particular discipline. You can look at a methodology as a structured process defining the who, what, where, when, and why of one's operations, and the procedures to use when defining problems, solutions, and courses of action.

When employing a standard set of processes, you must ensure the framework you adopt adheres to accepted industry standards or best practices, and takes into account the requirements of the business—ensuring continuity between expectations and the services delivered by the IT organization. Consistently using a repeatable and measurable set of practices allows an organization to quantify more accurately its progress to facilitate adjustment of processes as necessary for improving future results. The most effective IT organizations build an element of self-examination into their IT service management (ITSM) strategy to ensure processes can be incrementally improved or modified to meet the changing needs of the business.

With IT's continually increased role in running successful business operations, having a structured and standard way to define IT operations aligned to the needs of the business is critical when meeting expectations of business stakeholders. This alignment results in improved business relationships in which business units engage IT as a partner in developing and delivering innovations to drive business results.

The Bottom Line

Systems management can be intimidating when you consider that the problems described to this point could happen even in an ostensibly "managed" environment. However, these examples just serve to illustrate that the processes used to manage change in your environment must be reviewed periodically and updated to accommodate changes in tools and technologies employed from the desktop to the datacenter.

Likewise, meeting the expectations of both the business and compliance regulation can seem an impossible task. At the end of the day, as technology evolves, so must IT's thinking, management tools, and processes. This makes it necessary to embrace continual improvement in those methodologies used to reduce risk while increasing agility in managing systems, keeping pace with the increasing velocity of change.

Systems Management Defined

Systems management is a journey, not a destination. That is to say, it is not something you achieve at a point in time. Systems management encompasses all points in the IT service triangle, as displayed in Figure 1.1, including a set of processes and the tools and people that implement them. Although the role of each varies at different points within the IT service life cycle, the end goals do not change. How effectively these components are utilized determines the ultimate degree of success, which manifests itself in the outputs of productive employees producing and delivering quality products and services.

FIGURE 1.1   The IT service triangle includes people, process, and technology.

At a process level, systems management touches nearly every area of your IT operations. It can continually manage a computing resource, such as a client workstation, from the initial provisioning of the OS and hardware to end-of-life, when user settings are migrated to a new machine. The hardware and software inventory data collected by your systems management solution can play a key role in incident and problem management, by providing information that facilitates faster troubleshooting.

As IT operations grow in size, scope, complexity, and business impact, the common denominator at all phases is efficiency and automation, based on repeatable processes that conform to industry best practices. Achieving this necessitates capturing subject matter expertise and business context into a repeatable, partially or fully automated process. At the beginning of the service life cycle is the service provisioning, which from a systems management perspective means OS and software deployment. Automation at this phase can save hours or days of manual deployment effort in each iteration.

After resources are in production, the focus expands to include managing and maintaining systems, via ongoing activities IT uses to manage the health and configuration of systems. These activities may touch areas such as configuration management, by monitoring for unwanted changes in standard system and application configuration baselines.

As the service life cycle continues, systems management can affect release management in the form of software upgrades. Activities include software-metering activities, such as reclaiming unused licenses for reuse elsewhere. If you can automate these processes to a great degree, you can achieve higher reliability and security, greater availability, better asset allocation, and a more predictable IT environment. These translate into business agility, more efficient, less expensive operations, with a greater ability to respond quickly to changing conditions.

Reducing costs and increasing productivity in IT service management are important because efficiency in operations frees up money for innovation and product improvements. Information security is also imperative because the price tag of compromised systems and data recovery from security exposures can be large, and those costs continue to rise each year.

Microsoft's Strategy for Service Management

Microsoft utilizes a multi-faceted approach to IT service management. This strategy includes advancements in the following areas:

▶ Adoption of a model-based management strategy (a component of the Dynamic Systems Initiative, discussed in the next section, "Microsoft's Dynamic Systems Initiative") to implement synthetic transaction technology. ConfigMgr delivers Service Modeling Language (SML)-based models in its compliance settings feature (previously known as desired configuration management or DCM), allowing administrators to define intended configurations.

▶ Using an Infrastructure Optimization Model as a framework for aligning IT with business needs and as a standard for expressing an organization's maturity in service management. The "Optimizing Your Infrastructure" section discusses the IO Model further. The IO Model describes your IT infrastructure in terms of cost, security risk, and operational agility.

▶ Supporting a standard Web Services specification for system management. WS-Management is a specification of a SOAP-based protocol, based on web services, used to manage servers, devices, and applications. (SOAP stands for *Simple Object Access Protocol*.) The intent is to provide a universal language that all types of devices can use to share data about themselves, which in turn makes them more easily managed. Microsoft has included support for WS-Management beginning with Windows Vista and Windows Server 2008, and it is leveraged by System Center.

▶ Integrating infrastructure and management into OS and server products, by exposing services and interfaces that management applications can utilize.

▶ Building complete management solutions on this infrastructure, either through making them available in the OS or by using management products such as Configuration Manager, Operations Manager, Service Manager, and Virtual Machine Manager.

▶ Continuing to drive down the complexity of Windows management by providing core management infrastructure and capabilities in the Windows platform itself, thus allowing business and management application developers to improve their infrastructures and capabilities. Microsoft believes that improving the manageability of solutions built on Windows Server System will be a key driver in shaping the future of Windows management.

Microsoft's Dynamic Systems Initiative

A large percentage of IT departments' budgets and resources typically focuses on mundane maintenance tasks such as applying software patches or monitoring the health of a network, without leaving the staff with the time or energy to focus on more exhilarating (and more productive) strategic initiatives.

DSI is a Microsoft and industry strategy intended to enhance the Windows platform, delivering a coordinated set of solutions that simplifies and automates how businesses design, deploy, and operate their distributed systems. Using DSI helps IT and developers create operationally aware platforms. By designing systems that are more manageable and automating operations, organizations can reduce costs and proactively address their priorities.

DSI is about building software that enables knowledge of an IT system to be created, modified, transferred, and operated on throughout the life cycle of that system. It is a commitment from Microsoft and its partners to help IT teams capture and use knowledge to design systems that are more manageable and to automate operations, which in turn reduce costs and give organizations additional time to focus proactively on what is most important. By innovating across applications, development tools, the platform, and management solutions, DSI will result in

- ▶ Increased productivity and reduced costs across all aspects of IT

- ▶ Increased responsiveness to changing business needs

- ▶ Reduced time and effort required to develop, deploy, and manage applications

Microsoft is positioning DSI as the connector of the entire system and service life cycles.

Microsoft Product Integration

DSI focuses on automating datacenter operational jobs and reducing associated labor though self-managing systems. Here are several examples in which Microsoft products and tools integrate with DSI:

- ▶ Operations Manager uses the application knowledge captured in management packs to simplify identifying issues and their root causes, facilitating resolution and restoring services or preventing potential outages, and providing intelligent management at the system level.

- ▶ Configuration Manager uses model-based configuration baseline templates in its compliance settings feature to automate identification of unwanted shifts in system configurations.

▶ Service Manager uses model-based management packs. You can easily add new models describing your own configuration items or work items to track their life cycle. Each data model is stored in one or more management packs that make up the model.

▶ Visual Studio is a model-based development tool that leverages SML, enabling operations managers and application architects to collaborate early in the development phase and ensure applications are modeled with operational requirements in mind.

▶ Windows Server Update Services (WSUS) enables greater and more efficient administrative control through modeling technology that enables downstream systems to construct accurate models representing their current state, available updates, and installed software.

SDM AND SML: WHAT'S THE DIFFERENCE?

Microsoft originally used the System Definition Model (SDM) as its standard schema with DSI. SDM was a proprietary specification put forward by Microsoft. The company later decided to implement SML, which is an industrywide published specification used in heterogeneous environments. Using SML helps DSI adoption by incorporating a standard that Microsoft's partners can understand and apply across mixed platforms. SML is discussed later in the "The Role of Service Modeling Language in IT Operations" section.

DSI focuses on automating datacenter operations and reducing total cost of ownership (TCO) through self-managing systems. Can logic be implemented in management software so that the software can identify system or application issues in real time and then dynamically take actions to mitigate the problem? Consider the scenario in which without operator intervention, a management system moves a virtual machine running a line-of-business application because the existing host experiences an extended spike in resource utilization. This is now a reality, delivered in the live migration feature of Virtual Machine Manager. DSI aims to extend this type of self-healing and self-management to other areas of operations.

In support of DSI, Microsoft has invested heavily in three major areas:

▶ **Systems designed for management:** Microsoft delivers development and authoring tools, such as Visual Studio, that enable businesses to capture the knowledge of everyone from business users and project managers to the architects, developers, testers, and operations staff using models. By capturing and embedding this knowledge into the infrastructure, organizations can reduce support complexity and cost.

▶ **An operationally aware platform:** The core Windows operating system and its related technologies are critical when solving everyday operational and service challenges. This requires designing the operating system services for manageability. In addition, the operating system and server products must provide rich instrumentation and hardware resource virtualization support.

▶ **Virtualized applications and server infrastructure:** Virtualization of servers and applications improves the agility of the organization by simplifying the effort involved in modifying, adding, or removing the resources a service utilizes in performing work.

THE MICROSOFT SUITE FOR SYSTEMS MANAGEMENT

End-to-end automation could include update management, availability and performance monitoring, change and configuration management, service management, and rich reporting services. Microsoft's System Center focuses on providing you with the knowledge and tools to manage and support your IT infrastructure. The objective of System Center is to provide systems management tools and technologies, thus helping to ease operations, reduce troubleshooting time, and improve planning capabilities.

The Importance of DSI

There are three architectural elements behind the DSI initiative:

▶ Developers have tools (such as Visual Studio) to design applications in a way that makes them easier for administrators to manage after those applications are in production.

▶ Microsoft products can be secured and updated in a uniform way.

▶ Microsoft server applications are optimized for management, to take advantage of System Center Operations Manager.

DSI represents a departure from the traditional approach to systems management. DSI focuses on designing for operations from the application development stage, rather than a more customary operations perspective that concentrates on automating task-based processes. This strategy highlights that Microsoft's Dynamic Systems Initiative is about building software that enables knowledge of an IT system to be created, modified, transferred, and used throughout the life cycle of a system. DSI's core principles of knowledge, models, and the life cycle are key in addressing the challenges of complexity and manageability faced by IT organizations. By capturing knowledge and incorporating health models, DSI can facilitate easier troubleshooting and maintenance, and thus lower TCO.

The Role of Service Modeling Language in IT Operations

A key underlying component of DSI is the eXtended Markup Language (XML)-based specification called the Service Modeling Language. SML is a standard developed by several leading information technology companies that defines a consistent way for infrastructure and application architects to define how applications, infrastructure, and services are modeled in a consistent way.

SML facilitates modeling systems from a development, deployment, and support perspective with modular, reusable building blocks that eliminate the need to reinvent the wheel when describing and defining a new service. The end result is systems that are easier to develop, implement, manage, and maintain, resulting in reduced TCO to the organization. SML is a core technology that will continue to play a prominent role in future products developed to support the ongoing objectives of DSI.

NOTE: SML RESOURCES ON THE WEB

SML functionality and configuration management within Configuration Manager is implemented using compliance settings. For more information about SML, view the latest draft of the SML standard at http://www.w3.org/TR/sml/. For additional technical information about SML from Microsoft, see http://www.microsoft.com/download/en/details.aspx?displaylang=en&id=24838.

IT Infrastructure Library and Microsoft Operations Framework

ITIL is widely accepted as an international standard of best practices for operations management. MOF is closely related to ITIL, and both describe best practices for IT service management processes. The next sections introduce you to ITIL and MOF. Warning: Fasten your seatbelt because this is where the fun begins!

What Is ITIL?

As part of Microsoft's management approach, the company relied on an international standards-setting body as its basis for developing an operational framework. The British Office of Government Commerce (OGC) provides best practices advice and guidance on using IT in service management and operations. The OGC also publishes the IT Infrastructure Library, commonly known as ITIL.

ITIL provides a cohesive set of best practices for ITSM. These best practices include a series of books giving direction and guidance on provisioning quality IT services and facilities needed to support IT. The documents are maintained by the OGC and supported by publications, qualifications, and an international users group.

Started in the 1980s, ITIL is under constant development by a consortium of industry IT leaders. ITIL covers a number of areas and is primarily focused on ITSM; it is considered to be the most consistent and comprehensive documentation of best practices for ITSM worldwide.

ITSM is a business-driven, customer-centric approach to managing IT. It specifically addresses the strategic business value generated by IT and the need to deliver high quality IT services to one's business organization. Here are the key objectives of ITSM:

▶ Align IT services with current and future needs of the business and its customers.

▶ Improve the quality of IT services delivered.

▶ Reduce long-term costs of providing services.

MORE ABOUT ITIL

The core books for version 3 (ITIL v3) were published on June 30, 2007. With v3, ITIL has adopted an integrated service life cycle approach to ITSM, as opposed to organizing itself around the concepts of IT service delivery and support.

ITIL v2 was a targeted product, explicitly designed to bridge the gap between technology and business, with a strong process focus on effective service support and delivery. The v3 documents recognize the service management challenges brought about by advancements in technology, such as virtualization and outsourcing, and emerging challenges for service providers. The v3 framework emphasizes managing the life cycle of the services provided by IT and the importance of creating business value, rather than just executing processes.

There are five core volumes of ITIL v3:

▶ **Service Strategy:** This volume identifies market opportunities for which services could be developed to meet a requirement on the part of internal or external customers. Key areas here are service portfolio management and financial management.

▶ **Service Design:** This volume focuses on the activities that take place to develop the strategy into a design document that addresses all aspects of the proposed service and the processes intended to support it. Key areas of this volume are availability management, capacity management, continuity management, and security management.

▶ **Service Transition:** This volume centers on implementing the output of service design activities and creating a production service (or modifying an existing service). There is some overlap between Service Transition and Service Operation, the next volume. Key areas of the Service Transition volume are change management, release management, configuration management, and service knowledge management.

▶ **Service Operation:** This volume involves the activities required to operate the services and maintain their functionality as defined in service level agreements (SLAs) with one's customers. Key areas here are incident management, problem management, and request fulfillment.

▶ **Continual Service Improvement:** This volume focuses on the ability to deliver continual improvement to the quality of the services that the IT organization delivers to the business. Key areas include service reporting, service measurement, and service level management.

Philosophically speaking, ITSM focuses on the customer's perspective of IT's contribution to the business, which is analogous to the objectives of other frameworks in terms of their consideration of alignment of IT service support and delivery with business goals in mind.

Although ITIL describes the what, when, and why of IT operations, it stops short of describing how a specific activity should be carried out. A driving force behind its development was the recognition that organizations are increasingly dependent on IT for satisfying their corporate objectives relating to both internal and external customers, which increases the requirement for high quality IT services. Many large IT organizations realize that the road to a customer-centric service organization runs along an ITIL framework.

ITIL also specifies keeping measurements or metrics to assess performance over time. Measurements can include a variety of statistics, such as the number and severity of service outages, along with the amount of time it takes to restore service. You can use these metrics or key performance indicators (KPIs) to quantify to management how well IT performs. This information can prove particularly useful to justify resources during the next budget process!

What Is MOF?

ITIL is generally accepted as the "best practices" for the industry. Being technology-agnostic, it is a foundation that can be adopted and adapted to meet the specific needs of various IT organizations. Although Microsoft chose to adopt ITIL as a standard for its own IT operations for its descriptive guidance, Microsoft designed MOF to provide prescriptive guidance for effective design, implementation, and support of Microsoft technologies.

MOF is a set of publications providing both descriptive (what to do, when, and why) and prescriptive (how to do) guidance on ITSM. The key focus in developing MOF was providing a framework specifically geared toward managing Microsoft technologies. Microsoft created the first version of the MOF in 1999. The latest iteration of MOF (version 4) is designed to further

▶ Update MOF to include the full end-to-end IT service life cycle.

▶ Let IT governance serve as the foundation of the life cycle.

▶ Provide useful, easily consumable best practice-based guidance.

▶ Simplify and consolidate service management functions (SMFs), emphasizing workflows, decisions, outcomes, and roles.

MOF v4 now incorporates Microsoft's previously existing Microsoft Solutions Framework (MSF), providing guidance for application development solutions. The combined framework provides guidance throughout the IT life cycle, as shown in Figure 1.2.

At its core, the MOF is a collection of best practices, principles, and models. It provides direction to achieve reliability, availability, supportability, and manageability of mission-critical production systems, focusing on solutions and services using Microsoft products and technologies. MOF extends ITIL by including guidance and best practices derived from the experience of Microsoft's internal operations groups, partners, and customers worldwide. MOF aligns with and builds on the ITSM practices documented within ITIL, thus enhancing the supportability built on Microsoft's products and technologies.

MOF uses a model that describes Microsoft's approach to IT operations and the service management life cycle. The model organizes the ITIL volumes of service strategy, service design, service transition, service operation, and continual service improvement, and includes additional MOF processes in the MOF components, which are illustrated in Figure 1.3.

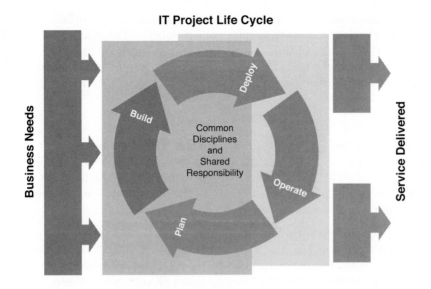

FIGURE 1.2   The IT life cycle

FIGURE 1.3   The IT life cycle, as described in MOF v4, has three life-cycle phases and one functional layer operating throughout all the other phases.

The activities in Figure 1.3 can occur simultaneously within an IT organization. Each area has a specific focus and tasks, and within each area are policies, procedures, standards, and best practices that support specific service management-focused tasks.

Configuration Manager can be employed to support tasks in the different top-level MOF components. Look briefly at each of these areas to see how you can use Configuration Manager to support MOF:

▶ **Plan:** This phase covers activities related to IT strategy, standards, policies, and finances. This is where the business and IT collaborate to determine how IT can most effectively deliver services enabling the overall organization to succeed.

Configuration Manager delivers services that support the business, enabling IT to change to meet business strategy and support the business in becoming more efficient.

▶ **Deliver:** This phase represents activities related to envisioning, planning, building, testing, and deploying IT service solutions. It takes a service solution from vision through deployment, ensuring you have a stable solution inline with business requirements and customer specifications.

Inventory management enables you to keep a handle on your hardware and software inventory, assisting with managing costs and planning for operating system and software upgrades.

Using a connector, Configuration Manager provides configuration item data about the computers it manages to Service Manager, enabling that information to be used in the Service Manager configuration management database (CMDB).

▶ **Operate:** This phase focuses on activities related to operating, monitoring, supporting, and addressing issues with IT services. It ensures that IT services function in line with SLA targets.

Configuration Manager's System Center Operations Manager Configuration Pack contains configuration items to manage Operations Manager server roles.

You can incorporate a structure into the software updates capability to assess the current situation, identify new updates, evaluate and plan for deployment, and put the actual update deployment into effect, reducing the support and operations costs of implementation by using a process.

▶ **Manage:** This layer, operating continuously though the three phases, covers activities related to managing governance, risk, compliance, changes, configurations, and organizations. It promotes consistency and accountability in planning and delivering IT services, providing the basis for developing and operating a flexible and durable IT environment.

The Manage layer establishes an approach to ITSM activities, which helps to coordinate the work of the SMFs in the three life cycle phases.

Configuration Manager's compliance settings capability enables you to manage compliance of your systems, identifying non-compliant systems so that you can take actions for remediation.

You can find additional information about the MOF at http://technet.microsoft.com/library/cc506049.aspx.

MOF Does Not Replace ITIL

Microsoft believes that ITIL is the leading body of knowledge of best practices. For that reason, it uses ITIL as the foundation for MOF. Instead of replacing ITIL, MOF complements it and is similar to ITIL in several ways:

▶ MOF (now incorporating MSF) spans the entire IT life cycle.

▶ Both MOF and ITIL are based on best practices for IT management, drawing on the expertise of practitioners worldwide.

▶ The MOF body of knowledge is applicable across the business community (from small businesses to large enterprises). MOF also is not limited only to those using the Microsoft platform in a homogenous environment.

▶ As is the case with ITIL, MOF has expanded to be more than just a documentation set. MOF is now intertwined thoroughly with System Center, Configuration Manager, Service Manager, and Operations Manager.

In addition, Microsoft and its partners provide a variety of resources to support MOF principles and guidance, including self-assessments, IT management tools that incorporate MOF terminology and features, training programs and certification, and consulting services.

Total Quality Management: TQM

The goal of Total Quality Management (TQM) is to continuously improve the quality of products and processes. It functions on the premise that the quality of the products and processes is the responsibility of everyone involved with the creation or consumption of the products or services offered by the organization. TQM capitalizes on the involvement of management, workforce, suppliers, and even customers, to meet or exceed customer expectations.

Six Sigma

Six Sigma is a business management strategy, originally developed by Motorola, which seeks to identify and remove the causes of defects and errors in manufacturing and business processes. The Six Sigma process improvement originated in 1986 from Motorola's drive toward reducing defects by minimizing variation in processes through metrics measurement. Applications of the Six Sigma project execution methodology have since expanded to incorporate practices common in TQM and Supply Chain Management; this includes customer satisfaction and developing closer supplier relationships.

Service Management Mastery: ISO 20000

You can think of ITIL and ITSM as providing a framework for IT to rethink the ways in which it contributes to and aligns with the business. ISO 20000, which is the first international standard for ITSM, institutionalizes these processes. The ISO 20000 helps companies to align IT services and business strategy and create a formal framework for continual service improvement and provides benchmarks for comparison to best practices.

Published in December 2005, ISO 20000 was developed to reflect the best practice guidance contained within ITIL. The standard also supports other ITSM frameworks and approaches, including MOF, CMMI, and Six Sigma. ISO 20000 consists of two major areas:

▶ Part 1 promotes adopting an integrated process approach to deliver managed services effectively that meets business and customer requirements.

▶ Part 2 is a "code of practice" describing the best practices for service management within the scope of ISO 20000-1.

These two areas—what to do and how to do it—have similarities to the approach taken by the other standards, including MOF.

ISO 20000 goes beyond ITIL, MOF, Six Sigma, and other frameworks in providing organizational or corporate certification for organizations that effectively adopt and implement the ISO 20000 code of practice.

Optimizing Your Infrastructure

According to Microsoft, analysts estimate that more than 70% of the typical IT budget is spent on infrastructure—managing servers, operating systems, storage, and networking. Add to that the challenge of refreshing and managing desktop and mobile devices, and there's not much left over for anything else.

GARTNER STUDY ON DESKTOP TOTAL COST OF OWNERSHIP

Gartner's RAS Core Research Note G00208726 (November 16, 2010) states while declining hardware and software costs have an impact on TCO, how desktop PCs are managed remains the most critical factor in reducing total cost of ownership. A well-managed desktop PC can cost 43% less to keep than an unmanaged one!

Microsoft describes an Infrastructure Optimization Model that categorizes the state of an IT infrastructure, describing the impacts on cost, security risks, and the capability to respond to changes. Using the model shown in Figure 1.4, you can identify where your organization is and where you want to be:

▶ **Basic:** Reactionary, with much time spent fighting fires

▶ **Standardized:** Gaining control

▶ **Rationalized:** Enabling the business

▶ **Dynamic:** Being a strategic asset

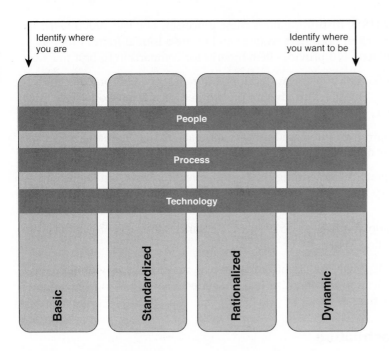

Identify where
you are

Identify where
you want to be

People

Process

Technology

Basic

Standardized

Rationalized

Dynamic

FIGURE 1.4   The Infrastructure Optimization Model.

Although most organizations are somewhere between the basic and standardized levels in this model, typically you would prefer to be a strategic asset rather than fighting fires. After you know where you are in the model, you can use best practices from ITIL and guidance from MOF to develop a plan to progress to a higher level. The IO Model describes the technologies and steps organizations can take to move forward, whereas the MOF explains the people and processes required to improve that infrastructure. Similar to ITSM, the IO Model is a combination of people, processes, and technology.

You can find more information about infrastructure optimization at http://www.microsoft.com/technet/infrastructure.

ABOUT THE IO MODEL

Not all IT shops will want or need to be dynamic. Some choose, for all the right business reasons, to be less than dynamic! The IO Model includes a three-part goal:

▶ Communicate that there are levels.

▶ Target the wanted levels.

▶ Provide reference on how to get to the wanted levels.

Realize that infrastructure optimization can be by application or by function, rather than a single ranking for the entire IT department.

Items that factor into an IT organization's adoption of the IO Model include cost, ability, and whether the organization fits into the business model as a cost center versus being an asset, along with a commitment to move from being reactive to proactive.

From Fighting Fires to Gaining Control

At the basic level, your infrastructure is hard to control and expensive to manage. Processes are manual, IT policies and standards are either nonexistent or not enforced, and you don't have the tools and resources (or time and energy) to determine the overall health of your applications and IT services. Not only are your desktop and server management costs out of control, but you are also in reactive mode for security threats and user support. In addition, you tend to use manual rather than automated methods for applying software deployments and patches.

Does this sound familiar? If you can gain control of your environment, you may be more effective at work! Here are some steps to consider:

► Develop standards, policies, and controls.

► Alleviate security risks by developing a security approach throughout your IT organization.

► Adopt best practices, such as those found in ITIL, and operational guidance found in the MOF.

► Build IT to become a strategic asset.

If you can achieve operational nirvana, this can go a long way toward your job satisfaction and IT becoming a constructive part of your business.

From Gaining Control to Enabling the Business

A standardized infrastructure introduces control by using standards and policies to manage desktops and servers. These standards control how you introduce machines into your network. For example, you could use directory services to manage resources, security policies, and access to resources. Shops in a standardized state realize the value of basic standards and some policies but still tend to be reactive. Although you now have a managed IT infrastructure and are inventorying your hardware and software assets and starting to manage licenses, patch management, software deployments, and desktop services are not yet automated. For security, the perimeter is now under control, although internal security may still be a bit loose. Service management becomes a recognized concept, and your organization is taking steps to implement it.

To move from a standardized state to the rationalized level, you need to gain more control over your infrastructure and implement proactive policies and procedures. You might also begin to look at implementing service management. At this stage, IT can also move more toward becoming a business asset and ally, rather than a burden.

From Enabling the Business to Becoming a Strategic Asset

At the rationalized level, you have achieved firm control of desktop and service management costs. Processes and policies are in place and beginning to play a large role in supporting and expanding the business. Security is now proactive, and you respond to threats and challenges in a rapid and controlled manner.

Using technologies such as lite-touch and zero-touch operating system deployment helps you to minimize costs, deployment time, and technical challenges for system rollouts. Because your inventory is now under control, you have minimized the number of images to manage, and desktop management is now largely automated. You also are purchasing only the software licenses and new computers the business requires, giving you a handle on costs. Security is proactive with policies and control in place for desktops, servers, firewalls, and extranets. You have implemented service management in several areas and are taking steps to implement it more broadly across IT.

Mission Accomplished: IT as a Strategic Asset

At the dynamic level, your infrastructure helps run the business efficiently and stay ahead of competitors. Your costs are now fully controlled. You have also achieved integration between users and data, desktops and servers, and the different departments and functions throughout your organization.

Your IT processes are automated and often incorporated into the technology, allowing IT to be aligned and managed according to business needs. New technology investments yield specific, rapid, and measurable business benefits. Measurement is good—it helps you justify the next round of investments!

Using self-provisioning software and quarantine-like systems to ensure patch management and compliance with security policies allows you to automate your processes, which in turn improves reliability, lowers costs, and increases your service levels. Service management is implemented for all critical services with SLAs and operational reviews.

According to IDC Research (October 2006), few organizations achieve the dynamic level of the Infrastructure Optimization Model—due to the lack of availability of a single toolset from a single vendor to meet all requirements. Through execution on its vision in DSI, Microsoft aims to change this. To read more about this study, visit http://download.microsoft.com/download/a/4/4/a4474b0c-57d8-41a2-afe6-32037fa93ea6/IDC_windesktop_IO_whitepaper.pdf.

MICROSOFT INFRASTRUCTURE OPTIMIZATION HELPS REDUCE COSTS

The April 21, 2009, issue of *BizTech* magazine includes an article by Russell Smith about Microsoft's Infrastructure Optimization Model. Russell makes the following points:

Although dynamic or fully automated systems that are strategic assets to a company sometimes seem like a far-off dream, infrastructure optimization models and products can help get you closer to making IT a valuable business asset.

Microsoft's Infrastructure Optimization is based on Gartner's Infrastructure Maturity Model and provides a simple structure to evaluate the efficiency of core IT services, business productivity, and application platforms.

Though the ultimate goal is to make IT a business enabler across all three areas, you will need to concentrate on standardizing core services: moving your organization from a basic infrastructure (in which most IT tasks are carried out manually) to a managed infrastructure with some automation and knowledge capture.

A 2006 IDC study of 141 enterprises with 1,000 to 20,000 users found that PC standardization and security management could save up to $430 per user annually; standardizing systems management servers could save another $46 per user.

For additional information and the complete article, see http://www.biztechmagazine.com/article.asp?item_id=569.

Overview of Microsoft System Center

At the Microsoft Management Summit (MMS) in 2003, Microsoft announced System Center, envisioned as a future solution to provide customers with complete application and system management for enterprises of all sizes. (See http://www.microsoft.com/presspass/press/2003/mar03/03-18mssystemcenterpr.mspx for the original press release.) The first phase was anticipated to include Microsoft Operations Manager (MOM) 2004—later released as MOM 2005—and SMS 2003.

NOTE: WHAT IS SYSTEM CENTER?

System Center is a brand name for Microsoft's systems management products, and as such has new products and components added over time. System Center represents a means to integrate system management tools and technologies to help you with systems operations, troubleshooting, and planning.

Different from the releases of Microsoft Office (another Microsoft product family), Microsoft has historically released System Center in "waves"; the components were not released simultaneously. The first wave initially included SMS 2003, MOM 2005, and System Center Data Protection Manager 2006; 2006 additions included System Center Reporting Manager 2006 and System Center Capacity Planner 2006.

The second wave included Operations Manager 2007, Configuration Manager 2007, System Center Essentials 2007, Virtual Machine Manager 2007, and new releases of Data Protection Manager and Capacity Planner. Next released were updates to Virtual Machine Manager (version 2008), Operations Manager 2007 R2, Configuration Manager 2007 R2 and R3, DPM 2010, System Center Essentials 2010, and Service Manager 2010. Think of these as rounding out the second wave.

Microsoft has also widened System Center with its acquisitions of Opalis (rebranded for System Center 2012 as System Center Orchestrator) and AVIcode, incorporated into System Center 2012 Operations Manager as Application Performance Monitoring (APM). Microsoft's Enrollment for Core Infrastructure (ECI) agreement helps bundle the necessary software components together to help manage growth as you begin virtualizing your Windows Server environment and leverages System Center.

With System Center 2012, Microsoft is moving from the wave approach and releasing the System Center components simultaneously. System Center 2012 also includes the first version of a common installer. The components include Configuration Manager, Operations Manager, Virtual Machine Manager, Orchestrator, Data Protection Manager,

App Controller, Endpoint Protection, and Service Manager. System Center Advisor, previously code-named Atlanta, promises to offer configuration-monitoring cloud service for Microsoft SQL Server, Exchange, and Windows Server deployments; expect the list of monitored products to grow over time. (Advisor is a software assurance benefit and is not included in the licensing for System Center.) Microsoft's System Center 2012 cloud and datacenter solutions provide a common management toolset for your private and public cloud applications and services to help you deliver IT as a service to your business.

System Center builds on Microsoft's DSI, introduced in the "Microsoft's Dynamic Systems Initiative" section, which is designed to deliver simplicity, automation, and flexibility in the datacenter across the IT environment. Microsoft System Center products share the following DSI-based characteristics:

▶ Ease of use and deployment

▶ Based on industry and customer knowledge

▶ Scalability (both up to the largest enterprises and down to the smallest organizations)

Figure 1.5 illustrates the relationship between the System Center 2012 components and MOF.

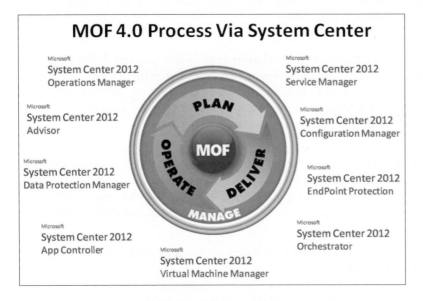

FIGURE 1.5   MOF with System Center applications.

Reporting in System Center

The data gathered by Configuration Manager is collected in a self-maintaining SQL Server database and comes with numerous reports available using Microsoft SQL Server Reporting Services (SSRS). Using the native functionality of SSRS, report output can be exported to a variety of formats, including Report Server file shares, web archive format, Excel, and PDF. You can schedule and email reports, enabling users to open these reports independent of the tool.

System Center 2012 introduces the concept of integrated reporting for System Center, available with the data warehouse shipping with Service Manager. This data warehouse utilizes SQL Server Analysis Services and incorporates consolidated reporting for Service Manager, Configuration Manager, and Operations Manager. Data for the individual products is available in separate data marts.

Operations Management

System Center 2012 Operations Manager provides the monitoring component of delivering IT as a service, helping you to manage your datacenter and cloud environments by

▶ Delivering flexible and cost effective enterprise-class monitoring and diagnostics while reducing the total cost of ownership by leveraging commodity hardware, configurations, and heterogeneous environments

▶ Helping to ensure the availability of business-critical applications and services through market-leading .NET and JEE application performance monitoring and diagnostics

▶ Providing a comprehensive view of datacenters, and private and public clouds

System Center 2012 Operations Manager also adds extensively to those network monitoring capabilities available with OpsMgr 2007 R2 by incorporating EMC Smarts technology.

In 2010, Gartner Group placed Operations Manager in its Magic Quadrant for IT Event Correlation and Analysis.

Service Management

Using Service Manager implements a single point of contact for all service requests, knowledge, and workflow. System Center 2012 Service Manager incorporates processes such as incident, problem, change, and release management.

Service Manager's CMDB includes population from Configuration Manager, Operations Manager, Virtual Machine Manager, and Orchestrator via connectors, enabling it to consolidate information throughout System Center. As an example, Service Manager fills a gap in Operations Manager: What occurs when OpsMgr detects a condition that requires human intervention and tracking for resolution? Until Service Manager, the answer was to create a ticket or incident in one's help desk application. Now, within the System Center framework, OpsMgr can hand off incident management to Service Manager. The Configuration Manager connector enables Service Manager to incorporate the inventory information captured by ConfigMgr.

Enhancements to the 2012 version include a service catalog, release management, and the System Center data warehouse.

Protecting Data

System Center 2012 Data Protection Manager (DPM) is a disk-based backup solution for continuous data protection supporting Windows servers such as SQL Server, Exchange, SharePoint, virtualization, and file servers—as well as Windows desktops and laptops. DPM provides byte-level backup as changes occur, utilizing Microsoft's Virtual Disk Service and Shadow Copy technologies.

This version of DPM incorporates a number of enhancements over the previous version, including

▶ Centralized management

▶ Centralized monitoring

▶ Remote administration

▶ Remote recovery

▶ Role-based management

▶ Remote corrective actions

▶ Scoped troubleshooting

▶ Push to resume backups

▶ SLA-based alerting

▶ Consolidated alerts

▶ Alert categorization

▶ PowerShell

Virtual Machine Management

Virtual Machine Manager (VMM) is Microsoft's management platform for heterogeneous virtualization infrastructures. VMM provides centralized management of virtual machines across several popular platforms, specifically Windows Server 2008 and 2008 R2 Hyper-V, VMware ESX 3.x, and Citrix XenServer. VMM enables increased utilization of physical servers, centralized management of a virtual infrastructure, delegation of administration in distributed environments, and rapid provisioning of new virtual machines by system administrators and users via a self-service portal.

System Center 2012 Virtual Machine Manager includes the capability to build both Hyper-V hosts and host clusters as it moves to being a private cloud product for management and provisioning rather than just a virtualization management solution. This provisioning involves deploying services using service templates, in addition to simply configuring storage and networking.

VMM enables you to

▶ Deliver flexible and cost-effective Infrastructure as a Service (IaaS). You can pool and dynamically allocate virtualized datacenter resources (compute, network, and storage) enabling a self-service infrastructure, with flexible role-based delegation and access control.

▶ Apply cloud principles to provisioning and servicing your datacenter applications with techniques like service modeling, service configuration, and image-based management. You can also separate your applications and services from the underlying infrastructure using server application virtualization. This results in a "service-centric" approach to management in which you manage the application or service lifecycle and not just datacenter infrastructure or virtual machines.

▶ Optimize your existing investments by managing multihypervisor environments such as Windows Server 2008 R2 Hyper-V, Citrix XenServer, and VMware vSphere 4.1 using a single pane of glass.

▶ Dynamically optimize your datacenter resources based on workload demands, while ensuring reliable service delivery with features like high availability.

▶ Achieve best-of-breed virtualization-management for Microsoft workloads such as Exchange and SharePoint.

Deploy and Manage in the Cloud

System Center 2012 App Controller, previously code-named Concero, is a self-service portal built on Silverlight, enabling IT managers to more easily deploy and manage applications in cloud infrastructures. App Controller provides a single console for managing multiple private and public clouds while provisioning virtual machines and services to individual business units. Using App Controller with VMM, datacenter administrators can provision not only virtual machine OS deployments, but also, leveraging App-V, deploy and manage down to the application level, minimizing the number of virtual hard disk (VHD) templates necessary to maintain.

Orchestration and Automation

System Center 2012 Orchestrator is based on Opalis Integration Server (OIS), acquired by Microsoft in December 2009. The product provides an automation platform for orchestrating and integrating IT tools to drive down the cost of datacenter operations while improving the reliability of IT processes. Orchestrator enables organizations to automate best practices, such as those found in MOF and ITIL, by using workflow processes that coordinate the System Center platform and other management tools to automate incident response, change and compliance, and service life cycle management processes.

The IT process automation software reduces operational costs and improves IT efficiency by delivering services faster and with fewer errors. Orchestrator replaces manual, resource-intensive, and potentially error-prone activities with standardized, automated processes. The product can orchestrate tasks between Configuration Manager, Operations Manager, Service Manager, Virtual Machine Manager, Data Protection Manager, and third-party management tools. This positions it to automate any IT process across a heterogeneous environment, providing full solutions for incident management, change and configuration management, and provisioning and service management.

Cloud-Based Configuration Monitoring

System Center Advisor promises to offer configuration-monitoring cloud service for Microsoft Windows Server, Exchange, and SQL Server deployments. Microsoft servers in the Advisor cloud analyze the uploaded data and then provide feedback to the customer in the Advisor console in the form of alerts about detected configuration issues. System Center Advisor's mission statement is to be a proactive tool to help Microsoft's software assurance customers avoid configuration problems, reduce downtime, improve performance, and resolve issues faster. The web-based console is written with Silverlight and is similar to the look and feel of the Microsoft InTune console, Microsoft's cloud-based management service for PCs.

Endpoint Protection

The product previously known as Forefront Endpoint Protection, Microsoft's enterprise antimalware suite has a name change and is moving into System Center. Its integration with Configuration Manager enables administrators to better deploy, monitor, and maintain antimalware software and updates, and provides a single infrastructure for client management and security.

Configuration Manager integration enables System Center 2012 Endpoint Protection to provide a single infrastructure for deploying and managing endpoint protection. You have a single view into the compliance and security of client systems through antimalware, patching, inventory, and usage information.

The Value Proposition of Configuration Manager

Configuration Manager helps you empower your employees to use those devices and applications they need to be productive, while maintaining corporate compliance and control. With blurred boundaries between work and life, people expect consistent access to corporate services from wherever they are, on any device they use—including desktops, laptops, smart phones, and tablets.

Configuration Manager helps you embrace this trend without giving up the control needed to protect your corporate assets. Using ConfigMgr, user experiences can be delivered and managed based on corporate identity, network connectivity, and device type—enabling you to meet the demand for consistent, anywhere access to corporate services. The product provides a unified infrastructure for mobile, physical, and virtual environments, and helps you manage everything in one place using the processes you already have established. This infrastructure also extends to include critical endpoint security and service management technologies necessary to protect and support your workers; while providing simplified administrative tools and improved compliance enforcement mechanisms to help to make IT more efficient and effective.

The value of Configuration Manager lies in these areas:

▶ Empowering individuals to be productive from anywhere on whatever device they choose. This includes the wide range of devices that connect to Exchange ActiveSync, including Windows Phone, Symbian, iOS, and Android-based devices. Through the new application model, the best application experience can be delivered to users based on their identity, their device, and their connection.

▶ Streamlining operations with a unified infrastructure, integrating client management and protection across mobile, physical, and virtual environments. Improved capabilities such as endpoint protection integration, role-based administration, and virtualization scenario support can simplify both infrastructure and processes for IT.

▶ Driving organizational efficiency for IT with improved visibility and enforcement options for maintaining system compliance. This means fewer mouse clicks to accomplish tasks and higher degrees of automation in activities such as patch management and settings enforcement.

Summary

The purpose of this chapter was to introduce the challenges of systems management and discuss what System Center 2012 Configuration Manager brings to the table to meet those challenges. Systems management is a process that touches many areas within ITIL and MOF, such as change and configuration management, asset management, security management, and indirectly, release management. The functionality delivered in ConfigMgr can help you meet these challenges more easily and efficiently.

The chapter discussed ITIL v3, which is an internationally accepted framework of best practices for IT service management. ITIL describes what should be accomplished in IT operations, although not actually how to accomplish it, and how the processes are related and affect one another. To provide additional guidance for its own IT and other customers, Microsoft uses ITIL as the foundation of its own operations framework, the Microsoft Operations Framework. The objective of MOF is to provide both descriptive (what to do and why) as well as prescriptive guidance (how to do it) for IT service management as they relate to Microsoft products.

Microsoft's management approach, which incorporates the processes and software tools of MOF and DSI, is a strategy or blueprint intended to build automation and knowledge into datacenter operations. The company's investment in DSI includes building systems designed for operations, developing an operationally aware platform, and establishing a commitment to intelligent management software.

Configuration Manager is a tool for managing systems in a way that increases the quality of service IT delivers while reducing the operational cost of service delivery. Together with Operations Manager, Service Manager, and the other System Center components,

ConfigMgr is a critical component in Microsoft's approach to system management that can increase your organization's agility in delivering on its service commitments to the business.

Systems management is a key component in an effective service management strategy. Throughout this book, you see this functionality described and demonstrated, as the authors hope to illustrate the full value of Configuration Manager as a platform for improving the automation, security, and efficiency of service support and delivery in your IT organization.

The next chapter includes an overview of ConfigMgr terminology and discusses key concepts, feature dependencies, and what's new in this version of ConfigMgr.

CHAPTER 2

Configuration Manager Overview

Chapter 1, "Configuration Management Basics," discussed the challenges of system and configuration management. This chapter covers the history of System Center Configuration Manager (ConfigMgr). The chapter also discusses key concepts and terminologies found in later chapters of this book to help ConfigMgr administrators become familiar with the lexicon.

System Center 2012 Configuration Manager includes a significant number of changes. Even seasoned ConfigMgr administrators will discover concepts they were once familiar with are now different. This chapter covers those changes. To assist in planning a new ConfigMgr implementation or migration of an existing infrastructure, the chapter also includes outlines feature dependencies.

The History of Configuration Manager

Starting with Systems Management Server (SMS) 1.0 and ending with System Center 2012 Configuration Manager, Microsoft has released five major versions of its systems and configuration management product. After SMS 1.0 (code-named *Hermes*) came versions 1.1, 1.2, 2.0, and—as Microsoft moved to incorporating the release year as part of the name of the product—SMS 2003. Microsoft rebranded the following version, 2007, as System Center Configuration Manager. Microsoft's newest release, version 2012, continues with the System Center moniker as System Center moves toward becoming a single integrated product. Figure 2.1 shows the timeline of releases.

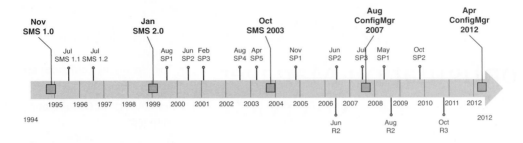

FIGURE 2.1   SMS and Configuration Manager releases.

Systems Management Server 1.x

Microsoft began its journey into the configuration management space in 1994 with the SMS 1.0 release. Subsequent releases in the 1.x product line with versions 1.1 and 1.2 released in 1995 and 1996, respectively. Although these two "dot" releases were planned initially as service packs; the added features were significant enough to become product releases.

However, the 1.x versions of the product failed to receive wide adoption. Requirements such as installing the site server on a backup domain controller (BDC) made deployment cumbersome. In addition, SMS 1.x's management scope supported control of an entire domain only. Inventory functions were executed using login scripts. Administrators received numerous complaints from end users about prolonged logon times, yet another reason for the product's slow adoption.

Systems Management Server 2.0

Microsoft released SMS 2.0 in early 1999, complete with a new user interface (UI) utilizing the Microsoft Management Console (MMC). The first service pack (SP) became available 8 months later. SMS 2.0 was a complete rewrite of Microsoft's configuration management product and unfortunately did not pass through the quality control gates it should have. The product was plagued with bugs and became a relatively stable platform only with SP 2, released in 2000. By the time Microsoft released a third service pack in 2001, the SMS 2.0 platform had truly stabilized.

SMS 2.0 addressed many concerns Microsoft's customers had with SMS 1.x. You now could install a site server on a member server instead of a domain controller. The inventory process was moved to agent components rather than running in login scripts. In addition, the management scope was defined by subnets instead of the entire domain.

Despite these enhancements, the product had several significant failings:

▶ The client agent was not designed for a mobile workforce and did not consider low bandwidth situations, and at a time when laptops were becoming prevalent.

▶ Lack of Active Directory (AD) integration although the product was released just before Active Directory with Windows 2000 became available.

Neither SP 4, released in 2002, nor SP 5 (2003), addressed these areas, as these updates were primarily bug fixes rather than adding new functionality. However, the shortcomings in SMS 2.0 positioned Microsoft to release a product that addressed them—SMS 2003.

Systems Management Server 2003

Microsoft released the next major version of SMS in November 2003. The release was so late in 2003, it could have been named SMS 2004! This release added integration with Active Directory along with functionality supporting a mobile workforce.

The SMS server infrastructure remained largely the same with the inclusion of Internet Information Server (IIS), which arguably raised complexity but brought significant benefits (such as communication over HTTP and the use of the Background Intelligent Transfer System, also known as BITS). In addition, SMS 2003 included significant improvements to the SMS agent, discussed in the "Advanced Client" section. A legacy client was maintained to support older operating systems such as Windows 98 and Windows NT 4.0. Windows 95 support was dropped entirely. Another significant change was revamping the reporting interface into SMS Web Reporting, removing the complicated and obtuse Crystal reports.

Most of the changes in this version were not noticeable in the console. The UI looked almost identical to that of SMS 2.0.

Active Directory Integration

Aside from the general inference of using AD's capabilities (such as discovering AD clients), those organizations willing to extend their schema for SMS could leverage AD to optimize the way SMS 2003 operated. This was known as *Active Directory Integration*. There were numerous benefits from extending the schema, such as AD site boundaries, global roaming, and advanced security (meaning the large number of service accounts previously required were no longer necessary). Although most of these capabilities were minor, they improved the overall experience.

One substantial change in SMS 2003 from its predecessor was the introduction of a concept called *roaming*. Roaming came in two flavors: global and regional.

▶ **Global roaming:** Clients retrieve site information from AD enabling them to know the site they are in, communicate with the resident management point (MP) for that site, and receive information pertaining to the distribution points (DP) of that site. Global roaming was only available to organizations that extended the AD schema.

▶ **Regional roaming:** Clients are unaware of any site they may have roamed into and continue speaking to their default MP. As long as the client has roamed into a site lower in the hierarchy than their assigned site, the default MP can inform the client of the closest DPs.

Advanced Client

SMS 2003 included two types of clients: the Advanced Client and the Legacy Client. The Legacy Client was simply the previous version of the client, left in the product for compatibility reasons for those older operating systems unable to run the new client.

The Advanced Client was touted as designed for mobility; however, it was more advanced than the Legacy Client in nearly every way. Regardless of running on a desktop or laptop, the Advanced Client provided a number of benefits over the Legacy Client:

▶ AD site-aware clients could retrieve site system information from Active Directory.

▶ Instead of storing configuration data and other information in a file system, the Advanced Client used Windows Management Instrumentation (WMI).

▶ Clients no longer uninstalled when moving out of site boundaries. They remained persistent to their assigned location unless otherwise reassigned by an external process, removing the burden of managing client travel behavior.

▶ If the clients were roaming, the program execution behavior would change to support potential low bandwidth situations.

▶ Inventory data format used eXtensible Markup Language (XML).

▶ Integration with BITS provided a reliable, intelligent method of transferring files between the server and client.

These capabilities paved the way for functionality that exists in ConfigMgr 2007 and the 2012 version.

Additional Functionality Releases

To stay competitive, Microsoft continued to release functionality incrementally into SMS 2003 with service packs and a new branding called R2 (Release 2).

The first two service packs (released in 2004 and June 2006, respectively), were largely hotfix rollups with performance optimization. Functional changes were minor, adding support for newer operating systems. Microsoft announced that rather than adding new capabilities in service packs, new functionality would be included in *feature packs*, an example being the Operating System Deployment (OSD) Feature Pack released as a free download in November 2004.

Microsoft released the first full update to SMS 2003 with an R2 release in late 2006. SMS 2003 R2 was built on SMS 2003 SP 2 with two additional features:

▶ Scan Tool for Vulnerability Assessment

▶ Inventory Tool for Custom Updates (ITCU)

SMS 2003 SP 3, released in 2007, was the last maintenance release for the product. Along with another hotfix rollup, SP 3 included Asset Intelligence (a product developed from an acquisition of AssetMatrix). Asset Intelligence normalized more than 400,000 software titles into a legible format, easing the burden of tracking and reporting on licensing data. SP 3 also included an extension to OSD for deploying the Vista operating system—though considering the adoption rate of Vista, that is hardly worth noting!

System Center Configuration Manager 2007

The next release of the product saw a change in branding. No longer called Systems Management Server, the software was aligned into the System Center product line and renamed *Configuration Manager*. ConfigMgr 2007 was released in August 2007.

In this version, the Legacy Client was finally dropped, along with support for operating systems prior to Windows 2000. All the familiar feature packs released for SMS 2003 were included as part of ConfigMgr 2007, removing the requirement to layer installation after installation to get all the features.

ConfigMgr 2007 was the first version to use public key infrastructure (PKI) for securing client-to-server communications. This security mode was known as *native mode*. With the use of native mode and PKI, it was possible to manage clients that rarely connected over virtual private networks (VPN) or came into the office. The utilization of Internet-based client management (IBCM) enabled managing ConfigMgr 2007 clients over a regular Internet connection.

Out of band (OOB) management and improved Asset Intelligence functionality were the highlights of the first service pack, released in May 2008. Just a year after the release to manufacturing (RTM) of ConfigMgr 2007, Microsoft released ConfigMgr 2007 R2, which included a number of changes:

- ▶ **Application virtualization:** This supported running virtual applications sequenced through the Application Virtualization (App-V) platform.

- ▶ **Client status reporting (CSR):** This separate tool analyzed and reported on client health.

- ▶ **OSD improvements:** OSD enhancements included support for unknown computers, improvements to task sequences allowing alternative credentials for running command lines, and network bandwidth efficiency gains with multicast deployments.

- ▶ **SQL Reporting Services support:** This enhancement enabled using SQL Reporting Services (SSRS) for ConfigMgr reports, including the ability to convert most reports to the Reporting Services format.

Microsoft released ConfigMgr 2007 R3 in October 2010, introducing another wave of new features and improvements. This release included power management through ConfigMgr, eliminating the need to use third-party products to manage and report on computer power consumption. There also were several other improvements:

- ▶ **Performance:** Performance in scalability was improved to support up to 100,000 clients per primary site and 300,000 clients in a hierarchy.

- ▶ **Delta discovery:** AD discovery was modified to provide a delta discovery method that picks up only changes such as additions, deletions, and modifications, reducing the load on the site server running the discovery.

▶ **Dynamic collection updates:** Under certain conditions (first-time discovery, OSD provisioned, initial hardware inventory scan, or ConfigMgr client upgrade), collections can be enabled to dynamically add new resources as they are discovered.

▶ **Prestaged media:** Prestaging media enables a PC manufacturer to load an image it is provided with to a PC during the build process.

In December 2010 (post R3), Microsoft released Forefront Endpoint Protection 2010, integrating it into ConfigMgr to provide malware and security protection.

ConfigMgr is a system that continuously improves and evolves. The requirement to support every new Windows operating system is difficult enough to manage; in addition, a configuration management system developed by Microsoft is expected to manage (to some extent) every product Microsoft ever released! From the 1.x releases that installed software and ran inventory by logon script to the most advanced agent capable of installing the latest security updates, delivering whole operating systems, and self-healing, ConfigMgr has had a long career managing the rich Microsoft ecosystem.

The product has grown immensely complex over the years. At one point, it was expected that a ConfigMgr administrator could learn the entire product to an expert level. Today, with all the features that extend ConfigMgr beyond simple inventory management and software delivery, it is easy to become buried in the details.

System Center 2012 Configuration Manager

The current Information Technology (IT) climate is not what it was when SMS 1.x, 2.0, 2003, or even ConfigMgr 2007 was released. In today's environment, IT administrators confront the challenges of an environment with users operating on more than one device, often multiple types of devices, all of which require management.

System Center 2012 Configuration Manager, released in April 2012, brings waves of changes to the systems management platform, injecting new life into a product whose legacy now dates back over 15 years. This newest version includes some radical changes requiring adoption of new concepts and thinking to support today's flexible work style. By understanding relationships of users to devices and following the intent of managing software, ConfigMgr aims to optimize both the administrative experience and end user experience.

Terminology in Configuration Manager

Microsoft has added many new terms in System Center 2012 Configuration Manager with which you need to become familiar. In addition, the meaning of some terms has changed. Before beginning to understand how to deploy and operate ConfigMgr, familiarize yourself with the terminology and concepts that define System Center 2012 Configuration Manager discussed in the following sections.

Site Hierarchy

Any organization with more than one site connected together automatically has a *site hierarchy*. All site hierarchies include at least one primary site. A site hierarchy with more than one primary site must include a central administration site (CAS). Hierarchies can also include secondary sites.

Previous versions of ConfigMgr gave the site hierarchy the flexibility to be immensely deep and complex (although not recommended). System Center 2012 Configuration Manager supports a simplistic, flat hierarchy. Starting from the top, the hierarchy for a large organization generally goes three tiers deep, as indicated in Figure 2.2.

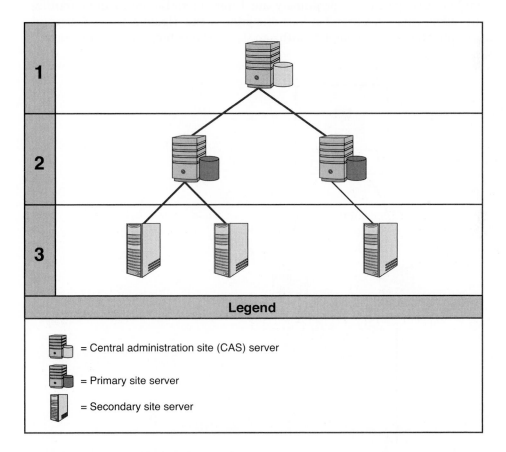

FIGURE 2.2   Site hierarchy depth diagram.

A secondary site can exist in a tiered hierarchy with another secondary site, effectively creating more than three tiers. However, all secondary sites communicate with their primary site for database replication. Although you can adopt this topology, few reasons exist for secondary sites in ConfigMgr 2012. Chapter 4, "Architecture Design Planning," provides detail for creating an optimized hierarchy.

REASONS AGAINST COMPLEX HIERARCHIES

Complex hierarchies generally are not recommended due to the amount of time administrative functions such as setting up applications and packages take to reach the client at the bottom of the hierarchy. Data sent from that client also takes a long time to reach the top of the hierarchy.

Site

A *site* is the core role of ConfigMgr. Depending on your organization's requirements, the hierarchy may be as simple as a single primary site. Large enterprises may require starting with a central administration site and at least one primary site. Figure 2.3, a new diagram view in the ConfigMgr console complete with site status, shows how a typical hierarchy might look.

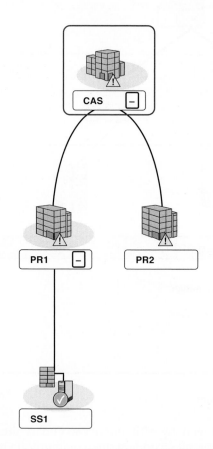

FIGURE 2.3   Hierarchical view of the Odyssey implementation.

Central Administration Site

The *central administration site* is an entirely new type of site used to manage all other sites, facilitate site-to-site communication, and manage reporting. The CAS does not support clients nor process any client data. The CAS is a required site whenever you connect multiple primary sites.

In previous versions of the product, this concept was known as a central site; although it was not technically restricted from supporting clients. A central site was the top-level primary site of a site hierarchy.

Primary Site

Every implementation of System Center 2012 Configuration Manager requires at least one *primary site*, which is a site to which clients can be assigned and that can be administered using the Configuration Manager console. Because this is a required site, the real question is whether you need to require multiple primary sites. This is an important decision you must make while installing a primary site because it cannot be added to a CAS later if initially built as a stand-alone primary site.

CAUTION: MULTIPLE PRIMARY SITES REQUIRE CAS DURING INITIAL INSTALLATION

Remember that multiple primary sites require a CAS to connect them together. Before installing the first site, know your hierarchy requirements and plan accordingly! If a primary site server is installed as a stand-alone site, it can never be joined to a CAS. It requires a complete reinstall to join to the CAS as part of the installation process.

Microsoft has maintained similar scalability for the primary site as in the most recent version of ConfigMgr 2007. Each primary site can support up to 100,000 clients, now with 400,000 clients supported in the hierarchy (assuming default settings are used for all ConfigMgr features). Unlike version 2007, however, the 2012 version can have multiple management points without the added complexity of using Network Load Balancing (NLB).

Here are areas to consider when planning for additional primary sites:

▶ **Scale:** Each primary site supports up to 100,000 clients.

▶ **Redundancy:** An additional primary site reduces the impact against the total client base if a single primary site were to have a failure.

▶ **Local connectivity:** Administrators can connect the console to any primary site.

▶ **Bandwidth constraints:** Sending deployment content can be managed to reduce the contention on a wide area network (WAN) connection.

Secondary Site

Secondary sites perform the same role as in earlier versions of ConfigMgr with several caveats:

▶ The 2012 secondary site now requires a SQL Server database.

▶ Secondary sites also automatically receive the proxy management point and distribution point roles.

Secondary sites are always a child site of primary site and can be administered only by a primary site. Clients cannot be assigned directly to secondary sites. Because administrative consoles can connect only to a central administration or primary site, secondary sites are typically used in locations that do not have administrators.

Secondary sites can help control bandwidth utilization by managing the flow of client information sent up the hierarchy. In addition, secondary sites can be tiered to help control content distribution to remote sites. The software update point role can be positioned on a secondary site server to provide local access to clients scanning for compliance without needing to talk to a primary site server. However, a hierarchy with secondary sites adds a layer of complexity that often is not necessary.

Use of a secondary site should be considered carefully. The authors recommend simplicity when designing your hierarchy. More information on secondary sites is available in Chapter 4.

Site Systems

Each site can perform a wide variety of roles based on the site type. Any computer, either server or workstation, hosting a site system role is referred to as a *site system* server. Some site system roles are required for operation of the site. Although roles can be transferred to other site servers in some cases, here is a list of site system roles that must exist in each site:

▶ **Component server:** This is any server running the ConfigMgr Executive service.

▶ **Site database server:** This is a server with Microsoft SQL Server installed, hosting the ConfigMgr site database.

▶ **Site server:** This main role contains components and services required to run a central administration, primary, or secondary site.

▶ **Site system:** This role supports both required and optional site system roles. Any server (or share) with an assigned role automatically receives this role.

▶ **SMS Provider:** This is a WMI provider operating as an interface between the ConfigMgr console and the site database.

In addition to default roles, System Center 2012 Configuration Manager includes optional roles to support other capabilities:

▶ **Application catalog web service point:** This role relays software information from the Software Library to the Application Catalog website.

▶ **Application catalog website point:** This is an optional role required for presenting available software to users.

▶ **Asset intelligence synchronization point:** This role synchronizes Asset Intelligence data from System Center Online by downloading Asset Intelligence catalog data and uploading custom catalog data.

▶ **Distribution point:** The DP holds application source files for clients to access.

▶ **Fallback status point (FSP):** The FSP provides an alternative location for clients to send up status messages during installation when they cannot communicate with their management point.

▶ **Management point:** The MP facilitates communication between a client and site server by storing and providing policy and content location information to the client, and receiving data from the client such as status messages and inventory.

▶ **Mobile device and AMT enrollment point:** This optional role facilitates enrollment of Intel's Active Management Technology (AMT)-based computers and mobile devices.

▶ **Mobile device enrollment proxy point:** This role allows the management of mobile device enrollment through ConfigMgr.

▶ **Out of band service point:** Use this role to allow out of band management of AMT-based computers.

▶ **Reporting services point:** This role is used to integrate reporting through SQL Server Reporting Services and is required if using reports.

▶ **Software update point (SUP):** The SUP provides software update management for ConfigMgr clients by integrating with Windows Server Update Services (WSUS).

▶ **State migration point:** When using OSD, the state migration point holds the user state data for migration to the new operating system.

▶ **System health validator point:** This role runs only on a Network Access Protection (NAP) health policy server. It validates NAP policies from the ConfigMgr client.

Table 2.1 illustrates the site system roles available for each type of site and specifies whether the role is a hierarchy role (H) or site role (S).

TABLE 2.1   Site System Roles

ConfigMgr Roles	CAS	Primary	Secondary	Stand-Alone Primary	Site/ Hierarchy
Application catalog web service and website points		X		X	H
Asset intelligence synchronization point	X			X	H
Distribution point		X	X	X	S
Endpoint protection point	X			X	H

ConfigMgr Roles	CAS	Primary	Secondary	Stand-Alone Primary	Site/Hierarchy
Enrollment point		X		X	S
Enrollment proxy point		X		X	S
Fallback status point		X		X	H
Management point		X	X	X	S
Out of band service point		X		X	S
Reporting services point	X	X		X	H
Software update point	X	X	X	X	S
State migration point		X	X	X	S
System health validator point	X	X	X	X	H

Senders

Senders are installed as a part of the ConfigMgr site server to manage connectivity to other sites, ensuring data integrity and error recovery during transmissions. Senders operate multiple threads in parallel to boost the transfer of data (assuming the sender is not throttled). Changing the concurrent threads and retry settings, displayed in Figure 2.4, are available options for each site.

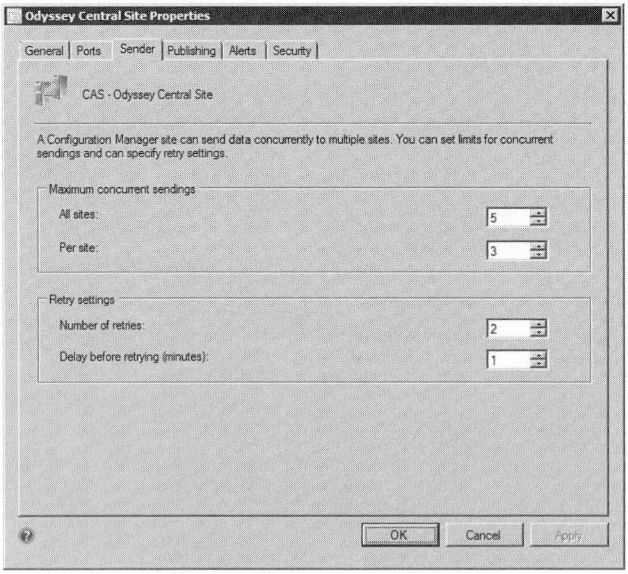

FIGURE 2.4   Changing concurrent threads and retry settings for the sender.

UNDERSTANDING MAXIMUM CONCURRENT THREADS

When the number of connected sites exceeds the maximum concurrent threads default of five, data queues up—waiting for an available thread to free up before sending to the next site.

Addresses

An *address* helps manage the communication between two sites by controlling data flow through schedules and bandwidth rate limits. By default, an address (shown in Figure 2.5) is created from the parent to child and child to parent whenever a site server is added to the hierarchy.

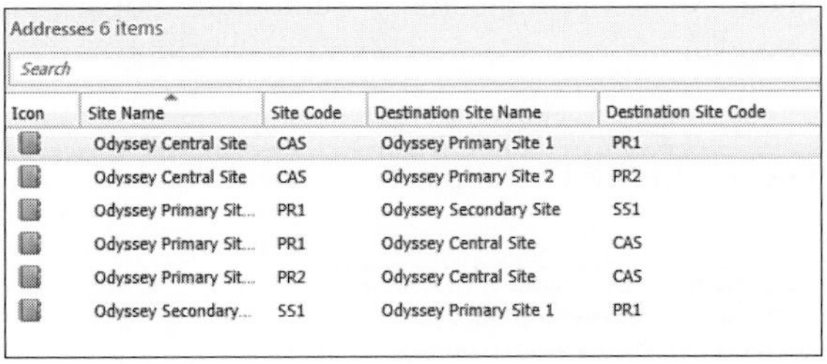

Icon	Site Name	Site Code	Destination Site Name	Destination Site Code
	Odyssey Central Site	CAS	Odyssey Primary Site 1	PR1
	Odyssey Central Site	CAS	Odyssey Primary Site 2	PR2
	Odyssey Primary Sit...	PR1	Odyssey Secondary Site	SS1
	Odyssey Primary Sit...	PR1	Odyssey Central Site	CAS
	Odyssey Primary Sit...	PR2	Odyssey Central Site	CAS
	Odyssey Secondary...	SS1	Odyssey Primary Site 1	PR1

Addresses 6 items · Search

FIGURE 2.5   Addresses used in the Odyssey hierarchy.

Configuration Manager Discovery Types

Knowing the available resources in a network is one of the benefits of having a configuration management system. System Center 2012 Configuration Manager uses a variety of discovery methods to gather resource information. Here are the seven types of discovery methods:

▶ Active Directory Forest

▶ Active Directory Security Group

▶ Active Directory System

▶ Active Directory System Group

▶ Active Directory User

▶ Heartbeat

▶ Network

The Active Directory Forest Discovery method is new with this release and discovers trusted forests, AD sites, and Internet Protocol (IP) subnets. In addition, this discovery method can automatically create AD site boundaries as well as IP subnet boundaries as they are discovered.

AD discovery methods can target specific LDAP paths. The discovery can search for resources recursively down that path if specified to do so. Optionally, ConfigMgr can expand groups and discover members of groups. In certain AD discovery types, you can specify attributes of the discovered resources as part of the information to retrieve.

Polling schedules are defined to run at set intervals. By default, most discovery methods run once a week. AD discovery methods also support delta discovery to help get newly discovered resources into the ConfigMgr database quickly.

TIP: HEARTBEAT DISCOVERY IS THE ONLY REQUIRED DISCOVERY

When a device installs the ConfigMgr client, it sends a heartbeat discovery record bringing the new resource into the database. Other discovery methods are not required and should be enabled with caution. For example, if computer records are not well maintained in AD, enabling any of the AD discoveries will fill the database with records of computers that may not exist.

Figure 2.6 shows the available discovery methods in the Detail pane.

	Active Directory Forest Discovery	Disabled	PR2	Configures settings that Configuration Manager uses to find Active...
	Active Directory Forest Discovery	Disabled	PR1	Configures settings that Configuration Manager uses to find Active...
	Active Directory Forest Discovery	Enabled	CAS	Configures settings that Configuration Manager uses to find Active...
	Active Directory Group Discovery	Disabled	PR2	Configures settings that Configuration Manager uses to find groups...
	Active Directory Group Discovery	Disabled	PR1	Configures settings that Configuration Manager uses to find groups...
	Active Directory System Discovery	Enabled	PR1	Configures settings that Configuration Manager uses to find comput...
	Active Directory System Discovery	Disabled	PR2	Configures settings that Configuration Manager uses to find comput...
	Active Directory User Discovery	Disabled	PR2	Configures settings that Configuration Manager uses to find user ac...
	Active Directory User Discovery	Enabled	PR1	Configures settings that Configuration Manager uses to find user ac...
	Heartbeat Discovery	Enabled	PR2	Configures interval for Configuration Manager clients to periodically...
	Heartbeat Discovery	Enabled	PR1	Configures interval for Configuration Manager clients to periodically...
	Network Discovery	Disabled	SS1	Configures settings and polling intervals to discover resources on th...
	Network Discovery	Disabled	PR2	Configures settings and polling intervals to discover resources on th...
	Network Discovery	Disabled	PR1	Configures settings and polling intervals to discover resources on th...

FIGURE 2.6   Discovery methods as seen in the System Center 2012 Configuration Manager console.

Configuration Manager Agent

The System Center 2012 Configuration Manager agent, known as the *client*, resides on managed systems, servers, and workstations. The client checks in on a defined interval with the ConfigMgr MP to determine if new policies are available. This interval is by default 60 minutes, although you may expand it to 1,440 minutes (24 hours).

You can deploy the client in a number of ways. A common method of deployment is to prestage the client into an operating system image; although many other methods also exist such as manually installing, automatically pushing installs with the ConfigMgr server, using software update, using group policy, and script (logon or machine).

The ConfigMgr client performs a wide range of actions. It is responsible for collecting computer inventory, checking for security update compliance, facilitating remote control, managing the computer's power state, managing application state (installing or uninstalling software), reimaging the computer, and managing computer settings. The client also downloads and applies policies received from the ConfigMgr server and sends up status messages. In addition, the client is intelligent enough to stay bandwidth-sensitive. By utilizing BITS, the ConfigMgr client can examine the available network bandwidth and throttle transfers to minimize any performance impact to the user. The client is discussed further in Chapter 9, "Configuration Manager Client Management."

Configuration Manager Console

Using the System Center framework, the 2012 console features an intuitive interface complete with navigational shortcuts, temporary nodes, and rich search functionality.

The console utilizes a Navigation pane to help navigate, quickly moving the administrator between the following operational groupings:

- ▶ Administration

- ▶ Software Library

- ▶ Monitoring

- ▶ Assets and Compliance

An Outlook-styled ribbon provides access to common administrative tasks. As the object focus changes, the available options on the ribbon bar adapt to the object type, displaying relevant tasks in the console. Figure 2.7 shows an example of the ribbon.

FIGURE 2.7   Ribbon bar with context focused on software updates.

When you select an object that contains details, the Detail pane displays tabs pertinent to the object that help further categorize information to reduce overall clutter. Furthermore, the entire console is security context-aware. By using role-based administration, based on the assigned role, sections and tasks display only if access is granted to that role. In Figure 2.8, the Detail pane displays details and statistics for a security update.

For additional information on security and role-based administration, see Chapter 20, "Security and Delegation in Configuration Manager." The console is discussed in Chapter 8, "The Configuration Manager Console."

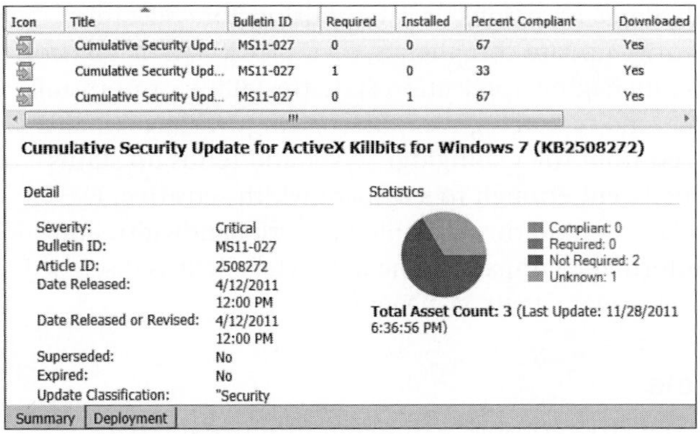

Icon	Title	Bulletin ID	Required	Installed	Percent Compliant	Downloaded
	Cumulative Security Upd...	MS11-027	0	0	67	Yes
	Cumulative Security Upd...	MS11-027	1	0	33	Yes
	Cumulative Security Upd...	MS11-027	0	1	67	Yes

Cumulative Security Update for ActiveX Killbits for Windows 7 (KB2508272)

Detail		Statistics
Severity:	Critical	■ Compliant: 0
Bulletin ID:	MS11-027	■ Required: 0
Article ID:	2508272	■ Not Required: 2
Date Released:	4/12/2011 12:00 PM	■ Unknown: 1
Date Released or Revised:	4/12/2011 12:00 PM	**Total Asset Count: 3** (Last Update: 11/28/2011 6:36:56 PM)
Superseded:	No	
Expired:	No	
Update Classification:	"Security	

Summary | Deployment

FIGURE 2.8   Detail pane-related information for a security update.

Collections

A *collection* is a logical grouping of either users or devices. A collection is used to target a group of objects for management such as security boundaries, client settings, or deployments. During a collection evaluation cycle, if a schedule is specified, the membership of the collection is updated with any new objects that match the criteria specified by a collection rule.

NOTE: COLLECTIONS NOW ARE EITHER USER- OR DEVICE-SPECIFIC

In previous versions of ConfigMgr, a collection could store both users and devices in the same collection.

A collection rule defines the membership of a collection. Here are the different types of rules:

▶ **Direct rule:** An object is added directly to the collection.

▶ **Query rule:** An object is added to the collection based on the result of a query.

▶ **Include rule:** Objects in other collections can be added using this rule.

▶ **Exclude rule:** Objects in other collections can be excluded using this rule.

Collections are discussed further in Chapter 13, "Distributing and Deploying Applications."

Queries

Queries, which are discussed in Chapter 17, "Configuration Manager Queries," request information from the ConfigMgr database. Specifying criteria in a query returns a filtered result of objects. Queries in ConfigMgr are written in WMI Query Language (WQL) and can return results from hundreds of different attribute classes ranging from inventory data to sites. Here is an example of a typical query to return devices with 1GB of RAM or greater:

```
select
    SMS_R_System.Name,
    SMS_G_System_X86_PC_MEMORY.TotalPhysicalMemory
from
    SMS_R_System
    inner join SMS_G_System_X86_PC_Memory on
    SMS_G_System_X86_PC_Memory.ResourceID = SMS_R_System.ResourceId
where
    SMS_G_System_X86_PC_Memory.TotalPhysicalMemory > 1048000
```

Alerts

System Center 2012 Configuration Manager provides near real-time monitoring, with alerts displaying within the console. The alerts are state-based, automatically updating as conditions change, covering technologies such as client health, deployments, software updates, and so on. Figure 2.9 shows a low free space alert with supporting information in the Detail pane.

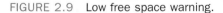

Icon	Alert State	Name	Type	Severity	Postpone Alert
⚠	Active	Warning low free space alert for dat...	Database free space warning	Warning	11/4/2011 4:16 PM
⚠	Active	Warning low free space alert for dat...	Database free space warning	Warning	11/4/2011 9:14 PM
⚠	Active	Warning low free space alert for dat...	Database free space warning	Warning	11/4/2011 3:21 PM

Warning low free space alert for database on site: PR1

General Information

Name:	Warning low free space alert for database on site: PR1
Type:	Database free space warning
Feature Area:	Database free space
Severity:	Warning
Condition:	Generate a warning alert if the free space on disk that contains the database file is greater than 5 GB and less than 10 GB.
Alert Text:	Database files disk space free GB between 10 and 5
Status:	Enabled
Comment:	

Status information

Alert State:	Active
Postpone Alert:	11/4/2011 4:16 PM
Date Created:	11/4/2011 4:16 PM
Closed By:	
Date Modified:	11/4/2011 4:40 PM
Modified By:	System
Occurrence Count:	1

FIGURE 2.9   Low free space warning.

Status System

Roles and components of Configuration Manager generate status messages indicating health. You can examine, query, filter, and configure statuses. Site status gives administrators a broad view of health for each role of the ConfigMgr site such as management points, distribution points, or the ConfigMgr database. Component status gives a detailed view of each component of the site (such as distribution manager, inbox manager, site backup, and so on) and its relative health. Chapter 21, "Backup, Recovery, and Maintenance," discusses the status system.

Status Summarizers

A *status summarizer* changes the status of a component if a threshold is breached. It also manages the interval for summarizing application deployment status and application statistics.

Status Filter Rules

Status filter rules specify criteria for finding certain status messages and taking action such as writing the status to the event log or replicating the status to the parent site.

Status Reporting

Status reporting configuration manages *status reporting* for server and client components. You can modify reporting and logging to increase or decrease the detail level. Logging is turned off by default. Enabling this feature writes the information to the event log.

> **CAUTION: IMPACT OF CHANGING REPORTING AND LOGGING VALUES**
>
> Improperly changing reporting and logging values may cause an unexpected increase in processing requirements of the ConfigMgr site server. Inversely, reducing the reporting level may cause you to miss important status information.

Managing Applications

As users become increasingly more technically savvy, expectations of the user experience when interacting with IT also changes. Previously, it was feasible to manage environments as a collection of computers when there was a one-to-one relationship between a user and a computer. You could rely on each user having only a single device. Users now have multiple devices and tend to be extremely mobile. To support these changes, the concept of software distribution has evolved into a state-based system that has the intelligence of understanding the user-to-device relationship. These concepts are discussed in Chapter 12, "Creating and Managing Applications."

The application model of System Center 2012 Configuration Manager is significantly improved from the software distribution model used in ConfigMgr 2007. For example, the evaluation processing that occurred in ConfigMgr 2007 operated at the collection level with complex queries driving the intelligence behind targeting software to the right devices. In this version, much of that intelligence is held within applications, allowing the evaluation process to occur at the client. Collections are still a necessary part of targeting; however, because the evaluation is no longer at the collection level, complex queries are not required for application management.

Applications

Applications are models of software that contain far more than source files and program execution instructions. Models define the properties of software. They contain the deployment types to support local installations, virtual applications, and mobile applications. Because these models are state-based, the "state" of the application can be detected. This means that ConfigMgr can detect if the software is installed before attempting an installation and detect if the software has been uninstalled and needs to be reinstalled. The inverse is also true if the requirement is to uninstall software.

Application Catalog

System Center 2012 Configuration Manager offers a self-service website where users can browse and request software, called the *Application Catalog*. Users can specify their primary device to ensure that critical software is always installed and available.

Global Conditions and Requirement Rules

Requirement rules are contained in applications and instruct the client to evaluate properties in real time. Before the client even begins to download content, it first runs through the evaluation.

A *global condition* is the foundation of a requirement rule. It can be defined by script, WMI query, registry, and much more. ConfigMgr comes with a handful of defined global conditions such as CPU speed, operating system, total physical memory, AD site, and so on.

For example, say an application requires a minimum of 500MB to install. You could add a requirement rule that uses the provided "Free disk space" global condition. The rule would specify the condition as requiring at least 500MB. When the client is instructed to install the software, it first evaluates its available drive space, and, assuming it meets conditions, installs the software. Figure 2.10 illustrates how a requirement rule is constructed.

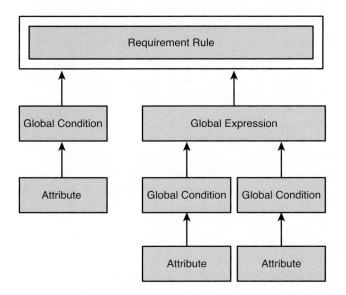

FIGURE 2.10   Requirement rule relationship with global conditions and expressions.

Global Expressions

A *global expression* contains a logical grouping of different global conditions and their associated values. Instead of repeating the same core global conditions in each application, you could create a global expression that defines those core conditions and use it in a requirement rule.

For example, if all the computers in your Finance department were in the same OU, you could create a global expression named **Finance Dept**, require the device belong to the Finance OU, and require the device to be the primary device. Here is what this expression would look like:

```
Organizational unit (OU) One of {OU=Finance,DC=odyssey,DC=com} AND Primary device
➥Equals True
```

Dependencies

As you begin to develop a software library, you might find that one application relies on (is dependent upon) another application. If, for example, an application were dependent on the Internet Explorer 9 browser, a *dependency* could specify that before installing the application, Internet Explorer 9 must first be installed.

Packages

A *package* can contain source files and programs. *Programs* are instructions telling the client how to execute a script; these can range from shell commands to full scripts. In some cases, source files do not need to be included if not required by the executing program. For example, a package to defragment a hard drive would not require any source files because the program calls an existing executable.

Packages were used for software deployment in previous versions of ConfigMgr. System Center 2012 Configuration Manager uses packages predominantly for scripting situations and uses applications for software installations. Packages are described in Chapter 11, "Packages and Programs."

Deployments

A *deployment* is a set of instructions for the ConfigMgr client to evaluate and execute. Deployments typically refer to applications or packages; although, they also include task sequences, software updates, and configuration baselines. Because deployments are state-based, administrators need to deploy to a collection only once, leveraging requirement rules to manage the deployment state.

Available deployment types are constrained based on the type of collection targeted. For example, if the target collection is a user collection, the software update deployment type is not an available option because software updates are targeted to devices.

NOTE: DEPLOYMENT IS A NEW TERM

In earlier versions of ConfigMgr, a deployment was referred to as an advertisement.

Deployment Type

Deployment types exist within applications to facilitate different installation methods. A *deployment type* specifies installation files, commands, and programs, based on established criteria, which are used to install the correct type of software. Here is the information typically held by a deployment type:

▶ Application dependencies

▶ Command for installation

▶ Command for uninstallation

▶ Content location

▶ Detection method for verifying if the application is installed

▶ Installation method

▶ Requirement rules

Here are the deployment types used by System Center 2012 Configuration Manager:

▶ Microsoft Installer (MSI)

▶ Script Installer

▶ Application Virtualization

▶ Mobile Cabinet (CAB)

Software Center

Software Center is a separate user interface installed with the 2012 client, designed to provide the user with a friendlier interaction. With Software Center, a user can

▶ Access the Application Catalog to request software.

▶ View the status of software requests.

▶ Manage settings to define business hours for interaction with software updates.

▶ Define power management settings.

▶ Manage remote control settings.

Content Management

Content management refers to the technologies in ConfigMgr responsible for storing, distributing, and maintaining content.

Distribution Point

A *distribution point*, discussed in Chapter 13, is a site role that stores content and facilitates the transfer of content to devices. A site could contain multiple DPs to help offset a large volume of content transfer to devices or situate content closer to a group of devices reducing impact on traffic over the WAN.

In bandwidth-sensitive locations, content distribution to a DP can be throttled. In addition, you could schedule DPs to transfer content during optimal times of the day. You could also prestage content to the distribution point.

In ConfigMgr 2012, distribution points have been simplified to a single type. Branch DPs, PXE shares, and DP shares no longer exist. However, the DP is now much more robust, supporting additional options to enable it to handle PXE, multicast, and so on.

Distribution Point Groups

A logical grouping of distribution points is a *distribution point group (DPG)*. For ease of administration, you can send content to a DPG instead of individually selecting DPs. This sends the content to all members of the DPG. Any new members of a DPG can automatically receive the distributed content. Figure 2.11 shows how three distribution points are managed as a single distribution group.

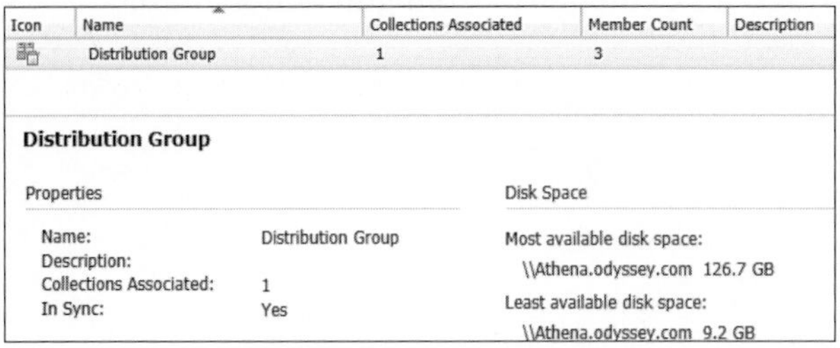

Icon	Name	Collections Associated	Member Count	Description
	Distribution Group	1	3	

Distribution Group

Properties		Disk Space	
Name:	Distribution Group	Most available disk space:	
Description:		\\Athena.odyssey.com 126.7 GB	
Collections Associated:	1	Least available disk space:	
In Sync:	Yes	\\Athena.odyssey.com 9.2 GB	

FIGURE 2.11   Distribution group with three members.

Collections can also be associated to distribution point groups. Whenever content is distributed to the collection, all associated members of the DPG receive the content. See Chapter 13 for additional information.

Content Library

The *content library* is a single instance storage file structure that stores all content on a distribution point. Because it leverages single instance storage, all unique files are stored only once no matter how many times the same file is referenced by a package. Furthermore, even if the file is referenced by multiple packages on the distribution point, it is still stored once potentially bringing reduction of file storage requirements.

NOTE: SMSPKG IS STILL REQUIRED IN CONFIGMGR 2012

Earlier versions of ConfigMgr stored content in SMSPKG folders. Even with a content library, ConfigMgr 2012 relies on the SMSPKG folder when an advertisement for a legacy package is set to the **Run program from distribution point** option.

Software Update Management

Configuration Manager includes the capability to manage client software update compliance, much as you would with WSUS. However, ConfigMgr offers greater capability to control and manage the deployment of software updates, providing a rich console to manage compliance through monitoring and reporting. See Chapter 14, "Software Update Management," for additional information.

Compliance Settings

If you are familiar with desired configuration management (DCM), think of compliance settings in System Center 2012 Configuration Manager as the next generation of DCM. These settings assess the configuration compliance of devices such as the service pack level of the operating system (OS), if applications are installed, whether specific software updates have been applied, and so on. Optionally, some configuration settings can be remediated to return settings back to the correct value thereby providing true configuration drift management. Chapter 10, "Managing Compliance," discusses how this works.

Configuration Item

A *configuration item* is a unit of compliance that defines the required value of a specified setting. It can contain multiple settings and multiple rules to evaluate settings. A configuration item is one of the following four types:

▶ Application configuration item

▶ Operating system configuration item

▶ Software updates configuration item

▶ General configuration item

Configuration Baseline

A *configuration baseline* is a collection of configuration items as well as other configuration baselines, defining an overall compliance status. Configuration baselines can be deployed to collections, instructing the devices in the collection to assess compliance based on the specified conditions. For the configuration baseline to evaluate as compliant, all the included items must be compliant.

BITS

BITS is a component of IIS that manages file transfers in a more advanced manner than a standard copy job. When the ConfigMgr client requests files from BITS, BITS handles the transfer asynchronously, freeing the ConfigMgr client to move on to other tasks. Being bandwidth-sensitive, BITS continuously monitors the available bandwidth during the transfer and throttles the transfer as required. Though BITS can help manage bandwidth, it only monitors the local NIC—it does not monitor the bandwidth of the network.

In addition, BITS supports checkpoint restarts. If a network connection is lost during transfer, BITS stops the transfer and resumes where it left off after the connection is available again.

Software Metering

Software metering is a component of the ConfigMgr client that passively collects software usage statistics based on a defined rule set. Rules are defined either manually or automatically based on ConfigMgr inventory data. The usage statistics from software metering can be used in reports to help administrators understand

- The number of licenses actively in use
- The most active time of day for software use
- The regular users of software
- Whether software is still in use

Figure 2.12 shows the details of software metering information for Notepad usage.

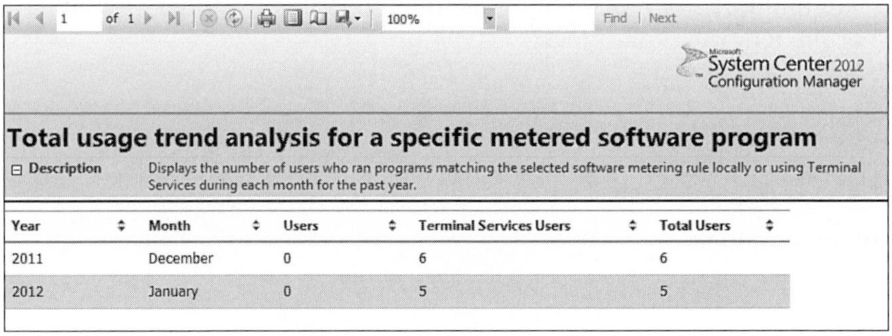

Year	Month	Users	Terminal Services Users	Total Users
2011	December	0	6	6
2012	January	0	5	5

FIGURE 2.12 Software metering trend usage report for Notepad.

Network Access Protection

Maintaining the health of an environment is more than having a secure perimeter. Because any laptop or desktop is a potential carrier for malware payload, it is critical that you ensure your devices are healthy. Network Access Protection (NAP) works on the premise that unhealthy clients, those that fail to meet certain compliance standards, are restricted from accessing the network.

Instead of simply quarantining an unhealthy client, NAP enables remediation of a noncompliant state. ConfigMgr's role is to examine the software update compliance status and deliver the statement of health to the network policy server (NPS), and assuming the client is noncompliant, remediate the client health by installing the appropriate software updates.

BranchCache

BranchCache is a software-based WAN optimization technology designed to reduce bandwidth usage. Environments composed of supported operating systems can leverage the data-caching benefits of BranchCache. ConfigMgr can utilize BranchCache on applications, packages, and task sequences.

Say you deploy an application to a group of computers in a remote office. When Branch-Cache is utilized, the first client to retrieve the application content from a BranchCache-enabled DP caches it locally, making it available to other clients in its local subnet. Whenever another client requests the same content, it refers to the first client for the application; reducing the requirement to traverse the WAN to retrieve the same content. After that client retrieves the content, it also caches the content for other local clients.

Reporting

Reporting in System Center 2012 Configuration Manager is fully integrated into SSRS. Reports and subscriptions can be managed directly from the ConfigMgr console. Outside the console, ConfigMgr uses Report Builder 2.0 (as shown in Figure 2.13) for authoring reports. Visual Studio remains an option for authoring reports, offering the highest flexibility. With System Center 2012, Microsoft introduces an integrated data warehouse to the System Center suite, implemented with Service Manager. See Chapter 18, "Reporting," for additional information.

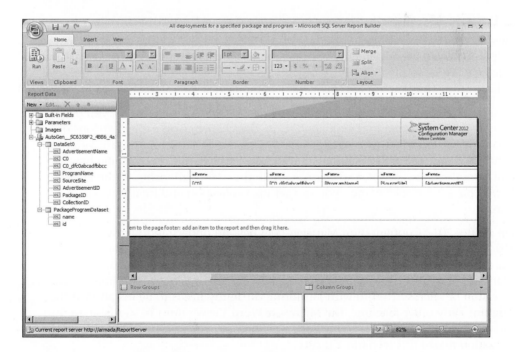

FIGURE 2.13   Using Report Builder 2.0 to edit a ConfigMgr report.

What's New in This Version

System Center 2012 Configuration Manager brings an impressive list of new features and capabilities. The following sections focus on the improvements to existing features, new features, and new concepts.

HETEROGENEOUS MANAGEMENT

Under development but not slated for release with System Center 2012 Configuration Management RTM is cross platform management functionality. Here are some highlights:

- ▶ Built and supported by Microsoft, uses a fully customizable CIMOM server to provide the equivalent of Windows WMI service
- ▶ Anticipated support for Red Hat, SUSE, Solaris, HP-UX, and AIX
- ▶ Subset of ConfigMgr functionality, including inventory with reporting, software distribution, and update management

---

64-Bit Site System Requirements

System Center 2012 Configuration Manager requires an x64 operating system for site system server roles. A notable exception to this is the distribution point that can still run on some x86 operating systems—specifically Windows Server 2003 and Windows 7.

User-Centric Management

System Center 2012 Configuration Manager is written with user-centric management in mind. This is not an abandonment of managing devices; it simply makes the translation of device to user an automatic one. During a deployment, the administrator targets the user while ConfigMgr handles the translation to the device.

If you are a ConfigMgr administrator for any earlier version of the product, you do this every day—just manually. Think about this: The challenge on earlier versions of ConfigMgr is delivering software to a group of users, but before you can start, you must have that list of users! The list is usually a list of devices passed through some type of magical formula (query, script, and so on) to map the user relationship to the device. When you have the device names, you can set up a collection and finally advertise software.

System Center 2012 Configuration Manager goes beyond understanding user device affinity (UDA). It uses UDA in ways that manages software deployment behavior for primary devices and secondary devices. To illustrate this concept, imagine you are deploying an application such as Microsoft Word to a user. While the user is on their primary machine, a full version of Microsoft Word with authoring capability needs to be installed. If the user logs into any other machine, the Microsoft Word Viewer must be available to read authored documents. Integration with other technology such as Microsoft Application Virtualization makes this scenario a reality.

Applications and Packages

System Center 2012 Configuration Manager divides application management into two areas: applications and packages.

A package contains source files (in most cases) and "programs." The programs in this case are commands issued by the ConfigMgr agent. The commands issued are not limited to just software installations, although this is the primary use case. You can also use a package without source files with a program that simply runs a command, such as copying files from one location to another. This still exists in System Center 2012 Configuration Manager, largely for backward compatibility.

Applications, on the other hand, employ a new concept for application management that seeks to understand dependencies and build models around it. This is known as an *application model*. This includes numerous advantages over the legacy deployment method. Features such as global conditions and expressions remove the burden of managing requirements from the query and the installation package. The application model itself holds the requirements of the application instead.

Dependency intelligence has moved to the agent. The agent checks the requirements (OS type, hardware, disk space, and so on) before it handles the installation request. This improves things on several layers:

▶ The processing burden is removed from the site server.

▶ Deployment speed is improved because there is no evaluation required by a query to determine if a computer goes in or out of a collection.

▶ The burden of writing requirements into the installer package is removed.

The application model can also be instructed on how to manage superseded applications and application uninstalls.

Hierarchy Changes

The hierarchy model in ConfigMgr has changed to become a flat, simplified infrastructure, redesigned with additions such as role-based administration that make segmentation of responsibilities easier to manage. In previous versions, the primary site was the boundary that separated the management of objects belonging to the site. There were ways to separate security for workstations and servers, but this is not an easy process and often felt like a hack.

In a multiple-tiered hierarchy, processing of data discovery records (DDRs) is processed one time. After processing the DDR, the data is shared in the hierarchy by database replication. This replication process makes the same data available throughout the entire hierarchy instead of only at higher-level sites (such as a central site) as it was previously.

New Configuration Manager Console

The ConfigMgr console has moved away from the MMC framework and uses the System Center framework, bringing it into alignment with the same look and feel as other components in System Center. The new console has significant usability enhancements such as easier navigation, search functionality, and role-based administration (RBA) support. With RBA support, the console displays only the objects to which an administrative user has access. One neat feature is the new geographical view, which displays a hierarchy over a Bing map along with site status, as shown in Figure 2.14.

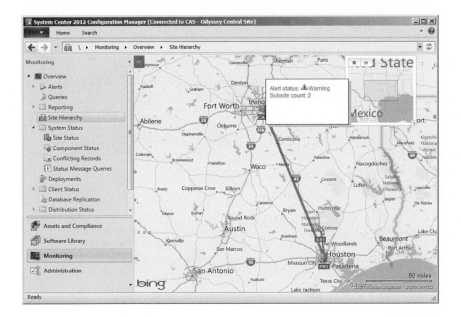

FIGURE 2.14   Site hierarchy on a Bing map.

Enhancements to BITS

BITS continues to provide bandwidth management capabilities. In ConfigMgr 2012, BITS throttling can be managed by client settings. Because client settings can be applied to collections, BITS settings can be selectively managed allowing the management of devices that may operate continuously over suboptimal bandwidth conditions.

Application Catalog

The Application Catalog website point and Application Catalog web services point are new roles that together offer a new end user experience. The Application Catalog is a self-service portal designed to enable users to install available software. If the software installation is of a type requiring approval, the request goes to the administrator first. The interaction with the ConfigMgr client no longer requires complicated backend cycles of collection evaluations and client policy retrieval to initiate the software installation process. Instead, installations happen almost instantaneously.

Extended Mobile Device Management

ConfigMgr 2012 unifies the management of mobile devices into a single pane of glass with the mobile device proxy enrollment point. Mobile device management (MDM) is delivered in an in-depth (client-based) and a light (clientless) model. Building on the in-depth management features of ConfigMgr 2007 R3, secure, over-the-air enrollment is now part of the feature set.

Table 2.2 displays the features available in both types and which devices are supported. *Light management* refers to devices managed through the Exchange ActiveSync Connector, whereas *depth management* includes devices such as Windows Mobile 6.1, Windows Phone 6.5, and Symbian (Nokia). It also includes Windows Mobile 6.0 and Windows CE 6.0, but with limited features.

TABLE 2.2   Available Features in Mobile Device Management

Features	Light	Depth
Inventory	X	X
Over the Air Enrollment		X
Remote Wipe	X	X
Settings	X	X
Software Distribution		X

Managing with depth gives administrators several more options above light management, namely over-the-air enrollment and software distribution. For devices that cannot run the ConfigMgr client, System Center 2012 Configuration Manager includes the Exchange Server connector. This connector uses the Exchange ActiveSync protocol to find and manage devices that connect to an Exchange environment bringing together mobile device management into a single pane of glass. The Exchange Server connector provides the ability to manage settings, collect inventory, and remotely wipe devices. See Chapter 15, "Mobile Device Management," for additional information.

Management Point Enhancements

You now can install more than one management point in the same site. The client automatically selects the best MP based on its capability and proximity. Because a site can have multiple management points, this increases the number of clients each site can support. Having more than one MP also adds a layer of resiliency by providing a redundant site role.

Boundary Changes

In previous versions of the product, the concept of a boundary defined the logical perimeter of a site. Any clients in the boundary of the site would typically become clients of that site. In System Center 2012 Configuration Manager, the boundary is a hierarchy-wide object. When defined, it is available at every site.

With the addition of forest discovery, introduced in the "Discovery" section of this chapter, ConfigMgr can inspect the entire AD forest and read information about all the domains, sites, and subnets. Boundary groups can be created using the discovered information. Having the ability to keep boundary information up to date in an efficient manner is critical to maintaining client saturation and ensuring deployments work smoothly, particularly with roaming clients.

> **NOTE: DIFFERENCE IN BOUNDARIES AND BOUNDARY GROUPS**
>
> Boundaries, in and of themselves, cannot be used for assigning clients to sites or finding content servers. Instead, boundaries are added to boundary groups; the boundary group handles this function.

Fallback Site

If a client does not reside in a defined boundary, typically the client remains unassigned. With the introduction of a fallback site, a default site can be defined for this scenario. Clients that do not reside in a boundary group would simply be assigned to the fallback site.

Centrally Managed Client Settings

System Center 2012 Configuration Manager manages client settings centrally. Any changes committed to the client settings affect all clients in the entire hierarchy. You can apply granularity to client settings by creating custom client settings and then applying them to groups of users or devices by assigning the customized settings to collections.

Role-Based Administration

A much-needed shift in managing security is introduced in this version of ConfigMgr. Role-based administration looks at security and permissions as roles instead of the confusing and complicated use of class and instance rights. By using a combination of security roles and security scopes, you can apply permissions to groups of securable objects by assigning the role to a collection that holds these objects. Because security is available throughout the hierarchy, an administrator with an assigned role can connect their console to any site and expect to receive the same set of permissions assigned to them no matter which site they are in. See Chapter 20 for additional information.

Backup and Recovery

Recovery is completely integrated in the ConfigMgr console, no longer requiring a separate utility. With the benefit of a database-replicated infrastructure, the recovery process can draw from data that is globally available from other sites to help reconstruct the site server. Even without a backup, data loss is minimized because the same data has been replicated elsewhere in the hierarchy. Chapter 21 discusses this in more detail.

Collection Changes

Configuration Manager takes advantage of a feature from previous versions known as *collection limiting* and enforces its use. Any new collection must be limited to some other collection. Collections can no longer contain a mixture of users and devices. Collections update faster because they execute collection member evaluations through an incremental process (by default, every 10 minutes). Because objects are globally available, a collection at any site can contain the objects from the entire hierarchy. System Center 2012 Configuration Manager also adds two new collection rules, Include Collections and Exclude Collections, making it much easier to include or exclude objects from another collection, as shown in Figure 2.15.

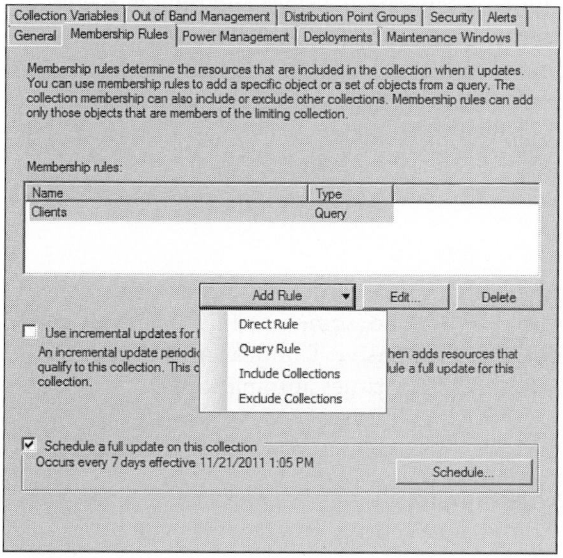

FIGURE 2.15   New collection rules for including and excluding objects from other collections.

Folders

Subcollections no longer exist in ConfigMgr and are replaced with folders. Because the scenario for creating subcollections was usually for organizational purposes, subcollections were removed from the product.

Include and Exclude Rules

Subcollections were also useful in helping to control the expansion of a deployment. That functionality is available and addressed with the addition of include and exclude collection rules. These rules are specifically designed to either include the members of another collection or exclude them in much the same way that a subcollection is used to control deployment.

Client Health Status Enhancements

Over the years, the ConfigMgr client has become more durable and less prone to break. Even with the increased stability, the effort to maintain overall client health is demanding. Dependency on other services such as WMI or BITS is a challenge to overall client health. For example, WMI has a notorious reputation of becoming corrupt. Unfortunately, without those services running, the client cannot operate all its components properly. As if that were not enough, there is the persistent tampering that some "power" users may feel inclined to do. Often, the root cause is not the ConfigMgr client.

Monitoring and Reporting

Reporting on client status is not a novel concept. Client status reporting was introduced with SMS 2003 as an add-on product. It required a separate database and offered reporting only through Microsoft Excel spreadsheets. Client status reporting was provided in ConfigMgr 2007 R2 as well with some additional enhancements such as database integration, status message examination, and native ConfigMgr Web reporting. With System Center 2012 Configuration Manager, client health is completely integrated into the console utilizing new features such as alerting administrators when client health drops below an acceptable threshold.

Remediation

Every seasoned ConfigMgr administrator uses some type of script or process to keep clients running, which is a laborious process to maintain. Even so, some administrators rely on manual remediation, which is time consuming and expensive. ConfigMgr 2012 looks to help solve some of those problems by remediating client issues automatically.

Compliance Settings Changes

System Center 2012 Configuration Manager has improved on what was formerly known as DCM and labeled it *compliance settings*. Compliance settings receive new benefits available in the ConfigMgr 2012 framework such as reporting, monitoring, and enhanced security.

Overall, the ease of creating and managing baselines has improved with additions such as creating configuration items while browsing a "gold" device. Enhanced versioning is included, which allows version-specific configuration items to be included in baselines. After baselines are deployed, dashboards and reporting help easily determine the level of compliance for the collection.

The 2012 product adds a missing feature of managing configuration drift. Automatic remediation of registry and WMI settings can revert a value back if they are detected as changed. Even a scripted discovery can have a corresponding scripted remediation response.

Compliance settings broaden the target range by enabling user, device, and mobile management.

Remote Control Improvements

Remote Control is finally made usable during times when the user is not in front of the device. CTRL-ALT-DEL is supported (again), a popular feature that was lost in ConfigMgr 2007 due to using the Windows Vista RDP, which allows administrators to get to the logon dialog, as shown in Figure 2.16.

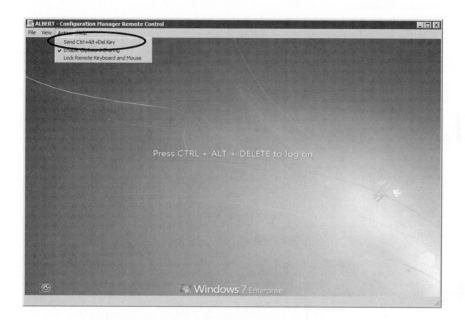

FIGURE 2.16   CTRL-ALT-DEL command is again available.

Hardware Inventory Improvements

Any administrator who has heard of the sms_def.mof file probably understands the tedium and testing required to extend hardware inventory. Extending hardware inventory required understanding the obscure language used to write the SMS_Def.mof file and often required trial and error to manage. In System Center 2012 Configuration Manager, extending hardware inventory is now built into the console (see Figure 2.17) rather than editing a SMS_Def.mof file. Extending classes to inventory is as simple as clicking a box. In addition, you can export and import inventory settings.

CAUTION: TESTING IS STILL REQUIRED

Even though the operation of adding and removing inventory is simplified, the selection may still yield unexpected results. Approach extending hardware inventory with care, and test every new selection.

FIGURE 2.17   New way to configure hardware inventory.

Power Management Improvements

Power management, a feature introduced in ConfigMgr 2007 R3, is included as part of System Center 2012 Configuration Manager. By inventorying the current power settings using hardware inventory and reporting on those settings, ConfigMgr administrators can configure those power management settings that they want enforced to a certain collection of computers. System Center 2012 Configuration Manager includes these changes:

▶ The capability to copy power management settings between collections

▶ Excluding virtual machines from power management

▶ A new report showing computers excluded from power management

▶ The capability to enable users to exclude their computers from power management

Power management is enabled as part of Client Settings in the Administration workspace of the console, and the power management plan is applied to a device collection. Configuration Manager provides three power plans out-of-the-box:

▶ Balanced

▶ High Performance

▶ Power Saver

You can create your own power management plan by selecting Customized Peak or Customized Non-peak, clicking **Edit** in the collection, and giving the customized power management plan a name. Table 2.3 provides an overview of the possible settings, which can be enabled individually or set differently for computers running on battery power and computers that are plugged in.

TABLE 2.3   Possible Settings of a Power Plan

Name	Description
Turn off display after (minutes)	Length of time before the display is turned off for an inactive computer.
Sleep after (minutes)	Length of time before an inactive computer goes to sleep.
Require a password on wakeup	Specify if you want the computer to lock after it wakes up.
Power button action	Specify what the Power button on the computer will do when pressed: sleep, hibernate, shut down, or nothing.
Start menu Power button	Specify what the Power button in the start menu will do: sleep, hibernate, shut down, or nothing.
Sleep button action	Specify what the Sleep button will do: sleep, hibernate, shut down, or nothing.
Lid close action	What occurs when user closes the lid of laptop (sleep, hibernate, shut down, or do nothing).
Turn off hard disk after (minutes)	Length of time before inactive computer turns off hard disk.
Hibernate after (minutes)	Length of time before inactive computer goes into hibernate mode.
Low battery action	Specify computer action when battery is low (sleep, hibernate, shut down, or do nothing).
Critical battery action	Specify computer behavior when battery is at critical level: sleep, hibernate, shut down, or do nothing.
Allow hybrid sleep	Specify if computer should write a hibernate file when it goes to sleep, so settings are preserved in case of power loss during sleep.
Allow standby state when sleeping action	When you set this setting, a computer either can hibernate or turn off.
Required idleness to sleep (%)	Specify the percentage of idle time of the processor required before entering sleep. This option applies only to computers running Windows Vista and not for Windows 7.
Enable Windows wake up timer for desktop computers	You can enable the Windows wake up timer, when the computer wakes up it remains awake for 10 minutes, making it possible to install software or software updates, and for the computer to receive policy from ConfigMgr.

FOR THE SAME COMPUTER

When a computer belongs to multiple collections each having its own power management settings, which power management plan will be applied can be unpredictable. The Computers with Multiple Power Plans report can help identify the computers receiving more than one power plan.

Software Updates Improvements

Software updates in System Center 2012 Configuration Manager has been overhauled to address some of the problems that make managing software updates painful for administrators today: manual cleanup of expired content (including content), lack of auto-approval, expiring superseded updates, poor end user experience, and lack of decent reporting.

Functional Changes

System Center 2012 Configuration Manager adds new features to help ease the administrative burden of patching devices, whether manual or automatic. One such change to the interface is the ability to perform granular searches of software updates. When the right criteria are set, the criteria can be saved to be reused later. Other functional changes include the ability to configure superseded updates so that software updates do not automatically expire after being superseded; this allows the deployment of superseded updates if required.

Automated Administration

Utilizing software update groups and automatic deployment rules, you can automate the entire software update process. Software update groups are state-based. When deployed to a collection, any updates added to the software update group are deployed automatically. Using automatic deployment rules, software updates matching specified criteria can be added to a software update group automatically and pushed out.

Software Center Integration

With Software Center (see Figure 2.18), users have the ability to schedule the most convenient times for software updates to install. By scheduling their business hours, users can instruct the software update process to occur only after hours, minimizing any potential productivity loss. The ConfigMgr client is also intelligent enough to group future deadlines together so that any pending software updates can be installed as a group, minimizing the amount of reboots that would normally be required.

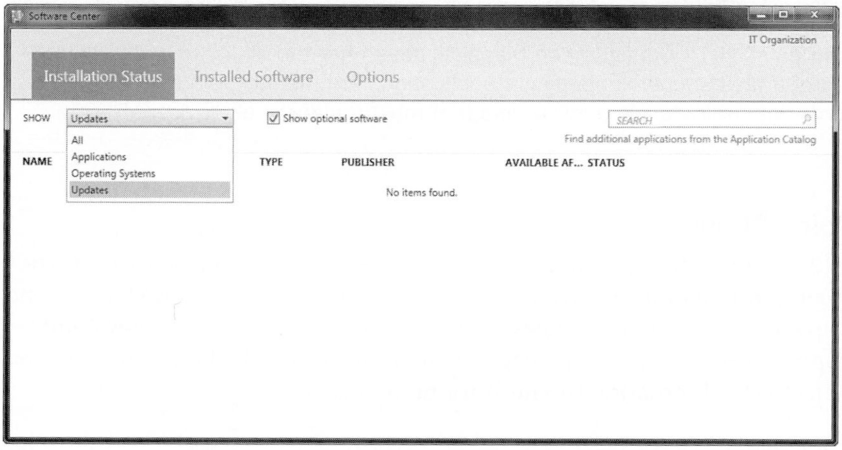

FIGURE 2.18   Software Center showing updates.

Improved End User Experience

Software Center is a new interface for users to request software and manage (to a limited degree) settings for interaction with ConfigMgr, effectively empowering users with self-service. Enabling users to manage themselves relieves some burden for IT administrators by reducing unnecessary support calls.

Content Library

The content library has been added to ConfigMgr as a replacement for traditional file storage. It uses single instance storage to help reduce drive space requirements. The content library of a site holds content for all the DPs.

Operating System Deployment

First released as a feature pack for SMS 2003, Microsoft continues to make enhancements to OSD. Software updates can now be applied using component-based servicing (CBS) to offline Windows imaging (.wim) format images. Pre-execution hooks (now called prestart command files) were supported in ConfigMgr 2007 but cumbersome to implement. The Task Sequence Media Wizard in System Center 2012 Configuration Manager includes the ability to add prestart command files directly to media.

ConfigMgr also provides the ability to manage some of the new features of 2012 such as defining user device affinity and installing applications. New features of the User State Migration Tool (USMT) version 4 have also been included. Chapter 19, "Operating System Deployment," discusses OSD in detail.

NOTE: APPLICATIONS SHOULD NOT BE INSTALLED WITH TASK SEQUENCES

Although System Center 2012 Configuration Manager does offer the ability to install applications as a part of a task sequence, because applications are meant to be state-based, you should reserve this for installing applications that must reside on all devices.

Distribution Point Changes

System Center 2012 Configuration Manager brings much needed improvements to distribution points, ranging from administrative ease to bandwidth control. ConfigMgr 2012 no longer offers multiple distribution point types. As mentioned in the "Distribution Point" section of this chapter, only one type is available, which can be installed on either servers or workstations, effectively eliminating the need for branch DPs.

Managing Distribution Points as Groups

DPs are now managed as a group of DPs, called distribution point groups. This is a manageable unit providing the capability to control content to groups instead of a specific DP, removing the need to target multiple DPs per application or package.

Prestaged Content

Distribution points accept prestaged content to help get files to remote distribution points without the concern of over saturating a WAN link. Unlike ConfigMgr 2007, the tools for managing prestaged content are integrated.

Added Bandwidth Control

Distribution points are now bandwidth-sensitive allowing the same kind of control over bandwidth, throttling, and scheduling common with secondary site servers. BranchCache integration gives administrators far better control over how to distribute content to devices.

PXE Role Integration

Along with multicast, the PXE role, which is a site role in ConfigMgr 2007, is integrated into the distribution point site system role. Instead of a visible Preboot eXecution Environment (PXE) share to store boot images, images are automatically held in the PXE store.

Content Validation

Sometimes packages in ConfigMgr 2007 would go out of sync with the content of the source location. Whenever this happens, the content hash fails to match up properly causing clients to fail installing software because they would not obtain content. System Center 2012 Configuration Manager includes content validation, which can be scheduled or run manually to verify integrity.

System Center 2012 Endpoint Protection Integration

Endpoint Protection, known previously as Forefront Endpoint Protection, has been integrated into System Center 2012 Configuration Manager. Unlike most of the other features of ConfigMgr that are integrated into the ConfigMgr agent, Endpoint Protection uses its own agent.

Endpoint Protection supports the detection and remediation of malware, spyware, and rootkits. A full set of policies scan schedules, definition update source locations, exclusion settings, default actions, and so on. In addition, Endpoint Protection can manage basic Windows Firewall settings such as enabling or disabling the firewall state, blocking incoming connections, and user notification of program blocking.

More information on Endpoint Protection is available in Chapter 16, "Endpoint Protection."

Feature Dependencies of System Center 2012 Configuration Manager

ConfigMgr includes 13 optional roles that can be installed to provide a variety of additional functionality such as distribution points, management points, reporting services points, and so on. Each of these roles may have dependent technologies.

For example, BITS is required for distribution points. Because BITS is a part of IIS, IIS is required for a distribution point. Other roles such as software update points require WSUS because it is a core component to the way patch management works in ConfigMgr. Table 2.4 outlines the dependencies required for each role in System Center 2012 Configuration Manager.

TABLE 2.4   System Role Dependencies in System Center 2012 Configuration Manager

Optional ConfigMgr Roles	.NET Framework (Full Version)	ASP.NET	BITS Server	IIS	NAP Policies	PKI	Remote Differential Compression	SQL Database	.WCF	WebDav	Windows Update Agent	Windows Deployment Services	WSUS
Application Catalog web service point	X	X		X					X				
Application Catalog website point	X	X		X									
Asset Intelligence synchronization point	X												
Distribution point			X	X		X[2]	X						
Endpoint protection point	X							X					
Enrollment point	X			X				X					
Enrollment proxy point	X			X									
Fallback status point				X									
Management point				X		X[2]			X				
Out of band service point	X			X		X							
Reporting services point				X				X					
Software update point						X[2]		X[1]			X		X
State migration point				X									
System health validation point					X								
PXE												X	
Multicast												X	

[1] Required by WSUS

[2] Required for Internet-based management

Summary

The landscape of configuration management continually evolves. To stay current with these changes, System Center 2012 Configuration Manager has evolved as well into a user-centric configuration management platform. While increasing capability and performance, the ConfigMgr infrastructure has simplified to reduce the administrative burden. ConfigMgr is a completely scalable architecture, which can run in complex scenarios as a widely distributed system or as a simple, stand-alone server.

The shift of ConfigMgr to a state-based system introduces a new paradigm of configuration management. Instead of managing software, administrators manage applications with enough intelligence built in to handle most deployment scenarios. When the intent of how to manage the application is set (installed, uninstalled, and so on), the state-based deployment can continuously ensure the application follows those requirements. The new console includes monitoring and alerting views, which relieves the requirement of constantly going out of the console to gather information from queries, reports, spreadsheets, and so on.

A state-based system, with simplified architecture, easier administration, administrative task automation, and a better end user experience, makes System Center 2012 Configuration Manager an evolutionary leap from its past legacy.

2

CHAPTER 3

Looking Inside Configuration Manager

This chapter examines the inner workings of System Center 2012 Configuration Manager (ConfigMgr). It describes the design concepts and working principles of ConfigMgr, along with information about how the product utilizes core Windows technologies, specifically Active Directory (AD) and Windows Management Instrumentation (WMI). It also discusses the various components of ConfigMgr, how they communicate with each other, and how they work together to implement product features. The chapter looks inside the site database, which is the heart of ConfigMgr. It shows how to view the inner workings of ConfigMgr through its status messages and logs, as well as through other tools for viewing database and process activity. This chapter focuses on depth rather than breadth. The authors have chosen some of the most important feature sets and data structures to use as examples throughout the chapter, rather than try to provide a comprehensive account of all ConfigMgr functionality.

If you are simply planning to get ConfigMgr up and running, you may find some of the material in this chapter unessential. However, you will find a basic understanding of the product architecture and knowledge of techniques for viewing the inner working of ConfigMgr invaluable for troubleshooting purposes. If you have not decided whether to extend the AD schema, you will want to review the "Schema Extensions" section of the chapter. The "SQL Replication Crash Course" and "Configuration Manager Database Replication" sections may also be helpful for hierarchy and site system planning. Should you want a deeper understanding of what is going on behind the scenes with ConfigMgr; the material in this chapter can help you grasp the architectural principles of the product and guide you into exploring its inner workings.

Design Concepts

System Center 2012 Configuration Manager (ConfigMgr) delivers a variety of configuration management and system support services via a flexible and distributed architecture. The product utilizes standards-based network protocols and object models for its internal working and interaction with client systems. ConfigMgr components store and use data about ConfigMgr infrastructure and activity, the environment, and managed systems in the site database. Sites in a hierarchy replicate data for effective management across the environment.

ConfigMgr 2012 builds on the core functionality of ConfigMgr 2007 and adds an enhanced feature set that includes native 64-bit code, role-based administration, simplified hierarchy design, user centric management, advanced power management, and client status reporting.

In this latest release of its systems management software, Microsoft emphasizes security and compliance, scalability, and operational simplicity. This chapter focuses on some key architectural principles System Center 2012 Configuration Manager uses to support these goals:

▶ **Integration with core services:** Rather than reproducing existing functionality, ConfigMgr leverages the rich set of services provided by Windows Server and other Microsoft products. This chapter describes some ways ConfigMgr utilizes Active Directory and WMI. Other chapters present various other integration points. For example, Chapter 14, "Software Update Management," describes Windows Server Update Services (WSUS) integration, Chapter 18, "Reporting," discusses the use of SQL Server Reporting Services, and Chapter 19, "Operating System Deployment," describes Windows Deployment Services integration.

▶ **Distributed database:** System Center 2012 Configuration Manager has replaced many of the inboxes used in ConfigMgr 2007 and previous versions of Systems Management Server (SMS) with SQL replication. Database replication provides efficient communications and eliminates redundant processing.

▶ **Flexible distributed component architecture:** System Center 2012 Configuration Manager, like ConfigMgr 2007, implements specific features and functionality as individual threads within the executive service. These threads can run on a single server or across many servers. ConfigMgr 2012 improves on communication between components by replacing many file based exchanges with database updates. This provides high scalability and allows administrators to adapt their deployment to their environment.

ConfigMgr leverages key elements of the Windows platform to implement much of its functionality. The two most important Windows components are AD and WMI. The next sections look in depth at how ConfigMgr uses these technologies.

Active Directory Integration

Active Directory is the central information store used by Windows Server to maintain entity and relationship data for a wide variety of objects in a networked environment. AD provides a set of core services, including authentication, authorization, and directory services. ConfigMgr takes advantage of the AD environment to support many of its features. For information about Active Directory in Windows Server 2008 R2, see http://www.microsoft.com/windowsserver2008/en/us/active-directory.aspx.

ConfigMgr can use AD to publish information about its sites and services, making it easily accessible to Active Directory clients. To take advantage of this capability, you must extend the AD schema to create classes of objects specific to ConfigMgr. Although implementing ConfigMgr does not require extending the schema, it is required for certain ConfigMgr features. Extending the schema also greatly simplifies ConfigMgr deployment and operations. The "Schema Extensions" section discusses extending the AD schema. Chapter 4, "Architecture Design Planning," discusses the benefits and feature dependencies of the extended schema.

Schema Extensions

All objects in AD are instances of classes defined in the AD schema. The schema provides definitions for common objects such as users, computers, and printers. Each object class has a set of attributes that describes members of the class. As an example, an object of the computer class has a name, operating system, and so forth. Additional information about the AD schema is available at http://msdn.microsoft.com/en-us/library/ms675085.aspx.

The schema is extensible, allowing administrators and applications to define new object classes and modify existing classes. Using the schema extensions provided with Configuration Manager eases administration of your ConfigMgr environment. The ConfigMgr schema extensions are relatively low risk, involving only a specific set of classes not likely to cause conflicts. Nevertheless, you need to test any schema modifications before applying them to your production environment.

> **NOTE: SCHEMA EXTENSIONS AND CONFIGMGR 2012 UPDATES**
>
> There are no changes to the schema extensions from ConfigMgr 2007 to 2012. If you extended the Active Directory schema for ConfigMgr 2007, you do not need to run the System Center 2012 Configuration Manager schema extensions.

After you extend the AD schema and perform the other steps necessary to publish site information to AD, ConfigMgr sites can publish information to AD.

The next sections describe the process for extending the schema and configuring sites to publish to AD, as well as the AD objects and attributes created by the schema extensions.

Tools for Extending the Schema

You can extend the schema in either of two ways:

▶ Running the ExtADSch.exe utility from the ConfigMgr installation media

▶ Using the LDIFDE (Lightweight Data Interchange Format Data Exchange) utility to import the ConfigMgr_ad_schema.ldf LDIF file

To use all the features of ConfigMgr 2012, you must use Active Directory with Windows Server 2003 or later; Windows 2000 domains are supported with reduced functionality; most notably, Active Directory Forest Discovery does not work with Windows 2000 domains. If you are extending the schema on a Windows 2000 domain controller, you must use the LDIF file.

Using ExtADSch   Using ExtADSch.exe is the simplest way to extend the schema and until ConfigMgr 2007 was the only way to extend the schema. ExtADSch.exe creates the log file extadsch.log, located in the root of the system drive (%*systemdrive*%), which lists all schema modifications it has made and the status of the operation. Following the list of attributes and classes that have been created, the log should contain the entry `Successfully extended the Active Directory schema`.

Using LDIFDE   LDIFDE is a powerful command-line utility for extracting and updating directory service data on Active Directory servers. LDIFDE provides command-line switches, allowing you to specify a number of options, including some you may want to use when updating the schema for ConfigMgr. Table 3.1 includes the options that you are most likely to use.

TABLE 3.1   LDIFDE Command-Line Switches and Descriptions

Switch	Description
-i	Turns on Import Mode. Required for updating the schema.
-f	Filename. (Used to specify the location of the ConfigMgr_ad_schema.ldf file.)
-j	Log file location.
-v	Turns on Verbose Mode.
-k	Ignore Constraint Violation and Object Already Exists errors. (Use with caution. May be useful if the schema is previously extended for ConfigMgr.)

The options vary slightly, depending on the Windows Server version you are running. You can see a complete listing of LDIFDE syntax by entering this command:

```
ldifde /?
```

You can also find detailed information about using LDIFDE at http://technet.microsoft.com/en-us/library/cc731033.aspx. Here is an example of a typical command to update the schema for ConfigMgr:

```
ldifde -i -f ConfigMgr_ad_schema.ldf -v -j SchemaUpdate.log
```

The verbose logging available with LDIFDE includes more detail than the log file generated by ExtADSch.exe. The ConfigMgr_ad_schema.ldf file allows you to review all intended changes before they are applied. You can also modify the LDF file to customize the schema extensions. As an example, you can remove the sections for creating classes and attributes that already exist as an alternative to using the –k switch referred to in Table 3.1.

CAUTION: BE CAREFUL WHEN EDITING THE LDF FILE

Do not attempt to edit the LDF file unless you have a thorough understanding of LDF, and remember to test all modifications before applying them to your production environment.

Extending the Schema

Each AD forest has a single domain controller with the role of schema master. All schema modifications are made on the schema master. To modify the schema, you must log on using an account in the forest root domain that is a member of the Schema Admins group.

NOTE: ABOUT THE SCHEMA ADMINS GROUP

The built-in Schema Admins group exists in the root domain of your forest. Normally there should not be any user accounts in the Schema Admins group. Only add accounts to Schema Admins temporarily when you need to modify the schema. Exercising this level of caution will protect the schema from any accidental modifications.

The ConfigMgr schema modifications create four new classes and 14 new attributes used with these classes. Here is what the created classes represent:

▶ **Management points:** Clients can use this information to find a management point.

▶ **Roaming boundary ranges:** Clients can use this information to locate ConfigMgr services based on their network location.

▶ **Server locator points (SLPs):** ConfigMgr 2007 clients can use this information to find a SLP. This class is created but it is not used in System Center 2012 Configuration Manager. SLP functionality is now integrated into the management point and the SLP no longer exists as a separate site system role.

▶ **ConfigMgr sites:** Clients can retrieve important information about the site from this AD object.

REAL WORLD: TIPS AND TECHNIQUES ABOUT CHANGING THE SCHEMA

Exercise caution when planning any changes to the AD schema, particularly when making modifications to existing classes because this could affect your environment.

When you modify the schema, you should take the schema master offline temporarily while you apply the changes. Regardless of the method used to extend the schema, review the logs to verify that the schema extensions were successful before bringing the schema master back online. This way, if there is a problem with the schema modifications, you can seize the schema master role on another domain controller and retain your original schema!

Before actually extending the schema for System Center 2012 Configuration Manager, run the `dcdiag` and `netdiag` command-line tools, which are part of the Windows Support Tools. These tools validate that all domain controllers (DCs) are replicating and healthy. Because it may be difficult to validate the output of these tools, you can output the results to a text file using the following syntax:

```
Ddcdiag >c:\dcdiag.txt
```

Search the output text file for failures and see if any domain controllers are having problems replicating. If any failures are present, do not update the schema. Upgrading the schema when domain controllers are not healthy or replicating correctly will cause them to be orphaned as AD is revved to a higher version. The machine will then need to be manually and painfully cleaned out of AD.

Viewing Schema Changes

If you are new to ConfigMgr and are extending the schema and curious about the details of the new classes, the Schema Management MMC snap-in enables you to view their full schema definitions. Before adding the snap-in to the management console, you must install it by running the following command from the command prompt:

```
regsvr32 schmmgmt.dll
```

> **TIP: REGSVR32 REQUIRES ADMINISTRATIVE RIGHTS**
>
> On domain controllers running Windows 2008 or Windows 2008 R2 Server, you may need to launch the command prompt using the **Run as Administrator** option to register the schema management dll.

After installing the snap-in, perform the following steps to add Schema Management to the MMC:

1. Select **Start**, choose **Run**, and then enter **MMC**.

2. Choose **Add/Remove snap-in** from the File menu of the console.

3. Click the **Add** button and then choose **Active Directory Schema**.

4. Choose **Close** and then click **OK** to complete the open dialog boxes.

The left pane of the schema management tool displays a tree control with two main nodes—classes and attributes. If you expand out the classes node, you will find the following classes defined by ConfigMgr:

▶ mSSMSManagementPoint

▶ mSSMSRoamingBoundaryRange

▶ mSSMSServerLocatorPoint

▶ mSSMSSite

Clicking a class selects it and displays the attributes associated with the class in the right pane. The list of attributes for each class includes many attributes previously defined in AD, in addition to those attributes specifically created for System Center 2012 Configuration Manager. You can right-click a class and choose **Properties** to display its property page. For example, Figure 3.1 shows the general properties of the mSSMSSite class. For an explanation of these properties, click the **Help** button on the Properties page.

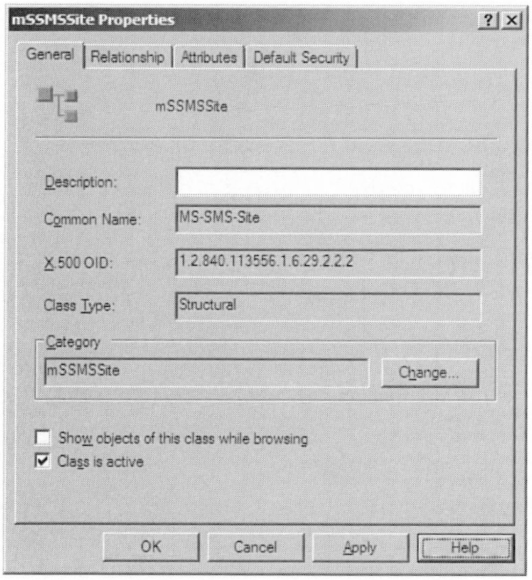

FIGURE 3.1   General properties of the schema class representing ConfigMgr sites.

You can see the 14 ConfigMgr attributes under the Attributes node in the schema management console. The names of each of these attributes start with *mS-SMS*. You can right-click an attribute and choose **Properties** to display its property page. Figure 3.2 shows the properties of the mS-SMS-Capabilities attribute.

TIP: VERIFY SCHEMA EXTENSIONS WHEN EXTENDING THE SCHEMA

ExtADSch.log file is created at the root of the system drive on the computer that the extensions were installed from. You should check this log for failures. Seeing Event ID 1137 in the Directory Service event log alone does not confirm the schema was extended properly; several experiences in the field have found failures in the logfile in what seemed to be a successful schema extension.

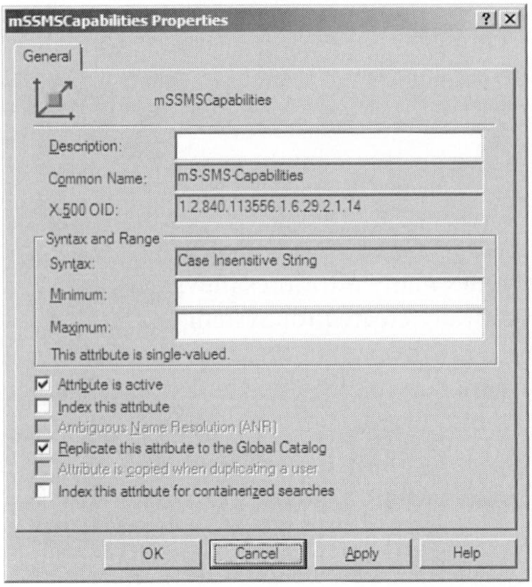

FIGURE 3.2   General properties of the schema attribute representing site capabilities.

Additional Tasks

After extending the schema, you must complete several tasks before ConfigMgr can publish the objects it will use to Active Directory:

▶ **Create the System Management container where the ConfigMgr objects will reside in AD:** If you previously extended the schema for ConfigMgr 2007, the System Management container will already exist. Each domain publishing ConfigMgr data must have a System Management container.

▶ **Set permissions on the System Management container:** Setting permissions allows your ConfigMgr site servers to publish site information to the container.

▶ **Configure your sites to publish to AD:** You can specify one or more AD forests to which each site will publish. Publishing to a forest other than the sites server's local forest requires a cross-forest trust.

The next sections describe these tasks.

Creating the System Management Container   You can use the ADSIEdit MMC tool to create the System Management AD container. If you do not already have ADSIEdit installed, you can install the tool yourself.

On Windows Server 2008, add ADSIEdit using Server Manager. Configuring the domain controller server role automatically adds ADSIEdit to the Administrative Tools program group.

To create the System Management container from ADSIEdit, perform the following steps:

1. Right-click the Root ADSI Edit node in the tree pane, select **Connect to**, and then click **OK** to connect to the default name context.

2. Expand the default name context node in the tree pane. Then expand the node showing the distinguished name of your domain (this will begin with DC=<*domain*>) and right-click **CN=System node**.

3. Select **New** and then choose **Object**.

4. Select **Container** in the Create Object dialog box and click **Next**.

5. Enter the name **System Management** and then click **Next** and **Finish**, completing the wizard.

Figure 3.3 shows ADSIEdit with the tree control expanded to the CN=System node and the Create Object dialog box displayed.

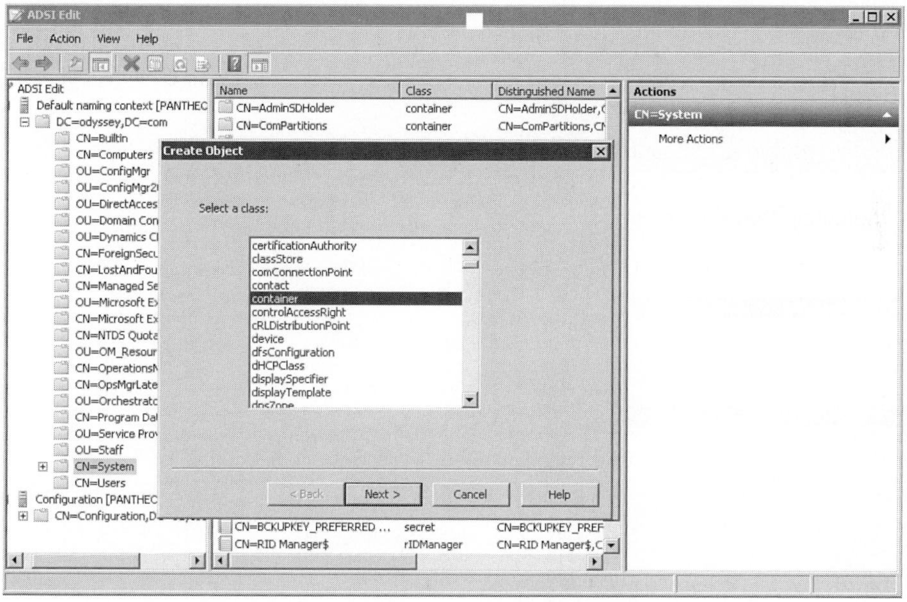

FIGURE 3.3   Using ADSIEdit to create the System Management container.

Setting Permissions on the System Management Container   You can view the System Management container and set permissions on it using the Active Directory Users and Computers (ADUC) utility in the Windows Server Administrative Tools menu group. After launching ADUC, enable the **Advanced Features** option from the View menu. You can then expand out the domain partition and System container to locate System Management.

By default, only certain administrative groups have the rights required to create and modify objects in the System Management container. For security reasons, you should create a new group and add ConfigMgr site servers to it, rather than adding them to the built-in administrative groups. Perform the following steps to grant the required access to the ConfigMgr site server security group:

1. Right-click the System Management container, choose **Properties**, and then select the Security tab.

2. Click the **Add** button, and select the group used with your ConfigMgr site servers, as shown in Figure 3.4.

3. Check the box for **Full Control**, as displayed in Figure 3.5, and choose **OK** to apply the changes.

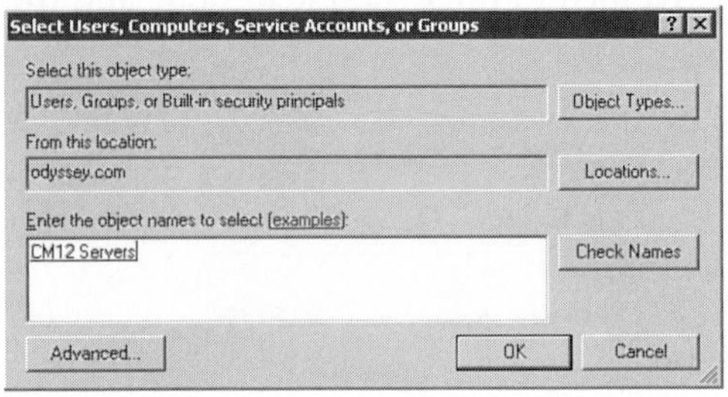

FIGURE 3.4   Selecting the Site server security group.

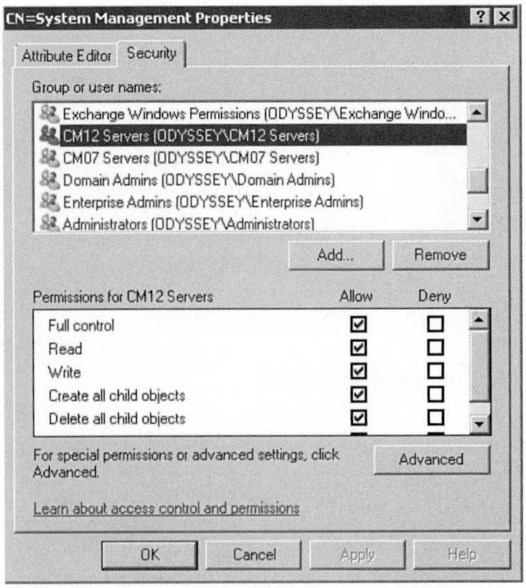

FIGURE 3.5   Assigning permissions to the System Management container.

Configuring Sites to Publish to Active Directory   Perform the following steps to configure a ConfigMgr site to publish site information to AD:

1. In the ConfigMgr 2012 console, select the Administration workspace.

2. Expand **Site Configuration -> Sites**. In the Sites pane, highlight the desired site, and click **Properties** on the ribbon bar.

3. Select the **Publishing** tab, and then select the check box next to each forest to which the site will publish, as shown in Figure 3.6.

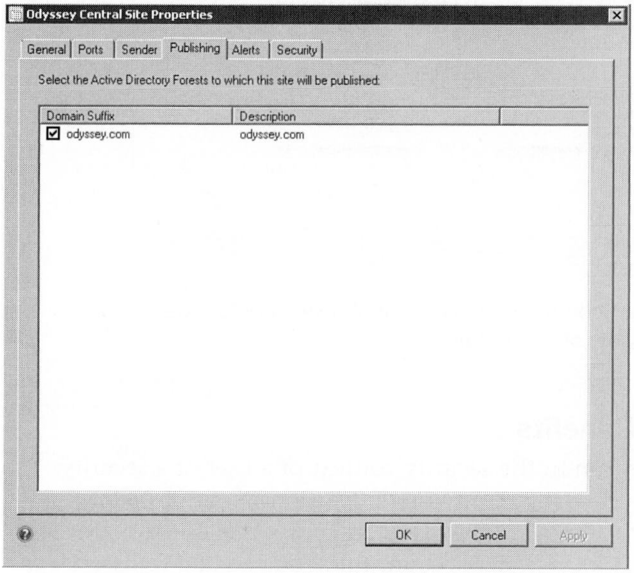

FIGURE 3.6   Configuring a site to publish to AD.

After extending the schema and taking the other steps necessary to enable your sites to publish to AD, you should see the ConfigMgr objects displayed in the System Management container. Figure 3.7 shows the ConfigMgr objects viewed in Active Directory Users and Computers.

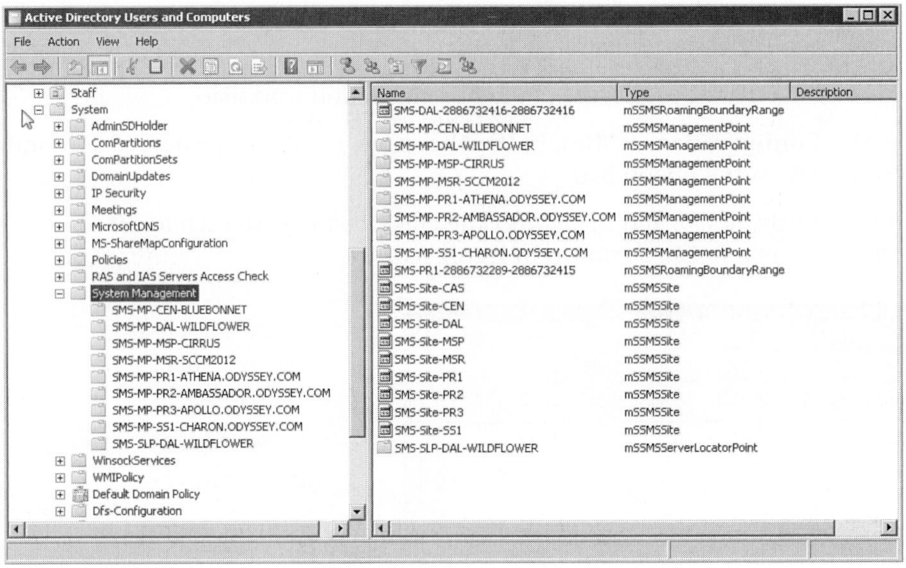

FIGURE 3.7   The System Management container displayed in Active Directory Users and Computers. You can use ADSIEdit to view object details.

Additional Active Directory Benefits

In an AD environment, all processes run in the security context of a user or a security context supplied by the operating system. System Center 2012 Configuration Manager uses Active Directory to authenticate administrative users and authorize user account for administrative roles. Each system has a computer account that you can add to user groups and grant access to resources. ConfigMgr makes extensive use of system and computer accounts to connect securely to network services and client systems, as well as providing security contexts for its internal operations. Using system accounts greatly simplifies administration. You can use additional AD accounts to supplement the available system accounts. Chapter 20, "Security and Delegation in Configuration Manager," discusses authentication, access control, and accounts used in ConfigMgr.

Here are other ways ConfigMgr can take advantage of AD:

▶ Discovering information about your environment; including the existence of potential client systems, users, and groups. Chapter 4 discusses how you can use this information to plan user-centric management. Before implementing AD discovery methods, evaluate your AD data to ensure it is reliable and up to date. Importing obsolete records for users and computers that no longer exist or have changed may cause problems with various ConfigMgr operations. Chapter 9, "Configuration Manager Client Management," provides details about configuring the discovery process.

▶ Assigning and installing clients using group policy, also described in Chapter 9.

▶ Using certificates and certificate settings deployed through AD. For example, if you use the System Center Updates Publisher (SCUP) to deploy custom software updates, you can use AD to deploy the required certificates to the trusted store on client computers.

A WMI Primer

If the SQL Server database is the heart of ConfigMgr, consider WMI its lifeblood. WMI has been the core management infrastructure for all Windows desktop and server operating systems beginning with Windows 2000. WMI is the Windows implementation of Web-Based Enterprise Management (WBEM). WBEM is a set of standards intended to provide the basis for cross-platform interoperability of technologies to exchange management data and access management interfaces across distributed computing environments.

The Distributed Management Task Force (DMTF) supports WBEM. This group is an industry consortium created to promote standardization and integration of enterprise and Internet management technology. For more information about WBEM in general and the DMTF, see http://www.dmtf.org/standards/wbem. Although much of the architectural material in this chapter is common to all implementations of WBEM, the next sections exclusively focus on WMI and its role in ConfigMgr:

▶ **WMI architecture:** This includes describing the WMI feature set, reviewing the major components of WMI, and discussing how they interact.

▶ **WMI object model:** The WMI object model and its implementation are discussed, with several tools you can use to manage WMI and look into its inner workings.

▶ **ConfigMgr use of WMI:** Configuration Manager's use of WMI is discussed, with examples of how you can look inside ConfigMgr through its WMI interfaces.

WMI Feature Set and Architecture

WMI makes it much easier to write programs and scripts that interact with local resources on Windows systems. WMI serves as an abstraction layer between management applications and scripts and the physical and logical resources they manage. WMI exposes managed resources through a COM (Component Object Model) API (application programming interface). Programs written in C/C++ can call these resources directly, or you can access them through intermediate layers by applications such as scripts, Windows forms, or web forms. WMI presents a consistent and extensible object model to represent a wide variety of system, network, and other resources. Here are some examples of what you can do with WMI:

▶ Rename the built in administrator account.

▶ Compile a list of printers that support color printing.

▶ Receive an alert each time a new device connects to a USB port.

Using an object model removes much of the complexity that would otherwise be required to access and manipulate these resources. Some examples of resources you can manage through WMI include hardware devices, running processes, the Windows file system and registry, and applications and databases.

Here are several ways you can invoke WMI services:

▶ Locally on a machine

▶ Remotely through a DCOM (Distributed COM) connection

▶ Remotely using a WS-Management (Web Services for Management) connection

WS-Management is a SOAP (Simple Object Access Protocol)–based specification published by the DMTF. SOAP is a standard for invoking objects remotely over an HTTP (Hypertext Transfer Protocol) or HTTPS (Hypertext Transfer Protocol over Secure Socket Layer) connection. The main advantage of SOAP is that it works across many existing network firewalls without requiring additional configuration. You can find a complete description of WS-Management and related specifications at http://www.dmtf.org/standards/wsman.

WMI supports requests from management applications to

▶ Retrieve or modify individual data items (properties) of managed objects.

▶ Invoke actions (methods) supported by managed objects.

▶ Execute queries against the data set of managed objects.

▶ Register to receive events from managed objects.

ABOUT WMI QUERY LANGUAGE

WMI provides its own query language that allows you to query managed objects as data providers. WMI Query Language (WQL) is essentially a subset of SQL (Structured Query Language) with minor semantic changes. Unlike SQL, WQL does not provide statements for inserting, deleting, or updating data and does not support joins. WQL does have extensions that support WMI events and other features specific to WMI. WQL is the basis for ConfigMgr queries, whereas SQL is used for ConfigMgr reports. Queries and reports are discussed in Chapters 17, "Configuration Manager Queries," and 18, respectively.

One important advantage of WQL is that a WQL query can return WMI objects as well as specific properties. Because management applications such as the ConfigMgr console interact with WMI objects, WQL queries can return result sets that you can use within the ConfigMgr infrastructure. For example, ConfigMgr collections are based on WQL queries. For more information about WQL, see http://msdn.microsoft.com/en-us/library/aa394606.aspx.

Here is how WMI handles requests from management applications:

1. Management applications submit a request to the WMI infrastructure, which passes the request to the appropriate provider. The next section describes WMI providers.

2. The provider then handles the interaction with the actual system resources and returns the resulting response to WMI.

3. WMI passes the response back to the calling application. The response may be actual data about the resource or the result of a requested operation.

Figure 3.8 shows the basic data flow in WMI.

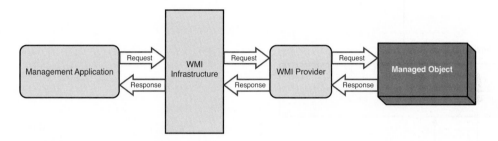

FIGURE 3.8   How WMI accepts a request from a management application and returns a response from a managed resource.

WMI Providers

WMI providers are analogous to device drivers in that they know how to interact with a particular resource or set of resources. In fact, many device drivers also act as WMI providers. Microsoft supplies several built-in providers as part of Windows, such as the Event Log provider and File System provider. You will see providers implemented in the following ways:

▶ As DLLs (Dynamic Link Libraries)

▶ As Windows processes and services

Just as the WMI infrastructure serves management applications through a COM interface, providers act as COM servers to handle requests from the WMI infrastructure. When a provider loads, it registers its location and the classes, objects, properties, methods, and events it provides with WMI. WMI uses this information to route requests to the proper provider.

The WMI Infrastructure

Figure 3.9 displays the main logical components of the WMI infrastructure. The core of the WMI infrastructure is the Common Information Model Object Manager (CIMOM), described in the "Inside the WMI Object Model" section. CIMOM brokers requests between management applications and WMI providers, and communicates with management applications through the COM API, as described earlier in the "WMI Feature Set and Architecture" section. CIMOM also manages the WMI repository, an on-disk database used by WMI to store certain types of data. Beginning with Windows XP, WMI also includes an

XML (eXtensible Markup Language) encoder component, which management applications and scripts can invoke to generate an XML representation of managed objects.

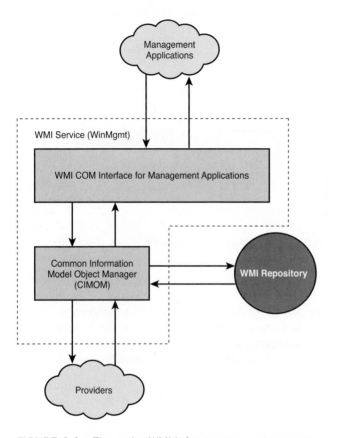

FIGURE 3.9   The major WMI infrastructure components.

Most files used by WMI are stored on the file system by default under the %*windir*%\ System32\Wbem folder. The WMI repository is a set of files located by default under %*windir*%\System32\Wbem\Repository. The exact file structure varies slightly depending on the Windows version. WMI uses a customized version of the Jet database engine to access the repository files.

The executable containing the WMI service components is Winmgmt.exe. The physical implementation of the WMI infrastructure varies, depending on the version of Windows. In Windows 2000, Winmgmt runs as a separate Windows service. In this implementation, WMI providers are loaded into the Winmgmt process space, which means that a fault in one provider can crash the entire WMI process. This can cause repository corruption, which is a common cause of WMI problems in earlier Windows implementations. Using a single process space also means that providers share the security context of the Winmgmt process, which is generally the highly privileged Local System account. Newer versions of Windows achieve greater process isolation by loading providers into one or more instances of WMIPrvse.exe. All WMI service components beginning with Windows XP run inside shared service host (SVCHOST) processes. Beginning with Windows Vista, Microsoft introduced several significant enhancements in WMI security and stability, including the ability to specify process isolation levels, security contexts, and resource limits for provider instances. These enhancements are also available as an update for Windows XP and Windows Server 2003 systems at http://support.microsoft.com/kb/933062.

Configuration parameters for the WMI service are stored in the system registry subtree `HKEY_LOCAL_MACHINE\Software\Microsoft\WBEM`. The keys and values in this section of the registry specify WMI file locations, logging behavior, the list of installed provider, the default namespace for script, and other WMI options. You will rarely need to edit these options directly. As with any modification of the registry, you should use extreme caution as changes to the registry can destabilize your system.

WMI also provides detailed logging of its activities. Prior to Windows Vista, log entries were written in plain text to files in the %*windir*%\System32\Wbem\logs folder. In Windows Vista, Windows 7, and Windows Server 2008 and 2008 R2, most of these logs no longer exist, and Windows Event Tracing makes log data available to event data consumers, including the Event Log Service. By default, event tracing for WMI is not enabled. The "Managing WMI" section discusses logging and event tracing options for WMI and describes how to configure tracing for WMI.

Some WMI providers, such as the ConfigMgr provider, also log their activity. The "Viewing Detailed Process Activity" section discusses logging by the ConfigMgr WMI provider.

Inside the WMI Object Model

Understanding the WMI object model is essential if you will write programs or scripts that interact with WMI. It is also helpful for ConfigMgr administrators who want a better understanding of ConfigMgr objects such as collections and client settings. The DMTF's Common Information Model (CIM) is the basis for the WMI object model. CIM defines a core model that provides the basic semantics for representing managed objects and describes several common models representing specific areas of management, such as systems, networks, and applications. Third parties develop extended models, which are platform platform-specific implementations of common classes. You can categorize the class definitions used to represent managed objects as follows:

▶ Core classes represent general constructs that are applicable to all areas of management. The `Managed Element` class is the most basic and general class and is at the root of the CIM class hierarchy. Other examples of core classes include

    ▶ `Component`

    ▶ `Collection`

    ▶ `CIM_StatisticalInformation`

Core classes are part of the core model and are the basic building blocks from which other classes are developed.

► Common classes represent specific types of managed objects. Common classes are generalized representations of a category of objects, such as a computer system or an application. These classes are not tied to a particular implementation or technology.

► Extended classes are technology-specific extensions of common classes, such as a Win32 computer system or ConfigMgr.

WMI classes support inheritance, meaning you can derive a new class from an existing class. The derived class is often referred to as a child or subclass of the original class. The child class has a set of attributes available to it from its parent class. Inheritance saves developers the effort of needing to create definitions for all class attributes from scratch. Developers of a child class can optionally override the definition of an inherited attribute with a different definition better suited to that class. A child class can also have additional attributes not inherited from the parent.

Typically, core and common classes are not used directly to represent managed objects. Rather, they are used as base classes from which other classes are derived. The "Looking Inside the CIMV2 Namespace" section of this chapter presents an example of how a class inherits attributes from its parent class.

A special type of WMI class is the `System` class. WMI uses system classes internally to support its operations. They represent things such as providers, WMI events, inheritance metadata about WMI classes, and more.

WMI classes support three types of attributes:

► *Properties* are the characteristics of the managed objects, such as the name of a computer system or the current value of a performance counter.

► *Methods* are actions that a managed object can perform on your behalf. As an example, an object representing a Windows service may provide methods to start, stop, or restart the service.

► *Associations* are actually links to a special type of WMI class, an association class, which that represents a relationship between other objects. The "Looking Inside the CIMV2 Namespace" section examines the associations that link a file share security descriptor to the share and to the security principals specified in its access control lists.

You can also modify WMI classes, properties, and methods by the use of qualifiers. A qualifier on a class may designate it as abstract, meaning the class is used only to derive other classes and no objects of that class will be created. Two important qualifiers designate data as static or dynamic:

► **Static data:** Supplied in the class or object definition and stored in the WMI repository

► **Dynamic data:** Accessed directly through the provider and represents live data on the system

The CIM specification also includes a language for exchanging management information. The Managed Object Format (MOF) provides a way to describe classes, instances, and other CIM constructs in textual form. In WMI, MOF files are included with providers to register the classes, properties, objects, and events they support with WMI. The information in the MOF files is compiled and stored to the WMI repository. Examples of information in MOF format are included in the next section.

TIP: ACRONYM USAGE

Chapter 1, "Configuration Management Basics," discussed the Microsoft Operations Framework, often referred to as MOF. There is no relationship between the Microsoft Operations Framework and Managed Object Format, although both use the same acronym.

Namespaces organize WMI classes and other elements. A namespace is a container, much like a folder in a file system. Developers can add objects to existing namespaces or create new namespaces. The `Root` namespace defines a hierarchy organizing the namespaces on a system. The "Managing WMI" section describes the WMI Control tool, which allows you to specify the default namespace for connections to WMI. Generally, the default namespace will be `Root\CIMV2`. This namespace defines most of the major classes for Windows management. The next section looks at several classes in that namespace. Because ConfigMgr is all about Windows management, it is not surprising that it uses this namespace extensively. ConfigMgr also defines its own namespaces, discussed in the "Looking Inside Configuration Manager with WMI" section.

If you are familiar with relational databases such as SQL Server, you may find it useful to consider an analogy between WMI and a database system. Table 3.2 presents some corresponding WMI and database concepts.

TABLE 3.2   Analogous WMI and Database Concepts

WMI Concept	Database Concept
WMI Infrastructure	Database Engine
Namespace	Database
Class	Table
Instance	Row
Attribute	Column

This section presented the major concepts of WMI and the CIM model, which are essential to understanding ConfigMgr WMI activity. If you are interested in learning about other aspects of CIM, a good place to start is the tutorial at http://www.wbemsolutions.com/tutorials/CIM/index.html. The full CIM specification can be found at http://www.dmtf.org/standards/cim. Documentation for WMI is available at http://msdn.microsoft.com/en-us/library/aa394582.aspx.

Managing WMI

This section is intended to illustrate the options available for configuring WMI rather than being a "how-to" guide to administering WMI. You will rarely need to modify the WMI settings directly during day-to-day ConfigMgr administration. However, understanding the available options can help you understand the inner workings and functionality of WMI.

The Windows WMI Control is a graphical tool for managing the most important properties of the WMI infrastructure. Only members of the local Administrators group can use the WMI Control. To run this tool, perform the following steps:

1. Launch the Computer Management MMC snap-in. The exact procedure will vary depending on the version of Windows you are running. Generally you can right-click **Computer** or **My Computer**, and choose **Manage**.

2. Expand the **Services and Applications** node in the tree pane. For server operating systems, expand the **Configuration** node.

3. Right-click **WMI Control** and choose **Properties**.

The WMI Control opens to the General tab. As shown in Figure 3.10, the General properties confirm you have successfully connected to WMI on the local machine, display some basic properties of your system, and specify the installed version of WMI.

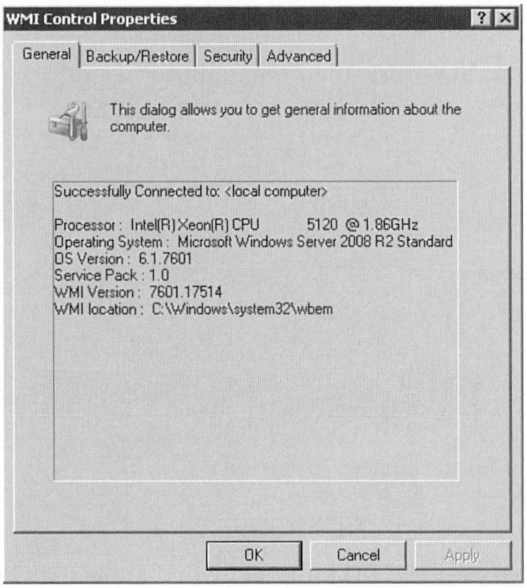

FIGURE 3.10   The General tab of the WMI Control showing a successful connection to WMI on the local machine.

NOTE: ABOUT MANAGING WMI ON A REMOTE MACHINE

You can use the WMI Control tool to manage WMI on the local machine or on a remote machine. To connect to WMI on a remote machine, you follow the same procedure previously described in this section, with one additional step. Immediately after step 1, right-click the Computer Management node at the top of the tree, and choose **Connect to Another Computer**. Then enter the name or IP address of the computer you want to manage and click **OK**. After connecting to the remote machine, complete steps 2 and 3 in the procedure.

In addition to administrative privilege on the remote machine, you need appropriate DCOM permissions (described later in this section). In addition, DCOM network protocols must not be blocked on the remote machine or on any intermediary devices.

You can manage WMI security from the Security tab of the WMI Control tool. WMI uses standard Windows access control lists (ACLs) to secure each of the WMI namespaces that exist on your machine. A namespace, as described more precisely in the "Inside the WMI Object Model" section of this chapter, is a container that holds other WMI elements. The tree structure in the Security tab shows the WMI namespaces, as displayed in Figure 3.11.

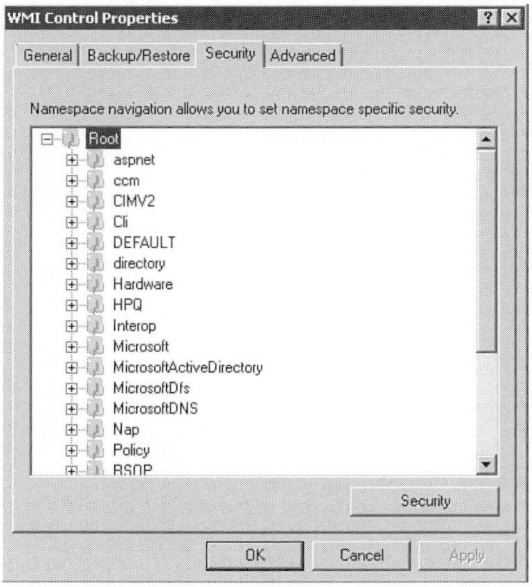

FIGURE 3.11   The Security tab of the WMI Control tool, displaying the top-level WMI namespaces.

The namespace is the most granular level in which to apply ACLs in WMI. The process of setting security on WMI namespaces, and the technology behind it, is very similar to the process of setting NTFS (NT File System) security. If you click a namespace to select it and click **Security**, you see a dialog box similar to the one displayed in Figure 3.12.

NOTE: ABOUT THE SMS ADMINS GROUP

ConfigMgr automatically creates a local group named SMS Admins on each computer where you install the SMS Provider, and assigns the appropriate WMI permissions to this group. All administrative users configured as part of role-based administration are automatically added to this group, as is the site server computer account.

The dialog box in Figure 3.12 allows you to add security principals to the discretionary ACL (DACL) of the WMI namespace. The DACL specifies who can access the namespace and the type of access they have. With Windows XP and earlier operating systems, this was the only namespace access control implemented in WMI. Beginning with Windows Vista, enhancements to WMI, mentioned previously in the "WMI Feature Set and Architecture" section, added a system access control list (SACL) for WMI namespaces. The SACL specifies the actions audited for each security principal.

TIP: ABOUT AUDITING

As with other auditing of object access in Windows, auditing access to WMI namespaces requires the effective value of the group policy setting Audit Object Access to be enabled. The Windows Security event log records the events specified in the auditing settings.

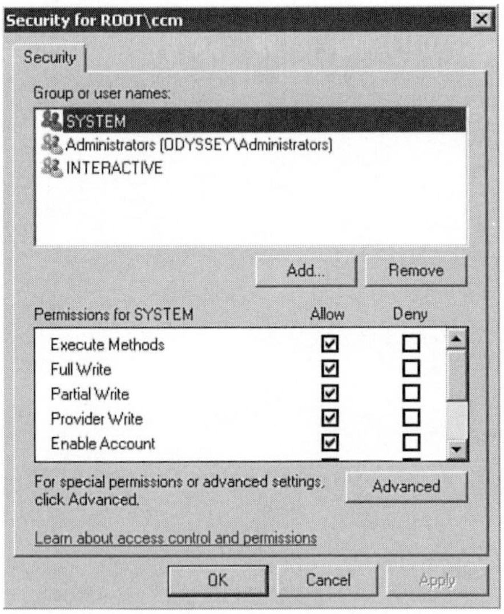

FIGURE 3.12   The WMI Security dialog box for the CCM namespace (the root namespace of the ConfigMgr client).

To specify auditing on a WMI namespace, follow these steps:

1. From the Security dialog box, as shown in Figure 3.12, click the **Advanced** button.

2. In the Advanced Security Settings dialog box, click the **Auditing** tab.

3. Click the **Add** button and then enter the name of the user, group, or built-in security principal (see Figure 3.13). Click OK.

4. Complete the selections in the Auditing Entry dialog box, and click **OK**.

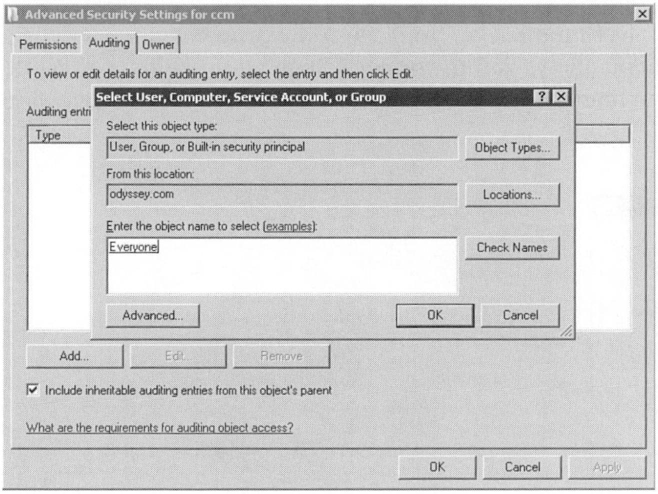

FIGURE 3.13   Specifying a user, computer, or group for WMI control security.

REAL WORLD: USING AUDITING TO TROUBLESHOOT WMI CONNECTIONS

You can use auditing as a troubleshooting tool in the following ways:

▶ Auditing for access failures to help determine whether security problems are causing a WMI problem

▶ Auditing for access success to help determine whether there is a successful connection

Be judicious in auditing, as excessive auditing consumes unnecessary system resources and generates noise in the Security event log.

Figure 3.14 shows the entries to enable auditing for all access failures by members of the CM12 Servers group.

The remaining tabs of the WMI Control tool allow you to change the default namespace for WMI connections, and provide one of several methods of backing up the WMI repository. Windows system state backups also back up the repository. Prior to Windows Vista, the WMI Control tool also contained a Logging tab that allowed you to specify verbose, normal, or no logging, as well as choose the WMI log location and maximum log size. In Windows Server 2008, Windows Server 2008 R2, Windows Vista, and Windows 7, you can enable logging and configure log options in the Windows Event Viewer. To enable WMI Trace Logging in these versions of Windows, perform the following steps:

1. Open Event Viewer.

2. On the View menu, select **Show Analytic and Debug Logs**.

3. In the tree control, expand **Applications and Service Logs -> Microsoft -> Windows -> WMI Activity**.

4. Right-click **Trace** and then select **Enable Log** from the context menu. Choosing **Properties** from the same menu allows you to configure logging properties for WMI. You can now view, filter, and manage the WMI log from this node in the Event Viewer tree.

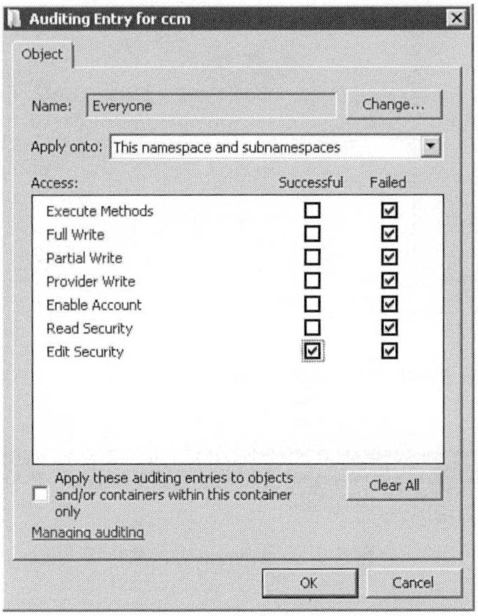

FIGURE 3.14   The WMI Auditing Entry dialog box displaying auditing enabled for all access failures by members of the ConfigMgr Site Servers group.

You can read more about WMI logging at http://msdn.microsoft.com/en-us/library/aa394564.aspx.

You should be aware that User Account Control, first introduced in Windows Vista, applies to privileged WMI operations. This can affect some scripts and command-line utilities. For a discussion of User Account Control and WMI, see http://msdn.microsoft.com/en-us/library/aa826699.aspx.

Additional command-line tools are available for managing WMI, which you can download from http://msdn.microsoft.com/en-us/library/aa827351.aspx. These tools include a MOF compiler, a command-line tool for performing WMI operations, and more. Another great resource for working with WMI is the WMI Diagnosis Utility (WMIDiag). WMIDiag is a Visual Basic script that tests the WMI functionality on the system and repairs many

WMI problems. You can obtain the WMIDiag from the Microsoft download site (http://www.microsoft.com/en-us/download/details.aspx?id=7684), or go to www.microsoft.com/downloads and search for WMIDiag. The WMI Diagnosis Utility documentation provides a wealth of information about WMI.

> **TIP: TROUBLESHOOTING REPOSITORY ISSUES**
>
> SMS 2.0 was one of the first applications to take advantage of WMI. At one time, SMS was often the only WMI management application running on many Windows machines. In those days, it was a common practice among SMS administrators to simply delete the repository when WMI errors were detected, and then restart WMI to re-create the repository. This is no longer a safe practice, as many applications depend on data stored in the repository. Moreover, WMI errors can result from many other problems in your environment and may have nothing to do with WMI. Beginning with Windows Vista and Windows Server 2008, you can run the command `winmgmt /verifyrepository` to check the consistency of the repository. If this command reports that the repository is inconsistent, you can run `winmgmt /salvagerepository` to attempt to rebuild the repository. You can find information about these and other command options at http://blogs.technet.com/b/askperf/archive/2008/07/11/wmi-troubleshooting-the-repository-on-vista-server-2008.aspx. WMIDiag can also help you diagnosis most WMI problems, and in many cases it provides detailed instructions on how to correct those problems.

Looking Inside the CIMV2 Namespace

Windows provides a basic tool called WBEMTest that allows you to connect to a WMI namespace and execute WMI operations. However, there are a number of tools from Microsoft and third parties with more intuitive graphical interfaces for displaying and navigating WMI namespaces. This section uses the Microsoft WMI Administrative Tools to look into the Root\CIMV2 namespace. These tools include the WMI CIM Studio and the WMI Object Browser. To download the latest WMI Administrative Tools, search for **WMITools** at www.microsoft.com/downloads. After downloading, run the WMITools.exe executable file to install the tools.

You can use CIM Studio to explore the classes in a namespace and view the properties, methods, and associations of each class. Perform the following steps to launch CIM Studio and connect to the CIMV2 namespace:

1. Select **Start -> All Programs -> WMI Tools -> WMI CIM Studio**.

2. CIM Studio opens a web browser and attempts to run an ActiveX control.

    If your browser blocks the control, select the option **Allow Blocked Content**.

3. Verify that root\CIMV2 displays in the **Connect to namespace** dialog box and then click **OK**. Notice that you can also browse to other namespaces on the local computer or a remote computer.

4. Click **OK** to accept the default logon settings.

When you open CIM Studio and connect to a namespace, the Class Explorer in the left pane contains a tree structure that displays the base classes in the selected namespace. Figure 3.15 displays the left pane with some of the root classes of the CIMV2 namespace.

Notice that most of the class names in Figure 3.15 begin with CIM or Win32. Class names starting with CIM indicate that the class is one of the core or common classes defined in the DMTF CIM schema. Classes with names beginning with Win32 are those extended classes that are part of the Win32 schema defined by Microsoft for managing the Win32 environment.

FIGURE 3.15   The root classes of the CIMV2 namespace displayed in CIM Studio.

The Win32_LogicalShareSecuritySetting Class

This section uses the Win32_LogicalShareSecuritySetting class to illustrate how you can use CIM Studio to understand a class of managed objects. Figure 3.16 shows the Win32_LogicalShareSecuritySetting class displayed in CIM Studio. This class represents the security settings on a Windows file share. The expand tree shows the root class, CIM_Setting, and the classes derived from each successive subclass.

Looking at the tree structure, you can see that Win32_LogicalShareSecuritySetting is derived from Win32_SecuritySetting, which in turn is derived from CIM_Setting. The Class View in the right pane displays the properties of the Win32_LogicalShareSecuritySetting class. To the left of each property name, you will see one of the following icons:

▶ A yellow downward-pointing arrow indicates the property is inherited from the parent class.

▶ A property page indicates the property is defined within the class.

▶ A computer system indicates that the property is a system class. You can also recognize system classes by their names, which always start with a double underscore (__).

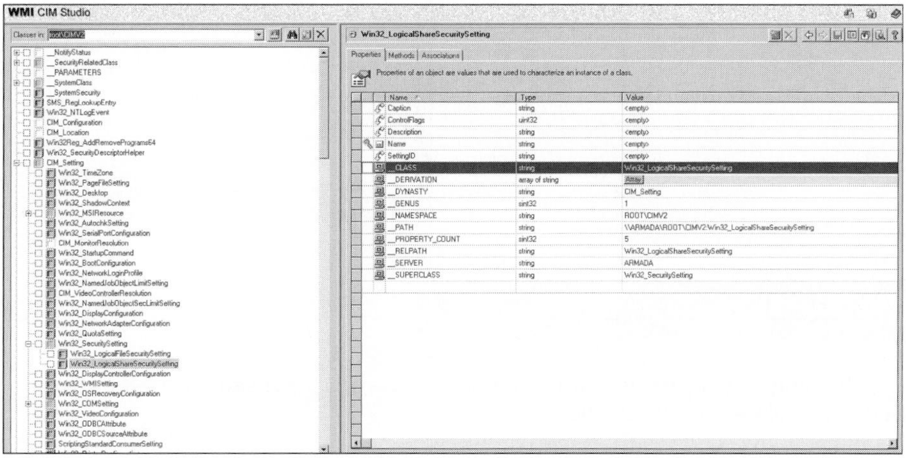

FIGURE 3.16   The `Win32_LogicalShareSecuritySetting` class displayed in CIM Studio.

For example, each WMI class has certain System properties, such as __PATH, __DYNASTY, __SUPERCLASS, and __DERIVATION. Here are some points to keep in mind:

▶ The __PATH property shows the location of the class in the namespace hierarchy. Management applications and scripts use the __PATH property to connect to the class.

▶ __DYNASTY, __SUPERCLASS, and __DERIVATION are all related to class inheritance and represent the root class from which the class is derived its immediate parent, and the entire family tree of the class, respectively.

Clicking the Array button next to __DERIVATION displays the array of parent classes from which the class is derived. The array is essentially the inheritance information already observed by traversing the tree, as shown in Figure 3.17.

The remaining properties of `Win32_LogicalShareSecuritySetting` are the ones that actually represent characteristics describing instances of Windows file share security settings. You can see that except for the name, all these properties are inherited. An object that has nothing unique about it except its name would not be very interesting, but there is more to the `Win32_LogicalShareSecuritySetting` class than the class properties. The most interesting attributes of `Win32_LogicalShareSecuritySetting` are on the remaining tabs of the CIM Studio Class View pane.

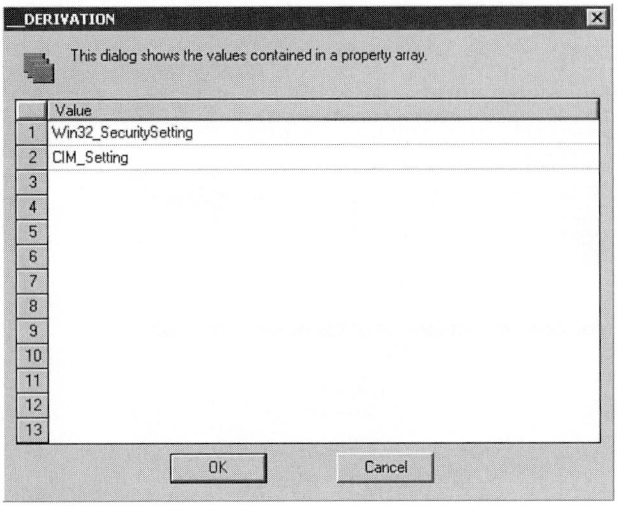

FIGURE 3.17   The array of classes from which the `Win32_LogicalShareSecuritySetting` class is derived, as displayed in CIM Studio.

Clicking the **Methods** tab displays the two methods (GetSecurityDescriptor and SetSecurityDescriptor) of the `Win32_LogicalShareSecuritySetting` class, as shown in Figure 3.18.

Getting Additional Information

These methods let you work with the permissions on the actual file share. Clicking the Help button on the toolbar in the upper-right corner of Class View in Figure 3.18 provides additional information about the class.

A SAMPLE HELP ENTRY

The help entry for Win32_LogicalShareSecuritySetting returns the following information:

```
security settings for a logical file
Caption
A short textual description (one-line string) of the CIM_Setting object.

ControlFlags
Inheritance-related flags.  See SECURITY_DESCRIPTOR_CONTROL

Description
A textual description of the CIM_Setting object.

Name
The name of the share

SettingID
The identifier by which the CIM_Setting object is known.
```

```
uint32 GetSecurityDescriptor(
[out] object:Win32_SecurityDescriptor Descriptor
);
```

Retrieves a structural representation of the object's security descriptor.
The method returns an integer value that can be interpreted as follows:
0 - Successful completion.
2 - The user does not have access to the requested information.
8 - Unknown failure.
9 - The user does not have adequate privileges.
21 - The specified parameter is invalid.
Other - For integer values other than those listed above,
refer to Win32 error code documentation.

Descriptor
<description missing>

```
uint32 SetSecurityDescriptor(
[in] object:Win32_SecurityDescriptor Descriptor
);
```

Sets security descriptor to the specified structure.
The method returns an integer value that can be interpreted as follows:
0 - Successful completion.
2 - The user does not have access to the requested information.
8 - Unknown failure.
9 - The user does not have adequate privileges.
21 - The specified parameter is invalid.
Other - For integer values other than those listed above,
refer to Win32 error code documentation.

Descriptor
<description missing>

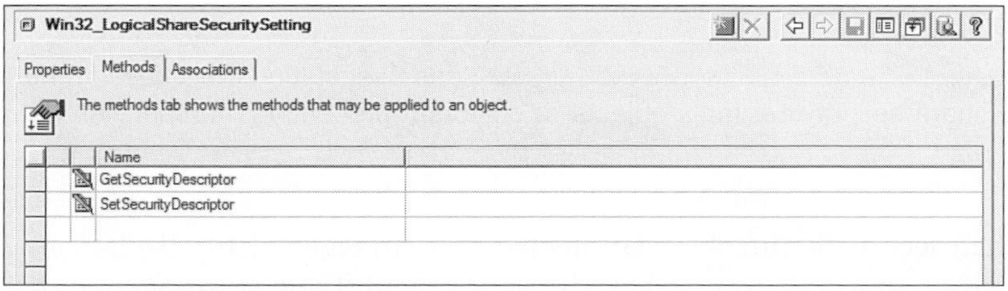

FIGURE 3.18   The `Win32_LogicalShareSecuritySetting` class methods, displayed in CIM Studio, allow management applications to retrieve or modify security on file shares.

Putting It All Together

The Win32_LogicalShareSecuritySetting example in the "A Sample Help Entry" sidebar shows that the GetSecurityDescriptor method returns the current security descriptor of the file share as an object of type Win32_SecurityDescriptor. The SetSecurityDescriptor method accepts a Win32_SecurityDescriptor object as input and replaces the security descriptor on the share with information supplied in the security descriptor object. The example also lists the status codes returned by these methods.

The information on the Class View Associations tab, shown in Figure 3.19, provides the key to understanding the implementation of Win32_LogicalShareSecuritySetting.

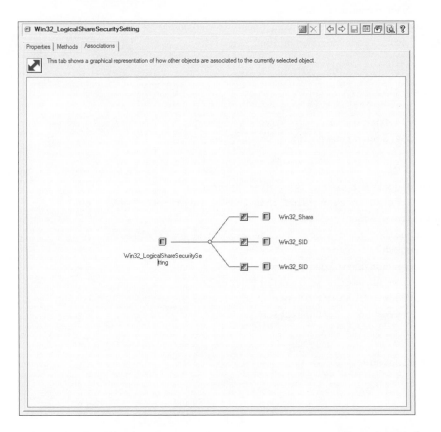

FIGURE 3.19   The Win32_LogicalShareSecuritySetting class associations, displayed here in CIM Studio, link the share security setting's objects to objects representing the share and the share's ACL entries.

The Win32_LogicalShareSecuritySetting Associations tab (refer to Figure 3.19) displays an association with the Win32_Share class as well as associations with the two instances of the Win32_SID class. Class icons marked with a diagonal arrow represent the association classes linking other classes together. If you hover your mouse cursor over the Class icons for each of the association classes linking Win32_LogicalShareSecuritySetting to Win32_SID class instances, you can see that one is a `Win32_LogicalShareAccess` class instance and the other is a `Win32_LogicalShareAuditing` class instance.

▶ Instances of the `Win32_LogicalShareAccess` association represent access control entries (ACEs) in the DACL (that is, share permissions).

▶ The `Win32_LogicalShareAuditing` instances represent ACEs in the SACL (audit settings) on the share. You can double-click any of the classes shown on this tab to navigate to it in Class View.

Because objects of the `Win32_LogicalShareSecuritySetting` class allow you to work with live data on the system, you would expect this to be a dynamic class. You can verify this by returning to the Properties or Methods tab, right-clicking any attribute, and selecting **Object Qualifiers**. The `Win32_LogicalShareSecuritySetting` object qualifiers are shown in Figure 3.20, including the dynamic qualifier, which is of type boolean with a value of true.

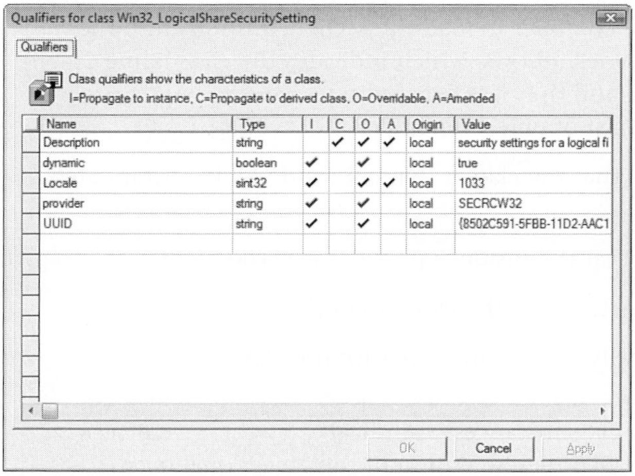

FIGURE 3.20   The `Win32_LogicalShareSecuritySetting` class qualifiers displayed in CIM Studio.

From the Class View, you can also use the Instances button to display all instances of the class, and you can open the properties of an instance by double-clicking it. The "Hardware Inventory Through WMI" section discusses how to use another of the WMI Administrative Tools, the WMI Object Browser, to view class instances. Just above the toolbar are icons that launch the MOF generator and MOF compiler wizards, as shown earlier in Figure 3.16. To launch the MOF compiler, you must check the **Class** icon next to the class and double-click the **Wizard** icon. The MOF language defining the `Win32_LogicalShareSecuritySetting` class is as follows:

```
#pragma namespace("\\\\.\\ROOT\\CIMV2")

//*******************************************************************
//* Class: Win32_LogicalShareSecuritySetting
```

```
//* Derived from: Win32_SecuritySetting
//*************************************************************************
[dynamic: ToInstance, provider("SECRCW32"): ToInstance, Locale(1033): ToInstance,
UUID("{8502C591-5FBB-11D2-AAC1-006008C78BC7}"): ToInstance]
class Win32_LogicalShareSecuritySetting : Win32_SecuritySetting
{
    [key, read: ToSubClass] string Name;
    [Privileges{"SeSecurityPrivilege", "SeRestorePrivilege"}: ToSubClass,
    implemented, ValueMap{"0", "2", "8", "9", "21", ".."}]
    uint32 GetSecurityDescriptor([OUT] Win32_SecurityDescriptor Descriptor);
    [Privileges{"SeSecurityPrivilege", "SeRestorePrivilege"}: ToSubClass,
    implemented, ValueMap{"0", "2", "8", "9", "21", ".."}]
    uint32 SetSecurityDescriptor([IN] Win32_SecurityDescriptor Descriptor);
};
```

The first line of the MOF entry, `#pragma namespace ("\\\\.\\ROOT\\CIMV2")`, is a prepro-
cessor command instructing the MOF compiler to load the MOF definitions into the
`Root\CIMV2` namespace. A comment block follows, which indicates the class name `Class:`
`Win32_LogicalShareSecuritySetting` and the class derivation `Derived from: Win32_`
`SecuritySetting`. Next is a bracketed list of object qualifiers:

▶ The dynamic qualifier indicates that the class is dynamic and will be instantiated at
   runtime.

▶ The provider qualifier specifies that the instance provider is SECRCW32.

▶ The locale qualifier indicates the locale of the class, 1033 (U.S. English).

▶ The UUID qualifier is a Universally Unique Identifier for the class.

Each of these qualifiers propagates to class instances, as indicated by the `toinstance`
keyword. Refer to Figure 3.20 to see a GUI representation of the object qualifiers.

The next section contains the class declaration `Win32_LogicalShareSecuritySetting :`
`Win32_SecuritySetting`. This declaration derives the `Win32_LogicalShareSecuritySetting`
class from the `Win32_SecuritySetting` base class. The body of the class declaration
declares locally defined class properties and methods. The Name property (the name
of the share) is declared to be of type String and designated as a key value, indicating that it uniquely identifies an instance of the class. The GetSecurityDescriptor and
SetSecurityDescriptor methods are both of type uint32, indicating that each method
return an unsigned 32-bit integer. GetSecurityDescriptor has an output parameter of
type Win32_SecurityDescriptor, whereas SetSecurityDescriptor has a corresponding input
parameter of the same type. Immediately preceding each of these method definitions, you
will see the following method qualifiers specified:

▶ *Privileges* requests the access privileges required to manipulate Win32 security
   descriptors.

▶ *Implemented* is a Boolean value indicating the method is implemented in the class.

▶ *Valuemap* specifies the method's return values. The "A Sample Help Entry" sidebar lists the meaning of each of these values.

In addition to the locally implemented properties and qualifiers, the `Win32_LogicalShareSecuritySetting` class inherits properties and qualifiers defined as part of its parent class, `Win32_SecuritySetting`.

Before continuing, you may want to explore several other classes in the `Root\CIMV2` namespace:

▶ Work your way up the inheritance tree from the `Win32_LogicalShareSecuritySetting` class and see where each of the inherited properties of the class originates. In addition, notice that if you bring up the object qualifiers on the parent classes, you can see these are qualified as abstract classes.

▶ The immediate sibling of the `Win32_LogicalShareSecuritySetting` class is the `Win32_LogicalFileSecuritySetting` class. Notice the differences in the properties and associations for this class. Share security and file security have many characteristics in common but a few important differences. Seeing how they are both derived from the `Win32_SecuritySetting` class demonstrates the power and flexibility of class inheritance.

▶ Expand the `CIM_StatisticalInformation` root class and then the `Win32_Perf` class. The two branches of Win32_Perf show how a variety of performance counters are implemented as managed objects.

This section looked at several of the default classes in the `Root\CIMV2` namespace and discussed how to use CIM Studio to explore a WMI namespace. The "WMI in ConfigMgr" section describes how ConfigMgr uses the classes in `Root\CIMV2` and as well as its own namespaces and classes.

WMI in ConfigMgr

ConfigMgr uses WMI extensively for both client and server operations. The ConfigMgr client uses WMI for internal control of its own operations and for gathering hardware inventory. ConfigMgr also uses WMI as an interface to the site database. The next sections discuss how ConfigMgr uses WMI on the client and then describe the use of WMI in ConfigMgr server operations.

ConfigMgr Client Namespaces

ConfigMgr 2012 creates and uses several namespaces in addition to adding classes to the `Root\CIMV2` namespace. The primary namespace created by the ConfigMgr client is the `Root\CCM` namespace. Together with several namespaces under `Root\CCM`, this namespace holds the configuration and policies that govern the operation of the ConfigMgr client. The `Root\CIMV2\SMS` namespace contains additional system-wide objects used by ConfigMgr. The hardware inventory process described in the next section of this chapter uses a policy stored in the `Root\CCM\Policy\Machine\actualconfig` namespace to specify what inventory data to retrieve from managed objects defined in the `Root\CimV2` namespace. The "Additional Client Operations Through WMI" section discusses additional uses of the `Root\CCM` namespace.

Hardware Inventory Through WMI

The ConfigMgr client agent gathers hardware inventory data by querying WMI. The Client Agent settings determine which object classes are reported as part of the client inventory. For the majority of hardware inventory policy definitions, enabling or disabling what is reported from the clients to the ConfigMgr infrastructure is done from the console, via Client Agent settings. Modifications can be applied on as site wide basis by editing the Default Client Agent settings. To modify the hardware inventory settings for a subset of the environment (servers for example), create and modify a custom client setting, then assign it to a collection consisting of the appropriate systems. Chapter 9 describes client settings and inventory customization through the ConfigMgr console. Chapter 9 also discusses the changes in client inventory from ConfigMgr 2007. Appendix B, "Extending Hardware Inventory," provides a detailed discussion of inventory customization.

The configuration.mof file defines classes used by the hardware inventory client agent to collect inventory. The CAS or top-level primary site imports the class definitions from the configuration.mof file and replicates them throughout the hierarchy. The configuration.mof file that ships with ConfigMgr provides a standard set of WMI classes, such as the Win32 classes. In some cases, a custom data class might be required. For example, an application or device driver may act as a WMI provider and create custom classes. You can also create data classes to provide inventory data that is accessible through existing WMI providers, such as data from the client's system registry. In those cases, the administrator must import a custom mof file into the default client agent settings.

To apply inventory settings from a custom mof file, navigate to **Administration -> Client Settings**, and either select the **Default Client Settings** or create or a Custom Client Device Settings object. On the Properties page, choose **Hardware Inventory** and click **Set Classes -> Import**.

ConfigMgr clients download client settings as part of their machine policy retrieval cycle. Any changes are compiled and loaded into the WMI repository. The ConfigMgr client stores its machine policy in the `Root\CCM\Policy\Machine\actualconfig` WMI namespace. You can use the WMI Object Browser from the WMI Administrative Tools to examine some to the inventory-related objects in this namespace. To launch the WMI Object Browser and connect to the `Root\CCM\Policy\Machine\actualconfig` namespace, follow these steps:

1. Select **Start -> All Programs -> WMI Tools -> WMI Object Browser**.

   The WMI Object Browser opens a web browser and attempts to run an ActiveX control.

If your browser blocks the control, select the option **Allow Blocked Content**.

2. Change the entry in the Connect to namespace dialog box to **Root\CCM\Policy\ Machine\actualconfig** and then click **OK**.

3. Click **OK** to accept the default logon settings.

You can locate objects of a specified class by clicking the **Browse** button (the binocular icon on the toolbar above the left pane). Select **InventoryDataItem** from the available classes, as shown in Figure 3.21. Click **OK** to display a list of the items that will be inventoried.

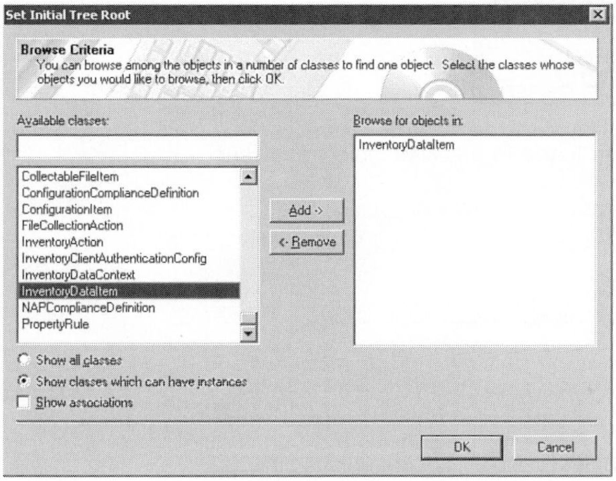

FIGURE 3.21   Browsing for InventoryDataItem in the WMI Object Browser.

InventoryDataItem is the class representing inventory items specified in the machine policy. Figure 3.22 lists several of these instances in the Root\CCM\Policy\Machine\ actualconfig namespace.

Figure 3.22 has the columns resized to hide the Key (1) column, which displays an object GUID (Globally Unique Identifier), and to display the more interesting information in Key(2) and Key (3).

Selecting the instance that refers to the Win32_DiskDrive class in the Root\CIMV2 namespace and double-clicking this entry displays the instance properties, as shown in Figure 3.23.

The Namespace and ItemClass properties tell the hardware inventory agent it can retrieve inventory data for this class from Win32_DiskDrive objects in the \\Root\CIMV2 namespace. The Properties property contains a list of properties to inventory from each instance of \\Root\CIMV2\Win32_DiskDrive. Here are the properties listed:

Availability, Caption, Description, DeviceID, Index, InterfaceType, Manufacturer, MediaType, Model, Name, Partitions, PNPDeviceID, SCSIBus, SCSILogicalUnit, SCSIPort, SCSITargetId, Size, SystemName

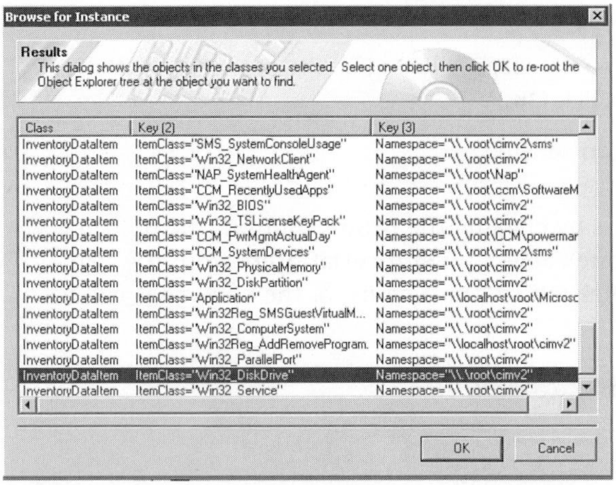

FIGURE 3.22   InventoryDataItem instances listed in the WMI Object Browser.

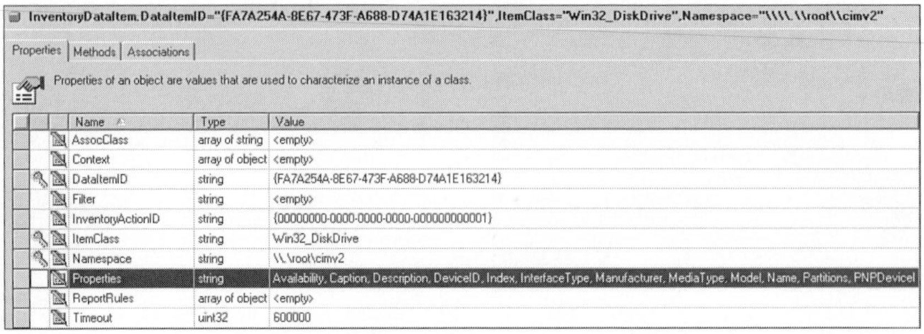

FIGURE 3.23   Properties of the Win32_DiskDrive instance of the `InventoryDataItem` as displayed in the WMI Object Browser.

`Win32_DiskDrive` objects have many other properties besides these. The property list in the machine policy settings instance corresponds to the properties selected in the applicable client settings object. To view these settings in the console, navigate to the Administration workspace and select **Default Client Agent Settings** -> **Properties** -> **Hardware Inventory** -> **Set Classes**. Classes that are checked will be collected and reported upon. Figure 3.24 shows the client agent hardware inventory settings for **Disk Drives (Win32_DiskDrive)**.

Another InventoryDataItem instance in the `Root\CCM\Policy\Machine` namespace— Win32Reg_AddRemovePrograms—configures inventory settings for reporting on items of the `Win32Reg_AddRemovePrograms` class in the `\\Root\CIMV2` namespace. Here is the MOF code for Win32Reg_AddRemovePrograms:

```
#pragma namespace("\\\\.\\ROOT\\CIMV2")

//**************************************************************************
//* Class: Win32Reg_AddRemovePrograms
//* Derived from:
//**************************************************************************
[dynamic: ToInstance, provider("RegProv"), ClassContext("local|HKEY_LOCAL_MACHINE\\
Software\\Microsoft\\Windows\\CurrentVersion\\Uninstall")]
class Win32Reg_AddRemovePrograms
{
        [key] string ProdID;
        [PropertyContext("DisplayName")] string DisplayName;
        [PropertyContext("InstallDate")] string InstallDate;
        [PropertyContext("Publisher")] string Publisher;
        [PropertyContext("DisplayVersion")] string Version;
};
```

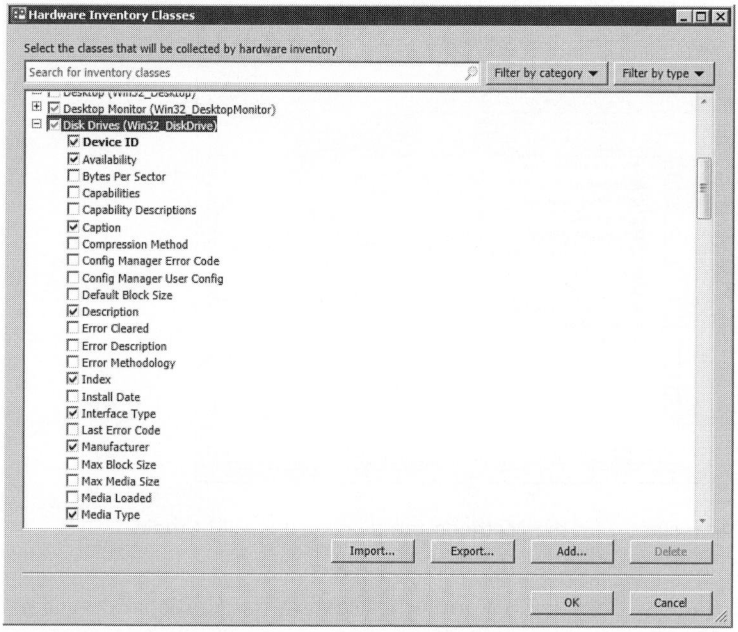

FIGURE 3.24   Client Settings Specifying Disk Drive Properties to Inventory.

The System Registry provider (RegProv) exposes registry data to management applications. The Win32Reg_AddRemovePrograms class uses the Registry provider to retrieve the information stored under HKEY_LOCAL_MACHINE\Software\Microsoft\Windows\CurrentVersion\ Uninstall in the local registry dynamically. Each key under this location stores information about an item in Add/Remove Programs.

This example shows how the Registry provider exposes registry keys and values through WMI. You can use a mof compiler such as the one in CIM Studio to create classes representing various registry data, which you can then add to the ConfigMgr inventory. You can use similar methods to add data from any provider installed on the ConfigMgr client machines.

Additional Client Operations Through WMI

The ConfigMgr client creates WMI classes to represent its own components and configuration. The root of the ConfigMgr client namespace hierarchy is Root\CCM. The Root\ CCM namespace contains classes representing client properties, such as identity and version information, installation options, and site information. Two of the classes in this namespace expose much of the functionality available through the Configuration Management Control Panel applet:

▶ The SMS_Client WMI class provides methods, displayed in Figure 3.25, that implement client operations such as site assignment, policy retrieval, and client repair.

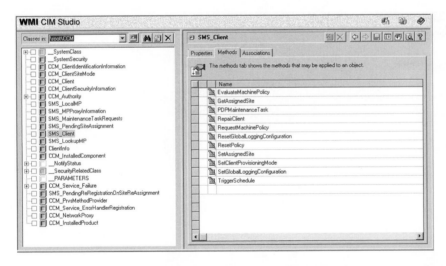

FIGURE 3.25   The SMS_Client class with the Methods tab displayed in CIM Studio.

▶ The CCM_InstalledComponent class defines properties such as name, file, and version information describing each of the installed client components. Figure 3.26 displays a list of the instances of the CCM_InstalledComponent class.

You will find managed objects for various client components in namespaces under Root\CCM. Figure 3.27 shows an instance of these classes, the CacheConfig class. The CacheConfig class in the Root\CCM\SoftMgmtAgent namespace contains settings for the client download cache, found on the Advanced tab of the Configuration Management Control Panel applet.

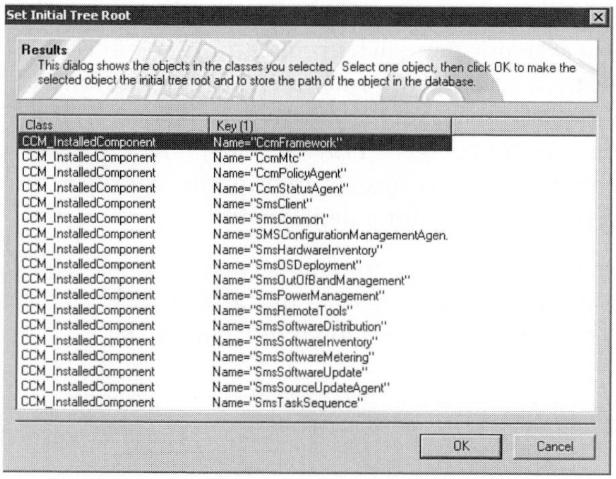

FIGURE 3.26   Instances of the `CCM_InstalledComponent` class listed in the WMI Object Browser.

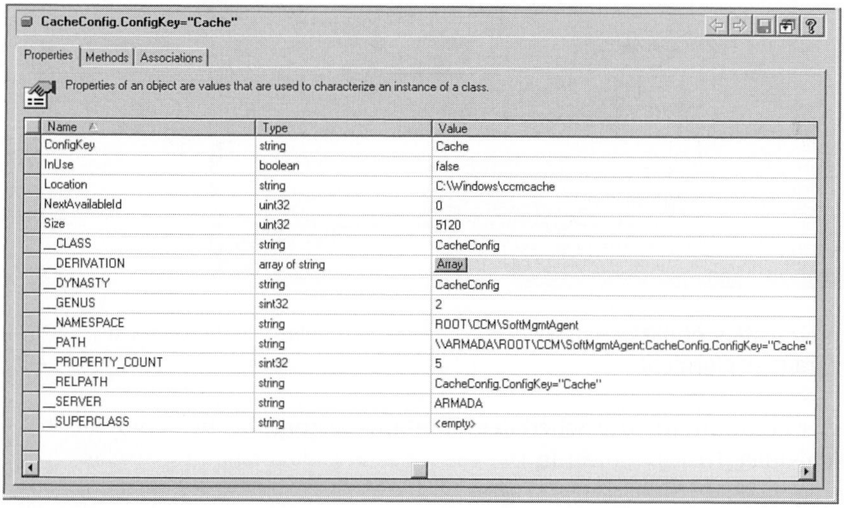

FIGURE 3.27   The properties of the `CacheConfig` class instance represent the client download cache settings.

The ConfigMgr client uses the `Root\CCM\policy` namespace hierarchy to store and process policy settings retrieved from the management point. The client maintains separate namespaces for machine policy and user policy.

During the policy retrieval and evaluation cycle, the policy agent, a component of the client agent, downloads and compiles policy settings and instantiates the requested policy settings in the `Root\CCM\policy\{machine|user}\RequestedConfig` namespace, where the value of *{machine|user}* is *machine* for systemwide policies or *user* for user specific policies. The Policy Evaluator component then uses the information in RequestedConfig to update the `Root\CCM\policy\{machine|user}\ActualConfig` namespace. Based on the policy settings in the actual configuration, the Policy Agent Provider component updates various component instances with their appropriate settings. As an example, consider some of the objects used by the client to process policy for a deployment:

▶ **The policy agent:** The policy agent stores the policy for an assigned deployment as an instance of the `CCM_SoftwareDistribution` class in the `Root\ccm\policy\<machine|user>\ActualConfig` namespace, as shown in Figure 3.28.

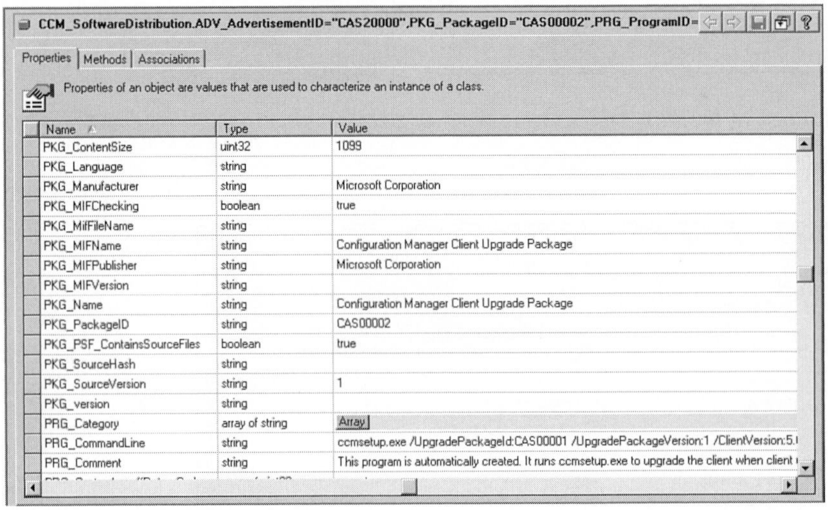

FIGURE 3.28   The properties of the `CCM_SoftwareDistribution` class instance for a ConfigMgr client upgrade deployment.

▶ **The Scheduler component:** The Scheduler maintains history for the deployment in a CCM_Scheduler_History object in the `Root\CCM\scheduler` namespace, as displayed in Figure 3.29.

This namespace can also contain schedule information for other components, including compliance evaluation schedules, software update schedules, and NAP schedules.

▶ **The Execution history:** The Execution Manager component uses the CCM_ExecutionRequestEx object in the `Root\CCM\SoftMgmtAgent` namespace, shown in Figure 3.30, to manage execution history for the deployment.

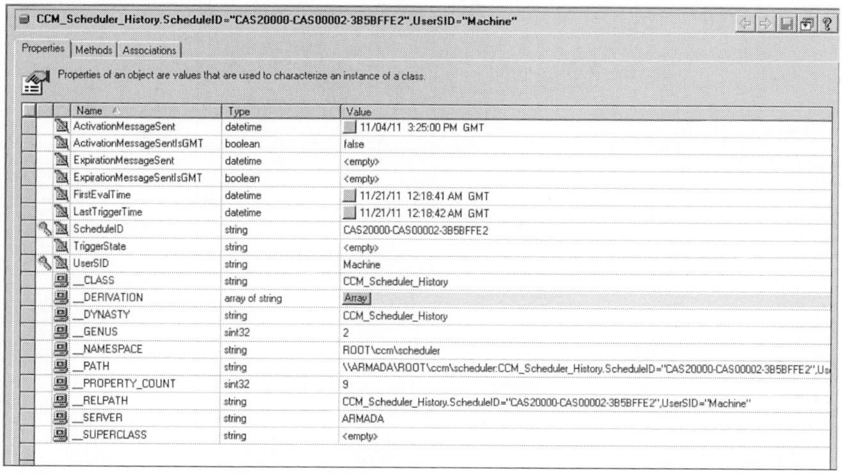

FIGURE 3.29   The Scheduler uses the CCM_Scheduler_History object to maintain history for a deployment.

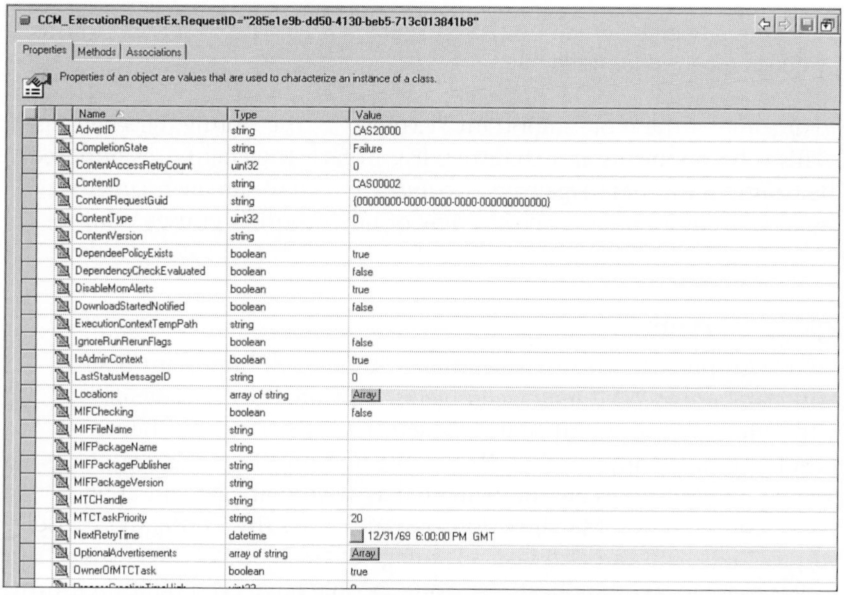

FIGURE 3.30   The CCM_ExecutionRequestEx object is used to manage execution history for the deployment.

▶ **The Software Distribution Client Configuration class:** Machine policy also controls the settings of various ConfigMgr client components. The CCM_SoftwareDistributionClientConfig class in the root\ccm\policy\ machine\actualconfig namespace, shown in Figure 3.31, contains the Software Distribution client agent settings.

	Name	Type	Value
	ADV_RebootLogoffNotification	boolean	true
	ADV_RebootLogoffNotificationCo	uint32	<empty>
	ADV_RebootLogoffNotificationFin	uint32	<empty>
	ADV_RunNotificationCountdownD	uint32	300
	ADV_WhatsNewDuration	uint32	14
	CacheContentTimeout	uint32	2592000
	CacheSpaceFailureRetryCount	uint32	18
	CacheSpaceFailureRetryInterval	uint32	14400
	CacheTombstoneContentMinDura	uint32	86400
	ComponentName	string	SmsSoftwareDistribution
	ContentLocationTimeoutInterval	uint32	28800
	ContentLocationTimeoutRetryCou	uint32	21
	DefaultMaxDuration	uint32	0
	DisplayNewProgramNotification	boolean	true
	Enabled	boolean	true
	ExecutionFailureRetryCount	uint32	1008
	ExecutionFailureRetryErrorCodes	array of uint32	Array
	ExecutionFailureRetryInterval	uint32	600
	LockSettings	boolean	false
	LogoffReturnCodes	array of uint32	Array
	NetworkAccessPassword	string	<empty>
	NetworkAccessUsername	string	<empty>
	NetworkFailureRetryCount	uint32	<empty>
	NetworkFailureRetryInterval	uint32	<empty>
	NewProgramNotificationUI	string	RAP
	PRG_PRF_RunNotification	boolean	true

FIGURE 3.31 Some of the properties of the `CCM_SoftwareDistributionClientConfig` class reflect client agent settings received from the site.

This section looked at some of the more important WMI classes the ConfigMgr client uses for its operations. This is by no means an exhaustive list; in fact, the client uses hundreds of WMI classes. The Configuration Manager server components have an even larger set of WMI classes. The next section presents an overview of how ConfigMgr uses WMI for server operations.

WMI on ConfigMgr Servers

The SMS Provider is a WMI provider that exposes many of the most important objects in the ConfigMgr site database as WMI managed objects. This provider is generally installed on either the site server or the site database server, as discussed in Chapter 4. The ConfigMgr console, auxiliary applications such as the Resource Explorer, Service Manager, and various ConfigMgr tools are implemented as WMI management applications. Chapter 8, "The Configuration Manager Console," discusses the ConfigMgr console. As with other WMI providers, you can also take advantage of the SMS Provider's objects in custom scripts or other management applications. Some people have even built their own console or web interfaces to replace console operations. The provider also implements the ConfigMgr object security model. Chapter 20 discusses the object security model and explains how to grant users access to the console and rights on various ConfigMgr objects and classes.

The SMS Provider namespace is `Root\SMS\site_<site code>`. You can use standard WMI tools to view ConfigMgr classes and objects.

This section uses ConfigMgr collections to illustrate how to drill down into the underlying WMI using PowerShell. (Chapter 11, "Packages and Programs," and Chapter 13, "Distributing and Deploying Applications," discuss collections.) The following PowerShell command connects to the `site_CAS` namespace on the site server Armada and displays the collection objects:

```
Get-WmiObject -class SMS_Collection -computer "Armada" -namespace "root\SMS\site_
CAS"
```

Here are several selected properties of one collection output by this statement:

```
IsBuiltIn                    : True
LimitToCollectionID          : SMS00001
LimitToCollectionName        : All Systems
MemberClassName              : SMS_CM_RES_COLL_SMSDM001
Name                         : All Mobile Devices
OwnedByThisSite              : True
```

Notice that the MemberClassName property shows the WMI class for all members of the collection. This statement displays the complete attribute set of all members of the All Mobile Devices collection:

```
Get-WmiObject -class  SMS_CM_RES_COLL_SMSDM001  -namespace root\SMS\site_CAS
```

TIP: WINDOWS POWERSHELL SCRIPTOMATIC

The Windows PowerShell Scriptomatic tool, created by Ed Wilson, allows you to browse WMI namespaces and automatically generate PowerShell code to connect to WMI objects. The tool is available for download from http://www.microsoft.com/download/en/details. aspx?displaylang=en&id=24121.

Figure 3.32 shows a PowerShell command to display the properties and methods of the SMS_Collection class, together with its output.

TIP: FORMATTING POWERSHELL OUTPUT

Several of the method definitions shown in Figure 3.32 are truncated and displayed with an elipsis (...). To see the entire definitions you can use the command: `Get-WmiObject -class SMS_Collection -namespace root\SMS\site_CAS|Get-Member|Format-List`

The `SMS_Collection` class methods allows you to perform operations such as pushing the ConfigMgr Client to collection members with the Create CCRs method and updating collection membership with the RequestRefresh method. When you perform these operations through the ConfigMgr console, you are actually invoking the methods of the `SMS_Collection` class. Figure 3.33 displays the `SMS_Collection` class associations.

```
PS C:\Users\bholt> Get-WmiObject -class SMS_Collection -namespace root\SMS\site_CAS|Get-Member|Format-Table


   TypeName: System.Management.ManagementObject#root\SMS\site_CAS\SMS_Collection

Name                          MemberType    Definition
----                          ----------    ----------
AddMembershipRule             Method        System.Management.ManagementBaseObject AddMembershipRule(System.Manageme...
AddMembershipRules            Method        System.Management.ManagementBaseObject AddMembershipRules(System.Managem...
AMTOperateForCollection       Method        System.Management.ManagementBaseObject AMTOperateForCollection(System.UI...
ClearLastNBSAdvForCollection  Method        System.Management.ManagementBaseObject ClearLastNBSAdvForCollection()
CreateCCRs                    Method        System.Management.ManagementBaseObject CreateCCRs(System.Boolean Include...
DeleteAllMembers              Method        System.Management.ManagementBaseObject DeleteAllMembers()
DeleteMembershipRule          Method        System.Management.ManagementBaseObject DeleteMembershipRule(System.Manag...
DeleteMembershipRules         Method        System.Management.ManagementBaseObject DeleteMembershipRules(System.Mana...
FindResourceSite              Method        System.Management.ManagementBaseObject FindResourceSite(System.Boolean I...
RequestRefresh                Method        System.Management.ManagementBaseObject RequestRefresh(System.Boolean inc...
CollectionID                  Property      System.String CollectionID {get;set;}
CollectionRules               Property      System.Management.ManagementObject#SMS_CollectionRule[] CollectionRules ...
CollectionType                Property      System.UInt32 CollectionType {get;set;}
CollectionVariablesCount      Property      System.Int32 CollectionVariablesCount {get;set;}
Comment                       Property      System.String Comment {get;set;}
CurrentStatus                 Property      System.UInt32 CurrentStatus {get;set;}
IncludeExcludeCollectionsCount Property     System.Int32 IncludeExcludeCollectionsCount {get;set;}
IsBuiltIn                     Property      System.Boolean IsBuiltIn {get;set;}
IsReferenceCollection         Property      System.Boolean IsReferenceCollection {get;set;}
ISVData                       Property      System.Byte[] ISVData {get;set;}
ISVDataSize                   Property      System.UInt32 ISVDataSize {get;set;}
LastChangeTime                Property      System.String LastChangeTime {get;set;}
LastMemberChangeTime          Property      System.String LastMemberChangeTime {get;set;}
LastRefreshTime               Property      System.String LastRefreshTime {get;set;}
LimitToCollectionID           Property      System.String LimitToCollectionID {get;set;}
LimitToCollectionName         Property      System.String LimitToCollectionName {get;set;}
LocalMemberCount              Property      System.Int32 LocalMemberCount {get;set;}
MemberClassName               Property      System.String MemberClassName {get;set;}
MemberCount                   Property      System.Int32 MemberCount {get;set;}
MonitoringFlags               Property      System.UInt32 MonitoringFlags {get;set;}
Name                          Property      System.String Name {get;set;}
OwnedByThisSite               Property      System.Boolean OwnedByThisSite {get;set;}
PowerConfigsCount             Property      System.Int32 PowerConfigsCount {get;set;}
RefreshSchedule               Property      System.Management.ManagementObject#SMS_ScheduleToken[] RefreshSchedule {...
RefreshType                   Property      System.UInt32 RefreshType {get;set;}
ReplicateToSubSites           Property      System.Boolean ReplicateToSubSites {get;set;}
ServiceWindowsCount           Property      System.Int32 ServiceWindowsCount {get;set;}
__CLASS                       Property      System.String __CLASS {get;set;}
__DERIVATION                  Property      System.String[] __DERIVATION {get;set;}
__DYNASTY                     Property      System.String __DYNASTY {get;set;}
__GENUS                       Property      System.Int32 __GENUS {get;set;}
__NAMESPACE                   Property      System.String __NAMESPACE {get;set;}
__PATH                        Property      System.String __PATH {get;set;}
__PROPERTY_COUNT              Property      System.Int32 __PROPERTY_COUNT {get;set;}
__RELPATH                     Property      System.String __RELPATH {get;set;}
__SERVER                      Property      System.String __SERVER {get;set;}
__SUPERCLASS                  Property      System.String __SUPERCLASS {get;set;}
ConvertFromDateTime           ScriptMethod  System.Object ConvertFromDateTime();
ConvertToDateTime             ScriptMethod  System.Object ConvertToDateTime();
```

FIGURE 3.32   The SMS_Collection class Properties and Methods.

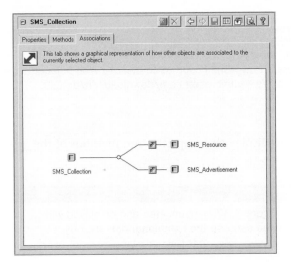

FIGURE 3.33   The SMS_Collection class associations link a collection to its members (class SMS_Resource), and deployments (SMS_Advertisement) assigned to the collection.

The following PowerShell commands create an object representing the Odyssey Computers collection and enumerate all associated objects of type SMS_Resource, writing the results to a text file:

```
$MyCollection = Get-WmiObject -class SMS_Collection -computer "Armada" -namespace
"root\SMS\site_CAS" | where {$_.Name -eq "Odyssey Computers"}
$MyCollection.GetRelated()|Where {$_.__SUPERCLASS -eq "SMS_Resource"} |Out-File
"OdysseyCollectionComputers.txt"
```

Several blogs referenced in Appendix C, "Reference URLs," provide additional examples of how you can use PowerShell with ConfigMgr. Microsoft has announced plans to release a PowerShell provider for ConfigMgr by the end of 2012. This provider will extend the usefulness of PowerShell for managing ConfigMgr operations.

The smsprov.mof file contains the MOF language defining the Root\SMS namespace and the classes it contains. You can find the smsprov.mof file in the bin*<platform>* folder under the ConfigMgr installation folder. You can also export MOF definitions for instances of the following ConfigMgr object types directly from the console:

▶ Device Collections are found in the Assets and Compliance workspace.

▶ User Collections are found in the Assets and Compliance workspace.

▶ Queries are found in the Monitoring workspace.

To export objects definitions to MOF files, right-click the workspace node to export multiple object or right-click a single object to export, choose **Export**, and complete the wizard to choose the instances to export and file location as well as to enter descriptive text. You can use a similar process to import objects from MOF files. You can use this process to copy objects between hierarchies. For example, you might develop and test queries in your lab environment and import them into production.

This section showed how the SMS Provider exposes Configuration Manager server components and database objects as WMI-managed objects. The "Root\CCM Namespace," "Hardware Inventory Through WMI," and "Additional Client Operations Through WMI" sections discussed how the ConfigMgr client uses WMI to maintain its configuration and policy and to gather inventory data. The ConfigMgr SDK, which was in prerelease when writing this chapter, is available for download from http://www.microsoft.com/download/en/details.aspx?id=29559 (or search for **ConfigMgr SDK** at www.microsoft.com/downloads). It provides extensive documentation and sample code for using WMI to manage ConfigMgr programmatically, with managed code or scripts.

Components and Communications

ConfigMgr's code design is based on a componentized architecture, where sets of related tasks are carried out by logically distinct units of executable code, that work together to implement higher-level functionality. Most ConfigMgr code resides in dynamic link libraries (DLLs) in the bin\<*processor architecture*> folder under the ConfigMgr installation folder. Although most components run as threads of the SMS Executive service, some run as separate services. You can install all the components on the site server, or you can alternatively distribute many components to other servers.

Many of the thread components use folders known as *inboxes* to receive files from other components within the site. Inboxes may consist of a single folder or a folder subtree. Components maintain open file system change notification handles on their inboxes. A component can notify another component that is has work to do by dropping a file in its inbox. The operating system then returns a file change notification event to the component owning the inbox. In ConfigMgr 2012, many components no longer write directly to other components' inbox folders. Instead, these components apply changes directly to the database. The Database Notification Monitor component detects the change and creates a zero byte file in the appropriate inbox to serve as a wake up call. Some components also use in-memory queues for faster communications with other components on the local machine. Some components also maintain outbox folders in which they place files to be processed by other components. Many components additionally operate a watchdog cycle, in which they wake up at regular intervals to perform specific work. Unlike early SMS versions in which watchdog cycles introduced latency into various operations, time-sensitive processing does not depend on watchdog cycles.

Table 3.3 displays many of the ConfigMgr components with a description of their principal functions, the folders they use to communicate with other components, and the log files they maintain. To view the actual components installed on each server expand the `HKEY_LOCAL_MACHINE\SOFTWARE\Microsoft\SMS\Components` registry key. The actual inboxes installed and their folder locations are found under `HKEY_LOCAL_MACHINE\SOFTWARE\Microsoft\SMS\Inbox Source\Inbox Instances`. Most components log details of their activities. Appendix A, "Configuration Manager Log Files," discusses logging options and log file locations for specific components. The Component Type column indicates whether the component runs as its own process or as a thread of the Executive service, and if it is monitored by the Site Component Manager. The components installed on a ConfigMgr site system will vary depending on the site roles assigned to the server and the code revision you are running.

TABLE 3.3   Component Names and Descriptions

Component Name	Display Name	Description	Directory Used	Log File
SMS_SITE_COMPONENT_ MANAGER	Site Component Manager (Component not installed by Site Component Manager)	Installs and manages components on site systems	INBOX: sitecomp. box	sitecomp.log
Monitored Service Components				
SMS_EXECUTIVE	Executive Service	Host process for thread components		Smsexec.log
SMS_SITE_SQL_BACKUP	SMS Site SQL Backup Service	Backup process for site database		smssqlbkup.log
SMS_SITE_VSS_WRITER	SMS Writer Service	Manages volume snapshots for backups		smswriter.log
Monitored Thread Components				
SMS_AI_KB_MANAGER	Asset Intelligence Knowledge Base Manager	Maintains Asset Intelligence data in the site database	INBOX: aikbmgr.box	aikbmgr.log
SMS_ALERT_NOTIFICATION	Alert Notification Manager	Processes instruction files for alerts, sends e-mail, maintains database triggers	INBOX: notictrl.box	NotiCtrl.log
SMS_AMT_PROXY_COMPONENT	Advanced Management Technology (AMT) Proxy	Handles provisioning, maintenance, and requests for Intel AMT clients	INBOX: amtproxymgr.box	amtproxymgr.log
SMS_AWEBSVC_CONTROL_ MANAGER	Application Catalog Web Service	Maintains Application Catalog web service		awebsctl.log
SMS_CERTIFICATE_MANAGER	Certificate Manager	Maintains certificates	INBOX: certmgr.box	CertMgr.log
SMS_CLIENT_CONFIG_MANAGER	Client Configuration Manager	Carries out client push installation and maintains the Client Push Installation account	INBOX: ccr.box	ccm.log

Component Name	Display Name	Description	Directory Used	Log File
SMS_CLIENT_HEALTH	Client Health	Processes client health (.POL) files		Chmgr.log
SMS_COLLECTION_EVALUATOR	Collection Evaluator	Updates collection membership	INBOX: colleval.box OUTBOX: coll_out. box (used for sending to child sites)	colleval.log
SMS_COMPONENT_MONITOR	Component Monitor	Maintains registry setting for discovery components		compmon.log
SMS_COMPONENT_STATUS_SUMMARIZER	Component Status Summarizer	Processes component status summarization rules	INBOX: Compsumm. box	compsumm.log
SMS_DATABASE_NOTIFICATION_MONITOR	Database Notification Monitor	Watches the database for changes to certain tables and creates files in the inboxes of components responsible for processing those changes	This component writes to many inbox folders	smsdbmon.log
SMS_DESPOOLER	Despooler	Processes incoming files from parent or child sites	INBOX: despoolr.box	despool.log
SMS_DISCOVERY_DATA_MANAGER	Discovery Data Manager	Processes discovery data and enters it into the site database	INBOXES: ddm.box; Auth\ddm.box	ddm.log
SMS_DISTRIBUTION_MANAGER	Distribution Manager	Copies packages to distribution points	INBOX: distmgr.box	distmgr.log
SMS_ENDPOINT_PROTECTION_MANAGER	Endpoint Protection Manager	Manages endpoint protection configuration	INBOX: epmgr.box	EPMgr.log
SMS_HIERARCHY_MANAGER	Site Hierarchy Manager	Processes and replicates changes to the site hierarchy	INBOX: hman.box	Hman.log
SMS_INBOX_MANAGER	Inbox Manager	Maintains inbox files		inboxmgr.log

Component Name	Display Name	Description	Directory Used	Log File
SMS_INBOX_MONITOR	Inbox Monitor	Monitors the file count in various inboxes		inboxmon.log
SMS_INVENTORY_DATA_LOADER	Inventory Data Loader	Loads hardware inventory data from clients into the site database	INBOXES: dataldr.box; Auth\dataldr.box	dataldr.log
SMS_INVENTORY_PROCESSOR	Inventory Processor	Converts hardware inventory to a binary format used by the data loader	INBOX: Invntry.box	invproc.log
SMS_LAN_SENDER	Standard Sender	Initiates intersite communications across TCP/IP networks	INBOX: schedule. box\outboxes\LAN	sender.log
SMS_MIGRATION_MANAGER	Migration Manager	Schedules migration tasks	INBOX: mmctrl.box	Migmctrl.log
SMS_MP_CONTROL_MANAGER	Management Point Control Manager	Manages certificate usage for the management point and monitors management point availability		mpcontrol.log
SMS_MP_FILE_DISPATCH_MANAGER	Management Point File Dispatcher	Transfers files from management point outboxes to site server inboxes	INBOX: MP\ OUTBOXES OUTBOXES: See note	mpfdm.log
SMS_OBJECT_REPLICATION_MANAGER	Object Replication Manager	Creates CIXML representations for the ConfigMgr object for replication to primary child sites	INBOX: objmgr.box	objreplmgr.log
SMS_OFFER_MANAGER	Offer Manager	Manages advertisements	INBOX: offermgr.box	offermgr.log
SMS_OFFER_STATUS_SUMMARIZER	Offer Status Summarizer	Populates advertisement status summary information in the site database	INBOX: OfferSum. box	offersum.log

Component Name	Display Name	Description	Directory Used	Log File
SMS_OUTBOX_MONITOR				
SMS_PACKAGE_TRANSFER_MANAGER	Package Transfer Manager	Transfers packages to distribution points	INBOX: PkgTransferMgr.box; OUTBOXES: PkgTransferMgr.box\outboxes	PkgXferMgr.log
SMS_POLICY_PROVIDER	Policy Provider	Generates policies for ConfigMgr components	INBOX: policypv.box	policypv.log
SMS_PORTALWEB_CONTROL_MANAGER	Application Catalog Web Portal Manager	Configures web portal service		Portlctl.log
SMS_REPLICATION_CONFIGURATION_MONITOR	Replication Configuration Monitor		INBOX: rcm.box	Rcmctrl.log
SMS_REPLICATION_MANAGER	Replication Manager	Processes inbound and outbound files for intersite communications	INBOX: Replmgr.box	replmgr.log
SMS_RULE_ENGINE	Rule Engine	Processes automatic deployment rules for software updates	INBOX: RuleEngine.box	Ruleengine.log
SMS_SCHEDULER	Scheduler	Converts replication manager jobs to sender jobs	INBOX: Schedule.box	sched.log
SMS_SITE_CONTROL_MANAGER	Site Control Manager	Maintains site control data	INBOX: sitectrl.box	sitectrl.log
SMS_SITE_SYSTEM_STATUS_SUMMARIZER	Site System Status Summarizer	Processes status messages for the local site and applies summarization rules	INBOX: SiteStat.Box\repl	sitestat.log
SMS_SOFTWARE_INVENTORY_PROCESSOR	Software Inventory Processor	Loads software inventory data from clients into the site database	INBOXES: sinv.box; Auth\sinv.box	sinvproc.log

Component Name	Display Name	Description	Directory Used	Log File
SMS_SOFTWARE_METERING_PROCESSOR	Software Metering Processor	Processes software metering information from clients and updates metering data in the site database	INBOX: swmproc.box	swmproc.log
SMS_SRS_REPORTING_POINT	Reporting Services Point	Configures SQL Server Reporting Services		srsrp.log
SMS_STATE_MIGRATION_POINT	State Migration Point	Maintains user state data		smpmgr.log
SMS_STATE_SYSTEM	State System	Processes and summarizes state messages	INBOX: Auth\statesys.box	statesys.log
SMS_STATUS_MANAGER	Status Manager	Processes status messages and writes status information to the site database	INBOX: Statmgr.box; SMS_EXECUTIVE to SMS_STATUS_MANAGER in-memory status message queue	statmgr.log
SMS_WSUS_CONFIGURATION_MANAGER	WSUS Configuration Manager	Maintains WSUS settings and checks connectivity to upstream server	INBOX: WSUSMgr.box	WCM.log
SMS_WSUS_CONTROL_MANAGER	WSUS Control Manager	Verifies WSUS component health, configuration, and database connectivity		WSUSCtrl.log
SMS_WSUS_SYNC_MANAGER	WSUS Synchronization Manager	Synchronizes updates with upstream server	INBOX: wsyncmgr.box	wsyncmgr.log

Unmonitored Service Component

Component Name	Display Name	Description	Directory Used	Log File
SMS_SITE_BACKUP	Site Backup Agent	Performs the site backup task		Smsbkup.log (in site backup folder)
Unmonitored Thread Components				
SMS_OFFLINE_SERVICING_MANAGER	Offline Servicing for Operating System Images	Manages Software Updates for offline OS images		OfflineServicingMgr.log
SMS_NETWORK_DISCOVERY	Network Discovery Agent	Performs network discovery	Drops DDRs in DDR.box	netdisc.log
SMS_WINNT_SERVER_DISCOVERY_AGENT	Server Discovery Agent	Performs discovery on ConfigMgr site systems	Drops DDRs in DDR.box	ntsvrdis.log

Here is additional information regarding some of the components described in Table 3.3:

▶ The Site Component Manager monitors the Site Control inbox (sitectrl.box) for changes to site properties that require adding, removing, or altering a component on a site system. This is in addition to monitoring its own inbox.

▶ The Discovery Data Manager, Inventory Data Loader, Software Inventory Processor, and State System components maintain trusted inboxes under the inboxes\auth folder for signed files.

▶ The Management Point File Dispatcher transfers files from its inboxes (MP outbox folders) to the inboxes of other components. To accomplish this, it uses the inboxes of the following components as its outboxes: Client Configuration Manager, Discovery Data Manager, Distribution Manager, Inventory Processor, Software Metering Processor, State System, and Status Manager.

The core components that maintain a ConfigMgr site are the Executive Service, Site Component Manager, Site Control Manager, and Site Hierarchy Manager:

▶ The Executive Service is the host process in which most other components run. The Executive Service exists on every ConfigMgr site system other than the site database server.

▶ The Site Component Manager is a separate service that configures and manages other components.

▶ The Site Hierarchy Manager and Site Control Manager work together to maintain the site settings. Each ConfigMgr site maintains site control information in the ConfigMgr database for that site.

Site control information includes the parent site, sender addresses, client and server components, and various other site properties. Site control data is stored in the site database and replicated as global data to all sites in the hierarchy.

Here is an example where an administrator makes a change to a site property using the ConfigMgr console, showing how ConfigMgr components interact:

1. The console application reads the current site control file and calculates a delta based on the settings applied by the administrator. The console code then invokes the CommitSCF method of the SMS_SiteControlFile WMI object to apply the changes in the database.

2. The SMS Provider executes the method against the database. The CommitSCF method inserts the changes into the SiteControl table. Inserting data into the SiteControl table fires the SMSDBMON_SiteControl_SiteControl_AddUpd_HMAN_ins trigger. This creates a new entry in the TableChangeNotifications table.

3. The Database Monitor reads the TableChangeNotifications and processes the change notification.

4. The Database Monitor drops an empty site control file in the Hierarchy Manager inbox to notify Hierarchy Manager of the site changes.

5. Hierarchy Manager updates related tables in the site database.

Figure 3.34 illustrates these steps.

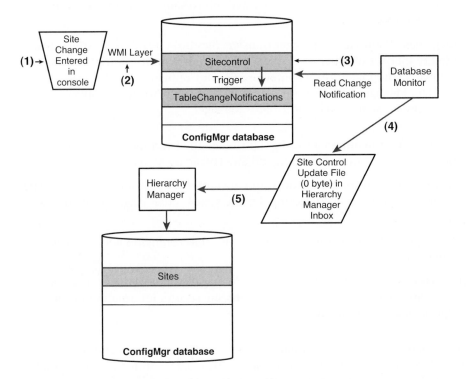

FIGURE 3.34   Illustrating changes made to a site property.

After the site control information in the database is updated, ConfigMgr uses SQL replication to replicate this data as global data.

Most of the remaining components work together, implementing specific feature sets. An important example of this is file-based replication between sites. Here is what will occur when a ConfigMgr component has file data to replicate to another site:

1. The component with data to replicate to another site copies the file(s) to one of the subfolders of the Outbound folder in the Replication Manager's inbox. The subfolders are named high, normal, or low to indicate the priority of the replication job. The file names begin with the destination site code for routing purposes.

2. The Replication Manager compresses the file(s) to its process folder and moves them to its ready folder. Replication Manager then creates a job file under the Scheduler inbox.

3. The Scheduler processes the instruction file and creates instruction and package files in the tosend folder (inboxes\schedule.box\tosend). It then transfers the files to the appropriate sender.

4. The Sender copies the files to the SMS_SITE share on the destination site server. This share is the despooler\receive inbox.

5. At the destination site, the Despooler validates the signature from of the source site server, decompresses the files, and moves them to the Replication Manager inbox.

6. The Replication Manager moves the file to the appropriate inbox of the component for which the file is intended. The Replication Manager also initiates any replication to additional sites that may be required.

The "Viewing Detailed Process Activity" section looks into the inner workings of these processes.

Inside the ConfigMgr Database

The ConfigMgr site database is a SQL Server database that contains data about your ConfigMgr infrastructure and objects, the client systems you manage, and other discovered resources. The default name of the site database is CM_*<site code>* (where *<site code>* indicates the primary site the database is associated with). Although the exact number of objects in a ConfigMgr site database varies, there are generally several thousand objects. Management applications, including the ConfigMgr console, use WMI to access the database.

ConfigMgr Tables and Views

SQL Server stores data in tables. If you are new to SQL, you can think of a table as similar to a spreadsheet with rows and columns of data. A view is a window into the data. A view retrieves data from one or more tables and presents it to the user or calling application. Microsoft's Configuration Manager developers provide an extensive set of database views that presents the underlying data tables in a consistent way. The views abstract away many of the details of the underlying table structure, which may change with future product releases. The reports in ConfigMgr use SQL views. Chapter 18 presents numerous examples of reports based on the SQL views. You can use the views to understand the internal structure of the database. The next sections present a subset of these views and provide information about how the views are organized and named.

Most of the Configuration Manager SQL views correspond to ConfigMgr WMI classes. In many cases, the views also reflect the underlying table structure, with minor formatting changes and more meaningful field names. Many views also combine related data from multiple tables.

Most ConfigMgr administration tasks do not require you to work directly with SQL statements. You can enter SQL statements directly into ConfigMgr reports and database maintenance tasks. Chapter 18 discusses reports, and Chapter 21, "Backup, Recovery, and

Maintenance," discusses database maintenance tasks. To understand the internal structure and operation of the database, however, requires looking at it with SQL tools.

Using SQL Server Management Studio

The primary user interface for administering SQL Server 2008 is the SQL Server Management Studio. To access the Configuration Manager views, follow these steps:

1. Launch the SQL Server Management Studio from **Start -> All Programs -> Microsoft SQL Server 2008 -> SQL Server Management Studio**.

2. After connecting to the site database server SQL instance, expand the *<servername>*database\CM_*<site code>*\views in the tree control in the left pane.

CAUTION: DO NOT MODIFY THE SITE DATABASE DIRECTLY

The site database is critical to the functioning of your site. This section presents tools you can use to view the site database. This information can be useful for understanding how Configuration Manager works and for using ConfigMgr data in reporting. Do not attempt to create, delete, or modify any database objects, or to modify data stored in the database, unless asked to do so by Microsoft support personnel. Remember to test all modifications before applying them to your production environment.

Viewing Collections

The "WMI on Configuration Manager Servers" section of this chapter looked in some detail at the `Collection` WMI object. This object provides access to the properties and methods of the ConfigMgr collections defined in the site database. The SQL view v_Collection provides access to much of the same data. Figure 3.35 shows the tree control expanded in the left pane to display the column definitions for v_Collection, whereas the view on the right displays some of the column values visible when opening the view. These columns correspond to `SMS_Collection` WMI class properties (refer to Figure 3.32). Notice that the MemberClassName column provides the name of the view for the collection membership. These views correspond to the WMI objects specified in the MemberClassName property of the `SMS_Collection` WMI class.

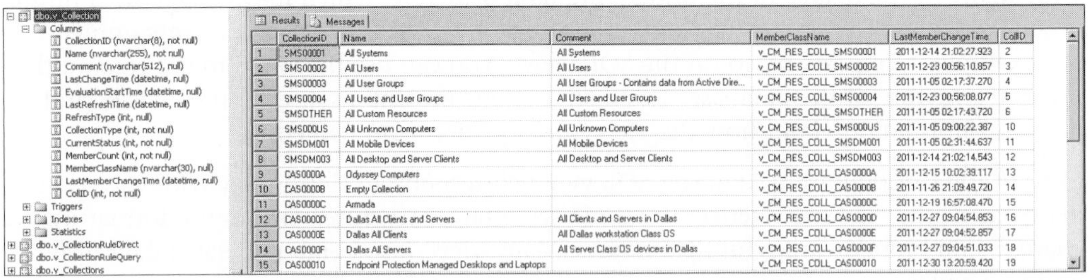

FIGURE 3.35   The v_Collection SQL view displays the descriptive properties of the site's ConfigMgr collections.

The v_Collection view is one of several views referencing ConfigMgr objects. Similar views include v_Advertisement, v_Package, and v_Roles. The naming conventions for views generally map to the corresponding WMI classes, according to the following rules:

▶ WMI class names begin with SMS_, and SQL view names begin with v or v_.

▶ View names more than 30 characters are truncated.

▶ The WMI property names are the same as the field names in the SQL views.

Site Properties

Basic ConfigMgr site properties are stored in the Sites table and exposed though several views and stored procedures. As an example, v_site displays the basic configuration of the current site and its child sites. The sysreslist table stores information about the site systems. An example of a stored procedure that retrieves data from the sites and sysreslist tables is GetMPLocationForIPSubnet, which displays management point information for an IP subnet. The SMSData table includes additional site details, exposed through v_identification.

The tables and views discussed so far relate to the ConfigMgr objects and infrastructure. The database also contains a wealth of data gathered by various discovery methods and client inventory. Chapter 9 discusses discovery and inventory. Discovery and inventory data is stored in resource tables and presented in resource views. The naming conventions for resource views are as follows:

▶ Views displaying current inventory data are named v_GS_*<group name>*.

▶ Views displaying inventory history data are named v_HS_*<group name>*.

▶ Views containing discovery data are named v_R_*<resource type name>* for data contained in WMI scalar properties and v_RA_*<architecture name>*_*<group name>* for data contained in WMI array properties.

▶ Inventory data for custom architectures is presented in views named v_G*<resource type number>*_*<group name>* and v_H*<resource type number>*_*<group name>*. Custom architectures are created by adding IDMIF files to the inventory as described in Chapter 9.

Other Views

Several views are included that present metadata on other views and serve as keys to understanding the view schema. The v_SchemaViews view, displayed in Figure 3.36, lists the views in the view schema family, and shows the type of each view.

Here is the SQL statement that generates the V_SchemaViews view:

```
CREATE VIEW [dbo].[v_SchemaViews] As SELECT CASE
    WHEN name like 'v[_]RA[_]%' THEN 'Resource Array'
    WHEN name like 'v[_]R[_]%'  THEN 'Resource'
    WHEN name like 'v[_]HS[_]%' THEN 'Inventory History'
```

```
    WHEN name like 'v[_]GS[_]%' THEN 'Inventory'
    WHEN name like 'v[_]CM[_]%' THEN 'Collection'
    WHEN name like '%Summ%'  THEN 'Status Summarizer'
    WHEN name like '%Stat%' THEN 'Status'
    WHEN name like '%Permission%' THEN 'Security'
    WHEN name like '%Secured%' THEN 'Security'
    WHEN name like '%Map%' THEN 'Schema'
    WHEN name = 'v_SchemaViews' THEN 'Schema'
ELSE 'Other'
END
As 'Type', name As 'ViewName' FROM sysobjects
WHERE type='V' AND name like 'v[_]%'
```

If you examine the SQL statement, you can see that the selection criteria in the CASE statement use the naming conventions to determine the type of each view.

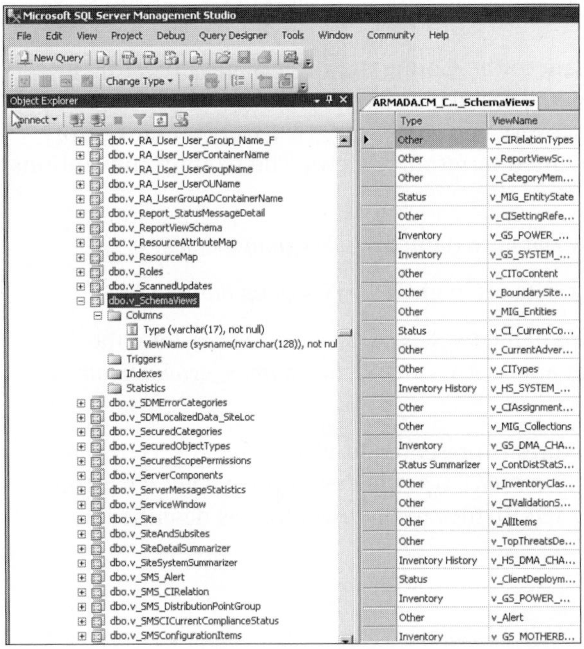

FIGURE 3.36   V_SchemaViews provides a list and categorization of ConfigMgr views.

The v_ResourceMap view presents data from the DiscoveryArchitectures table, which defines the views representing discovery data. Table 3.4 displays the data provided by the v_ResourceMap view.

ConfigMgr uses the fields in Table 3.4 in the following manner:

▶ The ResourceType field is the key used throughout the resource views to associate resources with the appropriate discovery architecture.

▶ The DisplayName field is a descriptive name of the discovery architecture.

▶ The ResourceClassName indicates the view that contains basic identifying information for each discovered instance of the architecture.

TABLE 3.4   The v_ResourceMap View

ResourceType	DisplayName	ResourceClassName
2	Unknown System	v_R_UnknownSystem
3	User Group	v_R_UserGroup
4	User	v_R_User
5	System	v_R_System
6	IP Network	v_R_IPNetwork

As an example, the v_R_System represents discovery data from the System_DISC table. This view provides the unique Resource ID of each computer system discovered by ConfigMgr as well as basic system properties such as the NetBIOS name, operating system, and AD domain. Each resource view containing system information includes the Resource ID field, allowing you to link resources such as hard drives and network cards with the system to which they belong.

The v_ResourceAttributeMap view displayed in Figure 3.37 presents resource attribute types extracted from discovery property definition data in the DiscPropertyDefs table.

FIGURE 3.37   v_ResourceAttributeMap lists the attributes used in resource views.

TIP: COLUMN NAMES HAVE A "0" APPENDED

The ConfigMgr development team appends many of the column names with "0" to avoid possible conflicts with SQL reserved words.

The v_GroupMap view lists the inventory groups and views associated with each inventory architecture. Table 3.5 displays some v_GroupMap entries. Each inventory architecture represents a WMI class specified for inventory collection in the client agent settings.

Each entry in Table 3.5 specifies the resource type, a unique GroupID, the inventory and inventory history views that present the group data, and the Management Information Format (MIF) class from which the inventory data for the group is derived.

The v_GroupAttributeMap lists the attributes associated with each inventory group, and the v_ReportViewSchema view provides a list all classes and properties.

This section examined several of the SQL views that Microsoft provides. You can learn a considerable amount about the internal structure of ConfigMgr by using SQL Server Management Studio to explore the database on your own. You may want to look at the views, the underlying tables, and some of the stored procedures ConfigMgr uses. The examples in this section show how you can analyze and understand these objects.

Viewing Detailed Process Activity

The "WMI in ConfigMgr," "Components and Communications," and "Inside the ConfigMgr Database" sections described the ConfigMgr technical architecture. This section presents some tools you can use to view the inner working of ConfigMgr in detail. The section includes a detailed example to illustrate the use of these tools.

System Center 2012 ConfigMgr provides two built-in mechanisms that allow you to view and analyze ConfigMgr operations in detail:

▶ ConfigMgr components generate status messages to report milestone activity and problem occurrences. System administrators can view status messages and use them in queries and reports. You can also configure the status message system to invoke automated actions in response to specified status messages.

▶ ConfigMgr components generate extensive logs that give additional detail about their activity.

Both the status message system and logging are highly configurable and provide valuable windows into the system.

Digging into ConfigMgr logs is one of the best ways to gain a deep understanding of ConfigMgr internals. Much of the material in this chapter is drawn from analyzing log files. Chapter 21 covers configuring the status message system. Appendix A discusses the various ConfigMgr logs in detail. This part of the chapter discusses the use of status messages and logs for looking at the inner working of ConfigMgr.

TABLE 3.5   The v_GroupMap View (Partial Listing)

ResourceType	GroupID	DisplayName	InvClassName	InvHistoryClassName	MIFClass
5	1	System	v_GS_SYSTEM	v_HS_SYSTEM	SYSTEM
5	2	Workstation Status	v_GS_WORKSTATION_ STATUS		MICROSOFT|WORKSTATION_ STATUS|1.0
5	10	CCM_ RecentlyUsedApps	v_GS_CCM_RECENTLY_ USED_APPS		MICROSOFT|CCM_ RECENTLY_USED_APPS|1.0
5	13	Add Remove Programs	v_GS_ADD_REMOVE_ PROGRAMS	v_HS_ADD_REMOVE_ PROGRAMS	MICROSOFT|ADD_REMOVE_ PROGRAMS|1.0
5	14	Add Remove Programs (64)	v_GS_ADD_REMOVE_ PROGRAMS_64	v_HS_ADD_REMOVE_ PROGRAMS_64	MICROSOFT|ADD_REMOVE_ PROGRAMS_64|1.0
5	21	CD-ROM	v_GS_CDROM	v_HS_CDROM	MICROSOFT|CDROM|1.0
5	22	Computer System	v_GS_COMPUTER_ SYSTEM	v_HS_COMPUTER_SYSTEM	MICROSOFT|COMPUTER_ SYSTEM|1.0
5	23	Disk	v_GS_DISK	v_HS_DISK	MICROSOFT|DISK|1.0
5	24	Partition	v_GS_PARTITION	v_HS_PARTITION	MICROSOFT|PARTITION|1.0
5	25	Logical Disk	v_GS_LOGICAL_DISK	v_HS_LOGICAL_DISK	MICROSOFT|LOGICAL_ DISK|1.0

The ConfigMgr logs are text files, and you can view them in Windows Notepad or your favorite text editor. Most administrators prefer to use the ConfigMgr Trace Log Tool (CMTrace) rather than a text editor to display log files. The log viewer formats log entries, provides search and highlighting features, and provides error lookup. You can optionally turn on an auto-refresh feature to update the displayed log in near real time.

NOTE: CONFIGURATION MANAGER TRACE LOG TOOL (CMTRACE)

Microsoft's Configuration Manager Trace Log Tool (CMTrace) for System Center Configuration Manager eases the ability to view log files. CMTrace.exe can be found in the tools directory on the root on the ConfigMgr 2012 installation media. Previous versions of this tool do not work with ConfigMgr 2012 logs.

Process Monitor is a tool you can use to capture detailed process activity on Windows systems. It provides extensive filtering options that allow you to drill down on activity related to specific folders, view only the operation of selected threads, and so forth. More information on Process Monitor and a link to download this useful tool are available at http://technet.microsoft.com/en-us/sysinternals/bb896645.aspx.

The SQL Server Profiler allows you to capture detailed activity on your SQL Server. The profiler provides extensive filtering options that allow you to record the specific SQL activity in which you are interested. You can use this tool though the SQL Server Profiler user interface or use the ConfigMgr stored procedures spDiagStartTrace and spDiagStopTrace to capture activity ConfigMgr SQL activity. SQL Server Profiler ships with Microsoft SQL Server; the SQL Online Books describe its use in detail.

The "Components and Communications" section presented an example of how ConfigMgr components work together to process a site change. This section takes a closer look at WMI and SQL activity associated with the same site change as captured in logs and other tools. In this example, an administrator uses the ConfigMgr console to modify a site component. This results in the following sequence of events:

1. The console application invokes the SMS Provider WMI object for the modified site control item. The SMS Provider log file (smsprov.log) shows this activity.

2. The provider implements code that applies the update to the database. You can use either the SQL Server Profiler tool or the ConfigMgr SQL logging option to capture the SQL statements the provider uses.

3. The database contains special stored procedures, known as triggers, which automatically carry out additional processing when the update occurs. The triggers write records for auditing purposes and to provide notification to the Database Notification Monitor (SMSDBMON) component. You can use SQL Management Studio to locate and understand the triggers.

4. SMSDBMON processes the data and notified additional components of the change. The Database Notification Monitor log (smsdbmon.log) shows SMSDBMON polling the database for changes. The Process Monitor tool shows file system activity by the Database Notification Monitor thread as it writes to other components' inboxes.

5. Additional threads carry out work to complete the site change. These threads record their activity in status messaged and logs.

Here is a detailed look at the activity just described.

Figure 3.38 shows a portion of the smsprov.log file as displayed in the log viewer.

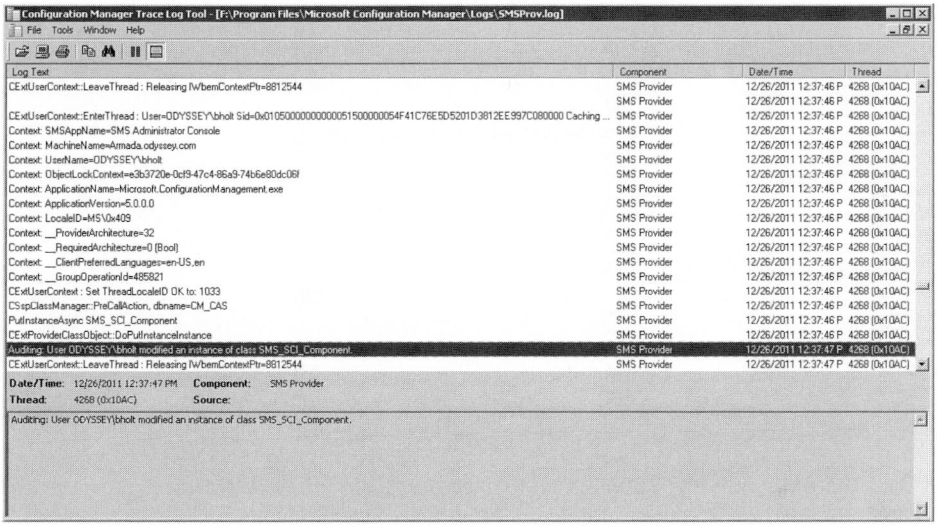

FIGURE 3.38   Smsprov.log displayed in the Log Viewer (SMS Trace).

The smsprov.log file shows calls to the SMS Provider from management applications. The bottom pane of the log viewer displays the details of the highlighted log entry. The entry in Figure 3.35 shows that the user ODYSSEY\bholt modified an instance of class SMS_SCI_SiteDefinition. The SMS_SCI_SiteDefinition, displayed in Figure 3.39, provides an interface to binary data stored in the SiteControl table.

Using the SQL Server Profiler lets you see SQL requests sent to the SQL Server database. (For information about the SQL Server Profiler, see http://msdn.microsoft.com/en-us/library/ms187929.aspx.)

TIP: USING SQL LOGGING TO CAPTURE SQL ACTIVITY

An alternative to using the SQL Server Profiler to capture SQL activity is to enable SQL logging, as described in Appendix A. This adds details of SQL commands directly into the logs for components that access the database. Turning SQL logging on or off requires you to restart the Executive service.

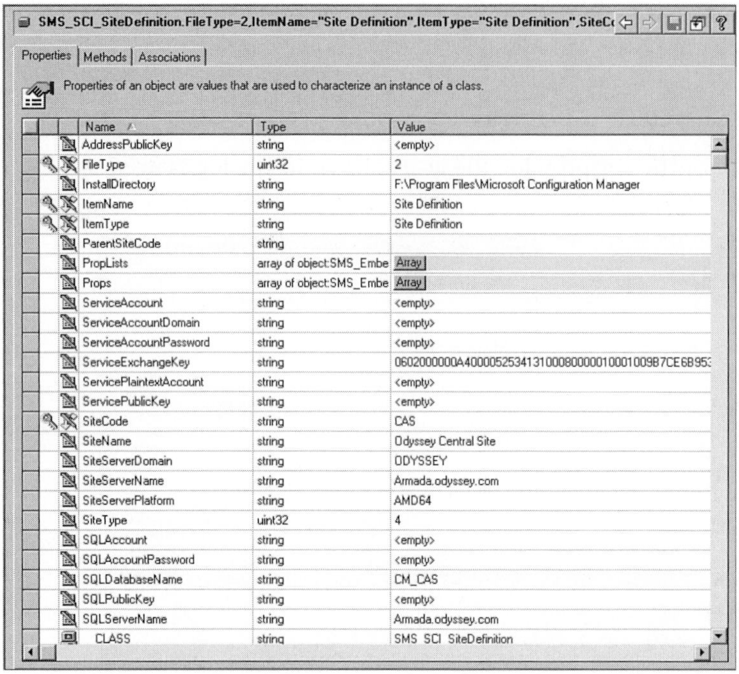

FIGURE 3.39   The SMS_SCI_SiteDefinition WMI class displayed in the WMI Object Browser.

The following SQL commands show the application SMS Provider inserting data into the vSMS_SC_SiteDefinition_Properties view:

```
IF NOT EXISTS (select 1 from vSMS_SC_SiteDefinition_Properties where ID = 0 and Name
= N'Comments'
)
insert into vSMS_SC_SiteDefinition_Properties (ID, Name, Value1, Value2, Value3)
values (0, N'Comments', N'Central Administration Site (CAS)', N'', 0)
 ELSE update vSMS_SC_SiteDefinition_Properties set ID = 0, Name = N'Comments',
Value1
= N'Central Administration Site (CAS)', Value2 = N'', Value3 = 0  where ID = 0 and
Name = N'Comments'
```

You can use SQL Server Management Studio to view the underlying tables for a view. Figure 3.40 shows that vSMS_SC_SiteDefinition_Properties is based on the SC_SiteDefinition_Property table.

Figure 3.41 shows the SC_SiteDefinition_Property table in the Object Explorer tree on the left with the text of the SMSDBAudit trigger in the right text pane. A trigger is a special type of SQL stored procedure that runs automatically when changes are made to table data. The SMSDB Audit trigger (SMSDBAuditTrigger_SC_SiteDefinition_Property_INS_UPD_DEL) inserts a row into the SCCM_Audit table when the data in the SC_SiteDefinition_Property table changes.

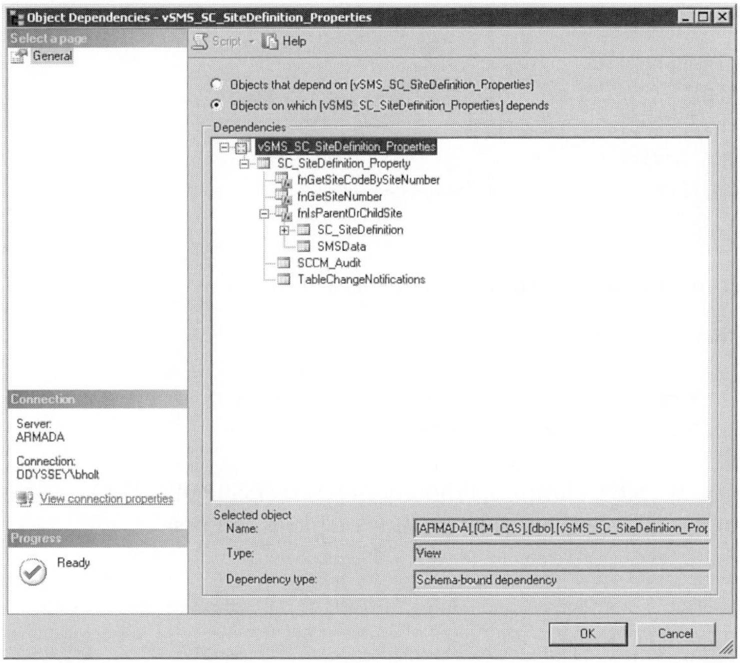

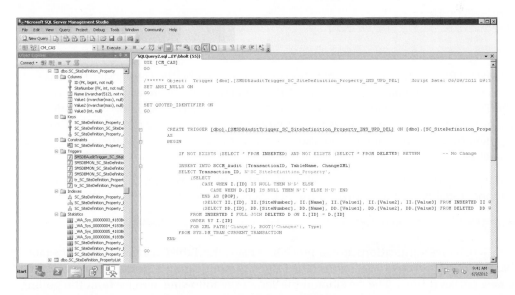

FIGURE 3.40   The Site Definition Properties View depends on the SC_SiteDefinition_Property table.

FIGURE 3.41   The SC_SiteDefinition_Property Table displaying a trigger definition.

The following query displays entries in the SCCM_Audit table associated with changes made by the SMS Provider:

```
SELECT [ID], [TransactionID], [TableName], [By_Machine], [By_User]
    , [By_Component], [ChangeXML], [ChangeTime]
  FROM [CM_CAS].[dbo].[SCCM_Audit]
  WHERE By_Component = 'SMS Provider' and TableName = 'SC_SiteDefinition_
PropertyList'
```

The ChangeXML column from the site description change is as follows:

```
<Changes><Change OP="U"><NewValue><row ID="68" SiteNumber="0" Name="Comments"
Value1="Central (CAS) site" Value2="" Value3="0" /></NewValue>
<OLDValue><row ID="68" SiteNumber="0" Name="Comments" Value1="CAS site"
Value2="" Value3="0" /></OLDValue></Change></Changes>
```

Another trigger, SMSDBMON_SC_SiteDefinition_Property_SQLServerSSBPORT_UPD_HMAN_upd, inserts data into the TableChangeNotifications table as follows:

```
BEGIN
    INSERT INTO TableChangeNotifications(Component,TableName,ActionType,Key1,Key2,
Key3)
        SELECT all
N'SQLServerSSBPORT_UPD_HMAN',N'SC_SiteDefinition_Property',2,IsNULL(convert(nvarchar
(256),SiteNumber),N''),N'',N'' FROM inserted WHERE Name = 'SSBPort' AND
UPDATE(Value3) AND (dbo.fnIsParentOrChildSite(SiteNumber) != 0 OR SiteNumber =
dbo.fnGetSiteNumber())
    IF @@ERROR != 0 ROLLBACK TRAN
END
```

The SMSDBMON prefix indicates that this trigger is owned by the ConfigMgr Database Notification Monitor component. Many of the database tables have triggers that write to the TableChangeNotifications table when changes occur. The Database Notification Monitor log (smsdbmon.log) shows the activity of the maintenance thread, which maintains these triggers. The same thread also maintains the various site maintenance tasks in the database.

The Database Notification Monitor polling thread regularly executes the spGetChangeNotifications stored procedure shown in this SQL Server Profiler trace:

```
[SMS_DATABASE_NOTIFICATION_MONITOR] exec spGetChangeNotifications
```

The spGetChangeNotifications stored procedure reads the TableChangeNotifications table in batches of up to 1000 transactions. The Database Notification Monitor then processes any new entries it finds. The smsdbmon file shows the following activity from the polling thread:

```
RCV: UPDATE on SiteControl for SiteControl_AddUpd_HMAN [CAS  ][9811]
RCV: UPDATE on SiteControl for SiteControl_AddUpd_SiteCtrl [CAS  ][9812]
```

```
SND: Dropped F:\Program Files\Microsoft Configuration Manager\inboxes\
hman.box\CAS.SCU  [9811]
SND: Dropped F:\Program Files\Microsoft Configuration Manager\inboxes\
sitectrl.box\CAS.CT0  [9812]
SQL>>>delete from TableChangeNotifications where RecordID in (9811,9812)
```

Notice the Database Notification Monitor receives notifications that site control data has been updated and drops files in the Hierarchy Manager and Site Control Manager inboxes. These are zero byte files; however, Windows generates a directory change notification when the file is created. ConfigMgr components subscribe to change notifications for their inboxes. The SQL command in the final log entry deletes the change notification entries after processing the changes. This is why you cannot directly view the output of the associated trigger in the TableChangeNotifications table as was possible with the SCCM_Audit table.

To see even more detail of the process activity that carries out the site modification, use Process Monitor to capture the file system activity of the SMSExec process during the site change. Here is a partial listing for some Process Monitor event details during the site change, with comments added:

```
***SMSDBMON file drops files in HMAN and SITECTRL inboxes***
Event Class:      File System
Operation:        CreateFile
Result:  SUCCESS
Path:    F:\Program Files\Microsoft Configuration Manager\inboxes\hman.box\CAS.SCU
Event Class:      File System
Operation:        CreateFile
Result:  SUCCESS
Path:    F:\Program Files\Microsoft Configuration Manager\inboxes\sitectrl.box\CAS.
CT0
*** SMSEXEC thread 5248 detects a Directory Change Notification***
*** Thread ID 5248 matches a thread ID in the Hierarchy Manager log***
Name:    smsexec.exe
Event Class:      File System
Operation:        NotifyChangeDirectory
Result:  SUCCESS
Path:    F:\Program Files\Microsoft Configuration Manager\inboxes\hman.box
TID:     5248
Duration:         27.4709051
Filter:  FILE_NOTIFY_CHANGE_FILE_NAME, FILE_NOTIFY_CHANGE_DIR_NAME
```

Several threads detect the file system changes. The Hierarchy Manager does much of the processing and will serve as an example of ConfigMgr process activity. The Hierarchy Manager Log (Hman.log) now shows:

```
Processing site control file: Site CAS
```

The actual processing is performed by executing SQL statements against the database. With SQL Tracing enabled, the log then shows a large number of SQL SELECT statements retrieving data from tables and views such as SC_SiteDefinition, vSMS_SC_SiteDefinition_Properties and vSMS_SC_Component_Properties. After retrieving data about the site, Hierarchy Manager logs the following entry:

```
Update the Sites table: Site=CAS Parent=
```

This is followed by a number of SQL statements, including updates to the SysReslist table and calls to the spUpdateSites stored procedure, which updates the Sites table. Hierarchy Manager then updates the SiteControlNotification table to create a site control notification for the site. Finally, the thread raises the following status message:

```
Hierarchy Manager successfully processed "F:\Program Files\Microsoft Configuration
Manager\inboxes\hman.box\CAS.SCU", which represented the site control file for site
"Odyssey Central Site" (CAS).
```

Process Monitor can display registry access as well as file access. You could use Process Monitor to see the details of Hierarchy Manager retrieving the registry values it uses to construct a connection string to the site database and accessing the SQL client libraries to initiate the database connection.

SQL Replication Crash Course

A major change in System Center 2012 ConfigMgr is the use of SQL Server replication for intersite communications. SQL Server replication largely replaces the inbox structure and file transfer methods of data exchange used in ConfigMgr 2007 and SMS. ConfigMgr sites are now able to process data and replicate it to other sites rather than requiring multiple sites to process the same data files. When you add a site to an existing hierarchy, ConfigMgr automatically configures SQL replication during site installation.

ConfigMgr uses two types of database replication:

▶ Snapshot replication is used for initial replication when a new site is created in a hierarchy.

▶ The ConfigMgr Database Replication Service uses the SQL Server Service Broker for ongoing data replication.

SQL Server also supports other types of replication that are not used by ConfigMgr and are not discussed in this chapter.

When you add a new site to the hierarchy, the initial snapshot replication uses the SQL Server bulk copy program (BCP) to export site data to a file. ConfigMgr then uses file-based replication to replicate the database extract to the parent site and loads it into the database through the BCP process.

The SQL Server Service Broker provides messaging services for SQL Server applications. Some advantages of the Service Broker include

▶ **Asynchronous messaging:** When an application submits a message to a Service Broker queue, the application can continue to process other work and leave the message delivery details to the Service Broker.

▶ **Transactional processing:** Applications can send a set of related messages as a transaction. The transaction will not be committed until all messages are successfully processed, and can be rolled back if one of the messages fails.

▶ **Message sequencing:** The Service Broker handles the details of providing messages to the receiver in the correct order.

▶ **Database engine integration:** The Service Broker is part of the database engine, which improved performance and leverage the existing connection and security context.

Here are some of the key objects that Service Broker uses for message delivery:

▶ **Messages:** These are units of data. Each message has a specific message type. For example one of the message types defined by ConfigMgr is a notification that and Alert variable has changed.

▶ **Queues:** Queues receive messages and hold them for delivery.

▶ **Conversations:** These are asynchronous, reliable, long-running exchanges of messages. Each conversation has a priority so that messages in higher priority conversations will be processed before lower priority conversations.

▶ **Services:** Services are the endpoints for conversations. A service implements the set of tasks required to produce or consume messages.

ConfigMgr uses SQL Server change tracking to detect changes to the database tables that are in scope for replication. SQL Server change tracking is a new feature introduced with SQL Server 2008. Applications can enable database tables for change tracking. After a table is enabled for change tracking, the database engine maintains information about changes to the table. Applications can access the information to determine what rows in the table have changed and can then query the table to retrieve the modified data. Executing the following query against the ConfigMgr database displays a list of tables that are enabled for change tracking:

```
select name from sys.tables where object_id in (select object_id
from sys.change_tracking_tables) order by name
```

These tables contain data that will be replicated to other sites if changes occur. The list will generally contain several hundred tables and will vary depending on the whether the site's role in the hierarchy and the number of locally updated objects. Some ConfigMgr data is local to the site and not replicated. Tables containing local data are not enabled for change tracking. Chapter 5 discusses ConfigMgr replication scopes and planning considerations related to replication.

Configuration Manager Database Replication

Several ConfigMgr components work together to replicate data between sites. The code that carries out replication resides in several places:

▶ The Executive service

▶ Stored procedures defined in the site database

▶ Managed code in .NET assemblies

ConfigMgr creates several Service Broker objects for its own use. Figure 3.42 displays the ConfigMgr Service Broker Queues and Services nodes in the tree pane along with the corresponding sections of the default Service Broker report.

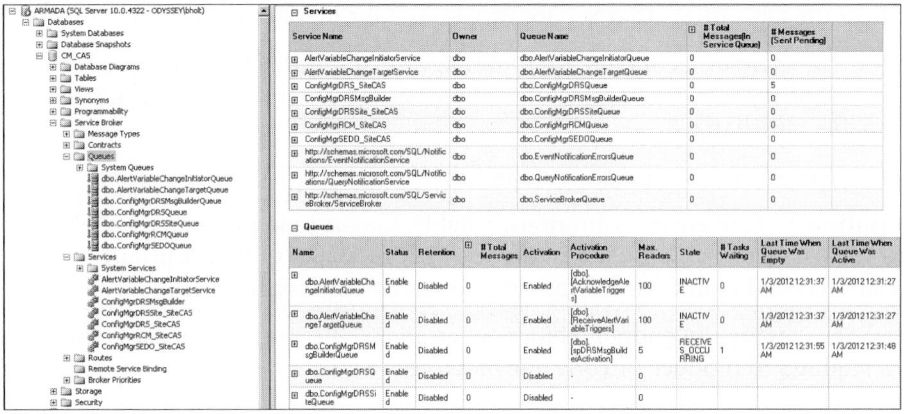

FIGURE 3.42   Service Broker Objects in the CAS site database.

The SQL statements used to create these objects reveal how they work together. Here is the procedure to display the SQL language used to create an object:

1. Right-click on the object in the Object Explorer tree.

2. Select **Script {objecttype} as -> CREATE to" -> New Query Editor Window"** where objecttype may be "Service," "Queue," and so on.

The queue used by the data replication service (DRS) to replicate global data is the ConfigMgrDRSQueue queue. The ConfigMgr DRS is implemented as managed code and runs within the Common Language Runtime (CLR) component of the .NET Framework integrated into SQL Server. CLR integration allows procedural language code to run in close proximity to the database engine, which provides performance advantages and other optimizations. Figure 3.43 shows the ConfigMgr managed code assemblies, together with the functions and procedures that depend on the MessageHanderService assembly.

The code for the MessageHanderService, contained in *<ConfigMgrInstallPath>*\bin\x64\
messagehanderervice.dll, implements much of the DRS functionality. For more information on SQL Server CLR integration, see http://msdn.microsoft.com/en-us/library/
ms131089.aspx.

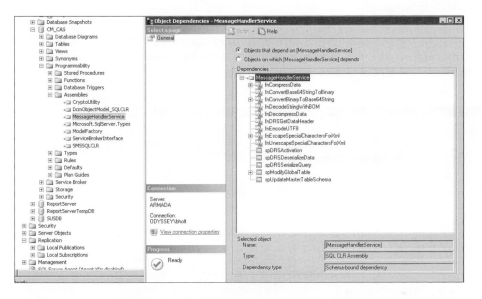

FIGURE 3.43   Managed code assemblies in the CAS site database and message handler
service dependent objects.

NOTE: ENABLING CLR INTEGRATION

CLR integration is disabled by default in SQL Server. ConfigMgr Setup will enable CLR integration. You should consider the impact on other databases if ConfigMgr will be sharing a
SQL Server instance.

Here is the object definition for the ConfigMgrDRSQueue:

```
CREATE QUEUE [dbo].[ConfigMgrDRSQueue] WITH STATUS = ON ,
RETENTION = OFF  ON [PRIMARY]
```

The ConfigMgrDRS_SiteCAS service uses the ConfigMgrDRSQueue and is defined as
follows:

```
CREATE SERVICE [ConfigMgrDRS_SiteCAS]  AUTHORIZATION [dbo]  ON QUEUE
[dbo].[ConfigMgrDRSQueue] ([CriticalPriority],
[HighPriority],
[LowNormalPriority],
[LowPriority],
[NormalPriority])
```

Related service broker objects define the various DRS message types, broker priorities, local routes and routes to other sites, and contracts. As an example, the route to site PR2 is defined as

```
CREATE ROUTE [ConfigMgrDRSRoute_SitePR2]    AUTHORIZATION [dbo]    WITH  SERVICE_NAME
  = N'ConfigMgrDRS_SitePR2' ,    ADDRESS  = N'TCP://Ambassador.odyssey.com:4022'
```

A contract specifies the broker priorities for various message types. Figure 3.44 shows the CriticalPriority contract. All message types specified as critical priority will be delivered before messages of lower priorities in the same queue.

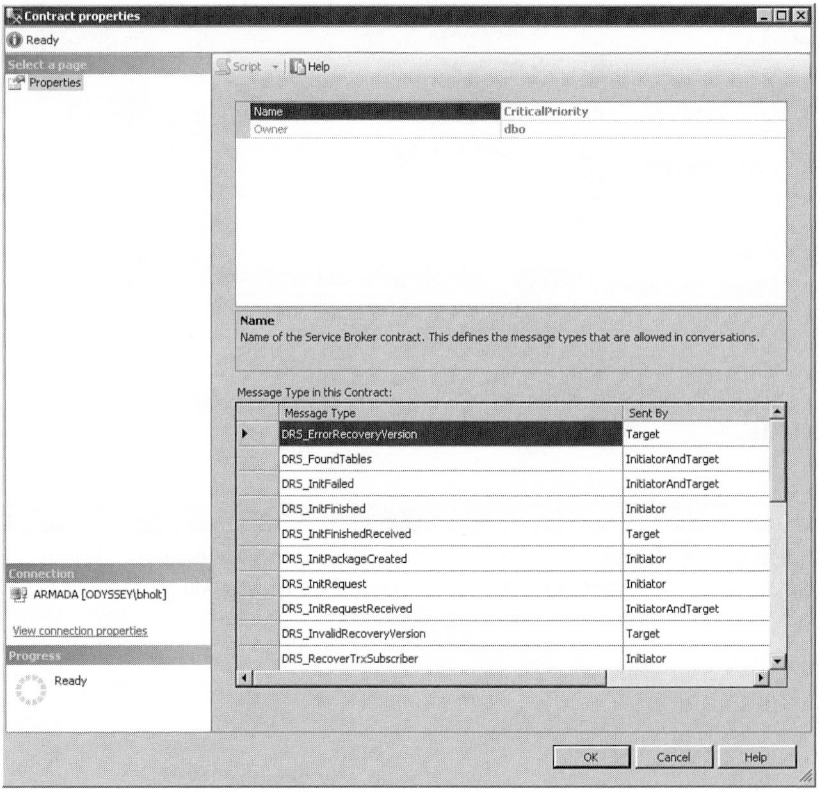

FIGURE 3.44   The message broker critical priority contract.

Table 3.6 shows the priority, service name, contract, message type, and message body for some typical messages from the ConfigMgrDRSQueue. For purposes of this discussion, the message body has been cast into a human readable form. The actual messages contain additional metadata including the conversation group ID and sequencing information.

TABLE 3.6 Sample Message Data from ConfigMgrDRSQueue

Priority	service_name	service_contract_name	message_type_name	casted_message_body
7	ConfigMgrDRS_SiteCAS	HighPriority	DRS_SyncStart	<DRS_SyncStart SourceSite="PR2" SyncID="21AC43A3-9A35-48D2-BE92-40FDE527335D" ReplicationGroup="Alerts" StartTime="2012-01-05T00:40:24.467" BuildNumber="7678"/>
7	ConfigMgrDRS_SiteCAS	HighPriority	DRS_SyncData	<DRS_SyncData BuildNumber="7678" LastSyncVersionToSource="98540" ThisVersion="230384" SyncID="21AC43A3-9A35-48D2-BE92-40FDE527335D" ReplicationGroupID="8" MessageID="B214790C-717E-4BB7-83B6-2F851114C47C"><Operation Type="U" TableName="AlertVariable_G1" Context=""><row ID="23" Value_Int="9" LastChangeTime="2012-01-05T00:39:29.573"/></Operation></DRS_SyncData>
7	ConfigMgrDRS_SiteCAS	HighPriority	DRS_SyncEnd	<DRS_SyncEnd SourceSite="PR2" SyncID="21AC43A3-9A35-48D2-BE92-40FDE527335D" ReplicationGroup="Alerts" LastSyncVersionFromSource="230384"/>

Priority	service_name	service_contract_name	message_type_name	casted_message_body
5	ConfigMgrDRS_SiteCAS	NormalPriority	DRS_SyncData	`<DRS_SyncData BuildNumber="7678" LastSyncVersionToSource="98544" ThisVersion="356796" SyncID="DCBA3151-830F-4AB6-93A6-2D197686487F" ReplicationGroupID="3" MessageID="9A6BC0AA-A096-4D67-A028-6B764492E2ED"><Operation Type="U" TableName="SEDO_LockableObjects" Context=""><row ID="154" LockID="7735F1D5-E343-42A4-8D1D-429024D859DA" ObjectID="580B2320-7903-4DEC-BF3B-1AA7775776BB" ObjectVersion="DA1FC089-EA1F-4FF0-8860-BA24BB70B780" ObjectTypeID="1" OrigSiteNum="0"/></Operation><Operation Type="U" TableName="SMSPackages_G" Context=""><row PkgID="DAL00006" Name="Report Viewer 2008" Version="" Language="" Manufacturer="Microsoft" Description="" Source="C:\Packages\SD\Install - Report Viewer 2008" SourceSite="PR1" RefreshSchedule="" LastRefresh="1970-04-10T06:35:00" ShareName="" PreferredAddress="" StorePkgFlag="2" ShareType="1" Permission="15" UseForcedDisconnect="0" ForcedRetryDelay="2" DisconnectDelay="5" IgnoreSchedule="0" Priority="2" PkgFlags="1" MIFFilename="" MIFPublisher="" MIFName="" MIFVersion="" SourceVersion="1" SourceDate="2012-01-03T11:52:16" SourceSize="2865" SourceCompSize="0" UpdateMask="268697632" Action="1" Hash="0817602173640594 FC0D7636927CA6DF9" ImageFlags="0" UpdateMaskEx="557056" HashVersion="2" NewHash="4B41F72B69B91928E9B3A04410F B26F6B860F261" ImagePath="" Architecture="" PackageType="0" AlternateContentProviders="" SourceLocaleID="1033" DefaultImage="1" SEDOComponentID="4DAC422F-A2E5-4475-B90E-E420F67EC02B" TransformReadiness="0" TransformAnalysisDate="1980-01-01T00:00:00"/></Operation></DRS_SyncData>`
5	ConfigMgrDRS_SiteCAS	NormalPriority	DRS_SyncEnd	`<DRS_SyncEnd SourceSite="PR1" SyncID="DCBA3151-830F-4AB6-93A6-2D197686487F" ReplicationGroup="Configuration Data" LastSyncVersionFromSource="356803"/>`

The ConfigMgr SMS_REPLICATION_CONFIGURATION_MONITOR (RCM) executive thread component identifies the data replication, connects to the database, and initiates DRS synchronization. Figure 3.45 shows a sample of RCM database activity. The SQL Server Profiler template used to capture these events, ReplicationActivity.tdf, is included as online material for this book, see Appendix D, "Available Online," for information.

EventClass	ApplicationName	FileName	ObjectName	TextData
SP:StmtStarting	SMS_REPLICATION_CONFIGURATION_MONITOR		spGetSSBDialogHandle	SET @Handle = @ConversationHandle; ...
SP:StmtStarting	SMS_REPLICATION_CONFIGURATION_MONITOR		spGetSSBDialogHandle	GOTO SUCCESS;
SP:StmtStarting	SMS_REPLICATION_CONFIGURATION_MONITOR		spGetSSBDialogHandle	IF (@@TRANCOUNT > 0)
SP:StmtStarting	SMS_REPLICATION_CONFIGURATION_MONITOR		spGetSSBDialogHandle	COMMIT TRANSACTION;
SP:StmtStarting	SMS_REPLICATION_CONFIGURATION_MONITOR		spGetSSBDialogHandle	RETURN @RetVal;
SP:StmtStarting	SMS_REPLICATION_CONFIGURATION_MONITOR		spDRSInitiateSynchronizations	SEND ON CONVERSATION @Handle MESSAG...
Broker:Convers...	SMS_REPLICATION_CONFIGURATION_MONITOR	ConfigMgrDRSMsgBuilder	565B4CBC-293A-E111-AA39-00155D0A8106	CONVERSING
Broker:Message...	SMS_REPLICATION_CONFIGURATION_MONITOR	ConfigMgrDRSMsgBuilder		
Broker:Convers...	SMS_REPLICATION_CONFIGURATION_MONITOR	ConfigMgrDRSMsgBuilder	595B4CBC-293A-E111-AA39-00155D0A8106	CONVERSING
SP:StmtStarting	SMS_REPLICATION_CONFIGURATION_MONITOR		spDRSInitiateSynchronizations	END TRY
SP:StmtStarting	SMS_REPLICATION_CONFIGURATION_MONITOR		spDRSInitiateSynchronizations	FETCH NEXT FROM Groups INTO @Replic...
SP:StmtStarting	SMS_REPLICATION_CONFIGURATION_MONITOR		spDRSInitiateSynchronizations	WHILE @@FETCH_STATUS=0
SP:StmtStarting	SMS_REPLICATION_CONFIGURATION_MONITOR		spDRSInitiateSynchronizations	SET @Contract = dbo.fnDRSGetPriorit...

FIGURE 3.45   SQL Server Profiler Trace Showing RCM Component Activity.

Here are some SQL stored procedures that carry out much of the work for the RCM:

▶ **spDRSInitiateSynchronizations:** RCM drives the replication process by calling this procedure for each message priority. spDRSInitiateSynchronizations extracts changed data from the ReplicationData table, constructs the appropriate message type and calls the spGetSSBDialogHandle to retrieve a handle for a dialog on the message builder queue, ConfigMgrDRSMsgBuilder. The procedure then uses the dialog handle to insert the message into the ConfigMgrDRSMsgBuilder queue.

▶ **spGetSSBDialogHandle:** This procedure first attempts to retrieve a handle from the Service Broker dialog pool (dbo.SSB_DialogPool) that matches the contract and conversation required for the message. If there is not an existing handle the procedure verifies that a valid route exists, and then creates a new handle in the dialog pool and initializes a new dialog. ConfigMgrDRSMsgBuilder returns a dialog handle to the calling procedure.

▶ **spDRSMsgBuilderActivation:** This is the activation stored procedure for the ConfigMgrDRSMsgBuilder queue. This means that the procedure automatically fires when there are messages in the queue. The procedure performs various checks and then calls the procedure spDRSSendChangesForGroup. spDRSSendChangesForGroup updates replication metadata table and then calls additional procedures to obtain an handle on the site or global DRS message queue and insert the message into the queue.

You can view the full text of these procedures using the same method described in the beginning of this section to script the object broker object definition language to a query editor window.

TIP: VIEWING REPLICATION STATUS WITH SPDIAGDRS

The SQL stored procedure spDiagDRS provides detailed status of the replication queues, message activity and replicated data at your site. To execute this procedure, locate dbo. spDiagDRS under **Programmability** -> **Stored Procedures** in the site database, right-click and choose **Execute Stored Procedure**. You can optionally enter values for specific values for the table, column, and value you wish to examine. For example, you would enter **BoundaryGroup**, **Name**, and **Headquarters** to view the replication status or the boundary group named Headquarters. Leave these parameters blank to view general replication status.

File-Based Replication

ConfigMgr uses file-based replication for certain operations such as transferring package content to distribution points in child sites. Chapter 5, "Network Design," describes the scenarios that use file replication and the relevant configuration options. The "Components and Communications" section presented an overview of how file-based replication works. This section uses the transfer of the file content to illustrate in more detail how file-based replication works. ConfigMgr components work together to prepare file content, schedule replication, and execute Windows file copy operations.

Again processing begins when the Database Notification Monitor detects a change in the site database. In this case, an administrator has initiated distribution of a package to a distribution point at a secondary site. The Database Notification Monitor log shows DBMON dropping a package notification file in the Distribution Manager inbox:

```
RCV: INSERT on PkgNotification for PkgNotify_Add [PR100003  ][72057594037942821]
SMS_DATABASE_NOTIFICATION_MONITOR 1/10/2012 12:57:45 PM 3652 (0x0E44)
SND: Dropped F:\Program Files\Microsoft Configuration Manager\inboxes\distmgr.box\
PR100003.PKN
   [72057594037942820] SMS_DATABASE_NOTIFICATION_MONITOR 1/10/2012 12:57:45 PM 3652
(0x0E44)
```

Here are some status messages showing Distribution Manager processing the request to distribute a package to a child site:

```
Distribution Manager is beginning to process package "MOFComp" (package ID =
PR100003).
Distribution Manager is preparing to send the compressed image of package "PR100003"
to child site "SS1".
Distribution Manager instructed Scheduler and Sender to send package "PR100003" to
child site "SS1".
```

The Distribution Manager log shows additional detail about the processing between the time that Distribution Manager began preparing to send the compressed image and the time it instructed the Scheduler and Sender to send the package.

```
Needs to send the compressed package for package PR100003 to site SS1 1/10/2012
12:57:57 PM 4892 (0x131C)
Sending a copy of package PR100003 to site SS1 1/10/2012 12:57:57 PM 4892 (0x131C)
The reporting site of site SS1 is this site. 1/10/2012 12:57:58 PM 4892 (0x131C)
Use drive F for storing the compressed package. 1/10/2012 12:57:58 PM 4892 (0x131C)
Incremented ref count on file F:\SMSPKG\PR100003.SS1.PCK, count = 1 1/10/2012
 12:57:59 PM 4892 (0x131C)
Setting CMiniJob transfer root to F:\SMSPKG\PR100003.SS1.PCK 1/10/2012 12:57:59
PM 4892 (0x131C)
Incremented ref count on file F:\SMSPKG\PR100003.SS1.PCK, count = 2 1/10/2012
12:57:59 PM 4892 (0x131C)
Decremented ref count on file F:\SMSPKG\PR100003.SS1.PCK, count = 1 1/10/2012
12:57:59 PM 4892 (0x131C)
Created minijob to send compressed copy of package PR100003 to site SS1.  Transfer
 root = F:\SMSPKG\PR100003.SS1.PCK. 1/10/2012 12:57:59 PM 4892 (0x131C)
```

This shows Distribution Manager creating the compressed package F:\SMSPKG\PR100003.
SS1.PCK. Distribution Manager then notifies the Scheduler and Sender by dropping a JOB
file in its inbox. The details of the notification process are not logged but can be seen
through Process Monitor events such as the ones shown in Table 3.7.

TABLE 3.7   File Operations That Initiate Intersite Replication

Operation	Details	Component
CreateFile	\\ATHENA.ODYSSEY.COM\SMS_PR1\inboxes\ schedule.box\0000005F.JOB	Distribution Manager
WriteFile	\\ATHENA.ODYSSEY.COM\SMS_PR1\inboxes\ schedule.box\0000005F.JOB	Distribution Manager
ReadFile	\\ATHENA.ODYSSEY.COM\SMS_PR1\inboxes\ schedule.box\0000005F.JOB	Scheduler

The component names shown in Table 3.7 are not displayed in the Process Monitor
output but are determined by matching the thread IDs (TIDs) to the TIDs in the log files.

Here is an extract from the Scheduler log showing the Scheduler creating an instruction
file for the Sender:

```
<Activating JOB 0000005F> [Software Distribution for MOFComp, Package ID = PR100003]
1/10/2012 12:58:12 PM 5844 (0x16D4)
    Destination site:  SS1, Preferred Address: *, Priority: 2 1/10/2012 12:58:12 PM
5844 (0x16D4)
    Instruction type:  MICROSOFT|SMS|MINIJOBINSTRUCTION|PACKAGE 1/10/2012 12:58:12
 PM 5844 (0x16D4)
```

```
    Creating instruction file:
\\ATHENA.ODYSSEY.COM\SMS_PR1\inboxes\schedule.box\tosend\0000005F.Iem 1/10/2012
12:58:12 PM 5844 (0x16D4)
    Transfer root:  F:\SMSPKG\PR100003.SS1.PCK 1/10/2012 12:58:12 PM 5844 (0x16D4)
    Instruction (and package) file created.  Mark job active. 1/10/2012 12:58:12 PM
5844 (0x16D4)
    <JOB STATUS - ACTIVE> 1/10/2012 12:58:12 PM 5844 (0x16D4)
<Updating JOB 0000005F> [Software Distribution for MOFComp, Package ID = PR100003]
1/10/2012 12:58:12 PM 5844 (0x16D4)
    Destination site:  SS1, Preferred Address: *, Priority: 2 1/10/2012 12:58:12 PM
 5844 (0x16D4)
    Created new send request ID:  2002NPR1 1/10/2012 12:58:13 PM 5844 (0x16D4)
```

The following excerpts from the LAN Sender log show the major phases of the sending operation. First, the Sender connects to the Scheduler's outbox (\..\schedule.box\ outboxes\LAN) to check for sender instructions. The Sender then finds the send request and establishes a connection to the destination site.

```
Connecting to F:\Program Files\Microsoft Configuration Manager\inboxes\
schedule.box\outboxes\LAN.
COutbox::TakeNextToSend(pszSiteCode)
Retrieved the snapshot for priority 2, there are 1 files in the snapshot.
Found send request.  ID: 2002NPR1, Dest Site: SS1
Created sending thread (Thread ID = 1AF4)
Trying the No. 1 address (out of 1)
Passed the xmit file test, use the existing connection
```

The next major phase of the sender operation is to locate the package and instruction files and verify that they are not already on the destination server:

```
Package file = F:\SMSPKG\PR100003.SS1.PCK
Instruction file = F:\Program Files\Microsoft Configuration Manager\inboxes\
schedule.box\tosend\0000005F.Iem
Checking for remote file \\CHARON.odyssey.com\SMS_SITE\2002NPR1.PCK
```

The final major phase of the sending process is to actually transmit the data, together with package instructions that will allow the Despooler component at the receiving site to unpack and correctly route the files:

```
Attempt to create/open the remote file \\CHARON.odyssey.com\SMS_SITE\2002NPR1.PCK
Created/opened the remote file
Attempt to write 1024 bytes to \\CHARON.odyssey.com\SMS_SITE\2002NPR1.PCK
at position 0
Wrote 1024 bytes to \\CHARON.odyssey.com\SMS_SITE\2002NPR1.PCK at position 0
Sending completed [F:\SMSPKG\PR100003.SS1.PCK]
Finished sending SWD package PR100003 version 1 to site SS1
```

TIP: USING NAL LOGGING TO CAPTURE NETWORK ACTIVITY

If you are interested in seeing even more detail of ConfigMgr network activity, you can enable Network Abstraction Layer logging. Appendix A describes NAL logging.

Other processes not detailed here due to space considerations include the receiving end of the site join, processing file signatures and hashes, and content status updates applied to the site database.

Summary

This chapter discussed the internal working of Configuration Manager. It looked at how ConfigMgr sites publish information in Active Directory and how ConfigMgr clients use directory information. The chapter then discussed how ConfigMgr clients and servers use WMI. It examined some of the internal storage of the ConfigMgr database, and how ConfigMgr processes and threads work together to implement key features. The chapter also examined how sites replicate data and content. Finally, the chapter presented examples of how you can use ConfigMgr status messages and logs along with some other tools to drill down into the inner workings of Configuration Manager.

The next chapter discusses how to leverage Configuration Manager features to design solutions and deliver value to your organization.

PART II

Planning, Design, and Installation

IN THIS PART

Architecture Design Planning

Part 1 of this book discussed basic configuration management principles and described the feature set and inner workings of System Center 2012 Configuration Manager (ConfigMgr). To use ConfigMgr successfully, you must design an infrastructure, configuration standards, and workflow appropriate to your environment and business goals. This chapter addresses planning and design considerations that are critical for using ConfigMgr to effectively manage your environment and deliver high-quality services to users.

Developing the Solution Architecture

Information Technology (IT) is at the heart of nearly every business process and organizational activity today, and IT departments are increasingly responsible for delivering the applications and data users need without limiting geographic mobility or device types. The services IT provides must be secure, reliable, and scalable. Each IT department has its own style and methods for meeting these challenges.

Microsoft designed System Center 2012 Configuration Manager to be flexible and configurable, enabling you to deploy it in a way that matches your organization's business needs and the working model of your IT department. To get the most out of ConfigMgr, you need to consider your organizational goals, your current environment, and the pain points in your IT service delivery. You can then leverage the appropriate solution scenarios to improve the quality of your IT services.

Establishing Business Requirements

What are the major challenges facing your IT organization today? What additional challenges are you likely to encounter in the coming years? You should focus on these areas as you plan your Configuration Manager architecture. You can use Configuration Manager to deliver a wide variety of services; focus on those features that are most important to your organization. Here are some of the major challenges common to most IT departments:

▶ **Aligning IT services with business goals:** Many organizations start with an enterprise service catalog that defines the essential services the enterprise delivers to its customers. All IT activities should support these enterprise services, directly or indirectly. Whether you have a formal enterprise service catalog, you should consider what the primary goals and activities of your organization are and how IT projects support organizational priorities. You can use ConfigMgr with service management tools to optimize your infrastructure to support critical services.

▶ **Compliance requirements:** Most organizations are subject to various regulations such as the Sarbanes-Oxley Act (SOX) or the Federal Information Security Management Act (FISMA). These regulations require IT to maintain and validate effective controls around information systems. IT must also track compliance with intellectual property laws, including software licensing agreements and privacy laws. ConfigMgr offers features to automate compliance tracking, configuration lockdown, patch deployment, and license management.

▶ **Security requirements:** In a time when intellectual property is the most important asset for most organizations, businesses are faced with an array of threats ranging from cyber-punks to sophisticated state-sponsored cyber attacks. Financially motivated cyber crime alone is estimated to be the largest criminal activity in the world in economic terms. Survival and competitive advantage require an effective information security program. You can use ConfigMgr to provide endpoint protection and network access protection, remediate vulnerabilities, and manage security setting across a variety of devices.

▶ **Embracing consumerization:** Computer technology has become a part of everyday life, and workers expect and demand to use the devices, applications, and services they are familiar with in the workplace. Gartner Group has called the consumerization of IT an "irreversible megatrend," one that IT departments need to accept while managing the security, compliance, and support challenges it presents. System Center 2012 Configuration Manager's new user-centric content delivery, including the Application Catalog and Software Center, along with support for mobile devices, is a powerful tool for enabling users to work with the flexibility they require.

▶ **Controlling costs:** Supporting personal computer (PC) hardware and software and providing access to basic services like printing, email, and content sharing has consumed major part of IT budgets in the past. Efficient and scalable support practices are essential to meet the increased pressure to reduce costs in today's business environment. ConfigMgr shines in the area of cost control, with automated OS and software deployment, tools for optimizing hardware assets and software licenses, remote troubleshooting tools, power management, and more.

▶ **Harnessing the cloud:** Advances in virtualization and distributed computing have led to a new generation of on-demand applications and services. Although ConfigMgr is just beginning to address management of cloud-based services, its support for virtual application delivery and managing user experience, as well as server infrastructure management, can play a supporting role in private cloud deployments.

Assessing Your Environment

This chapter focuses on infrastructure and solution delivery planning. To apply the material presented here in an effective manner, you need a good understanding of your environment and organization. Here are some factors to consider as you begin your planning:

▶ Regulatory compliance requirements affecting your organization, as well as organizational security and auditing policies.

▶ Organizational structure is especially important for planning user-centric management and communicating with the business about your rollout and the services you will offer.

▶ Configuration Management processes in place, especially if your organization has an enterprise Configuration Management Database (CMDB) with which you may want to integrate data stored in ConfigMgr.

▶ Change management and release management processes that you need to consider when planning for software distribution, software updates, and OS deployment.

▶ IT administrative policies and service level agreements (SLAs).

▶ Various IT groups you may need to interact with, such as network and database administrators.

▶ Your data center facilities and server infrastructure.

▶ Server and client virtualization technologies in use.

▶ Operating systems and device types in your environment, including mobile devices.

▶ Your network topology and Active Directory (AD) configuration.

▶ Enterprise storage architecture, particularly if you are considering using a SAN backend for software distribution files.

▶ Enterprise services such as monitoring and backups that are necessary for supporting your ConfigMgr infrastructure.

Decision points to consider regarding your environment incorporate information related to a number of areas:

▶ The business dynamics of your solution

   ▶ **Your business objectives:** Review your company's mission statement and strategic goals. How can better systems management support company goals? Is cost cutting a major imperative? Do departments have specific requests for better support or easier access to software and content?

   ▶ **The services and solutions you plan to deliver:** Consider your user requirements. Do users have difficulty getting support? Do they need access to certain applications from a variety of devices and locations?

   ▶ **Geographic, language, and cultural considerations:** Start by identifying the geographic locations with large numbers of users. Consider whether your users need a localized experience. Are there users in remote locations with little access to IT support? Do users travel frequently?

   ▶ **Organizational structure:** Do various business units have their own "shadow IT" for user support? How are licensing costs handled? Are you likely to deal with mergers and acquisitions, or with frequent changes in physical locations?

Based on this assessment, you may choose to design your solution around efficiency and cost-savings, focusing on features such as power management and remote support, or you might focus on productivity gains through robust software delivery and user-centric management. You may also find that deploying services to remote locations or supporting multiple languages are priorities. If you expect a high level of organizational change, you may want to look at the flexibility that virtualization provides and place a premium on maintaining a good lab environment where you can test changes before implementing them.

▶ Dynamics of your IT environment

   ▶ **Business, regulatory, and IT policies that govern operations:** What regulations and policies govern your systems? How is compliance measured? Are IT and business personnel often asked to provide evidence to auditors that ConfigMgr could automate?

   ▶ **Security requirements:** How much priority does the organization place on security relative to usability and cost? Are there requirements for ConfigMgr security features, such as endpoint security and network access protection (NAP)? Are there other security controls in place on your network and systems that you need to consider? Is there a requirement to send security events to a security information and event management (SIEM) system?

   ▶ **Administrative model:** Who will be responsible for ConfigMgr administration? Where are administrators located? Will some administrators need limited, delegated access?

   ▶ **Support considerations:** Who will support AD? SQL Server? Networking? End users and end user devices?

ConfigMgr can automate many of the repetitive tasks that may be consuming your IT resources. Reach out to IT stakeholders and help them address the inefficiencies in their processes, and make sure your design conforms to and supports IT department policies and security controls.

▶ Your technical environment

  ▶ **Network environment:** What does your network topology look like? What network infrastructure and security devices are in place? What ports and protocols are allowed through these devices? How are change requests handled?

  ▶ **Active Directory environment:** Do you have multiple AD forests? Will you support computers in workgroups?

  ▶ **Server and Data Center infrastructure:** Is server infrastructure centralized in a few large data centers or is it distributed? Are some data centers better connected than are others, or do they have better physical security? What are the hardware standards? Is virtualization preferred?

  ▶ **Installed client base and hardware refresh cycle:** What is the hardware and operating system (OS) mix for the installed PC base? How are new systems imaged? What mobile devices are in use? Is there a need to support embedded systems? How often are systems replaced? Are users allowed to bring their own systems? Is there a planned OS upgrade?

  ▶ **Existing SQL Server deployment:** Will you be using existing SQL servers? Do these systems meet ConfigMgr requirements? Are SQL servers clustered? Are SQL reporting services deployed?

  ▶ **Storage and backup infrastructure:** What storage technologies are in use? How is data replicated between storage systems?

Details of your design such as optimum server placement, hardware configuration, and client installation methods depend on the IT infrastructure and services you have in place.

Planning for Licensing

Microsoft is making significant licensing changes with System Center 2012. With System Center Endpoint Protection now being released with Configuration Manager, this section calls out specifics on that as well. The System Center 2012 suite has two product editions, differentiated by virtualization rights only:

▶ **Datacenter:** Used for highly virtualized environments

▶ **Standard:** Used for lightly virtualized or nonvirtualized environments

These product editions include System Center Endpoint Protection in addition to the other System Center 2012 components. The only difference between the two editions is the number of operating system environments (OSEs) that you can manage per license.

Datacenter allows unlimited number of OSEs per license; Standard Edition allows the management of up to two OSEs per license.

The new licensing model can be simplified by separating it into Server Management Licenses (MLs) and Client Management Licenses. Server MLs are physical processor-based and each license covers up to two physical processors. Both product editions include rights to run each server management license associated with System Center, plus a run-time instance of SQL Server Standard edition when utilized for the SQL engine used by the System Center components.

There is also a Client Management Suite, which is an additional licensing suite for customers that want to utilize additional functionality. This includes Service Manager, Operations Manager, Data Protection Manager, and Orchestrator licenses for machines managed by those products.

Client MLs cover managed devices that run nonserver OSEs. This includes the standard Configuration Manager client ML and Virtual Machine Manager Client ML. Endpoint protection has a specific System Center 2012 Endpoint Protection Client Subscription License (SL) available in addition to two other Client MLs. To manage endpoint protection on your clients, they must be managed by Configuration Manager, so two separate Client MLs are required:

- ▶ System Center 2012 Configuration Manager Client ML
- ▶ System Center 2012 Endpoint Protection Client ML

These two Client MLs are included in the Core CAL suite. A Client Access License (CAL) is a license giving a user on a networked computer the right to access the services of the server. Microsoft offers several CAL suites for its customers; these suites combine CALs for some of the most popular products into several packages. The Enterprise CAL suite includes an additional Client ML, the System Center Client Management Suite Client ML.

If you are licensed to use a CAL suite, you are licensed to use endpoint protection, which is available as a per-user or per-device subscription as well as in the Core CAL and Enterprise CAL suites. The subscription includes all antimalware updates and product upgrades during the subscription period. Microsoft makes available volume licensing information on its CAL suites at http://www.microsoft.com/calsuites/en/us/products/default.aspx, describing the Server CAL and highlighting whether a specified Server CAL is included as part of the Core CAL suite or Enterprise CAL suite. Here is information on the current CAL suites:

- ▶ **Core CAL Suite:** Provides capabilities that users need to do their job
- ▶ **Enterprise CAL Suite:** Provides everything in the Core CAL, plus additional benefits for Enterprise customers

The most current list of Microsoft CAL suite technologies is included in the Licensing Core CAL and Enterprise Suite Volume Licensing Brief, available at www.microsoft.com by searching for **Licensing Core CAL and Enterprise Suite docx** (http://download.microsoft.com/download/3/D/4/3D42BDC2-6725-4B29-B75A-A5B04179958B/Licensing_Core_CAL_and_Enterprise_Suite.docx).

Qualifying Software Assurance customers wanting to move to the new licensing model can avail themselves of a license migration grant from Microsoft. Customers with active device subscriptions to use Forefront Endpoint Protection to protect their servers can continue to use the FEP service for the remainder of the agreement and then transition to the new model.

Hierarchy Planning

When you have a good understanding of your objectives and environment, your first planning task is to design your ConfigMgr hierarchy. A hierarchy may consist of a single stand-alone primary site or multiple sites joined together. The "Planning Your Hierarchy Structure" section discusses considerations for using a single site or more than one site. Unlike Configuration Manager 2007, System Center 2012 Configuration Manager does not allow you to restructure your hierarchy later by changing the parent-child relationships of primary sites. It is therefore worth investing time up front to design a hierarchy that is optimal for your organization.

Chapter 2, "Configuration Manager Overview," introduces Configuration Manager hierarchies. Sites in a hierarchy share replicated data, security policy, and a variety of objects such as the software library, boundaries, and boundary groups. The top-level site in a hierarchy may be a single primary site or a central administration site (CAS). Some site server roles provide services to the entire hierarchy, whereas others function within a specific site. The "Site Servers and Site Systems Planning" section of this chapter discusses site system placement.

A System Center 2012 Configuration Manager hierarchy cannot contain ConfigMgr 2007 sites; however, a separate ConfigMgr 2007 hierarchy can exist alongside your new hierarchy. You cannot upgrade a ConfigMgr 2007 hierarchy to System Center 2012 Configuration Manager. System Center 2012 Configuration Manager does provide tools for migrating from ConfigMgr 2007. Because the hierarchy design principles are quite different between the two versions, you will not want to replicate your existing hierarchy design in your new architecture. Chapter 7, "Migrating to System Center 2012 Configuration Manager," discusses the migration process.

Configuration Manager Sites

Each Configuration Manager system is part of a site. Every site has a site server, a site database, and a three-character alphanumeric site code. The site code must be unique in the hierarchy. System Center 2012 Configuration Manager has three types of sites: the CAS, primary sites, and secondary sites. The following sections describe these sites.

CAUTION: CHOOSE SITE CODES CAREFULLY

Be aware of the following restrictions when using site codes:

▶ Avoid using reserved names such as AUX, CON, NUL, PRN (see http://msdn. microsoft.com/en-us/library/aa365247.aspx for the list of reserved file names) or using SMS when choosing site codes.

▶ Avoid reusing site codes previously used in your ConfigMgr hierarchy. Site codes are stored in the site databases of other sites in the hierarchy and in some configurations saved in AD and WINS. If you were to reuse a site code, you may discover that all references to the old site were not fully removed or are re-introduced from a restored backup. This could cause problems resolving the site.

Central Administration Site

If you install a CAS, it is the top-level site in the hierarchy. All replicated data in the hierarchy is visible at the CAS, which makes it ideal for reporting. If you have more than one primary site, you must install a CAS. The CAS does not support clients directly and therefore does not support system roles that exclusively provide client services. The CAS can have only primary sites as child sites.

Primary Sites Versus Secondary Sites

ConfigMgr clients are assigned to *primary* sites, and they receive policy from their assigned sites. *Secondary* sites are used at remote locations to provide ConfigMgr services locally to clients assigned to primary sites in the hierarchy; they cannot have clients assigned to them. Secondary sites are administered from their parent site. In ConfigMgr 2007, secondary sites did not have their own site database. The new version of ConfigMgr requires that all sites have a site database and participate in database replication. The CAS and primary site databases must be hosted on a SQL Server instance. A secondary site database can be hosted on either SQL Server Express or SQL Server. You can install the site database on either the default instance or a named instance of SQL Server. However, the improved content distribution capabilities in System Center 2102 Configuration Manager have greatly reduced the need for secondary sites, and you should avoid them in most implementations.

Hierarchy-wide Site System Roles

Certain site systems provide services to the entire hierarchy. Here are the site systems that synchronize with Microsoft services on the Internet; configure them at the top-level site in your hierarchy, either the CAS or single primary site:

▶ **The asset intelligence synchronization point:** This site role allows you to request on-demand catalog synchronization with System Center online or schedule automatic catalog synchronization.

▶ **The top-level software update point:** Additional SUPs are required at child primary sites that use software updates; these are optional at secondary sites. The "Software Update Planning" section of this chapter discusses the operation of software update points.

▶ **The endpoint protection point:** ConfigMgr uses the endpoint protection point to accept the System Center Endpoint Protection license terms and to configure the default membership for Microsoft Active Protection Service.

You should assign these roles to servers at a well-connected Internet point of presence.

You may install multiple instances of some hierarchy-wide site server roles; although this often is not needed. Here are the servers that provide hierarchy-wide client services and that you may deploy at multiple primary sites in the hierarchy:

▶ **Application catalog web service point:** This role feeds data to the application catalog website point.

▶ **Application catalog website point:** This system provides users with access to the software in your application catalog. This role should therefore have high connectivity from all locations where end user systems reside.

▶ **Fallback status point:** Fallback status points must be in network locations that are easily reachable for clients that are having trouble communicating with a management point.

These two server roles are hierarchy-wide and may be deployed at the CAS as well as additional sites:

▶ **System health validator point:** This role is part NAP. One or more system health validator points may reside at any site. Chapter 14, "Software Update Management," discusses NAP.

▶ **Reporting services point:** This role is generally most useful at the top-level site where all replicated data in the hierarchy is available for reports. You may deploy multiple reporting services points in a single site to facilitate access for administrators. You may also deploy reporting services points at any primary site in the hierarchy to report on data available at that site. Some organizations use dedicated sites for reporting at the top of their ConfigMgr 2007 hierarchy. This is not necessary or possible in ConfigMgr 2012. Chapter 18, "Reporting," further describes considerations for the reporting services point placement.

Planning Your Hierarchy Structure

Network connectivity was often the reason for creating additional Configuration Manager 2007 sites. A major change in System Center 2012 Configuration Manager is that new content distribution options allow a single site to span geographic locations separated by wide area network (WAN) links more efficiently. The "Planning Content Management" section of this chapter discusses content distribution. Partitioning of administrative rights or client settings were other common reasons for creating additional ConfigMgr 2007 sites. In ConfigMgr 2012, sites no longer serve as boundaries for security and client settings. A well-designed System Center 2012 Configuration Manager hierarchy is likely to contain fewer sites than a typical ConfigMgr 2007 hierarchy. Your goal should be a hierarchy that is smaller, flatter, and less complex, and therefore easier to manage.

The top site in your hierarchy will be either a primary site or a CAS. Many organizations may choose to use a single primary site, and optionally one or more secondary sites. Because a primary site can no longer have another primary site as a child site, you need a CAS if you choose to have more than one primary site. Here are reasons you may choose to create additional sites:

▶ A single primary site can support up to 100,000 clients. If you anticipate supporting more than 100,000 clients, you need additional primary sites.

▶ An additional primary site distributes processing load and reduces the impact of a primary site failure. Chapter 21, "Backup, Recovery, and Maintenance," describes options for site recovery.

▶ You may choose to install an additional site to support Internet-based clients. The "Planning for Internet-Based Client Management" section discusses both single-site and multiple-site options to support Internet-based clients.

▶ Locations that will be using different language versions of the Configuration Manager client and server software should generally be separate sites.

▶ You may choose to install a primary or secondary site to manage content distribution across WAN links. System Center 2012 Configuration Manager distribution points provide new capabilities for managing network bandwidth more efficiently than in ConfigMgr 2007, which reduces the need for secondary sites. A separate site may be desirable, however, to minimize the client traffic such as inventory data and status messages from locations with large numbers of clients. If you are considering a secondary site for network reasons, you should carefully consider the discussion of inter-site traffic and content distribution in Chapter 5, "Network Design."

Planning Boundaries and Boundary Groups

System Center 2012 Configuration Manager *boundaries* define network locations in which client systems may reside. As discussed in Chapter 2, boundaries are defined at the hierarchy level and are no longer used to define sites. Boundary groups aggregate boundaries for efficient management. Boundaries have two functions:

▶ **Automatic site assignment:** If you choose to use automatic site assignment, you need to configure one or more boundary group for automatic site assignment. During automatic site assignment, the client determines whether its current network location corresponds to a boundary that is configured for site assignment. If the client is within such a boundary, it assigns itself to the appropriate site; otherwise, automatic assignment fails. Chapter 9, "Configuration Manager Client Management," describes site assignment.

▶ **Selection of protected site systems:** Protected site systems are distribution points or state migration points that are associated with boundary groups. Clients within a boundary that is associated with a protected site system will use that system preferentially as a content source. Protected distribution points are the default configuration in ConfigMgr 2012.

Boundaries must be added to a boundary group before they can be used. Site assignment is configured on boundary groups rather than individual boundaries. Similarly, protected site systems are associated with boundary groups. Here is how boundaries are defined:

- ▶ Active Directory site

- ▶ Internet Protocol (IP) subnet

- ▶ IP range

- ▶ IPv6 prefix

- ▶ Combination of the preceding elements

AD site and IP subnet boundaries suffer from the same major shortcoming: They do not work correctly with the Classless Inter-Domain Routing (CIDR) method commonly used in networking today. CIDR uses variable length subnet masks (VLSM) to provide more flexible addressing than the older class A, B, and C IP subnets. Both AD site and IP subnet boundaries assume the use of a specific subnet mask based on the legacy "class" assignment of the specified subnet. Here is an example of the problems you can run into using these types of boundaries.

An AD site used as a boundary contains the IP subnet of 192.168.14.0–192.168.15.255 or 192.168.14/23. ConfigMgr calculates the subnet ID as 192.168.14.0. If you now have a client with an IP address of 192.168.15.27 with a subnet mask of 255.255.255.0, or 192.168.15.27/24, the calculated subnet ID is 192.168.15.0. Although the client's IP address is clearly within the range specified in AD, the subnet ID comparison does not match and the client is not assigned during discovery.

In addition, clients unable to retrieve site information from your AD, such as workgroup clients or clients in domains that do not have a trust relationship with your site server's domain, cannot use AD sites as boundaries. For these reasons, IP ranges or IPv6 prefixes are usually the best choice for defining boundaries.

In ConfigMgr 2007, AD site boundaries were often used to avoid the duplicate effort of maintaining subnet information in two places—AD and ConfigMgr. The new AD Forest Discovery feature in System Center 2012 Configuration Manager allows you to import subnet information from AD and automatically create boundaries based on the corresponding IP address ranges. Chapter 9 includes details of how to configure AD Forest Discovery for boundary creation.

Boundary groups are used in content distribution to control the distribution points from which a client in a given network location will retrieve content. Because boundaries are hierarchy-wide, the distribution point boundaries are independent of sites, and a DP can be shared between sites. This feature allows you to optimize content delivery based on network considerations. When clients are not within the boundaries of a distribution point with the required content, they will use the deployment option you specify for slow or unreliable networks. This behavior is defined differently for different deployment types:

▶ On the Content tab of application deployment types

▶ On the Distribution Points tab of a package deployment

▶ On the Download Settings tab of a software update deployment

Chapter 5 discusses network considerations for the placement of protected site systems. Chapter 13, "Distributing and Deploying Applications," discusses content deployment.

Overlapping boundaries are those that include the same network locations. Overlapping boundaries were explicitly not supported in ConfigMgr 2007; however, for ConfigMgr 2012, the story has changed.

▶ Overlapping boundaries still are not supported for automatic site assignment. If you use boundaries for automatic site assignment, it is important to plan and maintain boundaries that are appropriate to your network topology and do not overlap. Automatic site assignment can have unpredictable results when a client is located within the boundaries of more than one site.

▶ Overlapping boundaries are now supported for content distribution. For clients that happen to fall into multiple boundaries groups, ConfigMgr returns a complete list of all distribution points associated with all the client's assigned boundary groups. The client then follows its normal DP location rules to select the best DP from the list returned.

Choosing Client Discovery and Installation Methods

Before you can use ConfigMgr to manage a system, you must discover the system and install the client. Chapter 9 discusses client discovery and installation in detail. This section introduces some basic considerations relevant to your overall planning. Here are the methods you can use to install the ConfigMgr client agent:

▶ **Client push installation** occurs when the site server makes a network connection to a potential client and invokes the client installation process. Client push installation requires prior discovery of the system. You can enable client push installation on a site-wide basis or push the client to individual systems or collections. Client push installation has a number of dependencies you must configure, and you are limited to setting installation properties on a site-wide basis. Client push allows you to control installation entirely from within ConfigMgr, which may simplify administration if collaboration with AD administrators requires additional effort. Client push requires firewall exceptions and the use of administrative rights. These requirements make client push a less desirable option in terms of security.

▶ **Software update point-based installation** uses your existing software updates infrastructure to install the client. Software update point-based installation does not require prior discovery of the system. Software update point-based installation may be a good choice if you currently deploy software updates through Windows Server Update Services (WSUS).

▶ **Manual installation** occurs when an administrator logs onto the system and runs the CCMSetup client installation program manually. Manual installation does not require prior discovery of the system. Manual installation has few dependencies and is a great way to install a few test clients; however, it is not scalable.

▶ **Logon script installation** is essentially equivalent to manual installation, except that a logon script initiates CCMSetup. Logon script installation provides a high degree of control over installation properties. Because you have limited control over when a logon script runs, you must plan carefully to avoid excessive network traffic. In an AD domain, you can maintain logon scripts centrally and assign them through group policy. Managing logon scripts in a workgroup environment requires more overhead since scripts need to be copied to each system and assigned through local policy.

▶ **Group policy installation** uses group policy software assignment to invoke the Windows Installer package for the client. Group policy installation provides a high degree of control over installation properties; however, you have limited control over when the installation runs and must plan carefully to avoid excessive network traffic. Group policy is not available for workgroup clients.

▶ **Upgrade installation** uses your existing software distribution infrastructure to upgrade the client. Upgrade installation requires prior discovery and site assignment of the system.

Chapter 2 describes the available discovery methods. Here are the discovery methods Configuration Manager uses to discover potential clients:

▶ **Active Directory System Discovery** executes a Lightweight Directory Access Protocol (LDAP) query to retrieve information from a domain controller about the computers in the domain. If you use Active Directory System Discovery, ensure your Active Directory database is well maintained and obsolete computer accounts are regularly purged.

▶ **Network Discovery** uses various network protocols to enumerate IP subnets and hosts. Chapter 5 describes Network Discovery in detail.

You can configure each discovery method at one or more sites in your hierarchy. When an object is discovered, the discovery method creates a DDR (data discovery record) file with basic data about the object. The CAS or a primary site processes the DDR, inserting the discovery data into the site database and replicating it throughout the hierarchy.

Active Directory System Discovery provides an excellent way to discover computers that are part of an AD domain. One caveat with Active Directory System Discovery is that ConfigMgr generates discovery records for stale computer objects; these are old computer accounts representing machines that are no longer on the network. To address this issue, System Center 2012 Configuration Manager provides new Active Directory System

Discovery options to discover only computers that have logged into a domain in a given period of time, and/or to only discover computers that have updated their computer account password in a given period of time.

Network Discovery has the advantage of discovering potential client systems that are not part of AD domains. Network Discovery can also retrieve other information about your network. You must configure Network Discovery carefully to avoid consuming excessive bandwidth. If you use Network Discovery, you may want to configure each site to discover a portion of your network based on bandwidth considerations. Chapter 5 discusses Network Discovery in detail.

System Center 2012 Configuration Manager provides additional Active Directory discovery methods that retrieve information about users and the environment. Here are the discovery methods you may choose to use to supplement discovery of potential clients:

▶ Active Directory Forest Discovery retrieves information about AD sites and IP ranges and makes these objects available for defining boundaries. Forest Discovery requires network connectivity and access permissions to a domain controller in the target forest.

▶ Active Directory Group Discovery retrieves information about security groups and distribution groups, and optionally enumerates the users and computers in each group.

▶ Active Directory User Discovery retrieves information about AD users.

If you use any of the Active Directory discovery methods, you generally want to run them at a single site with the best possible connectivity to a domain controller. If possible, you should choose the least heavily loaded site server and domain controller that meet this requirement. You should avoid scheduling Active Directory discovery at times when the domain controller or network is under a heavy load.

You can configure the Active Directory User Discovery and Active Directory System Discovery methods to discover any AD attributes of the discovered objects. As you plan your user-centric management, consider what attributes can help you to deliver appropriate content to your users. Figure 4.1 provides an example of selecting user attributes that describe the user's role in the organization and linguistic preference. Of course, you must have these attributes populated in AD before you can use them.

Defining Your Client Architecture

The ConfigMgr client consists of a set of core components and optional components that you may install and enable to provide additional functionality. The set of components you install and the component settings define your client architecture. Client architecture shapes the experience for your users and affects performance, security, and capacity planning for ConfigMgr. This section presents an overview of the planning considerations around client settings and other client options. Chapter 9 describes these settings and options in detail.

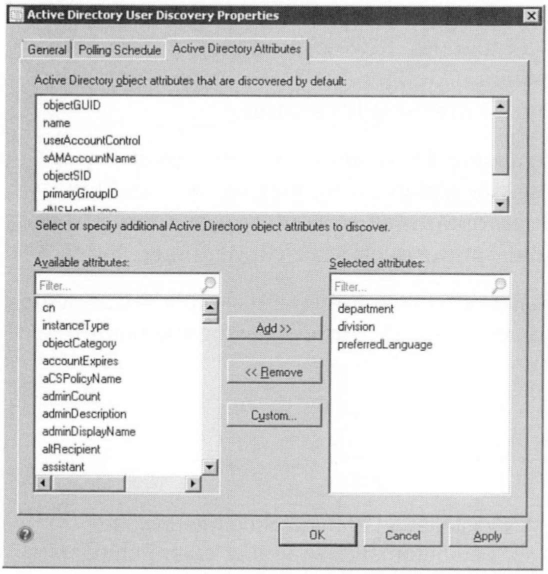

FIGURE 4.1   Active Directory Attributes for User Discovery.

In ConfigMgr 2007, client settings were site-wide. In System Center 2012 Configuration Manager, you define the default client architecture for your hierarchy. You may also apply custom settings to collections of systems or users. This provides enhanced flexibility in managing client settings.

Here are the settings that govern the behavior of the core client components:

▶ **Client policy settings:** These determine the frequency of policy polling and whether user policy will be applied on intranet and Internet clients.

▶ **Computer agent settings:** These settings affect the user experience for software deployments, including notification and reminders. New computer agent settings allow you to specify a default application catalog website and add the application catalog site to the Internet Explorer trusted zone, and to brand the Software Center with your organization name. Several security-related settings are also configurable for the computer agent.

▶ **Computer restart settings:** These settings determine the time allowed prior to a mandatory shutdown and the notifications provided to the user.

▶ **State messaging settings:** State messaging settings specify the frequency of client state messages.

▶ **User and device affinity settings:** These settings determine how devices will be assigned to users. User device affinity enables the new user-centric content delivery model in System Center 2012 Configuration Manager. Options include allowing users to define their primary devices or automatically configuring user device affinity based on usage data.

Background Intelligent Transfer Service (BITS) settings are also configurable as client settings. Although BITS is not a ConfigMgr component, BITS settings play an important role in determining ConfigMgr network behavior. Configurable BITS settings control bandwidth utilization and scheduling. Chapter 5 discusses BITS settings.

Various client installation options are also available. Installation options to which you should pay particular attention include cache size and location, logging level and log size, and location. Additional client installation options allow you to specify the sites and systems the client will use and security-related options such as certificate usage.

Selectively enable additional components based on your requirements. Table 4.1 presents some client settings for optional components you should consider during the planning phase.

TABLE 4.1   Client Settings

Component	Settings
Endpoint Protection	Configurable options for installation and initial update include system restart behavior and automatic removal of other antimalware programs.
Network Access Protection	Allows you to specify whether you will use NAP and set health state evaluation policies. NAP is a powerful security feature and can prevent clients from connecting to your network. You should therefore plan your NAP deployment carefully.
Hardware Inventory	ConfigMgr can inventory almost every detail of system resources and configuration. Client settings allow you to configure inventory options, which previously required customizing the smsdef.mof and config.mof files. Hardware inventory consumes resources on the client, server, and network. You should therefore consider the inventory you need to effectively manage and report on your environment, as well as inventory frequency.
Power Management	Specify whether to allow users to exclude devices from power management.
Remote Tools	Remote Tools settings control how support personnel can access the system remotely. Settings include user notification and user control options. You should consider these settings carefully in light of privacy regulations and company policies. Overly intrusive notification can be annoying to users.
Software Inventory	ConfigMgr can inventory file system data and file properties. Inventory settings specify the locations and file extension included in the inventory. Software inventory consumes resources on the client, server, and network. You should consider what file information you need for management and reporting, the level of detail you require, and the inventory frequency. You can also collect specific files. File collection should be used sparingly and for small files, such as configuration files.
Software Updates	Options include installing multiple updates that are approaching their installation deadlines at the same time.

The following optional components have schedule settings only:

▶ Compliance settings (schedule is for compliance evaluation)

▶ Software deployment (schedule is for the re-evaluation task)

▶ Software metering

Here are scheduling options for recurring operations:

▶ **Simple schedule:** Specifies frequency only (in days, hours, or minutes). The operation occurs when the client applies the policy specifying the schedule and repeats at regular intervals thereafter.

▶ **Custom schedule:** Specifies the frequency and initial start time.

Using a simple schedule avoids large numbers of clients executing tasks simultaneously, thereby reducing the impact of scheduled operations, whereas a custom schedule allows you to avoid times with peak activity in your environment or when other scheduled operations take place. A custom schedule can also make it easier to identify when scheduled operations take place for troubleshooting purposes.

The client architecture should also consider requirements for multilanguage support. If you need to support languages other than English, you need to deploy the appropriate International Client Packs (ICPs) to your clients.

Virtual desktop infrastructure (VDI) is a technology in which users connect remotely to a virtual desktop hosted on a server. Organizations are increasingly using VDI to provide device agnostic access to remote users. By keeping the operating environment and data inside the data center, VDI allows IT to provide security and manageability while allowing the user to choose and manage their physical device.

ConfigMgr is capable of managing virtual desktops as well as physical devices. System Center 2012 Configuration Manager provides significant optimizations for the VDI environment. ConfigMgr provides a random offset for common scheduled operations so that large numbers of virtual machines are not performing resource-intensive operations like hardware inventory or malware scans simultaneously. Virtual desktops may be configured as persistent or nonpersistent.

▶ Persistent virtual desktops save changes at shutdown, may be assigned to unique users, and are managed much like a physical PC.

▶ Nonpersistent virtual desktops do not save changes and essentially form a pool of identical systems users draw from for a standardized environment.

Nonpersistent virtual desktops present special management challenges in areas such as tracking software license compliance and updating malware signatures. ConfigMgr addresses these challenges by assigning special attributes to virtual desktops to provide them with a unique identity and metadata that describes the virtualization attributes of each system. Application deployment rules can leverage these attributes to handle deployments appropriately.

Planning for User-Centric Management

Like most systems management products, ConfigMgr 2007 emphasized management of devices. System Center 2012 Configuration Manager retains and expands device management capabilities, and introduces a new paradigm of user-centric management. User-centric features enable administrators to deliver content to users, regardless of the device they log on to, and gives users more control over ConfigMgr features.

Administrators now have the option to specify collections of users or AD user groups as deployment targets. Users receive such deployments on any client system onto which they log on. The new user affinity feature associates users with their primary systems. Each user may have more than one primary device, and users can share a primary device. You want to consider how to set user affinity in your environment. Here are the ways you can set user affinity:

▶ Generate a file with computer assignment information. This can be a good option if you keep records on system provisioning.

▶ Allow users to select their own primary device.

▶ Let ConfigMgr make these assignments automatically from usage data.

▶ Have administrators set the device manually.

▶ Specify the user during OS deployment or mobile device enrollment.

User affinity lets you specify different deployment options for the user's primary device. For example, you might choose to install an application on the user's primary device and stream a virtualized version of the same application to the user when he logs onto a different machine.

Users can also use the Software Center web portal to select applications you make available to them from the Application Catalog. In this way, users can provision their own software quickly and easily without the need of a support call or local administrative rights. You may also choose to give users control over their remote control and power management settings, set preferences such as preferred hours for software installation and maintenance operations, and wipe their managed mobile devices in case of loss or theft.

Planning Content Management

Content includes files for applications, packages, software updates, and operating system deployment. Delivering content efficiently to users across various network locations and device types is one of the most important functions of Configuration Manager. Chapter 2 introduces ConfigMgr content management. This section offers guidance on deploying content management in your environment.

The content distribution infrastructure for each site consists of the content source location(s), the site server, and a set of distribution points. Figure 4.2 shows an example of a content distribution infrastructure.

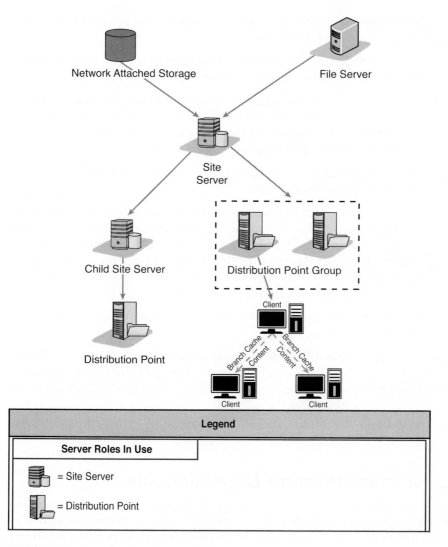

FIGURE 4.2   Content distribution infrastructure.

You may choose to specify existing locations as the source for your content, or copy source files to a specific location. In either case, you want the source folders to have good network connectivity to the site server. Content source locations should be secure to prevent unauthorized changes. If existing shares are used to source content, they should be managed with the understanding that changes to content may result in updates propagating to client systems.

A new feature in System Center 2012 Configuration Manager is the content library. The content library is a single instance store of all content files located on the site server. The site server checks to see if a file already exists in the content library before downloading it and sending it to distribution points.

The placement of distribution points (DPs) is especially important in site planning. Here is how you generally want to use distribution points:

▶ Deploy one or more DPs at the primary network location of the site. Adding distribution points provides load balancing and redundancy.

▶ Deploy protected distribution points strategically to serve remote locations. Associate these distribution points with boundary groups consisting of the network locations they are intended to serve. Optionally you may allow clients outside the associated boundary groups to retrieve content from the protected DPs.

▶ If you support Internet-based clients or mobile device clients, place HTTPS-enabled DPs in locations accessible to these clients.

▶ Use distribution point groups (DPGs) to simplify administration of content distribution. You can add each DP to one or more groups. You can then associate DPGs with collections so that all members of the group automatically receive content required by any deployments to those collections. DPGs can also include DPs from multiple sites for content deployment across the hierarchy. When a DP is added to a group, it automatically receives all content assigned to the group.

▶ Consider using BranchCache functionality for content distributions with limited connectivity to your primary locations.

▶ Enable prestaged content on specific distribution points if you prefer to use a different mechanism to distribute some or all content to those DPs. Prestaging content adds to administrative overhead but may be desirable to conserve network resources.

Chapter 5 examines the network considerations for content distribution in detail. Chapter 13 describes the operational aspects of content management.

Planning for Infrastructure Dependencies

System Center 2012 Configuration Manager integrates with many of the basic services in your network and Windows server environment. Chapter 2 introduced these dependencies. Chapter 5 discusses network infrastructure in detail. This section considers two other core services with substantial planning considerations, Active Directory and Certificate services.

Active Directory Considerations

Active Directory is a prerequisite for System Center 2012 Configuration Manager. The next sections consider two specific issues relating to AD—whether to extend the AD schema and requirements for dealing with systems in multiforest scenarios and workgroups.

Extending the AD Schema
Chapter 3, "Looking Inside Configuration Manager," describes the ConfigMgr AD schema extensions in detail. This section explains the benefits of extending the schema and the design implications of not extending the schema.

The AD schema contains a template for each class of AD objects. Schema extensions add new classes of AD objects or modify the set of attributes for existing objects. ConfigMgr schema extensions do not modify any default object classes, making the risk of conflict with other application extremely low. ConfigMgr sites publish information about site systems, boundaries, and configuration to the extended schema. Global roaming and NAP are features that require the schema extensions. You can use ConfigMgr's NAP capabilities to prevent clients that do not comply with specified security patch requirements from connecting to the network. NAP requires the client to retrieve health state reference information stored in the attributes of the mSSMSSite AD object. See Chapter 14 for a discussion of Network Access Protection.

The schema extensions also enable clients to retrieve much of their management information from AD. Here are some tasks that are simpler with the extended schema:

▶ **Client installation and site assignment:** Clients can query AD to retrieve installation properties such as the size of the download cache. Clients can also retrieve information about boundaries from AD and use this information for automatic site assignment. If you do not extend the schema, you need to supply this information as part of your client installation. This requires you to manually install clients and supply information as part of your client setup, or use client push installation. Chapter 9 describes installation options.

▶ **Locating the management point:** Clients can use Active Directory to identify management points. In System Center 2012 Configuration Manager, the server locator point functionality available in previous versions is now part of the management point. Without the schema extensions, you must provide this information in other ways, such as supplying this information via the command line or manually creating special Domain Name System (DNS) or Windows Internet Naming Service (WINS) entries. Chapter 9 describes client installation command-line options. Details of how to configure these DNS and WINS entries are available in the "Planning for Service Location by Clients" section at http://technet.microsoft.com/en-us/library/gg712701.aspx.

▶ **Custom Transmission Control Protocol (TCP)/Internet Protocol (IP) Port information:** If a site has been configured to use nonstandard ports for client communications, this information can be provided through the schema extensions. Without the schema extensions, changing network ports for ConfigMgr communications requires deploying a script to all clients or re-installing the clients. Chapter 5 discusses port customization.

Applying the schema extensions and configuring your sites to publish to AD is the preferred choice for most environments. One caveat is that if you have multiple ConfigMgr hierarchies managing clients in the same forest, managing site information in AD can be difficult. If clients from more than one hierarchy exist on the same subnet, extreme care is required to avoid overlapping boundaries. If you have an active ConfigMgr 2007 hierarchy using automatic site assignment and you publish your ConfigMgr 2012 boundaries to AD, site assignment may not work correctly on the 2007 clients. In this situation, you should use manual site assignment for ConfigMgr 2007.

Multi-Forest and Workgroup Considerations

A ConfigMgr hierarchy can manage clients in more than one AD forest as well as workgroup clients. You can deploy site systems across multiple forests. All site servers must reside in the same AD forest or in forests with AD trusts. Hierarchies and sites that span multiple forests require additional configuration to specify the security context for communication between servers. Site systems in workgroups are not supported.

You can add forests to your hierarchy from the Administration workspace by right-clicking **Active Directory Forests** under the Hierarchy Configuration node and choosing **Add Forest**. Figure 4.3 shows the Add Forest dialog, which allows you to configure a forest for forest discovery and publishing. If the new forest trusts the site server's forest, you have the option of granting the site server computer account appropriate rights in the target forest and using that account for discovery and publishing. You also have the option to specify an account with appropriate access. You must extend the AD schema in each forest to which you will publish. By default, the site server will publish to its local domain in its own forest and to the root domain in other forests. You can also specify a domain for publishing.

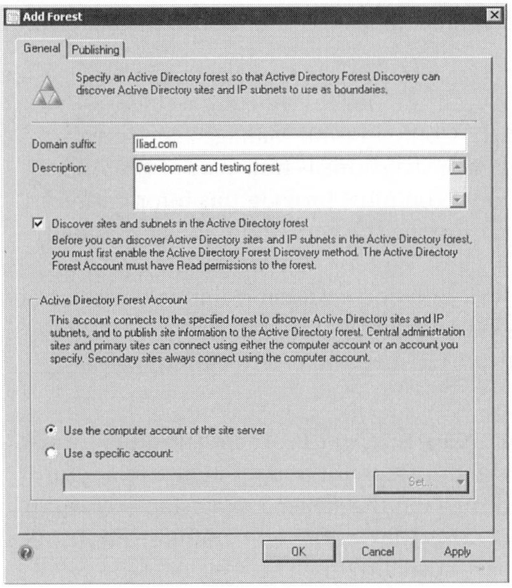

FIGURE 4.3   The Add Forest dialog.

Deployments to user collections and user device affinity depend on Active Directory User Discovery. This means you cannot use these features unless you have a site in the user's AD forest. These user-centric features are not available for users in workgroups or untrusted forests. If you use Configuration Manager mobile device enrollment and you have users in untrusted forests, you must configure an enrollment point in the user's forest to support this feature.

Workgroup clients cannot take advantage of the AD schema extensions, and you cannot use group policy with workgroup clients. This means that workgroup clients do not have access to AD services for certificate deployment and establishing trusted certificates. You should manually install the site server signing certificate on workgroup clients.

NOTE: ABOUT DISJOINT NAMESPACE AND SINGLE LABEL DOMAINS

Disjoint namespaces occur when a system's NetBIOS name or primary DNS suffix does not match the Active Directory DNS domain name. ConfigMgr supports disjoint namespaces on domain controllers or site systems. Special configuration is required for these situations; refer to the product documentation for details. Single label domains are domain names that do not contain a dotted extension such as .com or .net. ConfigMgr does not support single label domains.

Planning Certificate Services

Certain ConfigMgr functionality requires a properly configured public key infrastructure (PKI). You may use any PKI implementation supporting x.509 version 3 certificates with ConfigMgr; however, a Microsoft Enterprise PKI will be the easiest to use and supports the broadest range of functionality. Here are the ConfigMgr features that depend on PKI:

▶ HTTPS (hypertext transfer protocol secure) provides encryption and authentication for network communications. Servers that accept HTTPS connections require a web server certificate, and clients configured to use HTTPS require a client computer certificate. Chapter 5 contains additional information about ConfigMgr HTTPS communications.

▶ Mobile device management (MDM) requires an enrollment certificate on each device for mutual authentication and SSL communications with site systems. The Exchange Server Connector does not require PKI certificates. Chapter 15, "Mobile Device Management," provides details on MDM.

▶ Out of band (OOB) management has special certificate requirements as explained in the "Out of Band Management Planning" section of this chapter.

NOTE: ADDITIONAL CRYPTOGRAPHIC CONTROLS IN CONFIGURATION MANAGER

Here are some cryptographic controls System Center 2012 Configuration Manager servers and clients use to protect communications between systems that do not specifically depend on PKI:

▶ The site server signs policies. This ensures that the client can trust that the policy is from a trusted source and has not been tampered with. Policies containing sensitive information may also be encrypted.

▶ Publishers sign software updates. Clients will not install a software update without a valid signature.

▶ Clients may be configured to sign inventory data.

▶ Clients sign configuration data for compliance settings.

▶ Servers use certificate-based authentication for intrasite and intersite communications.

▶ The distribution manager service creates a hash of all content downloads. Clients use the hash contained in the signed software distribution policy to verify content authenticity and integrity before installing software.

▶ Operating system deployment (OSD) uses encryption to protect user state data, deployment media, and multicast packages.

In general, clients and servers use self-signed certificates for encryption and signing if a PKI is not available. In a PKI environment, systems use PKI certificates in place of self-signed certificates. Microsoft provides a complete reference on ConfigMgr cryptographic controls at http://technet.microsoft.com/en-us/library/hh427327.aspx.

The next section of this chapter, "About PKI," briefly introduces basic PKI concepts. The "Planning to Use PKI with Configuration Manager" section discusses how ConfigMgr uses PKI and how you should plan to deploy a PKI solution or leverage your existing PKI for ConfigMgr.

About PKI

Public key cryptography is the principal cryptographic standard for secure communications on the Internet and on private networks. The algorithms behind public key cryptography allow messages to be encrypted and decrypted using a *key pair*. The keys in the pair are numbers mathematically related such that a message encrypted with one of the keys in the pair can be decrypted only with the other key. Each user (or system) that uses public key cryptography has a unique key pair. One of the keys in the pair is kept secret. This is the *private key*. The other key, the *public key*, is published to make it available to other users. You can use key pairs in two different ways:

▶ You can encrypt a message with a user's public key and send it to the user. Only the user with the matching private key can decrypt and read it.

▶ You can sign a message by encrypting it with your private key. Users who have your public key can decrypt and read the message. Because the recipients know that the message was encrypted with your private key, they can be confident that you are the sender and the message has not been tampered with.

On a small scale, it would be possible for all users to know each other's public keys. This is not practical on a larger scale. To allow the use of public key cryptography in large environments including the Internet, PKI technology was developed. PKI provides a framework for securing both session-based and messaging communications using a hierarchy of certificate authorities (CAs). At the top of a PKI hierarchy is the root CA, a system whose public key is known and trusted by all parties who will participate in that PKI. A CA is used to issue binary objects known as certificates to other systems or users. Certificates can be issued for specific purposes and validate the identity of the certificate holder. Because a compromised root CA would compromise the integrity of an organization's entire PKI, the root CA is generally kept offline and not used to issue certificates directly to users and systems. A set of subordinate CAs receive certificates from the root, which allow them to also issue certificates.

Planning to Use PKI with Configuration Manager

The HTTPS protocol provides client-to-server communications that are mutually authenticated, signed, and encrypted. Internet clients must use HTTPS, and all clients are more secure if configured to use HTTPS. You must deploy the required certificate to each client and site system that will use HTTPS.

NOTE: ABOUT CRL CHECKING

Certificate authorities are a high value target for hackers. In fact, there have been cases in which well-known Internet root certificates have been compromised. The certificate revocation list (CRL) allows administrators to revoke certificates that might have been compromised. ConfigMgr clients check the CRL by default to protect against accepting revoked certificates. By default, clients do not perform CRL checking while validating signatures on software updates. These settings are configurable. CRL checking introduces some latency in communications and is a potential source of communication failure in the event that the CRL server is unreachable. You should consider whether the added security benefit outweighs the potential performance and availability impact in your environment.

All systems must trust the CAs that issue the certificates. Certificates issued by certain well-known public authorities are trusted by default on all Windows computers and many mobile devices. If you use your own PKI, you must ensure that your CA certificates are added to the trusted store on all systems. In an AD forest, you can use AD services to achieve this. You also need to deploy the certificates required by each site system and client. Using Microsoft Certificate Services with an enterprise CA simplifies these operations. Chapter 20, "Security and Delegation in Configuration Manager," discusses certificate requirements in detail and provides step-by-step procedures for certificate deployment using a Microsoft enterprise CA.

NOTE: COMMUNICATION WITH THE FALLBACK STATUS POINT (FSP)

All communications with Internet-based clients and Internet-based device clients require PKI certificates on the clients and site systems, except for sending status messages to the FSP. Status messages sent to the FSP are essentially a call for help when a client is having problems contacting the site, so HTTP is used in case certificate-related issues are causing the problem.

System Center 2012 Configuration Manager provides auto-enrollment capability for mobile devices. Auto-enrollment simplifies management by allowing devices to self-provision certificates and supports the greatest range of device management functionality. Auto-enrollment requires a Microsoft enterprise CA.

TIP: ABOUT ENCRYPTING COMMUNICATIONS BETWEEN SERVERS

Server-to-server communication is signed to prevent tampering but is not encrypted. To secure communications between servers, you should consider using IP Security (IPSec). Chapter 20 discusses the use of IPSec on ConfigMgr.

Site Planning

After defining your sites, you can begin to plan the site infrastructure and the services at each site. The major tasks involved in site planning include determining the site systems to deploy, hardware sizing for each site system, and planning for site operations. These areas are discussed in the next sections.

Site Servers and Site Systems Planning

The server infrastructure is the foundation of your site. Chapter 2 introduces Configuration Manager system roles. This section presents the key issues to consider when you decide how to distribute system roles among servers and develop specifications for server hardware.

The minimum server requirement for a ConfigMgr site is a single site server. You can configure the site server for all the site system roles deployed at your site, or you can assign some roles to other servers. You should consider the optimal placement of site servers as part of the planning process. Here are some reasons for assigning site system roles to servers other than the site server:

- ▶ **Network topology:** For those sites that span WAN links, you may want to make distribution points available at each physical location. Chapter 5 discusses network considerations for DP placement.

- ▶ **Security:** You may want to move client-facing roles such as the management point (MP), distribution point, and software update point (SUP) off the site server to avoid allowing clients to access the site server directly. You will definitely want to do this if you support Internet clients, in which case it is best to deploy the servers accessible from the Internet in a DMZ (demilitarized zone, also known as a perimeter network).

- ▶ **Scalability:** For large sites, you may want to distribute the computing load between multiple systems. If you install multiple MPs in a site, the client selects one automatically. If the client has a valid PKI certificate, it chooses a MP that supports HTTPS if one is available. Multiple MPs also provide redundancy. For large sites, you may need to use Network Load Balancing (NLB) clusters with certain site systems.

- ▶ **Management:** Many organizations have SQL database servers already deployed and supported by database administrators (DBAs). If this is the case, it may make sense to move the site database to one of these servers. SQL Server is the only site system that supports failover clustering. To take advantage of clustering, you must move the database off the site server.

▶ **Performance:** In general, you may get better performance if you install SQL Server on your site servers and keep the ConfigMgr database local to the site server. ConfigMgr is a database-intensive application. If the database is not on the site server, it is essential you have good connectivity between the site server and SQL Server system. Co-locating the site database on the site server requires additional server memory and disk capacity. If you co-locate the database on the site server, limit the memory for SQL Server to between 50 and 80 percent of available address-able system memory.

NOTE: SECONDARY SITES AND DATABASE PLACEMENT

At secondary sites, the site database must be located on the site server.

The SMS Provider is a Windows Management Instrumentation (WMI) provider that serves as an interface to between applications such as the ConfigMgr console and the site database. Chapter 3 describes WMI and WMI providers. The CAS site and each primary site require one or more instances of the SMS Provider. Secondary sites do not require or support the SMS Provider. You can install the provider on the site server, the site database server, or another server-class computer. Here are the system requirements for the SMS Provider:

▶ The provider must be installed on a system in a domain with a two-way trust with the domains of the site server and the site database server.

▶ You cannot install the provider on a system that holds a site system role or provider instance from a different site.

▶ The operating system requirements for the provider are the same as for the site server. The provider requires 650MB of free disk space for Windows Automated Installation Kit (WAIK) components installed with the SMS Provider.

Here are some points to consider when choosing a location for the SMS Provider:

▶ Locating the provider on the site database server provides the best performance but uses database server system and network resources. This option is not available if the site database resides on a clustered SQL Server instance.

▶ Locating the provider on the site server may provide better performance than using a system other than the site server or site database server but uses server system and network resources.

▶ Locating the provider on a server other than the site server takes the load off those critical systems, but may reduce performance due to the network communications overhead involved. This configuration also introduces another potential failure point in your environment. Using a separate system for the provider allows you to create additional provider instances.

You may want to have more than one provider instance if you expect a large number of simultaneous connections from the console and other applications. Having additional instances can also increase availability. If your site has multiple provider instances, you cannot control which instance is used for a given connection. In the event that one provider is down, a connection request may still be routed to that provider, which will result in a failure. Having more than one instance allows you to retry the connection if a failure occurs.

Capacity Planning

Both distribution points and software update points may require substantial storage. The storage requirements for distribution points depend on the number and size of software packages and OS images they host. Storage considerations for software update points are covered in the "Software Update Planning" section of this chapter. Heavily used distribution points and software update points have a large amount of network traffic; you will want to provision them with the fastest network card that your network infrastructure will support.

The site database at the CAS site can support a hierarchy with up to 50,000 clients using SQL Server Standard Edition and up to 400,000 clients using SQL Server Enterprise Edition. The size of the site database depends on many factors, including

▶ The number of clients.

▶ Client inventory customizations—extending the inventory could increase the database size by several megabytes per client.

▶ Status message configuration and retention.

▶ The number of sites—SQL replication metadata can consume a significant amount of database space.

Here are some additional factors to take into account for capacity planning:

▶ A CAS can support up to 25 child primary sites, and each primary site can support up to 250 secondary sites. It is not likely that you will want to test these limits, as a smaller number of sites are generally desirable.

▶ A primary site with the SQL database on the site server can support up to 50,000 clients. A primary site with a dedicated SQL database server can support up to 100,000 clients.

▶ A management point can support up to 25,000 clients at a primary site and up to 2,500 clients at a secondary site. For sites with larger numbers of clients, you should deploy additional management points.

▶ A distribution point can support up to 4,000 clients, assuming high I/O and network performance. You may need more DPs depending on the number and size of your applications and packages.

▶ A dedicated software update point running WSUS 3.0 Service Pack 2 (SP 2) can support up to 100,000 clients. A SUP that performs other site system roles can support a maximum of 25,000 clients. If the number of clients exceeds the capacity of a single SUP, you can configure an NLB cluster to distribute the load across multiple servers.

▶ The features you support make a difference. Endpoint protection in particular uses a large amount of database storage. Inventory customizations may also result in additional database use. These factors may reduce the number of clients your site can support.

▶ You should consider the amount of content you expect to support and make sure your site servers, DPs, and SUPs have adequate storage for content.

These numbers are based on the supported configurations described at http://technet. microsoft.com/en-us/library/gg682077.aspx, and additional guidance on WSUS found at http://technet.microsoft.com/en-us/library/gg712696.aspx#BKMK_SUMCapacity. Because many variables affect capacity requirements, it is important to validate your capacity plan during your proof of concept. This is especially true of the sizing for your SQL Server database. The "Proof of Concept" section of this chapter discusses the proof of concept phase. Keep in mind that future service packs could increase capacity requirements, as might growth and changes in your organization. It is generally more expensive to add capacity after your initial deployment, especially if you use physical servers for site systems.

Developing the Server Architecture

As with all Windows Server installations, use only hardware components listed in the Windows Server Catalog. The catalog is located at http://www.windowsservercatalog. com/. For maximum supportability, it is best to use hardware bearing the Windows Server Hardware logo. Virtualization of all site systems roles is supported on Windows Server 2008 and 2008 R2 and Hyper-V Server 2008 and 2008 R2. You can find information about supportability on other virtualization products at http://www.windowsservercatalog.com/ svvp.aspx. Directly attached volumes on a storage area network (SAN) are supported, provided all hardware components are supported.

All System Center 2012 Configuration Manager site system roles except for distribution points must be installed on systems running a 64-bit OS. Site systems cannot by deployed on server core or foundation server instances. Here are the minimum recommended hardware specifications for ConfigMgr site systems:

▶ 2.0GHz Pentium III processor

▶ 1.0GB of RAM

▶ 5GB free disk space; 15GB if you will support OSD

You can find hardware sizing recommendations for specific site systems at http://technet. microsoft.com/en-us/library/hh846235.aspx. For production systems, you should meet (and generally exceed) the recommended minimum specifications. For systems that handle large amount of HTTPS traffic, you should consider a cryptographic accelerator card. ConfigMgr does not support server clustering. If you use a dedicated SQL database server, you may use server clustering for high availability.

Planning for Solution Scenarios

After you determine the solutions you will deliver, you must plan the infrastructure and processes you will need. The following sections describe specific planning considerations for specific ConfigMgr services.

Software Update Planning

All software is subject to possible bugs or design flaws that may introduce security vulnerabilities or other defects into your environment. Software vendors, including Microsoft, regularly release updates or patches to their software to address these problems. Software updates may also introduce new or enhanced functionality to software products. Testing software updates and deploying them to a large number of systems in a timely manner is an increasingly important challenge for all IT organizations. This section presents the major planning considerations for ConfigMgr software updates. Chapter 14 considers software updates in depth.

Patch management is a vital component of an enterprise security policy. The average time from the publication of a vulnerability to the appearance of an exploit has gone from several months in the 1990s to just several days. Zero day exploits, which appear before a patch is released, are increasingly common. You should therefore plan for both standard releases and emergency releases of software updates.

System Center 2012 Configuration Manager provides options for automated or manual patch deployment. Automated patch deployment allows you to create predefined rules to deploy patches. Here are some examples of rules for automated deployments:

▶ Deploy all Windows 7 patches of severity "critical" to the IT Department W2K7 Systems collection, allow the user do delay mandatory installation and reboot up to one week. Do not install if clients have a slow or unreliable network connection.

▶ Deploy all Windows 7 or Office 2010 patches to the Patch Testing collection. Deploy and install as soon as possible and reboot the systems if required.

An important consideration in deploying software updates is testing. Any change to systems may have unintended consequences. Ideally, you would test patches against all your standard configurations before deployment. You need to weigh the risks of deploying patches without extensive testing against the risks of delay in patching your systems. In some cases regulatory compliance may require testing all patches before deployment to production systems. On the other hand, regulations sometimes require deploying certain patches within a given time frame. The Payment Card Industry Data Security Standard (PCI DSS) version 2.0, for example, includes a requirement to install critical security patches within one month of release.

To test patches prior to production implementation, create test collections of machines with a representative cross-section of your hardware and software configurations. Your test plan should include procedures to deploy updates to test collections and monitor both the deployment process and the impact on test machines.

Another factor you should consider in patch deployment is licensing. ConfigMgr automatic deployment rules include options to automatically accept any license agreements, or to deploy only updates with no license agreements or for which the license agreement has already been approved. If unsure which option is appropriate in your organization, consult with your license compliance or legal department.

An important planning consideration for software updates is which products, classifications, and languages to support. This determines the storage requirements for software updates. The software update point component properties at the top site in your hierarchy determine which updates will be retrieved from the Microsoft site. Figure 4.4 shows the Classifications tab of the Software Update Point Component Properties page.

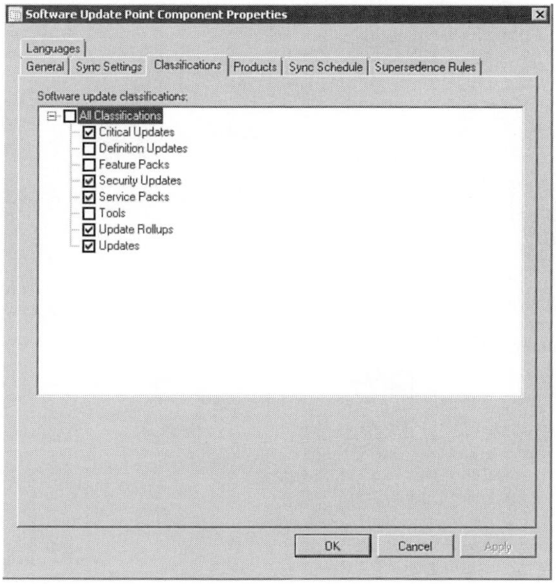

FIGURE 4.4   The Classifications tab of the Software Update Point Component Properties page.

Software Updates Architecture

The active SUP at the top-level site in your hierarchy is generally configured to synchronize with the Microsoft Updates Internet site. The active SUP at every other site synchronizes with the active SUP at its parent site.

▶ Client systems connect to the SUP to run vulnerability scans.

▶ The client then retrieves any required patches from the distribution point and applies the patches to the client system.

Each ConfigMgr primary site that provides software update services to clients must have an active SUP. The SUP is an optional system role in a secondary site. If a secondary site does not have an active SUP, clients at the site will use the SUP at the parent site. The advantage of configuring an active SUP at a secondary site is it reduces network bandwidth consumption on the link between the site and its parent.

How Software Updates Work

Intranet clients run vulnerability scans from the active SUP at their local site. If the active SUP is not configured to accept connections from Internet clients, you can configure a separate Internet-based SUP. Internet-based SUPs at secondary sites are not supported and do not work, although the user interface allows you to configure them. Figure 4.5 shows some options for software updates synchronization and client support.

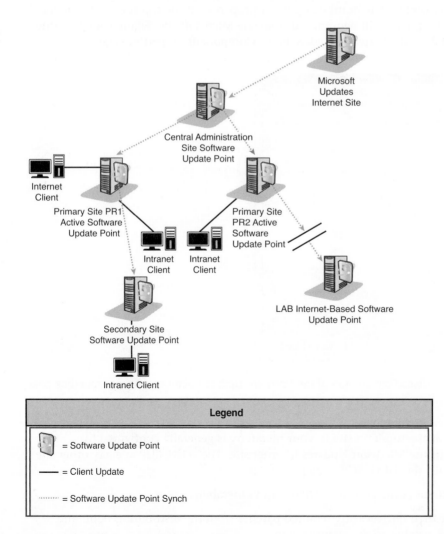

FIGURE 4.5   Software updates synchronization architecture.

In this figure, the active SUP for the primary site PR1 is configured to accept both intranet and Internet client connections. The LAB SUP acts as an Internet SUP. It is disconnected from the active SUP at site PR2 and is synchronized manually.

NOTE: ABOUT ENVIRONMENTS WITH STANDALONE WSUS

Do not configure the WSUS functionality on your SUP outside of ConfigMgr. ConfigMgr overwrites any settings configured in WSUS. You also should remove any group policy for WSUS that might affect ConfigMgr clients. Clients with WSUS settings set by group policy cannot be managed by ConfigMgr software updates.

Planning for Internet-Based Clients

Most organizations have users working from home or remote offices without a direct connection to the enterprise network. Mobile workers also use laptops or tablets at locations that are on the network and at remote locations. In other cases, systems such as kiosk computers or point-of-sale systems require remote management. As long as these computers have a connection to the Internet, Configuration Manager Internet-based client management (IBCM) can provide content distribution and other key services to those clients.

NOTE: ABOUT VIRTUAL PRIVATE NETWORK (VPN) AND DIRECTACCESS CONNECTIONS

Many organizations implement a virtual private network to allow users to connect to the enterprise network over the Internet. To establish a VPN connection, client computers or other devices authenticate with a gateway on your network and establish an encrypted session (or tunnel) through which private communications can take place. You can use VPN connections to support all ConfigMgr 2007 features.

VPN services require a significant investment in infrastructure and support. Even if you have a VPN in place, there are reasons why it may not be an ideal vehicle for delivering ConfigMgr services:

▶ Some client systems may not meet the security standards appropriate for unrestricted access to your corporate network. With IBCM, you can manage these systems without exposing internal resources.

▶ IBCM clients use a client certificate to mutually authenticate with site systems. This prevents most man-in-the-middle attacks, which are a particular risk on insecure wireless networks such as coffee shops and airports. Not all VPN implementations provide this level of security.

▶ VPN clients systems are manageable only after the user establishes a VPN connection. IBCM clients are manageable any time the system connects to the Internet.

▶ Managing the VPN address space as part of your boundaries may present additional challenges.

The Windows Server 2008 R2 DirectAccess feature provides security for connecting to corporate networks over the Internet without requiring a VPN. If your network is configured to allow DirectAccess, clients can use this method to connect Windows Server 2008

R2 site systems. Clients on the Internet that connect using the Windows Server 2008 R2 Direct Access feature communicate with their assigned site in the same manner as intranet clients. Direct Access does not support OSD and supports only server-initiated actions over IPv6. You can find information about DirectAccess at http://technet.micro-soft.com/en-us/network/dd420463.

Depending on your business requirements and existing infrastructure, a VPN-based solution or DirectAccess may be the best way to manage computers that must connect through the Internet. VPN supports all ConfigMgr's features, whereas IBCM and Direct-Access support only a subset. Consider the capabilities of each solution when deciding how to meet the needs of your Internet-based clients.

Here are the ConfigMgr features supported by IBCM:

- ▶ Hardware and software inventory, including file collection
- ▶ State and status reporting
- ▶ Software distribution
- ▶ Software updates
- ▶ Software metering

A new feature in System Center 2012 Configuration Manager is that Internet-based software distribution can now include task sequences. IBCM does not support other ConfigMgr features such as client deployment, OSD, Remote Tools, and NAP.

Sites supporting Internet-based clients must be primary sites. Certificates must be deployed to servers and clients. The systems that directly support Internet-based clients must be accessible from the Internet via HTTP/HTTPS. Systems that may provide services for Internet clients include the following:

- ▶ **Management point:** The MP is the only required role, providing policy to clients and receiving inventory, state, status, and other data from clients.
- ▶ **Distribution points:** One or more DPs are required for software deployment. These distribution points must be site systems rather than server shares.
- ▶ **Fallback status point:** The FSP is recommended to allow clients that are having problems contacting the management point to report status to the site.
- ▶ **Software update point:** The SUP is required for software updates.

Each of these systems require configuration to accept connections from the Internet, and the site system properties must include a fully qualified domain name (FQDN) that is resolvable from the Internet. Internet-facing site systems cannot be protected site systems. Deploying Internet-facing site systems requires additional planning from a security perspective. Chapter 5 discusses network placement of site systems that support Internet clients.

Out of Band Management Planning

One of the most exciting developments in desktop technology in recent years is Intel's Advanced Management Technology (AMT), based on the vPro technology. For many years, server vendors have offered OOB management capability using a dedicated network connection, network card, and processor. Server administrators can remotely access keyboard, video, and mouse (KVM) functionality directly, without depending on the operating system. Due to cost, this type of configuration is generally not practical for desktop systems. Intel's introduction of network cards and chipsets supporting AMT, while not providing the hardware redundancy of the server class solutions, brings the similar management functionality to desktop systems. Additional functionality allows management applications, such as ConfigMgr, to perform management tasks even when the operating system is not loaded. This section looks at the ways ConfigMgr takes advantage of AMT features. For more information about AMT and vPro technologies, see www.intel.com/vpro.

ConfigMgr OOB management uses Windows remote management technology (WS-MAN) to connect to the management controller on a computer. Here are some supported use cases for System Center 2012 Configuration Manager OOB management:

► **Remote helpdesk functions:** You can launch the OOB Management console from the ConfigMgr console to connect to systems and perform functions including

   ► Changing the power state of sleeping systems

   ► Watching the boot sequence before the operating systems loads

   ► Managing system BIOS settings

   ► Booting the system from a boot image on the network

   ► Redirecting IDE drives to network locations or other devices

► **Powering up sleeping systems:** This capability enables software distribution, software updates, and OSD

   ► ConfigMgr updates can be scheduled or done on demand

   ► Provides better security than Wake on LAN, including Kerberos authentication and encryption

► **Support for 802.1X authentication:** 802.1X is an industry standard network authentication protocol suite used to restrict network connections to authorized systems. An inherent problem with NAP or network access control (NAC) solutions that rely on health statements generated within the operating system environment is the "lying endpoint" problem. If the NAP/NAC software is compromised or a root kit compromises the OS, the endpoint may present a false "clean" health state assertion to the NAP or NAC server. Modules in the Intel firmware can inspect the integrity of key system components to mitigate the lying endpoint problem.

If you plan to use OOB management, your desktop infrastructure and PKI deployment must meet several requirements to support it. Even if you do not plan to use this functionality immediately, you may want to plan for it in your new hardware purchases. Table 4.2 lists the key dependencies to plan for should you want to use OOB management.

TABLE 4.2   Dependencies for Using OOB Management

Requirement Type	Details
Client hardware	Intel Centrino, Core Duo vPro, or i-series chipset.
	Intel AMT firmware versions 3.2.1 or later. The Intel HECI driver must also be installed.
	A supported network card such as the Intel 82566DM.
PKI	A provisioning certificate signed by a well-known CA or a custom firmware containing the thumbprint for a certificate issued by your CA. You can manually enter a certificate thumbprint on the AMT BIOS configuration screen for testing or small-scale deployments.
	OOB management requires a Microsoft enterprise certificate authority.
	Each AMT managed computer requires a web server certificate installed in the management controller memory. This requires a certificate template enabled for auto-enrollment. 802.1X support requires an additional client certificate.
Configuration Manager setup	Site systems must be configured with the OOB service point and enrollment point roles.
	Computers supporting OOB management must be discovered and provisioned.
	An AMT Provisioning and Discovery account must be configured.
Active Directory	A container or organizational unit (OU) for computer objects representing AMT managed systems.
	A universal security group containing the computer accounts of AMT managed systems.
	Appropriate rights for the site server on the container and security group.
Network infrastructure	Appropriately configured DHCP scope.
	Firewall rules configured to allow provisioning and management.
	For 802.1X functionality, an appropriate authentication infrastructure (see Chapter 14).

You must *provision* the management controller on each client system before ConfigMgr can connect to the management controller for OOB management. The provisioning process configures the management controller with the information it needs about the management server and installs a web server certificate in the management controller protected memory to support HTTPS connections from management applications.

The management controller firmware contains a set of "thumbprints" representing CAs authorized to sign provisioning certificates. The enrollment point site system must have a certificate signed by one of these CAs to authenticate to the management controller and carry out the provisioning process. By default, AMT-enabled systems trust a small number of public certificate vendors to sign provisioning certificates. The exact list of vendors varies depending on the AMT version installed. You may purchase a provisioning certificate from one of these vendors to install on the enrollment point. Alternatively, you may request a custom firmware from your system vendor with the thumbprint of your internal CA installed. Custom firmware is likely to be more expensive than purchasing a provisioning certificate, but restricting provisioning only to your internal CA adds a measure of security. For testing purposes, you can also manually enter a thumbprint through the AMT BIOS setup utility.

Provisioning the management controller with a computer certificate requires a Microsoft enterprise CA. 802.1X support requires provisioning an additional client certificate. You must configure the certificate template for auto-enrollment. OOB management requires additional AD, DHCP, and firewall configuration. The planning and initial effort to enable your ConfigMgr environment for OOB management is significant, but this feature greatly extends your management capabilities.

> **NOTE: CONFIGURATION MANAGER WAKE-ON-LAN AND POWER MANAGEMENT SUPPORT**
>
> In addition to OOB management, System Center 2012 Configuration Manager can use Wake on LAN (WOL) technology to "wake up" computers from certain sleep states and perform various operations. WOL is an older technology that provides a subset of AMT functionality and is less secure. WOL is, however, supported on a wider range of computer hardware and has fewer infrastructure dependencies than OOB management. Chapter 9 describes ConfigMgr WOL functionality.
>
> Chapter 2 introduces ConfigMgr power management capabilities. Power management provides many of the same wake-up capabilities as OOB management without the certificate and hardware requirements. You should evaluate each of these technologies and decide which best meets your requirements.

Testing and Stabilizing Your Design

Implementing and supporting System Center 2012 Configuration Manager requires a phased approach in transforming your initial vision into a working production system. Planning for your architectural design should include a plan to test your solution before deploying it to your production environment, and to stabilize and customize your solution as you begin the deployment phase. Building, testing, and stabilizing your solution includes several major activities:

- ▶ The first step is building a proof of concept (POC) implementation. A POC is a trial deployment that implements the essential features of your solution but is not designed to be part of your production environment.

▶ Later in your implementation, you carry out a pilot deployment in your production environment. The pilot is a controlled implementation to a selected subset of your production systems.

Throughout the POC and pilot phases, you monitor and test your solution. Based on the test results, you may need to make adjustments and customizations so that the final solution can work well in your production environment.

Depending on the size and culture of your organization, you may follow a more or less structured approach to plan and build your solution. For any deployment, you want to test the basic functionality you plan to use before deploying to production. You may require more or less extensive testing and formal release management processes, based on

▶ **The size and complexity of your environment:** Deploying ConfigMgr in a large, complex environment calls for more extensive testing than a smaller deployment.

▶ **The feature set you plan to use:** Some ConfigMgr features such as OOB management and OSD have network and service infrastructure dependencies you need to consider when testing and building your solution. Similarly, some features such as NAP and software updates impact clients more directly than lower impact ConfigMgr services such as inventory and reporting. Features that have a higher impact on clients introduce greater risk to your production environment. You need to account for those risk factors in testing and incorporate risk avoidance or mitigation strategies as you build your solution.

▶ **The extent to which your solution is customized and integrated with other elements of your environment:** Relatively generic deployments may largely consist of deploying features that are well tested out-of-the-box. These features may just need basic validation in your environment. In contrast, every customization and integration point should be thoroughly tested and documented as part of your solution build.

The Proof of Concept

To prove your design is conceptually sound, you need to implement the essential features of your solution in a test environment. The primary goals of the POC include

▶ Providing evidence that the proposed technical solution is feasible and it addresses the business requirements. It is important to validate your processes and documentation as well as the technical design.

▶ Furnishing an opportunity for the support team to gain knowledge of the product.

▶ Identifying and addressing any gaps or weaknesses in the original design.

Here are the key requirements for an effective proof of concept:

▶ A POC environment that adequately reflects your production environment

▶ A test plan that validates each element of your functional requirements

▶ A communications plan that allows you to share lessons learned effectively, and applies the results to improving your design, documentation, and processes

You should specify the design, goals, and metrics for the POC as part of the following planning documents:

▶ **Functional Specification:** This provides a detailed description of the feature set and explains how each feature should look and behave. It also describes the overall architecture and design of each feature. This document will identify what ConfigMgr features you need to configure, and the infrastructure requirements each feature depends on.

▶ **Master Project Plan (MPP):** The MPP generally includes a deployment plan, capacity plan, security plan, and test plan among other elements. One goal of the POC will be to validate each element of the MPP. The test plan in the MPP is largely carried out during the POC phase.

Building the Proof of Concept Environment

Ideally, your POC environment would be an exact replica of your production environment; however, in practice this is not feasible. This makes it necessary to identify the critical systems, infrastructure, and activities that adequately represent the production environment. Organizations using the Microsoft Operations Framework (MOF) or other Information Technology Infrastructure Library (ITIL) practices can leverage information from the enterprise CMDB to help identify the relevant configuration items (CIs) that need to be replicated in the test environment. The CMDB includes details about both the individual CIs and the relationships between them. You should review your functional specification and master project plan and use the CMDB to map the dependencies relevant to the CIs in your ConfigMgr deployment. Here are some examples of how you might use the CMDB to plan your test environment:

▶ The CMDB is the starting point for enumerating the client configurations you need to test. Although it may not be possible to test every configuration, your test environment should include as complete a sample of platforms as possible. At a minimum, you should include all operating system versions found in your production environment and the major hardware platforms you will be supporting. If you plan to use ConfigMgr to manage mobile devices such as smartphones, you should include devices on each carrier network as well.

▶ Your MPP calls for ConfigMgr sites in various locations such as Brussels and Beijing. The CMDB contains information about these sites including local area network (LAN) and WAN characteristics, Windows language and locale settings, the number and type of clients systems, information about the local IT and vendor support organizations, and possibly legal and regulatory requirements affecting the sites.

One way to replicate the network environment of these sites accurately in your POC would be with a distributed test environment, which would include systems physically located at these sites. An alternative method is to configure the physical or virtual network infrastructure to introduce bandwidth throttling, latency, and transient communications anomalies between sites to simulate your actual network characteristics and conditions.

▶ Your functional specification calls for delivering OOB management to laptop and desktop computers supporting Intel Advanced Management Technology (AMT). The CMDB can help you identify all AMT capable models in your environment so that you can include them in testing.

▶ Your functional specification includes a requirement to provide reports on software license compliance for all your standard desktop applications. You can use the CMDB to identify those applications you need to report on and the available license data to incorporate in the reports.

If you do not already have an enterprise CMDB, you need to use other means to gather data about your environment. Start with the existing documentation about your network, client and server hardware, and other elements of your environment. You may want to employ an asset discovery tool to update your documentation and fill in any gaps. If you have an existing ConfigMgr 2007 deployment, you can leverage ConfigMgr discovery methods and asset intelligence for this purpose. The information and data collection methods you assemble may be useful to you later if you decide to develop a CMDB. Microsoft System Center Service Manager provides full CMDB functionality.

You can carry out a POC in a physically isolated lab or in a controlled environment with connectivity to your production network. Here are advantages and disadvantages to each:

▶ Using an isolated lab provides the greatest safety and frees you from the need to consider possible impact on the live environment. However, this can take longer to set up because you must duplicate infrastructure services.

▶ Implementing a POC in a test environment connected to your production network can save time and money because you can leverage existing infrastructure services rather than having to duplicate them in the test environment, The downside is that caution needs to be exercised at all times to avoid making changes that affect your live environment.

The following sections discuss each of these environments.

Proving the Concepts in a Pure Lab Environment
Generally, you deploy the POC in a lab environment isolated from your production network. Testing in an isolated lab gives you the freedom to try things out without having to worry about risks to your production environment. If your organization does not already have a suitable lab in place, you should consider building one. The test environment should mirror your live environment as closely as possible.

▶ Ideally, you should deploy ConfigMgr server roles on hardware identical to what you use in production. You could accomplish this by "borrowing" the actual hardware you use for your production site systems to use as part of the POC. This approach allows the most realistic testing but requires you to tear down at least part of the POC environment when you move the production hardware to the live environment.

▶ In addition to the site systems, you should have a mix of clients in the POC environment representing a cross section of the hardware, operating systems, and applications you encounter in your live environment. The network infrastructure and core services should also replicate the essential features of your production environment. Although this may be expensive, it can save you from greater costs later if you encounter unexpected problems in the production environment.

In general, it is a good idea to keep the POC environment available if possible. This gives you an environment for future testing of hotfixes, service packs, upgrades, new packages, and operating system images, and any additional functionality you may decide to deploy. The POC environment is also a great place for training and experimentation. A properly designed lab environment allows development and testing your solution without affecting production systems. Everyone working in the lab should understand that test systems could become unstable and require reinstallation. It is not uncommon for an unstable lab environment to be a source of frustration, but keep in mind that many of the problems that arise in the lab would otherwise have occurred in your production environment! As it is often necessary to roll back a test server to a previous state, you should maintain frequent backups or snapshots of all servers. Here are several approaches:

▶ For virtual machines, reverting to a snapshot of the original build or a more recent baseline snapshot is generally the most efficient way to roll back to a previous configuration.

▶ For physical machines, you may be able to leverage ConfigMgr operating system deployment to capture configuration baselines and redeploy them as necessary. If you use this method, you must plan a different strategy to restore a ConfigMgr site server or other site systems required for OSD.

▶ You can perform a bare metal restore or apply a standard server image and then restore your site from backup or reinstall SQL Server and ConfigMgr. It may be helpful to maintain images of standard server configurations because machines are often "wiped" or reformatted. Developing scripted installations can help with this process, and you can use them in your production environment as well.

Regardless of how you manage recovery in your lab environment, you must to follow the site recovery process described in Chapter 21 when restoring a site server that is part of a ConfigMgr hierarchy.

VIRTUALIZATION IN A TEST ENVIRONMENT

When designing a test environment, you should consider the respective advantages of physical or virtual hardware. Virtualization can dramatically lower the costs of building a test environment. Virtualization allows you to take snapshots of a virtual machine and later roll the machine back to the exact state it was in at the time of the snapshot. Reverting a test system to a snapshot requires much less time and effort than restoring a physical machine from a backup. Virtualization enables quick and efficient provisioning of large numbers of client systems for test purposes.

If you use a clustered configuration for the SQL Server database server in production, you want to test the effects of a cluster failover. For this type of testing, virtual machines may not accurately represent the functioning of physical hardware you have in production.

Similarly, if you use NLB clustering for any of your servers roles, virtual machines (VMs) sharing the same network interface card (NIC) or sharing a NIC with other VMs might not adequately reflect the behavior in the live environment. OSD and OOB management are examples of functionality you need to test on physical hardware. To test OS deployment adequately, you should deploy images and task sequences to hardware that realistically reflect the target hardware in your production environment.

The standard methods for provisioning VMs and deploying base images to them differ significantly from the methods used with physical hardware. Adequate testing of driver installation requires a representative population of physical hardware devices in the test environment. OOB management using Intel AMT requires special hardware support, as described in Chapter 9. Backup and recovery processes are also different for VMs and physical machines. You should ensure the backup and recovery processes you test are valid for your production environment.

An optimum test environment may include both virtual and physical systems. System Center 2012 Configuration Manager requires certain infrastructure dependencies for installation and for certain features to work. Chapter 2 covers feature dependencies. Your POC environment generally needs the following services to be in place:

▶ AD is a required dependency for System Center 2012 Configuration Manager. The AD environment for your POC should closely resemble your production AD. The "Active Directory Considerations" section of this chapter discusses creating the AD environment for your POC.

▶ DNS is required for AD and for many ConfigMgr features. Using AD-integrated DNS meets this requirement when you deploy AD in the POC environment. If you use a non-AD-integrated DNS, you need to configure DNS servers in the POC environment.

▶ WINS is required for certain functionality if you do not use AD schema extensions or you have clients that cannot take advantage of AD schema extensions.

▶ PKI is required for certain features such as HTTPS communications and OOB management.

You should also deploy any security software you use in production, such as antimalware and host intrusion detection software, to the POC environment. Network-based security controls such as firewalls and intrusion detection systems should also be in place and configured consistently with those in your production environment.

You can use several approaches in creating a suitable AD implementation in a POC environment. The first method is often referred to as the *peel off method*. In this scenario, you add a domain controller (DC) to each production domain you want to replicate in your POC, peel the DC off from production, and move it to the POC environment. A variation on the peel-off method is to clone an existing DC instead of actually removing it from the domain and transferring it to the lab. To clone a DC on physical hardware, you may be able to use your backup software following procedures described in the backup vendor's documentation. You may also be able to use imaging software or P2P (physical-to-physical) migration tools. If you have a DC running as a VM, the cloning process may be even easier. You probably just need to shut down the DC and use your virtualization software's management tools to clone the image. You can then copy the cloned image to the lab and bring the new VM online on a host connected to the lab environment.

The major alternative to the peel off method is standing up a new AD forest in the POC environment and reproducing the essential elements of your production AD in the new forest. When your POC forest is in place, you can use the LDIFDE command or other tools to export the objects you need from your production AD and import them into the lab. You should transfer any relevant group policy objects (GPOs) from the production environment to the POC environment. GPOs control many settings that affect ConfigMgr, such as security and network settings. At a minimum, you want to import the default domain policy and default domain controller policy from your production environment. You can use either scripts or the Group Policy Management Console (GPMC) to copy GPOs.

Proving the Concepts in an Environment Connected to Your Production Network

Although there are many advantages to having an isolated lab environment for your POC, you may also consider doing POC testing on systems connected to your production network. Here are the advantages to this approach:

▶ Costs are lower because you do not need to create a separate network infrastructure.

▶ The time to deploy the POC environment is substantially less because you typically can leverage existing services such as DNS, WINS, Dynamic Host Configuration Protocol (DHCP), and backup services. In a lab environment, you would need to install and configure these services independently of your production deployment.

▶ It may be difficult or impossible to reproduce certain features of your environment in a test lab adequately. Enterprise monitoring solutions, PKI infrastructure, and production security services are examples of services you may have deployed in production that would be prohibitively expensive to duplicate in a lab.

If you use a POC environment connected to production, you generally need to create a separate AD environment for the POC. This is particularly true if you use the schema extensions to publish site information to AD. You cannot use the peel off method in this circumstance, so you need to stand up a separate AD forest from scratch. If you have an existing ConfigMgr 2007 or Systems Management Server (SMS) 2003 deployment in production, you also must make sure that the site boundaries of your POC ConfigMgr sites do not overlap with the site boundaries of your production deployment, and that you do not use the same site code for more than one site!

The Pilot Deployment

When you complete the POC, you can begin the pilot phase. The pilot is a limited deployment of your actual production infrastructure and services. You typically install a single primary site and a few clients during the pilot phase. If your hierarchy includes a CAS site, you must install it at this time. The pilot is the beginning of your production build-out and should follow the methodologies described in Chapter 6, "Installing System Center 2012 Configuration Manager," and Chapter 7. From an architecture design planning perspective, the importance of the pilot is that this is when your deployment initially interacts with production systems and actual users. Your test plan for the pilot phase should include

▶ Testing integration with production systems, including AD, DNS, monitoring, and backup/restore functions. Pay particular attention to validating any integration points you cannot reproduce in the POC environment.

▶ Soliciting user input to validate that the user experience is what you envisioned. Often a brief survey and an open door policy for user suggestions and complaints can provide useful feedback from the user perspective.

Summary

This chapter discussed the overall design of your ConfigMgr architecture. You should start by identifying your business goals and ConfigMgr features to use to support them. You then must identify the likely technical challenges and how you can address them. The chapter then presented design considerations for your hierarchy, sites, and key infrastructure services. The chapter also examined some specific feature sets that require additional planning. Finally, it described to validate your design in the proof of concept and pilot environments.

The next chapter provides a detailed discussion of network design considerations for ConfigMgr.

Network Design

Chapter 4, "Architecture Design Planning," described the Configuration Manager application architecture and discussed how you can design a Configuration Manager (ConfigMgr) topology and infrastructure to support the services you want to deliver to your users. This chapter discusses how to deploy your solution in your network environment with the following goals in mind:

▶ **Security:** An appropriate network design can minimize the exposure of your ConfigMgr servers and services to attack and protect communications between systems.

▶ **Availability:** Client systems need to locate and access ConfigMgr services reliably from any supported network location.

▶ **Performance:** Clients should experience as little impact as possible from latency and bandwidth constraints.

▶ **Resource utilization:** ConfigMgr should live within your network without consuming an excessive amount of network resources or adversely affecting other network activity.

To develop an effective network design, it is essential to understand your network environment, the types of data exchanged between ConfigMgr sites and systems, the ports and protocols used, and the options for tuning network communications. After describing ConfigMgr communications in detail, this chapter examines how network considerations affect your site design and operations. The chapter also discusses how you can use ConfigMgr to discover your network topology and resources, and provides some tips on troubleshooting common network problems.

Understanding Your Network

Chapter 4 introduced planning considerations for your architectural design. The information gathered in the architectural design phase can provide much of the basis for network design considerations as well. Here are the key decision criteria for deploying ConfigMgr in a network environment:

▶ At which locations will you provide services? This is the starting point of your network planning. You want to provide effective and efficient services to every location.

▶ What client systems are at each location? Enumerate the devices at each location and device characteristics in terms of operating systems, Active Directory (AD) services, hardware capabilities, and mobility.

▶ What users are at each location? You should understand the applications that you need to deliver across the network based on user need as well as special requirements such as language support.

▶ How is your network connected? Gathering network topology diagrams and engaging your network support team are essential to planning how your systems communicate.

▶ What are the usage patterns for network resources? Gathering statistics about average and peak network utilization is essential for proper planning around bandwidth throttling and scheduling communications.

▶ What local data center resources are available at each location? The available options for site system placement depend on the availability of existing servers or data center infrastructure.

▶ Will you support mobile device client such as smartphones, or Internet-only clients? If so, you need to consider where you will deploy systems to support these clients.

You should consider the network requirements of System Center 2012 Configuration Manager in the context of your network environment. The next section describes the overall movement of data in ConfigMgr.

Configuration Manager Data Flow

When planning your ConfigMgr network infrastructure, you should consider the data flow between systems. The purpose of ConfigMgr communication is to deliver policy and content to your users and managed systems, and to gather information from those systems that can help you better manage and report on your environment. The primary data flow to managed systems is as follows:

▶ *Policy* originates as administrators use the ConfigMgr console to define client settings and schedule operations on managed systems. The console inserts policy into the site database through the SMS Provider. If you have more than one site in your hierarchy, the policy data is replicated among your sites. Policy flows to the client through the management point(s).

▶ *Content* includes applications, software updates, operating system (OS) and boot images, migrated user state data, and ConfigMgr components. Content flows from the source locations you configure to distribution points and other site systems where it is available to the client. You may use intermediate systems to make content distribution more efficient. Because content is the largest component of your ConfigMgr data flow in total bytes, you should pay close attention to planning efficient content acquisition and distribution.

ConfigMgr provides your Information Technology (IT) organization with a wealth of data about your environment, which can be used to support ConfigMgr operations and to support other IT goals. This data is replicated to the CAS site or the single primary site for management and reporting. The data ConfigMgr retrieves includes

▶ Discovery data, hardware and software inventory, software metering data, Asset Intelligence data, and client health data sent by ConfigMgr clients to various client facing systems, primarily management points (MP). The site systems send this data to the site server, which inserts client data into the database.

▶ Depending on the discovery methods you enable, site servers may query AD for information about AD objects. Similarly, the site server may use various network protocols to discover your network topology and systems.

▶ Status messages, state messages, and alerts generated by site systems and clients.

Additional data flows to consider involve the Asset Intelligence synchronization point and the software update point (SUP) at the top of your hierarchy. These systems have the capability to synchronize with Microsoft systems on the Internet and make downloaded content available throughout the hierarchy. Asset Intelligence data is inserted into the database and propagates through the hierarchy using database replication. The software update infrastructure provides software updates and endpoint protection engine and definition updates to clients throughout the hierarchy. If you use ConfigMgr to manage endpoint protection, the endpoint protection point must also connect to Microsoft systems on the Internet to enable licensing and configure membership in the Microsoft Active Protection Service.

When planning your ConfigMgr infrastructure and operations, it is important to understand the details of these data flows. ConfigMgr clients and servers use a variety or protocols to communicate with each other across the network. The following sections discuss the network communications between server roles within a site, the communications of ConfigMgr clients with servers in the site, and communications between sites. The discussion includes details of the network protocols ConfigMgr systems use and the ports over which they operate. Understanding the characteristics of these protocols is useful for planning purposes. Knowing what ports are in use can help you with configuration and troubleshooting.

Intrasite Server Communications

As previously described in Chapter 2, "Configuration Manager Overview," a ConfigMgr site contains of a set of servers carrying out various system roles. In the simplest configuration, the ConfigMgr primary site server holds all deployed site system roles. Designs that are more complex may involve moving certain roles to other servers within that site. Assigning roles to multiple servers brings network considerations into play for intrasite communications. This section discusses the flow of information between site systems and the network protocols used. For information on how network considerations affect your decision of how to distribute server roles, see the "Server Placement" section of this chapter.

The site server, SMS Provider, and site database form the core of the ConfigMgr site. All other site systems communicate with these systems.

ConfigMgr site systems use various protocols to communicate with each other. The most important protocols include the following:

▶ ConfigMgr site systems use standard SQL Server communication protocols to talk to SQL Server.

▶ The site server and some other systems use the Remote Procedure Call (RPC) protocol to invoke remote functionality on other systems.

▶ Most file transfer operations use the Server Message Block (SMB) protocol.

▶ The Background Intelligent Transfer Service (BITS) and various other services use Hypertext Transfer Protocol (HTTP)/Secure Hypertext Transfer Protocol (HTTPS).

The following sections discuss specifics of these protocols.

Communications with SQL Server

With System Center 2012 Configuration Manager, SQL Server connectivity uses standard SQL Server Transmission Control Protocol/Internet Protocol (TCP/IP) communications. Port 1433 is used by default with the default SQL Server instance. For named instances, the default port is dynamic and is not 1433. If you use a named instance, you must configure SQL Server to listen on a static port. Chapter 6, "Installing System Center 2012 Configuration Manager," describes SQL Server configuration options.

The primary site server, SMS Provider, and management point all make intensive use of SQL Server. The reporting services point and enrollment point also access the database directly. Although ConfigMgr supports Named Pipes connections to SQL Server, you should use the Named Pipes protocol for troubleshooting only.

NOTE: ABOUT NAMED PIPES

Named Pipes uses NT LAN Manager (NTLM) authentication only and does not support Kerberos authentication. Kerberos provides mutual authentication of the client and server, whereas NTLM authenticates only the client. TCP/IP also provides better performance under challenging network conditions, such as across a wide area network (WAN) link.

The ConfigMgr console accesses the site database using the SMS Provider, which is an intermediate Windows Management Instrumentation (WMI) layer used for database communication. Figure 5.1 shows the systems that communicate with SQL Server. The figure does not show other communications involving these site systems, such as communications with the site server or with clients. The figure also does not show the reporting services point, which uses SQL communications to connect to the reporting database.

Communications Using RPC

RPC is an industry-standard protocol used to invoke code across process boundaries, generally between processes on different machines. The calling process initiates an RPC call on TCP or UDP port 135 and receives a response on a dynamically allocated TCP port. The default RPC response port range is 49152 through 65535. You can configure your server to use a different port range using the `netsh` command:

```
netsh int <ipv4|ipv6> set dynamic <tcp|udp> start=<number> num=<range>
```

You may want to use a different range for tighter control over the ports uses or to conform to network firewall policies. The site server initiates RPC connections for configuring site systems. For example, the site server can use an RPC connection when you add a new role to a site system.

Communications Using SMB

SMB protocol is the core protocol for Windows file, printer, and port sharing, and for interprocess communications mechanisms such as Named Pipes and Mail Slots. ConfigMgr processes rely on file exchanges along with data exchanges within the site database to communicate with each other, as described in Chapter 3, "Looking Inside Configuration Manager." Most site systems also pass status message and state message files back to the site server using SMB. SMB traffic involves a series of requests and responses, which can involve multiple round trips between the communicating systems. This means that network latency can substantially affect certain SMB communications.

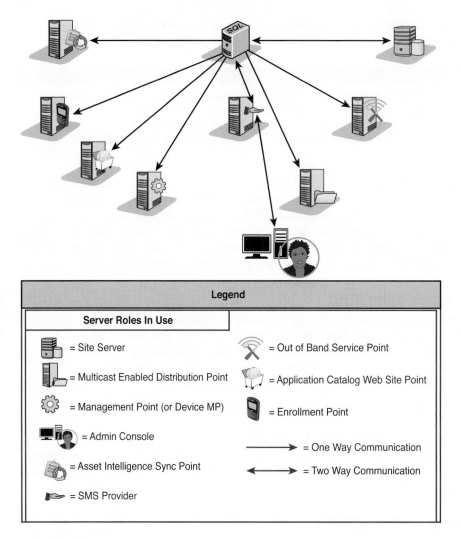

FIGURE 5.1   SQL Server communications.

NOTE: NETWORK LATENCY VERSUS BANDWIDTH

Network latency is the delay in transmitting data from one point to another. Several factors can contribute to latency. For example, delays may be introduced by packets queuing up on network devices by long distances such as round trips to satellites. The quickest way to measure latency is to ping a remote node and note the response time in the reply. Bandwidth is the total amount of data that your network can handle in a given amount of time and is determined by the capacity of components such as network cards, cabling, and switches. You can use tools such as netperf, available at http://www.netperf.org/netperf/, to measure bandwidth. Latency and bandwidth are the two primary measures of network performance.

The largest file transfers between site systems involve distributing deployment content (including OSD image files) to distribution points. System Center 2012 Configuration Manager introduces these major enhancements for deployment content distributions:

▶ The new Package Transfer Manager component provides the same scheduling and bandwidth throttling options for sending deployment content from the site server to distribution points within the site that are available for transferring content between sites. These options are not needed and therefore not available for distribution points co-located on the site server.

▶ ConfigMgr 2012 also provides an important new option to enable a distribution point for prestaged content. This allows you leverage an existing enterprise data replication solution to copy content to your distribution points or to bypass the network altogether by distributing content on media such as cloned drives or backup tapes.

Site servers use SMB protocol to transfer deployment content to remote distribution points within the site as well as to remote sites. The new configurable scheduling and bandwidth throttling options for distributing content within a site reduce the need for secondary sites. Packages are sent between sites using the sender mechanism, described in the "Site-to-Site Communications" section. Secondary sites were often created in ConfigMgr 2007 to take advantage of the bandwidth throttling and scheduling.

To configure distribution point settings, navigate to the Distribution Points node in the Administration workspace of the ConfigMgr console, and double-click the distribution point to open its Properties page. Figure 5.2 shows the Schedule tab on the Distribution Point Properties page. You can use scheduling to specify sending limits and the data priorities allowed by day and time.

Figure 5.3 shows the Rate Limits tab, which allows you to specify the percentage of available network capacity to allocate for transfers to the distribution point. When transfer rate limits are in effect, the site server times how long it takes to send each block of data and pauses before sending the next block for an interval determined by the maximum transfer units setting. In general, this results in the sender using all available bandwidth the designated percentage of time, which is roughly equivalent to using the allowed percentage of overall bandwidth.

NOTE: ABOUT DISTRIBUTION POINTS ON SITE SERVERS

The Property page Schedule tab and Rate Limit tab in Figures 5.2 and 5.3 are not displayed for distribution points that are installed on the site server.

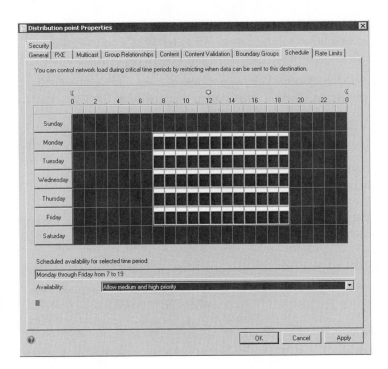

FIGURE 5.2   Distribution point schedule.

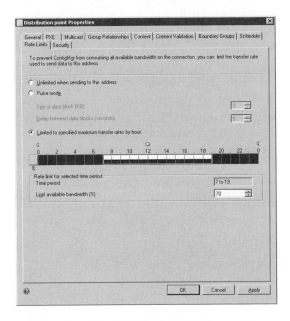

FIGURE 5.3   Distribution rate limits.

> **CAUTION: USE CARE WHEN ADJUSTING DISTRIBUTION POINT SETTINGS**
>
> Changing the distribution point settings shown in Figures 5.2 and 5.3 can affect overall site function. If you are already seeing backlogs in any of the inboxes or sluggish site server processing, adjusting these settings may make overall performance worse. Identify and diagnose any communications issues before making changes, and monitor intrasite communications closely as changes are applied.

The sender calculates available bandwidth by sending test packets to the destination site and measuring the response time. In some cases, factors other than bandwidth availability might cause a delay in receiving acknowledgments, resulting in calculations of available bandwidth that may be unrealistically low. For example, if the destination site system is heavily loaded or if network latency is a factor, the elapsed time before an acknowledgment is received may be high even though there is ample bandwidth. In cases of networks having very low bandwidth or those that may frequently be near saturation with other traffic, you may find the pulse mode option to be more useful in limiting network utilization by the sender. Pulse mode sends blocks of data of a specific size at fixed intervals. The default for pulse mode is 3KB blocks at 5-second intervals.

Replication of Deployment Content Refresh Data

When you initially deploy content to a distribution point, ConfigMgr provides two mechanisms specifically designed to minimize the amount of network traffic generated as content changes are replicated. These mechanisms are delta replication and binary differential replication:

▶ Using file-based delta replication, when a package is updated, all modified files are added to a delta compressed package file. The source site server maintains deltas for up to five versions of a package in addition to the full compressed package file. If the target distribution point or site already has one of the previous five versions of the package, only the required deltas are sent.

▶ Binary differential replication works similarly to delta replication, with two exceptions:

   ▶ A binary comparison of the files is made.

   ▶ Only the portions of the files that have changed are sent, not the entire file.

Binary differential replication is highly advantageous for content consisting of very large files, such as Windows Installer packages or OS images.

For deployments with many small files, binary differential replication may not be worth the overhead it incurs. You can enable the option to use binary differential replication on a per-package basis. Chapter 12, "Creating and Managing Applications," and Chapter 13, "Distributing and Deploying Applications," discuss options for configuring packages and sending them to distribution points. It is important to incorporate these considerations into your operational processes for software distribution.

NOTE ABOUT THE CONTENT LIBRARY

Chapter 4 introduced the content library. The content library makes replication more efficient since duplicate files are not replicated.

Site System Communications Using HTTP and HTTPS

HTTP and HTTPS are among the protocols used for communication between various site systems, including the site server and the software update point. At the highest-level site in your hierarchy configured with a software update point, the SUP connects to the Internet over HTTP if you configure it to retrieve updates from directly from Microsoft. If the server cannot connect to the Internet directly, you can specify a proxy server for the Internet connection. If Internet connectivity is not available for the SUP or if you choose not to have this system synchronize directly from the Internet, you can manually stage updates by importing them from a .cab file. Chapter 14, "Software Update Management," describes configuring the SUP.

Other Server Communications

In addition to communications between site systems, ConfigMgr requires the following basic network services:

- ► Active Directory Domain Services
- ► Global Catalog (GC) services
- ► DNS (Domain Naming Service)
- ► NetBIOS name resolution (in some configurations)

If you have configured any of the Active Directory discovery methods, you should consider the volume of network traffic between the site server and domain controller (DC) while AD discovery is running when determining which site servers and domain controllers to use for discovery. Avoid times with peak network activity when scheduling full discovery since this may generate significant network traffic. Subsequent delta discovery results in minimal network impact. Chapter 9, "Configuration Manager Client Management," discusses Active Directory discovery methods.

Client to Server Communications

ConfigMgr is designed to use Internet standard protocols for most client communications. In addition, nearly all client communication ports are configurable. ConfigMgr supports both HTTP and HTTPS for most client to server communications. For security reasons, HTTPS is the preferred protocol. Clients provisioned with the certificate required for mutually authenticated HTTPS communications select site systems using HTTPS whenever such systems are available. Chapter 20, "Security and Delegation in Configuration Manager," describes how to configure systems for HTTPS communication.

Client Ports and Protocols

Data sent across the network using the TCP or UDP protocol is transmitted in discrete units of data called *packets*. Each packet includes the following:

► A body that contains the actual data

► A header with addressing and other control information

The header includes the IP addresses of the source and destination machines as well as the port numbers of the source and destination services or applications. A port number is a number from 1 to 65535 used to identify the application. An application or service "listens" on a specific port if it has registered with the operating system to receive packets addressed to that port. Like many services, ConfigMgr services have standard ports on which they listen by default.

Table 5.1 lists the communications protocols and ports used by various applications and services. You can also find information regarding the communication protocols and ports used by ConfigMgr at http://technet.microsoft.com/en-us/library/hh427328.aspx#BKMK. The table provides some details not included in the online reference.

NOTE: USING INTERNET PROXIES

You can configure systems to connect to the Internet through a proxy server. For Internet connections, you must use the default ports, which are based on Internet standards, whether you configure systems to use a proxy server.

As Table 5.1 shows, you can configure custom ports for many ConfigMgr services as an alternative to using the default ports. The next section presents the planning considerations for port customization.

Reasons for Changing Ports

Here are reasons you may choose to use custom rather than standard ports for client-to-server communications:

► Custom ports may be necessary for ConfigMgr to work with your network firewall policies.

► You may need to use a custom website for ConfigMgr instead of the default site on your Internet Information Services (IIS) servers. Although it is not a best practice to share IIS servers with other applications, if you do have another application using the default site ConfigMgr requires a custom site. You may also choose to use a custom site due to company policies and standards regarding the use of default sites.

Chapter 9 provides details of how to customize client communications.

TABLE 5.1   Communication Protocols and Ports

From Component	Direction	To Component	Description	UDP Port	TCP Port
Application catalog website point	->	Application catalog web services point	HTTP	—	80[1]
Application catalog website point	->	Application catalog web services point	HTTPS	—	443[1]
Application catalog web services point	->	Distribution point	HTTP	—	80[1]
Application catalog web services point	->	Distribution point	HTTPS	—	443[1]
Asset intelligence synchronization point	->	Internet	HTTPS	—	443
Client without HTTPS certificate (or with certificate if no HTTPS-enabled server is available)	->	IIS-enabled site systems[2]	HTTP	—	80[1]
Client with HTTPS certificate	->	IIS-enabled site systems with HTTPS certificate[2]	HTTPS	—	443[1]
Client	->	Distribution point	SMB	—	445
Client	->	Distribution point	Multicast Protocol	63000–64000	—
Client	->	Distribution point (enabled as PXE service point)	Dynamic Host Configuration Protocol (DHCP)	67, 68	—
Client	->	Distribution point (enabled as PXE service point)	Trivial File Transfer Protocol (TFTP)	69[3]	—
Client	->	Distribution point (enabled as PXE service point)	Boot Information Negotiation Layer (BINL)	4011	—
Client	->	Software update point	HTTP	—	80 or 8530[4]

From Component	Direction	To Component	Description	UDP Port	TCP Port
Client	->	Software update point	HTTPS	—	443 or 8531[4]
Client	->	State migration point	SMB	—	445
Client	->[5]	System Heath Validator	DHCP	67, 68	—
Client	->[5]	System Heath Validator	IPSec	500	80, 443
ConfigMgr console	->	Client	Remote Control (control)	2701	2701
ConfigMgr console	->	Client	Remote Control (data)	2702	2702
ConfigMgr console	->	Client	Remote Assistance RDP (Remote Desktop Protocol) and Real-Time Communications (RTC)	—	3389
ConfigMgr console	->	Client	RPC Endpoint Mapper	—	135
ConfigMgr console	->	Internet	HTTP	—	80
ConfigMgr console	->	Provider	RPC Endpoint Mapper	135	135
ConfigMgr console	->	Provider	RPC	—	DYNAMIC
ConfigMgr console	->	Reporting services point	HTTP	—	80[1]
ConfigMgr console	->	Reporting services point	HTTPS	—	443[1]
ConfigMgr console	->	Site server	RPC (initial connection to WMI to locate provider system)	—	135
Distribution point (enabled as PXE service point)	->	SQL Server	SQL over TCP	1434 (for named instances only)	1433 for default instance; DYNAMIC for named instances
Domain joined systems	->	Domain controller	Lightweight Directory Access Protocol (LDAP)	—	389

5

From Component	Direction	To Component	Description	UDP Port	TCP Port
Domain joined systems	->	Domain controller	LDAP (Secure Sockets Layer [SSL] connection)	636	636
Domain joined systems	->	Domain controller	Global Catalog LDAP	—	3268
Domain joined systems	->	Domain controller	Global Catalog LDAP SSL	—	3269
Domain joined systems	->	Domain controller	RPC Endpoint Mapper	135	135
Domain joined systems	->	Domain controller	RPC	—	DYNAMIC
Domain joined systems	->	Domain controller	Kerberos	88	—
Endpoint protection point	->	Internet	HTTPS	—	443
Management point	->	SQL Server	SQL over TCP	1434 (for named instances only)	1433 for default instance; DYNAMIC for named instances
Mobile device client	->	Enrollment point or proxy enrollment point	HTTP	—	80
Mobile device client	->	Enrollment point or proxy enrollment point	HTTPS	—	443
Out of band service point	->	Enrollment point	HTTPS	—	443
Out of band service point	->	AMT Management Controller	Intel(R) AMT SOAP/HTTPS (Discovery, provisioning, and Power management)	—	16993
Out of band Management Console	->	AMT Management Controller	Intel(R) AMT SOAP/HTTPS (WS-Man and SOAP messaging)	—	16993
Out of band Management Console	->	AMT Management Controller	Intel(R) AMT Redirection/TLS (Serial over LAN (SOL); IDE redirection (IDE-R))	—	16995

From Component	Direction	To Component	Description	UDP Port	TCP Port
Provider	->	SQL Server	SQL over TCP	1434 (for named instances only)	1433 for default instance; DYNAMIC for named instances
Reporting Services Point	->	SQL Server	SQL over TCP	—	1433 for default instance; DYNAMIC for named instances
Site server	->	Client	Wake On LAN	9[1]	—
Site server	<->	Site server	SMB	—	445
Site server	<->[6]	Site Systems: Asset Intelligence synchronization point, distribution point, fallback status point, reporting services point, SMS Provider, state migration point, system health validator point	SMB	—	445
Site server	<->[6]	Site systems: See list above	RPC Endpoint Mapper	135	135
Site server	<->[6]	Site systems: See list above	RPC	—	DYNAMIC
Site server	<->[6]	Software update point	SMB	—	445
Site server	<->[6]	Software update point	HTTP	—	80 or 8530[4]
Site server	<->[6]	Software update point	HTTPS	—	443 or 8531[4]
Site server	->	SQL Server	SQL over TCP	1434 (for named instances only)	1433 for default instance; DYNAMIC for named instances
Software update point (top level site)	->	Internet	HTTP	—	80

5

From Component	Direction	To Component	Description	UDP Port	TCP Port
Software update point	->	Windows Software Update Services (WSUS) synchronization server	HTTP	—	80 or 8530[4]
Software update point	->	WSUS synchronization server	HTTPS	—	443 or 8531[4]
Site server	->	Client	Client push installation	—	135
Site server	->	SQL Server	SQL over TCP	1434 (for named instances only)	1433 for default instance; DYNAMIC for named instances

[1] You can define an alternative port in ConfigMgr for this value. If you define a custom port, substitute that port when defining the IP filter information for your IPSec policies.

[2] IS-enabled site systems include the application catalog website point, distribution point, management point, fallback status point, and state migration point. The fallback status point does not support HTTPS.

[3] The TFTP Daemon system service does not require a username or password and is an integral part of Windows Deployment Services (WDS). TFTP is designed to support diskless boot environments. The daemons listen on UDP port 69, but they respond from a dynamically allocated high port. Enabling this port allows the TFTP service to receive incoming requests but does not allow the server to respond to the requests. (Allowing a response requires configuring the TFTP server to respond from port 69.)

[4] You can install WSUS on the default website (port 80) or on a custom website (port 8530). You can change this port after installation. If the HTTP port is 80, the HTTPS port must be 443. If the HTTP port is something other than 80, then the HTTPS port must be 1 higher (for example, 8530 and 8531).

[5] The client requires the ports used by the Network Access Protection (NAP) enforcement client, such as DHCP and IPSec. No port is required for 802.1x enforcement.

[6] Communication between a site server and site systems is bidirectional by default. The site server initiates communication to configure the site system, and then most site systems will connect back to the site server to return status information. (Distribution points do not send back status information.) Selecting **Require the site server to initiate connections to this site system on the site system** properties page keeps the site system from initiating communication to the site server.

> **TIP: SPECIFYING DIFFERENT PORTS**
>
> If you utilize custom ports or custom websites, you should use them consistently throughout your hierarchy. Using different ports or websites at different sites can cause problems as clients roam from one site to another.
>
> Regardless of whether you change the default HTTP and HTTPS ports, it is always a good idea to specify alternative ports to increase the availability of these services.

Initial Communication

The initial communication between the client and the ConfigMgr hierarchy occurs during client installation. Chapter 9 discusses client installation methods in detail. For purposes of this discussion, there are two general types of client installation methods:

- ▶ Server initiated (client push)

- ▶ Client initiated (all other methods)

Client push installation includes a preinstallation phase in which the site server connects to the client to initiate installation:

- ▶ In the client push installation method, the server makes an initial connection to the admin$ share on the prospective client computer using Windows file-sharing protocols. Administrative access to the client is required to connect to the admin$ share.

- ▶ The server also establishes a WMI connection to the client using the Distributed Component Object Model (DCOM) through TCP port 135.

  DCOM is a Microsoft standard for communication between software components, either on a local computer or across a network.

- ▶ The site server uses these connections to copy the required setup files to the client and then installs and starts the ccmsetup service. Additional requirements for client push installation are covered in Chapter 9.

After the preinstallation phase is complete, the installation proceeds in a manner similar to other installation methods.

Regardless of the client installation method used, the first network-related task for the new client is to locate and contact a MP for its assigned site. From this point onward, the MP will be the primary point of contact between the client and its site. Unless client installation source files are staged locally, the setup process uses BITS to pull the files from the CCM_CLIENT website on the MP. After the client is installed, it continues to communicate with the management point using HTTP or HTTPS, and generally uses BITS to download policy and component updates and to send client information to the site, including inventory, metering data, state messages, and status messages.

Identifying and Contacting the Client's Assigned Site

There are four general ways for the client to determine the site to which it is assigned and locate a management point for that site:

▶ Depending on the installation method used, the site code and initial management point may have been supplied as command-line arguments. The management point may be specified using an IP address, a fully qualified domain name (FQDN), or a simple name.

▶ Clients that are members of AD domains can retrieve this information by querying AD, provided the site publishes data to the client's AD forest.

▶ If the required information is not available in AD, you can configure DNS to provide management point information to clients. DNS does not support automatic site assignment and requires that you supply the domain suffix of the MP as a client installation property.

▶ Each primary site publishes the first MP configured for HTTP communications in the site to WINS. Clients can use this WINS entry to find their initial management point.

When possible you should either supply site and management point information as part of the client installation properties or use AD to provide these settings. If your client installation methods do not provide the settings, you need to use DNS or WINS to provide them to clients that cannot retrieve the information from AD, these being workgroup clients or clients in untrusted forests or forests to which your sites do not publish. After the client has contacted its initial management point, it downloads and caches a list of available management points.

Chapter 9 describes the process of assigning clients to sites in detail.

Client Protocols

The ConfigMgr client uses the HTTP or HTTPS protocol to communicate with several site systems, including the management point and the software update point. These two roles are among the systems having the highest volume and frequency of communication with ConfigMgr clients. Clients communicate with the management point more frequently than with any of the other ConfigMgr site systems.

▶ Client systems poll the management point regularly for policy updates. The default polling interval is every hour.

▶ Clients send state, status, inventory, metering, and discovery data to the management point. State information is sent every 5 minutes by default. Inventory, metering, and heartbeat discovery data is sent every 7 days by default. Clients use the SMB protocol to send status messages.

▶ You can configure the schedules for clients to pull policy and send state, inventory, metering, and heartbeat discovery data as described in Chapter 9. Choosing a *simple* schedule for inventory causes the network load to spread over time because not all clients will send inventory at the same time. A *custom* schedule provides more control over the timing of inventory collection but may have considerable impact when inventory runs.

▶ Initial inventory on new clients is considerably larger than regular inventory updates, which send only a delta (changes since the previous version) over the network.

The frequency and size of client downloads of software updates from the SUP depends on how you configure software updates and the client configuration. Many individual software updates are relatively small (several megabytes or smaller). Some can be quite large, however, including service packs, which can be hundreds of megabytes or even larger. If you use ConfigMgr as a source for endpoint protection updates, the SUP infrastructure also downloads and distributes engine and definition updates.

TIP: MORE ABOUT SOFTWARE UPDATES

You can find additional information about software updates in Chapter 14.

Microsoft generally releases critical security updates for its products monthly on the second Tuesday of the month, known as Patch Tuesday. Typically, after evaluating and approving the Patch Tuesday updates for your environment, you can make them available as a group for distribution to your clients.

System Center 2012 Configuration Manager is designed to minimize the network impact of software updates:

▶ The Software Updates agent uses selective download technology to download only the individual files that the client requires from a software updates package.

▶ Supersedence information is provided to help administrators avoid deploying updates superseded by a newer update.

Even with these enhancements, software updates can require significant network bandwidth. You will want to consider this requirement when planning your software updates strategy. If you manage endpoint protection settings, you should avoid configuring clients to scan network drives unless you have identified a clear requirement for scanning network drives.

Clients use HTTP/HTTPS or the SMB protocol to pull data from distribution points and state migration points:

▶ Clients downloading content to their local cache from a distribution point will use BITS over HTTP or HTTPS.

▶ Clients running the package directly from the distribution point use SMB. Although this option is still available in ConfigMgr 2012, it is generally deprecated in favor of other deployment options.

Depending on the size of the software package, downloads from distribution points may be quite large. Clients do not use either binary differential replication or delta replication; therefore, changes to a package the client has cached will trigger a full download to the client.

Clients use state migration points less frequently, generally during operating system upgrades or hardware replacement. The amount of traffic sent to and from the state migration point depends on the amount of user data to be preserved. For more information about user state migration, see Chapter 19, "Operating System Deployment."

The remaining site systems handle relatively little client traffic, but use a variety of protocols:

▶ If you enable ConfigMgr for NAP, clients will pass a statement of health (SoH) to the system health validator (SHV) point when making a new DHCP request or a new Internet Protocol Security (IPSec) connection to the network. When connected, the client will periodically submit a new SoH to the SHV. The default interval for system health to be reevaluated is 24 hours. Chapter 14 discusses NAP.

▶ The fallback status point responds to client requests using HTTP communications only.

▶ The site server connects to the client when Wake On LAN (WOL) functionality is required for patch deployment or other activities. The default port for WOL is UDP port 9. The WOL port is configurable; Chapter 9 describes WOL configuration.

▶ If administrators use the ConfigMgr Remote Tools, the machine on which the console is running contacts the client directly. Remote tools use the Remote Desktop Protocol (RDP) on port 3389.

Planning for Network Access Protection

In addition to standard ConfigMgr traffic, NAP generates the traffic described in Table 5.2. If you use firewalls that block this traffic, you must reconfigure them for NAP to work with ConfigMgr. You will also need to identify ports used by the client to the system health validator point. ConfigMgr does not use the ports listed in the table directly; they are established by NAP and dependent on the enforcement client being used.

TABLE 5.2   TCP Ports Required by Firewalls to Support NAP

Function	TCP Port	Description
Site server publishing health state reference to AD domain services	389 (LDAP) or 636 (LDAPS)	Writing to AD domain services.
SHV point querying AD for ConfigMgr health state reference	3268 (Global Catalog lookup) or 3269 (secure Global Catalog lookup)	Reading from a global catalog server.
Installing System SHV point and ongoing configuration	445, 135	SMBs to install; RPCs for configuration.
Status messages from SHV point to site server	445	SMBs.

Site-to-Site Communications

Sites in a ConfigMgr hierarchy must share configuration information, client data such as inventory and discovery data, status information, and so on. ConfigMgr 2012 uses two mechanisms to replicate data between sites: SQL Server replication and file-based replication. This differs from ConfigMgr 2007, which used file-based replication only. This section describes the data sites exchange through each type of replication and presents some tuning considerations for file-based replication. Chapter 3 provides an in-depth look at the inner workings of both file-based replication and SQL Server replication.

Database Replication

Sites share most data through SQL Server replication. Sites replicate the following types of data:

- ▶ Administrators create objects that are replicated as global data, including

    - ▶ Configuration objects representing site and site server configuration, security role and scopes, and rules for alerts and collections

    - ▶ Configuration items for compliance settings

    - ▶ Metadata for software distribution and software updates objects

    - ▶ Operating system images

        The replicated database object for an OS image does not contain the actual image file. Chapter 19 describes distribution of OS images in detail.

- ▶ ConfigMgr clients and site systems generate objects that are replicated as site data, such as

    - ▶ Hardware inventory

    - ▶ Software inventory and software metering data

    - ▶ Status messages, status summaries, and alerts

    - ▶ Data related to client health and license compliance

    - ▶ Local evaluation of collection membership

The replication scope is either global data or site data:

- ▶ Global data replicates to all sites in the hierarchy. Primary sites and the central administration site (CAS) maintain a complete copy of all global data, whereas secondary sites maintain a subset of global data.

- ▶ Site data replicates from a primary site to the CAS only.

- ▶ Secondary sites participate in SQL replication only by receiving replicated data from their parent primary site. Data from clients at secondary is replicated by file-based transfers only.

ConfigMgr uses the SQL Server Service Broker for replication between sites. The default port for the SQL Server Service Broker is TCP port 4022. Database replication between sites in different forests requires a forest trust. This means it is not possible to create a hierarchy with site servers in separate forests without trusts, although clients and site systems in untrusted forests are supported.

File-Based Replication

In ConfigMgr 2007, sites carried out all data exchanges through file transfers. ConfigMgr 2012 still uses file transfers for some types of data, including

▶ Deployment content for software distribution.

▶ Client discovery data records (DDRs) are sent to the client's assigned site if a different site receives them from the client.

▶ Client status messages received by the fallback status point and sent to the client's assigned site.

▶ Data sent from a secondary site to its parent primary site.

Sites exchange file data by means of *senders*. Senders use the SMB protocol to transfer files between sites. Here are the sender settings you can configure for each site:

▶ **Maximum Concurrent Sendings (All Sites):** Senders can use multiple threads to send more than one job at a time. This setting controls the maximum number of sendings (from 1 to 999) that the sender can execute simultaneously. Increasing this number speeds up site-to-site communications but could potentially consume more bandwidth.

▶ **Maximum Concurrent Sendings (Per Site):** This is the number of sendings (from 1 to 999) that could execute simultaneously to a single site.

Always set this setting to a lower value than Maximum Concurrent Sendings (All Sites) to avoid the possibility that all of a sender's threads will be occupied sending to a site that is unavailable.

▶ **Number of Retries:** Specifies the number of times (from 1 to 99) that the Sender will retry a failed sending.

▶ **Delay Before Retrying (Minutes):** Specifies the delay (from 1 minute to 99 minutes) before retrying a failed sending attempt.

If you have sufficient server resources and available network bandwidth, you might want to increase the number of threads allowed by the Maximum Concurrent Sendings setting from the default value. Each thread can process only one file at a time. Before increasing this setting, obtain a baseline of network utilization and server performance data for key server resources such as the processor and network interface to verify additional capacity is available. You should closely monitor the change to ensure that server and network performance are not adversely affected.

Addresses connect sites in the file replication topology. Each address specifies a source and destination site, the destination site server name, and the security context of the connection. You can also specify a schedule and rate limits for the address. The scheduling and rate limit options are identical to those for distribution points. The "Communications Using SMB" section described these options. The address properties and the sender properties of the source site together define the operational parameters for file replication.

NOTE: ABOUT BANDWIDTH THROTTLING BETWEEN SITES

If you implement bandwidth throttling between sites, the sender will send all data serially between those sites, regardless of the number of concurrent sendings configured on the sender.

Data Priorities

Address and Distribution Point schedules provide the option to restrict transfers to specified data priorities during peak hours. ConfigMgr data is classified by priority:

▶ High

▶ Medium

▶ Low

You can configure the priority as a property of the distribution settings of certain content such as packages and boot images. Chapter 13 describes distribution settings. You should identify any links between sites or between distribution points that are near saturation during peak hours, and consider using scheduling priorities together with content distribution settings to minimize the impact of file transfers on your environment.

NOTE: ABOUT LATENCY BETWEEN SITES

Restrictions on sending between sites during certain hours can introduce substantial latency in file replication. It is important to keep this in mind when working with deployment content. If updates are made to a package before a child site has received previous updates to the same package, redundant files may be sent between sites. Binary differential replication also does not work between sites until all targeted sites have received at least one version of the package.

Chapter 6 describes how to configure addresses and senders.

Fast Network and Slow Network Boundaries

Some ConfigMgr services such as software deployment can consume substantial network bandwidth. Effectively delivering these services across slow, congested, or unreliable network segments requires careful planning. Chapter 4 discussed the concepts of boundaries and boundary groups. This section describes how you can use boundary groups to optimize content delivery to clients.

System Center 2012 Configuration Manager uses boundary groups to define protected site systems. Protected site systems include distribution points or state migration points. When a client is within the boundary group, it will access content from the appropriate protected site systems. ConfigMgr 2007 introduced fast and slow boundaries. Administrators could configure specific options for clients in slow boundaries when distributing software. ConfigMgr 2012 improves this functionality by defining a connection speed, fast or slow, to each protected site system within the boundary group properties. Figure 5.4 shows the References tab on the Boundary group Properties page. This tab displays the site systems associated with the boundary group and allows you to add and remove systems. The Change Connection button toggles the connection speed between fast and slow.

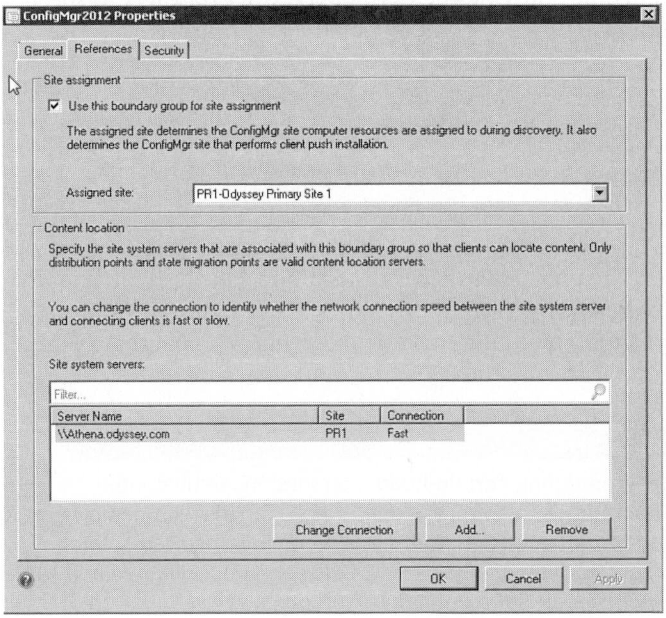

FIGURE 5.4   The Boundary group property page References tab.

Chapter 6 discusses boundary group configuration. Using boundary groups to define fast and slow connections provides the following advantages over the functionality in ConfigMgr 2007:

▶ Easier management by treating boundaries with similar network properties as a unit rather than managing them individually

▶ More flexible and granular control over content distribution by defining connection speeds to specific site systems rather than a single connection speed for all site systems

Options are available to control how software deployment and operating system deployment take place based on the connection speed property. As an example, a deployment might specify that clients will download content from the distribution point and run content locally over a fast connection but will not receive the deployment over slow or unreliable network connections. For more information about software deployment and operating system deployment, see Chapters 13 and 19.

Fast, slow, reliable, and unreliable are all relative terms. Although the user interface (UI) suggests that a fast network shares a local area network segment with the ConfigMgr site systems, you should take this suggestion as a general guideline and not necessarily a definitive criterion. You should base your decision of whether to define a particular boundary as fast or slow on your software distribution model and how you want clients within that boundary to behave within that model. In addition to overall speed and reliability, here are some additional factors you might consider:

▶ Available bandwidth, including peak usage times

▶ Potential impact of software distribution on other business processes sharing the link

▶ The business value of delivering the higher level of service you intend to provide to fast network clients

Use of BITS

The Background Intelligent Transfer Service optimizes file transfers based on network conditions. This optimization includes the following:

▶ Automatically adjusting the rate of the transfer, based on available bandwidth

▶ File transfers that occur quietly in the background, using only bandwidth that is not required by other applications

▶ The ability to suspend and resume transfers interrupted by transient network conditions

▶ Rudimentary consistency checking

▶ Options for tuning BITS-enabled transfers using group policy or ConfigMgr client settings

The next sections look in depth at the BITS feature set, its use by ConfigMgr, and configuring BITS background transfers.

ConfigMgr makes extensive use of BITS to efficiently use network bandwidth and deal with network connections that are unreliable or not always available. BITS 2.5 or higher is a required ConfigMgr 2012 component. BITS supports downloads over both HTTP and HTTPS.

TIP: ADVANTAGE OF USING BACKGROUND TRANSFERS

If you have ever initiated a large file transfer and had your computer come to a crawl, you can appreciate the concept of background transfers. BITS throttles the bandwidth used such that file transfers will take only bandwidth not used by other applications. Foreground applications thus remain responsive to the user and other services can operate without interruption. The transfers occur asynchronously, meaning that the rate can vary over time.

Instead of a steady stream of data, you can consider the data as being "drizzled" across the network. This also allows an interrupted transfer to pick up where it left off when connectivity is restored.

BITS Versions for ConfigMgr Clients

BITS has been a component of Windows operating systems beginning with Windows XP. Microsoft has released several versions of BITS, each with added functionality. Here are the versions supported by ConfigMgr 2012:

▶ **BITS Version 2.5:** Included on all systems running Windows Server 2008, Windows Vista, and Windows XP Service Pack (SP) 3. Version 2.5 can also be installed on machines running Windows Server 2003 SP 1 or SP 2 or Windows XP SP 2 64 bit.

▶ **BITS Version 3.0:** Available on Windows Server 2008 and Windows Vista operating systems only.

▶ **BITS Version 4.0:** Available natively in Windows 7 and Windows Server 2008 R2, can be downloaded and installed on Windows Vista SP 1 or SP 2 and Windows Server 2008 SP 2.

One problem with earlier versions of BITS is that the system is only aware of the traffic passing through the NIC. Even if the network segment to which the machine is connected is quite congested, if there is little or no network activity on the local machine it would appear to BITS that most of the bandwidth supported by the card is available. Under these conditions BITS transmits data at a high rate, potentially causing additional network congestion problems. BITS 2.5 and higher versions get around this limitation by pulling usage statistics from the Internet Gateway Device (IGD). Certain conditions must be met to pull statistics from the IGD:

▶ Universal Plug and Play (UPnP) must be enabled.

▶ The device must support UPnP byte counters.

▶ UPnP traffic (TCP 2869 and UDP 1900) is not blocked by any firewall device or software.

▶ The device must respond to GetTotalBytesSent and GetTotalBytesReceived in a timely fashion.

▶ The file transfer must traverse the gateway.

NOTE: ERROR 16393 IF BITS CANNOT RETRIEVE INFORMATION FROM IDG

If BITS cannot retrieve counter data from the IDG, the following event is logged:

```
Event ID 16393 Source: Microsoft-Windows-Bits-Client

BITS has encountered an error communicating with an Internet Gateway
Device. Be sure to check that the device is functioning properly. BITS
will not attempt to use this device until the next system reboot. Error
code: %1.
```

Modifying BITS Functionality Through Group Policy

BITS typically manages the use of network bandwidth intelligently without additional configuration. If you find that BITS-enabled transfers are consuming more bandwidth than desired or want to provide extra protection for other business-critical network activity, you can configure group policy to limit the bandwidth BITS will consume. The setting is specified in Kbps, and its name varies depending on the version of Windows you are running.

▶ For Windows Server 2003 group policy, the setting is called Maximum network bandwidth that BITS uses.

▶ For Windows Server 2008 group policy, the setting is Maximum network bandwidth for BITS background transfers.

In both versions, you can find this under **Computer Configuration -> Policies -> Administrative Templates -> Network -> Background Intelligent Transfer Service**. The setting, shown in Figure 5.5 for Windows Server 2008 group policy, allows a limit for a specific time interval (such as working hours) and a different limit for outside that interval. All versions of BITS supported by ConfigMgr also have a timeout for inactive transfers (default 90 days) configurable through group policy.

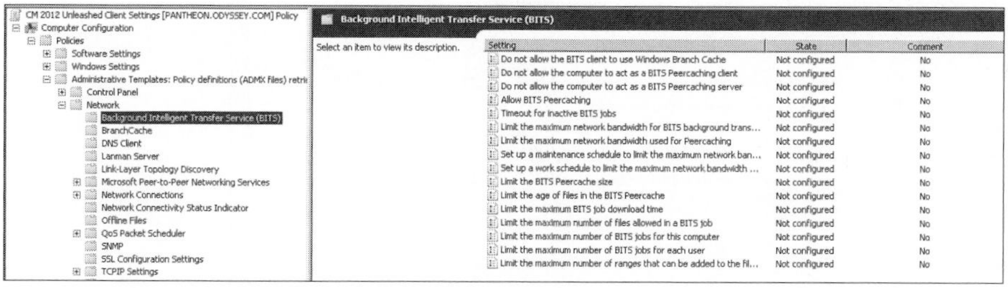

FIGURE 5.5   Group policy settings for BITS.

BITS 3.0 and BITS 4.0 each introduce several new group policy options. These allow you to control setting such as the maximum active download time for BITS jobs, the number of jobs allowed per user and per machine, and the maximum number of files per job. Microsoft provides a complete list of group policy settings for each BITS version at http://msdn.microsoft.com/en-us/library/aa362844.aspx.

Group policy settings are only available in AD domains. Although group policies are generally applied at the domain or organizational unit (OU) level, BITS-related policies are examples of a policy that you might consider implementing at the site level. An AD site is generally a region of high network connectivity. By applying the BITS-related policies to the site, you can control the behavior of all systems in your AD forest based on network location, regardless of their domain or OU membership.

Modifying BITS Functionality Within ConfigMgr

You can also define ConfigMgr client settings for BITS that specify

▶ A daily start and stop time for a throttling window

▶ The maximum network bandwidth for BITS background transfers during the throttling window

▶ Whether to allow transfers outside the throttling window, and how much bandwidth to allow for such transfers

Figure 5.6 shows the client agent property page for BITS settings. Chapter 9 provides additional details of available client settings.

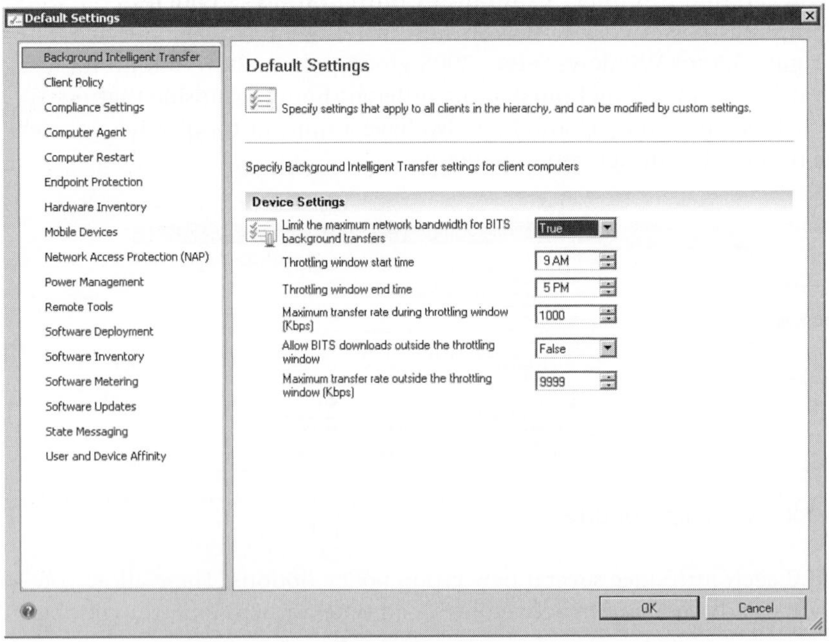

FIGURE 5.6   Setting the maximum network bandwidth for BITS background transfers.

Comparative Advantages of Group Policy and ConfigMgr Settings for BITS

Unlike group policy settings, the settings on the Computer Client agent apply to clients that are in workgroups or untrusted domains. In ConfigMgr 2007, these were global settings for all clients in the site; however, System Center 2012 Configuration Manager allows you to apply specific client settings based on collection membership. Through ConfigMgr, you can also assign BITS settings specifically to BranchCache-enabled distribution points. Group policy allows you to control the behavior of BITS for clients in specific domains, OUs, individual computers, or AD sites. You can achieve even more granular control of group policy by WMI filtering and/or security group filtering. These filtering techniques selectively apply group policy objects (GPOs) to users or computers based on the results of WMI queries or security group membership. An excellent resource on group policy management is available online at the TechNet Windows Server Group Policy home page (http://technet.microsoft.com/en-us/windowsserver/bb310732).

> **TIP: GROUP POLICY MANAGEMENT REFERENCES**
>
> For your convenience, these URLs are included as live links in Appendix C, "Reference URLs."

As mentioned in the "BITS Versions for ConfigMgr Clients" section of this chapter, Windows Server 2008 and Windows Server 2008 R2 group policy provide a wider range of BITS-related options for BITS versions 3.0 and 4.0 than that available through the ConfigMgr settings. Because there are different options available through group policy and ConfigMgr settings, you may choose to use both to control BITS behavior.

> **CAUTION: AVOID CONFLICTS IN GROUP POLICY AND CONFIGMGR BITS SETTINGS**
>
> If using both group policy and ConfigMgr settings to govern BITS functionality, be careful to avoid applying both methods to the same systems. The domain policies override locally stored ConfigMgr settings and may produce unpredictable results. If systems requiring ConfigMgr BITS settings reside in AD containers that have BITS policies applied, you can use WMI filtering or security group filtering to block application of group policy objects containing BITS settings. In any case, you should plan and test such configurations carefully.

Systems with Multiple Interfaces and File Integrity Checking

On client systems with multiple physical or virtual interfaces, BITS uses the GetBestInterface function to select the interface with the best route to the server it needs to access. When the file transfer is complete, BITS verifies that the file size is correct. However, BITS does not perform a more extensive file integrity check to detect corruption or tampering that may have occurred.

ConfigMgr and BranchCache

System Center 2012 Configuration Manager leverages the BranchCache functionality provided by the Windows 7 and Windows Server 2008 R2 operating systems. BranchCache is also available on Vista and Windows Server 2008 with BITS 4.0 installed. BranchCache provides caching of content from remote servers at a local site, so each client at the site does not have to transfer the content across a WAN link. BranchCache supports two modes: Hosted Cache mode and Distributed Cache mode. BranchCache also supports both the SMB or HTTP protocol suites. ConfigMgr 2012 uses the Distributed Cache mode only for HTTP transfers using the BITS protocol. The following discussion therefore pertains to BranchCache in Distributed Cache mode using BITS.

BranchCache provides two important advantages for users who are located at sites across a WAN link from the main office:

▶ **Client latency is reduced:** Because content is downloaded from the local subnet, the time required to retrieve the content is greatly reduced. In addition, BranchCache downloads content in 64KB blocks and makes each block available to the application as soon as it is downloaded and verified, rather than waiting for the entire download to complete.

▶ **WAN utilization is improved:** Because a package may be downloaded to the local site once and used by many clients, the amount of traffic across the WAN is reduced. In addition, the BranchCache feature utilizes the BITS 4.0 protocol, which provides network friendly optimizations such as bandwidth throttling and resumption of interrupted transfers. For more information about BITS, see the "Use of BITS" section of this chapter.

Here are the requirements for BranchCache in ConfigMgr:

▶ One or more distribution points installed on a Windows Server 2008 R2 computer with the BranchCache feature enabled in the operating system. These DPs can provide BranchCache-enabled deployments to clients.

▶ Windows 7 and Windows Server 2008 R2 clients can cache content they retrieve from distribution points that support BranchCache and share the content locally so that other clients do not need to source it from the server. Windows Vista and Windows Server 2008 clients with BITS 4.0 installed can access content from other BranchCache clients; however, these clients cannot run such content from the network or access it through SMB.

To enable Windows 7 and Windows Server 2008 R2 clients to cache content for use on the local subnet, you must enable BranchCache and configure the BranchCache settings on the clients. Although you can configure BranchCache on individual systems, it is easier to manage them through AD group policy. As with other group policy settings, you can apply BranchCache policy selectively as appropriate in your environment. You should configure the following settings in the BranchCache policy under **Computer Configuration -> Policies -> Administrative Templates -> Network -> BranchCache:**

▶ **Turn on BranchCache:** (Enabled)

▶ **Set BranchCache Distributed Cache Mode:** (Enabled)

▶ **Configure BranchCache for network files:** This setting specifies the minimum latency for caching to occur. The client will use the BranchCache feature when it does not receive content from a remote source within the specified interval. The default value is 80ms. Setting a higher value causes more WAN downloads to occur but use less disk space, I/O, and network throughput on the client systems acting as cache repositories.

▶ **Set percentage of disk space used for client computer cache:** The default setting allows up to 5 percent of the client disk space for caching. The cache is located under %*systemroot*%\ServiceProfiles\NetworkService\AppData\Local\PeerDistRepub.

You must also configure Windows Firewall or your third-party firewall software to allow BranchCache transfers and the Web Services Dynamic Discovery (WS-Discovery) protocol used to discover cached content.

When a BranchCache-enabled client attempts to access content from a server not on the local subnet, the client first determines the latency of the connection. If the latency exceeds the configured threshold, the client attempts to discover the content on the local subnet. The first BranchCache-enabled client on the subnet to access the content learns it is not available locally and retrieves it from the remote server. The client then caches the content and makes it available to other clients on the subnet. When other clients later try to access the content, local clients will respond that it is available in cache and the content will be sourced locally. Peer-to-peer BranchCache sharing may be appropriate for software distribution at network locations where there is no local DP and for software update content distribution at network locations where there is no local SUP.

Here are some points to keep in mind when considering BranchCache functionality:

▶ Microsoft designed BranchCache to handle large file transfers efficiently. When a high latency connection is detected, the client downloads a SHA-256 hash of the original files that it uses to determine if matching files are available at the local site. The hash is on the order of 1/2,000 of the original file size. Because there is some overhead in downloading the hash and discovering whether matching content is available locally, content smaller than 64KB is not cached.

▶ The hash is protected on the source system by the same authentication and access controls as the original content and can be downloaded only to authorized systems.

▶ Hash verification validates content integrity and ensures proper versioning.

▶ BranchCache protects data confidentiality using AES-128 encryption. The encryption key is based on the hash and can therefore be derived by authorized clients only.

▶ Client computers running Windows Vista SP 2 or Windows Server 2008 SP 2 with BITS 4.0 installed can also take advantage of BranchCache functionality.

For more information on BranchCache, see http://technet.microsoft.com/en-us/network/dd425028.aspx.

Server and Site Placement

To optimize ConfigMgr's use of your network, you should consider the placement of servers holding various site roles. Here are some guidelines to help with your planning:

▶ For improved security, consider moving client-facing roles off the site server and segregating client-facing and nonclient-facing roles. You can then use firewall policies or other mechanisms to restrict connections to critical systems such as site servers. Chapter 20 provides additional information about protecting site systems.

▶ The site server should have a high bandwidth and highly available connection to the site database server. Chapter 4 discusses considerations for site database placement. The site server also needs good connectivity to a domain controller. If you enable any of the AD discovery methods, the site servers that run discovery need adequate available bandwidth to domain controllers in each of the target forests.

▶ CAS and primary sites require one or more instances of the SMS Provider. Secondary sites do not support provider instances. You can install the provider on the site server, the site database server, or another server with highly available network connectivity to these systems and to all systems running the ConfigMgr console. The optimum provider placement for network performance is on the site database server. Because the SMS Provider uses system and network resources, you should consider the available resources when you select the provider location.

▶ The reporting services point needs good connectivity to the CAS or single primary site database server.

▶ You can configure management points to use the site database or a replica of the site database. In either case, good connectivity to the database is required.

▶ Consider deploying additional client-facing site systems at locations with a large number of clients and slow or unreliable network connections.

▶ If you support Internet-only clients or mobile device, the systems these clients will access should be in a DMZ (demilitarized zone, also known as a *perimeter network*). In general, do not place the site server and site database server in an Internet-accessible DMZ. For more information on placement of Internet facing systems, see the "Deploying Servers to Support Internet-Based Clients" section of this chapter.

▶ The placement of distribution points is especially important. For clients across a WAN link from the site server, consider placing distribution points in a region of high connectivity to the clients.

▶ Deploying a secondary site at the remote location to take advantage of intersite communication features such as scheduling and compression was often advantageous in ConfigMgr 2007 hierarchies. The enhanced DP functionality in ConfigMgr

2012 often makes this unnecessary. Chapter 4 discusses the decision to create additional sites.

▶ You may still want to consider using secondary sites at the remote location with limited connectivity and larger numbers of clients to take advantage of compression, scheduling, and throttling for client data such as inventory and status messages. For example, you might use a secondary site to provide services on a ship at sea with satellite only communications.

Chapter 4 discusses additional considerations for site system planning and hierarchy design.

Deploying Servers to Support Internet-Based Clients

Chapter 4 introduced Internet-based client management (IBCM), and it presented the supported features and required client-facing site system roles for IBCM. Internet-based clients require mutually authenticated HTTPS communication with all site systems except the fallback status point. ConfigMgr HTTPS communication requires a public key infrastructure (PKI). Chapter 4 also includes PKI planning considerations. For Internet clients to access site systems, the clients must resolve the FQDN for each of those site systems from the Internet. The previous version of ConfigMgr required native mode sites for HTTPS communications; ConfigMgr 2012 provides more flexibility by allowing you to configure this option for individual clients and site systems. Chapter 20 discusses the advantages of HTTPS and describes certificate deployment for HTTPS communications.

For security reasons, systems accessible to Internet-based clients, including mobile devices that connect over the Internet, should always be deployed in a DMZ/perimeter network. Here are scenarios supported by Microsoft for site and server placement:

▶ A site that does not support intranet clients and spans the perimeter network and intranet. The site server is in the intranet. All site systems that accept connections from clients connecting over the Internet are in the perimeter network.

▶ A site that does not support intranet clients and is in the perimeter network only.

▶ A site supporting both Internet and intranet clients, which spans the perimeter network and intranet. All site systems that accept connections from clients connecting over the Internet are in the perimeter network. A second MP, SUP, fallback status point (FSP), and additional DPs, along with other site systems, are in the intranet for those clients connecting over the intranet.

▶ A site that supports Internet clients and resides on the internal network. Internet clients connect to site systems using a web proxy.

▶ A site that supports both Internet and intranet clients, and bridges the perimeter network and the intranet. Internet- and intranet-based clients may share the same management points.

5

When designing your solution, your primary consideration will be the level of security necessary. Providing services through the Internet potentially exposes you to unauthorized access. You should involve any necessary resources to ensure that proper security risk management and secure network design principles are followed.

Each of the scenarios Microsoft supports involves three security zones:

▶ Internet (least secure)

▶ Perimeter network (more secure)

▶ Internal network (most secure)

The purpose of the perimeter network is to protect your internal network, where your most valuable systems and data reside. If a host in the perimeter network is compromised, it is the job of the inner firewall, the one between the perimeter network and the internal network, to protect your high-value assets. One basic principle of network security is that it is a risk to allow any connections to be initiated from a less secure zone to a more secure zone. Internet-based clients must be able to initiate connections to site systems to receive ConfigMgr services. The specific traffic the outer firewall must allow for each site system is described at http://technet.microsoft.com/en-us/library/gg712701.aspx#Support_Internet_Clients. As you step through the supported scenarios, focus on the allowed protocols at the inner firewall. The options that allow inbound connections are likely to be less secure than those that do not.

Solutions that bridge the perimeter network and the internal network introduce a special type of risk. In this case, you do not have a dedicated inner firewall. If one of the bridging hosts is compromised, it could be used to attack the internal network. If you choose to implement this model, you should take particular care to harden the systems as much as possible, monitor them closely, and verify that you have disabled routing between the network cards. Many organizations have security policies that forbid using servers to bridge security zones.

Take your own secure network architecture into account as you consider each of the scenarios Microsoft supports for deploying servers to support Internet clients because you may need to adapt these scenarios to meet your own security requirements. Carefully consider the relative advantages of each model.

Using a Dedicated Site for Internet Clients

The first option to consider is whether to have a dedicated site for Internet clients. Using a dedicated site provides some options that simplify your security planning. If you use a dedicated Internet-only site, you should have only an Internet-based management point. The most secure configuration is a dedicated site, totally within the perimeter network, that is absolutely separate from the hierarchy supporting intranet clients. This configuration, shown in Figure 5.7, does not require connectivity between the Internet-accessible systems and your internal network.

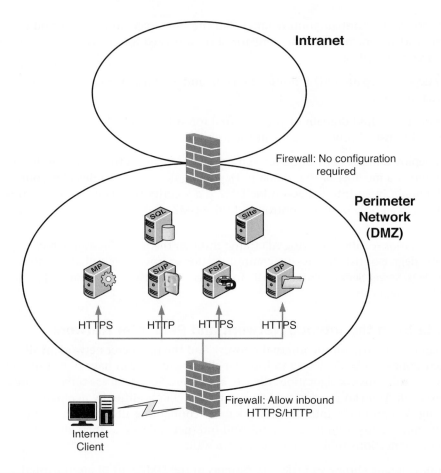

FIGURE 5.7   A dedicated site within the perimeter network is separate from the hierarchy supporting intranet clients.

Complete isolation requires a separate, untrusted AD forest and a dedicated ConfigMgr site in the perimeter network. This is the most secure configuration but has some limits in terms of functionality. This configuration does not support clients that connect both as Internet and intranet clients. Even if you have mobile clients that sometimes connect directly to your network, or clients that sometimes establish a VPN connection, you will need to configure them as Internet-only clients, which will have the more limited IBCM management capabilities. A trust relationship with the user's forest is required for user based policy features. A trust relationship requires modifications to the firewall policy of the inner firewall, which weakens security.

Allowing Site-to-Site Communications Across an Inner Firewall

A dedicated site for Internet clients can also reside in the perimeter network but be joined to a parent site in your internal network. This configuration requires you to allow site-to-site communications across your inner firewall. Because site hierarchies cannot span untrusted AD forests, this configuration requires that the site servers in the DMZ and on the internal network are members of the same forest or of trusted forests. Here are some ways you can accomplish this:

▶ You can deploy a separate AD forest in the DMZ and establish a trust with the forest on internal network.

▶ You can deploy a child domain of your internal forest in the DMZ. Child domains automatically trust all other domains in the forest.

▶ You can deploy domain controllers for you internal domain in the DMZ, and make your site server a member of that domain. Deploying domain controllers for your internal domain in an Internet accessible DMZ is a security risk. You can reduce this risk by using read-only domain controllers in the DMZ.

Each of these scenarios requires allowing AD traffic through the inner firewall, which introduces some degree of risk. Site-to-site communications across a firewall also require that you allow SQL Server Service Broker traffic to support database replication and SMB traffic for file-based replication.

Having a Site Span the Internal Network and Perimeter Network

You can configure a site to span the internal network and the perimeter network. A site that spans these zones can be dedicated to Internet clients only or can have both Internet and intranet clients. In this configuration, the site server and SQL database server are in the internal network. You can provide services to intranet clients either by deploying separate client-facing systems in the internal network or by configuring site systems in your DMZ to accept connections from both intranet and Internet clients and then allowing outbound client connections though the internal firewall.

In this scenario, you may choose to make site systems in the DMZ part of an untrusted forest. Using an untrusted forest eliminates the need to modify the inner firewall policy for AD traffic; however, it also prevents your Internet-based clients from receiving user based policy. To eliminate the need for DMZ-based site systems to access the SQL database on the internal network, you can deploy a replica of the SQL database in the DMZ. Chapter 6 describes configuration of database replicas.

Using Web Proxies and Proxy Enrollment Points

As an alternative to deploying site systems in a DMZ, you can use a web proxy, such as ISA Server and Forefront Threat Management Gateway, to publish internal site systems to the Internet. Here are the configuration options for using a web proxy:

▶ You can configure the proxy for SSL bridging. In this configuration, the proxy server terminates the connection and inspects the inbound packets before sending them on to the site system. SSL bridging does not support mobile device clients enrolled by ConfigMgr.

▶ You can configure the proxy for tunneling. Here the proxy creates a tunnel from the Internet-based client to the internal site system. This option should only be used if your security requirements are minimal.

If you support ConfigMgr mobile device enrollment you should deploy a proxy enrollment point to receive requests from mobile devices on the Internet rather than allowing them to communicate directly with the enrollment point.

Intermittently Connected Users

Users who do not connect to the enterprise network or who connect only occasionally present a special configuration management challenge, which ConfigMgr addresses through use of BITS. If a client's network connection to its distribution point drops while a download is in progress, the download could resume the next time the client establishes a connection to that distribution point. This allows effective software distribution services to users such as home office users who intermittently establish a VPN connection to the corporate network. Those individuals using laptops both at the office and away from the office also benefit from the ability to resume interrupted downloads. System Center 2012 Configuration Manager allows suspended BITS downloads to resume from any BITS-enabled distribution point. This allows even highly mobile users such as airline pilots, who may connect only briefly at various points along their route, to receive content using multiple distribution points.

> **NOTE: ABOUT DIRECTACCESS**
>
> The DirectAccess feature in Windows Server 2008 R2 provides security for connecting to corporate networks over the Internet without requiring a VPN. It provides an additional option for clients to connect site systems. DirectAccess does not support OS deployment or server-initiated actions such as remote control. You can find information about DirectAccess at http://technet.microsoft.com/en-us/network/dd420463.

ConfigMgr also provides IBCM, which allows you to provide some services to users who never connect directly to your network. IBCM allows you to provide services over the Internet, including software distribution and software updates to Internet-only clients. You will also receive inventory and status from those clients. Clients that sometimes connect to the corporate network can also take advantage of IBCM services, including the ability of BITS downloads to take place partially over the intranet and partially over the Internet. IBCM does not support OS deployment, client deployment, NAP, and ConfigMgr Remote Tools. For more information on Internet-based clients, see Chapter 4.

Network Discovery

ConfigMgr can use a variety of network protocols to probe your network and gather data about the objects it discovers into the site database. Network Discovery can be used to identify potential ConfigMgr clients. Network Discovery can also be used to add network topology data and information about nonclient network devices to your database for use in queries, collections, and reports. ConfigMgr 2012 Network Discovery is similar to that in ConfigMgr 2007, except that it is no longer used to discover resources supporting out of band management.

To configure Network Discovery, double-click **Network Discovery** in the Administration workspace under **Overview** -> **Site Hierarchy** -> **Discovery Methods**. As displayed in Figure 5.8, there are three levels of discovery:

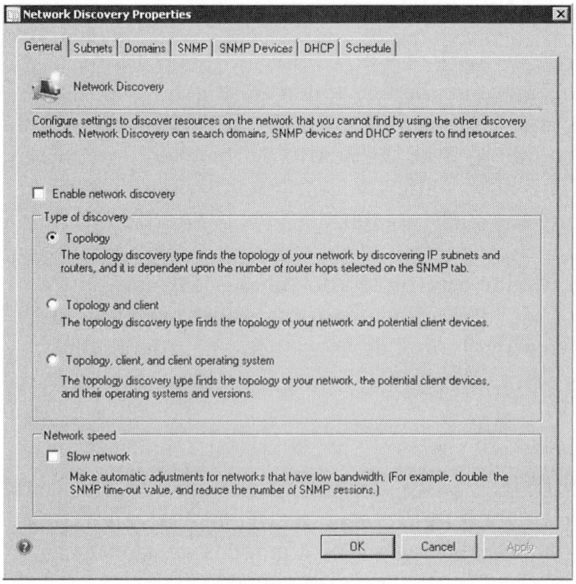

FIGURE 5.8   Levels of Network Discovery.

▶ Topology

▶ Topology and client

▶ Topology, client, and client operating systems

NOTE: ABOUT NETWORK DISCOVERY RESOURCE UTILIZATION

Network Discovery can have a major impact on your network and site systems. Scheduling Network Discovery to run during off-peak times helps avoid overloading network or server resources. If you have a large number of machines, you should perform initial discovery in phases. You may choose to discover a few subnets at a time, or you may choose to first discover topology only, then clients, and later add operating system discovery. You should limit the number of new resources you expect to discover to no more than 5,000 at a time.

If discovery will traverse slow network segments, check the **Slow network** option on the General tab to throttle the number of concurrent network request and adjust timeout values.

The Subnets, Domains, and SNMP Devices tabs determine the initial scope of discovery. Figure 5.9 displays the Subnets tab. The local subnet and the site server's domain are discovered by default. You can add subnets, domains, or SNMP devices using the starburst icon (circled in Figure 5.9) on the respective tabs. You can also remove or modify existing subnets or domains.

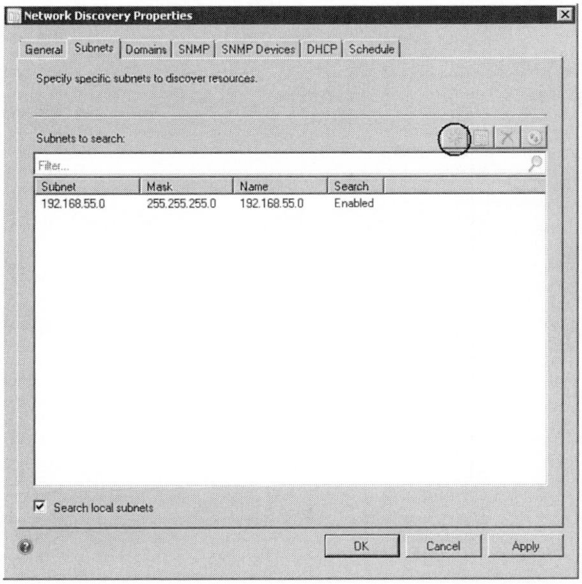

FIGURE 5.9   Specifying subnets for Network Discovery.

Discovering Network Topology

Network Discovery uses Simple Network Management Protocol (SNMP) to query network infrastructure devices for basic information about your network topology. The discovery process generates DDRs for network devices and subnets. A DDR is a small file with identifying information about an object that is processed and stored in the ConfigMgr database.

The properties for SNMP discovery are configured on the SNMP tab of the Network Discovery Properties sheet, shown in Figure 5.10. All SNMP devices are configured with a community string, named *public* by default. To connect to an SNMP device, you must add its community string to the list of communities to discover. The maximum hops specified on the SNMP tab controls how far discovery traverses the network. If the number of hops is set to 0, only those devices on the site server's local subnet are discovered. If the number of hops is more than 0, Network Discovery queries the routing tables of the local router to retrieve a list of subnets connected to it and the IP addresses of devices listed in the ipRouteNextHop of the router. These subnets and devices are considered one hop away. Network Discovery continues to perform the same process based on the routing data of the devices on the next hop, until it reaches the maximum number of hops. Additional subnets and devices on those subnets are discovered if one of the following occurs:

▶ The subnet is specified on the Subnets tab.

▶ The subnet information is retrieved from a device specified on the SNMP Devices tab.

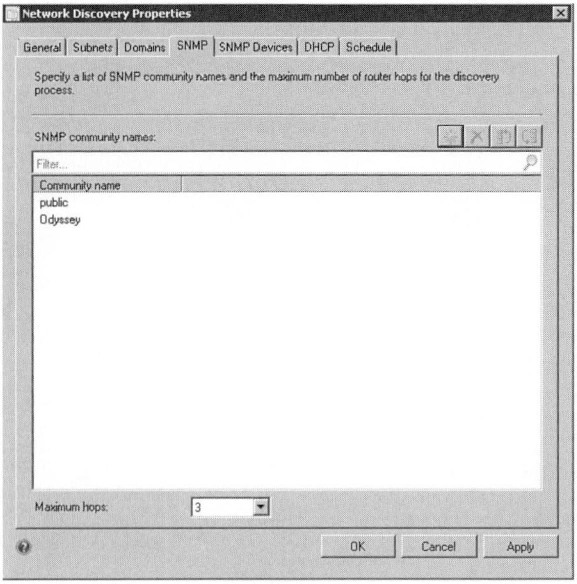

FIGURE 5.10   Specifying SNMP community strings for Network Discovery.

Because a router can be connected to many subnets, the scope of Network Discovery could increase dramatically with each higher value of the maximum hops setting. On the local subnet, Network Discovery can connect to the router using Router Information Protocol (RIP) or by listening for Open Shortest Path First (OSPF) multicast addresses, even if SNMP is not available on the router.

Network Discovery can also retrieve information from Microsoft DHCP servers. The Network Discovery Properties DHCP tab lists the DHCP servers to query. By default, Network Discovery uses the site server's DHCP Server, although the site server typically is not configured as a DHCP client and you need to add DHCP servers manually using the starburst icon. Figure 5.11 displays an example of this.

The site server will establish an RPC connection to each of the specified DHCP servers to retrieve subnet and scope information. Subnets defined on the DHCP servers are added to the list of available subnets for future network discovery but are not enabled for discovery by default. For each active lease on the DHCP server, the network discovery process also attempts to resolve the IP address to a name. For more information on Microsoft

DHCP, see the Microsoft DHCP FAQ at http://www.microsoft.com/technet/network/dhcp/dhcpfaq.mspx#EUG.

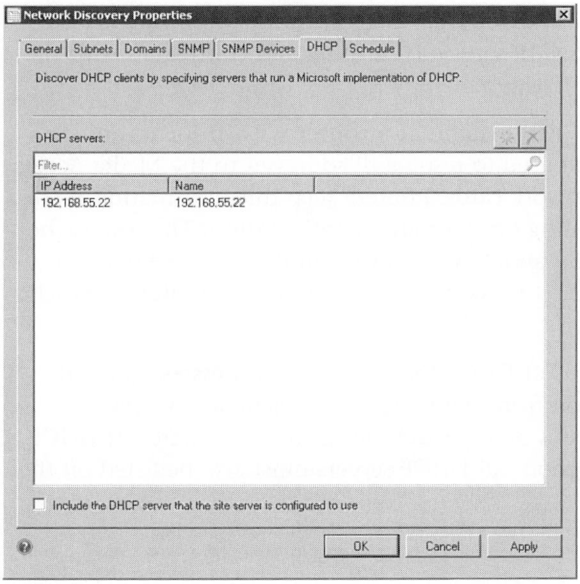

FIGURE 5.11   Specifying DHCP servers to be used by Network Discovery.

Topology and Client Discovery

To discover potential ConfigMgr clients, Network Discovery attempts to identify as many devices as possible on the IP network. An array of IP addresses from the ipNetToMedia-Table of SNMP devices is used to identify IP addresses in use, and Network Discovery pings each address to determine if it is currently active. If the device replies to the ping, Network Discovery attempts to use SNMP to query the device. If Network Discovery can access the device's management information through SNMP, it will retrieve any routing table or other information the device holds about other IP addresses of which it is aware. Each IP address is resolved to a NetBIOS name if possible.

Network Discovery also retrieves the Browse list for any domains specified on the Domains tab. The Browse list is the same list used to display machines in the Windows Network Neighborhood and can be enumerated with the Net View command. As with other discovered devices, Network Discovery then attempts to ping the device to see if it is active.

Discovering Topology, Client, and Client Operating Systems

In addition to the discovery process for topology and clients, if client operating system discovery is specified, Network Discovery attempts to make a connection using LAN Manager calls to determine whether the machine is running Windows and, if so, the version of Windows it is running.

For Network Discovery to create a DDR for a discovered device, the IP address and subnet mask of the device must be retrieved. Network Discovery retrieves the subnet mask from one of the following:

▶ **The device itself if it is manageable through SNMP:** Windows machines are only manageable through SNMP if the SNMP service is running and configured with the required community information. This is generally not the case.

▶ **The Address Resolution Protocol (ARP) cache of a router with information about the device:** ARP is a protocol used to resolve IP addresses to the Media Access Control (MAC) addresses of the network cards. Routers keep this information cached for a finite amount of time, depending on the router configuration. The ARP cache generally does not have information about every device on the attached network segment. This makes retrieving subnet mask information from the router ARP cache a hit-or-miss operation.

▶ **The DHCP server:** If you use Microsoft DHCP for all your IP address assignment, retrieval of subnet mask information from the DHCP server generally works well. Any machines with static IP addresses or any machines using non-Microsoft DHCP must be discovered by another method. All DHCP servers must also be listed on the DHCP tab.

Troubleshooting ConfigMgr Network Issues

ConfigMgr depends on basic network services such as connectivity and name resolution to work properly. Network-related issues are a common source of problems that can affect ConfigMgr service delivery. The last part of this chapter provides a brief overview of some general network troubleshooting methods, followed by a discussion of how to troubleshoot some specific ConfigMgr issues potentially caused by network problems. When troubleshooting, it is important to keep an open mind. Some issues caused by incorrect security settings, for example, can produce similar symptoms to network issues.

Among the common network-related issues that can affect ConfigMgr are the following:

▶ Network configuration issues

▶ Basic connectivity problems

▶ Name resolution issues

▶ Blocked or unresponsive ports

▶ Timeout issues

The following sections briefly describe a few of the many tools and techniques for troubleshooting these types of issues.

Network Configuration Issues

If you suspect that the TCP/IP networking on one of your systems is not working correctly, you can log on to the system and enter the following at the command prompt (Start -> Run, and then type **cmd**):

```
Ipconfig /all
```

You should see a list of the installed network adapters with IP addresses and other IP configuration data. If no IP address or only an autoconfiguration IP address is displayed, the network components are either not configured or not functioning properly. If this occurs when the IP address configuration is set to obtain an IP address automatically, this means the machine was unable to contact a DHCP server. For more information on configuring TCP/IP, see http://go.microsoft.com/fwlink/?LinkId=154884.

If the machine has one or more valid IP addresses, you can test TCP/IP functioning by entering the following two commands at the command prompt:

▶ Ping 127.0.0.1

▶ Ping <IP address of this machine>

In both cases, you should see a series of replies, such as the following:

```
Reply from 127.0.0.1: bytes=32 time=9ms TTL=128
```

If you receive a request timed out message, TCP/IP networking on the machine is not working properly.

The NetDiag.exe utility, which you can download from Microsoft's website, can be used to diagnose (and in some cases fix) a wide variety of network configuration issues. For more information on NetDiag, see http://technet.microsoft.com/library/Cc938980.

Basic Connectivity Problems

Basic connectivity problems occur if

▶ Systems are not physically connected.

▶ There is a hardware or software problem on one of the systems or an intermediate device.

▶ The packets are not correctly routed between the systems.

To start troubleshooting basic connectivity, log on to one of the affected systems and ping the system with which it has problems communicating. To do this, open a command prompt (Start -> Run, and then type **cmd**) and enter the following command:

```
ping <IP address of target system>
```

In most cases, you should get a response showing the time it took to get a reply to the ping request and other statistics. If the system is not responding, you may get one of the following messages:

▶ **Request timed out:** This simply means that you did not get a response in the expected time. In some cases, the target system may have been configured not to respond to a ping. You can test this on the target system by pinging its own IP address to make sure it is responding. If you suspect that the ping request timed out because of slow network conditions, you can try increasing the timeout value from the default value of 1 second. As an example, `ping -w 5000 <IP address of target system>` will wait 5,000 milliseconds (5 seconds).

▶ **Destination Host Unreachable or Destination Network Unreachable:** This is generally a response from a router indicating that no route is defined to the host or subnet.

Other return values are possible, indicating specific errors. For more information on the ping command, see http://technet.microsoft.com/en-us/library/cc732509.aspx.

You can drill deeper into connectivity issues using commands such as `tracert` and `pathping`, described at http://technet.microsoft.com/library/Cc940095.

Name Resolution Issues

Most ConfigMgr components rely on DNS for name resolution. In some cases, ConfigMgr also uses NetBIOS name resolution. Again, you can use the `ping` command as a quick test of name resolution. At the command prompt, enter

▶ `Ping <FQDN of target system>`

For example: `Ping armada.odyssey.com`

▶ `Ping <hostname of target system>`

For example: `Ping armada`

▶ `Ping <NetBIOS name of target system>`

For example: `Ping \\armada`

In each case, these commands should return a response showing the correct IP of the target system, such as the following:

`Pinging armada.odyssey.com [192.168.5.4] with 32 bytes of data:`

If DNS name resolution fails, you can troubleshoot this with the `NSlookup` command described at http://support.microsoft.com/kb/200525. To troubleshoot NetBIOS name resolution using `Nbtstat` and other methods, see KB article 323388 (at http://support.microsoft.com/kb/323388). It's also useful to test pinging the known IP address of the target machine—if that works then you have narrowed the issue to some sort of name resolution-related issue.

An additional DNS problem that sometimes occurs is an incorrect referral. Incorrect referrals occur when a hostname is used instead of a FQDN, and the wrong domain name is appended due to the DNS suffix search order. This typically results in Access Denied errors. If you see unexpected Access Denied errors, try pinging the site system using both the hostname and the FQDN to make sure they resolve to the same address.

Blocked or Unresponsive Ports

A common source of connectivity problems involves ports blocked by intermediate devices such as routers or firewalls. In other cases, the port may simply not be listening on the system to which you are trying to connect. To identify problems with specific ports, first refer to Table 5.1 to determine the ports used by the failing service. You can then attempt to connect to the specific port on the target system using the `telnet` command. For example, to verify that you can connect to the Trivial File Transfer Protocol (TFTP) Daemon service (port 69) on PXE enabled distribution point Charon.Odyssey.com, open a command prompt (Start -> Run, and then type **cmd**) and enter the following:

```
Telnet Charon.Odyssey.com 69
```

If telnet is successful, you will receive the telnet screen with a cursor. If the connection fails, you will receive an error message.

When a connection to a port fails, first verify that the service is listening on the appropriate port. On the machine that should receive the connections, enter the command `netstat -a` to list all connections and listening ports.

▶ If the port is not shown, verify that all system requirements and prerequisites are met.

▶ If the port displays as enabled, check all network firewall logs for dropped packets.

Refer to your network team or vendor firewall documentation for procedures for checking firewall logs. Also, check the Windows Firewall logs and settings (see http://technet. microsoft.com/en-us/network/bb545423.aspx) and any third-party security software that performs intrusion detection and prevention.

Additional tools are available for troubleshooting port status issues, such as the following:

▶ The PortQry command-line utility, downloadable from http://www.microsoft.com/ en-us/download/details.aspx?id=17148.

▶ PortQryUI, which you can download from http://www.microsoft.com/en-us/ download/details.aspx?id=24009. PortQryUI provides equivalent functionality to PortQry through a graphical user interface (GUI).

Going to http://www.microsoft.com/downloads and searching for **PortQry** brings up links for each of these tools.

TESTING CLIENT–TO–MANAGEMENT POINT CONNECTIVITY

To test client connectivity to a MP, you can try entering the following URLs in the client's web browser:

▶ http://<MP>/sms_mp/.sms_aut?mplist

▶ http://<MP>/sms_mp/.sms_aut?mpcert

▶ https://<MP>/sms_mp/.sms_aut?mplist

▶ https://<MP>/sms_mp/.sms_aut?mpcert

Note that <MP> is either the IP address or the name of the management point. If a name is used, the name should be one of the following:

▶ The NetBIOS name

▶ Either the short name or the FQDN for intranet clients, depending on how the management point name is specified in the site properties

▶ The FQDN for Internet clients

In each case, the URL ending in mplist in the preceding examples should return an XML-formatted list of management points or a blank page, whereas the URL ending in mpcert should return a string of characters corresponding to the management point certificate. Any error messages or other unexpected return values indicate a problem communicating with the management point.

Timeout Issues

The response times you see from the `ping` command can help you to confirm network performance problems that could be causing connections to time out. In some cases, timeouts are configurable; however, if timeouts are a frequent problem, you should review your server placement and network configuration to see if improvements are possible.

Identifying Network Issues Affecting ConfigMgr

Almost all ConfigMgr functionality depends on adequate network services. The next sections look at some of the features most often affected by network issues. These features include site system and client installation, software distribution, and data synchronization across the hierarchy. Chapter 3 introduces the two major features of ConfigMgr for troubleshooting:

▶ The Status Message System

▶ The ConfigMgr logs

The following sections discuss some indicators of possible network issues that you may see in the status messages and logs. In addition to troubleshooting, you can use this information to configure proactive monitoring for ConfigMgr, helping to spot many problems before they impact service delivery.

The discussion is by no means an exhaustive list of possible network issues. It does cover some of the more common issues, and should give you an idea of how to use these tools effectively.

Network Issues Affecting Site Configuration

When there is a problem installing or configuring a site system, this will generally show up in the Site Component Manager status. In the ConfigMgr console Monitoring workspace, select **System Status -> Component Status**. Right-click **SMS_SITE_COMPONENT_ MANAGER**, choose **View Messages -> All**, and specify the time interval over which you want to view messages. If network problems are preventing a site system installation, you typically see status messages similar to the ones detailed in Table 5.3.

TABLE 5.3   Site Component Manager Status Messages Indicating Network Problems

Severity	Message ID	Description
Error	1037	Site Component Manager could not access site system "\\APOLLO. ODYSSEY.COM." The operating system reported error 2147942453: The network path was not found.
		Possible cause: The site system is turned off, not connected to the network, or not functioning properly.
		Solution: Verify the site system is turned on, connected to the network, and functioning properly.
		Possible cause: Site Component Manager does not have sufficient access rights to connect to the site system.
		Solution: Verify that the site server's computer$ account has administrator rights on the remote site system.
		Possible cause: Network problems are preventing Site Component Manager from connecting to the site system.
		Solution: Investigate and correct any problems on your network.
		Possible cause: You took the site system out of service and do not intend on using it as a site system any more.
		Solution: Remove this site system from the list of site systems for this site. The list appears in the Site Systems node of the Administrator console.
Error	1028	Site Component Manager failed to configure site system "\\ APOLLO.ODYSSEY.COM" to receive Configuration Manager Server Components.
		Solution: Review the previous status messages to determine the exact reason for the failure. Site Component Manager cannot install any Configuration Manager Server Components on this site system until the site system is configured successfully. Site Component Manager will automatically retry this operation in 60 minutes. To force Site Component Manager to retry this operation immediately, stop and restart Site Component Manager using the Configuration Manager Service Manager.

5

Severity	Message ID	Description
Error	578	Could not read registry key "`HKEY_LOCAL_MACHINE\SOFTWARE\` `Microsoft\SMS`" on computer APOLLO.ODYSSEY.COM. The operating system reported error 53: The Network Path Was Not Found. Resolution: Troubleshoot name resolution.

You will find additional information in the log file sitecomp.log. If you have enabled NAL logging, network problems are indicated by errors such as `ERROR: NAL failed to access NAL path....` Appendix A, "Configuration Manager Log Files," discusses NAL logging.

Network Issues Affecting Client Installation

When client push installation is enabled, the Client Configuration Manager component on the site server is responsible for installing the client on those systems that are discovered and targeted for installation. When an installation attempt fails, a client configuration request (.CCR) file is copied to the folder *<ConfigMgrInstallPath>*\inboxes\ccrretry. box (where *<ConfigMgrInstallPath>* indicates the folder in which ConfigMgr is installed, by default *%ProgramFiles%*\Microsoft Configuration Manager).

It is not unusual for a client installation to take more than one attempt, and you may see some files in the ccrretry.box folder as part of normal operations. However, a large backlog of files in this location may indicate a problem pushing out the client software. Problems will also show up under the status for Client Configuration Manager (in the Monitoring workspace of the console, select **System Status** -> **Component Status**. Right-click **SMS_CLIENT_CONFIG_MANAGER**).

NOTE: ABOUT OFFLINE CLIENTS

You may see a backlog of CCR retries and numerous status messages indicating client installation failures, which occur simply because the machines were temporarily disconnected or shut down when Client Configuration Manager attempted contacting them. The Client Configuration Manager may also be attempting to reach machines that are permanently offline but previously discovered by ConfigMgr. This is a particularly common issue with Active Directory System Discovery. If your AD contains machine accounts for computers that no longer exist, Active Directory System Discovery will discover these machines, and client push (if enabled) will attempt to install the client on them. Your change control process should include removal of stale computer accounts from Active Directory.

Chapter 21, "Backup, Recovery, and Maintenance," discusses additional considerations for managing discovery data.

Table 5.4 lists some messages that indicate possible network issues.

TABLE 5.4   Client Configuration Manager Status Messages Indicating Network Problems

Severity	Message ID	Description
Warning	3014	Client Configuration Manager cannot connect to the machine ALBERT. The operating system reported Error 5: Access is denied.
		Possible cause: The client is not accessible.
		Solution: Verify that the client is connected to the network and that the service account or (if specified) the Client Remote Installation account has the required privileges, as specified in the ConfigMgr documentation.
		Possible cause: A remote client installation account was not specified in the ConfigMgr console, the account is not valid, is disabled, or has an expired password.
		Solution: Ensure one or more valid and active remote client installation accounts are specified in the ConfigMgr console, that the account names and passwords are correct, and that the account has the required administrator rights on the target machines.
Warning	3010	In the past %3 hours, Client Configuration Manager (CCM) has made %1 unsuccessful attempts to install on client %2. CCM will continue to attempt to install this client.
Error	3011	Client Configuration Manager (CCM) failed to complete the SMS installation on client.
Warning	3015	Client Configuration Manager cannot find machine %1 on the network.

%1, %2, and so forth represent replaceable parameters. The actual values will be supplied a run-time.

You may find additional information in the log files ccm.log on the site server and ccmsetup.log on the client (the ccmsetup log only exists if the attempted installation progressed far enough for the setup process to start on the client).

Table 5.5 lists log entries that can help identify network issues.

TABLE 5.5   Log File Entries Indicating Network Problems with Client Installation

Log File Name	Log File Entry	Description	Troubleshooting Steps
ccm.log	The network path was not found (Error Code 53).	Unable to resolve or contact client	Follow basic network troubleshooting between the site server and client (note: the client may simply have been offline).

Log File Name	Log File Entry	Description	Troubleshooting Steps
ccm.log	The network name cannot be found (Error 67).	Unable to connect to client	Verify that File and Printer Sharing for Microsoft Networks is enabled on the client and not blocked by firewall or security software.
ccmsetup.log	Failed to send HTTP request (Error 12029).	Error communicating with management point	Review the LocationServices log to identify the MP. Test the connection to the MP.
ccmsetup.log	Failed to successfully complete HTTP request.	Error communicating with management point	Review the LocationServices log to identify the MP. Test the connection to the MP.

Missing or Incorrect Service Principal Name Registration

Service principal names (SPNs) provide information used by clients to identify and mutually authenticate with services using Kerberos authentication. Services use Active Directory SPN registration to make the required information available to clients. Missing or incorrect SPN registration is a common cause of problems with client communications with site systems, such as failure to download content or client approval problems. HTTP 401 errors in client log files, including the Datatransferservice.log and ccmexec.log, may indicate problems with SPN registrations. To register the required service principal names properly, refer to the following documentation:

▶ If you are running the SQL Server service using a domain account on the site database server or other roles requiring SQL Server, you must follow the instructions at http://technet.microsoft.com/en-us/library/hh427336.aspx#BKMK_ManageSPNforDBSrv to register the SPN. If the SQL Server service is configured to run under the local system account, you do not need to manually register the SPN. However, running SQL Server in the local system context is not recommended for security reasons.

▶ For site systems that require IIS, if the system is registered in DNS using a CNAME (a DNS alias rather than the actual computer name), you will need to register the SPN using the procedure described at http://support.microsoft.com/kb/929650/en-us.

Network Issues Affecting Software Distribution

Software distribution relies on networking to send content to distribution points and for clients to download policy from management points and content from distribution points. Chapter 4 described planning considerations for deploying site systems to support software distribution. Figure 5.12 shows the principal network exchanges involved in these software distribution scenarios:

▶ The three client systems shown in the lower-left portion of the figure reside on the same subnet and use BranchCache to share content.

▶ The client on the lower right retrieves content from a local distribution point. In this scenario, scheduling and bandwidth throttling between distribution points are available.

In this figure, the directional arrows indicate the principal direction of data transfer. This may differ from the direction previously shown in Table 5.1, which indicates the system initiating the connection.

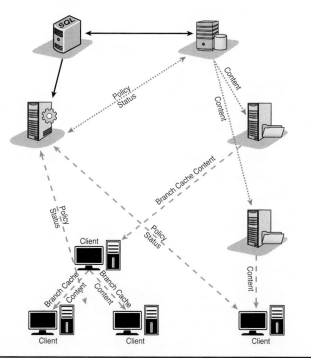

Legend	
Server Roles In Use	**Network Protocols In Use**
= Site Server	- - - - - = HTTP / HTTPS
= Site Database Server	———— = SQL over TCP
= Management Point	·········· = SMB / RPC
= Distribution Point	

FIGURE 5.12   The major systems for software distribution and data flow between them.

You will find status information relating to the general functioning of content deployment under the Monitoring workspace in the distribution status node. Chapter 13 discusses distribution status. You can view distribution status messages from the SMS_ DISTRIBUTION_MANAGER component at **System Status -> Component Status**.

The client-to-management point connection includes policy downloads and status uploads.

Table 5.6 shows Distribution Manager status messages that may indicate network problems preventing content distribution.

TABLE 5.6   Distribution Manager Status Messages Indicating Possible Network Problems

Severity	Message ID	Description
Error	2302	Distribution Manager failed to process package %1 (package ID = %2).
Error	2307	Distribution Manager failed to access the source directory %1 for package %2.
Error	2328	Distribution Manager failed to copy package %1 from %2 to %3.
Error	2332	Distribution Manager failed to remove package %1 from distribution path %2.
Error	2344	Failed to create virtual directory on the defined share or volume on distribution point %1.

Additional details are available in Distmgr.log.

The Status Message Queries node provide several queries you can use to view client status messages that may indicate network problems, such as Clients That Failed to Start a Specific Deployed Program or Clients That Reported Errors or Warnings During Inventory File Collection. Detailed troubleshooting of inventory and software deployment problems often requires looking at the client logs. Table 5.7 shows some key entries to check in the client logs. Chapter 9 describes the services associated with these logs.

ConfigMgr provides an option to enable Network Abstraction Layer (NAL) logging, which adds detailed logging of network connection processing to the log for components that use network resources. NAL logging increases the log size substantially and logs many apparent errors that may be misleading; however, it can also be an essential tool for network troubleshooting. In general, you should only enable NAL logging when you need it to troubleshoot a specific issue. Appendix A discusses how to enable NAL logging.

TABLE 5.7   Client Log File Entries Related to Locating and Retrieving Advertised Content

Log File Name	Log File Entry	Description	Troubleshooting Steps
LocationServices.log	Distribution Point=<server name>	Informational. Shows what DP is used for the package, based on the PackageID.	A UNC (Universal Naming Convention) path (e.g., \\<servername>\<share>\<packageID>) indicates an SMB connection. Transfer details will be in FileBITS.log. A URL (e.g., http://<servername>/<p ackageID>) indicates a BITS download. Transfer details will be in DataTransferService.log.
LocationServices.log	Retrieved <local|proxy|default> Management Point	Informational. Shows the MP systems.	None.
PolicyAgent.log	Received delta policy update with <number of> assignments	Informational. Shows the policy download occurred and the number of assignments.	None.
CAS.log	Failed to get DP location...	Possible boundary issue.	Review the LocationServices log.
CAS.log	Download failed for content...	Error communicating with distribution point (DP).	Review the log for additional details. Follow basic network troubleshooting between the client and the DP.
CAS.log	Download failed for download request...	Error communicating with distribution point.	Check BITS functionality on the client; reinstall BITS if necessary.
DataTransferService.log	ERROR (0x80070422)	BITS communication failure.	Follow basic network troubleshooting between the client and DP.
FileBITS.log	Encountered error while copying files	SMB error.	Review the log for additional details. Follow basic network troubleshooting between the client and the DP.

5

KEEPING BOUNDARIES CONSISTENT WITH NETWORK CHANGES

As changes occur in your network topology, such as new or modified IP subnets, it is important to modify your ConfigMgr boundaries and boundary groups to reflect these changes. Failure to update the ConfigMgr boundaries in your boundary groups to reflect network changes is a common cause of problems with software distribution and automatic site assignment. Use appropriate change control procedures to ensure ConfigMgr stays up to date with your network environment.

If you are using Active Directory for your site boundaries, you can monitor the Windows System event log for specific event IDs based on the version of Windows Server:

▶ For Windows Server 2003 and Windows Server 2008 domain controllers (DCs), look for Event ID 5807, Type: Warning, Source: NETLOGON on each DC.

▶ On Windows 2000 domain controllers, the Event ID will be 5778.

This event indicates that one or more computers have connected to the domain controller from an IP address that is not part of a defined Active Directory site. For information on troubleshooting and remediating this issue, see http://support.microsoft.com/kb/889031.

Network Issues Affecting Site Communications

Problems with site-to-site communications can cause problems such as new or modified objects at parent sites not replicated to child sites, and data from child sites not updated at the parent site. An indication of problems with site communications is often a backlog of files in the folders used by the site-to-site communications components:

▶ *<ConfigMgrInstallPath>*\inboxes\schedule.box\outboxes*<sender name>* is the outbox for the sender (where *<sender name>* is the name of the sender; for the standard sender, this will be LAN).

Files used by the sender are queued here for processing. A backlog of send request (.srq) files may indicate that the sender is having problems processing requests or a problem connecting or transferring data to another site.

▶ *<ConfigMgrInstallPath>*\inboxes\schedule.box\requests stores send requests before sending them to the sender.

▶ *<ConfigMgrInstallPath>*\inboxes\schedule.box\tosend stores package and instruction files to transfer to another site.

If you find a backlog of files in any of these folders, check the sender log (sender.log) for errors. You may also view the SMS_LAN_SENDER status in the ConfigMgr console, under the Monitoring workspace, System Status -> Component Status node.

ConfigMgr provides alerts for critical issues affecting SQL replication. You should regularly review the alerts in the Monitoring workspace under Alerts -> Overview. The primary tool for troubleshooting SQL replication issues is the Replication Link Analyzer. You can run the Replication Link Analyzer from the Monitoring workspace. This tool detects and attempts to fix common replication problems, and provides an option to save analysis and remediation logs for further diagnosis.

Several SQL stored procedures provide detailed information about replication status. Perhaps the most important of these is spDiagDRS. Chapter 3 introduced SQL stored procedures, including spDiagDRS.

Summary

This chapter described how System Center 2012 Configuration Manager uses the network. It discussed the data flow and protocols used by ConfigMgr as well as configuring the network components. It then considered how you could apply this knowledge to optimize your operations and server placement for effective network utilization. The chapter looked at some of the details of BITS and BranchCache, enabling key technologies for ConfigMgr, and described how Configuration Manager Network Discovery can gather data about your network and potential clients. Finally, it discussed network troubleshooting, and ways to identify network issues that may affect some specific ConfigMgr components and services.

The next chapter discusses ConfigMgr installation and configuration.

CHAPTER 6

Installing System Center 2012 Configuration Manager

The installation experience of System Center 2012 Configuration Manager is vastly improved and simplified from previous versions of the product. The new installation process consolidates the mini-installation processes that were often run separately into a simple unified experience. Though simplified, the installation experience requires you to plan, design, and validate your objectives for System Center 2012 Configuration Manager.

If you've read the planning exercises in Chapter 4, "Architecture Design Planning," and Chapter 5, "Network Design," you know that installing Configuration Manager (ConfigMgr) properly is much more than dropping the DVD—physically or virtually—into a system and running a setup program. ConfigMgr is a wide and deep product, meaning it has many in-depth capabilities that you must properly plan for as well as properly implement.

The authors strongly recommend you review Chapters 4 and 5 as a prerequisite to reading this chapter. Chapter 4 provides detailed information and guidance on planning activities and decisions that will influence the choices you make during the installation steps discussed in this chapter. This chapter takes you through the foundational steps of installing a site hierarchy, primary stand-alone sites, site servers, required components, and performing the initial site configuration.

Configuring Pre-Installation Requirements

The successful installation of System Center 2012 Configuration Manager sites depends on the correct installation and configuration of all required external components.

The preceding chapters provide extensive information on the dependencies and requirements prior to performing the installation. The authors recommend creating a checklist of requirements based on the information in those chapters.

TIP: CHECKING DEPENDENCIES FOR INSTALLATION

Chapter 2, "Configuration Manager Overview," outlines the dependencies required for each role in System Center 2012 Configuration Manager.

The following sections summarize the requirements specific to the installation tasks for System Center 2012 Configuration Manager sites and the roles you can install during setup. A management point and distribution point are the only supported roles available for selection during the installation. As a central administration site (CAS) does not support the management point or distribution point role, these role options are not available if you are installing the CAS. A CAS by itself provides no value; you must configure at least one primary site before you can install and manage System Center 2012 Configuration Manager clients.

Windows Components

There are several mandatory Windows components you must have in place prior to starting the System Center 2012 Configuration Setup Wizard:

▶ **Operating System Version:** You must use a 64-bit architecture version of one of these operating systems:

   ▶ Windows Server 2008 (Standard, Enterprise, and Datacenter editions)

   ▶ Windows Server 2008 R2 (Standard, Enterprise, and Datacenter editions), with or without Service Pack (SP) 1

▶ **Minimum Hardware Requirements:** The minimum hardware requirements are in addition to the supported hardware requirements of the operating system. Here are the minimum hardware requirements specific to System Center 2012 Configuration Manager:

   ▶ Processor: 733Mhz Pentium III (2.0Ghz or faster recommended)

   ▶ Memory: 256MB (1024MB or more recommended)

   ▶ Free disk space: 5GB (15GB recommended)

▶ **Operating system roles:** The minimum operating system role requirement for a System Center 2012 Configuration Manager site with the management and distribution point is the Web server (IIS) role.

NOTE: ABOUT SIZING

Chapter 4 discusses how you can plan for requirements specific to your needs and environment. Sizing information is available at http://technet.microsoft.com/en-us/library/hh846235.aspx.

Table 6.1 provides details of the additional operating system role services and features required for the typical System Center 2012 Configuration Manager site.

TABLE 6.1   Operating System Roles and Features Requirements

Operating System Feature	Role Services for IIS Role	Additional Features
.NET Framework 3.5 SP1 with WCF activation* .NET Framework 4.0 Full installation	**Common HTTP Features:** Static Content Default Document **Application Development:** ASP.NET (and automatically selected options) **Security:** Windows Authentication IIS 6 Management Compatibility: IIS 6 Metabase Compatibility	Remote Differential Compression BITS Server Extensions (and automatically selected options), or Background Intelligent Transfer Services (BITS) (and automatically selected options)

Required for the Application Catalog web services point site role

For information on requirements, see http://technet.microsoft.com/en-us/library/gg682077.aspx.

TIP: BEST PRACTICES FOR PLANNING YOUR INSTALLATION

Create a matrix of your site systems by role and plan to configure the prerequisites by role type. Also, realize that the hardware requirements are for a minimum installation; plan to add additional resources based on the production demands of the System Center 2012 Configuration Manager site(s).

The authors recommend planning to baseline a proof of concept site and scaling that based on scenario testing in the controlled environment.

Supported SQL Server Requirements

All System Center 2012 Configuration Manager site types have a database engine requirement. Here are the supported database requirements for the server assigned the site database role:

▶ **SQL Server Version:** The following versions and editions are required and supported:

  ▶ SQL Server 2008 SP 2 (Standard and Enterprise) with Cumulative Update (CU) 7

  ▶ SQL Server 2008 R2 SP 1 (Standard, Enterprise) with CU 4

  ▶ SQL Server Express 2008 R2 SP 1 (Standard, Enterprise) with CU 4 is supported only for secondary sites.

NOTE: SQL EDITION LIMITATIONS

If SQL Server Standard edition is installed for the central administration site, the hierarchy is limited to managing a maximum of 50,000 clients. Upgrading the database server to the Enterprise edition after site installation does not change this limit. Plan to install the Enterprise edition of SQL Server if your hierarchy must support more than 50,000 clients.

Similarly, a primary site supports a maximum of 50,000 clients if the site server is co-located with the site database server. A primary site supports up to 100,000 clients if the database server is a remote server, but the entire hierarchy is limited to 50,000 clients if the CAS has SQL Server Standard edition installed.

▶ **SQL Server Requirements:** Here is the required configuration for the supported editions and versions of SQL Server (for additional information, see Chapter 4):

  ▶ **Database collation:** SQL_Latin1_General_CP1_CI_AS. Each site must use the same collation.

  ▶ **SQL Server features:** The Database Engine Services is the only required feature for each database site server.

  ▶ **Authentication method:** Windows authentication is required.

  ▶ **SQL Server Instance:** Install a dedicated instance of SQL Server for each site.

  ▶ **SQL Server memory:** In implementations scenarios with the site server role and the database role co-located, dedicate at least 50% of the memory to SQL Server (http://technet.microsoft.com/en-us/library/gg682077. aspx#BKMK_SupConfigSQLSrvReq).

  ▶ **SQL Server Reporting Service (SSRS):** Optional but must be installed for the reporting services point role.

  ▶ **SQL Server ports:** System Center 2012 Configuration Manager supports only static ports (default or custom). In the case of SQL Server named instances, which use dynamic ports by default, you must manually configure a static port. Information on static ports for a named instance is available at http://support.microsoft.com/kb/823938.

  ▶ **SQL Server memory:** You must set a memory limit for the SQL Server instance; a warning is displayed during the prerequisite check if the default configuration is unlimited. This setting is important because failing to configure it normally leaves SQL Server to consume almost all the available memory by default. The authors recommend you set this to a value that leaves the operating system and other applications co-hosted on the server with enough memory to function at their recommended levels.

> **TIP: ACCOUNT TYPE FOR THE SQL SERVER SERVICE**
>
> You can configure the SQL Server service to use an Active Directory (AD) domain account or the local system account. The SQL product team recommends using a domain account as a security best practice. Using a domain account requires you to register the service principal name (SPN) manually for the account. Information on SPN registration is available at the http://technet.microsoft.com/en-us/library/hh427336.aspx. The Local System account option registers the SPN automatically. If the SPN is not configured properly for the AD account assigned as the SQL service account, System Center 2012 Configuration Manager may not function correctly. The authors recommend ensuring the SPN registration is configured properly before proceeding with your System Center 2012 Configuration Manager installation.

Validating and Configuring Active Directory Requirements

System Center 2012 Configuration Manager installation has mandatory and optional AD requirements:

▶ **Mandatory:** All site systems must be members of an AD domain. You must use a domain user account that is a local administrator on the site server for the installation.

▶ **Optional:** You can extend the AD forest schema to support the publishing of System Center 2012 Configuration Manager data. Though the schema extension is optional, there are many benefits and feature dependencies discussed in Chapter 4. The schema extension step and configuration is discussed in Chapter 3, "Looking Inside Configuration Manager." (There are no changes in the schema if you previously extended it for ConfigMgr 2007.) A recommended best practice is to use an AD security group for the delegation required after extending the schema.

Windows Server Update Services

You must install Windows Server Update Services (WSUS) SP 2 on the site system that is to be configured as the software update point (SUP). Specific to System Center 2012 Configuration Manager hierarchies, the requirement for WSUS has changed from ConfigMgr 2007; you must install and configure a SUP on the CAS before you can enable the SUP role on child primary sites.

Prerequisite Checker

ConfigMgr 2007 included a prerequisite check with the Setup Wizard. System Center 2012 Configuration Manager has three options for running a prerequisite check:

▶ Invoke the prerequisite check from the setup splash screen (Assess Server Readiness on the Installation wizard start page).

▶ Invoked as part of the setup routine.

▶ Use the new stand-alone prerequisite checker option.

ConfigMgr 2012 uses the same executable for the prerequisite checks. The following sections discuss the differences in these approaches.

Splash Screen Prerequisite Check

The splash screen method is initiated from the setup media splash screen by selecting the **Assess Server Readiness** link, as illustrated in Figure 6.1.

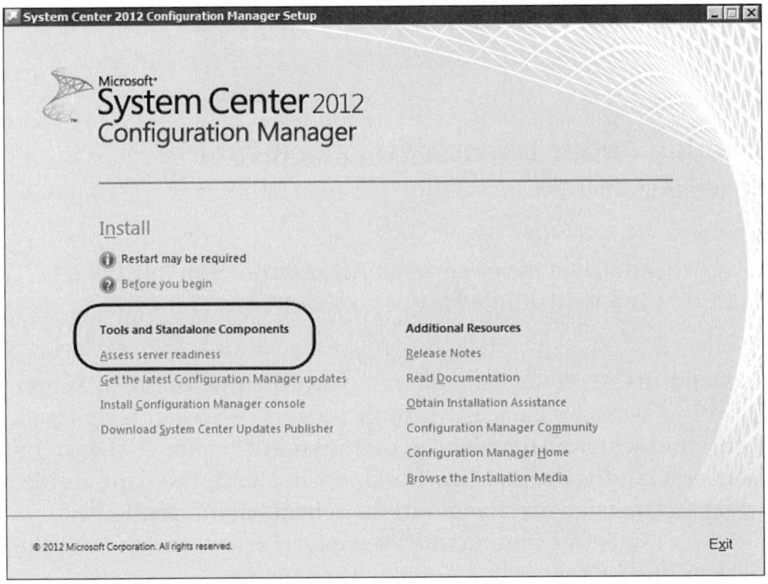

FIGURE 6.1   Assess server readiness GUI initiation.

The prerequisite checker is a stand-alone tool unlike the previous version of the product, which has the tool integrated into setup. The tool generates three log files on the root of the system drive. The primary log file with the full check details is ConfigMgrPrereq.log. Figure 6.2 shows a sample of this log file.

The assess server readiness link starts the prerequisite checker with a special switch /local, and checks the local computer's state for the prerequisites of the following System Center 2012 Configuration Manager roles:

▶ Site server

▶ SQL Server

▶ SDK server (Site provider)

▶ Management point (MP)

▶ Distribution point (DP)

▶ Reporting services point (RSP)

▶ Fallback status point (FSP)

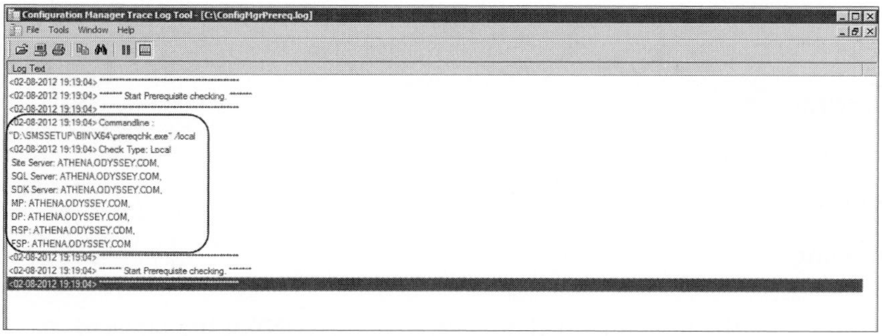

FIGURE 6.2   Prerequisite check log file.

The checks performed are the prerequisites required for the roles discussed in the "Configuring Pre-Installation Requirements" section.

The parameters used with this method are not optional and always start a graphical user interface (GUI), as illustrated in Figure 6.3.

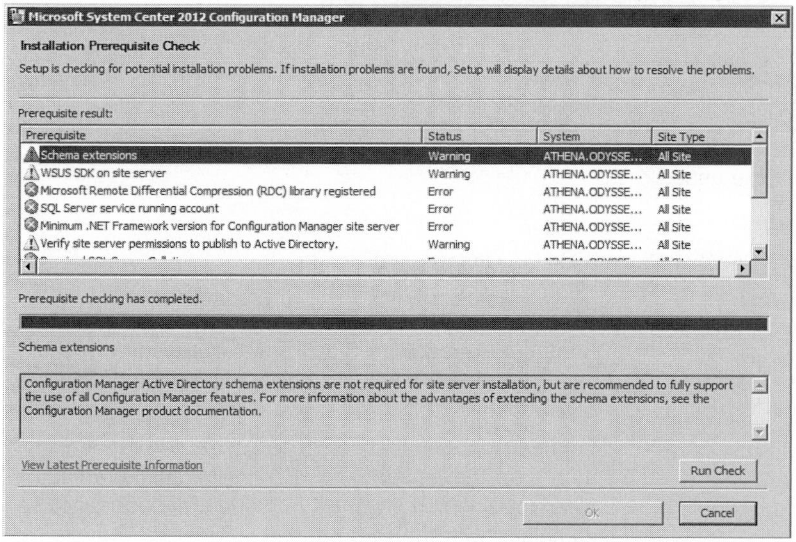

FIGURE 6.3   Prerequisite check results GUI.

Stand-Alone Prerequisite Checker

The other option is to run the prerequisite checker from a command prompt. This option provides the most flexibility and in addition allows you to target a remote computer. The prerequisite checker verifies the minimum requirement of each site type listed in the relevant installation. Here are the checks you can either run on the local machine or target a remote machine:

▶ Configuration Manager console

▶ CAS

▶ Primary site

▶ New secondary site

▶ Upgrade to secondary site

▶ Management point

▶ Distribution point

The tool requires you to use the fully qualified domain name (FQDN) of the targeted machine. Run the tool at the command prompt with a /? switch to invoke the help menu and correct syntax, as shown in Figure 6.4. See Table 6.2 for the full command-line options.

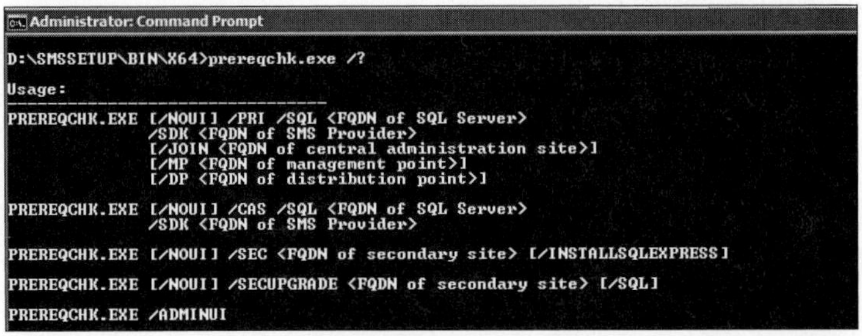

FIGURE 6.4   Prereqchk.exe usage.

TABLE 6.2   Prerequisite Checker Command-Line Options and Usage

Usage Switch	Notes
/NOUI	Runs the Prerequisite Checker without displaying the user interface. You must specify this option before any other options.
/PRI or /CAS	Verifies that the local computer meets the requirements for the primary site or central administration site. You can specify only one option, and it cannot be combined with the SEC option.

Usage Switch	Notes
/SEC *<FQDN of secondary site>*	Verifies that the specified computer meets the requirements for the secondary site. This option cannot be combined with the /PRI or /CAS option.
/SECUPGRADE *<FQDN of secondary site>*	Verifies that the specified computer meets the requirements for the secondary site upgrade. This option cannot be combined with the /PRI or /CAS /SEC option.
[/INSTALLSQLEXPRESS]	Verifies SQL Express can be installed on the specified computer. This option can be used only after the /SEC option.
/SQL *<FQDN of SQL Server>*	Verifies that the specified computer meets the requirements for SQL Server to host the Configuration Manager site database. This option is required when you use the /PRI or /CAS option.
/SDK *<FQDN of SMS Provider>*	Verifies that the specified computer meets the requirements for the SMS Provider. This option is required when you use the /PRI or /CAS option.
/JOIN *<FQDN of central administration site>*	Verifies that the local computer meets the requirements for connecting to the central administration server. This option is valid only when you use the /PRI option.
/MP *<FQDN of management point>*	Verifies that the specified computer meets the requirements for the management point site system role.
/DP *<FQDN of distribution point>*	Verifies that the specified computer meets the requirements for the distribution point site system role.
/ADMINUI	Verifies that the local computer meets the prerequisites for the Configuration Manager console. This option cannot be combined with any other option.

Warnings generated by the prerequisite check do not prevent you from initiating the installation. The authors recommend you ensure warning issues are addressed before continuing with the installation.

Using the Prerequisite Files Downloader

A mandatory part of setup is to check for updated prerequisite components. The updated prerequisite components check requires an Internet connection to download the files required by the setup routine. You have an option to download the prerequisite components to a local drive and specify the location of the files without an Internet connection requirement during the installation.

The download component option was available in the previous version of the product by running the setup.exe with a /download switch. System Center 2012 Configuration

Manager has a new download tool, setupdl.exe, which you can find in the installation media at \SMSSETUP\BIN\X64. Perform the following steps to download the files to a local folder:

1. Create a folder on a local drive.

2. Run the command prompt in administrator mode.

3. Navigate to the setupdl.exe file and run it.

4. Browse to the folder you created for the prerequisite files, and start the download.

Performing Site Installations

The "Configuring Pre-Installation Requirements" section discussed prerequisites and dependencies you must consider and perform before invoking the System Center 2012 Configuration Manager Setup Wizard. The remainder of the chapter discusses installing System Center 2012 Configuration Manager sites and the initial post installation configurations.

ABOUT THE SYSTEM CENTER UNIFIED INSTALLER

As part of System Center 2012, Microsoft provides a unified installer for all the components. The installed configuration is just a minimal configuration for deploying System Center and does not provide for redundancy; thus, the authors do not recommend it for a production deployment. The installer uses Orchestrator runbook technology, running the installer requires you to install System Center 2012 Orchestrator. The installer is an interesting starting point for Microsoft to develop something more sophisticated going forward; at a minimum, standardize the setups across the System Center components, or to develop a full-fledged installer.

Use of the unified installer is not required and definitely not intended to replace the detailed individual setup programs for those organizations requiring a customized setup process. Documentation for the installer is available at http://technet.microsoft.com/en-us/library/hh751290.aspx.

You can install and implement System Center 2012 Configuration Manager in two different modes. These two modes require you to install specific Configuration Manager site types and with a specific installation order:

▶ Create a hierarchy

▶ Create a stand-alone site

A hierarchy supports the CAS, child primary, and secondary site types. In a hierarchy, a primary site must always join an existing CAS. Here is the order in which you must install a hierarchy:

1. Install a CAS, following the steps discussed in the "Installing the Central Administration Site" section.

2. Install one or more child primary sites by following the steps in the "Installing Primary Sites" section.

3. Based on your design and needs, optionally install secondary sites under the child primary sites, following the steps in the "Installing Secondary Sites" section.

A stand-alone site supports one primary and one or more secondary sites under the primary site. Here is the order in which you must install a stand-alone site implementation:

1. Install a primary site by following the steps discussed in the "Installing Primary Sites" section.

2. Based on your design and needs, optionally install secondary sites under the primary site by following the steps in the "Installing Secondary Sites" section.

Installing the Central Administration Site

The CAS site is new to System Center 2012 Configuration Manager. If you plan to build a hierarchy with more than one primary site, you must install this site type first. Here is a checklist of activities you must perform before starting the installation:

1. Install a supported operating system.

2. Install and configure the prerequisites for the CAS.

3. Optionally extend the AD schema and configure the delegation required.

4. Document the site code and site name for the CAS.

5. Optionally run the stand-alone prerequisite checker.

The authors recommend installing the prerequisites relevant to the CAS on the server or servers allocated to the CAS site installation. Table 6.3 lists the supported roles for a CAS and the prerequisites of each role.

ABOUT PREREQUISITES

The authors recommend installing all prerequisites for the CAS role except the NAP health policy server (which you should install when the CAS server is nominated for this specific role). The database server and SSRS requirements are required only if the CAS server will host the SQL Server components.

The minimum WSUS installation required is the console. If you perform a full installation of WSUS, you must cancel the Windows Server Update Services Configuration wizard because this is not required.

TABLE 6.3   Supported Site Roles for CAS and Prerequisites

Site Role	Prerequisites - Operating System	Prerequisites - Application Installation
Asset Intelligence synchronization point	.NET 3.5 SP 1	.NET 4.0 Framework (Full Installation)
Reporting services point	Required prerequisites for SSRS	SQL Server Reporting Services (SSRS) .NET 4.0 (Full Installation)
Endpoint Protection point	.NET 3.5 SP 1	N/A
Software Updates point	Default Web Server (IIS) Configuration and Application Development: ASP.NET (and automatically selected options) Security: Windows Authentication Performance: Dynamic Content Compression IIS 6 Management Compatibility: IIS 6 Metabase Compatibility	Windows Update Services 3.0 SP 2 (Console or Full Installation)
Site server	Remote Differential Compression	N/A
Database server	Required prerequisites for SQL Server	System Center 2012 Configuration Manager Supported version of SQL Server
Site provider	650MB of free disk space for automatic installation of Windows Automated Installation Kit (WAIK)	N/A
System health validator point	Network Access protection (NAP) health policy server	N/A

TIP: LOG FILE READER

The System Center 2012 Configuration Manager installation media has an updated stand-alone log file reader, CMTrace.exe. The log file reader is located in \SMSSETUP\TOOLS. CMTrace.exe is great for reading the log files generated by the installation and configuration process. The previous version of the log file reader, Trace32, does not work with System Center 2012 Configuration Manager log files.

With the prerequisites successfully installed, it is time to install the CAS. Perform the following steps:

1. Log on to the server (Armada in this example) using a domain user account with local administration privileges.

2. Start the installation from the System Center 2012 Configuration Manager media splash screen. Double-click **splash.hta**, and select **Install**.

3. Here are the significant wizard pages you must configure to install a CAS:

   ▶ **Before You Begin:** This page lists the items you must check before you begin the installation. Click **Next** to continue.

   ▶ **Getting Started:** Select **Install a Configuration Manager central administration site**, as shown in Figure 6.5.

   ▶ **Prerequisite Licenses:** You must accept the terms to continue with the installation, as displayed in Figure 6.6.

   ▶ **Prerequisite Downloads:** You have two options: **Download required files** or **Use previously downloaded files**. You must specify either a UNC file path or local file path to an existing folder. Figure 6.7 shows the second option where setupdl.exe is used to download the prerequisite files to a local folder. This option is useful in situations where there is no Internet access during the installation process.

   ▶ **Server Language Selection:** Select the supported languages appropriate for your environment. This setting can be changed post installation. Figure 6.8 shows the supported languages available for selection.

   ▶ **Client Language Selection:** Select the System Center 2012 Configuration Manager client supported languages appropriate for your environment. This setting can be changed post installation. Figure 6.9 shows the supported languages wizard page.

   ▶ **Site and Installation Settings:** Type a unique three-character site code, provide a site name, and specify the installation folder. You cannot change these settings without reinstallation. Figure 6.10 shows the site settings page.

   ▶ **Database Information:** Type server name, instance, and database name for the site server hosting the CAS database role. Figure 6.11 shows the default selection when the database server is co-located on the site provider server. Also shown is the SQL Server service broker port. (This is the service used for replication in the hierarchy.)

   ▶ **SMS Provider Settings:** Accept or specify the SMS Provider setting and click **Next**. Figure 6.12 shows the SMS Provider settings page. Chapters 4 and 5 discuss aspects of the SMS Provider.

   ▶ **Settings Summary:** Review the summary of settings selected, and click **Next** to begin the built-in prerequisite check.

   ▶ **Complete Installation:** The final wizard page is the Completion page, as displayed in Figure 6.13. You have a link to the installation log files on this page.

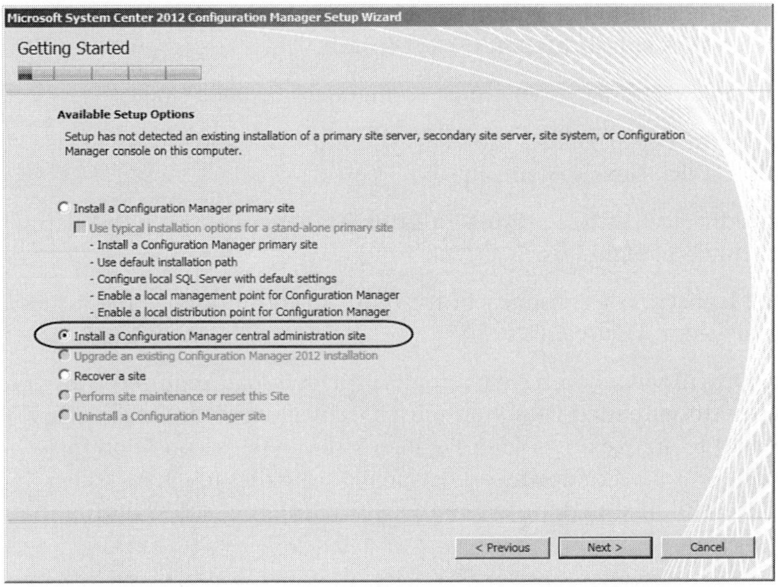

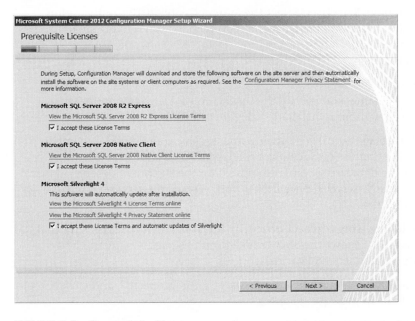

FIGURE 6.5   Getting started with the CAS installation.

FIGURE 6.6   Prerequisite Licenses.

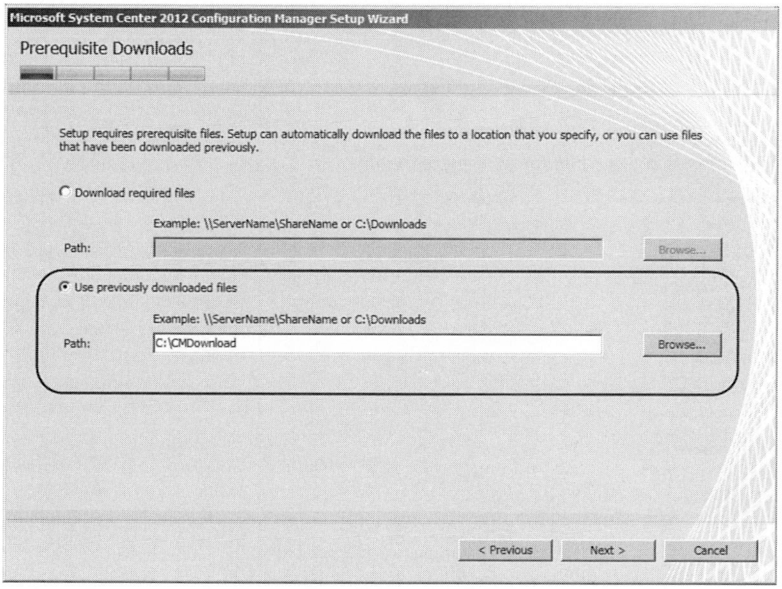

FIGURE 6.7   Prerequisite Downloads.

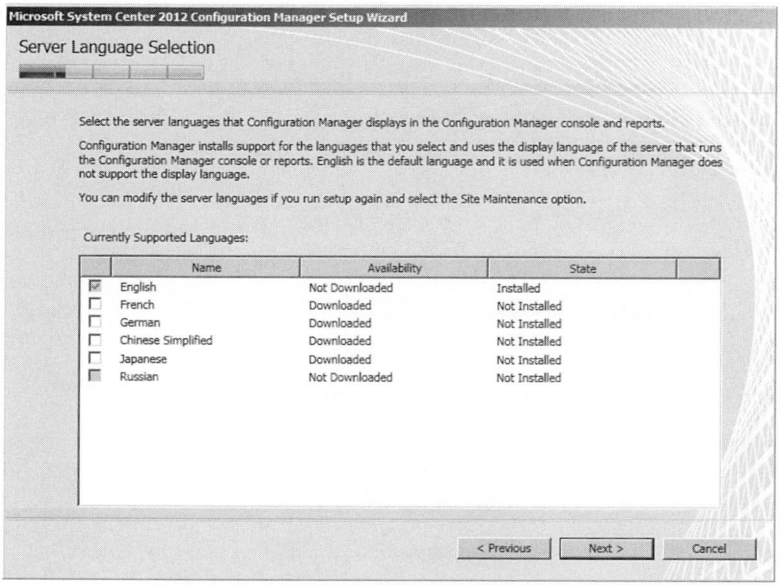

FIGURE 6.8   Server Language Selection.

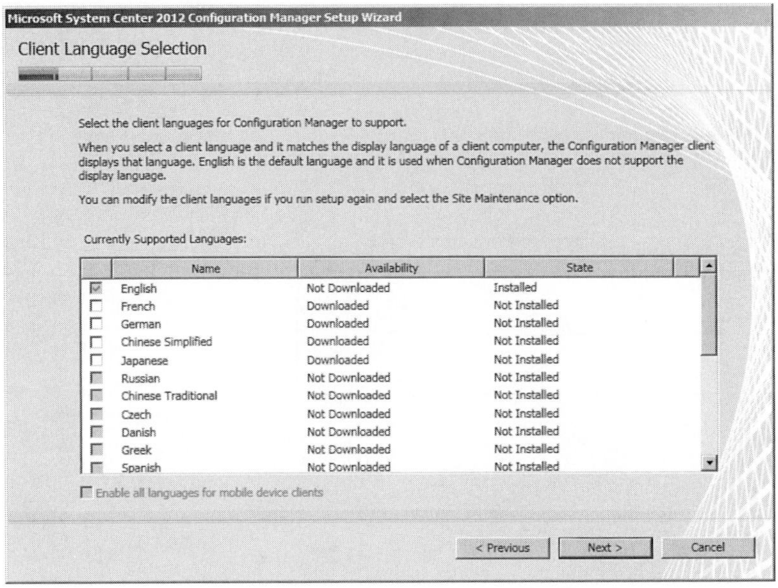

FIGURE 6.9   Client Language Selection.

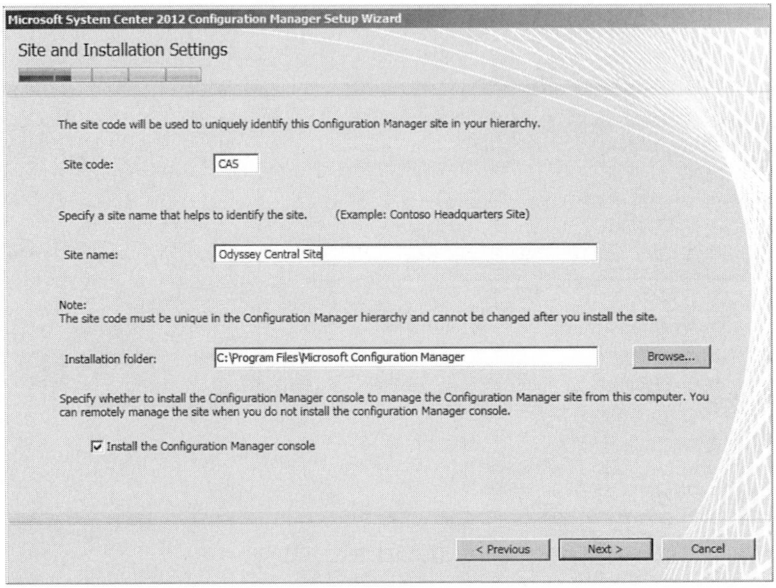

FIGURE 6.10   Site and Installation Settings.

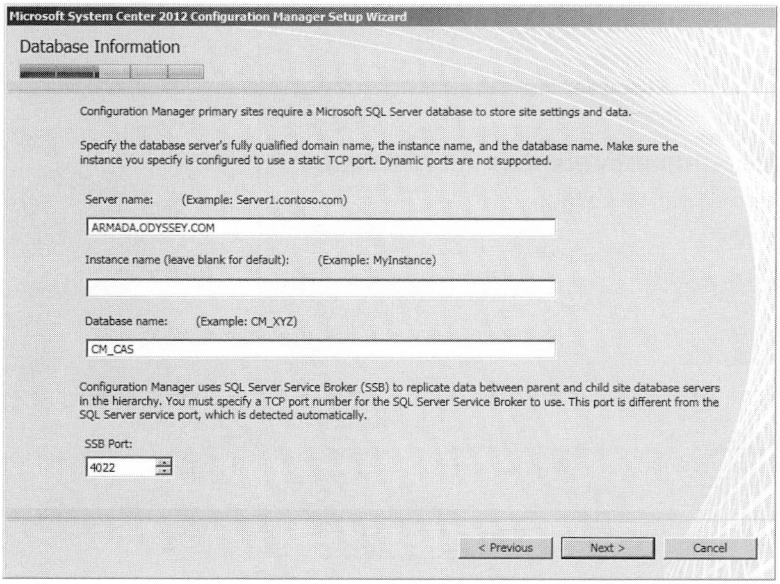

FIGURE 6.11   Specify the database information.

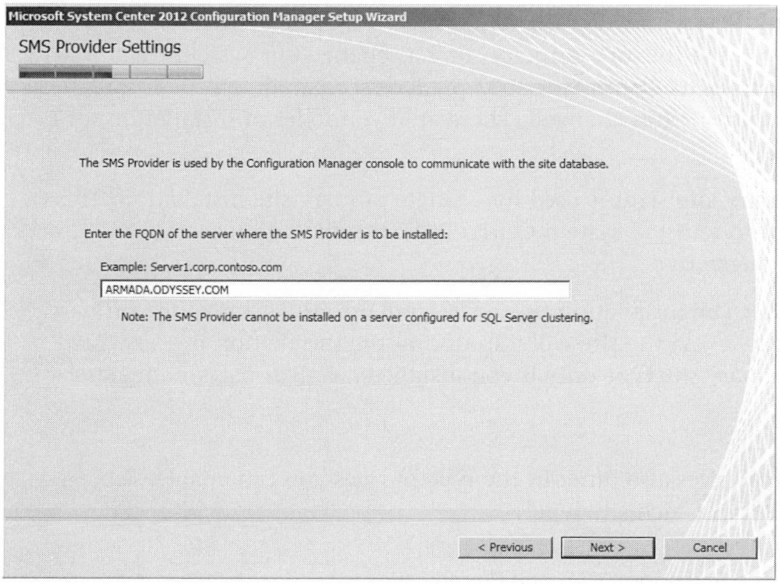

FIGURE 6.12   SMS Provider selection.

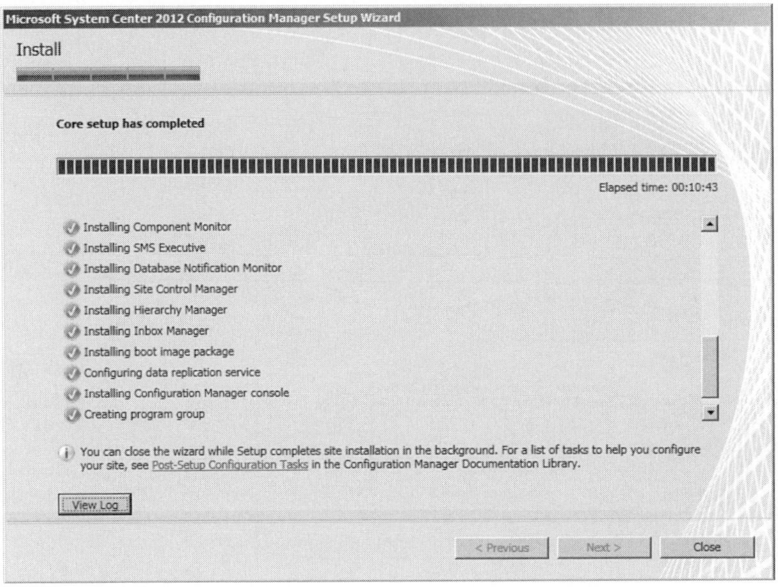

FIGURE 6.13   Installation complete.

Installing Primary Sites

As discussed in Chapter 4, the role of a primary site has changed in System Center 2012 Configuration Manager from its ConfigMgr 2007 predecessor. Similarly, the installation process of the primary site has changed. There are two modes of installation for a primary site:

▶ **Stand-alone primary site:** This is used for a single primary site installation. This mode requires you to reinstall System Center 2012 Configuration Manager if you decide to build a hierarchy.

▶ **Child primary site:** The installation process is similar to the stand-alone primary site, but you specify a CAS the site will join during the installation process. You can install this primary site type only if you installed a CAS as part of a hierarchy deployment.

The two modes of primary sites also differ in the type of roles you can enable. Table 6.4 lists the supported roles for of each site type.

TABLE 6.4   Supported Site Roles for a CAS and Prerequisites

Site Role	Stand-Alone Primary	Child Primary
Application catalog web service point	Yes	Yes
Application catalog website point	Yes	Yes
Asset intelligence synchronization point	Yes	No

Site Role	Stand-Alone Primary	Child Primary
Distribution point	Yes	Yes
Fallback status point	Yes	Yes
Management point	Yes	Yes
Endpoint protection point	Yes	No
Enrollment point	Yes	Yes
Enrollment proxy point	Yes	Yes
Out of band service point	Yes	Yes
Reporting services point	Yes	Yes
Software update point	Yes	Yes
State migration point	Yes	Yes
System health validator point	Yes	Yes

Here is a checklist of activities you must perform before starting the installation of either type of primary site:

1. Install a supported operating system.

2. Install and configure the minimum prerequisites for a primary site.

3. Optionally extend the AD schema and configure the delegation required.

4. Document the site code and site name for the primary site.

5. Optionally run the stand-alone prerequisite checker.

6. Applicable to a child primary only: document the CAS site code and FQDN of the CAS site provider.

TIP: ABOUT PREREQUISITES

The authors recommend installing all the prerequisites for the primary role based on the design of the environment. In scenarios in which all roles are hosted on a single server, installing the prerequisites in advance can reduce errors during additional site role installation.

Using an example in which the minimum requirement for the primary site is the ability to manage clients, perform hardware and software inventory, distribute software, and read default reports, you can find the minimum required roles and their prerequisites listed in Table 6.5. A full list of the requirements for all roles supported by the primary site is at http://technet.microsoft.com/en-us/library/gg682077. aspx#BKMK_SupConfigSiteSystemReq.

TABLE 6.5   Supported Site Roles for Primary Prerequisites

Site Role	Prerequisites - Operating System	Prerequisites - Application Installation
Site server	.NET 3.5 SP 1 Remote Differential Compression	N/A
Distribution point	**Default Web Server (IIS) Configuration and Application Development:** ISAP Extensions **Security:** Windows Authentication **Performance:** Dynamic Content Compression **IIS 6 Management Compatibility:** IIS 6 Metabase Compatibility IIS 6 WMI Compatibility **Features:** Remote Differential Compression BITS Server Extensions (and automatically selected options) Windows Deployment Services (required for PXE or multicast)	N/A
Reporting services point	Required prerequisites for SSRS	SQL Server Reporting Services (SSRS) .NET 4.0 Full Installation
Management point	**Default Web Server (IIS) Configuration and Application Development:** ISAP Extensions **Security:** Windows Authentication **Performance:** Dynamic Content Compression **IIS 6 Management Compatibility:** IIS 6 Metabase Compatibility IIS 6 WMI Compatibility **Features:** Remote Differential Compression BITS Server Extensions (and automatically selected options)	N/A

Site Role	Prerequisites - Operating System	Prerequisites - Application Installation
Software update point	**Default Web Server (IIS) Configuration and Application Development:** ASP.NET (and automatically selected options) **Security:** Windows Authentication **Performance:** Dynamic Content Compression **IIS 6 Management Compatibility:** IIS 6 Metabase Compatibility	Windows Update Services 3.0 SP 2 (Console or Full Installation) .NET 4.0 Full Installation
Database server	Required prerequisites for SQL Server	Supported full version of SQL Server
Site provider	650MB of free disk space for automatic installation of WAIK	N/A
Application catalog web service point	**Default Web Server (IIS) Configuration and Application Development:** ASP.NET (and automatically selected options) **Security:** Windows Authentication **Performance:** Dynamic Content Compression **IIS 6 Management Compatibility:** IIS 6 Metabase Compatibility WCF activation (sub feature of .NET 3.5 SP 1) HTTP Activation Non-HTTP Activation	NET 4.0 Full Installation
Application catalog website point	**Default Web Server (IIS) Configuration and Application Development:** ASP.NET (and automatically selected options) **Security:** Windows Authentication **Common HTTP Features:** Static Content Compression Default document **IIS 6 Management Compatibility:** IIS 6 Metabase Compatibility	NET 4.0 Full Installation

9

Stand-Alone Primary Site

With the prerequisites successfully installed, it is time to install the first primary site type, the stand-alone primary. Perform the following steps:

1. Log on to the server (Athena in this example) with a domain user account with local administration privileges.

2. Start the installation from the System Center 2012 Configuration Manager media splash screen. Double-click splash.hta, and select **Install**.

3. Here are the significant wizard pages you must configure to install a stand-alone primary site:

   ▶ **Getting Started:** Select **Install a Configuration Manager primary site**, as shown in Figure 6.14.

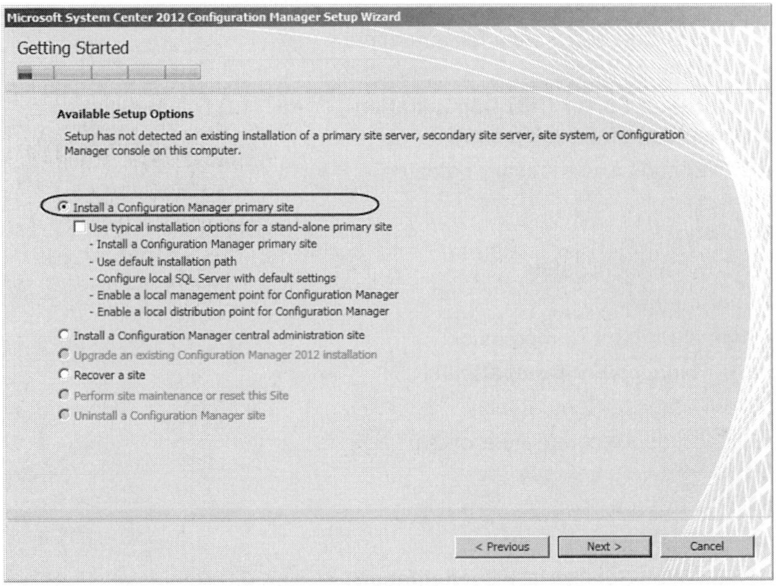

FIGURE 6.14   Getting Started stand-alone primary installation.

   ▶ **Prerequisite Downloads:** You have two options: **Download required files** or **Use previously downloaded files**. You must specify either a UNC file path or local file path to an existing folder.

   ▶ **Server Language Selection:** Select the System Center 2012 Configuration Manager supported languages appropriate for your environment. This setting can be changed post installation.

   ▶ **Client Language Selection:** Select the System Center 2012 Configuration Manager client supported languages appropriate for your environment. This setting can be changed post installation.

▶ **Site and Installation Settings:** Type a unique three-character site code, provide a site name, and specify the installation folder. You cannot change these settings without a reinstallation. Figure 6.15 shows the site settings page.

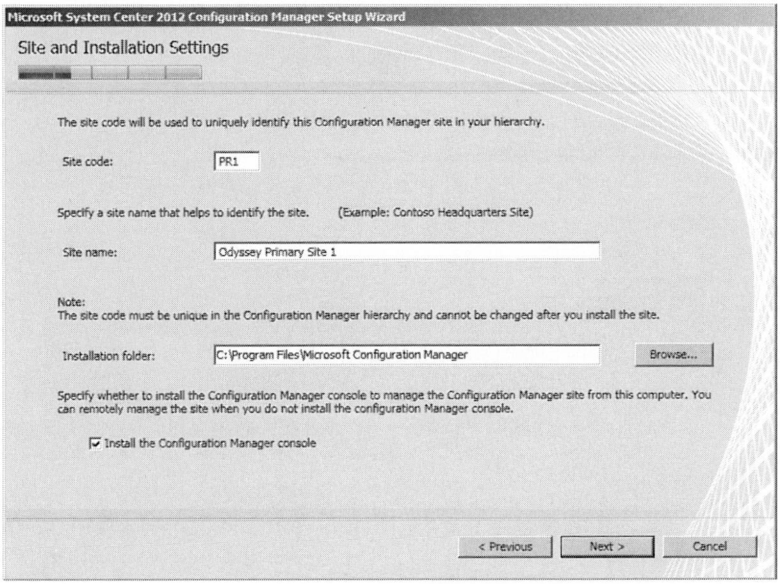

FIGURE 6.15   Stand-alone primary site and installation settings.

▶ **Primary Site Installation:** Select **Install the primary site as a stand-alone site.** Figure 6.16 shows the primary site type installation page. A warning message displays letting you know the primary site cannot be part of a hierarchy without a reinstallation. Click **Yes** to continue.

▶ **Database Information:** Type server name, instance, and database name for the site server hosting the stand-alone primary site database role. Figure 6.17 shows the default selection when the database server is co-located on the site provider server. Also shown is the SQL Server Service Broker port (this is the service used for replication).

▶ **SMS Provider Settings:** Accept or specify the SMS Provider setting and click **Next.**

▶ **Client Computer Communication Settings:** Select whether clients communicate over HTTPS only (requires PKI certificate authentication to be configured to support this setting) or set the communication protocol on each site system. Figure 6.18 shows the second option.

▶ **Site System Roles:** You can install the management point and distribution point roles. Select the required roles and click **Next.** Figure 6.19 shows both optional roles selected.

▶ **Prerequisite Check:** Review and resolve any blocking issues, and click **Begin Install**.

▶ **Complete Installation:** The final wizard page is the completion page. There is a link to the installation log files on this page.

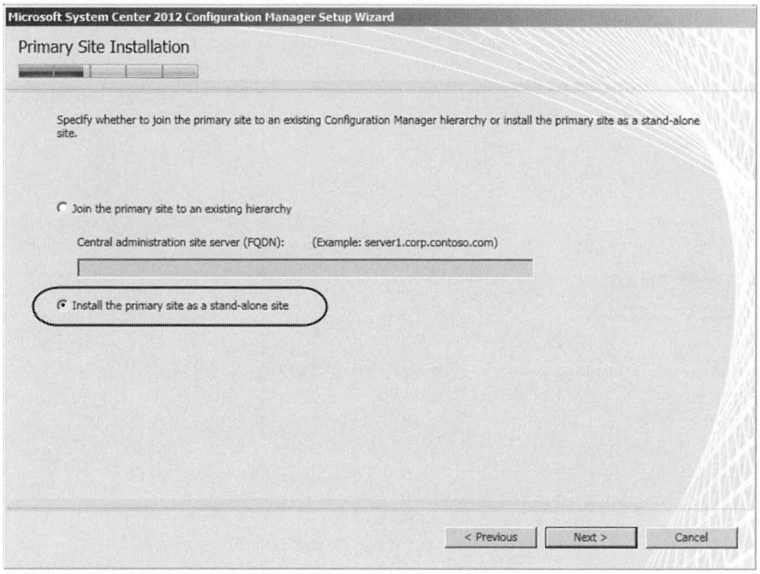

FIGURE 6.16   Stand-alone primary site selection.

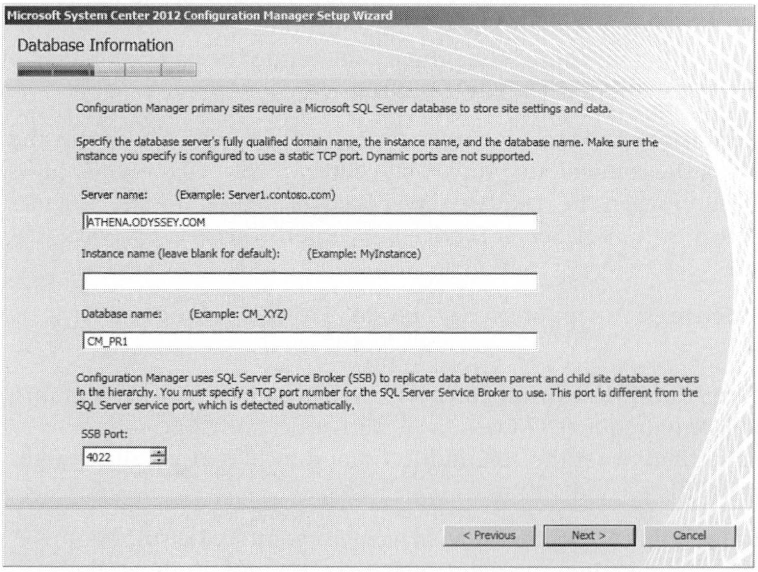

FIGURE 6.17   Stand-alone primary site database information.

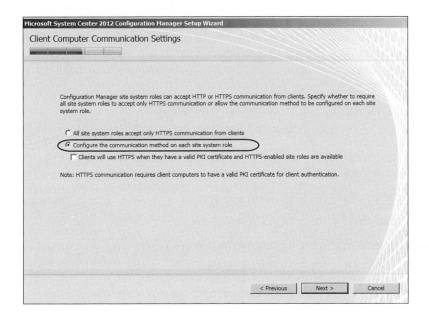

FIGURE 6.18   Primary site client communication protocol.

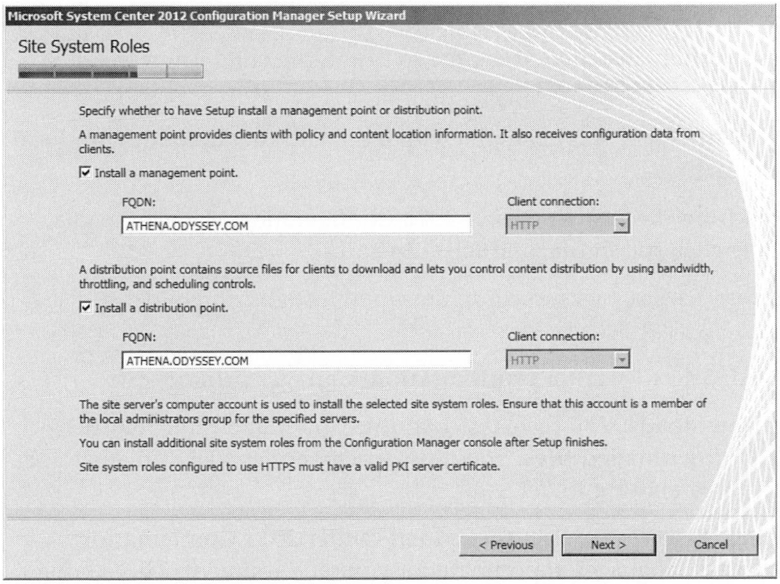

FIGURE 6.19   Primary site available site roles selection.

Child Primary Site

Installing a child primary site requires the same prerequisites and checklist as a stand-alone primary site, plus an additional checklist of activities. Here is the list of additional prerequisite activities you must perform before starting the child primary site installation wizard:

1. Document the CAS site code and FQDN of the CAS site provider.

2. Verify the SQL collation on the child primary assigned database server is the same as the CAS database.

3. The user account running the installation must have the following rights:

   ▶ Local administrator rights on the CAS site server

   ▶ Local administrator rights on the CAS database server

   ▶ Local administrator rights on the primary site server

   ▶ Local administrator rights on the primary site database server

   ▶ User assigned with the Infrastructure Administrator or Full Administrator role on the CAS

4. Document the site code and site name for the primary site.

5. Optionally run the stand-alone prerequisite checker with the **JOIN** option.

With the prerequisites successfully installed, it is time to install the child primary site. Perform the following steps:

1. Log on to the server (Athena in this example) with a domain user account with local administration privileges.

2. Start the installation from the System Center 2012 Configuration Manager media splash screen. Double-click splash.hta, and select **Install**.

3. Here are the significant wizard pages to configure when installing a child primary site:

   ▶ **Getting Started:** Select **Install a Configuration Manager primary site**.

   ▶ **Prerequisite Downloads:** You have two options: **Download required files** or **Use previously downloaded files**. You must specify either a UNC file path or local file path to an existing folder.

   ▶ **Server Language Selection:** Select the System Center 2012 Configuration Manager supported languages appropriate for your environment. This setting can be changed post installation.

   ▶ **Client Language Selection:** Select the System Center 2012 Configuration Manager client supported languages appropriate for your environment. This setting can be changed post installation.

▶ **Site and Installation Settings:** Type a unique three-character site code, provide a site name, and specify the installation folder. You cannot change these settings without a reinstallation.

▶ **Primary Site Installation:** Select **Join the primary site to an existing hierarchy**, and type the FQDN of the target CAS. Figure 6.20 shows the join hierarchy primary site type installation page.

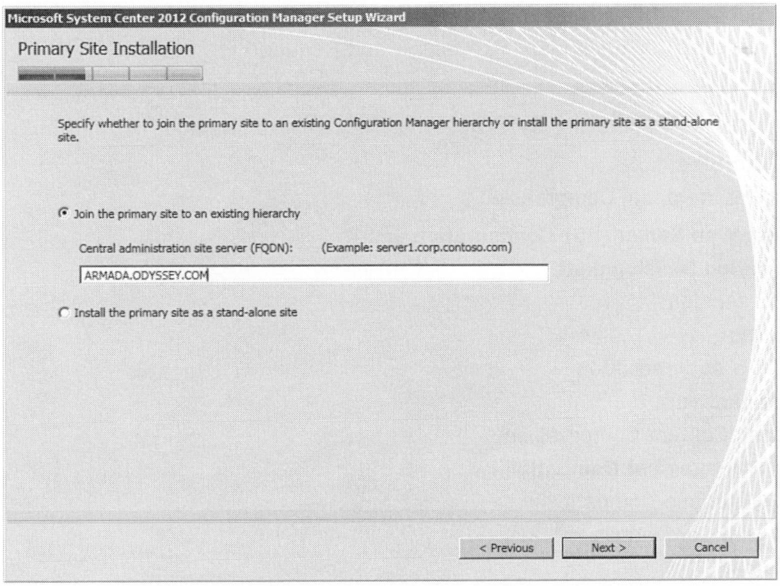

Microsoft System Center 2012 Configuration Manager Setup Wizard

Primary Site Installation

Specify whether to join the primary site to an existing Configuration Manager hierarchy or install the primary site as a stand-alone site.

○ Join the primary site to an existing hierarchy

  Central administration site server (FQDN):   (Example: server1.corp.contoso.com)

  ARMADA.ODYSSEY.COM

○ Install the primary site as a stand-alone site

< Previous   Next >   Cancel

FIGURE 6.20   Child primary site join CAS selection.

▶ **Database Information:** Type server name, instance, and database name for the site server hosting the child primary site database role.

▶ **SMS Provider Settings:** Accept or specify the SMS Provider setting, and click **Next**.

▶ **Client Computer Communication Settings:** Select whether clients communicate over HTTPS only (requires PKI certificate authentication to be configured to support this setting) or set the communication protocol on each site system.

▶ **Site System Roles:** You can install the management point and distribution point roles. Select the required roles, and click **Next**.

▶ **Prerequisite Check:** Review and resolve any blocking issues, and click **Begin Install**.

▶ **Complete Installation:** The final wizard page is the completion page. There is a link to the installation log files on this page.

Installing Secondary Sites

The final site type you can install is a secondary site. Unlike ConfigMgr 2007, System Center 2012 Configuration Manager secondary sites cannot be installed from the installation media. You must connect to a primary site or a central administration site to initiate the installation. A distribution point and a management point are automatically enabled as part of installation of a secondary site.

Table 6.6 lists the prerequisites for a secondary site installation.

TABLE 6.6   Supported Site Roles for Secondary Site Server and Required Prerequisites

Site Role	Prerequisites - Operating System	Prerequisites - Application Installation
Site server	.NET 3.5 SP 1 Remote Differential Compression	N/A
Distribution point	**Default Web Server (IIS) Configuration and Application Development:** ISAP Extensions **Security:** Windows Authentication **Performance:** Dynamic Content Compression **IIS 6 Management Compatibility:** IIS 6 Metabase Compatibility IIS 6 WMI Compatibility **Features:** Remote Differential Compression BITS Server Extensions (and automatically selected options) Windows Deployment Services (required for PXE or multicast)	N/A
Management point	**Default Web Server (IIS) Configuration and Application Development:** ISAP Extensions **Security:** Windows Authentication **Performance:** Dynamic Content Compression **IIS 6 Management Compatibility:** IIS 6 Metabase Compatibility IIS 6 WMI Compatibility **Features:** Remote Differential Compression BITS Server Extensions (and automatically selected options)	N/A

Site Role	Prerequisites - Operating System	Prerequisites - Application Installation
Database server	Required prerequisites for SQL Server	Supported full version of SQL Server
		*SQL Server Express 2008 R2 with SP 1 and CU4
Site Provider	650MB of free disk space for automatic installation of WAIK	N/A

SQL Server Express 2008 R2 with SP 1 and CU 4 are automatically installed if no supported version of SQL Server is installed on the server.

Here is the list of additional prerequisite activities you must perform before starting the Create Secondary Site Wizard:

1. Document the secondary site code and site name.

2. Add the primary site provider server computer account to the local administrators group on the secondary site server.

3. Optionally assign the secondary site provider server computer account security rights to publish to the system management folder when the Active Directory schema has been extended.

4. Here are the rights required for the user account running the installation:

   ▶ Local administrator rights on the secondary site server

   ▶ Local administrator rights on the primary site server

   ▶ Local administrator rights on the primary site database server

   ▶ User assigned with the Infrastructure Administrator or Full Administrator role on the CAS or secondary site parent primary site

5. Install and configure the required prerequisites listed in Table 6.6.

6. Optionally run the stand-alone prerequisite checker with the **SEC** option.

With the prerequisites successfully installed, it is time to install the secondary site. Perform the following steps:

1. Launch the Configuration Manager console, and connect to the secondary site's parent primary site (for a stand-alone primary) or the CAS.

2. Connect to the System Center 2012 Configuration Manager console and navigate to **Administration -> Site Configuration -> Sites** and select the parent primary site in the middle pane; then select **Create Secondary Site** from the ribbon bar, as shown in Figure 6.21.

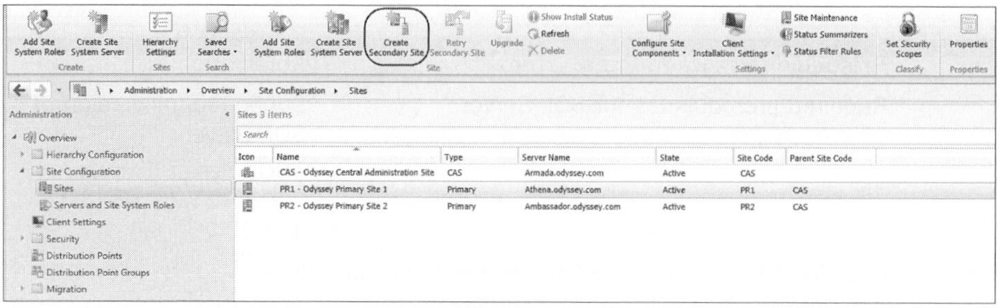

FIGURE 6.21   Create Secondary Site Wizard.

3. Here are the significant wizard pages you must configure to create a secondary site:

▶ **General:** Type a unique three-character site code, the fully qualified domain name, a site name, and specify the installation folder for the secondary site. You cannot change these settings without a reinstallation. Figure 6.22 shows the general page with configuration details for the secondary site in the Odyssey lab. Click **Next** to continue.

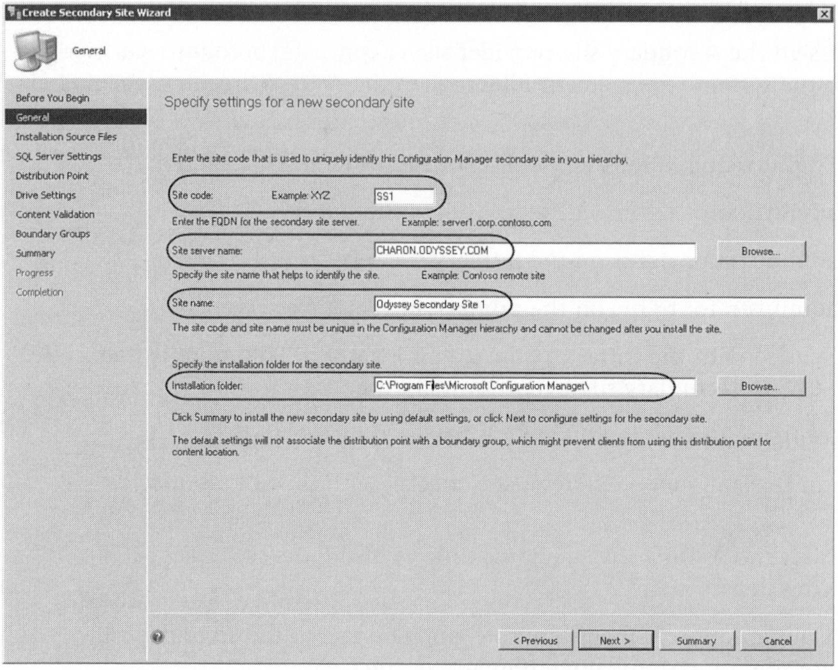

FIGURE 6.22   General page of the Secondary Site Wizard.

▶ **Installation Source Files:** You have three options:

Copy installation files over the network from the parent site server

Use the source files at the following location

Use the source files at the following location on the secondary site server (most secure)

The default option shown in Figure 6.23 is to copy the source files from the parent site. Accept the default or provide details for an alternative choice, and click **Next** to continue.

▶ **SQL Server Settings:** Accept the default option to install SQL Server Express using the default ports, as shown in Figure 6.24, or provide the details for a full supported SQL Server instance for the secondary site.

▶ **Distribution Point:** Review the distribution point options on this page. The authors recommend selecting the option to install IIS if required, as shown in Figure 6.25.

▶ **Drive Settings:** You have two configurable options: Drive space reserve and content placement options. Specify the minimum space to reserve on the distribution point drive(s). In addition, you can select the logical drives to use and a secondary location. The default, as shown in Figure 6.26, is to allow automatic configuration where the drive with the most free space is selected.

▶ **Content Validation:** Specify content validation configuration. The default settings, shown in Figure 6.27 are set to not validate. You can enable content validation on a schedule, and specify the priority for the content validation process.

▶ **Boundary Group:** Select or create boundary groups you want to assign to the distribution point of the secondary site and whether clients outside the assigned boundary groups can use the DP as a fallback.

▶ **Complete Installation:** The final wizard page is the completion page. This page completes the wizard and shows success if you have completed all mandatory sections. The installation process is not complete; the wizard gathers your secondary site installation properties and initiates the installation process. You must monitor the state and status of the installation by selecting the secondary site in the console and selecting **Show Install Status**, as shown in Figure 6.28. Use the status window to track the installation of the secondary site.

NOTE: INSTALLATION SOURCE FILES

The option to use the source files from another location or a location on the secondary site server requires you to copy the full System Center 2012 installation media. The default option to copy the files from the parent site automatically compresses the media and performs a copy of the compressed files to the secondary site server. You may want to copy from the parent if the secondary site location has a local copy of the media and thereby reduce network impact during the secondary site installation.

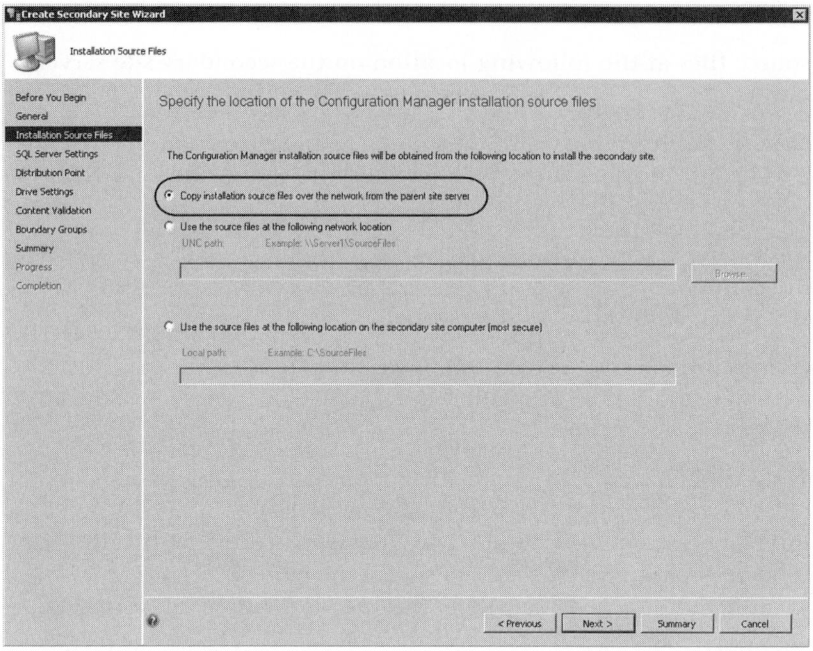

FIGURE 6.23 Installation Source Files.

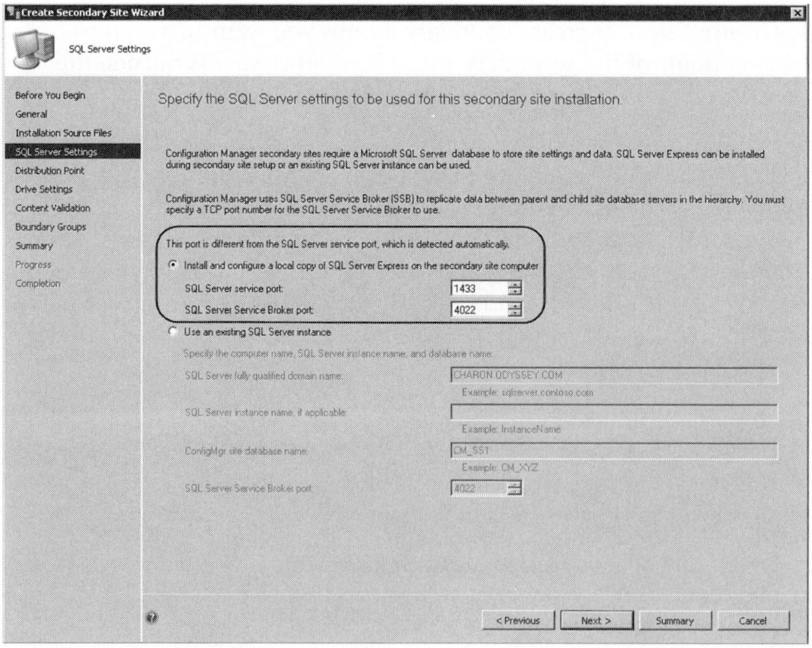

FIGURE 6.24 SQL Server Settings.

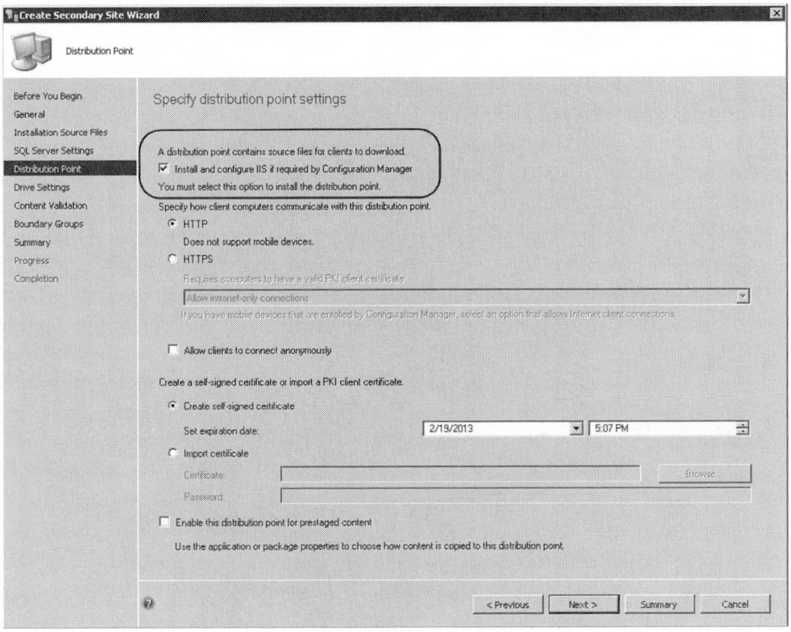

FIGURE 6.25   Distribution point settings.

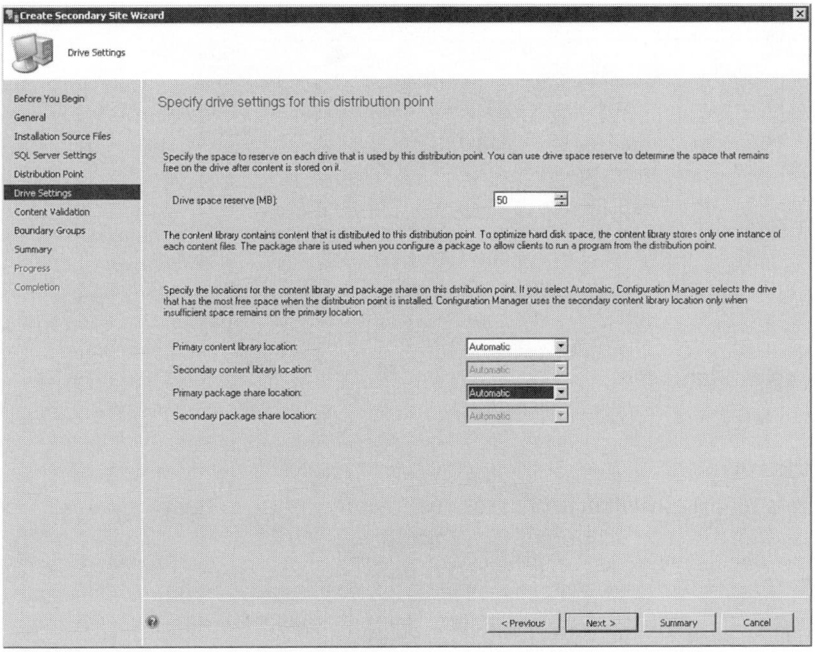

FIGURE 6.26   Content drive settings.

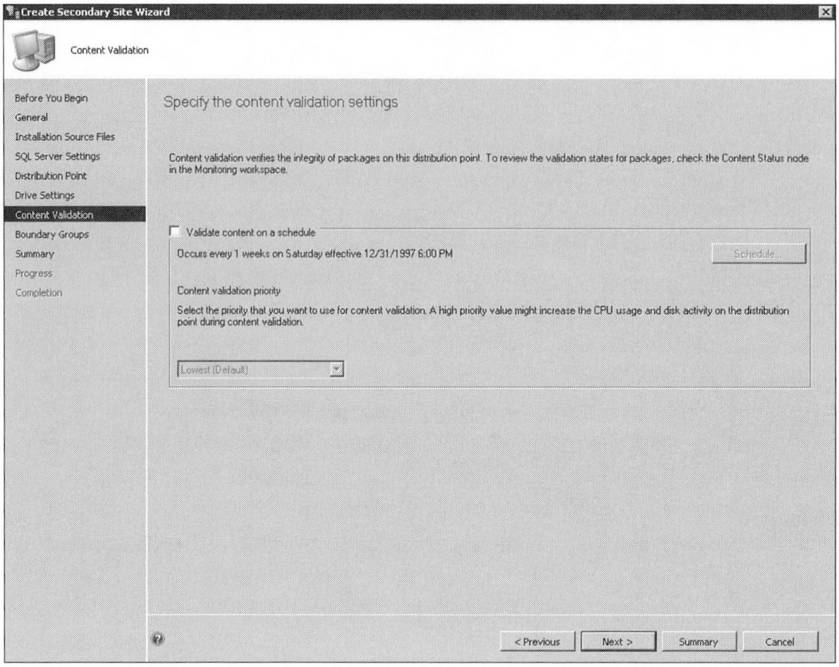

FIGURE 6.27   Content Validation.

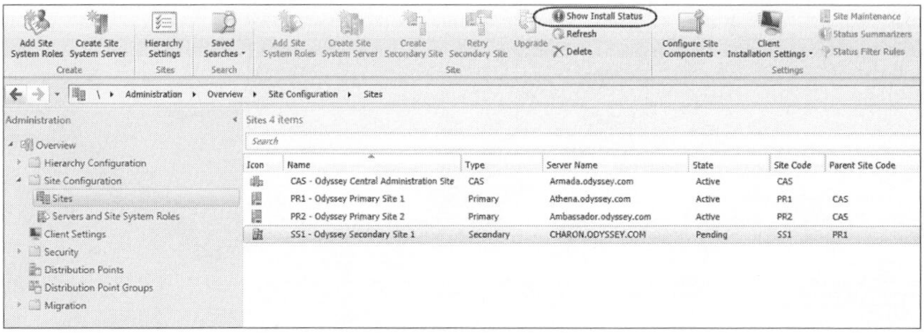

FIGURE 6.28   Show Install Status.

Installation Validation

The installation wizards report either success or failure. You must also validate reported success status, discussed in the next sections.

Console

You can validate the successful installation of a System Center 2012 Configuration Manager site, using the System Center 2012 Configuration Manager console. Two nodes can be used to validate the status of the site and components selected during the installation of the System Center 2012 Configuration Manager site:

- Site Status
- Component Status

These status nodes are located in the Monitoring workspace; **Monitoring** -> **System Status** -> **Site Status** and **Monitoring** -> **System Status** -> **Site Component Status**. The two status nodes are illustrated in Figures 6.29 and 6.30.

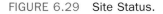

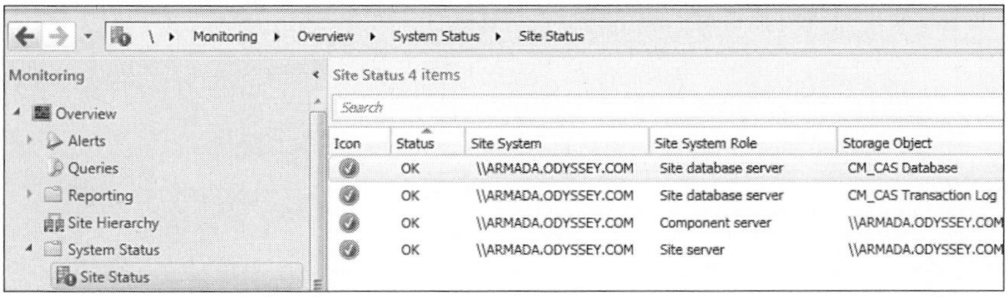
Monitoring ▸ Overview ▸ System Status ▸ Site Status
Monitoring
Overview
Alerts
Queries
Reporting
Site Hierarchy
System Status
Site Status
Site Status 4 items
Search
Icon
Status
Site System
Site System Role
Storage Object
OK
\\ARMADA.ODYSSEY.COM
Site database server
CM_CAS Database
OK
\\ARMADA.ODYSSEY.COM
Site database server
CM_CAS Transaction Log
OK
\\ARMADA.ODYSSEY.COM
Component server
\\ARMADA.ODYSSEY.COM
OK
\\ARMADA.ODYSSEY.COM
Site server
\\ARMADA.ODYSSEY.COM

FIGURE 6.29 Site Status.

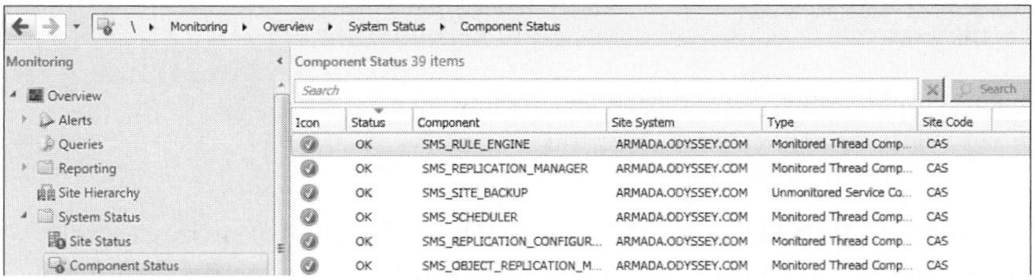
Monitoring ▸ Overview ▸ System Status ▸ Component Status
Monitoring
Overview
Alerts
Queries
Reporting
Site Hierarchy
System Status
Site Status
Component Status
Component Status 39 items
Search
Icon
Status
Component
Site System
Type
Site Code
OK
SMS_RULE_ENGINE
ARMADA.ODYSSEY.COM
Monitored Thread Comp...
CAS
OK
SMS_REPLICATION_MANAGER
ARMADA.ODYSSEY.COM
Monitored Thread Comp...
CAS
OK
SMS_SITE_BACKUP
ARMADA.ODYSSEY.COM
Unmonitored Service Co...
CAS
OK
SMS_SCHEDULER
ARMADA.ODYSSEY.COM
Monitored Thread Comp...
CAS
OK
SMS_REPLICATION_CONFIGUR...
ARMADA.ODYSSEY.COM
Monitored Thread Comp...
CAS
OK
SMS_OBJECT_REPLICATION_M...
ARMADA.ODYSSEY.COM
Monitored Thread Comp...
CAS

FIGURE 6.30 Site Component Status.

A healthy functioning site shows a status of **OK** for all configured and active components for the site. Review warnings and errors in the status nodes and resolve them before making the site available for use.

TIP: INVOKING CONFIGURATION MANAGER SERVICE MANAGER

ConfigMgr 2007 includes a tool to manage the individual component services of a site; this tool is still in System Center 2012 Configuration Manager and used for the same purpose. The tool is somewhat hidden and is invoked by right-clicking a component in **Site Status Components** -> **Start** -> **Configuration Manager Service Manager** (see Figure 6.31). The tool illustrated in Figure 6.32 is where you stop and start individual components of the System Center 2012 Configuration Manager site.

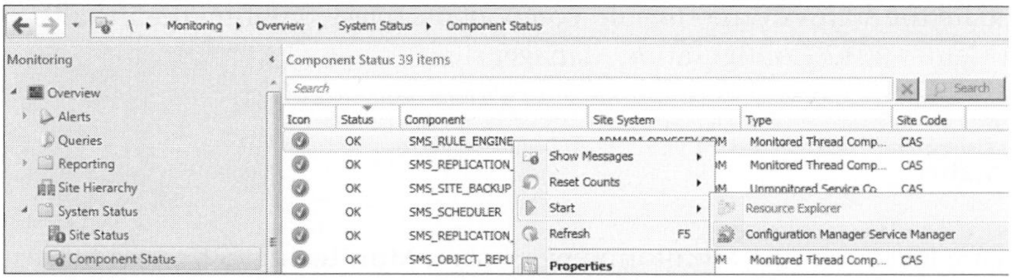

FIGURE 6.31   Start Configuration Manager Service Manager.

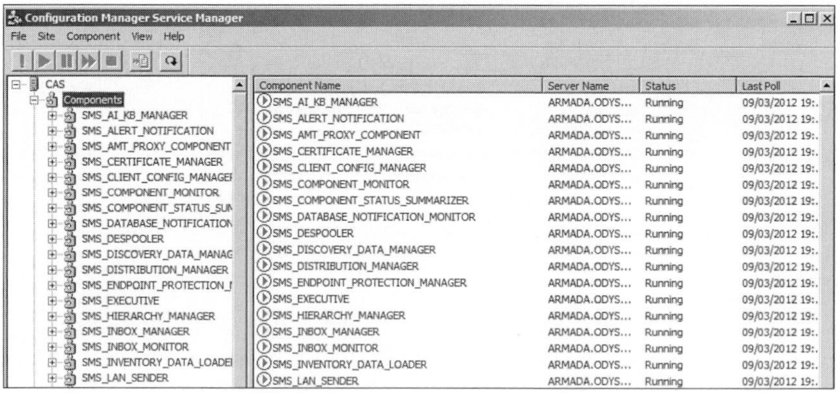

FIGURE 6.32   Configuration Manager Service Manager tool.

Log Files

System Center 2012 Configuration Manager provides extensive logging of processes and installation. The full list of System Center 2012 Configuration Manager log files is found in Appendix A.

The installation log files also provide a detailed look at the installation steps performed by the installation process.

Site Properties

The "Pre-Installation" and "Site Installation" sections discussed preparation and installation of the supported site types in System Center 2012 Configuration Manager. The rest of this chapter discusses the basic configuration you must perform before managing clients.

Initial Configuration

After you successfully install your Configuration Manager site, the authors recommend performing some initial configurations. The customizations discussed in the following sections focus on ensuring you can provide the following basic functionality:

▶ Reporting functionality

▶ Prepare System Center 2012 Configuration Manager for client management

Reporting Functionality

As the saying goes: *You can't manage what you don't measure.* System Center 2012 Configuration Manager's reporting capabilities provide the means to see and measure the various features and functionality of the product. The reporting role is an optional installation and highly recommended. The reporting role is typically installed and enabled on a CAS for the hierarchy implementation and on the primary site for a stand-alone implementation. For installation and a detailed discussion on the reporting functionality, see Chapter 18, "Reporting."

Prepare System Center 2012 Configuration Manager for Client Management

The basic client management functionality of a System Center 2012 Configuration Manager implementation requires you to configure and enable core infrastructure settings after installation.

The previous version of the product, ConfigMgr 2007, uses boundaries as the scope of management. All systems within the boundaries of a specific site can potentially be managed by that site. Boundaries in ConfigMgr 2007 serve two functions: client assignment to the site and content location for features such as software distribution and software updates management. These two functions cannot be separated in a ConfigMgr 2007 implementation, and overlaps with other sites in the hierarchy produce undesired client behavior and administrative nightmares.

System Center 2012 Configuration Manager simplifies the creation of boundaries and separates the two functions associated with boundaries. Separation of boundaries is implemented using boundary groups. Boundary groups, discussed in the "Configuring Boundary Groups" section, have a dependency on your creating standard boundaries. The manual steps to create a boundary are similar to the ConfigMgr 2007 process. The automated boundary creation method is new to System Center 2012 Configuration Manager and is a function of Active Directory Forest Discovery.

Active Directory Forest Discovery

Active Directory Forest Discovery is a new discovery method introduced in System Center 2012 Configuration Manager. Chapter 9, "Configuration Manager Client Management," discusses discovery methods in depth. This section discusses the use of Active Directory Forest Discovery in relation to site boundary creation. Figure 6.33 shows the properties of the Active Directory Forest Discovery for the hierarchy (this discovery method is configurable at all primary sites). You must enable this discovery method and select one or both automatic boundary creation methods if you want AD sites and subnets in your environment created as site boundaries in System Center 2012 Configuration Manager. The boundaries automatically created in the Odyssey forest are shown in Figure 6.34. (Note that all subnets are automatically converted to IP range boundaries.)

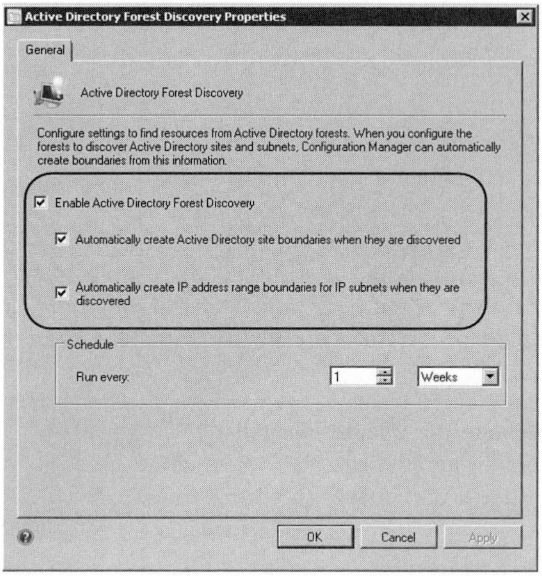

FIGURE 6.33   Active Directory Forest Discovery.

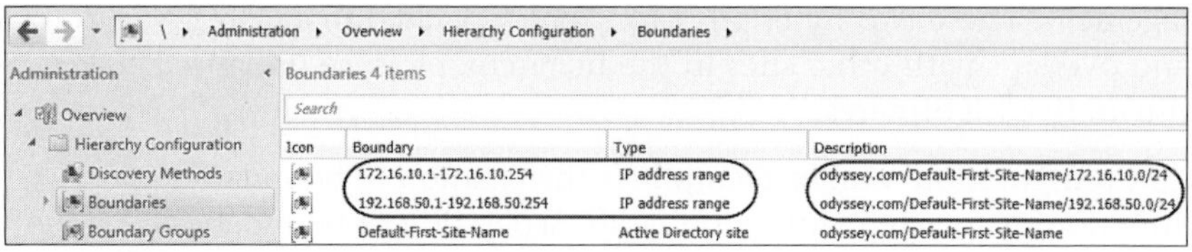

FIGURE 6.34   Detected boundaries.

Configuring Boundary Groups

In System Center 2012 Configuration Manager, boundaries—whether manually created or automatically created by Active Directory Forest Discovery—are not in use until you create a boundary group.

The authors recommend you create a boundary group for site assignments before deploying System Center 2012 Configuration Manager agents. Optionally, create a boundary group for content required by clients.

Follow these steps to create a boundary group for site assignment:

1. In the console, navigate to **Administration -> Hierarchy Configuration -> Boundary Groups**, and select **Create Boundary Group** from the ribbon bar, as shown in Figure 6.35.

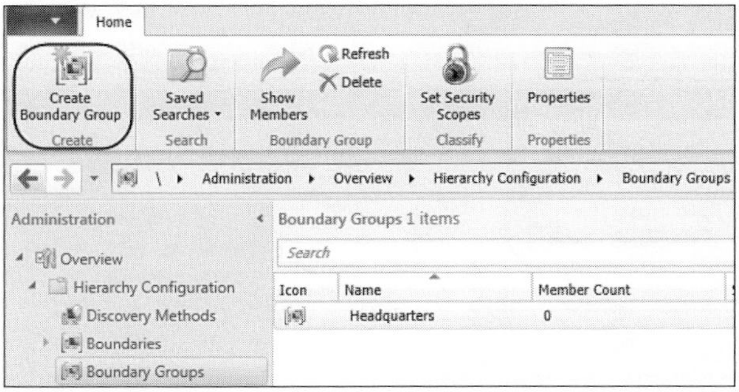

FIGURE 6.35   Create Boundary Group.

2. In the General section, type a name and description for the boundary group. Click **Add** in the Boundaries section, and select the relevant boundary/boundaries. Figure 6.36 shows an example.

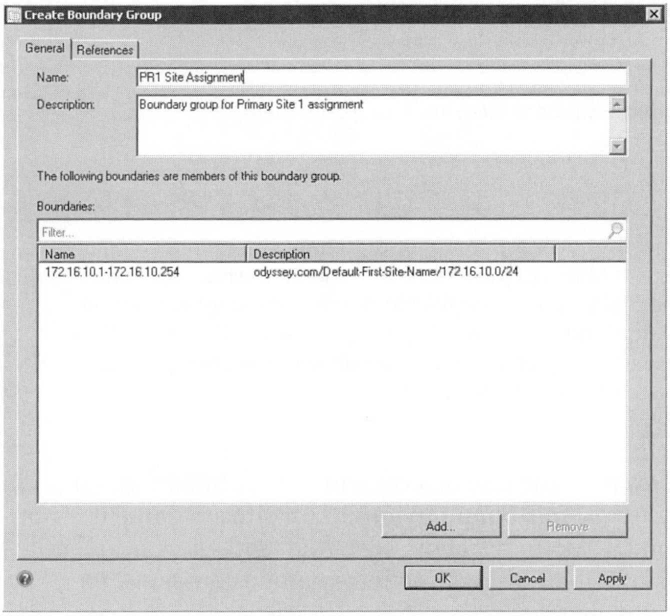

FIGURE 6.36   Create Boundary Group General tab.

3. To configure the boundary group type and association with a site, configure the properties under the References tab:

► **Site Assignment Boundary Group:** Select **Use this boundary group for site assignment**, and select the site associated with the boundary group, as illustrated in Figure 6.37.

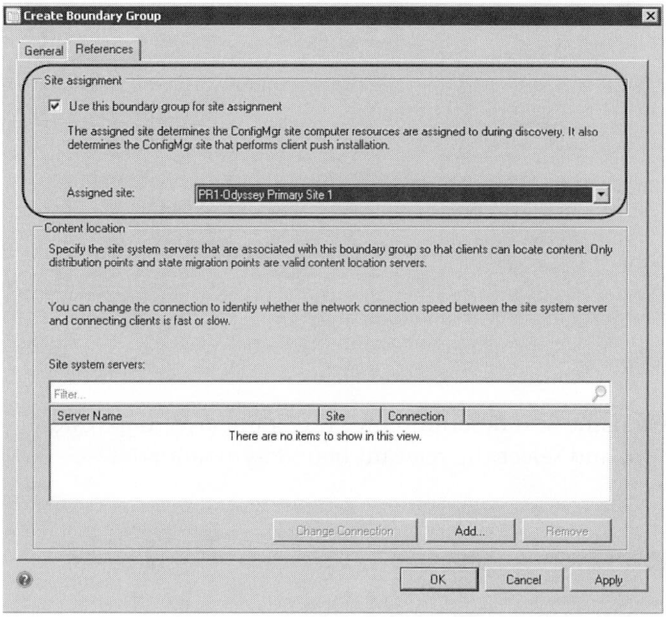

FIGURE 6.37   Create Boundary Group References tab for site assignment.

NOTE: SITE ASSIGNMENT BOUNDARY GROUPS

You must configure a site assignment boundary group for a primary site before you install a System Center 2012 Configuration Manager client in the scenario in which only one primary site is installed in the hierarchy or in a standalone primary site implementation. Client deployment will not complete if the site to which you try to assign the client does not have a site assignment boundary group configured or a fallback site configured for hierarchy implementations with more than one primary site.

▶ **Content Boundary Group:** In the case of a content-only boundary group configuration, make sure **Use this boundary group for site assignment** is not selected. Under the content location section, click **Add**, and select a content role site system(s). Figure 6.38 illustrates a boundary group configured for content only.

TIP: SEPARATE BOUNDARY GROUPS

You can combine site assignment and content location into a single boundary group; however, you lose the flexibility and improved separation introduced in System Center 2012 Configuration Manager. In addition, site assignment boundary groups cannot have overlapping boundaries, whereas content boundary groups support overlapping boundaries. The authors' recommendation is to plan for and implement boundary groups for site assignment and to create separate boundary groups for content location only.

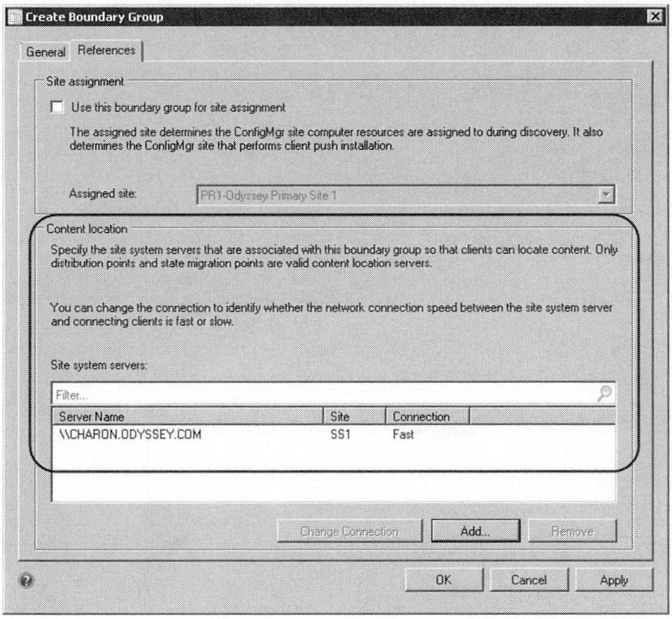

FIGURE 6.38   Create Boundary Group References tab for content.

Installing Optional Site Systems

This section discusses site system installation and uses the fallback status point and the out of band service point as examples of site roles you can install for your System Center 2012 Configuration Manager primary site or hierarchy.

Fallback Status Point

The fallback status point is the System Center 2012 Configuration Manager clients' emergency system. The FSP is typically used during client installation and during post installation when clients cannot communicate with their management points. You must assign a client a fallback status point during the client installation; so plan to install a fallback status point role before you deploy clients. To install and enable a fallback status point for a System Center 2012 Configuration Manager site, follow these steps:

1. In the console, navigate to **Administration -> Site Configuration -> Sites**. Select the System Center 2012 Configuration Manager site system you want to enable the FSP on in the middle pane. Select **Add Site System Roles** from the ribbon bar, as shown in Figure 6.39.

2. On the General page, as displayed in Figure 6.40, configure the options shown, and click **Next** to proceed to the role selection page:

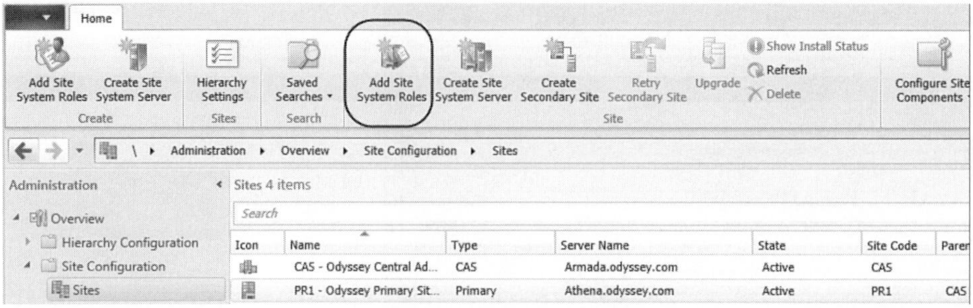

FIGURE 6.39   Add Site System Roles.

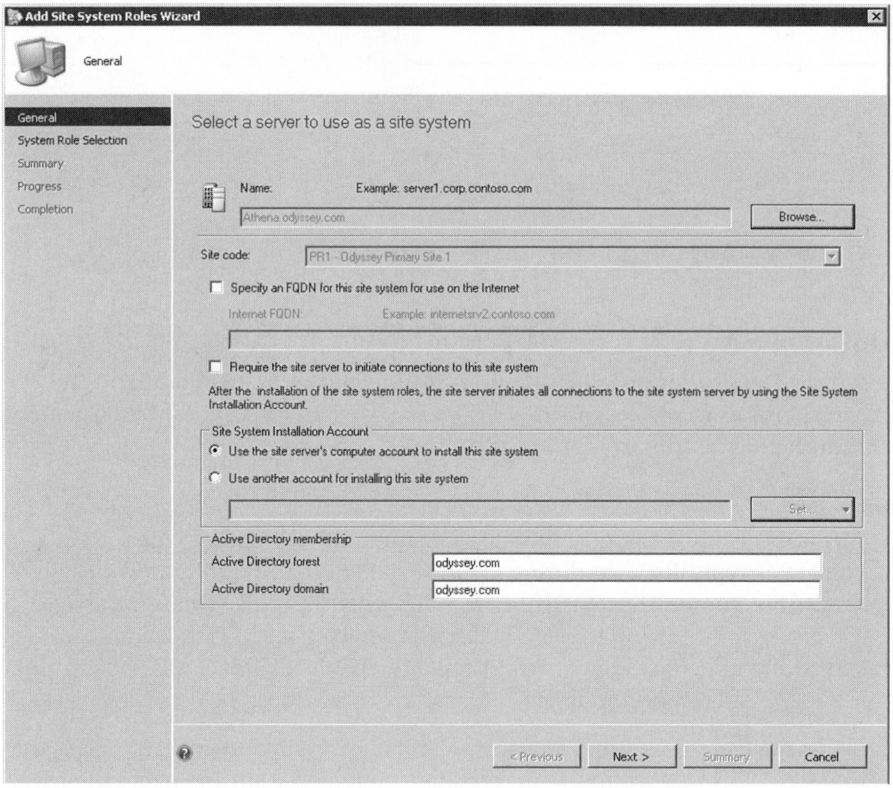

FIGURE 6.40   Add Site Roles Wizard General page.

▶ **Name:** This option is preselected. (You must specify a fully qualified domain name if you initiate the role creation by selecting the Add Site system Option.)

▶ **Site Code:** The site on which you will be enabling the role.

▶ **Specify an FQDN for this site system for use on the Internet:** FQDN in the case where a supported site system role will be accessed from the Internet.

> ► **Require the site server to initiate connections to this site system:** A security option where communication is controlled and initiated by the site provider.

> ► **Site system installation account:** Use the site system computer account to install the role or specify a domain user account.

3. Select the **Fallback status point** on the role selection, as shown in Figure 6.41, and click **Next**.

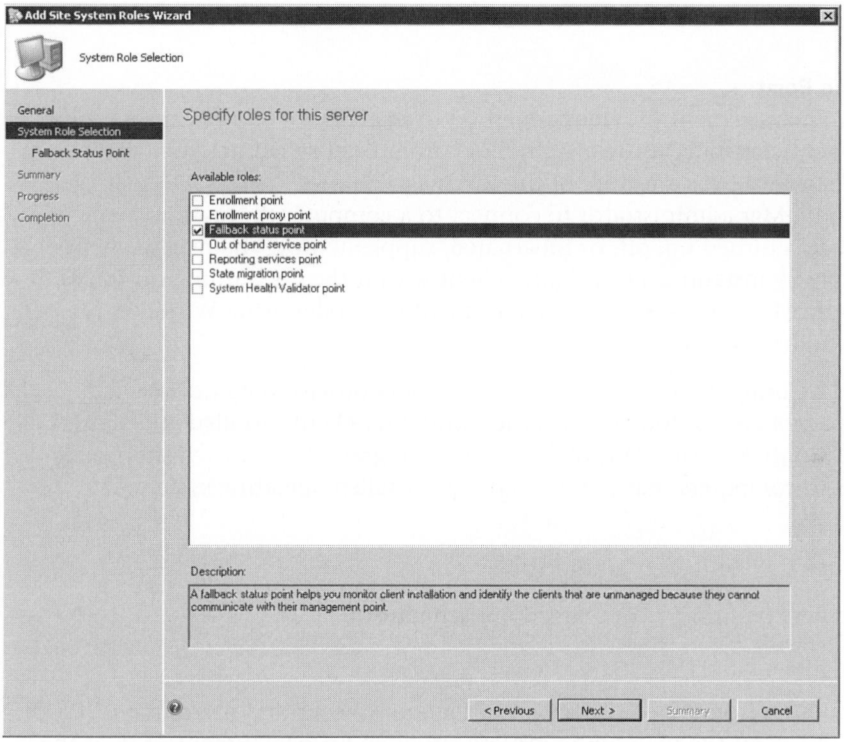

FIGURE 6.41   Role selection page.

4. The next page shows the fallback status point specific settings. Accept the default configuration, or edit the Number of state messages and throttle interval in seconds. (The defaults are 10000 and 3600, respectively.)

5. On the Summary page, review the settings, and click **Next** to proceed with role installation.

6. Review the FSPMSI.log file for the installation status.

TIP: FALLBACK STATUS POINT LOCATION AND CLIENT INSTALLATION

The fallback status point is the site role clients send messages to if communication to their assigned management point fails. Plan to install the fallback status point role on a separate site server from the management point. In addition, specify the FSP property in the client installation options of the site. If a fallback status point is installed, the client push installation method automatically assigns a fallback status point to a client during installation. Other installation methods require you to specify the FSP property, although this is not required if it is already specified in the client installation properties and the AD schema is extended.

Out of Band Service Point

Out of band (OOB) management provides a method to manage a computer through its onboard management controller using a technology from Intel called Active Management Technology (AMT), available as a feature of the Intel vPro chipset. Using OOB management enables a ConfigMgr administrator to connect to a computer through its management controller that is turned on, off, or hibernated, supplementing the management capabilities available by installing a ConfigMgr client within the OS running on top of the computer. ConfigMgr connects to the management controller using Windows remote management technology (WS-MAN).

System Center 2012 Configuration Manager supports OOB provisioning only on a computer that is part of an AD domain with the ConfigMgr client installed and successfully assigned to a ConfigMgr site. This differs from ConfigMgr 2007, which supported provisioning OOB to computers that did not have an installed operating system or ConfigMgr client.

With OOB configured, a ConfigMgr administrator can

- ▶ Power computers on or off either directly or scheduled.

- ▶ Restart computers.

- ▶ Boot the computer from a boot image using Preboot eXecution Environment (PXE) or from a location on the network to initiate either an OS deployment or boot the machine in an OS for troubleshooting purposes by using IDE redirection.

- ▶ Reconfigure the BIOS of a computer, using Serial over LAN functionality providing a terminal emulation session to the managed computer.

Chapter 4 discusses the infrastructure dependencies for OOB management, and Chapter 20, "Security and Delegation in Configuration Manager," provides detailed information on the security considerations including the public key infrastructure (PKI) requirements. You must enable two roles to support OOB management in System Center 2012 Configuration Manager.

Here are the two site roles to enable and the significant wizard pages to configure:

1. In the console, navigate to **Administration** -> **Site Configuration** -> **Sites**. Select the site system you want to enable the role on in the middle pane. Select **Add Site System Roles** from the ribbon bar.

2. On the System Role Selection, select the following for the respective role:

   ▶ **Enrollment point:** The options you must select are the enrollment point role, website name, port number, and virtual application name. Figures 6.42 and 6.43 show the default selections.

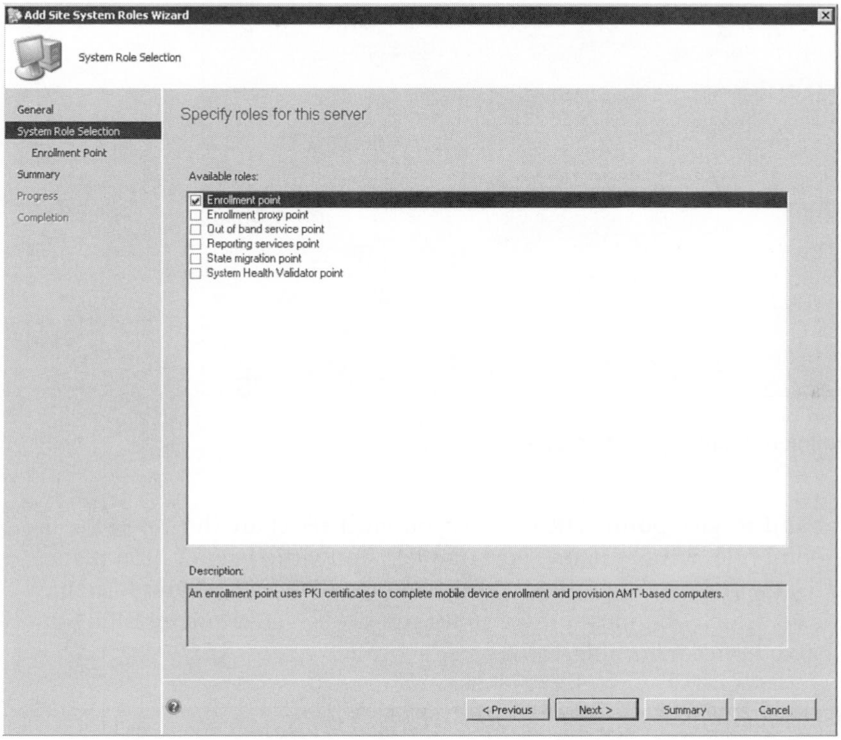

FIGURE 6.42   Enrollment point selection.

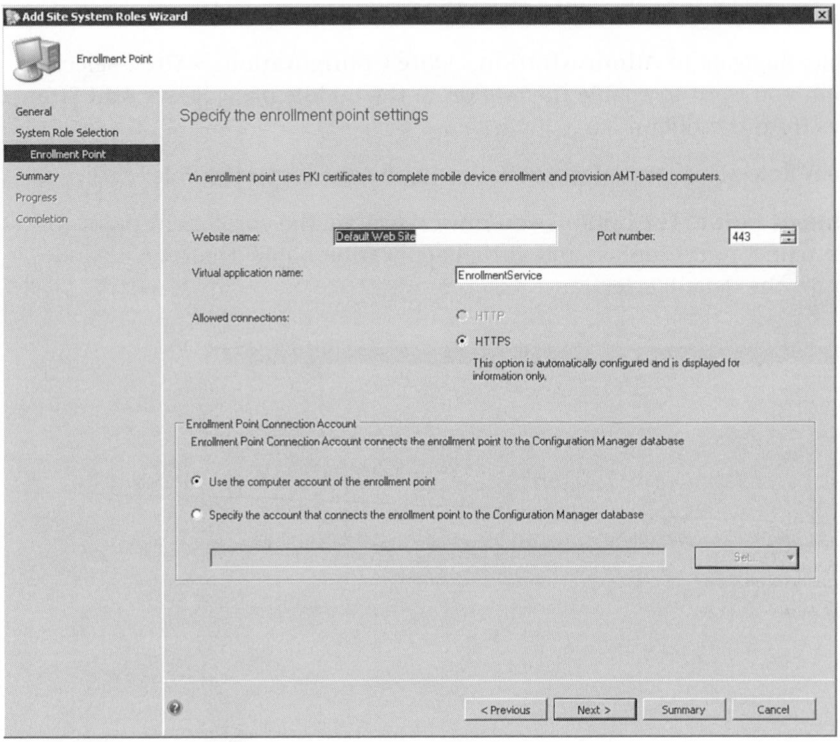

FIGURE 6.43   Enrollment point installation configuration.

▶ **Out of band service point:** The options you must select are the out of band service point role, website name, port number, and virtual application name. Figures 6.44 and 6.45 show default selections. Figure 6.46 illustrates selecting a certificate, which you must provision for the site server before installing the out of band service point role.

NOTE: OUT OF BAND SERVICE POINT CERTIFICATE

You must provision the certificate required for the out of band service point role before starting the role installation. Refer to Chapter 20 for information on provisioning the required certificate.

The site roles enabled form a subset of all the roles you can enable or configure on one or more site servers. The location of the roles and the specific settings depend on your planning and design, as discussed in Chapter 4.

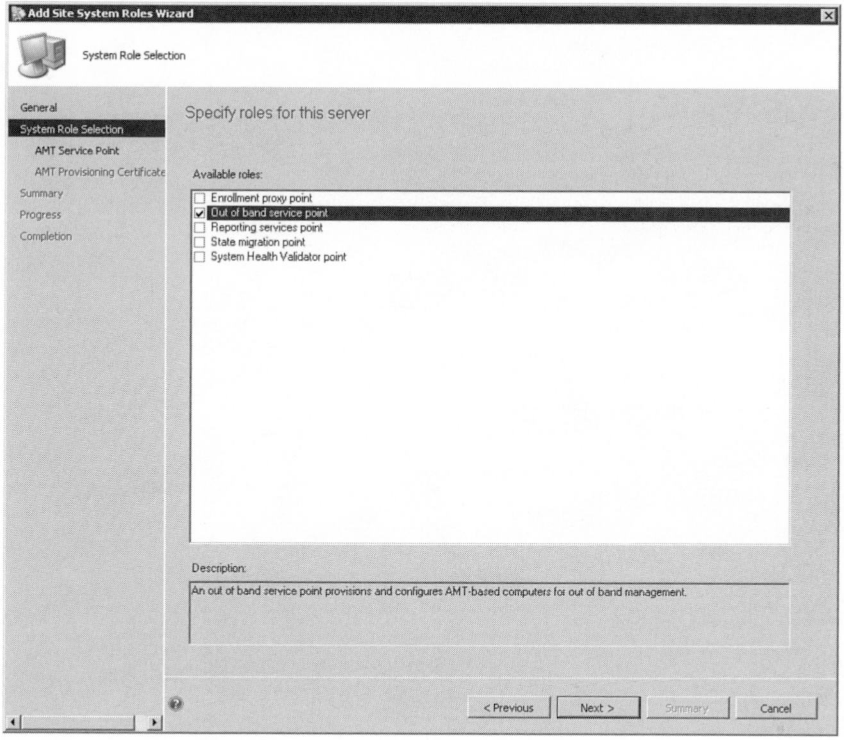

FIGURE 6.44   Out of band service point selection.

Fallback Site

New to System Center 2012 Configuration Manager is the fallback site role. This option is specific to hierarchies only. Clients that do not fall within a site assignment boundary group are assigned to the fallback site if one is configured for the hierarchy.

Perform the following steps to enable a primary site in a hierarchy as a fallback site:

1. In the console, navigate to **Administration -> Site Configuration -> Sites**. In the middle pane, select the site you want to enable as a fallback site. Select **Hierarchy Settings** from the ribbon bar, as shown in Figure 6.47.

2. Check the option to **Use a fallback site**, displayed in Figure 6.48, select a primary site from the hierarchy, and click **OK** to complete the configuration.

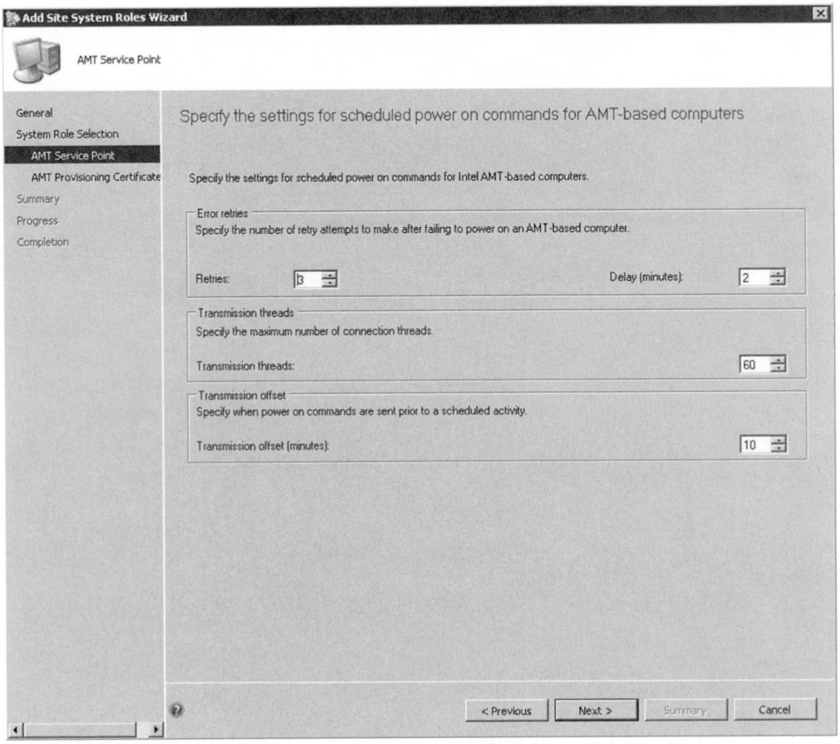

FIGURE 6.45   Out of band service point installation power on settings.

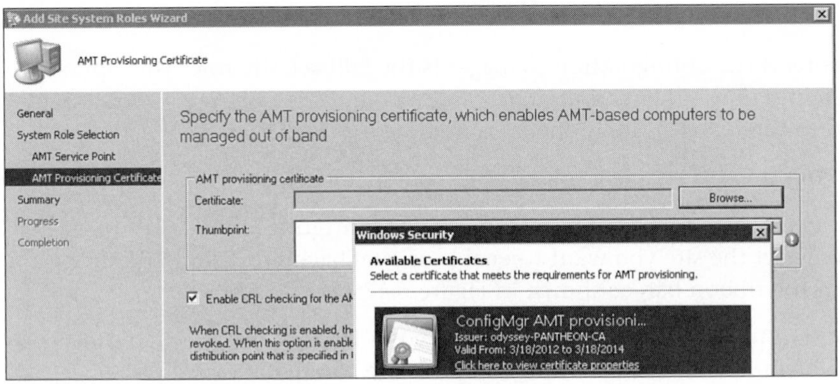

FIGURE 6.46   Out of band service point certificate selection.

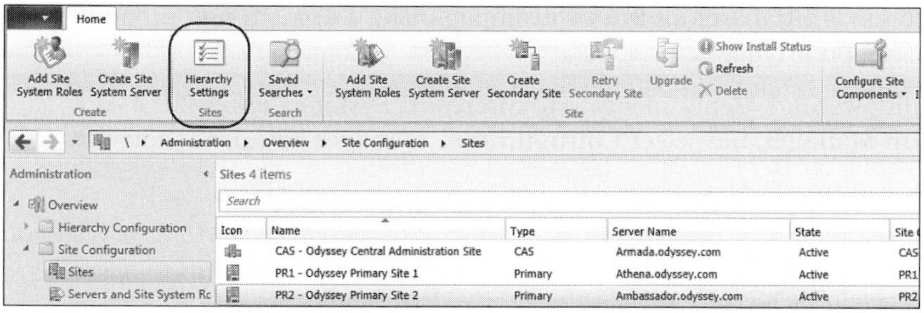

FIGURE 6.47   Hierarchy Settings.

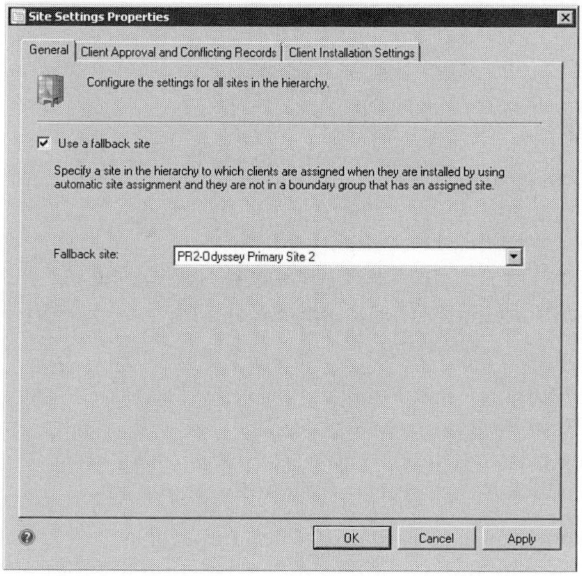

FIGURE 6.48   Enable fallback site.

Chapter 9 discusses client installation in detail.

Uninstalling Sites

System Center 2012 Configuration Manager has a supported uninstallation process. The next sections discuss uninstalling primary sites, secondary sites, and a full hierarchy with a CAS.

Uninstalling Primary Sites

The process used to uninstall a hierarchy joined or stand-alone primary site is the same. Follow these steps to complete the uninstallation of a primary site:

1. Log on to the server (Ambassador in this example) using a domain user account with local administration privileges.

2. From the Windows Start Menu, navigate to **Microsoft System Center 2012 -> Configuration Manager** and select **Configuration Manager Setup**, as shown in Figure 6.49.

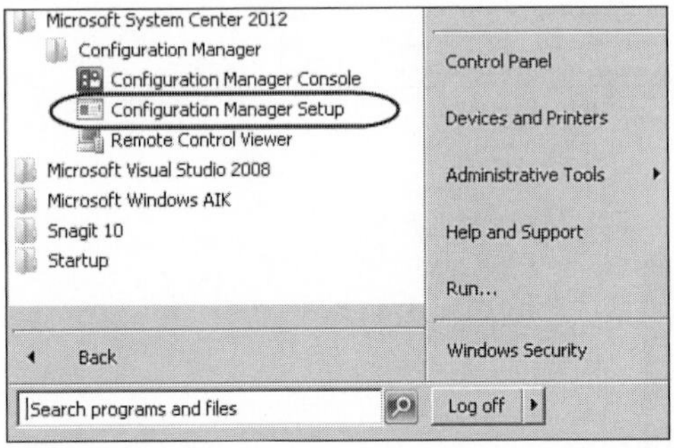

FIGURE 6.49   Initiate setup for uninstallation.

3. Here are the significant wizard pages to uninstall a primary site:

   ▶ **Getting Started:** Select **Uninstall a Configuration Manager site,** as shown in Figure 6.50.

   ▶ **Uninstall the Configuration Manager site:** You can choose to keep the primary site database or the ConfigMgr console, or both. The default, as shown in Figure 6.51, is to remove the primary site database and the console. Make your selection and click **Next**. Click **Yes** to confirm the uninstallation action.

   ▶ **Core setup has completed:** The final page is the Completion page, as displayed in Figure 6.52. The page includes a link to the installation log files.

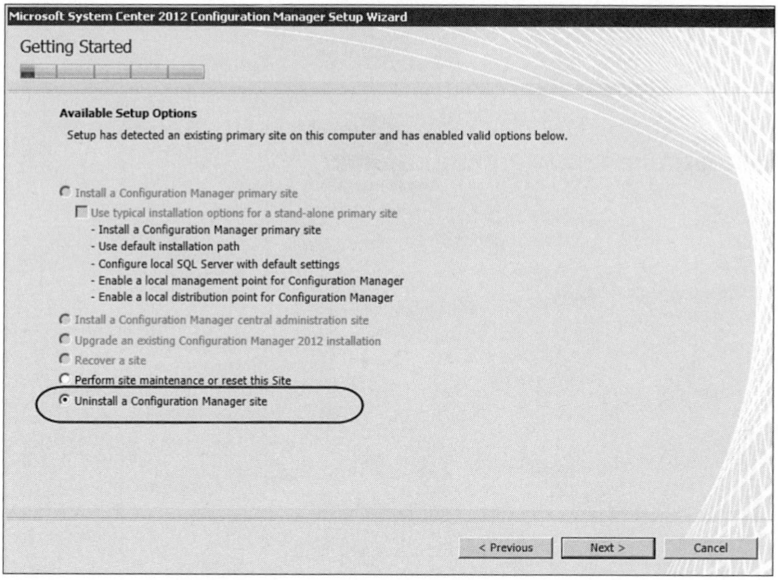

FIGURE 6.50   Uninstall a Configuration Manager site.

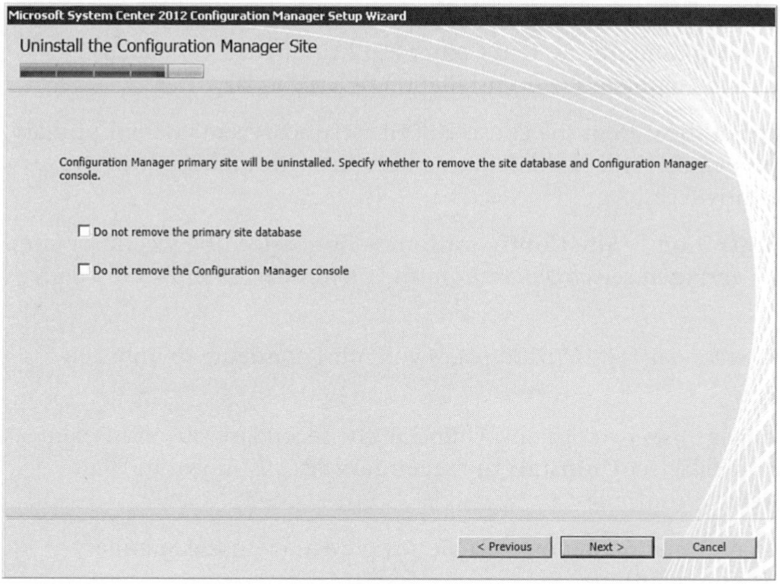

FIGURE 6.51   Uninstall primary site options.

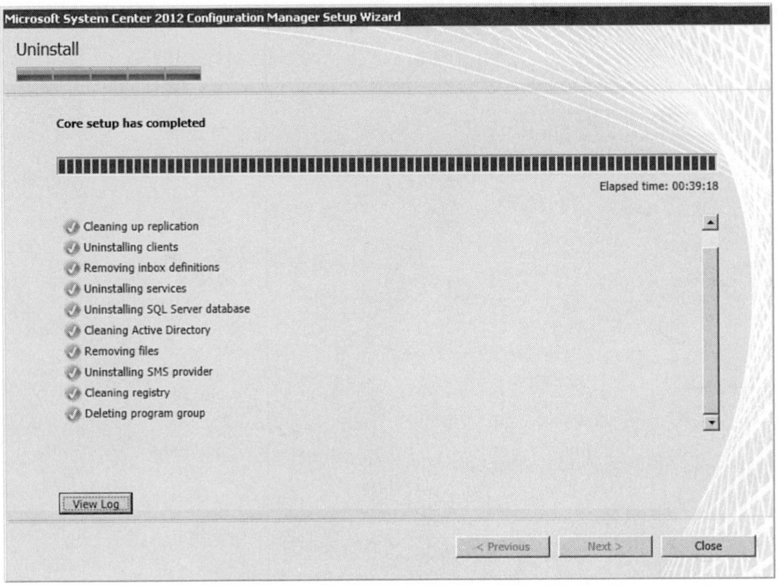

FIGURE 6.52   All primary site components uninstallation complete.

Uninstalling Secondary Sites

Secondary sites are uninstalled using the System Center 2012 Configuration Manager console. Follow these steps to complete the uninstallation of a secondary site:

1. Connect the console of the CAS or the console of the secondary site's parent primary site (Athena in this example) with a domain user account with Infrastructure or Administrative role privileges.

2. Navigate to **Administration -> Site Configuration -> Sites**, select the secondary site in the middle pane, and then select **Delete** from the ribbon bar, as shown in Figure 6.53.

3. Here are the Delete Secondary Site Wizard pages you must configure to uninstall a secondary site:

   ▶ **General:** This page lists two options: Uninstall the secondary site and Delete the secondary site. Select **Uninstall the secondary site**, as shown in Figure 6.54. Click **Next** to continue.

   ▶ **Summary:** A confirmation of your selection is presented on the Summary page. Click **Next** to continue.

   ▶ **Completion:** The completion page confirms successful initiation. Click **Close** to end the process. The secondary site state changes to deleting. Select the **Show Install Status** option from the ribbon to track the uninstallation process, as shown in Figure 6.55.

CAUTION: USE OF DELETE THE SECONDARY SITE OPTION

You must not use the **Delete the secondary site** option if you want to uninstall the secondary site. This option is used when a secondary site installation did not complete as expected or when the secondary site is still present in the console after successfully uninstalling the secondary site.

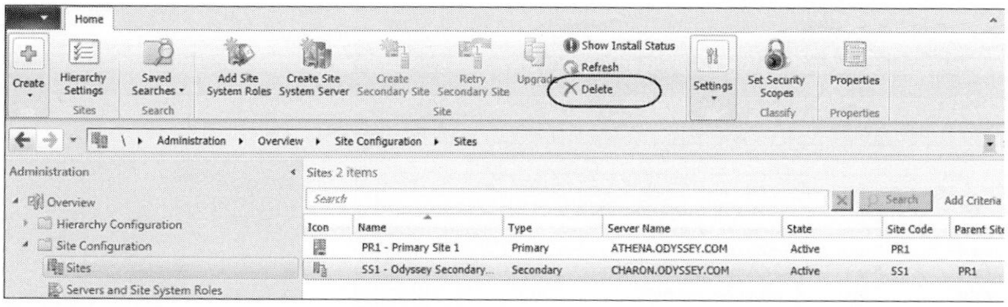

FIGURE 6.53   Initiate uninstall secondary site.

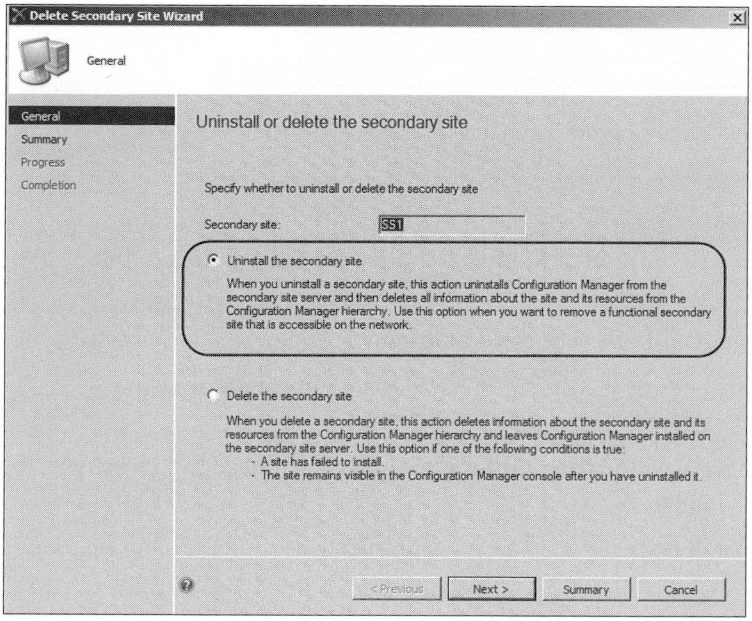

FIGURE 6.54   Uninstall the secondary site.

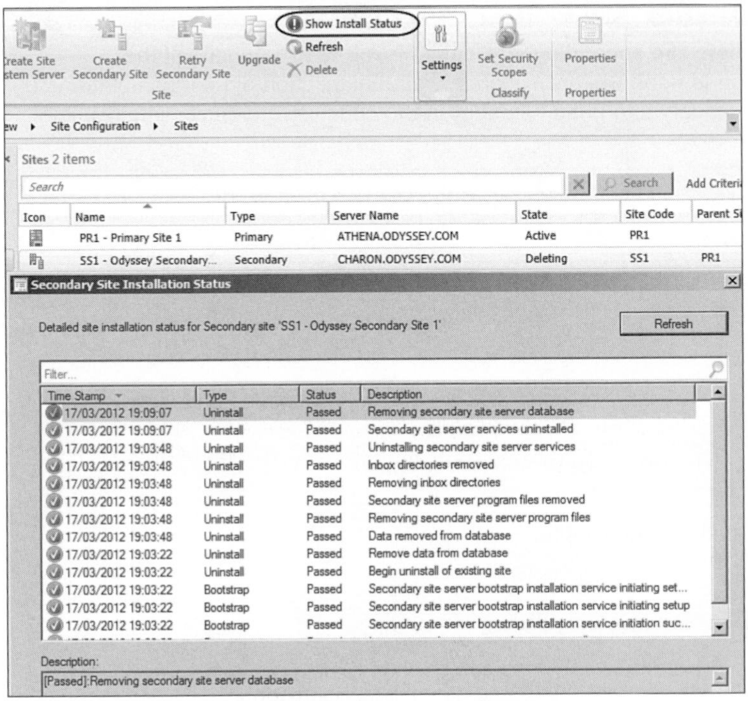

FIGURE 6.55   Show uninstall status of the secondary site.

Uninstalling a Full Hierarchy

The process you must follow to uninstall a full hierarchy requires you to follow these steps:

1. Uninstall all client agents using a supported method.

2. Uninstall all secondary sites in the hierarchy as discussed in the steps in the "Uninstalling Secondary Sites" section of this chapter.

3. Uninstall all primary sites as discussed in the steps in the "Uninstalling Primary Sites" section of this chapter.

4. The final site to uninstall is the CAS. The CAS is uninstalled using the same steps as a primary site.

NOTE: HISTORIC HIERARCHY DATA

System Center 2012 Configuration Manager collects valuable organization data about clients that you may find useful in future projects. You can back up and archive the hierarchy site databases before initiating the uninstallation processes. If you do not select the option to keep the site databases, all historic information is deleted as part of the uninstallation process.

Troubleshooting Site Installation

The installation of System Center 2012 Configuration Manager can present some technical challenges and issues. Table 6.7 provides information on troubleshooting resources, known issues, and resolutions.

TABLE 6.7   Troubleshooting Resources and Known Issues

Resource/Issue	Notes
Log file	System Center 2012 Configuration Manager provides detailed logging of the installation process. The logs specific to installation are listed in Appendix A.
Incorrect or missing dependency component configuration	Most of the common troubleshooting issues are associated with missing or incorrectly configured dependencies. You must ensure you have installed and configured the required prerequisites. Run the prerequisite checker and plan to resolve issues identified before processing with the installation. Plan to review the latest supported configuration information at http://technet.microsoft.com/en-us/library/gg682077.aspx.
Firewalls	Ensure that the required ports used by System Center 2012 Configuration Manager during and after the installation process are configured properly on firewalls (operating system or external appliances).
User and computer account rights	Ensure that the required rights have been assigned to users or computer accounts used in the installation and configuration processes.
SQL nondefault Instances	Ensure that you configure static ports for SQL server instances. The default instance is configured with a static port (default is 1433). All other instances are configured by default with a dynamic port.
Publishing in Active Directory	Delegate the required security rights to the System Management container. The installation process for hierarchies uses published data in this folder for the initial replication configuration.
Replication issues during hierarchy primary and secondary site installation	A primary site installation when joined to a hierarchy must perform an initial replication with the CAS. This replication process is also required for a secondary site. If this initial replication process is unsuccessful, the site will stay in a pending state and the console will show a read-only status.
	Ensure that all site provider servers have the right to publish to the System Management container using the computer account and are also in the local administrators group of both child and parent sites before starting the installation.
	Sites in a read-only or pending state may require a full reinstallation to resolve.

TIP: USER FORUMS AND BLOGS

Troubleshooting information on System Center 2012 Configuration Manager is available on Internet user forums. Use search engines such as Bing and Google to aid in your troubleshooting, as the product has many community leaders discussing the most up-to-date issues and how they were resolved.

Summary

This chapter discussed and provided guidance on preparing for System Center 2012 Configuration Manager installation, installing supported sites, post-installation configuration, uninstallation, and troubleshooting installation issues.

The next chapter provides a detailed discussion of how you migrate from previous versions of the product to System Center 2012 Configuration Manager.

CHAPTER 7

Migrating to System Center 2012 Configuration Manager

System Center Configuration Manager (ConfigMgr) has and continues to evolve with technological advances and organizational strategies in managing a diverse and dynamic environment. This version includes numerous changes to the product, discussed in Chapter 2, "Configuration Manager Overview."

Chapter 6, "Installing System Center 2012 Configuration Manager," discussed installing a new Configuration Manager 2012 stand-alone site or hierarchy. As Microsoft releases new versions of its systems management software, existing installations must determine how to best move to the most recent version of the product. If you have an existing ConfigMgr deployment, you should preserve much of the work put into that implementation when you move to this newest version. System Center 2012 Configuration Manager does not offer an in-place upgrade; environments running the previous version of ConfigMgr must migrate to the 2012 version.

This chapter discusses and provides guidance on the migration process. It provides background as why this is a migration and not an upgrade, discusses pre-migration considerations, the process of migrating your ConfigMgr 2007 infrastructure, migrating features and objects, client migration, and troubleshooting migration issues.

About Migration

Migration can be defined as *the movement of data and objects from one system to another*. The next sections discuss why you must migrate to System Center 2012 Configuration Manager from previous versions rather than perform an upgrade, and the benefits gained from this perceived constraint.

Migration Background and Introduction

Introducing new versions of software for existing users prompts the question, "In-place upgrade, or side-by-side installation?" The answer is usually, *It depends*. There are clear advantages and documented challenges to each.

The authors' experience with both approaches shows that when you have a choice between the two, side-by-side migration drives the implementation to use more of the new capabilities of the new version. More important, migration reduces the risk of potentially preserving undocumented and unsupported legacy configurations.

System Center 2012 Configuration Manager incorporates significant enhancements from ConfigMgr 2007. It includes architectural changes in the hierarchy and the move from a 32-bit to 64-bit software platform that also includes registry changes; these enhancements do not support an in-place upgrade. System Center 2012 Configuration Manager also introduces new capabilities and enhancements aligned with business requirements that required workarounds to implement with ConfigMgr 2007. A migration is an opportunity to revisit the original requirements of the business. A specific example of this is the use of secondary sites for network bandwidth management for content distribution; System Center 2012 Configuration Manager introduces network bandwidth management for distribution points, in most cases removing the need of secondary sites for content management.

The migration process is similar to moving to a new house from your current home. Moving to a new house provides both opportunities and challenges:

- ▶ Opportunities
    - ▶ Clearing out the old stuff you don't use
    - ▶ Getting new fixtures and furniture
    - ▶ Acquiring more space and better scenery
- ▶ Challenges
    - ▶ Organizing and coordinating the move
    - ▶ Packing and labeling what you are taking to the new house
    - ▶ Enlisting friends to help you or using a moving company

Moving to System Center 2012 Configuration Manager from ConfigMgr 2007 is in effect a new implementation, followed by moving supported objects from the existing ConfigMgr

2007 implementation. Implementation planning is covered extensively in Chapter 4, "Architecture Design Planning," and is a prerequisite to the overall migration process.

The successful migration from ConfigMgr 2007 to ConfigMgr 2012 is the combination of *art* (design, planning, and installation) and *science* (the technical mechanism used to move objects). The rest of the chapter discusses using these two methodologies when migrating to System Center 2012 Configuration Manager.

Migration, Not an Upgrade

The primary goal to migrate to a new version of an established platform is to preserve functional settings and configurations. This is possible with System Center 2012 Configuration Manager, because Microsoft includes migration tools built into the product that provide the means to effectively safely export and preserve previous configurations and objects from your existing ConfigMgr 2007 site or hierarchy.

The migration process centers on the capability to share distribution points (DPs) between your existing site and the new System Center 2012 Configuration Manager site.

Here is the supported approach for migrating from ConfigMgr 2007 to System Center 2012 Configuration Manager:

1. Provision new server(s) for the System Center 2012 Configuration Manager site or hierarchy. The authors recommend you use a new site or hierarchy design specific to System Center 2012 Configuration Manager, as discussed in Chapter 4.

2. Perform initial configuration specific to System Center 2012 Configuration Manager.

3. Establish a link to the existing ConfigMgr 2007 site or hierarchy.

4. Optionally share site roles (DPs); more on this in the "Planning the Migration" section.

5. Create migration jobs to migrate supported objects.

6. Upgrade the ConfigMgr 2007 client agents and assign to the System Center 2012 Configuration Manager site.

7. Decommission the ConfigMgr 2007 site and site systems. Optionally, you could rebuild servers and reuse them for ConfigMgr site roles.

The requirement for new servers is an opportunity to leverage private cloud principles. Private clouds are based on virtualization; using virtualization enables you to focus on providing computing and storage capacity rather than physical server hardware. System Center 2012 Configuration Manager is supported on virtualized systems and can remove the challenge to provision new physical hardware associated with side-by-side migrations. Another notable advantage is System Center 2012 Configuration Manager is designed to run on 64-bit architecture, thus making full use of the computer resources on modern physical servers.

> **NOTE: VIRTUAL VERSUS PHYSICAL SERVERS**
>
> The use of virtual servers for site roles introduces flexibility and in most cases reduces operational costs in management and maintenance. Although System Center 2012 Configuration Manager is highly scalable, using a virtualization platform means you should test and plan for performance impact for large environments. The authors recommend you test on a small scale and measure performance. Performing a detailed test provides you with factual data. You can use the data from this small scale to model what a medium or large deployment will require and to assist in determining whether to use virtualization or physical machines for System Center 2012 Configuration Manager roles.

Planning the Migration

Migrating from versions of the product before ConfigMgr 2007 is not directly supported. If you use an earlier version than ConfigMgr 2007, you have two options:

- ► Upgrade to ConfigMgr 2007; then migrate to System Center 2012 Configuration Manager.

- ► Perform a new installation of 2012 and rediscover objects.

Though both options are similar in principle, the move from ConfigMgr 2007 to System Center 2012 Configuration Manager is simplified with the assistance from the built-in migration functionality. This migration functionality of System Center 2012 Configuration Manager is discussed in the "Migration Jobs" section.

Central Site and Hierarchy Concepts in 2012

Chapter 4 provides detailed information on site concepts in System Center 2012 Configuration Manager. This section builds on the concepts in that chapter and specifically focuses on migration considerations.

ConfigMgr 2007 hierarchies addressed the following typical requirements:

- ► Scaling

- ► Centralized management

- ► Administrative separation (server management versus workstation management)

- ► Wide area network (WAN) bandwidth management

- ► Legal and political considerations

These requirements are still relevant when planning migrations to System Center 2012 Configuration Manager. Chapter 4 discusses these requirements and shows how System Center 2012 Configuration Manager 2012's new capabilities may remove the need for hierarchies for sites with less than 50,000 clients.

The System Center 2012 Configuration Manager hierarchy is based on centralized management; this can play a key role in the migration process. In 2012, the central administration site (CAS) provides a central point of communication and coordination without the overhead of direct client management. Though not mandatory, here is what establishing a CAS in either a new implementation or migration scenario provides:

▶ A controlled approach to collapsing existing hierarchies when resources prohibit this prior to the migration; for example, with a global implemented hierarchy with multiple primary and secondary sites, you could establish a CAS at your headquarters and then perform a migration by country and replace or remove unnecessary primary/secondary sites.

▶ A means to introduce new sites during disaster recovery scenarios for primary sites; the stand-alone primary site scenario does not provide the same flexibility as a CAS when provisioning additional or replacement sites.

▶ The ability to establish a hierarchy when the business needs change without rebuilding System Center 2012 Configuration Manager, as a stand-alone primary site cannot be converted into a CAS.

▶ Centralized security delegation; global security configuration is implemented at the CAS and local configuration at the site or collection level.

If used in a migration, the CAS can increase flexibility of the overall process and should be considered during the planning phase.

About Site Mode

ConfigMgr 2007 sites are implemented in mixed or native mode. Mixed mode sites only can manage clients connected directly to the corporate network (local area network [LAN] or WAN using a virtual private network [VPN]). Native mode sites can manage clients over the Internet without the need for a VPN connection using certificates from a trusted public key infrastructure (PKI).

In System Center 2012 Configuration Manager, the site mode functionality is part of the relevant site system (for example, DPs can service LAN-connected clients over HTTP and Internet-connected clients over HTTPS). Chapter 2 discusses site modes.

You should plan how to service Internet-based clients from a site role perspective rather than a native or mixed mode site perspective.

What Is Migrated

Like most of the product, the migration process introduces new terms and concepts. Table 7.1 provides an overview of the terms and concepts specific to migration in System Center 2012 Configuration Manager.

TABLE 7.1   Migration-Specific Terms and Concepts

Concept or Term	Notes
Source hierarchy	This is the source ConfigMgr 2007 hierarchy. Start with the top site (central site) in a full hierarchy or the primary site in cases in which only one primary site is installed.
Source sites	Sites identified after querying the source hierarchy. This would be one or more primary sites below the ConfigMgr 2007 central site in a hierarchy.
Data gathering	An ongoing process once a source hierarchy has been configured. This process identifies data you can migrate to ConfigMgr 2012.
Migration jobs	How you configure specific jobs to migrate supported discovered objects from the data gathering process.
Client migration	The process of migrating the ConfigMgr 2007 client to version 2012. Note: Use a supported client installation method to upgrade the ConfigMgr 2007 client.
Monitoring migration	The process of monitoring migration activities. Most of the monitoring is performed in the System Center 2012 Configuration Manager console. You can also use the log file generated by the migration process to monitor migration activities.
Stop gathering data	The process to stop or suspend data gathering from the source site.
Clean up migration data	The process to clean up the migration metadata. This does not clean up the data you have migrated but rather the configuration used to migrate the data in the first place (for example, clears the source hierarchy and starts again).
Shared distribution points	System Center 2012 Configuration Manager can use distribution points from ConfigMgr 2007 during the migration phase. The content metadata is migrated, but the actual content can be accessed by clients using the ConfigMgr 2007 DP until all clients have migrated. When migration is complete, you can upgrade the DPs.

Here are the supported objects the Migration Wizard can migrate from ConfigMgr 2007:

▶ Collections

▶ Advertisements

▶ Boundaries

▶ Software distribution packages

▶ Virtual application packages

- ▶ Software Updates
  - ▶ Deployments
  - ▶ Deployment packages
  - ▶ Templates
  - ▶ Software update lists
- ▶ Operating System Deployment
  - ▶ Boot images
  - ▶ Driver packages
  - ▶ Drivers
  - ▶ Images
  - ▶ Packages
  - ▶ Task sequences
- ▶ Desired Configuration Management
  - ▶ Configuration items
  - ▶ Configuration baselines
- ▶ Asset Intelligence customizations
  - ▶ Custom catalogs
  - ▶ Custom hardware requirements
- ▶ Software metering rules

What Is Not Migrated

The supported objects for migration have some constraints and rules. Table 7.2 lists the constraints and rules for the supported migrated objects.

TABLE 7.2   Migration Objects Constraints and Rules

Migrated Object	Constraints and Rules
Collections	Empty collections without objects associated are migrated as organization folders: 　Site code references in collections will be flagged. 　Users and devices cannot be part of the same collection. 　Nested empty collections are converted to folders.
Packages	All package source locations must use a UNC path.
OSD	The ConfigMgr 2007 client installation package is not migrated.
Advertisements	Advertisements are only available for selection when using collection migration.

Here are objects that cannot be migrated from ConfigMgr 2007 using the Migration Wizard:

▶ Queries

▶ Security rights and instances for the site and objects

▶ Configuration Manager 2007 reports from SQL Server Reporting Services (SSRS)

▶ Configuration Manager 2007 web reports

▶ Client inventory and history data

▶ Active Management Technology (AMT) client provisioning information

▶ Files in the client cache

Pre-Migration Activities

A successful migration to System Center 2012 Configuration Manager requires you to perform a number of activities before invoking the Migration Wizard. Here are those prerequisite activities:

▶ Complete the installation and configuration of the System Center 2012 Configuration Manager hierarchy (stand-alone site or CAS installed hierarchy).

▶ Ensure the ConfigMgr 2007 source site(s) is at the supported version.

▶ Prepare the ConfigMgr 2007 sources site(s) and System Center 2012 Configuration Manager destination site(s) for migration.

▶ Provision and configure the migration user account for the ConfigMgr 2007 source sites.

▶ Assign ConfigMgr 2007 source site database access rights to the migration account.

▶ Assign the Full Administrator role to the migration account in the destination System Center 2012 Configuration Manager hierarchy.

These activities are discussed in the following sections.

Install and Configure the Configuration Manager Hierarchy

The destination System Center 2012 Configuration Manager hierarchy should be fully configured before starting the migration process. You should test and validate the full functionality in scope for the implementation before invoking any of the migration wizards.

The migration process assumes a fully configured site is in place. Chapters 4, 5 ("Network Design"), and 6 cover planning and implementation in depth, and the authors recommend you review those chapters to ensure the System Center 2012 Configuration Manager site is ready to receive migrated data. The System Center 2012 Configuration Manager online documentation is an excellent source of information, and you can review the migration section at http://technet.microsoft.com/en-us/library/gg682006.aspx for additional information.

Ensure the ConfigMgr 2007 Source Site(s) Is at Supported Version

The only supported ConfigMgr 2007 version is ConfigMgr 2007 with Service Pack (SP) 2. Upgrade to ConfigMgr 2007 SP 2, and validate the site is fully operational before attempting to migrate to System Center 2012 Configuration Manager.

Prepare the ConfigMgr 2007 Site for Migration

The migration process is an opportunity to "clean house." You should plan to perform an audit of supported migration objects (see the "What Is Migrated" section earlier in this chapter). Here are examples of some recommended activities:

▶ Review advertisements and plan to remove redundant nonapplicable advertisements.

  ▶ Delete redundant advertisements.

  ▶ Create placeholder collections for redundant advertisements and avoid keeping old advertisements linked to live collections.

▶ Review collections in scope.

  ▶ Avoid mixed collections (that is, user and device combined collections).

  ▶ As a best practice, mark only query-based collections for migration.

  ▶ Review advertisements or deployments linked to the collections.

  ▶ Avoid site codes in query-based collections.

▶ Review the software updates catalog synchronization settings. Are all the synchronized categories still relevant to your environment today?

Prepare Sources Site(s) and Destination Site(s) for Migration

The migration process has a dependency on security credentials and infrastructure configuration, as described in Table 7.3.

TABLE 7.3 Migration User Account and Infrastructure Prerequisites

Site/Infrastructure	Required Settings
System Center 2012 Configuration Manager destination site (CAS or primary site)	Migration user account with the Full Administration role. A security best practice is to use the computer account instead of a user account.
ConfigMgr 2007 source sites (site provider)	A migration user account with Read permission to all source site objects. The account must optionally have Delete permission to the ConfigMgr 2007 `site` class if you plan to upgrade the distribution point.

Site/Infrastructure	Required Settings
ConfigMgr 2007 source sites (site database)	Read and Execute permissions to the source site database. In SQL, this is equivalent to assigning the following to the Windows Login account: db_datareader and smsschm_users on the site database for the source site.
	A security best practice is to use the computer account instead of a user account.
Shared distribution points	The ConfigMgr 2007 source site and the System Center 2012 Configuration Manager primary site or CAS must use the same client port number.
Firewall/network protocols	The following network protocols are used when gathering data to communicate between the source and destination sites: NetBIOS/SMB - 445 (TCP) RPC (WMI) - 135 (TCP) SQL Server - 1433 (TCP)
DCOM Security Group on the Source Site Provider	The migration user must be a member of Distributed COM Users local group.

A best practice is to create a dedicated migration user account; Microsoft recommends using the computer account. Additional information on security and privacy pertaining to migration is available at http://technet.microsoft.com/en-us/library/gg712336.aspx.

Creating a dedicated user account ensures you can limit the access rights to only what is required for the migration tasks. Plan to remove all access rights to the migration account when all migration tasks are complete.

Figure 7.1 provides a summary of the migration planning process tasks.

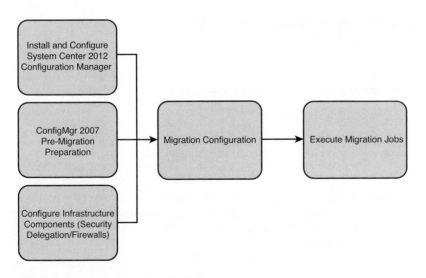

FIGURE 7.1   The migration planning process.

Coexistence Considerations

This section discusses coexistence considerations specific to migration. Chapter 4 provides details on coexistence when considering the implementation of System Center 2012 Configuration Manager. The two main areas of focus during the migration are

▶ Shared infrastructure

▶ Client management

These are discussed in the next sections.

Shared Infrastructure

System Center 2012 Configuration Manager allows you to use a ConfigMgr 2007 distribution point during the migration phase for clients. After the migration is complete, you can upgrade the distribution point. This shared infrastructure functionality minimizes data storage requirements and network bandwidth utilization.

ConfigMgr 2007 and System Center 2012 Configuration Manager publish information into the same Active Directory system folder when implemented in the same domain. As a part of the migration process, you should plan for new site codes for your System Center 2012 Configuration Manager hierarchy.

Client Management

You cannot manage ConfigMgr 2007 clients from a System Center 2012 Configuration Manager site.

Complete your infrastructure migration before migrating ConfigMgr 2007 clients. A small set of clients can be migrated to validate the process and functionality. A best practice is to use the Internet Protocol (IP) range or exclusive subnet boundaries for site assignment to avoid boundary overlaps between the old infrastructure and the new sites. Upgraded ConfigMgr 2007 clients can access distribution points that are configured as shared distribution points as long as their original site is still configured as the active source site (see Figure 7.2).

The following section discusses the technical process of moving objects, which is the science of migration.

Migrating Your Configuration Manager Infrastructure

This section focuses on the infrastructure considerations and configuration required to support a successful migration. Here are the activities you will be considering:

▶ Placement of site servers and site roles

▶ Temporary migration roles

▶ Security considerations

▶ Boundaries and what is changing

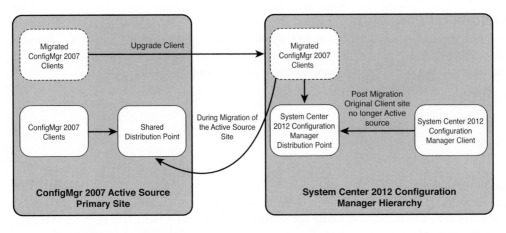

FIGURE 7.2   Migrated Client Management.

Site Servers and Site Roles

Chapter 2 and Chapter 4 discuss site servers and their roles in detail. You should review the discussion regarding site systems in Chapter 2. In addition to default roles, at a minimum you must also have these roles available:

▶ Software update point

▶ Distribution points

▶ Management points

▶ Reporting services point

▶ Fallback status point

Software Update Point

A software update point (SUP) must be configured to migrate software update objects supported by the Migration Wizard. The SUP must be installed and configured to synchronize the same catalog options as the source site(s). Table 7.4 illustrates the requirements in either a System Center 2012 Configuration Manager stand-alone primary or CAS scenario.

TABLE 7.4   Software Update Point Migration Requirements

Site Type	Required Settings
Stand-alone primary site	Configure classifications, products, and languages on the site server nominated as the software update point.
CAS hierarchy	Configure classifications, products, and languages on the site server nominated as the software update point. This needs to be configured on the CAS and the role enabled on the child primary site.

Figure 7.3 shows the ConfigMgr 2007 settings for the software update point, and Figure 7.4 shows the equivalent in System Center 2012 Configuration Manager.

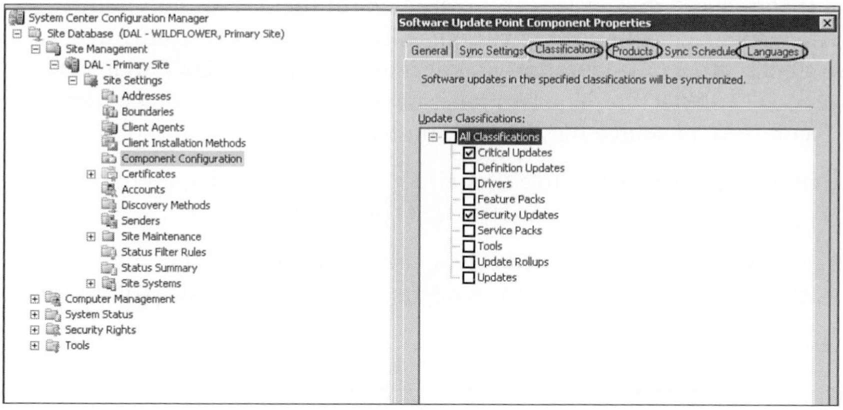

FIGURE 7.3   ConfigMgr 2007 SUP configuration.

NOTE: SOFTWARE UPDATE POINT IN A CAS SCENARIO

The software update point role is only available in a child primary site of a System Center 2012 Configuration Manager hierarchy after a software update point has been installed at the CAS.

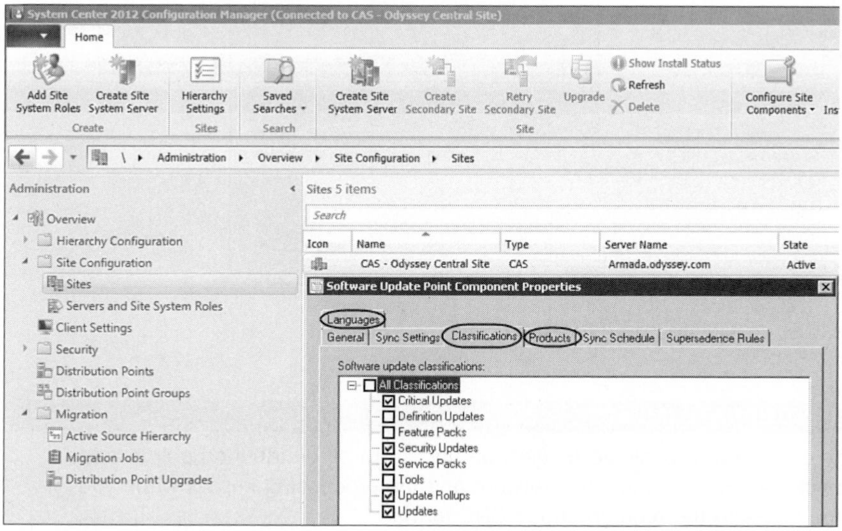

FIGURE 7.4   System Center 2012 Software update point configuration.

Distribution Point

Distribution points are primarily used for content management during the migration process. Migration process requirements for distribution points focus on how the source of the package files is configured in packages and placement of the distribution points in your infrastructure. Table 7.2 specified that all source locations must be configured as UNC paths. System Center 2012 Configuration Manager and ConfigMgr 2007 share the same type of source to DP architecture. The two types of configuration are source files stored locally (see Figure 7.5), or source files stored remotely (see Figure 7.6):

▶ **Local source files:** Configure the source files folder as a shared folder, and update all packages in scope of the migration to use the UNC path to the source.

▶ **Remote source files:** Do not use mapped drives; use a UNC path to the source files, and update all packages in scope of the migration to use the UNC path to the source.

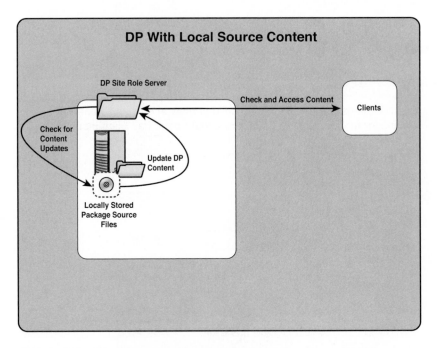

FIGURE 7.5   DP with source files stored locally.

CAUTION: CONTENT UPDATE IMPACT

Changing the source path of a package triggers an update to all distribution points associated with the package. Plan to minimize network and file processing impact when you change the source paths to the recommended UNC format.

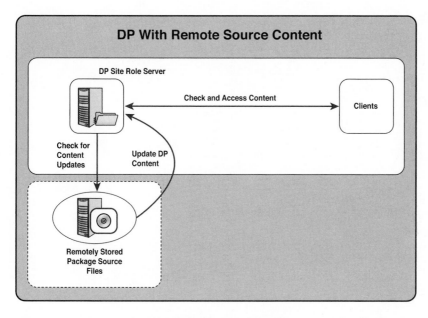

FIGURE 7.6   DP with source files stored remotely.

The architecture of distribution points implicitly mandate content is stored at least twice. Distribution points effectively copy the files from your original source location to the content store of the ConfigMgr 2007 or System Center 2012 Configuration Manager site. The migration process is an opportunity to review existing packages and remove redundant data (for example, when two versions of a package refer to the same source files on your local or remote file storage repository).

Management Point

Management points are the central point of communication for System Center 2012 Configuration Manager clients. You need to configure a management point in your hierarchy before you can manage migrated clients.

Reporting Services Point

The old saying goes *You can't manage what you don't measure.* This is true when you start your migration. There are a number of options available to track the status and validate the outcome of the migration. The options include but are not limited to log files, console objects validation, and reports. System Center 2012 Configuration Manager uses SSRS as its reporting engine. The migration process is supported with five built-in reports, displayed in Figure 7.7.

You must enable the reporting services point role as a prerequisite to making these reports available. Chapter 18, "Reporting," delves deeper into the reporting configuration for System Center 2012 Configuration Manager.

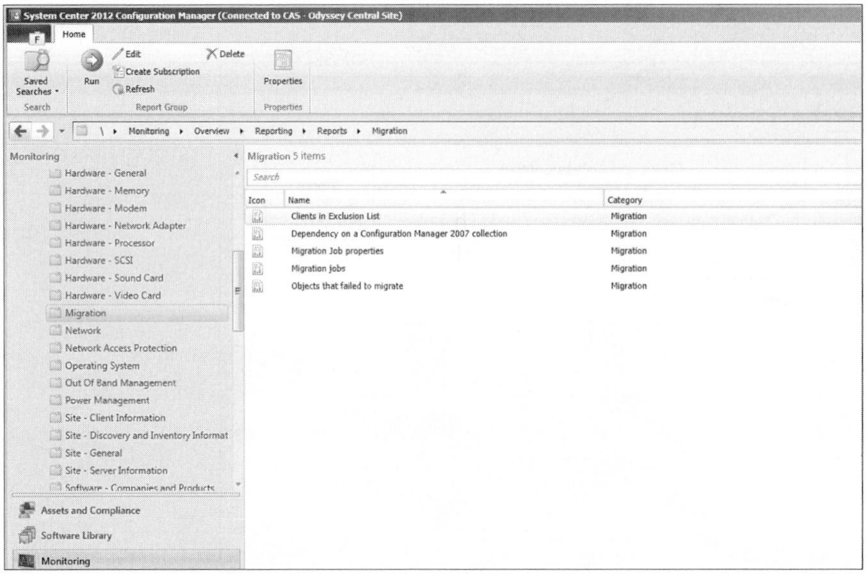

FIGURE 7.7   System Center 2012 Configuration Manager Migration Reports.

Fallback Status Point

A fallback status point (FSP) is the System Center 2012 Configuration Manager client emergency contact. Fallback status points provide a number of functions; the primary function during the migration is its use during client upgrades. Upgrade-initiated ConfigMgr 2007 and new System Center 2012 Configuration Manager clients will report success or failure information to the fallback status point specified in the installation properties. The authors recommend you establish a fallback status point before client deployments and upgrades as a best practice. See Chapter 4 for additional information on fallback status point considerations.

Security Considerations

Security, much like most of System Center 2012 Configuration Manager, includes significant enhancements and capabilities. The migration process has a dependency on the security configuration you choose to implement. The objects you migrate that fall into the global data category are replicated to all sites in the hierarchy. (See Chapter 5 for a discussion about global data.) The migration process provides you with the means to maintain security access as you intended by leveraging four built-in new security functions: collection limiting, security scopes, security roles, and administrative users; this is collectively known as *role-based administration* (RBA).

Collection Limiting

A significant enhancement in System Center 2012 Configuration Manager is the ability to scope your security boundaries by collection. ConfigMgr 2007 required you enforce security segregation by using primary sites. An example of security segregation is a hierarchy with two primary sites: one for workstation operating environments and one for server operating environments. Using the house analogy, you had to share the living space with your neighbors and put locks on everything you owned within the same room. The limitation of delegation by primary sites results in organizations implementing multiple sites for the sole purpose of security boundary management.

System Center 2012 Configuration Manager enables delegation at the collection level. Furthermore, you must specify a parent collection known as the *limiting collection* each time you create a new collection. Continuing with the house analogy, you now have a dedicated apartment inside an apartment block allowing you to have a single lock to the front door specific to you.

The migration process provides a means to collapse complex hierarchies into a System Center 2012 Configuration Manager single site or hierarchy. Collapsing sites require that you have defined a collection structure to represent your security model and effectively convert your primary sites into collections. The built-in collections (All Systems and All Users for devices and users, respectively) provide a fallback when custom collections have not been created prior to the migration.

Security Scopes

New to System Center 2012 Configuration Manager is the notion of *security scopes*. Security scopes are analogous to the locks you put on the things you own in your house. In System Center 2012 Configuration Manager, security scopes enable you to tag instances of objects with the notation of a universal key. In ConfigMgr 2007, everything was secured individually. Security scopes limit the objects on which administrators can perform an action. The action an administrator can perform on an object is defined by the security role the administrator is assigned. Security roles' impact on the migration process is discussed in the next section.

You want to plan and implement the intended security scopes in the destination System Center 2012 Configuration Manager stand-alone site or hierarchy as part of your migration process.

Here are objects that can be limited by security scopes:

▶ Antimalware policies

▶ Applications

▶ Boot images

▶ Boundary groups

▶ Configuration items

▶ Custom client settings

▶ Distribution points and distribution point groups

▶ Driver packages

▶ Global conditions

▶ Migration jobs

- ▶ Operating system images
- ▶ Operating system installation packages
- ▶ Packages
- ▶ Queries
- ▶ Sites
- ▶ Software metering rules
- ▶ Software update groups
- ▶ Software updates packages
- ▶ Task sequence packages
- ▶ Windows CE device setting items and packages

Here are the objects that cannot be limited by security scopes:

- ▶ Active Directory forests
- ▶ Administrative users
- ▶ Alerts
- ▶ Boundaries
- ▶ Computer associations
- ▶ Default client settings
- ▶ Deployment templates
- ▶ Device drivers
- ▶ Exchange Server connector
- ▶ Migration site-to-site mappings
- ▶ Mobile device enrollment profiles
- ▶ Security roles
- ▶ Security scopes
- ▶ Site addresses
- ▶ Site system roles
- ▶ Software titles
- ▶ Software updates
- ▶ Status messages
- ▶ User device affinities

Two security scopes are created by default when you install System Center 2012 Configuration Manager:

▶ **All:** Built-in security scope that grants access to all scopes. You cannot manually have objects assigned to this scope.

▶ **Default:** All objects are assigned to this scope; default is the only scope available during the migration if custom scopes have not been created.

Security Roles

Security roles are preconfigured administrative profiles with appropriate rights to perform actions on System Center 2012 Configuration Manager objects. You want to review the built-in security roles as part of your migration planning process.

Administrative users are those users or groups you assign limiting collections, security scope, and security roles to complete the role-based administration process. The migration process requires you to add the nominated account for the active source site hierarchy discovery as an administrative user assigned to the Full Administrator security role; this security role is assigned the default security scopes and limiting collections.

The migration process gives you the opportunity to implement the enhanced capabilities in role-based security in System Center 2012 Configuration Manager. Table 7.5 illustrates the differences in how the functionality is achieved in ConfigMgr 2007 versus System Center 2012 Configuration Manager.

TABLE 7.5   Security Delegations in ConfigMgr 2007 Versus System Center 2012 Configuration Manager RBA

Functionality	ConfigMgr 2007	System Center 2012 Configuration Manager
What types of objects can you see and what can you do to them?	Class rights	Security roles
Which instances can you see and interact with?	Object instance permissions	Security scopes
Which resources can you interact with?	Site specific resource permissions	Collection limiting

Figures 7.8 and 7.9 provide a graphical illustration of these differences. The Migration Wizard has security scoping options that automatically allow you to implement the role-based security on objects you migrate.

NOTE: MIGRATION AND SECURITY CONCIDERATIONS

The Migration Wizard prompts you for optional security settings, discussed in this section. Only the default security settings for collection limiting and scopes are presented if you have not created your organization's intended security model before starting the migration.

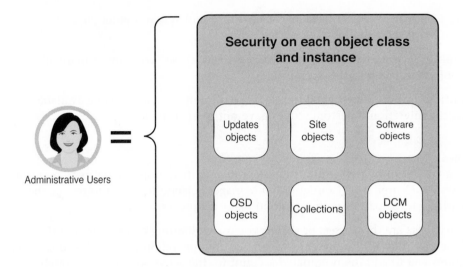

FIGURE 7.8   Role-based security in ConfigMgr 2007.

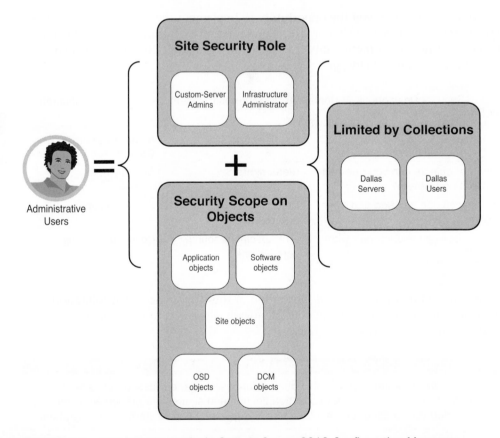

FIGURE 7.9   Role-based security in System Center 2012 Configuration Manager.

Boundaries and What's Changing

Chapter 4 discusses the changes in site boundaries from ConfigMgr 2007 to System Center 2012 Configuration Manager. A significant change is the ability to have one or more boundary groups for site assignment and a separate set of boundary groups for content management. The new separation of site assignment boundary groups from content management boundary groups can simplify your migration planning. The recommended approach during migration planning is not to configure any assignment boundary groups that overlap with your existing active ConfigMgr 2007 boundaries.

Figure 7.10 shows a boundary group properties page with the site assignment option enabled. Figure 7.11 shows a boundary group with the site assignment option disabled. In Figure 7.11, the configuration setting marks the boundary for content management only. The built-in System Center 2012 Configuration Manager migration tool converts ConfigMgr 2007 boundaries to content only boundary groups.

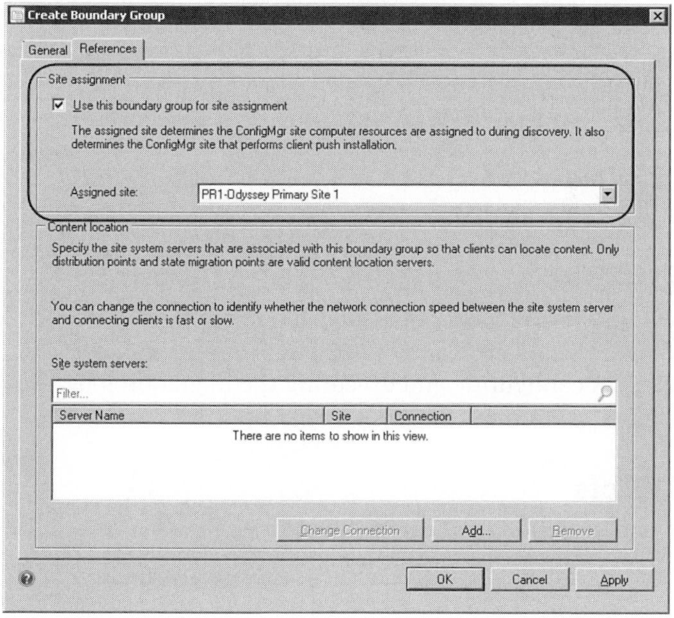

FIGURE 7.10   Site Assignment boundary group properties.

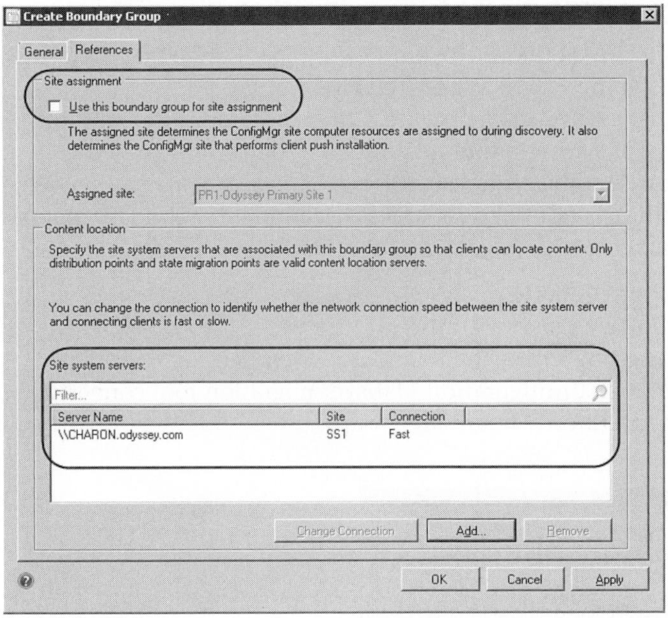

FIGURE 7.11   Content boundary group properties.

Performing the Migration

The "Planning the Migration" section of this chapter discussed activities you must consider and perform before invoking the system Center 2012 built-in migration wizards. The remainder of the chapter discusses configuring and executing the migration jobs, migrating the ConfigMgr 2007 clients, and troubleshooting migration.

Migrating Features and Objects

The technical migration process is mapped to two distinct streams:

▶ The supported objects linked to a collection; for example, software distribution

▶ The actual supported objects

The process is linked to either the targeted collection(s) or the objects that can be migrated independently. Figure 7.12 shows all the supported objects for migration and their unique mapping to the migration job streams.

Migrating by Feature and Dependencies

System Center 2012 Configuration Manager presents the built-in migration job wizards by collection or objects. A structured approach to migration is to organize the process by infrastructure-only objects such as boundaries and then by the features linked to collections.

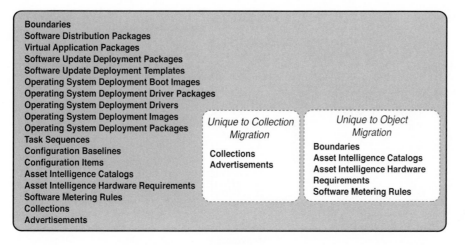

Boundaries
Software Distribution Packages
Virtual Application Packages
Software Update Deployment Packages
Software Update Deployment Templates
Operating System Deployment Boot Images
Operating System Deployment Driver Packages
Operating System Deployment Drivers
Operating System Deployment Images
Operating System Deployment Packages
Task Sequences
Configuration Baselines
Configuration Items
Asset Intelligence Catalogs
Asset Intelligence Hardware Requirements
Software Metering Rules
Collections
Advertisements

Unique to Collection Migration
Collections
Advertisements

Unique to Object Migration
Boundaries
Asset Intelligence Catalogs
Asset Intelligence Hardware Requirements
Software Metering Rules

FIGURE 7.12   Supported migration objects.

The first migration configuration required is data gathering from the active source hierarchy. The active source hierarchy is typically the top site of your ConfigMgr 2007 hierarchy.

Migration Dependencies Configuration

The migration jobs have several prerequisites that you must complete before invoking the built-in wizards in the System Center 2012 Configuration Manager console:

▶ **ConfigMgr 2007 migration account configuration:** This includes delegation rights in a local security group, the console, and SQL database access rights for the ConfigMgr 2007 site.

▶ **System Center 2012 Configuration Manager migration account:** This configuration consists of delegation rights to the migration account either on the CAS or stand-alone primary site.

ConfigMgr 2007 Migration User Account Configuration

Here are the steps to perform when a dedicated account is used for the migration tasks:

1. Create a dedicated Active Directory domain user, for example, a user named **CM12 Migration**.

2. Add the migration user account to the Distributed COM Users group on each primary site server provider server in your hierarchy. In Server Manager, navigate to **Configuration -> Groups -> Distributed COM Users -> Properties**, and add the migration user created in step 1, as shown in Figure 7.13. Click **Add**.

3. Grant the migration user Read and Execute rights in the database for all primary sites in the ConfigMgr 2007 hierarchy in scope. Figure 7.14 shows the SQL Server Windows user logon properties for the migration user in SQL Server Management Studio.

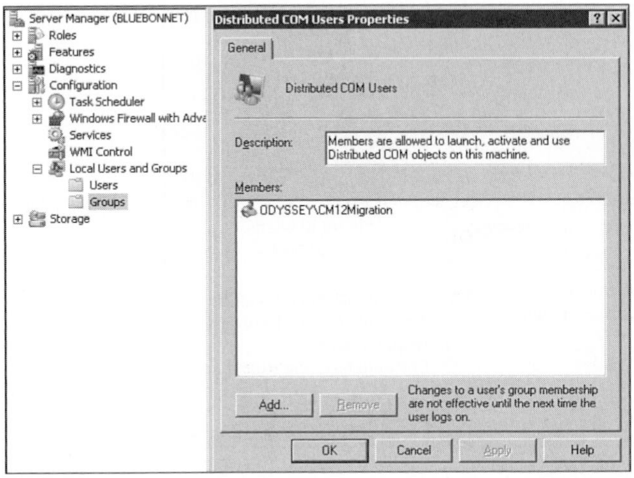

FIGURE 7.13   Distributed COM Users Properties.

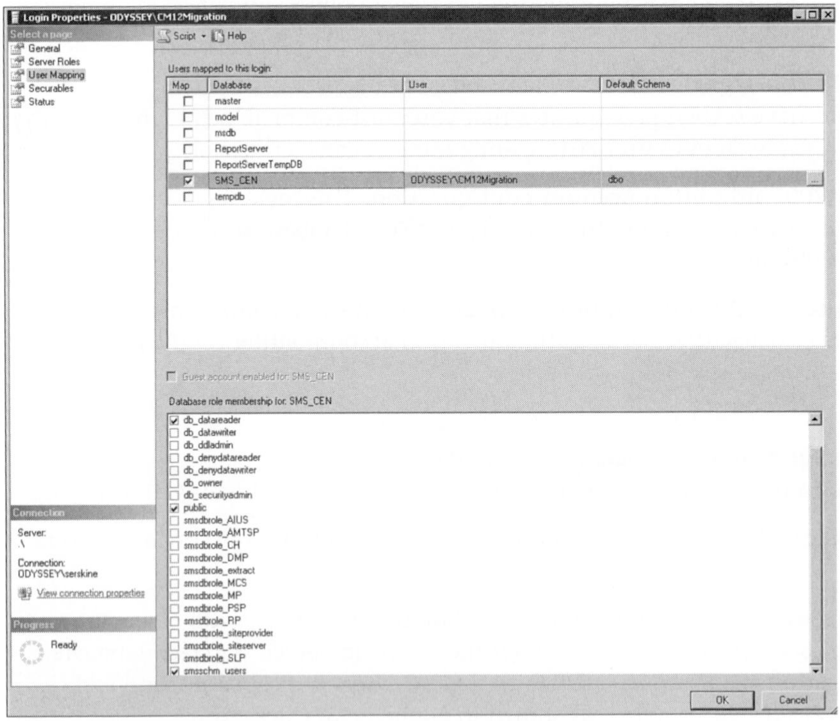

FIGURE 7.14   SQL Login Properties for the migration user.

4. Grant a minimum of Read object rights to the Migration user account in the ConfigMgr 2007 primary sites in scope of the migration. In the Configuration

Manager 2007 console, navigate to **Security Rights -> Manage ConfigMgr Users**. Add a new user by specifying the migration user you created.

5. When you add a new user, you can **Copy Rights from an Existing ConfigMgr User or User Group** if you have a user already configured appropriately for the site.

The minimum rights required are read site objects. Figure 7.15 shows a summary of user rights in the wizard. This example shows rights where the minimum rights are elevated and access restricted to the migration user as a business process.

REAL WORLD: MIGRATION USER CONFIGURATION

The ConfigMgr 2007 security rights assignment for objects can be challenging to configure and implement, and is potentially error prone. Grant the migration user full administrative rights by copying a user or group assigned the equivalent of full administrative rights (for example, the System account in a default installation). This approach reduces errors when assigning rights in the ConfigMgr 2007 environment. If the migration account does not have sufficient rights, the data gathering process and migration jobs will fail.

The SQL Read and Execute permission is implemented by assigning db_datareader and smsschm_users on the site database for the source site to the migration user account.

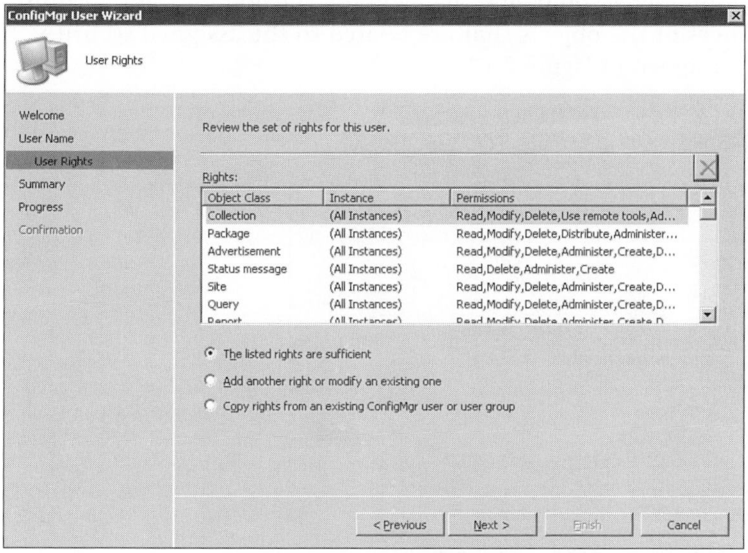

FIGURE 7.15   Summary of assigned rights.

System Center 2012 Configuration Migration User Account Configuration

To configure the migration user account, perform the following steps on the CAS or stand-alone primary site of the System Center 2012 Configuration Manager destination site:

1. Connect to the System Center 2012 Configuration Manager console, and navigate to **Administration -> Security -> Administrative Users**; then select **Add User or Group** from the ribbon bar, as shown in Figure 7.16.

FIGURE 7.16   Add an Administrative User.

2. Browse for the migration user account, and then add the Full administrator security role. Select **All instances of the objects that are related to the assigned security roles**, and click **OK**, as shown in Figure 7.17.

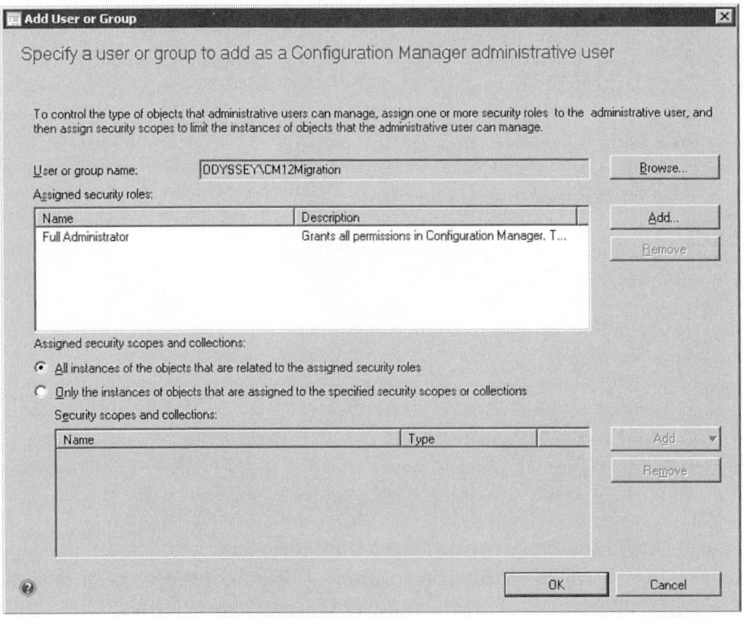

FIGURE 7.17   System Center 2012 Configuration Manager migration user role configuration.

Configuring the Active Source Site

After the migration user credentials are configured and have appropriate rights for the ConfigMgr 2007 and System Center 2012 Configuration Manager environments, you are ready to configure the Migration Wizard components starting with the active source site, which is the top site of the ConfigMgr 2007 hierarchy. Perform the following steps to configure this site:

1. Connect to the System Center 2012 Configuration Manager console, and navigate to **Migration -> Active Source Hierarchy**. In the ribbon bar, select **Specify Source Hierarchy**, as shown in Figure 7.18.

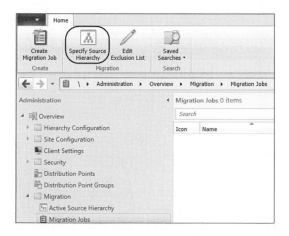

FIGURE 7.18   Specifying the Active Source Hierarchy.

The Specify Source Hierarchy page displayed in Figure 7.19 provides these settings:

▶ **Active Source Hierarchy:** The default value is **New Source Hierarchy** for a new site with no migration settings configured. Changing the active source hierarchy cancels all existing migration jobs for the current configured active source site.

▶ **Top-level Configuration Manager 2007 site server:** Specify the fully qualified domain name (FQDN) value to the top site of the ConfigMgr 2007 site; for example, **BLUEBONNET.ODYSSEY.COM**.

▶ **Source site access accounts (SMS Provider):** Select a new or existing user account that has been granted a minimum of read rights in the ConfigMgr 2007 site. Only user accounts are supported for this configuration.

▶ **Source site access accounts (Site SQL database):** Select a new or existing user account which has been granted a minimum of read and execute rights to the ConfigMgr 2007 SQL database. You can use the same account as specified for the provider access to simplify management of the migration user credentials. Figure 7.19 shows an example of the required fields configured for the Odyssey environment.

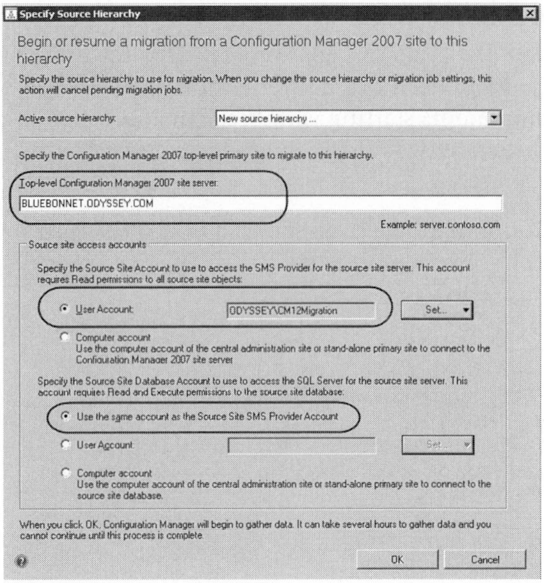

FIGURE 7.19   ConfigMgr 2007 active source site configuration.

2. The initial data gathering process starts when you complete the mandatory settings. The time the process takes to complete depends on the size of your ConfigMgr 2007 hierarchy. The authors recommend you perform a health check and clean up your ConfigMgr 2007 source site(s) before starting this process.

Figure 7.20 shows the completed process. CEN is the central site and DAL the primary child site in the ConfigMgr 2007 hierarchy specified as the active source site.

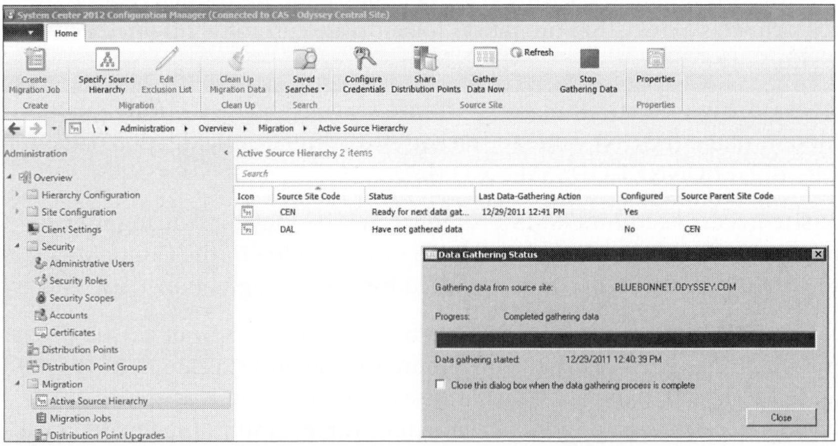

FIGURE 7.20   Data gathering completed for active source site.

Configuring Child Sites for Data Gathering

In a ConfigMgr 2007 site hierarchy with multiple child primary sites, you must configure credentials as a separate step before you can migrate objects from the child sites. The active source site configuration enables you to only migrate objects from that site. Perform the following steps for the child site(s) before attempting to configure migration jobs for objects configured at the child site(s):

1. Connect to the System Center 2012 Configuration Manager console, and navigate to **Migration -> Active Source Hierarchy**. Now select the child site (DAL in Figure 7.21) and click **Configure Credentials** in the ribbon bar.

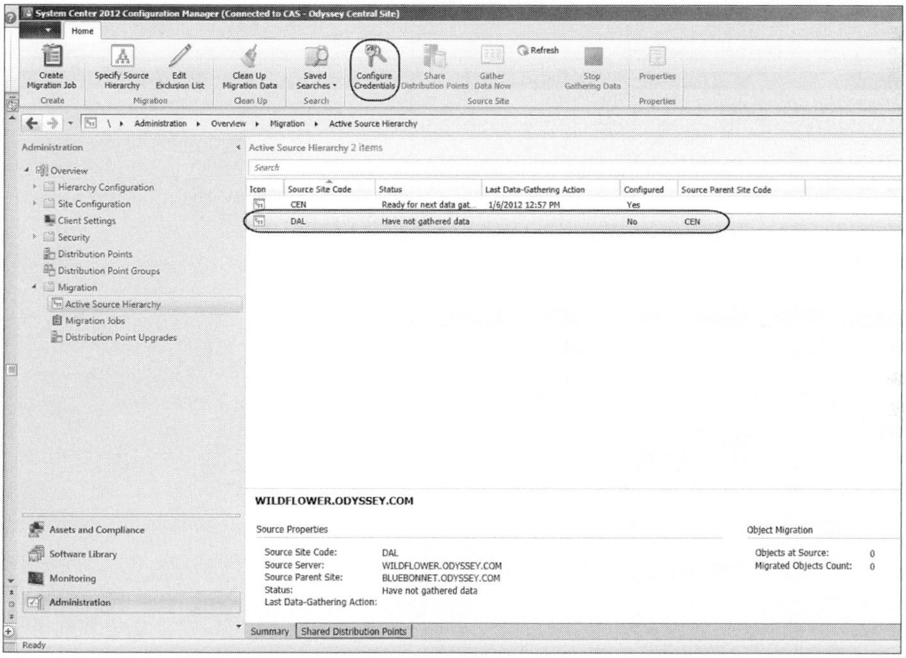

FIGURE 7.21   Configure child site credentials.

2. You are presented with the same settings as required for the active source site configuration except the requirement for the hierarchy and FQDN settings. If you have configured the same account for all sites, select **Existing Account** as shown in Figure 7.22.

3. Select the user account specified for the active source site. (You use the same migration user account for the child sites in your hierarchy in this scenario.) Use the same account for the site database access. Click **OK** to begin the data gathering process for the child site (see Figure 7.23).

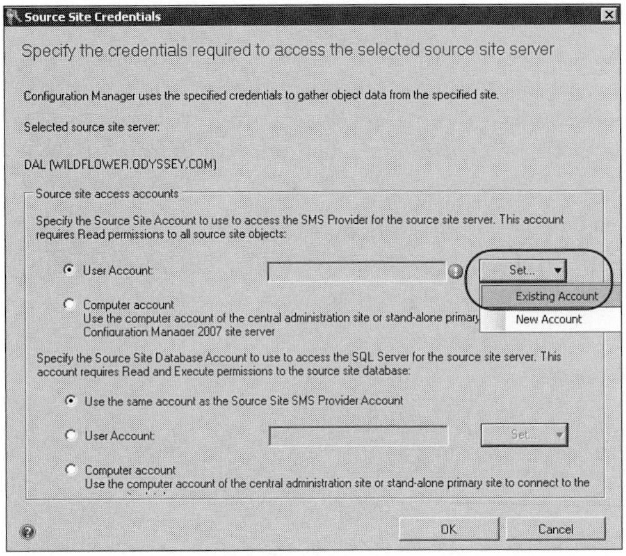

FIGURE 7.22   ConfigMgr 2007 child site using existing credentials.

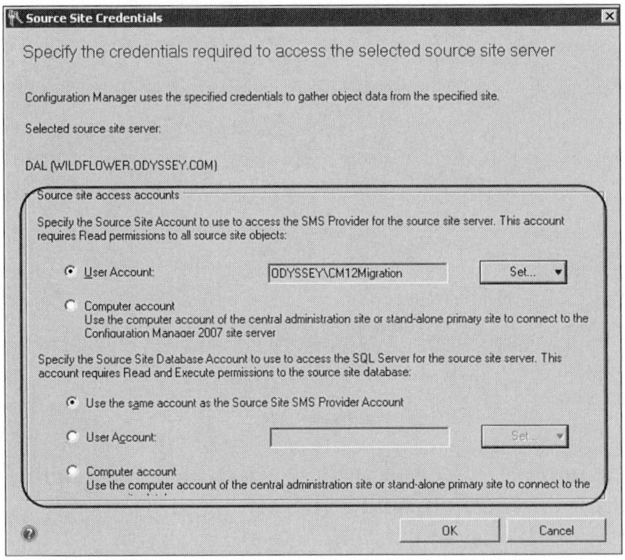

FIGURE 7.23   Completed Child ConfigMgr 2007 site credentials.

Figure 7.24 shows all the sites within the source hierarchy with all credentials successfully configured. The initial migration data gathering also returns the total number of objects for each site.

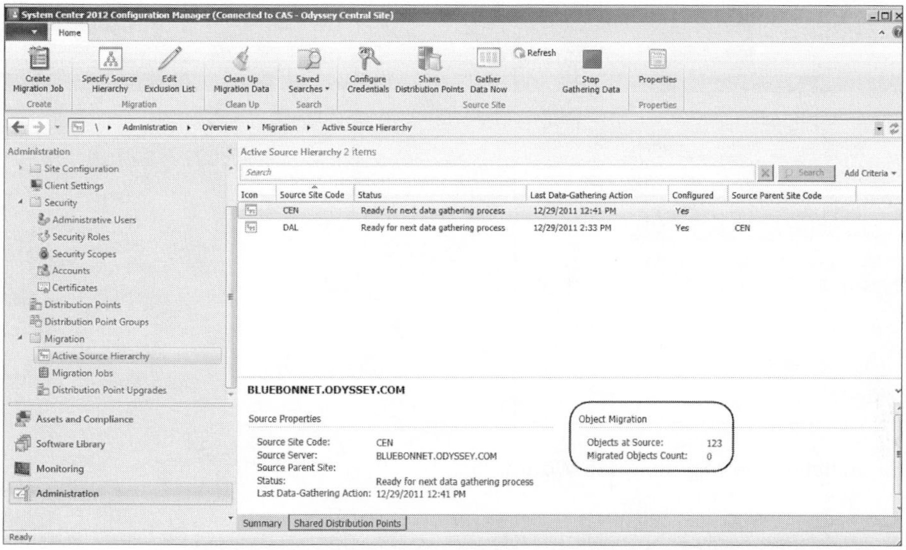

FIGURE 7.24   Completed source site and child site data gathering.

The next section discusses and provides configuration steps for the different migration jobs that are available.

Migration Jobs

There are three types of migration jobs. Each job type addresses a specific migration scenario:

▶ **Collection Migration:** Migrates supported objects associated with the selected collections or migrate the supported collections only

▶ **Object Migration:** Migrates supported objects

▶ **Objects Modified After Migration:** Migrates objects that have changed since either object migration or collection migration

The migration job type is specified when you invoke the Create Migration Job Wizard, as illustrated in Figure 7.25. The migration job type options are presented on the first page of the wizard, as displayed in Figure 7.26.

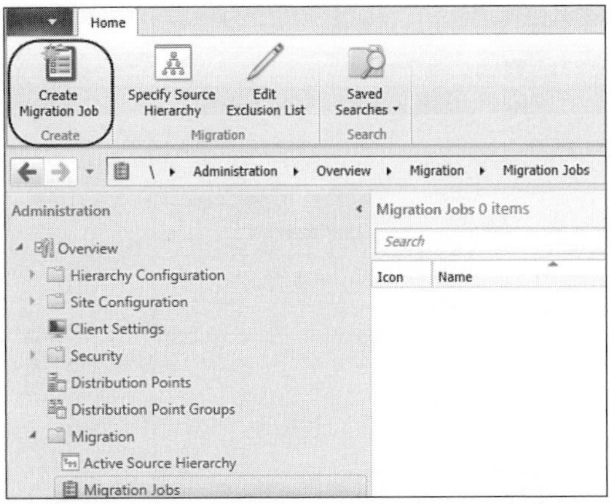

FIGURE 7.25   Initiating the Migrating Job Wizard.

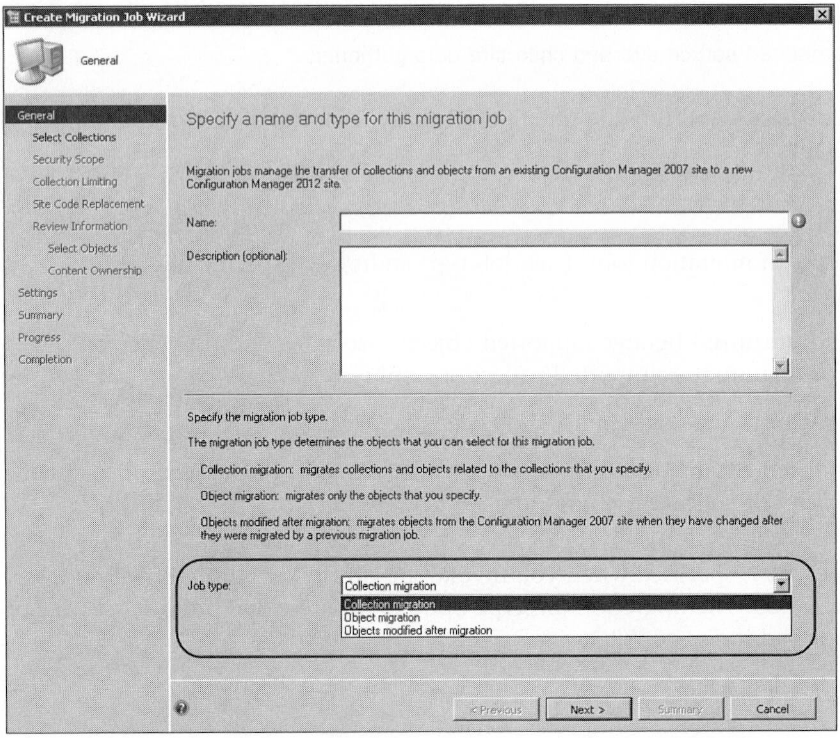

FIGURE 7.26   Selecting the migration job type.

Collection Migration Job

The collection migration operates in two modes: migrate collection only, and migrate the collection (s) and associated objects.

Here is the reasoning for the two collection migration options:

▶ **Collection Only:** This option provides a means to migrate collections as independent entities and effectively remove all objects linked to the collection, advertisements being an example. This option is useful for migrating collection definition queries and collections you create for organization structures; for example, an empty collection called **All Active Clients** with two subcollections called **Workstations** and **Servers**. The top collection in this example becomes a folder in System Center 2012 Configuration Manager.

NOTE: MIGRATING ADVERTISMENTS REQUIRES MIGRATING ASSOCIATED OBJECTS

The only way to migrate advertisements is by migrating associated objects. Advertisements cannot be migrated without a link to a collection.

▶ **Collection and Associated Objects:** The option that migrates the collection(s) and supported associated objects is best used when the ConfigMgr 2007 site has been adequately structured to support the migration by collection. Review your ConfigMgr 2007 environment to ensure you do not have overlapping and duplicate objects linked to collections. An approach will be to plan a collection structure dedicated to the migration.

Collection Only Migration

Here is how to configure and run a collection migration job that migrates only the specified collection with no associated objects:

▶ Connect to the System Center 2012 Configuration Manager console, and navigate to **Migration -> Migration jobs -> Create Migration Job** to start the wizard.

▶ Provide a name and optionally a description. Under Job type, select **Collection Migration**, as shown in Figure 7.27. Click **Next** after completing the required selection and mandatory options.

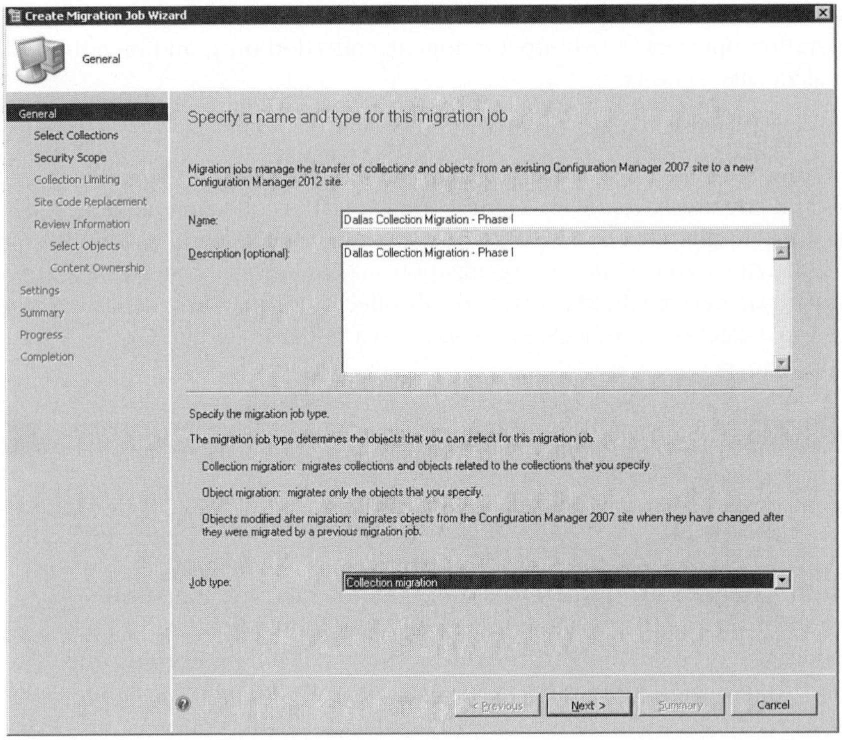

FIGURE 7.27   Select Collection Migration.

Here are the available wizard pages following the collection migration selection:

▶ **Select Collections:** This page presents you with a list of collections available for selection. Each collection is presented with information on its site code, collection type, and migration status, as shown in Figure 7.28. Select the collections in scope of the migration job being configured. Note a new collection with the source site code is created if you select a collection that already exists in the System Center 2012 Configuration Manager site. The list of collections that are not supported for migration can be viewed by clicking **View Collections That Cannot Migrate**.

Select the targeted collection(s) for migration, and uncheck **Migrate objects that are associated with the specified collections**.

▶ **Security Scope:** Objects in scope of the migration can be secured with a security scope. Security scopes do not apply to collections; only to objects associated with the collections.

▶ **Collection Limiting:** The collection limiting page is populated with available collections you have created if relevant to the objects migrated. An example in which you get this choice is when you have an advertisement targeted at a collection that is created from a higher-level site. The collection definition is available and evaluated at all System Center 2012 Configuration Manager sites; the migration job links the advertisement to all sites in the destination hierarchy. The collection limiting in the example scenario gives you the option to limit the advertisement to only the site(s) intended.

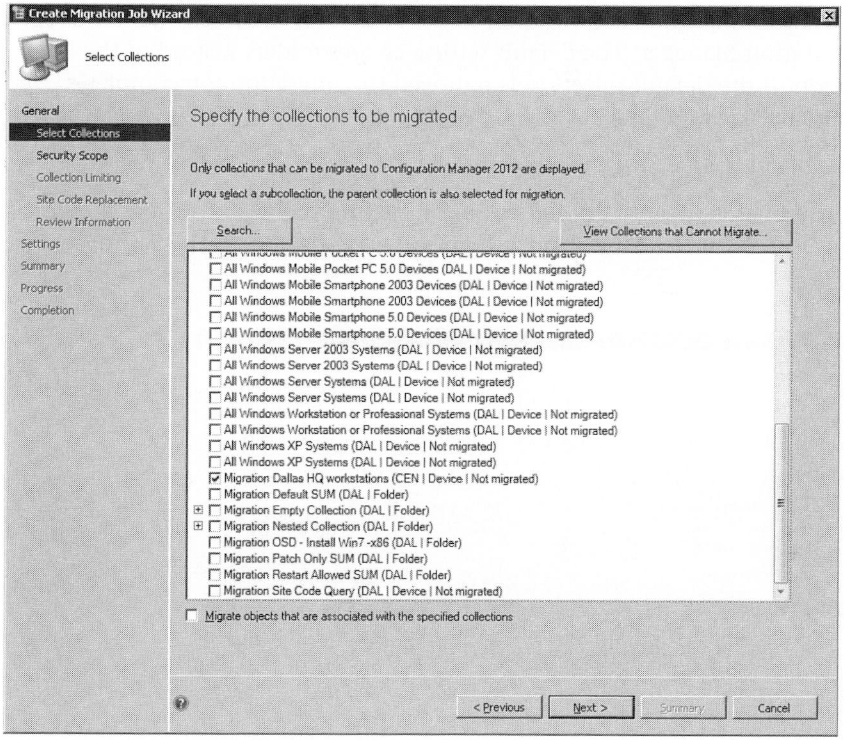

FIGURE 7.28   Collection selection with no associated objects.

▶ **Site Code Replacement:** Collections with site codes in the query are flagged, and you have the option to assign to one of the System Center 2012 Configuration Manage site codes in the hierarchy.

▶ **Review Information:** This page is only relevant when objects are selected and is not configurable for collection only migration.

▶ **Settings:** The settings page has three parts, scheduling, object conflict resolution, and additional object behavior settings.

    ▶ **Scheduling:** You can specify either not to run the job and effectively save the job for manual execution, run the job now (default), and schedule the job to run on a specified date and time (destination server time or UTC).

▶ **Object conflict resolution:** You can specify the behavior for overwriting update previously migrated objects. The default is not to overwrite updated objects.

▶ **Additional object behavior settings:** The only available option in the collection only migration is how to create the representation of empty nested collections that become organization folder structures in System Center 2012 Configuration Manager. The default setting creates folders instead of the collection. If the default selection is removed the migration job completes without creating any folders.

The Settings wizard page is shown in Figure 7.29.

▶ **Summary:** The final verification page before completing the wizard. The migration job is started if the **Run the Migration Job** option was selected on the Settings page.

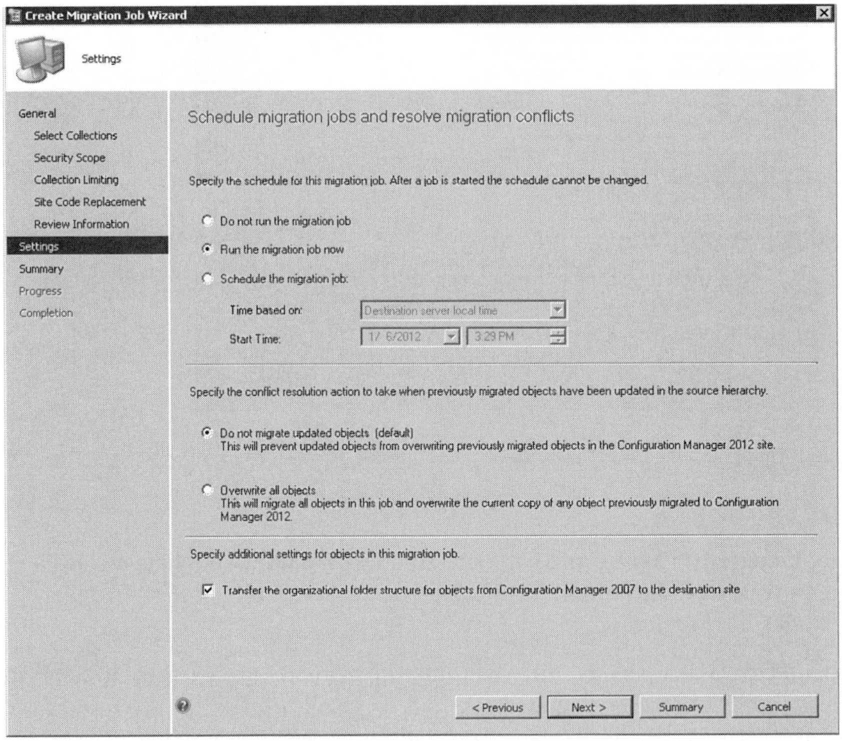

FIGURE 7.29 Settings page for collection only migration.

Collection Migration with Associated Objects

The option to migrate objects associated with collections is the only method to migrate advertisements specifically linked to collections. The wizard steps are the same as in collection only migration with the following exceptions and additional wizard pages:

▶ **Select Collections:** Select the targeted collection(s) for migration, and check the **Migration objects that are associated with the specified collections** option, as displayed in Figure 7.30.

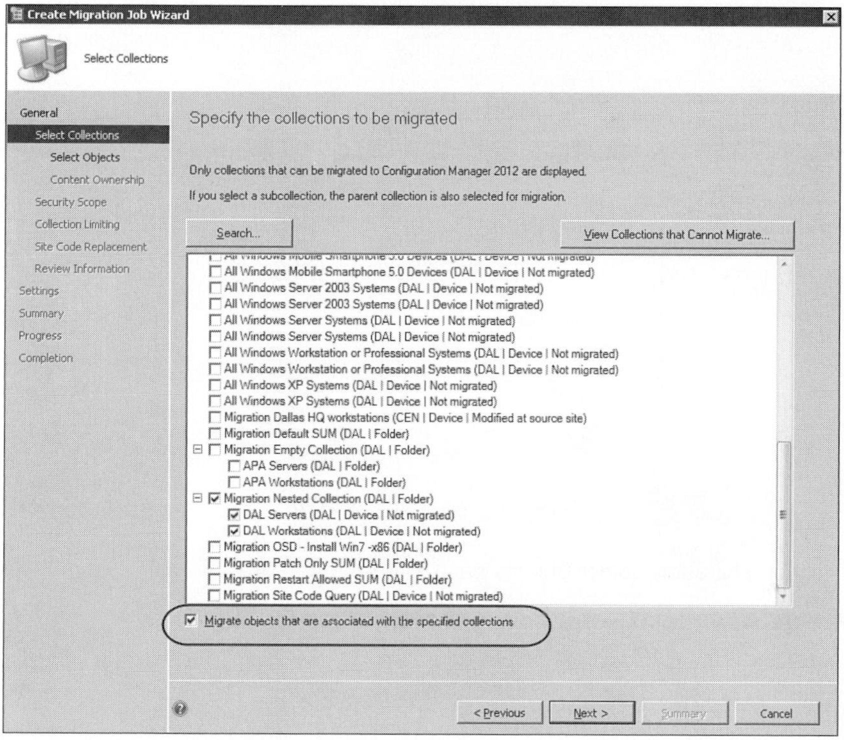

FIGURE 7.30   Collection migration with associated objects.

▶ **Select Objects:** By default, all supported objects associated with the collection(s) are selected, as shown in Figure 7.31. Deselected objects on this page are put on the migration exclusion list and not shown for future migrations. Note you can edit the exclusion list to make the objects available again.

▶ **Content Ownership:** You must assign ownership of the content associated with deployment objects. The CAS owns the metadata for the content, but a primary site must be selected as the content owner. A best practice to minimize network traffic associated with content transfer is ensure you select the closest available site in the System Center 2012 Configuration Manager destination hierarchy. Figure 7.32 shows the Content Ownership page with a list of available sites for selection.

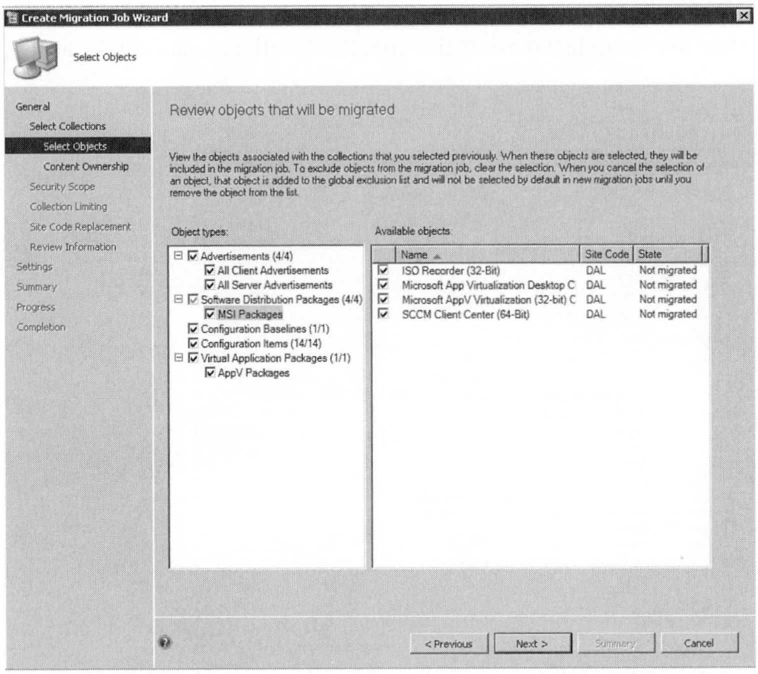

FIGURE 7.31   Collection Migration Select Objects page.

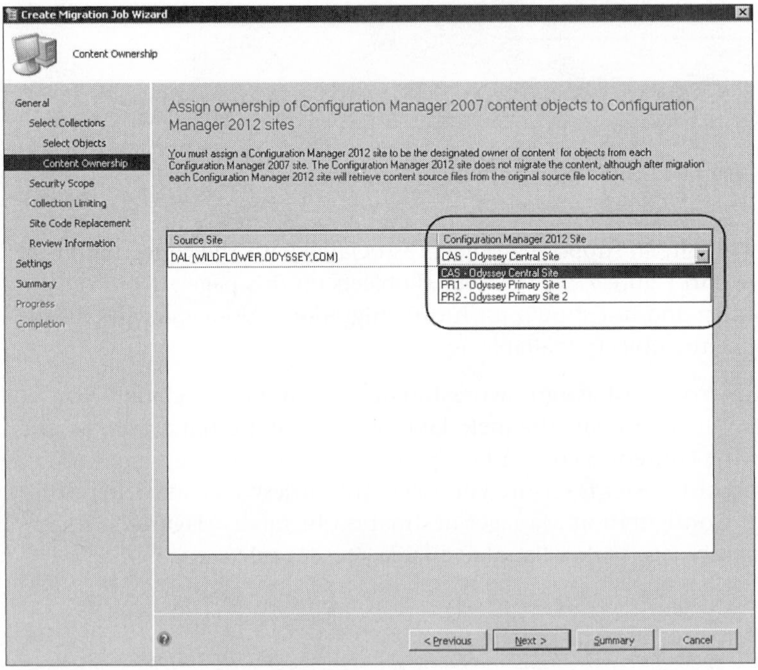

FIGURE 7.32   Content Ownership selection page.

▶ **Collection Limiting:** The collection limiting page is populated with available collections you have created if relevant to the objects migrated. Figure 7.33 shows the Collection Limiting page with the default selection of **All Systems** for devices. Creating custom collections in advance gives you the option to assign your intended limiting structure and leverage the full benefits of RBA in System Center 2012 Configuration Manager, as shown in Figure 7.34.

▶ **Review Information:** This page gives you the option to save information on the behavior of the objects selected when migrated to the System Center 2012 Configuration Manager site. Figure 7.35 shows you the Review Information page that is split into two panes, the collection behavior file save option and the object behavior file save option. This is a great resource to validate and document the transformation of objects during your proof of concept testing phase.

▶ **Settings:** The settings page has three parts, scheduling, object conflict resolution and additional object behavior settings. The first two parts are the same as discussed in the "Collection Migration Only" section.

An additional option is available to control program behavior for migrated advertisements. The default option is unchecked, as shown in Figure 7.36. The best practice is to leave the default setting as unchecked until the migration is complete.

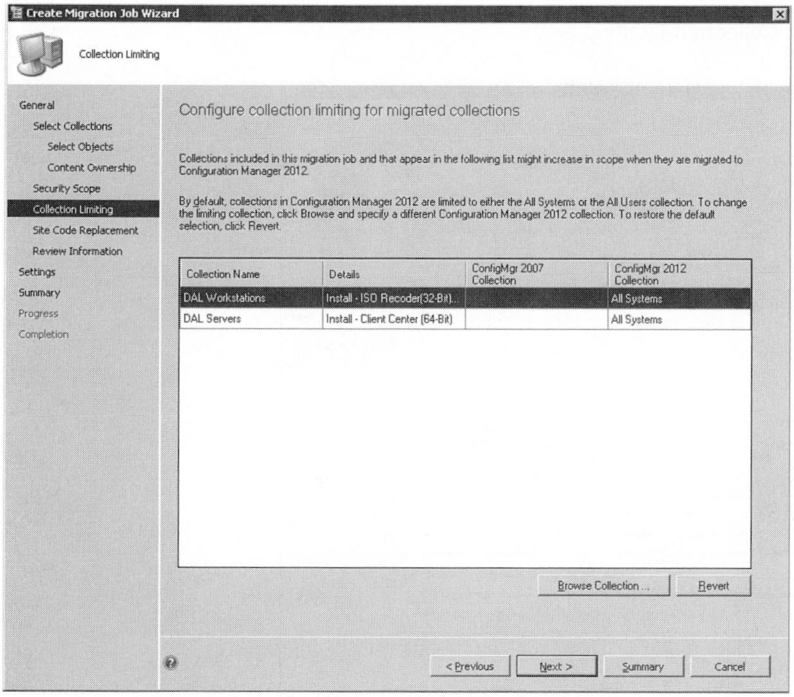

FIGURE 7.33   Default Collection Limiting.

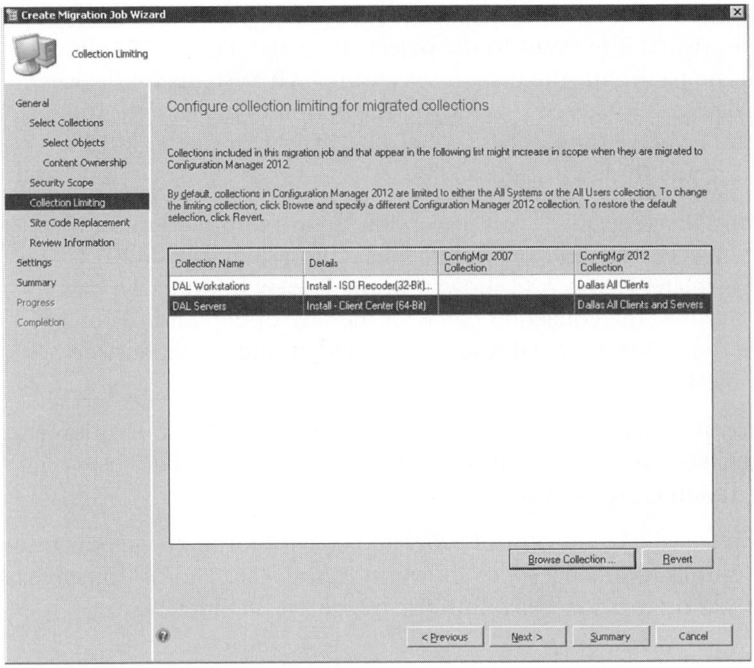

FIGURE 7.34   Custom Collection Limiting.

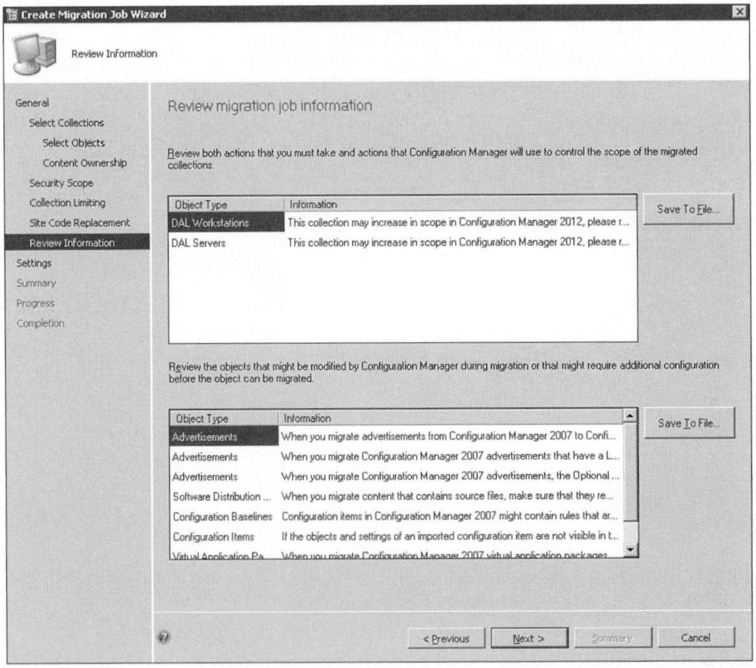

FIGURE 7.35   Review Settings page.

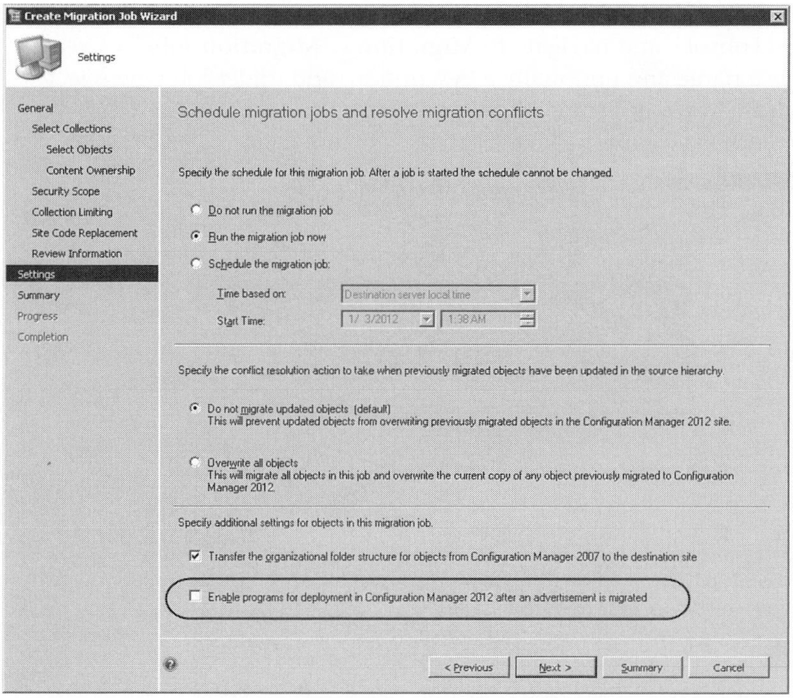

FIGURE 7.36   Settings page options for collection migration with objects.

▶ **Summary:** This is the final verification page before completing the wizard. The migration job is started if the **Run the Migration Job** option was selected on the Settings page.

Object Migration Job

You can use an object migration job to migrate the supported objects from your ConfigMgr 2007 sites without depending on collections. This migration method differs from the collection migration with associated objects, as the following object types are unique to this job type:

▶ Boundaries

▶ Asset Intelligence catalogs

▶ Asset Intelligence hardware requirements

▶ Software metering rules

The benefit to using this method to migrate objects is embracing the new user centric capabilities in System Center 2012 Configuration Manager. User-centric deployments target users instead of the devices typically in collections in the majority of ConfigMgr 2007 implementations.

To configure and run an object migration job, connect to the System Center 2012 Configuration Manager console, and navigate to **Migration -> Migration Jobs -> Create Migration Job**. Provide a name and optionally a description, and under Job type select **Object Migration**. This is shown in Figure 7.37.

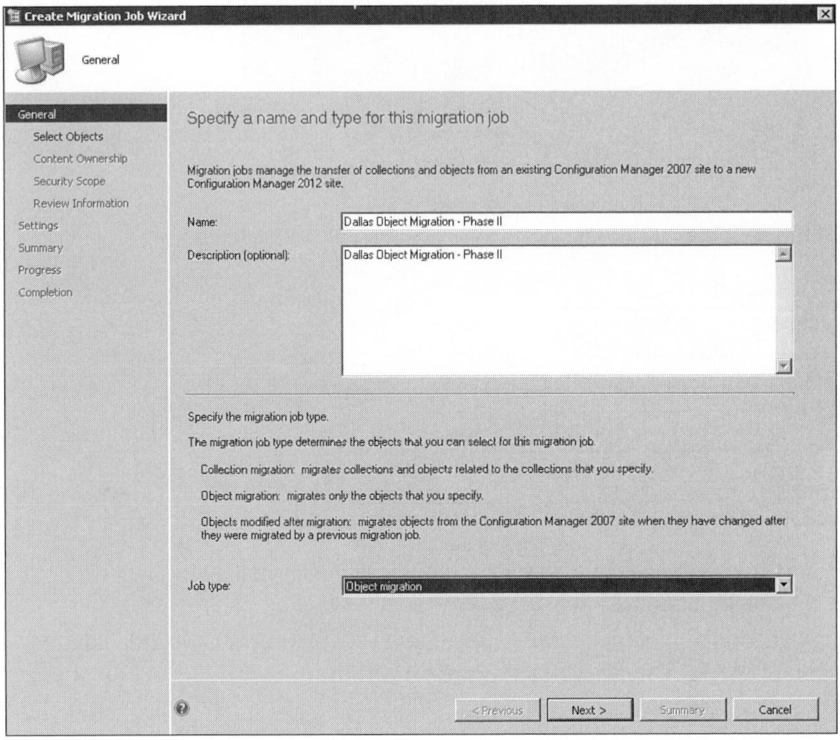

FIGURE 7.37   Object Migration start page.

Here are the available wizard pages following the object migration selection:

▶ **Select Objects:** This page presents you with a list of objects available for selection. The selection process is the same as discussed in the "Collection with Associated Objects" section. Figure 7.38 shows the Select Objects page. There are two special conditions for you to note:

   ▶ **Boundaries:** Boundaries are listed by ConfigMgr 2007 site, as shown in Figure 7.39. All the boundaries for the ConfigMgr 2007 site are migrated and a boundary group object is created in the targeted System Center 2012 Configuration Manager site. Plan to review your existing boundaries prior to including boundaries in your object selections.

   ▶ **Included objects:** When objects with dependent subcomponents are selected, for example a task sequence, you are presented with a dialog box confirming the included subcomponents automatically included, as shown in Figure 7.40.

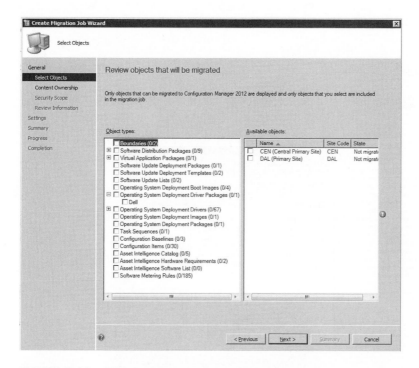

FIGURE 7.38   Object migration objects selection page.

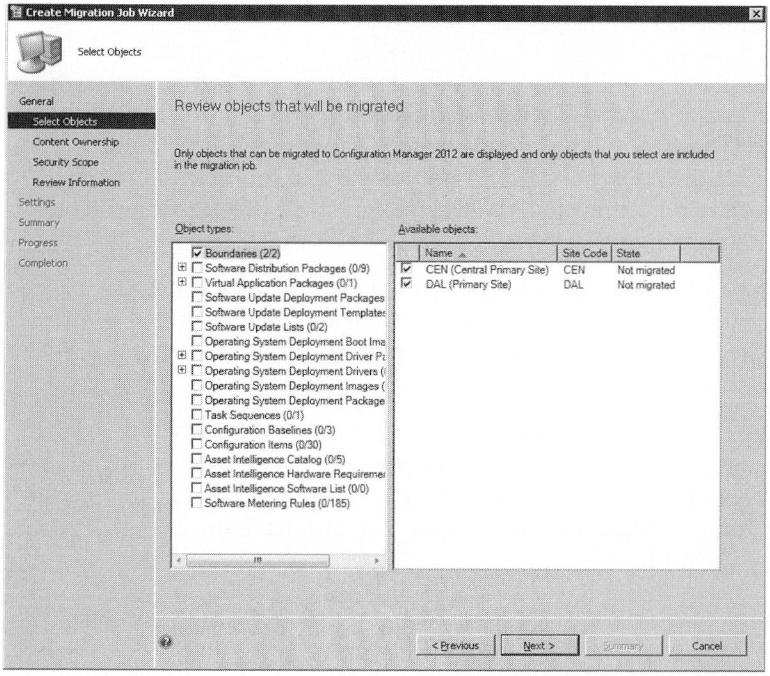

FIGURE 7.39   Object migration boundaries selection.

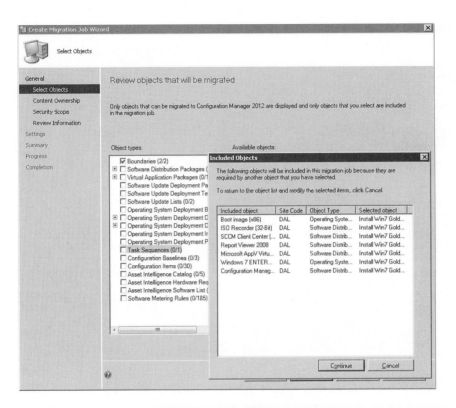

FIGURE 7.40   Object migration included objects.

▶ **Content Ownership:** You must assign ownership of the content associated with deployment objects. The CAS owns the metadata for the content, but you must select a primary site as the content owner. A best practice to minimize network traffic associated with content transfer is to ensure you select the closest available site in the destination hierarchy.

▶ **Security Scope:** The authors recommend that you plan and create your security scopes before the object migration job. For example, assuming the Dallas client administrators are responsible for operating system deployment objects, you can select **Dallas Clients** as the security scope, as shown in Figure 7.41.

▶ **Review Information:** This page provides you with information on the behavior of objects being migrated. The information on this page is an additional checklist, such as reminding you that custom boot images will be replaced with the default System Center 2012 Configuration Manager boot images. You also have the option to save this information to a text file.

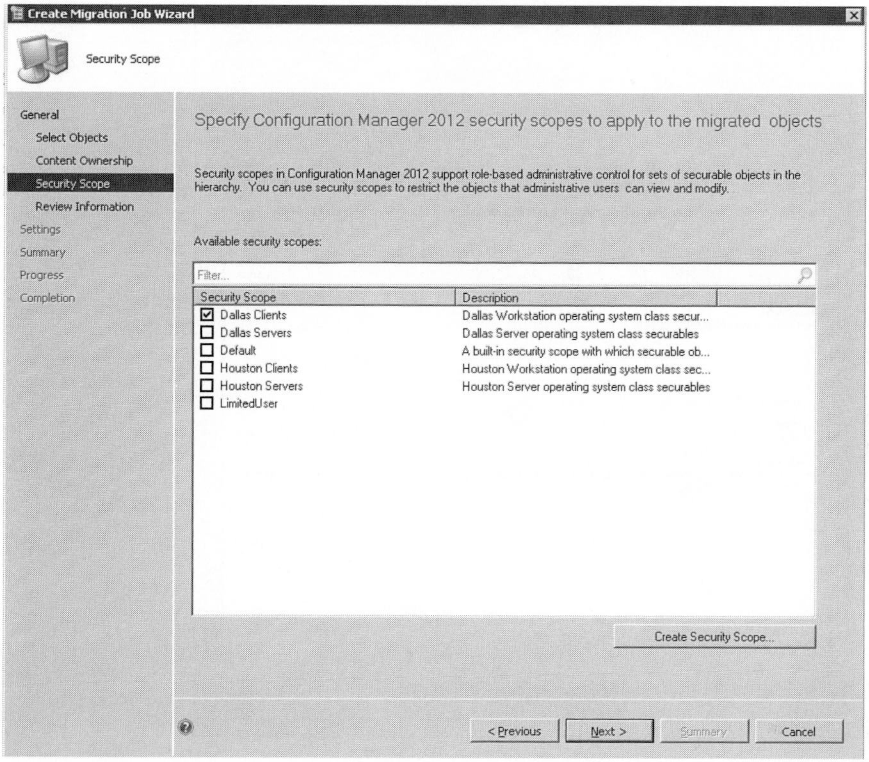

FIGURE 7.41   Object migration custom security scope.

▶ **Settings:** The settings page has three parts: scheduling, object conflict resolution, and additional object behavior settings.

  ▶ **Scheduling:** You can specify not to run the job and effectively save the job for manual execution, run the job now (default), and the final option is to schedule the job to run on a specified date and time (destination server time or UTC).

  ▶ **Object conflict resolution:** You can specify the behavior for overwriting update previously migrated objects. The default is not to overwrite updated objects.

  ▶ **Additional object behavior settings:** Here is where you can enable or disable the option to **Transfer the organizational folder structure for objects from Configuration Manager 2007 to the destination site**.

▶ **Summary:** This is the final verification page before completing the wizard. The migration job is started if the **Run the migration job** option was selected on the Settings page. Figure 7.42 shows the Summary page.

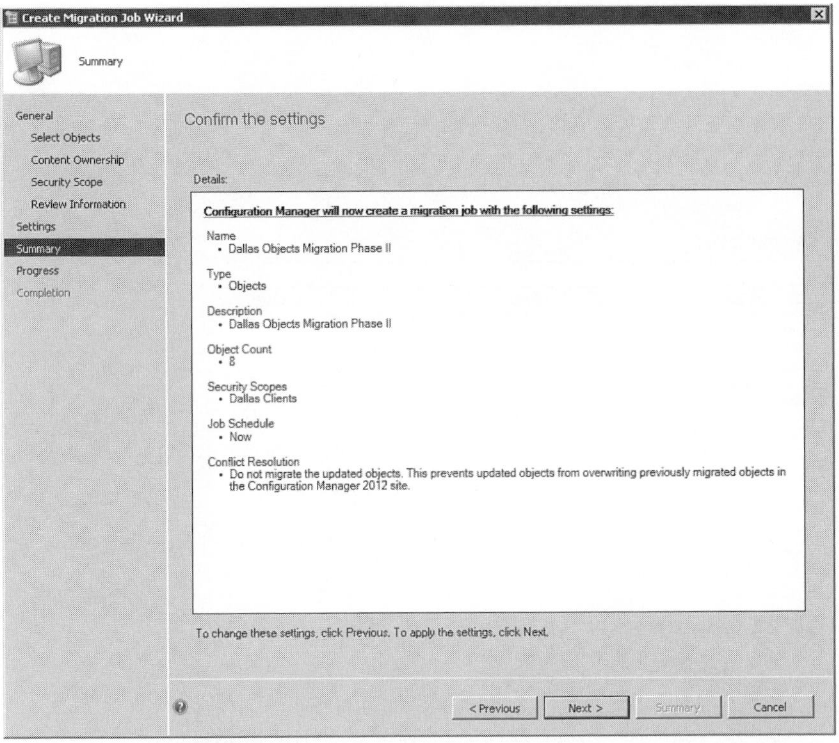

FIGURE 7.42   Object migration summary.

The built-in migration capabilities are designed to support a continual migration process. Objects and collections in your ConfigMgr 2007 source sites may change after a migration job has completed. The next section, "Objects Modified After Migration Job," discusses the built-in migration capabilities used to update migration objects that have changed at the ConfigMgr 2007 source site since the last successful migration.

CAUTION: EDITING AND DELETING MIGRATION JOBS

Migration jobs with a status of completed cannot be edited or deleted. You can edit the Settings page of a migration job that has not started. Migration jobs remain in the console until the active source hierarchy is changed and the Clean Up Migration Data process is run.

Objects Modified After Migration Job

This job type depends on a successful completion of the data gathering from the ConfigMgr 2007 source site after an object change. The data gathering job runs every 4 hours by default. The data gather process can be initiated outside the schedule set by using the **Gather Data Now** option for the source site, as shown in Figure 7.43.

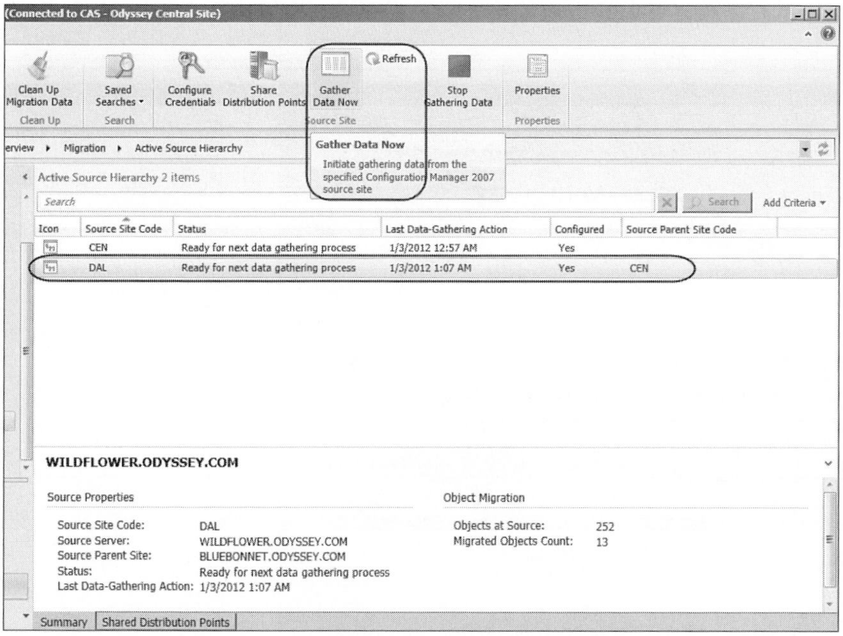

FIGURE 7.43   The Gather Data Now selection.

To configure and run an objects modified after migration job, connect to the System Center 2012 Configuration Manager console, and navigate to **Migration -> Migration jobs -> Create Migration Job**. Provide a name and optionally a description, and under Job type, select **Objects modified after migration**. This is shown in Figure 7.44.

Here are the available wizard pages following the Objects modified after migration selection:

▶ **Select Objects:** This page presents you with a list of objects available for selection. Only migrated objects that have changed at the source site are listed for selection. Figure 7.45 shows the Select objects page; note the State column of modified objects show a value of **Modified at source site**.

▶ **Content Ownership:** You must assign ownership of the content associated with deployment objects. You can change the content owner for the modified object.

▶ **Security Scope:** Assign a security scope.

▶ **Review Information:** This page provides with information on the behavior of objects being migrated. The information on this page is an additional checklist. For example, you are reminded that custom boot images will be replaced with the default System Center 2012 Configuration Manager boot images. You also have the option to save the review information to a text file.

▶ **Settings:** The settings page has three parts: scheduling, object conflict resolution, and additional object behavior settings.

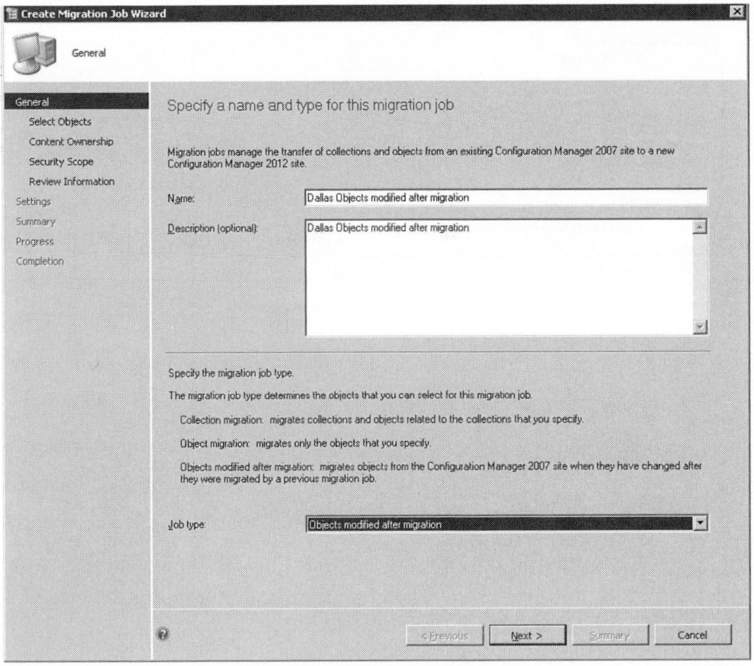

FIGURE 7.44   Selecting the objects modified after migration job type.

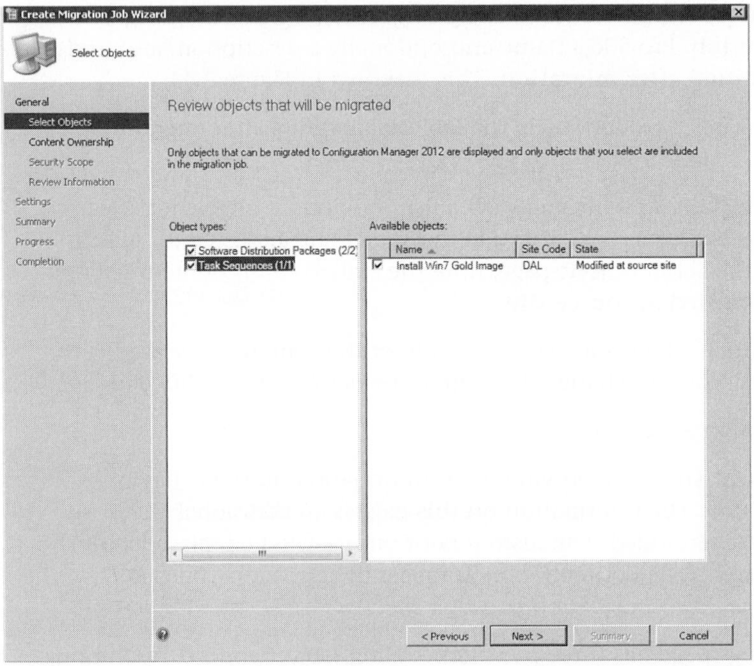

FIGURE 7.45   Objects modified after migration selection page.

▶ **Scheduling:** Specify not to run the job and effectively save the job for manual execution, run the job now (default), or schedule the job to run on a specified date and time (destination server time or UTC).

▶ **Object conflict resolution:** The only option available for this job type is **Overwrite all objects**, as shown in Figure 7.46.

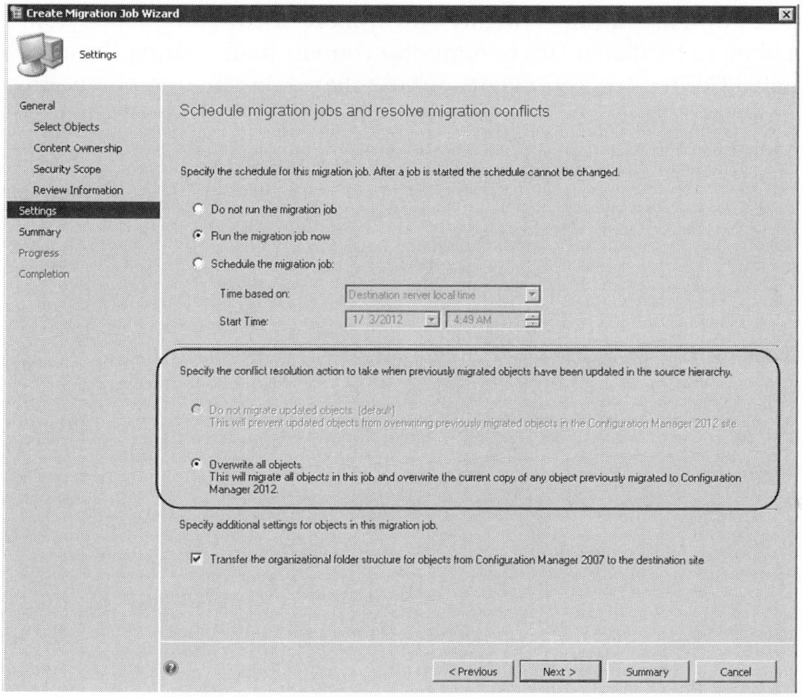

FIGURE 7.46   Settings - Overwrite all objects.

▶ **Additional object behavior settings:** The option to **Transfer the organizational folder structure for objects from Configuration Manager 2007 to the destination site** can be enabled and disabled here.

▶ **Summary:** This is the final verification page before completing the wizard. The migration job is started if the **Run the migration job** option was selected on the Settings page.

The content migrated objects depend on is not automatically distributed to the distribution points in the destination site. After migration, you must assign either a distribution point or a distribution point group. Assigning a distribution point or distribution point group copies content from the source location to the distribution points or distribution point groups. The built-in migration capabilities provide a means for upgraded ConfigMgr 2007 and new System Center 2012 Configuration Manager clients to access content on the original ConfigMgr 2007 distribution points from the active source hierarchy. This capability is called *shared distribution points*.

Shared Distribution Points

Use ConfigMgr 2007 distribution points during and after the migration to access content. The migration process offers you three options:

▶ **Share distribution points:** You can configure one or more distribution points from your source hierarchy to be shared DPs to minimize content traffic during the migration phase. Migrated ConfigMgr 2007 clients can use shared distribution points after they have been upgraded. Figure 7.47 shows how you enable the shared distribution point capability for a ConfigMgr 2007 source site.

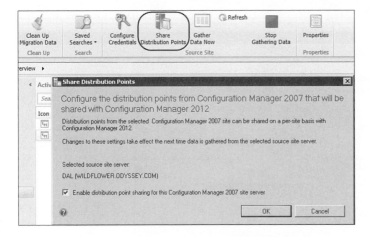

FIGURE 7.47   Enable shared distribution point.

▶ **Upgrade ConfigMgr 2007 distribution points:** You have the option to upgrade the shared distribution points as part of the migration process. Configured shared distribution points will be listed under the Shared Distribution Points tab for the configured ConfigMgr 2007 source site upgrade possibility status. Figure 7.48 shows a status of **No** for eligibility to upgrade. ConfigMgr 2007 distribution points can be upgraded only if the site server meets the following criteria:

▶ Any type of ConfigMgr 2007 distribution point.

▶ Must meet the supported requirements for a System Center 2012 Configuration Manager distribution point.

▶ Can be a secondary site but with no other site system roles.

▶ Cannot have a ConfigMgr 2007 client agent installed.

▶ Cannot be a ConfigMgr 2007 primary site.

See http://technet.microsoft.com/en-us/library/gg712275.aspx for additional information.

▶ **Upgrade ConfigMgr 2007 secondary sites:** A common scenario for secondary sites in ConfigMgr 2007 implementations is their use in content bandwidth management due to their scheduling capabilities. During the migration process, you can upgrade a shared distribution point that is co-located with a secondary site. The upgrade process removes the secondary site but preserves the original distribution point content. System Center 2012 Configuration Manager distribution points have built-in scheduling and thus are an excellent replacement for secondary sites that were established for the sole purpose of being content bandwidth managers. See http://technet.microsoft.com/en-us/library/gg712275.aspx for additional information.

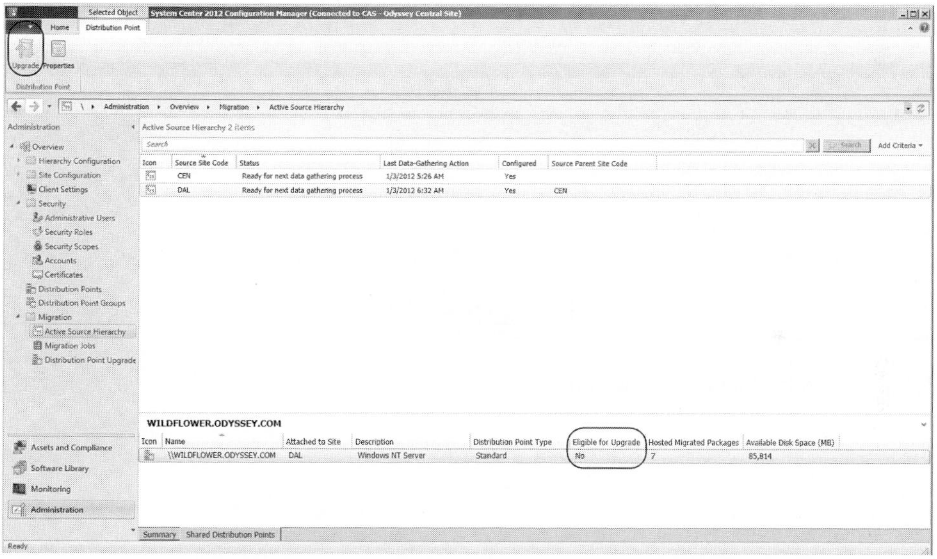

FIGURE 7.48   Shared distribution point status.

NOTE: SHARED DISTRIBUTION POINTS ACCESS

The migration process allows you to migrate from multiple hierarchies. When a hierarchy is migrated, you can change the source hierarchy. Shared distribution points from other hierarchies are no longer available if you change the source hierarchy.

Migration Clean Up

The built-in Clean Up Migration Data migration function is the step you must perform to complete the migration. Clean up is required if you want to migrate data from a different ConfigMgr 2007 hierarchy.

The cleanup process is in two parts:

▶ **Stop gathering data:** You must stop gathering data for all ConfigMgr 2007 source sites configured under the active source sites. The Clean Up Migration Data function fails if this step is not performed, as shown in Figure 7.49.

▶ **Clean Up Migration Data:** This process deletes all migration job configurations and removes all ConfigMgr 2007 source hierarchy information. You must stop the data gathering from the lowest child site configured in the active source hierarchy and repeat the process up the configured active source hierarchy. Clean Up Migration Data does not delete migrated objects; migration configuration and jobs are deleted for the configured active source hierarchy. Figure 7.50 shows the Clean Up Migration Data task.

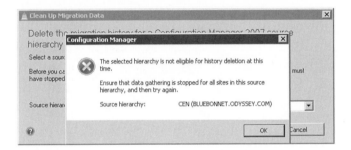

FIGURE 7.49   Clean Up Migration Data error.

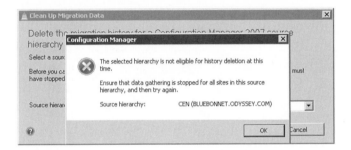

FIGURE 7.50   Clean Up Migration Data - stop gathering data.

Reports and clients are the two types of objects that you can migrate to System Center 2012 Configuration Manager from your ConfigMgr 2007 sites without using the built-in migration function. How you migrate reports and clients is discussed in the "Migrating Reports" and "Client Migration methods" sections.

Migrating Reports

System Center 2012 introduces a new set of reports built to run on SSRS. ConfigMgr 2007 legacy reports cannot be migrated. Chapter 18 covers the changes and enhancements in reporting. Here are the two areas in ConfigMgr 2007 to plan for during the migration:

▶ **Legacy Reports:** Reports created by the reporting point role; web reports based on Active Server Pages (ASP)

▶ **Custom Reports:** Any reports you have authored and published

Legacy Reports

Legacy reports are associated with the reporting point role in ConfigMgr 2007 implementations. Legacy reports were the only reporting option built into ConfigMgr 2007 prior to SP 1. With the introduction of R2, you could install a reporting service point role that leverages SSRS. In environments where the legacy reports have not been customized, the only action required during migration is a review of the built-in reports in System Center 2012 Configuration Manager.

SSRS Reports

If your ConfigMgr 2007 environment uses a reporting service point with no customized reports, review the new System Center 2012 Configuration Manager reports as part of your migration planning. These reports have been re-engineered to query the latest schema of the product. The default ConfigMgr 2007 SSRS reports cannot be migrated to System Center 2012 Configuration Manager.

Custom Reports

Here is the migration process for custom reports, legacy or SSRS-based:

▶ **Legacy Custom Reports:** Review the System Center 2012 Configuration Manager reports to see if your reporting criterion is in an existing default report. Create new custom reports if the default reports do not meet your needs.

▶ **SSRS Custom Reports:** Review the System Center 2012 Configuration Manager reports to see if your reporting criteria are in an existing default report. If your criteria are not met, test your report queries against the new database schema. If your report queries run with the correct results, you have the option of saving your RDL file and importing it into System Center 2012 Configuration Manager (see Chapter 18 for additional information on this topic).

Client Migration and Methods

System Center 2012 Configuration Manager supports an in-place upgrade of the existing ConfigMgr 2007 client. The supported methods for upgrade are the same as a standard installation of the client:

▶ Client push

▶ Group policy

▶ Manual installation

▶ Software distribution

▶ Software update-based

Regardless of the client upgrade method, you must ensure the ConfigMgr 2007 clients to be upgraded meet the minimum requirements for a System Center 2012 Configuration Manager client. You can find the most up-to-date information on the System Center 2012 Configuration Manager client requirements at http://technet.microsoft.com/en-us/library/gg682042.aspx.

Background and Client Migration Concepts

The goal of migrating ConfigMgr 2007 clients to System Center 2012 Configuration Manager is to retain as much existing client management information as possible.

Here is the information that is retained when a ConfigMgr 2007 client is upgraded:

▶ Unique identifier (GUID)

▶ Advertisement history

The following information is not retained:

▶ Files in the client cache

▶ Information about advertisements that have not yet run

▶ Desired configuration management (DCM) compliance data

▶ Inventory information

▶ Information stored in the Configuration Manager client registry, such as power schemes, logging settings, and local policy settings

Plan to migrate the information the client will depend on, such as advertisements, collections, and packages. The "Migration Jobs" section earlier in this chapter provides information on how to migrate the supported objects the upgraded client depends on.

REAL WORLD: CLIENT AUDIT AND HEALTH

Your migration is an excellent opportunity to perform an audit of the environment and validate the health of existing clients. Plan to perform an audit of the environment with the aim of validating that you have full coverage for all clients in scope, and check the health state of existing clients. Upgrading an unhealthy client will not necessarily resolve an underlining external issue (for example, WMI corruption). Although System Center 2012 Configuration Manager has significantly improved client health monitoring and remediation built-in functions, this will not fix existing issues with the ConfigMgr client. You should plan to resolve issues with existing clients before attempting to upgrade.

Client Migration Strategies for Your Network

Client migration typically has two parts:

▶ How you migrate

▶ When and how many clients you migrate

The ConfigMgr 2007 client migration methods are discussed in the "Client Migration and Methods" section. When and how many clients you migrate at a time requires that you plan and execute the upgrade process with minimal disruption to your existing operating environment.

The major impact is on the network infrastructure, due to the initial traffic generated by client activities after the upgrade of the ConfigMgr 2007 client. Consider the following strategies when executing your client migration phase:

▶ **Upgrade in batches:** Migrate in batches in line with the available bandwidth of your network infrastructure. A recommended best practice is to perform a pilot migration coordinated with the network team to get an actual measurement of the traffic generated. Use the actual measured network impact to guide you.

▶ **Minimize active targeted advertisements to the devices migrated and users aligned with the migrated devices:** A deployment freeze for all but essential activities is a method usually employed as an industry best practice during this phase.

See the documentation at http://technet.microsoft.com/en-us/library/gg712283.aspx for additional information.

Troubleshooting Migration Issues

The migration process can present some technical challenges and issues. Table 7.6 provides information on troubleshooting resources, known issues, and resolutions.

TABLE 7.6   Troubleshooting Resources and Known Issues

Resource/Issue	Notes
Log file.	The migration process is logged in the following log file: migmctrl.log (*<ConfigMgrInstallPath>*\ LOGS folder on the site server). This file is overwritten, so check it as soon as you encounter any issues.
Migration reports.	Enable the reporting services role for the System Center 2012 Configuration Manager to have access to the Migration reports.
Migration workspace.	Monitor individual migration jobs in the System Center 2012 Configuration Manager console at **Administration** -> **Migration** -> **Migration jobs**.
Gathering data fails for a ConfigMgr 2007 source site.	Check the security delegation for the configured migration account.
Content access fails for shared distribution point.	Ensure the source hierarchy for the shared distribution point is still the active source site.
Cannot delete migration jobs after migration.	Stop all data gathering for all sites configured under the active source site. Run the Data Clean Up task. You must stop data gathering from the lowest child site configured and work your way up the hierarchy to the top site.
You get a message saying No objects have been modified in Configuration Manager 2007 since they were migrated to Configuration Manager 2012 when you try to create a objects modified after migration job.	This occurs when you run a clean data migration to remove the active source site and try to migrate updated objects. The clean task removes all migration job history. You must use either a collection migration job or an object migration job in this case.

NOTE: ADDITIONAL TROUBLESHOUTING RESOURCES

Additional information on troubleshooting migration is available at http://technet.microsoft.com/en-us/library/gg712297.aspx.

Summary

This chapter discussed and provided guidance on the migration process. It provided background as to why this is a migration rather than an upgrade and discussed planning the migration, the process of migrating your ConfigMgr 2007 infrastructure, migrating features and objects, client migration, and troubleshooting migration issues.

The next chapter provides a detailed discussion of the System Center 2012 Configuration Manager console.

PART III

Configuration Manager Operations

IN THIS PART

The Configuration Manager Console

Configuration Manager's console has historically used the Microsoft Management Console (MMC) framework. The console has evolved over the years; with each product version, it received little touches to enhance the administrative experience. The Configuration Manager (ConfigMgr) 2007 console, which uses MMC 3.0, included drag and drop, dashboards on home pages, column sorting, search folders, and finally a search bar. Activities such as providing different user experiences still required customizing the console and somehow distributing the customized version to the appropriate individuals.

With System Center 2012 Configuration Manager, Microsoft removes the MMC-based console from the product. The new console that utilizes the System Center framework brings a fresh and intuitive look to the platform. By building the ConfigMgr console on this common framework, the console becomes aligned with the familiar look-and-feel of the other System Center components. Incorporating the Outlook style makes the console easier to navigate, search, and operate than with previous versions. In addition, role-based security controls the console experience, giving each security role a common set of views, tasks, and objects.

The ConfigMgr console is the administrative interface for managing all facets of the ConfigMgr infrastructure, applications, deployments, software updates, monitoring, and users and devices. As a key element of any ConfigMgr environment, the console is also the interface used to maintain the site and hierarchy—performing daily tasks to manage and configure sites, the site database, clients, and monitor the status of the hierarchy.

This chapter describes the core areas of the console and its many features. The chapter also covers console installation and deployment, including console prerequisites, security considerations, and troubleshooting.

Console Highlights

The new Configuration Manager console sports some nice features, which this chapter covers in detail. Here are the highlights:

▶ Similar operations are grouped together into intuitive, administrative workspaces rather than one gigantic, confusing tree structure.

▶ An Outlook style experience adds a similar type of navigation to ConfigMgr, coupled with context-sensitive ribbons displaying only the relevant actions.

▶ Supporting role-based administration (RBA), the console displays only what you have rights to see, removing much of the clutter and confusion often associated with a busy console.

▶ Search bars in nearly every facet of the console enable instant filtering to narrow down the scope of data to a manageable view.

▶ Temporary nodes help track various objects used in the console, allowing quick reference back to objects you already visited.

▶ Just like your favorite web browser, a temporary history is available of the areas you have visited while navigating the console, making it easy to go back to a previous view.

▶ In-console alerts brings near real-time status information, providing light monitoring functionality without leaving the console.

Touring the Console

As you open the System Center 2012 Configuration Manager console, notice it is divided into four main quadrants, reminiscent of Outlook:

▶ Navigation

▶ Lists

▶ Detail

▶ Bars

These are discussed in the next sections. In addition, the console contains other functionality that is similar to the behavior of Outlook. The navigation pane and ribbon bar are key elements of Outlook that you can immediately recognize in the new console.

Configuration Manager Console Panes

Console panes are areas that are themed to contain a certain type of object. There are three panes in the console, shown in Figure 8.1:

▶ **Navigation:** Area 1 in Figure 8.1 is the left side of the console, known as the Navigation pane (sometimes referred to as the *WunderBar*). The workspaces at the bottom quickly move you between administrative areas, whereas the folder list at the top is used to select specific nodes.

▶ **List:** Depending on the selected node, the List pane on the right side (Area 2 in Figure 8.1) displays charts, dashboards, or list of objects.

▶ **Detail:** When selecting certain items in the List pane, the Detail pane (Area 3) dynamically shows additional information about the selected item. Often, the Detail pane is broken out into multiple tabs containing more information.

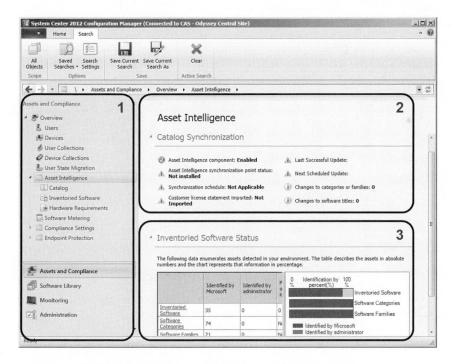

FIGURE 8.1   The panes of the Configuration Manager console.

NOTE: EVER WONDER HOW THE WUNDERBAR GOT ITS NAME?

WunderBar is the name used within Microsoft to refer to the Navigation pane. Before the WunderBar term was used, the Navigation pane was known as the "Combined Outlook Bar and Folder List." You can read more information about this and the ribbon bar at http://blogs.msdn.com/b/jensenh/archive/2005/10/07/478214.aspx.

Configuration Manager Console Bars

The ConfigMgr console also includes three bars, as displayed in Figure 8.2:

▶ **Ribbon:** The ribbon bar (Area 1), situated along the top of the console, is a context-sensitive list of commands available based on the selected object.

▶ **Address:** The Address bar, as shown as Area 2 in Figure 8.2, shows the node on which the console is currently focused. It is primarily designed to make navigation easier by providing a history of places already visited.

▶ **Search:** The Search bar (Area 3) provides a means to isolate the objects in the List pane by matching them against criteria, helping you to quickly find information.

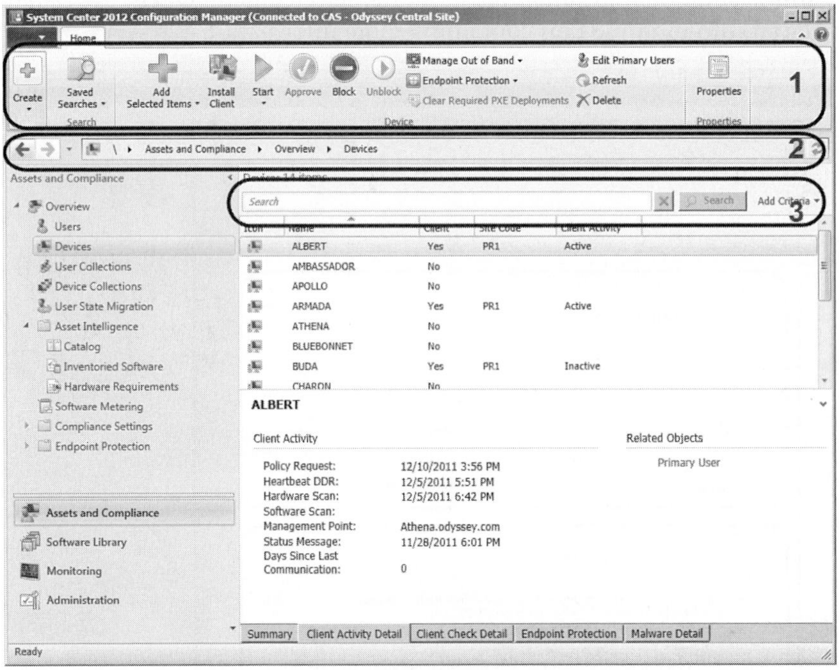

FIGURE 8.2   The ribbon, address, and search bars of the ConfigMgr console.

Backstage

The tab on the far left section of the ribbon bar is referred to as the *backstage*. The backstage contains a common set of commands that are available no matter where the focus is in the ConfigMgr console, providing a consistent set of commands, as shown in Figure 8.3.

▶ **Connect to a New Site:** Displays the Site Connection dialog box to connect to a different site server.

▶ **About Configuration Manager:** Displays the About System Center 2012 Configuration Manager dialog box.

▶ **Help:** Displays the help file.

▶ **Customer Experience Improvement Program:** Launches the Customer Experience Improvement Program dialog box, which you can use to enable or disable participation in the program.

▶ **Exit:** Closes the ConfigMgr console.

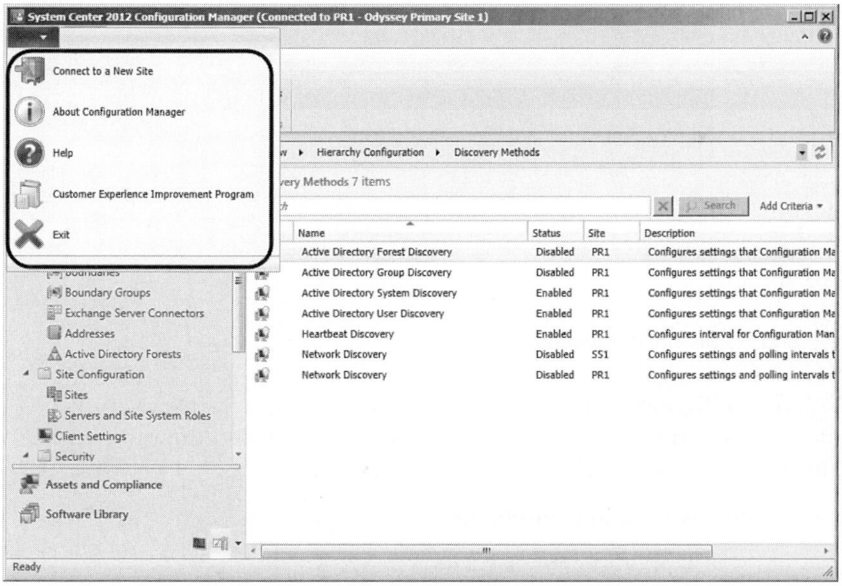

FIGURE 8.3   The backstage area of the console.

ConfigMgr Workspaces

The ConfigMgr console is categorized into four different workspaces:

▶ Assets and Compliance

▶ Software Library

▶ Monitoring

▶ Administration

Each workspace is designed for a specific purpose with similar functions grouped together. By selecting a workspace, the Navigation pane displays a different set of nodes in the folder list. The next sections discuss each of these workspaces.

Assets and Compliance Workspace

Displayed in Figure 8.4, the Assets and Compliance workspace includes collections for managing users and devices. In addition, you can manage user state migration, asset intelligence, and software metering from this workspace.

FIGURE 8.4   Assets and Compliance workspace.

Managing baselines and configuration items for compliance settings take place in this workspace. Endpoint protection policies that configure antimalware and firewall settings are also managed in this workspace.

Here are the main nodes for Assets and Compliance:

▶ Users

▶ Devices

▶ User Collections

▶ Device Collections

▶ User State Migration

▶ Asset Intelligence

▶ Software Metering

▶ Compliance Settings

▶ Endpoint Protection

Software Library Workspace

The Software Library workspace, as shown in Figure 8.5, places all the elements of managing applications, software updates, and operating system deployments into one area. This node is not just about managing content; it includes other activities such as managing the global conditions and requirement rules that drive the stateful behavior of applications, managing automatic deployment rules for software updates, and managing task sequences which provide a means to perform multiple steps on a client system (typically during use with operating system deployments). In addition, when users request applications through Software Center, these approval requests populate the Approval Requests node. Utilize this workspace to approve or deny application requests.

FIGURE 8.5   Software Library workspace.

You can manage all your software updates from this workspace, including synchronizing software updates and managing automatic deployment rules to update and deploy software updates. All the drivers, images, and task sequences that comprise operating system deployments exist in this workspace.

The Software Library workspace is separated into three main nodes:

▶ Application Management

▶ Software Updates

▶ Operating Systems

Monitoring Workspace

The Monitoring workspace, as the name suggests, is used to monitor information. The status of the ConfigMgr infrastructure (site, component, distribution, replication, and so on) can be viewed in various nodes. Client health information is also available. When these types of statuses are set to alert, the alert data populates the Alerts node, making management of these alerts (commenting, postponing, disabling, and so on) available. You can view status information in more ways than just text. This workspace includes diagram views displaying status, alert, and configuration data over a hierarchy diagram or geographical view. As you can see in Figure 8.6, a site hierarchy diagram view is available that graphically shows you the status of your hierarchy.

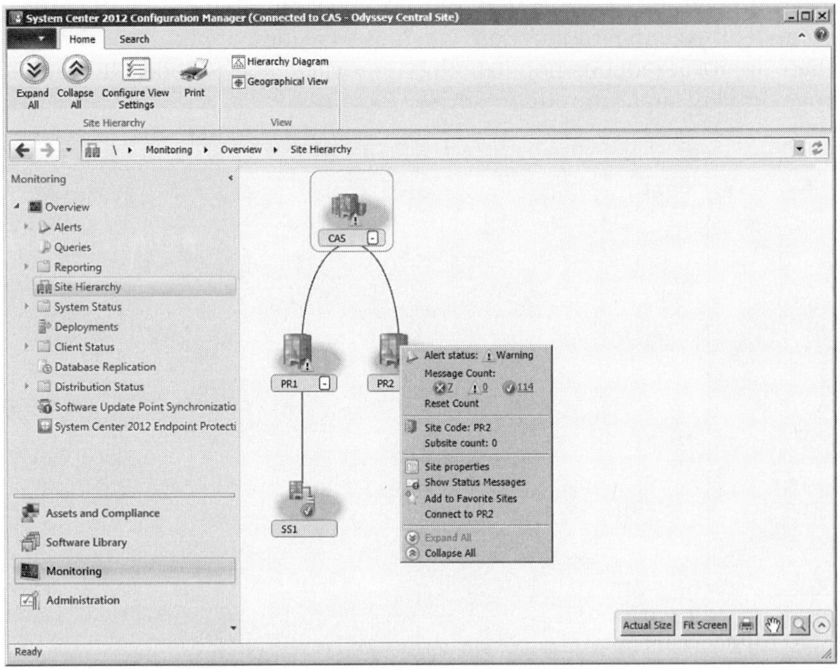

FIGURE 8.6   Hierarchy diagram view.

Although you might typically think of monitoring in terms of alerts and statuses, the System Center 2012 Configuration Manager Monitoring workspace contains far more than this traditional definition. For example, you can manage reports and create subscriptions from this workspace.

Queries are managed and executed here as well. Although collections and queries are often viewed as interrelated, it is important to note that they exist in different workspaces in the console.

Here are the main nodes in this workspace:

▶ Alerts

▶ Queries

▶ Reporting

▶ Site Hierarchy

▶ System Status

▶ Deployments

▶ Client Status

▶ Database Replication

▶ Distribution Status

▶ Software Update Point Synchronization Status

▶ System Center 2012 Endpoint Protection Status

Administration Workspace

The Administration workspace, as displayed in Figure 8.7, contains the nodes necessary for managing the ConfigMgr infrastructure, security, and settings. ConfigMgr infrastructure management consists of tasks such as managing distribution points, site boundaries, resource discoveries, and migration of data from ConfigMgr 2007. Custom ConfigMgr client settings can be created, assigned, and edited in this workspace.

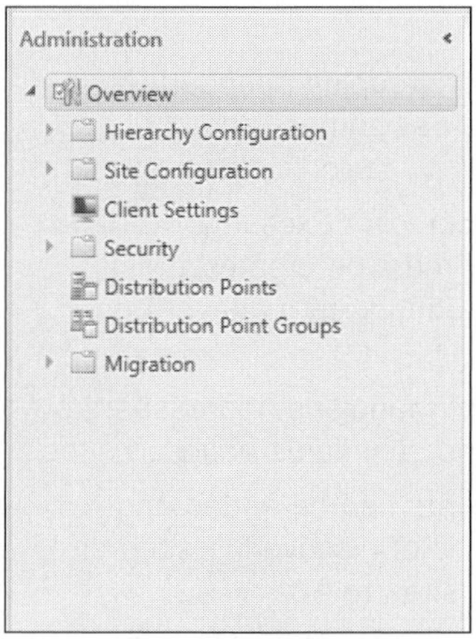

FIGURE 8.7   Administration workspace.

You can add administrative users to System Center 2012 Configuration Manager in this workspace. You can assign new roles, create scopes, and apply permission. In addition, certificates used in various components of ConfigMgr are managed in the Administration workspace.

This workspace consists of the following main nodes:

▶ Hierarchy Configuration

▶ Site Configuration

▶ Client Settings

▶ Security

▶ Distribution Points

▶ Distribution Point Groups

▶ Migration

Console Node Details

The main nodes in the Navigation pane often contain additional nodes. These subnodes provide access to functionality aligned with the current workspace theme. Table 8.1 describes the subnodes for each workspace covered in this chapter.

TABLE 8.1 Configuration Manager Console Nodes

Node	Subnode	Description
Administration		
Hierarchy Configuration	Discovery Methods	Settings for discovering resources are managed in this subnode. Heartbeat, network discovery, and the various Active Directory (AD) discovery methods are available.
	Boundaries	Use this subnode for creating and managing boundaries.
	Boundary Groups	This subnode is used for grouping boundaries together to manage site assignment and content location.
	Exchange Server Connectors	To manage mobile devices over Exchange ActiveSync, a connector must be created to link to Exchange. Use this subnode to manage these connections.
	Addresses	This subnode is used for managing addresses that control transfer rates and schedules between sites.
	Active Directory Forests	In this subnode, AD forests can be added and modified for the purposes of discovering sites and subnets and publishing sites to AD.
Site Configuration	Sites	Sites are added and modified in this subnode. Each site object provides access to settings such as Wake on LAN, communication ports, free disk space alerts, and sender retry.
	Servers and Site System Roles	Site servers and site system roles are managed in this subnode. Roles such as distribution points, management points, reporting services points, and state migration points (to name several) are added and deleted here.
Client Settings		Use this node to edit default client settings. Customized client settings can be created and modified.

Node	Subnode	Description
Security	Administrative Users	Administrative user accounts are listed in this subnode. They can be assigned to security roles and granted object security.
	Security Roles	This subnode defines the security roles that grant access to ConfigMgr. Permission over each class object can be defined per role.
	Security Scopes	Security scopes are created and managed in this subnode.
	Accounts	Use this subnode to view accounts and modify the account passwords used for various roles.
	Certificates	Boot media, Independent Software Vendor (ISV) proxy, and Preboot eXecution Environment (PXE) deployment certificates are managed in this subnode.
Distribution Points		Use this node to manage distribution points and configuration settings for each distribution point. You can also view relative information in the Detail pane such as distribution point (DP) capabilities (protected, PXE, multicast, and so on) as well as free drive space.
Distribution Point Groups		Manage the settings of distribution point groups in this node such as the associated collections, assigned content, and member distribution points.
Migration	Active Source Hierarchy	Define the ConfigMgr 2007 source hierarchy sites from which migration jobs use to pull data.
	Migration Jobs	Manage migration jobs in this subnode.
	Distribution Point Upgrades	Use this subnode to monitor shared distribution points from the active source hierarchy.
Software Library		
Application Management	Applications	Manage applications and their settings such as the deployment action and requirement rules. Chapter 13, "Distributing and Deploying Applications," discusses this functionality.
	Packages	Manage software packages and their associated programs.
	Approval Requests	When users request software through Software Center, administrative users approve or deny requests in this subnode.
	Global Conditions	Add, view, or modify global conditions. Chapter 12, "Creating and Managing Applications," covers this further.

Node	Subnode	Description
Software Updates	All Software Updates	Use this subnode to manage synchronization, configuration, download, and deployment of software updates. Chapter 14, "Software Update Management," discusses this functionality.
	Software Update Groups	Organize and manage software updates as groups in this section.
	Deployment Packages	Software update deployment packages are managed in this section.
	Automatic Deployment Rules	This subnode is used for the management of rules that indicate how to download and deploy software updates. Review Chapter 14 to learn more about automatic deployment rules.
Operating Systems	Drivers	Use this subnode for managing device drivers and catalogs.
	Driver Packages	Driver packages hold a collection of drivers. Create and manage driver packages in this subnode.
	Operating System Images	Intuitively named, WIM files are managed in this subnode.
	Operating System Installers	Use this subnode to manage Windows source files used to install operating systems.
	Boot Images	This subnode specifically manages the images used to boot machines.
	Task Sequences	Manage task sequences from this subnode. This, as well as the other subnodes in the Operating Systems node, is discussed in Chapter 19, "Operating System Deployment."
Monitoring		
Alerts		In this node, administrators can view alerts. Management of alerts such as adding comments, configuring, postponing and so on can also be done in this section.
	Subscriptions	Use this subnode to subscribe to alerts of interest.
Queries		Manage queries in this node. Refer to Chapter 17, "Configuration Manager Queries," for information on using and writing queries.
Reporting	Reports	This subnode is used to manage reports, report options, and report security.
	Subscriptions	Manage report subscriptions in this subnode.
Site Hierarchy		Use this node to view site data (status, message count, and so on) in both a hierarchical diagram and a geographical view.

Node	Subnode	Description
System Status	Site Status	Status information of system roles can be viewed and managed in this section.
	Component Status	Status information of components can be viewed and managed.
	Conflicting Records	Manage conflicting records in this subnode.
	Status Message Queries	Manage status message queries to view information about components, audit messages, and so on.
Deployments		View the deployment status of applications, packages, and operating systems.
Client Status	Client Health	View trends and summary information about client health. The client status update schedule can be modified from this subnode.
	Client Activity	View trends and summary information about client activity. The client status update schedule can be modified from this subnode.
Database Replication		View database replication site link status and summary information from this subnode. Detail tabs also provide database specific configuration information.
Distribution Status	Content Status	Information regarding content distribution status is available in this subnode.
	Distribution Point Group Status	View distribution point group status information from this subnode.
	Distribution Point Configuration Status	Information regarding the configuration of distribution points is available in this subnode.
Software Update Point Synchronization Status		Status information for the software update point synchronization can be viewed in this node.
System Center 2012 Endpoint Protection Status		This node provides status information malware, Endpoint Protection client health, and saturation status of definitions.
Assets and Compliance		
Users		Use this node to manage users and user groups.
Devices		Use this node to manage devices. Summary, client activity, and client health information is available from the Detail pane.
User Collections		Use this node to manage user collections. Summary, deployment, and assignment information is available from the Detail pane.

Node	Subnode	Description
Device Collections		Use this node to manage device collections. Summary, deployment, and assignment information is available from the Detail pane.
User State Migration		From this node, manage user state migration, used during operating system deployments. User State Migration enables transferring user customizations and data from a previous installation to the new system.
Asset Intelligence	Catalog	You can view the asset intelligence catalog, and create custom categories, families, and labels here as well.
	Inventoried Software	Manage inventoried software in this subnode by viewing the collected data, modifying its category or family classification, or specifying custom labels.
	Hardware Requirements	View hardware requirements for software titles. Custom hardware requirements can be created for unlisted software.
Software Metering		Manage the configuration rules for monitoring software usage.
Compliance Settings	Configuration Items	Manage configuration items used to define baselines as described in Chapter 10, "Managing Compliance."
	Configuration Baselines	Manage configuration baselines, which contain the configuration items that define evaluation criteria for compliance. Chapter 10 discusses compliance settings management in further detail.
Endpoint Protection	Antimalware Policies	Manage and deploy policies that control Endpoint Protection settings from this subnode.
	Windows Firewall Policies	Manage and deploy policies that control Windows Firewall settings from this subnode.

Console Deployment

The ConfigMgr console can be installed as a part of the CAS or primary site server installation. Unlike earlier versions, however, this is a choice and not a requirement. In most organizations, the administration and operation of ConfigMgr is typically not managed by a single individual. This is especially true in enterprises where the management may reside with entire teams.

During transitions from ConfigMgr 2007 to System Center 2012 Configuration Manager, it is likely that your administrative users will have to operate consoles for both environments. Because Microsoft fully supports installing both versions of the console on the same computer, this does not require a separate computer or virtual machine. Keep in mind that the 2012 console cannot manage a 2007 environment, however.

Console Placement

Regardless of whether the administration is one administrator or a group of administrators scattered across the globe, a best practice is to install the console locally on the administrator's desktop.

Depending on your hierarchy, there could be potential challenges to local console installations. For example, if the hierarchy is designed such that a site database server is not physically near the administrator and WAN latency is an issue, the console may perform poorly because it must retrieve content over a slow link.

You may want to install the console on a server with the SMS Provider and allow administrators access to console over Remote Desktop Services (RDP). The SMS Provider can be installed on the ConfigMgr site server, database server, or a separate server entirely. You can install additional SMS providers in a site, providing distributed load and high availability for console connections.

Regardless of the number of providers, if the SMS Provider is not on the same server as the database server, console performance will be affected by the speed and latency of the connection from the SMS Provider to the database.

NOTE: THE ROLE OF THE SMS PROVIDER

When a ConfigMgr console connects to a ConfigMgr site server, the console is actually connecting to the database. To be more specific, the console connects to the SMS Provider, a Windows Management Instrument (WMI) provider, which handles all reads and writes to the site database.

Often those using ConfigMgr may not be administrators. For example, help desk staff might use the console as a means to view configuration data of a device and connect through remote control to assist an end user. In situations such as these, it is far safer and easier to provide a local console than allow help desk staff to log on directly to the server. If bandwidth is a factor, the console could be loaded on the primary site server, allowing administrators to use Remote Desktop Connection to manage the site.

Supported Platforms

The ConfigMgr console can run on both workstations and servers. Table 8.2 shows the list of supported operating systems with respect to both 32- and 64-bit flavors.

TABLE 8.2   Supported Operating Systems for the ConfigMgr Console

Operating System	Version	X86	X64
Workstation			
Windows 7 (Enterprise and Ultimate)	RTM, Service Pack (SP) 1	X	X
Windows Vista (Business, Enterprise, and Ultimate)	SP 2	X	X
Windows XP Professional	SP 3	X	
Windows XP Professional for 64-bit Systems	SP 2		X
Server			
Windows Server 2003 R2 (Standard, Enterprise, and Datacenter)	SP 2	X	X
Windows Server 2008 (Standard, Enterprise, Datacenter)	RTM	X	X
Windows Server 2008 R2 (Standard, Enterprise, Datacenter)	RTM, SP 1		X

ConfigMgr Console Prerequisites

System Center 2012 Configuration Manager includes a nifty prerequisite checker that can help determine whether a computer meets the requirements to run the ConfigMgr console. You can find the utility `prereqchk.exe` located under SMSSETUP\BIN\X64 of the ConfigMgr source files or the %*ProgramFiles*%\Microsoft Configuration Manager\bin\x64 folder of an installed server.

When running `prereqchk.exe` with the ADMINUI switch, it runs through a scan of the specified system to determine if it meets the requirements for installing the console. Run the utility to scan for console prerequisites by issuing the following command:

```
prereqchk.exe /ADMINUI
```

After the utility runs, you can find the log of the prerequisite scan in the root of the system drive, named ConfigMgrPrereq.log. Here are the required components for the ConfigMgr console:

▶ .NET Framework 4.0 or higher

▶ Microsoft XML Core Services 6.0 (MSXML60)

▶ Windows Remote Management (WinRM) v1.1

For further information about the prerequisite checker, see the article at http://www.systemcenterblog.nl/2011/11/16/new-prerequisite-check-tool-shipped-with-rc-of-configuration-manager-2012/.

Installation Using the ConfigMgr Setup Wizard

When all prerequisites are met, the ConfigMgr console can be installed by launching the System Center Configuration Manager 2012 Setup Wizard. You can start the wizard by opening the splash.hta file, found in the root of the installation media.

> **TIP: LAUNCHING THE CONSOLE INSTALLATION WIZARD WITHOUT THE SETUP WIZARD**
>
> It is not necessary to use the ConfigMgr Setup Wizard to install the console because the console install is now separate from the rest of the product. Navigate to the \SMSSETUP\ BIN\I386 folder and click on `consolesetup.exe` to launch the console installation program.

To install the console, launch the System Center 2012 Configuration Manager Setup Wizard, and perform the following steps:

1. In the wizard, under the Tools and Standalone Components, click the **Install Configuration Manager console** link.

2. The Configuration Manager Console Setup Wizard launches (see Figure 8.8), indicating **This wizard will install the Configuration Manager 2012 console**. When you are ready, click **Next** to move forward.

3. On the Site Server page, as displayed in Figure 8.9, enter the site server fully qualified domain name (FQDN) name for the ConfigMgr console to connect to on its first launch. Click **Next**.

4. The Installation Folder page displays the default path, as shown in Figure 8.10, where the installation occurs. If the location is acceptable, click **Next**. Otherwise, click **Browse** to update the location, and click **Next** when complete.

5. When you arrive at the Ready to Install screen (see Figure 8.11), all settings required for setup have been entered. Use the Back button to review or change the settings if necessary. When ready, click **Install**.

   The Please Wait page includes a progress bar, as displayed in Figure 8.12, providing a visual indicator of the installation. The wizard also displays the installation steps on this page.

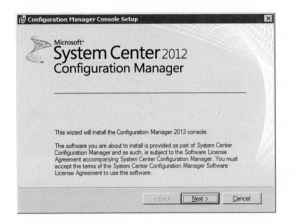

FIGURE 8.8   Console setup welcome screen.

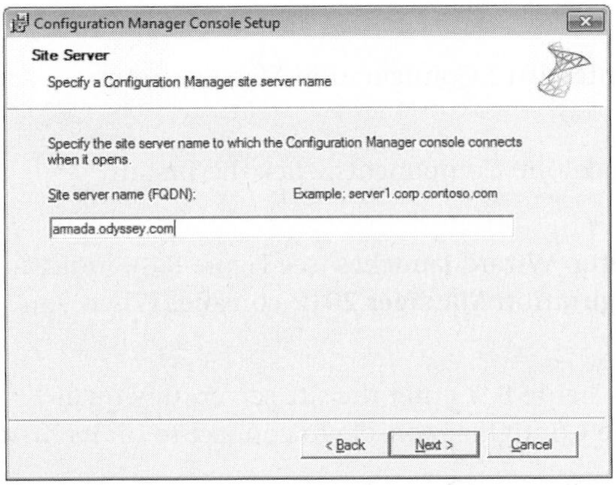

FIGURE 8.9   Site Server dialog screen.

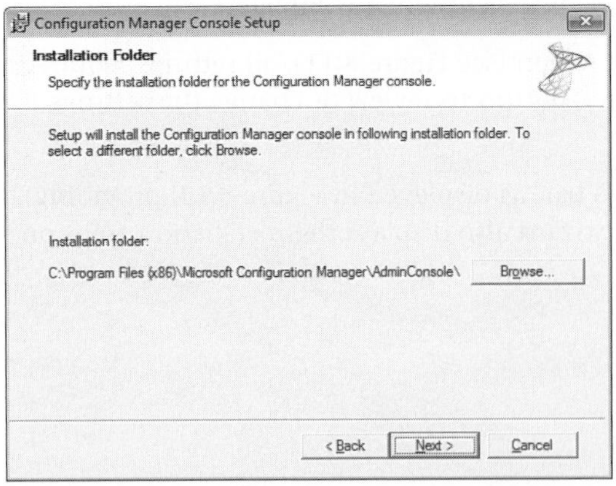

FIGURE 8.10   Installation folder path.

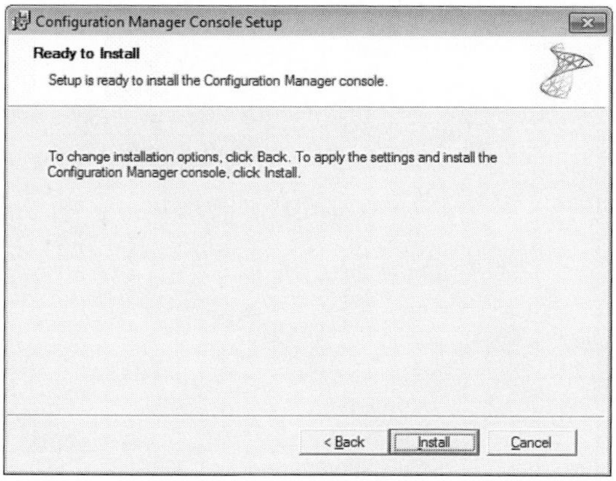

FIGURE 8.11   Ready to install.

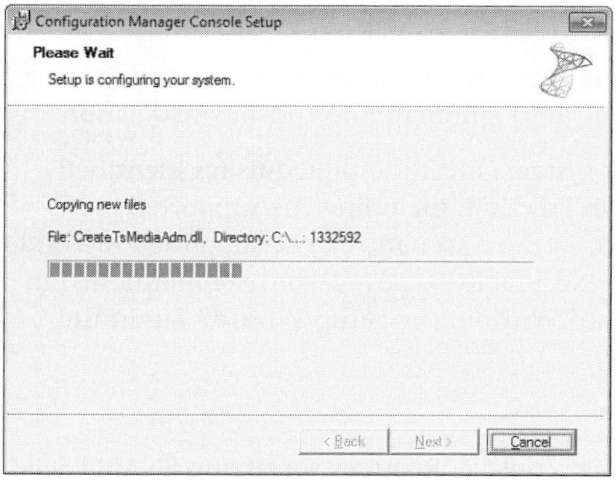

FIGURE 8.12   Installation progress.

6. When installation completes, the option to **Start the Configuration Manager console after you close the Setup Wizard** displays with the option to uncheck it, as indicated in Figure 8.13. Click **Finish** to complete the wizard.

FIGURE 8.13   Console installation completion.

Unattended Console Installation

In those situations in which multiple individuals manage administration and operation of the ConfigMgr infrastructure, it may be beneficial to automate the console installation.

Before installing the console, verify the target systems meet the prerequisites identified earlier in the "ConfigMgr Console Prerequisites" section, including the supported platform. (Generally, this should not be a problem in most scenarios.) The supported method for installing the ConfigMgr console uses the executable consolesetup.exe mentioned in the "Launching the Console Installation Wizard Without the Setup Wizard" Tip in the previous section.

The executable accepts the following switches:

- ▶ **/q:** Indicates a silent install the ConfigMgr console. Requires specifying ENABLESQM and DEFAULTSITESERVERNAME.

- ▶ **/uninstall:** Indicates to uninstall the ConfigMgr console.

- ▶ **DEFAULTSITESERVERNAME:** Specifies the site server FQDN for which the console connects upon launch.

- ▶ **ENABLESQM:** Value indicating the acceptance of joining the Customer Experience Improvement Program (CEIP). Accepts 0 for No and 1 for Yes.

- ▶ **TARGETDIR:** Specifies a different directory if the default directory of *%ProgramFiles%* \Microsoft Configuration Manager\AdminConsole is not acceptable.

- ▶ **LangPackDir:** If you want to install a language pack, use this switch to specify a directory where the language pack files are located.

Other than the switches that begin with a slash (/q and /uninstall), the other switches require the use of an equal sign (=) between the switch and the value. Here are some usage examples of using consolesetup.exe:

▶ `consolesetup.exe /q DEFAULTSITESERVERNAME=armada.odyssey.com ENABLESQM=0`

▶ `consolesetup.exe /q DEFAULTSITESERVERNAME=armada.odyssey.com ENABLESQM=1`
  `LangPackDir=c:\LangPacks`

▶ `consolesetup.exe /uninstall`

Role-Based Administration

The ConfigMgr console is context-sensitive based on the security of each administrative user. As you begin to assign permission to other users, notice the console displays only what the user can manage.

Introducing the "Show Me" Behavior

Despite that organizationally the ConfigMgr console is far improved and easier to navigate than in previous versions, it can still benefit from a touch of clarity. Known as "Show Me" in System Center 2012 Configuration Manager, the console displays only the relevant workspaces, panes, nodes, and objects that the administrative user can manage. By reducing the amount of clutter in the console, this removes some of the complexity of navigation. In ConfigMgr 2007, it is easy to become inundated by the myriad nodes and actions that comprise the tree. This is no longer the case with 2012.

The console is designed to reflect only what the administrative user is assigned to do. This behavior means specialized console customization is no longer required because the console automatically displays what is pertinent. This means you need to deploy only a single version of the console and let the assigned security do the rest. To illustrate this, Figure 8.14 shows the console when no restrictions are applied, a role known as Full Administrator. As you can see, the entire workspace and folder list are available.

In contrast, Figure 8.15 shows the console when role-based administration is utilized to grant an administrator a limited scope of permission. In this case, the administrator is assigned the following permissions:

▶ Application Administrator

▶ Software Update Manager

The console with the limited workspace shows only Application Management and Software Updates folders, whereas the console with the unrestricted access also shows an Operating Systems folder. Under the Software Library Overview, even the Navigation Index is scoped to show relevant content.

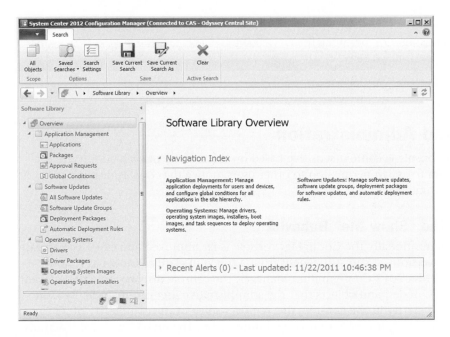

FIGURE 8.14   Unrestricted ConfigMgr console.

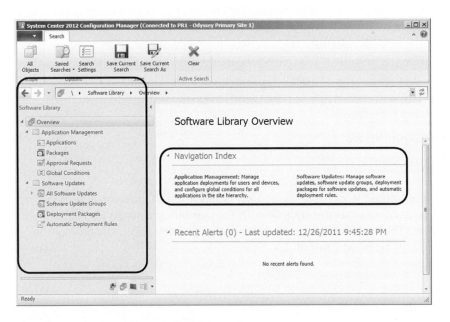

FIGURE 8.15   Restricted ConfigMgr console.

Behind the Scenes

For an administrative user to use the ConfigMgr console, that user must be assigned to at least one role, or the console will fail to connect. After a role is defined, when the console is opened, the objects that fall under the management of the administrative user is displayed and accessible. All other objects are hidden from view. The console displays content based on the assigned roles, scopes, and collections:

- ▶ **Roles:** Visible workspaces, nodes, folders, objects, and actions are defined by the administrative user's associated role.

- ▶ **Scopes:** Only the objects associated to assigned scopes can be managed.

- ▶ **Collections:** Only assigned collections can be viewed and managed.

The Three States of Interaction

Objects in the console exist in three states: shown, hidden, and disabled. Objects in a shown state do just as the name implies. If a user has permission to manage these objects, they display in the console. If the object is a folder or a node, the parent objects also display.

By default, objects are hidden. Only by granting access do objects appear. Hidden behavior is determined by the following rules:

- ▶ **Actions:** If an administrative user does not have permissions to perform the action, the action is not displayed.

- ▶ **Objects:** If an object does not belong to a security scope assigned to the administrative user, the object is not displayed.

- ▶ **Nodes:** Without access to manage items in the node, the node is not displayed.

- ▶ **Workspaces:** Without access to manage at least one node in the workspace, the workspace itself is not displayed.

Objects that are disabled display as grayed-out objects in the console and do not allow full interaction. This is typical whenever a user is granted read access to an object. Notice in Figure 8.16, all fields, including the IP address range drop-down, are grayed out. This is because the user's privileges in this example are not sufficient to modify the properties.

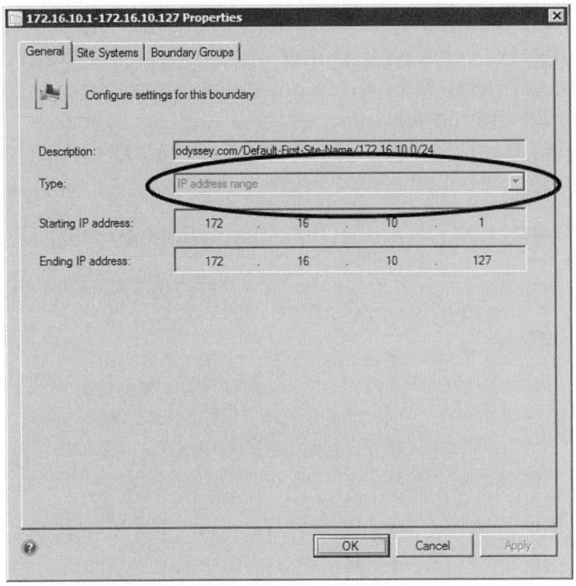

FIGURE 8.16   Grayed-out properties.

Connecting to a Site

During installation of the ConfigMgr console, a default site server is specified for the console to automatically connect to upon opening. When connected, you can connect to any site server you have access to. Accessing the backstage, you can use the **Connect to a New Site** dialog to provide a site server name.

Recent Connections

When the ConfigMgr console is installed on a modern operating system such as Windows 7 or Windows Server 2008, you can expect the rich Start menu and taskbar interaction that other applications enjoy such as pinning the application to the taskbar or the Start menu and utilizing Recent Connections. If you have favorite connections, Recent Connections can also be pinned to persist in the list. Figure 8.17 shows this interaction from the Start menu, whereas Figure 8.18 shows the taskbar interaction.

Clearing Recent Connections

If you enter the wrong server name or connect to many different servers, over time, the dialog drop-down menu may become crowded with unnecessary or unwanted entries. To remove one of the entries, simply hover the mouse pointer over the entry until the red X appears. Click the **X** (seen in Figure 8.19) to remove the entry.

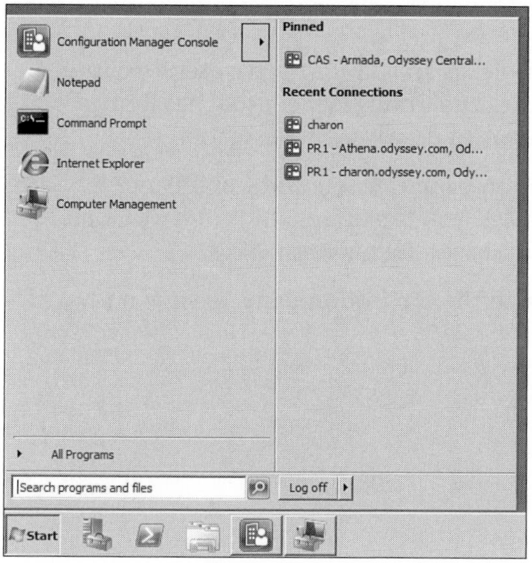

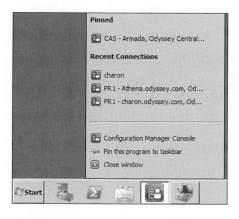

FIGURE 8.17   Recent connections on the Start menu.

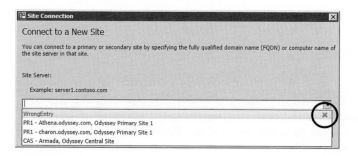

FIGURE 8.18   Recent connections on the taskbar.

FIGURE 8.19   Clearing recent connections from the drop-down list.

Personalizing the Console

There are few options for customizing the console, as an administrative user's security context drives what is available for view and use. The ConfigMgr console has limited personalization to suit your taste, all of which has to do with the Navigation pane.

The default order of workspaces in the Navigation pane is Assets and Compliance, Software Library, Monitoring, and Administration. You can arrange this order to something that makes more sense. To rearrange workspaces, follow these steps:

1. Click the arrow below the last workspace in the Navigation pane, as shown in Figure 8.20.

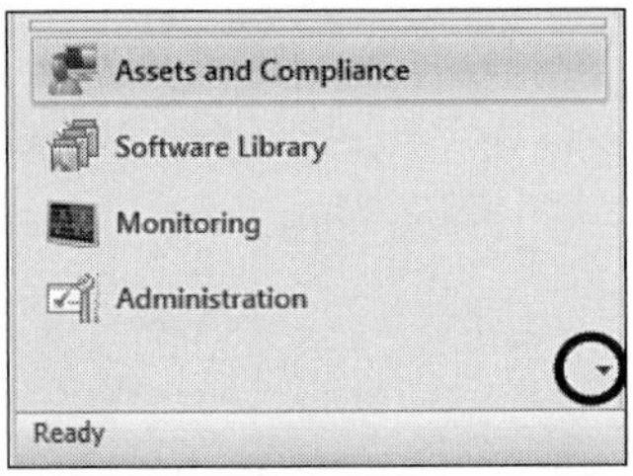

FIGURE 8.20   Navigation pane arrow.

2. When the menu opens, choose **Navigation Pane Options**.

3. This brings up the Navigation Pane Options window (see Figure 8.21); click the button to move, and then choose either **Move Up** or **Move Down**.

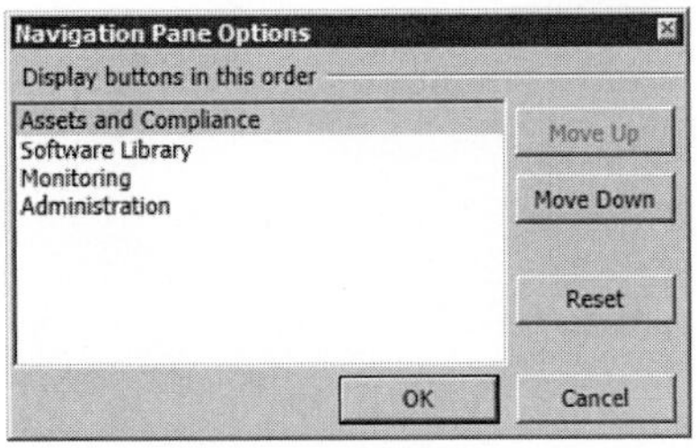

FIGURE 8.21   Navigation pane options.

4. After all the buttons are arranged in your order of preference, click **OK**.

TIP: RESETTING WORKSPACES

If you need to reset the arrangement of the workspace needs, follow the steps in the previous procedure to open Navigation Pane Options, and use the **Reset** button. This puts the workspaces back into the original order.

If the Workspaces pane overlaps the node list, you can collapse it. When collapsed, the workspaces are represented by only icons. You can collapse the Workspaces pane by moving the separator bar down. Using the **Show More Buttons** and **Show Fewer Buttons** is the equivalent of using the separator bar, as shown in Figure 8.22.

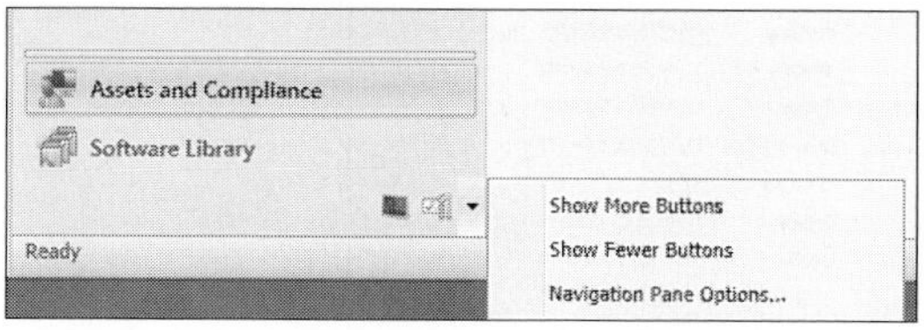

FIGURE 8.22   Console separator bar with Show More and Show Fewer buttons.

A vertical separator bar also exists between the Navigation pane and the List and Detail panes. The List and Detail panes have a horizontal separator bar as well for resizing.

The In-Console Alert Experience

Although not a new concept to most administrators, alerts are new to ConfigMgr. In comparison to status messages, alerts provide a number of features and improvements. As an example, alerts are state-based (meaning they update automatically as the condition changes), providing a near real-time monitoring experience and subscription capability. However, ConfigMgr alerts are limited in functionality and should not be considered a robust monitoring solution as provided by other tools such as System Center Operations Manager, which is designed to handle enterprise-level alerting, notification, and performance metric gathering.

Viewing Alerts

Alerts are located in the Monitoring workspace of the ConfigMgr console. The Overview node provides a list of recent alerts. Clicking the Alerts node displays the list of available alerts in the List pane and provide details of any highlighted alert in the Detail pane.

Alerts display with five different states. Figure 8.23 shows an example of some alerts with different states.

Available actions are based on the state of the alert. ConfigMgr assigns the following states for alerts:

▶ **Active:** When a specified condition is met

▶ **Canceled:** Specified condition is no longer met

▶ **Disabled:** Condition of an alert is not evaluated while in this state

▶ **Never Triggered:** Alert has been created but no condition has yet been met

▶ **Postponed:** The same as disabled with an expiration period to revert to an active state

Alerts 19 items						
Search					✕	🔎 Search
Icon	Alert State	Name	Type	Severity	Postpone Alert	Subscription
▷	Postponed	Warning low free space alert for dat...	Database free space warning	Warning	12/14/2011 12:23 AM	0
▷	Canceled	Replication link down between paren...	Site to site connectivity	Critical	11/18/2011 3:37 AM	0
▷	Canceled	Replication link down between paren...	Site to site connectivity	Critical	11/10/2011 5:39 PM	0
▷	Canceled	Replication link down between paren...	Site to site connectivity	Critical	11/10/2011 4:57 PM	0
ⓘ	Active	Warning low free space alert for data...	Database free space warning	Warning	11/4/2011 9:14 PM	0
▷	Never Triggered	Critical low free space alert for data...	Database free space critical	Critical	11/4/2011 9:14 PM	0
▷	Never Triggered	Database Replication component fail...	Database Replication component fail...	Critical	11/4/2011 9:14 PM	0
▷	Never Triggered	Database Replication component fail...	Database Replication component fail...	Critical	11/4/2011 4:16 PM	0
▷	Disabled	Warning low free space alert for dat...	Database free space warning	Warning	11/4/2011 4:16 PM	0
▷	Never Triggered	Critical low free space alert for data...	Database free space critical	Critical	11/4/2011 4:16 PM	0
▷	Canceled	Critical low free space alert for data...	Database free space critical	Critical	11/4/2011 3:21 PM	0
▷	Never Triggered	Database Replication component fail...	Database Replication component fail...	Critical	11/4/2011 3:21 PM	0

Warning low free space alert for database on site: CAS

General Information		Status information	
Name:	Warning low free space alert for database on site: CAS	Alert State:	Postponed
		Postpone Alert:	12/14/2011 12:23 AM
Type:	Database free space warning	Date Created:	11/4/2011 3:21 PM
Feature Area:	Database free space	Closed By:	ODYSSEY\moh
Severity:	Warning	Date Modified:	12/12/2011 11:23 PM
Condition:	Generate a warning alert if the free space on disk that contains the database file is greater than 5 GB and less than 10 GB.	Modified By:	ODYSSEY\moh
		Occurrence Count:	2
Alert Text:	Database files disk space free GB between 10 and 5		
Status:	Enabled		
Comment:			

FIGURE 8.23   Alerts displayed with various states.

Managing Alerts

Alerts that bubble up in the ConfigMgr console support a variety of actions. As mentioned in the previous section, the available actions are dependent on the state of the alert. For example, the Enable action is not available on an enabled alert. Here are the available alert actions, also shown in Figure 8.24:

▶ **Postpone:** Postponing an alert essentially ignores the alert for a specified period of time. When the time period has lapsed, the alert is updated to its current state. You can postpone only active alerts.

▶ **Edit Comments:** You can add or modify comments to provide additional context about an alert.

▶ **Configure:** Configuring an alert provides the ability to change the name, severity, and definition.

▶ **Enable:** Enables the selected alert.

▶ **Disable:** Disables the selected alert.

▶ **Refresh:** Refresh is not for a specified alert but rather refreshes the entire list of alerts.

▶ **Delete:** Deleting an alert removes it from the Alerts node and the list of recent alerts.

FIGURE 8.24   Available alert actions.

NOTE: USE THE DELETE ACTION WITH CAUTION

The three states (Postpone, Disable, and Delete) might be confusing at first because their descriptions are somewhat similar. Postpone and Disable are most alike—disabling an alert is much like postponing an alert without a time period. Delete, however, is different from either Postpone or Disable. Deleting an alert modifies the alert configuration, turning off the alert. This is quite different than disabling an alert because the disabled alert configuration remains the same and can be re-enabled. A deleted alert requires creating the alert configuration again.

Configuring Alerts

In contrast to viewing alerts, which is available in a single area of the ConfigMgr console (the Alerts node of the Monitoring workspace), alert configuration pages are scattered across the console. This creates a challenge in knowing where all the configuration areas are to create alerts. Table 8.3 displays the location and function of the alerts you can create.

TABLE 8.3   Alert Locations

Workspace	Node	Function
Administration	Sites	Low free disk space alerts on site database server. See Chapter 21, "Backup, Recovery, and Maintenance," for additional information.
Software Library	Applications	Deployment success or failure percentage meets a specified threshold. More information is available in Chapter 13.
	Software Update Groups	Deployment compliance fails to meet a specified threshold. More information is available in Chapter 14.
Monitoring	Database Replication	Replication link does not work for a specified duration. Additional information is available in Chapter 21.

Workspace	Node	Function
Assets and Compliance	Device Collections	Value falls below specified client check, remediation, and activity thresholds. Chapter 9, "Configuration Manager Client Management," contains additional information for setting up alerts.
		Antimalware alerts for Endpoint Protection. You can find more detail in Chapter 16, "Endpoint Protection."
	Compliance Settings	Baseline deployment compliance falls below a specified threshold. Additional information is available in Chapter 10.

Each alert configuration is slightly different but overall uses the same basic concept. The configuration requires the alert to be enabled and a threshold value to be specified. Refer to the individual chapters (as listed in Table 8.3) for additional information.

Subscribing to Alerts

Subscriptions specifically refer to malware alerts. An alert subscription sends an email whenever a malware condition is met.

Here's an example of setting up a subscription for System Center Endpoint Protection. Perform the following steps:

1. Navigate to the **Monitoring** workspace, drop down the **Alerts** node, and select **Subscriptions**.

2. On the ribbon bar, select the **Create subscription** button.

3. In the New Subscription window, provide a name for the subscription.

4. Specify the email address of the alert recipient. If there are multiple recipients, separate the email addresses with a semi-colon (;).

5. Select the email language.

6. Select the appropriate alerts and click **OK**.

Figure 8.25 shows a fully configured alert subscription.

Configuration Manager Service Manager

The Configuration Manager Service Manager console assists in managing the state of ConfigMgr components. The console, shown in Figure 8.26, has the ability to check the status, set logging, and control the running state.

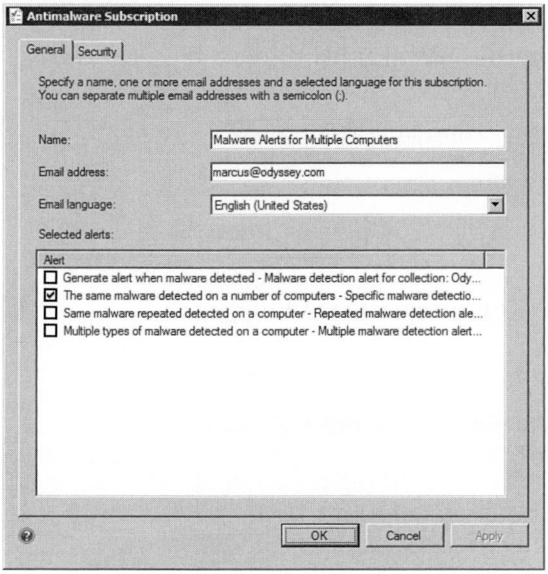

FIGURE 8.25   Alert subscription.

Although nearly all components should be in a running state, there are a handful of components that run only when initiated. For example, the SMS_SITE_BACKUP service remains stopped until the backup operation for ConfigMgr is initiated.

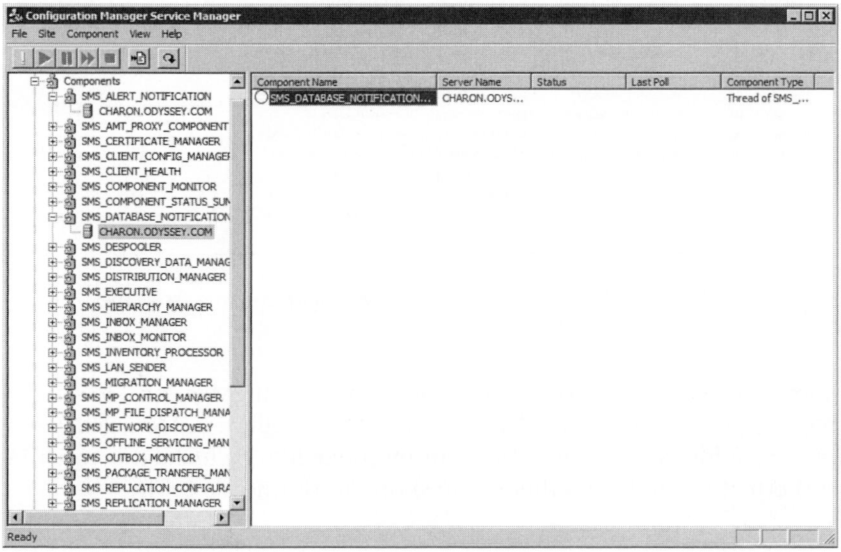

FIGURE 8.26   Viewing the Service Manager console.

Initiating the Configuration Manager Service Manager Console

Configuration Manager Service Manager can be launched either through the ConfigMgr console or directly by running the proper executable.

To launch Service Manager from the ConfigMgr console, perform these steps:

1. Select the **Monitoring** node in the Navigation pane.

2. Navigate to the **System Status** node, and select **Component Status**, as shown in Figure 8.27.

3. On the ribbon bar, click **Start**; then select **Configuration Manager Service Manager**.

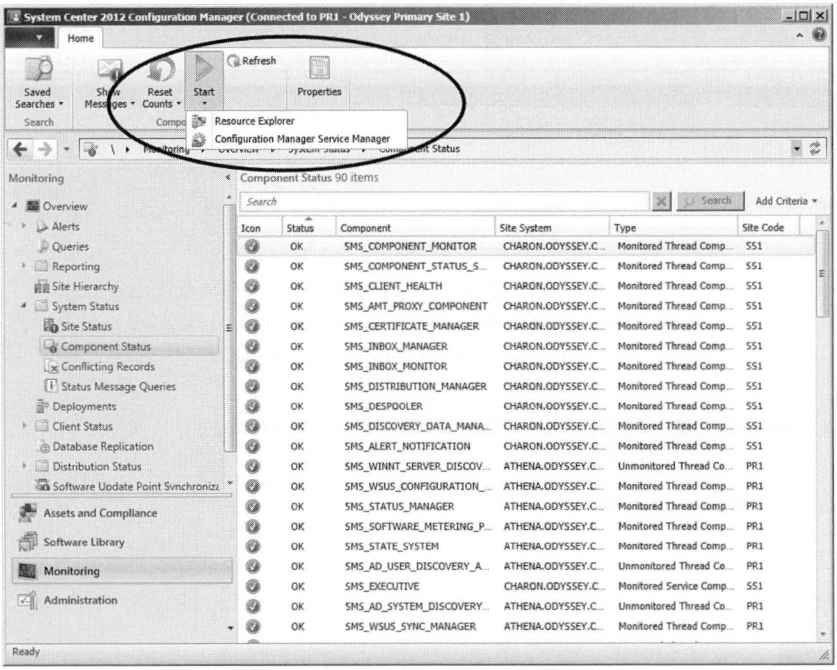

FIGURE 8.27   Launching the Configuration Manager Service Manager console from the ConfigMgr console.

Starting Configuration Manager Service Manager outside of the ConfigMgr console can be achieved by navigating to the *%ProgramFiles%*\Microsoft Configuration Manager\AdminConsole\bin\i386 folder and opening the **compmgr.exe** file. To make this easier in the future, create a shortcut to the file, as there is no shortcut for this file in the Start menu.

Unlike launching the Configuration Manager Service Manager console from the ConfigMgr console, you need to provide a site server name to connect to when the Service

Manager console initially opens. If you prefer to launch the console directed at a specific server, simply add the name of the site server after compmgr.exe. For example, here is how to open the Configuration Manager Service Manager connecting to the Athena site server:

```
%ProgramFiles%\Microsoft Configuration Manager\AdminConsole\bin\i386\compmgr.exe
athena
```

Operating the Configuration Manager Service Manager Console

You can perform several actions within the Configuration Manager Service Manager console. The components of ConfigMgr are managed in a similar fashion to standard Windows services, meaning that components can be started, stopped, paused, resumed, and queried.

Here are the options Configuration Manager Service Manager has for managing components. These are listed in order as displayed on the toolbar, as shown in Figure 8.28:

▶ **Query:** Use the query action to detect the current status of a component. This must be executed first because the availability of other commands is based on the current status.

▶ **Start:** Use the start action to start a component in a stopped state.

▶ **Pause:** If the desire is to preserve a component's runtime environment, pause the service. Data in the component log file persists when paused. Certain components do not support pausing.

▶ **Resume:** The resume action can be applied to any component in a paused state.

▶ **Stop:** When there is no concern regarding the preservation of a component's runtime environment or data in the component's log file, use the stop action to shut down the component.

▶ **Logging:** Displays the log control dialog to control whether logging is enabled or disabled, the name and location of the log filename, and the size of the log file.

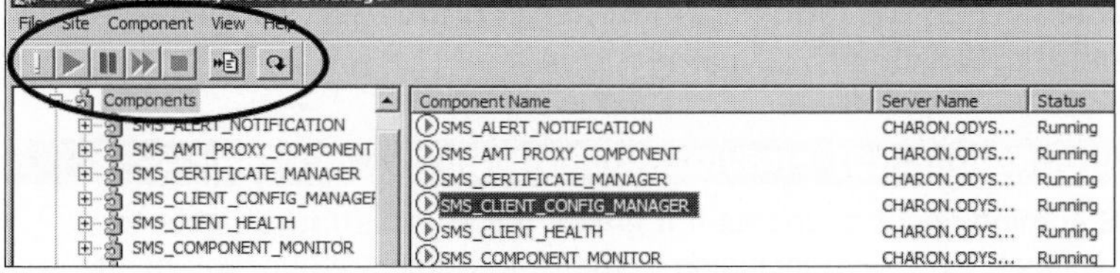

FIGURE 8.28   Service Manager console toolbar.

NOTE: COMPONENTS ACTIONS NOT AVAILABLE UNTIL AFTER QUERY

Unlike Windows services, you must first query a component to perform an action against it. Actions are available based on the component's status. For example, the resume action is only available when a component is paused.

The Configuration Manager Service Manager console supports the following general actions:

▶ **Clear status:** This action simply blanks the component status.

▶ **Site Refresh:** This action refreshes the list of components.

▶ **Connect:** Displays the Connect to Site dialog. The Service Manager console supports connecting to multiple sites.

▶ **Disconnect:** Displays the Disconnect from Sites dialog. This dialog box supports multiselecting sites and disconnecting from multiple sites at once.

TIP: PERFORMING ACTIONS AGAINST MULTIPLE COMPONENTS

While the components node is selected, you can select multiple components using **CTRL+click**, or select all components using **CTRL+A**. When multiple components are selected, using the query action checks the component status of the selected components.

In addition, the logging action displays a slightly modified log control dialog allowing the use of a same filename for all selected components.

Security Considerations

Despite all the advancements of the System Center 2012 Configuration Manager console, there is still some commonality between it and the ConfigMgr 2007 consoles. The security requirement for things such as the SMS Provider has not changed.

By default, a local group called SMS Admins is granted the permissions required to access the SMS Provider and the Common Information Model (CIM) repository. Whenever an administrative user is granted access to Configuration Manager, the user is added to the SMS Admins group, inherently receiving these permissions.

NOTE: SMS ADMINS GROUP DOES NOT PROVIDE ADMINISTRATIVE ACCESS

Although the name SMS Admins might sound as if it grants full administrative rights to ConfigMgr, this is not the case. Even with inclusion in the SMS Admins group, you must grant the administrative user database access as well. Think of it like an office building. The SMS Admins group is the key to the front, public space. When inside, you must be given access to the individual office suites.

SMS Provider Permissions

When running the ConfigMgr console locally (on the same server as the SMS Provider), it uses WMI to connect to the SMS Provider, and in turn the SMS Provider allows access to the site database. This is made slightly more complicated for remote connections by adding the requirement for DCOM permissions.

Because Configuration Manager still uses WMI and WMI relies on the Distributed Component Object Model (DCOM), it is vital that you understand the requirements for WMI. For information about remote WMI security requirements, see http://msdn.microsoft.com/en-us/library/aa393266%28v=VS.85%29.aspx.

DCOM Permissions

Administrative users running the console from their workstations, where the SMS Provider does not exist, require the Remote Activation DCOM privilege on any computer where the SMS Provider is installed and providing access to the ConfigMgr database. (In most cases, the SMS Provider is installed on the same server as the site server.)

By default, the local SMS Admins group has the following permissions applied:

- ▶ Local Launch
- ▶ Remote Launch
- ▶ Local Activation
- ▶ Remote Activation

For remote console access, only the Remote Activation privilege is required. Figure 8.29 shows a custom local group is provided only this privilege.

WMI Permissions

Along with DCOM permissions, WMI permissions are also required for ConfigMgr console access. By default, the SMS Admins group is given the appropriate permissions necessary to provide operability.

Permissions are applied to two different namespaces. Here are the privileges granted to the SMS Admins group in the Root\SMS WMI namespace:

- ▶ Enable Account
- ▶ Remote Enable

Figure 8.30 displays the permissions assigned to the same custom group (Limited SMS Admins, mentioned in the "DCOM Permissions" section) with the appropriate permissions granted to the Root\SMS namespace.

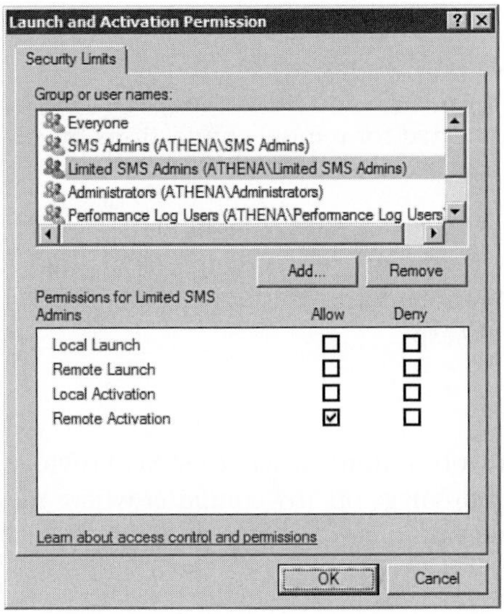

FIGURE 8.29   DCOM permissions with Remote Activation privilege.

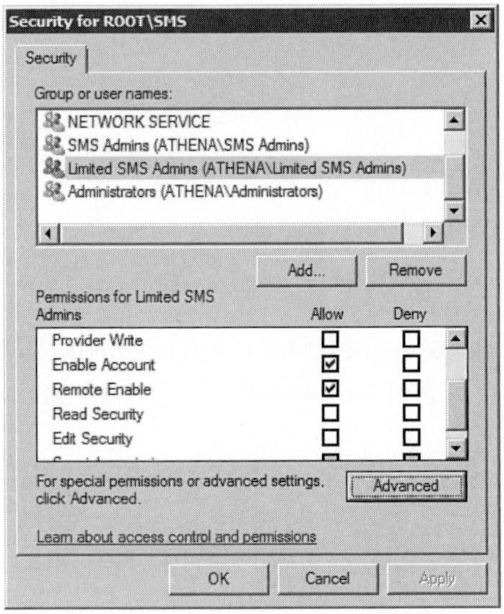

FIGURE 8.30   WMI permissions required on `Root\SMS` namespace.

The SMS Admins group is provided a slightly different set of permissions to the `Root\SMS\` `site_<site code>` WMI namespace:

▶ Enable Account

▶ Execute Methods

> ▶ Provider Writer

> ▶ Remote Enable

Figures 8.31 shows the same custom group (Limited SMS Admins) with the appropriate permissions granted to this namespace.

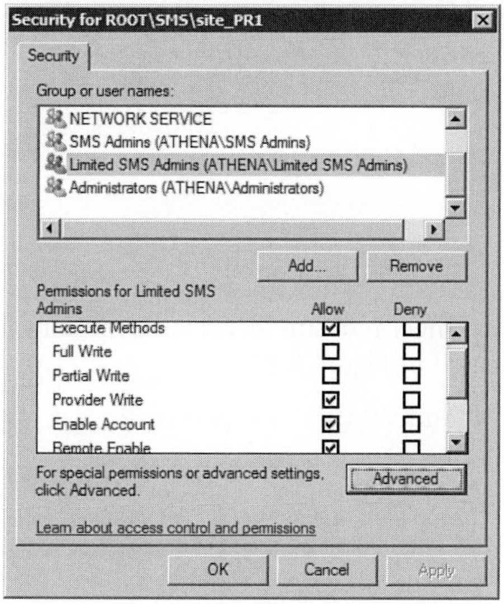

FIGURE 8.31   WMI permissions required on `Root\SMS\site_<site code>`.

Troubleshooting Console Issues

With a new role-based ConfigMgr console, the expected behavior may not always be the expected outcome. Console problems often are due to insufficient or inappropriately assigned security privileges. The next sections describe how to troubleshoot issues with the ConfigMgr console.

Console Logging

Administrators cherish the rich, detailed logging provided in ConfigMgr. The ConfigMgr console is no exception. Use the log to gain valuable insight and detail during console-related issues. The console logs to the SMSAdminUI.log file located in the following path:

`<%ProgramFiles%>\Microsoft Configuration Manager\AdminConsole\AdminUILog`

If the default logging level in the SMSAdminUI.log does not provide sufficient detail, you can increase the logging verbosity. To enable verbose logging, navigate to the following path, and then follow these steps:

`<%ProgramFiles%>\Microsoft Configuration Manager\AdminConsole\bin`

1. Open the file named **Microsoft.ConfigurationManagement.exe.config**.

2. Search for the following line `<source name="SmsAdminUISnapIn"` `switchValue="Error" >` and then change the value of `"Error"` to `"Verbose"`.

3. If the ConfigMgr console is open, restart the console for the setting to take effect.

CAUTION: DO NOT LEAVE SETTINGS AT VERBOSE

When logging levels are increased, the log size and activity to write logs also increase. If you enable verbose logging, be sure to change the logging level back to its default when finished.

Verify Security

The "Security Considerations" section discusses how DCOM and WMI permissions are applied with respect to console operation. Trying to connect to a site server with misconfigured security may lead to a similar failure, as indicated in Figure 8.32.

The next sections illustrate how to verify both DCOM- and WMI-related permissions.

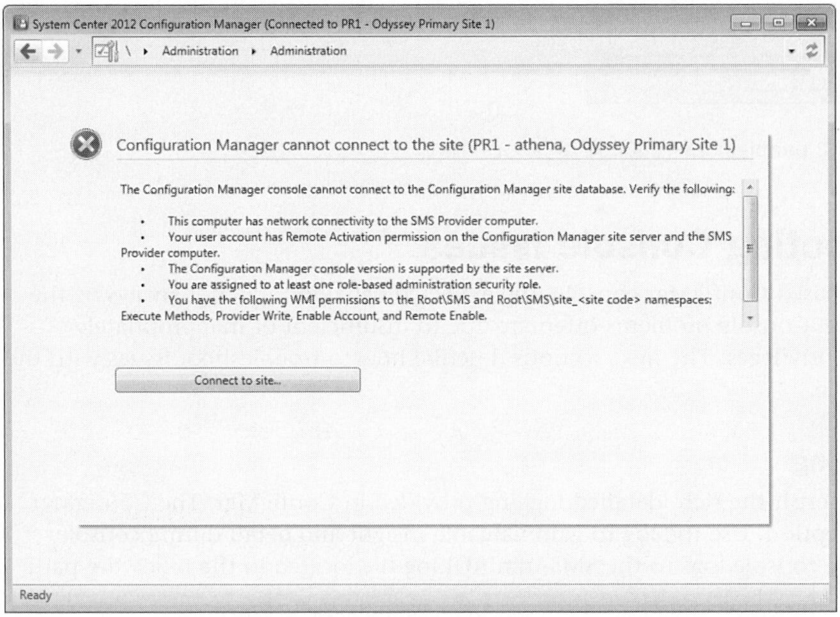

FIGURE 8.32   Failed connection to a site server.

Verify DCOM Permissions

At a minimum, the required DCOM permission is Remote Activation. To verify the Remote Activation permission, perform the following steps:

1. On the site server (and any SMS Provider computer), start the Component Services console. Click **Start -> Run** and then type **dcomcnfg.exe**.

2. Navigate to My Computer by expanding **Component Services** and then **Computers**.

3. Right-click on My Computer, and select **Properties** from the menu, as displayed in Figure 8.33.

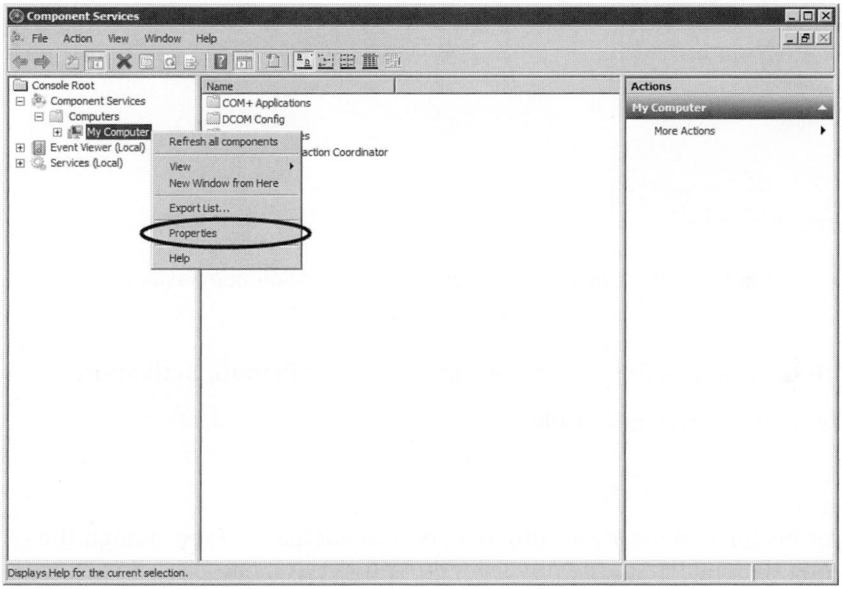

FIGURE 8.33   Opening the DCOM properties window.

4. Switch to the COM Security tab.

5. In the lower section titled Launch and Activation Permissions, click the **Edit Limits** button (see Figure 8.34).

   At this point, if permissions are correct (refer to Figure 8.29 in the "Security Considerations" section), the remaining steps are not necessary. If permissions are missing, proceed to step 6.

6. Click **Add** and specify the interested account or group. Click **OK**.

7. In the permission area, deselect all other values and select **Remote Activation**.

8. Click **OK** to close the Launch and Activation Permission dialog box, and click **OK** to close the My Computer Properties dialog box.

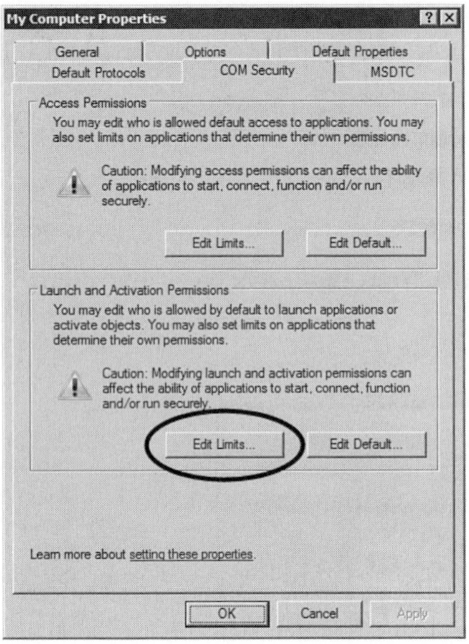

FIGURE 8.34   Opening the Edit Limits window for Launch and Activation permissions.

9. In the permission area, deselect all other values, and select **Remote Activation**.

10. Close the Component Services console.

Verify WMI Permissions

Validating WMI permissions occurs at two different WMI namespaces. Even though the namespaces are along the same path, the privileges differ for each namespace, and therefore the child namespace does not inherit from the parent. Note that the screenshots illustrate providing access to a custom local group (Limited SMS Admins).

To verify WMI permissions, perform the following steps:

1. On the site server (and any SMS Provider computer), start the Component Services console. Click **Start -> Administrative Tools**, and select **Computer Management**.

2. Expand the **Services and Applications** node, and right-click **WMI Control**.

3. Select **Properties** in the menu to launch the WMI Control Properties dialog, as displayed in Figure 8.35.

4. Switch to the Security tab, and expand the Root node. Select **SMS**, as shown in Figure 8.36, and click the **Security** button.

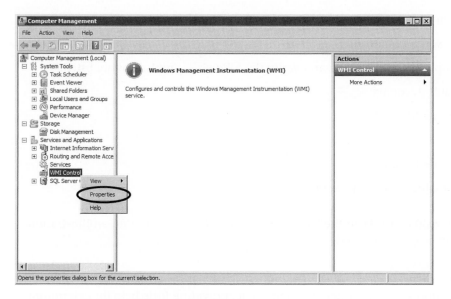

FIGURE 8.35   Launching WMI Properties.

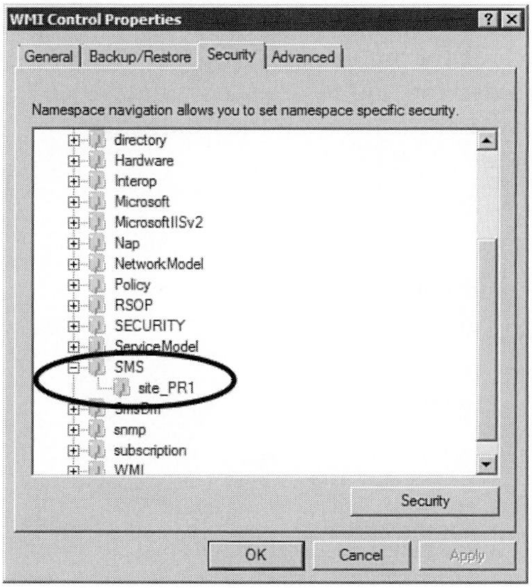

FIGURE 8.36   ConfigMgr namespaces in the WMI Control Properties dialog box.

5. Verify the following permissions are listed:

▶ Enable Account

▶ Remote Enable

6. Expand the SMS node, and select the site_<*site code*>_node below.

7. Click the **Security** button.

8. Select **Properties** in the menu and verify the following permissions are listed:

   ▶ Enable Account

   ▶ Execute Methods

   ▶ Provider Writer

   ▶ Remote Enable

9. Close all dialog boxes as necessary.

Refer to Figures 8.30 and 8.31 in the "Security Considerations" section for an illustration of the permissions applied properly.

Connectivity Issues

Console connection status messages are often vague, providing little help for determining issues. Even the SMSAdminUI.log might not provide additional value. Situations like these may leave you wondering in which layer the permissions issue is occurring.

It is helpful to filter out whether the problem is occurring both locally and remotely. Knowing this information helps isolate where to look for problems. To test this scenario, launch the console from the administrative user's desktop and record the results. When done, launch the console under the administrative user's context on the ConfigMgr server. Table 8.4 lists which component to examine.

TABLE 8.4   Testing Console Behavior

Local Fails	Remote Fails	Component
X	X	WMI, SMS
	X	WMI, DCOM

Common Problems with the ConfigMgr Console

Table 8.5 describes issues you might experience while using the ConfigMgr console.

TABLE 8.5   Console Problems and Resolutions

Error	Description
Error: Configuration Manager cannot to the site.	SMSAdminUI.log contains Insufficient Privilege to Connect, Error: Access Is Denied.
	When an administrative user does not have local administrator privileges to the ConfigMgr site server, they are most likely missing DCOM privileges. Ensure the user is a member of the Distributed COM Users local group.
Error: Configuration Manager cannot connect to the site.	SMSAdminUI.log contains Transport Error; Failed to Connect, Message: The SMS Provider Reported an Error.
	An administrative user who does not have access to the SMS Provider (generally through WMI permissions) will fail to connect to the site. Ensure the user is a member of the SMS Admins local group.
	If the user is a member of the SMS Admins local group, ensure that an administrative user context has been created for them with at least one role assigned.
Expected objects are not displayed in the console.	Ensure the administrative user has the correct security scopes and collections assigned, if limiting the user's access to certain objects.
Expected workspaces, nodes, or actions are not displayed in the console.	Ensure the administrative user has the correct security role assigned, granting access to the correct objects.

Summary

This chapter introduced you to the new System Center 2012 Configuration Manager console. It covered the new panes and ribbons, and included a table listing the nodes and their functions. It stepped through a console installation and discussed automating the console installation. This chapter described how to use the secondary console, Configuration Manager Service Manager, and actions to control the various ConfigMgr components.

The chapter ended with a troubleshooting section to help diagnose common console problems. The following chapter discusses managing clients.

CHAPTER 9

Configuration Manager Client Management

With your Configuration Manager (ConfigMgr) environment installed and configured, you can begin client management. The context in which *client* is used refers to the end device managed by System Center 2012 Configuration Manager. A ConfigMgr client refers to any system that has the ConfigMgr agent installed and configured. This can be a workstation or server operating system, mobile device, or cash register using Windows Embedded systems. ConfigMgr site servers can also (and usually do) have the ConfigMgr client installed. This chapter discusses discovery, client requirements, client installation and configuration, client settings, inventory, managing the client, client health, and Wake On LAN (WOL).

ConfigMgr can execute tasks on clients. This requires the System Center Configuration Manager agent software is installed on that client, which runs the agent as a Windows service. When installed, the ConfigMgr client, which communicates with the ConfigMgr backend infrastructure, can execute commands on behalf on ConfigMgr, such as running a hardware inventory or installing software. ConfigMgr must discover the device before the client can be installed.

Discovery

Discovery is used to locate potential clients prior to installing client software on those systems. Systems must be discovered before the client can be installed. The next sections discuss the different methods to discover the client.

CAUTION: NEED FOR A CLEAN ACTIVE DIRECTORY

System Center 2012 Configuration Manager offers six different discovery types:

▶ Active Directory Forest Discovery

▶ Active Directory Group Discovery

▶ Active Directory User Discovery

▶ Active Directory System Discovery

▶ Heartbeat Discovery

▶ Network Discovery

If you use one of the Active Directory Discovery methods and your Active Directory (AD) contains objects no longer used—such as obsolete groups, computers, and user accounts—these objects are imported into ConfigMgr. Although some discovery methods provide methods to prevent pollution, the authors recommend you clean up AD regularly.

Active Directory Forest Discovery

By enabling Active Directory Forest Discovery, you can discover IP subnets and AD sites that you can automatically add as boundaries, and find remote forests to which you can publish ConfigMgr site information for clients in that forest to use. You must discover a remote forest before you can publish information to it. Active Directory Forest Discovery is disabled by default. When enabled, it runs weekly by default. To configure Active Directory Forest Discovery, perform the following steps:

1. In the Administration workspace of the console, navigate to **Overview -> Hierarchy Configuration -> Discovery Methods**. Select **Active Directory Forest Discovery** and choose **Properties**.

2. On the General tab, as displayed in Figure 9.1, check the box to enable Active Directory Forest Discovery.

   You can specify whether to create Active Directory site boundaries from Active Directory and if you want to create IP address range boundaries for IP subnets.

   The default Active Directory Forest Discovery schedule can be modified from 1 week to a value between 1 hour and 4 weeks. For normal usage, a weekly schedule should be sufficient. For some scenarios, such as when in the midst of a huge migration that affects Active Directory, you may want to modify the schedule to a less or more frequent value.

To configure publishing to an Active Directory forest, perform the following steps:

1. Navigate to **Administration -> Overview -> Hierarchy Configuration -> Active Directory Forests**. Select the forest you want to configure, and choose **Properties**.

2. On the General tab of the forest's properties page, select whether to discover sites and subnets in that forest. You can also specify which account to use for the AD Forest Discovery, the computer account of the site server is used by default.

3. On the Publishing tab, as shown in Figure 9.2, select which sites will be published to the remote forest. By default, the information is published to the root of that forest; to override this behavior, specify a particular domain or server.

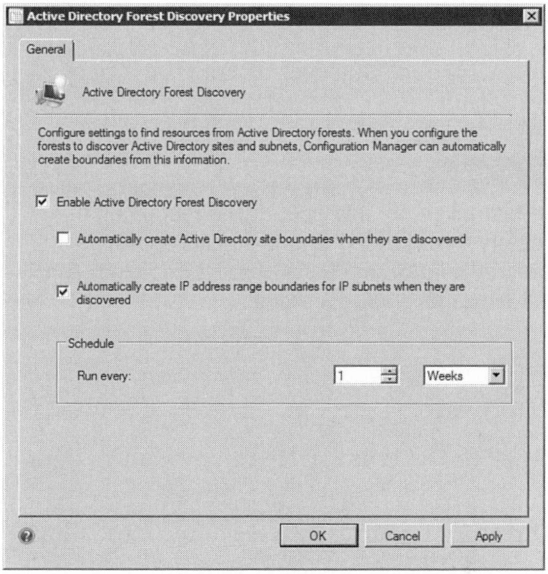

FIGURE 9.1   Active Directory Forest Discovery Properties.

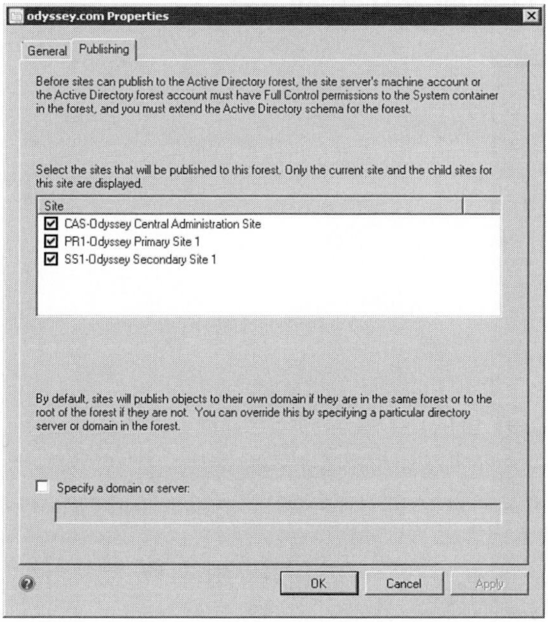

FIGURE 9.2   Active Directory Forest Publishing Properties.

Active Directory Group Discovery

Active Directory Group Discovery lets you discover AD groups and their memberships. It inventories groups, group membership, group membership relations, and basic information about the objects that are members of these discovered groups if these resources are not already discovered by other discovery methods.

You can specify a location in AD to search for AD groups in a specific container, or specify a specific group. These are security groups by default.

> **TIP: ABOUT DELTA DISCOVERY**
>
> Delta discovery discovers changes since the last inventory and uses fewer resources than a full discovery. It is available for Active Directory Group, User, and System Discovery. Delta discovery will search AD every 5 minutes by default for changed attributes since the last full discovery. Delta discovery cannot detect removal of resources from AD; this is only detected by a full discovery cycle.

Perform these steps to configure Active Directory Group Discovery:

1. In the Administration workspace, navigate to **Overview -> Hierarchy Configuration -> Discovery Methods**.

2. In the Navigation tree, select **Active Directory Group Discovery** and choose **Properties**.

   ▶ On the General page, as shown in Figure 9.3, check the box to enable Active Directory Group Discovery, which is disabled by default. To add a location or a group, select **Add** and then select **Groups** or **Location**.

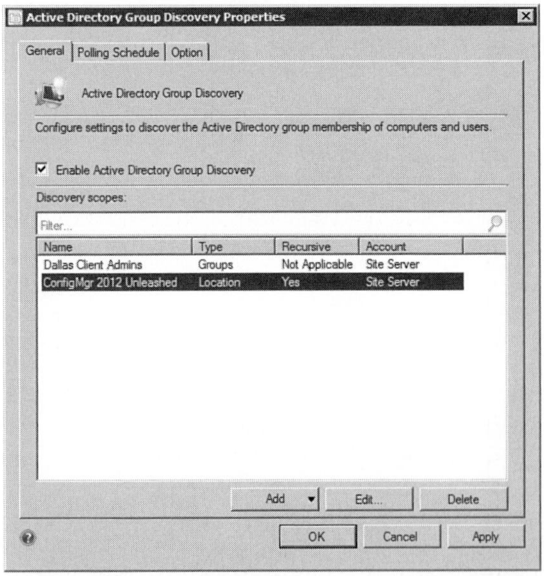

FIGURE 9.3   Active Directory Group Discovery Properties.

Selecting **Groups** opens the Add Groups dialog displayed in Figure 9.4. Specify a name to reflect the group you want to add, or use the **Browse** button to search for a group in AD. By default, the site server's computer account is used to search AD, but you can specify another account if necessary, for example when you want to specify a group in another AD. You can also specify a specific domain controller (DC) to use for the search to lessen the burden on other DCs serving users and devices; the default domain and forest is used by default.

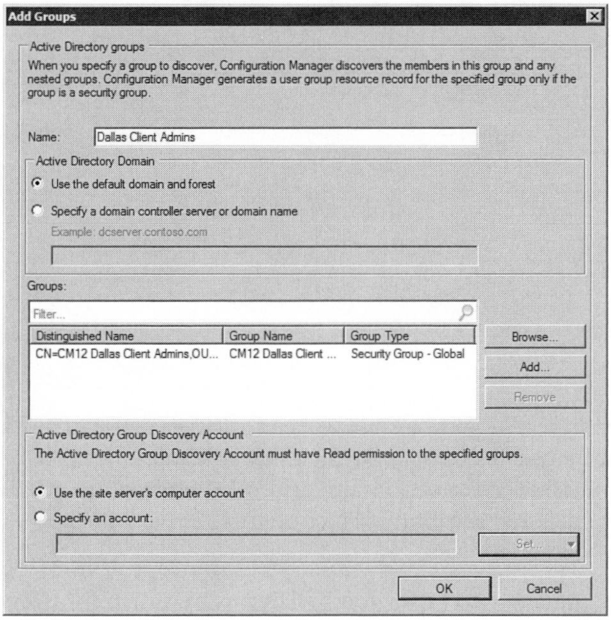

FIGURE 9.4   Active Directory Group Discovery Add Groups page.

Selecting **Location** opens the Add Active Directory Location dialog, as shown in Figure 9.5. Here you can specify a name to reflect the location you want to add and use the **Browse** button to search for an AD container. The search is recursive by default, meaning child objects of the selected container are also inventoried. The site server's computer account is used to search AD, but you can specify another account.

▶ Use the Polling Schedule tab to specify the full discovery polling schedule, which is set to run every 7 days. You can also specify whether you want to use delta discovery, enabled by default.

▶ The Option tab lets you exclude certain computers from discovery. This could be computers that have not logged on to a domain for a certain amount of time, 90 days by default, or computers for which the computer account was not updated for a certain amount of time, also 90 days by default. You can also enable discovery of members of distribution groups.

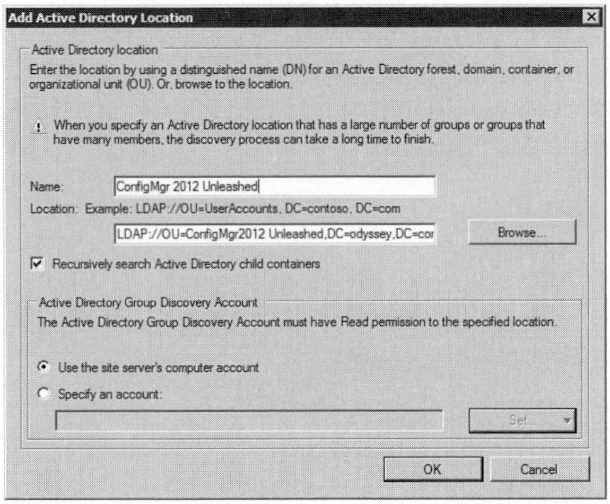

FIGURE 9.5   Active Directory Group Discovery Add Location page.

Active Directory User Discovery

Active Directory User Discovery discovers user accounts and their AD attributes. ConfigMgr discovers the username, unique username, domain, and AD container names attributes by default; you can specify additional attributes. To configure Active Directory User Discovery, perform these steps:

1. In the Administration workspace, navigate to **Overview -> Hierarchy Configuration -> Discovery Methods**.

2. In the Navigation tree, select **Active Directory User Discovery** and choose **Properties**.

   ▶ On the General tab, as displayed in Figure 9.6, enable Active Directory User Discovery. Use the starburst icon to specify an Active Directory container to search by providing the LDAP path manually or clicking the **Browse** button to search for a container. This search is recursive by default. You can specify if you want to discover users that reside within groups. By default, the site server's computer account is used to search AD; you can specify another account if needed.

   ▶ Use the Polling Schedule tab to specify the full discovery polling schedule, set to run every 7 days. You can specify whether you want to use delta discovery, enabled by default.

   ▶ Use the Active Directory Attributes tab, as shown in Figure 9.7, to add specific attributes belonging to the user object for inclusion with the discovery; select the attribute and click **Add**. If an attribute is not listed, select the **Custom** button, and type the name of the attribute.

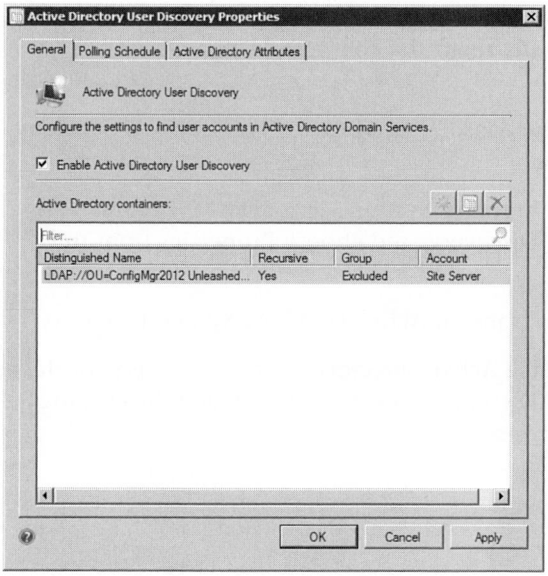

FIGURE 9.6   Active Directory User Discovery Properties.

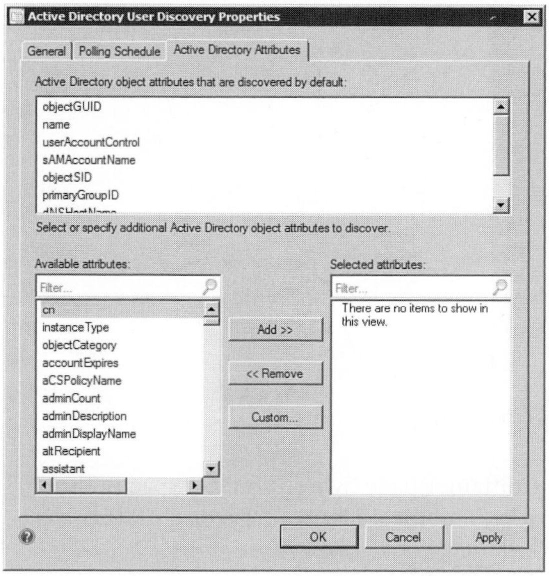

FIGURE 9.7   Active Directory User Discovery AD Attributes.

Active Directory System Discovery

Active Directory System Discovery polls the specified AD containers, such as domains and sites in a domain controller, to discover computers. This discovery method can also recursively poll the specified AD containers. Active Directory System Discovery connects to each discovered computer to retrieve details about the computer. Follow these steps to enable Active Directory System Discovery:

1. In the Administration workspace of the console, navigate to **Overview -> Hierarchy Configuration -> Discovery Methods**.

2. In the Navigation tree, select **Active Directory System Discovery** for the site code for which you want to enable System Discovery, and choose **Properties** from the ribbon.

   Here is information about the different tabs for Active Directory System Discovery:

   ▶ **General tab:** Use this tab to enable Active Directory System Discovery for the site. You must also specify the AD containers you want to search by clicking the starburst in the middle of Figure 9.8.

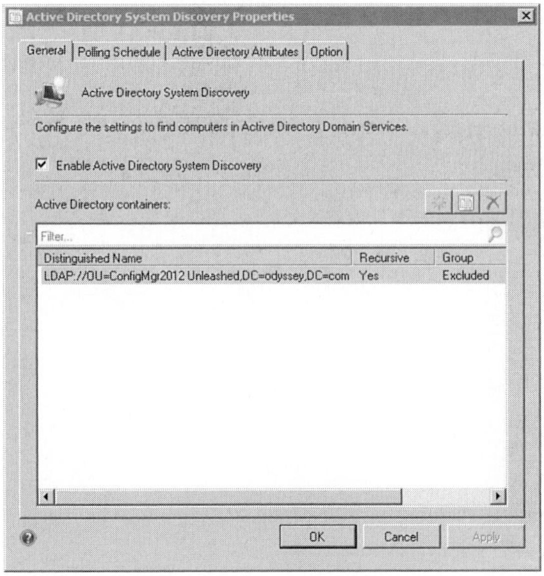

FIGURE 9.8   Active Directory System Discovery Properties.

This opens the Active Directory Container page, where you can specify the container to search during discovery. Provide a LDAP query, or click the **Browse** button to search for a container. You can specify a global catalog (GC) query to find an AD container within multiple domains. After specifying the path, you can specify the search options, which include recursively searching AD child containers and discovering objects within AD groups.

Recursively searching AD child containers will search any child container within the specified path. Discovering objects within AD groups will also discover objects within groups in the search path.

You can specify a service account to use for the discovery process. By default this is the site server's computer account, which should at least have Read permissions on the specified location; alternatively, you can specify a specific domain account with the same user rights.

Click **OK** after configuring the AD container properties to return to the Active Directory System Discovery Properties dialog.

▶ **Polling Schedule:** This tab enables you to modify how often ConfigMgr polls AD to find computer data. By default, a full discovery polling occurs every 7 days starting Thursday 1/1/1998, and delta discovery runs every 5 minutes. Both settings are modifiable.

▶ **Active Directory Attributes:** Here you can specify the AD properties of discovered objects to discover. Attributes discovered by default include name, sAMAccountName, and primaryGroupID. You can also specify attributes such as adminCount, department, and division, by selecting them from the available attributes list and clicking **Add**.

▶ **Option:** Use this tab to specify additional options, such as discovering only those computers that have logged on or updated their computer account password with the domain within a given period. These settings are disabled by default.

After you enable Active Directory System Discovery or discover clients using Active Directory Group Discovery, clients will begin to appear in the Devices node of the Assets and Compliance workspace that do not yet have the ConfigMgr client installed. This is easy to determine as the Client property is set to **No**.

Heartbeat Discovery

Heartbeat Discovery is enabled by default when a ConfigMgr site is installed. It is also the only discovery method that must be enabled, as ConfigMgr uses this discovery method to determine if clients are healthy and reachable. This discovery method runs on every ConfigMgr client and creates discovery data records (DDRs) containing information about the client including network location, NetBIOS name, and operational status. The DDR is copied to the management point (MP), where it is processed by the client's primary site. Heartbeat Discovery lets ConfigMgr determine whether clients are still reachable and healthy as a ConfigMgr client.

The ConfigMgr client sends a DDR for Heartbeat Discovery every 7 days by default. By using Heartbeat Discovery with the Delete Aged Discovery Data setting in the Site Maintenance task, you can configure when to delete an inactive client from the ConfigMgr site database. Site maintenance tasks are discussed in Chapter 21, "Backup, Recovery, and Maintenance." The ConfigMgr client logs Heartbeat Discovery actions in the InventoryAgent.log file, found in the %*windir*%\CCM\Logs folder.

To configure Heartbeat Discovery, perform these steps:

1. In the Administration workspace of the console, navigate to **Overview -> Hierarchy Configuration -> Discovery Methods**.

2. In the Navigation tree, select **Heartbeat Discovery** for the site code and then **Properties** to open the Heartbeat Discoveries Properties dialog, as shown in Figure 9.9.

3. On the **General** tab, specify whether you want to disable Heartbeat Discovery and the schedule to use.

   If you use sitewide client push installation, discussed in the "Client Push Installation" section of this chapter, configure the heartbeat schedule so that it runs less frequently than the client rediscovery period for the Clear Install Flag site maintenance task. The Clear Install Flag site maintenance task is discussed in Chapter 21. If you set the Clear Install Flag to a lower value than the client rediscovery value, ConfigMgr reinstalls the client even if it is running as expected.

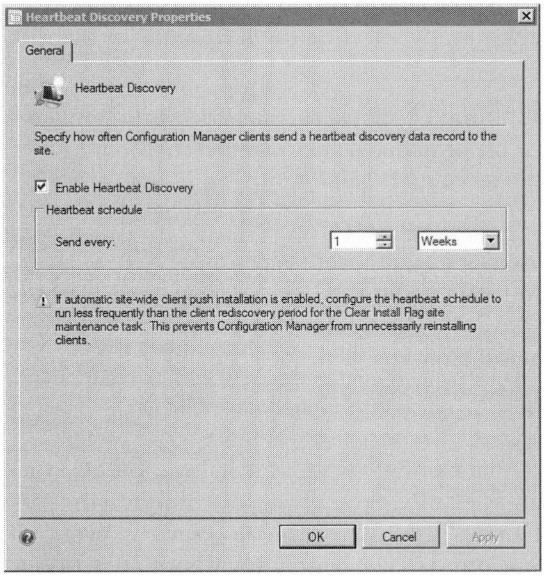

FIGURE 9.9   Heartbeat Discovery Properties.

For mobile devices, the DDR is generated by the MP of the mobile device. Disabling Heartbeat Discovery does not disable generation of DDRs for mobile devices by the MP. Chapter 15, "Mobile Device Management," explains how heartbeat discovery works for mobile devices.

Network Discovery

Network Discovery allows you to discover resources you cannot find using any of the other discovery methods. This enables you to search domains, SNMP services, and DHCP servers to find resources. Network Discovery is unique because, in addition to computers, it finds network devices such as printers, routers, and bridges. Network Discovery is disabled by default. Here's how to enable it:

1. In the Administration workspace of the console, navigate to **Overview -> Hierarchy Configuration -> Discovery Methods**.

2. In the Navigation tree, select **Network Discovery** for the site code for which you want to enable Network Discovery, and then choose **Properties** from the ribbon. Here is information on each of the tabs:

   ▶ **General:** This tab, displayed in Figure 9.10 and previously discussed in Chapter 5, "Network Design," has a check box to enable network discovery. You can also specify the type of discovery, which is **Topology** by default. Here are the available options:

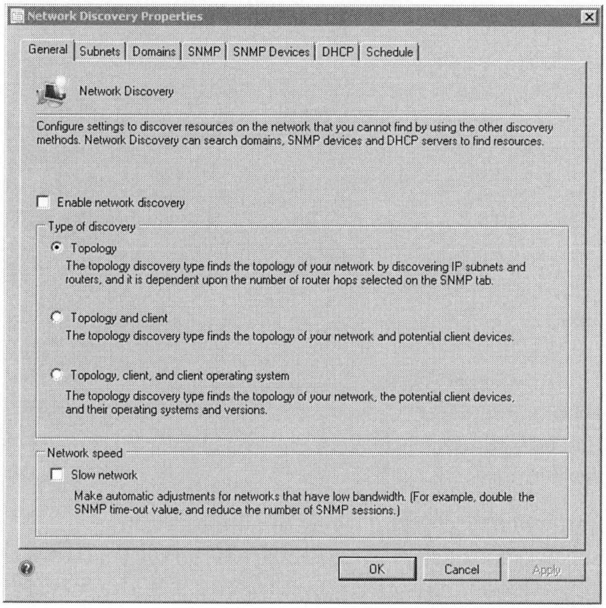

FIGURE 9.10   Network Discovery Properties.

   Topology: Topology finds the topology of your network by discovering IP subnets and routers using SNMP; although it does not discover potential clients. The number of subnets and routers discovered is dependent on the specified router hops on the SNMP tab.

   Topology and client: Selecting this option also discovers potential client devices.

Topology, client, and client operating system: Selecting this option causes operating systems and versions to be discovered as well.

You can specify that you have a slow network speed, which causes ConfigMgr to make automatic adjustments such as doubling the SNMP time-out value and reducing the number of SNMP sessions.

▶ **Subnets:** Specify the subnets to search. By default, only the subnet of the server that is running discovery is discovered; this can be disabled by removing the check mark from the **Search local subnets** check box. Clicking the starburst lets you specify a new subnet by providing its subnet address and subnet mask. You can modify subnet settings or disable a subnet by clicking **Edit**, the icon next to the starburst. You can also delete subnets or switch the order of appearance.

▶ **Domains:** Use this tab to specify the domains to search. Only the local domain is searched by default, which you can disable by removing the check mark from the **Search local domain** check box. Add additional domains by clicking the starburst to specify a domain name. Click **Edit** to modify the domain properties, or disable this option by deselecting **Enable Domain Search**. You can also delete domains from being searched or switch the order in which they are searched.

▶ **SNMP:** The SNMP tab lets you specify the SNMP community names and maximum number of router hops for the discovery process. The public community name is included by default. You can specify additional SNMP community names by clicking the starburst and specifying a new SNMP community name. You can modify the search order for the SNMP communities and delete earlier provided SNMP communities. Specifying maximum hops lets you indicate the number of hops used to search for discovered objects. Using hops lets you specify how many routers the process will pass through.

▶ **SNMP Devices:** This tab lets you specify specific SNMP devices to discover. If you know the Internet Protocol (IP) address or device name to be discovered, specify the information by clicking the starburst.

▶ **DHCP:** The DHCP tab enables you to specify one or more Microsoft DHCP servers to use to discover those clients receiving their IP address from a Microsoft DHCP server. You can also specify using the DHCP server that gave the site server its IP address by checking the check box for **Include the DHCP server that the site server is configured to use**.

▶ **Schedules:** Here you can specify one or more schedules when Network Discovery will run. Create a schedule by clicking the starburst. You can specify a schedule by identifying a start time and duration, and a recurrence schedule, which can be none, monthly, weekly, or using a custom interval.

CAUTION: DETERMINE IF YOU REALLY WANT TO ENABLE NETWORK DISCOVERY

Network Discovery should be a last resort to find potential ConfigMgr clients. Depending on the specified Network Discovery settings, you can get a considerable amount of information; determine whether you want use that information within ConfigMgr.

Manually Importing Clients into ConfigMgr

Clients can be manually imported into ConfigMgr using the ConfigMgr console or scripts to automatically create DDR files. You would manually import clients if not using unknown client support during operating system deployment (OSD). To import a client into ConfigMgr manually, perform these steps:

1. In the Assets and Compliance workspace of the console, navigate to **Devices**.

2. Select **Import Computer Information** from the ribbon bar to open the Import Computer Information Wizard.

3. In the Import Computer Information Wizard, you can select to import a single computer or import computers using a file:

   ▶ If you select **Import Single Computer**, provide the Computer Name and MAC address or SMBIOS GUID of the machine. You can also specify if you want to provide a reference computer for OSD to use when migrating settings from an old computer to this new computer.

   ▶ When you select **Import Computers Using A File**, you can browse for a comma separated values (CSV) file that you can create with an application such as Microsoft Excel. The minimum information to supply in the CSV file is the computer name and the SMBIOS GUID or MAC address of the machine. If you use column headings, check **This file has column headings**, as shown in Figure 9.11, to ignore the first line of the file.

   Map the values in the CSV file to the corresponding ConfigMgr fields. If you supplied the CSV fields in the order of Name, SMBIOS GUID, MAC Address, Source Computer, Variable1, and Variable 2, most of the import information is mapped automatically; all you must do is map the provided variables to a ConfigMgr variable. If you don't make this mapping, these values are ignored.

4. After you successfully supply the computer information with either CSV or the wizard, a data preview page indicates the expected result of the import. Click **Next** to supply the collection to which you want to add the computer resources (All Systems collection by default).

5. The Summary page shows what will be imported and where. Click **Next** to begin the actual import. When complete, close the Import Computer Information Wizard, and the new computers display in the specified collection.

9

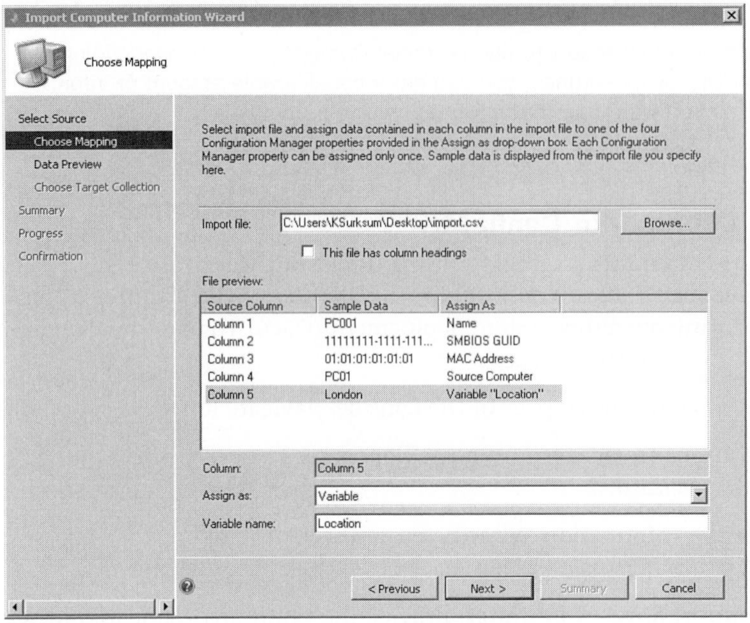

FIGURE 9.11   Choose CSV file mapping.

ConfigMgr Client Requirements

Before deploying the ConfigMgr client to devices, determine whether those devices are supported in terms of hardware and installed operating systems. Microsoft provides guidelines for supported hardware and supports the ConfigMgr client on a specific list of defined platforms. Before installing the client, you should inventory the systems in your environment. A tool that can assist with this task is the Microsoft Assessment Planning Toolkit (MAP).

ABOUT THE MICROSOFT ASSESSMENT PLANNING TOOLKIT

MAP is a solution accelerator providing an inventory, assessment, and reporting tool designed for technology migration projects such as Windows 7 migrations. MAP provides extensive hardware and software information. The Microsoft Assessment Planning Toolkit is available at no charge and can be downloaded from http://www.microsoft.com/download/en/details.aspx?id=7826. For frequently asked questions on MAP, see http://social.technet.microsoft.com/wiki/contents/articles/1643.aspx.

Hardware Dependencies

Microsoft provides minimal and recommended hardware requirements for the ConfigMgr client. However, if a supported operating system (OS) is running on a minimal hardware configuration, do not expect optimal performance. The authors suggest using the recommended hardware specifications listed in Table 9.1, allowing smooth operation of the ConfigMgr client.

TABLE 9.1   ConfigMgr Client Hardware Requirements

Component	Minimal Requirement	Microsoft Recommended
RAM	128MB	256MB, 384MB when using OSD
Processor	233MHz	300MHz or faster
Free Disk Space	350MB	5GB

Software Dependencies

Before installing the ConfigMgr client, verify you have at least version 3.1.4000.2435 of the Windows Installer. This version and higher allows you to use the Windows Installer update (.msp) files used by the client software.

In addition to the software mentioned here, other prerequisite software may be required, depending on the type of client. The ConfigMgr client installation process automatically installs this software as needed; although, you may want to install some prerequisite software before starting client installation. This could include BITS, which requires a restart, and .NET Framework, which takes a long time to install. Table 9.2 lists client software dependencies.

TABLE 9.2   Software Dependencies for the ConfigMgr Client

Dependent Software	Minimum Version Required
Microsoft Silverlight	4.0.50524
Microsoft Background Intelligent Transfer Service (BITS)	2.5
Windows Update Agent	7.0.6000.363
Microsoft Core XML Services	6.20.5002
Microsoft Remote Differential Compression (RDC)	
Microsoft .NET Framework 4 Client Profile	4.0
Microsoft Visual C++ 2008 Redistributable	9.0.30729.4148
Microsoft Visual C++ 2005 Redistributable	8.0.50727.42
Windows Imaging APIs	6.0.6001.18000
Microsoft Policy Platform	1.2.3514.0
Microsoft SQL Server Compact Edition	3.5 SP2
Microsoft Windows Imaging Components	

Supported Platforms

You can install the ConfigMgr client on the operating systems listed in Table 9.3.

TABLE 9.3   Supported Client and Server OS Versions

Operating System	Edition	Service Pack (SP)	System Architecture
Client Operating Systems			
Windows XP	Professional	SP 3	x86
Windows XP for 64-bit Systems	Professional	SP 2	x64
Windows XP	Tablet PC	SP 3	x86
Windows Vista	Business Edition Enterprise Edition Ultimate Edition	SP 2	x86, x64
Windows 7	Professional Enterprise Edition Ultimate Edition	RTM, SP 1	x86, x64
Server Operating Systems			
Windows Server 2003	Web Edition	SP 2	x86
Windows Server 2003	Standard Edition Enterprise Edition Datacenter Edition	SP 2	x86, x64
Windows Server 2003 R2	Standard Edition Enterprise Edition Datacenter Edition	SP 2	x86, x64
Windows Storage Server 2003 R2		SP 2	x86, x64
Windows Server 2008	Standard Edition Enterprise Edition Datacenter Edition	SP 2	x86, x64
Windows Server 2008	Standard Core Edition Enterprise Core Edition Datacenter Core Edition	SP 2	x64
Windows Server 2008 R2	Standard Edition Enterprise Edition Datacenter Edition	RTM, SP 1, SP 2	x64
Windows Server 2008 R2	Standard Core Edition Enterprise Core Edition Datacenter Core Edition	RTM, SP 1	x64
Windows Storage Server 2008 R2	Standard Edition Enterprise Edition		x64

The Configuration Manager mobile device legacy client can be installed on supported mobile devices. The available features depend on the platform and client type, discussed in Chapter 15.

ConfigMgr Client Installation

There are several methods for installing the ConfigMgr client on supported systems; the one you use depends on the particular rollout scenario. This approach lets Microsoft support most scenarios. For example, you can use your legacy non-Microsoft software distribution environment as a vehicle to roll out the ConfigMgr client. When installed, you can use the ConfigMgr client to uninstall the agent software for that legacy environment.

The next sections discuss the different ways to install the ConfigMgr client. Installing the mobile client is discussed in Chapter 15.

Manual Installation

When you install the ConfigMgr client manually, all that is required are the ConfigMgr client installation binaries. These are found on any site server and MP in a subfolder of the SMS-*<site code>* share, or provided by means of CD, DVD, or USB media. The CCMSetup.exe program copies all necessary installation prerequisites to the client computer and starts the Client.msi Windows Installer package to install the client. You cannot run Client.msi directly; CCMSetup.exe is required for a manual installation.

CCMSetup.exe and Client.msi support command-line options and properties you can use to change the installation behavior. First, specify the CCMSetup.exe command-line properties and then the Client.msi MSI properties, using the format CCMSetup.exe *<CCMSetup properties> <Client.msi properties>*. Table 9.4 and Table 9.5 list the available parameters for CCMSetup.exe and Client.msi.

TABLE 9.4   CCMSetup Command-Line Properties

Command-Line Property	Description	Example
/?	Opens a dialog box showing the command-line properties.	CCMSetup.exe /?
/logon	Using the logon property, you can specify stopping installation if a ConfigMgr client is already running on the system. This can be useful when using a login script to install the ConfigMgr client.	CCMSetup.exe /logon
/MP:*<servername>* or https://*<servername>*	Allows you to specify the MP for downloading necessary client installation files using BITS throttling when configured. When specifying multiple MPs, multiple MPs will be used to look up the CCMSetup source files.	CCMSetup.exe /MP: Apollo1,Apollo2, Apollo3

Command-Line Property	Description	Example
/source:*<path>*	Specify the source location from where to download the installation files using SMB, which can be local or a UNC path. Use this option if not using the MP to download files.	CCMSetup.exe /source:\\Armada\ client$
/UsePKICert	Specify using a public key infra-structure (PKI) certificate when one is available. If none is available, CCMSetup switches back to HTTP communications using a self-signed certificate.	CCMSetup.exe /MP:Apollo /UsePKICert
/NOCRLCheck	Allows you to specify not to check the Certificate Revocation List (CRL) for site systems.	CCMSetup.exe /NOCRLCheck
/uninstall	Uninstall the ConfigMgr client.	CCMSetup.exe /uninstall
/retry:*<minutes>*	Specify the retry interval in minutes if CCMSetup.exe cannot download the installation files. By default this is 10 minutes, and it will try until it reaches the limit specified in the downloadtimeout installation property.	CCMSetup.exe /retry:60
/noservice	Prevents CCMSetup from running as a service. In some scenarios, running CCMSetup.exe as a service isn't sufficient because the service doesn't have necessary rights to access network resources.	CCMSetup.exe /noservice
/service	Specify that CCMSetup should run as a service (default).	CCMSetup.exe /service
/forcereboot	Forces CCMSetup to restart the computer if needed to complete client installation.	CCMSetup.exe /forcereboot
/BITSPriority:*<priority>*	Specify the priority used to download the installation files, the following options are available: FOREGROUND HIGH NORMAL (default) LOW	CCMSetup.exe /BITSPriority: LOW

Command-Line Property	Description	Example
/downloadtimeout:*<minutes>*	How long CCMSetup will attempt to download the client installation files, 1 day (1440 minutes) by default.	CCMSetup.exe /downloadtimeout:200
/config:*<configuration file>*	Specify the name of a text file in the ccmsetup folder containing client installation properties. The mobileclienttemplate.tcf file in the *<ConfigMgrInstallDir>*\bin\platform folder can be used as a template for this text file.	CCMSetup.exe /config:mobileclient.txt
/skipprereq:*<filename>*	Skip installing a prerequisite program when the ConfigMgr client is installed	CCMSetup.exe /skipprereq: silverlight.exe

You can also provide MSI properties after setting ConfigMgr client installation properties or publish these properties in AD by configuring the client push installation method. More information and samples can be found at http://technet.microsoft.com/en-us/library/gg699356.aspx.

TABLE 9.5   Client.msi installation Properties

Installation Property	Description	Example
SMSSITECODE=<AUTO | ABC>	Tell the installation to determine the site code by querying Active Directory (AD) or the management point. When you specify a 3-digit site code, that site code is used.	CCMSetup SMSSITECODE=PR1
FSP=*<servername>*	Specify a fallback status point (FSP), used to receive state messages sent from the client computer before it is successfully joined to a ConfigMgr site.	CCMSetup.exe FSP=Apollo.odyssey.com
SMSCACHESIZE	Specify size of the temporary program download folder in MB or as a percentage when used in combination with the PERCENTDISKSPACE or PERCENTFEEDISKSPACE properties. By default, the maximum size of this folder is set to 5120MB.	CCMSetup.exe SMSCACHESIZE=80

9

Installation Property	Description	Example
SMSCACHEFLAGS	Configure the cache folder based on percentage of disk space, percentage of free disk space, the largest available disk, the disk with the most free space, on disks formatted with NTFS only, if the cache folder should be compressed, and whether the installation should fail if there is insufficient space to install the folder.	CCMSetup.exe SMSCACHEFLAGS= NTFSONLY;MAXDRIVSPACE
DISABLESITEOPT	Specify if end users with admin rights on the computer can change the ConfigMgr client assigned site from the Control Panel applet.	CCMSetup.exe DISABLESITEOPT=TRUE
DISABLECACHEOPT	Specify if end users with admin rights on the computer can change the cache folder settings for the ConfigMgr client from the Control Panel applet.	CCMSetup DISABLECACHEOPT=TRUE
SMSCACHEDIR	Specify the cache folder to use; by default, it is created in the *%windir%*\ccmcache folder.	CCMSetup.exe SMSCACHEDIR= "C:\Windows\Temp"
SMSCONFIGSOURCE	Specify where the ConfigMgr client should check for configuration settings. R stands for registry, P stands for installation properties, M stands for existing settings, and U stands for Upgrade. PU is used by default.	CCMSetup.exe SMSCONFIGSOURCE=PR
SMSDIRECTORYLOOKUP	Specify if the client can use WINS to find a MP that accepts HTTP connections. You have two options: NOWINS, which prevents the use of WINS, and WINSSECURE, where the client can use WINS but only if it has the trusted root key; this is used by default.	CCMSetup.exe SMSDIRECTORYLOOKUP= NOWINS

Installation Property	Description	Example
SMSMP	Specify one or more initial MPs for the client to use, separated by semicolons.	CCMSetup.exe SMSMP= apollo.odyssey.com; apollo2.odyssey.com
CCMINSTALLDIR	Specify where the ConfigMgr client should be installed.	CCMSetup.exe CCMINSTALLDIR= "C:\Unleashed"
CCMADMINS	Specify user account and groups that will be given access to the client settings and policies.	CCMSetup.exe CCMADMINS= "Odyssey\KSurksum; Odyssey\Unleashed Admins"
FSP	Specify an FSP to use.	CCMSetup.exe FSP=Apollo
DNSSUFFIX	Specify the DNS domain name to use when clients use DNS to find their MP. If you use this option, the SMSSITECODE cannot be set to AUTO.	CCMSetup.exe SMSSITECODE=PR1 DNSSUFFIX=odyssey.com
CCMEVALINTERVAL	Specify the interval for the Client Health evaluation tool to run. You can set an interval from 1 to 1440 minutes. By default, it will run once a day.	CCMSetup.exe CCMEVALINTERVAL=60
CCMEVALHOUR	Specify when the Client Health evaluation tool should run. You can set a value between 0 and 23. By default, 0 is used.	CCMSetup.exe CCMEVALHOUR=22
IGNOREAPPVVERSIONCHECK	Specify not to check for a minimal installed App-V version.	CCMSetup.exe IGNOREAPPVVERION CHECK=TRUE
CCMALWAYSINF	If the client always connects through the Internet and never via the intranet, set this option to 1.	CCMSetup.exe /UsePKICert CCMALWAYSINF=1 CCMHOSTNAME= apollo.odyssey.com SMSSITECODE=P01
CCMCERTISSUERS	Specify a list of certificate issuers, a list of trusted root CAs trusted by ConfigMgr.	CCMSetup.exe /UsePKICert CCMCERTISSUERS= "CN=ODYSSEY Root CA; OU= Servers; O=ODYSSEY; C=US | CN=Unleashed Root CA; O=Unleashed"

Installation Property	Description	Example
CCMCERTSEL	Specify the criteria to select a certificate if more than one is available. You can search for an exact or partial match in the Subject Name or Subject Alternative Name or search for the Object Identifier (OID) or distinguished name.	CCMSetup.exe /UsePKICert CCMCERTSEL= "SubjectStr:Odyssey.com"
SMSSIGNCERT	Specify the full path of the .cer filename that contains the exported self-signed certificate of the site server.	CCMSetup.exe /UsePKICert SMSSIGNSERT= *<path to filename>*
CCMCERTSTORE	Specify an alternative certificate store name, which you can use if the certificate is not located in the Personal default certificate store.	CCMSetup.exe /UsePKICert CCMCERTSTORE= "Unleashed"
CCMFIRSTCERT	When set to 1, specify you want to use the PKI certificate with the longest validity period.	CCMSetup.exe /UsePKICert CCMFIRSTCERT=1
CCMHOSTNAME	Specify the FQDN of the Internet-based MP.	CCMSetup.exe /UsePKICert CCMHOSTNAME= Apollo.odyssey.com
CCMHTTPPORT	Specify the HTTP port to use when communicating over HTTP.	CCMSetup.exe CCMHTTPORT=81
CCMHTTPSPORT	Specify the HTTPS port to use when communicating over HTTPS.	CCMSetup.exe CCMHTTPSport=444
SMSPUBLICROOTKEY	Specify the ConfigMgr trusted root key if it cannot be retrieved from AD.	CCMSetup.exe SMSPUBLICROOTKEY=*<key>*
SMSROOTKEYPATH	Use to reinstall the ConfigMgr trusted root key, by pointing to the full path of a file name.	CCMSetup.exe SMSROOTKEYPATH= *<full path to filename>*
RESETKEYINFORMATION	Use this property to remove the ConfigMgr trusted root key.	CCMSetup.exe RESETKEYINFORMATION= TRUE
CCMDEBUGLOGGING	When set to 1, you enable debug logging for client installation.	CCMSetup.exe CCMDEBUGLOGGING=1
CCMENABLELOGGING	If set to FALSE, logging is disabled; by default set to TRUE.	CCMSetup.exe CCMENABLELOGGING= FALSE

Installation Property	Description	Example
CCMLOGLEVEL	Specify the amount of detail written to the log file. By default this is set to 1 but can be set between 0 (most verbose) to 3 (least verbose).	CCMSetup.exe CCMLOGLEVEL=2
CCMLOGMAXHISTORY	After the ConfigMgr log file reaches a limit in size, it is renamed as a backup and a new log file is created. Setting this value allows you to specify how many backup log files to retain; by default set to 1.	CCMSetup.exe CCMLOGMAXHISTORY=2
CCMLOGMAXSIZE	Set the maximum size of the ConfigMgr log file before it is renamed as a backup. By default, set to 250000 and should at least be 100000.	CCMSetup.exe CCMLOGMAXSIZE=400000
CCMALLOWSILENTREBOOT	Specify the ConfigMgr client installation should reboot, even if a user is currently logged on.	CCMSetup.exe CCMALLOSILENTREBOOT
DISABLESITEOPT	Specify if you want end users with admin rights on the computer to change the ConfigMgr client assigned site from the Control Panel item.	CCMSetup.exe DISABLESITEOPT=TRUE

Here is sample syntax to install a ConfigMgr client manually in a site that has its properties published to AD:

```
CCMSetup.exe /MP:APOLLO SMSSITECODE=AUTO FSP=APOLLO
```

This example installs the ConfigMgr client using the management point installed on the Apollo machine. The site code, PR1 in this case, is determined by querying AD. The fallback status point also installed on the Apollo machine is used to send state messages until the client successfully joins the PR1 site.

Installing with Logon Scripts

Use login scripts to install the ConfigMgr client when a user is logging on. By specifying the /logon switch for the CCMSetup.exe installer, the client is only installed if it is not already installed. When you provide the /source property to CCMSetup, you can specify an installation source to use or specify an MP using AD, DNS, or WINS for the installation files.

Here is sample syntax to install the ConfigMgr client from a logon script:

```
CCMSetup.exe /logon /MP:APOLLO SMSSITECODE=PR1
```

Client Push

You can push the client to computer objects known to ConfigMgr; although these computers must belong to a domain. Begin by enabling Active Directory System Discovery or Network Discovery to find potential ConfigMgr clients. When clients are discovered, the ConfigMgr infrastructure can send the necessary installation files to the target machine and begin executing the ConfigMgr client installation remotely.

> **TIP: INSTALLATION PROPERTIES THAT ARE PUBLISHED TO AD**
>
> For information about the installation properties published to AD, see http://technet.microsoft.com/en-us/library/gg682121.aspx.

Enabling Client Push

After configuring your discovery methods or importing your computers using the Import Computer Information Wizard, you can specify how to push the ConfigMgr client to those devices after the client appears in the Devices node of the Assets and Compliance workspace.

Enable client push on a sitewide basis, or trigger it for specific collections or individual systems using manual push. There are several prerequisites to meet before you can successfully push a client to a remote computer:

▶ One of the specified client push installation accounts must be a member of the local Administrators group on the destination computer.

▶ The computer must have the ADMIN$ share enabled.

▶ The computer must be found by the site server and vice versa, using DNS name resolution.

▶ The computer must be discovered, or CCR files must have been created.

▶ The computer must be reachable by the site server.

▶ The computer must contact an MP so that it can download supporting files.

When using client push, the ConfigMgr site server connects to the client computer and verifies the client OS information, based on the information in a configuration request file (CCR) file, which contains the computer name and some additional information. The ConfigMgr site server then connects to the ADMIN$ share of the client computer and the registry via WMI to gather information about the client. It copies CCMSetup.exe and mobileclient.tcf from the *<ConfigMgrInstallPath>*\bin\i386 or x64 folder to the *%windir%/*ccmsetup folder on the client. From there it initiates a local installation of the ConfigMgr client on the computer.

Here is a sample MobileClient.tcf file, with all the options configured for the client to install successfully to the PR1 site:

```
[WINNT CLIENT FILES]
    bin\%cli_cpu%\MobileClient.tcf=MobileClient.tcf
    bin\%cli_cpu%\ccmsetup.exe=ccmsetup.exe

[SERVER PATHS]
    Server1=\\ATHENA.ODYSSEY.COM\SMSClient
    MP1=Athena.odyssey.com
    ServerRemoteName1=\\Athena.odyssey.com\SMSClient

[Site]
    Last TCF Update=11/28/2011 17:05:18
    SMSMPLIST=Athena.odyssey.com
    IISSSLState=480
    IISPreferedPort=80
    IISSSLPreferedPort=443
    IISPortsList=80
    IISSSLPortsList=443

SMSPublicRootKey=0602000000A40000525341310008000001000100 9B7CE6B953DE18D990E
F165CF7934E682AFA2545EB1657CD3F844DE352F1256703FAEDB52701637F0CB99008C0FF961
B9CB4B55769362DD174329CDDAEF620D7B58BB25D7345B992A700D4011AFB645D9EB4FDC5511
3FB1056EF83BED2B229717AA050C0C9477383FA2AAA76CEF64D3945E9478108E6FA56CC61C8C
4C2513E144A5180714957D245662DCB7A8851605E1D069BD249C8E656314DB8012E0A61F35E4
FA5808C15783C2CC8DF5F5F97C2E8793EEDCF09A951F93F5D963F29C7C071B4B15B74A32B501
2087137448F2664EE4CE85F229DE6EEBAA7390B6D5C46BD5458AB4447834AEDDD0DB945E916C
323174FADF0291E52F9C15A46591DFF67E1C1
    SelectFirstCertificate=1

[Client Install]
    Install=INSTALL=ALL SMSSITECODE=PR1

[IDENT]
    TYPE=Target Configuration File
```

When ConfigMgr determines that the CCMSetup.exe service is started successfully and the agent is running, it adds the CCR file to the *<ConfigMgrInstallPath>*\Inboxes\ccrretry. box folder for verification. This file is deleted after a second verification. Should something go wrong, the CCR file is renamed to the target name and placed in the same folder; ConfigMgr will try to reprocess the file every 60 minutes for 7 days, after which it is discarded.

TIP: CREATING THE CCR FILE ON YOUR OWN

You can also create the CCR file manually or by scripting. Create a text file containing these two lines:

```
[NT Client Configuration Request]
Machine Name=<NetBIOSName>
```

Save this file in the *<ConfigMgrInstallPath>*\Inboxes\Ccr.box\Inproc folder for it to be processed by ConfigMgr.

Enabling Automatic Sitewide Client Push

Enable automatic sidewide client push by configuring the Client Push Installation properties. Follow these steps:

1. In the Administration workspace of the console, navigate to **Overview -> Site Configuration -> Sites**.

2. In the navigation tree, select *<site code>* - *<site name>* in the Detail pane, then select **Client Installation Settings** from the ribbon bar, and finally select **Client Push Installation Properties** to open the page displayed in Figure 9.12.

3. Enable automatic sitewide client push installation by selecting the **Enable** check box on the General tab.

4. When enabled, you can specify the parameters to use for client push. A distinction is being made between server, workstations, and Configuration Manager site system servers. You can also specify whether automatic sitewide push installation should install the client software on domain controllers or prevent that installation unless explicitly specified in the Client Push Installation Wizard.

Here is information on the other tabs of the Client Push Installation Properties dialog displayed in Figure 9.12.

▶ **Accounts:** On this tab, you can specify one or more accounts ConfigMgr will use to initiate the installation; the account(s) specified should be local Administrator on the target computer. When installing the client software, ConfigMgr tries each account specified until it finds an account with local administrator privileges. Providing additional accounts allows you to specify credentials of one or more known local Administrator accounts.

You can select an account specified previously in ConfigMgr or provide a new account to use. When specifying a new account, you can key it in or browse for a user name and provide its password. Clicking the **Verify** button, as shown in Figure 9.13, lets you verify the account and password provided are correct.

Check whether you can provide the location of a network share; by clicking on **Test connection**, you can verify the provided account is valid by connecting to the network share with that account.

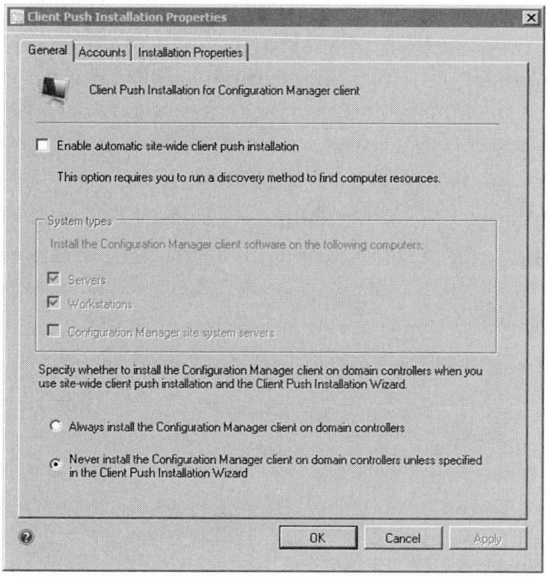

FIGURE 9.12   Client Push Installation Properties.

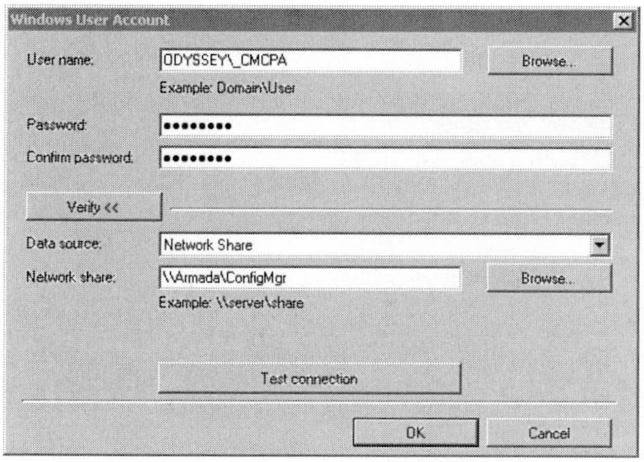

FIGURE 9.13   Specifying the Windows user account.

▶ **Installation Properties:** Here you can specify the installation properties used by the Client.msi Windows Installer file when installing the ConfigMgr client software. By default, SMSSITECODE=<*site code*> is already available.

CAUTION: CLIENT PUSH ONLY SUPPORTS DOMAIN JOINED CLIENTS

Client push is not supported for clients not joined to a domain. Workgroup clients cannot access the information published in AD by the client installation properties defined on the Client tab in the **Client Push Installation Properties** dialog box.

To prevent individual systems from receiving a ConfigMgr client when sitewide client push is enabled, add the computer name of these systems to a registry key on the primary site server. You may want to do this for temporary systems you eventually will not want to manage or for systems where you may not install any additional client software because of legal reasons. For additional information, see http://technet.microsoft.com/en-us/library/gg712273.aspx.

To push the ConfigMgr client manually to a collection or individual system, first specify a Client Push Installation account, or verify the computer account is the local administrator on those systems where you want to push the client. To push the ConfigMgr client on an individual system or collection, follow these steps:

1. In the ConfigMgr console, go to the Assets and Compliance workspace.

2. Navigate to **Devices**, and select a device in the Detail pane. Alternatively, navigate to **Device Collections** and select one of the collections.

3. Click on **Install Client** from the ribbon or right-click the context menu to start the Install Configuration Manager Client Wizard. This wizard provides three installation options, displayed in Figure 9.14, which you can select individually before continuing the installation:

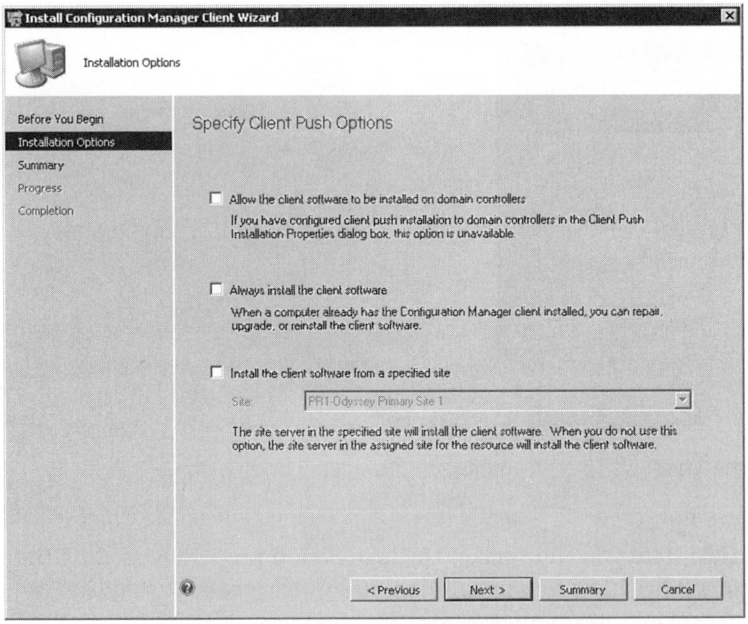

FIGURE 9.14   Install Configuration Manager Client Wizard.

▶ If you want to install the client software when the selected computer is a domain controller.

▶ Whether you always want to install the client software, even if the client software is already installed.

▶ You can specify if you want another site server than the site server in the assigned site for the resource to perform the installation. When enabled, you can choose a site server from a drop-down list.

4. Click **Next** on the Installation Options page to proceed to the Summary page showing your choices. After reviewing the Summary page, click **Next** to continue to install the ConfigMgr client onto the target system.

5. The Completion page displays when installation completes. Click **Close** to close the Install Configuration Manager Client Wizard.

Group Policy

The ConfigMgr client can be installed using the publish or assign functionality provided by Active Directory:

▶ When assigning the ConfigMgr client, the software is installed the first time the computer starts.

▶ When publishing the client, it appears in the Control Panel Programs and Features applet (Add or Remove programs on Windows XP) from where it can be installed.

Because group policy software installation supports only .msi files, you can specify only the CCMSetup.msi file, found in the *<ConfigMgrInstallPath>*\bin\i386 folder on the site server, without the ability to provide additional parameters. Here are several ways to provide the additional parameters:

▶ When the AD schema is extended and ConfigMgr publishes site information to AD, the client can query AD for the installation properties, which ConfigMgr pushes to AD based on the settings specified in the Client Push Installation Properties.

▶ If the AD schema is not extended, you can use Windows group policy to populate the ConfigMgr client properties in the registry using a group policy object (GPO); these properties are used later during ConfigMgr client installation. You can use the ConfigMgrInstallation.adm template located in the *<ConfigMgrInstallPath>*/Tools folder to make the necessary properties available in the GPO Management console.

CAUTION: BE CAREFUL WHEN USING ADM TEMPLATES

ADM templates are the old format of templates used to distribute group policy settings; the new format is ADMX. ADM files tattoo their settings in the registry, which means should you want to remove those settings, you have to delete them explicitly from the client's registry.

9

Software Update Point

If you have a WSUS infrastructure available within your organization, you can leverage it to install the ConfigMgr client on target computers. When you configure a software update point (SUP) site system in ConfigMgr, you can publish the ConfigMgr client software as an additional software update. For clients without the ConfigMgr client installed, you can point them to the SUP, which runs WSUS using a GPO.

Publish the ConfigMgr client to the SUP by configuring the Software Update-Based Client Installation properties. Follow these steps:

1. In the Administration workspace of the console, navigate to **Overview -> Site Configuration -> Sites**.

2. In the navigation tree, select *<site code>* - *<site name>* in the Detail pane, then select **Client Installation Settings** from the ribbon bar, and finally select **Software Update-Based Client Installation**, as shown in Figure 9.15, enabling ConfigMgr to publish the ConfigMgr client to the SUP.

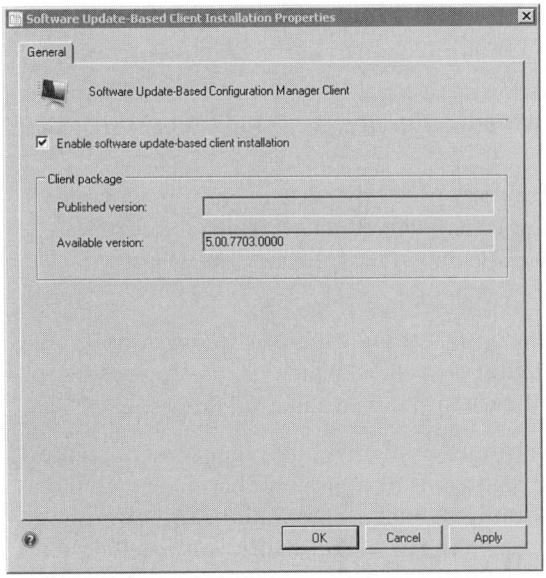

FIGURE 9.15   Software Update-Based Client Installation.

When using this method, you cannot provide any installation properties directly; you must either let the ConfigMgr environment push the settings to AD, or use a GPO to populate the necessary properties in the registry similar to ConfigMgr client deployment using group policy.

The SUP can be used to update ConfigMgr clients after they are installed; this takes place using the existing software updates functionality in ConfigMgr. More information is available in Chapter 14, "Software Update Management."

Client Approval

ConfigMgr can manage computers not using PKI certificates, but it must first approve these systems. By default, ConfigMgr automatically approves computers belonging to a trusted domain. You can specify that you want to configure each computer manually, or approve all computers automatically. This last option is not recommended because every computer with a ConfigMgr client can assign itself to one of your ConfigMgr sites.

To configure the Client Approval settings, perform the following steps:

1. In the Administration workspace of the console, navigate to **Overview -> Site Configuration -> Sites**.

2. On the ribbon, select **Hierarchy Settings** to open the Hierarchy Settings Properties page, displayed in Figure 9.16.

3. On the Client Approval and Conflicting Records tab of the Hierarchy Settings Properties page, specify which approval method to use for your site.

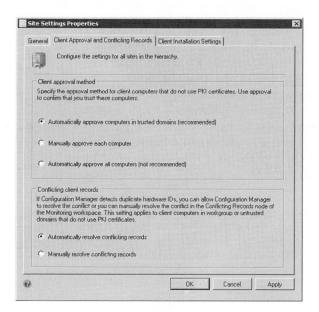

FIGURE 9.16   Client Approval and Conflicting Records.

Here's what you need to know about client approval:

▶ Clients communicating using HTTP and self-signed certificates must be approved before they can participate in the ConfigMgr hierarchy.

▶ AD clients from the local and trusted forests are approved automatically.

▶ Client approval is not necessary when you configure clients to always use HTTPS to communicate with your site or the clients use a PKI certificate to communicate to site systems, as they are already trusted by means of their installed certificate.

To approve a client, go to the Assets and Compliance workspace, and select the client either from the Devices node or by selecting it from a device collection. After selecting the device, click the **Approve** button on the ribbon to approve the client.

Blocking and Unblocking Clients

When you no longer want a client to participate in the ConfigMgr infrastructure, such as when the computer is stolen or missing, you can block the client. Select the client from the Devices node or in a device collection, and click the **Block** button on the ribbon. To unblock the client, click the **Unblock** button for the client to participate in the ConfigMgr hierarchy again.

Automatically Upgrading the Client

When a ConfigMgr 2007 client tries to be assigned to a ConfigMgr 2012 site, you can use the automatic client upgrade feature to upgrade it. Until the client is upgraded, features such as client settings, applications, and software updates are unavailable. Automatic client upgrade automatically creates a client upgrade package and program distributed to all available distribution points in the hierarchy, with a deployment targeted to all clients in the hierarchy, which can evaluate the deployment and apply it when applicable. Because you cannot restrict distribution of the upgrade package and the clients receiving the package, this method is not intended as the primary method to install or upgrade the client software. Chapter 7, "Migrating to System Center 2012 Configuration Manager," discusses approaches to client migration. Perform the following steps to configure the feature:

1. In the Administration workspace of the console, navigate to **Overview -> Site Configuration -> Sites**.

2. On the ribbon, select **Hierarchy Settings** to open the Hierarchy Settings Properties dialog shown in Figure 9.17.

3. On the Client Installation Settings tab, specify if you want to enable automatic upgrade of clients when new updates are available.

   ▶ Once enabled, configure whether to allow clients to use a fallback source location for content. You can also specify that you don't want the ConfigMgr client to run when the client is in a slow or unreliable network or when the client uses a fallback source location for its content.

   ▶ You can configure within how many days the clients should begin upgrading, which by default is set to 1 day, with a 31 days maximum. You should also specify the minimum version the client should have. If a client has a version below this specified version, it will be a candidate for an automatic upgrade.

You can also specify on this page if you want to distribute the ConfigMgr client installation package with its updates automatically to those distribution points enabled for prestaged content.

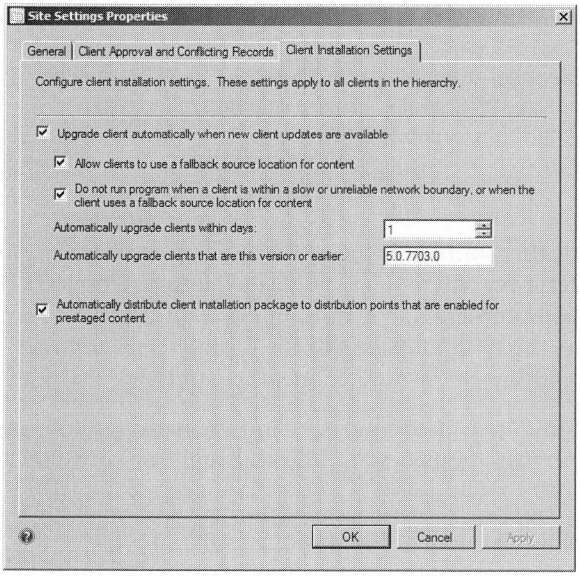

FIGURE 9.17   Client Installation Settings.

Troubleshooting Client Installation

Client installation can be problematic for many reasons; much depends on how you install the client, if the client is reachable, and if all prerequisite software is installable.

When using client push, ensure all prerequisites are met, that the site server can connect to the client machines, and that one of the configured Client Push Installation accounts can reach the machine on its ADMIN$ share. Test by performing a `net use` to a client machine using the credentials of the Client Push Installation account. Here are some possible reasons that can prevent the ConfigMgr infrastructure from connecting to the client:

- ▶ Incorrect firewall configuration.
- ▶ ADMIN$ share is unavailable.
- ▶ Client Push Installation account does not have required administrative rights.
- ▶ The Client Push Installation account is locked out or its password has expired.
- ▶ A pending reboot initiated by another software installation prevents installation of the ConfigMgr client software.
- ▶ A nonworking or corrupted DCOM or WMI configuration.

TIP: INFORMATION ON TROUBLESHOOTING CLIENT INSTALLATION AND WMI

Here are several blogs to assist with troubleshooting:

▶ Microsoft provides an in-depth article on troubleshooting client installation at http://blogs.technet.com/b/sudheesn/archive/2010/05/31/troubleshooting-sccm-part-i-client-push-installation.aspx. Although written for ConfigMgr 2007, the concepts are still valid.

▶ The System Center Configuration Manager team blog has an article on WMI trouble-shooting with some good tips for solving WMI issues. The article is available at http://blogs.technet.com/b/configmgrteam/archive/2009/05/08/wmi-troubleshooting-tips.aspx.

If the site server can connect to the client, the ConfigMgr infrastructure copies necessary files to the *%windir%*\ccmsetup folder from where the installation started. From this point forward, you can follow the installation progress in ccmsetup.log. This file provides detailed information about each step taken by the CCMSetup.exe executable, providing information about what went wrong should the client not install successfully.

Problems could be caused by incorrect configured site boundaries and boundary groups, or the ccmsetup bootstrapper being unable to find the necessary files to install the software prerequisites from a management point.

Configuration Manager provides reports to assist with failing client installations:

1. In the Monitoring workspace of the console, navigate to **Overview** -> **Reporting** -> **Reports** -> **Client Push**.

2. You see several reports available regarding client push installation.

    ▶ Client Push Installation Status Details

    ▶ Client Push Installation Status Details for a Specified Site

    ▶ Client Push Installation Status Summary

    ▶ Client Push Installation Status Summary for a Specified Site

3. Select one of the reports; clicking **Run** from the ribbon bar opens a page where you can provide criteria before running the report.

4. The reports provide guidance on where client push installation is failing and where to investigate to determine what is occurring. For example, if a prerequisite software installation is failing, you can start by examining what occurs when you manually install that software on a failing machine. By specifying verbose logging, you can check the log file to determine the root cause.

Problems may also occur with client push installation or client assignment after installing the client, leaving the ConfigMgr client in an unmanaged state.

TIP: MORE INFORMATION IN KB925282

Although written for ConfigMgr 2007, KB925282 (http://support.microsoft.com/kb/925282) has a good overview of the client push installation process and what can potentially go wrong.

Client Assignment

After the ConfigMgr client installs successfully, it must assign itself to a ConfigMgr site before it can be managed. ConfigMgr clients can be assigned only to primary sites, not secondary sites or the central administration site (CAS). If the client fails to assign itself to a site, it becomes unmanaged and stays unmanaged until it successfully assigns itself to a site. The client tries to assign itself to a site every 10 minutes. When assigned, it remains assigned to that site even if it roams to another site and will never automatically switch to a different site.

Here are the two ways for a client to assign itself to a ConfigMgr site:

▶ **Manually, based on provided parameters:** Manual client assignment can occur using the SMSSITECODE property during client installation or by providing the site code in the Configuration Manager Control Panel applet. Manual assignment is necessary when a client is already assigned, when it resides on the Internet, when DNS publishing is used to find the MP, or when the network location of the client does not fall within a boundary group configured for site assignment and no fallback site is configured.

▶ **Automatically, based on information the client can find in AD:** Automatic client assignment occurs by default when you install the client manually and SMSSITECODE=AUTO is provided during client installation. Automatic client assignment is also initiated by clicking **Discover** in the Configuration Manager Control Panel applet. When using automatic client discovery, the ConfigMgr client uses its AD site and own IP address to look up its site boundary configured in ConfigMgr and published to AD, or from a management point defined as a server locator point (SLP) if the necessary schema changes to AD for ConfigMgr have not occurred. If the client IP falls within a boundary group specified for site assignment on the ConfigMgr site, the client assigns itself to that site. If the client does not fall within a ConfigMgr site boundary group and a fallback site is specified in the hierarchy, the client is assigned to the fallback site. Chapter 6, "Installing System Center 2012 Configuration Manager," discusses configuring fallback site assignment.

After an intranet-based ConfigMgr client completes site assignment, it performs a site compatibility check to verify it is assigned to a ConfigMgr 2012 site and the client's OS and version are supported. Assignment will fail if the site is a ConfigMgr 2007 site or the OS and version are not supported. The site compatibility check checks if it can access a SLP when applicable and can access the site information in AD when published. If the client is configured for Internet-based client management, the site compatibility check does not occur.

The configmgrassignment.adm file is also available to configure client assignment. This ADM file is located in the *<ConfigMgrInstallPath>*/Tools folder on the site server and can be used to set these settings using GPO:

▶ Assigned Site by Specifying a Site Code

▶ Site Assignment Retry Interval in Minutes

▶ Site Assignment Retry Duration in Hours

After the client is successfully assigned to a ConfigMgr site, it uses the initial management point of its assigned site and composes a list of available MPs called the *MP list*, which it stores locally in WMI. The MP list contains the MPs specified during setup and the MPs matching the client's site code available in AD. After the client builds the MP list, it sorts the list putting HTTPS-capable MPs first in random order if configured with a PKI certificate, and HTTP-capable MPs in random order after which it determines the closest MP based on its AD forest membership. If the client is configured with a PKI certificate, it will try all the HTTPS-capable MPs first before trying an HTTP-capable MP. From that point, the ConfigMgr client tries to update the MP list every 25 hours, when CCMEXEC is restarted, or when it receives a new IP address resetting the order of MPs to use. If the client cannot contact an MP from the MP list, it uses an alternative method to search for an MP in the order listed here:

▶ **Active Directory:** The ConfigMgr site server publishes MP information to the Active Directory to which the client belongs.

▶ **DNS:** DNS information is published by the ConfigMgr site automatically if allowed or to DNS manually if automatic publishing is not allowed. For ConfigMgr clients to use DNS as a location mechanism for finding the MP, the DNS domain suffix must be provided during client installation using the DNSSUFFIX parameter.

▶ **WINS:** When the site server is configured to use WINS, it uses this information to publish the MP information

DNS and WINS are used when no MP was specified during client setup, and the AD schema has not been extended for ConfigMgr. The ConfigMgr client consults either DNS or WINS and adds the MPs published in DNS or WINS to its MP list.

Client Health

ConfigMgr 2007 Release 2 (R2) introduced an optional feature called Client Status Reporting (CSR). CSR provides current information on the status of client computers in a ConfigMgr hierarchy. The health of the client is essential because ConfigMgr can only manage healthy clients. There were some community-written scripts for ConfigMgr 2007 that admins could integrate in the startup or logon scripts of their clients; these performed checks and performed remediation actions when the ConfigMgr client was not healthy.

ConfigMgr 2012 includes this functionality out-of-the-box using a new feature called Client Health.

Each ConfigMgr client (except mobile clients) runs the Configuration Manager Health Evaluation scheduled task between 12:00 a.m. and 1:00 a.m. daily, by default. If the client is powered off or in sleep mode at that time, the task runs when the computer is booted or comes out of sleep mode. This scheduled task calls the Ccmeval.exe executable, evaluates the client health status, and sends the result to the site server using state messages. If it cannot deliver the message, it uses a fallback status point if one is deployed. Ccmeval.exe loads a configuration file named ccmeval.xml, found in the *%windir%*\CCM folder, which contains the Client Health evaluation rules. You can open Ccmeval.xml to see the checks and actions that occur, but Microsoft does not support modifying this file to include your own custom checks.

Here are the health checks that are performed:

- ▶ Verify WMI service exists.
- ▶ Verify/Remediate WMI service startup type.
- ▶ Verify/Remediate WMI service status.
- ▶ WMI Repository integrity test.
- ▶ WMI Repository Read/Write test.
- ▶ Verify BITS exists.
- ▶ Verify/Remediate BITS startup type.
- ▶ Verify/Remediate client and client prerequisites installation.
- ▶ Verify SMS Agent Host service exists.
- ▶ Verify/Remediate SMS Agent Host service startup type.
- ▶ Verify/Remediate SMS Agent Host service status.
- ▶ WMI Event sink test.
- ▶ Verify/Remediate Microsoft Policy Platform service startup type.
- ▶ Verity/Remediate Antimalware service startup type.
- ▶ Verify/Remediate Antimalware service status.
- ▶ Verify/Remediate Network Inspection service startup type.
- ▶ Verify/Remediate Windows Update service startup type.
- ▶ Verify/Remediate Windows Update service status.
- ▶ Verify/Remediate Configuration Manager Remote Control service startup type.
- ▶ Verify/Remediate Configuration Manager Remote Control service status.
- ▶ Verify/Remediate SQL CE database is healthy.

In addition to reporting about client health, the client health evaluation provides remediation by checking important WMI namespaces, classes, and instances, and reinstalls the ConfigMgr client when missing. It also tests whether it can read and write to WMI; if it cannot it rebuilds the repository and reinstalls the ConfigMgr client.

The client health mechanism can be configured to only perform checks versus attempting to remediate. To configure health-only scanning, open the registry and navigate to HKLM/ Software/Microsoft/CCM/CCMEval to change the NotifyOnly registry value from FALSE to TRUE.

Results are displayed in the Monitoring workspace of the ConfigMgr console under the Client Status node. From this node, you can configure the Client Status Settings (Figure 9.18), which specify the evaluation periods and retention of the client status history, and schedule Client Status Update.

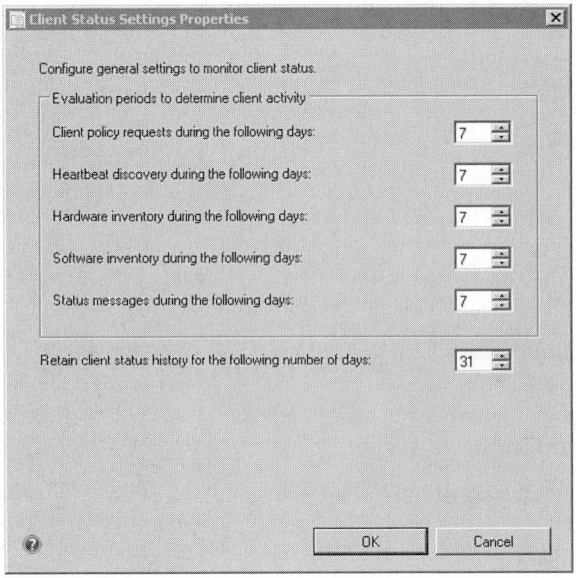

FIGURE 9.18   Client Status Settings Properties.

For example, when the software inventory evaluation period is set to 7 days, and the site server has not received software inventory data from a ConfigMgr client for more than 7 days, it will consider that client inactive for software inventory. The client is considered inactive when it is inactive for all the listed activities.

Each primary site runs a stored procedure called CH_UpdateAll that summarizes the client health and client activity information; this runs every day by default but is configurable. Follow these steps to configure the schedule:

1. In the Monitoring workspace of the console, navigate to Client Status.

2. Select **Schedule Client Status Update** from the ribbon bar to open its properties, as shown in Figure 9.19.

3. Here you can configure the recurrence schedule that by default is set to every 1 days but can be set to a value between 1 hours and 31 days.

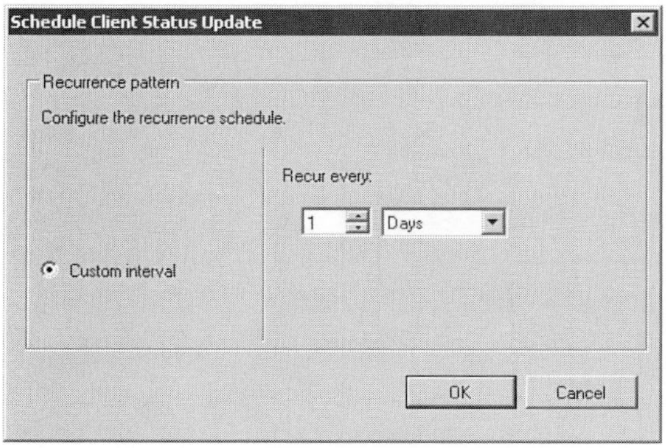

FIGURE 9.19   Schedule Client Status Update.

Be careful when modifying this setting to a more frequent value as it can decrease server performance if run too frequently. You can also update the Client Status by pressing the **Refresh Client Status** button in the ribbon bar which triggers the stored procedure and refreshes the charts with the latest information.

The Results pane of the Client Status node provides an overview with statistics and recent alerts. Clicking the corresponding regions in the chart creates a temporary collection containing the computer objects belonging to that selection. The Statistics node consists of one chart detailing Overall Client Status; this gives an overview of the status of clients, which can be one of the following statuses, as is shown in Figure 9.20:

▶ Active clients that passes client check or no results

▶ Active clients that failed client check

▶ Inactive clients that failed client check

▶ Inactive clients that failed client check or no results

▶ No Configuration Manager client installed; these are computer objects found by a discovery method or manual import that do not have the client installed.

The Statistics node also provides two pie charts: one for Client Activity, and one for Client Check. The Client Activity pie chart displays how many clients are active or inactive; by default it uses the All Desktop and Server Clients collection to determine this and a client activity period of 5 days. You can modify the amount of days by using the selection list next to Client activity period or Client check period, which contains selections between the last 5 days and last 90 days.

The Client Check pie chart, displayed in Figure 9.21, shows the client health status, based on the outcome of the Client Health scheduled task running on the client.

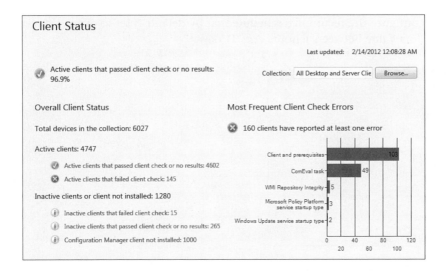

FIGURE 9.20   Client Status chart.

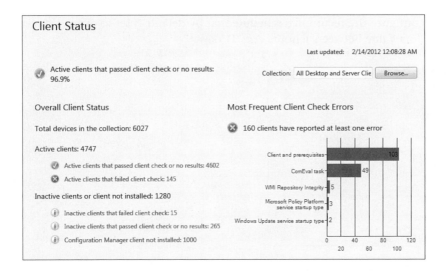

FIGURE 9.21   Client Check pie chart.

Here are the statuses the Client Check pie chart can have:

▶ Client check passed

▶ Client check failed

▶ No result

▶ No client installed

Client Settings

Client settings are centrally defined settings, accessible through the Administration workspace, that apply to all deployed ConfigMgr clients. These settings allow a ConfigMgr administrator to control the behavior and functionality of the client. In ConfigMgr 2007 and earlier versions of the product, client settings were specific to a single site; organizations often created multiple sites due to different client setting requirements. System Center 2012 Configuration Manager lets you specify client settings at a collection level, allowing you to define different settings as necessary.

While this is a major improvement, it could lead to conflicts when a client belongs to multiple collections that have client settings. To help manage these settings, ConfigMgr lets you specify priorities; those with a higher priority win over settings with a lower priority. Design these priorities carefully to maintain consistent client behavior, just as you would when designing group policy in Active Directory.

Another change in this version assists with Virtual Desktop Infrastructure (VDI) scenarios. Each ConfigMgr client now randomizes the scheduled times for hardware inventory, software inventory, software update scans, software update deployment evaluations, compliance settings evaluation, application deployment evaluations, and endpoint protection scans on virtual machines sharing the same host.

Each default ConfigMgr installation comes with default settings configured out-of-the-box. Default client settings, configured at the hierarchy level, are applicable to every user and device without custom settings. You can apply other settings (custom settings) to override the defaults. The default client settings have a priority of 10,000, meaning you could theoretically define 9,999 custom client device and user settings. Custom device settings, shown in Figure 9.22, contain settings related to devices and can be deployed to device collections, whereas custom user settings, displayed in Figure 9.23, contain settings related to users and can be deployed to user collections. Be careful when creating custom client settings: Keep them to the required minimum and give your custom client settings meaningful names so you know what each does.

Configure default settings by selecting the Administration workspace and choosing the **Client Settings** node. You can then open **Default Settings** by double-clicking it or choosing **Properties** from the right-click context menu or ribbon bar.

Some settings allow you to specify a simple or custom schedule. Here is information about each:

▶ A *simple schedule* allows you to specify the action should run regularly each number of days, hours, minutes, and so on. The client determines when to run this action based on its installation date and some coded randomization, which distributes the load on the ConfigMgr infrastructure. This option is preferred when the clients are VDI clients, as it minimizes the load on the host hosting the virtual machines because not all VMs run the same client action at exactly the same time.

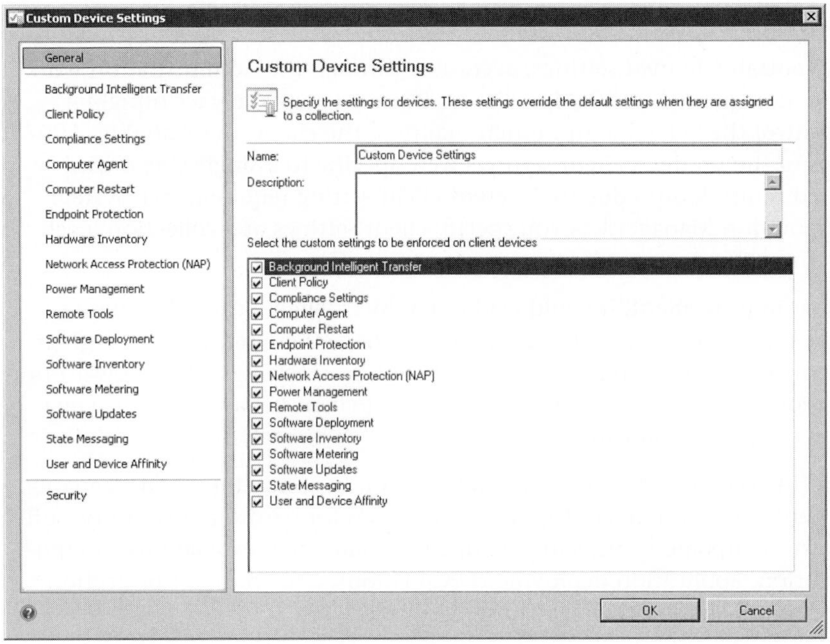

FIGURE 9.22   Custom Device Settings.

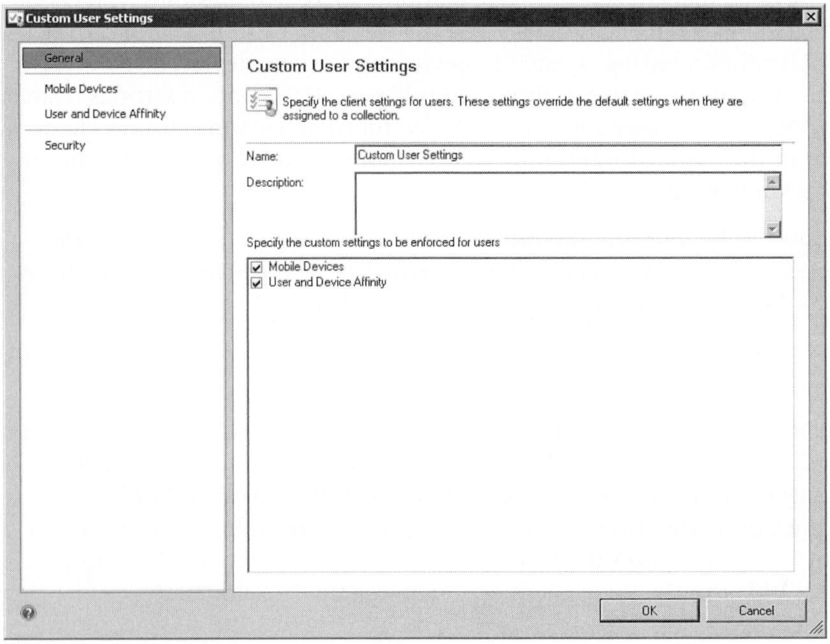

FIGURE 9.23   Custom User Settings

▶ With a *custom schedule*, you can specify the exact time to launch the action. This means each client receiving the schedule initiates that action at exactly the same time, which could create a high load on your ConfigMgr infrastructure. Consider a custom schedule when you have other processes running at specified intervals that require current information.

> **NOTE: MOBILE DEVICE SETTINGS**
>
> Chapter 15 discusses the user settings for mobile devices.

Defining Priority

Defining a priority lets you specify which settings apply when a client receives multiple custom user or client device settings. Settings with a lower priority number take precedence over settings with a higher priority number. Because the default client settings have the highest priority count (10,000), any defined custom client device or custom user settings will always take precedence over the custom default client settings.

You can use custom client settings to provide specific settings that are applied to members of one or more specific collections. For example, you can define another hardware inventory schedule for specific servers that you manage with ConfigMgr. The first custom client setting defined receives priority 1, the second priority 2, and so on. When created, you can adjust the priority of the custom client setting by increasing or decreasing its Priority, as shown in Figure 9.24, using the right-click context menu or the buttons on the ribbon.

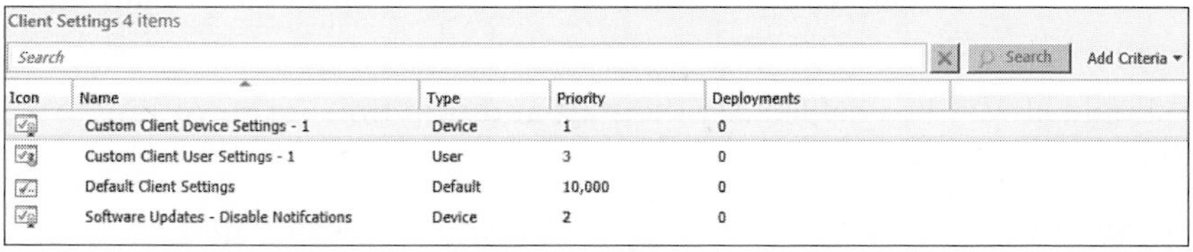

Client Settings 4 items				
Search				✕ 🔍 Search Add Criteria ▾
Icon	Name	Type	Priority	Deployments
☑	Custom Client Device Settings - 1	Device	1	0
☑	Custom Client User Settings - 1	User	3	0
☑	Default Client Settings	Default	10,000	0
☑	Software Updates - Disable Notifcations	Device	2	0

FIGURE 9.24   Client Settings.

You can deploy custom settings to one or more collections. Select the setting and choose **Deploy** from the ribbon bar, after which you can specify the collection to which the settings should be applied. Note that you can deploy only custom client device settings to device collections, and custom client user settings to user collections. The next sections describe the client settings.

Background Intelligent Transfer Device Settings

The Background Intelligent Transfer Service (BITS) device settings allow you to configure the behavior of BITS. BITS, introduced in Chapter 5, provides bandwidth throttling to control the transfer of packets on the network between ConfigMgr clients and their management points. DP traffic goes through an MP when using BITS. If you enable BITS, there are several options to control its behavior. These include providing start and stop times for a throttling window, allowing BITS downloads outside a defined throttling window, and maximum transfer rate during and outside the throttling window. Figure 9.25 shows the default options for BITS settings.

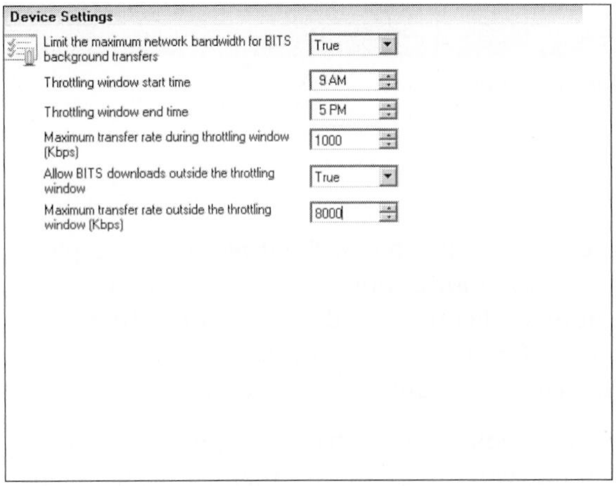

FIGURE 9.25   Background Intelligent Transfer Device Settings

After enabling BITS using the **Limit the maximum network bandwidth for BITS background transfers** setting, you can modify its settings.

▶ Specify the timeframe to enable BITS bandwidth throttling by specifying a start and stop time.

▶ If throttling should always be enabled, set the start and stop time for throttling to the same value.

▶ Specify the maximum transfer rate during the throttling window in Kbps.

▶ Define whether to use bandwidth throttling outside of the specified throttling window by specifying a maximum transfer rate in Kbps.

CAUTION: DO NOT SET CONFLICTING BITS GROUP POLICY OBJECTS

If you also configure BITS settings using group policy, GPO settings could overwrite the settings coming from ConfigMgr and vice versa, leading to unpredictable results when those settings differ.

Client Policy Device Settings

Client policy device settings are related to how the client deals with its received policy, which comes from its management point. Figure 9.26 displays the default settings.

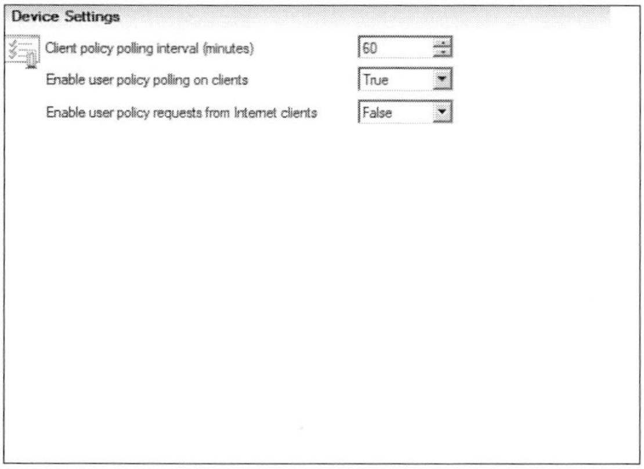

FIGURE 9.26   Client Policy Device Settings.

By default, a client requests policy from its management point every 60 minutes, which should be sufficient in most cases. You can modify the policy refresh interval to between 3 minutes and 24 hours (1440 minutes). When the **Enable user policy polling on clients** setting is set to False, users will not receive required applications or any other operations contained in user policies. Users will not receive revisions and updates for applications published in the application catalog, nor will they see notifications about their application approval requests.

User policy requests from Internet clients can work only when the **Enable user policy polling on clients** setting is set to True and the Internet-based management point can successfully authenticate the user using Windows Authentication.

Compliance Settings Device Settings

Using compliance settings device settings, you can enable or disable the functionality it provides, discussed in Chapter 10, "Managing Compliance." The ability to report and alert on compliance helps monitor and manage configuration drift. You can apply compliance settings to desktops, servers, mobile devices, and users, and can remediate Windows Management Instrumentation (WMI), registry, and script settings not compliant natively in ConfigMgr 2012. (In ConfigMgr 2007, you could configure remediation of noncompliant settings only.) Automated remediation can drastically reduce the time a noncompliant configuration stays out of compliance. Figure 9.27 shows the available compliance settings.

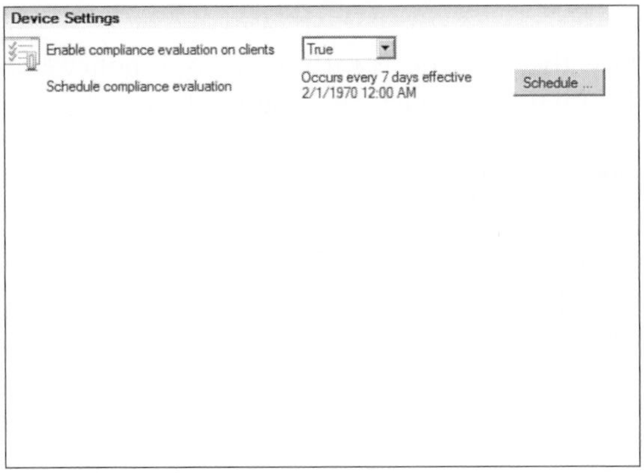

FIGURE 9.27   Compliance Settings Device Settings.

Computer Agent Device Settings

Computer agent device settings, displayed in Figure 9.28, enable you to define settings related to software distribution on the ConfigMgr client. These include specifying the notification interval for deployments, the default Application Catalog website point, and more. Here is information on these settings:

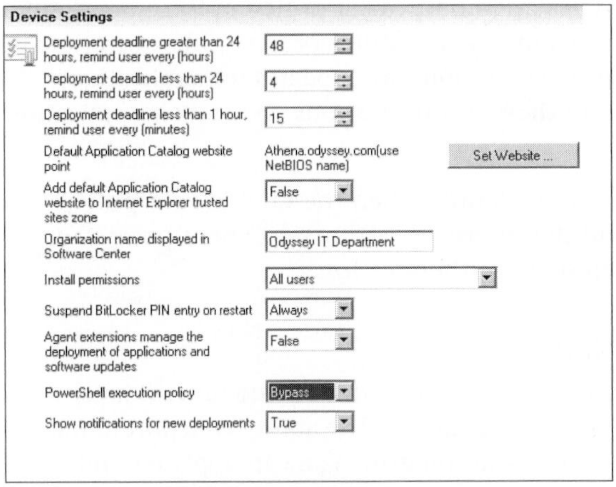

FIGURE 9.28   Computer Agent Device Settings

► **Deployment deadline:** You can specify the notification intervals before a deployment deadline is reached.

► By default, users are notified 48 hours in advance when the deployment deadline is greater than 24 hours; you can modify this value from 1 to 999 hours.

► If the deployment deadline is less than 24 hours but more than 1 hour, users are reminded every 4 hours; this can be modified from 1 to 24 hours.

▶ If the deployment deadline is less than 1 hour, users are notified every 15 minutes, this can be modified to a value between 5 and 25 minutes.

▶ **Application Catalog:** Here are settings related to the default Application Catalog:

 ▶ Specifying the server that hosts the Application Catalog website.

 The authors recommend using the NetBIOS name to prevent clients from receiving a credentials prompt when connecting to the website. You must specify the NetBIOS name on the website point properties and have a name resolution mechanism in place supporting short names; this could be WINS, specifying the necessary DNS domain suffix search list on the client, or using the DNS GlobalNames Zone (GNZ) feature.

 ▶ Using automatic detection, allowing clients to receive the closest Application Catalog.

 Automatic detection uses a service location request to a MP; this request occurs every 25 hours. The MP returns an Application Catalog website depending on the client's location. Automatic detection is preferred, as clients are pointed automatically to the Application Catalog website from their own site. You can specify different application catalogs for clients residing on the intranet and those on the Internet; Application Catalog website points configured for HTTPS take precedence over HTTP. You may decide not to use automatic detection when you want to specify manually which clients connect to what server, or not want to wait for 25 hours when the Application Catalog website point changes.

 ▶ Specifying the URL to a customized Application Catalog, allowing you to specify a URL to a custom website hosting Application Catalog functionality.

 ▶ When the Application Catalog website is not added to the trusted sites zone in Internet Explorer on the client, Internet Explorer Protected Mode may not allow you to install applications from the Application Catalog. In this case, add the Application Catalog website to the trusted sites zone in IE using a GPO. When using the **Add default Application Catalog website to Internet Explorer trusted sites zone** setting, ConfigMgr ensures only the current Application Catalog is added to the trusted sites zone. If you use other mechanisms to populate the trusted sites zones or other security zones for Internet Explorer, verify these do not conflict with the ConfigMgr settings.

CAUTION: USING THE APPLICATION CATALOG IN COMBINATION WITH ACTIVE X FILTERING IN IE9

When you use ActiveX filtering in Internet Explorer, you must exclude the Application Catalog ActiveX control from filtering using a GPO or a custom script modifying the registry; the filename to exclude is Microsoft.ConfigurationManager.SoftwareCatalog.Website. ClientBridgeControl.dll. For more information on ActiveX filtering, see http://ie.microsoft. com/testdrive/Browser/ActiveXFiltering/About.html.

6

▶ **Configure Install permissions:** Specify which users can initiate software installation, software updates, and task sequences, set to All users by default. When set to **No users**, required deployments for the computer are always installed at the deadline and users cannot initiate software installation from the Software Center or Application Catalog. Other options available are to enable this feature for Administrators and Primary users only, or for Administrators only.

▶ **Bitlocker PIN:** Enable the suspension of the Bitlocker PIN during restart if Bitlocker with PIN is enabled on the client by setting the **Suspend BitLocker PIN entry on restart** to Always.

▶ **Agent extensions manage the deployment of applications and software updates:** When using a third-party solution or the Software Development Kit (SDK) that hooks into ConfigMgr application, you must set **Agent extensions manage the deployment of applications and software updates** to True.

▶ **PowerShell:** If your clients run PowerShell 2.0 or higher, you can specify the PowerShell execution policy that identifies the execution policy to use during ConfigMgr actions. By default the setting is Restricted, which means the current PowerShell restriction settings on the client are used. If you set the setting to Bypass, ConfigMgr can use unsigned scripts during ConfigMgr actions.

▶ **Notifications:** Enable or disable notifications for new deployments by setting the **Show notifications for new deployment** setting to False.

Software distribution is covered in depth in Chapter 13, "Distributing and Deploying Applications."

Computer Restart Device Settings

Computer restart device settings allow you to specify the countdown interval for ConfigMgr-initiated restarts, as shown in Figure 9.29.

▶ Display countdown interval before log off and restart is 90 minutes by default and can be set to a value between 1 minute and 24 hours (1440 minutes)

▶ Display countdown interval before final log off and restart in minutes is 15 minutes by default and can be set to any value between 1 minute and 24 hours

Ensure the intervals specified are shorter in duration than the shortest maintenance window applied to your client, so the computer restarts during the window.

Endpoint Protection Device Settings

Endpoint protection device settings become available after configuring endpoint protection in ConfigMgr. Additional information on configuring this feature and setting the corresponding device settings is in Chapter 16, "Endpoint Protection."

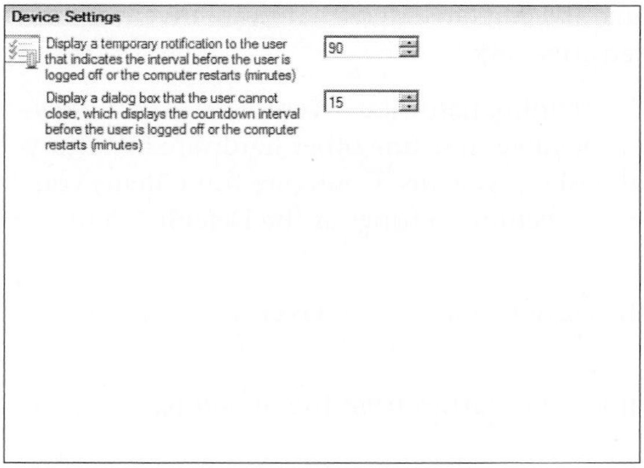

FIGURE 9.29   Computer Restart Device Settings.

Hardware Inventory Device Settings

Hardware inventory device settings allow you to enable or disable hardware inventory and define its settings, as displayed in Figure 9.30.

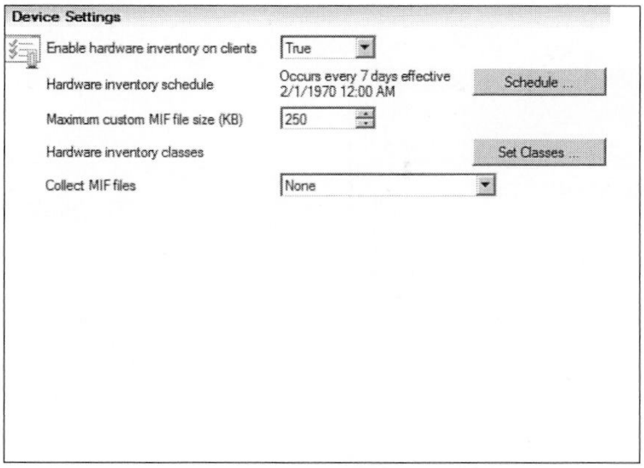

FIGURE 9.30   Hardware Inventory Settings.

When hardware inventory is enabled (default), you can specify its schedule. This is every 7 days by default, but you can specify a custom schedule. You can also specify how to collect specify management information files (MIFs), identify a maximum MIF file size, and define hardware inventory classes.

In ConfigMgr 2007, extending hardware inventory required modifying two managed object format (MOF) files. Those files, stored on the primary site server, were Configuration.mof, which defined the data classes, and SMS_Def.mof, which defined the reporting classes. Performing intricate manual edits to extend hardware inventory in ConfigMgr 2007 was a complex and fault sensitive task.

ConfigMgr 2012 simplifies configuring and extending hardware inventory. You can now set client settings more granularly, making it possible to define other hardware inventory settings for laptops, compared to traditional desktop systems. Configure those items you want to inventory by modifying the hardware inventory settings at the Default Client Settings level. Perform the following steps:

1. In the Administration workspace of the console, navigate to **Overview** -> **Client Settings**.

2. Select **Default Client Settings**, and choose **Properties** from the ribbon bar to open its properties.

3. Select the Hardware Inventory settings page and the **Set Classes** button to open a new window where you can set those inventory classes, displayed in Figure 9.31, which you will either enable or disable. Some of the classes are enabled with a black checkmark, meaning that the class and all its properties are inventoried.

   ▶ If the class has a gray check mark, the class and some of its properties are inventoried.

   ▶ When the class is not checked, it is not inventoried.

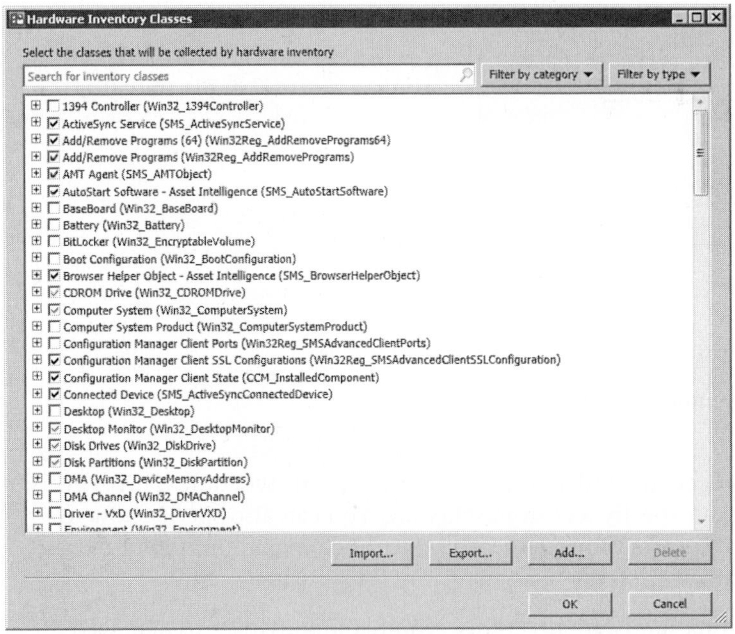

FIGURE 9.31   Hardware inventory classes

You can modify this list by defining custom client devices settings, allowing you to specify different selections for specific collections.

There are several ways to extend inventoried items:

▶ Import a MOF file using the import functionality, which allows you to browse for MOF files.

▶ Export the settings to a MOF file, which can be used to import into another ConfigMgr environment.

MIF files can be used to extend hardware inventory information. Alternatively, they could be used to transport information not available in the system. For example, you could write a tool that collects some information from an end user, writing its output in MIF format ready to be picked up by ConfigMgr inventory. The information stored in MIF files is sent to and stored in the site database, becoming available with the default client inventory data. There are two types of MIF files, NODIMIF and IDMIF.

CAUTION: BE CAREFUL WHEN USING MIF FILES

Data collected from NOIDMIF and IDMIF files is not validated, meaning that data could be used to overwrite valid data stored in the database, potentially breaking the functionality of the ConfigMgr site. The fact that this functionality is still available in ConfigMgr is mainly based on supporting customers that leverage this functionality. The authors recommend not using MIF files unless there is no other option that meets your requirements.

▶ **NOIDMIF:** These files are automatically associated with the client on which the NOIDMIF file is inventoried. For ConfigMgr to process the NOIDMIF file, place it in the %*windir*%\CCM\Inventory\noidmifs (default) folder.

▶ **IDMIF:** IDMIF files are not associated with the computer they are collected from, allowing you to collect inventory about non-ConfigMgr client devices. IDMIF files are collected only if they meet the maximum custom MIF file size specified value, which is less than 250KB by default. IDMIF files should be stored in %*windir*%\CCM\Inventory\idmifs folder to be picked up by ConfigMgr hardware inventory.

You can modify the MIF storage locations in the registry by modifying the registry keys specifying the locations of both files. The registry key is located under HKLM\Software\Microsoft\SMS\Client\Configuration\Client Properties and can be specified by modifying the NOIDMIF Directory and IDMIF Directory values.

The ConfigMgr client can scan the hardware currently installed on the client and report that information back to the ConfigMgr infrastructure. From the ConfigMgr console, a ConfigMgr user can start the Resource Explorer to view the inventoried hardware for a client. Inventory also takes hardware changes (*deltas*) into account, giving administrators the ability to determine if hardware changed between inventories. The hardware inventoried is defined centrally in the ConfigMgr settings, which can be adjusted to include additional hardware or omit certain hardware. When the client is not connected to the network during inventory, the inventory takes place, and data is uploaded when connectivity is resumed. If the client is offline during the scheduled time for inventory, inventory will take place when the client is online again.

Hardware inventory also inventories the software available through the Programs and Features Control Panel applet (Add and Remove Programs for older systems such as Windows XP). This typically suffices to determine the software installed on a client. However, not all software is advertised in the Programs and Features applet; you will use software inventory to obtain a full inventory of your software.

When standard hardware inventory does not provide all the necessary information, this could be because the hardware inventoried is not configured in the applied client settings, or that new hardware is available but unknown to ConfigMgr. However, you can modify your ConfigMgr configuration to enable inventory of extra or additional hardware, as discussed in Appendix B, "Extending Hardware Inventory."

Network Access Protection (NAP) Device Settings

ConfigMgr clients supporting NAP can use ConfigMgr for remediation when noncompliant, as determined by a system health validator (SHV) point. ConfigMgr clients should have the Network Access Protection Agent service started, and the backend infrastructure supporting NAP should be in place. Figure 9.32 shows the NAP settings.

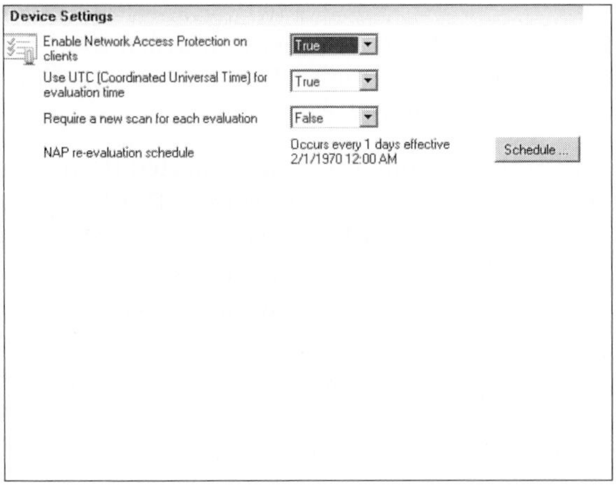

FIGURE 9.32   Network Access Protection Device Settings.

When the **Enable Network Access Protection on clients** setting is set to True, NAP evaluation is enabled on clients supporting a NAP infrastructure. You can specify using Coordinated Universal Time (UTC) as the specified NAP evaluation schedule, which is 12:00 a.m. daily by default and can be modified using a simple or custom schedule.

When **Require a new scan for each evaluation** is set to True, a client waits until scanning is completed to send its results for evaluation. This is the most secure setting but requires additional time before the client is permitted on the LAN. When False (default), the client is sent the result of the latest evaluation, reducing time for the evaluation process.

Power Management Device Settings

The power management settings specify whether power management by ConfigMgr is enabled or disabled, and if users can exclude their device from the defined ConfigMgr settings. Power Management settings are shown in Figure 9.33. Chapter 2, "Configuration Manager Overview," discusses power management.

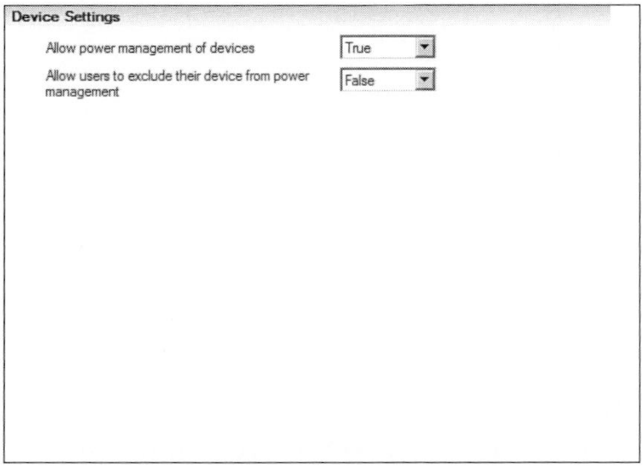

FIGURE 9.33   Power Management Device Settings.

Remote Control Device Settings

The Remote Control settings specify whether remote control on clients is enabled. You can specify if users can change the remote control policy and notification settings in the Software Center client applet, if remote control of an unattended computer is permitted, whether to prompt a user for remote control permission, and if users that are local Administrators on the client may use remote control. You can also configure an allowed Access level of Full Control, View Only, and No Access. You can specify permitted viewers by listing an AD group or user. Figure 9.34 shows the Remote Tools device settings.

You can use Remote Tools for remote management of client desktops for troubleshooting purposes, which is a common scenario in help desk environments. Using this functionality with ConfigMgr executes the utility from a central point, providing logging capabilities and report functionality. Remote Tools leverages the remote desktop protocol (RDP) functionality provided by the Windows OS. You can use Remote Tools in several ways, either completely taking over the desktop using Remote Desktop or assisting the end user using the Remote Assistance functionality, where both the end user and help desk look at the same desktop.

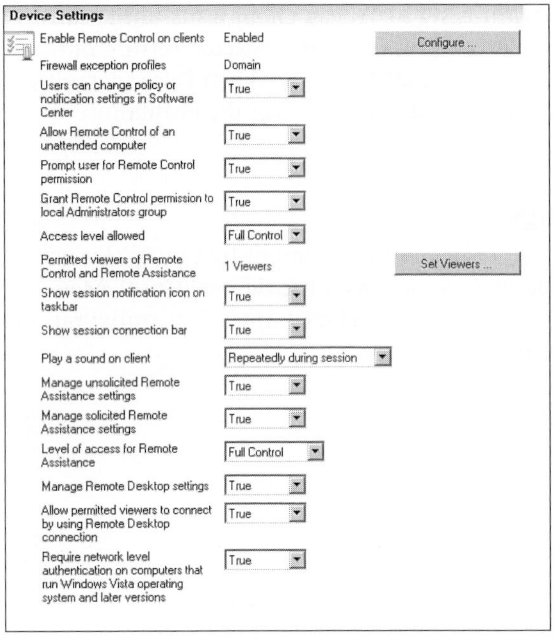

FIGURE 9.34   Remote Tools Device Settings.

Configuring Remote Control and Remote Assistance

Remote control behavior depends on the effective default or client device settings on the ConfigMgr client. The Remote Tools client settings allow you to enable Remote Control on clients. You can modify the Remote Tools client settings by navigating to **Administration -> Overview -> Client Settings** and selecting **Default Client Settings**, modifying custom device settings, or creating custom device settings from scratch. Open the Remote Tools section. Click **Configure**, which opens up the Remote Control and Windows Firewall Client Settings dialog box, and enable the check box for **Enable Remote Control on client computers**. When enabled, there are other settings you can configure:

▶ Specify whether ConfigMgr should configure the Windows firewall of the destination computer automatically with the correct rules to allow it to be remotely controlled. You can enable these rules for the Domain, Private, or Public Firewall profile, or a combination of these.

▶ If users can modify the policy or notification settings in the Software Center. When enabled, users can specify if they want to use the remote access settings specified by the ConfigMgr administrator, or if they prefer to override these settings with their own values. Figure 9.35 shows the settings a user can modify when this option is enabled.

▶ In the client settings, specify whether to enable remote control of an unattended computer.

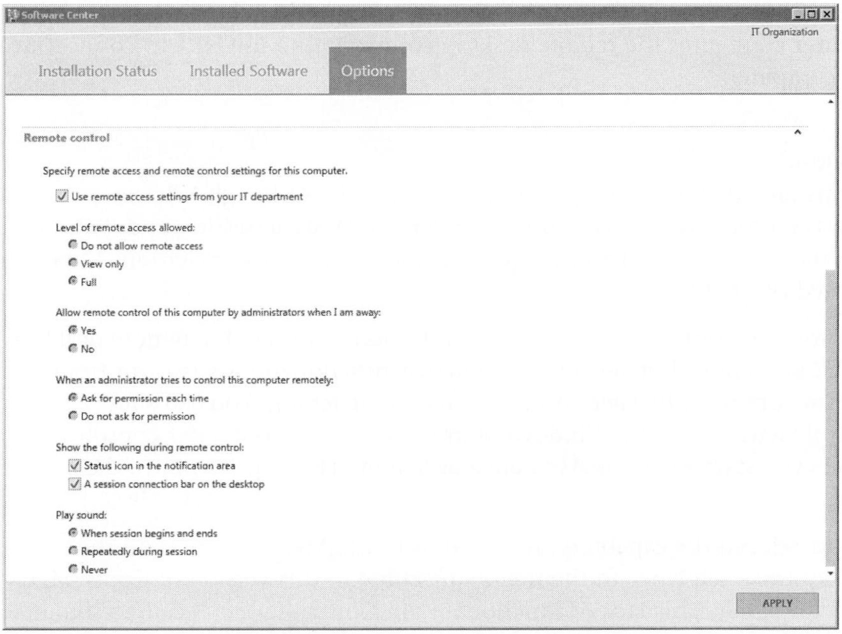

FIGURE 9.35   Remote Control Settings in the Software Center.

▶ Specify whether the user is prompted for remote control permission, so that if logged on, he is presented with a dialog box requesting permission to allow remote control.

▶ Specify who can initiate remote control by configuring the permissions, by allowing members of the local Administrators group or AD users and groups.

▶ Specify the types of notifications a user receives when Remote Control is active; enable a notification icon in the taskbar to be active during a remote session, or a connection bar. You can also configure a sound to be played on the client, at either the beginning or end of the session, or repeatedly during the session.

▶ The Remote Tools client settings also allow you to manage solicited and unsolicited Remote Assistance settings. When set to True, ConfigMgr manages remote assistance settings where the user at the client computer either requests (solicits) or doesn't request assistance.

▶ When the **Manage Remote Desktop settings** value is set to True, ConfigMgr manages the Remote Desktop settings of the client receiving the client settings.

▶ Setting **Allow permitted viewers to connect by using Remote Desktop connection** allows users specified in the Permitted viewers list to set up a remote connection.

▶ **Require network level authentication (NLA) on computers which run Windows Vista and later** configures the remote desktop connection to use NLA to connect to the remote computer.

Using Remote Control

Many organizations provide remote support to their end users. Although Windows includes several ways to provide this support using Remote Desktop session and Remote Assistance functionality, many companies require remote control of workstations to be managed and logged centrally.

Remote Control provides ConfigMgr administrators the ability to watch a remote desktop session locally, and take control of keyboard and mouse functionality to assist in troubleshooting or perform administrative actions on the remote machine. You can start the Remote Control viewer from the Windows Start menu or the ConfigMgr console. ConfigMgr also lets you start a Remote Assistance or Remote Desktop session to the remote computer.

Microsoft has re-introduced the capability, removed in ConfigMgr 2007, to send the CTRL+ALT+DEL keystroke sequence to the remote machine in this version of ConfigMgr; Figure 9.36 shows the result. This lack of functionality in ConfigMgr 2007 caused some angst, as it removed the ability to remote control logged or locked workstations and servers, or to lock a remote workstation or server using this keystroke sequence. Because you can now apply more granular client settings, you can also specify different remote control settings for workstations or servers, which was a sitewide setting in ConfigMgr 2007.

If the connection to the machine that is remotely controlled is disconnected, the remote computer is locked. Remote Control now also supports multiple monitors.

The notification bar is quite visible on the remotely controlled computer, displaying the account name of the user remotely controlling the computer. Remote control now uses only TCP port 2701; ports 2702 and 135 are no longer used. Should Kerberos authentication fail when you want to control a computer remotely, the system prompts if you want to use the less secure NTLM authentication mechanism.

Remotely Administering a Client Computer

You can remotely administer a client computer from the Assets and Compliance workspace by selecting the client computer from the Devices node or one of the Device collections. When selected, select **Start** and click **Remote Control** to start the Remote Control viewer window to let you administer the client computer remotely. The permissions you set using the Remote Tools client settings determine whether you can view or take over control of the keyboard and mouse of the remote machine.

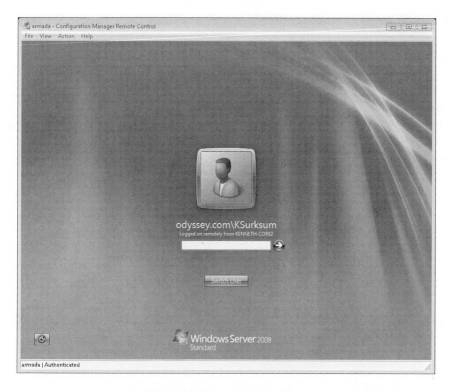

FIGURE 9.36   Configuration Manager Remote Control.

You can also start the Remote Control viewer from the command line. The executable is CmRcViewer.exe, located in the *<ConfigMgrInstallPath>*\AdminConsole\Bin\x64 folder. Supply two values when connecting to a client computer with this utility:

▶ The NetBIOS or FQDN of the client that you want to administer remotely

▶ The site server you want to use to sent state messages to

Here's an example of the syntax:

```
CmRcViewer.exe albert.odyssey.com \\ambassador.odyssey.com
```

Providing Remote Assistance

You can provide remote assistance to a client computer from the Assets and Compliance workspace by selecting the client computer from the Devices node or one of the Device collections. When selected, select **Start**, and click **Remote Assistance** to start the Remote Assistance Client.

> **NOTE: REQUIREMENT FOR PROVIDING REMOTE ASSISTANCE**
>
> To use the remote assistance functionality, Remote Assistance must also be installed on the machine running the ConfigMgr console.

Using Remote Desktop

You can use Remote Desktop to connect to a client computer from the Assets and Compliance workspace by selecting the client computer from the Devices node or from one of the Device collections. Then select **Start** from the ribbon bar, and click **Remote Desktop Client** to start a RDP session to the selected client.

Auditing Remote Control

Using Remote Control from ConfigMgr is advantageous because remote control actions are audited by ConfigMgr and can be retrieved using two reports:

▶ All computers remote controlled by a specific user

▶ All remote control information

Chapter 18, "Reporting," discusses ConfigMgr reporting in detail.

Software Deployment Device Settings

Software deployment device settings allow you to specify when software deployments are re-evaluated. Figure 9.37 displays the setting for software deployment.

FIGURE 9.37   Software Deployment Device Settings.

Selecting the **Schedule** button in Figure 9.36 allows you to change the default value (every 7 days effective 2/1/1970 12:00 AM) and whether it is a simple or custom schedule. Software deployment is described in more detail in Chapter 13.

Software Inventory Device Settings

The software inventory device settings allow you to enable or disable software inventory. Figure 9.38 shows the software inventory device settings.

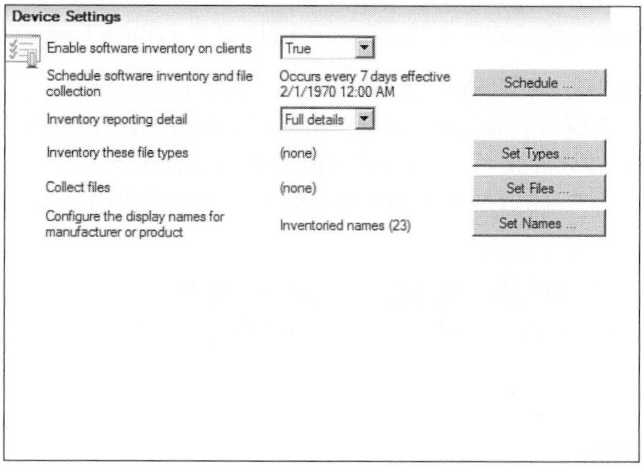

FIGURE 9.38   Software Inventory Device Settings.

Consider software inventory as a file inventory. Software inventory enables you to inventory certain files based on predefined search strings. This could be to inventory all executables, which could complement the inventory information coming from hardware inventory. When inventoried, information in the file header of the inventoried files is available in the ConfigMgr console—allowing a ConfigMgr administrator to report on software inventory or use the information to create dynamic collections for software distribution. Software inventory does not include deltas; it reflects the latest uploaded data. It also lets you upload specified files to the ConfigMgr hierarchy. For example, you could scan for .ini files matching a certain search query and upload those files to become part of that inventory, which you could then query using the Resource Explorer, discussed in the "Using the Resource Explorer" section.

To configure software inventory, perform the following steps:

1. In the Administration workspace of the console, navigate to **Overview -> Client Settings**. Select either the Default Client setting or Custom Device Settings. You can also create new Custom Device Settings.

2. In the Software Inventory section of Device Settings, configure software inventory:

   ▶ To enable Software Inventory, set the **Enable software inventory on clients** value to True, and specify a schedule defining when clients should execute software inventory.

   ▶ Setting inventory reporting detail lets you specify what to report about the inventoried files: You can inventory details about the file only, about the product associated with the file, or all information about the file using the Full Details option.

▶ Configure the types of files to inventory by clicking the **Set Types** button, as part of the **Inventory these file types** option, which opens the Configure Client Setting page:

Click the starburst to specify the files to inventory.

Specify a specific filename to inventory, or use the * or ? wildcard characters.

Specify where to look for the specified file, set to All Client Hard Disks by default, and whether to search in the subfolders of the specified location. You can also specify if you also want to search encrypted and compressed files, which by default is disabled, and whether you want to exclude the Windows folder from the search locations.

Figure 9.39 shows settings to search for all .exe files on all client hard disks including subfolders, excluding encrypted and compressed files, and the Windows folder.

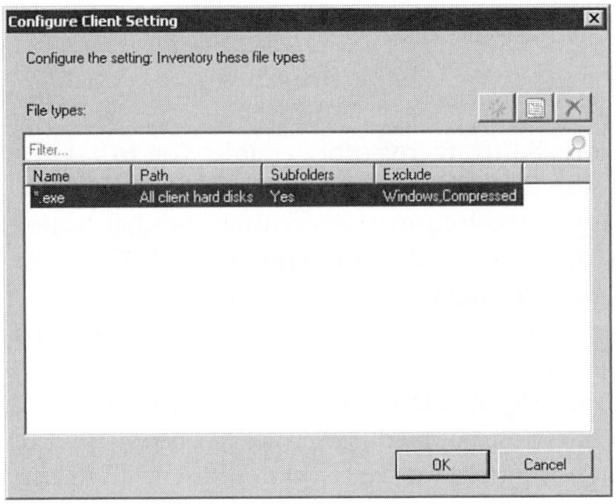

FIGURE 9.39   Software Inventory File Types settings.

▶ To collect files, select the **Set Files** button to bring up the Configure Client Setting dialog. Click the starburst to open the Collected File Properties dialog box, where you can specify the files to collect. Specify a filename, optionally making use of the * and ? wildcard characters, then the location, and whether you want to search in subfolders of the specified location. Specify whether to include encrypted and compressed files, which are excluded by default, and the total amount of files collected, by default set to 128KB. Collecting too many files could have a negative impact on network bandwidth capacity and the ConfigMgr infrastructure. Figure 9.40 shows collecting the hosts file, which resides in the %*windir*%\system32\drivers\etc folder.

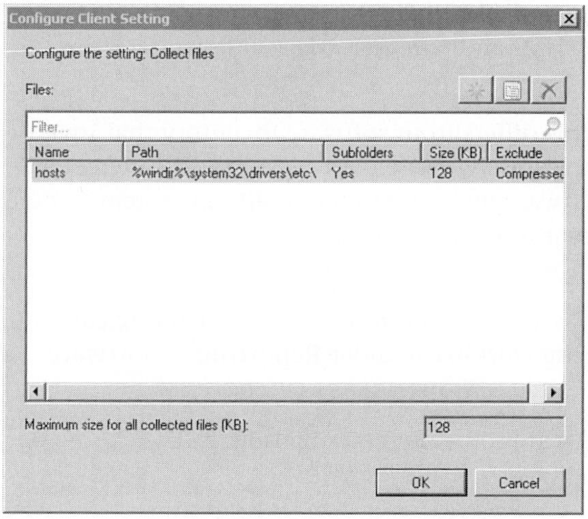

FIGURE 9.40   Software Inventory Collect Files settings.

Software Metering Device Settings

Software metering measures the actual use of software rather than just inventorying it. You can use software metering rules to collect file usage data. Figure 9.41 shows the settings that apply to configuring software metering.

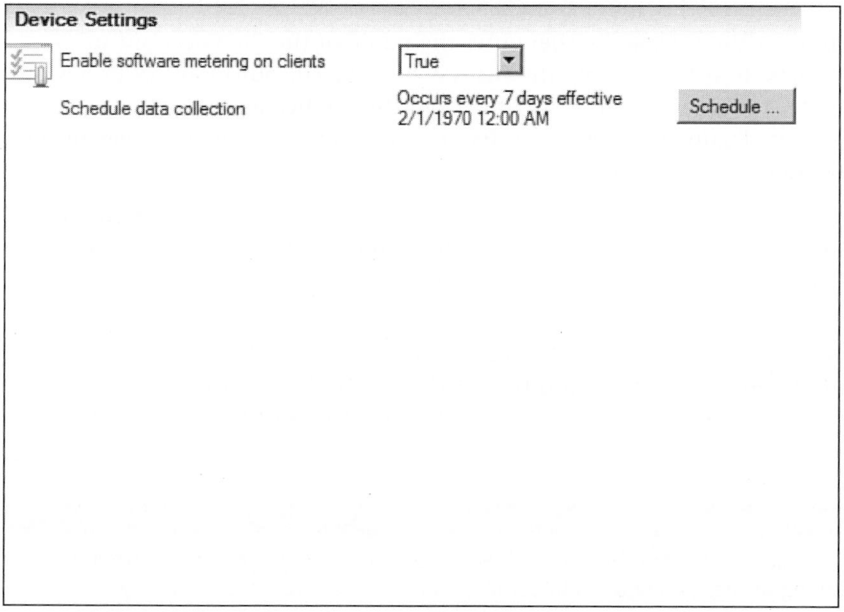

FIGURE 9.41   Software Metering Device Settings

Selecting the Schedule button, as shown in Figure 9.41, allows you to change the default value (every 7 days effective 2/1/1970 12:00 AM) and whether it is a simple or custom schedule.

Software metering collects file usage data; this differs from software inventory that inventories if data (software files such as executables) is available on a system. Software metering measures if the software is used. The software metering functionality in System Center 2012 Configuration Manager is similar to that in ConfigMgr 2007.

Enable software metering using the default client settings or with custom client device settings is described in the "Client Settings" section. Data from software metering can be viewed using the reports in the Monitoring workspace under **Reporting -> Software Metering**.

After enabling software metering, you can create software metering rules in the ConfigMgr console. Follow these steps:

1. In the Assets and Compliance workspace, navigate to **Software Metering.** You notice several rules created; although they are not enabled. ConfigMgr automatically creates a (disabled) software metering rule when 10% of computers in the hierarchy use a program, and stops automatic creation of rules when 100 rules are created. You can modify these settings by clicking Software Metering properties on the ribbon. You can also configure the data retention here, 90 days by default.

   To enable a software metering rule, select the rule, and click **Enable** in the ribbon.

2. Select **Create Software Metering Rule** from the ribbon to create a custom software metering rule. This opens the Create Software Metering Rule Wizard.

3. Provide a name for the rule, and either enter the name of the file you want to monitor or browse to it by selecting the **Browse** button. The advantage of browsing is ConfigMgr reads the details of the file from the file header and fills it in for you automatically. Figure 9.42 shows a software metering rule to meter usage of the Remote Desktop Client software.

4. Click **Next** to continue to the Summary page to review your software metering rule settings; click **Next** again to create the rule. Click **Close** in the Completion page to close the wizard.

In addition to having the information from software metering available with reports, you can create collections based on information provided by software metering. These collections are based on the `Software Usage Data` attribute class. Chapter 13 discusses creating collections.

TIP: MORE INFORMATION ABOUT SOFTWARE METERING

Minfang Lv, a ConfigMgr sustained engineer at Microsoft, provides insight in the working of software metering at http://blogs.msdn.com/b/minfangl/archive/2011/04/29/step-by-step-on-how-to-use-software-metering.aspx. Although written for ConfigMgr 2007, the article is still valid for System Center 2012 Configuration Manager.

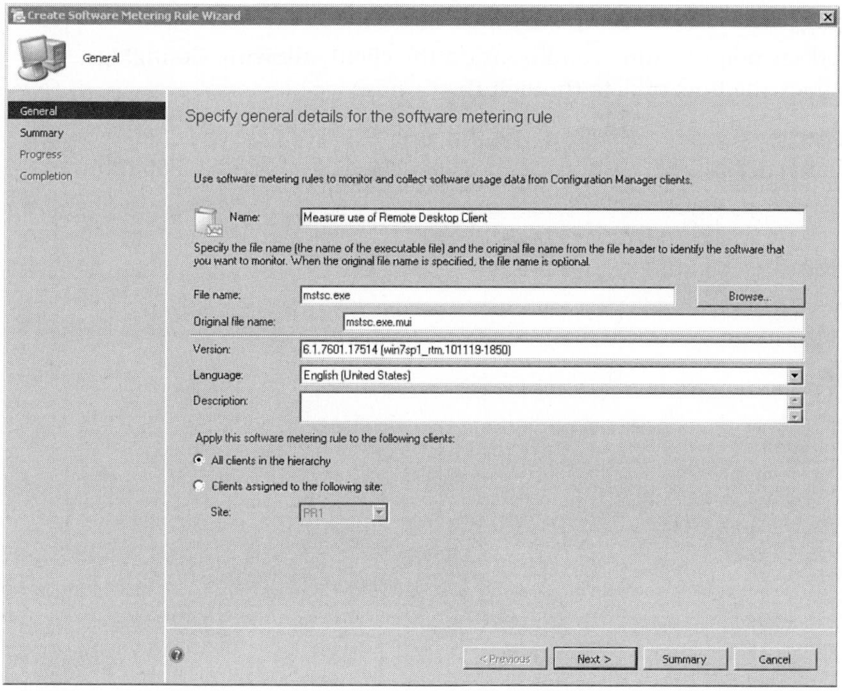

FIGURE 9.42   Create Software Metering Rule Wizard

Software Updates Device Settings

Software updates device settings allow you to specify how the client handles software updates coming from ConfigMgr; this is described in more detail in Chapter 14. Figure 9.43 shows the possible software updates client settings.

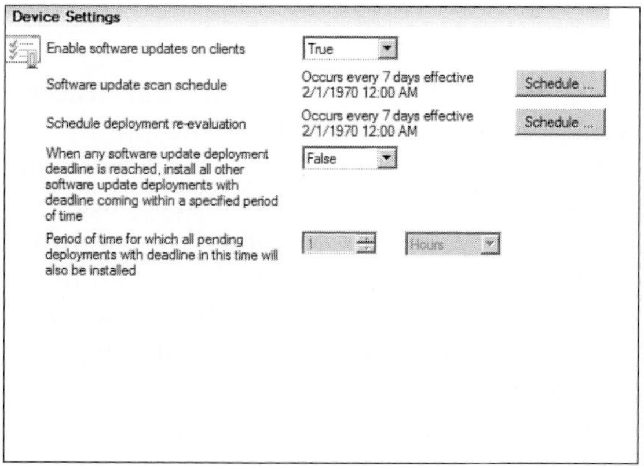

FIGURE 9.43   Software Updates Device Settings.

State Messaging Device Settings

State messaging reflects point-in-time conditions on the client, allowing ConfigMgr administrators to track the flow of data through the ConfigMgr hierarchy.

There is only one setting for state messaging, as shown in Figure 9.44. The State message reporting cycle, which defaults to 15 minutes, can be set between 1 and 43200 minutes (12 days).

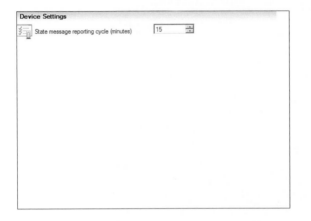

FIGURE 9.44   State Messaging Device settings.

State messages sent by ConfigMgr clients to their management point or fallback status point report the current state of ConfigMgr client operations. The result of collected state messages is shown in reports, and various data in the console depends on the state messages received, such as software updates, settings management, and NAP.

For more information about state messaging, see Steve Rachui's article at http://blogs. msdn.com/b/steverac/archive/2011/01/07/sccm-state-messaging-in-depth.aspx.

User and Device Affinity Settings

User and Device Affinity settings are available both in custom device settings and custom user settings, and allow you to specify the settings that relate to specifying the affinity between the user and the device being used. You can specify these settings for devices and for users. Device affinity can be used when defining deployment types within applications. Chapter 12, "Creating and Managing Applications," covers user and device affinity and how to use this information when deploying applications. When the default affinity settings are used, a user device affinity mapping is created after it uses the device for 48 hours (2880 minutes) within 30 days. You can also specify if you want ConfigMgr to automatically create user device affinities based on the specified data when setting the **Automatically configure user device affinity from usage data** setting to True.

The User and Device Affinity settings for users allow you to specify whether you want to enable a user to define their primary device. There is only one setting for user and device affinity for users, shown in Figure 9.45. When set to True, users can set their own device affinity in the Application Catalog.

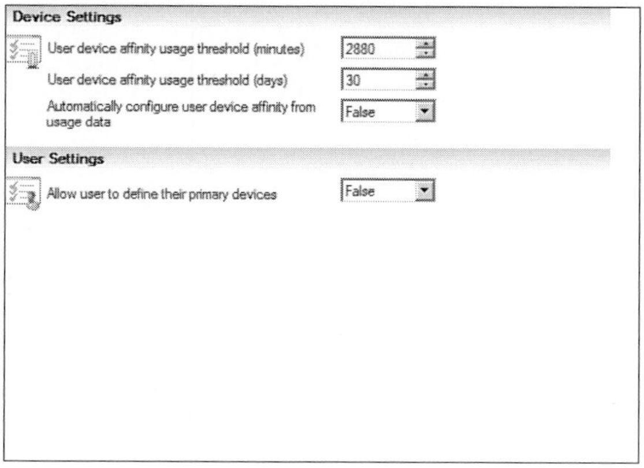

FIGURE 9.45   User and Device Affinity.

Using the Resource Explorer

The Resource Explorer is executed from the ConfigMgr console. It provides insight into hardware inventory, software inventory, and file collections taken from the client, within a single console. Here's how to start the Resource Explorer:

1. In the ConfigMgr console, click **Assets and Compliance Library** to open the workspace. Then select **Devices** or locate the device in one of the available collections.

2. Select the device for which you want to see information, and select **Start** -> **Resource Explorer** from the ribbon bar or right-click context menu.

   Here are the nodes shown by the Resource Explorer, displayed in Figure 9.46:

   ▶ **Hardware:** Hardware shows the inventoried hardware from the last hardware inventory. You can extend the list by enabling extra classes or properties, or adding extra data to the hardware inventory by extending it, described in Appendix B.

   ▶ **Hardware History:** This gives an overview of what changed between hardware inventory scans, and can provide information about changes to inventory.

   ▶ **Software:** Software provides insight into data coming from software inventory; it provides an overview of collected files, file details of inventoried files, information about when the last software scan was performed on the client, and information about which products were inventoried.

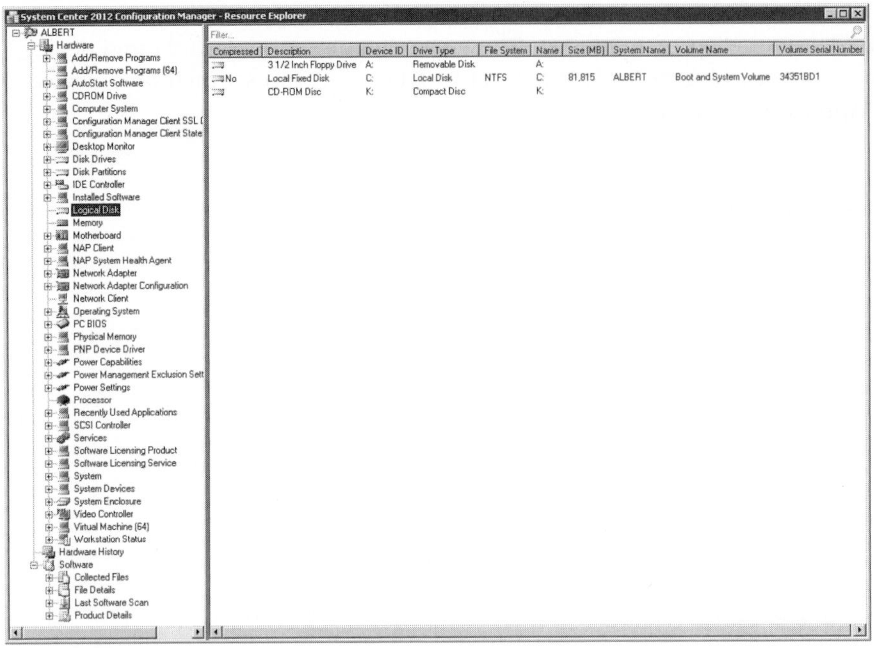

FIGURE 9.46 The System Center 2012 Configuration Manager Resource Explorer.

Wake On LAN

One of the challenges of updating a system with the latest updates or software is its power status; specifically, if the system is not powered on, how can it be maintained? The best time to update or deploy software to systems generally is at night when they are not in use. However, many users turn off their desktops when they leave for the day, and some systems go into a power saving hibernation mode when not used. Powered-down systems present a problem with no easy workaround and leave systems not patched or slammed with patches the moment users log into the network in the morning.

A solution to this is Wake On LAN. WOL is an industry standard for sending a remote signal over the network to a system to "wake" it when powered off or hibernated. The signal is a specially crafted network packet known as a magic packet. The network interface card (NIC) of the destination system receives this magic packet (also referred as a wake-up packet in the ConfigMgr console) and wakes up the system.

WOL Prerequisites

There are two ConfigMgr-specific and three external prerequisites to fully enable WOL capabilities in ConfigMgr.

Here are the ConfigMgr prerequisites:

▶ Enable hardware inventory.

▶ Install the ConfigMgr agent on destination systems.

The external prerequisites consist of

▶ Network interface cards must support WOL and the use of the magic packet.

▶ Enable WOL on NICs and in the BIOS of destination systems.

▶ If subnet-directed broadcasts (discussed in the next section) are used, configure the network infrastructure to forward subnet-directed broadcasts.

Two Types of WOL

ConfigMgr supports two types of WOL:

▶ **Unicast:** With unicast WOL, a single magic packet is sent to the IP address of the system. The IP address is taken from the hardware inventory of the destination system (hence the requirement to enable hardware inventory). Most network infrastructures do not require changes for this type of WOL to function. The magic packet is simply a specially crafted User Datagram Protocol (UDP) packet sent directly to the destination system's IP address.

The magic packet includes the Media Access Control (MAC) address of the system. The destination NIC compares the MAC address to its own before actually waking up the system; if the MAC address in the magic packet does not match the MAC address on the destination NIC, the NIC does not signal the system to wake up. This prevents a situation where the wanted destination system changes its IP address, but the magic packet is sent to a different system that acquired the old IP address of the destination system. In this case, there is no way to actually to wake up the destination system because its new IP address is unknown to ConfigMgr!

> **CAUTION: WOL RELIES ON ARP CACHE**
>
> A major weakness of the unicast method for WOL is its reliance on the Address Resolution Protocol (ARP) cache of the last Layer 3 device in the path to the targeted system. Although this device is usually a router or Layer 3 switch, it could be the primary site server if both systems are on the same subnet.
>
> If the ARP cache of this device no longer contains the MAC address of the target system, it must use an ARP request to discover the MAC address. However, because responding to an ARP request is a function of a running operating system, the magic packet cannot be delivered to the target. An exception to this scenario is when the network card and driver installed on a system have a feature called ARP Offload, the feature is enabled, and the system is running Windows 7.

▶ **Subnet directed:** With subnet-directed WOL, ConfigMgr broadcasts the magic packet to the IP subnet of the destination system. All NICs on that subnet receive the packet. Each compares the MAC address specified in the magic packet to its own; if there is a match, the NIC wakes up its system. This allows ConfigMgr to wake up those systems with changed IP addresses that remain on the same subnet. Subnet-directed WOL requires support from your network infrastructure as it must support subnet-directed broadcasts. These broadcasts are often disabled due to overhead or security concerns because enabling them opens the network to possible Distributed Denial of Service (DDoS) attacks such as the Smurf Attack. You can mitigate this by changing the default port used by subnet-directed WOL packets and configuring the network infrastructure to allow only subnet-directed broadcasts from your ConfigMgr site server.

Configuring WOL

Several configuration options are available for WOL in ConfigMgr. Customizations are performed from the Wake On LAN tab of the *<site>* Properties dialog box (see Figure 9.47), accessible from **Administration** -> **Overview** -> **Site Configuration** -> **Sites**. Right-click *<site code>* - *<site name>* in the Detail pane, and select **Properties**.

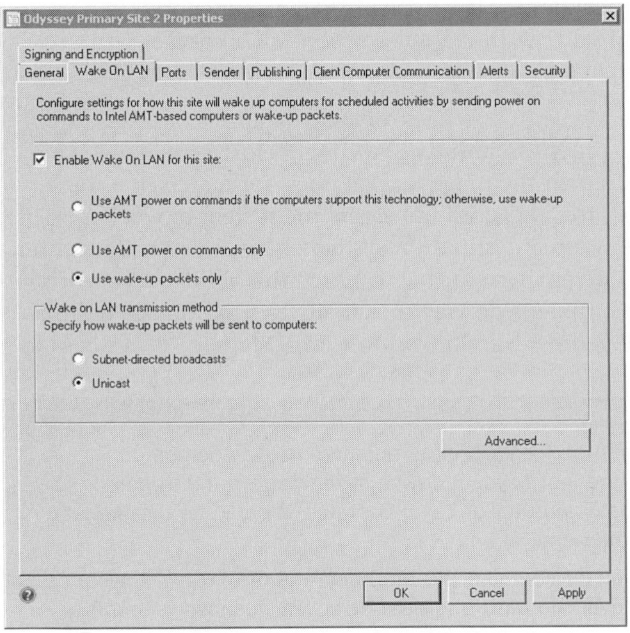

FIGURE 9.47   Wake On LAN settings for the site.

The Wake On LAN tab provides several approaches for how the site will wake up computers. When you enable WOL on the Wake On LAN tab, you first have to configure how you are going to power on your clients. The following options are provided:

▶ **Use AMT power on commands if the computer supports the technology, otherwise ise wake-up packets**

▶ **Use AMT power on commands only**

▶ **Use Wake-up packets only**

When choosing wake-up packets options, you can configure whether to use unicast or subnet-directed broadcasts. The power-on functionality of the Intel AMT technology is an alternative to the magic packets used by traditional WOL, but requires OOB management support on the destination system; OOB also must be fully configured and enabled in ConfigMgr.

To view the port used by ConfigMgr for the magic packet, select the Ports tab of the *<site>* Properties dialog box. ConfigMgr uses UDP port 9 by default. To change the port, double-click the **Wake On Lan (UDP)** entry in the list box, or select it and click the **Properties** button. The Port Details dialog box launches, allowing you to change this port number. Only a single port number is supported. Click the **Advanced** button to access advanced options, displayed in Figure 9.48. These options are mainly network and ConfigMgr throttling controls; only change them if you experience issues.

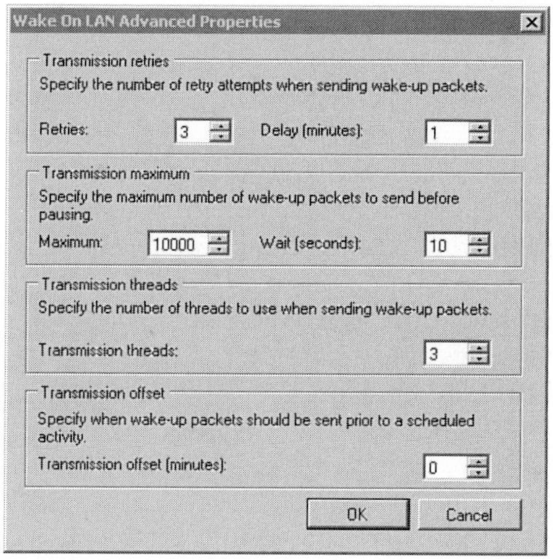

FIGURE 9.48   Wake On LAN Advanced Properties for the site.

Using WOL

ConfigMgr takes care of all the details for actually implementing WOL. You simply have to tell the system when to use it. ConfigMgr supports WOL for these activities:

▶ Application management package/program mandatory deployments

▶ Task sequence mandatory deployments

▶ Software update mandatory deployments

A check box is present on the Deployment Settings page of the deployment wizard for each type of these objects if (and only if) the intent or purpose of the deployment is set to **Required**, which cannot be changed after a deployment is created. When configured, ConfigMgr sends the WOL request to each applicable destination system at the scheduled mandatory time. The magic-packet is sent directly from the primary site server only—not a secondary site server or peer managed system. When the destination system wakes up, it initiates any applicable mandatory deployments.

The primary site server sends only WOL magic packets at the mandatory times specified in the deployment. If a deployment becomes mandatory on a system after the time scheduled for the deployment—for example, by adding it to a collection where a deployment is past its mandatory time—this system will not have a magic-packet sent to it for the deployment.

WOL is a great addition to the ConfigMgr toolset, although there are third-party tools that can enhance the functionality available in ConfigMgr. The two primary third party alternatives—Green Planet from Adaptiva and Night Watchman from 1E—fill some gaps and enable greater flexibility for both WOL and power management by providing peer-to-peer capabilities where peer systems harvest MAC addresses and send the WOL magic packets based upon both ConfigMgr and other events.

Summary

This chapter discussed how to import potential clients into ConfigMgr by using discovery methods or manually importing them. It also discussed the requirements of these potential clients for installing the ConfigMgr client, and the different methods available to install the client. After the client is installed, it needs to assign itself to a ConfigMgr site, and it needs to stay healthy. This chapter also discussed using different client device and user settings, which enables to define ConfigMgr settings on a granular level. The chapter ended with a discussion of how to manage the client, and how to leverage WOL using ConfigMgr to wake up clients.

PART IV

Software and Configuration Management

IN THIS PART

CHAPTER 10

Managing Compliance

Perhaps the most under-used Configuration Manager (ConfigMgr) 2007 feature was desired configuration management (DCM). DCM was a newly introduced feature enabling you to monitor, report, and take action on systems that do not meet specific, predefined settings.

Compliance settings is the evolution of DCM, although it is similar to what it was in ConfigMgr 2007. Compliance settings provide the ability to define, monitor, enforce, and report configuration compliance. Compliance settings handle the following four general scenarios that all IT organizations deal with in one form or another:

▶ **Regulatory compliance:** Given the impact of new regulatory laws in the United States that cover privacy and corporate responsibility, regulatory compliance is a key scenario for many Information Technology (IT) organizations. Examples of these laws include the Sarbanes-Oxley (SOX) Act of 2002, the Gramm-Leach-Bliley Act (GLBA), and the Health Insurance Portability and Accountability Act (HIPAA). Each of these regulations requires IT organizations to set specific security and privacy standards for corporate and user data, as well as for IT systems. The difficult part for IT occurs when trying to enforce and report on the enforcement of the standards set.

Most IT organizations have no way to enforce these policies, and rely on ad-hoc custom scripts or tools that provide on-demand results. In addition, these laws are not technical in nature. This leads to the actual technical requirements to fulfill the standards being subject to interpretation and varying between organizations: SOX for you is not necessarily SOX for someone else.

Even if your organization is not subject to specific regulatory compliance laws, it should still be subject to internal policies and standards. Validating your infrastructure's compliance against this internal governance is the same as validating it against governmental standards.

▶ **Pre-and post-change verification:** This scenario involves verifying the configuration of a system before and after planned changes. It is to your advantage to confirm you are applying changes only to systems in a specific state, that the planned changes occurred, and unintended changes did not take place.

▶ **Configuration drift:** Although obvious when pointed out to most IT administrators, typical IT organizations do not account for configuration drift or its implications on the state of the network.

Configuration drift starts the moment a system goes into production and is difficult to control. No matter how rigorously standard your build process is, as soon as multiple administrators begin logging in to a system to install applications, troubleshoot issues, "tweak" performance, or just make it look like they want it to, the system begins its drift from the standard. Over time, the drift for a particular system is unpredictable and has the potential to cause technical issues.

▶ **Time to resolution:** An overwhelming number of problems in the IT world are due to human error. These problems ultimately become the dreaded problem ticket that every on-call administrator loathes, particularly the one in the middle of the night or halfway through the fourth quarter of the Super Bowl (the American championship game in professional football). Stopping human error is all but impossible; however, identifying that human error quickly so that it can be resolved is the key to reducing the impact of such errors.

Individually or in combination, each of these scenarios places a burden on IT. There is little reward in successfully handling these scenarios because they do not directly address or contribute to business objectives. These are typically considered the "unfun" things in IT, and administrators do not look forward to dealing with them.

Although compliance settings management does not necessarily change the nature of these four scenarios, it goes a long way toward making the scenarios more manageable and less time-consuming, and integrating them into your existing processes.

The feature known as compliance settings is also a fundamental building block for other features in ConfigMgr, such as the awesome new application model (discussed in Chapter 11, "Packages and Programs," and Chapter 12, "Creating and Managing Applications"), software updates (discussed in Chapter 14, "Software Update Management"), and endpoint protection (discussed in Chapter 16, "Endpoint Protection"). Knowing this and your way around the compliance settings feature set can help in managing these other features also.

This chapter explores compliance settings, how to set it up, configure it, and use it to address these scenarios.

New and Improved in System Center 2012 Configuration Manager

This latest iteration of ConfigMgr adds many new and exciting bells and whistles. With compliance settings being the evolution of DCM, at its core it continues to do the same thing in the same way with many of the rough edges rounded off and some new functionality added, including

▶ Unified compliance and settings management across servers, desktops, laptops, and mobile devices

▶ Simplified administrator experience

  ▶ Role-based administration (as discussed in Chapter 8, "The Configuration Manager Console")

  ▶ Browse a reference system when creating configuration items

  ▶ Simplified baseline creation experience

▶ Deployment of baselines

  ▶ User and device targeting of baselines

  ▶ Define compliance service level agreements (SLAs) for baseline deployments and alert generation

  ▶ True per user evaluation and remediation

▶ Monitoring baseline deployment compliance status

  ▶ In console monitoring

  ▶ Updated reports to include remediation, conflict, and error reporting

▶ Automatic remediation for registry values, Windows Management Instrumentation (WMI) values, and script based compliance checks

▶ Configuration item revisioning

▶ Migration of existing Configuration Manager 2007 baselines and compliance items (configuration items)

▶ Simplified collection creation based on configuration item compliance. This was actually introduced in ConfigMgr 2007 Release 3 (R3) so it not necessarily new.

Configuring Compliance Settings

Unlike other major features of ConfigMgr, there are no server-side prerequisites (other than ConfigMgr itself) and there is no initial configuration for settings management:

you simply enable it or disable it using granular client settings as discussed in Chapter 9, "Configuration Manager Client Management." The client performs all processing and returns the results to the site server. This section discusses the quick setup of compliance settings and the rather straightforward configuration options available.

Here are the two client-side prerequisites for compliance settings:

▶ Clients must have the ConfigMgr 2012 Client agent installed.

▶ Clients must have the .NET Framework 2.0 installed.

NOTE: .NET FRAMEWORK VERSIONS

.NET Framework 3.5 requires and includes .NET Framework 3.0, which in turn requires and includes .NET Framework 2.0. Thus, if a system has any of the these .NET Framework versions installed, it meets the .NET Framework version requirement even if .NET Framework 2.0 is not explicitly listed in the installed programs list.

.NET Framework 4.0, although backward-compatible with these other versions, does not fulfill this requirement.

To enable compliance settings, edit or create a new set of client settings by navigating to the Administration workspace and selecting **Client Settings** in the navigation tree. Edit an existing set of client settings by selecting it in the workspace pane and choosing **Properties** from the ribbon bar or the right-click menu. To create a new set of client settings, select **Create Custom Client Device Settings** from the ribbon bar or right-click the context menu. For a complete discussion of client settings, see Chapter 9.

On any resulting client settings configuration dialog (shown in Figure 10.1), select **Compliance Settings** from the list on the left. There are two resulting options:

▶ The first option on this page is to **Enable compliance evaluation on clients**. That's all there is to actually enabling compliance settings; it is either on or off, based on this one little drop-down.

▶ The second option is to set the default evaluation schedule for assigned baselines (the "Configuration Baselines" section covers baselines in detail).

As with many other configurable schedules in ConfigMgr, you can choose to use a simple schedule that allows the client to determine exactly when the action occurs using a minimum interval. Alternatively, you can set a custom schedule that defines exactly when to perform the action.

The schedule set here is only the default schedule for newly assigned baselines; you can set a separate schedule for each baseline deployment when you create it.

When the client settings are deployed, the client compliance settings feature will be enabled on clients after the next machine policy refresh.

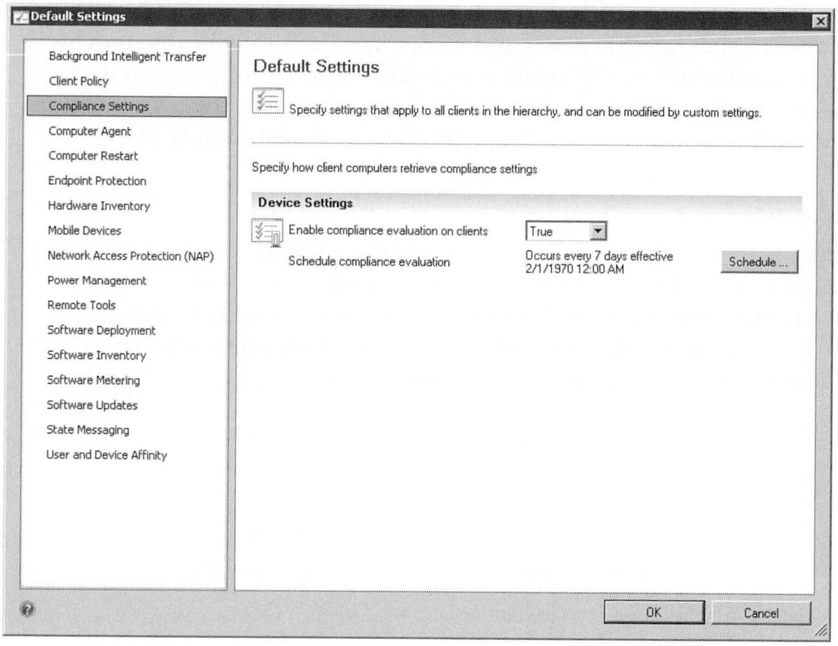

FIGURE 10.1   Compliance Settings client settings.

This is all that is required to configure the ConfigMgr site and server to use compliance settings. On its own, compliance settings work quite well, although it does not include a method to monitor the results. Consequently, you should also set up reporting as described in Chapter 18, "Reporting." Of course, just turning compliance settings on and enabling reporting doesn't tell ConfigMgr what to monitor or report on; you do this by creating configuration items and configuration baselines, as discussed in the next section.

Configuration Items and Baselines

You configure compliance by creating two object types:

▶ **Configuration items:** A collection of settings, values, and criteria that defines what is compared, checked, or evaluated on a target system.

▶ **Configuration baselines:** This is a grouping of multiple configuration items. Configuration items must be part of a configuration baseline to be assigned for evaluation on a collection of systems.

Instances of these two object types are often called *configurations* collectively because they define a specific system configuration.

Microsoft built compliance settings knowing that every IT environment is unique and that configuration standards and requirements in each IT environment are different.

10

Thus, compliance settings gives you the tools to create configuration items and baselines from scratch according to your specific needs and wants. The built-in editor is straightforward and easy to use, allowing you to create simple to complex configuration items, and anything in-between. The following two sections define the details of baselines and configuration items, including using the built-in editor to create and modify them.

Configuration Items

Configuration items encapsulate the checks that compliance settings makes against a system to determine its compliance. Collectively, these checks are called *evaluation criteria*. To view or edit the configuration items present in a site, navigate to the Assets and Compliance workspace, and in the navigation tree, select **Compliance Settings** -> **Configuration Items**. Figure 10.2 shows a typical list of configuration items in the console.

Icon	Name	Type	Device Type	Revision	Child	Relationships	User Setting
	Analysis services: Part 1	Application	Windows	4	No	Yes	No
	Analysis services: Part 2	Application	Windows	4	No	Yes	No
	Analysis services: Part 3	Application	Windows	4	No	Yes	No
	Engine: Part 1	Application	Windows	4	No	Yes	No
	Engine: Part 2	Application	Windows	4	No	Yes	No
	Engine: Part 3	Application	Windows	4	No	Yes	No
	Engine: Part 4	Application	Windows	4	No	Yes	No
	Integration services	Application	Windows	4	No	Yes	No
	Microsoft Windows Server 2008 R2 SP1 DHCP Server Role BPA Configur...	Application	Windows	4	No	Yes	No
	Microsoft Windows Server 2008 R2 SP1 DHCP Server Role BPA Configur...	Application	Windows	4	No	Yes	No
	Microsoft Windows Server 2008 R2 SP1 DHCP Server Role BPA Configur...	Application	Windows	4	No	Yes	No
	Microsoft Windows Server 2008 R2 SP1 Web Server (IIS) Role BPA Conf...	Application	Windows	4	No	Yes	No
	Replication	Application	Windows	4	No	Yes	No
	Reporting services	Application	Windows	4	No	Yes	No
	Setup	Application	Windows	4	No	Yes	No
	Win2003 Domain Controller HIPAA (200045)	Application	Windows	44	No	Yes	No
	Win2003 Domain Controller SOX (200048)	Application	Windows	51	No	Yes	No
	Win2003 Member Server HIPAA (200027)	Application	Windows	44	No	Yes	Yes
	Win2003 Member Server SOX (200030)	Application	Windows	44	No	Yes	Yes

Configuration Items 19 items

FIGURE 10.2   Configuration items in the console.

Similar to the other areas of the console, you can use search filters and saved searches to find specific configuration items or limit those displayed in the primary workspace pane. Here is notable criteria specific to filtering configuration items and described later in this section:

▶ **Revision:** This field indicates the highest revision number of the configuration item. The "Versioning" section includes a complete discussion of versioning and revision numbers.

▶ **Child:** Indicates that the configuration item is a child of another configuration item.

▶ **Relationships:** Indicates that the configuration item is a parent of another configuration item.

▶ **Type:** One of the four types of configuration items described next.

▶ **Device Type:** One of the two device types described next.

▶ **Categories:** The defined categories for the configuration item.

There are two different configuration item device types; each configuration item is applicable to one or the other:

▶ **Windows**

▶ **Mobile**

In addition, there are four configuration item types:

▶ **Application:** A configuration item of this type checks for the existence of an application and its associated settings. The application's existence can be assumed, checked by Windows Installer detection, or determined by a custom script.

▶ **Software Updates:** These configuration items check the patch or update level of a system. The only evaluation criterion for this configuration item type is the installation status of a specific software update. Software updates configuration items are a special type of configuration item not listed with the other configuration items in the console. You cannot directly create them like the three other types: the Software Update feature in ConfigMgr creates them for every update in the update repository. Thus, to use software updates configuration items, the ConfigMgr software update feature (discussed in Chapter 14) must be properly configured and working not only to define the software updates configuration item, but also to detect its installation status.

▶ **Operating System:** This type of configuration item checks for a specific operating system version and settings relevant to that version. The operating system version is set by choosing from a drop-down list of preconfigured operating systems or by directly setting the version values.

▶ **General:** This type of configuration item is only used for mobile devices; all mobile device configuration items are general configuration items. In ConfigMgr 2007, general configuration items could be created for Windows systems. This type was redundant though, and offered no real value or added functionality as compared to operating system configuration items.

To create a new configuration item, select **Create Configuration Item** from the ribbon bar or the right-click context menu: This results in the Create Configuration Item Wizard (shown in its initial, default state in Figure 10.3) with the following pages:

▶ **General:** On this page, you specify the name of the configuration item and can optionally supply a description. The order and existence of the other pages in this wizard depend upon the options chosen here and listed in Table 10.1.

10

TABLE 10.1   Create Configuration Item Wizard Pages

Windows	Windows Application	Mobile Device
General	General	General
Supported Platforms	Detection Methods	Mobile Device Settings
Settings	Settings	Supported Platforms
Compliance Rules	Compliance Rules	Platform Applicability
Summary	Supported Platforms	Summary
Progress	Summary	Progress
Completion	Progress	Completion
	Completion	

In addition, you specify the type of configuration item to create:

▶ **Windows:** Applicable to Windows systems only. If selected, one additional option is presented on the General page: **This configuration item contains application settings**. Choosing this option adds a Detection Methods page to the wizard and specifies that this configuration item is an application configuration item.

▶ **Mobile device:** Applicable to fully supported mobile devices. At RTM, this includes only Windows CE (version 5.0, 6.0, and 7.0), Windows Mobile 6.0, Windows Mobile 6.1, Windows Mobile 6.5, and Nokia Symbian Belle; it does not include devices managed using the Exchange ActiveSync connector. For the complete list of supported devices, see http://technet.microsoft.com/en-us/library/gg682077.aspx.

On the bottom of the General page, you assign categories to the configuration item to improve filtering and searching in the console and reports; although ultimately, categories serve no functional purpose. These categories cannot be exported or imported and only exist on the server. Four default categories are created at installation time:

▶ Client

▶ IT Infrastructure

▶ Line of Business

▶ Server

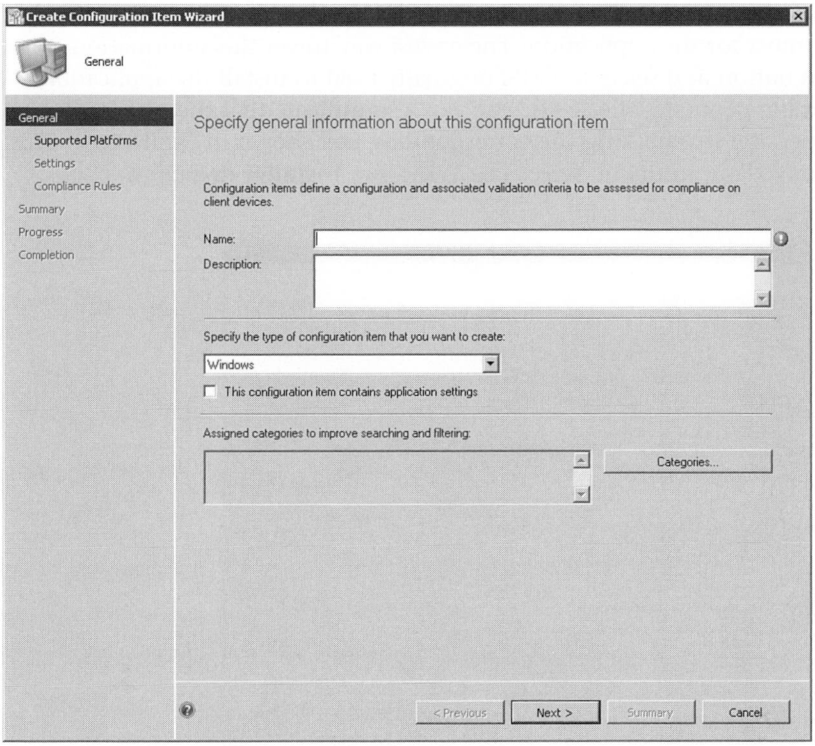

FIGURE 10.3   Create Configuration Item Wizard.

You can use these categories, delete them, or add new ones; no special functionality is associated with these categories.

▶ **Detection Methods:** This page is shown only if the configuration item is applicable to Windows and is an application configuration item that is specified by checking the **This configuration item contains application settings** check box on the General tab. Use this page to specify the criteria for detecting the application that this configuration item targets. If the application does not exist, the configuration item is not evaluated by the client. There are three possible detection methods as shown in Figure 10.4:

   ▶ **Always assume application is installed**: When this method is selected, the client assumes that the application is installed without a check. Choosing this option is essentially the equivalent of creating a general configuration item.

   ▶ **Use Windows Installer detection:** This method uses the list of products installed by Windows Installer to determine if an application is installed. If an application was not installed using an MSI, this method is not applicable.

10

Expected data for this method includes the Globally Unique Identifier (GUID) and the version number for the application. The easiest way to get this information is to click the **Open** button and select the MSI originally used to install the application. This automatically populates the fields. You can also indicate that the installation was installed per user by checking the corresponding box shown in Figure 10.4. This check box is grayed out until you select **Use Windows Installer detection**.

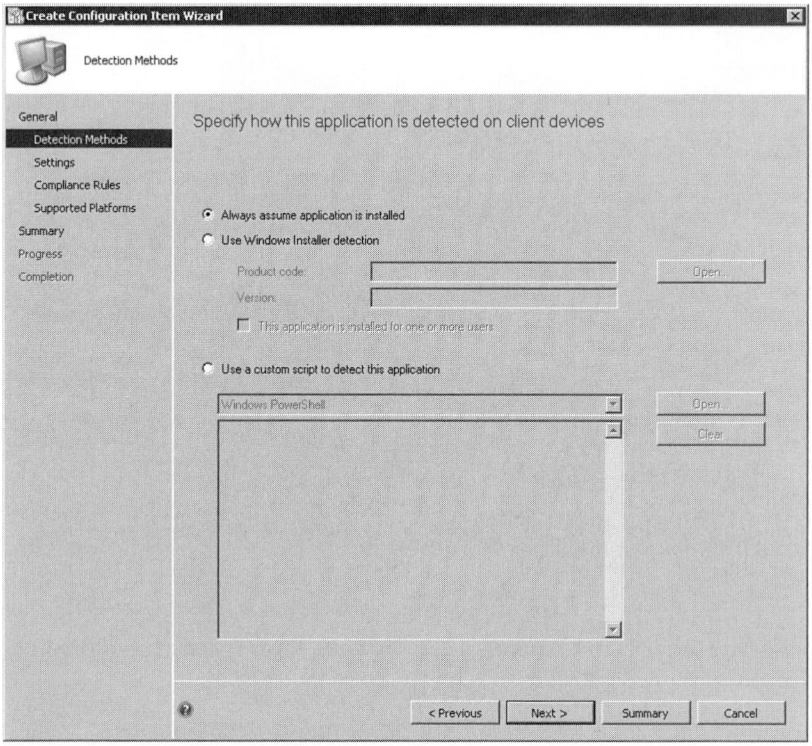

FIGURE 10.4   Detection Methods page in the Create Configuration Item Wizard.

TIP: MANUALLY DETERMINING A PRODUCT'S GUID

Although not always apparent, most software applications today are installed using a MSI; these are often hidden inside of executables and not directly accessible. During installation, the MSI is extracted from the executable to a temporary folder and then installed from that folder. The easiest way to determine the application's GUID and version if the MSI is hidden in this way—or not readily available for any reason—is to use WMI, and the easiest way to query WMI is the WMI Console (WMIC). WMIC is part of every Windows installation and invoked from the command line. The September 2006 issue of TechNet contains an excellent article on WMIC, titled "Gathering WMI Data without Writing a Single Line of Code," available at http://technet.microsoft.com/en-us/magazine/2006.09. wmidata.aspx.

Here's an example of a WMIC command to query for the GUID and version of all Microsoft Live products:

```
wmic product where "caption like '%Live%'" get name, IdentifyingNumber, version
```

This command outputs the product name, GUID, and version for every product that has **Live** in its name.

▶ **Use custom script to detect this application:** This method uses a custom script (VBScript-, Jscript-, or PowerShell-based) to detect the installation of an application. The script should return some text to indicate the successful detection of an installed application and no text to indicate failure. A simple example VBScript to detect the installation of the Internet Explorer Administration Kit 7 follows:

```
folderPath = "C:\Program Files\Microsoft IEAK 7"
Set fso = CreateObject("Scripting.FileSystemObject")
If fso.FolderExists(folderPath) Then
    WScript.Echo "IEAK 7 Found"
End If
```

NOTE: SCRIPT SUCCESS

Application detection scripts used in compliance settings are considered to be successful if they output anything to the standard output—often referred to as StdOut. The exact contents of the output are not evaluated; it is just that something is output. Conversely, if nothing is output, the script is considered unsuccessful.

▶ **Settings:** Use this page to configure the actual settings that you want the client to evaluate for compliance on targeted systems. For each setting, specify

▶ **Name**

▶ **Description**

▶ **Setting type**

▶ **Data type**

Note that not every setting has a data type. To create, edit, or delete a setting, use the corresponding fields and controls discussed in this section and listed in Table 10.2. Each setting and data type is fully described in the "Windows Settings" section.

When creating or editing a setting, you can also directly create or modify compliance rules (described next) on the Compliance Rules tab.

▶ **Compliance Rules:** Compliance rules dictate how a targeted client evaluates each setting in a configuration item. Without an associated compliance rule, settings are meaningless. Compliance rules cannot exist without an associated setting. Compliance rules are discussed in further detail in the "Compliance Rules" section.

10

▶ **Supported Platforms:** On this page, select which platforms this configuration item applies to using the check box tree; all supported versions of Windows are listed for Windows configuration items and supported mobile devices are listed for mobile device configuration items. If the client platform does not match, the configuration item is not evaluated.

For Windows application configuration items, one additional option exists at the bottom of this page: **This application runs only on computers that have 64-bit hardware**. This option indicates that the application is a 64-bit application that will not run on a 32-bit version of Windows, preventing the configuration item from being applicable and evaluated on 32-bit versions of Windows.

For non-application configuration items, you can manually specify a specific operating system version by inputting these operating system version values:

> ▶ Major version
>
> ▶ Minor version
>
> ▶ Build number
>
> ▶ Service Pack major version
>
> ▶ Service Pack minor version

▶ **Mobile Device Settings:** Use this page to select a group of settings that you want the client to evaluate for compliance on targeted mobile devices. Each chosen setting group adds an additional configuration subpage to wizard.

A check box at the bottom of this page, **Configure additional settings that are not in the default setting groups**, enables another subpage, titled Additional Settings for individually configuring settings. The name of this setting is a bit misleading however, as all possible, built-in settings are available from this new subpage including those in one of the default groups.

The "Mobile Device Settings" section discusses the available settings.

▶ **Platform Applicability:** This information-only page lists all mobile device settings chosen and configured on the Mobile Device Settings page that do not apply to all the platforms chosen on the Supported Platforms page. The only option available is to export the list to a report.

▶ **Summary:** A list of all choices made in the wizard for review before actual creation of the configuration item.

▶ **Progress:** Shows the progress of creating the configuration item.

▶ **Completion:** A completion results page listing any errors or warnings that occurred while the configuration item was created.

To edit a configuration item, select it in the console, and choose **Properties** from the ribbon bar or the right-click context menu. The properties dialog for a configuration item has tabs corresponding to the Create Configuration Item Wizard pages, based upon the type of configuration item outlined in Table 10.1. After creating a configuration item, you cannot change its type.

Windows Settings

Windows settings are configured on the Settings page of the Create Configuration Item Wizard when creating a Windows configuration item, or on the Settings tab in the properties dialog box for a Windows configuration item (shown in Figure 10.5). Settings define the criteria a client agent evaluates to determine compliance of a configuration item. If you are familiar with ConfigMgr 2007, settings are the combination of objects and settings from DCM.

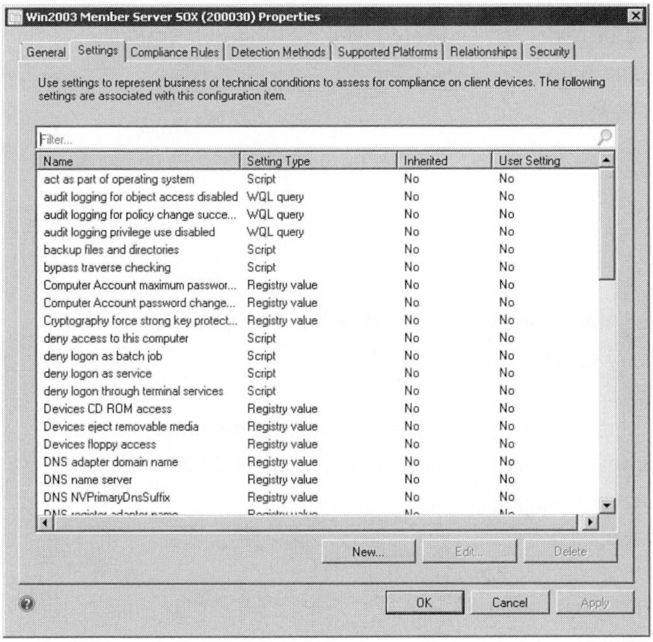

FIGURE 10.5   Configuration Item Settings.

Each configuration item can contain as many (or few) settings as you want to configure. There are ten different types of settings; these are listed in Table 10.2. Each type has its own (relatively) self-explanatory fields or options for which you must supply values.

TABLE 10.2   Configuration Item Settings Properties

Setting	Fields
Active Directory Query	LDAP prefix
	Distinguished name (DN)
	Search filter
	Search scope
	Property
	Query
Assembly	Assembly name
File system	Type
	Path
	File or folder name
	Include subfolders
	This file or folder is associated with a 64-bit application.
IIS Metabase	Metabase path
	Property ID
Registry Key	Hive
	Key
Registry Value	Hive
	Key
	Value
	This registry value is associated with a 64-bit application.
Script	Discovery script
	Remediation script
	Run scripts by using the logged-on user credentials.
	Run scripts by using 32-bit scripting host on 64-bit devices.
SQL query	SQL Server instance
	Database
	Column
	Transact-SQL statement
WQL query	Namespace
	Class
	Property
	WQL query WHERE clause
XPath query	Path
	eXtended Markup Language (XML) file name
	Include subfolders
	This file is associated with a 64-bit application.
	XPath query
	Namespaces

For file system settings, you can use a built-in browser by clicking the **Browse** button to directly find a wanted folder or file on the local system or a remote one. You can also use the Browse File System dialog box, as shown in Figure 10.6, to create value and existential compliance rules directly using the options in the lower right of the dialog.

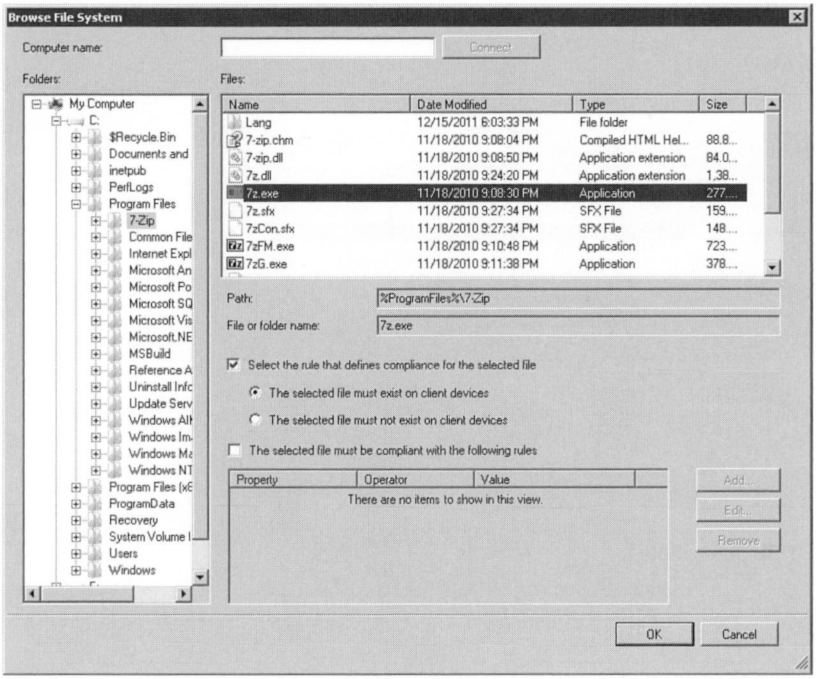

FIGURE 10.6   Browse File System dialog.

Similarly, for registry key and registry value settings, a registry browser is also included and accessible using the **Browse** button. From the Browse Registry dialog, as shown in Figure 10.7, you can locate registry keys and values on the local system or a remote one and also create compliance rules. You cannot create value compliance rules for registry keys because registry keys do not have a value; the corresponding fields will be hidden in the Browse Registry dialog if a registry key is chosen.

Most settings also have a data type that you must define; Table 10.3 shows the different data types available for each setting type. Note the lack of data types for the assembly, file system, and registry key settings; this is discussed in the "Compliance Rules" section.

10

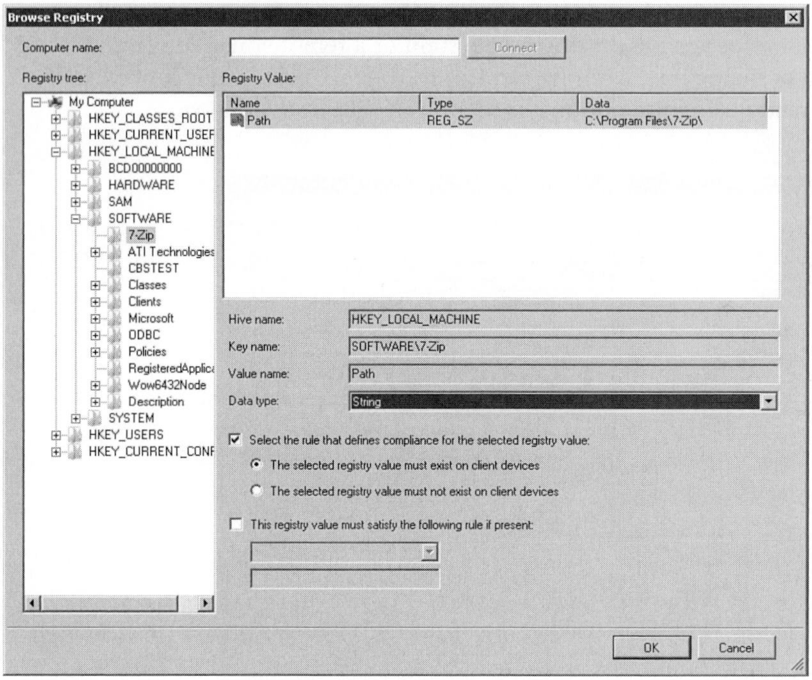

FIGURE 10.7   Browse Registry dialog.

TABLE 10.3   Data Types per Setting

Setting Type	String	Date and Time	Integer	Floating Point	Version	Boolean	String Array	Integer Array
Active Directory Query	X	X	X	X	X	X	X	X
Assembly								
File system								
IIS Metabase	X	X	X	X	X	X	X	
Registry Key								
Registry Value	X	X	X	X	X		X	
Script	X	X	X	X	X	X		
SQL query	X	X	X	X	X	X		
WQL query	X	X	X	X	X	X	X	X
XPath query	X	X	X	X	X	X		

The data type chosen for each setting directly determines the operators available in value type compliance rules for the configuration item; this is discussed in the "Compliance Rules" section and listed in Table 10.4 in that section.

The use of scripts is a powerful method in compliance evaluation; using scripts, you can evaluate anything on a Windows system. Scripts can be VBScript, JScript, or PowerShell, and can return any value you want them to according to Table 10.3. This returned value is then evaluated using compliance rules similar to the result of any setting. In addition to evaluation, you can optionally specify a script to directly remediate the noncompliance issue identified by the evaluation script. Script types are limited only by your scripting and web searching capabilities.

NOTE: USING POWERSHELL SCRIPTS

Unlike VBScript and JScript, PowerShell is not a core component on all versions of Windows. Should you use a PowerShell script, ensure PowerShell is installed on all the systems where the configuration item will be applicable. Also, verify the version in use. PowerShell 2.0 and 3.0 include many new features, cmdlets, and bug fixes that are not backward compatible.

Registry key, registry value, and script settings can be user-specific. This is the case when the registry key or registry value setting specifies HKEY_CURRENT_USER for the hive or the script setting has the option **Run scripts by using the logged on user credentials** option checked. User settings are evaluated for the currently logged-in user only, and they are clearly denoted on the Settings tab in the compliance item's properties dialog by a User Setting column, as shown in Figure 10.8. Each configuration item containing a user setting is also called out the console by the User Setting column.

Compliance Rules

Compliance rules define how the settings in a configuration items are evaluated on a client system. Each compliance rule is specific to a single setting and defines the exact criteria to use when evaluating that setting on the client system for compliance. Settings that match the criteria in the compliance rule are marked as compliant for that client system.

There are two compliance rule types:

▶ **Value:** This compliance rule type checks the setting's value against a value defined in the configuration item. Based upon the data type chosen for the setting, different comparison operators are available, as shown in Table 10.4.

10

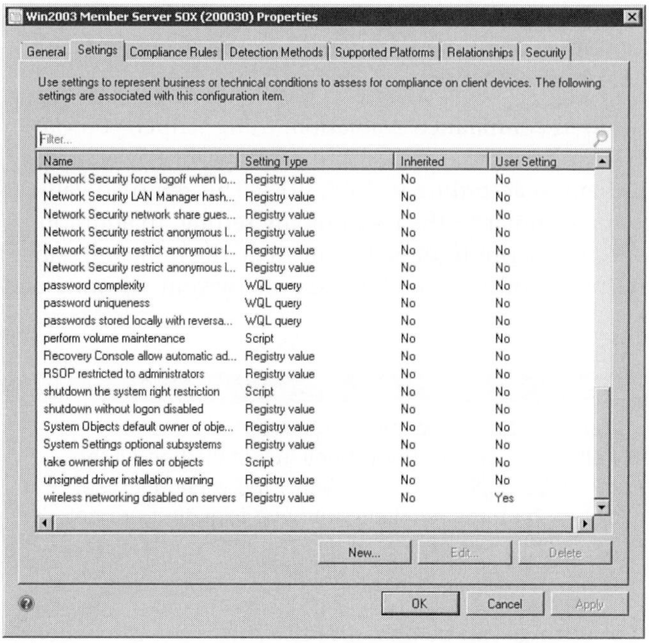

FIGURE 10.8   The Settings tab of a compliance item.

TABLE 10.4   Comparison Operators for Different Data Types

Integer, Date and Time, Floating Point, and Version	String	String Array, Integer Array
Equals	Equals	All of
Not equal to	Not equal to	
Greater than	Begins with	
Less than	Does not begin with	
Between	Ends with	
Greater than or equal to	Does not end with	
Less than or equal to	Contains	
One of	Does not contain	
None of	One of	
	None of	

There are two additional options for value type compliance rules:

▶ **Remediate noncompliant rules when supported:** Changes compliance settings from a passive, reporting feature into a settings enforcement feature automatically changing the value of the setting on the client to the expected value. Remediation is supported only for registry values, WMI values, and scripts. More detail on remediation is covered in the "Remediation" section.

▶ **Report noncompliance if this setting instance is not found:** Makes this rule existential (described next) in addition to value-based.

▶ **Existential:** These rule types check for the existence or nonexistence of the specified setting. (The philosopher Søren Kierkegaard would be proud.) You can also configure existential rules to check for a specific number of instances of a setting; this is meaningless or invalid for many setting types, but given the right context, checking for multiple instances is valuable. For example, checking for multiple instances of the `Win32_LogicalDisk` class enables you to create a rule that checks for a specific number of logical disks in a system.

For the setting types that do not have a data type—assembly, file system, and registry key—you must also choose a property of the object represented by the setting to evaluate in a value compliance rule. These three setting types by themselves have no value to compare or evaluate; however, they represent objects that have properties, and it is one of these properties that is evaluated for compliance. If you are familiar with ConfigMgr 2007, these setting types were actually separated from the other settings and called *objects* for this exact reason. Table 10.5 lists the properties available for each of these setting types. Each of these properties also has a predefined data type used for the same purpose as setting data types: to determine the available operators used when evaluating the compliance rule, previously described in Table 10.4.

TABLE 10.5   Object Properties

Object	Properties	Property Data Type
Assembly	Version	Version
	Culture	String
	Public Key Token	String
File System	Date Modified	Date and Time
	Date Created	Date and Time
	Size (Bytes)	Integer
	Product Name	String
	File Version	Version
	Company	String
	SHA-1 Hash	String
	Attributes	File Attributes
	Permissions	File Permissions
Registry Key	Permissions	Registry Permissions

The attributes and permissions properties listed in Table 10.5 do not have corresponding operators in Table 10.4. This is because these are special data types that require a different kind of comparison than is provided by using simple operators. For attributes, the following attributes can be verified as on or off in a compliance rule:

▶ Archive

▶ Compressed

▶ Encrypted

▶ Hidden

▶ Read only

▶ System

For permissions property types, the access control list (ACL) of the file, folder, or registry key is evaluated. The dialog provided, shown in Figure 10.9 for a file, is flexible and can model any type of access control entry (ACE) possible by specifying a user or group name and the various permissions that should exist for that user or group. For permissions evaluation, there are two, nonintuitive options as well:

▶ **Exclusive:** Indicates that the permissions specified and only the permissions specified must exist on the file, folder, or registry key

▶ **Non-exclusive:** Indicates that the permissions specified must exist at a minimum but other additional permissions may be applied to the file, folder, or registry key

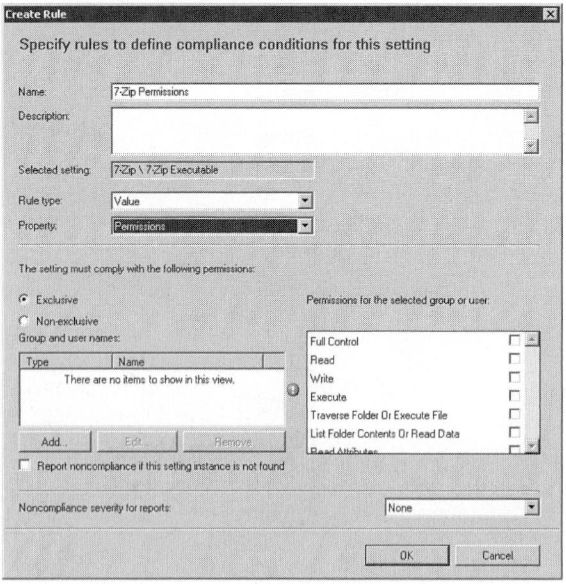

FIGURE 10.9   Permissions in a compliance rule.

Mobile Device Settings

The number of specific mobile device settings is too large to specifically list here; nearly all the settings are self-explanatory, so listing them provides minimal value.

The built-in settings are grouped into eight default setting groups:

▶ Password

▶ Email management

▶ Security

▶ Peak synchronization

▶ Roaming

▶ Encryption

▶ Wireless communication

▶ Certificates

Configuring a value for any of the built-in settings on one of the subpages in the Create Configuration Item Wizard automatically creates a compliance rule for that setting. As with Windows configuration items, settings without a compliance rule are not evaluated by the client. Two additional options are available for each setting group and are equivalent to the same options available for compliance rules in Windows configuration items:

▶ **Remediate noncompliant settings:** This setting automatically changes the value of the setting on the mobile device to the expected value.

▶ **Noncompliance severity for reports:** If the client agent determines that the mobile device does not meet the compliance rule, one of five different noncompliance severities is reported based on the chosen option:

 ▶ None

 ▶ Information

 ▶ Warning

 ▶ Critical

 ▶ Critical with event

You can also create new mobile device settings, similar to creating settings in a Windows configuration item. To create a new mobile device setting, check **Configure additional settings that are not in the default setting groups** on the Mobile Device Setting page of the Create Configuration Item Wizard. There are two types of custom mobile device settings:

▶ **Registry value:** This type is nearly identical to the Windows setting of the same name. You must specify the following values:

  ▶ Name

  ▶ Description

  ▶ Data Type

  ▶ Hive

  ▶ Key

  ▶ Value

▶ **Windows Mobile OMA URI:** Specifies the Open Mobile Alliance Uniform Resource Identifier for device provisioning. You can find more information on OMA on MSDN at http://msdn.microsoft.com/en-us/library/bb737369.aspx.

Child Configuration Items

You can organize configuration items into hierarchies by creating child configuration items. Child configuration items inherit all the evaluation criteria of their designated parent; these inherited criteria cannot be changed or removed in the child. You can add additional criterion, differentiating the child item from its parent.

One common use of child configuration items includes specialization of a more general configuration item. For example, you may create a generic configuration item that checks for organization-wide security standards. You could then create child configuration items to check for the more rigorous security standards of the Accounting and Human Resource departments. This scenario prevents duplication and reduces effort when an organization-wide setting requires changing because you need to update only the parent to update all child configuration items. If you are familiar with object-oriented programming, this concept is similar to class specialization through inheritance.

To create a child configuration item, select the desired parent configuration item, and choose **Create Child Configuration Item** from the ribbon bar or the right-click-context menu. This initiates the Create Child Configuration Item Wizard, which is nearly identical to the Create Configuration Item Wizard. Child configuration items are always the same type as their parent configuration item, so the wizard contains the pages for that type of configuration item (refer to Table 10.1). The General page of the Create Child Configuration Item Wizard does contain one additional option: the version of the parent configuration item. Versioning enables you to update a parent configuration item without affecting any dependent child configuration items. Configuration item versioning is covered in the "Versioning" section.

Configuration Baselines

As stated earlier, configuration baselines group configuration items together; the baselines are then deployed to collections for evaluation on members of that collection. You can add any number of configuration items to a baseline in any combination that makes sense for your purposes. You can also add software updates and other baselines to a baseline. Ultimately, a baseline is the aggregation of all the settings in configuration items that it contains.

To work with configuration baselines in the console, open Compliance Settings in the Assets and Compliance workspace, and select **Configuration Baselines**. You can use the console's built-in filtering and search capabilities to limit the baselines shown or find a particular baseline of interest. The following notable criteria are specific to filtering configuration baselines and described later in this section:

▶ **Revision:** Indicates the highest revision number of the configuration baseline. The "Versioning" section includes a complete discussion of versioning and revision numbers.

▶ **Compliance Count:** Indicates the number of systems that comply with the settings in the baseline.

▶ **Noncompliance Count:** Indicates the number of systems that do not comply with the settings in the baseline.

▶ **Failure Count:** Indicates the number of systems that encountered errors while evaluating the settings in the baseline.

▶ **Categories:** Includes the defined categories for the configuration baseline.

Double-clicking a baseline in the console or selecting one and choosing **Show Members** from the ribbon bar or right-click context menu creates a sticky node for that baseline under the Configuration Baselines node. Selecting a baseline sticky node lists the configuration items in that baseline.

To create a new baseline, choose **Create Configuration Baseline** from the ribbon bar or right-click context menu. Unlike almost every other object creation activity in ConfigMgr, creating a baseline does not have a wizard. Instead, a single-paged dialog is used, as shown in Figure 10.10.

Add your desired name and description for the new baseline at the top of this dialog and pick the desired categories at the bottom using the **Categories** button. Configuration items and baselines share the same set of categories from which to choose. Categories have no specific functional purpose outside of console organization.

The primary activity for creating a baseline is choosing the configuration data that it contains; these are collectively called the *evaluation conditions*. This is done using the **Add** button menu under the Configuration data list box, which has three choices when clicked:

▶ **Configuration Items**

▶ **Software Updates**

▶ **Configuration Baselines**

Each choice results in an object picker dialog, where you select the corresponding type of object to include in the baseline.

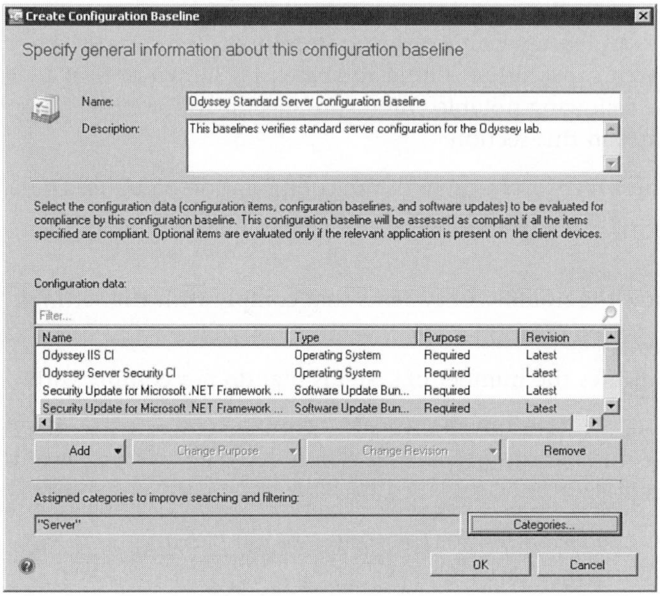

FIGURE 10.10   Create Configuration Baseline dialog.

You can change the configuration item revision included in the baseline by selecting the configuration item in the Configuration data list box and using the **Change Revision** button menu. This allows you to modify and test a configuration item without affecting those baselines to which it belongs. By default, the latest revision is included. Software updates and baselines always use the latest revision.

Application configuration items can have one of the following purposes:

▶ **Required:** The application defined in the configuration item must exist on the target system for it to be compliant. All settings in the configuration item are also evaluated for compliance.

▶ **Optional:** Settings in the configuration item are evaluated only for compliance if the application defined in the configuration item exists on a target system.

▶ **Prohibited:** The application defined in the configuration item must not exist on the target system for it to be compliant. All settings in the configuration item are ignored.

Software updates are always set to Required, meaning that they must exist on the target system. Baselines are also set to Required, although this has no real substantive meaning other than the configuration items in that baseline will be evaluated according to the evaluation conditions set in that baseline.

To modify a baseline including its evaluation conditions, select the baseline and choose **Properties** from the ribbon bar or right-click context menu to show the properties dialog box for the baseline. The Detail pane appears at the bottom of console when any baseline is selected. The Summary tab lists basic information about the baseline including deployment status and the following compliance statistics (which you can also add to the search filter as described earlier in this section):

▶ Compliance Count

▶ Noncompliance Count

▶ Failure Count

You can also disable a baseline; this prevents its evaluation on target systems even if the baseline is deployed as discussed in the next section. To disable a baseline, select it and then choose **Disable** from the ribbon bar or right-click context menu. Choose **Enable** from the same locations to re-enable it later.

Baseline Deployment

Deploying a baseline assigns it for evaluation on a selected set of client systems defined by a collection. Each baseline deployment has its own evaluation schedule; the schedule is by default set to the schedule defined in the Default Client Settings for the hierarchy (configuring client settings is discussed in the "Configuring Compliance Settings" section). To deploy a baseline, select the **Configuration Baselines** node or any configuration baseline; then choose **Deploy** from the ribbon bar or right-click context menu. This shows the Deploy Configuration Baselines dialog, displayed in Figure 10.11, where you configure the following properties for the deployment:

▶ Included configuration baselines

▶ Remediation for noncompliant rules when supported and remediation is outside maintenance windows

▶ Console alert generation based upon compliance percentage after a defined date and time

▶ System Center Operations Manager alert using the same criteria

▶ Target Collection

▶ Baseline evaluation schedule

In the spirit of System Center 2012 Configuration Manager's user-centric focus, you can target baselines to either device or user collections. When targeted at a user collection, user settings contained in the baseline are evaluated against the user currently logged in. Baselines without at least a single user setting do not make sense to deploy to users.

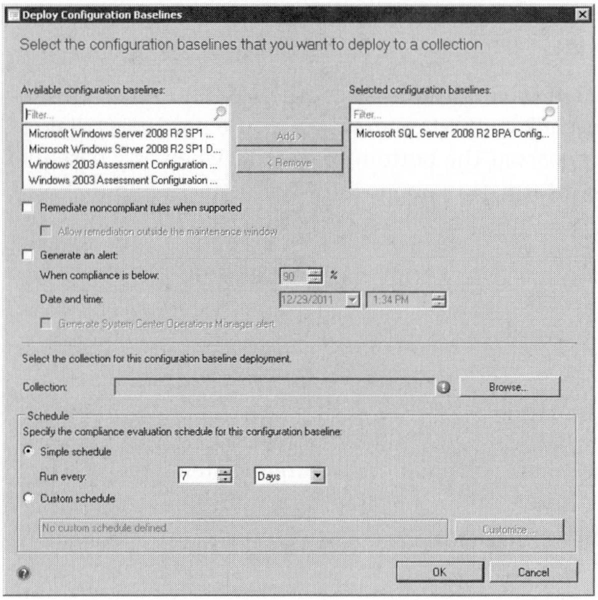

FIGURE 10.11   Deploy Configuration Baselines dialog.

Each baseline chosen has its own deployment created. To view all deployments for a specific baseline, select the baseline in the console. The Detail pane at the bottom has two tabs, including a Deployments tab; selecting this tab lists all deployments for the selected baseline.

To examine or modify baseline deployments, you can also open the Monitoring workspace and select the Deployments node. This node lists all deployments, not just baseline deployments. Use the console search and filtering capabilities to list or find the deployment you want to view or modify. Note that you cannot delete a baseline deployment from the Monitoring workspace. You must select the baseline in the Assets and Compliance workspace and delete its deployments from the Deployments tab of the Detail pane of the baseline.

To modify a deployment, select it and choose **Properties** from the ribbon bar or right-click context menu. This shows a dialog nearly identical to the Deploy Configuration Baselines dialog, as shown in Figure 10.10, where you can refine any of the deployments properties except the targeted collection. To change the targeted collection, you must create a new deployment for the baseline.

Baseline Monitoring

Using the Deployments node on the Monitoring workspace, you can monitor the evaluation status of any baseline deployment. For a quick summary, select a desired baseline and review the information in the Summary tab in the details pane, which includes compliance statistics viewed as a pie chart.

For more detailed information, click the **View Status** link in the Detail pane near the pie chart, select the baseline, and choose **View Status** from the ribbon bar or the right-click context menu, or double-click the wanted baseline. All these result in a new sticky node under the Deployments node for the baseline. Selecting this sticky node shows detailed information about the deployment status of the baseline in the deployment. The View pane shows four tabs, one for each compliance state, as discussed in the next section, "Compliance Evaluation." Listed under each tab are the compliance rules with systems in that state and a count of those systems. Selecting a compliance rule in the top pane lists the actual systems with that compliance state for that compliance rule in the **Asset Details** pane at the bottom.

Double-clicking a compliance rule in the top pane takes you to the Assets and Compliance workspace where a new sticky node is created under the Devices or Users node depending upon the collection type targeted by the baseline deployment. Figure 10.12 shows an example. This node resembles a collection and lists the applicable resources that, when selected, you can manage.

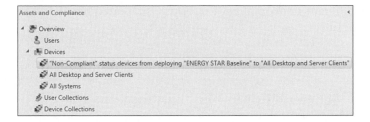

FIGURE 10.12   Compliance Rule Evaluation Status Sticky Node.

Double-clicking an asset from the Asset Details pane shows a dialog for that resource that lists each compliance rule on tabs for each applicable compliance state.

The information displayed here is summarized from information in the actual database. Summarizations are run automatically on a periodic basis and can be forced by choosing the **Run Summarization** option from the ribbon bar. The time of the last summarization displays in the upper right of the view pane along with links to Run Summarization and Refresh the view.

Compliance Evaluation

Clients receive new and updated compliance baseline deployments just like all other deployments and server-assigned actions in ConfigMgr: from the management point (MP) in a policy. The information needed for configuration settings compliance scans often takes more than one client policy refresh cycle to be fully staged to the client. During this period, the status of the scan will not match your expectations for the result of the scan; this is to be expected and should not be cause for alarm or an extensive troubleshooting exercise. Patiently wait for an extra policy refresh cycle; ConfigMgr will dutifully report its results in full.

Based on the applicable baseline deployments, clients evaluate the configuration items and settings contained in them using the corresponding compliance rules and based on the evaluation schedule defined. Actual evaluation starts randomly up to two hours after the defined time in the evaluation schedule to prevent overloading the MP.

Here are the four different compliance states for a baseline deployment:

▶ **Compliant:** The client system conforms to the compliance rules defined in the baseline's evaluation conditions as discussed in the "Baseline Deployment" section.

▶ **Error:** An error occurred on the client system while evaluating the baseline.

▶ **Non-Compliant:** The client system does not conform to the compliance rules defined in the baseline's evaluation conditions as discussed in the "Baseline Deployment" section.

▶ **Unknown:** The client system has not reported any status for the baseline.

If any compliance rule fails, the configuration item as a whole is marked as noncompliant for that system and one of five different noncompliance severities is reported based on the chosen option in the compliance rule:

▶ None

▶ Information

▶ Warning

▶ Critical

▶ Critical with event

The last severity type, Critical with event, also registers a message in the event log of the local client system.

The highest severity level for any failed compliance rule is used as the severity level for the configuration item. Results of these rules are sent back to ConfigMgr for reporting. Compliance rules that fail and are marked as Critical with event severity add an entry to the Windows application event log, such as the one shown in Figure 10.13. Based on these event log entries, you can configure an action using the Windows Task Scheduler (in Windows Vista and above) or use a tool such as System Center Operations Manager to generate an alert for further action.

Baseline and configuration item evaluation is a completely client-side task. The results are returned to the site using the state message mechanism built into ConfigMgr. State messages are asynchronous messages sent from the client to the management point to report information back to the site. State messages for compliance settings include eXtended Markup Language (XML) attachments to report specific details about the evaluation of configuration baselines and items. ConfigMgr consolidates these state messages in the database and makes the results available to end users in reports. For a detailed look at the state messaging system in ConfigMgr, review a blog post that is specific to ConfigMgr

2007 but also applicable to ConfigMgr 2012, at http://blogs.msdn.com/b/steverac/
archive/2011/01/07/sccm-state-messaging-in-depth.aspx.

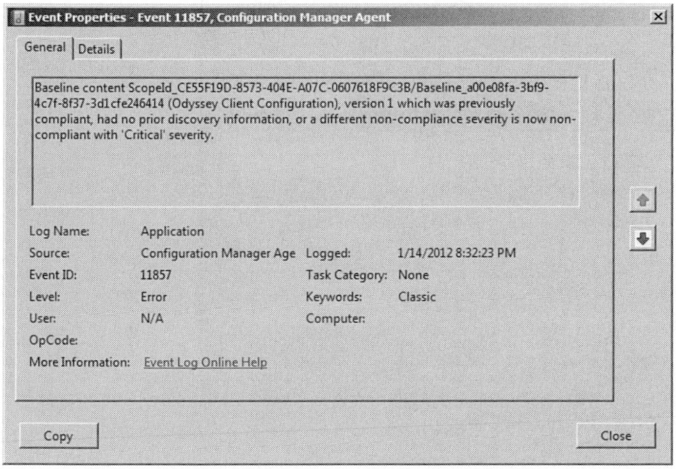

FIGURE 10.13   Noncompliance Event Log Entry.

ConfigMgr clients cache baseline evaluation results for 15 minutes. Unless a deployed
baseline has changed, the client will not re-evaluate the baseline until this 15-minute
caching interval expires, even if configured for a shorter evaluation period or you manually trigger its evaluation using the ConfigMgr Control Panel applet (described in the
"On-Demand Results" section).

Versioning

settings contains a fairly robust form of version control for its two main
iguration baseline and configuration items. Both object types have an associ-
number; every time one of these objects is updated, its version number is
and information about the update is stored including who updated it and
as updated. Version numbers are clearly shown in the console using the revi-
for both configuration items and baselines.

EGORIES AND REVISIONS

the categories of a configuration item or configuration baseline does not change
its version number.

In addition, entire previous versions of configuration items are also stored, enabling you
to roll back to them. You can directly reference a previous version of configuration items
in an evaluation condition as discussed in the "Configuration Baselines" section. To view
or manipulate previous versions of configuration items, select the wanted configuration
item, and choose **Revision History** from the ribbon bar or right-click context menu. This
shows the Configuration Item Revision History dialog, as shown in Figure 10.14.

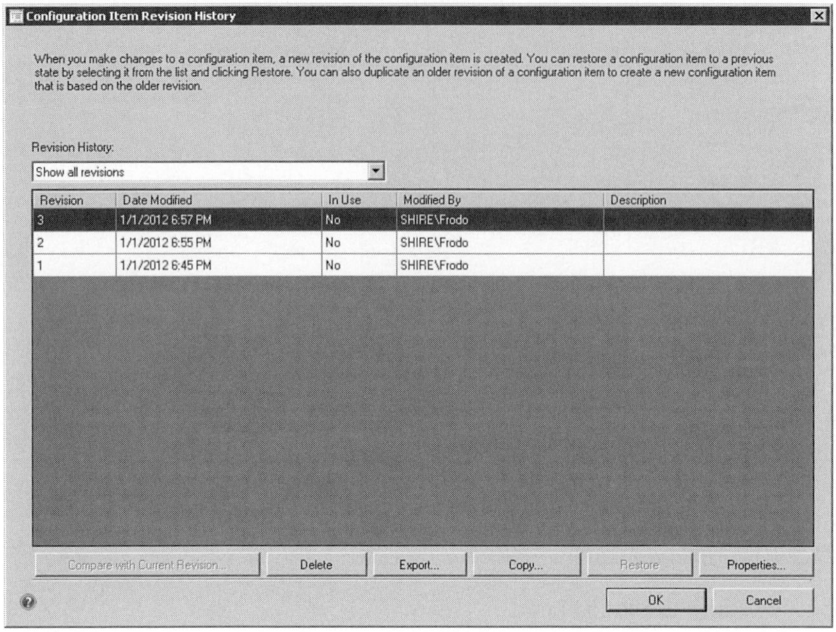

FIGURE 10.14   Configuration Item Revision History dialog.

From this dialog, you can see all previous versions of a configuration item, if the revision is in use, and who modified the configuration item to create the revision. In use configuration items are those referenced in a baseline. To display only in use configuration items, choose **Show Revisions in Use** from the Revision History from the drop-box at the top. You can also perform the following actions on a selected version in the Configuration Item Revision History dialog:

▶ **Compare with Current Revisions:** Only valid if the most recent revision is not selected, this option displays a dialog box showing all the differences between the selected version and the most recent version of the configuration item.

▶ **Delete:** Deletes the selected version of the configuration item.

▶ **Export:** Exports the selected version of the configuration item to a CAB file (see the "Exporting Configuration Items and Baselines" section for further information on these CAB files).

▶ **Copy:** Copies the selected version of the configuration item as a completely new configuration item.

▶ **Restore:** Copies the selected version of the configuration item as a new revision in the same configuration item while also making it the most recent version.

▶ **Properties:** Shows a read-only version of the Configuration Items Properties dialog box for the selected revision, allowing you to view its configuration and settings but not edit them.

> **NOTE: LOCKED CONFIGURATION BASELINES AND ITEMS**
>
> In ConfigMgr 2007, configuration baselines and items imported from a configuration pack or another hierarchy were "locked," so you could not edit them—to edit an imported baseline or configuration item, you first had to duplicate it. Because of the robust versioning capabilities in ConfigMgr 2012, this is no longer the case. Imported configuration baselines and items are fully editable; however, you can still roll back to previous versions as discussed in this section.
>
> Using the copy functionality on a configuration item or baseline does still has value for creating branches in the version history.

Configuration Packs

Microsoft understands there are many similarities and common requirements between IT organizations and has released a large number of configuration baselines to use as a starting point, as a reference, or as complete solutions. These baselines are encapsulated in configuration packs (CPs). Analogous to management packs in Operations Manager (OpsMgr), CPs are freely downloadable from Microsoft's System Center Marketplace at http://systemcenter.pinpoint.microsoft.com. Types of available CPs include the following:

▶ **Regulatory compliance:** Configuration packs intended for regulatory compliance, such as SOX, HIPAA, and the European Union Data Protection Directive (EUDPD).

▶ **Best practice:** CPs based on best-practice configurations used by Microsoft's internal IT department for major products such as Exchange, SQL Server, and Windows Server.

▶ **Third-party software and hardware:** As with the development of OpsMgr management packs, many third parties are starting to create and release CPs to help with your configuration enforcement efforts while using their products.

CPs designed for DCM in ConfigMgr 2007 are compatible with System Center 2012 Configuration Manager and continue to work as designed.

To import a baseline downloaded from the catalog, you must first extract it from the downloaded Microsoft Installer package. These packages do not actually install the configuration pack; they merely extract the necessary cabinet (.CAB) compressed file (similar to a self-extracting executable) to a folder of your choosing. Most CPs also include a Word document detailing the included configuration items and baselines. When these are extracted, perform the following steps to import the CP into ConfigMgr:

1. Open the Assets and Compliance workspace in the console.

2. Select Configuration Items or Configuration Baselines, and select **Import Configuration Data** from the ribbon bar or right-click context menu.

3. This opens the Import Configuration Data Wizard dialog. On the Select Files page, use the **Add** button to browse for the CAB files containing the desired CPs. You can

add multiple CPs to import simultaneously. Note the option at the bottom of the page: **Create a new copy of the imported configuration baselines and configuration items**. This option creates new copies of configuration items and baselines if you have previously imported them; without this option, the previously imported copy of the configuration items and baselines are overwritten possibly causing you lose any customizations you made to them.

4. Click **Next** to proceed to the Summary page, which displays all the configuration items and baselines in the CP and that ConfigMgr will import.

5. Complete the wizard.

Although the CPs available from Microsoft's Configuration Pack Catalog (search at http://systemcenter.pinpoint.microsoft.com/en-US/applications/search/configuration-manager-d10?q=) are quite useful, they do not cover every possibility and are somewhat generic at times. Eventually, you will want to create your own criteria by modifying the CPs provided by Microsoft, or creating your own to evaluate your systems. The next sections discuss this activity, known as *authoring*.

Exporting Configuration Items and Baselines

A final step after creating a new configuration item or baseline is to export it. Exporting gives you a way to share these with others, copy them to a separate ConfigMgr site, edit or view them in their native DCM Digest format, or back them up separate from ConfigMgr. Viewing the native XML is useful for reviewing and extracting scripts directly from a configuration item.

Exporting a configuration item or baseline creates a CAB file in the folder you specify; baseline exports include any contained configuration items. To export either object type, select it in the console, and choose **Export** from the ribbon bar or right-click context menu. The resulting CAB file is the equivalent of the Microsoft-supplied configuration packs and can be distributed and used in the same way.

Inside the CAB file of an exported baseline is an XML file for each configuration item and the baseline itself. You can actually create or edit these files outside of ConfigMgr if you are familiar with Service Modeling Language (SML)—an XML schema-based modeling language that provides a rich set of constructs for modeling complex IT services and systems using Microsoft's free Security Compliance Manager (SCM) or Silect Software's commercial product CP Studio. SCM and CP Studio are discussed in the "Compliance Authoring" section.

You can also directly view the XML of a configuration baseline or configuration item by selecting it in the console and choosing **View Xml Definition** from the ribbon bar or the right-click context menu. This opens the associated XML application on the local system (Internet Explorer by default) to show the XML for the chosen configuration item or baseline.

Compliance Authoring

The main purpose of the ConfigMgr console in compliance settings management is to deploy, organize, create, and edit configuration baselines and configuration items. The built-in toolset for these last two activities (creating and editing) is fairly complete, vastly improved from ConfigMgr 2007, and described fully in the "Configuration Items" and "Configuration Baselines" sections.

The biggest challenge when creating custom configuration items is translating the business requirement or user interface-based setting into items ConfigMgr expects and can act on. The most common place to store and query settings from is the Windows registry. Other locations include WMI, Active Directory, and SQL Server. Compliance settings using one of the setting types can evaluate all these and more.

How do you determine where to look in the first place? Many resources can help you with this endeavor. First and foremost is experience with Windows. An intimate knowledge of the registry and of where Windows stores values will make your task much easier. The ability to write custom scripts and use WMI will also help tremendously. As the old cliché goes, *There's no substitute for experience.*

Of course, even an intimate knowledge of these things does not mean you know every single registry key or WMI class available. For that, there is TechNet and the Internet. A number of excellent books are also available on these subjects.

NOTE: OUTSIDE-THE-BOX USES OF COMPLIANCE SETTINGS

Typically, you might think of compliance settings as a vehicle to detect drift, but that doesn't have to be the case. Forefront Endpoint Protection (FEP) in 2007, for example, used DCM to check for various conditions with full anticipation that the baseline evaluation would show failure. It actually wasn't a failure but instead the baseline contained multiple checks, all but one of which was intended to fail so that you could find the real condition.

Organization

Similar to the organization of individual policies within a group policy object, organizing settings within configuration items and configuration items within baselines is an important point of planning. Technically, no real organization is needed: You can just throw all your settings into a single configuration item and baseline and be done. The problem with this, though, is that should something go wrong and you have to troubleshoot an issue, the number of settings in the configuration item will get in the way.

In general, following the "keep it simple, stupid" or KISS principal (like most things in life) is beneficial. Organize like settings into a single configuration item; for example, put all of your Internet Explorer settings into a single configuration item. Then, if you need to isolate those settings, you can create a baseline only containing that configuration item or remove it altogether from a baseline leaving the rest of the referenced configuration items and their settings intact.

Putting too few settings, like one, in a configuration item provides great isolation but forces you to create and maintain a larger number of configuration items resulting in more complexity and thus overhead.

When you have these like-group configuration items, they are also easy to mix and match to build up your baselines—somewhat like LEGOS®. Think of the configuration items as building blocks representing atomic units of functionality. Combining these in different ways results in a diverse and comprehensive set of baselines that are easier to maintain and troubleshoot.

CAUTION: EVALUATION IMPACT ON CLIENT PERFORMANCE

Most evaluations are quick and have a negligible impact on client systems; however, it is possible to create complex configuration items or pack a baseline so full of configuration items it will affect the end user. Software updates compliance items in particular impact a client's performance, particularly when many are packed into a single baseline. Test carefully and fully before deploying a baseline to ensure the impact is not noticeable to your end users or is at least acceptable. Script-based configuration items can also greatly affect a client's performance. For this reason, System Center 2012 Configuration Manager added a one-minute timeout for all scripts.

Using Microsoft Tools

An excellent resource is the Microsoft-provided configuration packs. Microsoft has put a significant amount of work into creating them, and they provide great examples of how and where to find settings. Even if you do not actually intend to use them, it is still a good idea to download and install these CPs just to dissect them and use them as a reference. Many of the evaluation criteria are checked using custom scripts. You can easily copy these scripts and use them in your own configuration items as is or with simple modifications; it is usually much easier to modify someone else's working script than create your own from scratch.

Registry Monitor (RegMon) and Process Monitor (ProcMon) are some of the greatest all around Windows utilities available—these are available as free downloads from Microsoft's Sysinternals site at http://technet.microsoft.com/en-us/sysinternals/default.aspx. (All of the capabilities of RegMon are rolled into ProcMon, and RegMon does not run on Windows Vista or newer operating systems.) These tools monitor the registry and record every change made to it, letting you identify the exact location of any modification occurring to a system. As an example, suppose you wanted to create an evaluation criteria to determine if Remote Desktop is disabled but don't know where this setting is stored in the registry. After starting ProcMon, make the change in the GUI, and the registry change will be displayed in the ProcMon window.

Detailed use of ProcMon is beyond the scope of this book but is straightforward; the help file provided with ProcMon is excellent and in-depth. The book *Windows Sysinternals Administrator's Reference* (Microsoft Press, 2011) by Mark Russinovich and Aaron Margosis has an entire chapter devoted to ProcMon.

Security Compliance Manager (SCM)

SCM is a free tool from Microsoft available at http://www.microsoft.com/download/en/details.aspx?displaylang=en&id=16776. SCM is a completely separate tool for creating and managing baselines of settings. It does not actually have a way to apply baselines to systems and instead relies on ConfigMgr, group policy, or tools conforming to the National Institute of Standards and Technology's Security Content Automation Protocol (SCAP).

SCM includes a large number of baselines covering Windows, Office, and Internet Explorer configurations. You can also import settings from a group policy backup, an export from ConfigMgr 2007's DCM, or an export from ConfigMgr 2012's compliance settings. You can't directly create a new baseline, but all imported baselines as well as the built-in baselines are completely customizable; you must first duplicate a built-in baseline to modify it.

Using SCM's capability to import a group policy object (GPO) is an easy way to kick-start your development of baselines in ConfigMgr. The built-in SCM baselines are also a fast track to creating baselines in ConfigMgr. From SCM, you can then export any baseline for import into ConfigMgr's compliance settings.

CP Studio

CP Studio is a third party offering from Silect Software (http://www.silect.com) that, like SCM, enables authoring of configuration baselines and configuration items outside the ConfigMgr console. This separation allows users or admins without ConfigMgr console access to author baselines and configuration items. In addition, CP Studio provides a richer and often more intuitive set of authoring tools that fills multiple gaps in the built-in toolset, including a WMI browser and an integrated testing module that enables direct baseline evaluation and testing on targeted systems without going through ConfigMgr to do so. The supplementary capabilities all add up to a shorter development lifecycle and a faster time to production for your baselines.

Compliance Strategy

Compliance settings functionality is relatively straightforward: Create a baseline of settings and deploy those to a set of systems. However, what do you do then? The answer (of course!) is, *It depends*. It actually depends on what you are going to do with the data provided.

What are your business goals for using compliance settings? Are you simply filling a check box for the auditors? Do you want to use reports to help in troubleshooting? Do you want to notify the on-call admin when something is amiss? Or do you want nonstandard configurations corrected? Each baseline you create may fulfill one or more of these goals; therefore, the first step for each baseline is to identify its purpose, the target audience, and the delivery method for results. These criteria define what criteria to include in the baseline.

After you identify these requirements, you can then set out defining the settings and evaluation rules (as discussed previously in the "Configuration Items" section) and how you enable the target audience to consume the results of the baseline evaluation. The following sections discuss this last mile for the results after performing an evaluation.

Reporting

In addition to monitoring compliance settings results in the console as described in the "Baseline Monitoring" section, ConfigMgr reporting offers another way to view and distribute the compliance results of your deployed baselines. A variety of reports are included out-of-the-box to assist with this:

▶ List of rules conflicting with a specified rule for an asset

▶ Summary compliance by configuration baseline

▶ Details of remediated rules of configuration items in a configuration baseline for an asset

▶ Compliance history of a configuration item

▶ Compliance history of a configuration baseline

▶ List of unknown assets for a configuration baseline

▶ Details of conflicting rules of configuration items in a configuration baseline for an asset

▶ Rules and errors summary of configuration items in a configuration baseline for an asset

▶ Details of compliant rules of configuration items in a configuration baseline for an asset

▶ Details of errors of configuration items in a configuration baseline for an asset

▶ Details of noncompliant rules of configuration items in a configuration baseline for an asset

▶ List of assets by compliance state for a configuration item in a configuration baseline

▶ List of assets by compliance state for a configuration baseline

▶ Summary compliance of a configuration baseline for a collection

▶ Summary compliance by configuration items for a configuration baseline

With the excellent flexibility of SQL Reporting Services (SSRS) reporting, rich reporting is available through a web browser without giving any type of access to the console. This is great for middle- and upper-management or those annoying auditors who interrupt you every time they need to see this data. See Chapter 18 for an in-depth look at reporting in ConfigMgr.

Knowing is half the battle; therefore, reporting is also typically only half the battle. What you do with the information in a report is the other half. Actions can include alerting to make everyone aware of the issue and using an automated mechanism to correct the reported issues.

On-Demand Results

In addition to using the server-side reporting functionality in ConfigMgr and console monitoring, administrative users can also trigger client-side report generation. After you enable compliance settings in the console using client settings as described in the "Compliance Settings Configuration" section, a new tab is available in the ConfigMgr Control Panel applet on clients where it is enabled, titled Configurations (shown in Figure 10.15). Each baseline deployed to the client is included in the list box. Using the Evaluate button at the bottom of the page, users can trigger the evaluation of selected baselines. Using the View Report button, administrative users can display a report showing the most current evaluation results of the selected baseline. A typical use of this on-demand reporting is for IT personnel to locally troubleshoot or remediate identified noncompliance issues.

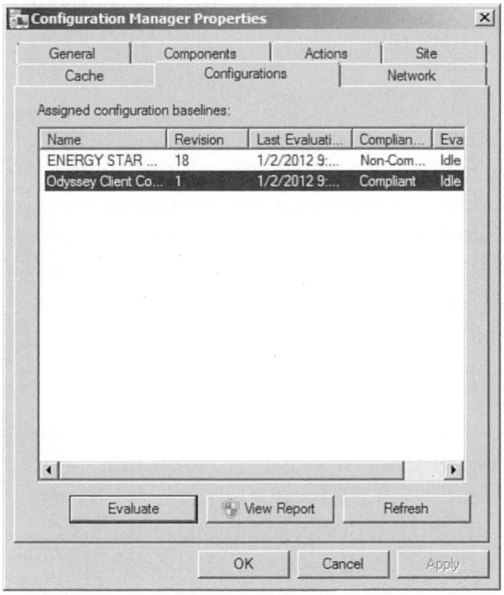

FIGURE 10.15   Configurations Control Panel Applet tab.

Alerting

Although ConfigMgr itself is not designed to be a real-time reporting or alerting system, it is perfectly reasonable to want the evaluation results of a baseline to raise a real-time alert. Like all alerting, how you use this alert in your organization and the process to handle it is up to you.

There are three forms of alerting for compliance settings in ConfigMgr 2012:

▶ **Using console alerts:** Console alerts are enabled individually on each baseline deployment and generate in-console alerts for deployed baselines under a specific percentage threshold for compliance evaluation after a specified date and time. You can review console alerts and their status in the Monitoring workspace under Alerts. For more information about console alerts, see Chapter 8, "The Configuration Manager Console."

▶ **Using Operations Manager (OpsMgr) on the server:** OpsMgr server alerts are directly generated by the ConfigMgr server according to the same criteria as in-console alerts. The OpsMgr agent must be installed on the ConfigMgr site server and the ConfigMgr management pack must be installed and properly configured in OpsMgr.

▶ **Using Operations Manager on the target system:** OpsMgr alerts on the target system rely on OpsMgr's abilities to scrape the event log and are generated when a compliance rule configured with the Critical with event severity is evaluated as noncompliant. This places an event in the Windows event log on the target system that is picked up using a custom monitor in OpsMgr.

Remediation

Knowing about an issue using an on-demand report or receiving an alert doesn't help if the issue identified is causing a security hole or service interruptions for users—what you want is to fix the issue as quickly as possible without human intervention. As was briefly touched on in the "Configuration Items and Baselines" section, remediation refers to the process of correcting an issue identified, and auto-remediation is having the issue corrected in an automated manner. In both cases, compliance settings identifies the issue using a baseline assigned to a system in your organization.

There are two built-in strategies for auto-remediation in ConfigMgr 2012:

▶ **Using the built-in remediation:** This type of remediation is new in System Center 2012 Configuration Manager. For the supported Windows configuration item setting types (WMI, registry value, and script), you can enable remediation in compliance rules referencing these settings. All settings in mobile device configuration items support remediation with a similar option in their configuration. Enabling this option causes baseline evaluation to modify the settings value on the target system to the expected value.

▶ **Creating collections:** For settings that do not support the built-in remediation or require more than just correcting a single value, you can build a collection and deploy a program, an application, or a software update to that collection. Perform the following steps to create these collections:

 1. Select the desired baseline from the console.

 2. From the details pane at the bottom, select the **Deployments** tab.

 3. Select the appropriate deployment, and choose **Create New Collection** from the ribbon bar or right-click context menu.

4. This results in a fly-out menu with the four compliance statuses as options. Choose the wanted compliance status for the new collection.

5. A Create Device Collection Wizard dialog is displayed; this is the same dialog as when you manually create a new collection except that all the information, including a query membership rule, is provided for you. Complete the wizard to create the new collection.

▶ After creating the collection, you deploy a package, application, or software update that corrects the issue to the collection. This could be as simple as reinstalling the antivirus software that an application administrator accidentally on purpose uninstalled. Alternatively, it could be a complex script delivered using a package. The actual actions performed are up to you and should correct any noncompliant issues that the baseline can identify. Those systems failing the compliance checks in the baseline automatically populate the collection, which in turn deploys your corrective action to them thus correcting the issue.

Troubleshooting

As with all automated systems, many assumptions are made about the environment in which the system is operating. When these assumptions no longer hold true, the system fails to operate as expected. Compliance settings management is an automated system and therefore operates on certain assumptions. When issues arise, troubleshooting is necessary to determine which assumption or assumptions are no longer true.

Troubleshooting compliance settings, like the rest of ConfigMgr, is largely a log file review exercise. Because compliance settings evaluation is a client activity, the logs for compliance setting processing are on the client in the client logs folder (*%SystemRoot%*\CCM\ Logs). Five log files are used by compliance settings to store activity; Table 10.6 describes these files. A complete list of log files is also available in Appendix A, "Configuration Manager Log Files."

TABLE 10.6   Compliance Settings Log Files

Filename	Description
ciagent.log	Provides information about downloading, storing, and accessing assigned configuration baselines
CITaskManager.log	Records information about configuration item task scheduling
dcmagent.log	Provides high-level information about the evaluation of assigned configuration baselines plus information regarding compliance settings processes
DCMReporting.log	Records information about reporting policy platform results into state messages for configuration items
DcmWmiProvider.log	Records information about reading configuration item synclets WMI

The Rules and errors summary of configuration items in a configuration baseline for an asset report is also of great value when troubleshooting an issue as it should clearly point out why the client is having issues.

In addition, issues involving the capability for ConfigMgr to evaluate a baseline or configuration item are reported through the ConfigMgr status message reporting mechanism. To view these status messages, perform the following procedure:

1. Navigate to the Monitoring workspace.

2. Expand System Status in the navigation tree, and select **Status Message Queries**.

3. From the list of status message queries on the right, select **All Status Messages**, and select **Show Messages** from the ribbon bar or right-click context menu.

4. In the All Status Messages dialog box, enter the wanted timeframe for which you would like to see status messages.

5. Review the displayed messages looking for the message IDs, as listed in Table 10.7.

TABLE 10.7   Compliance Settings Status Message IDs

Message ID	Description
11800	Indicates a download failure for a configuration item
11801	Indicates a hash failure for a configuration item
11802	Indicates that the .NET Framework 2.0 is not installed
11850	Indicates a download failure for SML content
11851	Indicates the policy could not be uncompressed
11853	Indicates the client computer has evaluated one or more assigned configuration baselines but cannot send the compliance results to its management point
11854	Indicates a compliance change from noncompliant to compliant or from unknown to compliant
11855	Indicates a compliance change to noncompliant with a noncompliance severity level of Information
11856	Indicates a compliance change to noncompliant with a noncompliance severity level of Warning
11857	Indicates a compliance change to noncompliant with a noncompliance severity level of Error
11858	Indicates that packages for SML content could not be uncompressed
11859	Indicates a failure in evaluating a configuration item
11860	Indicates a failure in evaluating SML content
11861	Indicates a failure in the SML discovery type process
11862	Indicates the SML discovery type is halted

Using the message IDs listed in Table 10.7, you can narrow down issues in compliance settings baseline and configuration item evaluation. These status messages also provide the ability to track and monitor the evaluation status of baselines in your site.

Summary

Compliance settings, with a little expertise, creativity, and hard work on your part, is an excellent tool that provides feedback about the configuration and compliance of Windows systems and mobile devices. With the new remediation features, it also enforces compliance ensuring standard configurations and settings across the enterprise. (*Resistance* is *futile.*) It does this while seamlessly integrating with the rest of ConfigMgr, providing a "single pane of glass" to manage your systems from cradle to grave, top to bottom, and every other cliché you can think of. Just having the ability to provide consistent and timely compliance reports to auditors is always critical for any type of review. Compliance settings does this and more.

Those familiar with group policy may now wonder which is the appropriate tool to configure systems in their organization. There is no clear answer to this question, and even Microsoft is still crafting the answer to this, but the authors suggest the answer is "*It depends.*" It depends on many different factors and your goals. One advantage with compliance settings is reporting. Group policy simply has no way to verify it is doing what is says it is doing. Actually, many ConfigMgr 2007 administrators used DCM to verify group policy in their enterprise.

Compliance settings efficiently fills a major blind spot in most organizations—configuration and compliance verification and enforcement—without having to implement any additional enterprise tools.

With the growing burden of IT audits and compliance regulations, compliance settings is a powerful feature set in ConfigMgr and System Center.

10

CHAPTER 11

Packages and Programs

One of the challenges of client/server administration and distributed computing is managing the software deployed to those systems. The ability to manage software includes

▶ Deploying software as required on workstations, servers, and Windows mobile devices

▶ Updating existing software packages

▶ Providing a comprehensive inventory of installed software packages

▶ Removing software from systems where it does not belong

These topics are discussed throughout the chapters of *System Center 2012 Configuration Manager Unleashed*. The first item in the list—software distribution—has been a core component of Systems Management Server (SMS) since Microsoft first released the product in 1994. This functionality has evolved over the various versions of SMS, and it continues to be a core capability in Microsoft's newest release of the software, System Center 2012 Configuration Manager (ConfigMgr). However, before deploying, updating, inventorying, or removing software, you will most likely need to package it for use by ConfigMgr. Software packaging is a core component of distributing software in ConfigMgr.

This chapter discusses how software packaging works in System Center 2012 Configuration Manager and provides examples of how to deploy software with ConfigMgr. Chapter 12, "Creating and Managing Applications," takes you through the application model, an enhanced method of software delivery and new in this version of ConfigMgr. Chapter 13, "Distributing and Deploying Applications," is the next logical step, where you distribute and deploy packages and applications.

NOTE: FOCUS ON THE APPLICATION MODEL

This chapter discusses packages, which have been used in the product since the first days of Systems Management Server. If you have worked with ConfigMgr/SMS for many years, you are probably most comfortable working with the package/program paradigm. Take the opportunity now to move to the new application model (covered in Chapter 12), and use only traditional packages when absolutely necessary.

About Packages, Programs, Collections, Distribution Points, and Deployments

This chapter and Chapters 12 and 13 focus on software deployment. This chapter starts by discussing some of the key terms associated with software deployment in ConfigMgr and how these capabilities interact with each other. The next sections discuss packages, programs, collections, distribution points, and deployments.

Packages

A software *package* consists of general information about the software to deploy, including the name, version, manufacturer, language, and where source files for the package are located (if that package has source files). Packages are created either from a package definition file (such as an MSI, SMS, or PDF file—discussed in more detail later in the "Creating a Package" section), or manually. Software packages within ConfigMgr can be a repackaging of the software packaged by a vendor or an unintended installation direct from the vendor. ConfigMgr uses the MSI installation file to automatically populate many of the software deployment settings available for the package and program. You can also create software packages without using package definition files. ConfigMgr provides the ability to deploy executables, batch files, VBScript, JavaScript, and command files, among others. If you can execute it, you can design a package to deploy it!

Programs, described in the next section, provide the specifics of how the software runs and are optional components of a package. The package also contains information about who can access it (security) and where it is distributed (distribution points).

ConfigMgr uses packages to distribute software, as well as to deploy changes to client configurations, such as registry changes.

Programs

A package contains one or more *programs*. These are commands specifying what should occur on a client when the package is received. A program can do just about anything;

it can install software, distribute data, run antivirus software, or update the client configuration.

Each package must contain at least one program if the package will perform any action other than to provide a pointer to the source files. Most MSI files provide six default programs when used for software distribution, each allowing the package to run in different ways:

▶ **Per-system attended:** This installation causes a program to install, expects user interaction, and is run once for the system on which it is targeted to install.

▶ **Per-system unattended:** This installation causes a program to install that expects to run without user interaction and is run once for the system on which it is targeted to install.

▶ **Per-system uninstall:** This installation performs an uninstallation of the program and is run once for the system on which it is targeted to uninstall.

▶ **Per-user attended:** This installation causes a program to install and expects user interaction and is run once for the user for whom it is targeted to install.

▶ **Per-user unattended:** This installation causes a program to install without user interaction and runs once for the user for whom it is targeted to install.

▶ **Per-user uninstall:** This installation performs an uninstallation of the program and is run once for the user for whom it is targeted to uninstall.

Each program specifies the command line used to run the program in the method described. As an example, a per-system unattended installation will include a switch to run the program without user intervention.

Collections

A *collection* represents resources within ConfigMgr. A collection is a logical grouping and can consist of computers, users, or security groups. In ConfigMgr 2012, a collection can contain devices or users, but not both. Collections provide a target for ConfigMgr functions such as software distribution. Collections can be either static (defined to specific resources) or dynamic (built either on a query you define or on an existing query that comes prebuilt with ConfigMgr). Chapter 13 discusses collections in detail.

Distribution Points

A *distribution point* (DP) is a ConfigMgr server role where packages are stored for later distribution, making it similar in nature to a file share containing software used for installations. Clients connect to DPs for installation source files (either run from the DP, or downloaded to cache, and then run). Chapter 13 includes additional information about distribution points.

Deployments

A *deployment* ties these concepts together. A deployment says to take a specific program within a package and make it available to a collection, and it specifies the distribution point(s) to use when deploying the program. Deployments are either Available (they show as available for the user to install) or Required (can also be made available for the user to install before the deadline, or can be installed silently at deadline time). In System Center 2012 Configuration Manager, deployment is a general term used for deploying multiple types of items, such as packages, applications, software updates, compliance settings, client agent settings, and more.

Combining the Use of Packages, Programs, Collections, and Deployments

Consider a package containing multiple programs. That package is sent to a distribution point and deployed to a collection. Although this looks like a relatively complex way to distribute software, it is also a powerful approach. Let's break this down into a simple example of how these concepts work together.

You need to distribute an application called MyApp to the HR department this week. Perform the following steps:

1. Create a package for the application, and then create an unattended installation and (optionally, but recommended) an uninstallation program within the package.

2. Define a collection of the workstations used by the HR department personnel. The users of the HR application are all located in the corporate office, which has a single distribution point used when distributing software from ConfigMgr.

3. Create a deployment that ties this all together. The deployment ties the package and the program (MyApp unattended installation) to the collection (the HR workstations) and the distribution point used for installing the software (corporate distribution point).

Knowing how these concepts combine is critical for understanding how ConfigMgr deploys software. Chapter 13 provides additional information on how ConfigMgr distributes software.

Creating a Package

Because the focus of this chapter is software packaging, the next sections walk through the steps to create a package in ConfigMgr and provide examples of the process.

Packages can come in many flavors:

▶ Packages that use a definition file.

    You can create ConfigMgr packages either with a definition file or without. A *definition file* provides the answers to the majority of the questions required to create a package.

SMS 1.x definition files had an extension of PDF (Package Definition File). With SMS 2.0, you created the definitions in files using either a PDF or SMS (Systems Management Server) extension. Although these two types of definition files still exist and you can use them with ConfigMgr to create a package, they are relatively uncommon now.

The package definition file most commonly used by System Center 2012 Configuration Manager is the MSI file. The next section of this chapter includes an example of using an MSI file.

▶ Packages that you can create without a definition file.

▶ A package that does not need to have source files as part of the package. This is often used when ConfigMgr is used to run a program already stored on the system.

The goal remains the same, regardless of how it is achieved. ConfigMgr takes these different types of packages and integrates them to create Configuration Manager packages. To illustrate how this is accomplished, the next sections step through an example using a relatively simple package to deploy.

Creating a Package from the Package Definition Wizard

7-Zip (http://sourceforge.net/projects/sevenzip/) is a handy freeware archiving utility that you can use with .zip, .iso, .7z, and many other archive types. This chapter uses the Windows installer distributable of 7-Zip to walk through the process of creating a package from a definition. Download the latest version (in .msi format) for both x86 and x64 (for example, 7z922.msi and 7z922-x64.msi).

Creating the ConfigMgr package for 7-Zip is straightforward and only requires several steps:

1. Download and save the installation file(s) to a share that is accessible by the site server. (ConfigMgr requires you specify a UNC path in the package.) For this example, the source path is \\armada\ConfigMgr\Packages\Software\7-Zip.

2. From the ConfigMgr console, navigate to **Software Library -> Overview-> Application Management -> Packages**, and select **Create -> Create Package from Definition** from the ribbon. The wizard appears, as shown in Figure 11.1.

3. On the **Create Package from Definition Wizard**, click **Browse** and navigate to the .msi. Choose the x86 version for this example. Figure 11.2 shows the imported package definition metadata for 7-Zip version 9.22. Click **Next** to continue.

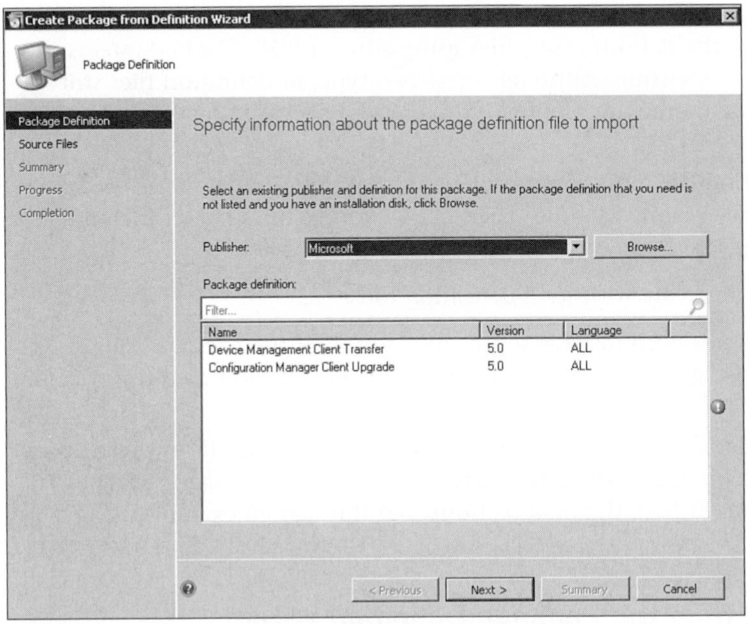

FIGURE 11.1   Selecting the publisher and file to import in the Create Package from Definition Wizard.

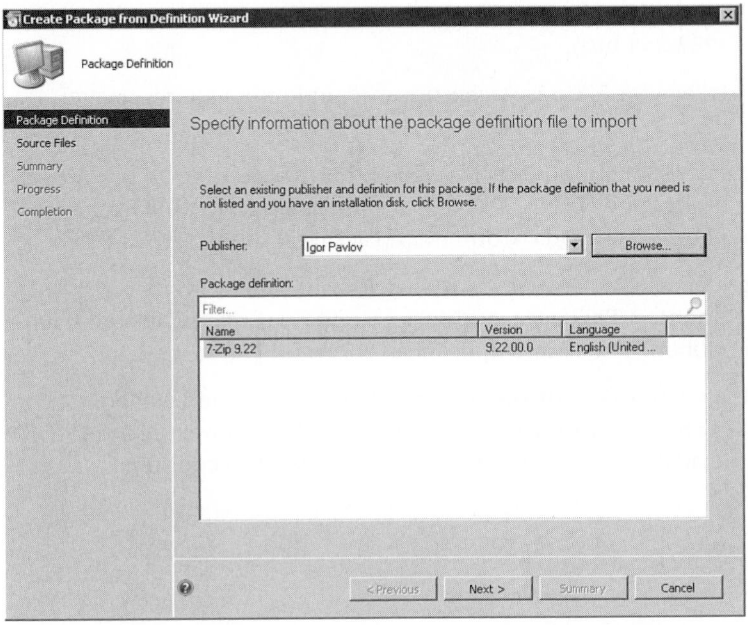

FIGURE 11.2   Specifying Package Definition metadata.

4. The next page of the wizard identifies three different ways you can manage source files:

▶ **This package does not contain any source files:** This may be useful in a configuration where ConfigMgr is running a program already stored on the system.

▶ **Always obtain files from a source folder:** This option is the one most commonly used.

▶ **Create a compressed version of the source files:** This may be useful when you need to decrease storage requirements or don't expect the package to change.

Select the second option for this package—**Always obtain files from a source folder**—as shown in Figure 11.3. Click **Next** to continue.

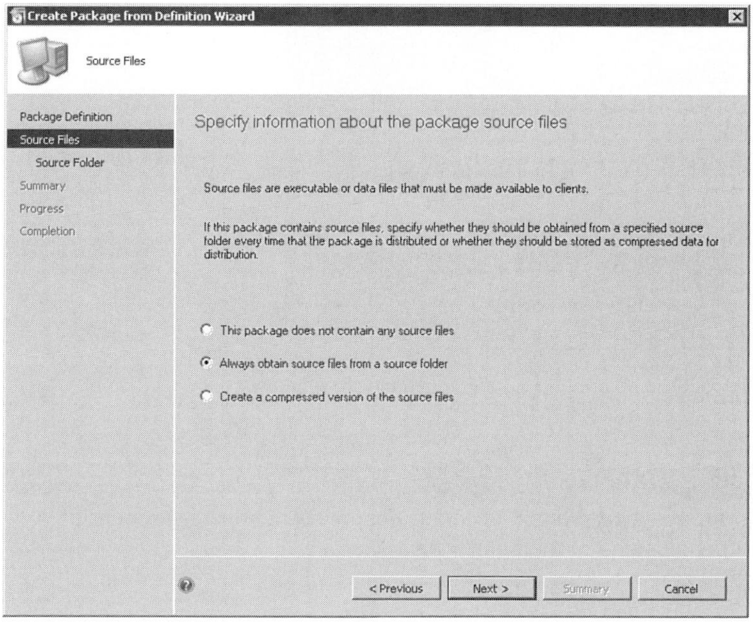

FIGURE 11.3   Specify how source files are created in the Create Package from Definition Wizard.

5. The wizard next verifies the location of the source files. This step appears if the option selected on the previous page of the wizard specified source files were part of the package; if the package did not contain any source files, this page does not appear.

Specify the package source location, choosing either **Network path** or **Local folder**. As a best practice, always try to use network path. Applications (discussed in Chapter 12) require UNC paths. If you decide to convert a package to an application using the Package Conversion Manager discussed in Chapter 12, a UNC path will be required. Specify the path to the source installation folder. Keep in mind that the contents of the selected folder and all subfolders will be sent to each targeted distribution point, so try to keep source files organized, reducing any chance for extra files and folders to be distributed for a package. Figure 11.4 shows the desired source path for 7-Zip. Click **Next** to continue.

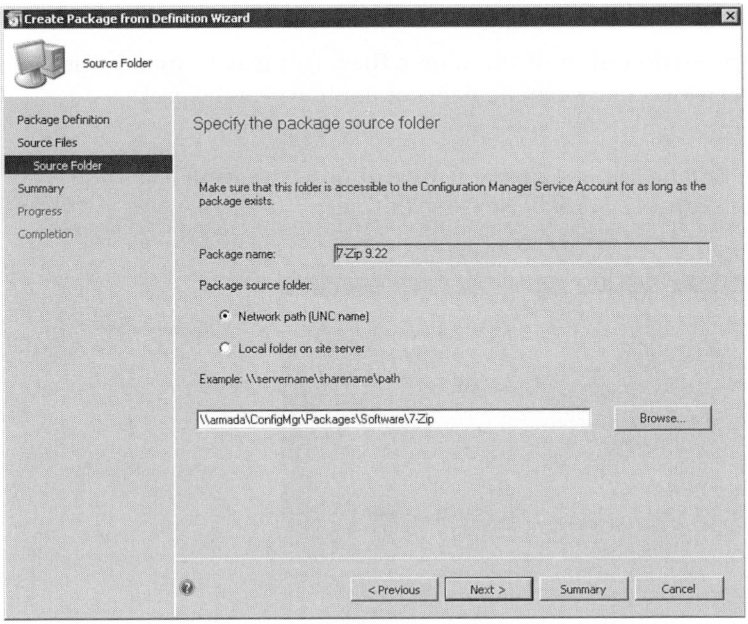

FIGURE 11.4   Specifying package source folder.

NOTE: CONFIGMGR PROCESSES USE LOCAL SYSTEM ACCOUNT

ConfigMgr processes run as the Local System account. Ensure the computer account of the site server has Read permissions to the source files share.

---

6. Review the Summary page of the Create Package from Definition Wizard, displayed in Figure 11.5, which lists the options chosen to create the package. These include the name of the package, how to handle source files, and the location of the source folder. Click **Next** to create the desired package.

7. The Progress page appears for several moments and then automatically changes to the Completion page. Review the status of this page (as shown in Figure 11.6), and then click **Close**. Using the information in the .msi file, the wizard now creates a set of installation options for the program, including Per-system attended, Per-system unattended, Per-system uninstall, Per-user attended, Per-user unattended, and Per-user uninstall, as displayed in Figure 11.8.

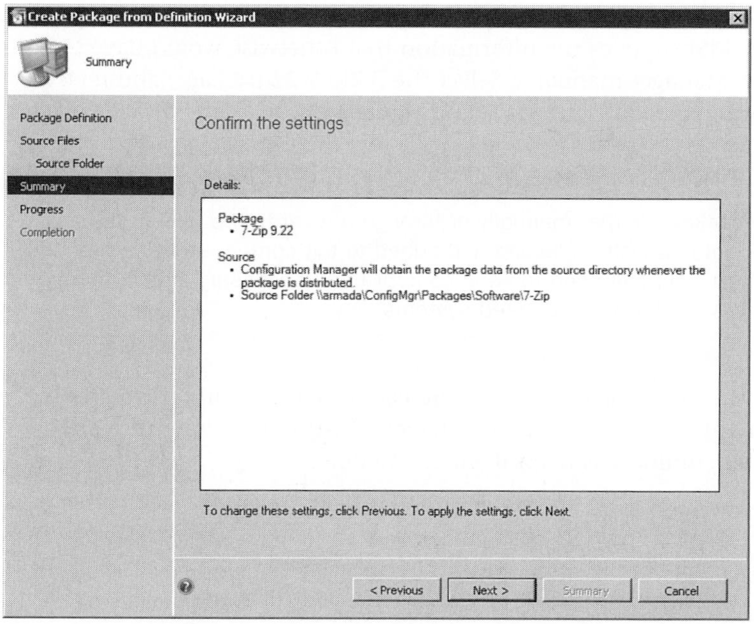

FIGURE 11.5   The Summary page of the Create Package from Definition Wizard.

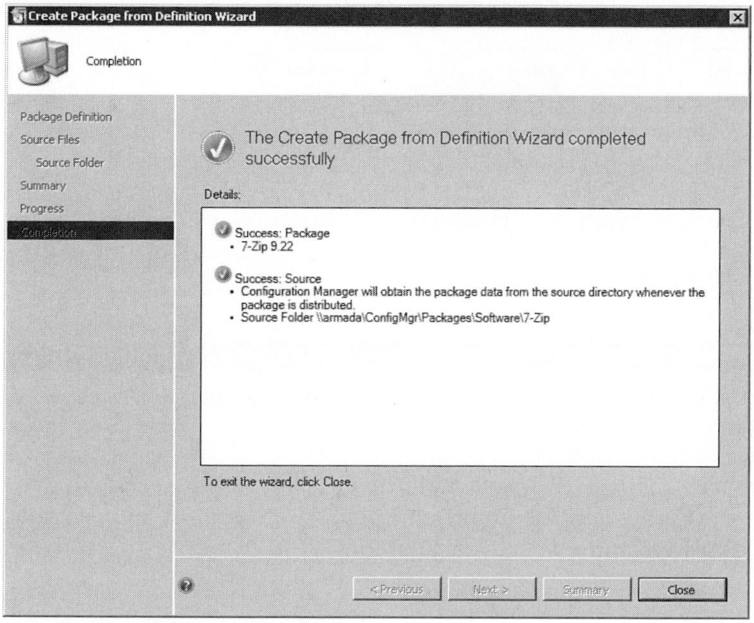

FIGURE 11.6   Completion page of the Create Package from Definition Wizard.

Using an MSI file for the package definition greatly simplifies the process of creating the 7-Zip package because the MSI supplies the information that otherwise would have to be specified to Configuration Manager manually. Select the 7-Zip 9.22 package, and review the Summary and Programs panes in Figure 11.7 and Figure 11.8.

NOTE: CONTENT AUTOMATICALLY ADDED TO STORE AT CREATION

When you create a new package (either manually or through a wizard), the files in the content source path are automatically collected and added to the content store on the site that owns the package. You still need to send content to all necessary distribution points to ensure content is available for targeted systems.

The Summary tab, as shown in Figure 11.7, shows the PackageID (helpful for trouble-shooting), as well as Content Status. Although you haven't distributed content to any distribution points yet, this summary is helpful when you do.

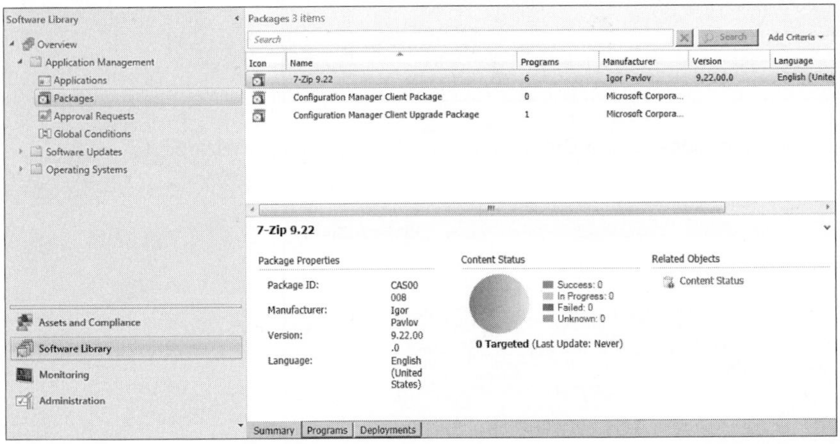

FIGURE 11.7   Package Summary information.

TIP: SELECTING ADDITIONAL COLUMNS FOR VIEWING

You can also right-click the column header to display additional package data.

The Programs tab, as shown in Figure 11.8, displays all the programs for the selected package. Because you ran the Create Package from Definition Wizard against an .msi, you can see the six programs that were automatically created for 7-Zip.

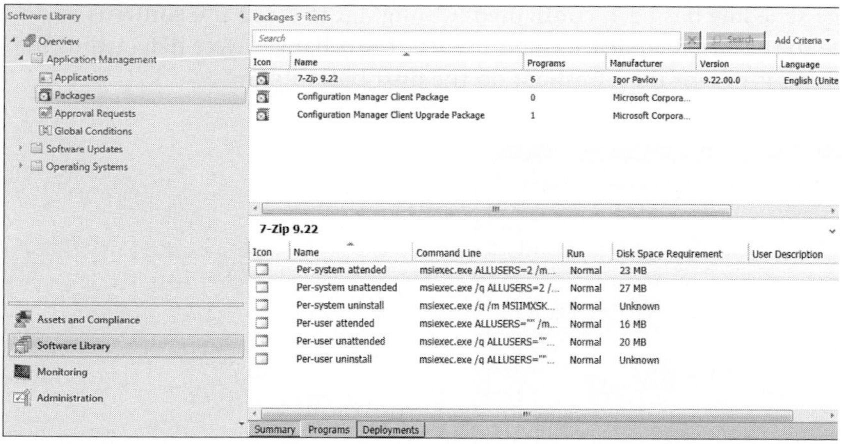

FIGURE 11.8   Programs associated with a package.

Package Properties

Now that you have created the package and program using the wizard, view the properties of the package and program to ensure all settings are configured as wanted. Populate as many fields as possible on the General tab, as shown in Figure 11.9. This information will be helpful to a user who needs to choose a software installation from Software Center or the Application Catalog.

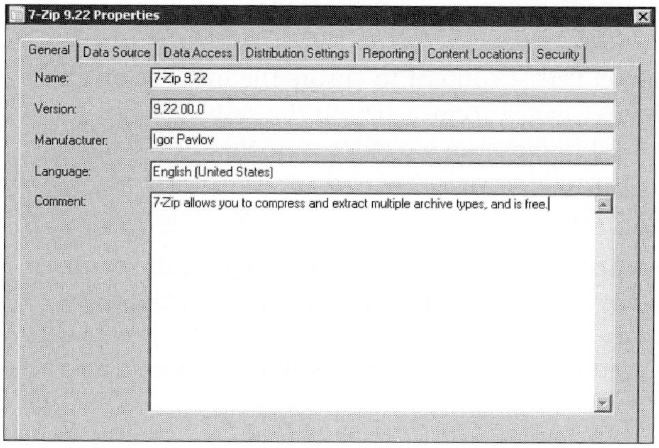

FIGURE 11.9   The General tab.

Figure 11.10 shows the Data Source tab. From this tab, you can see the package source location, as well as the current source version. If the contents of the source folder update on a regular basis, consider enabling the **Update distribution points on a schedule** check box. When a schedule has been configured, ConfigMgr re-sends the contents of the package source to the specified distribution points. If no changes were detected in the source folder, nothing is re-sent (or refreshed) on the distribution points.

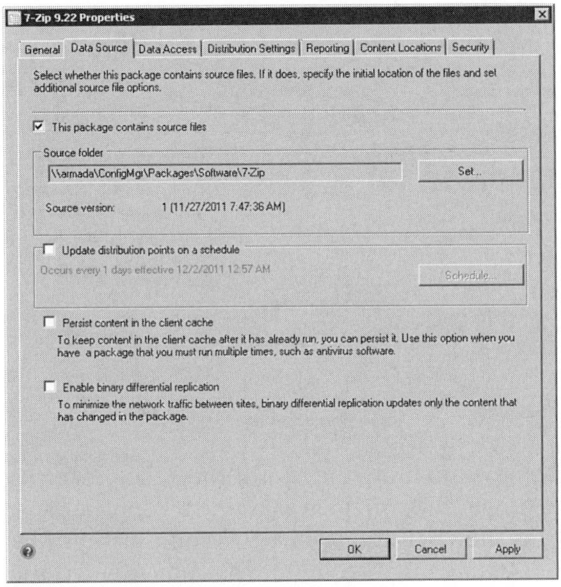

FIGURE 11.10   The Data Source tab.

Enable the following options on the Data Source tab as required:

▶ **Persist content in the client cache:** Persist content to ensure the installation source remains in the local cache (%*windir*%\ccmcache) on the system. This option is perfect for software that may need to rerun on a regular basis that not require a content update. Use this option sparingly because the package source size affects the size of available cache.

▶ **Enable binary differential replication:** Use binary differential replication for packages that contain large files, such as the installation .wim file for OSD. Use this option sparingly because the binary differential algorithms require additional overhead for calculating which bits need to be transferred to distribution points for each file in the package source.

The Data Access tab configures two important settings, as shown in Figure 11.11.

Use this tab to configure how the package is stored on distribution points.

▶ **Copy the content in this package to a package share on distribution points:** Enabling this check box instructs ConfigMgr to copy the package contents to the SMSPKGD$ share (where **D** is the drive letter for the share), giving you the same distribution point experience as ConfigMgr 2007. You can also enable the check box to use a custom named share for the package, just as you could in ConfigMgr 2007.

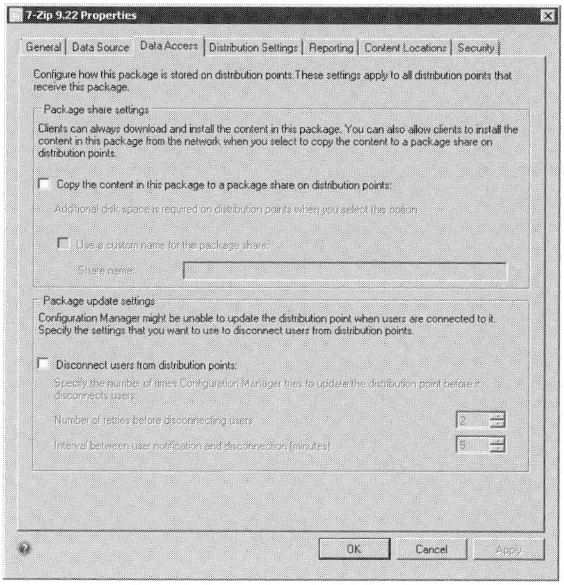

FIGURE 11.11   The Data Access tab.

NOTE: PACKAGE SHARE CAUSES DUPLICATE CONTENT ON DISTRIBUTION POINT

One of the greatest features of System Center 2012 Configuration Manager is the single instance store for content. When you select the option to copy the content to a package share, ConfigMgr will do just that and make a copy of all required files and place them on the share. All content in package shares will be in addition to the content in the content store, thus increasing your distribution point size. However, if you plan to configure any deployment to run from a distribution point, you must enable this check box.

▶ **Disconnect users from distribution points:** If you use deployment options to run the content from the distribution point, and an application install hangs, the target system may keep files open on the distribution point share for an extended period of time. Enable this check box, and configure the retry and notification settings.

Figure 11.12 displays the Distribution Settings tab and configuration.

▶ **Distribution priority:** Use this setting to control the order in which multiple packages are sent to distribution points. For example, you may want to configure more critical packages (such as antivirus, security patches, and so on) to a high priority so that it would have priority to be sent to child sites and distribution points faster than a package of low priority, such as a portable document format viewer application.

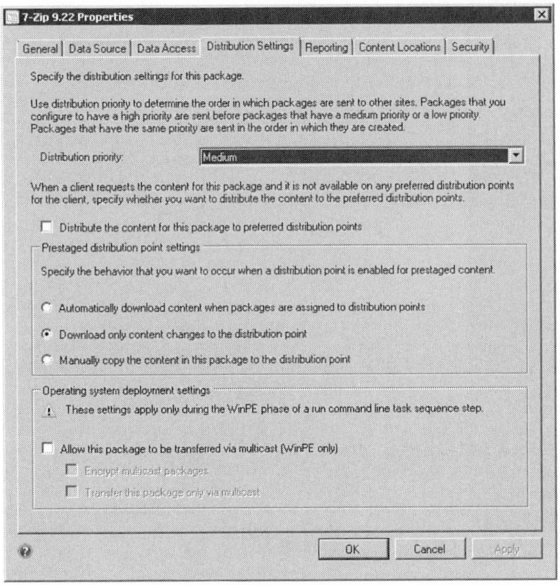

FIGURE 11.12   The Distribution Settings tab.

▶ **Distribute the content for this package to preferred distribution points:** A client has a "preferred" distribution point (DP) when it is in the boundaries of a defined DP. In this situation, when a client in a preferred DP boundary requests a package that is not on the DP, the content is automatically deployed to the preferred DP, to fulfill the request for the client. This can be a great option for content that you want to avoid deploying to all DPs, such as a MUI language package.

▶ **Prestaged distribution point settings:** If you selected the **Enable this distribution point for prestaged content** check box, the following settings affect content distribution:

  ▶ **Automatically download content when packages are assigned to distribution points:** This setting causes the DP to perform normally and not follow any prestaged content rules—content will be distributed to any targeted DP.

  ▶ **Download only content changes to the distribution point:** This option requires you to export content and then extract content manually on the DP for the initial distribution. Subsequent update distribution point's actions send delta updates to the package. A scenario to consider would be when you're ready to deploy the next version of Microsoft Office. The source installation is approximately 1GB currently. Due to WAN availability, you may choose to manually transfer content to the distribution point the first time (either over a

WAN file copy, or actually shipping media that contains content to the remote DP). After you have prestaged the initial payload, update DPs work normally, as expected.

▶ **Manually copy the content in this package to the distribution point:** This setting prevents ConfigMgr from copying any content to the DP and requires you to export content from the Admin console and then extract content to a new DP.

▶ **Operating system deployment settings:** Configure this section to enable multicast, require encryption, and/or only allow the package to be transferred via multicast. As mentioned in the dialog in Figure 11.12, this section applies only while the system is running WinPE.

The Reporting tab (Figure 11.13) displays status Management Information Format (MIF) matching information. Because the Windows installer package is now imported, the **Use these fields for status MIF matching** option is enabled, with all text fields complete.

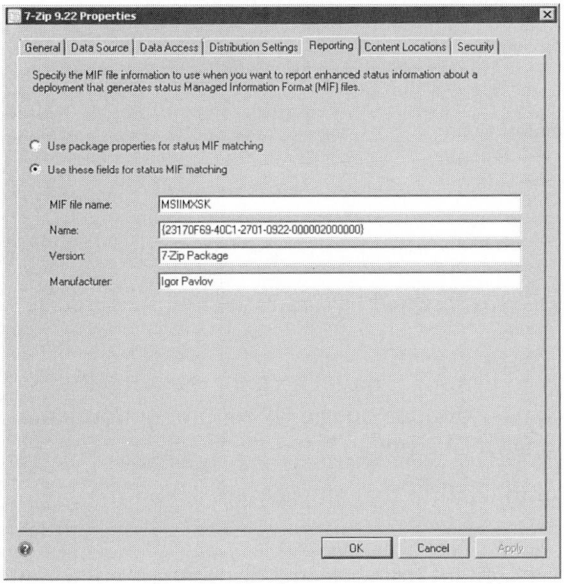

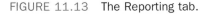

FIGURE 11.13   The Reporting tab.

The default setting for this dialog is **Use package properties for status MIF matching** and is a good default setting. Only enable the **Use these fields for status MIF matching** radio button if you can complete the MIF matching information, such as the MIF file-name. Choosing the wrong MIF filename (and the other text box configurations in the dialog) may cause ConfigMgr to consume the wrong MIF file and incorrectly report instal-lation status to the site server. If you have software that requires this to correctly report status, consider moving to the new application model, discussed in Chapter 12. With the application model, you can write additional detection rules to determine whether software is installed.

Figure 11.14 shows the Content Locations tab.

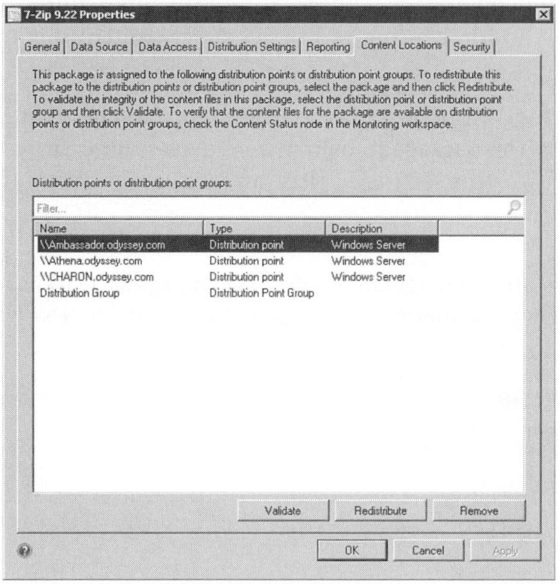

FIGURE 11.14   The Content Locations tab.

The Content Locations tab enables you to see the targeted DPs and DP groups, as well as perform the following actions:

▶ **Validate content:** Instruct ConfigMgr to perform a hash check for the wanted package on the selected DP. Review SMSDPMon.log on the DP for more information. This option can be initiated only to one DP at a time.

▶ **Redistribute content:** Use this option to confirm that all packages are on the targeted DPs when needed.

▶ **Remove content:** This option removes content from selected distribution points and from all DPs in a selected DP group.

The Security tab displays all users and user groups who have rights to a package, as well as their operational rights. **Cancel** the dialog (or click **OK** if you have made changes you want to keep) and proceed to view/change the Program properties.

Program Properties

With the package created, the next step is configuring the program the package will use. Notice from Figure 11.8 that there are six programs for the package. These programs were automatically created because you used the Create Package from Definition Wizard and were created from a Windows installer file. For this example, you want a system-based, unattended installation. The Per-system unattended program deploys the 7-Zip installation on a per-system basis and runs without user intervention. If you never plan to use some of the programs, such as Per-user unattended, consider deleting them to remove clutter. Right-click the program named **Per-system unattended** (located in **Software Library -> Overview -> Application Management -> Packages**), select the 7-Zip package, as shown in Figure 11.8, and open the **Properties** page, as shown in Figure 11.15.

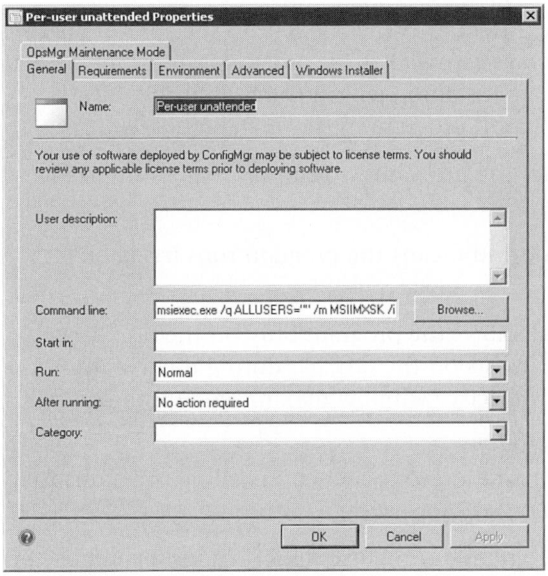

FIGURE 11.15   The General tab of Program Properties.

Properties for each program include the following tabs:

▶ General

▶ Requirements

▶ Environment

▶ Advanced

▶ Windows Installer

▶ OpsMgr Maintenance Mode

Each of these tabs defines how the program will function. Review the content of each, using the 7-Zip package as an example.

The General tab (shown in Figure 11.15) has a variety of fields automatically populated with information, based on the package definition file used to create the 7-Zip package:

▶ **Name:** The Name field is prepopulated and cannot be changed.

▶ **User description:** This is the first field you can modify. This field is a 127-character text field used to give a description of the program.

▶ **Command line:** This field is a text field that can have up to 255 characters. It provides the command line that installs the 7-Zip application. For the 7-Zip application, the field uses the following syntax:

```
msiexec.exe /q ALLUSERS="" /m MSIIMXSK /i "7z922.msi"
```

▶ **Start in:** An optional 127-character text field, this specifies either the absolute path to the program you are installing (such as c:\install_files\program.exe) or the folder relative to the distribution point you are installing within (such as install_files). This defaulted to blank for the 7-Zip installation program.

▶ **Run:** This drop-down specifies whether the program will run normal, minimized, maximized, or hidden.

  ▶ **Normal:** This is the default mode and means the program runs based on system and program defaults.

  ▶ **Minimized:** Running minimized shows the program only on the task bar during installation. The window exists on the task bar during the installation process; however, it is not the active window maximized on the user's workstation.

  ▶ **Maximized:** This is a good configuration to use when installing programs that require user intervention. It's also good for package testing.

  ▶ **Hidden:** This mode hides the program during installation and is a good option for fully automated program deployments.

The 7-Zip installation program defaulted to the Normal configuration.

▶ **After running:** This field is a drop-down selection determining what occurs after the program completes. Here are the options:

  ▶ **No action required:** The 7-Zip installation program defaulted to **No action required**, which means that no restart or logoff is required for the program (the case in the 7-Zip installation).

  ▶ **Configuration Manager restarts computer:** The option to have ConfigMgr restart the computer is useful when you deploy a program that requires a reboot but the reboot is not initiated as part of the program.

  ▶ **Program controls restart:** Select this option if the program requires a reboot and the program actually performs the restart program.

  ▶ **Configuration Manager logs user off:** Use this option to log off the user after installation.

It is important to note that both the ConfigMgr restarts computer and ConfigMgr logs user off options take place forcefully after a grace period. This means that if either of these options is used, any applications running on the clients will not have the opportunity to save their data or state.

▶ **Category:** Category is a drop-down selection used to help find specific programs in ConfigMgr when deployed to the Application Catalog. This field defaults to blank, but you can create a new category by typing in the text for the category's name.

NOTE: USE CARE WHEN ENTERING A NEW CATEGORY

Category entry is a one-way street. Enter a category and click **Apply**, and that category cannot be removed (at least not in a supported way). Always check to see if a category already exists, and when entering a new category, double-check your spelling! (You can remove the category from a program by selecting the category that is blank from the drop-down.)

Configuring the Installation Program

You may want to make changes to the program's configuration on the **General** tab for the 7-Zip installation. First, add a comment explaining what the program will do. Next, change the properties on the per-system unattended command line, as follows:

```
msiexec.exe /q ALLUSERS="" /m MSIIMXSK /i "7z922.msi" /l %temp%\7z922_install.log
```

This command line runs the installation silent and logs to %*windir*%\temp\7z922_install. log (if run using the local system account). Run the program as hidden, keep the **After running setting** of **No action required**, and specify a **Category** setting of **Utility**.

Now, move to the **Requirements** tab for the program. Figure 11.16 shows the default configuration for the 7-Zip program previously created using the package definition file. The Requirements tab tells Configuration Manager the requirements for running the program:

▶ **Estimated disk space:** The estimated disk space required to run the program.

▶ **Maximum allowed run time (minutes):** The amount of time the program is permitted to run. Enter your worst-case scenario for the time required to install the application. It is important to enter an accurate number because maintenance windows use this number to determine if there is a large enough window to run the installation. With the default setting of Unknown, ConfigMgr monitors the installation for a maximum of 120 minutes. So if you have only a 90-minute maintenance window, the program would never run.

▶ **Only on specified client platforms:** If the program can run only on specified platforms, select the allowed platforms. When possible, avoid specifying platforms as narrow as **All Windows 7 SP1 (32-Bit)**, unless you know the software will run only on Windows 7 Service Pack (SP) 1 (and not SP 2.) Try instead to use the **All Windows 7 (32-bit)**. Software generally continues to install and execute successfully when an operating system upgrades to a new service pack. For example, if you limit your favorite portable document (PDF) utility installation to an All Windows 7 SP1 collection and then deploy Service Pack 2, you cannot install the application on the SP 2 system until you modify the supported platforms defined in Figure 11.16.

▶ **Additional requirements:** This is an optional field for specifying additional requirement information for users (up to 127 characters). Text appears on client computers in **Software Center**.

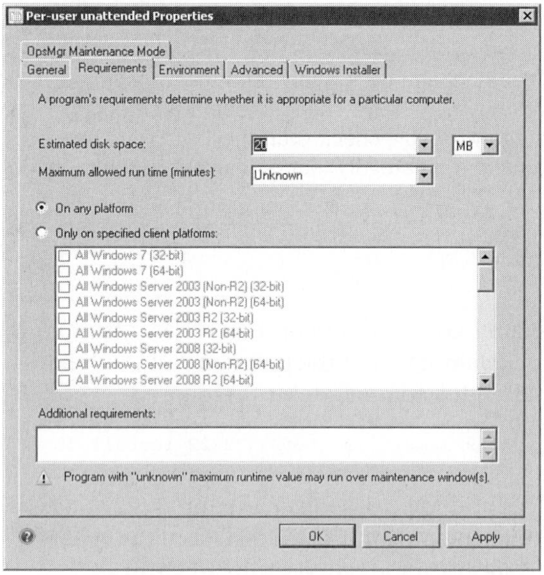

FIGURE 11.16   The Requirements tab.

The **Estimated disk space** setting defaults to 20MB when the package definition file for the 7-Zip is used. Although the actual amount of disk space may vary from the amount defined with the package definition file, the default generally provides a good starting point. This setting can be in KB, MB, or GB, and it defaults to Unknown for program installations. The setting is for informational purposes only and appears in the properties of the installation in Software Center.

The **Maximum allowed run time (minutes)** setting defines how long the program is expected to run. There can be considerable variation in how a program runs; this depends on the speed of the system ConfigMgr is installing it on, the size of the program, and the network connectivity between the system and the source files used for the installation. In this example, the setting defaulted to Unknown. However, based on previous installations of 7-Zip, it should complete within 5 minutes. ConfigMgr requires a setting between 15 and 720 minutes (or choose Unknown), so set this value to 15 minutes. Choose the maximum run time carefully because it affects the following:

▶ During program installation, the ConfigMgr client monitors the installation until the maximum time is reached. If the installation has not completed by the maximum allowed time, ConfigMgr sends a status message stating that the maximum run time has been reached, and that ConfigMgr will no longer monitor it. (This in turn frees up ConfigMgr to deploy additional software, if required.)

▶ Before a program runs, ConfigMgr checks to see if any maintenance windows have been defined, and if so, verifies that the available window is larger than the Maximum allowed run time. If the available window is not large enough, the client waits for an available window for deployment (unless you configured the deployment to ignore maintenance windows).

▶ The **OpsMgr Maintenance Mode** tab uses the Maximum allowed run time setting as the timeout for the maintenance mode duration.

Two options are available for platforms on which ConfigMgr can run the program:

▶ **On any platform:** This is the default configuration and works well for programs that are not platform-specific.

▶ **Only on specified client platforms:** This type of installation is for client-specific platforms. As an example, the 7-Zip client actually has two different installation files based on the client platform (amd64, i386). In this situation, you would separately package each of the different program types and use this option to allow each program to run only on a specific client platform. When possible, avoid scoping a supported platform down to the service pack level.

▶ **Additional requirements:** Add additional text in this box for the user to view from Software Center. No items are evaluated from this setting, but it is additional information for the user.

HIDE NON-APPLICABLE SOFWARE WITHOUT CREATING SPECIFIC COLLECTIONS

The **Only on specified client platforms** (also known as "Restricted Platforms") setting allows you to easily control which client systems see a deployment, based on the operating system and architecture. For example, if you know that an application runs only on XP 32-bit, enable the restricted platform, and target a collection that contains XP 32-bit as well as Windows 7 32-bit. For machine-targeted deployments, the restricted platforms are evaluated when the client receives policy and will not run unless the restrictions are met. The deployment also appears only in Software Center if the current operating system meets the required platform restriction. User-targeted software (including software that appears in Application Catalog) is evaluated at run time. If a user initiates the example described on a Windows 7 system from the Application Catalog, the user receives a notification that the requirements were not met to install the wanted software on this computer.

For the 7-Zip program, change the properties on the **Requirements** tab to set the Estimated disk space to 5MB and the Maximum allowed run time (minutes) to 15. Also, specify that this program can run only on the following platforms: **All Windows 7 (32-Bit)**, **All Windows Vista (32-Bit)**, and **All Windows XP (32-Bit)**. This configuration allows the software to be installed on the described platforms, regardless of service pack.

The Environment tab for this program (as shown in Figure 11.17) identifies when a program can run. Here are the options:

▶ **Only when a user is logged on:** This installation type is used when the program ConfigMgr is installing needs to have the user logged in to install.

▶ **Whether or not a user is logged on:** This is the most common option and always runs the program using the local system account (run with administrative rights).

▶ **Only when no user is logged on:** The installation type does not install until the user logs out of the system.

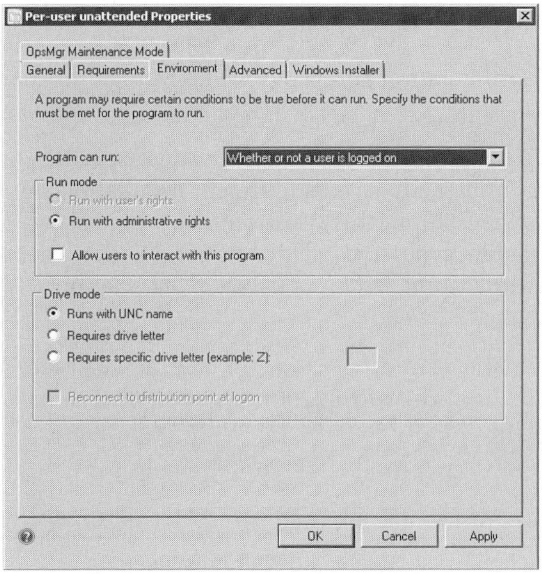

FIGURE 11.17   The Environment tab.

The conditions under which a program can run directly tie into the Run mode options:

▶ **Run with user's rights:** This option is only available if the option **Only when a user is logged on** is chosen for when the program can be run.

▶ **Run with administrative rights:** This is the default option and is available in any of the three configurations that determine when a program can run. If you choose this option, a check box is available to allow users to interact with the program.

▶ **Allow users to interact with this program:** Use the Allow users to interact with this program option in those situations in which the user needs to interact with the program. The option is also an excellent troubleshooting method to use when packages are not installing correctly. With this option selected, the user interface is visible to the user logged in to the system, and the user can interact with the program. As an example, you can choose this option if the program requires the user to make a selection or click a button. If a program runs without this option selected and the program requires user intervention, it waits for the user interaction (which never occurs) and eventually times out when the maximum allowed run time has occurred (defined on the Requirements tab of the program; if undefined, the program times out after 12 hours).

TIP: DEPLOYING SOFTWARE WITH ADMINISTRATIVE RIGHTS

At first glance, deploying a package with administrative rights seems like a no-brainer. Using this approach, you can install the software regardless of what level of permissions are available to the user logged in to the system. However, this can cause some difficulties when installing a program that writes data to the registry (in HKEY_CURRENT_USER), or if the package tries to access files the account does not have rights to access. If this situation occurs, try running with the user's rights instead. If that does not work, create two different programs—one that runs under the user access and allows access to the registry and a second that runs with administrative rights. Next, link the programs together with a Run this program first option. Sometimes this requires repackaging the application (see the "Repackaging Software" section for details) to determine the portion of the application that requires administrator rights to install. Another option involves using the task sequencing engine to deploy packages that need to perform Registry edits or run something in a user context. You can do this by running a command line with a run as statement.

The Drive mode that the program runs under includes the following configurations:

- ▶ **Runs with UNC name:** This is the default setting, which runs the program using the UNC (Universal Naming Convention) name. For example, \\athena\SMSPKGE$\ PR100004 would be the distribution point when you create a package for the PR1 site and store it on the E: drive of the system. A client runs only from the UNC path if the deployment is configured to **Run from distribution point**, and the package share settings have been configured on the Data Access tab of the Package properties. By default, content is downloaded from a distribution point to the client cache and run from there (normally *%windir%*\ccmcache\).

- ▶ **Requires drive letter:** The program requires a mapped drive to install but allows ConfigMgr to use any available drive letter.

- ▶ **Requires specific drive letter (example: Z):** The program requires mapping a specific drive letter for installation. (If you choose this option, an additional box is provided for specifying the letter to be mapped.) If the drive letter is not available on the client system, the program will not run.

- ▶ **Reconnect to distribution point at logon:** This last setting specifies that the client reconnects to the ConfigMgr distribution point when logging in to the system. This option is only available if the program runs only when a user is logged on, with the user's rights, and requires either a drive letter or a specific drive letter (for example, the drive letter Z).

For the 7-Zip program, configure the Environment tab (refer to Figure 11.17).

The Advanced tab for the program, shown in Figure 11.18, specifies a variety of configurations, such as whether other programs run prior to this one, whether this program is run once for the computer or for each user, where program notifications are suppressed, how disabled programs are handled on clients, and how the program integrates with install software task sequences.

▶ **Run another program first:** This is the first option available on the **Advanced** tab. These are program dependencies, and specifying this option causes another program to be run before this program runs. By default, the check box is cleared. For example, a software package has several separate programs requiring installation before the package can be installed. This program has five levels of dependency—the original program will not run unless program #2 has run, and program #2 will not run unless program #3 has run, and so on.

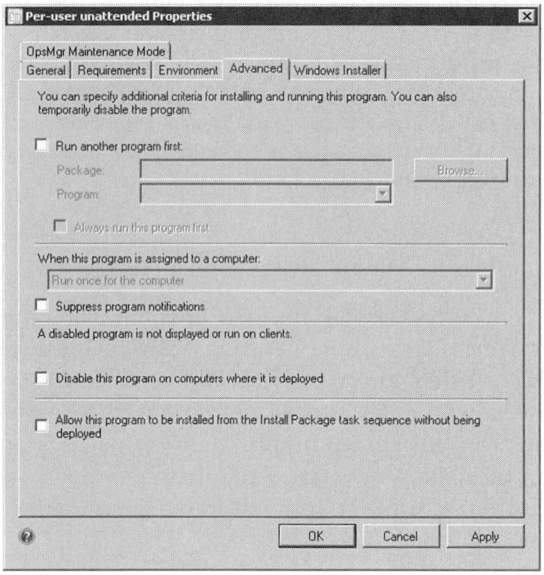

FIGURE 11.18   The Advanced tab.

If you choose this option, you must specify a package and a program. The option **Allow this program to be installed from the Install Software task sequence without being deployed** is relevant when discussing task sequences within ConfigMgr. Task sequences are a list of customizable tasks or steps sequentially performed. A task sequence can be deployed to a device collection; for example, a program can be deployed to a collection. Task sequences provide a more elegant solution for many situations, including those where multiple dependencies exist for a single program. Task sequences are discussed in more detail in Chapter 19, "Operating System Deployment."

If you specify the option to **Run another program first**, the **Always run this program first** option is also available (defaults as unchecked). If this option is checked, the program it is dependent on runs regardless of whether it previously ran on the same system.

An alternative to the **Run another program first** option is to create a task sequence and build in the logic to determine which commands should run. You can also leverage applications with defined dependencies, discussed in Chapter 12, for any prerequisite software.

▶ **When this program is assigned to a computer:** This is a drop-down with two choices:

   ▶ **Run once for the computer:** This is the default setting.

   ▶ **Run once for every user who logs in:** This option causes the program to run for each user who logs in to the computer.

▶ **Suppress program notifications:** When checked, the option causes any notification area icons, messages, and countdown notifications to not display for the program. This is useful for programs that may be running when someone uses the system, if there is no requirement for notification that the program is running. You can override this setting by the client setting **Show notifications for new deployments** in the Computer Agent section. Review Chapter 9, "Configuration Manager Client Management," for more information about customizing client settings.

▶ **Disable this program on computers where it is deployed:** This check box determines how ConfigMgr handles the program. The option defaults to unchecked, but if checked, it specifies that deployments containing this program are disabled. When checked, this option also removes the program from the list of available programs that the user can run, and the program will not run on the systems where it is assigned.

   This approach is useful when there is a need to temporarily halt a deployment because the change applies to all deployments of the program, and the program is disabled when policies are retrieved by the client.

▶ **Allow this program to be installed from the Install Software task sequence without being deployed:** The final check box on the Advanced tab determines how the Install Software task sequence in OSD handles the program. The option is unchecked by default. You should check this option for any programs used within an OSD task sequence that are not currently deployed to a collection.

For the 7-Zip program, accept the default configurations.

The Windows Installer tab for the program provides installation source management. If the program requires repair or reinstallation, the MSI file automatically accesses the package files on a distribution point to reinstall or repair the program.

The available fields on the screen shown in Figure 11.19 are the Windows Installer product code and the Windows Installer file. You can define these by clicking the **Import** button and specifying the MSI file used for the program. Choosing the MSI file populates both of these fields.

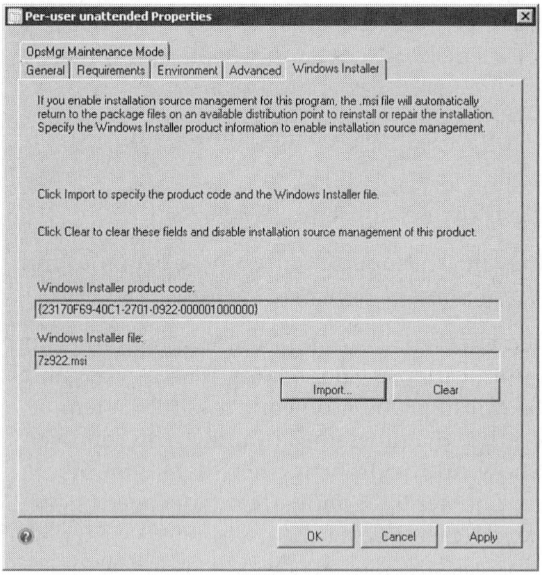

FIGURE 11.19   The Windows Installer tab.

For the 7-Zip program, click **Import**, select the Windows installer file used for the installation (7z922.msi), and click **Open**. The product code and filename will be automatically populated (refer to Figure 11.19).

The added benefit to this feature is that when a device moves to a different location, ConfigMgr automatically modifies the source path on the local system if the system is in a different boundary group that has content available for the software.

The final tab determines the OpsMgr Maintenance Mode configurations for the program. Two options are available on this tab, as displayed in Figure 11.20:

▶ **Disable Operations Manager alerts while this program runs:** Selecting this option places the computer in OpsMgr maintenance mode while the program is running. The duration of the maintenance mode is defined by the Maximum allowed run time (minutes) setting defined on the Requirements tab (refer to Figure 11.16). In previous versions of OpsMgr, this option does not actually perform the steps required to truly disable Operations Manager alerts while the program is running. The option pauses the OpsMgr health service but does not put everything into maintenance mode, meaning heartbeat alerts are still generated. Fortunately, with System Center 2012 Operations Manager, this check box should be fully functional, providing the wanted results for enabling full maintenance mode on a system.

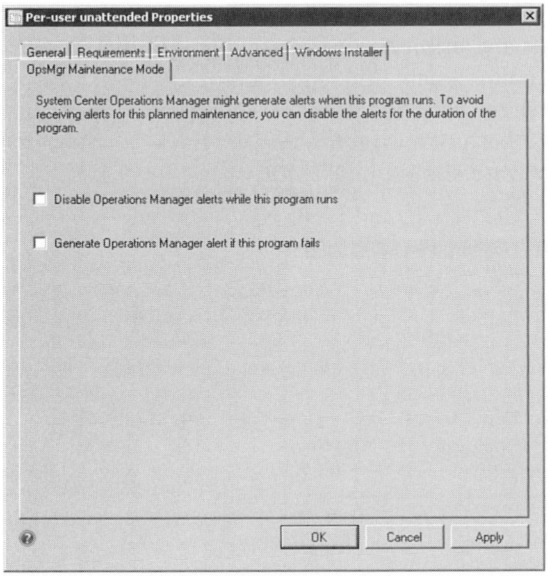

FIGURE 11.20   The OpsMgr Maintenance Mode tab.

▶ **Generate Operations Manager alert if this program fails:** If this option is checked, it creates an event in the application log containing the package name, program name, advertisement ID, deployment comment, and failure code or MIF failure description. You can configure the application event to create an alert in Operations Manager that alerts on the situation. A good example of when to use this feature is for critical software deployments such as service pack packages.

Packaging the 7-Zip application with a package definition file demonstrates many of the configurations used when manually creating a package and a program. Although using a package definition file (an MSI, PDF, or MIF file) is the recommended approach, what takes place when a package definition file is not available? Drawing on the information just used to create the 7-Zip package, the next section discusses the process for creating packages and programs manually, using the Microsoft Word Viewer installation as an example.

Creating a Package with the New Package Wizard

Microsoft Word Viewer is a free application to view and print Word documents that you can download from www.microsoft.com/downloads. Follow these steps using the Create Package and Program Wizard to create a package for the Microsoft Word Viewer:

1. Similar to when you created a package using a package definition file, from the ConfigMgr console, navigate to **Software Library -> Overview-> Application Management -> Packages**, and select **Create -> Create** from the ribbon bar.

2. On the Package page, specify a variety of fields, each of which is your personal preference for the package. These fields are visible in the ConfigMgr console as well as Software Center and Application Catalog. Enable the check box **This package contains source files**, and click **Browse** to select the source files location. From this dialog, you can select a network (UNC) path or a local folder. When possible, select a network path. The first page of the wizard should look similar to Figure 11.21.

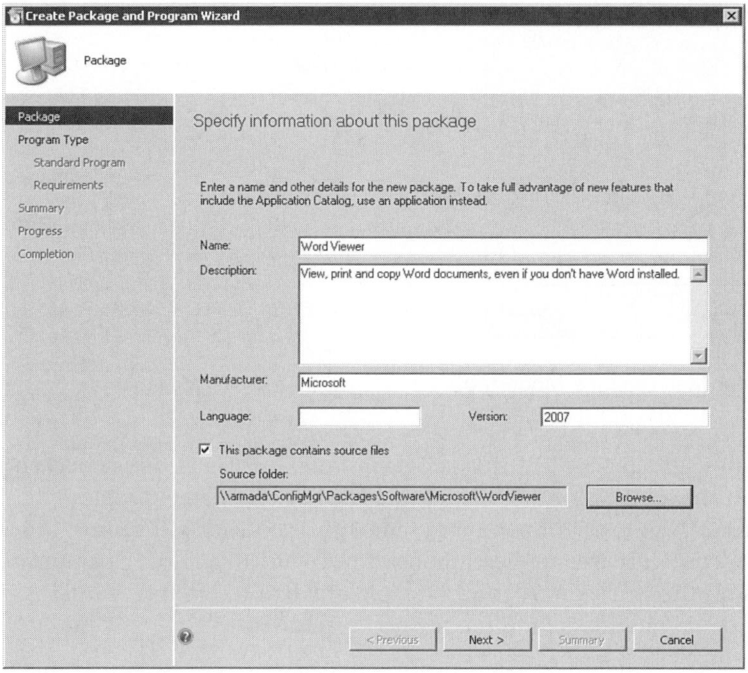

FIGURE 11.21   The Package page of the Create Package and Program Wizard.

3. On the Program page, you have three options:

▶ **Standard program:** This is a standard program used to deploy software to a computer system.

▶ **Program for device:** Use this option for creating a package to deploy to supported mobile devices.

▶ **Do not create a program:** Use this option if you are using a package to access the source files on a distribution point. This type of package (with no program) is often used with operating system deployment, for running scripts, utilities, and so on.

Select **Standard program**, and click **Next**.

4. On the Standard Program page, enter required information (Name and Command line), and modify any other required settings, as shown in Figure 11.22.

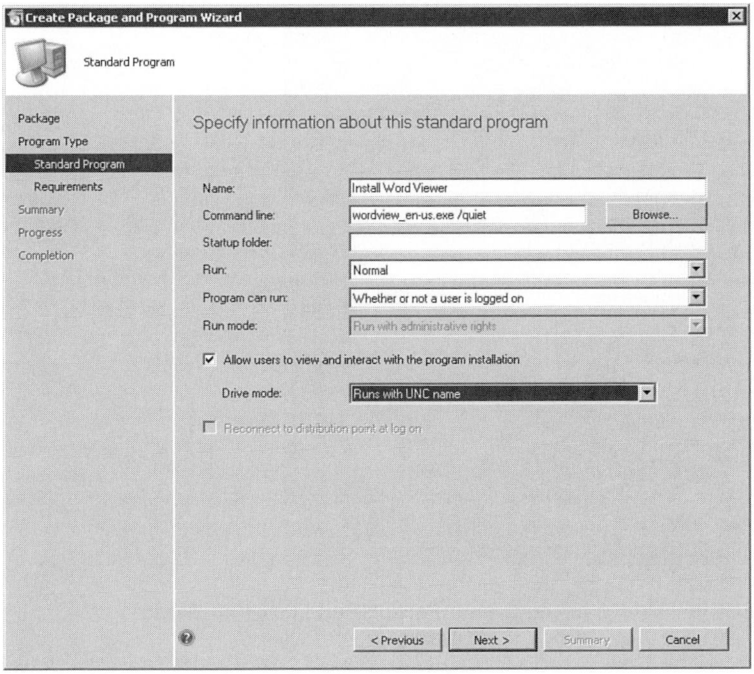

FIGURE 11.22   The Standard Program page of the Create Package and Program Wizard.

5. On the Requirements page, select if another program must run first, as well as platform restrictions, estimated disk space, and maximum allowed run time, as shown in Figure 11.23.

In the example, select **All Windows 7 (32-bit), All Windows Vista (32-bit),** and **All Windows XP (32-bit)** for the specified platforms.

6. Review the Summary page, and if everything looks good, click **Next**, confirm the Package and Program Wizard completed successfully, and then click **Close**.

From this point, refer to the "Creating a Package from the Package Definition Wizard" section for a refresher on how to view and modify the properties of the package and program. If you need to create a new program for an existing package, simply right-click the wanted program, and select **Create Program** from the context menu.

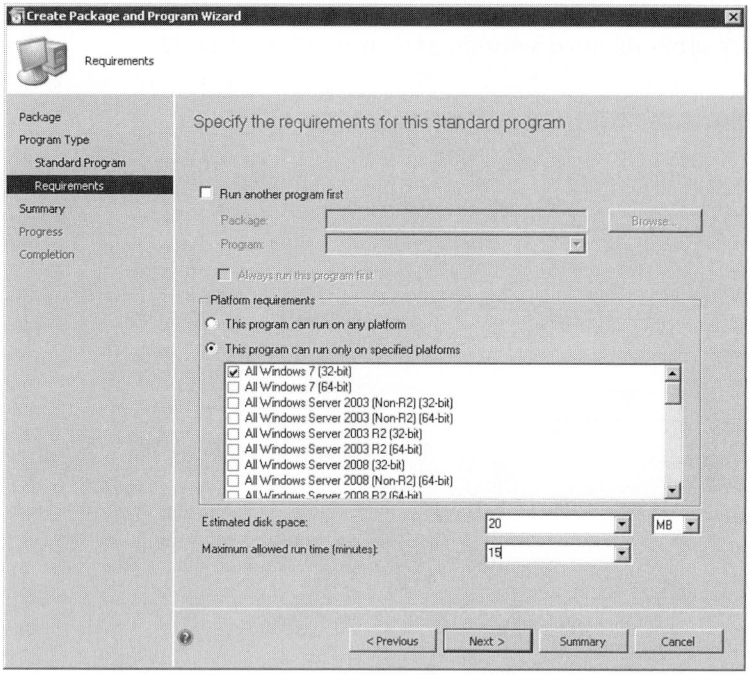

FIGURE 11.23   The Requirements page of the Create Package and Program Wizard.

Custom Packages

The majority of the packages needed by most organizations have existing package definition files because most major packages now install from MSI files. For those packages that do not have package definition files but do have setup files, the Word Viewer client example illustrates that you can manually create packages by performing some additional steps. You can often install simple applications with a batch file or a script. For more complex applications, work with the vendor to find a supported, documented process for performing an unattended deployment of the application.

SITE FOR SOFTWARE PACKAGING AND DEPLOYMENT GUIDANCE

A great place for general guidance on software deployment is the IT Ninja site (http://itninja.com/software). IT Ninja provides information on how to distribute software, including examples for Adobe Reader, Microsoft Office, and Visual Studio .NET. You now can deploy nearly all software using packages that run the various command-line configurations.

Repackaging Software

What do you do for the few applications that cannot be packaged using normal methods? There are some packages you cannot package using standard processes, but you can repackage them. Software repackaging takes an existing application installation and converts it to an MSI package. You would take a snapshot of a system before and after installing the software on a system and then convert the results into the MSI package. Review the IT Ninja website (http://itninja.com/software) and browse for **repackagers**. In addition, check out myITForum (http://www.myitforum.com), and participate in the community for suggestions on the best software packager. Flexera's AdminStudio (http://www.flexerasoftware.com/products/adminstudio-suite.htm) is currently one of the most popular software packaging suites and provides significant integration with ConfigMgr 2007 and System Center 2012 Configuration Manager.

Avoiding Common ConfigMgr Software Packaging Issues

Several common issues may occur when creating software packages in ConfigMgr. These relate to issues in understanding the options available within ConfigMgr and when testing software packages. A key point to remember when it comes to ConfigMgr and software deployment is that almost always ConfigMgr will do exactly what you tell it to do. If you deploy a less-than-desirable package, you will probably receive less-than-desirable results. Always test, retest, and test again.

Program and Package Properties

One key consideration when developing software packages in ConfigMgr are the options available when creating a package and a program. These options—such as the ability to require another package to install prior to installation, and placing restrictions on the program such as the platforms it installs on—provide increased capabilities when packaging software with ConfigMgr.

To better understand these options, this chapter includes details in the "Creating a Package from the Package Definition Wizard" and "Creating a Package with the New Package Wizard" sections on all available package and program configurations.

Testing, Testing, Testing

The most commonly overlooked method of avoiding issues with ConfigMgr packaging is to test for as many contingencies as possible. If you are creating a software package to deploy to 1,000 workstations, you almost certainly will run into unexpected configurations. Effective testing processes can limit the risks of program failures or unexpected complications.

To test software packages, you need a testing lab (also discussed in Chapter 4, "Architecture Design Planning"). This lab includes computers representative of those systems to which you will deploy the software package. However, it is often difficult to get nonproduction versions of actual systems for testing purposes.

One method to address this is to use a virtual lab environment for software package testing. With a product such as Hyper-V or VMware, you can run multiple computers without requiring an entire lab of physical hardware. One of the major benefits of a virtual environment is the ability to return a computer quickly to an earlier configuration.

This capability makes it easy to roll an operating system back to its previous state (prior to deploying the software package). This is beneficial when testing software packages, as you often need to go through multiple testing iterations. Build your virtual test systems with the same procedure as building a physical system. Virtual lab environments also have the benefit of a smaller physical footprint, so less hardware is required for creating the lab.

Alternatively, physical lab environments provide real examples of those computers where you would deploy the package. In some cases, only a physical lab environment will identify issues such as a driver conflict existing between the software package and a set of computers running on a specific hardware platform. Your physical lab computers should be actual production systems taken from the groups where you are deploying software packages, and should represent the types of hardware that exist in your environment.

The authors' recommended approach for creating a lab environment is a hybrid between a physical lab and a virtual lab. Using some of both types of systems minimizes the number of systems required, while providing many of the benefits of a physical lab.

Another important factor to consider when testing software packages is what exactly to test. You should create a set of tests identifying the types of conditions to test before releasing the package. Here are some examples of this:

▶ Installing the software package where there is not enough disk space

▶ Deploying to an unsupported platform

▶ Deploying where the program is already installed

▶ Deploying with other software packages installed that may cause conflicts

The exact set of tests will vary depending on your package, but identifying potential failure conditions ahead of time and testing for those conditions significantly increase the likelihood of creating a functional software package.

Summary

This chapter discussed the various methods available for deploying software in a Windows environment and explained the benefits of using Configuration Manager to deploy software. It described how various components in ConfigMgr come together to provide a software deployment solution, and it provided examples for how to create packages in ConfigMgr both with and without a package definition file. The chapter also discussed programs and packages and available configuration options, as well as tips for avoiding common issues when creating packages. The chapter concluded with a discussion of tips for avoiding common ConfigMgr packaging issues. The next chapter takes the traditional package and program and shows you how to use the new application model to create "smarter" applications with System Center 2012 Configuration Manager. And stay tuned for Chapter 13, which takes what you learn in Chapters 11 and 12 and deploys applications to systems.

CHAPTER 12

Creating and Managing Applications

Application and deployment types provide the System Center 2012 Configuration Manager (ConfigMgr) administrator with the tools to manage and deploy software for client devices within the enterprise. ConfigMgr 2007 software deployment primarily focused on deploying to a computer rather than users, depending heavily on collections to ensure proper targeting. This changes with System Center 2012 Configuration Manager, where application deployment is designed around deployment toward users, as well as improved machine targeting. You can still use collections to target users and devices, but given the evaluate-at-installation time features of applications, you can allow the client to determine programmatically the best command (deployment type) to run rather than creating a different collection for each variation of system!

ConfigMgr 2012 gives you the ability to associate a user with one or more devices he uses everyday, known as a primary device. You can also deploy applications based on the user's need. For example, you can control the application such that it is installed physically on the user's primary device and virtually on any other device where the user might work.

You control application deployment behavior using deployment types. A deployment type is quite similar to a program in Configuration Manager 2007. As with programs, applications can have multiple deployment types. Using a deployment type, you can control if, when, and how to install the application.

This chapter discusses the features of application management in System Center 2012 Configuration Manager, and using deployment types to control deployment behavior.

WHAT'S NEW IN 2012

This entire chapter is dedicated to a new feature in System Center 2012 Configuration Manager, called *applications*. Even if you are an advanced ConfigMgr 2007 administrator, take the time to absorb this chapter to learn how to take advantage of one of the most important new features in ConfigMgr.

ConfigMgr Applications Overview

Think of an application as an enhanced way to deliver software to a user or computer. An application is a container that may contain multiple methods of installation, based on user state or computer state. Before diving into creating a new application, start by learning some of the key terms and how they work together to deliver software.

About Applications

An *application* is the container used to deliver software, and contains the basic information for the application, such as name, version, application owner, localization information (for how the application is displayed in the Application Catalog), and how and where the content for the application is distributed. It also includes any references/dependencies on other applications, as well as if the application replaces an existing application. Here are the actions you can perform on an application:

▶ Distribute application content to distribution points.

▶ Deploy the application, either required or optional to devices or users.

▶ Create one or more deployment types.

▶ Simulate deployment, to validate deployment types.

▶ Export an application (with or without content) so that you can import it into a different environment, or save it to disk should you later need to restore it.

▶ Create a prestaged content file so that you can transport the content to remote locations (without using wide area network [WAN] connectivity).

▶ Set security scopes to ensure team members have the appropriate access to the application. Chapter 20, "Security and Delegation in Configuration Manager," provides information about security scopes.

▶ Monitor content distribution.

▶ Monitor deployment status.

The application is the shell; to install software, you need a deployment type, which is the key component of the application.

About Deployment Types

Deployment types (DTs) are a major component of the application. You can almost compare a DT to a program, used with packages in both ConfigMgr 2007 and ConfigMgr 2012. Just as a program contains the installation command line and any platform requirements (such as Windows 7 x86), a DT contains this same basic info, and much more. Here's a brief list of some of the most important information this chapter discusses for DTs:

▶ Content source location (Universal Naming Convention [UNC] path to source installation files).

▶ Install and uninstall command lines.

▶ Detection method(s), used to confirm if an application is installed, confirm dependencies, and determine supersedence. Detection methods are also used on a regular interval (once every 7 days by default) to re-evaluate installation status on each system.

▶ End-user experience configuration, to determine when to display notifications, logon requirements, and so on.

▶ Requirement rules, used to determine the requirements for a DT to proceed with the installation.

▶ Success and failure return code information, to give you more control over the installation process.

▶ Dependency information, in case the application depends on other applications being installed first (for example, .NET Framework).

You can have multiple deployment types for one application. As an example, say you have software with different installations for x86, x64, or different versions of Windows. After the DT is built properly and the application deployed, the DTs are evaluated to determine which one is appropriate to install on a system (for example, an x86 Windows 7 will install only the x86 version of the software). This example is basic but helps convey the process. Requirement rules are flexible and can leverage just about anything on a system, as well as SQL or LDAP queries, primary user information, and more.

WHAT IS A PRIMARY USER?

A *primary user* is the main user of a device. A device can have more than one primary user. (Think of one device in a call center used on multiple shifts, for example.) A primary user can be defined for a device during operating system deployment (OSD), manually through the ConfigMgr console, or configured to create the relationship automatically based on login events on a system. The ConfigMgr administrator can also enable the user to define his own association through the Application Catalog, a web-based portal used for application delivery. For more information about primary users, see the "About User Device Affinity" section.

With the RTM version of System Center Configuration Manager 2012, there are five types of DTs available. Here is a brief explanation of each:

▶ **Microsoft Application Virtualization:** When creating virtual applications with the Microsoft App-V sequencer, the output contains a manifest file that contains specific application information. You can use this deployment type to import that manifest file into ConfigMgr 2012. The Create Deployment Type Wizard displays the result of the import, where the wizard's information fields are populated automatically by information in the file.

▶ **Windows Installer:** You can use this deployment type for any Windows Installer file, better known as a MSI file. Similar to the manifest file of a virtual application, ConfigMgr 2012 retrieves the information it will automatically display in the Create Deployment Type Wizard.

▶ **Script Installer:** Using this deployment type, the administrator can specify a script to be deployed on devices to run an installation or make specific configuration changes. The script can be anything from a complex Visual Basic file to a simple batch file. An installation that uses an executable (.exe, .msu, and so on) is also considered a script installer.

▶ **Windows Mobile Cabinet:** Windows Mobile Cabinet (CAB) files are used primarily to deploy software to mobile devices that are fully managed. (CAB files are not for mobile devices inventoried through the exchange server connector. See http://technet.microsoft.com/en-us/library/gg682022.aspx for additional information.) This deployment type creates the deployment files for those CAB files. As with the Microsoft Application Virtualization and Windows Installer deployment types, this DT reads the information inside the CAB file and automatically displays the results in the Create Deployment Type Wizard.

▶ **Nokia SIS File:** Use a Nokia Symbian Installation source (SIS) file to populate some fields of the Create Deployment Type Wizard automatically.

A discussion of DTs includes requirements and global conditions.

About Requirements

Requirements are component of a DT and are used to determine if a DT is *installable* for a system. Requirements are optional—if you don't have a requirement rule, the DT is applicable to any system that evaluates it. You use requirements to determine *which* DT to install, if any. For example, you can have one application with four deployment types, with the following requirements for each:

1. Operating system is Windows 7 x86 and primary user = TRUE

2. Operating system is Windows 7 x64 and primary user = TRUE

3. Operating system is Windows XP x86 and primary user = TRUE

4. Operating system is Windows 7 x86 or x64

The first three DTs are obvious as far as whether a DT is installable. Requirements are evaluated in order of priority, so if the operating system is Windows 7 x86 and the primary user = FALSE, DT #4 will be installable. In this example, the first three DTs are Windows Installer-based DTs, and DT #4 is an App-V DT. The requirements for this application will ensure that the full install will apply only to systems where primary user = TRUE. If the system is Windows XP x86 and the primary user = FALSE, none of the DTs are applicable, and if a user attempts to install, he will receive the message that requirements have not been met to install the application.

About Global Conditions

Requirements are defined by using a *global condition*. A global condition can be based on operating system name and/or architecture, total physical memory, free disk space, Active Directory site, organizational unit (OU), primary user, and more. You can use one or more global conditions to create requirements for a DT. Technically, a requirement is not necessary for a DT, but is highly recommended to ensure software is delivered to appropriate devices and/or users. The "About User Device Affinity" section provides additional information about the primary user global condition.

About Detection Methods

Create a *detection method* to determine if a deployment type is installed on a device. A detection method is required and should be unique to the DT. To use a deployment type properly, a detection method must be defined. When a device evaluates an application, it checks to see if it is already installed, based on the detection method. In addition, if an application is deployed as Required (mandatory), the ConfigMgr client agent re-evaluates the application installation (based on detection method) on a weekly basis, by default. This re-evaluation interval is configured through Client Settings. See Chapter 9, "Configuration Manager Client Management," for more information.

About User Device Affinity

User device affinity is a new feature in System Center 2012 Configuration Manager. It allows the administrators to associate a user with his primary devices. A *primary device* is the typical daily work device of the user such as a workstation or laptop. A device can be associated to more than one user, and a user can be associated to more than one device. Chapter 9 discusses how to configure Client Settings for user device affinity.

The benefit of user device affinity is the ConfigMgr administrator can deploy applications to users without needing to know the name of the device a user is working on. It also gives administrators more control in deploying the application, as rules can be created related to user device affinity as part of the deployment. As an example, assume you have an application for Microsoft Project. It has two deployment types: the first DT installs Project with the full MSI, and the second DT installs the App-V application for Project:

▶ You create an additional requirement rule for the full MSI version and require primary user = TRUE.

▶ You also set this DT as the first DT available.

▶ When a user attempts to install the software (or you send it as Required), the application will evaluate the first deployment type, and for where primary user = TRUE, install the MSI version of Project.

▶ If primary user = FALSE, then the App-V application for Project will be installed.

You can create a user device affinity in multiple ways, including

▶ Importing a CSV file containing two columns: users and devices.

▶ The user specifies his own primary device in the Application Catalog.

▶ Manual selection by the administrator to select the user and primary device.

▶ A user device affinity can be set during OSD.

▶ For mobile devices, the affinity can be set during enrollment.

▶ The site itself can determine affinities between users and devices based on gathered usage information. After the detection by the site, the affinity has to be approved by the administrator.

Here is information an affinity can hold:

▶ Single user to a single device

▶ Single user to many devices (such as a desktop and a mobile device)

▶ Many users to a single device (such as a shared desktop by the same department)

The previous sections describe many of the key components to an application. To combine those components, consider this: An *application* is a container of one or *more deployment types*. Each DT may contain one or more *requirements* to determine if an installation can occur on a device, as well as a *detection method* to determine or confirm if the application is installed. Now, let's walk through the process to create applications.

WHAT ABOUT ADVERTISEMENTS, PACKAGES, AND PROGRAMS?

System Center 2012 Configuration Manager continues to support packages and programs used in Configuration Manager 2007. In addition, a deployment that uses packages and programs might be more suitable than using an application when deploying any of the following:

▶ Scripts that do not install an application on a computer (such as a script to defragment a disk drive)

▶ "One-off" scripts that do not need continual monitoring

▶ Scripts that run on a recurring schedule and cannot use global evaluation

▶ Application installations that update on a frequent basis

▶ Applications that may not have very good detection methods

When you migrate from Configuration Manager 2007 to 2012, you can migrate existing packages and deploy them in your System Center 2012 Configuration Manager hierarchy. (Application virtualization packages are automatically migrated to be an application.) After migration is complete, your migrated packages appear in the Packages node in the Software Library workspace. You can modify and deploy these packages in the same way as you did using Configuration Manager 2007 software distribution.

The Import Package from Definition Wizard remains in System Center 2012 Configuration Manager for importing packages, as discussed in Chapter 11, "Packages and Programs." Advertisements are converted to deployments when migrated from Configuration Manager 2007 to a System Center 2012 Configuration Manager hierarchy. Advertisements are completely removed—deployment is the new term in ConfigMgr 2012. Packages can use some new features of this version, including distribution point groups and the new monitoring functionality.

You will also find three new logs on client systems for applications: AppintentEveal.log, AppEnforce.log, and AppDiscovery.log. Information on log files is available in Appendix A, "Configuration Manager Log Files."

About Creating Applications

The next sections walk through the process to create applications using the Create Application Wizard. Be aware that although the wizard is an excellent approach to get you up and running, there are several configurable properties available only after you create an application using the wizard. The following sections walk through the creation process and then analyze the property pages for full detail.

Creating a Windows Installer (MSI)-Based Application

The first example creates a Windows Installer-based application, using 7-Zip (www.7-zip. org) as the sample application. The .msi files for both x86 and x64 are already downloaded and saved to the share \\armada\ConfigMgr\Packages\Software\7-Zip.

Perform the following steps to start the Create Application Wizard:

1. Open the Configuration Manager console, and select the **Software Library** workspace.

2. In the workspace, expand Application Management.

3. Right-click the **Applications** node.

4. Select **Create Application** from the menu.

When the wizard starts, it opens the General page with two options, as shown in Figure 12.1:

▶ To automatically detect the application information using existing content

▶ To manually define the information

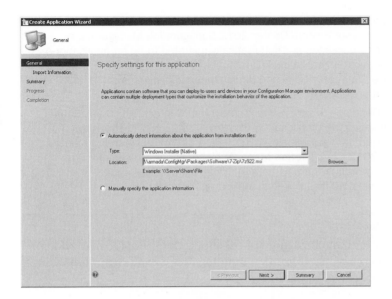

FIGURE 12.1   The General page of the Create Application Wizard.

The following scenario describes how to create an application for 7-Zip using existing Windows Installer content:

1. Using the wizard, specify or browse to the location of the application MSI file you want to use for the application. The path to the file must be a UNC path. Create the x86 DT first; for this example, enter **\\armada\ConfigMgr\Packages\Software\7-Zip\7z922.msi** for the path.

> **TIP: CREATING THE APPLICATION AND DEPLOYMENT TYPE IN ONE STEP**
>
> When you create a Windows Installer-based application using the Create Application Wizard, you actually create the application and one deployment type. The wizard extracts metadata from the .msi to populate the properties of the application, and uses the source location to create the first deployment type.

2. After specifying the path to the content file, click **Next**. You may receive a warning that the .msi file could not be verified. Click **Yes** to import this file.

3. After clicking **Next** on the General page, the wizard imports the application information from the specified MSI file, as displayed in Figure 12.2.

4. After the information is successfully imported, click **Next** to see the results. As displayed in Figure 12.3, the information collected is the name of the application and the installation program. The installation program is a default command line for a silent, unattended Windows Installer installation. This information will be used to create the first deployment type for this application.

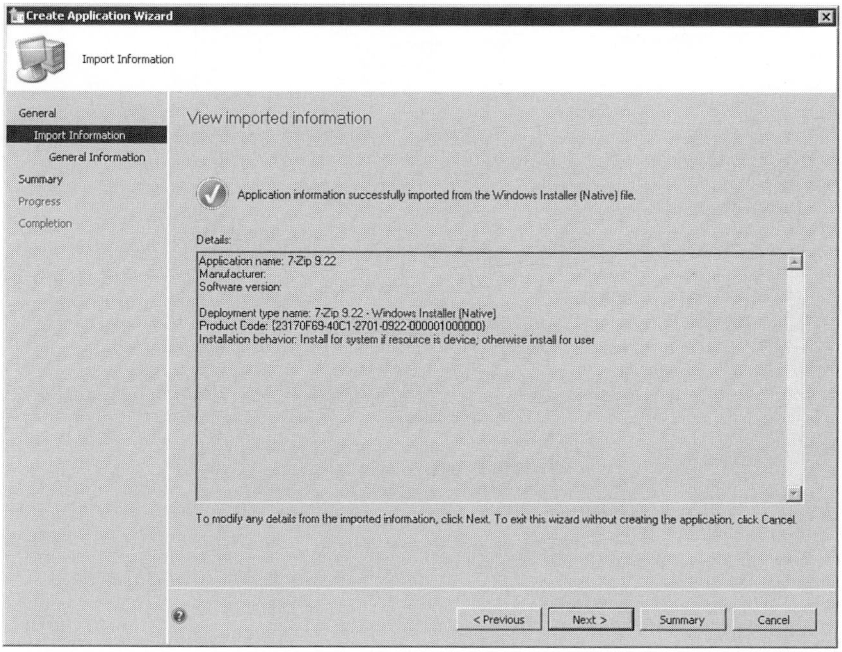

FIGURE 12.2   The Import Information page of the Create Application Wizard.

5. The imported information may be minimal with just the name, installation program, and install behavior displayed in the General Information screen. The information here is used to populate the application information and the minimal-required information for the DT. Edit this information as required.

For 7-Zip, the installation should always install using system rights, so be sure to select **Install for System**.

REAL WORLD: APPLICATIONS OFTEN NEED TO BE INSTALLED WITH ADMINISTRATOR RIGHTS

Administrators will often take the default application deployment type option to **Install system if resource is device; otherwise install for user**, which will cause many installations to fail if the user running the installation (from the Application Catalog) is not an administrator on the system.

---

6. Figure 12.3 displays an example of the information you would add for 7-Zip. Continue the wizard to the Summary page and review the information, as shown in Figure 12.4; then select **Next** to create the application and deployment type.

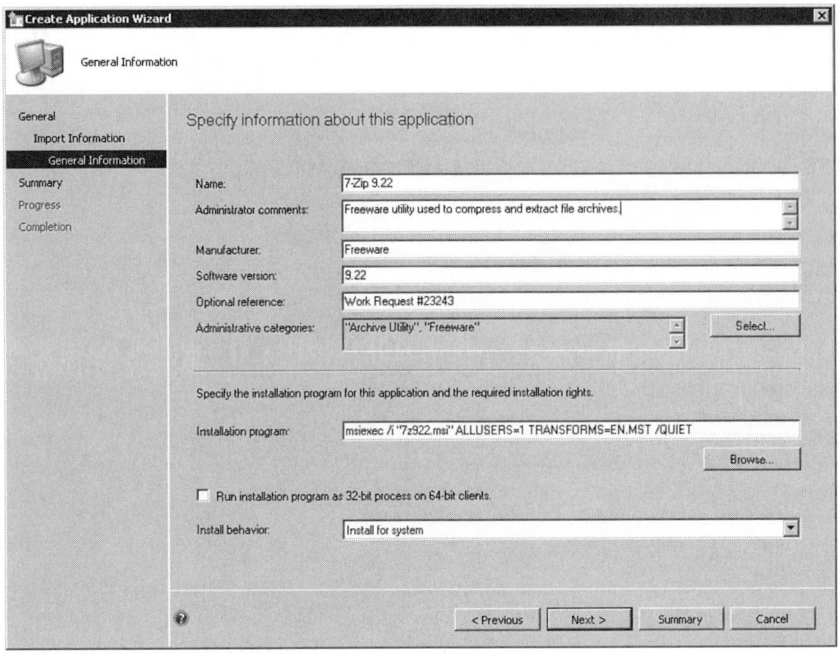

FIGURE 12.3   Use of the additional information fields in the Create Application Wizard.

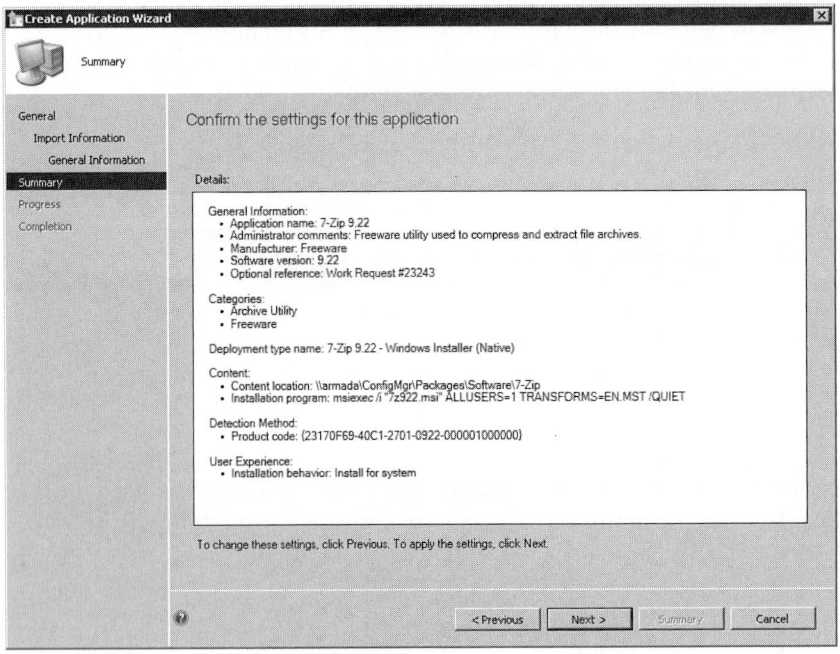

FIGURE 12.4   Summary page of the Create Application Wizard.

7. The last page of the wizard is the Completion page, as displayed in Figure 12.5; it shows the successful completion of the application or any errors with additional information about why the process did complete correctly. Clicking **Close** completes the Create Application Wizard.

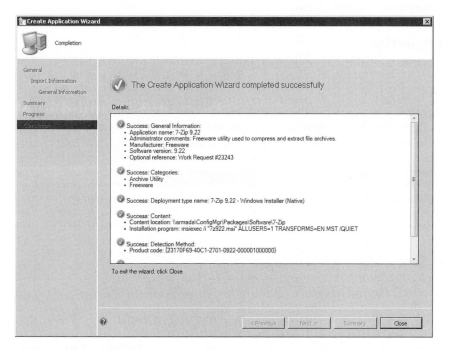

FIGURE 12.5   Completion page of the Create Application Wizard.

After closing the wizard, select the Applications node to view all applications. Figure 12.6 shows the application in the top frame, and you can select one of three tabs in the bottom frame. Figure 12.6 also shows the deployment type in the bottom frame.

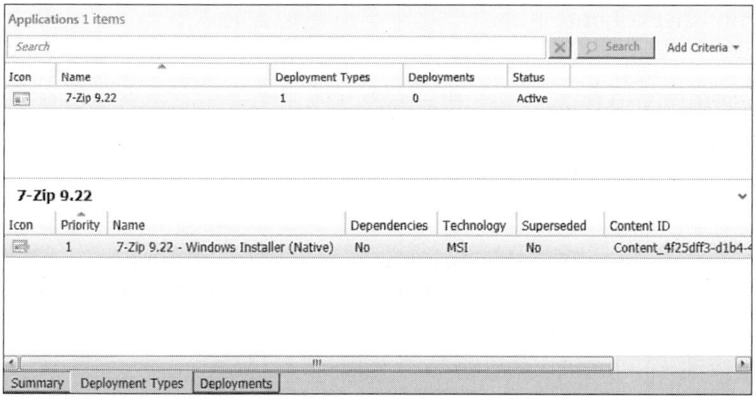

FIGURE 12.6   Application summary information after the Create Application Wizard.

As you walked through the Create Application Wizard, you may have noticed only several configurable options were available. When you use the wizard, ConfigMgr sets many defaults. Now view the details of the application and deployment type to ensure the defaults are configured properly. Start by selecting the application in the console, and then click **Properties** from the ribbon bar.

Application Properties

Improved functionality sometimes introduces complexity. A Configuration Manager application is somewhat more complicated than a traditional package and program, but the benefits significantly outweigh the cost. As mentioned in the "About Applications" section, the application is the container for deploying software (also known as an application). The configurations within an application enable you to provide the best user experience for application delivery. Let's take a detailed look at the properties of an application.

TIP: ABOUT THE FIGURES IN THIS SECTION

Figures in this section are displayed with additional configured settings rather than what appears as default.

The General Tab

The General tab provides basic information about the application (7-Zip in this example), as shown in Figure 12.7. Here is a brief description of each property on the General tab:

▶ **Name:** The name of the application. This is the name used in Software Center. As mentioned in the previous section, choose wisely and be slightly generic for this setting, as you may have multiple DTs to handle specific installation scenarios, such as x86 vs. x64.

▶ **Administrator comments:** Information that is only available in the Configuration Manager console. This is a property where you could add additional information visible only to administrators.

▶ **Manufacturer:** The manufacturer of the software. This field appears in Software Center, under the Publisher column.

▶ **Software version:** Enter a user-friendly software version, as the version here is what the end user sees in Software Center.

▶ **Optional reference:** This is property is only available to administrators. Take advantage of this field and add information such as a work order or request ID for software deployment.

▶ **Administrative categories:** Administrative categories are used in the application catalog. An administrator can create a new category, or select an existing application category if desired.

▶ **Date published:** This is an additional field for administrators, which appears in Software Center. Use this property in your environment to stamp when an application is deployed.

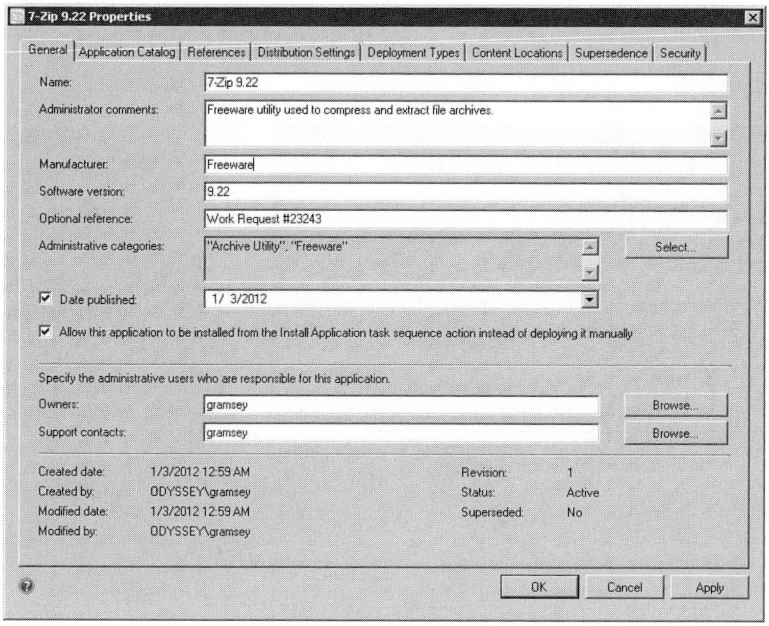

FIGURE 12.7   The Application General tab.

▶ **Allow this application to be installed from the Install Application task sequence action instead of deploying it manually:** This is descriptive text for a check box! By enabling this check box, you allow this installation to occur during a task sequence (TS).

▶ **Owners:** You can enter an owner into this field, or click the **Browse** button to select a user or AD group from Active Directory.

▶ **Support contacts:** Similar to Owners, you can enter an owner into this field, or click the **Browse** button to select a user or AD group from Active Directory.

Additional data appears at the bottom of the General tab: the created and modify dates, current revision, current status (active or retired), and if the application is superseded.

It is also important to mention that applications are version-controlled; meaning when an application is created, the previous version is saved and can be restored or revised when required. You can right-click an application and select **Revision History** (or simply select the application, and then choose **Revision History**) to show or select previous versions of the application.

The Application Catalog Tab

The Application Catalog tab, shown in Figure 12.8, displays all the properties used to enhance the user experience when searching/selecting an application from the Application

Catalog. Some of the properties are also used when the application is visible in Software Center.

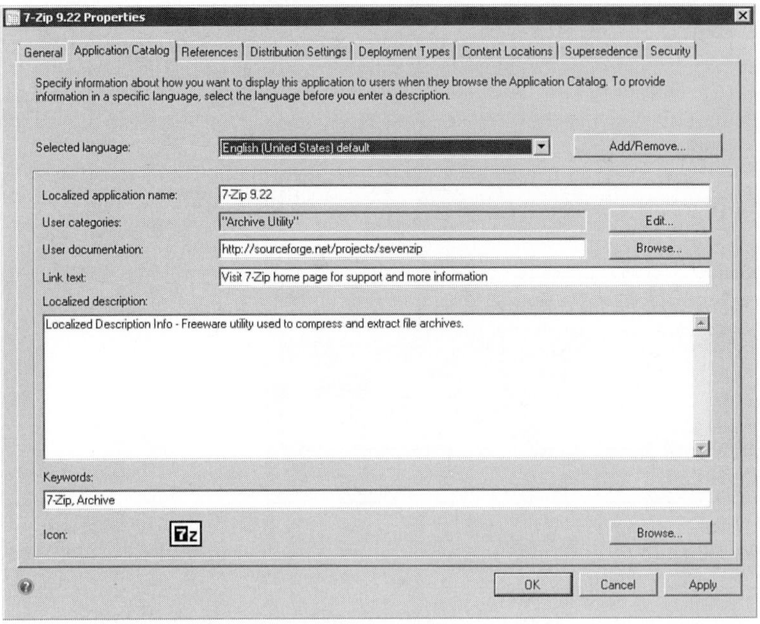

FIGURE 12.8   The Application Catalog tab.

Here is a brief description of each property on the Application Catalog tab:

▶ **Selected language:** The Application Catalog supports multiple languages. If you configure multiple languages here, the custom language text appears when a user with the appropriate language settings in Internet Explorer launches the Application Catalog. If the user has Internet Explorer language settings configured for a language not enabled for the Application, the user will see whichever language is marked as default (English by default). Notice that all items on this tab are localized. For each language that you want to support, populate the remaining information in the frame.

▶ **Localized application name:** This is the friendly name of the application that will appear in both Software Center and Application Catalog. This name is also searchable in both locations.

▶ **User categories:** Use these categories to help end users locate software quickly in the Application Catalog such as Web Browsers, Utilities, Human Resources, and so on. Categories appear in the left frame in the Application Catalog.

▶ **User documentation:** This is a great field that allows you to enter a web URL or import a file. A link will be visible in Software Center and Application Catalog when viewing the details of an application. Clicking the link either launches the web URL or opens the file. If uploading files, be sure to use a common document type that will be available on all systems.

▶ **Link text:** Provide a localized entry for what will occur when the user clicks on the user documentation. The example in this section tells the user that the link will navigate to the 7-Zip home page.

▶ **Localized description:** Populate this field to provide additional details to the user about the application. This field is searchable from Software Center and Application Catalog.

▶ **Keywords:** Separate keywords with a space. Add information such as file extensions, and generic terms for the product, like "archive," "word processor," and so on. You can search for these keywords in Application Catalog.

▶ **Icon:** Click the **Browse** button to either select a standard icon or import an icon from an .ico, .msi, .exe, or .dll file. This icon appears only in the Application Catalog.

Table 12.1 lists the settings appearing in Software Center and/or Application Catalog.

TABLE 12.1   List Properties and Visibility to the End User

General Tab and End-User Visibility

	Visible in Software Center	Visible in Application Catalog
Name	N	N
Administrator Comments	N	N
Manufacturer	Y (as 'Publisher')	N
Software Version	Y	
Optional Reference	N	N
Administrative Categories	N	N
Date Published	Y	N
Allow this application to be installed from the Install Application Task sequence action instead of deploying it manually	N	N
Owners	N	N
Support Contacts	N	N

Application Catalog Tab and End-User Visibility

	Visible in Software Center	Visible in Application Catalog
Selected Language	Y	Y
Localized Application Name	Y	Y
User Categories	N	Y

Application Catalog Tab and End-User Visibility

	Visible in Software Center	Visible in Application Catalog
User Documentation	Y	Y
Link Text	N	Y
Localized Description	Y	Y
Keywords	N	Y
Icon Image	N	Y

The References Tab

The References tab displays two types of application relationships, both of which are self-explanatory:

▶ **Applications that depend on this application**

▶ **Applications that supersede this application**

This tab helps you see whether changes you make to this application will affect another application. You will also see which revisions of this application are being referenced. The information in this tab also includes fine print, telling you that either there are no items in the list, or you do not have permission to view all items. Depending on how you have role-based administration (RBA) configured, you may find that some administrators cannot see all applications based on the configured scopes.

The Distribution Settings Tab

The Distribution Settings tab, displayed in Figure 12.9, helps you manage how an application is distributed to targeted distribution points (DPs). Here are the settings:

▶ **Distribution priority:** This setting controls the order in which multiple packages, applications, and other content are sent to DPs. You may want to configure more critical content (such as antivirus, security patches, and so on) to a high priority, giving it priority to be sent to child sites and distribution points faster than content of low priority such as a portable document format viewer application.

▶ **Distribute the content for this package to preferred distribution points:** A client's preferred DPs are those that exist in the boundary group that is defined for the boundary matching the clients location. In this situation, when a client in a preferred DP boundary requests content not on the DP, it is automatically deployed to the preferred DP to fulfill the request for the client. This could be an excellent option for content you do not want to deploy to all DPs, such as a MUI language package. (If content for an application or package is configured to download from remote or fallback DPs, this setting is ignored.)

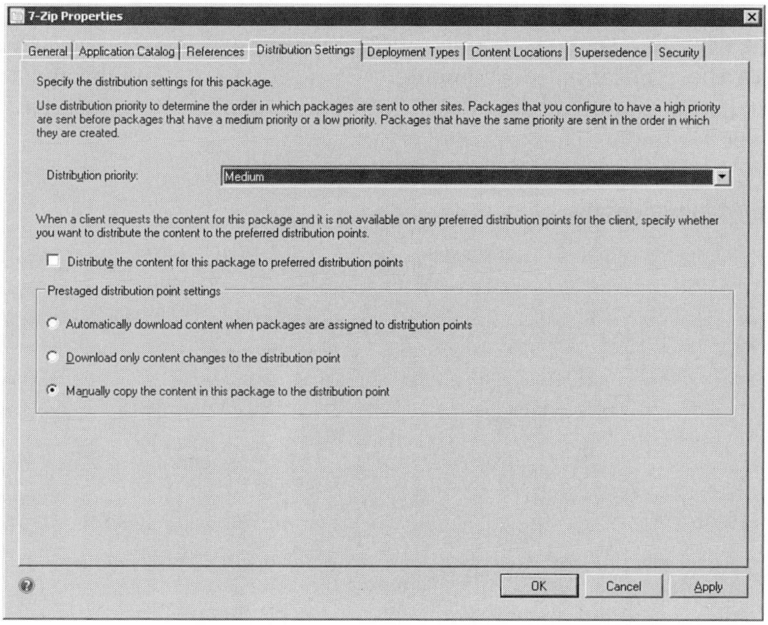

FIGURE 12.9   The Distribution Settings tab.

▶ **Prestaged distribution point settings:** If you select the **Enable this distribution point for prestaged content** check box on the Distribution Point properties, the following settings affect content distribution:

   ▶ **Automatically download content when packages are assigned to distribution points:** This setting causes the DP to perform normally and not really follow any prestaged content rules—content will be distributed to any targeted DP.

   ▶ **Download only content changes to the distribution point:** This option requires you to export content, and then extract content manually on the DP for the initial distribution. Subsequent update distribution point actions will send delta updates to the package.

   Here's an example: You are ready to deploy the next version of Microsoft Office. The source installation is around 1GB. Due to WAN availability, you may choose to manually transfer content to the distribution point the first time (either over a WAN file copy, or actually shipping media that contains content to the remote DP). After you prestage the initial payload, update DPs will work normally, as expected.

   ▶ **Manually copy the content in this package to the distribution point:** This setting prevents ConfigMgr from copying any content to the DP, and requires you to export content from the console and then extract content to the DP each time for this package.

The Deployment Types Tab

Deployment types are the heart and soul of the application; these are used to determine the best method to deploy the application to a computer system. Each DT contains one source files path and installation command for the application deployment. Figure 12.10 shows the deployment type for the 7-Zip application.

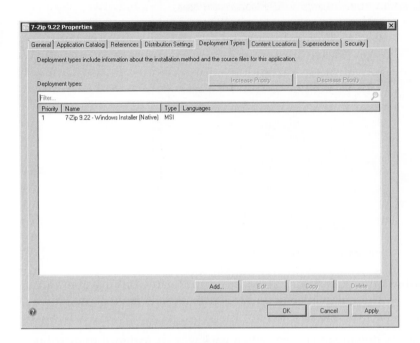

FIGURE 12.10   The Deployment Types tab.

The next sections describe the DT created with the Create Application Wizard for Windows Installer-based software. The "Creating Deployment Types" section contains additional information about creating deployment types.

Deployment Type - General   Select the DT, and click **Edit** to display the DT properties. Figure 12.11 shows the General tab of the DT. Notice the DT name is changed from 7-zip 9.22 - Windows Installer (Native) to 7-Zip 9.22 - Windows Installer x86—this provides some clarity to the administrator once a second DT is created for x64.

From this tab, you have the following options:

▶ **Name:** The DT name will be visible only in the ConfigMgr client logs, through the admin console for DT properties, deployment status, and through the Reporting Services point.

▶ **Technology:** Displays the technology used to create the DT (Windows Installer, script-based, and so on). Note that the Technology property is informational only—you can create a DT by using the wizard based on a Windows Installer file, but change all the other properties so that it really doesn't use any Windows Installer information.

▶ **Administrator comments:** Here is where the administrator can add comments about the DT; this is only visible to ConfigMgr administrators.

▶ **Languages:** This is another informational box where you can multiselect supported languages for this DT. If you actually want to restrict the application installation to specific languages, enable that under the Requirements tab with a custom rule.

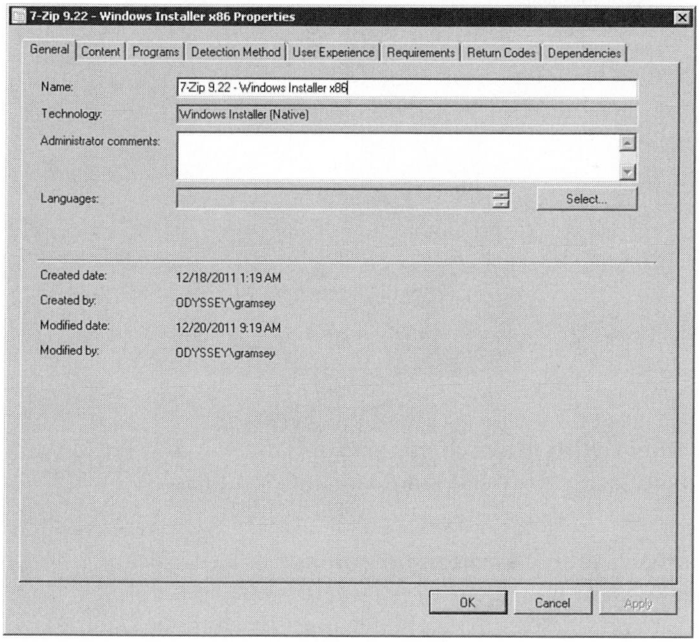

FIGURE 12.11   The Deployment Type General tab.

Deployment Type - Content   The Content tab contains installation source information and distribution settings, as shown in Figure 12.12. Here are the settings provided by the Content tab:

▶ **Content location:** The UNC source path to the content. All files in this path (including subfolders) are captured and stored in the content store, sent to DPs, and downloaded to clients for installation. For content, less is more—keep content source as small as possible.

▶ **Persist content in the client cache:** When you enable this setting and deploy the application to a target collection, clients that use this deployment type (based on the requirement rules) will download and keep the installation source in the local ConfigMgr Cache folder (%*windir*%\ccmcache). By default, client cache size is configured to 5GB, so use this option sparingly.

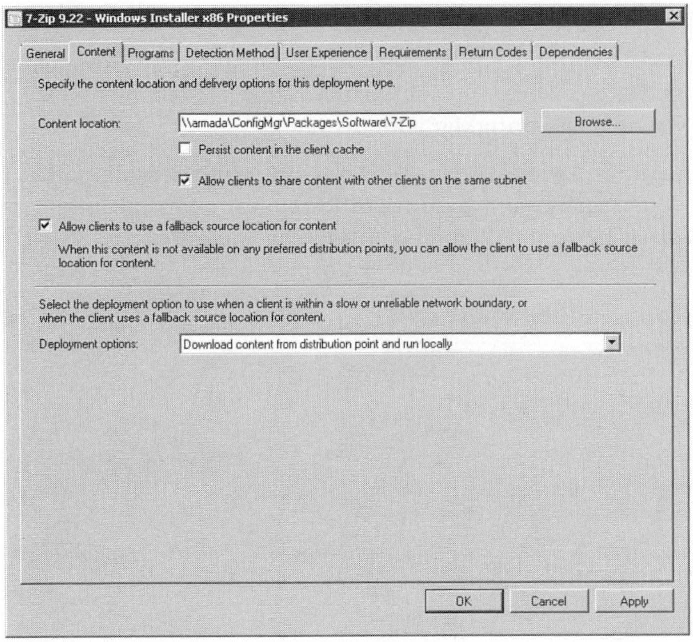

FIGURE 12.12   The Deployment Type Content tab.

▶ **Allow clients to share content with other clients on the same subnet:** Enable this check box to leverage BranchCache (provided BranchCache is configured for your environment).

▶ **Allow clients to use a fallback source location for content:** If a client cannot locate content for this deployment in its defined boundary group, this check box allows the client to search other locations. The DP must be configured with the option **Allow fallback source location for content**. Review Chapter 13, "Distributing and Deploying Applications," for more information regarding distribution points.

▶ **Deployment options:** If the client is located in a boundary considered slow or unreliable (by the DP Groups property), you can choose to not download content, or to download and run locally.

Deployment Type - Programs   The Programs tab (shown in Figure 12.13) defines the install and uninstall properties for a windows-installer or script-based deployment type. The Programs tab provides the following settings:

▶ **Installation program:** The command line to install the software. This command will be run from the root of the content source location, shown in Figure 12.12. Remember, this path should be relative to the content source location.

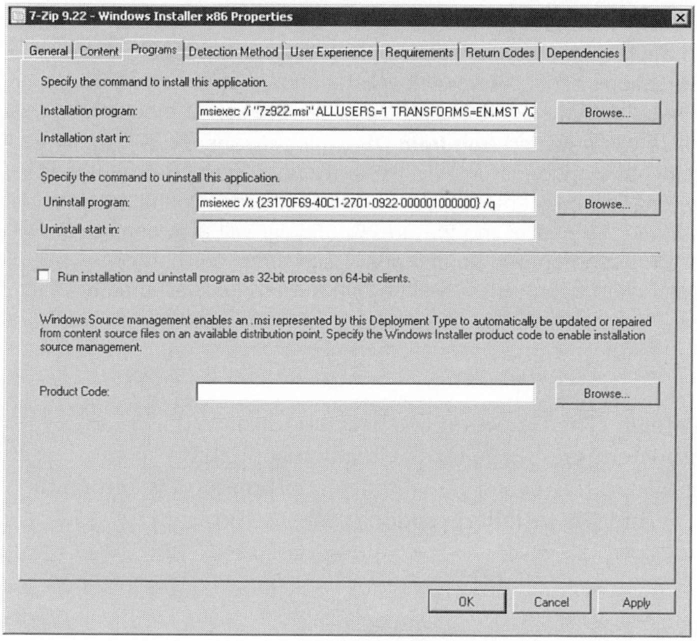

FIGURE 12.13   The Deployment Type Programs tab.

▶ **Installation start in:** If the installation requires a specific path to run, specify the path here. Most modern installations do not require this configuration, so this is usually left blank.

▶ **Uninstall program:** Specify the unattended uninstall command line. If you use the Create Deployment Type Wizard, and specify a Windows Installer program, the uninstall command is added automatically. Review and test the command line to verify the uninstall works as expected. Always include the uninstall command when possible. This is used to allow the user to remove optional software from Software Center, as well as any uninstall deployments from the site. Uninstall of previous applications can also be used with supersedence.

▶ **Uninstall start in:** If the uninstall requires a specific path to run, specify that here.

▶ **Run installation and uninstall program as a 32-bit process on 64-bit clients:** Enable this check box if the application is a 32-bit installation, which means it will install to %*ProgramFiles(x86)*%. This setting helps ConfigMgr properly install and uninstall the 32-bit application on a 64-bit system. The ConfigMgr client agent on a 64-bit system will not use the Program Files (x86) file path or the HKLM\Software\ Wow6432Node registry path by default.

▶ **Product Code:** The product code is used for Windows source management. You can specify a Windows Installer product code here; an easier method would be to click **Browse** and import the .msi file to ensure the product code is accurate.

WHAT IS WINDOWS SOURCE MANAGEMENT?

Many Windows Installer-based applications support self-healing, and/or the repair feature. Normally, when either of these actions occur, the original installation files are required. When these applications are installed from ConfigMgr, the source location is a subfolder of %*windir*%\ccmcache\. (Unless you selected **Run from DP**, which means the DP share UNC path is the source location—this option is only available for packages.) Both of these locations are not ideal for the long term. By entering a valid product code, ConfigMgr can manage the source location for you. As part of the feature, ConfigMgr will also configure the system to use the closest DP based on site boundaries. Each time your network address changes, the ConfigMgr client agent will verify the Windows Installer source is leveraging the nearest DP.

Deployment Type - Detection Method   The Detection Method tab (displayed in Figure 12.14) specifies how ConfigMgr determines if the DT is already installed. If you run through the Windows Installer wizard to create a DT, the detection method is automatically created based on the MSI (Windows Installer) product code, as shown in Figure 12.14.

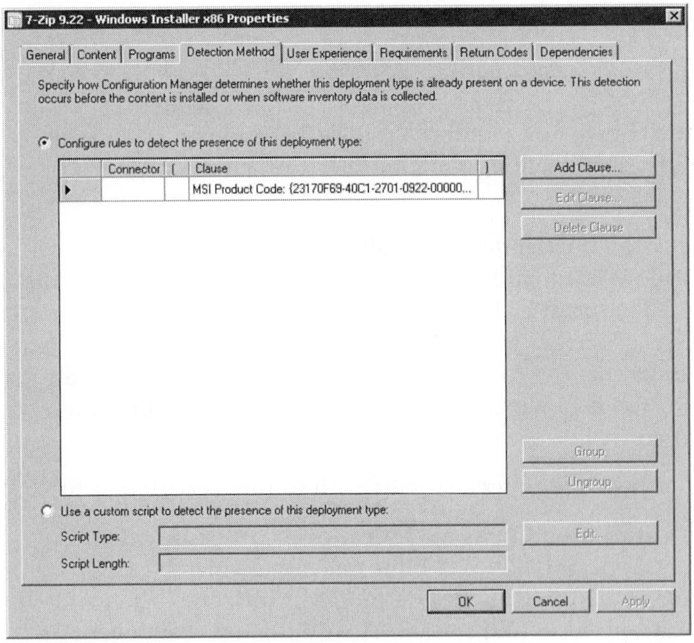

FIGURE 12.14   The Deployment Type Detection Method tab.

Every DT must have a detection method. The application depends on the detection method to provide the proper state of the application. Recall that by default, every 7 days the client performs an Application Deployment Evaluation Cycle for required installations. If an application is found required but not installed (based on the detection method),

ConfigMgr automatically initiates an installation. For more information on creating detection methods, see the "Creating Detection Methods" section.

Deployment Type - User Experience   The User Experience tab (shown in Figure 12.15) defines how the application installation interacts with the user. Here are the settings provided by the User Experience tab:

▶ **Installation behavior:** Choose the proper selection to determine the rights used to install the software:

   ▶ **Install for user:** Install using the rights of the current user.

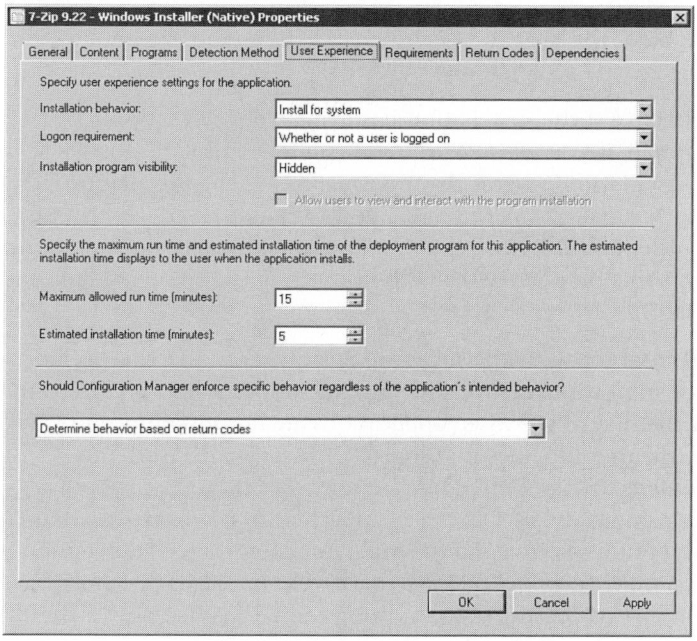

FIGURE 12.15   The Deployment Type User Experience tab.

   ▶ **Install for system:** Install using the rights of the SMS Agent Host service (Local System account).

   ▶ **Install for system if resource is device; otherwise, install for user:** If the application is targeted to a collection of devices, install for system; if the application is targeted to a collection of users (or user groups), install for user.

▶ **Logon requirement:** Determines when the installation can occur; this will be either **Only when a user is logged on or only when no user is logged on**. A required (mandatory) deployment will wait for the appropriate state before starting the installation.

▶ **Installation program visibility:** Defines how the installation should appear to the user during the installation process.

  ▶ **Normal:** This default mode indicates the program runs based on system and program defaults.

  ▶ **Minimized:** Running minimized shows the program only on the task bar during installation. The window exists on the task bar during the installation process, although it is not the active window maximized on the user's workstation.

  ▶ **Maximized:** This is a good configuration to use when installing programs requiring user intervention. It is also good for package and application testing.

  ▶ **Hidden:** This mode hides the program during installation, and is recommended for fully automated program deployments.

  These settings are only effective if the installation has available information to show to the user. For example, if you use a Windows Installer command line with the /passive switch, an installation progress bar appears during the installation, if program visibility is set to Normal or Maximized. If you use the /quiet switch, the installation is completely silent, and no information appears during the installation, regardless of the setting for this property. This visibility setting is also dependent on the next setting on this tab.

▶ **Allow users to view and interact with the program installation:** Use this option when the user needs to see and/or interact with the installation. This option is also an excellent troubleshooting method to use when applications are not installing correctly. With this option selected, the user interface is visible to the user logged in to the system, and the user can interact with the program. As an example, you will choose this option if the program requires the user to make a selection or click a button. If a program runs without this option selected and the program requires user intervention, it waits for the user interaction (which will never occur) and eventually times out when the maximum allowed runtime has occurred. This setting can be enabled only if the **Logon requirement** is configured to **Only when a user is logged on**.

▶ **Maximum allowed run time (minutes):** This setting defines the maximum time program is expected to run. There can be considerable variation in how a program will run; it depends on the speed of the system ConfigMgr is installing it on, the size of the program, and the network connectivity between the system and the source files used for the installation. In this example, the setting defaulted to 120 minutes. However, based on previous installations of 7-Zip, it should complete within 5 minutes. ConfigMgr requires a setting between 15 and 720 minutes, so set this value to 15 minutes. Choose the maximum run time carefully, as it will affect the following behavior:

  ▶ During program installation, the ConfigMgr client monitors the installation until the maximum time is reached. If the installation has not completed by the maximum allowed time, ConfigMgr sends a status message stating that the maximum run time has been reached, and that ConfigMgr will no longer monitor it. (This in turn frees up ConfigMgr to deploy additional software, if required.)

▶ Before a program will run, ConfigMgr will check to see if any maintenance windows have been defined, and if so, verify that the available window is larger than the Maximum allowed run time. If the available window is not large enough, the client will wait for an available window for deployment, unless you configured the deployment to ignore maintenance windows.

▶ **Estimated installation time (minutes):** This is the expected installation time, and appears to the user when selecting an application to install from Software Center.

▶ **Should Configuration Manager enforce specific behavior regardless of the application's intended behavior?:** This drop-down specifies if ConfigMgr should manage any operating system restart and also provides this information to the user through Software Center or Application Catalog. Here are the available settings:

  ▶ **Determine behavior based on return codes:** This setting handles reboots based on the codes configured on the Return Codes tab. The end user will see a message similar to **Might require a reboot** in Software Center and Application Catalog. Although a bit vague, it is the most flexible. By leveraging this setting, the user will receive a notification that a reboot is required (if required), if the installation returns a defined return code. This is a good user experience.

  ▶ **No specific action:** This setting tells ConfigMgr and the end user that no reboot should be required after installation.

  ▶ **The software install program might force a device restart:** This setting advises that ConfigMgr will not be controlling the reboot, and the actual installation may force a restart without warning. For example, if your Windows Installer command line includes the argument `/ForceRestart`, the installation process will force a restart. Although this is least desirable, ConfigMgr will at least expect a restart to occur. With any other setting, if the application forces a restart, ConfigMgr will return a failure status message of an unexpected system restart.

  ▶ **Configuration Manager client will force a mandatory device restart:** This is the preferred setting if you know that an application requires a restart. To leverage this setting, ensure the software installation does not force a restart of its own. After the installation exits, ConfigMgr will either notify the user that a restart is required or proceed to restart the computer. This decision is based on the user interaction, which is configured when you create a deployment (discussed in Chapter 13).

TIP: CONFIGURE THE RESTART OPTION CORRECTLY

Take time to configure the restart option correctly to avoid surprising the user with an unexpected restart.

Deployment Type - Requirements   The Requirements tab defines the required settings for the DT to be installed on a system. For this example (and by default when you use the Create Application Wizard), there are no requirements. This tab is similar to the Requirements tab on a program (described in Chapter 11), in that you can specify requirements for an installation to specific operating systems (such as Windows 7 x86).

Let's create the basic requirement for 7-Zip (x86). Select the **Add** button to display the Create Requirement dialog, and configure it as shown in Figure 12.16.

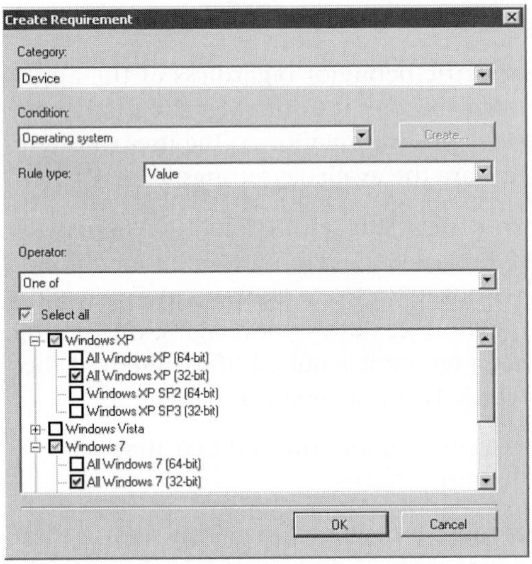

FIGURE 12.16   The Deployment Type Create Requirement dialog.

As shown in the figure, you can configure this DT to support all Windows XP (32-bit) and all Windows 7 (32-bit). Click **OK** to save the platform restriction. The Requirements tab for an application contains many more features than traditional programs. The "Managing and Creating Global Conditions" section includes detailed steps on how to create requirements.

Deployment Type - Return Codes   The Return Codes tab shown in Figure 12.17 contains the defined installation return codes for the DT. Default return codes include the most popular windows installer return codes. You can update this as required. Click **Add** to create a new return code entry for this deployment type.

Deployment Type - Dependencies   Use the Dependencies tab to specify required prerequisite applications for this application. See the "Adding Dependencies" section later in this chapter for more information.

Now you are finished with the properties of the deployment type. When you click **OK**, you will again be positioned on the Application properties.

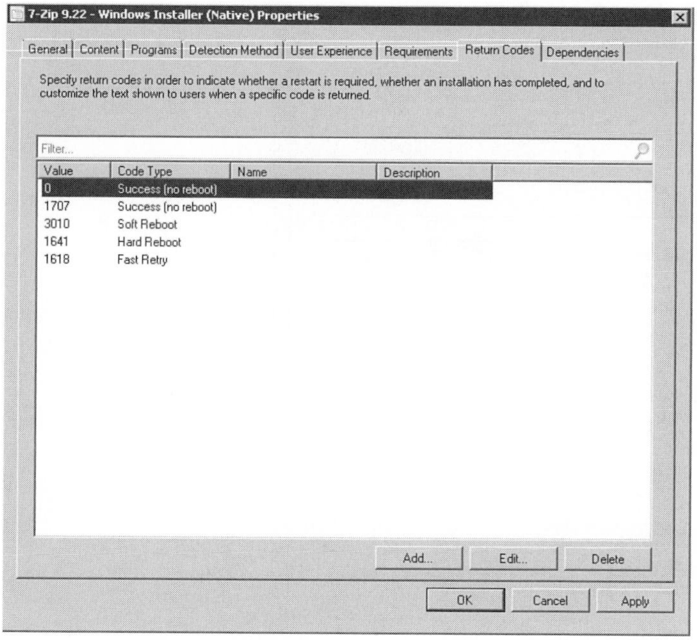

FIGURE 12.17   The Add Return Code dialog.

The Content Locations Tab

The Content Locations tab (see Figure 12.18) for the application displays all targeted distribution points (DPs) and DP groups. Content distribution is discussed in detail in Chapter 13.

The Supersedence Tab

Use the Supersedence tab to supersede an existing application with a new application, or a newer version of the application. You can use supersedence to automatically upgrade systems that have an existing application, or to require the latest version on one targeted collection while still supporting the previous version on a different collection. See the "Superseding Applications" section for more information.

After walking through the process of creating a new application, as well as viewing all the property pages for an application and deployment type, it is time to dive a little deeper into some of the components of an application.

Creating Deployment Types

DTs are a major component of every application. The "Application Overview" section provides an overview of DTs. The "Creating a Windows Installer (MSI)-Based Application" section walks through the process of creating a new application for a Windows Installer installation, creating a DT to install 7-Zip for the x86 version of the 7-Zip installation. The next sections create a DT for the x64 installation, and ensure it will install only on x64 platforms.

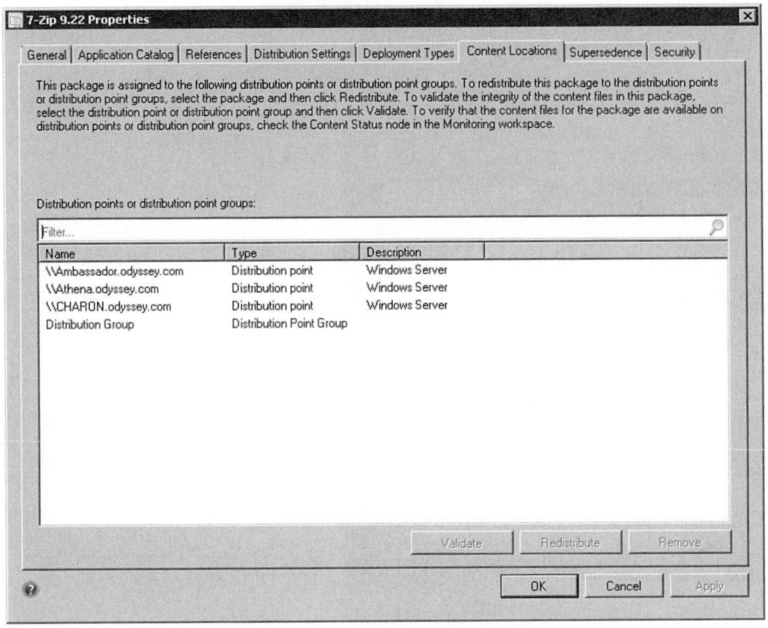

FIGURE 12.18   The Content Locations tab.

Creating a Windows Installer-Based Deployment Type

Perform the following steps to start the Create Deployment Type Wizard:

1. Open the Configuration Manager console, and select the **Software Library** workspace.

2. In the workspace, expand Application Management.

3. Right-click the **Applications** node.

4. Select the 7-Zip application.

5. Right-click the 7-Zip application, and select **Create Deployment Type** from the context menu.

6. Click the **Add** button.

7. In the Create Deployment Type Wizard, select **Windows Installer (Native)** as the type. **Browse** to the .msi file, and click **Next**.

8. The Import Information dialog will display a successful import. Click **Next** to continue.

9. The next page is the General Information page, shown in Figure 12.19. This wizard provides a subset of settings for the DT. The defaults are modified, so the x64 installation would be a similar installation experience to the x86 DT previously created

in the "About Creating Applications" section. The information on this page is used to populate the minimal-required information for the DT. Edit this information as required. Here is a basic description of each field:

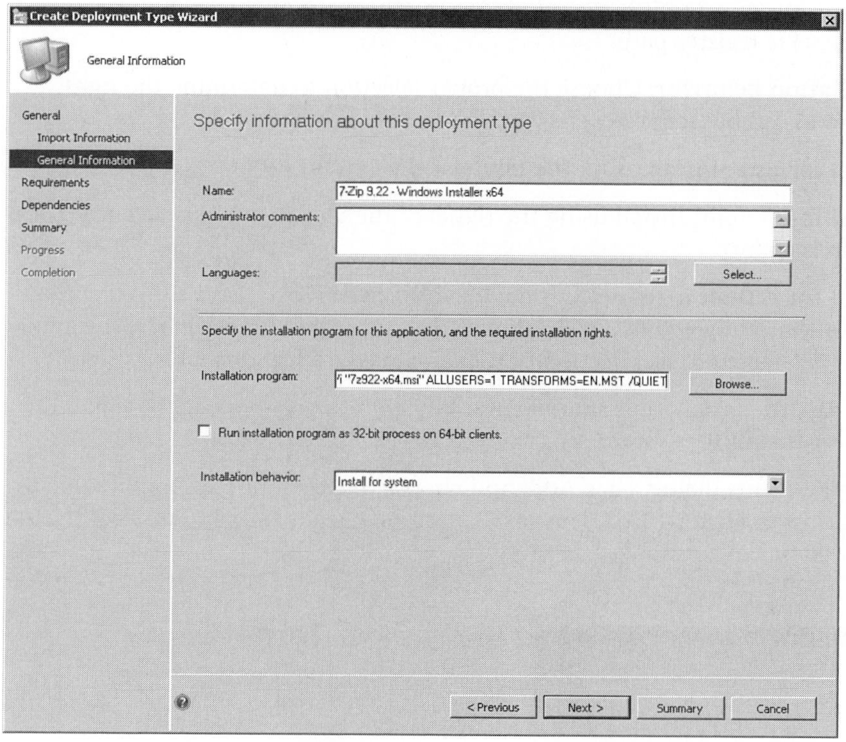

FIGURE 12.19   The General Information page of the Create Deployment Type Wizard.

▶ **Name:** The name of the deployment type. This example contains x64 in the DT Name, which will simplify troubleshooting.

▶ **Administrator comments:** Information that is only visible in the System Center 2012 Configuration Manager console.

▶ **Languages:** This is an informational box where you can multiselect supported languages for this DT. To restrict the application installation to specific languages, enable that under the Requirements tab with a custom rule.

▶ **Installation program:** The command line to install the software. The default for a windows installer program uses the /q switch, for a quiet installation. Modify this installation command if your installation requires additional parameters like public properties or transforms. This command will run from the root of the content source location, shown in Figure 12.19. Remember, this path should be relative to the content source location.

▶ **Run installation program as a 32-bit process on 64-bit clients:** Enable this check box if the application is a 32-bit installation, meaning it will install to *%ProgramFiles(x86)*. This setting helps ConfigMgr properly install and uninstall the 32-bit application on a 64-bit system. By default, the ConfigMgr client agent on a 64-bit system does not use this path or the `HKLM\Software\Wow6432Node` registry path.

▶ **Installation behavior:** Choose the proper selection to determine the rights used to install the software:

Install for user: Install using the rights of the current user.

Install for system: Install using the rights of the SMS Agent Host service (Local System account).

Install for system if resource is device; otherwise, install for user: If the application is targeted to a collection of devices, install for system; if the application is targeted to a collection of users (or user groups), install for user.

For 7-Zip, the installation should always install using system rights, so be sure to select **Install for system**, as shown in Figure 12.19.

10. For the Requirements dialog, click **Add**, and choose the appropriate supported platforms, as shown in Figure 12.20. This installation of 7-Zip is for x64, so select the desired x64 platforms to support.

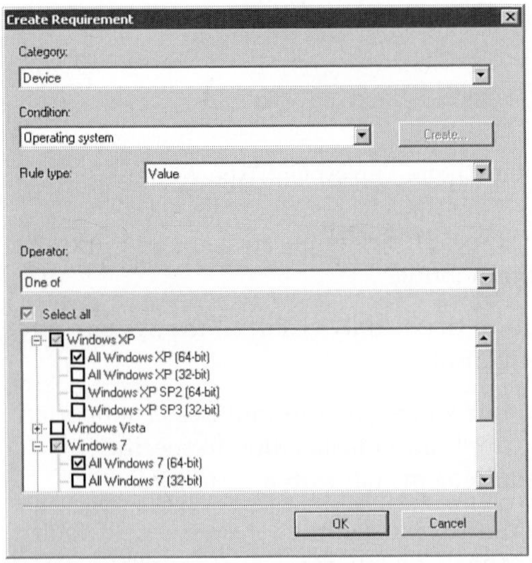

FIGURE 12.20   The Create Requirement dialog for the Requirements page of the wizard.

11. The next page of the wizard is the Dependencies page. 7-Zip does not have any dependent applications (such as .NET Framework, for example), so leave this page blank, and click **Next** to view the Summary page.

12. Click **Next** to create the DT. The Completion page will confirm success.

Notice the Deployment Types tab of the 7-Zip 9.22 application. You now have two deployment types, as shown in Figure 12.21.

An additional feature regarding deployment types is Priority. Figure 12.21 shows the x86 installation is priority 1, and x64 is priority 2. When you deploy an application, the client evaluates each DT in order of priority. The first DT that meets the requirements is run. If possible, place the DT that you expect will run the most as priority 1.

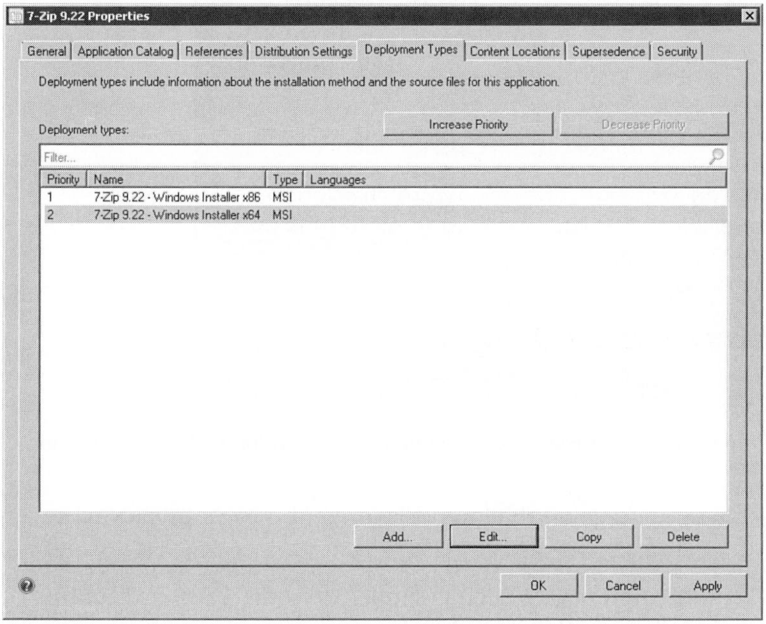

FIGURE 12.21 The Deployment Type tab of the 7-Zip application.

Now that you have created a new deployment type, review the "Application Properties" section to determine if you need to make additional changes to the DT. Recall that the wizard shows a limited set of options for the DT. View the properties to make additional changes.

Creating an Application Virtualization Deployment Type

An App-V DT is the easiest DT to create. You can use the Create Application Wizard to create a new application with an App-V DT, or you can choose an existing application and add a DT. Follow these steps to add a new DT to an existing application:

1. From the Application properties, select the Deployment Types tab, and click **Add** to create a new DT.

2. For DT type, select **Microsoft Application Virtualization**. For Location, browse to the .xml file for the App-V package; this is shown in Figure 12.22.

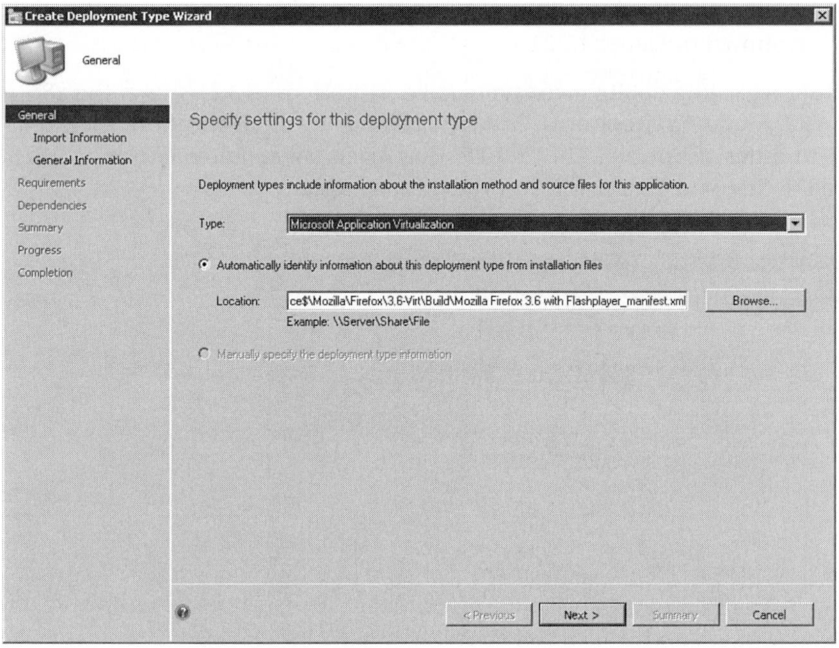

FIGURE 12.22   The General page of the Create Deployment Type Wizard for an App-V application.

3. You will receive a success message on the Import Information page. Click **Next** to continue the wizard.

4. Next is the General Information page, which is similar to Figure 12.19, except the command line is missing. Because this is an App-V application, an installation command line is not required. Modify required information, and click **Next** to proceed to the next page of the wizard.

5. The Requirements page already contains requirements for this App-V application. The information is included in the .xml file you imported for the DT. You can click **Add** to add additional requirements.

6. Continue the wizard by clicking **Next** on each remaining page to save the DT. When the DT is complete, select to **Edit** the DT. The General, Requirements, and Dependencies page are similar to the Windows Installer DT created in the "About Creating Applications" section earlier in this chapter. This section will review the tabs that are customized for App-V applications, namely Content and Publishing.

TIP: ALWAYS ENSURE APP-V CLIENT IS INSTALLED BEFORE APP-V APPLICATION

Create an application that installs both the x86 and x64 version of the App-V client, and make that application a dependency for this new App-V application so that if the App-V client is not installed, it will be required and automatically install before the desired App-V application installation.

---

7. Review the Content tab to see that the operating system requirements were success-fully imported from the manifest, shown in Figure 12.23. The Content tab for an App-V DT provides the following settings:

> **App-V manifest location:** The UNC source path to the App-V application manifest. Notice the location is read-only. To update the source location for the manifest file as well as the sequenced application, you must select **Update Content** from the Deployment Type properties (either right-click or the ribbon bar), and walk through the wizard to select a different manifest.

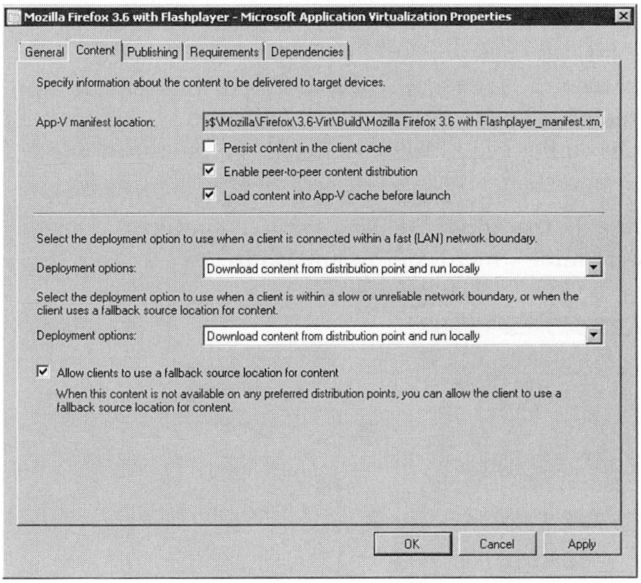

FIGURE 12.23   The Content tab for an App-V Deployment Type.

> **Persist content in the client cache:** When you enable this setting and deploy the application to a target collection, clients that use this deployment type (based on the requirement rules) will download and keep the installation source in the local ConfigMgr Cache folder (%*windir*%\ccmcache), configured to 5GB by default.

> **Enable peer-to-peer content distribution:** Enable this check box to leverage BranchCache (provided BranchCache is configured for your environment).

▶ **Load content into App-V cache before launch:** With this check box disabled and the download content option configured, a ConfigMgr client will download the content to its local cache, publish the icon(s), and exit. With the check box enabled, when content is downloaded the ConfigMgr client will call the App-V command to preload content to App-V cache immediately (instead of waiting until the first launch). The problem when the check box is cleared is if the software is downloaded to ConfigMgr cache but the user does not launch the application for the first time until *after* the cache has been cleaned on the client, the launch will fail. A best practice would be to enable this check box to precache the application to the App-V cache.

▶ **Deployment options:** If the client is located in a fast network (as defined in the boundary group configuration), you can configure the application to be streamed from the DP or to download the content first. If the client is located in a boundary considered slow or unreliable (by the DP Groups property), you can choose to not download content, to download and run locally, or to stream content from the DP.

▶ **Allow clients to use a fallback source location for content:** If a client is unable to locate content for this deployment in its defined boundary group, this check box allows the client to search other locations. To allow clients to access source from a different boundary group, the Boundary Group properties tab for the DP must be configured to **Allow fallback source location for content**.

8. The Publishing tab is also unique to the App-V DT. Review the Publishing tab in Figure 12.24. Use this tab to determine which icons to publish to the end user.

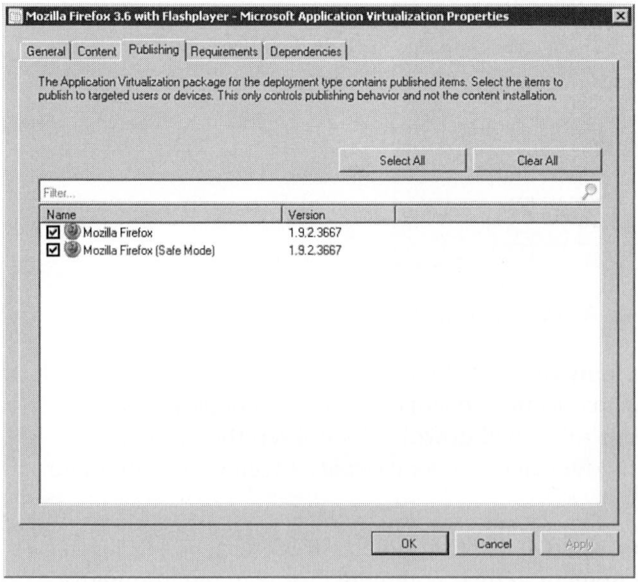

FIGURE 12.24   The Publishing tab for an App-V Deployment Type.

9. Select the Requirements tab, and select the **Add** button to add a new requirement. In the Create Requirement dialog, select a category of **User**, and verify the Condition is Primary Device equals True.

Creating a Script-Based Deployment Type

When you hear the word "script," you may think of something written in VBScript, PowerShell, or some other scripting language. When you work with applications, a script-based installer will be a familiar type. This could be an .exe, .bat, .com, .vbs, or any other type of command that you would run from a command line to install software (other than Windows Installer, covered in the "About Creating Applications" section of this chapter). This section walks through the process to add a new DT to an existing application. The steps are similar to the process for creating a new Windows Installer-based DT, but there are significant differences. Follow these steps to create a script-based DT for the Microsoft Word Viewer application:

1. From the Application properties, select the Deployment Types tab, and click **Add** to create a new DT.

2. For DT type, select **Script Installer (Native)**.

3. Notice the source location property is disabled because you selected Script Installer (Native) instead of Windows Installer. Click **Next** to display the General Information tab of the wizard, and fill out as much information as possible.

4. Click **Next** to advance to the Content page. Figure 12.25 shows the content page after manually adding the content location and installation program. If you have worked with different types of installations in the past, you know that there are no standard install arguments for all executables, batch files, and other script-based installations. That is why you should always work with the application vendor to either request a Windows Installer package, or provide a document that gives you the correct install/uninstall arguments. For this installation, as you don't currently know the proper uninstall command, leave it blank.

TIP: ALLOW USERS TO UNINSTALL APPLICATIONS FROM SOFTWARE CENTER

Include the proper uninstall when possible to allow the user to leverage Software Center to uninstall an application.

5. The Detection Method page prompts you to create a valid detection method. Another advantage to a Windows Installer application is that you get the detection method for free (based on the Windows Installer product code); these must be built for a script-based installation. For this step, you create a basic detection rule. The "Creating Detection Methods" section provides a detailed look at detection methods. Click the **Add Clause** button as shown in Figure 12.26, and select **File System** as the setting type. Then click the **Browse** button, and browse to wordview.exe on a test system with the Word Viewer installed.

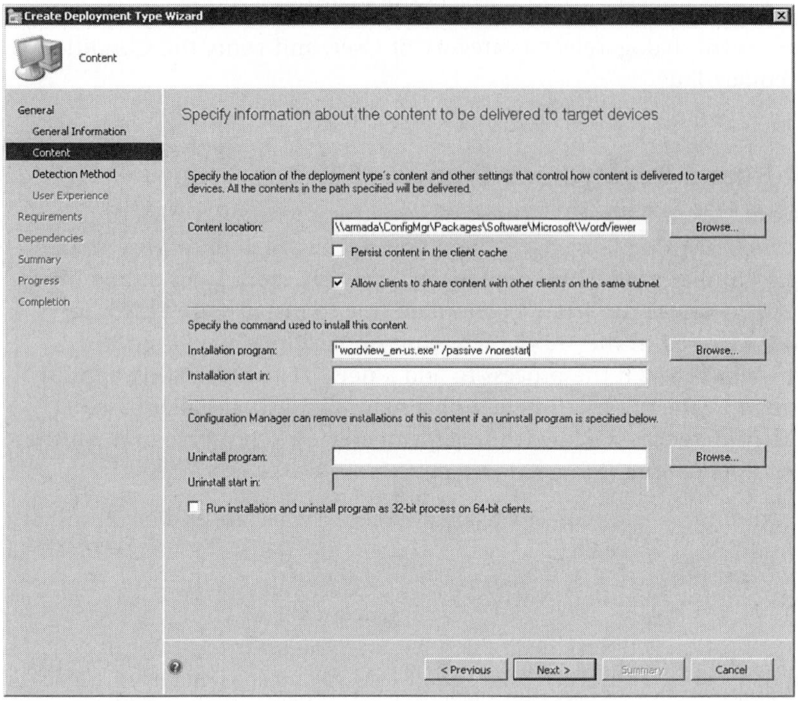

FIGURE 12.25 The Content page of the Create Deployment Type Wizard for a Script Installer.

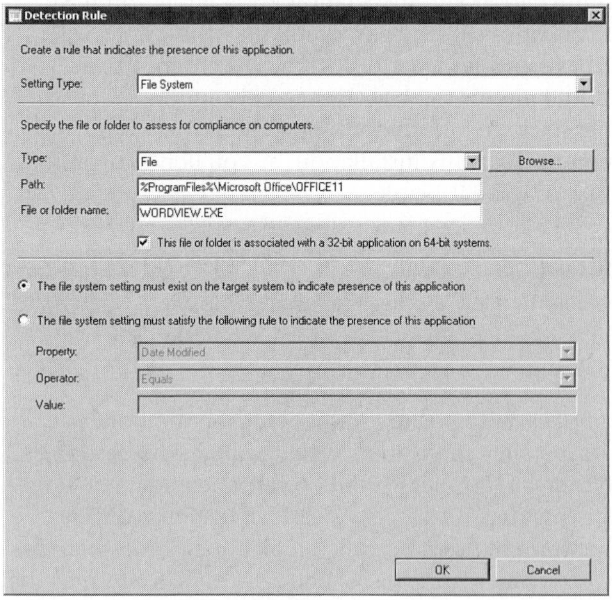

FIGURE 12.26 The Detection Rule dialog from the Detection Method page of the Create Deployment Type Wizard for a Script Installer.

TIP: ALWAYS VERIFY WINDOWS INSTALLER DETECTION METHODS

Some admins combine one or more applications into a single installer, often referred to as a *wrapper*. Use additional caution when writing detection methods based on wrapped installations. For example, if your wrapper program is a Windows Installer program, and your detection method looks for that program, you are guaranteeing that only the wrapper is installed on the client, not the actual software! Depending on your environment, this may or may not be your desired state. Always take a second look at detection methods to ensure you are truly detecting install status. As stated previously in the "Deployment Type - Detection Method" section, the application deployment evaluation cycle will validate application installation on a regular interval. (Default is 7 days—see Chapter 9 for more information.) If a required application state is evaluated as missing, ConfigMgr initiates another application installation.

You can see that looking to see whether the file exists in the specified path is a basic rule. You could enable the option to look for a specific file date or version, but this example just checks if the file exists. Detection methods are covered in more detail in the "Creating Detection Methods" section.

6. The User Experience page provides the standard settings for user experience (refer to Figure 12.15).

7. The Requirements page is the same as discussed with Figure 12.16. The "Managing and Creating Global Conditions" section presented an in-depth look at requirements, also known as global conditions. This optional field is left blank for this example. Leaving this option blank implies that the installation will install on all operating systems and platforms targeted with the installation.

8. The Dependencies, Summary, and Progress pages are the same as when creating a DT for a Windows Installer-based application, so they are skipped in this section.

Recall that requirements (also known as global conditions) were not added, so this application will become available to any targeted system. If you had a different installation for Server and created a second DT with a priority of 2 for the server DT, for example, it would never run, as DTs are evaluated in priority order. This means that when a system evaluates the requirement rules for a DT, if there is none, that DT is deployed with all other lower-priority DTs in the application ignored. Always put the least restrictive DT at the highest number of priority to ensure all other DTs are evaluated for applicability first.

Creating a DT for a script-based installer is similar to a Windows Installer DT. The challenge with script-based DT is you need to determine the proper detection method, as well as install and uninstall command-line arguments. Work with your packaging team and third-party application vendors to ensure you have the right information. In addition, test, test, test!

Creating Detection Methods

To this point, this chapter has discussed simple detection methods. Now it is time to dive a little deeper to understand the importance of a proper detection method, as well as how to create complex detection methods.

The purpose of a detection method is to determine if the software is installed. A detection method is not used to determine if ConfigMgr installed the application—only to determine if it is installed. Software can be installed and uninstalled in non-standard ways. If you are currently deploying the application to a collection of devices (either available or optional), the current state of the application is evaluated on each targeted system on a regular interval, 7 days by default, which can be configured using the Client Settings node. In addition, for user-targeted applications, when a user installs an application from the Application Catalog, that application appears in Software Center and is evaluated on the same interval as device-targeted applications.

That evaluation is called the *Application Deployment Evaluation Cycle* and can be triggered from the client (similar to hardware inventory) or configured using Client Settings. If an application is required, and not installed when the Application Deployment Evaluation Cycle runs, ConfigMgr automatically triggers a re-install. You can think of required applications as a type of desired state. If you have a required deployment for an application, ConfigMgr will ensure the application is installed as desired.

Detection methods are important because they report the current state of the application (installed, not installed, or required). Correctly configured detection methods are all-important, as they can cause software to be reinstalled. Software automatic reinstallation is a great thing, unless your detection methods are not correct, and then they can be a nightmare. *Incorrect detection methods can cause an incorrect application state (installed or not) as well as cause repeated attempts to install the application.* As with everything you do in ConfigMgr, test, and then test again.

Detection Methods for Windows Installer Applications

Applications that use Windows Installer generally have a simple detection method, based on the Windows Installer application product code. When you use the Create Application Wizard or Create Deployment Type Wizard and select a Windows Installer application, the detection method is automatically configured to use the Windows Installer product code. Most of the time, this auto-generated detection method will be sufficient, but there are some caveats:

▶ **Duplicate Product Codes:** Application product codes should be unique and usually are for official software installations. The authors have encountered duplicate product codes for some applications that have been repackaged. For example, the packager created PackageA, and then reused PackageA to create PackageB and failed to generate a new product code. Another example would be that the packager created a major revision to PackageA (from revision 2.1 to revision 3.0, for example) and reused the same product code. In traditional package and program software distribution, these errors wouldn't be as obvious. However, in the new application model, using these invalid product codes as a detection method can cause an incorrect installation state.

▶ **Repackaged Applications:** When you repackage an application into the Windows Installer format, the newly packaged application will have a product code. This will not always tell you if the actual application is installed, especially if other users have had the ability to install the application with the original source.

▶ **Wrapper Installers:** These are similar to a repackaged application, but usually the application installation is intact so the wrapper simply calls the installation executable with the proper command-line arguments. Then the wrapper may launch additional actions (such as installing a licensing file) to complete the installation. Wrappers have their place, but not always as a detection method.

As you can see, launching the wizard to create a Windows Installer DT could save you some steps but might cause additional pain in the future. Be sure you know the origin of the installer (from vendor, repackaged, and so on) and are aware of additional steps that the installation performs.

When working with these special-case installers, you may consider adding additional detection clauses to the detection method. For example, you may want to confirm a file exists, is of a specific version, or uses a specific registry value. The next section discusses additional detection methods.

Here are the basic steps for adding a Windows Installer detection method:

1. From the Deployment Type Properties dialog, select the Detection Method tab, and click **Add Clause**.

2. Choose the appropriate setting type. In this case, select **Windows Installer**, and click the **Browse** button.

3. Navigate to the desired .msi file and select **Open**. The product code appears, as shown in Figure 12.27.

    By default, the rule looks for only the product code. The rule in Figure 12.27 was modified to require a minimum version with the product code.

4. Click **OK** to save the detection rule.

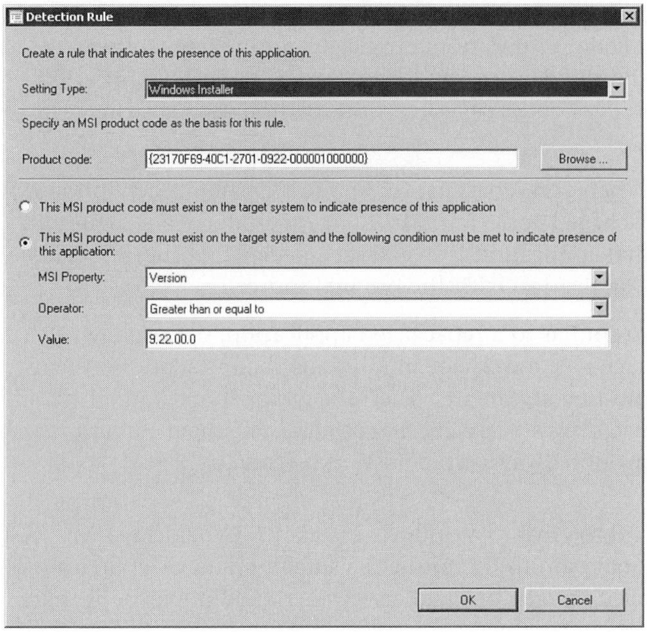

FIGURE 12.27   The Detection Rule dialog.

Other Detection Methods

In addition to the Windows Installer detection method, there are built-in methods based on file system and registry properties. This section walks through examples of each.

Here are the basic steps for adding a file-based detection method:

1. From the Deployment Type Properties dialog, select the Detection Method tab, and click **Add Clause**.

2. Choose the appropriate setting type. In this case, select **File System**, and click the **Browse** button.

3. You now see a Browse File System dialog. You can browse the current computer, or a different computer (provided you have administrative rights and the system is online) by entering a computer name and then clicking **Connect**. Expand the computer information in the left frame, find the desired file as shown in Figure 12.28, and then click **OK**.

4. The Detection Rule dialog will appear with the file and folder information populated, as shown in Figure 12.29.

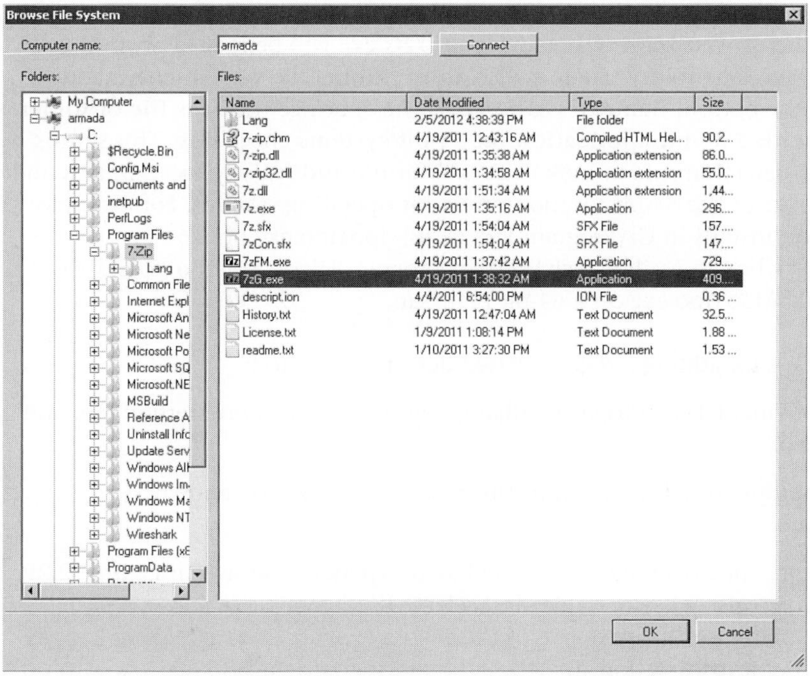

FIGURE 12.28   The Browse File System dialog for detection methods.

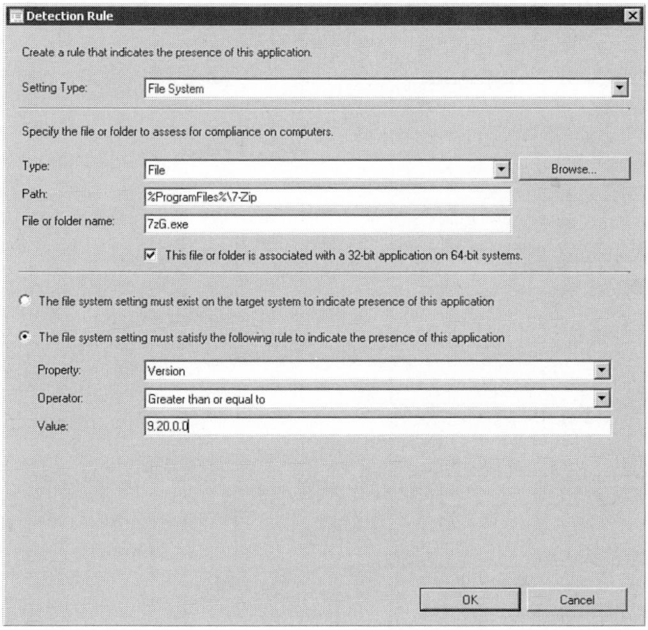

FIGURE 12.29   The Detection Rule dialog for a File System-based rule.

5. The middle section of Figure 12.29 automatically populates based on the file selected with the **Browse** button. It shows that 7zG.exe will be looked for in the %*ProgramFiles*%\7-Zip\ folder. There is also an additional file version check added and shown in the bottom frame of Figure 12.29. Also, notice the **This file or folder is associated with a 32-bit application on 64-bit systems** check box. This setting enables the DT detection rule to look in the 32-bit file and registry location first and if not found looks in the 64-bit location on 64-bit operating systems. For example, if an application installs in C:\Program Files(X86)\foo\foo.exe on a 64-bit system, enable this check box to easily check both C:\Program Files(X86)\foo\foo.exe and C:\Program Files\foo\foo.exe on a 64-bit platform.

Here are the basic steps for adding a registry-based detection method:

1. From the Deployment Type Properties dialog, select the Detection Method tab, and click **Add Clause**.

2. Choose the appropriate setting type. In this case, select **registry**, and click the **Browse** button.

3. The Browse experience is similar to the file-based experience shown in Figure 12.29. Select the proper registry key or value, and select **OK**. Figure 12.30 shows a basic registry rule, looking for the existence of the `HKLM\Software\7-Zip` registry key. As mentioned earlier in this section, the check box to include the x86 registry path on x64 systems is enabled. You can also specify specific registry name and value properties if desired.

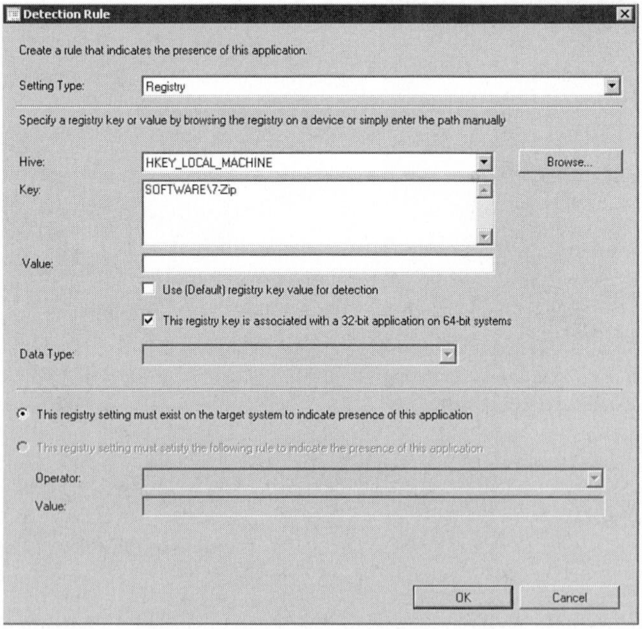

FIGURE 12.30   The Detection Rule dialog for a registry system-based rule.

Creating detection methods is fairly straightforward and uses a similar process to ConfigMgr compliance settings as well as System Center Updates Publisher. The challenge is working with your packaging team (or reverse-engineering a product install) to determine which detection rules you should create for a deployment type.

You can also group multiple clauses, as well as change connectors between ANDs and ORs, as shown in Figure 12.31.

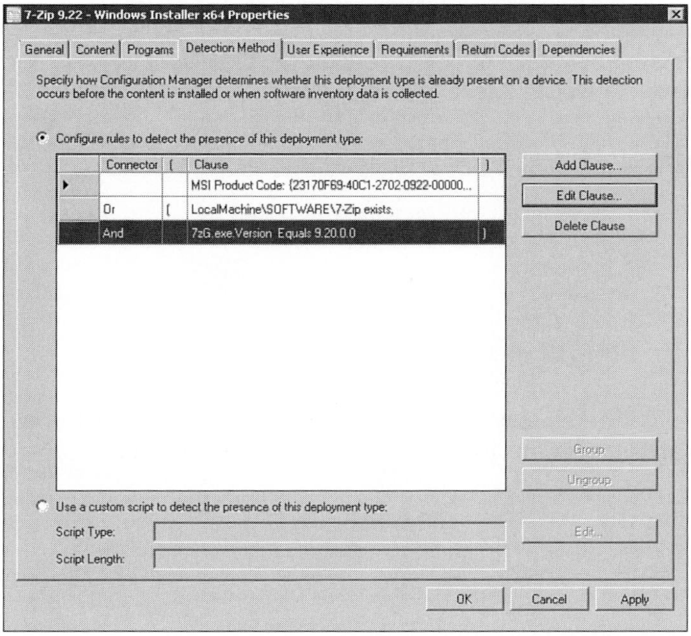

FIGURE 12.31   Grouping detection clauses.

From Figure 12.31, select the last two rows in the grid and select **Group**, and then toggle the **Or** to an **And**. Also, change the first **And** to an **Or**, as shown in Figure 12.31. This enables ConfigMgr to look for either the product code, or the combination of registry key and file path with version. 7-Zip is a perfect example for why you may want to create a detection method, as shown in this figure. The 7-Zip installer is available as both an .msi and an .exe, so the product code may or may not exist, depending on the installer used.

Custom Script Detection Methods

The final detection method to discuss is a custom script. The possibilities are endless when using a custom script. Most of your applications need standard detection methods (Windows Installer product code, file, or registry), but eventually you will encounter an application requiring a more complex way to determine installation state.

You write a custom script that ConfigMgr can use to determine if the software is installed. Be sure to return text from the script to confirm that the software is installed. If no text is returned, ConfigMgr understands that to be "not installed." The next two sections provide sample scripts for leveraging a custom script detection method.

Custom Detection Method Script with PowerShell

From the Deployment Type Properties dialog, enable the **Detection Method** option to create a custom script, and then click the **Edit** button. Select **PowerShell** as the script type, and review Figure 12.32.

TIP: MODIFY THE POWERSHELL EXECUTION POLICY IF REQUIRED

Depending on your environment, you may need to use Client Settings to adjust the PowerShell Execution Policy (under Computer Agent group).

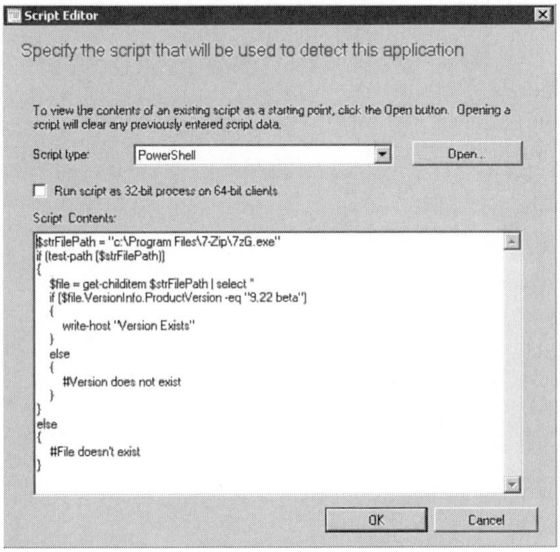

FIGURE 12.32   Custom Detection Method - Script Editor for PowerShell.

Figure 12.32 is a sample PowerShell script that checks for the existence of a file, and then verifies the file version. Notice the `write-host` "`Version Exists`" line of the code. If all the tests (file exists, and version is correct) pass, text is written to standard output. Text being written to standard output is what signifies TRUE for the script detection. As long as the script returns text, ConfigMgr considers the application installed. You see the two lines that begin with **#**; these are comment lines, so that text isn't printed but is in the script for clarity. Here is the text of the PowerShell script in Figure 12.32:

```
$strFilePath = "c:\Program Files\7-Zip\7zG.exe"
if (test-path) ($strFilePath))
{
    $file = get-childitem $strFilePath | select *
    if ($file.VersionInfo.ProductVersion -eq "9.22 beta")
    {
```

```
        write-host "Version Exists"
    }
    else
    {
        #version does not exist
    }
}
else
{
    #file doesn't exist
```

Custom Detection Method Script with VBScript

Enable the Detection Method option to create a custom script, and then click the **Edit** button. Select **VBScript** as the script type, and review Figure 12.33.

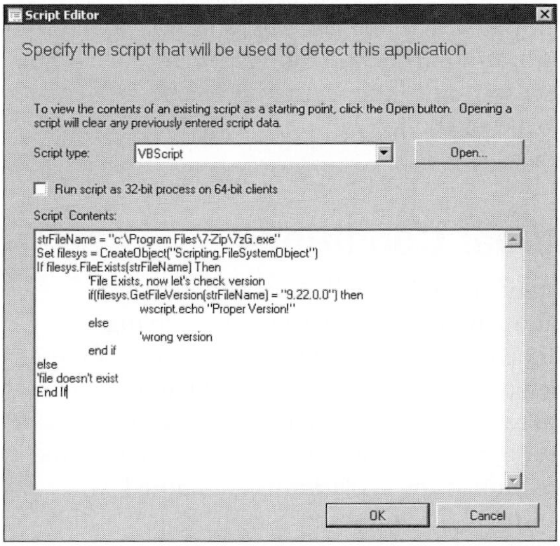

FIGURE 12.33   Custom Detection Method - Script Editor for VBScript.

Figure 12.33 is a sample Visual Basic script that checks for the existence of a file and then verifies the file version. Notice `wscript.echo "Proper Version!"` line of the code. If all the tests (file exists, and version is correct) pass, text is written to standard output, which signals to ConfigMgr that the application is installed. You see the two lines that begin with '; these are comment lines and not printed—they are in the script for clarity. Here is the text of the VBScript in Figure 12.33:

```
strFileName = "C:\Program Files\7-Zip\7zG.exe"
Set filesys = CreateObject("Scripting.FileSystemObject")
if filesys.FileExists(strFileName) Then
    'File exists, now let's check version
```

```
    if(filesys.GetFileVersion(strFileName) = "9.22.0.0") then
        wscript.echo "Proper Version!"
    else
        'wrong version
    end if
else
'file doesn't exist
```

TIP: AVOID SMART QUOTES FOR VBSCRIPT AND POWERSHELL

When you type or paste text into a document editor, you often receive smart quotes (" ");
these curve the quotes around whatever is being quoted (both single and double quotes).
Smart quotes cause scripts to break. If you encounter smart quotes, simply paste the
code into a text editor (such as Windows Notepad) and replace all smart quotes with standard quotes. Remember to replace for both single and double quotes.

The Script Editor dialog also has an **Open** button, which you can use to browse to a script
file to import. You can also enable the script to run in the 32-bit environment on a 64-bit
system. Some applications install to the 32-bit section of the registry. This check box
allows you to determine in which environment your script will run. Note that this check
box has no effect on 32-bit operating systems.

Managing and Creating Global Conditions

Global conditions are used to build requirements for DT installation. You may hear
the terms global conditions, requirements, and requirement rules used interchange-
ably. Requirements determine which DT will be deployed to a system. The more you use
requirements, the more you will see how they may greatly reduce the number of collections needed for software deployment. You may have used the Supported Platforms dialog
of Program properties to ensure software installs only on a specific operating system and
service pack. If you did, you recall that after you had those platforms configured, you
could deploy software to a collection of all systems, and only the systems that met the
platform requirements actually installed the software. Think of global conditions taking
this concept to the next level.

TIP: COLLECTION VS. GLOBAL CONDITION

Deployments still require a target collection, so you will always use a collection for targeting. Global conditions may help you reduce the number of collections you target. For
example, in ConfigMgr 2007, if you wanted to deploy AppA to all systems in the HR OU,
you would create a collection (based on discovery information) of all systems in the HR
OU, and deploy AppA to that collection. In ConfigMgr 2012, you can create requirement
rules on the deployment type in AppA to ensure it only installs on systems in the desired
OU. You can then target a larger collection of systems than just the HR OU, which means
you may no longer need a collection for HR OU. You can think of taking many of the query-
based collection membership rules from ConfigMgr 2007, and implementing them as
global conditions.

Let's start with reviewing the built-in global conditions. From the Deployment Type Properties dialog, select the Requirements tab, and then select **Add**. There are three categories to choose, discussed in the following sections.

Device Global Conditions

Device conditions contain information specific to the client device. Here are the built-in device conditions:

▶ **Active Directory site:** Use this condition to specify the DT can only run for systems that are part or not part of any specific AD site or sites.

▶ **Configuration Manager site:** For this condition, specify the DT can only run for systems that belong or not belong to a specific site code or codes.

▶ **CPU speed:** You can use CPU speed to specify a CPU speed requirement. The value provided is in Mhz.

▶ **Disk space:** With this condition, you can specify an amount of free disk space that must be met to run the deployment type for the application. The system drive can be selected, a specific drive, or any drive. The value is specified in megabytes and operators such as Equals, Not equals, Greater than, Less than, and so on can be used.

▶ **Number of processors:** Use this condition to specify the number of processors the device should have to run this deployment type.

▶ **Operating system:** For this condition, specify that the deployment type can only run on a specific operating system—for example, only on the Windows 7 64-bit operating systems.

▶ **Operating system language:** With this condition, the operating system language or languages can be configured as a requirement for the DT.

▶ **Organizational Unit (OU):** Use the **Add** button with this condition to add a specific organization unit so the deployment type will only run on devices that belong to that OU. If you have child OUs that also need to be included for this condition, select the **Include child OUs** option.

▶ **Total physical memory:** With this condition, you can specify how much memory is required in order to run the deployment type for the application. The value is entered in megabytes.

Figure 12.34 displays an example of using a built-in device condition, which shows a device requirement where total memory is at least 4GB (4096MB).

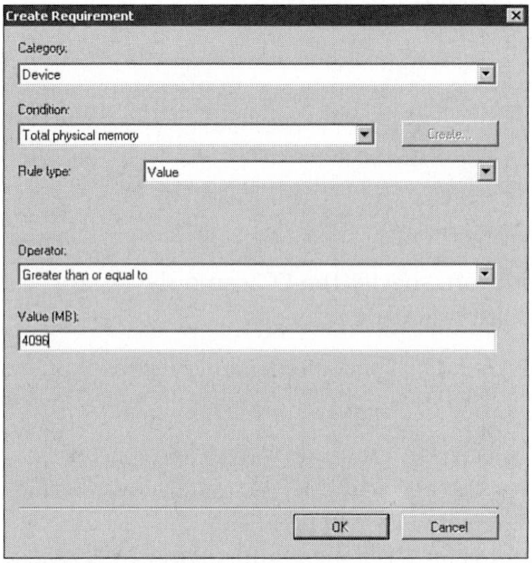

FIGURE 12.34 Device Requirement Rule (Global Condition).

User Global Conditions

Only one user global condition currently exists: Primary Device. You can set the requirement to TRUE or FALSE so that the appropriate software will install (or not install) based on whether the user is considered the primary user of the device.

Custom Global Conditions

If device and user conditions do not meet your needs, you can create custom conditions. Custom global conditions can contain LDAP queries, WQL queries, file and registry queries, and many other custom configurations. If you are familiar with creating configuration items for compliance settings (formerly known as desired configuration management), this process is similar. You can build multiple queries into one custom global condition. In addition to using the Create Deployment Type Wizard, you can create global conditions from the Global Conditions node under **Software Library** -> **Application** in the ConfigMgr 2012 console.

Perform the following steps to create a custom condition (also known as a global condition):

1. From the Create Requirement window, select **Custom** from the list of categories.

2. Select **Create** -> **New** condition in the condition field.

   This opens a new window where you can create your new custom conditions. In the upper section of the window, the following fields are available:

   ▶ **Name:** Use this field to specify a name for the global condition.

   ▶ **Description:** Specify a description for the global condition.

> ▶ **Device type:** Use the drop-down list to specify if the condition is for a Windows, Windows Mobile, or Nokia device.

> ▶ **Condition type:** Use the drop-down list to specify if the condition is a single setting, or an expression (a group of settings).

You can configure the actual condition in the lower section of the window. Based on the settings type, multiple options are available. Here are the available types:

> ▶ **Active Directory query:** Use this settings type to create a LDAP query condition. For example, the output of the query can be a specific Active Directory group.

> ▶ **Assembly:** Specify an assembly from the global assembly cache that will be used as the condition for the deployment type.

> ▶ **File system:** The File system settings type allows you to specify that a specific file or folder should be present on the device as the condition.

> ▶ **IIS Metabase:** This settings type allows you to build a condition based on specific property ID of an IIS metabase.

> ▶ **Registry key:** Use this settings type to specify that a certain registry key should be present on a device in order to run the deployment type of the application. You can specify multiple registry hives such as HKEY_LOCAL_MACHINE, or you can click the **Browse** button to browse through the local registry of the system from which you are running the ConfigMgr console.

> ▶ **Registry value:** This settings type is similar to the registry key settings type, but allows you to specify a key and value requirement.

> ▶ **Script:** You can use the script settings type to add a script that queries and returns data to ConfigMgr 2012. Use the **Add script** button to add a script as the condition. The script must be in PowerShell, Visual Basic Script, or the Java script language.

> ▶ **SQL query:** Use the SQL query settings type to execute a SQL query against a SQL database. You can specify the SQL instance, the database name, a column, and the actual SQL statement. If you already have an SQL query file, you can upload that by clicking the **Open** button. You cannot specify alternate rights; the query will be run under the Local System account.

> ▶ **WQL query:** WQL queries can be used to query the Windows Management Instrumentation (WMI). WMI contains information about the operating system and where hardware is stored. For example, if your application is software required for a specific video card, you can write a WQL query to query for that specific video card including the type and model.

> ▶ **XPath query:** This settings type can be used to add an eXtended Markup Language (XML) script that queries and returns data to ConfigMgr 2012. You can specify the path for the file and the filename, as well as the XPath query.

3. Select the desired settings, and click **OK** to save the global condition.

When the global condition is created, it becomes available in the Create Requirements window under the Custom category. You can use this window to specify if the result of the condition should be TRUE, FALSE, or contains a value. Here are some examples of custom global conditions:

▶ **File System Condition:** This example demonstrates how to create a global condition based on a file system check. Figure 12.35 shows a global condition that will use *%ProgramFiles%\ACME Corp\Licensefile.lic*.

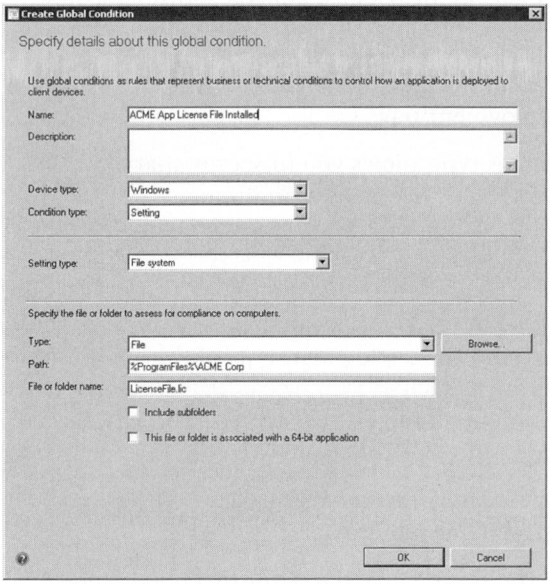

FIGURE 12.35   The Create Global Condition dialog.

After you have saved the global condition, you can add the requirement to your application, as shown in Figure 12.36.

Figure 12.36 shows that the requirement will pass only if the license file has a date modified of 4/7/2011 11:12:41 PM. You can just create a requirement for a file exists. If you want to verify more than just existential, here is a list of file properties you can use for the custom file system global condition:

▶ File Size

▶ File Version

▶ Date Created

▶ Date Modified

▶ Company

▶ Product Name

▶ SHA-1 Hash

▶ File Attributes

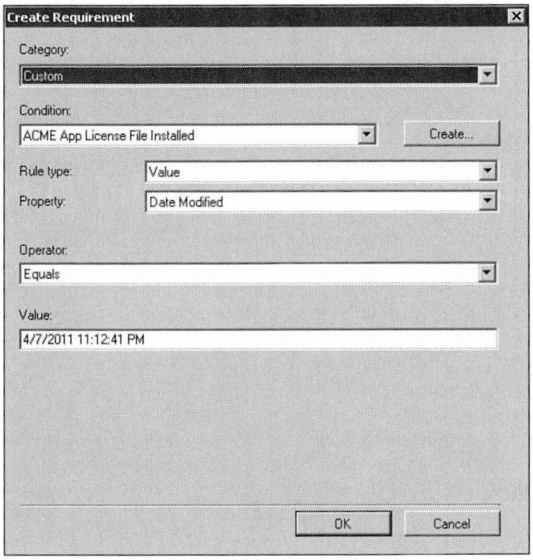

FIGURE 12.36   The Create Requirement dialog.

▶ **WQL Query Condition:** WMI queries can add flexibility to global conditions. This example demonstrates creating a global condition that allows you to create requirement rules to deploy software to specific computer models.

Figure 12.37 shows how to create a global condition that will dynamically make the computer model available to you, based on the Model property of the Win32_ComputerSystem WMI Class.

The condition created in Figure 12.37 will run a WQL query in the root\cimv2 namespace, Select Model from Win32_ComputerSystem. Leave the Where clause empty so that this condition will be dynamic.

Next, create a new requirement for the DT in your application. Figure 12.38 shows how to leverage the global condition created in Figure 12.37.

As shown in Figure 12.38, select the custom condition named **Computer Model** with the operator **Contains** followed by the computer model for the **Value**. Note that some computer manufacturers pad the Model property with extra spaces, so use **Contains** instead of **Equals** when possible. Now this requirement rule will only be met of the computer model property contains **Latitude E6420**.

Global conditions allow you to perform targeted software deployments, without the need of custom collections for each deployment. As always, test, and then test again to verify the condition works as expected.

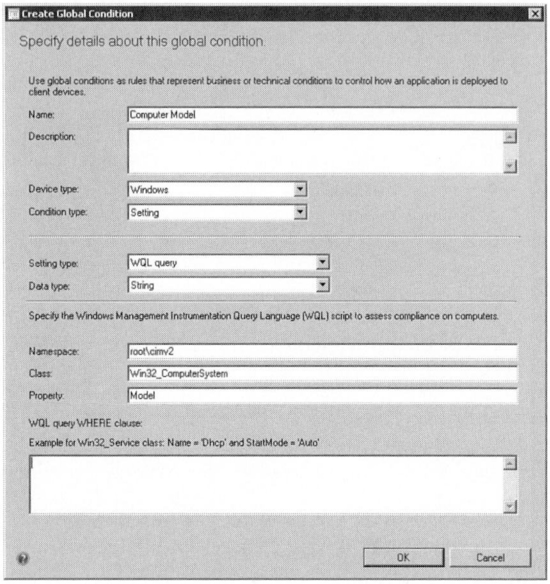

FIGURE 12.37   The Create Global Condition dialog for a WQL query.

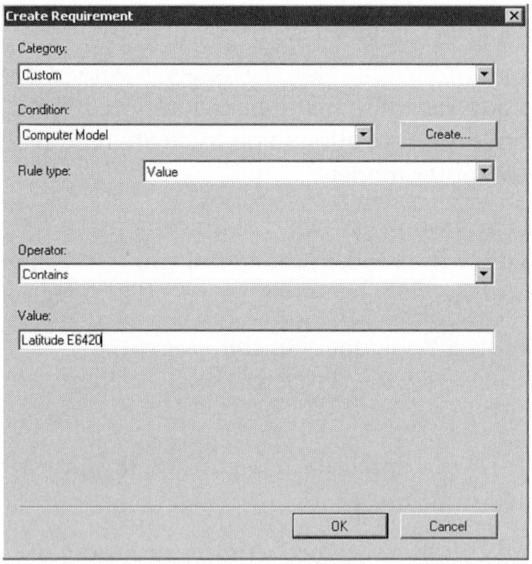

FIGURE 12.38   The Create Requirement dialog for the Custom Computer Model condition.

More About Managing Applications

Applications are a large part of ConfigMgr 2012. This chapter has included an extensive amount about creating applications. The next sections describe additional features to leverage applications to their fullest potential.

Adding Dependencies

You often will encounter applications that have prerequisite software requirements. For example, the ConfigMgr 2012 console requires .NET Framework 4.0 full installation. With traditional package/program deployment, you would use the **Run another program first** feature. This feature has long existed in ConfigMgr (and Systems Management Server), and works well to install prerequisite software. The feature is missing one thing: the ability to determine if the prerequisite software is already installed. With the **Run another program first** feature, ConfigMgr might run the prerequisite software again (depending on advertisement and program rerun properties), even if the software were actually installed.

Dependencies in System Center 2012 Configuration Manager applications are smarter. When an application has a dependency, the detection rules and requirement rules run to determine which DT needs to install, if any. If the dependent application is already installed (as defined by the detection rules), ConfigMgr skips that installation, checks additional dependencies, and then runs the desired application installation. Here are some items to remember about application dependencies:

- ▶ An application can be dependent only on another application (not a package/program).

- ▶ A package/program cannot be dependent on an application.

- ▶ Application dependencies are honored during OSD. (Package/program dependencies are not honored, and must be called out separately in a task sequence.)

- ▶ The order in which dependent applications install is nondeterministic. If dependent applications require a specific install order, create the dependency for each application, instead of one application with all dependencies defined.

- ▶ Create separate dependency groups for each application requirement. When you create a dependency group, only one application from the group must be installed to consider the requirement satisfied.

If one or more of the constraints mentioned here makes your task much harder to complete, consider using a task sequence. Although task sequences are categorized under operating system deployment, you can create a generic task sequence to install software in a well-defined sequence. One major caveat: Task sequences can be deployed only to devices.

Let's use the example of installing the ConfigMgr admin console. You have a .NET 4.0 full installation application and the ConfigMgr 2012 admin console application. The .NET 4.0 installation is a prerequisite installation for the ConfigMgr admin console installation. Perform the following steps to create the dependency:

12

1. From the Deployment Type dialog for the ConfigMgr console application, select the **Dependencies** tab.

2. Click the **Add** button to display the Add Dependency dialog.

3. Enter a group name for the installation; for this example call it **.NET Framework 4.0 Full** and click the **Add** button to display the Specify Required Application dialog.

4. Select the required application. For this example, select the **.NET Framework 4.0 x86 and x64 application** as shown in Figure 12.39, and click **OK**.

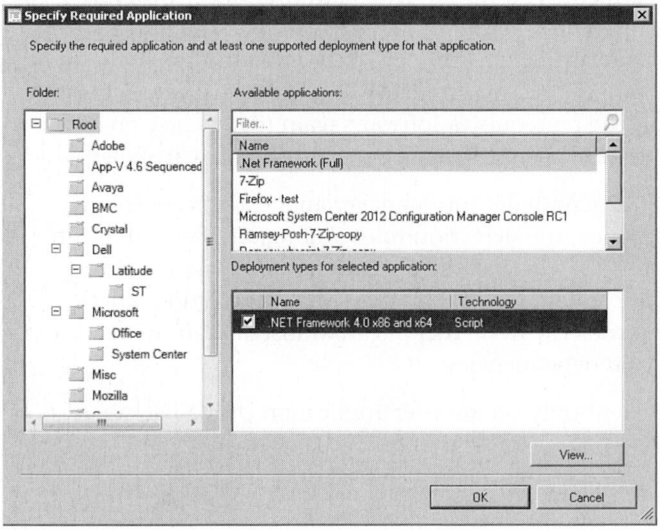

FIGURE 12.39   The Specify Required Application dialog for Application dependencies.

5. The Add Dependency dialog displays the dependency information, as shown in Figure 12.40.

6. By default, the **Auto Install** check box is enabled. This check box allows you to deploy the required software automatically (when required) to the targeted systems.

7. Click **OK** to the Add Dependency Wizard, and then **OK** again to save the Deployment type and Application.

Now when you deploy the ConfigMgr admin console, ConfigMgr automatically installs the .NET framework version 4.0 requirement first if needed.

Another example for a dependency is an App-V application. In ConfigMgr 2007, you had to deploy the App-V client to systems prior to attempting to install an App-V application on a system. With this version, simply create a dependency from the App-V application to the App-V client installation application, so that if the client does not already exist, it will be installed just in time for the App-V application.

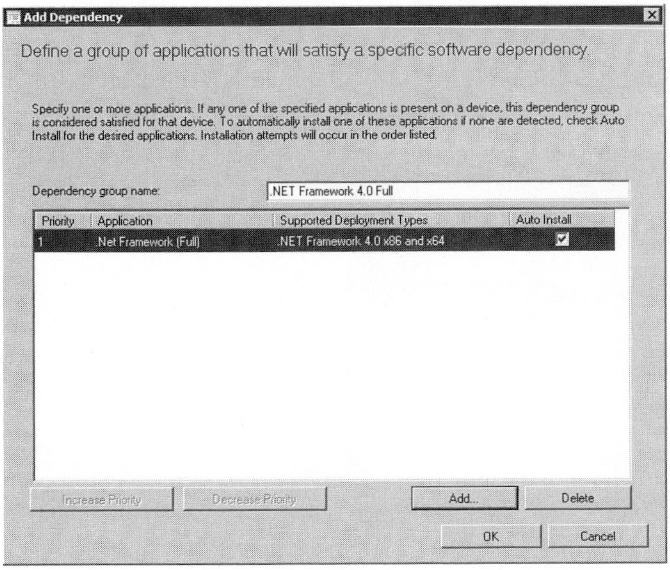

FIGURE 12.40   The Add Dependency dialog for the deployment type.

Managing Revision History

Revision history is another new concept to ConfigMgr 2012. Each time you modify an application (and click **OK** to save changes), ConfigMgr creates a new revision of the application. This concept allows you to "go back" easily to a previous application configuration state. Technically, when you "restore" a revision, ConfigMgr creates a duplicate of the desired revision, and assigns it the latest revision number. Figure 12.41 shows a sample application revision history for 7-Zip.

Figure 12.41 shows that only the last revision is currently referenced. You can select and delete any revision that does not have a reference. Each primary site also has a site maintenance task, Delete Unused Application revisions, that will remove any revision not referenced and at least 60 days old.

To revert to a previous version, select the desired version in the console and select **Restore**. You will notice that newer versions do not disappear. When you select a revision to restore, ConfigMgr clones the desired revision into a new revision.

You may also see that older revisions still have assigned references. You can view the revision to identify the reference. You can then go to the reference and reconfigure it to a newer revision if desired. You cannot delete a revision that is currently referenced.

One important caveat to remember when working with revision history is distribution point content. Say for example that you have a new application, with a DT that has a content source path. You send that content to the DPs, and notice that its size is 8GB. You know that is incorrect, and investigate to find that you are using the wrong source path, so you change the source path for the DT. This will increment the revision history. More important, the previous version of the application remains in the revision history, and as long as it is in revision history, that extra 8GB of content will remain on the DPs.

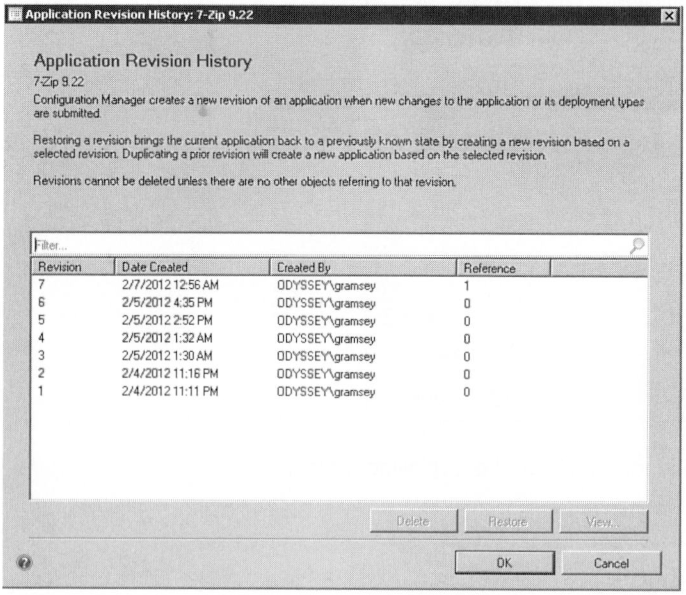

FIGURE 12.41   The Application Revision History dialog.

When you complete testing and are ready to deploy an application to production, consider implementing a standard process to clean up any old revision history entries so that you start as clean as possible in production.

Exporting and Importing Applications

System Center 2012 Configuration Manager gives you the ability to export objects from the ConfigMgr console and import them into a different infrastructure. This is an excellent approach to migrate objects between two different ConfigMgr infrastructures. Follow these steps to export one or more objects:

1. From the Software Library workspace, select the Applications node.

2. Select one or more applications, and then right-click and select **Export**.

3. Enter a path for the destination to export, and be sure to include the .zip file extension. Review Figure 12.42 for more information.

   You can choose the option to export all dependencies, supersedence relationships, and global conditions. You can also choose to export the content for the selected applications and dependencies.

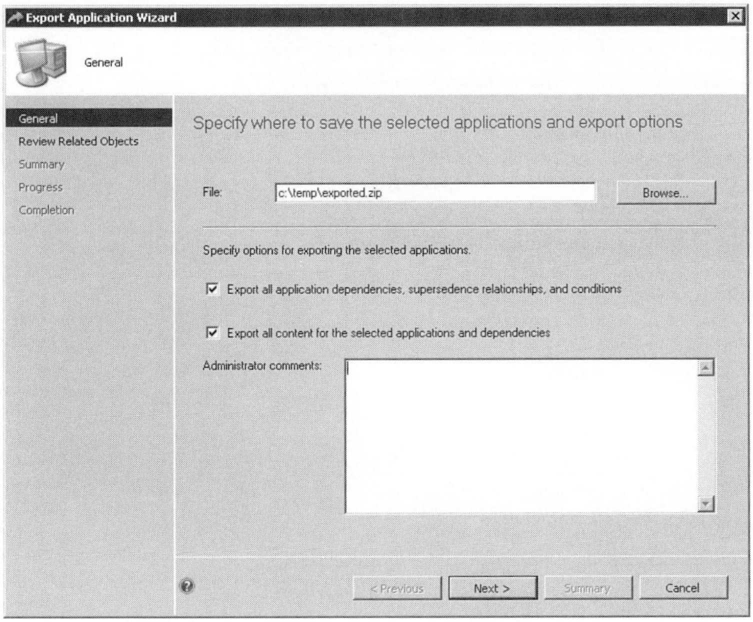

FIGURE 12.42   The Export Application Wizard.

4. Continue through the additional pages to complete the Export Application Wizard.

5. You can now copy the .zip file and associated content folder(s) to a new infrastructure, and import the contents as desired.

Superseding Applications

Use supersedence when you move to a new revision of a product. For example, you have FooApp version 1.0, and are currently deploying to multiple collections. When FooApp 2.0 releases, create a new application for FooApp 2.0. After you have verified success, you can supersede FooApp version 1.0 with FooApp version 2.0. Note that supersedence does not automatically execute an evaluation and installation. The new application must be deployed to a target collection to upgrade the application.

However, if an application was previously deployed as required, that software may automatically re-install. Notice that Figure 12.43 shows the **Uninstall** check box enabled. This instructs ConfigMgr 2012 to uninstall the previous version first, based on the uninstall command-line argument for uninstall in the superseded application, and then install the new version. If you do not enable the check box to uninstall, ConfigMgr will run the replacement DT without uninstalling the previous application first. In some situations, this is expected, and the installation process will upgrade the existing application. As always, test, and then retest before deploying to production.

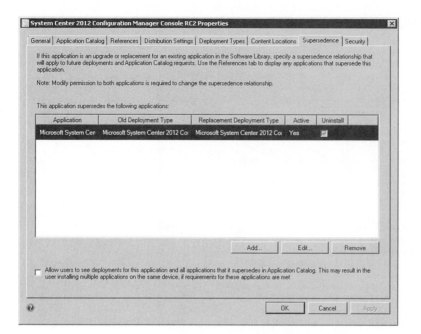

FIGURE 12.43   The Supersedence tab of the deployment type.

If you have more than one DT in either the old application or the new application, you will select the desired old DT and new DT to map together which DTs should run together. Be aware that you don't need to re-deploy an old version of software to take advantage of supersedence. For example, myApp version 1.0 has been in production for a year, and you just upgraded to ConfigMgr 2012. You can create an application for myApp version 1.0 (with proper detection rules, uninstall commands, and so on), and then create myApp version 2.0 and supersede myApp 1.0. When you deploy myApp 2.0, it will detect that 1.0 is installed (even though 1.0 actually was never deployed with ConfigMgr 2012) and follow the defined supersedence rules.

Retiring and Deleting Applications

When you know that you will no longer need to create new deployments for an application, right-click the application and select **Retire**. When you retire an app, you can no longer create deployments for that app, unless you **Reinstate** it first. Retiring an application does not affect existing deployments, only new deployments.

To delete an application, you must remove all references to it. References such as dependent applications, active deployments, and dependent task sequences can affect the ability to delete an application.

Remember that you can export an application (with or without associated content) and store the application on a file share, in case you need to restore it at a later point.

Package Conversion Manager

Package Conversion Manager (PCM) is a feature download from Microsoft. If you migrate packages/programs from ConfigMgr 2007, or have already created many packages/programs in ConfigMgr 2012, you will want to look at this tool to help you move quickly to the application model. Additional information about PCM is available at http://technet.microsoft.com/en-us/library/hh531583.aspx.

PCM can help you migrate legacy packages/programs to the new application model in ConfigMgr 2012. After analysis, you will find some packages can be converted automatically, others manually, and some may not be eligible to convert at all.

After installing PCM, restart the ConfigMgr console and browse to the Packages node so that you see packages in the Detail pane. Right-click the title row to show the following additional package property columns: **Readiness Issues**, **Last Analyzed / Converted**, and **Readiness**. These three columns will be populated by PCM. Next, select one or more packages, and select **Analyze Package** from the ribbon bar. After several moments, PCM will refresh the view and add information to the three new columns. Figure 12.44 shows the results of PCM analysis (with some standard columns removed to improve readability).

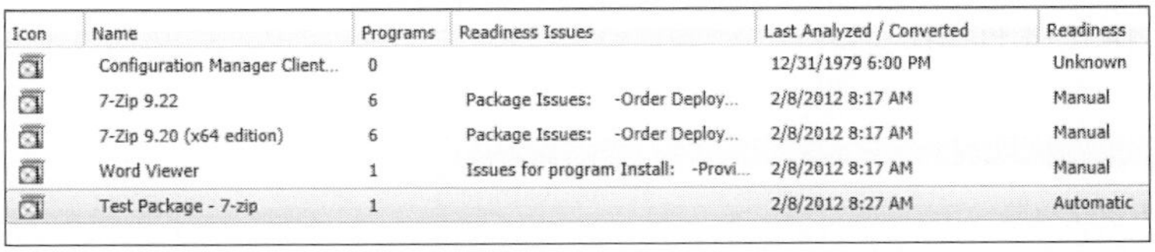

Icon	Name	Programs	Readiness Issues		Last Analyzed / Converted	Readiness
	Configuration Manager Client...	0			12/31/1979 6:00 PM	Unknown
	7-Zip 9.22	6	Package Issues:	-Order Deploy...	2/8/2012 8:17 AM	Manual
	7-Zip 9.20 (x64 edition)	6	Package Issues:	-Order Deploy...	2/8/2012 8:17 AM	Manual
	Word Viewer	1	Issues for program Install:	-Provi...	2/8/2012 8:17 AM	Manual
	Test Package - 7-zip	1			2/8/2012 8:27 AM	Automatic

FIGURE 12.44   The Packages node with Package Conversion Manager readiness information.

Figure 12.44 shows there are three packages that need manual intervention, one package that can be migrated automatically, and one program that is unknown. Here are some suggestions for some common reasons for the different states of readiness:

▶ **Automatic:** This means that you have one program, it is a Windows Installer-based installation, and you have populated the Windows Installer product code in the program properties. Your goal is to get as many packages to this scenario as possible. PCM will use the Windows Installer product code as the detection rule for the application.

▶ **Manual:** You will probably have a large number of packages that require manual intervention during the conversion process. Remember that applications require detection methods, while packages/programs do not, so you must intervene to add this information during the conversion process. As programs are treated as DTs, if you have more than one program, PCM needs you to specify the priority for deployment types. Should you have more than one DT, you will probably want to add requirement rules during the program conversion process.

▶ **Unknown:** This usually occurs because there are no programs in the package.

▶ **Converted:** The package has been converted.

Review PcmTrace.log for detailed information. You will find it in the user's profile *%temp%* folder.

Many of your current packages may appear as manual after PCM analysis. You can dive into each of those packages to try to get them to support an automatic conversion (for example, remove extra programs, add Windows Installer product code, and so on).

To convert packages with a readiness state of automatic, select them all and select **Convert Package** from the ribbon bar. A progress dialog will appear for a few moments and then display the results of the conversion.

Converting a package with a readiness state of manual does require a little effort, but is significantly easier than doing it without PCM. Here is an example of a manual conversion with the PCM. Perform the following steps:

1. Select the package and choose **Fix and Convert** from the ribbon bar.

2. The first page of the Package Conversion Wizard provides you a list of **Items to Fix**, shown in the lower part of Figure 12.45.

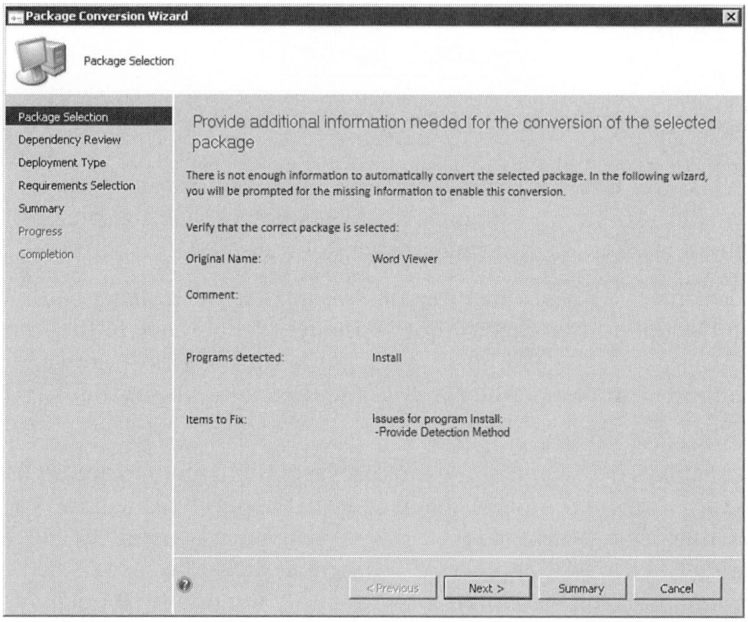

FIGURE 12.45   The Package Conversion Wizard, Package Selection page.

3. In this example, the only item to fix is to create a detection method. Because this application is an .exe, there is no Windows Installer product code to import into the program, so you must provide a manual detection method.

4. Click **Next** to view the Dependency Review page. If the program used the **Run another program first** feature, dependent programs would appear here and require conversion before this package conversion can continue. The sample program does not have a dependency, so click **Next** to view the Deployment Type page.

5. The Deployment Type page tells you that every deployment type must have a detection method. Click the **Edit** button to add a DT.

6. On the dialog that appears, click **Add**, and the Detection Rule dialog (previously shown in Figure 12.30) will appear. Add the appropriate detection rule, and click **OK** to return to the Package Conversion Wizard shown in Figure 12.45.

7. Figure 12.45 shows there is only one DT for this package. If you have more than one, you also have the ability to change priority at this point. Recall that DTs are evaluated in priority order: The first DT that meets the requirements of the system will be the DT used to deploy software to the system.

8. The next page shows the Requirements selection. Requirements are optional, so configure them as needed for your application.

9. Click **Next** to proceed through the Summary, Progress, and Completion pages to view the status of the conversion process.

Using PCM helps you move from packages/programs to applications. You still need to identify the proper detection rules, which may be the hardest part of migrating to the new application model. However, PCM helps you with a workflow to get to the application model.

Figure 12.46 shows the Package Conversion Manager Dashboard. From here, you can see the status of your environment.

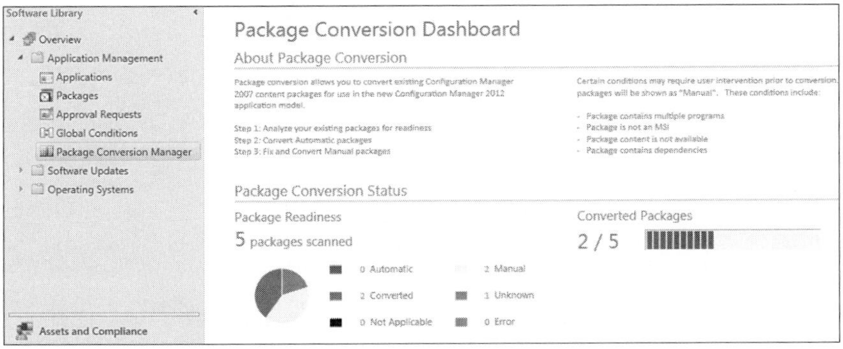

FIGURE 12.46   The Package Conversion Manager Dashboard.

Summary

This chapter walked you through the new process of creating applications with ConfigMgr 2012, explaining how applications are made of deployment types, and deployment types have detection and requirement rules; and how you can leverage these tools to deploy software using fewer collections. You also learned about the application state and how required applications can be reinstalled based on detection rules.

You also learned how to use custom scripts for detection methods, as well as to create and leverage global conditions. You learned how to export and import applications, as well as revision history, dependency, and supersedence. The chapter also demonstrated Package Conversion Manager. The next chapter shows you how to deploy applications and packages to users and systems.

CHAPTER 13

Distributing and Deploying Applications

In Chapter 11, "Packages and Programs," and Chapter 12, "Creating and Managing Applications," you learned about packages and applications; in later chapters, you will learn about software updates, mobile device management, endpoint protection, and operating system deployment. All these object types have at least three things in common:

▶ **Deployable:** All are objects that you deploy to one or more systems. As you deploy, you also want to monitor the status of that deployment.

▶ **Target group:** To leverage any of these objects, you must target a group of systems or users. In Configuration Manager (ConfigMgr), these target groups are called *collections*.

▶ **Content availability:** Almost everything you deploy has associated content that must be available for the ConfigMgr client to install.

As an example, to deploy Microsoft Office, you must have a package or application that has the associated content for the installation. You then send the content to the desired distribution points, create a collection of systems to target, and finally create a deployment. At this time, you then move to monitoring. You may need to monitor the distribution status of content to the distribution points, as well as the status of the deployment.

WHAT'S NEW IN 2012

ConfigMgr 2012 adds the ability to create a collection rule to *include* and *exclude* collections, as well as some additional features for dynamic collections. Many properties of the distribution point have been enhanced, including better status reporting and content validation. You can also simulate deployment of an application to verify the requirement rules and detection methods are correct. Software deployment now supports a basic approval process, plus the ability to easily configure the uninstall process for an application.

Creating and Managing Collections

Collections may very well be the most important object in ConfigMgr. Collections are used for software distribution, patching, settings management, client settings, power management, and more. Collections in ConfigMgr 2012 consist of two distinct types:

▶ Devices (computers, mobile devices, and such)

▶ Users (username, active directory user groups, and so on)

Collections may also be the most dangerous object in ConfigMgr. When you modify the rules of an existing collection, you may significantly increase the number of devices or users in a collection. If the collection has mandatory software deployments, settings management configurations, or even operating system deployment mandatory assignments, you could quickly create a "resume-generating event." As a rule, always use extreme caution when modifying collection membership.

COLLECTIONS AND DEPLOYMENTS REPLICATE ACROSS ALL PRIMARY SITES

If you have multiple primary sites in your environment, you may have noticed that each primary site shows the membership information for its site plus a member count showing the total count of members in the hierarchy for this collection. This information is important because when you create collections and target deployments from one site, the collection and rules are updated and evaluated at all primary sites and the deployment is replicated. When possible, use the CAS for creating collections and targeting deployments. The CAS is the only site that displays all clients to you for a collection.

To create a new collection, select **Assets and Compliance** in the ConfigMgr console, choose the Devices or Users collection node, and select **Create Device Collection** or **Create User Collection** from the ribbon bar. For this example, you create a new device collection. Figure 13.1 shows an example of the Create Device Collection Wizard.

Figure 13.1 shows the name of the collection, as well as the limiting collection. All collections in ConfigMgr 2012 require a limiting collection. This filters the collection to ensure only resources in the limiting collection are available in the current collection. Click **Next** to view the Membership Rules page, shown in Figure 13.2.

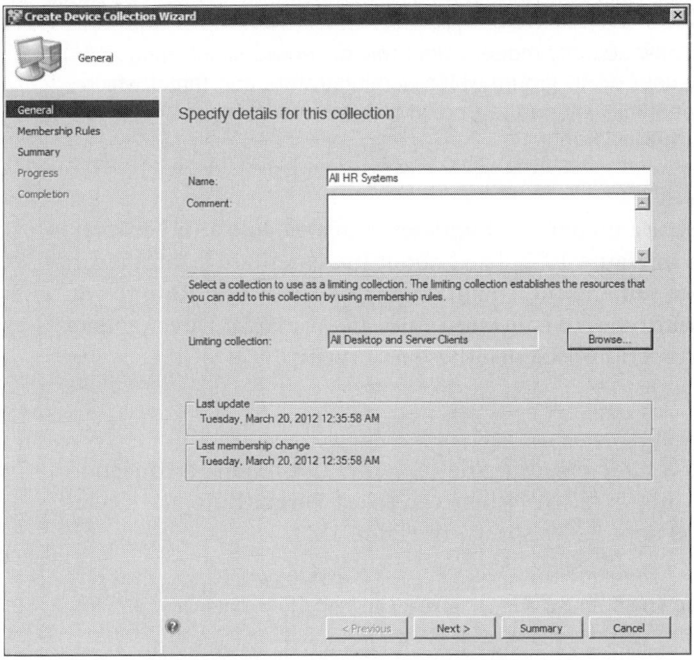

FIGURE 13.1   The General page of the Create Device Collection Wizard.

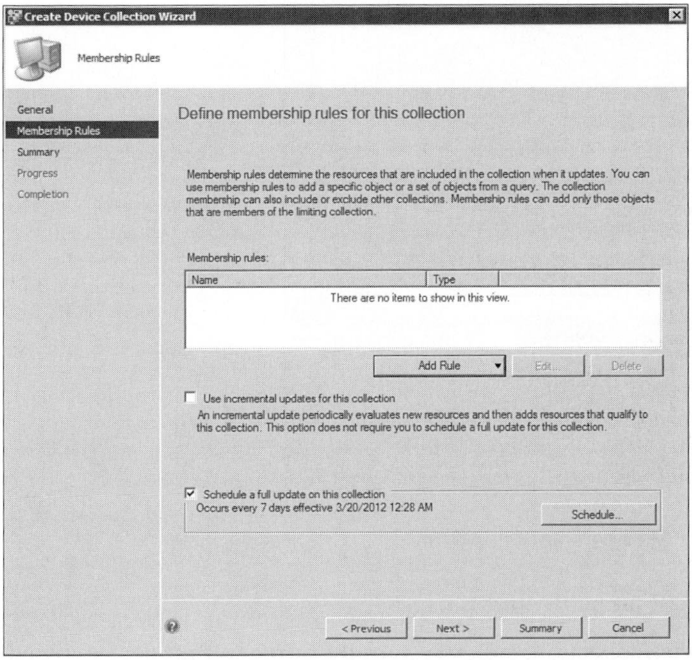

FIGURE 13.2   The Membership Rules page of the Create Device Collection Wizard.

> **TIP: LIMIT ADMINISTRATIVE ACCESS TO REDUCE RISK**
>
> ConfigMgr 2012 introduces a new security model called role-based administration (RBA). With RBA, you can control (by user or AD group) which administrators can target which systems, as well as limit functionality within the ConfigMgr console. If desired, you can limit a user to a collection of test systems.

You can add membership rules, use incremental updates, and schedule a full collection membership update, as shown in Figure 13.2. The "About Incremental Updates" section discusses the difference between full and incremental updates. Click **Add Rule** to add a collection membership rule. Four types of collection rules are available: Direct, Query, Include, and Exclude. The next sections describe these rule types.

Direct Rule

A direct rule (sometimes called a *static rule*) is a rule that does not require a collection update schedule (incremental, full, or both). When you select **Direct Rule**, the Create Direct Membership Rule Wizard appears, as shown in Figure 13.3.

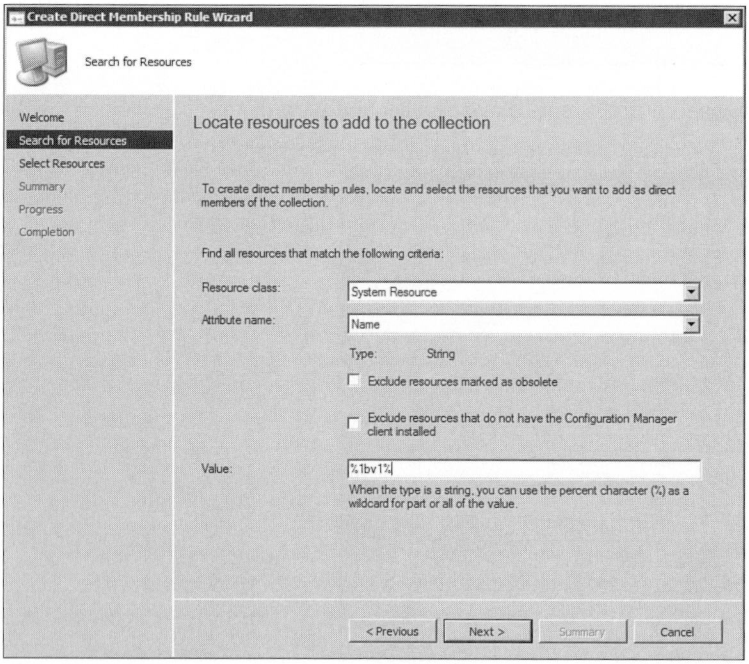

FIGURE 13.3   The Create Direct Membership Rule Wizard

Here is a brief description of each property on this page:

▶ **Resource class:** For a device collection, select **System Resource** to find devices based on discovery and inventory information.

▶ **Attribute name:** Choose the desired attribute. For this example, choose **Name**.

▶ **Exclude resources marked as obsolete:** When you rebuild a system or reinstall the client, you might encounter a duplicate record. This is because ConfigMgr has marked the old record obsolete. When a record is marked as obsolete, you cannot deploy software to it. Unless you are going to troubleshoot obsolete clients based on a collection, be sure to exclude obsolete records from your collections. Otherwise, you may see systems in your collection that are no longer valid, causing confusion when troubleshooting software delivery.

▶ **Exclude resources that do not have the Configuration Manager client installed:** Devices that fit into this category are devices discovered through Active Directory (AD) or some other means but do not appear to have the ConfigMgr client installed. Enable this check box as well.

▶ **Value:** Enter a device name (usually a computer name), or a partial name, and use the % sign as a wild card, or use the wildcard by itself for a full list of items to choose from.

Click **Next** to display resources that meet the criteria specified in Figure 13.3, and then select one or more devices in the Select Resources page of the wizard. Complete the wizard, and wait several moments to view the collection membership in the console. You may have to refresh the view to see the new collection members.

MULTIPLE PRIMARY SITES CAUSE SLIGHT COLLECTION MEMBERSHIP DELAY

As introduced in Chapter 2, "Configuration Manager Overview," ConfigMgr 2012 uses SQL replication to replicate data across a multisite hierarchy. When you have a central administration site (CAS) and multiple primary sites, the collection membership rule is replicated from the CAS to all primaries for each primary site to evaluate that rule. Should the collection membership change on a primary site (due to the new collection rule, or any other reason), the new membership information is replicated back to the CAS. In the authors' experience, the delay in seeing the membership change on the CAS is usually 4 to 5 minutes. Collection membership is not complete on the CAS until the primary child sites evaluate the membership rule(s) and replicate the results back to the CAS.

Query Rule

A query rule (sometimes called a *dynamic rule*) is a rule that requires a collection update schedule (incremental, full, or both) to update the membership information automatically based on the criteria of the query rule. When you select **Query Rule**, you see a dialog similar to Figure 13.4.

From here, you can import a query statement from the available Queries node (see Chapter 17, "Configuration Manager Queries") or select **Edit Query Statement** to modify the default query rule (which selects all systems, limited to the collection defined in Figure 13.1). When you import a query, you are copying the query statement to the collection. This means the statement in the collection is not linked to the query rule. Should you later modify the query rule (from the query,) the query rule for the collection will not change. Chapter 17 provides additional information about building complex queries. This example walks through the process of creating a rule for all systems that have Adobe Reader installed. Follow these steps:

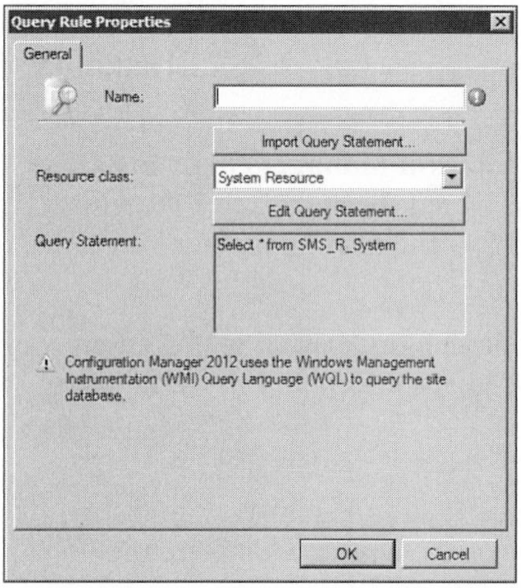

FIGURE 13.4   The Query Rule Properties dialog.

1. Enter a query rule name, and then click **Edit Query Statement** to modify the default query.

2. On the Query Rule Properties dialog, select the **Criteria** tab, and then click the starburst icon to create a new rule.

3. In the Criterion Properties dialog, select **Simple value** as the criterion type, and then click the **Select** button.

4. In the Select Attributes dialog, choose **Add/Remove Programs** for the Attribute Class, **Display Name** as the Attribute, and click **OK**.

5. In the Criterion Properties dialog, change the operator to **is like**.

6. For the Value property, enter **Adobe Reader%**, as shown in Figure 13.5.

7. Click **OK**.

If you have x64 systems in your environment, you may need to write an additional query-based rule depending on whether the application has a native 64-bit installation or it also uses the x86 installation files. For this example, create a second query rule, but select **Add/ Remove Programs (64)** for the attribute class.

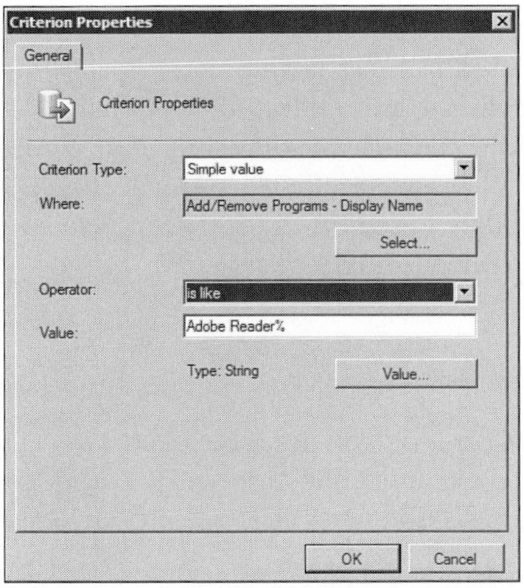

FIGURE 13.5   The Criterion Properties dialog.

After saving the rule, notice the Query Statement Properties dialog displays both rules with an *and* join. It would be unlikely for an application to appear in both Add/Remove Programs and in Add/Remove Programs (64). Select the **and** join, and press the &| icon to switch it to an **or**, as shown in Figure 13.6.

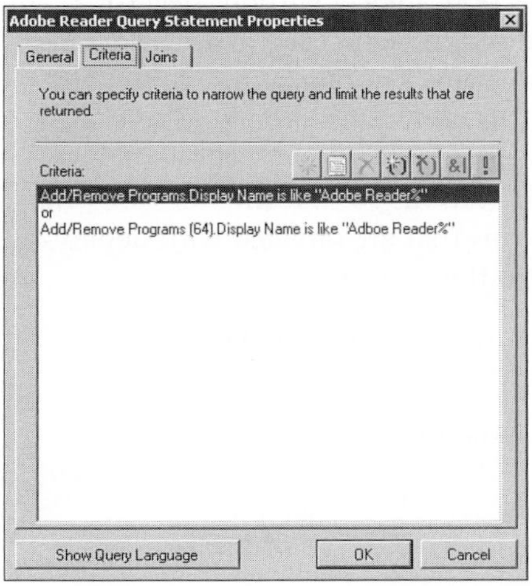

FIGURE 13.6   The Query Statement Properties dialog.

You can also see the additional actions and parameters you can add to the query criterion. For example, you can group using parenthesis, switch *and* to *or*, or change to a *not* query.

Include Rule

The *include rule* is a new rule type in ConfigMgr 2012 used to include all members of a different collection. For example, you may have two collections, one for all New York systems and one for all Los Angeles systems. You could make a third collection named All US Systems and create two include rules, one for New York and one for Los Angeles. This allows the All US Systems collection to dynamically update based on the rules for the New York and Los Angeles collections. Membership of this collection will be updated if the membership of an included collection has changed.

Exclude Rule

The *exclude rule* is also new to ConfigMgr 2012 and performs as you would expect. This rule type will ensure that systems defined in the desired exclude collection will never be a member of this collection. Membership of this collection is updated if the membership of the excluded collection changes.

> **NOTE: EXCLUDE RULES ALWAYS WIN**
>
> If you create a collection with both include and exclude rules and a system is a member of both the include and exclude collections, the exclude collection rule wins.

About Incremental Updates

Incremental updates allow you to add systems to a collection quickly without need of a full collection membership update. You may have noticed in Figure 13.2 that the default collection interval update is every 7 days, compared to every 24 hours with ConfigMgr 2007. In addition, the **Use Incremental updates for this collection** property is disabled by default. The general idea is that as you move to ConfigMgr 2012, you will use fewer collections and rely more on requirement rules for applications so that the rules are evaluated at the client. Use incremental updates on collections that are targeted with deployments to quickly deliver (or make available) software to the user or device.

To perform a manual collection membership update, simply select the collection, and choose **Update Membership** from the ribbon bar.

Here are the classes that do not support incremental updates:

- ▶ SMS_G_System_CollectedFile

- ▶ SMS_G_System_LastSoftwareScan

- ▶ SMS_G_System_AppClientState

- ▶ SMS_G_System_DCMDeploymentState

- ▶ SMS_G_System_DCMDeploymentErrorAssetDetails

- ▶ SMS_G_System_DCMDeploymentCompliantAssetDetails

- ▶ SMS_G_System_DCMDeploymentNonCompliantAssetDetails

▶ SMS_G_User_DCMDeploymentCompliantAssetDetails (for collections of users only)

▶ SMS_G_User_DCMDeploymentNonCompliantAssetDetails (for collections of users only)

▶ SMS_G_System_SoftwareUsageData

▶ SMS_G_System_CI_ComplianceState

▶ SMS_G_System_EndpointProtectionStatus

▶ SMS_GH_System_*

▶ SMS_GEH_System_*

If you need to use any of these classes, configure the full collection membership update to occur on an interval that meets your requirements.

> **TIP: BE CONSERVATIVE WITH INCREMENTAL UPDATES**
>
> You may encounter evaluation delays when the incremental update feature is enabled on a large number of collections. The suggested maximum is approximately 200 collections, but the exact number depends on multiple factors. The article at http://technet.microsoft.com/en-us/library/gg699372.aspx provides additional documentation.

User Collections Versus Device Collections

Although the examples in this chapter have focused on device collections, all software deployments (except for task sequences and software updates) can be targeted to user collections. Consider the following when targeting deployments:

▶ User-targeted deployments appear in the Application Catalog.

▶ Device-targeted deployments appear in Software Center.

▶ Deployments that appear in Software Center are evaluated when the policy is downloaded from the management point.

▶ Deployments that appear in Application Catalog are evaluated only when the user selects to install the application.

▶ Application approval requests can be enabled only with user-targeted deployments of applications (through the Application Catalog).

About Distribution Points

Distribution points play a key role in the delivery of packages, programs, endpoint protection updates, applications, software updates, and operating system deployment (OSD). You use DPs to make content available to clients. To prevent clients from traversing networks in undesirable paths, you leverage boundary groups to help specify which DP (or DPs) a client should use. This section walks through the process of creating DPs,

DP groups (DPGs), sending content to DPs, and monitoring DP status, as well as advanced configuration and troubleshooting.

TIP: NEW FEATURES OF CONTENT DISTRIBUTION IN CONFIGMGR 2012

There are enough changes in content distribution with ConfigMgr 2012 that it *is* worth a moment to remind you of the highlights. Content is king, and ConfigMgr 2012 does a good job of getting content where you need it, when you need it, and validating it moving forward. Here are some highlights from the authors:

▶ **Single instance store:** If multiple objects (packages, applications, software updates, and so on) use the same source file, ConfigMgr 2012 sends that file to each distribution point one time. Any additional requirement for that file is handled with multiple references to the same file on the DP. Depending on your environment, you may see a significant reduction in size for your package source.

▶ **Sender-capable DPs:** No more branch DPs or server DP shares; in ConfigMgr 2012, all DPs are created equally. All DPs support throttling, the single instance store, and status reporting. (DPs on workstation operating systems do not support Preboot eXecution Environment [PXE] or multicast, because the operating system [OS] does not support those core components.)

▶ **No more thumbs.db issues:** When a user with Write permission browses to a DP share on a Windows 7 system, he can accidentally modify the source for any package by simply viewing the contents. Win7 creates a thumbs.db that contains thumbnails of images in the folder. More information is available at http://gregramsey.wordpress.com/2012/02/13/interesting-issue-with-thumbs-db/). ConfigMgr 2007 generates a package hash based on the package source files folder. ConfigMgr 2012 does the same, as well as a hash for each file in a package source. The thumbs.db issue occurs if someone with Create rights browses to a DP package source on a system that is configured to create thumbnails for each file. This new file would cause the computed package source to be different from the hash ConfigMgr expected. Due to the single instance store and the way ConfigMgr 2012 handles each file for a package, this issue no longer exists (unless you choose the option to make a package share for a package).

▶ **.PCK files no longer stored in SMSPKG folder on site servers:** ConfigMgr 2012 uses compressed .pck packages to send content to DPs, but the .PCK files are no longer stored on each site. .PCK files are used for sending content to DPs, but after the content is extracted to the content library, the .PCK file is removed. This may be the reason you can find more free disk space on your site servers.

▶ **Hash validation:** ConfigMgr 2012 DPs can be configured to validate the hash of each file on a DP to verify its integrity on a regular interval, and if the hash is not correct, report failure.

▶ **Content status information in the console:** ConfigMgr 2012 does a great job of displaying the status of content to the admin. You can look for each package object, individual DP, as well as per DPG. You can think of this as more of a compliance view; the view status determines if a DP is compliant, meaning that it has all the intended content, and file hashes are verified.

▶ **Send an entire task sequence to a DP or DPG:** ConfigMgr 2012 allows you to select a task sequence and select **Distribute Content** so that you can ensure all package references for an OS deployment have been distributed to the desired DPs.

▶ **Replacement of Copy Packages Wizard:** Simply add DPs to a DPG to ensure that the new DP has all content referenced in the DPG.

▶ **Replacement of PreloadPkgOnsite utility:** The utility for ConfigMgr 2007 was handy but was still a challenge (and not completely supported) to properly preload all content types (packages, OS images, and so on) on a DP. ConfigMgr 2012 has a Prestage Content Wizard that allows you to extract any type of content from one location, transfer it via network or even offline media (thumb drive, DVD-ROM, external hard disk, and such) to a remote location, and import content.

Installing Distribution Points

Chapter 6, "Installing System Center 2012 Configuration Manager," discussed how to install and configure distribution points along with a primary or secondary site. This section describes the process of installing a DP on a remote server or workstation. DP role requirements are discussed in Chapter 6.

Follow these steps to create a DP:

1. In the console, navigate to **Administration -> Overview -> Site Configuration** and select **Servers and Site Systems**; then select **Create Site System Server.**

2. In the Create Site System Server Wizard, enter the fully qualified domain name (FQDN) of the new DP, as well as the site that will manage the DP. This is the standard wizard page for installing site systems discussed in Chapter 6. Click **Next**.

3. On the System Role Selection page, select **Distribution Point**.

4. On the Distribution Point page, configure the DP settings for your environment. Here is a brief description of each property on this page, shown in Figure 13.7:

    ▶ **Install and configure IIS if required by Configuration Manager:** Enable this setting to install Windows components required for a DP automatically. (This option does not install required components on Windows Server 2003 systems; you must install the components separately.) Chapter 6 describes required components.

    ▶ **Specify how client computers communicate with the distribution point:** Choose HTTP or HTTPS for client communication with the DP. Chapter 5, "Network Design," discusses PKI requirements for HTTPS.

    ▶ **Allow clients to connect anonymously:** Enable this check box only if you need anonymous connections to the DP. The ConfigMgr client uses the Local System account and the Network Access account to connect to the DP. However, there are scenarios in which may you need to grant anonymous access, for example, the Windows Installer repair functionality on Windows XP that attempts to connect using anonymous. Review http://technet.microsoft.com/en-us/library/gg682115.aspx#BKMK_ InstallDistributionPoint, under the "To modify the distribution point properties" heading, to determine if you must enable anonymous access.

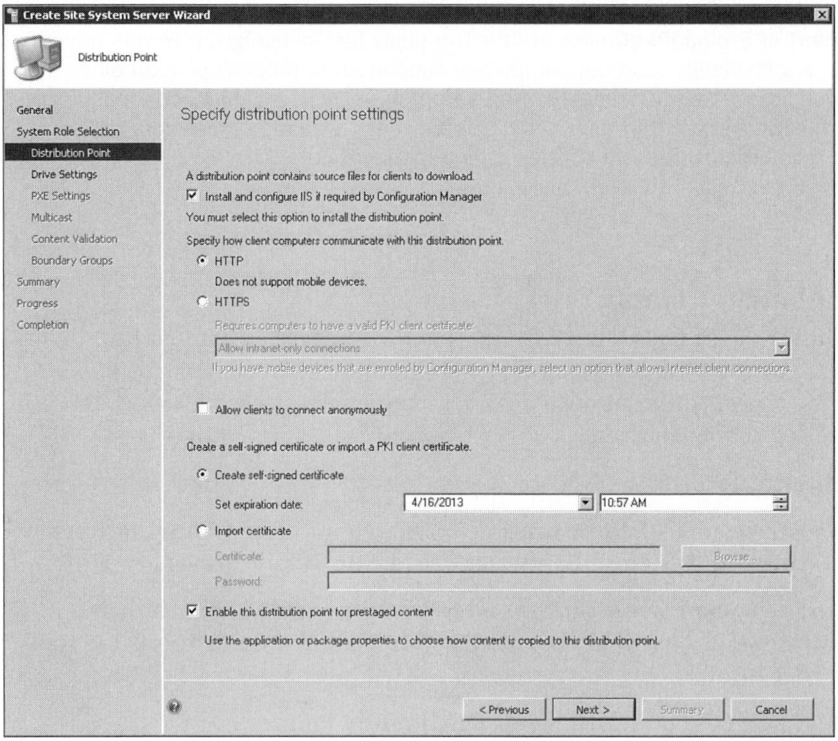

FIGURE 13.7 Specifying distribution point settings in the Create Site System Wizard.

▶ **Create a self-signed certificate or import a PKI client certificate:** This certificate is used to authenticate the DP to a MP so that the DP can send status messages to the MP. Clients that boot with PXE to connect to the MP during OSD also use this certificate. When all your management points are configured for HTTP, create a self-signed certificate. If your management points are configured for HTTPS, import a PKI certificate. For additional information about this certificate, see http://technet.microsoft.com/en-us/library/hh272770.aspx.

▶ **Enable this distribution point for prestaged content:** Enable this check box for more granular control when content can transfer over the WAN link, on a per-content package basis (package, application, operating system image, and so on). With this check box enabled, you can create prestaged content files, copy them to a remote location, and import the files into the local DP. After enabling this check box, review the information in the "Prestaging Content" section for more information.

5. On the Drive Settings page displayed in Figure 13.8, specify the amount of free space to reserve on the disk, as well as the preferred location for the content library and package share.

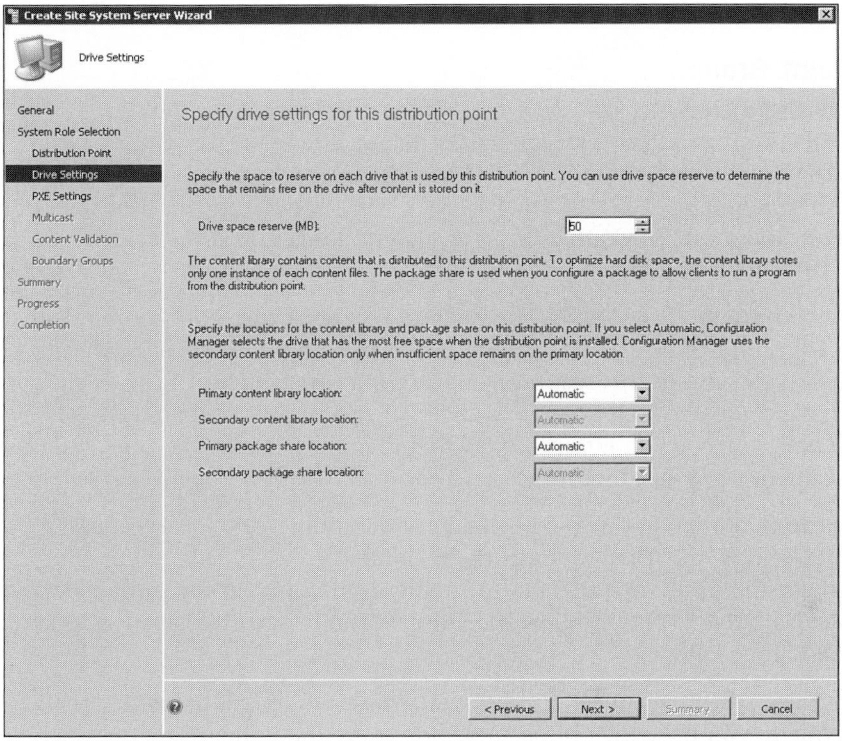

FIGURE 13.8   The Distribution Point Properties-Drive Settings page.

6. Configure the PXE Settings page as described in Chapter 19, "Operating System Deployment."

7. Configure the Multicast page as described in Chapter 19.

8. On the Content Validation page, enable content validation, and configure a recurring schedule for when the server is at low utilization. Also, note that the time is local to the site server. You can review the schedule on the DP from scheduled tasks. See the "Validating Content" section for more information.

9. On the Boundary Groups page, create or add an existing boundary group that will be supported by this DP. Enable the **Allow fallback source location for content** check box to allow clients to fall back to this site to obtain content when content is not available for the system from a local DP.

10. Complete the wizard.

11. After the DP installs successfully, navigate to **Administration -> Overview -> Hierarchy Configuration -> Addresses**. View the properties of the address you just configured, and modify throttling methods as necessary to reduce risk of WAN saturation.

Distribution Point Groups

Although DPGs are also included in ConfigMgr 2007, they deserve a fresh look in ConfigMgr 2012. DPG configurations are global data that can be managed with scopes to limit visibility of DPGs to different admin roles, if wanted. If you worked with ConfigMgr 2007, you may also be familiar with the Copy Packages Wizard used for packages, update packages, OS images, and more. In ConfigMgr 2012, you no longer need the Copy Packages Wizard: DPGs to the rescue.

Say, for example, you have multiple DPs in Europe, and you want to ensure content is available on each DP. Simply create a DPG named **All Europe DPs** and add each DP to the group. As you will see later in this section, you can send content to a DPG (which is highly recommended, compared to sending to individual DPs when possible). Now six months later, you have a new DP in Europe. By adding the new DP to All Europe DPs, the new DP automatically receives all content previously sent to the All Europe DPs DPG.

It is also important to note that a DP can be a member of multiple DPGs. For example, you may have a DPG called All DPs used to distribute content to every DP in your environment but also have the All Europe DPs that contains a subset of DPs for Europe. You could add a scope for each DPG to allow the Europe Admins security group to send content only to All Europe DPs.

You can also associate a DPG to a collection so that any time you target the desired collection with a deployment, you have the option to deploy content automatically to associated groups. This is demonstrated in the "Deploying Packages and Applications" section.

Follow these steps to create a DPG:

1. In the console, navigate to **Administration -> Overview** and select **Distribution Point Group**. Now select **Create Group**.

2. In the **Create New Distribution Point Group** wizard, enter a name and description.

3. On the Collections page, click the **Add** button, and select a collection to associate with this DP group (if desired).

4. Select Members, and click the **Add** button to select the desired DPs to add to the new DPG.

5. Click **OK** to save the DPG.

Associating Collections with Distribution Point Groups

Another new feature in ConfigMgr 2012 is the ability to associate a collection with a DPG. When distributing content, you can target a collection associated with a DPG. This in turn targets all DPs in the DPG with the content.

For example, you have a collection named All Devices in Europe (which obviously contains all devices in Europe). You also have a DPG, All Europe DPs, that is associated with the All Devices in Europe collection. Next, you have an application that needs to be deployed to All Devices in Europe. When you create the deployment, you can choose to deploy content automatically to the associated DPG for the target collection. You can use this process to ensure that content is distributed to all DPs necessary for the deployment. You can review DP and collection association by viewing the properties of the collection or DP.

To associate a DP, view properties for the desired collection, and select the Distribution Point Groups tab. Then click **Add** and choose the DPs or DPGs you want to associate to the collection, as shown in Figure 13.9.

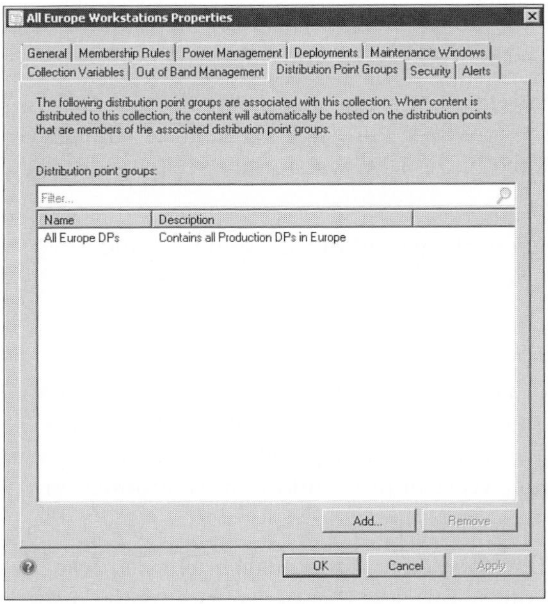

FIGURE 13.9 Associating a DP group to a collection.

You can also view the properties of a DP (from the administration group) and manage associations from the Group Relationship tab.

Sending Content to Distribution Points

Several types of content exist in ConfigMgr, these are applications, packages, software updates, and several types of OS deployment packages (image package, driver package, and so on). To send content to the distribution points, perform the following steps:

1. Navigate to the desired object (you can also multiselect), select it, and then choose **Distribute Content** from the ribbon bar.

2. On the General page, you see a check box near the bottom of the screen. It is enabled if the object has associated dependencies (such as dependent applications, programs configured to run another program first, and so on). Enable this check box to automatically distribute any dependency.

3. On the Content Distribution page, click the **Add** button and choose one of these options:

   ▶ **Collections:** Choose this option to select a collection that has been associated with a DP group. Don't be alarmed if you don't see any collections in this view; you will see only collections that have been associated.

   ▶ **Distribution Point:** Choose this option to selectively choose one or more DPs. When possible, leverage DPGs instead.

   ▶ **Distribution Point Group:** Choose this option to choose one or more DP groups. By choosing this option, if you later add a new DP to an existing DPG, all content that has been distributed to the DPG will automatically be distributed to the new DP.

4. Click **Next** through the remaining pages of the wizard to view summary and progress information.

Monitoring Distribution Point Status

Content is a key element of ConfigMgr. You have to know that content is exactly where you want it to be. ConfigMgr 2007 does a good job with reports and distribution status messages. ConfigMgr 2012 takes things to the next level to help you identify current state of a DP as well as that of DPGs. There are three types of distribution status information available to you in the admin console:

▶ **Content Status:** Provides DP information focused on the actual content (a package, application, software update package, and so on). Use this status to verify the distribution of one piece of content.

▶ **Distribution Point Group Status:** Provides DP information focused on the overall health of a DPG. Use this status to verify the status of all content associated with a DPG.

▶ **Distribution Point Configuration Status:** Provides DP information focused on each individual DP. Use this status to verify the state of a single DP.

These are discussed in the following sections.

Content Status

For clients to install software, the content must be available. Use this information to view DP status for a specific package, application, or other content. Perform the following steps:

1. In the console, navigate to **Monitoring -> Distribution Status** and select **Content Status**.

2. The Detail section lists all content that has been targeted to any distribution point.

3. You can quickly search for specific content, or you can right-click on the title bar, select **Group By -> Type**, right-click a type and select **Collapse All** to group content, as shown in Figure 13.10.

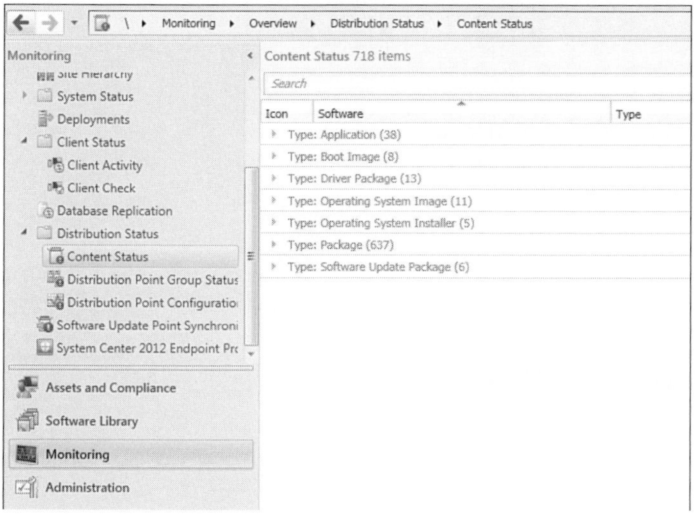

FIGURE 13.10   Content Status grouped by type.

4. After you select the wanted content, you can see the number of DPs targeted, the computed size, as well as compliance for that content state on targeted DPs. Review the summary at the bottom for more information, as displayed in Figure 13.11.

   In the summary, the Completion Statistics provides an overview. You can also see a property called Last Update, which displays the last time any status message was received for any DP for the selected content. Click the **View Status** link to view content status detail (see Figure 13.12). Also, notice you can filter the Asset Details frame by entering a DP server name into the filter box in this figure. Here are brief descriptions for each state:

   ▶ **Last Update:** The last time any status message was received for any DP.

   ▶ **Success:** This can be based on several conditions:

   Content has been distributed successfully to the DP.

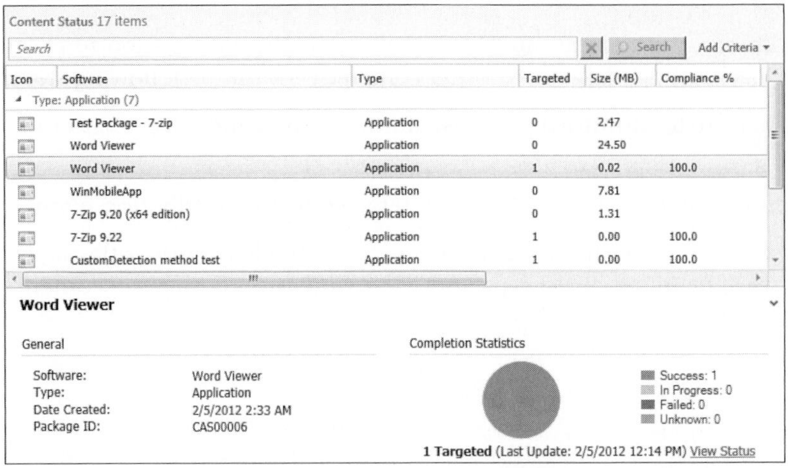

FIGURE 13.11 Content Status summary for Word Viewer application.

FIGURE 13.12 Completion statistics details.

Content hash has been successfully verified. (If you have content validation enabled for a DP, a new status message is generated for each validation success or failure.)

▶ **In Progress:** Content is currently being transferred to one or more DPs. (Review details for more information.)

▶ **Failed:** Content distribution failed for one or more DPs. (Review details for more information.)

▶ **Unknown:** No status has been reported for one or more DPs.

5. Right-click an asset in the Asset Details section; then select **More Details** from the context menu to display additional information about content status, as shown in Figure 13.12.

Distribution Point Group Status

DP Group status works just as its name implies; it reports the overall status for content targeted through a DP group. When you begin working with DPGs, you will find some additional value in DP group status. For example, if you have a team that handles OSD, you could create a group of DPs for OSD (even if it has the same DPs as a member of other DP groups). When this DP group is established and DPs targeted with DPGs, the OSD admin can monitor this group to determine that all required content for OSD is on targeted DPs. Figure 13.13 shows DP group status for two DP groups. You can see the group All Standard DPs has six DPs with 636 items assigned (packages, application content, software update packages, task sequence information, and so on). You can also see the overall distribution status for that DP group is Success. You also see the OSD Only DP group and the errors reported in the summary section at the top of the figure.

Icon	Distribution Point Group	Description	Members	Assigned Content	Overall Distri
	All Standard DPs		6	636	Success
	OSD Only		10	54	Error

OSD Only

General

Distribution Point Group: OSD Only
Description:
Assigned Content: 54

Distribution Statistics

Success: 50
In Progress: 1
Failed: 3
Unknown: 0

10 Members View Status

FIGURE 13.13   Distribution Point Group Status.

Similar to DP status, click the **View Status** link to drill in to identify issues.

Distribution Point Configuration Status

Review the DP configuration status to review specific information for a single DP. Notice the timestamp associated with each message. If you recently installed the DP, you may find *normal* warnings/errors that occur during the DP installation process; these older status messages are eventually purged from the database. You will find helpful information about hash validation, and progress for content being sent to DPs.

Updating Content on Distribution Points

When you modify source content, you must update content on DPs to make it available to clients. A common misconception is that you also must update DPs if you modify metadata for the object. For example, if you modify the command-line arguments of a program or deployment type, you do not need to update DPs (unless of course the source was updated with new files). Only update content when the content source is actually modified. Updating content in ConfigMgr 2012 distributes any new files. Recall that due to the single instance store, a unique binary file is distributed only one time.

TIP: REMEMBER TO UPDATE DISTRIBUTION POINTS

You may have noticed in ConfigMgr 2012 when you create a package or deployment, the content (according to the content source path) is immediately copied into the content store on the CAS (or single primary site server). In ConfigMgr 2007, you may have been in the habit of creating a package, modifying the package source, and then adding DPs, which works fine in that version. In ConfigMgr 2012, remember to update distribution points after you make a change to content source, even when you haven't sent content to DPs.

Here are the types of objects for which you can update distribution points: packages, deployment packages, driver packages, OS images, OS installers, and boot images. Notice you cannot update distribution points on an application, but you can add DPs. When you need to update DPs for an application, choose the wanted deployment type, and select **Update Content**. As a reminder, you can add new DPs for a task sequence (which sends all task sequence associated content to the DP), but you cannot update content for all DPs for a task sequence.

Refreshing Content on Distribution Points

In ConfigMgr 2007, you may have used refresh distribution points occasionally to ensure the package source share has the correct content (often because of hash mismatch errors). In ConfigMgr 2012, you should not need to refresh content often, unless you receive a status message error about a hash value check failure; see the "Validating Content" section. If this is necessary, simply view the properties of the package, select the **Content Locations** tab, highlight the wanted distribution point, and click **Redistribute**.

Removing Content from Distribution Points

Removing content from DPs occurs automatically when an object is deleted. To remove the content from a defined list of DPs, follow these steps:

1. Right-click the object containing the content (package, deployment type, and so on), and select **Properties**.

2. Click the **Content Locations** tab.

3. Select the wanted DP and select the **Remove** button.

To remove content from multiple DPs, you must follow this process to remove each DP, one at a time. If you deployed content to a DP group, choose the wanted DP group and select **Remove** to remove from all DPs that were targeted through the DPG. Keep an eye on the forum posts for a solution on performing this operation on multiple DPs using PowerShell.

The content does not immediately disappear from each DP; ConfigMgr automatically cleans up the excess content on a regular interval (approximately every 4 hours). Recall that files from one package may be used in a different package due to the single instance store. ConfigMgr runs a process to remove content no longer needed by any package.

Validating Content

As mentioned in Chapter 6, you can enable content validation on a weekly or daily basis or at multiple intervals. When ConfigMgr validates content, it enumerates all content that should be on the DP, and for each item it performs a hash check on each required file and compares that information with the information stored in ConfigMgr.

When content is validated, the information is reported back to the site server, whether pass or fail. ConfigMgr reports only the data; there is no built-in method to automate the process to attempt to re-send to DPs, or to revalidate. Also, note that the time you config-ure for content validation is local to the site server time. For example, if your primary server is in Chicago, and you configure content validation for a server in Bangalore to be **Every day at 6:00pm**, that time is local to Chicago, so the actual run time will be at 5:30 a.m. each day in Bangalore (due to the 12h 30m time difference). The task is configured as a scheduled task on the DP system, and modification of that task should occur from the primary site server through the Content Validation dialog.

Using BranchCache

BranchCache is a relatively new technology first released with Windows 7 Enterprise or Ultimate, Windows Server 2008 R2, and with a hotfix made available for Windows Vista. BranchCache allows you to leverage a peer-to-peer model securely to share content between systems. This is especially helpful in the scenario where you have multiple systems in a remote office with no distribution point. You can enable BranchCache to reduce the number of systems crossing the WAN link to download source content. For a comprehensive look at BranchCache, review the whitepaper at http://www.microsoft.com/download/en/details.aspx?displaylang=en&id=5772.

Here is the procedure for installing and configuring BranchCache:

1. On the server, add the Windows feature named BranchCache.

2. On the client systems, enable a GPO with the following configuration (you can find the BranchCache GPO in the **Computer Configuration** -> **Administrative Templates** -> **Network** -> **BranchCache** folder):

    ▶ Turn on BranchCache = Enabled.

    ▶ Set BranchCache Distributed Cache mode = Enabled.

    ▶ Configure BranchCache for Network Files = Enabled.

Modify the Round trip latency value from 80 to 0 so that all content will be cached using BranchCache.

▶ Set percentage of disk space used for client computer cache = Enabled, and modify the value to 20.

This is optional. By default, only 5% of disk space can be used by BranchCache.

As an alternative to enabling a GPO in step 2, you can run the following commands on each client using traditional software distribution to enable and configure BranchCache:

```
cmd.exe /c netsh branchcache set service mode=DISTRIBUTED
cmd.exe /c netsh branchcache smb set latency latency=0
cmd.exe /c set cachesize size=20 percent=TRUE
```

When BranchCache is enabled, review the detailed guide mentioned earlier in this section to validate tests and measure bandwidth savings. After BranchCache is configured, there is one setting you need to enable on each deployment. Under Distribution Settings, enable **Allow clients to share content with other clients on the same subnet**.

Preferred Distribution Points

ConfigMgr 2007 has a feature for branch DPs that enables the site to automatically distribute content to the branch DP whenever a client in that DP's boundary requests it. ConfigMgr 2012 has taken that feature and made it available for all DPs. Consider the scenario in which you have a large number of DPs and a large number of packages. Depending on your environment, you may just want to send everything to all DPs to ensure that content is available when needed. On the other hand, you may have a limited amount of space and be fairly certain that many packages (or other content) will not be required everywhere.

Let's say you have packaged all MUI language packs for Windows 7. Rather than distribute all European language MUIs to a Cleveland DP (where it's unlikely most of them will ever be needed), you can distribute the content to the parent site of the Cleveland DP and enable the check box to **Distribute the content for this package to preferred distribution points**, as shown in Figure 13.14. With this enabled, when a client requests content and the content is not available in the boundaries of a DP, ConfigMgr will distribute the content to the DP so that it will now be available locally for all managed systems. If you have configured the application to allow fallback to a remote DP, this setting wins over the **Distribute the content for this package to preferred distribution points** setting.

Prestaging Content

You may have some locations with slow connectivity or even costly connectivity. ConfigMgr 2012 gives you the ability to create a prestaged content file from one server and then mail it to another server and import the prestaged content. You can also copy the content over the WAN provided your WAN is robust. To enable prestaged content, first enable the check box, as shown in Figure 13.15. Enabling this check box instructs

ConfigMgr to obey the property configurations of the package or application (refer to Figure 13.15).

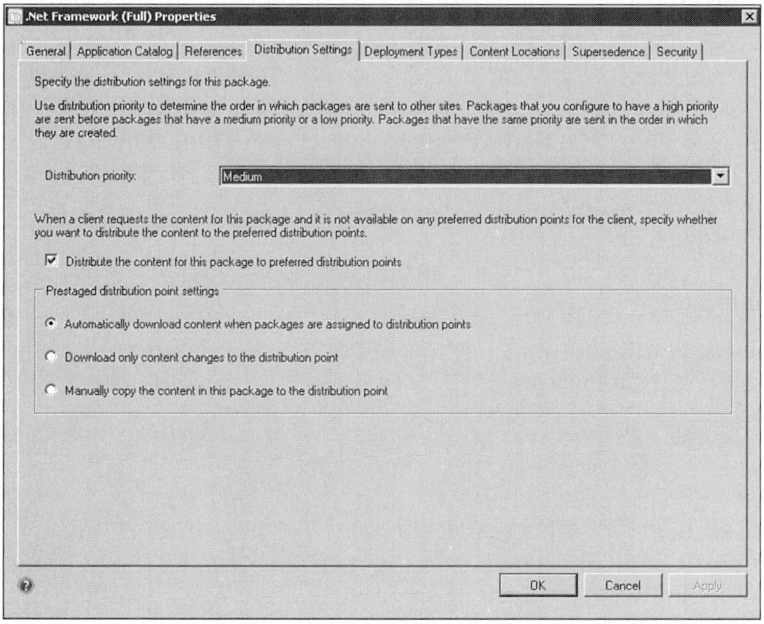

FIGURE 13.14   Enable preferred DP content distribution.

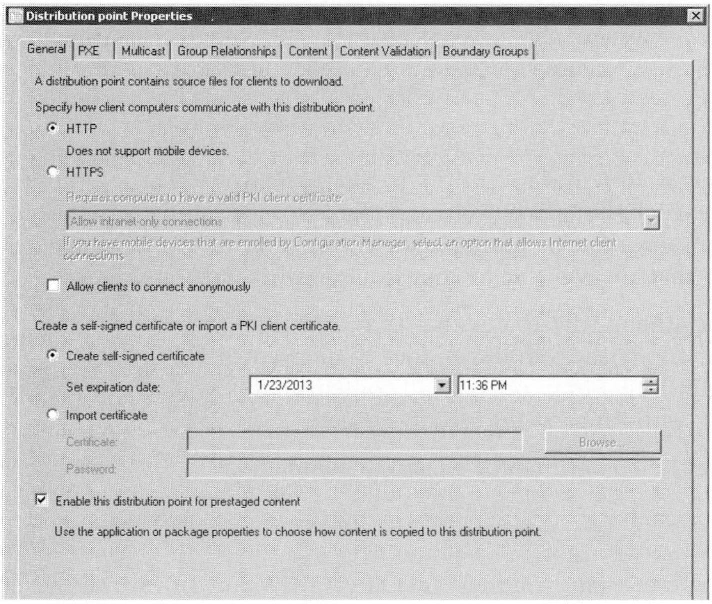

FIGURE 13.15   Enable prestaged content for a distribution point.

Figure 13.14 also displayed the package settings available for configuring how prestaged content will be managed. Here is a brief description of each option:

▶ **Automatically download content when packages are assigned to distribution points:** Configures a package to work as normally expected. From the ConfigMgr admin console, you distribute software, and software arrives on the DPs.

▶ **Download only content changes to the distribution point:** Use this setting to allow minor updates to occur to the DP using the standard content distribution processes. Here's an example: You deploy Office 2010 and later realize you have additional updates to deploy. Using this setting, you could deploy the base install (the largest size for content) of Office 2010 and require the initial package be installed by using prestaged content. Any subsequent changes could be sent using the normal distribution point process.

▶ **Manually copy the content in this package to the distribution point:** The setting ensures that ConfigMgr does not use any WAN for content transfer and relies completely on importing prestaged content.

Creating Prestage Content

You can use prestage content to export package source from the content library. This allows you to manually transfer content from one location to a remote location, insert the media, and import the content into a new distribution point. Perform the following steps to create the prestage content file:

1. Select one or more package objects, and choose **Create Prestage Content File** from the ribbon bar to start the wizard.

2. On the General page of the wizard, choose a path to store the compressed content, enable the check box to export all dependencies if wanted, and add any additional administrator comments.

3. Review the Content page to confirm the content you want to prestage is selected. If you need to add or remove content, cancel the wizard and return to step 1. On the Content Locations page, click the **Add** button, and choose one or more distribution points to be used as the source for the prestage content process, shown in Figure 13.16. Try to select DPs that are available to your local network when possible.

   Figure 13.16 shows that Athena.odyssey.com has three of the four wanted packages available, and Ambassador.odyssey.com has all four of the wanted packages. The Athena distribution point is first in priority, so all content that is available from Athena is collected first, with Ambassador used as needed.

4. Review the Content page, and continue the wizard to completion.

Importing Prestage Content

To successfully import prestaged content, you must first target the wanted DPs with the package, using one of the prestaged content settings for the package.

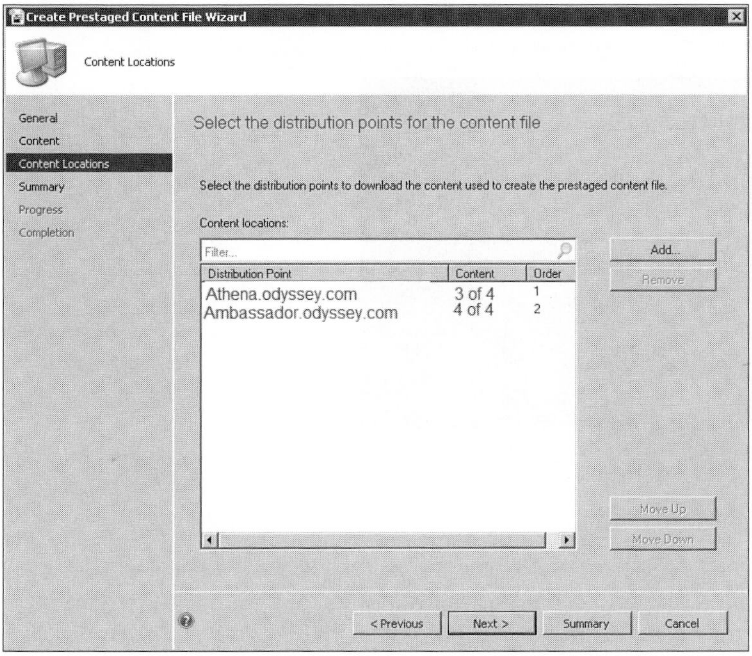

FIGURE 13.16   Create Prestaged Content File Wizard.

TIP: VERIFY PRESTAGE CONFIGURATION

Before beginning the import process, verify the package properties are configured properly, as described previously in this section. If a package is configured to **Automatically download content when packages are assigned to distribution points**, the prestage process will not work as expected, as content will be sent to the DP as it normally does, without prestaging.

After you use the ConfigMgr console to send content to DPs, you see status messages (under **Monitoring -> Distribution Status -> Content Status**) that state the distribution point is waiting for prestaged content. At this time, transport the prestaged content to the desired location. (This could be a simple file copy over the WAN or a process of copying the prestaged content to media and shipping it to the remote location.) Follow these steps on the distribution point to import prestaged content:

1. Copy the extracted content to c:\temp\.

2. Open a command prompt, and navigate to the SMS_DP$\sms\Tools folder.

3. Run this command: `extractcontent /p:c:\temp\mycontent.pkgx /i`

4. Review the output (run `extractcontent.exe /?` for more options).

Figure 13.17 shows an example of the output from content prestage.

FIGURE 13.17   Extract Content example.

Importing and Exporting Content

ConfigMgr 2012 allows you to export objects easily from one ConfigMgr 2012 environment to another or export for backup and archival purposes. When you export content, you can choose to export only the object, or the object and the package source.

Perform the following steps to export content:

1. Select one or more package objects, and choose **Export** from the ribbon bar to start the wizard.

2. From the General page, enter a file path for the location to store the exported content. Enter a file extension of **.zip**, as shown in Figure 13.18.

Here is a brief description of each of the options in Figure 13.18:

▶ **Export all application dependencies, supersedence relationships, and conditions:** As described, this export includes all dependence and supersedence information, and global conditions. For packages, this includes packages referenced with the **Run another program first** option. For task sequences, this includes all packages, applications, driver packages, and more referenced in a task sequence (all objects that appear under the References area for a task sequence). Without this check box enabled, you are exporting only the selected object.

▶ **Export all content for the selected applications and dependencies:** This second check box is specific to source files that are referenced by an object. Enabling this check box may significantly increase the size of the exported content.

3. Review the information on the Review Related Objects page, and walk through the rest of the wizard to completion. You will find a file with extension .zip in the export directory, and if you elected to export content, you'll find one or more subfolders that contains the actual content source for all selected objects.

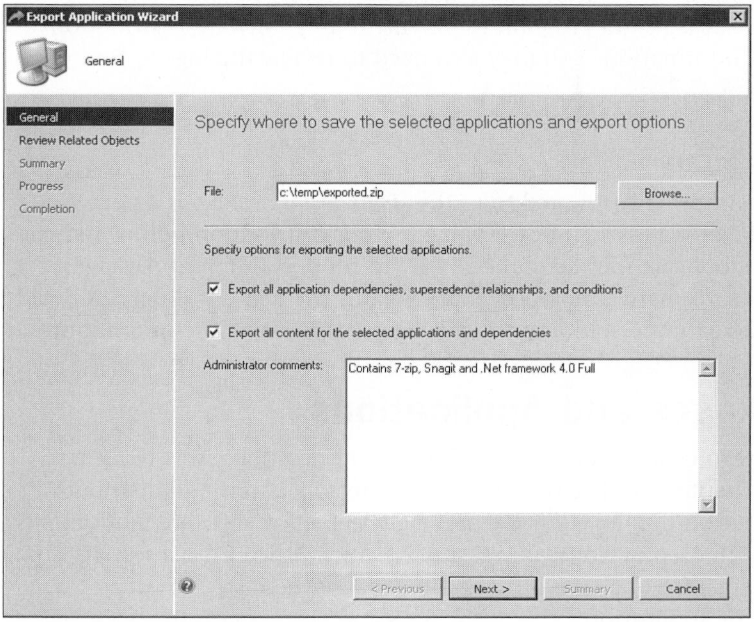

FIGURE 13.18   Export Application Wizard.

Perform the following steps to import the content to a different ConfigMgr 2012 environment:

1. Select an object node (Application, Package, and so on) and select **Import** (or **Import Application**, depending on your location) from the ribbon bar.

2. Select the UNC path to the exported content (for example, \\\<servername>\<share>\ myExportedApps.zip).

TIP: ENSURE THE COMPRESSED .ZIP FILE IS IN THE PROPER LOCATION

When you import, the content is extracted from the .zip file to the current directory, and that becomes the package source location for the object (application, package, program, and so on). Before you import, be sure to place the .zip and required subfolders in the proper location and import using the UNC path that you want to have for the content source location, or plan to move content and change paths after import.

3. Review the File Content page; if some of the content were previously imported, you may have additional options to skip or overwrite.

4. Continue through the wizard to completion.

Troubleshooting Content Distribution

Most troubleshooting for content distribution occurs in the ConfigMgr console, as mentioned in the "Monitoring Distribution Point Status" section. You also want to review the Software Distribution-Package and Program Deployment and Software Distribution-Content reports for more information. You may also need to review the logs to find more information.

About the Content Library

The Content Library, also informally referred to as the *single instance store*, is a new feature in ConfigMgr 2012 that adds significant value to your distribution points and reduces the need to send duplicate files across the WAN to support different packages. Kent Agerlund created an informative blog post that explains the content library in detail at http://blog.coretech.dk/kea/understanding-the-new-content-library-store-in-5-minutes/.

Deploying Packages and Applications

Chapter 11 described how to create packages, and Chapter 12 described how to create applications. So far, this chapter has discussed how to create collections and distribute content to wanted distribution points. Now you are ready to deploy software. Both applications and packages use the Deploy Software Wizard. As you will see in this section, some options will only be available for one type or the other. Follow these steps to deploy a ConfigMgr 2012 package or application:

1. In the console, navigate to **Software Library -> Overview -> Packages** and select the wanted package. (You can select the wanted program as well.) Alternatively, navigate to the Applications node and select an application.

2. Select **Deploy** from the ribbon bar to start the General page of the Deploy Software Wizard, shown in Figure 13.19. Edit the following properties as required:

   ▶ **Software:** If deploying a package, click **Browse** and choose the wanted program to deploy. (This will be filtered to show only the programs for the current package.) If deploying an application, the application name appears in the dialog.

   ▶ **Collection:** Choose the desired target collection. Notice the Member Count property for each collection; this shows you the total count of members in a collection. If you are in an environment with multiple primary sites, you may not see all collection members from a primary site. (But you will see all from the CAS.) Therefore, when you deploy software, you will always see the total member count so that you know how many systems you can impact.

   ▶ **Use default distribution point groups associated to this collection:** This option is enabled if you associated a DP group to the targeted collection. Simply enable the check box to populate the content distribution information automatically on the next page of the wizard.

▶ **Automatically distribute content for dependencies:** Choose this option to distribute all packages that would be required for the **Run another program first** feature for a program. If the program specified for this option references a different package, enable this check box to ensure the dependent package is also distributed. If deploying an application, any dependent application (discussed in Chapter 12) is distributed with this check box enabled. This automatic process occurs only at deployment creation time. If the dependent package is updated later, it must be updated using the Update Content wizard.

▶ **Comments:** Optional comments for administrators. Information entered here does not appear to the end user.

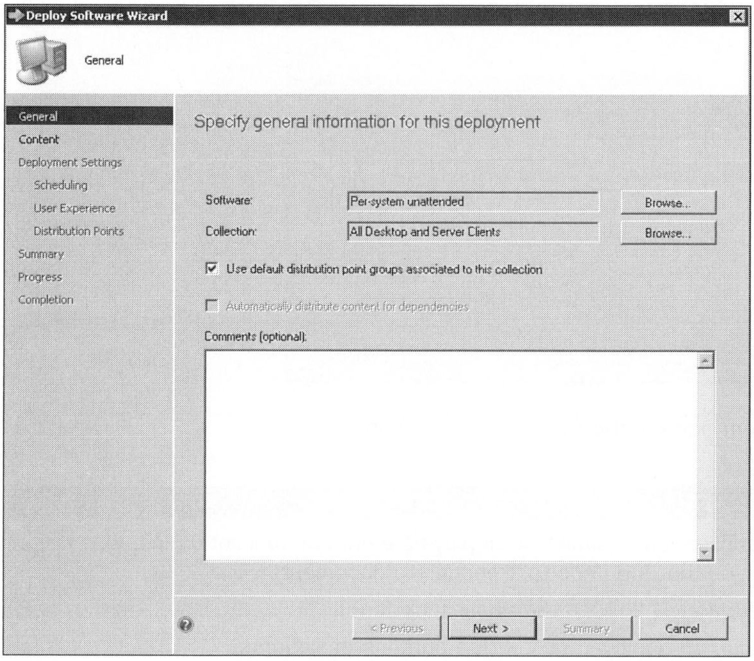

FIGURE 13.19   The General page of the Deploy Software Wizard.

3. The top frame of the Content page, shown in Figure 13.20, displays when content is currently distributed. The bottom frame will show any distribution points you add. If you associated to a collection as shown in Figure 13.18, the DP group is shown. You can add additional DPs and DPGs by clicking the **Add** button and browsing to a DP or DP group.

4. The information on the Deployment Settings page will differ depending on whether the application is targeted to users or devices, an application, or package, and whether the software is required or available. All options with explanations are listed here:

▶ **Action:** For packages, this option will always be set to **Install**. For applications, you can choose **Install** or **Uninstall**.

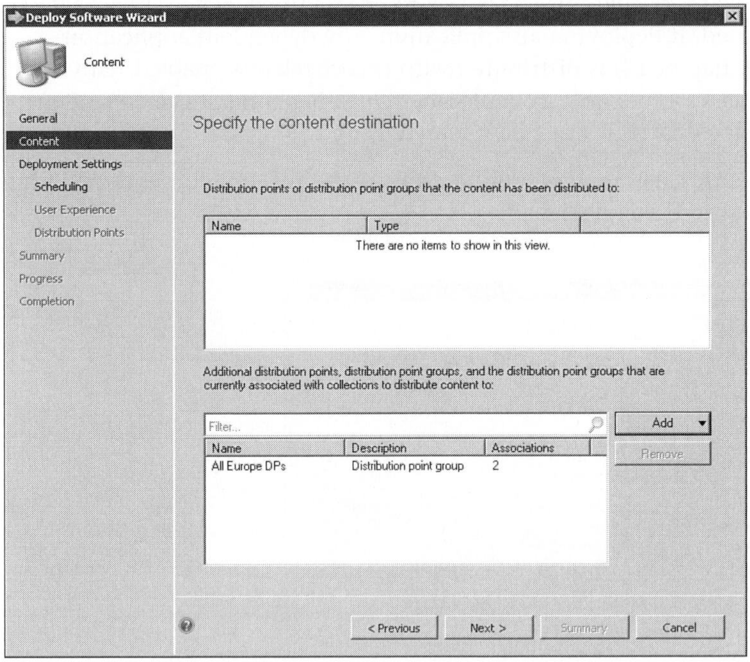

FIGURE 13.20   The Content page of the Deploy Software Wizard.

NOTE: ABOUT THE UNINSTALL ACTION

Deploying an uninstall application is similar to deploying a normal application install. There are some differences that are important enough to document:

▶ Uninstall is only supported through the application feature.

▶ Uninstall actions can be deployed only with a purpose of Required.

▶ Dependent applications are not uninstalled during this process.

▶ Requirement Rules are not checked for an Uninstall; if a detection rule determines the software is installed, the uninstall rule is initiated, regardless of requirement rules.

▶ If a system is targeted with a required deployment for both install and uninstall, install wins.

▶ **Purpose:** Choose **Required** or **Available**. After a deployment is created, the purpose cannot change; you must delete the deployment and create a new one to change the purpose.

> ▶ **Deploy automatically according to schedule whether or not a user is logged on:** This setting applies only to required applications targeting a user-based collection (and has no impact on packages). This setting instructs ConfigMgr to use the primary user device affinity (discussed in Chapter 12) to target the machine even while no user is logged on. ConfigMgr maps the user to the computer and deploys the required software. In other words, this setting allows you to deploy required software to a user collection based on user-primary device association.

> ▶ **Send wake-up packets:** This property is enabled for Required deployments; when Wake On LAN is enabled and properly configured for your environment, ConfigMgr sends wake-up packets to wake sleeping systems at deployment start time.

> ▶ **Require administrator approval if users request this application:** This property is enabled for available applications that target a user-based collection. This allows the user to see the application in the Application Catalog and submit a request for approval to install. After approval is granted by the administrator, the user can navigate back to the Application Catalog to install the application.

5. Use the Scheduling page to define when the application should be available and when it will be required (if a required deployment). By default, all times are configured to UTC time. When configuring this page for a package, you can specify an expiration time for the deployment.

TIP: NO EXPIRATION TIME FOR APPLICATIONS

Recall when you deploy an application as a required deployment, the intent is for all targeted and applicable systems to have the software installed. Therefore, applications do not have expiration times.

6. The User Experience page, displayed in Figure 13.21, allows you to configure behavior outside of maintenance windows as well as how or if the user will be notified of an installation or required restart.

> ▶ **User notifications:** This option is only available for applications. The options are self-describing; however, there is one client setting that can affect end-user notifications. Review the client setting under Computer Agent (discussed in Chapter 5) called **Show notifications for new deployments**.

> If this setting is set to False, targeted clients never receive a system tray notification for new software or system restarts for packages, applications, and software updates. To manage notifications for packages, you must configure a property on the program. The Advanced tab for the program has a property named **Suppress program notifications**. Checking this check box prevents system tray notifications. With the check box unchecked, the end user receives notifications if the Computer Agent setting **Show notifications for**

new deployments is set to True. This same configuration is required for task sequences to handle end user notifications.

▶ **Allow the user to run the program independently of assignments:** This setting displays only for programs. When enabled, this allows the deployment to appear in Software Center.

The last two options on this page are used to manage software installations and system restarts. By default, packages and applications adhere to maintenance windows. To bypass maintenance windows for a deployment, modify these settings as desired.

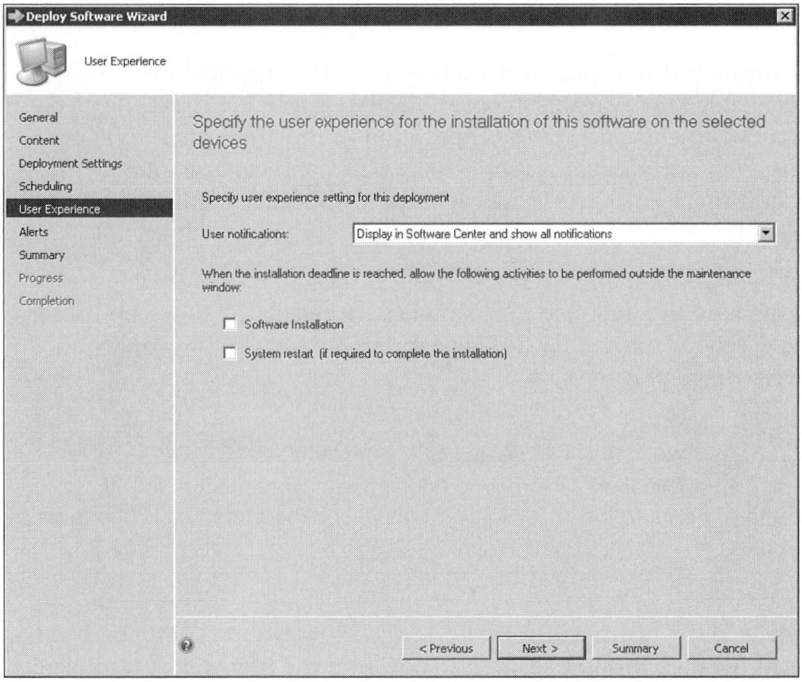

FIGURE 13.21   The User Experience page of the Deploy Software Wizard.

7. The packages version of the Deploy Software Wizard has an additional property page for distribution points, shown in Figure 13.22.

Here is a brief description of each option on the Distribution Points page:

▶ **Deployment Options (for a Fast or LAN Network):** When a system is on a network that has a DP configured as a fast boundary, the client will use the options defined for this property. By default, content is downloaded from the DP, and then run from the local cache. You have one additional option to **Run program from distribution point**. If you choose this option, you must enable the option **Copy the content in this package to a package share on distribution points** on the Data Access tab for the package, discussed in Chapter 11. (Enabling this check box instructs all DPs to copy the required content from the single instance store to a DP share.)

▶ **Deployment Options (for slow or undefined boundary, or fallback location):** Use this option to specify whether clients should download and install content from remote locations.

▶ **Allow clients to share content with other clients on the same subnet:** Use this setting to enable the deployment to support BranchCache.

▶ **Allow clients to use a fallback source location for content:** If a client is unable to locate content for this deployment in its defined boundary group, this check box allows the client to search other locations. To allow clients to access source from a different boundary group, the DP properties, Boundary Groups tab must be configured to **Allow fallback source location for content**.

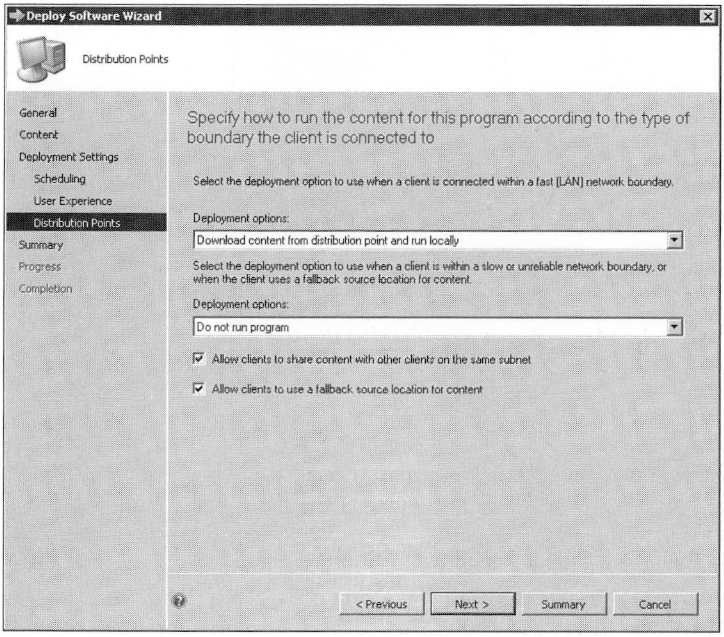

FIGURE 13.22   The Distribution Points page (for Packages Only) of the Deploy Software Wizard.

As mentioned previously in this section, the Distribution Points page in this wizard is only available for packages. Distribution point configuration for applications is part of the application deployment type. Chapter 12 discusses the settings specific to each deployment type.

8. Continue through the rest of the wizard to monitor progress and view completion.

End User Experience

This section provides a brief overview of the end user experience. It will help you determine when to target devices, and when to target users. There are two main views from the end user perspective:

▶ **Software Center:** This is a client-based application that can be accessed from **Start -> Programs -> Microsoft System Center 2012 -> Configuration Manager -> Software Center**. This application displays all device-targeted applications that meet the requirements to install on the system.

▶ **Application Catalog:** The Application Catalog is a rich web-based portal that allows the user to request software, install software, and manage user-device affinity (if granted by the admin). It displays all user-targeted applications. The catalog can be accessed directly by the URL, or by clicking the link **Find additional applications from the Application Catalog** in Software Center, as shown in Figure 13.23.

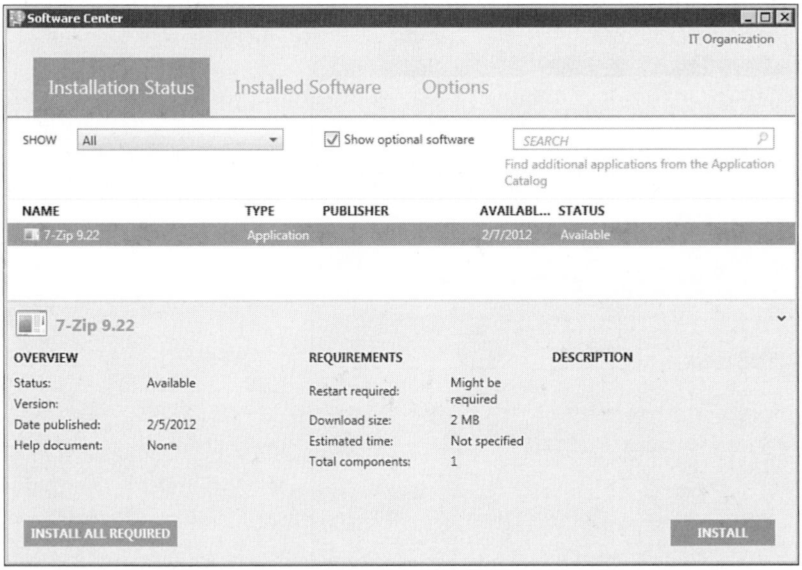

FIGURE 13.23   Showing Installation Status in the Software Center.

Software Center

Figure 13.23 is an example of software that appears in Software Center. The highlighted **Installation Status** tab shows all available software that has been targeted to the device.

This same view shows packages, applications, software updates, and operating system deployment task sequences. You can search, hide optional software, and use the SHOW drop-down box to filter to show only OS deployment, applications (including packages), or software updates. The user selects the wanted application and clicks the **Install** button to start the installation. The **Status** column informs the user of status, such as downloading, installing, installed, and so on. Virtually all information on this page is searchable, and if a help document exists for an application, you can link to it directly from here.

The user can also view the Installed Software tab to review applications installed on the system. The Options tab (shown in Figure 13.24) enables the user to specify when software installs on the system. The user can specify work hours in the Work information section, and then enable the check box under Computer maintenance to **Automatically install or uninstall required software and restart the computer outside of the specified business hours.** When this option is enabled, required software with a deadline in the future automatically installs at the next available user-defined window instead of waiting for the deadline, which could cause the installation to occur at a time more convenient for the user. If the user configured a local business hour installation window for 10:00 PM tonight, and the deadline is at 5 PM today, the software will run at the deadline instead of waiting for the user-defined window. The Computer maintenance section also has a check box, enabled by default, to **Suspend Software Center activities when my computer is in presentation mode.** You can enable presentation mode on Windows 7 or newer systems by pressing [Windows Key]+X on mobile systems, or in Control Panel under Windows Mobility Center -> Presentation Settings.

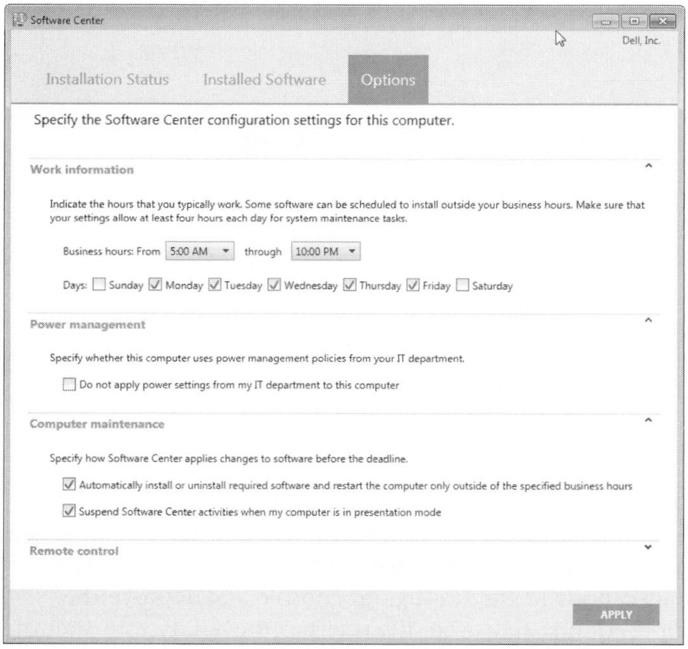

FIGURE 13.24   The Options tab in the Software Center.

TIP: SOFTWARE CENTER IS FOR DEVICE-TARGETED DEPLOYMENTS

All deployments targeted to a device appear in Software Center unless you configured the deployment not to appear in Software Center in the User Experience page of the Deploy Software Wizard (refer to Figure 13.21). All deployments shown in Software Center have already been evaluated based on supported platform rules (for package/program and task sequences) and requirement rules (for applications). Consequently, the Software Center view shows only the software that has met the requirements to install on the current system.

Application Catalog

Figure 13.25 is an example of software that appears in the Application Catalog. You can easily search, view more details, and filter by category.

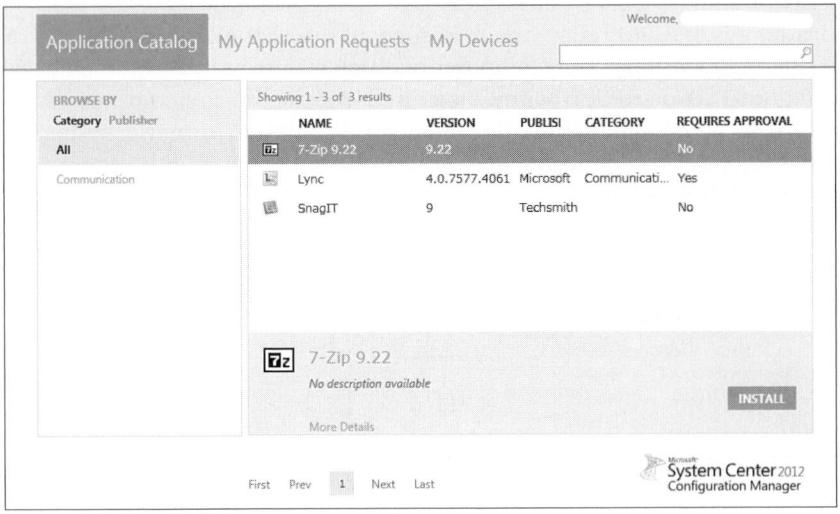

FIGURE 13.25   Viewing the Application Catalog.

As shown in this figure, the Lync installation requires approval. If you select the Lync application, the Install button changes to **Request**. Click **Request** and the view changes to allow the user to enter a justification for the software, as shown in Figure 13.26.

After submitting the request, the user can select the My Application Requests tab to view the status of the request. When the request has been submitted, the ConfigMgr admin (or delegated authority) can navigate to the **Software Library** -> **Overview** -> **Application Management** -> **Approval Requests** node in the ConfigMgr console and approve the application request. After the application is approved, the user has the ability to install the software on any device based on the requirements of the application.

TIP: APPLICATION CATALOG IS FOR USER-TARGETED DEPLOYMENTS

All deployments targeted to a user appear in the Application Catalog. Because these deployments are targeting users, no evaluations are run in advance to verify the installation is supported on the current device.

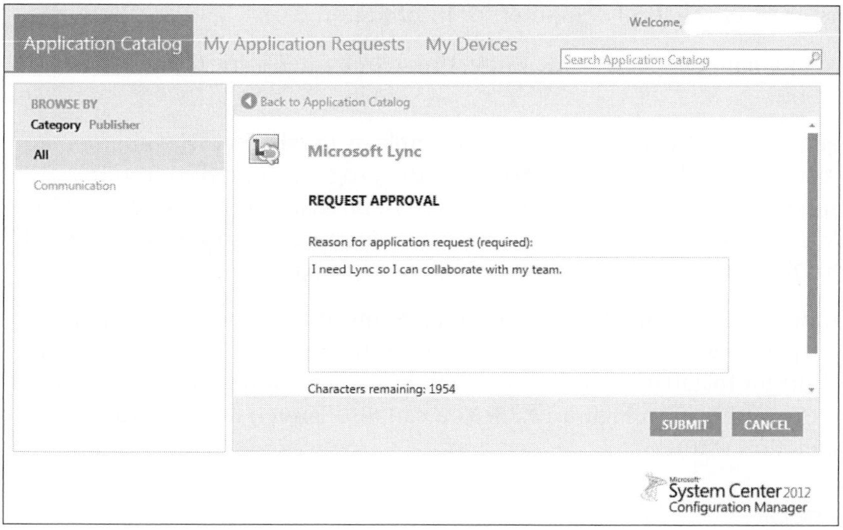

FIGURE 13.26   The Request Approval page of the Application Catalog.

Here is a brief walkthrough of the user experience when installing software from the Application Catalog:

1. The user selects the software and clicks **Install** (refer to Figure 13.25).

2. The user receives a dialog asking to confirm software installation (see Figure 13.27), and clicks **Yes** to continue.

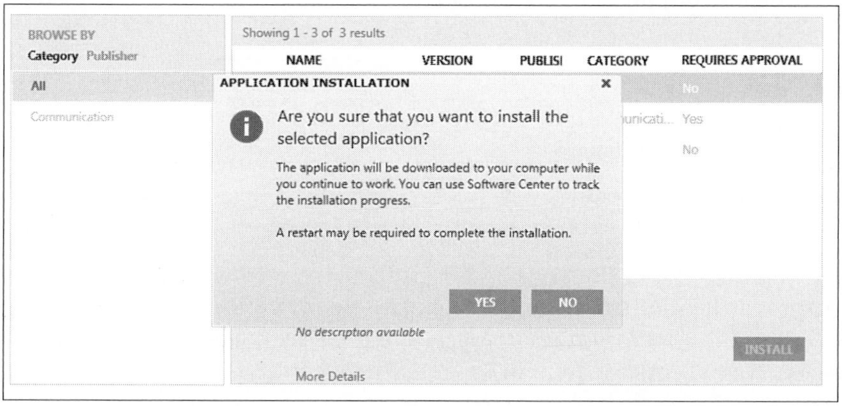

FIGURE 13.27   The Application Catalog installation confirmation.

3. Two additional dialogs appear that are similar to Figure 13.27, but these are informational only:

▶ The first queries the local computer for information.

▶ The second dialog appears while evaluating requirements for the software installation.

For a package/program, the requirement is as simple as to whether the program can run on the current platform. (For example, the program is marked to run only on Windows 7, but the user attempts to install on Windows Server 2008 R2.) Alternatively, it can be a complex requirement rule for an application, such as verifying a specific OU or specific amount of memory or disk space.

4. When the evaluation is complete, you see a dialog informing you the installation has started. Depending on how notifications are configured, you may see a system tray notification for installation progress. When the installation is complete, you see a success dialog, as shown in Figure 13.28. You can also launch Software Center to monitor installation status.

FIGURE 13.28   The Installation Success dialog in the Application Catalog.

5. If there were a failure during the requirements evaluation step, the end user would receive an error dialog, displayed in Figure 13.29.

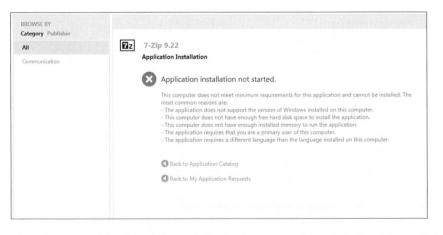

FIGURE 13.29   The Application installation not started dialog in the Application Catalog.

Because an application can have a large set of complex requirement rules, it can be difficult to inform the user specifically which rule (or rules) failed, so a dialog similar to Figure 13.29 would appear and give examples of why the application installation didn't start. Note these are examples and not specific to the requirement rules written for the application.

Monitoring and Troubleshooting Deployments

Most monitoring and troubleshooting for deployments occur in the ConfigMgr console. Navigate to **Monitoring -> Deployments** to view all deployments. You can right-click the header row and choose **Group By -> Feature Type** to organize this view by feature. Figure 13.30 shows an example of the Summary page for an application deployment.

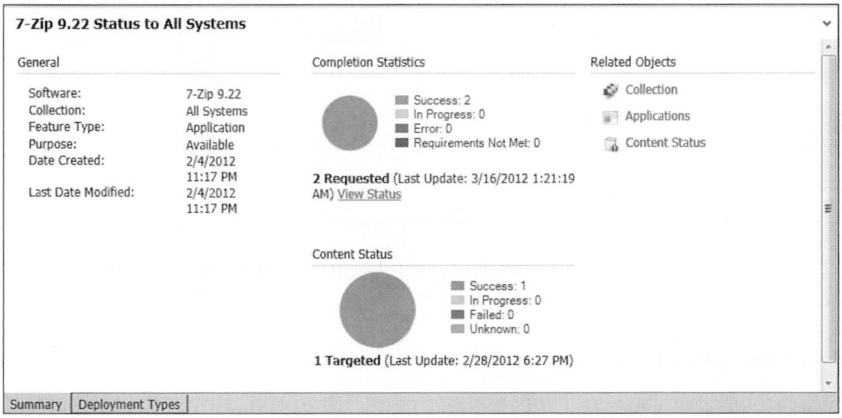

FIGURE 13.30   Summary page of application deployment monitoring.

The summary information in Figure 13.30 gives you a great overview of the deployment status. In one view, you can see the content status (to confirm content is on the DPs), deployment status, as well as created and modified dates for the software. Also, notice the links to Related Objects to take you quickly to other parts of the console you may need for troubleshooting.

You can also click the Deployment Types tab at the bottom to view the status of each deployment type if the deployment is for an application. Back on the Summary page; click the **View Status** link in the Completion Statistics section. A Deployment Status page appears, as shown in Figure 13.31.

The Deployment Status page provides a considerable amount of detail for the deployment. The top-right corner shows the summarization time. If the view has been open for a long time, click **Refresh** to see if an update summarization has occurred. If not, click the **Run Summarization** link to trigger summarization for this deployment across your hierarchy.

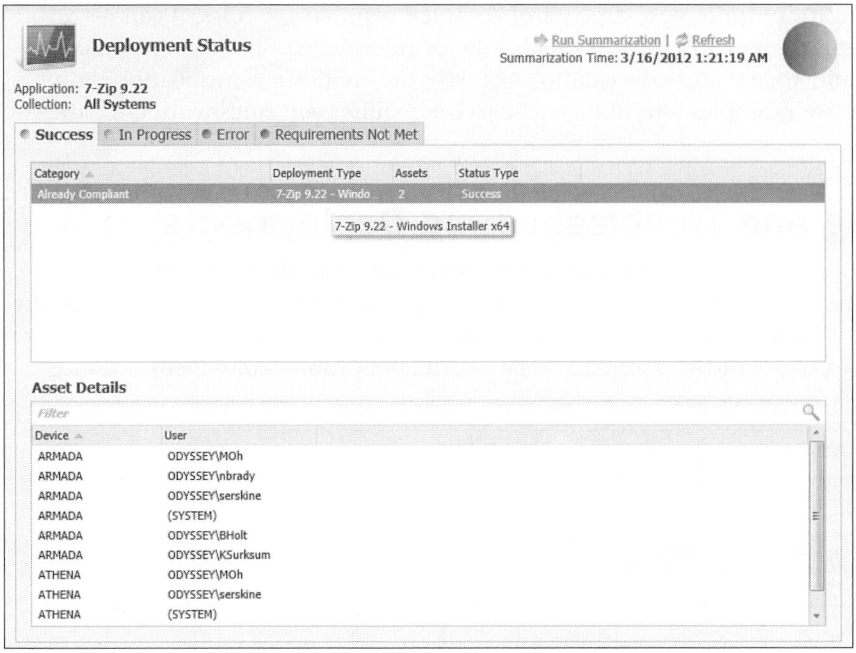

FIGURE 13.31   Deployment Status details page of application deployment monitoring.

You also see tabs for each category:

▶ **Success:** The installation returned a success exit code; for applications, the deployment state will be re-evaluated on an interval (default is 7 days), so you will probably see many Already Compliant messages on the Success tab.

▶ **In Progress:** The installation is currently in progress downloading, waiting for a maintenance window, or installing.

▶ **Error:** An error occurred during the installation, which could be a failure exit code or a fatal error from the installer.

▶ **Requirements Not Met:** The installation was evaluated against the system and ConfigMgr determined that the target system does not meet the platform requirement or the deployment type requirements.

You may notice from Figure 13.31 that the status information is grouped by category, so if you have 500 errors, ConfigMgr groups like errors together so that you can manage these like systems in one view.

You also want to review the Software Distribution-Package and Program Deployment and Software Distribution-Application Monitoring reports for additional information.

Simulated Deployments

As discussed in Chapter 12, the new application capability is quite versatile. ConfigMgr 2012 also has a new feature allowing you to simulate a deployment to determine the amount of systems that will run each deployment type. With a simulated deployment, clients can download and evaluate policy and return state messages you can monitor.

To create a simulated deployment, right-click an application and select **Simulate Deployment**. A dialog similar to Figure 13.32 appears. Choose the target collection and the intended action (**Install** or **Uninstall**). No schedule is required; clients can download and evaluate policy on their next polling interval.

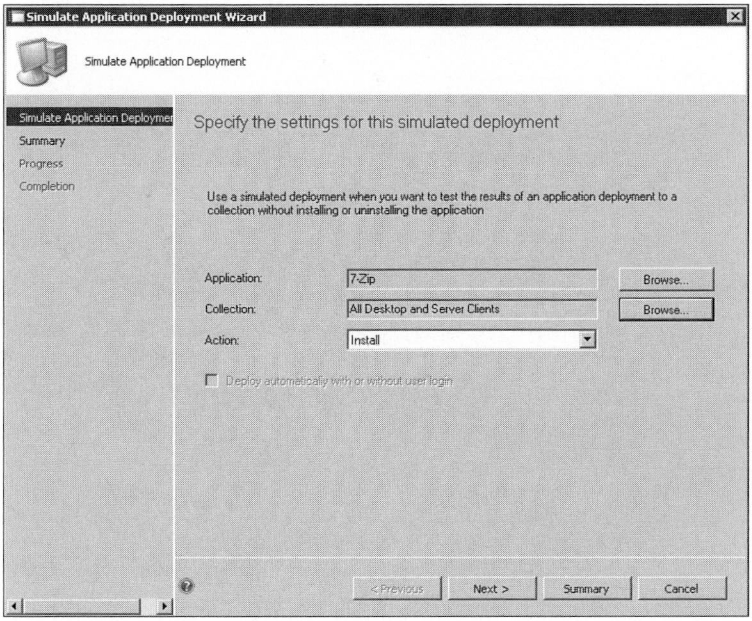

FIGURE 13.32   The Simulate Application Deployment page.

Summary

This chapter focused on collections, content, deployment, and deployment monitoring. The previous two chapters focused on packages and applications. The chapter went through the process of creating the collection, distributing the content, and deploying software. It also discussed how to monitor deployment status and how to simulate an application deployment.

Another important concept from this chapter is the Application Catalog and Software Center. You need to know where your deployment will appear and how to configure notifications to work for your environment.

CHAPTER 14

Software Update Management

Maintaining software updates and patch compliance is an important maintenance activity in any Information Technology (IT) organization. This capability has been available for some time with Microsoft's systems management product beginning with the Inventory Tool for Microsoft Updates (ITMU) as an add-on with Systems Management Server, although it was not actually incorporated into the product until Configuration Manager (ConfigMgr) 2007. Software updates in ConfigMgr 2007 was not without its faults though; although it worked well in general, it required some additional care and feeding. Software updates in ConfigMgr 2007 had a great deal of flexibility, but this flexibility led to confusion because there were too many ways to accomplish the same tasks. In System Center 2012 Configuration Manager, the product team built upon the strengths of software updates in ConfigMgr 2007 while streamlining and simplifying the process and adding several new features such as automatic update approval and update filtering. If you are familiar with software updates in ConfigMgr 2007, you should be able to find your way around with little difficulty. If you are coming from a competing product or stepping up from Windows Server Update Services (WSUS), you may have a bit of a learning curve.

System Center 2012 Configuration Manager enables you to seamlessly scan for and deploy updates for every supported Microsoft operating system (OS), most Microsoft server products, and selected Microsoft desktop applications such as Microsoft Office. You can also scan and deploy patches for supported third-party products using the software update capabilities in ConfigMgr.

This chapter shows how ConfigMgr handles patching using its built-in software updates mechanism. It also touches on integrating the Network Policy Server (NPS) role built into Windows Server 2008 and later versions. You can use NPS to ensure all your clients are up to date, including those that touch the network occasionally. The chapter describes how to find those updates applicable to your organization, download them, and successfully deploy them in a flexible, cohesive manner using ConfigMgr.

> **NOTE: ABOUT WAKE ON LAN**
>
> Wake on LAN (WOL) is regularly used to enable software updates after hours, although it is not specifically covered in this chapter—it is a generic client function in ConfigMgr and not limited to software updates. Chapter 9, "Configuration Manager Client Management," discusses WOL.

What's New in 2012

The core functionality of software updates management in System Center 2012 Configuration Manager is largely unchanged from ConfigMgr 2007; however, based on customer feedback, Microsoft has incorporated many improvements to simplify the process, fill in some gaps, and generally improve the update management experience. Here is what the improvements include:

- ▶ Superseded update support
- ▶ Role-based administration (RBA) integration
- ▶ Granular client agent settings
- ▶ Simplified workflow for update deployment
- ▶ Automated update deployment
- ▶ Improved end user experience
- ▶ In-console alerts and monitoring
- ▶ Content library cleanup

If you used the software updates management feature in ConfigMgr 2007, these changes will be welcome improvements. If you come from a stand-alone implementation of WSUS, these improvements will ease your migration pain. Each of these improvements—and more—are discussed in this chapter.

Planning Your Update Strategy

Deploying patches successfully with any tool requires planning and preparation. There are numerous aspects to consider, many of which depend on your specific environment and user requirements. Here are items to consider when developing your patch management strategy:

▶ **Scope:** Start by determining which systems and applications to patch. Although not updating all systems or applications for a particular flaw may pose a security risk, there may be specific reasons not to patch a particular piece of software (for example, third-party vendor support, as described in the next bullet).

▶ **Third-party support:** Check with your application vendors before applying patches. Many vendors do not support their products if you apply a Windows patch not yet tested with that product. Vendors may also issue patches to a product because a Microsoft patch caused it to break. This is vendor-dependent and varies from vendor to vendor.

Depending on the severity of the flaw that a patch addresses, you may have to weigh the risk of not applying it versus the possibility of breaking the application or going out of compliance with the vendor's recommended Windows patch level. Only you, in coordination with your user population and other IT support staff, can decide to apply the patch.

▶ **Patch testing:** Testing patches before deploying them to your production systems is highly recommended. If you do not have a full test environment available, do not let that deter you from testing. At a minimum, identify a group of systems for each patch category as guinea pigs. You might categorize this by operating system (such as Windows 7 workstations or Windows 2008 R2 servers) or hosted application (such as PeopleSoft servers or Finance department workstations).

Deploy patches to your identified test systems before the scheduled production rollout of the patches, leaving sufficient time to troubleshoot and resolve any problems caused by the patches.

▶ **Coordination and scheduling:** As Windows patches typically require a reboot, they do not lend themselves to deployment during business hours. Coordinate with other IT staff, server administrators, application administrators, your users, and management to establish maintenance windows defining acceptable times to reboot servers and workstations. Although maintenance windows are useful for all types of system maintenance, they are a definite requirement for patch management.

Do not necessarily limit yourself to a single maintenance window for all your systems, because deploying everywhere at once increases the risk of a single bad patch affecting your entire environment. In addition, rebooting all your systems within in a short period will most likely result in unexpected side effects from resource dependencies or other contention-type issues. As an example, if you patch your Domain Name System (DNS) servers and they all reboot at the same time, clients cannot resolve Internet Protocol (IP) addresses until those servers are operational. This could then cause other applications that rely on resolving IP addresses to fail.

There also may be application-specific jobs that run at particular times. Rebooting the system running the job or a remote system referenced by the job may cause that job to fail. Examples of scheduled jobs include accounting reports, payroll processing, and database maintenance.

Many organizations include patch management in their established change control process or create a process to deal with the many ramifications of updates and patches.

▶ **Notification:** Always issue fair warning to anyone potentially affected by a patch update or system reboot. Even when coordinating maintenance windows, sending additional notifications to other administrators and users to let them know what will transpire prevents a lot of finger pointing and many sleepless nights.

Consider using multiple notifications from different sources and different channels. Notifications from an IT manager, CIO, and such are also highly recommended because they carry additional political weight and garner more attention. As an example, an email blast from the IT manager and an announcement on the company intranet or newsletter not only goes a long way in preventing the "I didn't know" excuse, but also actually invalidates it!

▶ **Political policies and support:** IT professionals all know the risks of not patching systems and applications. To implement a successful patching strategy, you must have the political support in your organization to establish a policy that dictates and enforces applying patches. Without such a top-down policy, you will continue to face opposition to patching, not only from users but also within IT. A policy enforced by your CIO (or equivalent) will eliminate any quibbling over patching.

Compliance regulations in the United States such as the Health Insurance Portability and Accountability Act (HIPAA), Sarbanes-Oxley Act of 2002 (SOX), and Gramm-Leach-Bliley Act (GLBA) are another driver for patching, eliminating any question about its necessity. Although none of these compliance laws specifically require patching, this is one of the first things auditors check.

Based on the information listed here, plus other factors that may be unique to your own organization or environment, consider developing a patch strategy and policy document including things such as a timeline, rollback process, and testing procedure. Update this document monthly to indicate which patches are in scope, and distribute it as part of your notification process.

The recommendations in this section are applicable no matter which tool you use to update and patch your systems. The following section begins a practical discussion of software updates in System Center 2012 Configuration Manager, including how it works and how to implement it in your organization to mitigate one of the largest security risks today in IT.

Incorporated Tools

ConfigMgr, rather than reinventing the wheel, often uses existing components or products from other Microsoft teams. Software updates is no exception; it uses the Windows Update Agent (WUA) and WSUS. Building on existing technology frees up Microsoft's ConfigMgr development team from creating and testing components that perform the same functions. It also ensures consistent patch-scanning results between ConfigMgr, WSUS, and Windows Update manual patching.

The Windows Update Agent

The WUA, in Windows operating systems since Windows 2000 Service Pack (SP) 1, provides a standard method to detect and report patch applicability on all Windows systems for Windows itself, Windows components, other Microsoft products such as Office, and third-party products. System Center 2012 Configuration Manager uses the WUA to detect which patches are necessary on a system and install them after ConfigMgr delivers the updates. This approach eliminates using separate scanning tools and frees up the ConfigMgr administrator from maintaining these tools (which was quite burdensome prior to ConfigMgr 2007). Microsoft updates the agent regularly to ensure it can properly detect the need for the latest available patches.

You can configure the Windows Update Agent manually or through group policy to detect, download, and apply necessary patches automatically. This is important to remember because although ConfigMgr uses the WUA, the WUA maintains its own functionality that can still be enabled. This often leads to confusion by administrators and users alike, mysterious reboots, or unwanted update installation.

The WUA is embodied in a Windows service: "Windows Update" on Windows Vista systems and above, and "Automatic Updates Service" prior to Windows Vista. Do not disable this service because this will completely disable software updates functionality on a system. Instead, configure the WUA using group policy as discussed in the "Group Policy Settings" section.

Windows Software Update Services

WSUS is Microsoft's separate, stand-alone server-based product for distributing updates to Windows systems. WSUS also uses the WUA to scan for patch applicability and subsequently install updates delivered by WSUS. However, WSUS is somewhat limited in that it is not integrated into a larger, more capable system management product such as ConfigMgr, does not have customizable reporting, and does not allow fine-grained control of update delivery.

ConfigMgr integrates WSUS's update catalog download and distribution capabilities, but not its update download and distribution capabilities. This enables Microsoft to maintain and support a single update catalog containing all Microsoft supported updates, which is used for Windows Update, WSUS, and ConfigMgr, while also allowing each update service to deliver updates in its own way. For ConfigMgr, this means delivering updates to clients through its robust distribution point capabilities.

Knowing WSUS's role when integrated into ConfigMgr is important to prevent wasted work and confusion. This essentially equates to never going into the WSUS admin console to approve updates when WSUS is integrated into ConfigMgr. ConfigMgr takes control of WSUS and configures it as needed.

CAUTION: DO NOT APPROVE OR DECLINE UPDATES IN WSUS

Approving or declining updates directly in the WSUS console will have unexpected and difficult-to-reverse effects on software updates in ConfigMgr.

With ConfigMgr 2007 and the use of either Forefront Client Security (FCS) 2007 or Forefront Endpoint Protection (FEP) 2010 prior to update rollup 1, it was necessary to directly approve virus definition updates in the WSUS console. With the addition of automatic deployment rules in System Center 2012 Configuration Manager and the incorporation of System Center 2012 Endpoint Protection, this is no longer necessary.

Preparing for Software Updates with ConfigMgr

You must prepare ConfigMgr and your Windows infrastructure for the software updates functionality. Although relatively straightforward to install and configure, you must make several decisions and be patient because the initial synchronization process can take some time to complete. Preparation tasks include the following:

▶ Installing WSUS

▶ Adding software update points

▶ Preparing for synchronization

▶ Configuring the agents

▶ Establishing group policies

The following sections discuss these areas.

Prerequisites for Software Updates

WSUS is the only prerequisite to enable software updates in ConfigMgr. At a minimum, you must install the WSUS Software Development Kit (SDK) on the primary site server for the site where you are enabling software updates; this is accomplished by installing the WSUS administrator console. You must also install the WSUS server component on either the site server or another accessible server that meets the requirements for WSUS, as listed at http://technet.microsoft.com/en-us/library/dd939928(WS.10).aspx:

▶ Windows Server 2008 R2, Windows Server 2008 (with SP 1 or SP 2), or Microsoft Windows Server 2003 with SP 2

▶ Microsoft .NET Framework 2.0

▶ Internet Information Services (IIS) 6.0 or later

WSUS 3.0 Service Pack 2 is required for System Center 2012 Configuration Manager. In addition, because ConfigMgr 2012 supports only 64-bit site systems, you must use the 64-bit version of WSUS on one of the supported 64-bit editions of Windows Server listed in this section.

WSUS also requires a SQL Server database. Generally, you use the same SQL Server installation for WSUS that you use for ConfigMgr. You can create a separate SQL Server instance for ConfigMgr to allow for granular resource control; however, this is not required as the instance of WSUS does not manage any client data and requires little overhead on the database server, regardless of the size of the ConfigMgr installation.

Microsoft recommends installing WSUS on a dedicated server for larger sites. A WSUS instance on a shared site system can handle up to 25,000 clients whereas a WSUS instance on a dedicated site server can handle up to 100,000 clients; for sites that are larger, you should deploy a Network Load Balanced (NLB) cluster to scale out the capacity of WSUS or provide high availability. If you do implement WSUS on an NLB cluster for high availability, remember that WSUS is only part of the equation for software updates in ConfigMgr. You must also make other applicable parts of ConfigMgr highly available including the distribution points (DPs) and management points (MPs) by adding multiple systems hosting each of these roles.

Every ConfigMgr primary site must have its own WSUS instance; this is optional for secondary sites to offload work and network traffic from the primary site WSUS server.

WSUS installation is straightforward and wizard-driven. For Windows Server 2008 R2, use the Add Roles functionality from the Server Manager console. For Windows Server 2008 and 2003, you must download the WSUS installer from Microsoft. Use the following guidance to complete the installation on any of these platforms:

▶ Choose to **Store Updates Locally** on the system, as shown in Figure 14.1. This setting allows WSUS to download and store license terms for specific software updates in the update content folder that you choose; ConfigMgr separately handles the actual download and deployment of updates. During the update synchronization process, ConfigMgr looks for applicable license terms in the content folder. If it cannot find the license terms, it will not synchronize the update. In addition, clients must also have access to the applicable license terms to scan for update compliance.

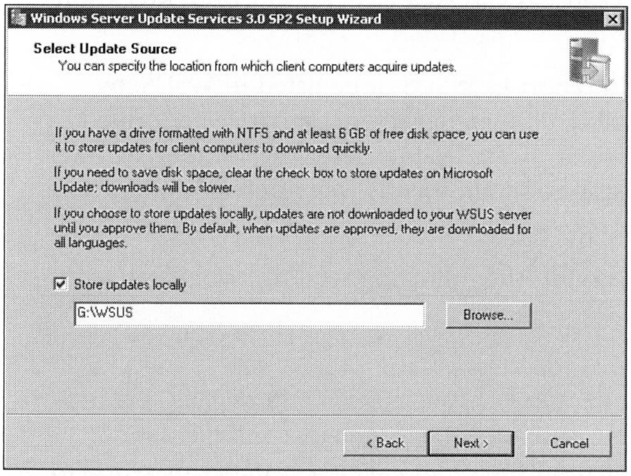

FIGURE 14.1   WSUS Update Source.

If using a dedicated system for WSUS, use the default website to host WSUS. If you host any other ConfigMgr roles on the system, create a dedicated IIS site; this is generally recommended by Microsoft and the authors although not necessarily a standard best practice or technical requirement. The port numbers for a dedicated site are 8530 and 8531 for Secure Socket Layer (SSL) connections.

A dedicated website keeps things nice and tidy and prevents any confusion over which website handles the WSUS responsibilities. One exception to this recommendation is for networks with tight port controls where having a single port for all ConfigMgr related traffic is desirable or technically easier to accomplish. Note that using a dedicated website does slightly increase complexity, as you now are enabling a nonstandard port for traffic. Thus, in the name of simplicity, many choose to use the default website without introducing or experiencing any technical issues.

▶ Click **Cancel** to skip the Configuration Wizard that launches at the end of installation. WSUS does not require manual configuration because ConfigMgr 2007 takes over the control and configuration of WSUS after you install a software update point (SUP).

You may use an existing WSUS server installation as a SUP for ConfigMgr; however, you should first delete the update catalog and associated metadata from WSUS to reset WSUS back to a clean state, allowing ConfigMgr to properly manage and control it. In addition, because ConfigMgr takes complete control over the WSUS configuration, you should not configure any clients not managed by ConfigMgr to use this WSUS installation, as this is not a supported configuration. There are various scripts available on the Internet that can help you clean up the WSUS metadata; however, it is far easier and quicker to simply uninstall and reinstall WSUS. This guarantees that you have a supported configuration.

Performing any administrative tasks directly in the WSUS console is strictly unsupported and it is difficult (at best) to back out changes. It is acceptable to go into the WSUS console to review updates or the synchronization status, but you should not perform tasks such as approving or declining updates because it can adversely affect ConfigMgr's software update management capabilities.

In addition, do not expect your systems to report to WSUS or be listed in WSUS; by default, WSUS is completely ignorant of all update management activities performed by ConfigMgr. As mentioned in the "Windows Software Update Services" section, WSUS is strictly used for its update catalog and distribution abilities as well as client update scanning; clients do not report to WSUS or retrieve updates directly from WSUS itself.

The software update point site role, discussed in the following section, completely configures and manages WSUS.

Software Update Points

Software update points are the site role in ConfigMgr that manage, configure, and communicate with WSUS. They are installed on top of an existing instance of WSUS as described in the previous section. A SUP is required to enable software update management functionality; adding a SUP as a role to a site system is similar to adding any ConfigMgr role to any other site system. The next sections discuss SUP placement, configuration, and update configuration.

Software Update Point Placement

There are three scenarios for SUP installation representing the three types of sites. Each of these has its own caveats for when you should (or should not) install a SUP:

▶ **Top-level site:** For software updates to be enabled, the central administration site (CAS) or stand-alone primary site must have a SUP installed. This is slightly different from ConfigMgr 2007 where child primary sites could have a SUP installed even if their parent did not.

▶ **Child Primary Site:** Although not strictly required, clients assigned to a child-primary site without a SUP will not receive updates. Unless that is your intention, install a SUP at every child primary site.

> **NOTE: CLIENTS AND SUPS**
>
> If a primary site does not have an active SUP, then clients managed by that site will not scan for update compliance or receive updates from ConfigMgr.

▶ **Secondary Site:** Secondary sites do not strictly require a SUP. Placing a SUP at a secondary enables clients in that secondary site's boundaries to retrieve their update catalog from this (presumably local) SUP, preventing them from traversing the wide area network (WAN) to do so. However, after the initial catalog synchronization, subsequent catalog synchronizations are deltas and are typically quite small. Without a local SUP on a secondary, clients retrieve the update catalog directly from the SUP in the client's assigned primary site.

There is no definitive guidance on whether to place a SUP at a secondary as this truly depends upon the network link to the site and the number of clients at that site. If you are unsure, start without the SUP and monitor the bandwidth usage. If the traffic becomes a burden, add a SUP to the secondary site.

SUPs should be installed top-down—in other words, the CAS first (if you have one), primary sites next, and finally any secondary sites in your hierarchy. To install a SUP, perform the following steps:

1. Navigate to the Administration workspace.

2. In the navigation tree, under Overview, expand **Site Configuration**, and select **Servers and Site System Roles**. All currently installed site systems display on the right.

3. To use an existing site server, right-click it, and choose **Add Site System Roles** to launch the Add Site System Roles Wizard, as shown in Figure 14.2.

If you use a remote installation of WSUS on a system that is not currently a site system, you must first make the system a site system by right-clicking the **Servers and Site System Roles** node in the navigation tree and selecting **Create Site System Server**.

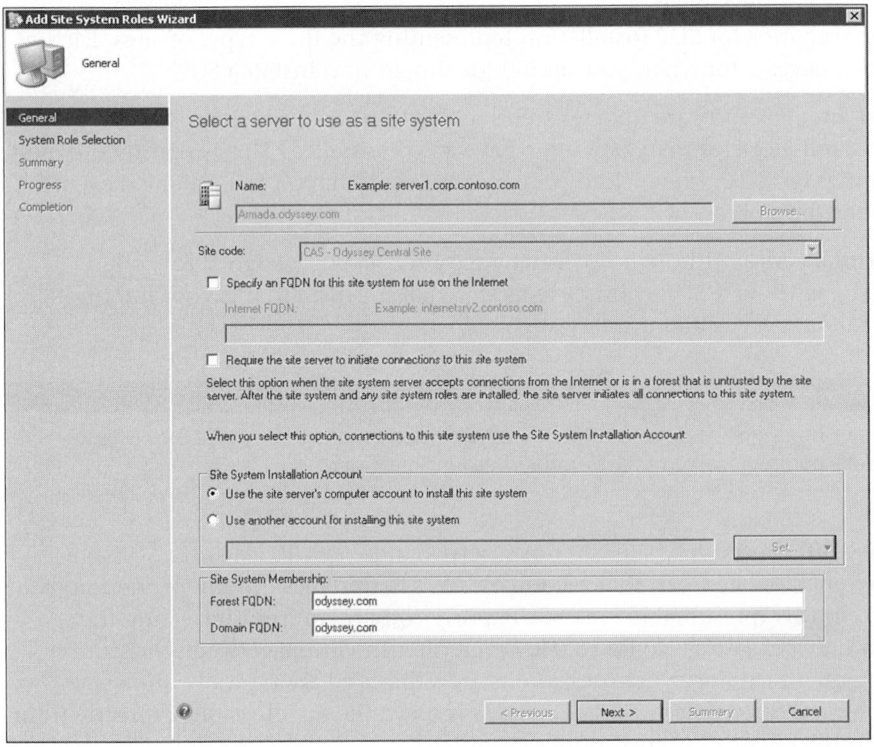

FIGURE 14.2   Add Site System Roles Wizard.

4. On the System Role Selection page of the Add Site System Roles Wizard or the Create Site System Server Wizard, select **Software update point**. This adds two subpages to the wizard: Software Update Point and Active Settings.

5. On the Software Update Point page (shown in Figure 14.3), choose the appropriate proxy settings for your environment. There are two different times that software updates may use a proxy server:

▶ When downloading the update catalog. (This is actually performed by WSUS, so this setting configures the equivalent setting in WSUS.)

▶ When automatically downloading the actual updates using the new automatic deployment rules, covered in the "Automatic Deployment Rules" section.

Many proxy servers require separate authentication; the bottom portion of this page enables you to enter the necessary credentials depending upon the type of proxy server in use and your organization's standards. In general, the authors recommend you use a dedicated, service type account and follow the rules of least privilege for this account.

Because non-top-level sites synchronize their update catalog from their parent site (see the "Update Synchronization" section for a complete discussion of this), you may need to configure a different proxy server for non-top-level sites in your hierarchy so that they can communicate with their parent site's SUP. This is based upon your actual network configuration and proxy server placement.

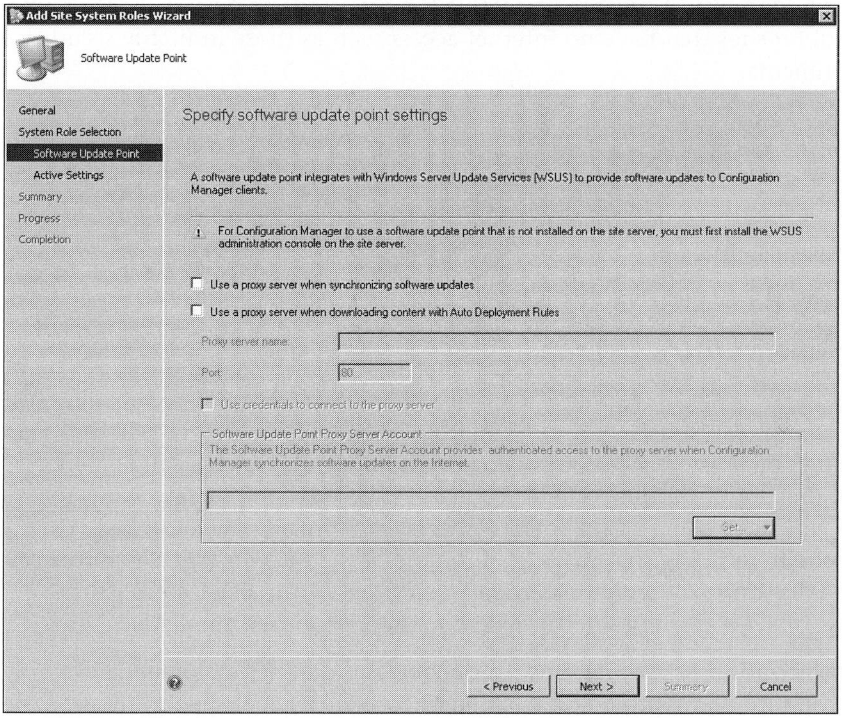

FIGURE 14.3   Software Update Point page.

6. On the Active Settings page, choose whether to make this SUP the active SUP for the site. Only one active SUP is permitted in a site. The active SUP is responsible for all update catalog activity including synchronizing the catalog from Microsoft or the parent site as well as making the catalog available to clients assigned to the site. The only time non-active SUPs are useful is when using an NLB of SUPs. On the bottom of this page, choose the website hosting WSUS on the system to which you are installing the SUP, as discussed in the "Prerequisites for Software Updates" section.

If you choose to make the SUP active, you must also select which website WSUS is using: default or custom. Six pages are also added to the wizard:

▶ **Synchronization Source:** There are two settings to configure on this page: where to synchronize the update catalog from and whether clients should report events to WSUS. Table 14.1 lists the three synchronization source options and their applicability to the three site types. Only top-level sites are allowed to synchronize directly from Microsoft Update; and only child primary and secondary sites are allowed to synchronize from an upstream server. Upstream servers are always the parent site's SUP; this is not configurable. You cannot synchronize from a stand-alone WSUS server.

As discussed in the "Update Synchronization" section, choosing **Do not synchronize from Microsoft Update or the upstream software update point** is useful for sites that have no Internet access such as those in highly secure environments.

TABLE 14.1   Software Update Point Synchronization Source

Source	Top-Level Site	Child Primary Site	Secondary Site
Synchronize from Microsoft Update.	X		
Synchronize from an upstream server.		X	X
Do not synchronize from Microsoft Update or the upstream software update point.	X		

Enabling one of these WSUS reporting event options is not typical. Enabling one of these options causes clients to report their scan and update status to WSUS similar to using a stand-alone WSUS server outside of ConfigMgr. You gain little from doing this other than the use of the built-in WSUS reporting, which falls short of ConfigMgr's robust reporting. It can also lead to issues because in general going into the WSUS console is not recommended.

▶ **Synchronization Schedule:** This page enables automatic catalog update synchronization and provides the schedule to perform that synchronization. The authors recommend enabling this option, using the default simple schedule of every 7 days. There is little impact from increasing the frequency of this schedule, and decreasing it could cause you to miss one of Microsoft's periodic scheduled update releases. Ultimately, you should configure this schedule per your organization's standards and software update rhythm as well as Patch Tuesday.

You also enable alerts for failed update synchronization on this page. For a top-level site, these alerts will be for any update synchronizations on any SUP in the hierarchy.

NOTE: MICROSOFT UPDATE RELEASE SCHEDULE AND PATCH TUESDAY

For the last 5 years, Microsoft has ardently stuck to releasing security and critical updates only on the second Tuesday of every month. This has become lovingly known as *Patch Tuesday*. Although Microsoft occasionally releases updates at other times to fix ultra-critical issues, this not a regular occurrence and should not directly affect your synchronization schedule. Critical updates not released on Patch Tuesday are often called *out-of-band updates* and typically fix zero-day security holes. To handle these out-of-band updates, run a manual update synchronization when appropriate following the instructions in the "Update Synchronization" section.

There is actually a lesser known, second wave of updates also released every month. This update release occurs on the fourth Tuesday of the month and is for stability and compatibility updates. On occasion, some of these updates do make it into the update catalog.

▶ **Supercedence Rules:** On this page, configure when you want ConfigMgr to expire superseded updates; ConfigMgr cannot and does not deploy expired updates even if they are configured to deploy to client systems.

The two self-explanatory options are to immediately expire an update after it has been superseded, or wait for a defined number of months to expire the update. This option allows you to continue to deploy superseded updates while the newer update is still in testing (or lost) in your update approval process. This is completely new functionality in System Center 2012 Configuration Manager; with ConfigMgr 2007, superseded updates were immediately expired and thus could not be deployed.

▶ **Classifications:** On this page and the two following it, define the subset of the WSUS update catalog applicable for your organization and its systems, this subset of the update catalog is actually all that is downloaded. Settings on these three pages directly change settings in the underlying WSUS instance and directly correspond to the same settings in WSUS.

On this page specifically, you define which of the standard update classifications to include in the update catalog:

> Critical Updates
>
> Definition Updates
>
> Feature Packs
>
> Security Updates
>
> Service Packs
>
> Tools
>
> Update Rollups
>
> Updates

One notable absence from this list is drivers. Although a standard update classification in WSUS, System Center 2012 Configuration Manager does not support deploying drivers using the software updates feature set, so this class is

14

not listed. This is a change from ConfigMgr 2007 where the drivers classification was listed and it was possible, although not supported, to deploy driver updates.

▶ **Products:** This page contains the list of products you want to include in the update catalog. The initial list of products is outdated, only contains Microsoft updates, and does not contain a list of current products or versions. However, this list of products is synchronized every time the update catalog itself is retrieved, so you should revisit the configuration of the SUP to add products to your catalog download after initial catalog configuration and synchronization. For this reason, it is best to uncheck all products during initial configuration and wait for the initial synchronization to complete. This prevents the catalog from containing any updates initially minimizing the synchronization time while also updating the product list. An initial synchronization is initiated immediately following the completion of the wizard (see the "Update Synchronization" section for instructions on how to monitor or verify synchronization).

NOTE: PRODUCTS AND CLASSIFICATIONS CHOSEN FOR THE UPDATE CATALOG

Including a product in the update catalog does not mean you must deploy updates related to that product or that those updates will be automatically downloaded or applied. Inclusion in the update catalog enables ConfigMgr to detect those systems requiring the update. By itself, this should be not be a concern, as it does not cause any real overhead or adversely affect the client systems in any way; however, it will affect your reports. Whether you choose to deploy the updates based on this information is up to you.

Be careful which products and classifications you choose for inclusion. There are some updates such as Internet Explorer 9 or Windows 7 SP 1 that might not be approved for your organization and could cause havoc to your environment (or your career) if accidentally deployed.

▶ **Languages:** The final page is for setting the update languages you want to include in your catalog. By default, multiple languages are selected. To prevent catalog bloat, you should ensure you choose the minimum set of languages applicable to your environment.

TIP: WHAT'S IN THE UPDATE CATALOG

Not every update and hotfix Microsoft releases is in the WSUS update catalog. In fact, only a small percentage of those released are actually included. The WSUS catalog is intended for updates Microsoft thinks should be readily available to the public and users or administrators of their products. This of course includes security-related and critical updates that directly affect Microsoft products. Each product group, in coordination with the maintainers of the WSUS update catalog, determines which updates should be included. For updates not included, you can use either software distribution or the System Center Updates Publisher (SCUP) discussed in the "System Center Update Publisher" section.

After completing the wizard, ConfigMgr installs the SUP with the desired parameters. Should you want to change the proxy server settings after the SUP is installed, navigate to the Server and Site Systems node under **Overview -> Site Configuration -> Servers and Site System Roles** in the Administration workspace's navigation tree, select the site server from the list on the right, right-click **Software Update Point** in the Detail pane at the bottom, and select **Properties**. Switching a SUP from or to active or configuring it for participation in an NLB is covered in the next section. To set any other settings, including revisiting the list of products selected after the initial synchronization, see the "Software Update Point Configuration" section.

To verify correct installation and initial communication between the SUP and WSUS, check WCM.log and WSUSCtrl.log in the server's log files directory for any errors. WSUSCtrl.log will have three lines similar to the following if the installation completed successfully:

```
Successfully connected to local WSUS server
There are no unhealthy WSUS Server components on WSUS Server Armada.odyssey.com
Successfully checked database connection on WSUS server Armada.odyssey.com
```

Software Update Point Configuration

Some initial configuration of the SUP is required to ensure that the update catalog matches the needs of your organization. These settings are not actually SUP-specific; they are site-wide settings because every SUP in a site must share these settings. Child and secondary sites will also inherit these settings from their parent.

NOTE: WHEN TO HAVE MORE THAN ONE SUP IN A SITE

The only time it makes sense to have more than one SUP in a site is if you configure an NLB for multiple SUPs to provide high-availability or additional client capacity. Additional non-active SUPs serve no purpose.

To configure these site-wide SUP settings, open the Administration workspace, and select **Sites** under **Overview -> Site Configuration** in the navigation tree. The list of currently manageable sites displays on the right. Right-click the site you want to configure, and choose **Configure site-wide components** if the site is a CAS or **Configure Site Components** otherwise. Finally, choose **Software Update Point**. Alternatively, select the site, push **Configure Site Components** from the ribbon bar at the top, and then choose **Software Update Point**.

If the site is a top-level site—CAS in a multisite hierarchy or primary site in a hierarchy without a CAS—the resulting Software Update Point Component Properties dialog will have seven tabs. If the site is a child primary, this dialog will have three tabs, and if the site is a secondary site, it will have only two tabs. This is described in Table 14.2.

TABLE 14.2   Software Update Point Component Properties Tabs

Tabs	Top-Level Site	Child Primary Site	Secondary Site
General	X	X	X
Sync Settings	X	X	X
Classifications	X		
Products	X		
Sync Schedule	X		
Supersedence Rules	X		
Languages	X	X	

The settings in each of the tabs in Table 14.2 correspond directly to the like-named pages of the initial software updates installation wizard as listed in step 5 of the "Software Update Points" section. The only exception to this is the General tab on which you can configure one of the following settings related to the site's active SUP:

▶ None

▶ Active software update point on the site server

▶ Active software update point on the remote server

▶ Use Network Load Balancing cluster for active software update point

The General tab on top-level sites also contains settings to configure the client communication port numbers, one for non-SSL and one for SSL communication as well as allowing intranet-only client connections or both intranet and Internet client connections. If allowing Internet client connections, the underlying instance of WSUS must also be configured to accept SSL connections. A convenient check box exists on the General tab of top-level sites to do this for you.

Update Synchronization

Each SUP, using its underlying WSUS instance, synchronizes updates from its configured source according to the defined schedule; this update process populates the update catalog in ConfigMgr. For top-level sites, this is typically Microsoft Update. For child primary or secondary sites, this is always the site's parent SUP. It is not possible to automatically or directly synchronize from any other source such as a stand-alone WSUS server. Successful update synchronizations on a parent site, whether manually or automatically initiated, will trigger synchronizations on that site's child primary or secondary sites; this is clearly shown in the wsyncmgr.log on the site system:

```
Sending sync notification to child site(s): PR1, PR2
```

To initiate synchronization manually on a top-level site, navigate to the **Software Library** workspace, and expand **Overview -> Software Updates** in the navigation tree. Then either right-click **All Software Updates** and choose **Synchronize Software Updates** from the context-menu or select **All Software Updates** in the tree and choose **Synchronize Software Updates** from the ribbon. To verify or monitor the synchronization process (manual or automatic), open wsyncmgr.log from the ConfigMgr logs folder.

You cannot initiate a catalog synchronization on a child site directly from the ConfigMgr console. The best you can do is to initiate synchronization in the WSUS console for that site; however, this is not a full ConfigMgr catalog synchronization, so you should not consider this a complete process for synchronizing child and secondary sites. A better strategy is to initiate the synchronization manually from the top-level site in the ConfigMgr console as discussed in the previous paragraph; this in turn synchronizes all child and secondary sites and ensures that all sites are properly synchronized.

After each successful catalog synchronization where new or updated updates are added to the catalog, the catalog's version number is incremented. Comparing this version number between the multiple sites in your hierarchy may be useful if you suspect a synchronization issue. This version number displays in wsyncmgr.log after each catalog synchronization whether the version incremented or not:

```
Set content version of update source {8F3ABFA6-EC00-4EE2-986E-663E07DF4285} for site
➥CAS to 1
```

Child sites show their own version as well as that of the parent site from where they synchronize:

```
Successfully synced site with parent CAS, version 1
Set content version of update source {8F3ABFA6-EC00-4EE2-986E-663E07DF4285} for site
➥PR2 to 1
```

A successful synchronization contains lines similar to the following snippet, taken from an initial synchronization on a CAS:

```
1: Found local sync request file
2: Performing sync on local request
3: Synchronizing WSUS server Armada.odyssey.com
4: Synchronizing WSUS server armada.odyssey.com ...
5: sync: Starting WSUS synchronization
6: sync: WSUS synchronizing categories
7: sync: WSUS synchronizing categories, processed 822 out of 822 items (100%)
8: sync: WSUS synchronizing categories, processed 822 out of 822 items (100%)
9: Done synchronizing WSUS Server armada.odyssey.com
10: Synchronizing SMS database with WSUS server Armada.odyssey.com
11: Synchronizing SMS database with WSUS server armada.odyssey.com ...
12: sync: Starting SMS database synchronization
```

14

```
13: requested localization languages: en
14: Syncing all updates
15: requested update classifications: Critical Updates, Definition Updates, Feature
16: Packs, Security Updates, Service Packs, Tools, Update Rollups, Updates
17: sync: SMS synchronizing categories
18: sync: SMS synchronizing categories, processed 0 out of 165 items (0%)
19: sync: SMS synchronizing categories, processed 165 out of 165 items (100%)
20: sync: SMS synchronizing categories, processed 165 out of 165 items (100%)
21: sync: SMS synchronizing updates
22: Removing unreferenced updates...
23: sync: SMS performing cleanup
24: Done synchronizing SMS with WSUS Server armada.odyssey.com
25: Sync succeeded. Setting sync alert to canceled state on site CAS
```

One notable thing to point out relevant to this log snippet is that catalog synchronization actually happens in two parts:

▶ The first part is the actual update catalog synchronization by WSUS (lines 3–9).

▶ The second part is the ConfigMgr database synchronization of the update catalog from WSUS (lines 10–25). This second step in the synchronization process uses the information from the WSUS catalog to create configuration items (as discussed in Chapter 10, "Managing Compliance"), which are in turn used for the compliance evaluation processes in ConfigMgr.

This log snippet from wsyncmgr.log does not show any updates, as it is an initial synchronization without any products chosen. When products are chosen, each update is clearly listed as it is synched from WSUS to the ConfigMgr database. During an initial synchronization, this could be a lengthy list (and process). The log also lists updates that were skipped because they are expired, superseded, or require interaction.

If the site system hosting the SUP in a top-level site is not connected to the public Internet (meaning it cannot synchronize its catalog directly from Microsoft Update), you could export the catalog from a WSUS server with access to Microsoft Update and import this catalog into the disconnected SUP. You could also use this method to synchronize the top-level SUP from a stand-alone WSUS server to skirt the requirement of having to synchronize from Microsoft Update. As this is a manual process, the authors do not recommend this approach unless it is required; however, if your environment is highly secure, Internet access may of course be restricted or completely non-existent.

You can also view complete SUP catalog synchronization status for the complete hierarchy on any system from the **Software Update Point Synchronization Status** node in the Monitoring workspace, as shown in Figure 14.4. This view shows all relevant catalog synchronization information including error codes, catalog version numbers, synchronization source, and synchronization times.

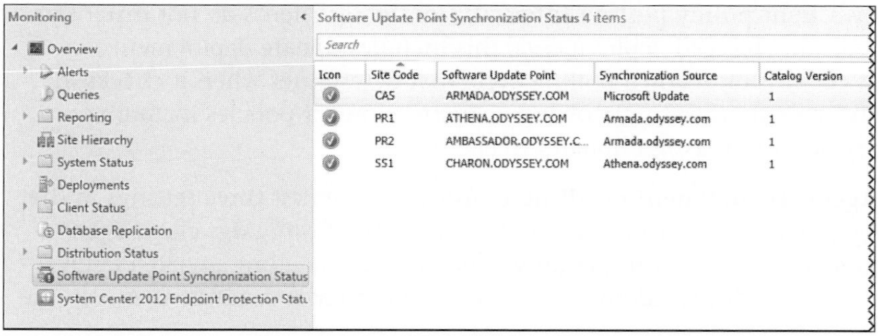

FIGURE 14.4   Software Update Point Synchronization Status.

Manual Update Synchronization

Both WSUS 2.0 and 3.0 use the same catalog format; this makes it possible to use either version to export the catalog manually using the same commands. To do so and then import the catalog on your SUP, follow these steps:

1. On the Internet-connected WSUS server, open a command prompt and run the following command:

```
WSUSutil export <export filename.cab> <export log filename>
```

   WSUSutil is typically located in the *%ProgramFiles%*\Update Services\Tools folder. The export process takes from 10 to 20 minutes to run (potentially more), depending on your hardware. WSUSutil writes to the log file after the export completes. The file is in eXtended Markup Language (XML) format.

2. Copy the export file to the SUP using whatever method is appropriate for your environment.

3. Open a command prompt on the destination WSUS server, and run WSUSutil import:

```
WSUSutil import <import filename.cab> <import log filename>
```

   The import process is more extensive than the export process and may take over 1 hour to complete, so be patient. As with the export process, WSUSutil does not write to the XML log file until the import completes.

Client Settings

The following granular client settings (discussed in Chapter 9) directly affect software updates functionality from the managed system's or user's perspective:

▶ **Background Intelligent Transfer (BITS):** Like all other content in ConfigMgr, software updates must be delivered to clients. The various BITS settings enable you to throttle this content delivery from BITS enabled distribution points, minimizing user and network disruption.

▶ **Client Policy, Client policy polling interval:** ConfigMgr clients do not instantly know about new or changed deployments; this includes update deployments. Instead, each client is on its own polling cycle that determines when it checks in with the management point to discover new instructions or policies including update deployments that assign updates to clients.

▶ **Computer Agent, Deployment deadline reminders:** The first three settings in the Computer Agent section determine at what intervals the ConfigMgr client agent displays reminders to users about pending deployments including update deployments. Reminders are displayed only if the deployment has a deadline that is in the future.

▶ **Computer Restart:** These two settings determine the grace period given before a system restart is automatically initiated when a restart is required, and a final countdown interval for a final restart notification before the restart is actually initiated. These two values are not cumulative; for example, if you leave the default values of 90 and 15 minutes respectively, the restart will happen in 90 minutes and the notification will happen at 75 minutes or 15 minutes before the 90-minute countdown expires.

▶ **Computer Agent, Show notifications for new deployments:** This enables or disables displaying a notification to the end user about a pending deployment according to the deadline reminders. This setting affects all deployment types including application and operating system deployments—there is no separate setting for these.

▶ **Software Updates:** The settings in this section directly affect the ConfigMgr client agent behavior in respect to software update activities and include the following:

    ▶ **Enable software updates on client:** Enables or disables software updates on clients.

    ▶ **Software update scan schedule:** Sets the schedule that clients scan for new updates using the update catalog hosted on the site's SUP.

> **NOTE: CLIENTS USE THE UPDATE CATALOG FROM WSUS**
>
> The fact that clients directly communicate with the WSUS instance corresponding to the site's active SUP to retrieve their update catalog is discussed several times in this chapter (including the "Windows Software Update Services" and "Prerequisites for Software Updates" sections) but is worth reinforcing and specifically mentioning here because it is a primary source of confusion. Just as important, and discussed many times in this chapter, is that clients do not download updates from WSUS; instead, they download them directly from ConfigMgr using any available DP.
>
> As an additional point of clarification, the difference between updates and the update catalog (also called *update metadata*) is worth calling out. The update catalog contains information about updates including (but not limited to) their name, applicability rules, and where they can be downloaded from. This update catalog is what is actually downloaded

by WSUS and made available to clients for use during update applicability scanning. The catalog does not contain the actual file(s) used to patch the target systems.

Updates are the actual binary files installed by the client and are downloaded from DPs as requested by the clients and not WSUS or the SUP.

> ▶ **Schedule deployment re-evaluation:** Sets the schedule when clients re-evaluate the installation status of previously deployed and installed updates. Missing updates are immediately reinstalled from the local cache, or downloaded again from a DP if necessary.

> ▶ **When any software update deployment deadline is reached, install all other software update deployments with deadline coming within a specified period of time:** Somewhat confusing in ConfigMgr 2007, this setting groups multiple update deployments together into a single deployment if scheduled to occur within the period of time specified by the next setting. This minimizes the impact on the end user and decreases the number of reboots that would be necessary with multiple, separate update deployments.

> ▶ **Period of time for which all pending deployments with deadline in this time will also be installed:** The period of time to consider update deployments for grouping according to the description of the previous setting.

▶ **State Messaging:** Client agent update scan and installation results are returned to the ConfigMgr site using state messages; to minimize network traffic and the impact on the site server, state messages are not sent individually but instead held on a client and sent only on the interval specified here. There is no way to trigger the sending of state messages from the client to the server except to restart the client agent.

Group Policy Settings

Using a domain-based group policy object (GPO) is the standard way to configure WSUS and the WUA. Here are some typical questions when you are installing and configuring software updates:

▶ Is it necessary to create a domain-based GPO to support ConfigMgr software updates?

▶ What should be done with in-place Windows Updates domain GPOs?

You do not need to create a domain GPO to support ConfigMgr software updates. However, if you choose to create a domain GPO to support ConfigMgr client agent installation (see Chapter 9 for additional information on client installations) or use an existing domain GPO, you must configure the Windows Updates server option to point to the active SUP in the site, as shown in Figure 14.5. If you used an alternative website to host your WSUS instance, be sure to include the port at the end of the address specified; for example, **athena.odyssey.com:8530**. The reason for setting this policy in your GPO is that the ConfigMgr agent creates a local group policy on clients, pointing them to the SUP; however, a domain-based GPO overrides the local group policy settings, causing software updates to fail on the client if the GPO does not specify the SUP as its update server. In addition, an effective GPO must not disable the Windows Updates service or the WUA.

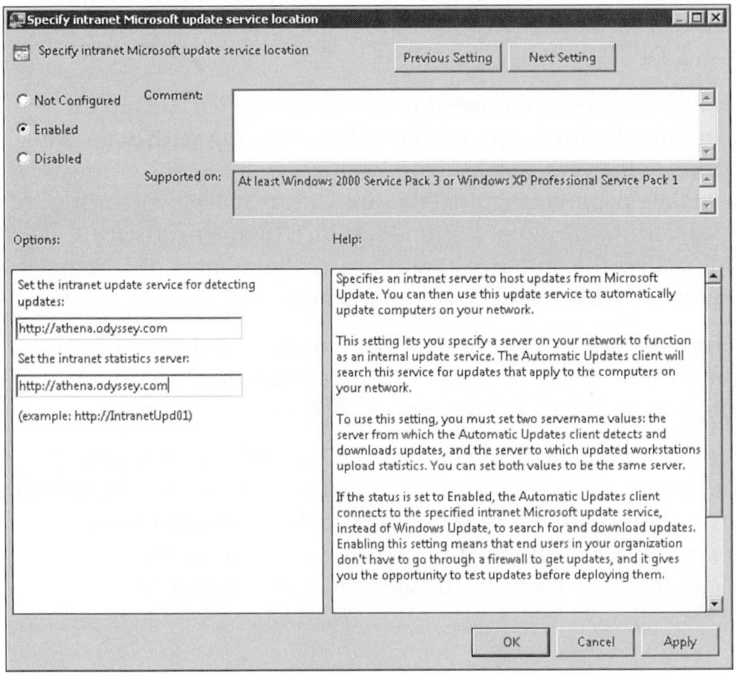

FIGURE 14.5   Microsoft Update Service Location GPO.

How do the rest of the settings in the Windows Updates Group Policy section affect software updates in ConfigMgr? The short answer is, *They don't*. These settings effectively control how the Windows Update Agent automatically handles updates. The key word in the statement is *automatically*; with ConfigMgr in the mix, the WUA doesn't (and shouldn't) automatically do anything. It's not that it can't do any work automatically, it's that the WSUS server itself does not have any updates for it, so it effectively does no work; recall that all updates are delivered via the content distribution mechanism in ConfigMgr and not WSUS. When a ConfigMgr client wants to do anything related to software updates, it directly controls the WUA to achieve the desired result: This includes update scans, re-evaluations, and installation. Thus, all of the other settings are essentially harmless or have no effect.

Here are several things of which you should be aware:

▶ If you set the Configure Automatic Updates setting to **Disabled**, the WUA will not automatically update itself from WSUS. This is important because WUA updates are periodically sent out by Microsoft and picked up by WSUS. These are listed as infrastructure updates in WSUS, are automatically approved by WSUS, and thus automatically pushed out to all client systems communicating with a WSUS instance if the Configure Automatic Updates setting is enabled on the client.

This may or may not be your desired outcome. It is generally recommended you set this setting to **Disabled** and distribute an updated WUA using software distribution in ConfigMgr.

Allowing WSUS to perform this task does not give you control over how WSUS pushes out these updates for the WUA; clients will download the updated WUA using BITS directly from WSUS, and each client that checks in gets it as soon as it checks in. Depending on your network infrastructure and SUP topology, this might be undesirable. There are other infrastructure updates that do not need to be approved in WSUS but are still made available to clients, so the users may also get prompted for these directly by the WUA and separate from ConfigMgr.

▶ A ramification of leaving the Configure Automatic Updates setting at **Enabled** is that WUA can detect when a restart is pending on the local system and display an additional warning to the interactive user, which could be confusing. By default, if an update deployment suppresses restarts, ConfigMgr displays an alert to the user, as displayed in Figure 14.6.

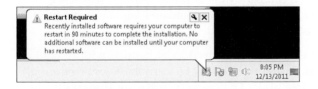

FIGURE 14.6   Restart Required Notification balloon.

▶ Leaving this group policy setting at **Not Configured** in a GPO doesn't change anything, it just leaves the actual setting as is whether it was set manually on the system or using another group policy. The ramifications discussed in this section still apply.

NOTE: IMPACT OF DISABLING THE CONFIGURE AUTOMATIC UPDATES SETTING

Setting the Configure Automatic Updates setting to **Disabled** does not disable the Windows Update service in Windows 7 or the Automatic Updates service in XP. (These are the WUA service itself, just different names in the different versions of Windows.) It merely disables automatic functionality of the WUA including scanning. The Automatic Updates service must be running for software updates in ConfigMgr to work properly. The authors recommend using a group policy to set this service to **Automatic**.

If you don't set the Configure Automatic Updates setting to **Disabled**, WUA isn't actually automatically installing updates, but it is still trying to help or actually getting in the way depending on how you look at it. (Moreover, with users being users, this will undoubtedly generate at least several help desk calls.)

▶ If you use a GPO to deploy the ConfigMgr client agent via WSUS, you should utilize Windows Management Instrumentation (WMI) filtering, security group filtering, or another mechanism to prevent these GPOs from being applied to managed systems.

CAUTION: ROAMING CLIENTS

If a client roams out of its normal location, it's possible that it may receive an alternate group policy that contains a different WSUS location. It's also possible that a roaming client may roam to a peer primary site or secondary site that contains a SUP. In this case, the ConfigMgr client agent configures itself to use this SUP. If the two settings match, then there is no issue; however, if the two settings do not match, as described earlier in this section, then the client cannot participate in the software update process.

Software Update Building Blocks

One of the redesign focuses for software updates in System Center 2012 Configuration Manager was to simplify the workflow by reducing the number of different supporting objects and nodes in the console. This resulted in eliminating search folders, update lists, and update deployments and the cluttered category view of the repository. Replacing these objects in the console is the *update group*. In addition, update templates have been removed from the console and cannot be directly created.

The following sections describe each of the objects you need to be familiar with to deploy updates successfully to your environment using the ConfigMgr console. These sections all correspond to a node in the navigation tree under **Overview** -> **Software Updates** in the Software Library workspace.

All Software Updates

This node contains the master list of all updates available in the local update catalog. It is roughly equivalent to the Update Repository in ConfigMgr 2007 but vastly simplified while at the same time much more powerful and flexible.

Clicking **All Software Updates** in the navigation tree displays a full list of updates from the currently synchronized catalog, as shown in Figure 14.7. The information displayed in this list about the updates is customizable by right-clicking the list header and selecting those columns you would like to add. An excellent column to add is the Unique Update ID column because this is what is typically referenced in any log files tracking the software update process.

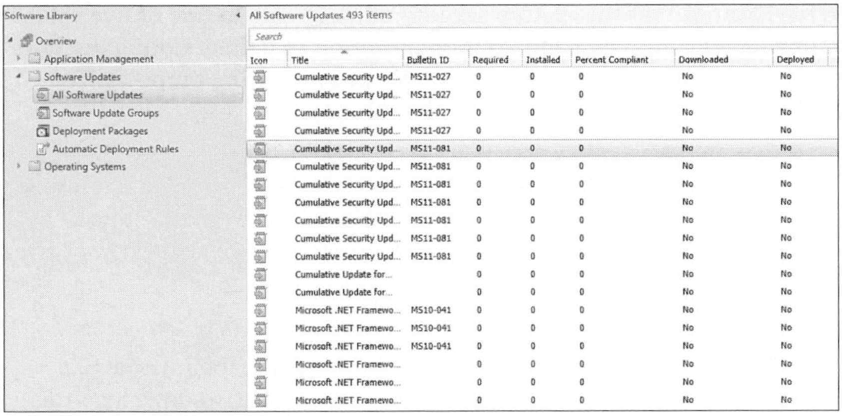

FIGURE 14.7 All Software Update List.

The arrow color in the icon next to each icon in Figure 14.7 indicates the status of the update as listed in Table 14.3.

TABLE 14.3 Update Icon Color

Arrow Color	Meaning
Green	Normal
Grey	Expired
Red	Invalid
Yellow	Superseded
Blue	Metadata Only

Selecting an update in the list displays either Summary or Deployment information in the Detail pane at the bottom, depending upon which tab you have selected in the Detail pane. Double-clicking an update, right-clicking, and choosing **Properties**, or selecting an update and then choosing Properties from the ribbon bar displays detailed information about that update, organized on seven tabs:

▶ **Software Update Details:** This tab displays information about the update such as its Bulletin ID, revision date, and description.

▶ **Maximum Run Time:** By default, all updates have a maximum run time of 5 minutes. This is changed from ConfigMgr 2007 where this value is 20 minutes. This value is used to calculate whether there is enough time to install the update within the time remaining in a maintenance window (discussed in the "Maintenance Windows" section).

▶ **Custom Severity:** You can set the custom severity of an update to one of five values, the meaning of which is up to you and your organization to define. ConfigMgr does not use these values in any way but you can you them for filtering purposes. The five values available are

   ▶ None

   ▶ Low

   ▶ Moderate

   ▶ Important

   ▶ Critical

▶ **Content Information:** This read-only tab contains information about the actual update file(s), whether they have been downloaded, and the URL to download them from. Normally, ConfigMgr handles the download of the files listed here; however, if you find that you need to review the location that ConfigMgr is using or want to download the file yourself, you can reference this tab. If you select a line in this list box and press **CTRL+C**, the entire line is copied to the Windows clipboard where you can then paste it into Notepad to extract the URL.

▶ **Custom Bundle Information:** *Bundles* are groups of updates that are installed together normally because they are tightly related or have inter-dependencies. This tab is read-only.

▶ **Supersedence Information:** This tab lists any updates that this update supersedes or any updates that superseded it. This tab is read-only.

▶ **Security:** This ubiquitous security tab lists ConfigMgr security for this update object. You cannot change the security of an object from this tab. See Chapter 20, "Security and Delegation in Configuration Manager," for detailed information on setting ConfigMgr security.

You can select multiple updates to modify either their Maximum Run Time or Custom Severity at one time.

You can sort the list of updates by clicking any displayed header. You can also filter the list of updates to display only those that you are interested in working with or examining. The first filtering technique is a simple text search: Type in the word or phrase you want to search for in the Search box above the update list's header, and then click the **Search** button. This evaluates and filters content from any displayed column that contains text. Columns such as Required that contain a count, Downloaded that contains a Boolean value, and Date released that contain a date are not considered to contain text and are not evaluated by the simple text search functionality. To clear the filter, click the X button next to the Search button.

You can create advanced filters by combining multiple criteria and multiple columns using the Add Criteria link to the left of the Search button above the update list's header. This drops down a list where you can select which categories you want to filter the update list on, as shown in Figure 14.8. Select those categories you want to include in your filter, and click **Add**. This adds an advanced filter section underneath the Search input box where you can define the values to search for by clicking the value next to the category and choosing an available value from the resulting list, as shown in Figure 14.9. You can also add criteria to the filter by pressing the **Add Criteria** button on the ribbon bar under the Search section.

FIGURE 14.8   All Software Update Criteria.

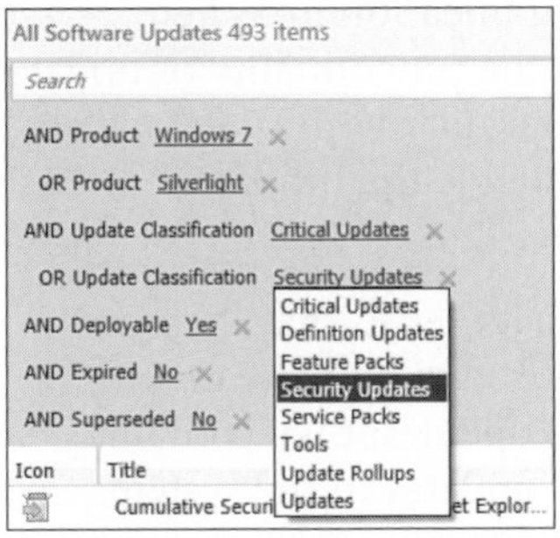

FIGURE 14.9   All Software Update Criteria Selection.

To filter the currently displayed list of updates using your custom filter, press the **Search** button. To add multiple values, as shown in Figure 14.9, for the Product category or Update Classification category, return to the Add Criteria drop-down and add them. To clear a specific category from the filter criteria, click the X next to it. To clear the entire filter, click the X to the left of the Search Button or the **Clear** button on the ribbon bar.

Using the ribbon bar under the Search section, as shown in Figure 14.10, you can save your search criteria, access recent searches and use a handful of built-in searches that are automatically populated under the Saved Searches option. Using the Search Settings button, you configure the maximum number of updates that any search returns. By default, this is set to 1,000. Saved Searches is also available from the Home tab of the ribbon bar when you select **All Software Updates** in the navigation pane.

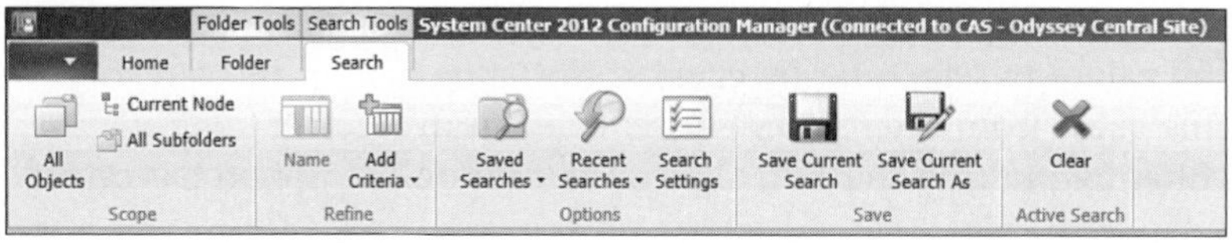

FIGURE 14.10   All Software Update Search Ribbon Bar.

An additional feature for organizing updates is subfolders of the **All Software Updates** node. You create and manage these subfolders using the **Folder** tab on the ribbon bar or right-clicking the **All Software Updates** node. You can apply filters to any subfolder the same way that you did for the **All Software Updates** node. You must manually move updates into the subfolders that you create. They are roughly equivalent in nature to update lists from ConfigMgr 2007 because they are static, have no real functionality, and exist only to organize updates manually.

Filters are the best choice for organizing updates; they are dynamic, persistent, easily modified, and self-defining. Both filters and subfolders are part of the global data replicated to all sites in a hierarchy, making them available at every site.

Software Update Groups

Update groups are one key to the software update workflow simplification in System Center 2012 Configuration Manager. Update groups streamline the functionality of update lists and update deployments into a single object. If you aren't familiar with these objects from ConfigMgr 2007, don't worry; the only thing you are missing is the headache that these two separate object types caused.

As the name implies, update groups reference a set of updates together so that they can be deployed together with the same parameters. Note the use of the word *reference* in the previous sentence. Update groups do not contain the actual updates; they contain a list of references to updates and are used to organize and assign updates to the systems managed by ConfigMgr. Updates must also be downloaded and available to clients in an accessible deployment package (see the "Deployment Packages" section). There is no link between update groups and deployment packages: An update in one of these objects has no bearing on whether it actually is in the other. Of course, for updates to be successfully deployed, the updates must be in both. The console attempts to ensure that updates are in fact contained in both object types, but ultimately there is nothing to guarantee this!

Create software update groups by selecting updates from the **All Software Updates** node or one its subfolders (if you created any). Filtering can help you narrow down which updates you want to include in a particular group. After selecting the wanted updates, choose **Create Software Update Group** from the right-click context menu or the **Home** tab of the ribbon bar. This launches the Create Software Update Group dialog. Using the simple dialog shown in Figure 14.11, enter the wanted name and description for the new update group. New update groups appear under the **Software Update Groups** node in the navigation tree.

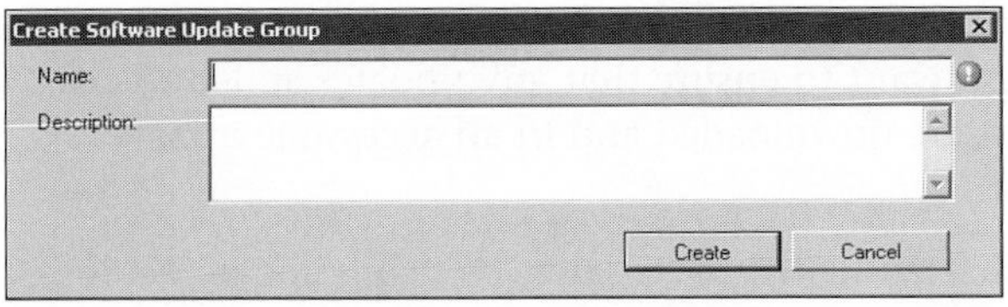

Create Software Update Group   ⊠

Name: [   ] ⓘ

Description: [▲]
[   ]
[▼]

[Create]   [Cancel]

FIGURE 14.11   Create Software Update Group dialog.

Here's how to maintain an update group:

▶ Select the wanted updates from the **All Software Updates** node, and choose **Edit Membership** from the right-click context menu or the **Home** tab of the ribbon bar.

  You cannot add an update that is not downloaded to a software group that has a deployment. This prevents deployment failures caused by the update not actually being available to clients even though it is assigned. First, download the update using the **Download** option from the ribbon bar or the update's right-click context menu and follow the Download Software Updates Wizard to download the update placing it into a new or existing deployment package. Deployments are discussed in "Update Deployments" and deployment packages are discussed in the "Deployment Packages" section.

▶ To remove updates from an update group, choose the update group in the console, and select **Show Members** from the right-click context menu or the **Home** tab of the ribbon bar or double-clicking the update group.

  This creates a sticky node (shown in Figure 14.12) under the **All Software Updates** node in the navigation tree listing all the updates in the update group, similar to clicking the **All Software Updates** node. You can then use the same filtering techniques and review the list of updates or delete them by selecting **Delete** from the right-click context menu or the **Home** tab of the ribbon bar.

FIGURE 14.12   Software Update Group Sticky Node.

Adding an update to an update group does not imply any functionality unless that update group already has a deployment. You also want to ensure that any updates added to an update group with an active deployment are downloaded and in an accessible update package.

Software update groups are more than just static lists of updates; by using update deployments, you directly assign an update group to a set of systems. Although they do not have a formal node under **Software Updates**, update deployments do exist as discussed in the next section.

NOTE: COMPLIANCE GROUPS

There is an informal concept in ConfigMgr 2012 known as *compliance groups*. Essentially, this is a software update group that has no corresponding deployment. Using a compliance group, you can evaluate the compliance of a set of updates against all systems in the console or a specific collection using the built-in reports.

Update Deployments

Update deployments are the primary, active object in software updates. All other objects are just groupings of other objects or settings and are generally passive. Update deployments on the other hand are active objects; they actually assign the updates to clients and cause updates to be installed on managed systems. Without any update deployments, software updates is purely a reporting feature set in ConfigMgr.

There are two types of update deployments:

▶ **Individual:** These assign a specific update to a collection using a defined set of parameters.

▶ **Group:** Group update deployments assign the updates referenced by an update group to a specific collection, also using a defined set of parameters.

An update group or individual update may have multiple update deployments. This small twist on the functionality from ConfigMgr 2007 makes update groups and updates much easier to work with and fundamentally more useful.

To create an update deployment, select an individual update or a set of updates from those listed under the **All Software Updates** node, and choose **Deploy** from the right-click context menu or from the ribbon bar, or choose an existing **Software Update Group** and then choose **Deploy** from the right-click context menu or from the ribbon bar. This launches the Deploy Software Updates Wizard with the following significant pages:

▶ **General:** On this first page, as shown in Figure 14.13, you set the Deployment Name, the collection that the deployment assigns updates to, and the update group from which the deployment assigns updates. Only device collections can be targeted by an update deployment. There are three possibilities for the update group:

▶ If you create the deployment using an existing update group, then that update group is used and automatically populated on this page.

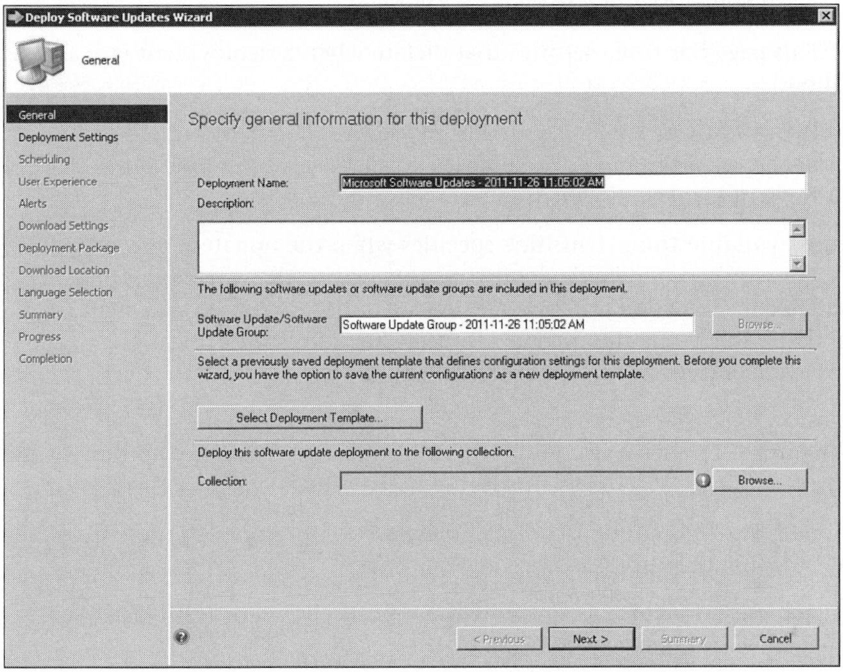

FIGURE 14.13   Deploy Software Updates Wizard General page.

▶ If you create a new deployment from a selected set of updates, then a new update group is also created; a default name is populated on this page but is editable.

▶ If you create a new deployment from a single selected update, no update group is actually created. The update deployment is associated to the single update.

You can also select a deployment template on the **General** page. These are discussed in the "Deployment Templates" section.

▶ **Deployment Settings:** This page lets you set the type of deployment and the detail level of state message returned to the site from the client.

  ▶ **Type of deployment:** Either **Required** or **Available**. Required updates are mandatory and automatically installed by ConfigMgr. Available updates are optional and at the discretion of the end user of a system to install. If you set the deployment to **Required**, you can also enable Wake-on-LAN for the deployment using the check box provided.

▶ **State message detail level:** The default is **Normal**, which causes all state messages relating to this deployment to be sent by the client to the site. The other option, **Minimal**, sends only state message relating to the success of deploying the updates and critical error messages.

▶ **Scheduling:** This page has three settings that dictate when a deployment is available and its deadline:

   ▶ **Schedule evaluation:** This sets whether to use the client's local time or Coordinated Universal Time (UTC) for the available and deadline times. The default is client local time, which is generally recommended.

   ▶ **Software available time:** This time specifies when the updates are available to clients. For required update deployments, this time is the time when updates are available for downloading by the clients. For both required and available updates, this is the time when end users begin to see notifications of the updates availability if notification is enabled.

   ▶ **Installation deadline:** Deadlines are only applicable to required update deployments; they specify the time when the referenced updates automatically are installed on the targeted clients if not already installed.

▶ **User Experience:** Three different sets of parameters are configurable on this page, each directly affecting the end user's experience:

   ▶ **User visual experience:** This sets how the user receives notification of available updates as summarized in Table 14.4.

TABLE 14.4   User Experience

Tabs	Required Update Deployment	Available Update Deployment
Displays in Software Center and show all notifications	X	X
Displays in Software Center, and show only notifications for computer restarts	X	X
Hides in Software Center and all notifications	X	

▶ **Deadline behavior:** Only applicable for require update deployments, the two check boxes in this section enable update installation or necessary system restarts outside of defined maintenance windows (discussed in the "Maintenance Windows" section).

▶ **Device restart behavior:** Only applicable for required update deployments, the two check boxes in this section suppress system restarts on servers and workstations.

▶ **Alerts:** You can configure two types of alerts:

> ▶ **Configuration Manager alerts:** In this section, you configure ConfigMgr console-centric alert parameters based upon client compliance percentage after a specified date and time. See Chapter 8, "The Configuration Manager Console," for information about alerts.

> ▶ **Operations Manager alerts:** This section enables OpsMgr alert suppression or alert generation for update failures. Unlike ConfigMgr 2007, the OpsMgr agent is now properly put into maintenance mode using these settings.

▶ **Download Settings:** The options on the page enable update download when the client is located on a slow boundary, using a fallback source location, or when the content is not available on a preferred distribution point. The most common use of these options is to prevent clients from downloading content when connected to the network using a known slow link such as a virtual private network (VPN).

Also configurable on this page is the use of BranchCache for downloading updates from local peer systems. Chapter 5, "Network Design," provides additional information about BranchCache.

▶ **Deployment Package:** On this page, you select an existing deployment package for downloading updates or create a new package to which to download the updates. Only updates not already downloaded are downloaded into the specified package.

NOTE: UPDATE DEPLOYMENTS ARE NOT LINKED TO UPDATE PACKAGES

There is no correlation between the update package used and the update deployment. This means the update deployment does not have a dependency on a specific update package. Updates can be spread across multiple update packages or contained within a single update package. It is the client's job to find updates; the client can locate and download updates from any available update package.

▶ **Download Location:** Specifies where to download any updates not already downloaded. The two options on this page are

> ▶ **Download software updates from the Internet:** This option downloads updates directly from Microsoft Update.

> ▶ **Download software updates from a location on my network:** This option downloads the necessary updates from a local source location. To download updates manually, you should use the URL listed on the Content Information tab of the updates as previously described in the "All Software Updates" section.

At the end of the wizard, ConfigMgr automatically downloads the necessary updates from the specified location and places them into the package specified on the previous step. The updates are actually downloaded on the system where the ConfigMgr

14

console is running, using the credentials of the user running the console. This is important for several reasons:

> ▶ It means that only the system running the console needs to actively connect to the Internet.

> ▶ It uses the proxy settings of the user that is running the console.

▶ **Language Selection:** Select which language version of the updates you want to download. This acts as a further filter from the languages you chose to include in your update catalog. Just because your update catalog contains information about updates for multiple languages does not mean that you actually have to download the corresponding versions of the update!

▶ **Summary:** This is a traditional summary page with one added function: to create an update template using some or all of the settings specified in the wizard. If you click the **Save As Template** button, a dialog box pops up where you can save the settings you just entered in the wizard to reuse the next time you create a deployment. This is the only way to create an update template, which you cannot modify after creation.

▶ **Progress:** A typical progress page, showing the download of any necessary updates.

▶ **Completion:** The final page gives a complete report of the update deployment creation including any other objects that may have been created along the way including an update group, deployment package, and update template as well as the result of downloading any applicable updates. Pay close attention to this summary box if everything did not complete successfully, so that you know where to begin troubleshooting.

The Deployment Package, Download Location, and Language Selection pages appear only as part of the wizard if the any of the updates selected have not been previously downloaded. Because of these three pages, this wizard appears to imply that update packages and update groups are somehow linked. This is not the case; the wizard is simply ensuring that all updates referenced by this update group have been downloaded and are available to clients. It does this because if any update is not downloaded, the update deployment cannot be completely successful.

As mentioned earlier in this section, update deployments exist only in the context of an update group or specific update. Thus to view or edit an existing update deployment, you must first select the update group or update to which that the deployment belongs. Update deployments particular to the update group or update are displayed at the bottom in the Detail pane by selecting the **Deployment** tab. After selecting the deployment that you are interested in from the Detail pane, you can Enable, Disable, Delete, or view the Properties of the deployment from the corresponding buttons on the **Deployment** tab of the ribbon bar or the right-click context menu of the deployment. The properties displayed in the update deployment's Properties dialog correspond to those configured using the Deploy Software Updates Wizard and are organized on tabs with the same names as pages of the wizard. There are no tabs corresponding to the download of the updates or placement of the updates in the package; the download of the updates is a one-time activity that has no connection to the actual update deployment. See the note in this section titled "Update Deployments Are Not Linked to Update Packages" for further details.

If an individual update is also part of an update group that has an applicable deployment, that update group's update deployment also appears in the list of deployments for that individual update. This means that when you select an update, a comprehensive list of all update deployments assigning that update to clients is displayed in the update's deployment tab in the Detail pane at the bottom, as shown in Figure 14.14.

NOTE: UPDATE DEPLOYMENT LIMIT

There is a hard limit of 1,000 updates in an update deployment. This limit is explicitly enforced to prevent server-side and client-side performance degradation.

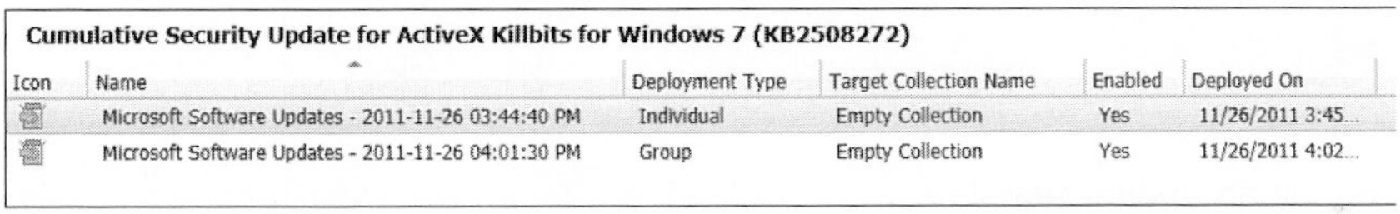

Cumulative Security Update for ActiveX Killbits for Windows 7 (KB2508272)					
Icon	Name	Deployment Type	Target Collection Name	Enabled	Deployed On
	Microsoft Software Updates - 2011-11-26 03:44:40 PM	Individual	Empty Collection	Yes	11/26/2011 3:45...
	Microsoft Software Updates - 2011-11-26 04:01:30 PM	Group	Empty Collection	Yes	11/26/2011 4:02...

FIGURE 14.14 Multiple update deployment for an individual update.

Update Templates

The product team chose to hide this object type because it does not have any explicit functionality of its own although it is still useful. The only time you see update templates referenced is during the Deploy Software Updates Wizard as discussed in the "Update Deployments" section. Update templates store a distinct set of parameters that you can reuse when creating an update deployment. Instead of respecifying the parameters each time you create an update deployment, you pick a previously created update template that already has all these parameters defined.

Because update templates are hidden objects, the only way to create one is to initiate the Deploy Software Updates Wizard. At the end of the wizard, you can save all the choices you made during the wizard to a template for later reuse using the **Save As Template** button, as displayed in Figure 14.15. When created, you cannot edit an update template. You can, however, delete or rename templates from the Select a Template dialog box shown when you click the **Select Deployment Template** button on the General page of the Deploy Software Updates Wizard, as shown previously in Figure 14.13.

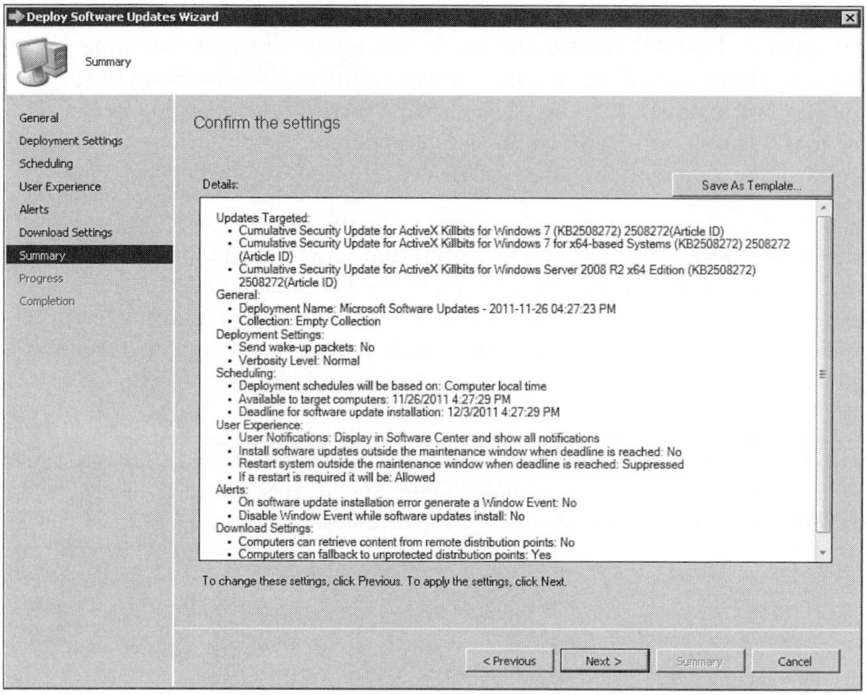

FIGURE 14.15   Creating an update template.

WHY TEMPLATES ARE HIDDEN

Although many have questioned the hiding of templates, it truly improves the workflow and perceived functionality of software updates. Specifically, a common source of confusion in ConfigMgr 2007 is that update templates are not linked in any way to the update deployments that you create using them and vice versa. This means if you change a setting in an update template, it affects only update deployments created after you make the change, not any of the update deployments previously created using the template. Although this may sound obvious, it caused many forum posts, endless questions, and explanations, as well as countless hours of lost work and disruptions to end users. By hiding update templates and not providing a way to edit them, the confusion should be eliminated and their true purpose readily apparent.

Deployment Packages

Similar to software distribution packages (covered in Chapter 11, "Packages and Programs"), deployment packages are simply the collection of files needed for a set of updates. From an administrative perspective, this is the only update object type in this version of ConfigMgr that did not change from ConfigMgr 2007.

You manage update packages identically to software distribution packages—they must have a source folder and be available to clients by assigning them to distribution points.

You cannot directly create a deployment package from the console; you can only create one using the Deploy Software Updates Wizard (described in the "Update Deployments" section) or the Download Software Updates Wizard.

You can launch the Download Software Updates Wizard by selecting either a single or multiple updates from one of the various times that updates are displayed in a list such as when the All Software Updates node in selected in the navigation tree. You can also select an update group from the Software Update Groups node in the navigation tree. After selecting the wanted updates or update group, select **Download** from the Home or Update Group tab on the ribbon bar or from the right-click context menu.

There are six pages in the Download Software Updates Wizard:

▶ Deployment Package

▶ Download Location

▶ Language Selection

▶ Summary

▶ Progress

▶ Completion

The purpose of each page in this wizard is identical to that of the like-named pages in the Deploy Software Updates Wizard, covered in the "Update Deployments" section. Essentially, these pages are inserted into that wizard when updates need to be downloaded during the course of creating an update deployment.

There is no specific, technical reason to put an update into any given package and not another. Clients that require an applicable update assigned to them using an update deployment will download that update from any available package. Deployment packages are not linked to update deployments in any way. In addition, clients do not need to download an entire package; they can download a single update from a package.

A common failure for software updates is not ensuring that all applicable update packages are properly replicated and available on DPs where clients will request the updates contained in those update packages. Thus, a strategy for dividing for update packages and making them available (or not available) on DPs is highly recommended. In general, unless your DPs are tight on space or you have severe bandwidth limitations, making all your update packages available on every DP is recommended. The authors also recommend organizing your deployment packages by the release date of updates such as the year or half year. Organizing your deployment packages by operating system causes wasted space, as some updates are applicable to multiple operating systems. Note that this wasted space is only applicable to the package source locations. With the new single-instance store in ConfigMgr 2012 for DPs, only a single copy of each file is replicated and stored on DPs.

Automatic Deployment Rules

Automatic deployment rules (ADRs) fill a large gap in software update functionality that existed in ConfigMgr 2007, as there was no way to automatically download and assign updates. For the normal monthly update process, this is not actually a large burden and was more of a perceived shortcoming particularly when compared to the built-in functionality of stand-alone WSUS.

When it came to Forefront Client Security (FCS) and Forefront Endpoint Protection (FEP) 2007 definition updates however, this burden is tangible and excessive because they are updated multiple times every day. See Chapter 16, "Endpoint Protection," for additional information on System Center Endpoint Protection, which is the successor to FCS and FEP.

As the name implies, ADRs automatically create update deployments. To create an ADR, select the **Automatic Deployment Rules** node in the navigation tree and choose **Create Automatic Deployment Rule** from the ribbon bar or the right-click context menu. This launches the Create Automatic Deployment Rule Wizard, which is similar to the Deploy Software Update Wizard described in the "Update Deployments" section. It contains the following pages (only pages with different options or meanings or those not existing in the Deploy Software updates Wizard are described in detail):

▶ **General:** On this first page, you name the ADR, select a collection to target, select using an existing software update group or creating a new one, and enabling the ADR at the end of the wizard. If you choose to add to an existing update group, a new one is created the first time the ADR is evaluated and reused for each subsequent evaluation of the ADR. If you choose to use a new update group, then a new update group is created for every evaluation of the ADR.

As update deployments can target only device collections, you can select only a device collection on this page. You can also use an existing update template to populate most of the settings in this wizard by pressing the **Select Deployment Template** button.

▶ **Deployment Settings:** On this page, you enable Wake-on-LAN for the generated deployment and set the state message detail level. You also configure the ADR to approve automatically any license agreements on applicable updates. Few updates have license agreements, but the ones that do must be approved before ConfigMgr can deploy them.

▶ **Software Updates:** ADRs populate an update deployment with references to updates based on a pre-defined filter similar to console filters described in the "All Software Updates" section. A subset of the filter criteria is displayed on this page, where you select and define the criteria for finding the updates for inclusion in the update deployment.

This page acts similar to the Rules Wizard in Microsoft Outlook—checking a criteria field in the top of the page adds that criteria to the bottom of the page, with a corresponding link enabling you to select of the option to filter on from those that are available.

For properties in this dialog that allow you to enter free text as a filter criteria like the title, you can prefix the string with a minus sign "-" to indicate that the string not be included. For example, entering -**Itanium** in the title property criteria excludes all updates that include Itanium in their title property.

▶ **Evaluation Schedule:** This page sets when you want the ADR rule to be evaluated. For convenience it also shows the SUP synchronization time so you can coordinate the two times—it doesn't make sense to run an ADR evaluation more frequently than the SUP synchronization time because there will be no new updates to find. You can also disable the automatic, scheduled evaluation of an ADR, leaving it to be initiated manually.

▶ **Deployment Schedule:** This page is identical to the like-named page on the Deploy Software Updates Wizard except that you cannot specify absolute times. You can only specify times relative to the time the ADR is evaluated.

▶ **User Experience**

▶ **Alerts**

▶ **Download Settings**

▶ **Deployment Package**

▶ **Download Location:** Although this page is identical to the one in the Deploy Software Updates Wizard, it has a different impact. With the Deploy Software Updates Wizard, updates are immediately downloaded at the end of the wizard. With ADRs, updates cannot be downloaded until the ADR evaluation time. This means that the console user's credentials and context cannot be used to download the updates. Instead, the credentials and (optional) proxy server specified on the SUPs configuration (described in the "Software Update Point Placement" section) are used by the SUP itself to download the updates.

▶ **Language Selection**

▶ **Summary**

▶ **Progress**

▶ **Completion**

To view or edit an ADR, select the **Automatic Deployment Rules Node** in the navigation tree, select the ADR of interest, and select **Properties** from the ribbon bar or the right-click context menu. This displays a Properties dialog for the ADR where all the settings from the Create Automatic Deployment Rule Wizard are available and organized on tabs named the same as the wizard's pages as listed here.

Also available from the ribbon bar or right-click context menus are the options to Delete an ADR, Enable and Disable an ADR, and manually evaluate an ADR that does not have an evaluation cycle or that you want to run out of cycle using the **Run Now** button.

Maintenance Windows

Deployments are somewhat limited in that they do not define an exact time that updates should or must be installed; they merely define a time when updates become mandatory. This could easily cause disruption to your users and your servers if updates install at various times after the deadline.

Maintenance windows solve this dilemma. In general, maintenance windows prevent the ConfigMgr client from undertaking any action that could disrupt the end user or hosted services on a system. This includes preventing software updates deployments, software distribution advertisements, and restarts initiated by ConfigMgr for software updates.

Edit these schedules by right-clicking any collection and choosing **Properties**. This displays the collection's Properties dialog box, which contains a Maintenance Windows tab for viewing and manipulating maintenance windows. The interface for creating maintenance window schedules, displayed in Figure 14.16, is quite flexible and allows you to specify settings such as every third Tuesday of the month.

TIP: MAINTENANCE WINDOWS AND SOFTWARE DISTRIBUTION

Maintenance windows also affect software distribution deployments. In the same way that they delay the installation of updates in a deployment, they also delay the execution of required software and application deployments. Be aware of this when setting up your collections and maintenance windows. If necessary, you can configure your required application deployments to ignore maintenance windows by using the **Schedule** tab on the deployment.

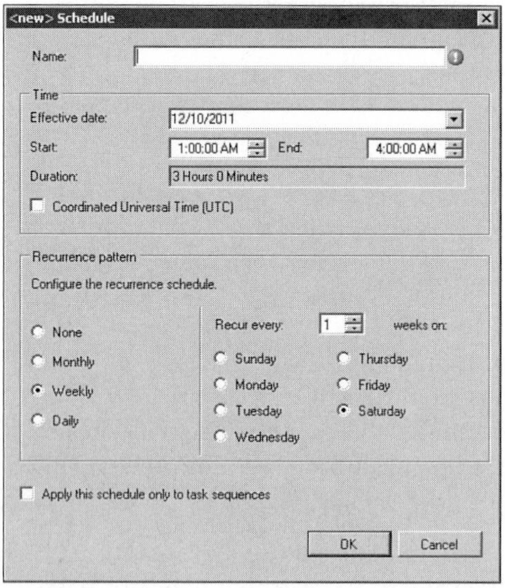

FIGURE 14.16   Maintenance Window Schedule dialog box.

Scheduling with Maintenance Windows

Maintenance windows prevent updates in a required deployment from installing on a system outside the window's configured times. This causes any required deployment past its deadline to wait until the next configured maintenance window before installing its updates.

Maintenance windows are calculated by the client agent without respect to the collection to which a deployment is assigned. If the client is a member of any collection that has a maintenance window, the agent schedules deployment installation at the start of the next occurrence of any assigned maintenance window.

You can create multiple maintenance windows on a single collection. Any system belonging to multiple collections is also subject to the maintenance windows of those collections; the effective maintenance windows for any given system is the cumulative or combined schedule specified in all the maintenance windows of all the collections of which a system is a member.

Maximum Runtimes

Another check performed by the client agent is the maximum runtime for each applicable update in a deployment. If the sum of these maximum runtimes is greater than the maintenance window allows for, the client agent will not install all applicable updates. The final reboot, if the deployment is configured not to suppress it, is also accounted for when determining which updates fit inside the maintenance window—maximum runtime for a reboot is hard-coded to 15 minutes. The maximum run time for the assigned updates (and reboot) are recalculated after each update is installed. If the maintenance window ends before all updates are installed, the remaining updates are culled based on their maximum runtime.

To view or edit the maximum runtime for any update, find the update (under the All Software Update node or an opened sticky node for a software update group), right-click it, and choose **Properties**. This opens a Properties dialog box for the update with a Maximum Run Time tab, shown in Figure 14.17; the value listed is editable. You can also multi-select updates to change their maximum runtimes in the same way. All updates have a maximum runtime of 5 minutes by default.

Note that clients begin downloading updates as soon as the deployments are available. This typically prevents the time required by clients to actually download updates from affecting the time available in the maintenance window.

Bypassing Maintenance Windows

Configure specific deployments to ignore or bypass configured maintenance windows by selecting the **Software update installation** check box under the Deadline behavior section on the **User Experience** tab of a deployment, as shown in Figure 14.18. Use this option carefully if you have gone through the trouble to define and set up maintenance windows, because it can disrupt your carefully planned update scheduling. However, in the case of zero-day updates, this disruption may be necessary and warranted.

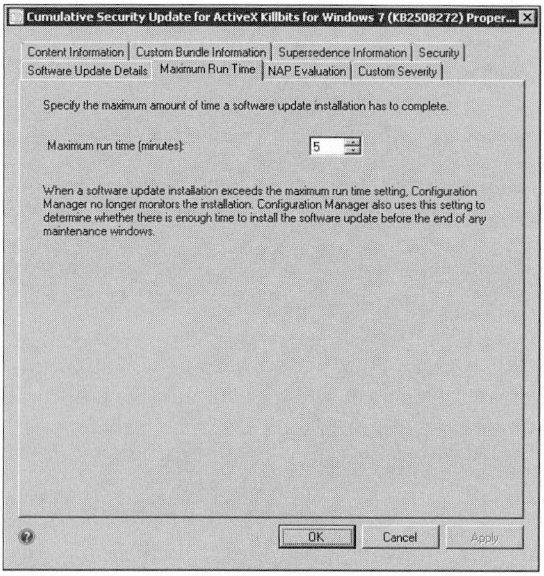

FIGURE 14.17   Maximum Run Time tab.

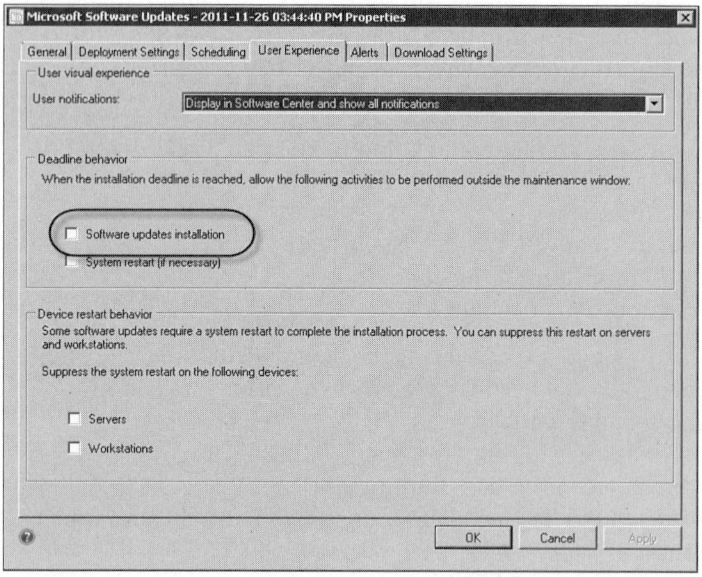

FIGURE 14.18   Bypassing Maintenance Windows.

Superseded Updates

A common issue in ConfigMgr 2007 is dealing with superseded updates. Some organizations with a rigorous configuration control process do not allow new updates for immediate deployment to the enterprise. However, when Microsoft publishes new updates that supersede older updates, you have a "Catch 22" situation: ConfigMgr does not allow deployment of the older superseded updates, but the organization's strict configuration policy does not allow deployment of the new updates.

System Center 2012 Configuration Manager addresses this issue by the choice made on the SUP's configuration known as supersedence rules, described fully in the "Software Update Point Placement" section.

The Software Updates Process in Action

Although software update management is streamlined from ConfigMgr 2007, the background software update process is largely unchanged and still involves many moving parts. What happens when and "whodunit" is important not only conceptually but also in practice when managing software updates in ConfigMgr. The cyclical process described here assumes that you have a properly configured ConfigMgr site as well as a properly working WSUS instance and SUP:

1. If the SUP is configured to update from the Internet, the update catalog is synchronized from Microsoft Update by the WSUS instance. Alternatively, the catalog could be synchronized from a manual import. Updates included in the catalog are based on the classifications, products, and languages configured on the SUP's component properties. To modify or review these, see the "Software Update Component" section earlier in this chapter.

   The update catalog is also now available for clients to perform update applicability or compliance scanning.

2. The update catalog is synchronized to the ConfigMgr database.

3. Based on the client's software update scan schedule as described in the "Client Settings" section, the ConfigMgr agent triggers the client's WUA to download the update catalog from the WSUS instance corresponding to the SUP the client is configured to communicate with, cache the catalog locally, and scan the system for update applicability. The entire update catalog is not downloaded every time; only the changed portion of the catalog is downloaded—this is typically called the *delta*. To kick-start client update compliance scanning, initiate a Software Updates Deployment Evaluation Cycle from the tab of the ConfigMgr Control Panel applet or use an equivalent method.

   Scan results are stored in WMI, using the undocumented `ccm_updatestatus` class in the `root\ccm\softwareupdates\updatesstore` namespace, and sent to the ConfigMgr site using state messages by the ConfigMgr agent. State messages are XML messages cached on the client for 15 minutes (by default) and submitted in bulk to the client's site MP. They relay point in-time information about the client to the site. For a detailed look at the state messaging system in ConfigMgr, review http://blogs.msdn.com/b/steverac/archive/2011/01/07/sccm-state-messaging-in-depth.aspx, this is specific to ConfigMgr 2007 but also applicable to ConfigMgr 2012.

TIP: STATE MESSAGE RESYNCH

In ConfigMgr 2007, the state message system seemed to be a weak link in the software update process on occasion. This often required a complete resynchronization of the software update compliance information using a simple script. Whether this plays out in ConfigMgr 2012 is yet to be seen, but the following VBScript (taken from the ConfigMgr 2007 SDK) can initiate this resynchronization:

```
' Initialize the UpdatesStore variable.
dim newCCMUpdatesStore


' Create the COM object.
set newCCMUpdatesStore = CreateObject ("Microsoft.CCM.UpdatesStore")


' Refresh the server compliance state by running the
➥RefreshServerComplianceState method.
newCCMUpdatesStore.RefreshServerComplianceState
' Output success message.
wscript.echo "Ran RefreshServerComplianceState."
```

---

4. The software updates administrator or in-place ADRs assign updates to managed systems by creating deployments of individual updates or software update groups. Assigned updates must also be placed into an update package; ADRs do this automatically, and the Update Deployment Creation Wizard also does this when manually creating an update deployment. Clients receive update deployments using the normal policy delivery process in ConfigMgr. You can kick-start this process by initiating a Machine Policy Retrieval & Evaluation Cycle from the Actions tab of the ConfigMgr Control Panel applet or using an equivalent method. When a client receives a policy containing a new update deployment, it initiates a software update evaluation scan that evaluates all the newly assigned updates for applicability.

5. If the deployment has a deadline, then at its defined available time, clients assigned to the deployment begin to download updates referenced in that deployment previously determined as applicable to them.

REAL WORLD: ONLY APPLICABLE UPDATES ARE DOWNLOADED AND APPLIED

Here is an important caveat: Not every update in a deployment is downloaded or installed; only those that the client needs based upon the WUA scan of the system are downloaded and installed. Given this caveat, you can freely mix updates for different products and languages in a single software update group or deployment package without any negative ramifications or impacts. The client simply ignores those that are not applicable to it.

For those deployments without a deadline time, updates are not downloaded until the end user triggers their installation.

Updates aren't actually downloaded from the deployment, as the deployment only contains a list of referenced updates. The updates are downloaded from any available update package that contains the update. Similar to not installing every update in the update deployment, clients do not download every update in an update package. They download only the specific updates that they need as determined by the most recent update scan performed by the WUA that are also referenced, and thus assigned, by the update deployment.

6. If the deployment has a deadline, clients trigger another update scan by the WUA at that defined deadline to ensure that nothing has changed since the last update scan. Newly applicable updates are downloaded as needed and the WUA is again triggered to install the applicable updates. If the deployment does not define a deadline, then updates are installable once manually triggered by the user.

    When the deadline is reached for a mandatory deployment, client computers create a state message for each software update in the deployment. Here are the software update enforcement states that provide information about the software update installation:

    ▶ Enforcement state unknown

    ▶ Enforcement started

    ▶ Enforcement waiting for content

    ▶ Waiting for another installation to complete

    ▶ Waiting for maintenance window before installing

    ▶ Restart required before installing

    ▶ General failure

    ▶ Pending installation

    ▶ Installing update

    ▶ Pending system restart

    ▶ Successfully installed update

    ▶ Failed to install update

    ▶ Downloading update

    ▶ Downloaded update

    ▶ Failed to download update

7. After all applicable updates are installed, another update compliance scan is performed by the client. If the updates require a reboot, a final update scan by the WUA is triggered after this reboot. The final scan reports effective update installation

results to ConfigMgr and ensures the compliance data in the ConfigMgr database is always current.

> **NOTE: TO REBOOT OR NOT TO REBOOT**
>
> Software update installation doesn't typically cause user or service disruption; reboots always do. Thus, delaying or preventing reboots is often a desirable practice. The primary issue with suppressing reboots in conjunction with software updates is that there have been known cases in which installing an update without a reboot also causes service disruption and other odd behavior on the system until the system is rebooted. Thus, the authors recommend rebooting a system as soon as possible after updates are installed to prevent this behavior from occurring. That doesn't mean you shouldn't suppress reboots in your update deployments; it means that you should consider this risk factor when determining how to configure you software update process.
>
> If you do suppress reboots, make sure that you have a process in place that eventually reboots systems where updates have been installed. Whether this is a regular forced reboot using a software deployment, a scheduled task, a workflow from System Center 2012 Orchestrator, manual, or something else is up to you and your organization, based on your priorities and needs.

Software Update Decisions, Design, and Workflow

There are three primary areas to choose or design for software updates in ConfigMgr and the actual administrative workflow for software updates follows their design:

▶ **Collections:** This is the "where" of software updates and defines the managed systems to which you want to deploy updates. Updates are always deployed to a collection and affect every system in that collection.

The authors recommend you create a separate set of device collections organized in a folder under the **Device Collections** node in the **Assets and Compliance** workspace. This set of collections should be used only for software updates and should be sufficiently granular to target the different types of updates you deploy as well as different update schedules using deadlines on the update deployments if you are not using maintenance windows.

When designing your collections, make sure they adequately separate your managed systems to model the various sets of updates you deploy. For example, if you don't always deploy every update to your Citrix servers, make a separate collection for them.

Remember also that collections are inclusive and all or nothing. There is no concept of conditionally excluding systems from a collection for different deployments or activities. If a one-off update is released that applies only to a portion of a particular collection, you have to create a new collection that includes only those systems that you want to assign that update to—there is simply no way to exclude systems. Knowing and considering this when designing your collections should help to prevent you from having to create additional collections though.

▶ **Updates:** This is the "what" of software updates. Specifically, which updates you want to detect and deploy in your environment. This is initially defined by the updates you include in your update catalog.

You can detect applicable updates by including them in your catalog but never deploying them. This means you should further refine the complete list of updates in the catalog by using the built-in console filtering capabilities and searches to download and assign only a subset of the updates. This refinement could include things such as including updates that are only applicable to at least one system, or instead including all updates for a specific operating system whether they are applicable to a single system or not. The possibilities for this refinement are endless and only limited by the filtering capabilities of the console; but they should be dictated by the needs of the environment or an in-place organizational policy.

The result of refining the update catalog is creating software update groups that are then deployed. This either is a manual process that you perform on a regular schedule as described in the "Software Update Groups" section or automatically with ADRs.

▶ **Deployments:** Deployments combine the above "where" and "what"—collections and updates—and add in the "when" and "how" in the form of schedules and various other properties described in the "Update Deployments" section. As with defining the updates through the creation of software update groups, creating update deployments is also either a regularly scheduled, manual activity (described in the "Update Deployments" section), or automatically done using ADRs.

Using ADRs greatly simplifies the administrative workflow in software updates in System Center 2012 Configuration Manager. With ADRs, software updates become primarily a "fire and forget" solution, similar to what many WSUS administrators are used to. This may not necessarily be desirable to you and your organization, however. The primary question is whether you want updates automatically selected and deployed to your organization, as this involves some risk. If you choose to use ADRs, then you should carefully plan the properties of the ADRs and follow up by regularly verifying and spot-checking the deployments they create.

TIP: MIXED APPROACH AVAILABLE FOR DEPLOYMENTS

You can use a mixed approach combining ADRs with manually created deployments. Software updates for Endpoint Protection and Windows Defender definitions, which are released quite frequently, is a cumbersome chore without using ADRs.

Compliance Scanning

Each system is responsible for scanning itself and reporting the results to ConfigMgr. The ConfigMgr agent initiates the actual compliance scanning, which is performed by the WUA at various times throughout the software update lifecycle, shown in Table 14.5. Clients use the metadata retrieved from their active software update point to perform compliance scanning. When retrieved, this update metadata is cached by the WUA for future use. The scan types in Table 14.5 are defined as follows:

▶ **Forced Scan:** A scan always occurs.

▶ **Unforced Scan:** Scan occurs only if the locally cached copy of the metadata is more than 24 hours old. This is called the time to live (TTL) of the update metadata and refers to how long a cached copy of the metadata is valid. Having a copy of the metadata less than 24 hours old implies that a scan has also occurred within the last 24 hours and does not need to be performed again.

Unforced scans are used to prevent excessive scans and unnecessary bandwidth usage. If an unforced scan is initiated and the TTL is less than 24 hours old, then the client does not actual perform a scan and nothing changes on the client itself.

▶ **Online Scans:** This type of scan uses the latest metadata available on the server and synchronizes the locally cached copy. If the metadata version on the server and client matches, an offline scan occurs.

▶ **Offline Scan:** The locally cached copy of the update metadata is always used.

TABLE 14.5   Client Update Compliance Scanning Times

Scan Time	Online Scan	Force Scan
Per the update scan schedule set in client settings	Yes	No
Forced from the Actions tab of the ConfigMgr Control Panel Applet	Yes	Yes
Per the re-evaluation scan schedule set in client settings	Yes	No
Before downloading update files for a required deployment	Yes	No
Before update installation of a required deployment	Yes	No
After update installation	No	Yes
After system restart following update installation	No	Yes

For the manually initiated scans from the Actions tab of the Control Panel applet, the update metadata is always refreshed.

During compliance scanning, the WUA marks each update with a compliance state. Here are the available compliance states:

▶ **Required:** This means that the update is still needed on the client system or that the update is installed but requires a restart.

▶ **Not Required:** The update is not applicable on the local system.

▶ **Installed:** The update is already successfully install on the local system.

▶ **Unknown:** There are many reasons for an unknown update status, including communication issues, client scan issues, or configuration issues. The wuahandler.log on the client is the first place on a client to go to verify proper configuration.

After compliance scanning completes, the compliance state of all updates whose state changed is sent to the server using state messages. State messages are stored by the ConfigMgr client agent for 15 minutes by default before they are sent in bulk; this value is configurable in the client settings on the State Messaging page. The only way to force a client agent to send queued state messages is to restart the client agent service. Because of this delay in sending the scan results from the client to the server, the actual state is not reflected on the server immediately.

End User Experience and Interaction

What does a user actually see when you deploy updates to their system? You may facetiously ask whether you actually care! You may not want the user to see anything. In that case, set the Notifications for new deployments setting on the Computer Agent Client Settings page (as described in the "Client Settings" section) to False. As described in Chapter 9, client settings are granular, so you can suppress deployment notification display on a per-collection basis based on your organization's needs.

Notifications

If deployment notification is disabled for a client per its deployed client settings, no notifications are ever displayed on the client. Users can still manually install available updates using the Software Center—launched from the Start Menu. If deployment notification is enabled, then notifications are displayed as outlined in Table 14.6.

TABLE 14.6   Update Notifications

Deployment Notification	Available Deployment	Required Deployment
Display in Software Center and show all notifications	A task bar notification icon (shown in Figure 14.19) and an initial balloon pop-up. The notification icon persists as long as the updates are applicable and available.	A task bar notification icon (shown in Figure 14.20) and an initial balloon pop-up. The notification icon persists as long as the updates are applicable and required. The notification balloon reappears based on the Deployment deadline reminders settings on the Computer Agent page of the client settings.

Deployment Notification	Available Deployment	Required Deployment
Display in Software Center, and only show notifications for computer restarts	No notification is displayed for updates.	No notification is displayed for updates.
Hide in Software Center and all notifications	N/A	No notification is displayed for updates.

FIGURE 14.19   Available updates notification balloon.

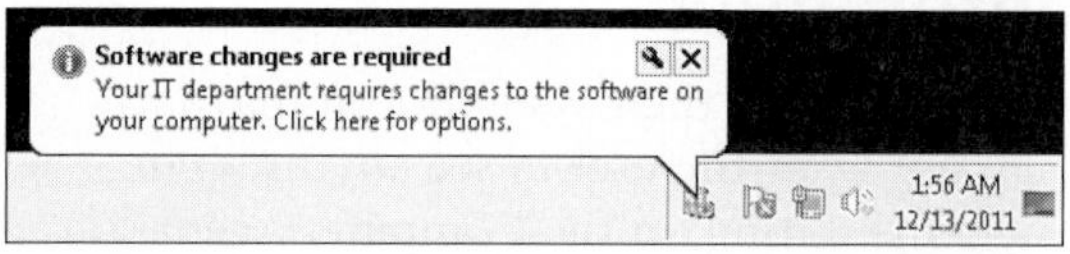

FIGURE 14.20   Required updates notification balloon.

CAUTION: DISABLING DEPLOYMENT NOTIFICATIONS

Disabling deployment notifications is not specific to any deployment type. This setting affects all deployment types including application and operating system deployments.

Updates and Software Center

Double-clicking the available updates notification bubble (shown in Figure 14.19) or the notification icon opens the Software Center shown in Figure 14.21. Double-clicking the required updates notification bubble (shown in Figure 14.20) displays the software changes dialog shown in Figure 14.22.

If notifications are disabled, or if you choose to do so, you can also launch the Software Center from the Start menu. The Software Center displays all applicable software updates on the Installation Status tab. Basic information is displayed about each update, including the following possible statuses:

▶ **Available:** The update is available for immediate installation.

▶ **Scheduled to install after:** A required update that is scheduled to install after the date and time specified in the status message.

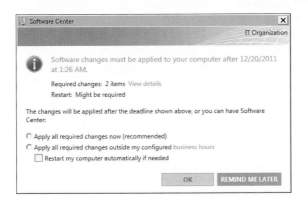

FIGURE 14.21   Software Center with available updates.

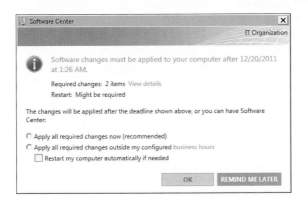

FIGURE 14.22   Software changes dialog.

▶ **Past due - will be installed:** A required update that is past its scheduled installation time. Updates are often in this status because of maintenance windows or failure to locate content.

▶ **Preparing to Download:** The client agent is finding an available location for the update's content.

▶ **Downloading:** The client agent is downloading the content from an available location. This status also includes a percent complete.

▶ **Waiting to install:** The update is preparing to install.

▶ **Installing:** The update is installing.

▶ **Pending verification:** The update is installed but being verified.

▶ **Installed:** The update is already installed and is verified as installed.

▶ **Requires restart:** The update requires a reboot to complete installation.

TIP: SOFTWARE CENTER DEPLOYMENT FILTERING

Use the SHOW drop-down in the upper-left corner of the Software Center to show all deployments or just a specific type including just update deployments.

If an update is actively downloading or installing and you have enabled notifications, an icon is present in the taskbar icon notification area with a tooltip that reads **Downloading and installing software**.

Update Installation

The end user of a system can always manually install available or required updates from the Software Center. Required updates are automatically installed after their deadline if they are still applicable. Alternatively, you can manually schedule required updates by selecting the update and choosing **SCHEDULE**. The resulting dialog box, shown in Figure 14.23, gives the user some self-explanatory options.

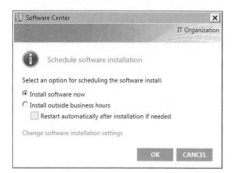

FIGURE 14.23   Schedule Software installation dialog.

To manually install updates from the Software Center, use the INSTALL button in the bottom right corner or the INSTALL ALL REQUIRED button in the bottom-left corner. You cannot multi-select a subset of the updates displayed; you must either install all of them or select updates one by one. Also, note that only updates are shown in the Software Center and not any software update groups. After you select the INSTALL or INSTALL ALL REQUIRED button, installation of the update(s) begins, and the Software Center displays the installation progress of each update in the Status column as it installs; this includes download progress. While an update is preparing to download or downloading, the INSTALL button turns into a CANCEL button. After an update is installed, the INSTALL button turns into an UNINSTALL button when an installed update is selected. Not all updates are actually uninstallable though; the button is grayed out when you select an update that cannot be uninstalled.

System Restarts and Restart Notifications

Restart notifications are valuable if you suppress restarts in required update deployments or the user chooses not to immediately restart the system after manually installing updates. Delaying or suppressing restarts ensures that users are not adversely disrupted by the restart. However, many updates require restarts to become effective so displaying a "nag" notification helps ensure that the system is eventually restarted. Three basic criteria must be met for ConfigMgr to display a restart notification and icon:

▶ Deployment notification is enabled for the client.

▶ User notification is not set to Hide in Software Center and all notifications.

▶ Installed update requires a reboot.

There are two types of restart notifications:

▶ A "nag" restart notification informing the user that a restart is desired to complete update installation. Figure 14.24 shows an example. This type of notification is displayed when one of the two following criteria is met:

  ▶ Installed update's deployment type is Available.

  ▶ Installed update's deployment type is Required, and the deployment has not yet reached its deadline. In this case, a restart is schedule for the actual deadline time and is reflected in the restart dialog.

  ▶ Installed update's deployment type is Required and restarts are suppressed in the deployment.

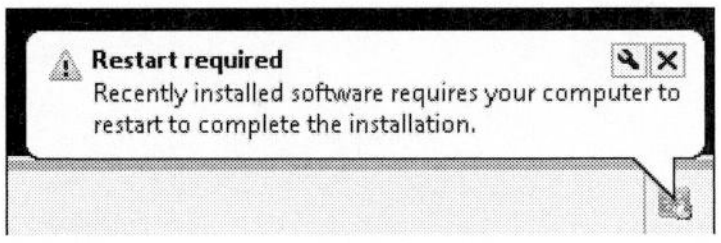

FIGURE 14.24   Restart notification.

▶ A restart notification informing the user that a restart is required and will be automatically initiated after a countdown. This notification (refer to Figure 14.6) is similar to the one shown in Figure 14.24 but also lists the amount of time until the restart is automatically initiated. This type of notification is displayed when the installed update's deployment type is Required and the deployment is past its deadline.

The countdown time used is set in the client settings on the Computer Restart page. An additional unclosable notification is displayed to the end user when the final restart countdown threshold is reached.

Right-clicking the restart notification icon shows two options:

▶ **Open restart window:** This opens the restart dialog shown in Figure 14.25 if a restart is wanted, or the one shown in Figure 14.26 if a restart is required. For desired restarts, you can choose to restart now or schedule a reminder for 1, 2, or 4 hours. For required updates, a simple countdown progress bar is shown along with RESTART and HIDE buttons.

▶ **Restart now:** Displays a restart dialog with a warning message, a RESTART, and a CANCEL button. Clicking RESTART on this dialog immediately initiates a system restart.

FIGURE 14.25   Restart Your Computer dialog.

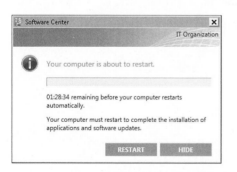

FIGURE 14.26   Restart Countdown dialog.

The Software Center also displays a RESTART button if the selected update requires a restart. Clicking RESTART in the Software Center has the same result as the Restart now option on the restart dialog, as shown in Figure 14.25.

Monitoring Software Updates

How do you know what software updates were installed where? Without this information, it is difficult to assure yourself, your boss, upper management, and the auditors that ConfigMgr is doing its part in keeping your enterprise compliant and safe. The next sections discuss how you can check individual update status and update deployment status in the console as well as using reporting for complete software updates tracking.

CAUTION: UPDATE COMPLIANCE STATUS DELAY

As mentioned in the "Compliance Scanning" section, state information for updates is not sent in real-time from clients back to the server. Instead, it is queued and sent based on the State Messaging client setting by each client. Thus, results for all compliance scans may be slightly delayed, so give your clients some breathing room to complete their state message transfer before hammering the Refresh button.

Individual Update Status

You can spot check individual updates in the console by selecting them under All Software Updates in the Software Library workspace. Each update listed in this view by default shows how many systems require its installation and an overall compliance percentage for all systems. A small pie chart also displays on the Summary tab in the Detail pane, showing the number of systems in each compliance state for the update (see the "Compliance Scanning" section for details on the various states). Multiselecting updates hides the Detail pane, so you cannot get a summarized pie chart from multiple updates in this view.

Update Deployment Status

The **Deployments** node in the Monitoring workspace lists all available deployments. Sort by the Feature Type column to quickly isolate all software update deployments in use; filtering narrows the results even more. Selecting a deployment here shows summarized information for the deployment in the Detail pane, including a combined pie chart showing the update compliance status for all updates in the deployment. If the deployment is for a single update, this view does not provide much value. If, however, the deployment is for a software update group, the pie chart adds value.

Double-clicking a deployment creates a sticky node under the Deployment node in the navigation tree. Selecting this sticky node shows detailed information about the compliance status of the updates in the deployment. The view pane shows four tabs, one for each compliance state. Listed under each tab is the number of systems for that compliance state and the actual systems with that compliance state are listed in the Asset Details pane at the bottom.

WSUS administrators should applaud this view of updates, as this summary of update compliance and status information is easy to access in WSUS but not in ConfigMgr 2007. The authors anticipate that this view will be the main hangout for ConfigMgr administrators interested in software updates status information. The information displayed here is summarized from information in the actual database. Summarizations are automatically run on a periodic basis and can be forced by choosing the **Run Summarization** option from the ribbon bar. The time of the last summarization is displayed in the upper right of the view pane along with links to Run Summarization and Refresh the view.

Reporting

Reports are the final source for monitoring and reporting on actual update status, compliance, and installation results. Reports are advantageous because the consumer of the update status information does not require access to the ConfigMgr console to view the data. As described in Chapter 18, "Reporting," reports are flexible and do not require specific ConfigMgr administrator involvement.

Out-of-the-box, ConfigMgr contains 31 specific software update reports. This should be sufficient for most organizations. The beauty of reporting services though is that you or another user can create custom reports for your specific needs and organization. Chapter 18 discusses creating custom reports.

A Super-Quick Walkthrough

This section provides a high-level outline of the steps to go through to deploy your first updates in a lab. If you used software updates management in ConfigMgr 2007, this process is much simpler and should be intuitive.

1. Install and configure WSUS discussed in the "Prerequisites for Software Updates" section.

2. Install and configure a SUP as discussed in the "Software Update Point Placement" section.

3. Synchronize the update catalog as discussed in the "Update Synchronization" section. Note that this takes a significant amount of time depending upon your Internet connection speed and performance of the system(s) used for WSUS and the SUP.

4. Configure your client agent settings as discussed in the "Client Settings" section. In general, for a lab environment, the default settings are all sufficient.

5. Use the **All Software Updates** node in the Software Library workspace to locate the updates that you would like to deploy to clients as described in the "All Software Updates" section and create update deployments from these updates as described in the "Update Deployments" section. Alternatively, create an ADR as described in the "Automatic Deployment Rules" section.

For a real production rollout, repeat step 5 every month or patch cycle interval or simply use ADRs.

Troubleshooting Software Updates

There are many points where the software update process can break down. Multiple components coordinate their efforts to make the process hum along normally; however, when something goes wrong, the first step is identifying the component that is having issues. Depending on the exact failure point, you can review a variety of log files for error messages. It is also important to track and report on the status of software updates to management. The next sections discuss how to monitor software updates as well as those areas that typically have issues and how to diagnose and (hopefully) fix them.

In addition to the information presented here, three excellent blog posts are available that review and step through the in-depth minutia of the software updates process as viewed through the log files:

- ▶ http://blogs.msdn.com/b/steverac/archive/2011/04/10/software-updates-internals-mms-2011-session-part-i.aspx

- ▶ http://blogs.msdn.com/b/steverac/archive/2011/04/16/software-updates-internals-mms-2011-session-part-ii.aspx

- ▶ http://blogs.msdn.com/b/steverac/archive/2011/04/30/software-updates-internals-mms-2011-session-part-iii.aspx

WSUS and SUP

The first component in software updates is WSUS. WSUS is significant because it acquires all information about available updates and distributes that catalog of updates to clients. Luckily, ConfigMgr takes over control of WSUS by using a SUP, and creates detailed log files of the WSUS operation. Here are the three main log files for WSUS and an SUP, located in *<ConfigMgrInstallPath>*\Logs:

- ▶ **WCM.log:** Provides information about the software update point configuration and connecting to the WSUS server for subscribed update categories, classifications, and languages.

- ▶ **WSUSCtrl.log:** Provides information about the configuration, database connectivity, and health of the WSUS server for the site.

- ▶ **wsyncmgr.log:** Provides information about the software updates synchronization process.

Most errors experienced with WSUS are configuration errors, including not matching the ports configured during installation of WSUS and then configured in the SUP.

Also common are Internet connectivity issues due to firewalls, proxy servers, or other mitigating factors. Always confirm that the system running WSUS has Internet connectivity if you are downloading the update catalog directly from Microsoft, and ensure that you have properly configured the proxy account if one is required.

In the course of writing this chapter, the authors encountered the following error on several occasions during the initial catalog synchronization process:

```
Not enough storage is available to process this command.
```

This was clearly an out-of-memory error on the CAS. The first time it was encountered, the wsyncmgr.log clearly displayed the error. The second time was somewhat more difficult to diagnose. The initial symptom was an error code 500—Internal server error— returned from the CAS to both child primary sites during their update synchronizations; this was also recorded in wsyncmgr.log on the child sites. Because by default IIS does not display detailed error information to remote systems and the log did not display the URL that was being accessed, it was necessary to find the URL by other means. This was easy enough to do by checking the IIS log on the CAS itself. It was then possible to use Internet Explorer to browse to the URL on the CAS; the page returned then revealed the same error message.

Two points from this troubleshooting exercise:

▶ ConfigMgr has many moving parts. Knowing them all and being comfortable digging through their various logs is crucial.

▶ A CAS server hosting its own SQL Server instance requires more than 4GB of memory. (Note that this is well below the minimum recommended memory for a CAS but due to resource constraints was all that was initially configured in the lab used to write this book.)

Downloading Updates

It is possible for an update download from Microsoft to fail. Recall WSUS does not download the updates in ConfigMgr; you must manually initiate download of all updates when not using ADRs. This is an interactive process; the ConfigMgr console initiates a connection to the Microsoft download servers using the credentials of the user currently logged in to the console. You can easily test connectivity for the current user by opening Internet Explorer and navigating to http://www.microsoft.com/downloads. (If a proxy server is required to connect to the Internet, configure the settings in Internet Explorer.) If the logged-in user does not have permission to perform the action, the download will not take place.

For ADRs, the site server hosting the SUP downloads the updates for you. This is done using the that system's Local System account which in turn uses that system's Active Directory computer account for its identity on the network. This is configurable as described in the "Software Update Point Placement" section.

The PatchDownloader.log file records download activity for updates and contains information about the update download process. The file is located in one of two places:

▶ **%ProgramFiles%\Microsoft Configuration Manager\Logs**: If you run the console on the site server.

▶ **%*ProgramFiles%*\Microsoft Configuration Manager Console\AdminConsole\ AdminUILog:** If you run the console remotely.

Client Update Scanning and Deployment

The WUA on the local system handles the process of scanning a client for applicable updates. The ConfigMgr agent initiates the scanning according to the defined schedules or any on demand requests; the WUA in turn reports to the ConfigMgr agent. The following client-side log files, located in the %*windir*%\CCM\logs folder, can help when investigating failures:

▶ **ScanAgent.log:** Provides information about the scan requests for software updates, the tool requested for the scan, the WSUS location, and so on.

▶ **UpdatesDeployment.log:** Provides information about the deployment on the client. This includes software update activation, evaluation, and enforcement.

▶ **UpdatesHandler.log:** Provides information about software update compliance scanning as well as download and installation of software updates on the client.

▶ **UpdatesStore.log:** Provides information about the compliance status for software updates assessed during the compliance scan cycle.

▶ **WUAHandler.log:** Provides information about when the Windows Update Agent on the client searches for software updates.

One of the main issues that can affect the scanning process is having a domain-based GPO override the Windows Updates settings. The WUAHandler.log file clearly indicates if this issue exists in your environment.

Beyond the Built-In Update Process

Although the built-in software update process is robust and flexible, it may not fit into every organization's update methodology or meet the specific or exact requirements for software update timing or procedures. To this end, there are two specific options to help fill the gap:

▶ **Task sequences:** These are built into ConfigMgr itself. Described in Chapter 19, "Operating System Deployment," task sequences enable a set of ordered tasks to be executed on a system. Using a custom task sequence and the built-in Install Software Update task, you can coordinate the deployment of software updates with other tasks on a single system such as reboots, software deployments, or other custom actions including scripts. Examples of other custom actions include shutting down line-of-business applications, pausing or disabling anti-virus or anti-malware protection, and initiating a backup.

▶ **Orchestration:** If further flexibility is needed, such as coordinating the software update activity among multiple machines in a cluster or a set of systems that host an application, using a product designed specifically for this is recommended.

Coordinating actions such as this among multiple systems is called *orchestration* and is the domain of one of Microsoft's newer System Center components: System Center 2012 Orchestrator. Its use is well beyond the scope of this book, however. For further information, check out *System Center 2012 Orchestrator Unleashed*, available at http://www.amazon.com/System-Center-2012-Orchestrator-Unleashed/dp/0672336103.

System Center Update Publisher

One shortfall of Microsoft's update catalog used by WSUS and ConfigMgr is that it does not contain any non-Microsoft updates. This isn't Microsoft's fault: How could they possibly keep up with or be responsible for tracking and providing the updates for the multitudes of other products used worldwide? However, Microsoft provides a great tool so that third parties including vendors and administrators can publish their own catalogs for use with ConfigMgr software updates—System Center Updates Publisher 2011.

SCUP is not actually included with ConfigMgr but is a separate and free download from Microsoft, available at http://www.microsoft.com/download/en/details.aspx?id=11940. Using this tool, you can import updates from non-Microsoft products into ConfigMgr or define your own for third-party products or in-house applications; these non-Microsoft updates sit side-by-side with the Microsoft updates in the ConfigMgr console and are managed and deployed the same as Microsoft updates contained in the WSUS catalog.

Interestingly, many administrators also use SCUP to deploy Microsoft updates not included in the WSUS catalog. Updates are updates, and managing them the same way—regardless of their source—has great value. In ConfigMgr 2007, some enterprising administrators even used SCUP to deploy and manage whole applications. This was useful because the update deployment model is state based and very similar to the new application deployment capabilities of System Center 2012 Configuration Manager.

SCUP Installation

You can install SCUP on any system with connectivity to your top-level SUP, including the site server or a remote workstation that also has the WSUS admin console installed (or full WSUS) and runs one of the following operating systems:

- ▶ Windows 7 SP 1
- ▶ Windows Server 2008 R2 SP 1
- ▶ Windows Server 2008 SP 2
- ▶ Windows Vista SP 2

A prerequisite for SCUP 2011 is a hotfix for WSUS, described in Microsoft KB article 2530678 at http://support.microsoft.com/kb/2530678. The SCUP installation provides a convenient link that opens a web page for this article. You should install this hotfix on every site system in your hierarchy that has a SUP.

SCUP uses a local SQL Server Compact Edition database so there is no need to provide any permissions or connectivity to a full SQL Server instance. SQL Server Compact Edition (CE) is a local, single-user, Microsoft Access-like database engine automatically installed with SCUP. For more information on SQL Server CE, see http://technet.microsoft.com/en-us/library/ms173037(v=sql.105).aspx. Using SQL Server CE as the database unfortunately has several negative ramifications in an enterprise:

▶ A single SCUP installation cannot be simultaneously opened by multiple users.

▶ It is initially configured only in the user's profile that installed SCUP and so is not sharable. You can remedy this in an unsupported manner using the information at http://myitforum.com/cs2/blogs/rzander/archive/2011/05/30/scup-2011-with-shared-database.aspx.

SCUP installation is quite straightforward; launch the downloaded Windows Installer package and follow the wizard.

SCUP Configuration

SCUP includes its own separate console and requires a small amount of initial configuration. After launching the SCUP console (shown in Figure 14.27), select the application menu from the ribbon bar, and then choose **Options**.

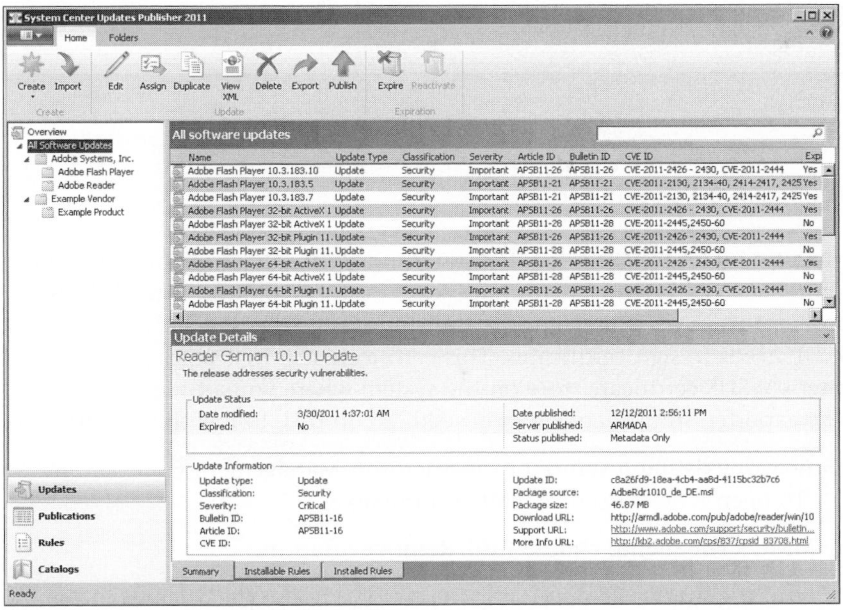

FIGURE 14.27   The SCUP Console.

There are five sections in the resulting Options dialog:

▶ **Update Server:** On this page (shown in Figure 14.28), you enable update publishing and configure the options that SCUP uses to connect to the SUP so that it can publish updates. You should specify the top-level site in your hierarchy.

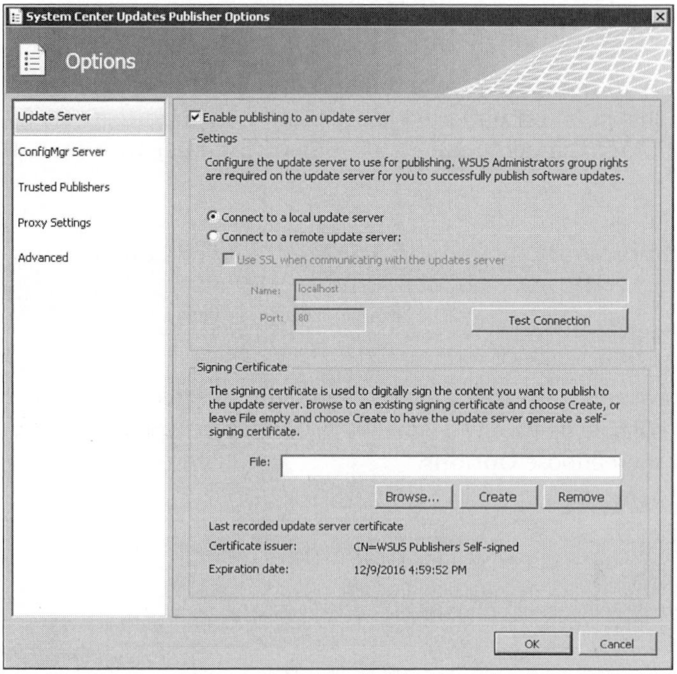

FIGURE 14.28   SCUP Update Server Options.

Publishing updates into a SUP also requires a signing certificate so clients can verify the source of updates delivered to them. The "easy button" solution is to click the **Create** button on this page, which automatically creates a self-signed certificate for use when SCUP needs to sign certificates. This certificate is initially stored in the local computer's WSUS certificate store on the system where you are running SCUP and should be exported from there when needed. To do this, follow these steps:

1. Open a new or existing instance of the Microsoft Management Console (MMC). To open a new instance, launch **mmc.exe**.

2. On the MMC's File menu, choose **Add/Remove Snap-in**.

3. On the resulting Add or Remove Snap-ins dialog, choose **Certificates** in the Available Snap-ins list box on the right, and press the **Add** button.

4. In the Certificates snap-in dialog, choose **Computer account**, click **Next**, leave Local computer selected on the next page, and click **Finish**.

5. Click **OK** on the Add or Remove Snap-ins dialog.

6. In the tree on the left, expand **Console Root -> Certificates (Local Computer) -> WSUS**, and select the resulting **Certificates** node.

7. The Detail pane on the right lists the certificate generated by SCUP and is named **WSUS Publishers Self-signed**. Right-click this certificate, and choose **All Tasks -> Export** to launch the Certificate Export Wizard.

8. In the Certificate Export Wizard, choose **No**, do not export the private key on the first page, **DER Encoded Binary** on the second page, enter an appropriate file name in the third page (with **.cer** for the filename extension), and finally finish the wizard by clicking **Finish** on the last page.

You can also choose to use a certificate generated by an internal public key infrastructure (PKI) or a public certificate authority such as Verisign. The only requirement is that the certificate is a code-signing certificate. Some public certificate authorities call these types of certificates "Microsoft Authenticode" certificates. Use the **Browse** button on this page to import an externally generated certificate.

NOTE: PUBLIC CERTIFICATE AUTHORITIES

If you choose to use a public certificate authority, ensure you are explicit when requesting the certificate and that you test your issued certificate thoroughly. Special use certificates like the one required for SCUP sometimes require you to jump through extra hoops when using a public certificate authority. What these hoops are is dependent on the public certificate authority itself.

For whichever certificate authority you choose to use, you must also add the certificate to the Trusted Publishers store on all systems running SCUP and all SUPs in your hierarchy. In addition, the certificate must also be in the computer's Trusted Publishers store on a client before it can install any updates signed by the certificate.

The certificate must also be trusted by any system including those hosting SCUP, SUPs, and clients. For self-signed certificates, this is easily accomplished by adding the certificate to the computer's Trusted Root Authorities store on those systems. Certificates issued by your internal PKI or a public certificate authority (CA) should already be trusted but you should verify this to make sure.

One last requirement on any client where you want to deploy updates published using SCUP is to enable the **Allow signed content from intranet Microsoft update service location** setting. This is typically set using a group policy and can be found under **Computer Configuration -> Administrative Templates -> Windows Components -> Windows Update** in the group policy object editor.

> **NOTE: CERTIFICATE MANAGEMENT**
>
> The ins and outs of managing certificates; certificate theory and practice; whether you should use a self-signed certificate, internal PKI, or public CA; detailed instructions for actual management of certificates in an enterprise; or anything PKI related are large topics on their own and well beyond the scope of this book.
>
> However, here are several recommendations to briefly address some of these points:
>
> ▶ Unless you already have a PKI established, using a self-signed certificate is sufficient for SCUP usage in most organizations.
>
> ▶ The best way to add a certificate to a certificate store en masse across your organization is to use group policy; a brief step-by-step example is located at http://technet.microsoft.com/en-us/library/cc770315(WS.10).aspx.

Updates from third parties will not use this certificate as their updates will be signed by their own signing certificate, so you or the WUA on managed clients can verify the update's source.

▶ **ConfigMgr Server:** Configure ConfigMgr integration on this page; specifically the top-level site with which SCUP should communicate—whether local or remote—when publishing updates. Enabling ConfigMgr integration allows SCUP to query the compliance status of updates and only fully publish them in ConfigMgr if actually requested by clients, and if they fall under a particular size. Prior to fully publishing updates, the two thresholds at the bottom of this page are checked:

   ▶ **Requested client count (threshold):** This is the minimum number of clients that must request an update.

   ▶ **Package source size threshold (MB):** This is the maximum size of the content for an update.

If either of these requirements is not met, then updates are only published in a metadata only fashion as described in the "Publication" section.

▶ **Trusted Publisher:** This page lists trusted certificates used to sign updates imported in third-party catalogs. You cannot add certificates here; you can only remove or view them.

▶ **Proxy Settings:** Configure proxy settings as necessary for SCUP to download third-party update catalogs and to connect to the SUP or ConfigMgr.

▶ **Advanced:** A handful of additional options exist on this page. In general, there is no need to change these.

   ▶ **Database file:** This is the SQL Compact Edition database file used by SCUP; it is read-only and is user-specific.

   ▶ **Add timestamp when signing updates:** This adds a timestamp from an authoritative Internet source when signing updates; this is useful because it makes updates deployable even after the certificate used to sign them has expired. With this option enabled, the updates are always deployable, as long as the updates were signed during the valid lifetime of the signing certificate. If this option is not chosen, updates signed by an expired certificate cannot be deployed.

▶ **Check for new catalog alerts on startup:** This option enables alerts when starting the console to notify you of updated update catalogs.

▶ **Enable certificate revocation checking for digitally signed catalog files:** Selecting this option verifies that the certificates used to sign imported update catalogs have not been revoked.

▶ **Always check the My Documents\LocalSourcePublishing folder for software update content before attempting to download from the specified Download URL:** Using this option enables you to manually download content referenced in update catalogs instead of SCUP automatically downloading the content. This option is useful for SCUP consoles not connected to the Internet.

▶ **Use a custom local source path:** Use this option to specify a custom local path string for manually downloaded content.

▶ **Software Update Cleanup Wizard:** This launches a wizard that searches for updates published in ConfigMgr that are not in the default WSUS catalog and are also not in the SCUP repository.

These are updates previously published by SCUP that have been deleted from SCUP and thus orphaned in ConfigMgr. If any updates meeting these criteria are found, you can select them to be cleaned up. Cleaning up an update expires it in ConfigMgr, making it no longer deployable. This is irreversible and should only be done on updates no longer needed.

Catalogs

Catalogs in SCUP contain the actual updates that you import and publish into ConfigMgr. You do not actually publish whole catalogs into ConfigMgr using SCUP; they are containers that make it easy to import and export groups of related updates from or to other SCUP publishers or user. Catalogs are managed from the Catalogs workspace in the SCUP console.

Third-party vendors can use SCUP to create update catalogs for their own products and then make these catalogs available to you for direct import and use in ConfigMgr using SCUP. There are two types of catalogs: those from Microsoft partners and directly listed in SCUP, and those from other sources.

You directly import catalogs from Microsoft partners in the SCUP console by going to the Catalogs workspace and choosing **Add Catalogs** from the ribbon bar. This launches the Add Partners Software Updates Catalogs dialog, listing available catalogs where you pick which update catalogs you wish to import into SCUP. The list of catalogs also includes download URLs, support URLs, and descriptions. Importing a catalog into SCUP is not the same as actually publishing the updates into ConfigMgr, so this step is harmless and reversible with respect to ConfigMgr.

Catalogs from other sources include:

▶ Commercial catalogs for third-party products directly from the vendors of those products

▶ Commercial, third-party update aggregators such as SCUPdates from Shavlik, which includes updates for other, frequently compromised third-party products such as Apple's iTunes, Oracle's Java Runtime Environment, and Mozilla's Firefox

▶ Community catalogs

▶ Your own, internal catalogs

To import one of these types of catalogs, navigate to the Catalogs workspace, and press the **Add** button on the ribbon bar. This launches the Add Software Update Catalog Wizard where you input five pieces of information:

▶ **Catalog Path:** The path to the CAB file containing the catalog. This can be a local path, a UNC, or a URL.

▶ **Publisher:** The name of the publisher of the catalog. You can use the name entered here to sort and filter updates in the SCUP console as well as the ConfigMgr console.

▶ **Name:** The name of the catalog.

▶ **Description:** An applicable description for the catalog.

▶ **Support URL:** A URL where support information for the catalog can be accessed.

After adding a catalog to SCUP, you must also import the updates in that catalog into SCUP to use them. You do this by selecting or multiselecting the update catalogs listed in the Catalogs workspace and choosing **Import** from the ribbon bar or right-click context-menu. This launches the simple Import Software Updates Catalog Wizard. There are no real options in this wizard except selecting additional or deselecting chosen catalogs for import.

During the update import process, you may be presented with a Security Warning dialog asking you accept content from the publisher. Choosing to **Always accept content from the publisher** trusts the publisher and accepts all future content from that publisher. You can view or remove the code signing certificate from that publisher in the Trusted Publisher page of the Options dialog, as described in the "SCUP Configuration" section of this chapter.

Also available from the Catalogs workspace are options to **Edit** and **Remove** a catalog from the ribbon bar or right-click context menus of the catalogs. You cannot actually edit a vendor-signed catalog; selecting the Edit option displays a dialog box with read-only information about the catalog. Removing a catalog does not remove the updates imported from that catalog.

Publications

Publications group updates for mass publishing into ConfigMgr, enabling their use and deployment or for export to a catalog that you can distribute to others. The use of publications is optional and of themselves have no real functionality; think of them as update lists.

You view existing publications from the Publications workspace in the console. To create a publication, choose the Publication tab in the ribbon bar, and choose **Create**. You can also create publications from selected updates in the Updates workspace by selecting those updates and choosing **Assign** or **Publish** from the ribbon bar or right-click context menu as described next in the "Updates" section.

Existing publications are listed in the navigation list box on the left—this is a simple list rather than a tree, as there is no hierarchy with publications. Selecting a publication displays the list of updates it contains. Additional options available from the Home tab of the ribbon bar for a selected publication include the following:

▶ **Export:** This exports all the selected publication's updates to a catalog in the form of a CAB file that you can then provide to other SCUP users.

▶ **Publish:** This actually publishes the selected publication's updates into ConfigMgr, making them available for compliance scanning or installation depending upon their publication type as discussed in the "Updates and Publication Types" section.

Here are the following options available on the Publication tab of the ribbon bar for a selected publication:

▶ **Edit:** Displays a simple dialog box where you can change the name of a Publication.

▶ **Delete:** Deletes the selected Publication.

These options are also available on the right-click context menu of a publication; however, the Edit option is listed as Rename.

Also available on the Home tab of the ribbon bar and right-click context menu for updates listed in a publication is the option to remove the selected update(s) from the publication and change the publication type for the selected updates.

Updates

All updates imported into SCUP and ready for publication into ConfigMgr are listed in the Updates workspace. Updates are organized under the All Software Updates node in the navigation tree by their publisher, and then by their applicable product. Using the Search box on the upper right of the update list, you can filter the list of updates currently displayed.

The Detail pane at the bottom displays detailed information about the selected update from the update list. If you select multiple updates, information from the first update selected is displayed in the Detail pane.

Update Operations

For each update, you can choose one of several different operations from the ribbon bar or the update's right-click context menu; most of these operations are valid and available when multiple updates are selected. Here are the options:

▶ **Edit:** This option, also accessible by double-clicking any update, displays the Edit Software Update Wizard where you can edit all aspects of the update. A detailed description of the many options available in this wizard is covered in the "Custom Updates" section. In general, modifying updates from a third-party vendor catalog is not recommended.

▶ **Assign:** This adds an update to an existing publication or to a new publication. Adding an update to a publication does not publish it to ConfigMgr.

▶ **Duplicate:** As its name implies, this creates an exact replica of an update; the new update's name is automatically prefixed with the text "Copy of".

▶ **View XML:** This option shows you the raw XML that defines an update. It is sometimes useful to see the raw XML for updates to view hidden options and identifiers not displayed in SCUP or ConfigMgr. Another benefit of this option is that you can review all of the rules associated with an update.

▶ **Delete:** This deletes an update from SCUP. If the update is published into ConfigMgr, this orphans the update and makes it unmanageable. To clean-up orphaned updates, use the Software Update Cleanup Wizard previously described in the "SCUP Configuration" section. Using the delete option is not recommended for updates in a catalog supplied by a third-party vendor; you should allow the vendor to do this for their catalog.

▶ **Export:** This exports the selected updates to a catalog in the form of a CAB file that you can then provide to other SCUP users.

▶ **Publish:** This publishes an update directly to ConfigMgr using one of the three publication types as described in the "Updates and Publication Types" section. Note that the update is not placed into a publication.

▶ **Expire:** This expires updates so that ConfigMgr can no longer deploy them. When the update's expiration is published to the SUP, it is irreversible, and your only course of action is to create a new update, possibly using the Duplicate option, if the update is still needed.

▶ **Reactivate:** This reactivates updates that are expired in SCUP but not published to ConfigMgr. Some vendors include expired updates in their catalogs so you can use them if the newer updates have not yet been approved for use in your organization. If this is the case, use this option to reactivate them and then publish them. As just mentioned with the Expire option, after an update is published as Expired to the SUP it cannot be reactivated, so you should only reactivate an update before you initially publish it.

CAUTION: UPDATE EXPIRATION

Before expiring any update, know the caveats listed in this section. Specifically, the reactivate option is not applicable to published updates that are expired: Expiring published updates closes the door on ever using them again.

Updates must be published either directly using the Publish option from the **All Software Updates** list in the Updates workspace or in the Publications workspace. Simply adding an update to a publication does not publish the update in ConfigMgr.

Updates can exist in multiple publications or none at all but are published only once to ConfigMgr if at all. Every occurrence of an update in a publication or the All Software Updates list shares the same publication type and date.

Updates and Publication Types

There are three types of update publications; these are actually set on a per update basis and are not set on or specific to an entire publication. In other words, each update, whether in a publication or not, may have a different publication type:

▶ **Metadata only:** This type of publication publishes only the metadata information for an update in ConfigMgr. This enables only compliance scanning for the update in ConfigMgr.

▶ **Full-content:** Full content publications publish both the update's metadata and the update's content, enabling ConfigMgr compliance scanning as well as update deployment.

▶ **Automatic:** You can use this type of publication only if you have ConfigMgr integration enabled and properly configured as described in the "SCUP Configuration" section. This hybrid publication type initially publishes only the metadata for an update. Then, based upon the ConfigMgr Server integration settings—Requested client count and Package source size threshold—SCUP automatically publishes the full-content of update.

To change the publication type of an update or multiple updates, select the update(s) in the Updates or Publications workspace; then from the Home tab of the ribbon bar or the right-click-content menu, choose one of the three different publication types.

Custom Updates

A primary use of SCUP is creating custom updates that sit alongside the Microsoft updates for your own line of business applications or even third-party applications in use in your environment.

The first step in creating your own custom updates is to create the folder structure in the navigation tree on the **Updates** workspace, starting with the vendor at the top level, and then adding a folder for the product.

1. Select the **All Software Updates** node, and choose **Create Vendor** from the right-click context menu, or choose **Vendor** from the drop-down menu shown when you select **Create** from the Folders tab of the ribbon bar. Enter the vendor name in the resulting dialog box.

2. Select the new vendor folder you just created, and choose **Create Product** from the right-click context menu, or choose **Product** from the drop-down menu shown when you select **Create** from the Folders tab of the ribbon bar. Enter the product name in the resulting dialog box.

Alternatively, you can use an existing vendor or product folder; vendor folders may contain multiple product folders and products may contain multiple updates. Updates are displayed in the Updates view on the right when a product folder is selected in the navigation tree.

The **Delete** and **Edit** options are available from the right-click context menu of a selected vendor or product folder and the ribbon bar; the **Edit** option shows a dialog box, where you can rename the folder.

Updates must be in one of the following forms:

▶ Windows executable (.exe)

▶ Microsoft Installer file (.msi)

▶ Microsoft Installer Patch file (.msp)

Windows Update (.msu) files are not directly supported because WSUS does not support them. To get around this limitation, use a wrapper technology such as IExpress. Some formal but dated Microsoft documentation exists for IExpress as do third-party walkthroughs and guides; you can find these by searching for IExpress on the Internet.

To create a new update, choose **Create** from the Home tab of the ribbon bar, and then select **Software Update** from the resulting drop-down. You do not have to select any specific node or node type in the navigation tree for this option to work. This launches the Create Software Update Wizard with the following pages and information to provide:

▶ **Package Information:** This page contains information about the update package you are creating.

   ▶ **Package source:** This is the location of the actual update file and must be one of the valid types just listed. This file is used only as a point of reference and to establish a file name; it is not actually captured or placed into the update created.

   ▶ **Use a local source to publish software update content:** If selected, this option designates that the content source used by ConfigMgr to download the actual update file specified in the Package source option is a local folder rather than a location specified by the next option. The local directory is My Documents\LocalSourcePublishing by default but is configurable on the Advanced page of the Options dialog, as discussed in the "SCUP Configuration" section.

This option is useful when creating updates for your own internal use and the SCUP console is installed on your site server.

▶ **Download URL (or UNC):** This field specifies the content source location used by ConfigMgr to download the actual update file specified in the Package source option. If the previous option is selected, this field is grayed out and is not fillable.

▶ **Binary Language:** The language of the update file specified in the Package source field.

▶ **Success return codes:** Codes returned from the update upon a successful installation. A typically success return code is 0, but this may vary. Manually test the update or consult the documentation of the vendor that created the update file to ensure you have accounted for all valid success return codes.

▶ **Success pending reboot codes:** Similar to the Success return codes, these codes are returned from a successful update installation that requires a reboot. Updates should never reboot the system on their own.

▶ **Command line:** The actual command-line options and properties to run the update on a target system. The specified options should suppress reboots, all user interaction, and fully automate installing the update. Consult the vendor's documentation for information on how to achieve this and then verify by manually testing the complete command line.

Do not include the update filename in this field, only the options or properties. For MSIs and MSPs, the proper options to make them silent and unattended are added automatically and should not be specified.

If the package source is an MSI or MSP, the last four fields are populated automatically for you, as the values are standard or extractable from the source file.

▶ **Required Information:** The information on this page defines the metadata published into WSUS, displayed in the ConfigMgr console, and used by ConfigMgr to determine if the update should be included in the catalog, including the following:

> ▶ Language
>
> ▶ Title
>
> ▶ Description
>
> ▶ Classification
>
> ▶ Vendor
>
> ▶ Product
>
> ▶ More Info URL

14

▶ **Optional Information:** Additional metadata is specified on this page. This information is displayed in the ConfigMgr console and can be used for filtering and sorting in the console but is not directly used by ConfigMgr. Each field's definition is subjective and definable for your own needs. Fields on this page include:

   ▶ Bulletin ID

   ▶ CVE ID

   ▶ Support URL

   ▶ Severity

   ▶ Impact

   ▶ Restart behavior

▶ **Prerequisites:** On this page, define the prerequisites that must already be in place on a target system for an update to be scanned for compliance. Valid prerequisites include other updates from SCUP and detectoids. *Detectoids* are high-level rules that the WUA can evaluate quickly. You can choose from a set of well-known WSUS detectoids but cannot create your own in SCUP. There are two groups of well-known WSUS detectoids: CPU Architecture and OS language.

▶ **Superseded Updates:** On this page, select which updates, if any, that are superseded by this new update. You can only choose updates in SCUP.

▶ **Installable Rules:** This page defines the update applicability rules; these rules are used by the WUA to scan the local system and determine if it requires the update. You combine rules on this page using typical Boolean logic constructs such as AND, OR, and NOT. For a brief discussion of rules, see the "Rules" section of this chapter.

   Using prerequisites is preferred to using installable rules when possible as prerequisites are essentially pre-evaluated and thus incur very little overhead.

▶ **Installed Rules:** Similar to the installable rules, these rules define how the WUA verifies the update is installed. In some cases, these rules may be identical to the installable rules; this is perfectly valid.

▶ **Summary**

▶ **Progress**

▶ **Confirmation**

In addition to individual updates, you can create update bundles. Although not that common, update bundles ensure a specific set updates is deployed at the same time. The WUA handles update bundles similar to updates.

You create a software update bundle by selecting **Create** from the Home tab of the ribbon bar, and then **Software Update Bundle** from the resulting drop-down. You do not have to select any specific node or node type in the navigation tree for this option to work. This launches the Create Software Update Bundle Wizard with the following pages, which are all identical to those in the Create Software Updates Wizard except the Optional Information and Bundle updates pages:

▶ **Required Information**

▶ **Optional Information:** This page differs from the one in the Create Software Wizard only because of the lack of the Impact and Restart behavior options.

▶ **Prerequisites**

▶ **Superseded Updates**

▶ **Bundle Updates:** Select the updates you want to include in the bundle on this page.

▶ **Summary**

▶ **Progress**

▶ **Confirmation**

Editing an update or update bundle displays the same editor used to create the update or update bundle with the word Create replaced by Edit in the wizard's title.

Rules

Rules are similar to the rules that you create in compliance settings, as described in Chapter 10. Rules are the checks that the WUA uses to determine if an update is required on a system and verify that an update has been successfully installed.

The rules workspace lists all previously saved rules. Note that just because a rule is used by an update does not mean it is saved. You must explicitly save a rule before it appears in this workspace; there are no default saved rules in SCUP.

Use the Rules workspace to construct and save reusable rules for use with the installable and installed rule's definitions in updates. You can also create rules directly in the software update wizard on the **Installable Rules** and **Installed Rules** pages using the small disk icon. To load a previously saved rule on these pages, first click the new rule button (looks like a yellow starburst) and choose **Saved Rule** from the Rule type drop-down.

You can create four different rule types:

▶ File

▶ Registry

▶ System

▶ Windows Installer

Each rule type is self-explanatory to configure and not covered in depth here. However, because they are nearly identical to the rules used in compliance settings, you can reference Chapter 10 for detailed explanations.

Quick Walkthrough

The user interface (UI) for SCUP 2011 was streamlined quite a bit from the previous version (SCUP 4.5), and moved to the new System Center UI framework which is straight-forward to use. Here is a quick, summarized walkthrough of the steps involved for publishing your first update:

1. Configure the initial options as discussed in the "SCUP Configuration" section.

2. Import a third-party catalog as discussed in the "Catalogs" section, or create your own updates as discussed in the "Custom Updates" section.

3. In the Updates workspace, select the update(s) you want to publish. Choose **Publish** from the ribbon bar and complete the basic wizard choosing the publication type for the selected updates.

4. After a catalog synchronization (described in the "Update Synchronization" section), the updates appear in the ConfigMgr console side-by-side with the Microsoft update. Filtering by the vendor or product is useful to view these published updates.

Using NAP to Protect Your Network

A Windows 2008 or Windows 2008 R2 server installed with the NPS role implements system health checks against Windows systems on the network. Those systems failing these health checks are subject to various actions, including

▶ Reporting

▶ Network access denial

▶ Quarantined with limited network access

The Network Access Protection (NAP) functionality included in System Center 2012 Configuration Manager extends the NAP functionality built in to Windows Server 2008 and 2008 R2, implementing a system health check based on the required software updates configured in ConfigMgr. NAP in System Center 2012 Configuration Manager is almost completely unchanged from NAP in ConfigMgr 2007 but is slightly streamlined: There is no dedicated section in the console, and there are no separate policies to configure; you simply enable required updates for evaluation. The next sections discuss this process.

NAP Prerequisites

ConfigMgr implements NAP using a separate site system role—the system health validator (SHV) point. Install this new role on a Windows Server 2008 or Server 2008 R2 system that has the NPS role already installed. (Installing and configuring the NPS role is beyond the scope of this book; for detailed information including step-by-step guides, see http://technet.microsoft.com/en-us/network/bb545879.aspx.) Perform the following steps on this system to install the SHV:

1. Navigate to the Administration workspace.

2. In the navigation tree, under Overview, expand **Site Configuration**, and select **Servers and Site System Roles**. All currently installed site systems display on the right.

3. To use an existing site server, right-click it, and choose **Add Site System Roles** to launch the Add Site System Roles Wizard, as shown in Figure 14.2.

   If you use a remote installation of NPS on a system that is not currently a site system, you must first make the system a site system by right-clicking the **Servers and Site System Roles** node in the navigation tree and selecting **Create Site System Server**.

4. On the System Role Selection page of the Add Site System Roles Wizard or the Create Site System Server Wizard, select **System Health Validator Point**. This adds a single, information-only subpage to the wizard: System Health Validator. After reviewing this page, finish the wizard.

The SHV point in ConfigMgr is actually a plug-in for the Windows Server NPS role and infrastructure. NAP compliance policies that you configure in ConfigMgr are communicated to and enforced by the NAP infrastructure.

To use NAP, you must extend AD for ConfigMgr (see Chapter 3, "Looking Inside Configuration Manager," for details). Extending AD is required because NAP uses the System container to store health state references. The site server publishes health state references used during client evaluation to ensure the most current policies are used. Because of NAP's reliance on AD, the small amount of configuration for the SHV point revolves around AD. To configure the SHV, open the Administration workspace, and select **Sites** under **Overview -> Site Configuration** in the navigation tree. The list of currently manageable sites displays on the right. Right-click the site you want to configure, and choose **Configure site-wide components** if the site is a CAS or **Configure Site Components** otherwise. Finally, choose **System Health Validator Point**. Alternatively, select the site, push **Configure Site Components** from the ribbon bar at the top, and then choose **System Health Validator Point**. This shows the System Health Validator Point Properties dialog, which has two pages and the following settings:

▶ **General:** This page configures general SHV parameters.

   ▶ **Active Directory query interval:** The interval the SHV queries AD for system health references. System health references are cached on the SHV for normal use.

   ▶ **Statement of health validity period:** On this section of the page, specify a Validity period in hours for a client's statement of health (SoH)—discussed in the "System Health" section. You may also specify a UTC date and time that the SoH must have been created after.

▶ **Health State Reference:** This page enables and configures settings for communicating with SHVs in a different forest. The accounts specified are used to publish and query health state information in AD in the System Management container. The following settings exist on this page:

  ▶ **Domain suffix**

  ▶ **Health state reference publishing account**

  ▶ **Health state reference querying account**

Health state references are used during compliance validation as discussed in the "Client Compliance" section.

On the client side, NAP works only with Windows Vista, Windows 7, Windows Server 2008, Windows Server 2008 R2, and Windows XP SP 3 (and above) clients. These are the only operating systems that include the NPS agent. Unfortunately, no download is available to make any other version of Windows work with NPS or NAP.

Agent Settings

By default, the NPS client agent is disabled in a ConfigMgr site and must be enabled. You can do this for the entire site or specific collections using the new granular client settings discussed in Chapter 9. Here are the settings available in the Network Access Protection section of a client settings object:

▶ **Enable Network Access Protection on clients:** Enables NAP enforcement on the clients to which this client settings object applies.

▶ **Use UTC (Coordinated Universal Time) for evaluation time:** This configures the client agent to assess computer system health according to UTC time rather than client local time. This setting is beneficial for those clients that roam between time zones, and ensures re-evaluations are performed on a fixed time scale rather than a variable one caused by the client moving between the time zones.

▶ **Require a new scan for each evaluation:** This option ensures cached evaluation results are not used when a client reconnects to a network in between configured evaluation times. Forcing an additional scan can cause delays in connecting to the network, which can adversely affect mobile systems; however, not re-scanning a mobile system when it reconnects to the network creates a small amount of risk that the system's health state changed since the last health scan and is now compromised.

▶ **NAP re-evaluation schedule:** This option lets you set either a simple or a detailed schedule of when you want to perform a system health check.

System Health

Those clients subject to the policies of the NPS report to the NPS using their built-in NPS client. The NPS client agent retrieves policies from the NPS and evaluates the health of a system against the checks defined in the policy encapsulating the results, known as an SoH. The SoH contains results from all the checks performed on the system, and the NPS client agent submits the SoH to the NPS. The NPS receives the SoH and compares it against the NPS policies:

▶ If the system appears compliant with the policies, it is allowed on the network.

▶ If deemed noncompliant, the system can be granted limited access to the network, allowing for correction of any issues that caused it to be considered noncompliant.

NPS policies, known as health policies, are based on SHVs. These SHVs plug in to the NPS server and enable performing specific checks on a client to validate its health. As an example, the built-in Windows Security SHV defines checks for the status of the Windows Firewall, existence of antivirus software, and other settings typically associated with the Windows Security Center. Each check results in one of two states: Pass or Fail. The status of a client as a whole may also be reported in one of three additional states:

▶ **Transitional:** This state indicates that the client is not ready to report its status. In the ConfigMgr context, this could mean the client agent is not yet enabled on the system.

▶ **Infected:** This state is primarily used by antivirus SHVs and is not used by the ConfigMgr client.

▶ **Unknown:** This is a catchall state often used to indicate client credential issues.

The health policies define which SHVs to use and what conditions must be met for a system to match a health policy. Here are the conditions that are possible in a health policy:

▶ Client passes all SHV checks.

▶ Client fails all SHV checks.

▶ Client passes one or more SHV checks.

▶ Client fails one or more SHV checks.

▶ Client reported as transitional by one or more SHVs.

▶ Client reported as infected by one or more SHVs.

▶ Client reported as unknown by one or more SHVs.

The ConfigMgr SHV point implements the SHV that plugs in to an NPS. The policies produced by this SHV instruct the NPS client agent to compare the exact patch status of a system against the applicable required updates configured in the ConfigMgr console. Perform the following steps to enable updates for NPS evaluation:

1. Select the **All Software Updates** node or any child folder that also displays updates including folders or software update group sticky nodes.

2. Select or multiselect the wanted updates in the list.

   Updates must be in a required deployment before you can enable them for NAP Evaluation. If you use multiselect, all selected updates must be in a required deployment. While selecting updates, you can use the full filtering and searching capabilities of the console as described in the "All Software Updates" section of this chapter.

3. From the ribbon bar or the right-click context menu, choose **Properties** and navigate to the **NAP Evaluation** tab. On this tab, shown in Figure 14.29, you enable the selected updates for NAP evaluation and set the time that the updates are considered for client health compliance checks by NAP.

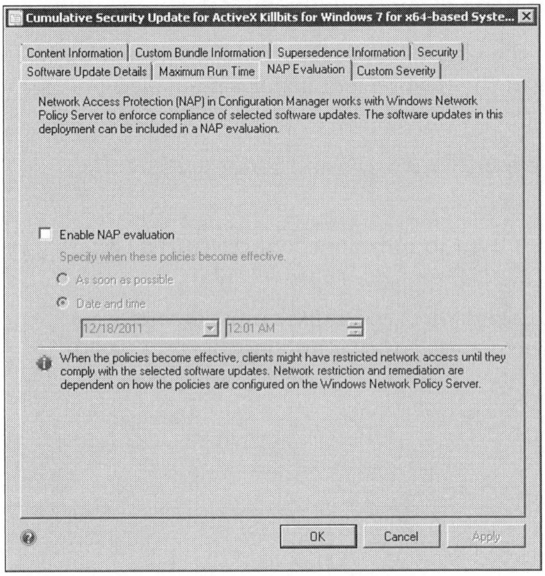

FIGURE 14.29   NAP Evaluation tab.

To review which updates are enabled for NAP evaluation, **NAP Evaluation** is provided as a possible criteria to filter the list of updates on in the console, as shown in Figure 14.30.

A System Health agent (SHA) is a component that plugs into the NPS agent on the client; each server-side SHV has a corresponding client-side SHA. SHAs perform the actual checks on a system and produce the Pass/Fail results that go into the client's SoH.

The ConfigMgr client implements the ConfigMgr SHA. This SHA performs the actual comparison of the current update status on the client with the mandatory deployments applicable to the system, adding the results to the SoH for that system.

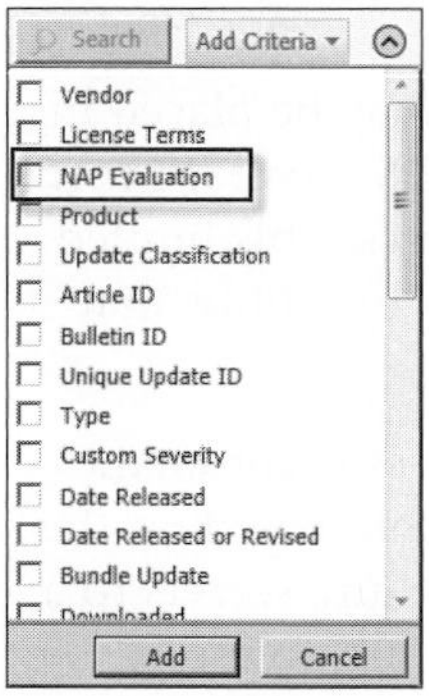

FIGURE 14.30   NAP Evaluation filter criteria.

Client Compliance

The ConfigMgr SHA first performs a series of nonconfigurable checks to determine the compliance state of the client. These checks include the following:

▶ **Is this a new client?** If a new client has not downloaded the policies yet, the client is marked as compliant.

▶ **Are the site code and site ID invalid?** If yes, the client is marked as Unknown.

▶ **Is the NAP client agent disabled?** If yes, the client is marked as compliant.

▶ **Is the SoH older than the "Validity" period?** If yes, mark the client as noncompliant.

▶ **Is the SoH older than the "Date created must be after" date?** If yes, mark the client as noncompliant.

The final two checks above use thresholds set on the System Health Validator Point Component Properties, as discussed in the "NAP Prerequisites" section.

If any of these checks succeed, the status updates in the SoH and the series of checks cease. If the client makes it through these checks, the SHA compares the configured NAP polices against the client. Unlike ConfigMgr 2007, client health policies are not explicitly defined in the console. As previously described in the "System Health" section, you simply enable individual or multiple sets of updates for NAP evaluation. This transparently creates the health policies for use by NAP, which are not exposed in any way in the ConfigMgr console.

In addition to actually evaluating the SoH submitted by the client, the SHV also retrieves health state references from AD that are periodically published by the ConfigMgr SHV point. Health state references enable the SHV to verify a client's site and if the client used the latest ConfigMgr NAP policies.

Remediation

If the ConfigMgr SHV deems a client system noncompliant, the system may be placed in a quarantine status based on the Network Policy configuration on the NPS server. In this quarantine status, the client system has limited access to network resources. This limited network connectivity, known as *remediation*, allows the client to correct conditions that caused it to be noncompliant.

With System Center 2012 Configuration Manager, the remediation process is automatic—the client automatically requests updates from ConfigMgr and installs them based on the NAP policies. The only required configuration is to add specific infrastructure servers to a remediation server group in the NPS. This group identifies which servers are accessible by systems placed into the quarantine status. You should add the following types of servers that host critical network services into this group:

▶ DNS servers for name resolution

▶ Domain controllers for authentication and group policy

▶ A global catalog server for locating Configuration Manager 2012 services

Do not place ConfigMgr servers in the remediation server group because access to these systems is dynamically granted.

TIP: UTILIZING REMEDIATION TO PROTECT AGAINST ZERO-DAY EXPLOITS

Although the obvious purpose for remediation is to prevent systems from accessing the network that are not patched up to a defined level, a not-so-obvious purpose is to deploy updates for zero-day exploits. In this case, you can use NAP to deploy updates by configuring a specific NAP policy for the update and making it effective immediately. As clients check in with your NPS infrastructure, they will immediately be out of compliance and fall into remediation, and automatically install the update. You must also ensure that the patch is available in a deployment package in this scenario.

Although it comes with some overhead in the form of the Windows Server NPS role, NAP increases the security posture of your network greatly by interrogating systems as they try to connect to the network and enforcing a minimum patch level. It can also help you deploy updates for those annoying (and upper-management attention-getting) zero-day exploits.

Summary

Although many tools exist for maintaining and deploying updates to Windows systems, software updates in System Center 2012 Configuration Manager implements a best of breed, single-stop-shop by integrating the process into a robust, cradle-to-grave, systems management tool. By using existing software tools such as WSUS and the WUA, ConfigMgr can leverage existing, known-good processes and code while extending them to new levels. This chapter discussed the ConfigMgr software update functionality, implementing it successfully within your organization, and taking advantage of supplementary tools such as SCUP and NAP. The combination of these tools gives you the flexibility to deploy updates in a manner that is user-friendly and meets the needs of your organization, large or small.

14

Mobile Device Management

As mobile devices continue to enter the enterprise at an ever-increasing pace, their proliferation elevates the priority for Information Technology (IT) to manage these devices. This challenge is fueled by additional information being distributed to these devices and users requesting access to more functions and services. Allowing use of these devices in a corporate setting can make users more mobile and efficient, saving time in their daily work.

For IT professionals, using mobile devices in a corporate environment presents challenges in managing risks and data:

▶ **Sensitive data:** Sensitive data is now accessible on mobile devices; this device might even be a personal phone.

▶ **Personal phones:** Not all organizations provide corporate mobile phones. Using a bring your own device (BYOD) strategy can make the line between business and private data and usage narrow and almost nonexistent as corporate and user data are on the same device.

▶ **Different device types:** Multiple types of devices may be used in a corporate setting, whether these are corporate or personal devices. Managing these different mobile platforms brings additional challenges because they have different feature sets. This makes it important to implement a clear policy and strategy on how these devices may be used.

These challenges are even more significant than managing laptops, as people tend to take mobile devices wherever they go. However, laptops are typically well protected by anti-virus software, firewalls, patch management, and in some cases even hard drive encryption. A mobile phone, which tends to be always with you and is exposed to daily threats, seldom has any of the protections extended to laptops. Its most common protection is to have a personal identification number (PIN) for the SIM card.

These are considerations for IT when implementing a mobile device strategy.

Planning for Mobile Device Management

You must understand the differences between the different mobile platforms when deciding how to implement mobile device management (MDM). The authors suggest you assess needs and risks before starting a mobile device management project. A good requirements specification on how the devices should be utilized is useful for this type of project. Many people look at the features of a mobile device management platform rather than the entire scenario; not realizing some mobile devices do not have the management capabilities that others have. Here are areas to consider:

▶ If you plan to store corporate data on mobile devices, assess the risks and classification of the data on those devices. Implementing a BYOD strategy should include considerations of data classification and different access methods for the different types of data in your environment. One approach is *sandboxed applications*, this "sandboxes" corporate data in a separate container that can be secured with passwords and other authentication mechanisms; non-business data is kept separately, and users can continue to use their devices for personal use.

Using this approach, should the device be lost or the employee leaves the company; you can wipe corporate data from the device while leaving personal data intact. The downside is this method often limits use of the phone for email and calendaring, often considered the greatest advantage of having an integrated device.

▶ Multiple device types can affect corporate support policies. Although these different types of devices may enable users to be more efficient on their chosen devices, it increases the complexity of managing them and makes this approach more expensive to support and maintain.

▶ Passwords are seldom used on devices today, even when they contain sensitive data. Users carry their personal life on the device, including pictures, messages, emails, and so on, without any concern of security. Adding corporate data to these devices makes them even more at risk. The authors advise adding a password policy to your devices to protect them from access, along with a wipe policy that destroys the data on the device if the wrong password is entered a certain number of times.

▶ Controlling applications on the devices is rather challenging because different vendors use different methods to make applications available. Windows Phone and Android each have their marketplace, and Apple has its App Store; this makes it almost impossible to control the applications users can run and download. Privacy between applications is also a challenge; some applications require access to other applications (such as calendar data) to run. If you are in a high-security environment in which you need to protect data, you should consider limiting access to these marketplaces. Blackberry has the most extended way to handle this today, whereas other vendors cannot even control this. This also should be considered in your requirements specification.

▶ You must consider a policy and strategy on how to back up devices. Some vendors offer backups to the cloud or locally to a personal computer. How is that backup secured, can it be backed up to any device, and is it encrypted?

Development of MDM software and mobile platforms will be an evolving process; Microsoft and others will continue developing their software, and partners will always extend the functionality further.

Overview of Mobile Device Management

Recognizing the challenges of managing mobile devices, Microsoft has taken the majority of features available in Mobile Device Manager 2008 and Configuration Manager (ConfigMgr) 2007 and consolidated them together into System Center 2012 Configuration Manager. This version of ConfigMgr also adds integration with Exchange ActiveSync functionality.

The approach presents two different levels of device management:

▶ **Light management:** This model uses Exchange ActiveSync, enabling broad support for different mobile platforms.

▶ **In-depth management:** The in-depth management model includes more functionality for device management. This model is supported only for a limited range of devices because it requires a client on the mobile device.

Each model has its own advantages. The light management model is applicable to more platforms, but its capabilities are limited. In-depth management provides more control, but the device set is currently limited to a subset of some older device types.

Light Management

The light management model is built on top of Exchange ActiveSync; it requires Exchange 2010 Server or Exchange Online through Office 365. This management model does not require a client on the device nor a public key infrastructure (PKI). Here are capabilities available with this model:

▶ **Inventory:** The Exchange Server Connector gives the System Center 2012 Configuration Manager administrator the ability to get a light limited inventory from Exchange on ActiveSync-enabled devices connected through the Exchange environment.

▶ **Controlling ActiveSync Policy:** The administrator can control the default Exchange ActiveSync policy through a single pane of glass.

▶ **Control:** You can use the ConfigMgr console to block devices from communication and wipe the device.

Exchange Server Connector

To configure the Exchange Server Connector, first identify some information about your Exchange environment, and if you use an on-premise or hosted Exchange solution.

▶ If you use an on-premise solution, obtain the name of the server(s) hosting the client access server (CAS) role.

▶ If using hosted Exchange, you need to know your hosted Exchange URL address.

Delegation of rights must be performed; use either the computer account of the site server or a specific account to perform the integration. This information is specified as account settings in the Add Exchange Server Wizard; see the "Account Settings" section for further information.

General Settings

To configure general settings, perform the following steps:

1. Navigate to the Administration workspace in the ConfigMgr 2012 console, expand Hierarchy Configuration, and select **Exchange Server Connectors**, as shown in Figure 15.1.

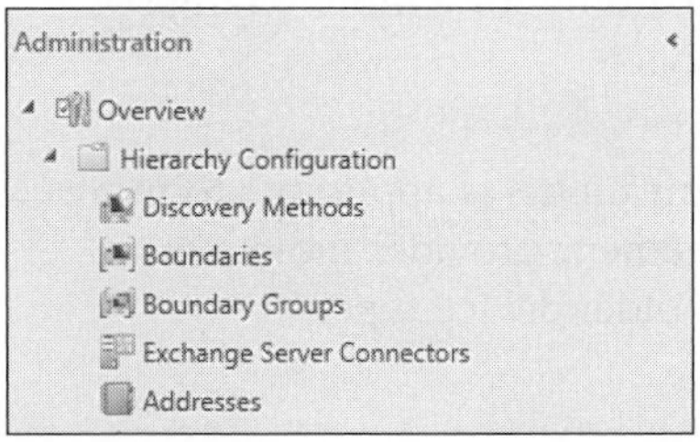

FIGURE 15.1   Navigating the console to the Exchange Server Connections node.

2. Under Exchange Server Connectors, right-click and open the **Add Exchange Server** Wizard.

3. Specify whether you are using an On-premise Exchange Server or Hosted Exchange Server, as shown in Figure 15.2.

   ▶ If using on-premise, enter the URL to your Exchange Client Access Server.

   ▶ If using Hosted Exchange, supply the URL of your hosted service.

When using the on-premise option, you can configure advanced configuration settings to specify the Exchange client access server the ConfigMgr server will use; if there are several client access servers and none are specified, ConfigMgr automatically selects an available server. If you want to use a proxy server for communication with the hosted Exchange Server, you can configure this under the proxy server option.

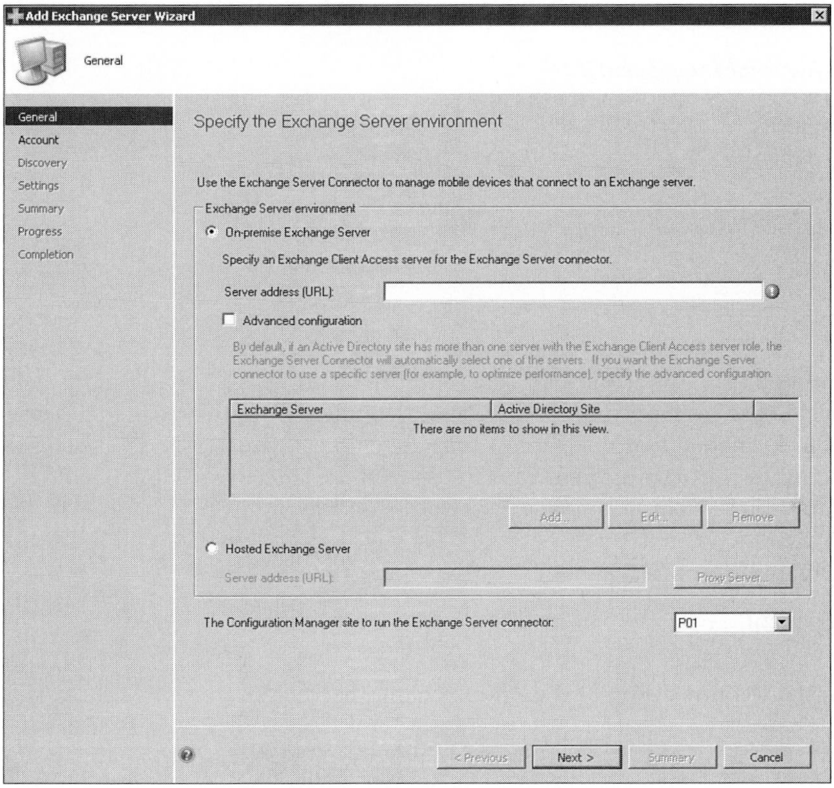

FIGURE 15.2   Specifying the Exchange Server environment.

Account Settings
To have full functionality with the Exchange Server Connector, specify an account with access to these Exchange PowerShell cmdlets:

▶ Set-ADServerSettings

▶ Get-ActiveSyncOrganizationSettings

▶ Get-ActiveSyncDeviceStatistics

▶ Get-ActiveSyncDevice

▶ Get-ExchangeServer

- `Get-Recipient`

- `Get-ActiveSyncMailboxPolicy`

- `Get-CASMailbox`

- `Set-ActiveSyncOrganizationSettings`

- `Set-CASMailbox`

- `Get-ActiveSyncDeviceAccessRule`

- `Set-ActiveSyncDeviceAccessRule`

- `New-ActiveSyncDeviceAccessRule`

- `Set-ActiveSyncMailboxPolicy`

- `New-ActiveSyncMailboxPolicy`

- `Remove-ActiveSyncDevice`

- `Clear-ActiveSyncDevice`

The authors recommend using the computer account of the ConfigMgr 2012 primary site server that you specified to perform these tasks. Should you decide to use the predefined management roles in Exchange that have access to these cmdlets, you must add the specified computer account or the account you want to use to these three management roles:

- Recipient Management

- View Only Organization Management

- Server Management

Figure 15.3 shows the Account dialog of the Add Exchange Server Wizard.

TIP: HOW TO ADD ACCOUNTS TO A ROLE GROUP

For information on adding accounts to a role group, see the Exchange documentation at http://technet.microsoft.com/en-us/library/dd638143.aspx.

Discovery Settings

When using a hosted Exchange solution, you must configure an account in the Discovery settings (refer to Figure 15.3). The Discovery page, displayed in Figure 15.4, has several options to configure:

- Timing of the full synchronization schedule

- Delta synchronization interval (240 minutes by default)

- The mobile devices to find

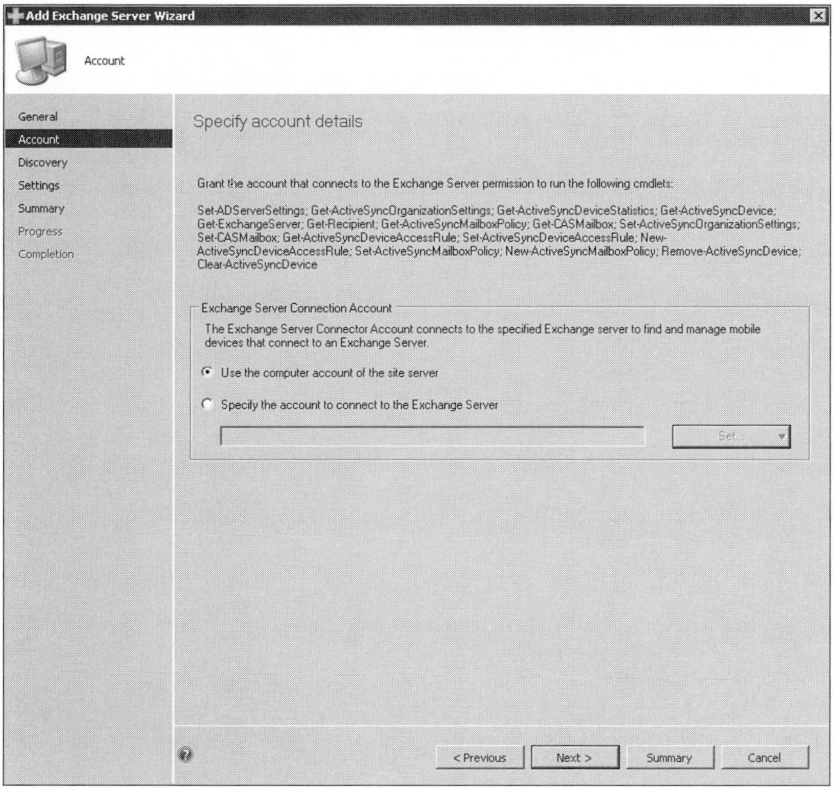

FIGURE 15.3   Specifying account settings.

This discovery finds new devices from Exchange but collects only a limited subset of values to decrease the performance impact on the Exchange Server. By default, the connector scans the entire Exchange organization for devices that have been active within 180 days. You have the option to change this or disable checking the age of the devices. For the scope, you can limit the discovery to one or multiple organizational units in Active Directory (AD), so only those users are discovered.

Settings

The settings available in the Exchange ActiveSync (EAS) Connector are limited to those settings available in Exchange, so this is a mirror of the settings in the default EAS Policy with the capability to manage them from System Center 2012 Configuration Manager. Should you want different settings for different users, this cannot be managed through ConfigMgr; you would have to use Exchange because ConfigMgr works only with the default policy for EAS.

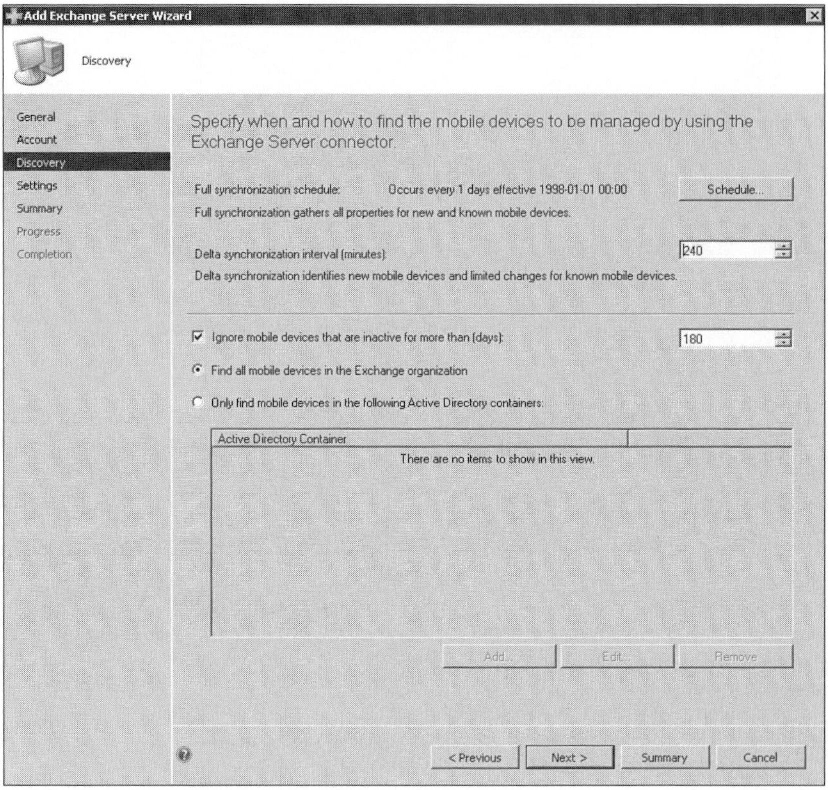

FIGURE 15.4   Specifying discovery settings.

As shown in Figure 15.5, you can specify settings for your mobile devices through the connector.

The Configure mobile devices general settings dialog, displayed in Figure 15.6, includes these options:

▶ Configure whether you should allow devices to participate in Internet sharing.

▶ Allow or disallow the device to synchronize with a computer.

▶ Specify whether a device that cannot be provisioned should be allowed to connect to the ActiveSync service.

▶ Configure the refresh interval, specifying how often the device updates its policy from the ActiveSync service.

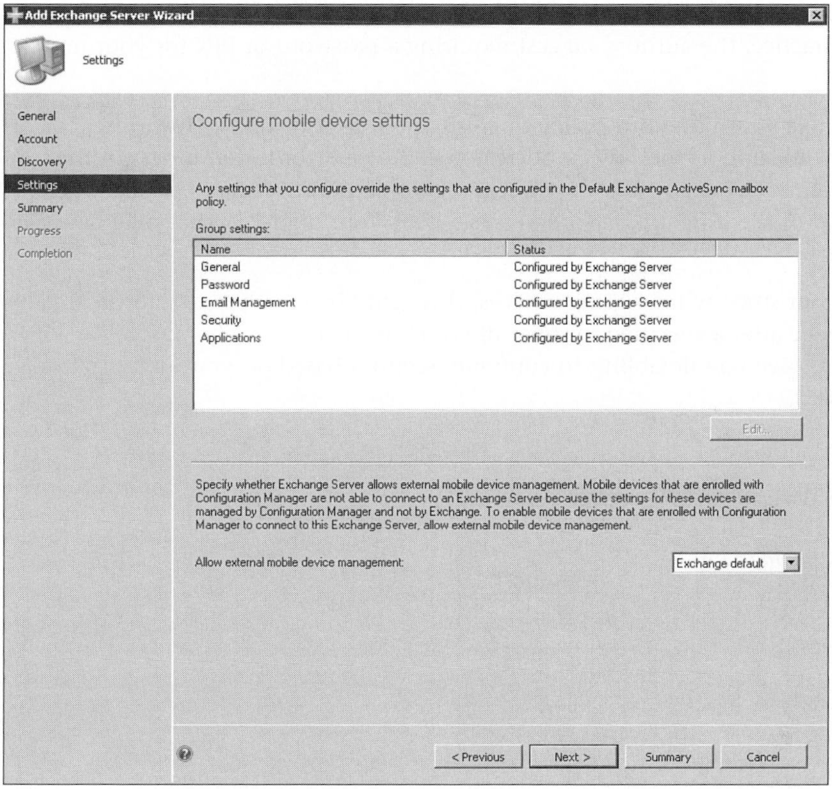

FIGURE 15.5   Specifying mobile device settings.

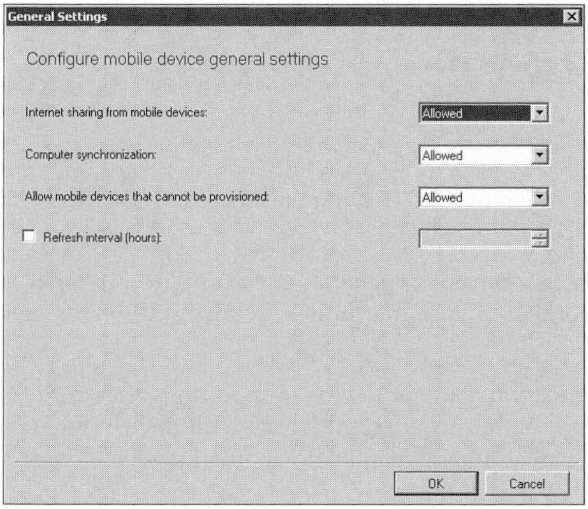

FIGURE 15.6   Specifying general device settings.

Figure 15.7 shows the Password Settings dialog, where you can control the settings for the device. As a best practice, the authors suggest requiring a password or PIN for your mobile devices.

▶ You can change your password policy or configure it as it is today. However, consider how to support locked-out devices and the password friendliness of the device. Sometimes a longer password is less secure then a short one because users may write down the longer password versus a short four-digit PIN that may be easier to remember.

▶ Determine your strategy for wiping devices; this could be whether you automatically wipe the device after a specified number of errors of the PIN or rely on remote wipe. These settings give you flexibility to configure security based on your organization's requirements.

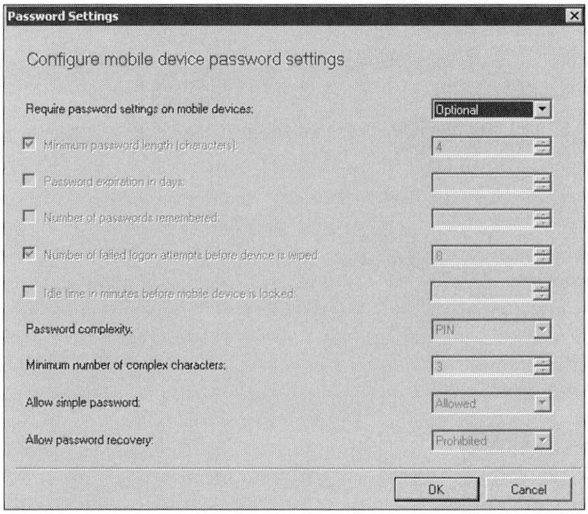

FIGURE 15.7   Specifying device password settings.

Email Management Settings, as displayed in Figure 15.8, let you configure basic settings for email functionality that are self-explanatory.

To control certain features on the devices in your policy, such as encrypting the storage card or prohibiting the camera or Bluetooth, configure that under Security Settings, as shown in Figure 15.9.

If you want to block or allow certain application on your devices, the settings shown in Figure 15.10 illustrate how you can do this. Note this does not work on all device types, and this does not give you the ability to block or allow applications on all devices—for example, Apple and Android devices.

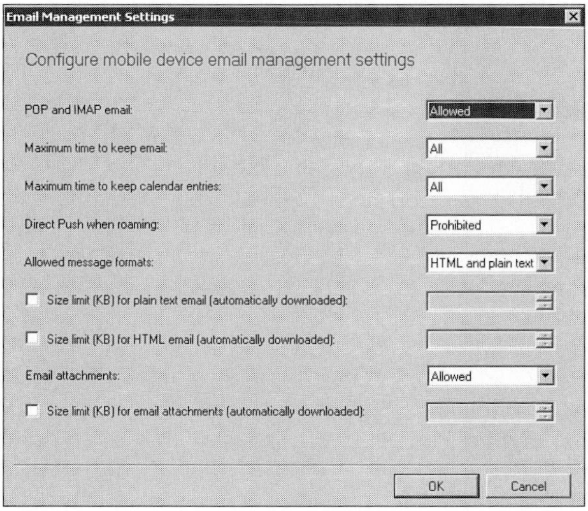

FIGURE 15.8   Specifying device email settings.

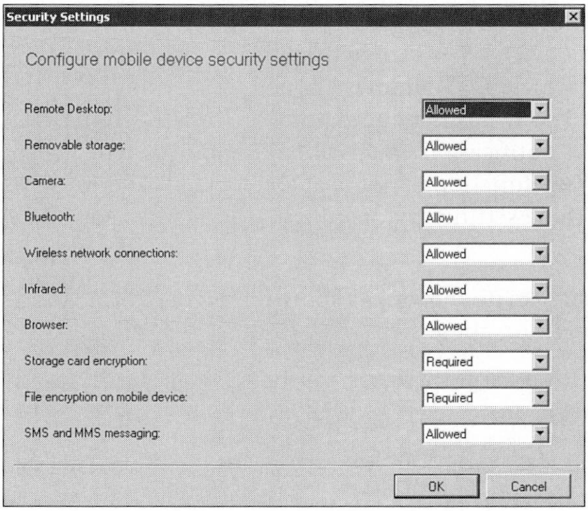

15

FIGURE 15.9   Specifying device security settings.

NOTE: TECHNET REFERENCE TO ACTIVESYNC SETTINGS

For additional information on settings for Exchange ActiveSync, see the documentation at http://technet.microsoft.com/en-us/library/bb123484.aspx. Some features also require an Exchange Enterprise Client Access License (CAL).

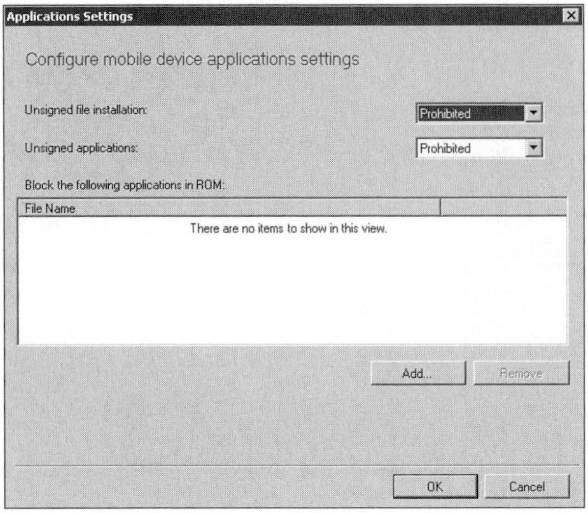

FIGURE 15.10   Specifying device application settings.

Access Rules

Access rules enable you to control which device types can communicate with the Exchange ActiveSync Service. In Figure 15.11, only Windows Phone (WP) is allowed, with all other devices put in quarantine. The two other alternatives are to allow or block access to the EAS service. You can also get notification emails about quarantined devices for the administrator to take action on. This function is not available when you create the Exchange ActiveSync Connector; access these settings by opening the Properties page for your connector.

To create additional access rules, select the **Create** button, as shown in Figure 15.11, to open the Create Access Rule dialog and perform these steps:

1. Choose the **Access level** you want to set, and then select either **Device family** or **Device model**. This is shown in Figure 15.12.

2. Select **Browse** (refer to Figure 15.12) for the option you are selecting, and the dialog displayed in Figure 15.13 or Figure 15.14 opens.

    Here you choose the specific device family or device model. The list will be populated with devices the Exchange Server Connector has identified; you cannot enter a new family or model until Exchange discovers it.

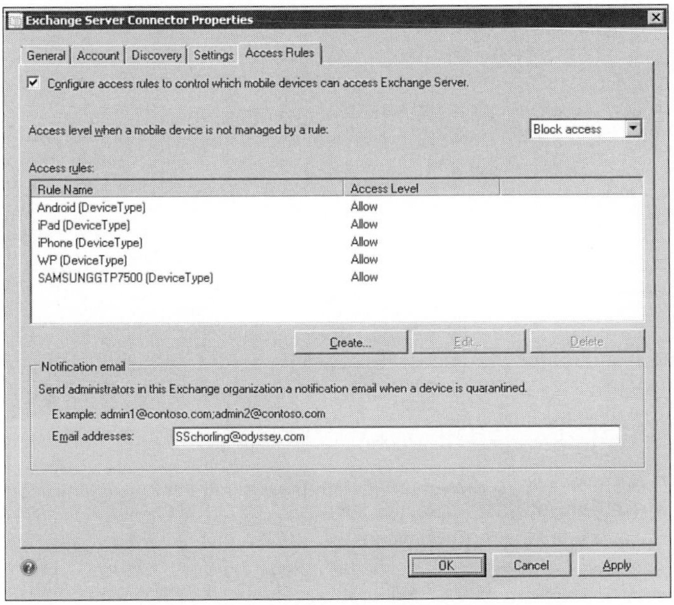

FIGURE 15.11   Setting up notification for access rules.

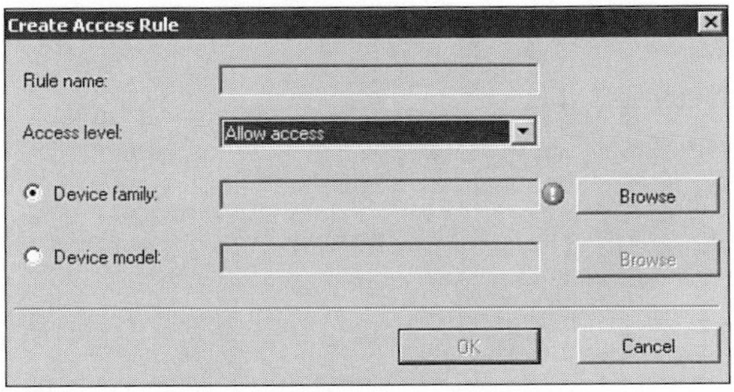

FIGURE 15.12   Creating an access rule.

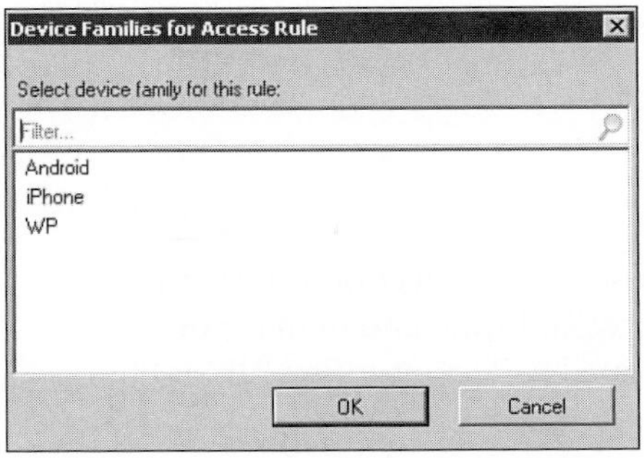

FIGURE 15.13   Specifying the device family for an access rule.

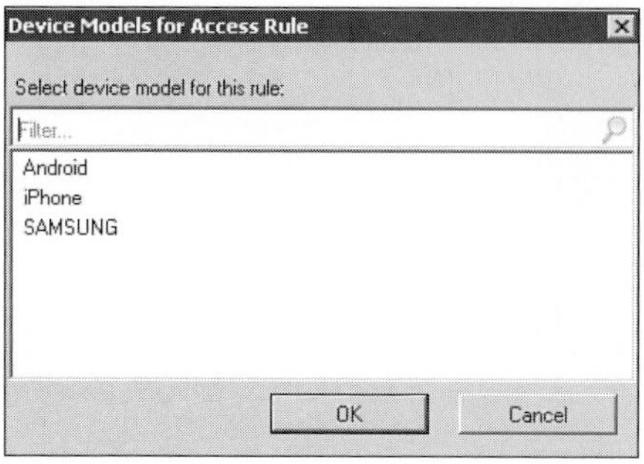

Device Models for Access Rule

Select device model for this rule:

Filter...

Android
iPhone
SAMSUNG

OK   Cancel

FIGURE 15.14   Specifying the device model for the access rule.

NOTE: ADDITIONAL OPTIONS FOR MICROSOFT THREAT MANAGEMENT GATEWAY OR ISA SERVER

If you use the Microsoft Threat Management gateway or Microsoft ISA Server to publish your Exchange ActiveSync, you can utilize these to control the devices allowed to communicate with Exchange ActiveSync, in which case the functionality is not restricted to Exchange 2010. The article at http://blogs.technet.com/b/exchange/archive/2008/09/05/3406212.aspx provides additional information.

Troubleshooting Light Management

Light Management relies on Exchange ActiveSync. From a Configuration Manager perspective, the only log file where you can track ongoing issues is EasDisc.log. This contains information about the Exchange Server Connector and is found under *<ConfigMgrInstallPath>*\Logs\.

Working with Devices

When working with devices, there are different areas where you will be navigating, discussed in the next sections. When working with those devices inventoried or connected to your environment, you will be navigating primarily under the Assets and Compliance workspace. You can use the collections and the functionality in the console such as the Resource Explorer and the right-click options to wipe or block devices.

The end user's mobile device experience will be based on the device itself or using the Application Catalog to manage and wipe their device.

Assets and Compliance

In System Center 2012 Configuration Manager, all assets and collection information is located under the Assets and Compliance workspace. To locate and manage devices, expand the Device Collections node to find a pre-created collection called All Mobile Devices, displayed in Figure 15.15.

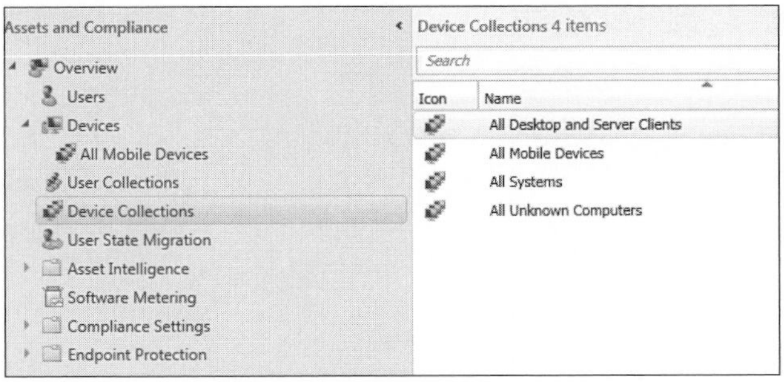

FIGURE 15.15   Assets and Compliance menu.

Resource Explorer
You can use the Resource Explorer to get additional information about a mobile device. From the ConfigMgr console, select the device, right-click, and start the Resource Explorer, as shown in Figure 15.16. The level of information available depends on whether the device is managed with the light or in-depth management method. Devices managed by the light management method have minimal information; this will be the same information stored in Microsoft Exchange about the device, meaning there is no information about installed applications. Figure 15.17 shows the Resource Explorer for a device managed with light management.

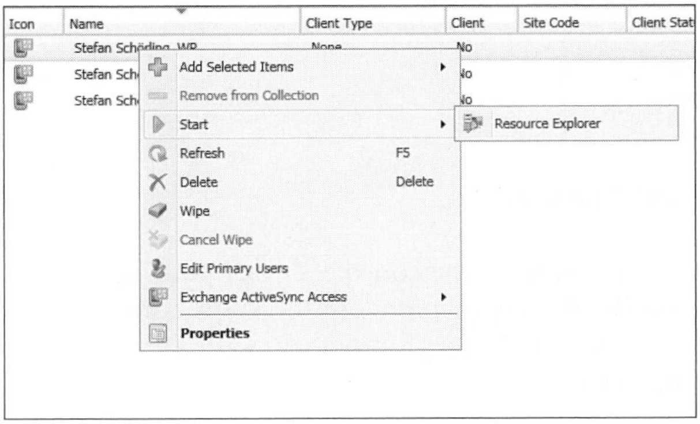

FIGURE 15.16   Opening the Resource Explorer.

Should you need to block a device from synchronizing via Exchange ActiveSync, you can block the device, as shown in Figure 15.18, and then later allow it to continue synchronizing again. This would be useful for lost devices that may be later found, rather than initiating a wipe request immediately. A wipe request erases all content on the phone.

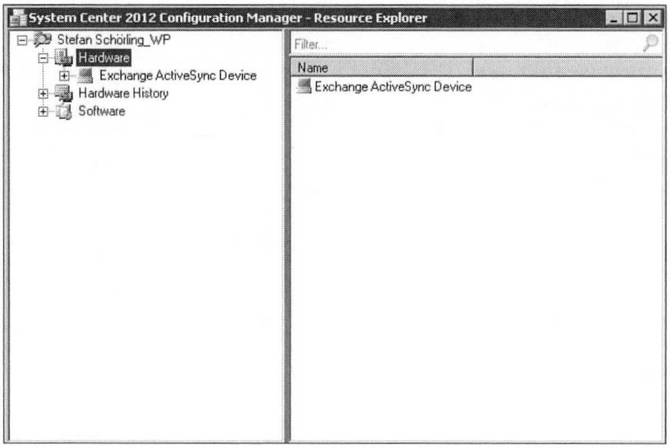

FIGURE 15.17   Viewing a light management device in the Resource Explorer.

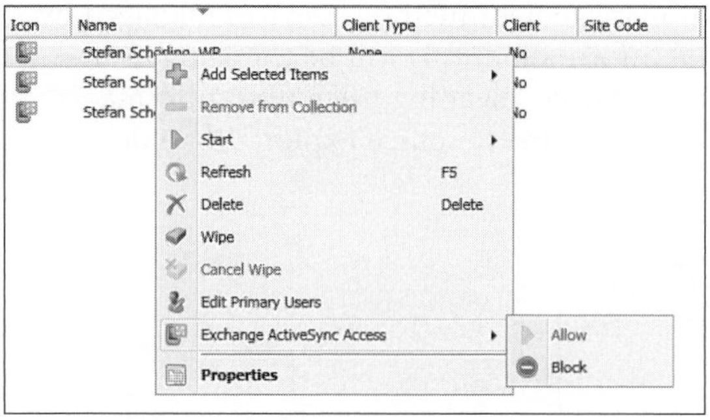

FIGURE 15.18   Blocking a device from synchronization.

Should you need to wipe a device, you can do so from the console. Locate your device in any collection, select it, and right-click on the device; then choose the **Wipe** command from the menu, as shown in Figure 15.19. Selecting Wipe prompts you with a warning (see Figure 15.20) if you want to wipe the device.

The device must be online or at some later point connect via ActiveSync to retrieve the command for a wipe. A stolen or offline device must get the wipe command after you initiate it to perform a wipe.

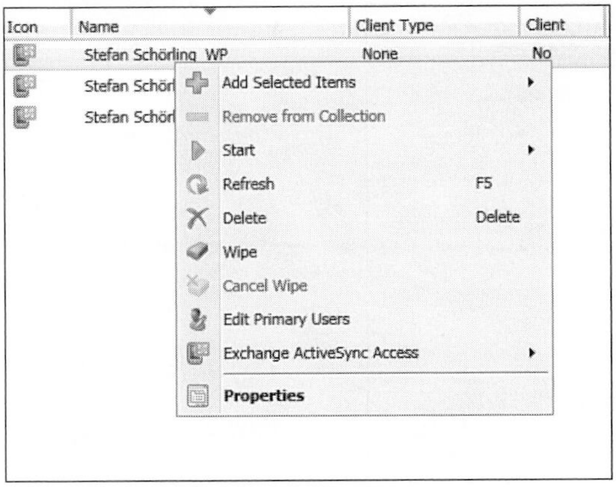

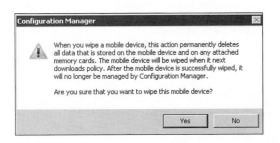

FIGURE 15.19   Initiate Wipe.

FIGURE 15.20   Warning before wiping a device.

End User Experience

Using the Application Catalog, end users can see their devices and initiate a wipe if they know they have lost their device. This is as easy as selecting their device and pressing **Wipe**, as shown in Figure 15.21. The users are prompted as to whether they want to continue (see Figure 15.22); the next time the device connects to Exchange, it receives the wipe command.

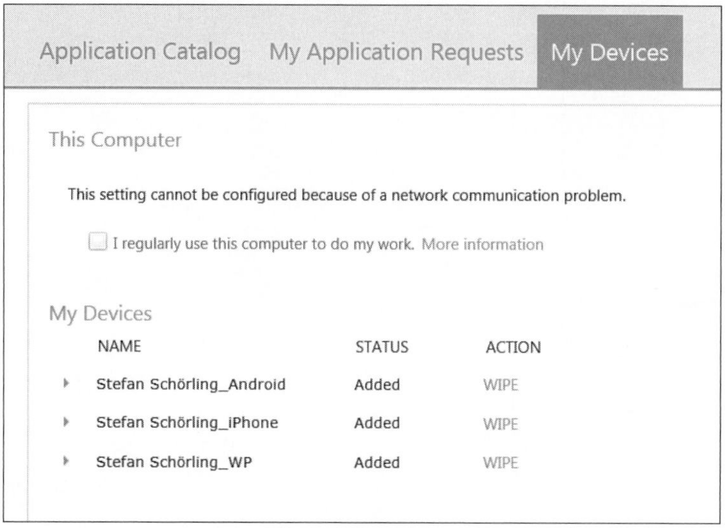

FIGURE 15.21   Selecting a device to wipe in the Application Catalog.

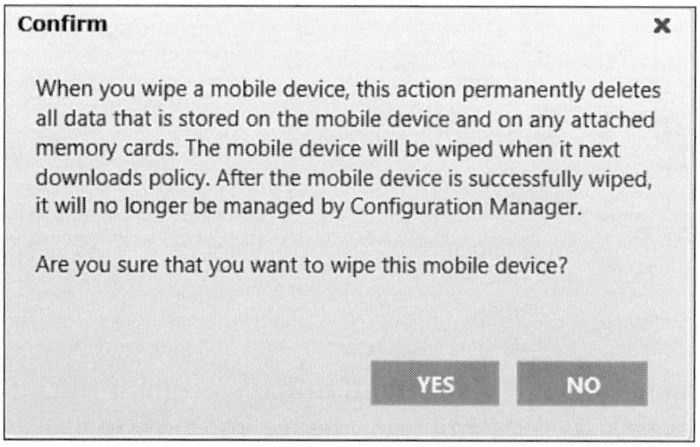

FIGURE 15.22   Confirming Application Catalog request to wipe a mobile device.

In-Depth Management

Configuration Manager's *in-depth management* management method gives you additional functions when managing mobile devices. Choose this type of management to perform software distribution or use settings management on mobile devices. Figure 15.23 illustrates components and architecture of the in-depth management management model.

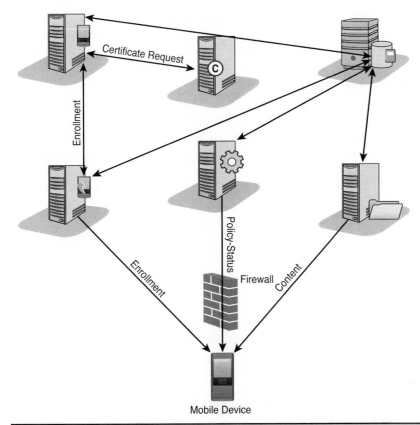

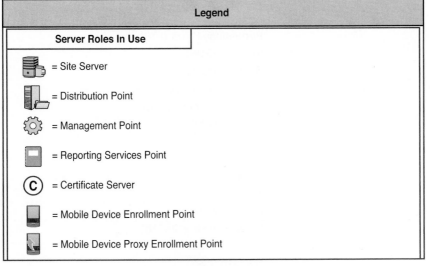

FIGURE 15.23   In-depth management architecture.

These devices are supported for enrollment with Configuration Manager and in-depth monitoring. The platforms have specific languages that are supported; the online support statement at http://technet.microsoft.com/en-us/library/gg682077.aspx#BKMK_SiteAndRoleScale provides a current list for Windows Mobile 6.1 and 6.5, Windows CE 6.0, and Nokia Symbian Belle Service Release (SR) 1.

Optionally, you can use the Configuration Manager legacy client, which provides support for Windows CE 5.0 to 7.0 and Windows Mobile 6.0. From a feature perspective, these legacy devices have only a subset of features available in the in-depth management model. They do not support remote wipe or settings management, and are limited in software deployment to packages described in Chapter 11, "Packages and Programs," rather than the new application model discussed in Chapter 12, "Creating and Managing Applications."

Table 15.1 lists the devices on which you can install the ConfigMgr mobile device legacy client.

TABLE 15.1   Supported Mobile Device OS Versions

OS	Processor Type	Version
Windows CE 5.0	ARM x86	Chinese Simplified (CHS) Chinese Traditional (CHT) English (WWE) French (FRE) German (DEU) Italian (ITA) Japanese (JPN) Korean (KOR) Portuguese-Brazil (PTB) Russian (RUS) Spanish (ESN)
Windows CE 6.0	ARM x86	Chinese Simplified (CHS) Chinese Traditional (CHT) English (WWE) French (FRE) German (DEU) Italian (ITA) Japanese(JPN) Korean (KOR) Portuguese-Brazil (PTB) Russian (RUS) Spanish (ESN)
Windows Mobile 6.0	ARM	

> **NOTE: FUNCTIONALITY ON MOBILE DEVICES**
>
> When the Configuration Manager client software is installed on supported mobile devices, only hardware inventory, software installation, and the compliance settings functionality are available. System Center 2012 Configuration Manager also supports managing clients using the Exchange Server Connector, but because the Configuration Manager client software is not installed on the mobile device, management is limited.

There are several considerations when configuring in-depth management. You should determine whether you want to expose your environment as Internet-facing, and potentially add additional servers to host the management point and distribution point roles because they will be facing the Internet.

Public Key Infrastructure

The in-depth management management method requires you to have a PKI in place and the required certificate templates for Configuration Manager configured. The PKI must be running Microsoft Certificate Services with an enterprise certificate authority (CA).

For mobile device management, different certificate templates must be configured and deployed in your CA infrastructure. Here are the roles you need to deploy a web server certificate to:

- ▶ Management point
- ▶ Distribution point
- ▶ Enrollment point
- ▶ Enrollment proxy point

You must also deploy a Client Authentication Certificate to the management point and distribution point. A certificate template must be created for issuing certificates to mobile devices. Users enrolling mobile devices must have Read and Enroll rights on this template.

It is also important that you configure the certificate with the external Internet fully qualified domain name (FQDN) as your mobile devices will use that name. Certificate setup and management is covered in Chapter 20, "Security and Delegation in Configuration Manager." PKI certificate requirements for ConfigMgr are also discussed at http://technet.microsoft.com/en-us/library/gg699362.aspx.

Heartbeat Discovery

Heartbeat discovery for mobile devices works differently than it does with computer clients. When working with mobile devices, the management point generates the data discovery records (DDR) for these devices.

Discovery activity is logged in the DMPRP.log file, which is located under %*ProgramFiles*%\CCM\Logs on the management point used by the device. If heartbeat discovery is disabled, the mobile devices are still discovered.

Also differing from normal heartbeat discovery is that if a mobile device is inactive and a DDR is not generated for it, the client's certificate will be revoked. This would require you to enroll the device again if you want to use it later. The revocation occurs when the Delete Aged Discovery Data task removes database records for mobile devices.

Mobile Device Management Site Roles

Using in-depth management requires installation of two additional roles; these are the enrollment and proxy enrollment point roles. These roles are used for the client to enroll certificates and be enrolled to the Configuration Manager site; the roles can be placed on the same site server or individual servers, although they need to be in the same site if you have several Configuration Manager sites. Typically, the proxy enrollment point is placed in a demilitarized zone (DMZ) and the enrollment point could be collocated with the site server unless you need to have it on a separate server from a scaling perspective.

Install the roles by adding them to the site server that will be hosting them; if there is a specific website you want to host the role under, specify this as shown in Figure 15.24. Details of the roles are shown in Figures 15.24 and 15.25.

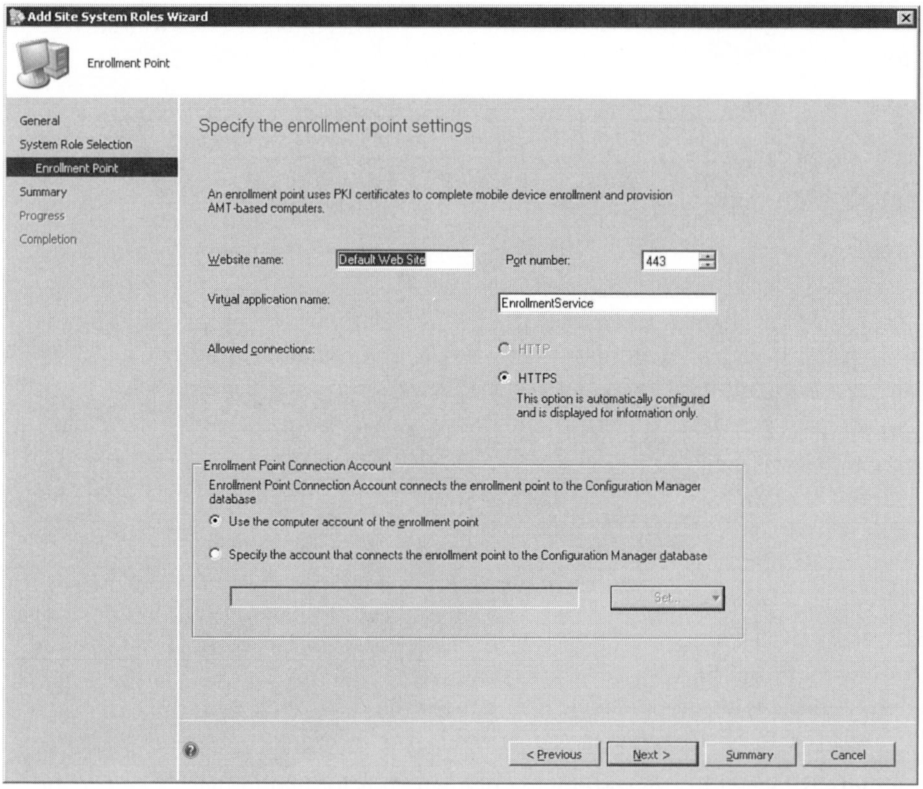

FIGURE 15.24   Enrollment Point Wizard.

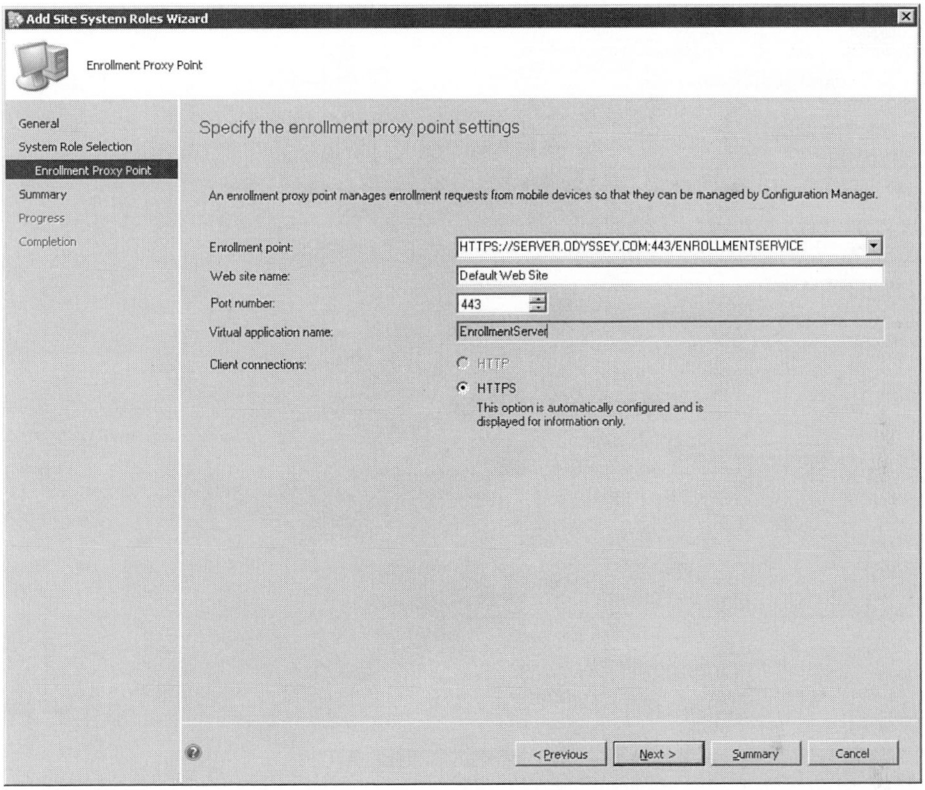

FIGURE 15.25   Enrollment Proxy Point Wizard.

The management and distribution points must be configured for Internet usage and device usage. That is done by first configuring the site server that is hosting the role as an Internet FQDN, as shown in Figure 15.26.

After this is configured, the management point needs to be reconfigured to use HTTPS, and you must select whether to allow Internet or intranet and Internet connections. The option you choose depends on your design. If you have only one management point in your environment and it will serve both internal and external clients, choose both types of connections; however, if you add an additional management point on another server, you could set it to allow only Internet-based clients. Open the Management Point Properties page to select the check box, as shown in Figure 15.27, allowing mobile devices to use this management point.

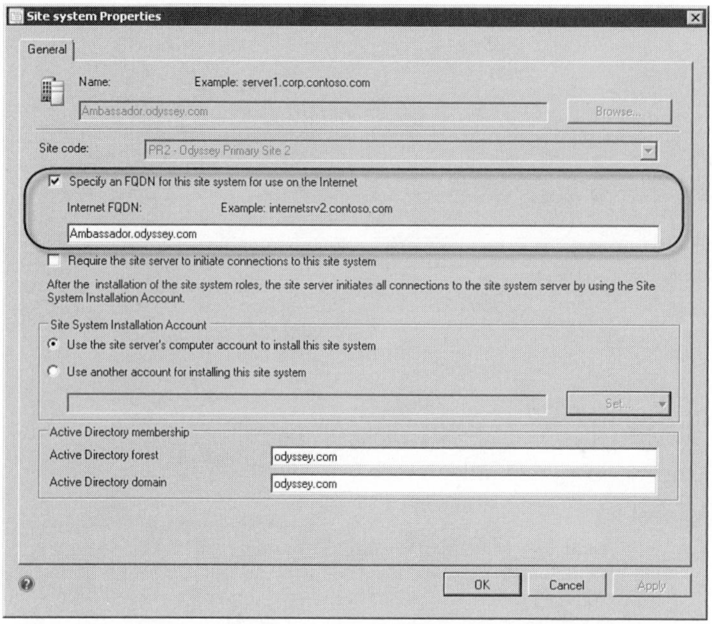

FIGURE 15.26   Setting the Internet FQDN.

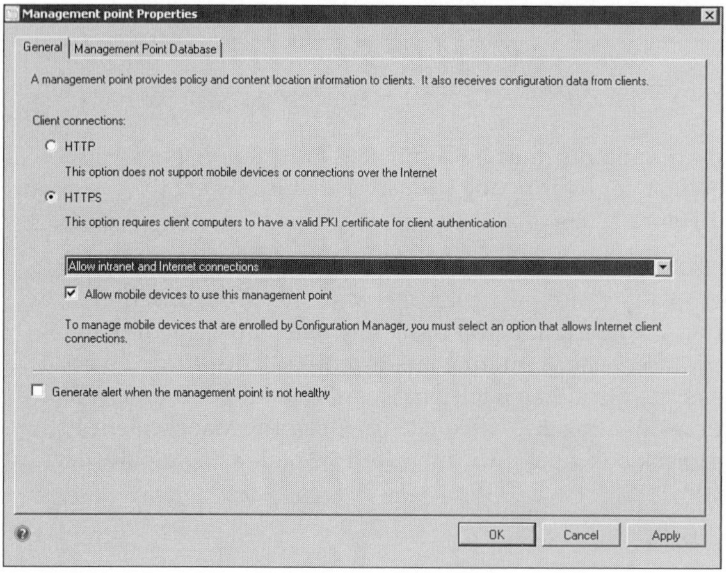

FIGURE 15.27   Defining the management point properties.

The distribution point would be configured in a similar manner as the management point except for the check box to allow mobile devices. Select whether the devices should connect only from the Internet/intranet or both Internet and intranet, as shown in Figure 15.28.

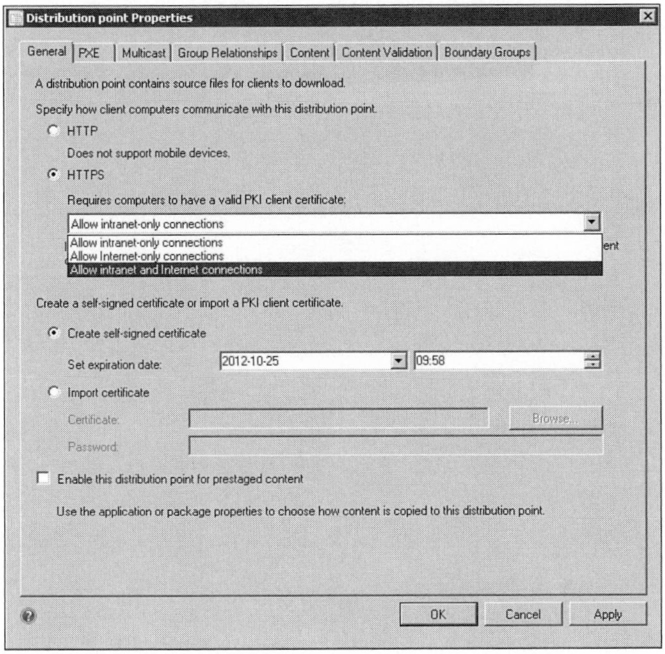

FIGURE 15.28   Distribution Point Properties.

For a mobile device client to auto enroll over the air to a ConfigMgr site, a CNAME record named configmgrenroll needs to be created for the domain you have as your user principal name (UPN) domain on your client accounts. The CNAME record should point to the server hosting the enrollment proxy.

Client Settings

Enrollment for mobile devices is controlled through the client user settings. Enrolling mobile devices is disabled by default. The authors recommend creating a new custom policy for granular control over who should enroll devices by assigning those settings to a collection that consists of only users that should have this ability. Perform the following steps:

1. Navigate to **Administration -> Client Settings**. Create a new custom client user setting, and check the Mobile Devices check box on the General page, as shown in Figure 15.29.

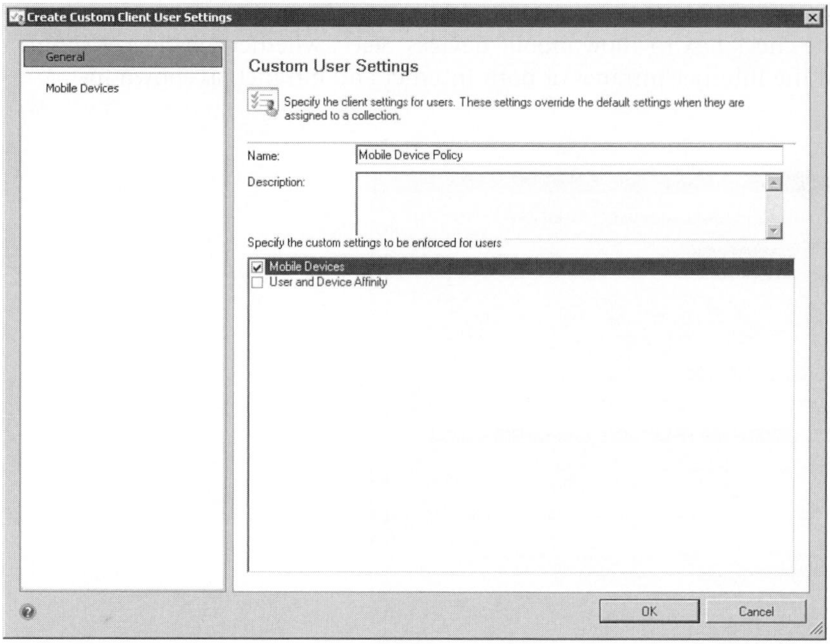

FIGURE 15.29 Create new custom client setting.

2. On the Mobile Devices page displayed in Figure 15.30, set **Allow users to enroll mobile devices** to **True**, and then click the button to **Set Profile** to assign a profile for enrollment.

3. On the Create Mobile Device Enrollment Profile page, choose **Create**, as shown in Figure 15.31, or choose from any existing profiles created earlier.

   Specify a **Name** for the profile a name, and choose a **Management site code**, as shown in Figure 15.32.

   If the list of management site codes is empty, this means you have not configured any management points to be enabled as device management points by enabling them for HTTPS and specifying the **Allow management for devices** option.

   You also need to configure the certificate settings by adding a certificate server and specifying a certificate template. PKI configuration is described in Chapter 20.

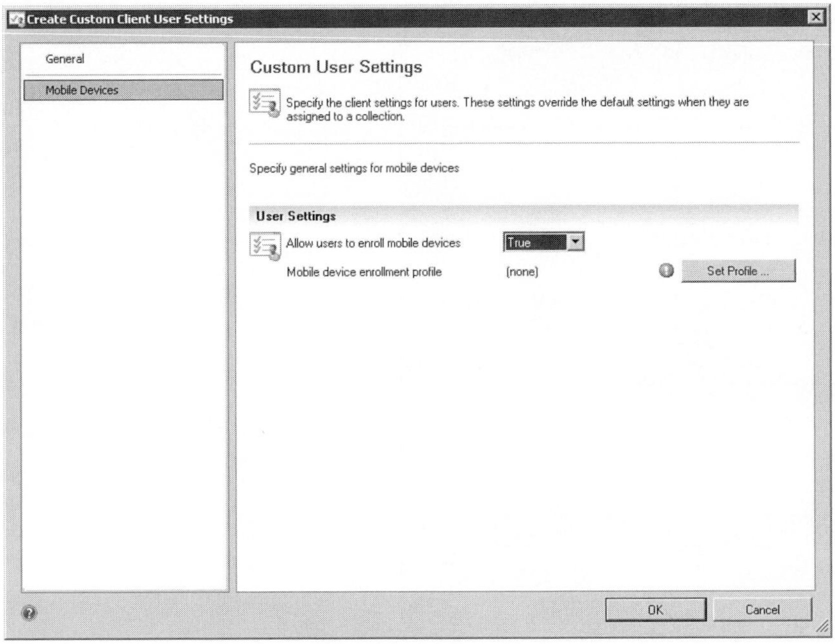

FIGURE 15.30   Allow users to enroll mobile devices.

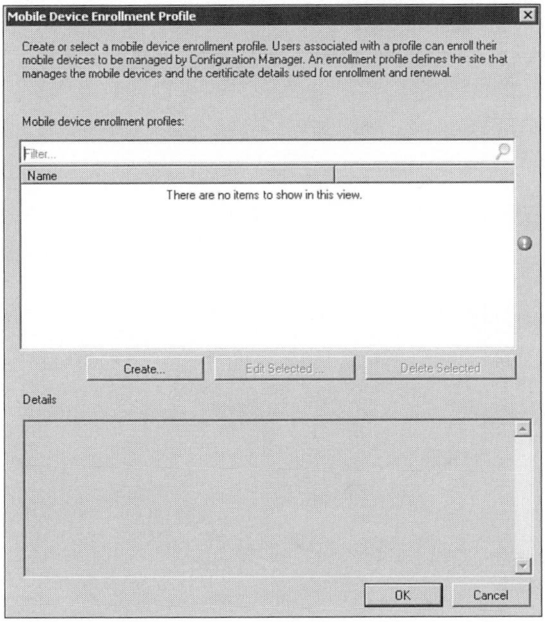

FIGURE 15.31   Create new mobile device enrollment profile.

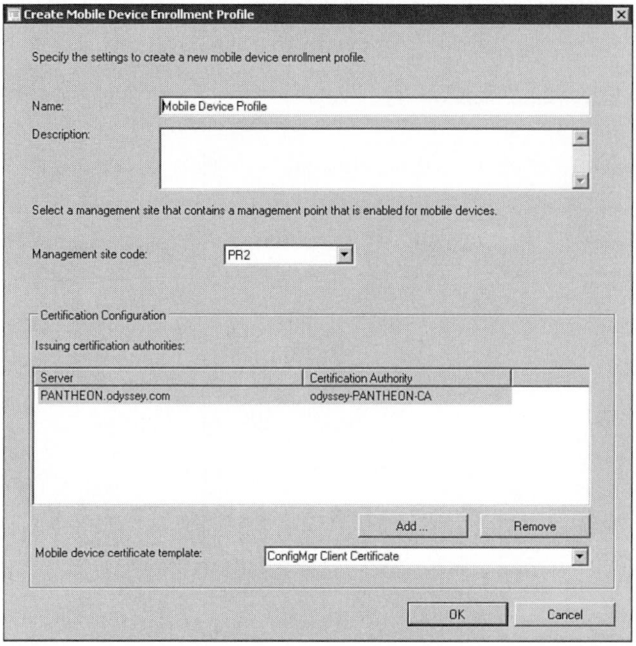

FIGURE 15.32   Specify the management site code and certificate template.

Mobile devices use a different polling interval, which is set to 8 hours by default and can be adjusted. You can also specify whether to enable the enrollment of mobile devices by users, and if so which enrollment profile to use. Figure 15.33 shows mobile device settings.

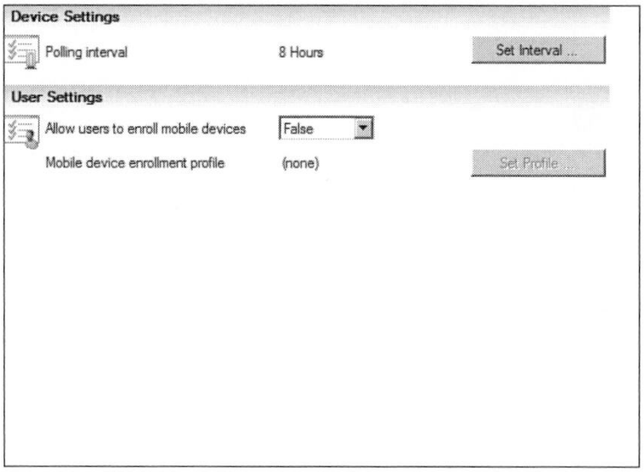

FIGURE 15.33   Default client settings mobile devices.

Enrolling Mobile Devices

After configuring your infrastructure, start enrolling mobile devices. You can do this over the air by providing the users with a link to your enrollment proxy point server. There are several ways to do this:

▶ Using https://*<FQDN>*/EnrollmentServer of your enrollment proxy internet address

▶ With the CNAME record previously discussed in the "Mobile Device Management Roles" section, using a link such as https://configmgrenroll.domain.topdomain/ EnrollmentServer

The benefit of using a CNAME is you don't need to update the link if you move the enrollment proxy server role. In addition, the enrollment process auto resolves to configmgrenroll your domain and top-level domain of your users' UPN account domain. As a best practice, the authors suggest that you use the same UPN suffix used for email to make it easier for the end user.

The enrollment proxy point validates the client and provides a prompt of a file, configmgrenroll.cab, as shown in Figure 15.34. This is the Mobile Device client; select **Save** to save it to the device, or **Menu**, and open and install the client. At the next prompt, accept the EULA to proceed, and then choose **Enroll** to enroll the device, or **Cancel** to enroll at a later stage, as shown in Figure 15.35.

FIGURE 15.34   Mobile Device client installation.

FIGURE 15.35   Mobile device enrollment.

After the client is installed, enroll the device by entering the user's Active Directory UPN name and password. The enrollment point URL is filled in automatically with the configmgrenroll URL. Although this can be changed manually, it is beneficial to use the configmgrenroll URL because it would cause less hardship for end users' enrolling devices. This is displayed in Figure 15.36.

The mobile device client should now be enrolled and show up in the ConfigMgr console under Device Collections shortly.

If you need to troubleshoot the client, its log files are located under the internal memory of the phone under Phone Memory\DeviceMgmt\Logs.

Software Deployment

Chapter 12 discusses creating and managing applications. This section covers those areas to consider that are specific when deploying software to mobile devices.

Using the in-depth management model lets you deploy software to mobile devices; both supported Nokia Belle devices and supported Windows devices. Nokia uses .sis format, whereas Windows Mobile uses .cab applications. Windows Mobile applications must be signed; if you have not already signed them with a code signing certificate, you can do that in the Create Application Wizard, as shown in Figure 15.37. The article at http://technet.microsoft.com/en-us/library/cc732597(WS.10).aspx provides information about acquiring a code signing certificate. This certificate must be trusted by the mobile device. Using compliance settings, you can deploy certificates along with other settings.

FIGURE 15.36   Mobile Device Enrollment Account Settings.

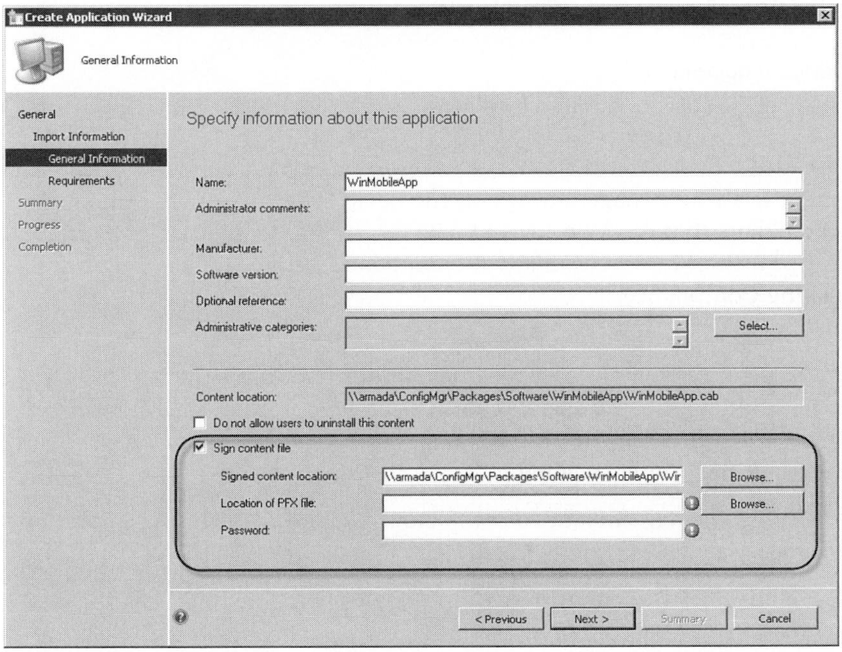

FIGURE 15.37   Adding a code signing certificate.

You can only deploy required applications to mobile devices because the client cannot see available applications for the device.

When deploying applications to mobile devices, you can set specific requirements related to these devices in the application model, for example, the operating system or free space on the mobile device. Figure 15.38 shows an example of available requirements.

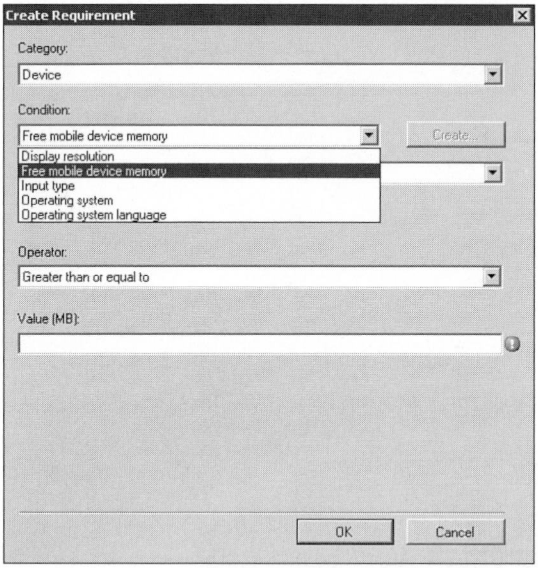

FIGURE 15.38   Device requirements.

Compliance Settings

In-depth management lets you manage settings on the devices. Settings management is supported only on clients that run Windows Mobile 6.1 and 6.5 or Nokia Symbian Belle (SR1) devices. For further information about compliance settings management, see Chapter 10, "Managing Compliance."

Reporting

When you install the Configuration Manager reporting services point, Configuration Manager reporting provides 29 reports related to mobile device management to assist you in your work with mobile device management.

Although Chapter 18, "Reporting," includes a complete list of the mobile device management reports, here are some of the more interesting reports:

▶ **Count of mobile devices by operating system:** This is a brief report providing a count of how many devices and different operating systems you have in your device management environment. Figure 15.39 shows a sample report.

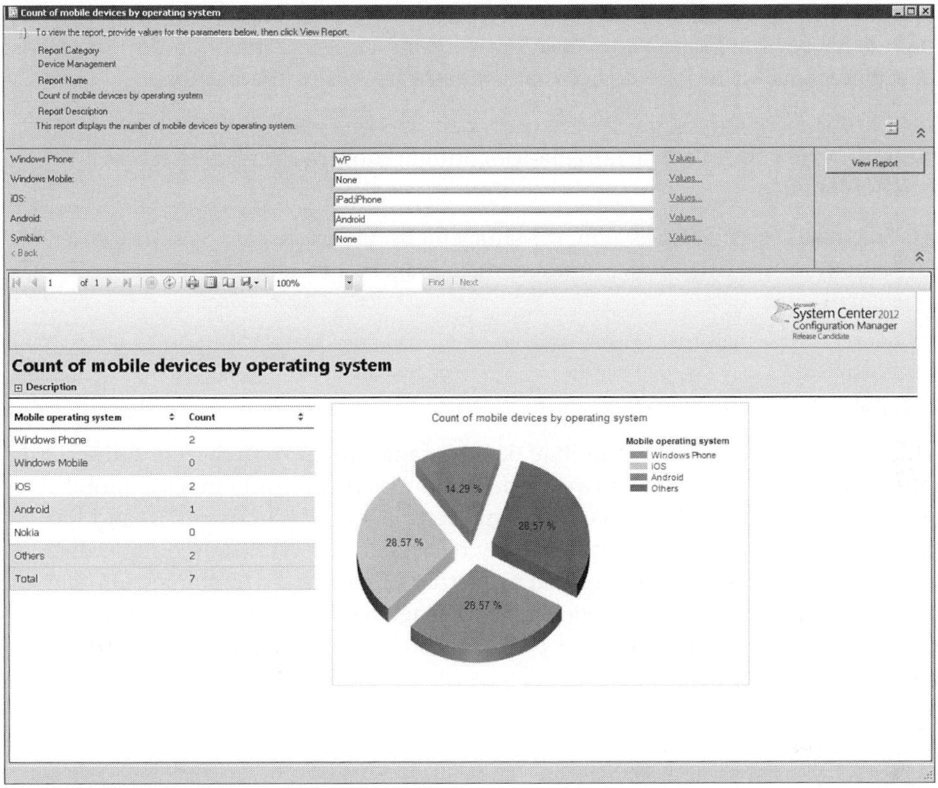

FIGURE 15.39   The Count of Mobile Devices by Operating System report.

▶ **Pending wipe request:** This report shows a list of devices that have a pending wipe to perform. This report is useful for following up on devices that were not wiped for some reason, such as compliance. They may be stolen and already offline for some reason.

▶ **Inactive mobile devices that are managed by the Exchange Server connector:** This is a report showing devices that have been inactive against the Exchange server, giving you a list of potential devices to remove or wipe from the system.

You may want to configure subscriptions for various reports to keep you up to date with device activity. Chapter 18 describes subscriptions.

Partner Extensibility

System Center 2012 Configuration Manager is built to allow vendors to extend the base functionality existing in the product. To extend your management capabilities further, you can add third-party add-ons and applications from different vendors to get additional features such extended hardware and software inventory, remote control, and so on. Here are several applications for mobile device management known to the authors:

▶ Athena MDM from Odyssey Software (now part of Symantec), http://www.odysseysoftware.com/products/athena-for-configuration-manager.aspx#sccm, provides details.

▶ Quest Software offers its QMX (Quest Management Xtensions) for System Center. For information, see http://www.quest.com/management-xtensions-device-management-cm/.

Summary

This chapter provides an overview of mobile device management with System Center 2012 Configuration Manager. It introduces two management methods for managing mobile devices in your enterprise, the light management method with Exchange 2010 and the in-depth management method managed natively by System Center 2012 Configuration Manager. The chapter discussed the required infrastructure and how to manage mobile devices in the ConfigMgr console. Mobile device management gives you the ability to manage your mobile devices from a single pane of glass through System Center 2012 Configuration Manager.

CHAPTER 16

Endpoint Protection

The addition of Microsoft System Center 2012 Endpoint Protection to Configuration Manager (ConfigMgr) is a logical step, given that it was previously available as an add-on for Configuration Manager 2007. Now system administrators can monitor and control the security state of their client computers natively from a single console and do so easily using the new role-based administration (RBA).

Microsoft has come full circle with this release by converging client management and security, and reducing cost through consolidating infrastructure. Your security team can now focus on end-to-end security tasks instead of updating antivirus definitions, and your administrators can manage, report, and react to everything that is client- and security-related using one common console.

Here are the highlights of endpoint protection in System Center 2012 Configuration Manager:

▶ **Licensing:** Microsoft requires you be licensed to use Endpoint Protection to manage clients in your ConfigMgr hierarchy. This requires the Core Client Access License (CAL). Chapter 4, "Architecture Design Planning," provides information on licensing.

▶ **Customizable:** The ability to define custom client settings allows you to target different device collections with unique Endpoint Protection client settings. Microsoft provides preconfigured malware policies to optimize the deployment process; these can be customized to a great degree.

▶ **Separate Client:** Endpoint Protection installs its own client (installed using scep-install.exe). This client is included with the ConfigMgr client source files, making it possible to be deployed quickly to those clients already managed by ConfigMgr. Here are capabilities of the System Center Endpoint Protection client (SCEP):

  ▶ Easy to deploy

  ▶ Can auto-uninstall some third-party antivirus software

  ▶ Malware and spyware detection and remediation

  ▶ Rootkit detection and remediation

  ▶ Critical vulnerability assessment and automatic definition and engine update

  ▶ Integrated Windows Firewall management

  ▶ Network vulnerability detection using the network inspection system

If you are familiar with Forefront Endpoint Protection (FEP) 2010 when installed in ConfigMgr 2007, you can notice some distinct differences between that version and the 2012 version. Here are some examples:

▶ You no longer have to run a separate program to install System Center Endpoint Protection because it is fully integrated within ConfigMgr; you just enable the site system role. This also means you can no longer install System Center Endpoint Protection by itself; it depends on ConfigMgr and is thus not a standalone product.

▶ The Endpoint Protection dashboard does not need to be installed separately; it can be viewed in the Monitoring workspace.

▶ Automatic deployment rules (ADRs) now take control of updating the definition updates via software updates, meaning you do not have to configure anything in the Windows Software Update Services (WSUS) console.

▶ Adding users with the correct permissions is now a breeze using RBA built-in roles; previously you had to undertake a complex process to grant the correct permissions necessary to do the job based on function.

▶ Installing the SCEP client agent on your clients is simple and efficient; there is no package or program to create or advertisement to deliver because the installer and its associated default antimalware policy is now included in the ConfigMgr client.

▶ Modifying collections to display endpoint protection-specific information is easy because there are new endpoint protection-specific columns that can be added to your view.

▶ Separate databases are no longer required (FEP hosted the FEP database and the FEP data warehouse). The endpoint protection information is now stored in the ConfigMgr site database. In addition, there are no additional SQL jobs running on a schedule as there were with FEP.

▶ Email notification is now near real-time, when previously it could be up to an hour before you would be notified about a malware threat.

Prerequisites for Endpoint Protection

You need to investigate prerequisites before implementing endpoint protection with System Center 2012 Configuration Manager; these can be a mixture of both internal and external dependencies as listed at http://technet.microsoft.com/en-us/library/hh508780.aspx.

Here are the external dependencies:

▶ WSUS is required if using the ConfigMgr software update point (SUP) role to deliver Endpoint Protection antimalware definition updates as discussed at http://technet. microsoft.com/en-us/library/hh237372.aspx.

▶ If you want to deploy firewall policies to Windows Server 2008 or Windows Vista Service Pack (SP) 1, you must install hotfix KB971800; see http://support.microsoft. com/kb/971800 for information.

Without this hotfix, applications and features such as SCEP that rely on the Remote Procedure Call service are blocked, and they cannot enforce the Windows firewall policy on the client.

▶ Client computers require Internet access if you synchronize endpoint protection and antimalware definition updates from Microsoft Update or the Microsoft Malware Protection Center.

Because most organizations already have Internet access on their client systems, this should not be a problem; you may however have to configure additional proxy settings on these clients depending how Internet access is configured at your site.

The internal dependencies are as follows:

▶ You must be running the endpoint protection point site system role on your central administration site (CAS) or standalone primary site.

The endpoint protection point site system role must be installed before you can use Endpoint Protection or configure Endpoint Protection client settings. It must be installed on one site system server only and at the top of the hierarchy on a central administration site or on a standalone primary site.

▶ The SUP site system role must be installed and configured if you use ConfigMgr for delivering definition and engine updates.

You must also specify that definition updates are selected in your classifications for the SUP role, or you cannot synchronize your endpoint protection definition (and engine) updates to your client computers.

▶ You must install and configure the reporting services point site system role to display and run endpoint protection reports.

SCEP comes with four built-in reports; these reports allow you to view infected computers in your organization or see top users by threats to determine who is spreading the malware. Using these reports requires installing and configuring the Reporting Services Point site system role.

▶ Security permissions must be defined to manage endpoint protection.

SCEP has its own security role, Endpoint Protection Manager. This built-in role grants permissions to define and monitor security policies. Associating administrative users with this role allows them to create, modify, and delete endpoint protection policies and deploy these policies to collections.

Planning and Considerations

Although enabling the endpoint protection point site system role is easy to perform, take time first to plan how you intend to roll out the SCEP agent across your hierarchy, and how you will configure it on your desktops, laptops, and servers. The authors strongly recommend you not configure the default client agent settings for endpoint protection, because this would apply to all computers across your hierarchy.

Creating Custom Client Settings and Antimalware Policies

As a best practice, you should create custom client settings for endpoint protection and target them to specific and applicable areas of your organization, using collections to assign these custom settings. You can create multiple custom client agent settings for endpoint protection to target computers with settings suited to its function and purpose.

You need to create separate antimalware policies for clients and servers; you don't want a standard desktop antimalware policy applied to your mission critical Microsoft SQL Server. What you do want is the antimalware policies intelligently configured to ignore or bypass certain Windows processes or file locations and file types, helping avoid unnecessary processor or disk load that would reduce server performance and impact end users.

Consider creating server role-specific antimalware policies that reflect and correspond to what those servers are running. Microsoft provides several predefined server specific antimalware policies; you can import them and customize them further to your needs. A good example of one of these policies is the built-in policy for Configuration Manager 2012, SCEP12_Default_ConfigMgr2012.xml. This policy combines default server workload policy settings with settings that are optimized for System Center 2012 Configuration Manager, in particular the settings for file and folder exclusions. The logic here is that server-specific roles do certain things repeatedly and consistently, and you want your antimalware solution to exclude certain processes and files that are regularly by that specific server role. Failing to add these exclusions can affect server performance and cause additional issues such as loss of communication and network issues.

Deciding from Where to Update and When

You should have a clear understanding of what options are available for definition updates retrieval, and decide where your Endpoint Protection clients can retrieve the definition updates.

▶ If you want to have total control and a single point of contact, you can force your client computers to get definition and engine updates from ConfigMgr and exclude all other sources of update retrieval.

▶ For additional flexibility, you can allow the clients to retrieve these updates from additional sources such as Microsoft Update or local network shares.

   Allowing your clients to update from sources other than ConfigMgr means they are protected, regardless of whether they talk to their management point. This is important because it could prevent a spread of malware—by containing it on the user's computer by receiving a definition update directly from Microsoft Windows Update.

As new malware is constantly created, when your SCEP client looks for definition updates is important. However, you need to determine how often is appropriate for your organization. If you configure a policy that has the client look for updates too often (say every 2 or 3 hours), it may be wasting bandwidth and CPU cycles because Microsoft releases the update definitions approximately three times per day. (Although Microsoft will release antivirus definition updates more often if necessary.) You also need to decide how often the SUP will synchronize with Microsoft. Assuming there are three definition updates per day, you could follow that release cycle and synchronize every 8 hours; however, most organizations would probably think that is extreme and opt for a single synchronization per day.

Deploying to a Test Collection First

As part of your initial setup of endpoint protection in your hierarchy, you should first deploy the agent to a test collection containing a group of test computers. This lets you verify that any custom client settings and custom malware policies function as intended before rolling those custom policies to the targeted computers. If your intended targets are specific server roles, your test computers should match those roles to verify that things work as you expected.

REAL WORLD: WHEN A DEFINITION OR ENGINE UPDATE CAUSES ISSUES

There is always a possibility that a definition update or engine update could cause a problem with your client. There have been cases in which antivirus firms have mistakenly sent out definition updates that caused blue screens in certain hardware scenarios. Be aware that this could happen or that a definition update may block files or computers vital to your business, and have a plan to restore access quickly. In this type of scenario, you can deploy a simple script through packages/programs to run `mpcmdrun.exe -remove-definitions` to roll clients back to the previous definition. Remember you would also have to prevent the client from installing that definition again by removing it from your deployable definitions.

16

Categorizing Client Remediation Status

Endpoint Protection in System Center 2012 Configuration Manager does not come with any of the collections its predecessor came with in Configuration Manager 2007. Those collections were used to sort computers with malware-related issues into predefined locked-query based collections. You could not edit or view the queries in those collections; however, third parties later released the contents of those queries online in Excel format in case you wanted to re-create the collections. You don't need to create those collections in System Center 2012 Endpoint Protection; the Endpoint Protection Status dashboard replaces this functionality by letting you see the malware and operational state of the entire selected collection. These items are clickable, allowing the administrator to drill down into reports or take recommended actions. Here are the malware remediation status items viewable in the dashboard:

- ▶ Remediation failed
- ▶ Full scan required
- ▶ Restart required
- ▶ Offline scan required
- ▶ Client settings modified by malware
- ▶ Malware remediated in the last 24 hours

In addition to the functionality in the dashboard, you can easily build collections based on the new endpoint protection classes; these are the same classes used in the predefined FEP 2010 collections, making those collections unnecessary as you can easily build your own.

Targeting Collections with Custom Antimalware Policy and Client Settings

You want to create separate custom antimalware policies and custom client settings to target individual collections. You can accomplish this by creating endpoint protection-specific folders, such as

- ▶ Endpoint Protection Managed Client Computers
- ▶ Endpoint Protection Managed Servers

You can populate these folders with collections, targeting those collections with separate custom client settings for SCEP, and more important, custom malware policies. As servers are critical to an organization, you most likely want to create multiple SCEP-managed server collections to separate many of the common server roles. For example, SQL Server systems should be treated differently for file and process exclusions in comparison to a Hyper-V host.

A suggested collection name for your Windows client computers is **Endpoint Protection Managed Desktops and Laptops**. You can create this device collection in the Endpoint

Protection Managed Client Computers folder. How the collection is populated is up to you; you can use queries or whatever criteria deemed appropriate for your hierarchy. However, you should not use these collections to target other deployments such as software updates or application installations. Use these collections for endpoint protection activities only.

Here are suggestions for a group of collections, as shown in Figure 16.1, based on common Windows Server roles:

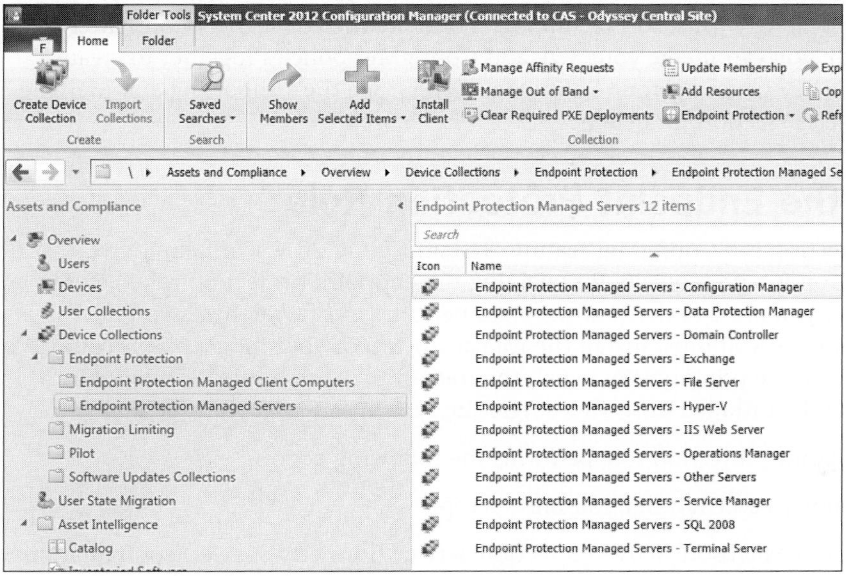

FIGURE 16.1   Endpoint Protection managed servers.

▶ Endpoint Protection Managed Servers - Domain Controller

▶ Endpoint Protection Managed Servers - Exchange

▶ Endpoint Protection Managed Servers - Operations Manager

▶ Endpoint Protection Managed Servers - Configuration Manager

▶ Endpoint Protection Managed Servers - SQL 2008

▶ Endpoint Protection Managed Servers - File Server

▶ Endpoint Protection Managed Servers - Service Manager

▶ Endpoint Protection Managed Servers - Data Protection Manager

▶ Endpoint Protection Managed Servers - IIS Web Server

▶ Endpoint Protection Managed Servers - Hyper-V

▶ Endpoint Protection Managed Servers - Terminal Server

▶ Endpoint Protection Managed Servers - Other Servers

Place these collections in the Endpoint Protection Managed Servers folder, and target them individually with specific antimalware policies that function best for that particular type of server role based on file and process exclusions. You may want to create a group of collections in a large global organization; in a small environment, target only those servers that are appropriate to your hierarchy, based on usage. The key point here is to target specific server roles with customized antimalware rule-sets configured to allow optimum performance and availability even while protected via endpoint protection. The SCEP client can handle servers in multiple collections targeted by multiple antimalware policies; however, the policy with the highest priority takes precedence. Don't be concerned about dealing with server technologies that are mixed (such as ConfigMgr that has SQL installed); you can merge your SQL and ConfigMgr policies together to create a new ConfigMgr Policy targeting your ConfigMgr servers. See the "Importing and Merging Antimalware Policies" section for details.

Installing the Endpoint Protection Role

As endpoint protection is a ConfigMgr feature, System Center 2012 Configuration Manager installation is a prerequisite for enabling the endpoint protection role. Before installing the role, you must understand its placement in your hierarchy. If you have a multiple site hierarchy, you must install the role at the top of your hierarchy on your CAS; if you have a standalone primary site, install the role on that site server. The endpoint protection role can be installed only on a single site system server in your hierarchy.

Enabling the endpoint protection role performs the following actions:

▶ Presents you with a EULA that you must accept

▶ Sets the default Microsoft Active Protection Service (formerly SpyNet) configuration for all antimalware policies

▶ Installs the SCEP client on the server hosting the role

NOTE: ABOUT THE SCEP CLIENT ON THE SERVER HOSTING THE ENDPOINT PROTECTION ROLE

When you install the endpoint protection point role, the SCEP client is installed on the server hosting this role. The client is used for downloading and hosting the definition file; a server component polls this client to get malware data into the database by converting malware IDs into names. This client does not have protection services or scans enabled, so it can coexist with an existing antimalware solution installed on that server. If you add this server to a collection managed by endpoint protection and select the option to remove any third-party antimalware solution, the third-party product is not removed. You must uninstall the third-party product manually.

The following example assumes a multiple site hierarchy, so you must install the endpoint protection role on the CAS. Follow these steps to install the endpoint protection role:

1. Navigate to the Administration workspace. In the navigation tree, under **Overview**, expand **Site Configuration**, and select **Servers and Site System Roles**. All currently installed site systems are displayed on the right.

2. Select the CAS site server, right-click, and choose **Add Site System Roles** to launch the Add Site System Roles Wizard, as shown in Figure 16.2.

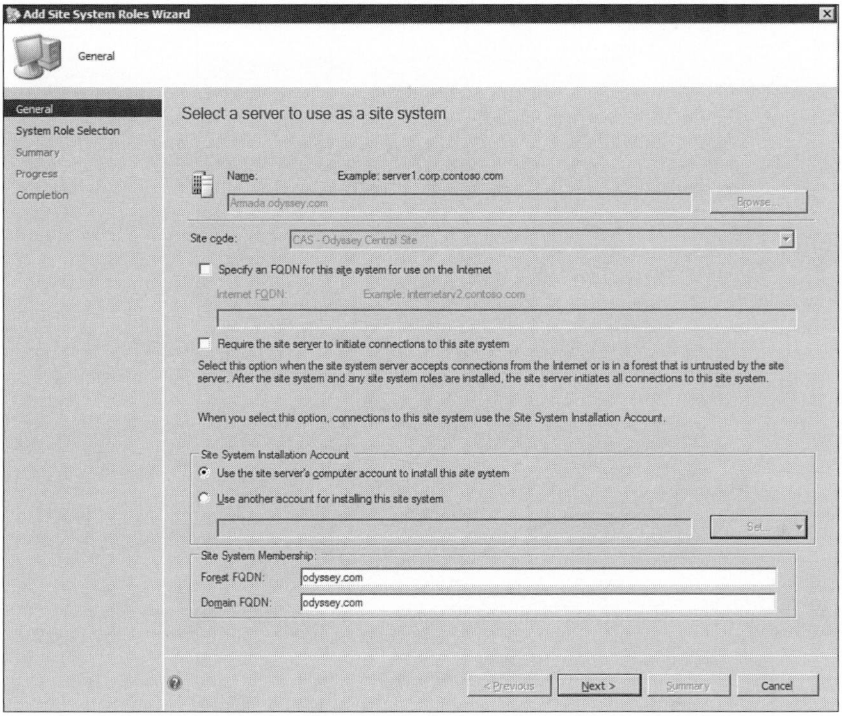

FIGURE 16.2   The Add System Roles Wizard.

3. On the System Role Selection page of the Add Site System Roles Wizard or Create Site System Server Wizard, select **Endpoint Protection Point**. If the software update point role is not already installed and configured, you are prompted that you should take the recommended actions of either

   ▶ Installing and configuring the SUP role prior to enabling the endpoint protection role

   Or

   ▶ Continuing anyway and adjusting the default antimalware policy not to retrieve updates from Configuration Manager

   Assuming the SUP role is previously installed and configured, there are now two subpages to the wizard: Endpoint Protection and Microsoft Active Protection Service.

4. On the Endpoint Protection page, as displayed in Figure 16.3, you must accept the license terms to continue with the wizard. Remember the SCEP 2012 license is separate from the System Center 2012 Configuration Manager license; if in doubt, talk to a Microsoft representative to determine if you are licensed to use the product.

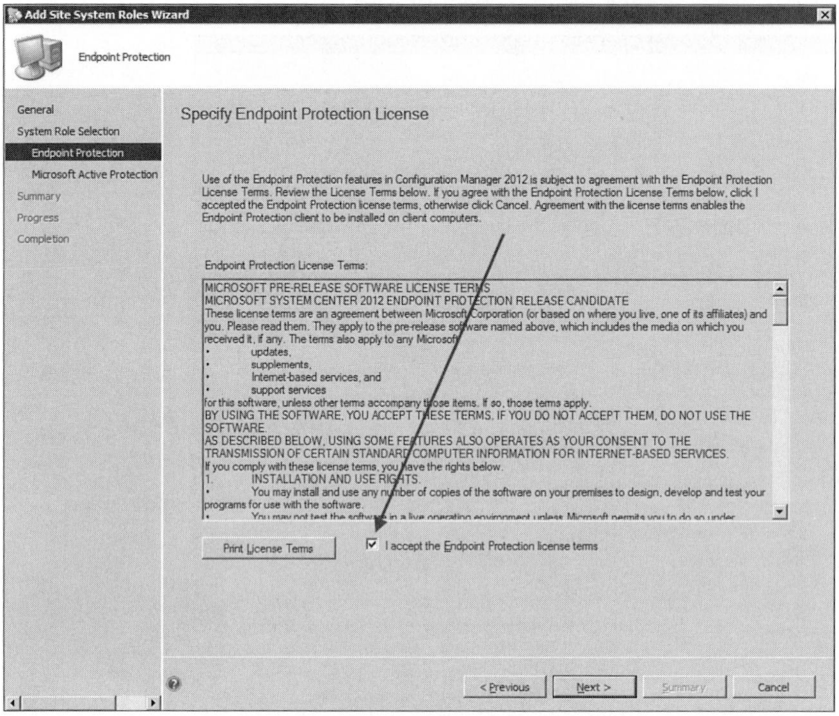

FIGURE 16.3   Accepting the Endpoint Protection License.

5. On the Microsoft Active Protection Service page, as shown in Figure 16.4, choose the appropriate Microsoft Active Protection Service settings. There are three options listed:

▶ I do not want to Join Microsoft Active Protection Service

▶ Basic membership

▶ Advanced membership

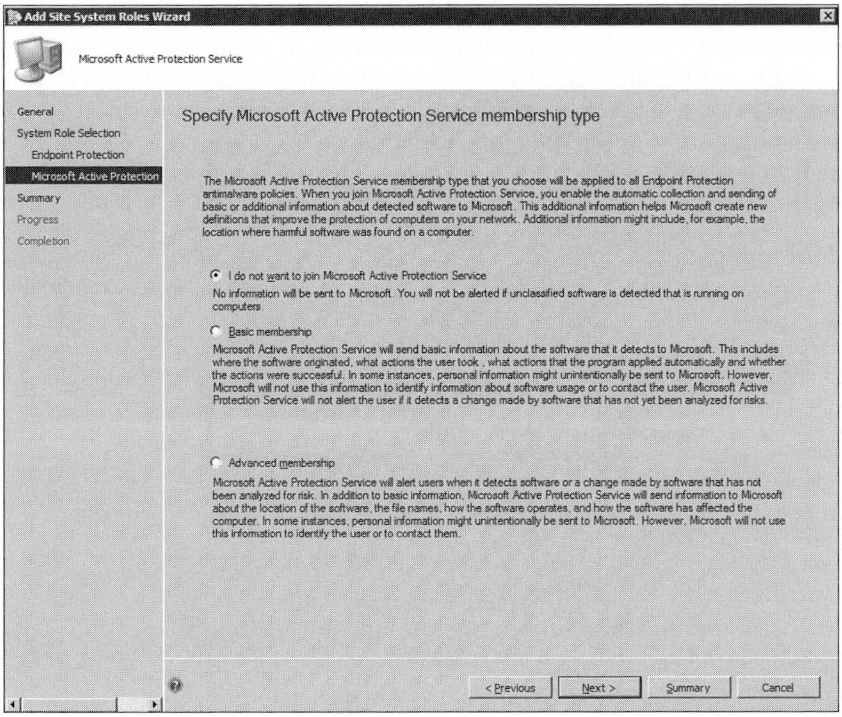

FIGURE 16.4   Selecting the Microsoft Active Protection Service membership type.

The Microsoft Active Protection Service (MAPS, formally SpyNet) allows you to opt-in or opt-out of automatically collecting and sending information to Microsoft about detected software; this information is used to create new definitions that can improve the level of protection for computers on your network. If you are concerned about privacy issues related to gathering data about program location or unintentional user-specific information and do not want to participate in this information exchange, select the first option. Note, however, that there are benefits to the other options.

Selecting the second option allows you to participate in information exchange with Microsoft. Basic information is sent such as where the software originated, what actions the user took, what actions were applied, and whether those actions were successful. MAPS will not alert the user if it detects a change made to software not yet analyzed for risks. Although some personal information might be sent unintentionally because of selecting this option, Microsoft commits to not using any of this information about the user or contacting the user.

With an advanced membership, MAPS sends more detailed information about detected software and alerts the user if it detects software that has not been analyzed for risks.

Microsoft recommends you at least choose a basic membership, as you have a higher level of protection than if you do not participate in MAPS. If malware enters your organization that is not yet identified by previous antimalware definitions, and it is exhibiting malware-like behavior, this information will be transmitted to the Microsoft Protection Center so that it can better understand what that malware is doing and its features. This may result in new antimalware definitions to protect you and other organizations from that malware.

Setting the MAPS setting here applies as the default level of membership for all subsequent antimalware policies that are created. You can override this as you create new policies.

6. Continue through the remaining pages of the wizard.

> **NOTE: ENDPOINT PROTECTION PRIVACY STATEMENT**
>
> Installing the endpoint protection role offers you the option to participate in the Microsoft Active Protection Service. To review Microsoft's privacy statement in relation to Endpoint Protection, see http://technet.microsoft.com/en-us/library/hh508835.aspx.

After completing the wizard, Configuration Manager installs the endpoint protection role with the specified parameters. To change the MAPS membership settings, navigate to the **Server and Site Systems** node under **Overview -> Site Configuration** in the Administration workspace's navigation tree, select the site server from the list on the right, right-click **Endpoint Protection Point** in the Detail pane at the bottom, and select **Properties**. You can then select the Microsoft Active Protection Service tab to revise your choices.

You can verify successful installation of the endpoint protection role by looking at the EPsetup.log file contained in the server's log files directory for any errors. You should see lines similar to the following:

```
SMSEP Setup Started....
Installing the SMSEP
Unable to query registry key
(SOFTWARE\Microsoft\Windows\CurrentVersion\Uninstall\Microsoft Security Client),
return (0x00000002) means EP client is NOT installed.
Installation was successful.
```

Configuring the SUP for Endpoint Protection

If you want to use the SUP role within ConfigMgr to synchronize and use software update ADRs to automatically download and deploy definition updates to your Endpoint Protection clients, you must configure it accordingly. The SUP role allows you to synchronize with Microsoft Windows Update on a predefined recurring schedule to enable you to protect your client computers with the latest antimalware definition and engine updates in an automated way. To automatically download and deploy these definitions using software updates, you need to create automatic deployment rules. However, before utilizing this new functionality, you must first configure the SUP as described in Chapter 14, "Software Update Management."

Configuring the SUP to Synchronize Definition Updates

To deliver endpoint protection engine and definition updates from the SUP, ensure it is configured to synchronize **Definition Updates** in the Classifications tab, as shown in Figure 16.5.

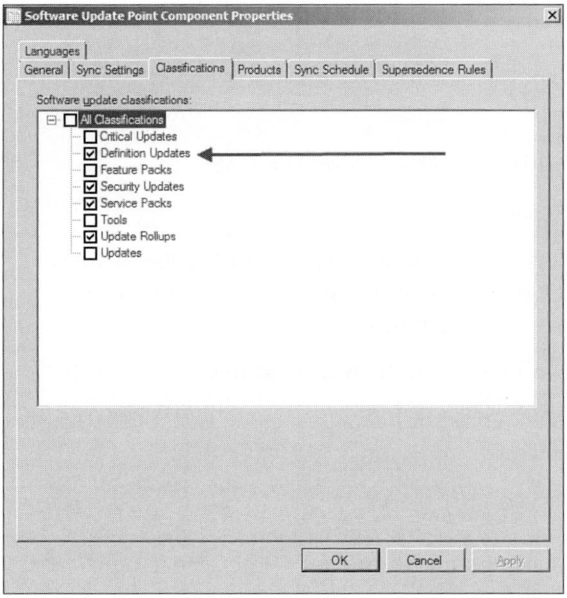

FIGURE 16.5   Configuring the SUP to synchronize definition updates in the Classifications tab.

In addition, you must select the **Forefront Endpoint Protection 2010** product listed in the Products tab, as shown in Figure 16.6. As these are definition updates and released several times per day, you probably want to synchronize with Microsoft Update at least once a day at a minimum to keep current with the latest antimalware definitions.

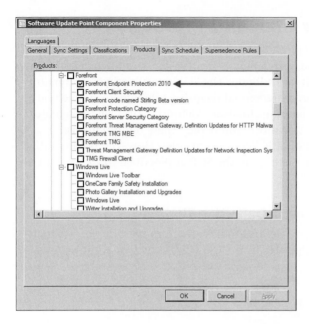

FIGURE 16.6   Selecting the Forefront Endpoint Protection 2010 product.

Perform these steps to configure the SUP with these changes on the CAS:

1. Navigate to the Administration workspace.

2. Select **Overview -> Site Configuration -> Sites,** select the CAS in the list of sites, and click **Settings** on the ribbon bar. Select **Configure Site Components** in the drop-down menu, and select **Software Update Point**:

   ▶ Select the **Classifications** tab, and check **Definition Updates**. Click **Apply**.

   ▶ Select the **Products** tab, and check **Forefront Endpoint Protection 2010** from the list of Forefront products listed.

   ▶ Select the **Sync Schedule** tab, and adjust the schedule to **Simple schedule** every **1 Days,** as shown in Figure 16.7. To control the actual time the sync takes place, choose **Custom schedule** and set the start time accordingly.

   ▶ After you click **OK,** synchronization is initiated as soon as possible, and then again based on the configured recurrence pattern.

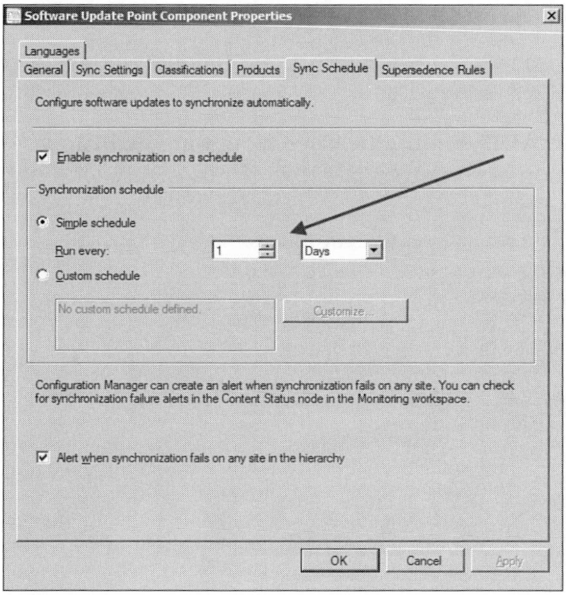

FIGURE 16.7   Sync Schedule set to run every 1 days.

Creating Auto Deployment Rules for Definition Updates

You want your SUP to use the new ADR feature because this eliminates the requirement to approve updates in WSUS manually. Auto deployment rules are scalable and not prone to human error. This feature instructs the SUP to automatically download and deploy specific software updates and on a recurring schedule. These updates are definition updates for endpoint protection because you want to push them out at least once per day to keep your clients current with antimalware definition files. You can configure multiple ADRs in your site to target several collections such as your server roles.

To configure an ADR for endpoint protection, perform these steps on the CAS:

1. Navigate to the Software Library workspace.

2. Select **Software Updates** and expand **All Software Updates**, right-click, and choose **Run Synchronization**. Verify that the synchronization is complete at the site by any of these methods:

   ▶ Review the **Software Update Point Synchronization Status** in the Monitoring workspace. Verify Synchronization status is **Completed**.

   ▶ Review the SMS_WSUS_SYNC_MANAGER; look for message ID **6702, WSUS Synchronization done**.

   ▶ Review the WSUSsyncmgr.log; look for **Sync Succeeded**.

16

3. Expand **Software Updates** and select **Automatic Deployment Rules**.

4. On the ribbon bar, click **Create Automatic Deployment Rule**. The Automatic Deployment Rule Wizard appears.

5. Give the rule a suitable name such as **ADR: Endpoint Protection Managed Client Computers**, and point it to a collection you want to target with this ADR, such as the **Endpoint Protection Managed Client Computers** collection. Prepending **ADR** to the name of the rule makes it easier to search for the deployment in the Deployments section of the Monitoring workspace. As you will be updating the endpoint protection definitions regularly, choose **Add to an existing Software Update Group**, as shown in Figure 16.8.

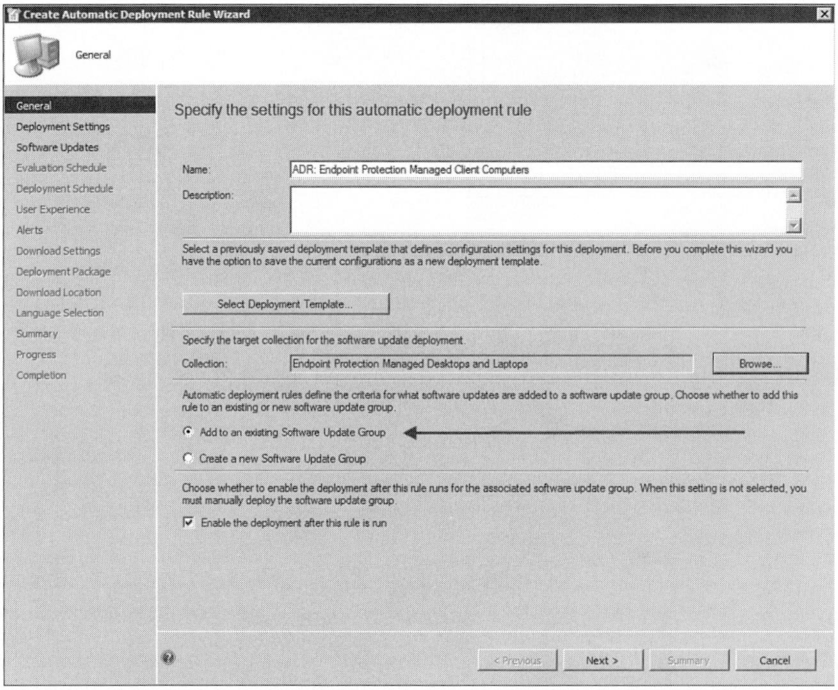

FIGURE 16.8   Add to Existing Software Update Group.

There is no option to browse to an existing software update group; it is not possible to select one. A software update group is created automatically with the name applied to this ADR when it successfully runs at least once, and is reused each time the ADR runs until you disable it. Choosing the other option (create a new software update group) is more suited to Patch Tuesday scenarios as you can then run compliance reports on that software update group, as it creates a new software update group each time it runs.

6. On the **Deployment Settings** page of the wizard, you can choose to **Use Wake-on-LAN** to wake up clients for required deployments. This is useful when you want to wake up computers to apply definition updates during the night so they are patched and ready for work hours in the morning. You could also wake computers with power management or AMT integration as needed instead of using this option. For state message detail level, choose one of these specifications:

  ▶ **Normal:** This sends all state message details about the deployment back to the server and is most applicable for standard software updates.

  ▶ **Minimal:** The minimal level is best suited for high frequency, low impact deployments such as definition updates, and returns only enforcement success and critical errors.

  Select **Minimal** from the Detail level drop-down list because this reduces state messages returned from the clients to the server, reducing network and Configuration Manager server load. Endpoint protection state messages are not subject to the 15-minute caching delay before sending to the management point.

7. At the **Software Updates** page, choose the criteria you want to check for when the ADR runs; as this ADR is limited to definition updates for endpoint protection, you can define the product to match that criterion. Similarly, you want to check for definition updates once per day. Set the date released or revised accordingly, as shown in Figure 16.9.

  ▶ **Date released or revised:** Last 1 day

  ▶ **Product:** Forefront Endpoint Protection 2010

8. In the **Evaluation Schedule**, click **Customize** and set it to run every **1 days**. Make sure that this ADR evaluation schedule does not exceed the SUP schedule, or the two will be out of sync. For example, there is no point evaluating for new definition updates every 2 hours if your SUP synchronizes only its catalog once per day.

9. In the **Deployment Schedule** screen, set time based on **UTC**. This allows all clients in the hierarchy to install the latest definitions at the same time. This setting is a recommended best practice. Note however that software update deadlines are randomized over a 2-hour period to prevent clients from requesting an update at the same time. For the **software available** option, select **2 hours** to allow sufficient time for the deployment definitions files to reach all distribution points, and select **As soon as possible** for the installation deadline, as shown in Figure 16.10.

10. On the **User Experience** page, you want to hide the definition update notifications from appearing because they occur frequently, and you don't want to irritate your users. Select **Hide in software center and all notifications** from the drop-down menu.

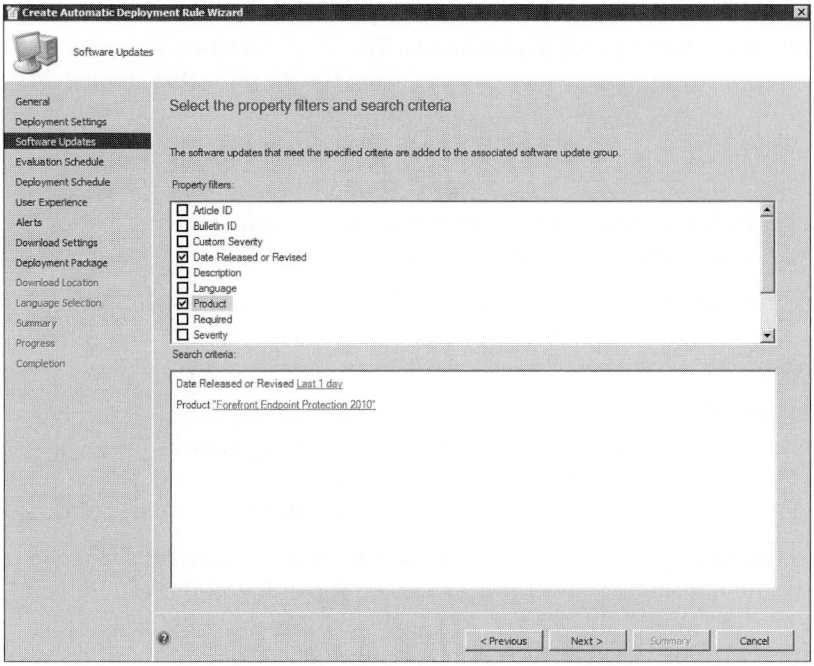

FIGURE 16.9   Software updates and date released or revised.

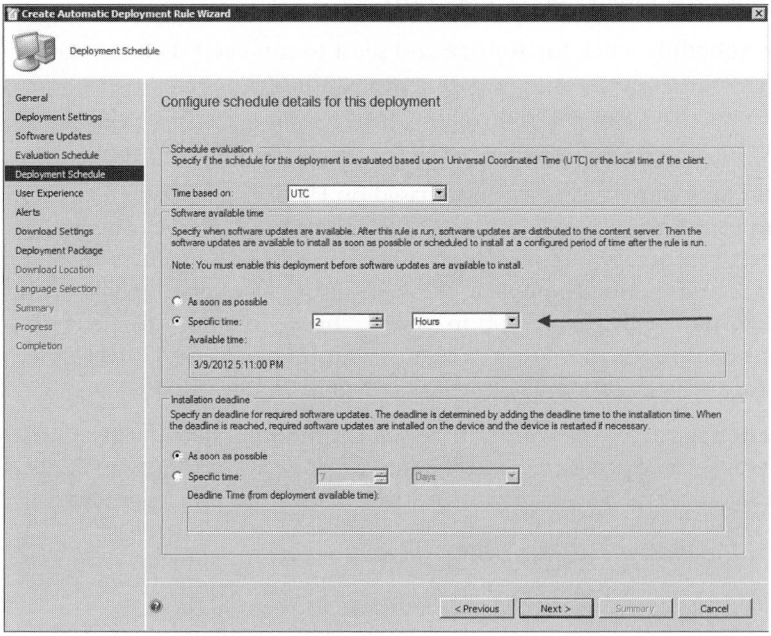

FIGURE 16.10   Deployment schedule.

11. On the **Alerts** page, enable the option to generate an alert, but consider setting the client compliance to a level that can work with your service level agreement (SLA). (Ninety percent might just be too aggressive!)

12. On the **Download Settings** page, it is important to download these definition updates even if on slow or unreliable networks because they offer your clients protection against malware. Select the option to download the updates for both choices provided.

13. There are two options on the **Deployment Package** screen:

    ▶ **Select Deployment Package:** Select this option if you have a deployment package already created to store the definition updates.

    ▶ **Create a New Deployment Package:** Select this option if you want to create a new deployment package. Give the package a suitable name such as **Endpoint Protection Definition Updates**, and point it to a previously created network folder. Ensure the path exists; otherwise, the wizard fails when it tries to download the definition updates because the network path will not exist.

    If running this wizard just to create this deployment package, after the package is created, retire (disable) this ADR and then create a new identical ADR from scratch, choosing the previously created deployment package.

14. Complete the rest of the wizard, reviewing the summary, as shown in Figure 16.11.

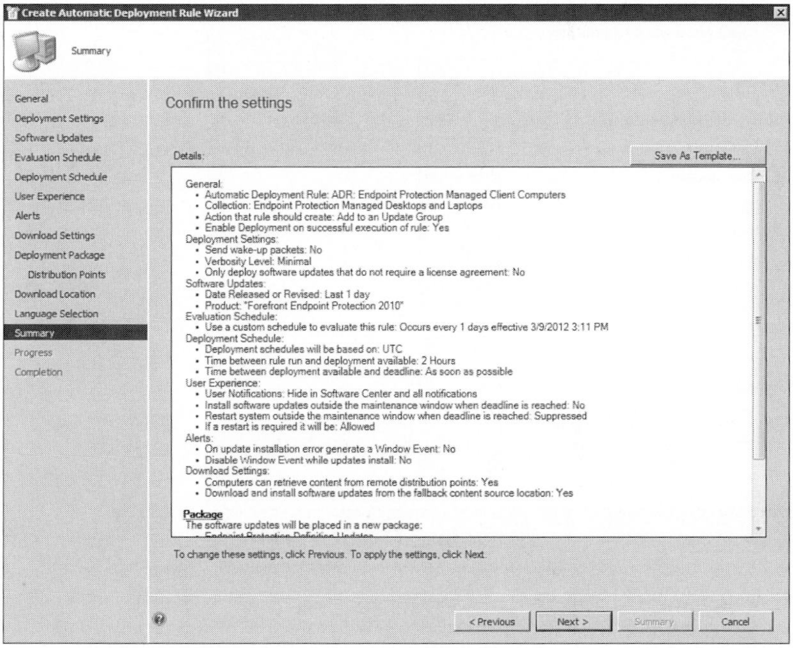

FIGURE 16.11   ADR summary screen.

After the ADR is created, you can run it manually to verify all the settings configured work correctly, or wait until it is scheduled to run. Successfully run ADRs have a Last Error Description of Success and Last Error Code 0x00000000. ADRs can also be disabled (or enabled if disabled) at any time. You cannot run a disabled ADR.

Working with Antimalware Policies

Antimalware policies define how the SCEP client is configured for key security behavior such as scheduled scans, scan settings, what actions to take if malware is found, real-time protection, behavior monitoring, exclusion settings, where to get the definition updates from, and much more. These topics are discussed in the following sections.

Understanding the Default Antimalware Policy

The default client antimalware policy is the policy applied to the client at initial client installation. The settings contained in this policy are broken into sections, each containing more configurable options as described below:

▶ **Scheduled Scans:** Here (as shown in Figure 16.12) you can define whether to run scheduled scans on client computers, and if you run the scheduled scan the type of scan to perform: Quick or Full.

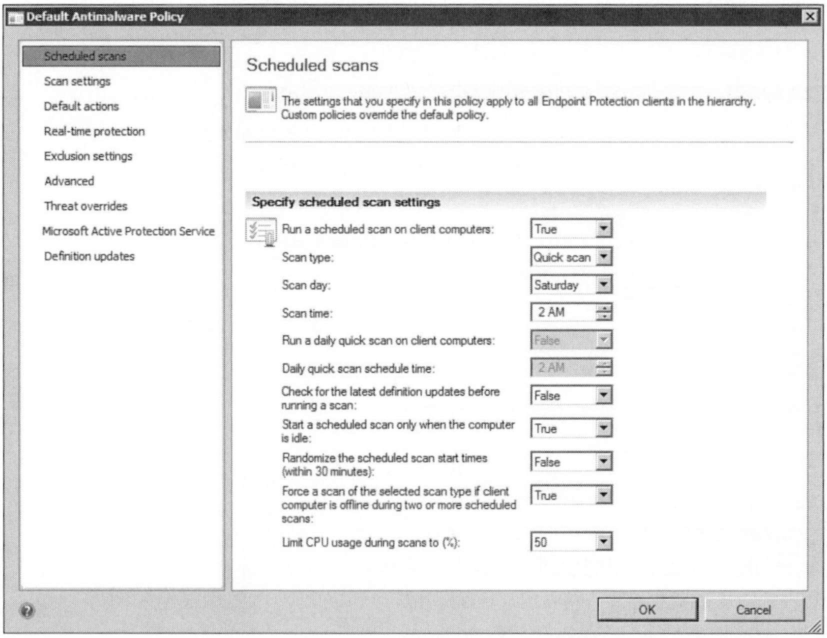

FIGURE 16.12   Default Antimalware Policy.

A Full scan obviously takes longer to perform because it scans everywhere; a Quick scan runs faster but does not check every file on the client computer. You can configure the day and time for the scan to occur if you choose the Full scan option; you can additionally enable a daily Quick scan and schedule when it should run. You can also configure checking for definition updates prior to running the scan and only running it when the computer is idle. If the client computer is offline for more than two consecutive scheduled updates, you can force it to get a definition update and limit the CPU usage to a definable percentage.

▶ **Scan Settings:** Here you can define whether to scan emails, email attachments, and archived files. If you want to scan removable storage devices such as USB drives, you can enable that option here as well. There is also an option to scan network drives when running a full scan; treat this option with care because a slow network with undefined network drives could literally take forever to complete and generate a substantial amount of network traffic.

You can give users some capabilities within the SCEP client by allowing them to configure CPU usage during scans and the ability to control scheduled scans.

▶ **Default Actions:** There are four alert levels defined for how Microsoft classifies malware based on monitoring behavior: severe, high, medium, and low. Should malware be detected, it is rated with one of these security levels, and action is taken based on that level. If malware is determined to be a severe risk, you can specify the default action to apply to that malware, such as removal instead of quarantining the malware.

▶ **Real-Time Protection:** This capability lets you scan files and processes in real time to ensure you are protected from suspicious files or processes you may encounter while using your computer. You can enable real-time protection by setting it to True, and also monitor file and program activity on your computer, either scanning incoming and outgoing files or limiting it to incoming or outgoing files. All downloaded files and attachments can be scanned, and behavior monitoring can be enabled (to look for malware-like activity). You can also enable network-based exploits protection and script scanning, and allow your users to configure these settings within the SCEP client agent.

▶ **Exclusion Settings:** Exclusion settings are important as they allow you to exclude files, file types, folders, and processes from scanning. You want to consider this, particularly on those servers where several files and folders are read or written to by known processes. You can set these options in the default policy, or import custom antimalware policies where the exclusions for the most common server roles are included along with some desktop roles such as high-performance or high-security. To add, remove, or review these settings, click **Set**, as shown in Figure 16.13.

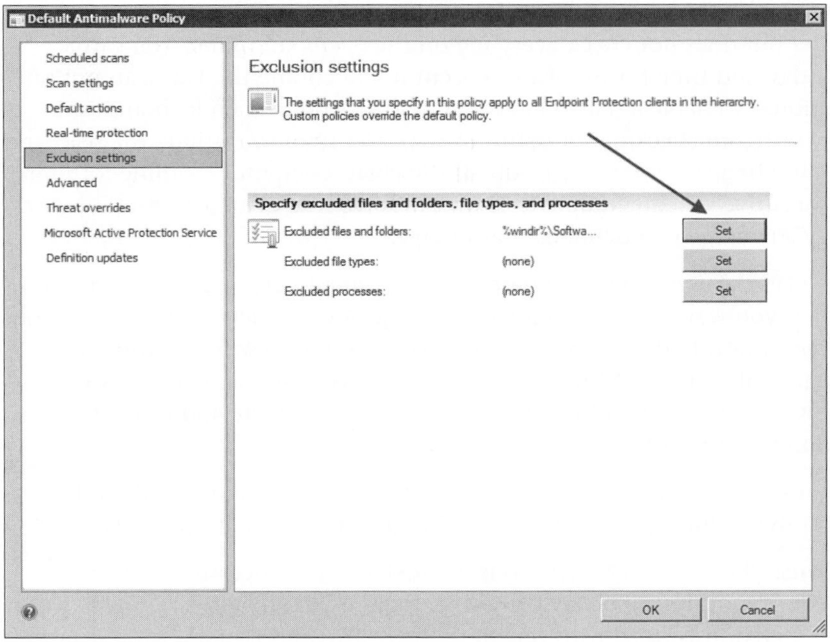

FIGURE 16.13   Exclusion settings.

▶ **Advanced:** These settings are for settings falling outside the other common sections. You can configure whether a system restore point is created before the computer is cleaned of malware, to show notifications to the end user when the user needs to perform certain actions such as running a full scan or downloading the latest definitions, or configure when quarantined files are deleted (default 14 days). You can grant users the ability to set the quarantined file deletion interval, exclude files, file types, and processes, and to view full history results.

▶ **Threat Overrides:** Here you can configure one of three actions (Allow, Remove, or Quarantine) to take when certain types of malware or specific viruses are detected. For example, if the W97M/Melissa.AF virus is detected, you can set the override action as Remove. This allows you to change the default action the Endpoint Protection client takes when a specific malware is detected.

▶ **Microsoft Active Protection Service:** Already discussed in the "Installing the Endpoint Protection Role" section, this is set when installing the endpoint protection role, but you can override this setting on each new policy you create. For example, if the default setting were set to Basic, you can configure one or more policies to have Advanced Membership. You can also allow your users to modify this setting.

▶ **Definition Updates:** Definition updates govern how current your SCEP agent will be. You can configure a variety of settings for definition updates including the interval in hours to check or a specific time to check daily (only configurable if the

interval-based check is disabled), and the action to take if more than two scheduled updates are missed if the computer is offline during a scheduled update (force
update). By clicking **Set Source**, you can also configure where to get the updates
from a list of five options: Configuration Manager, UNC file shares, WSUS, Microsoft
Update, and Microsoft Malware Protection Center. If you choose Configuration
Manager as the source of those updates in addition to specifying other sources, you
can configure the amount of hours before the client polls the other sources. Lastly,
if you specify a UNC path as an update source, you can specify the path by clicking
Set Paths, as shown in Figure 16.14.

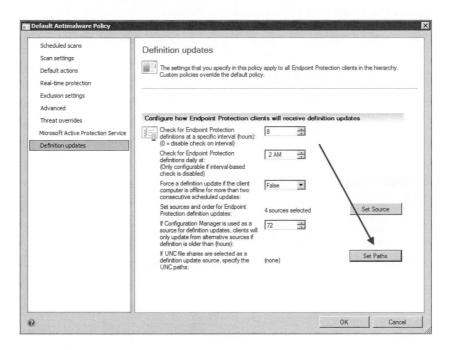

FIGURE 16.14   Set UNC paths for receiving definition updates.

Creating Custom Antimalware Policy

The statement "custom policies override the default policy" is repeated in every section of
each antimalware policy you configure for endpoint protection and is a reminder for you
to configure custom policies. Custom policies allow you to target the appropriate exclusions and suitable scan settings for your target computers, among many other antimalware
possibilities.

If you are uncertain about how to configure custom antimalware policy, Microsoft
provides samples that include examples for the most common Windows Server roles and
client computers. After creating your custom antimalware policy, deploy it to one or more
collections containing the computers you customized its settings for; otherwise, the policy
is not used and your computers could be at risk.

Importing and Merging Antimalware Policies

As mentioned in the "Planning and Considerations" section, Microsoft provides several predefined antimalware policies to make it easier for you to create custom antimalware policies. You can import any of these policies and later edit or merge them with another policy to create a new policy combining two or more targeted functions.

Importing Policy

To import a predefined antimalware policy, follow these steps:

1. Navigate to the Assets and Compliance workspace. In the navigation tree, expand **Overview -> Endpoint Protection -> Antimalware Policies**.

2. On the ribbon bar, select **Import**. A list of 25 ready-made policies displays, as shown in Figure 16.15.

3. Select a policy from the list and click **Open**.

4. When complete, the imported policy opens for you to review and edit. Make changes by clicking through the settings contained each section, and click **OK**. The imported policy now appears in your console.

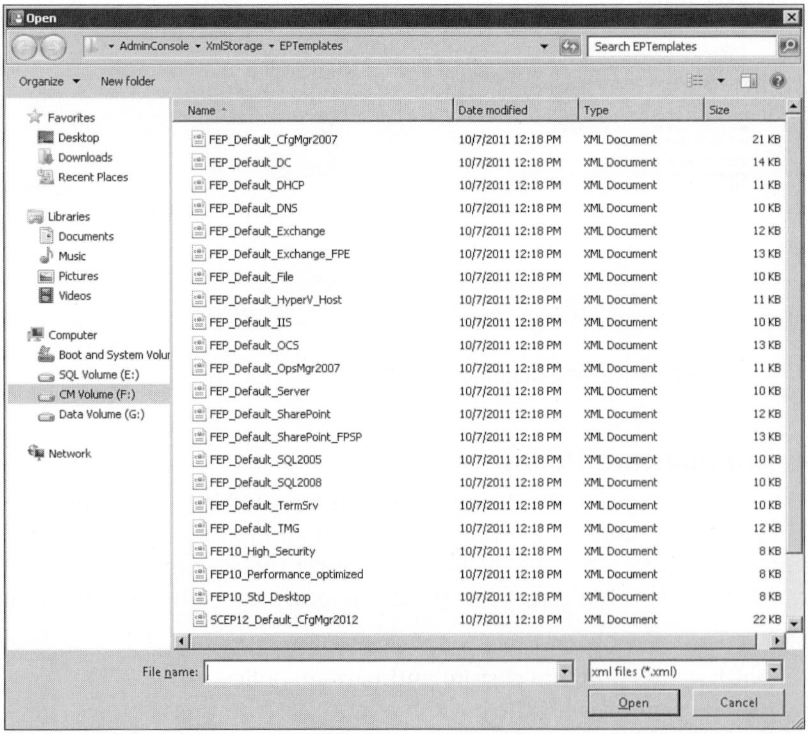

FIGURE 16.15 Importing antimalware policy.

Merging Policy

For an example of why you would merge policy, consider a server used for multiple functions. Say you have a policy targeted to your Configuration Manager server with exclusions set up for files and processes applicable to Configuration Manager. However, that server is also more than likely running SQL Server, which uses a separate policy. By merging those separately defined policies, you have one policy for all your Configuration Manager servers also running SQL Server. You can merge two (or more) policies together by selecting them in the console. To merge two antimalware policies together, follow these steps:

1. Navigate to the Assets and Compliance workspace. In the navigation tree, expand **Overview**, select **Endpoint Protection**, and select **Antimalware Policies**.

2. Select two or more policies that you want to merge, and click **Merge** on the ribbon bar, as shown in Figure 16.16.

3. You will be prompted to enter the **New Policy Name**. Provide it and select which of the two policies is the base policy. The base policy is the policy from which the overall antimalware policy settings are taken, to be merged with the exclusions of the other policy selected. Make any edits and click **OK**.

4. The merged policy appears in your console and is ready for deployment; the original policies also remain in the console.

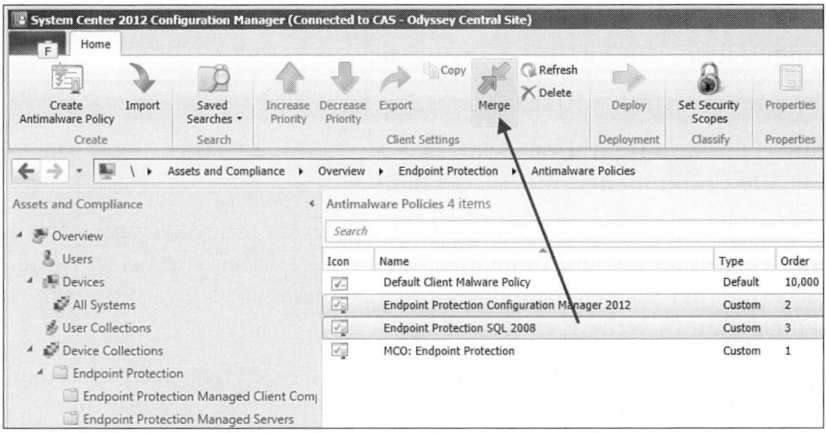

FIGURE 16.16 Merging two antimalware policies together.

Configuring Alerts for Endpoint Protection

Alerts, introduced in Chapter 8, "The Configuration Manager Console," let you know when specific security events have occurred in your hierarchy, and can notify your administrative users when a malware infection is detected. Alerts display in the Alerts node of the Monitoring workspace, and optionally can be emailed to specified users. How they are alerted to these security events is up to you to decide and configure accordingly.

The authors recommend configuring email notification because your administrators will not always be in front of the Configuration Manager console. Most administrators today have company-provided mobile phones with email capability and can receive these important notifications directly on their phone. The mail server itself would have to be monitored if this is the primary source of malware outbreak alerts because a potential outbreak might go unnoticed if the mail server were to go down at the same time.

Configuring Email Notification

If you have access to an SMTP server, you can optionally configure email notification alerts. An SMTP server can be specified only at the top-level site of your Configuration Manager hierarchy, meaning the CAS in a multisite hierarchy.

TIP: CONFIGURE ALERT SUBSCRIPTIONS TO RECEIVE EMAILS

Configuring email notification by itself will not keep your administrators alerted by email if a malware breakout occurs. You must also create one or more alert subscriptions to be notified by email of these specific alerts. You can specify different email addresses (recommended) to receive these email alerts. By having more than one person responsible for reading and reacting to these alerts, you are lessening the chances of malware breakout causing disruption to your business.

To configure email notification, perform the following steps:

1. Navigate to the Administration workspace.

2. Select **Overview -> Site Configuration -> Sites**. Select **Settings** on the ribbon bar, click **Configure Site Components**, and select **Email Notification**.

3. Fill in the FQDN or IP address of your SMTP server, and specify the SMTP port. If the SMTP server requires an account to login, specify it here; otherwise, select **None** (anonymous access). Enter the Sender address for email alerts. If you want users to reply to the sender address, verify it exists.

4. To test SMTP connectivity, click **Test SMTP server**, enter a Test email recipient email address, and click **Send test email**. If everything is configured correctly and the specified SMTP address and SMTP port are not blocked, you should see a message stating: `Testing email was sent successfully, please check your mailbox.` Check the mailbox of the test recipient to verify there is an email with this subject line from the email address you specified:

   `This is a Test Email for Alert Notification Sent from System Center 2012`
   `Configuration Manager.`

If things did not work properly, you may see a yellow exclamation mark indicating the server was not reachable or that the SMTP server could not verify the message was sent successfully.

NOTE: USING TELNET TO TEST SMTP SETTINGS FOR TROUBLESHOOTING

If you have issues configuring email alert notification, verify you can contact the SMTP server address you specified from your Configuration Manager server. One way to do this is using Telnet from a command prompt. Microsoft provides details describing how to test SMTP using Telnet from a command prompt. Follow the steps at http://technet.microsoft. com/en-us/library/aa995718%28EXCHG.65%29.aspx to verify you have proper connectivity and can send a test email using the address specified. This is an excellent way to determine if a firewall or other network issue might be blocking or interfering with SMTP communication.

When you receive an email notification alert, here is what is included as part of that email:

▶ The From address is the one you specified in the Email notification settings **Sender address for email alerts** option.

▶ The To address can contain one or more email addresses.

▶ The Subject of the email includes three important pieces of information:

  ▶ Description (Configuration Manager Malware Detected Alert).

  ▶ Type of alert—for example, Malware detection alert for collection.

  ▶ Collection Name is appended to the subject.

▶ Depending on the alert, the body of the email contains information about the breakout and may include the collection name, outbreak threshold, malware name and details, whether it was successfully remediated, and the infection percentage.

Here is an example of an email following an infection on one computer in the endpoint protection Managed Desktops and Laptops collection:

```
Configuration Manager Malware Detected Alert: Malware detection alert for
collection: Endpoint Protection Desktops and Laptops
From: EndpointProtectionAlerts@odyssey.com
To: nbrady@odyssey.com, jsandys@odyssey.com, kmeyler@odyssey.com
Configuration Manager Endpoint Protection has detected malware on one or more
computers in your organization

Collection name: Endpoint Protection Managed Desktops and Laptops
```

16

```
Malware Name: Virus:DOS/EICAR_Test_File
Number of infections: 3
Last detection time(UTC time): 1/2/2012 8:24:29 PM

These are the infections of this malware:
1. Computer name: buda.odyssey.com
Domain: ODYSSEY
Detection time(UTC time): 1/2/2012 8:24:29 PM
Malware file path: file:_C:\Users\NBrady\Desktop\test virus 123.txt
Remediation action: Remove
Action status: Succeeded
```

Configuring Alerts for Device Collections

By configuring alerts for a collection, you provide administrators with the ability to review malware activity in the dashboard and to receive emails for these alerts if email notification is configured. There are seven check boxes provided:

▶ Client Check

▶ Client Remediation

▶ Client Activity

▶ Malware Detection

▶ Malware Outbreak

▶ Repeated Malware Detection

▶ Multiple Malware Detection

Only malware alerts can be emailed, but all seven listed here are viewable in the Endpoint Protection dashboard. You can configure each of these alert thresholds individually. You cannot configure alerts for user collections. To configure alerts for device collections, follow these steps:

1. In the ConfigMgr console, navigate to the Assets and Compliance workspace.

2. In the navigation tree, under **Overview**, expand **Device Collections**, and select the **Endpoint Protection Managed Desktops and Laptops** collection.

3. Choose **Properties**, and click the **Alerts** tab, place a check mark in **View this collection in the Endpoint Protection Dashboard**.

4. Click **Add**, and select one or more alerts that you want to be notified about, as shown in Figure 16.17.

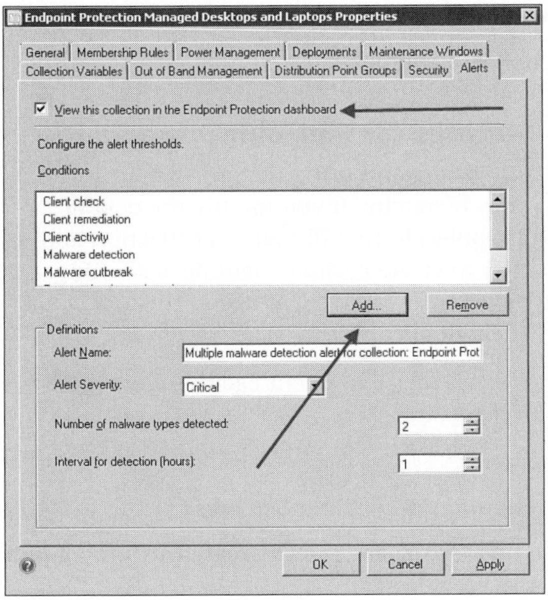

FIGURE 16.17   Adding alerts to a collection.

Configuring Alert Subscriptions

Alert subscriptions allow you to designate users to receive emails when a malware break-out (or similar event) occurs, provided you have configured email notification. You can specify multiple email addresses for each subscription you create (separating each email address using a semi-colon), and the subscription can contain one or more alert criteria. To configure alert subscriptions, follow these steps:

1. Navigate to the Monitoring workspace.

2. In the navigation tree, select **Overview -> Alerts -> Subscriptions**.

3. On the ribbon bar, select **Create Subscription**, and give the subscription a descriptive name that is no more than 255 characters, such as **Endpoint Protection Alert when Malware Detected**.

4. Select **Email language** from the drop-down menu provided.

5. Select an alert from the list; each collection that you enable for SCEP alerts is listed in the selected alerts list by default (provided you selected those alerts from the four available alerts for that collection). You need to select the type of alert and determine if it is applicable to the collection you want to monitor. The collection name is listed to the right of the listed alert. Four alerts are available:

   ▶ Generate alert when malware detected

   ▶ The same malware detected on a number of computers

▶ Same malware repeatedly detected on a computer

▶ Multiple types of malware detected on a computer

Configuring Custom Client Device Settings for Endpoint Protection

As a best practice, the authors recommend configuring and using custom client settings. Default client settings apply to all clients in your hierarchy. If you modify the default client settings and enable the SCEP client, this applies to the All Systems collection and thus all clients within that collection. It is better to create custom client device settings to target specific collections where you want to enable the SCEP client agent. Custom client settings are always a higher priority than the default client settings.

To configure custom client device settings to install the SCEP client agent, follow these steps:

1. Navigate to the Administration workspace.

2. In the navigation tree, expand **Overview**, and select **Client Settings**.

3. Right-click (or select the option on the ribbon bar) and select **Create Custom Client Device Settings**.

4. In the Create Custom Client Device Settings Wizard, give the settings a name such as **Custom Client Device Settings for Endpoint Protection**, and select **Endpoint Protection** from the available settings to be enforced on client devices, as shown in Figure 16.18.

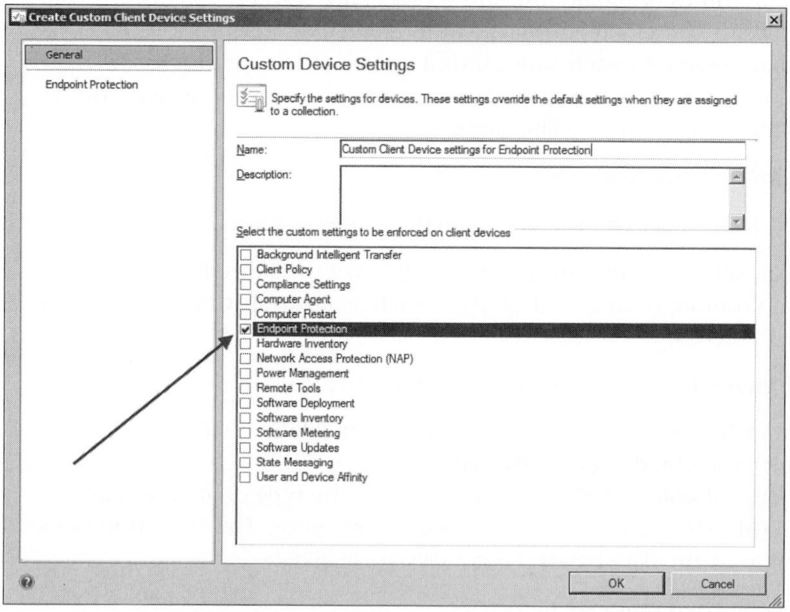

FIGURE 16.18   Selecting Endpoint Protection in custom client device settings.

5. Next, select **Endpoint Protection** in the left pane of Figure 16.18, and on the right side configure the options as appropriate. At a minimum, configuring the first two options to **True** means endpoint protection is managing the client computer and that the SCEP client is installed.

6. Click **OK** when complete; if necessary, adjust the priority of your custom client device setting by selecting it, right-clicking, and choosing to increase or decrease priority.

Deploying Endpoint Protection Custom Client Agent Settings

With your custom client device settings configured for endpoint protection, you must target these settings to one or more collections for them to be used. Perform the following steps to assign these custom client device settings to computers in a collection:

1. Open the ConfigMgr console, and navigate to the Administration workspace. In the navigation tree, expand **Overview**, and select **Client Settings**.

2. Right-click a previously created custom client device setting; then select **Deploy** from the available options. A Device Collection selection box appears, as shown in Figure 16.19.

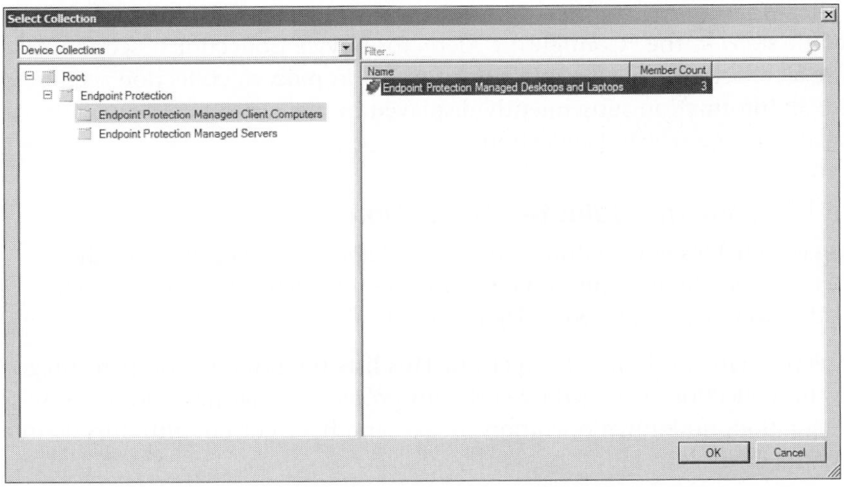

FIGURE 16.19   Deploying custom client device settings to a collection.

3. Select a device collection to which to deploy an endpoint protection custom device setting (you can deploy only client agent settings to device collections), and click **OK**.

4. When complete, any computers in the specified collection will receive this policy in their next policy update and the SCEP agent will be installed. If the SCEP client is already installed on any clients in this collection, the client is not reinstalled.

Monitoring Status in Endpoint Protection

In its simplest form, the Endpoint Protection dashboard is composed of three dynamic sections that allow you to ascertain the security health of your clients:

▶ Collection

▶ Security State

▶ Operational State

These sections of the dashboard show information related to the last reported endpoint protection status on the currently selected collection. You can force a summarization of this data by selecting **Run Summarization**, or you can schedule a recurring summarization (minutes, hours, and days) by selecting **Schedule Summarization**. Both options are available on the ribbon bar or by right-clicking **System Center 2012 Endpoint Protection Status**. Data listed in this dashboard is based upon the last summarization ran, so if you want current data, run a summarization before drilling further into the data. The next sections provide additional information on each of these views.

Configuring Collections to Appear in Collection View

To populate information in this dashboard, you must first configure one or more collections and enable them for viewing. To configure a device collection to show up on the dashboard, follow the steps in the "Configuring Alerts for Device Collections" section. After you configure a collection, you can select it from the drop-down collection section of your dashboard; all information subsequently displayed in the Security and Operational State sections is related to the selected collection.

Security State View for the Selected Collection

The Security State view enables you to find security applicable information about the overall Endpoint Protection client status and any malware remediation status. The left pane lists six clickable sections, displayed in Figure 16.20:

▶ **Clients protected with Endpoint Protection:** This lists the number and percentage of clients in this collection managed by endpoint protection that have no malware pending remediation, no known operations issues, and have current antivirus definitions (less than 7 days old).

▶ **At risk from active malware or known operational issues:** This lists clients with malware that is pending remediation, with known operational issues, without antivirus definitions, or with definitions older than 7 days.

▶ **Endpoint Protection client not yet installed:** Clicking this link shows any computer in the selected collection that has not reported their status yet or does not have the SCEP client installed.

▶ **Endpoint Protection client not supported on platform:** Operating systems not supporting the SCEP client are viewable by clicking here.

▶ **Configuration Manager client inactive:** This lists whether the Configuration Manager is inactive as defined in the activity settings defined in the Client Status Settings under **Monitoring -> Overview -> Client Status**.

▶ **Configuration Manager client not installed:** If the ConfigMgr client is not installed, any clients in this state are viewable by clicking here. The ConfigMgr client must be installed for the SCEP client to be managed.

Clicking any of the sections listed on the left side of Figure 16.20 opens a corresponding sticky node in your **Assets and Compliance** collections. Note the sticky node is not permanent; closing the console removes all sticky nodes from view.

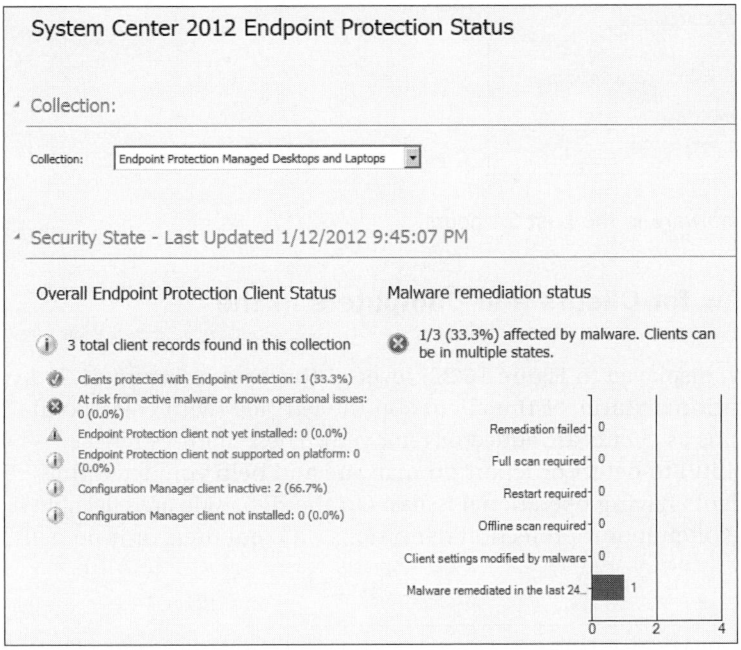

System Center 2012 Endpoint Protection Status

⊿ Collection:

Collection: | Endpoint Protection Managed Desktops and Laptops   ▾ |

⊿ Security State - Last Updated 1/12/2012 9:45:07 PM

Overall Endpoint Protection Client Status

ⓘ 3 total client records found in this collection

✓ Clients protected with Endpoint Protection: 1 (33.3%)
✗ At risk from active malware or known operational issues: 0 (0.0%)
⚠ Endpoint Protection client not yet installed: 0 (0.0%)
ⓘ Endpoint Protection client not supported on platform: 0 (0.0%)
ⓘ Configuration Manager client inactive: 2 (66.7%)
ⓘ Configuration Manager client not installed: 0 (0.0%)

Malware remediation status

✗ 1/3 (33.3%) affected by malware. Clients can be in multiple states.

Remediation failed 0
Full scan required 0
Restart required 0
Offline scan required 0
Client settings modified by malware 0
Malware remediated in the last 24... 1

0   2   4

FIGURE 16.20   Security state in the Endpoint Protection dashboard.

Malware Remediation Status

The right pane of the Security State area of the dashboard lists several additional sections pertaining to malware remediation. If any system is found in a state that matches one of the items on this list, a clickable blip is added to the evolving graph. Clicking the blip presents you with a sticky node in Assets and Compliance giving further details on the objects. All except the last item are clients at risk:

▶ Remediation failed

▶ Full scan required

▶ Restart required

▶ Offline scan required

▶ Client settings modified by malware

▶ Malware remediated in the last 24 hours

Top 5 Malware

The bottom right pane of the Security State area on the dashboard displays information about the Top 5 malware by number of computers in the last 24 hours, as shown in Figure 16.21. If malware were found in the last 24 hours, the results are listed and clickable. You can get more information about the malware by clicking its name.

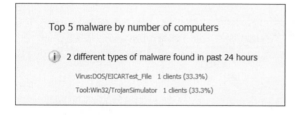

FIGURE 16.21   The top 5 malware in the past 24 hours.

Operational State View for Clients and Computers in the Selected Collection

The Operational State view, displayed in Figure 16.22, reverses the view in Figure 16.20 by putting the graph of **Operational status of the clients** on the left side (with corresponding growing/shrinking graphs as clients are added or removed). These statuses reflect the client's ability (or inability) to detect or report on malware and help you determine what is wrong with any clients having operational issues. On the right side are clickable sections that reveal the age of endpoint protection definitions on computers or if no definitions are found at all.

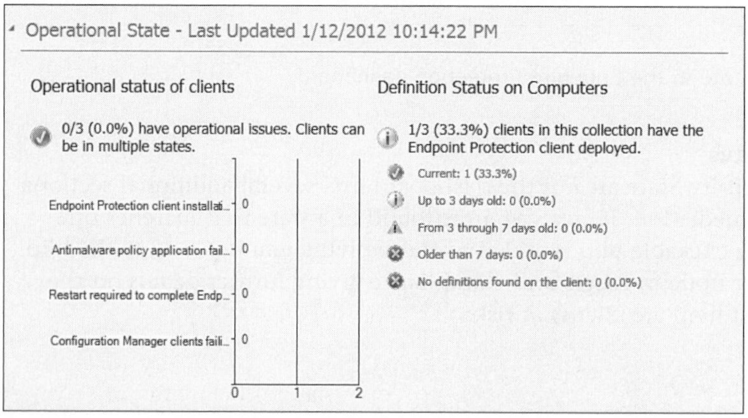

FIGURE 16.22   Operational State in the Endpoint Protection dashboard.

Monitoring Malware Details Using the Assets and Compliance Workspace

You can review information about malware in the Assets and Compliance workspace. To find malware details on a specific computer in the Assets and Compliance workspace, follow these steps:

1. Navigate to the **Assets and Compliance** workspace.

2. Select a device collection, select a computer, and then click the **Malware Detail** tab.

The Malware Detail tab lists information including the threat name, detection time, category, severity, action, state name, detection mode, process, path, and username. You can add or remove columns in this view to get more information if necessary.

You can select any of the malware listed and press CTRL+C to copy the details and paste the information into Notepad for review. The Path column lists all paths on which the malware was detected; this allows you to later verify that the malware is removed from the user's system by browsing the path in question on that computer.

Monitoring Endpoint Protection Details Using the Assets and Compliance Workspace

Knowing quickly if SCEP manages your computers is important, as is determining what endpoint protection policy is applied. To troubleshoot your clients and see this information in the console, follow these steps:

1. Navigate to the **Assets and Compliance** workspace.

2. Select a Device Collection, select a computer, and then click the **Endpoint Protection** tab.

Three key information glimpses are given:

▶ **Deployment Information:** This lists important details including EP Deployment State and Deployment Return code and description if available. EP Deployment State shows as Managed when SCEP is managing your client, or Unmanaged when it is not.

▶ **Remediation Information:** Here you can quickly see at-a-glance information pertaining to remediation status including whether a full scan is pending, manual steps are needed, or whether a rebooting is pending.

▶ **Policy Application Information:** Here you can determine if the custom antimalware policy you defined for your clients is being installed. EP Policy Name lists the policy applied and whether it succeeded in applying it or any return codes.

Performing On-Demand Actions for Malware

The ability to perform on-demand scanning (full or quick scan) or instruct the SCEP client to update its malware definition files (download definition) enables the administrator to initiate actions to protect the chosen client(s) from within the console.

16

You can select individual computers, multiple computers, or entire collections. To perform on-demand actions for malware, follow these steps:

1. Navigate to the **Assets and Compliance** workspace.

2. In the navigation tree, expand **Overview**, and select **Device Collections**.

3. Select a device collection managed by endpoint protection, and select one or more clients you want to scan.

4. Right-click the client, and select **Endpoint Protection**, as shown in Figure 16.23; then select to run a **Full Scan**, **Quick Scan**, or **Download Definition** as appropriate. Choosing to perform a scan advises you the client may encounter high CPU usage during the scan, and significant network traffic may result.

   These actions do not occur immediately; they start when the client receives the next policy, defined by the settings for Client Settings policy (60 minutes default).

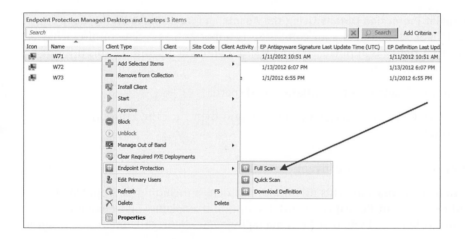

FIGURE 16.23   Performing a Full Scan on a client.

TIP: PERFORMING AN ON-DEMAND ACTION IMMEDIATELY

If you need a client computer to start the scan or definition download immediately rather than when it next checks for policy, you may want to obtain a third-party right-click tool to trigger the policy check on that computer. Alternatively, you can connect to that computer remotely and manually trigger a policy refresh.

Reporting in Endpoint Protection

Endpoint protection comes with six reports out-of-the-box; these reports enable you to drill down further to obtain more information about the malware problem. You can make these available to appropriate management using RBA (by configuring a user or group of users and an associated custom role) to constrain what reports the user or group has access to. Typically, the individuals reading the reports are not necessarily working within the console, so configuring users for access to these reports is a good idea. Here is information about the included reports:

▶ **Top Users by Threats:** This report shows the list of users with the most number of detected threats; it prompts you to enter a collection name and optionally a start and end date. The output lists any applicable users by threats, incident count, number of computers, and when the threat was detected. You can drill further into the report by clicking a **User Name**, which lists the Computer name and Threat name along with the severity level of the malware, its category, incident count, and detection date period. For information about the malware itself, click the **Threat Name** for a Malware Details report describing a particular threat in detail and the computers it has been found on, as displayed in Figure 16.24.

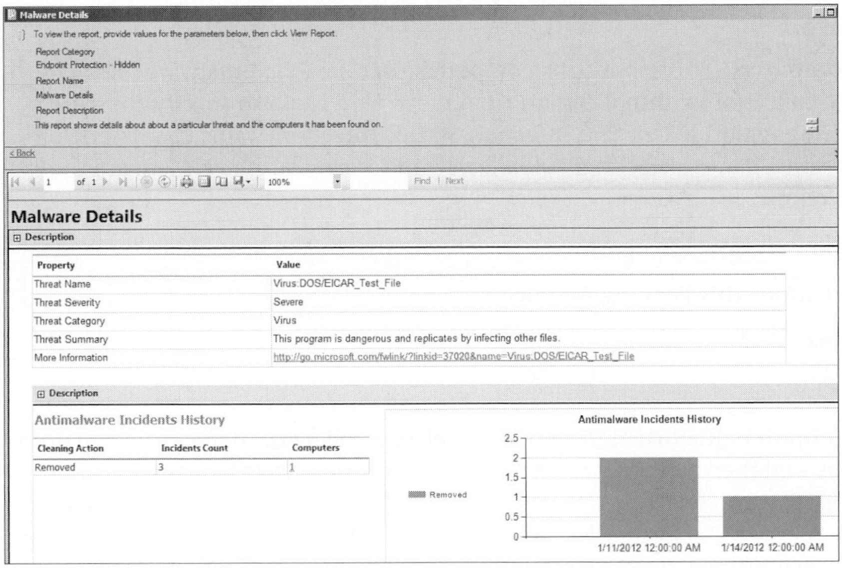

FIGURE 16.24   Malware Details report.

▶ **User Threat List:** This report shows the list of threats found under a particular user account. It is useful to identify those users endangering your organization through their activities; viewing or printing a report with usernames showing the malware threats they have on their computers is a good incentive for action for both the users involved and their managers.

▶ **Antimalware Activity Report:** Here you are prompted to enter the name of a collection you want the report to display information about, and to choose a timeframe from which you want to gather the data. The report gives an overview of antimalware quarantined or removed from computers in the selected collection, as displayed in Figure 16.25.

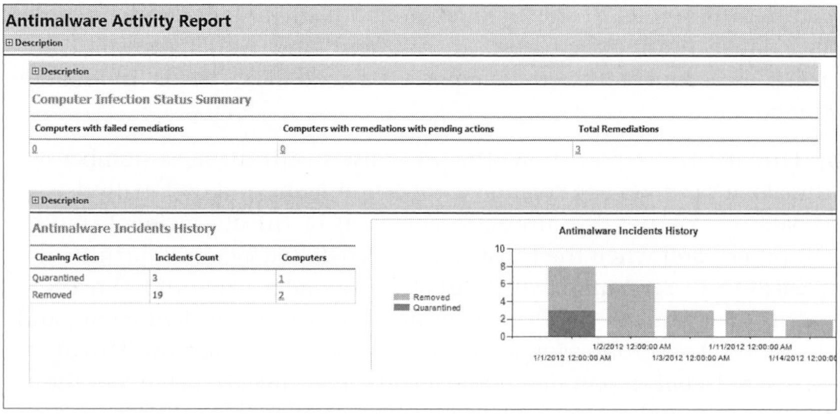

FIGURE 16.25   Antimalware Activity Report.

▶ **Infected Computers:** This report lists computers that have had malware on them on a specific collection within a certain timeframe. You can also specify the Threat name, Cleaning Action taken, and Infection Status. Infection Status can be one of three remediation states, selecting Null allows you to view all states. Here are the possible selections:

   ▶ Remediation Fail

   ▶ Remediation with Pending Actions

   ▶ Remediated

   ▶ Null

▶ **Infected Computers Report:** Here you must select a collection name from the drop-down choice, and then select a timeframe. The report preselects a one-week time-frame by default, but you can set the start date further back in time to capture data that is more relevant. You can select what cleaning action took place from a choice of Cleaned, Quarantined, Removed, Allowed, User Specified, No Action, Blocked, or Null. You can also select Infection status with the options of Remediation fail, Remediation with pending actions, and Remediated. If you want to target your report further, you can enter the Malware threat name in the threat field.

▶ **Dashboard Report:** Again, you enter the collection name from a drop-down menu to display a wide variety of endpoint protection information about the computers in that collection. You must also choose a timeframe from which you want to gather the data. The report gives a graphical overview of the state of endpoint protection for that collection much like the in-console Endpoint Protection dashboard, except in a report-friendly format.

Creating and Deploying Windows Firewall Policies

The firewall functionality provided by SCEP is basic but can be used to perform the following settings for the domain, public and private profiles of your client computers. If any firewall settings are configured via group policy, group policy wins:

▶ Turn Windows Firewall On or Off.

▶ Decide if incoming connections are allowed.

▶ Decide if users are notified when Windows Firewall blocks a new program.

To create a Windows firewall policy for SCEP, follow these steps:

1. Navigate to the Assets and Compliance workspace. In the navigation tree, expand **Overview**, and select **Endpoint Protection**.

2. Select **Windows Firewall Policies**.

3. Right-click and select **Create Windows Firewall Policy**; give it an appropriate name and description. Click **Next**.

4. Select the options you want to enable or disable from the screen, as displayed in Figure 16.26. Click **Next** to continue.

5. Continue through the wizard.

Follow these steps to deploy a Windows firewall policy:

1. Navigate to the Assets and Compliance workspace. In the navigation tree, expand **Overview**, and select **Endpoint Protection**.

2. Select **Windows Firewall Policies**, select the Windows firewall policy you created, right-click, and choose **Deploy**.

3. Select a target collection by clicking **Browse**. All computers in this collection receive the deployment in a random order over a 2-hour period to avoid network flooding. Click **Next** to continue.

4. For a compliance evaluation check, select the period you want the schedule to run. (The default is every 7 days.) Click **Next**.

5. Continue through the rest of the wizard.

16

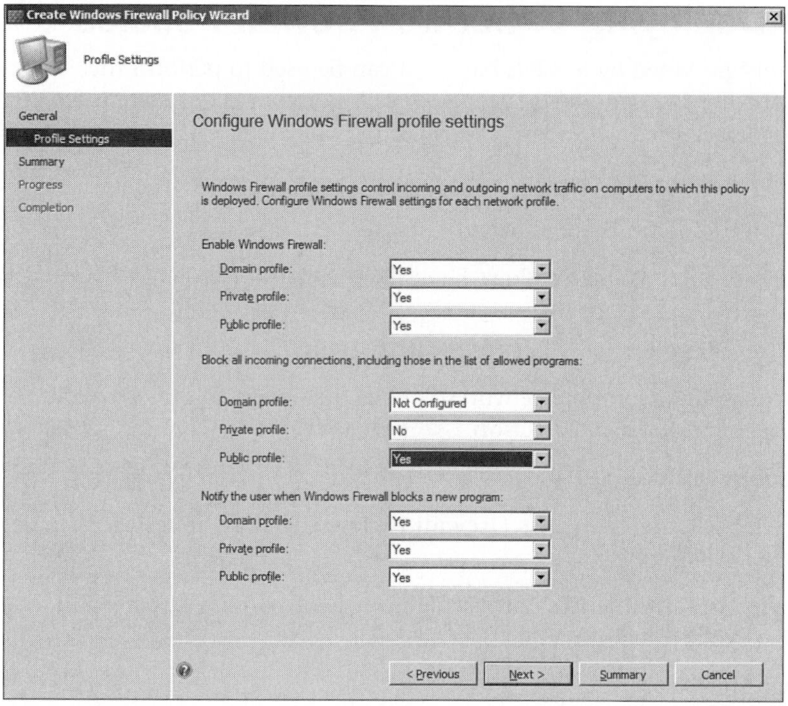

FIGURE 16.26   Configure Windows Firewall profile settings.

Understanding the Endpoint Protection Client

The Endpoint Protection client is the frontend application (associated with a system tray icon) that your users may interact with or see if malware is detected on their computer. When the client is in a healthy state, it has a green check mark, as shown in Figure 16.27.

If malware is detected while the computer is in use, the color changes to a dangerous red and flashes in the system tray to alert the user to the problem. Depending on the severity of malware found, the user could be prompted to take action such as to clean the computer by selecting the **Clean Computer** button, displayed in Figure 16.28. If the user takes no action, the Endpoint Protection client takes whatever action deemed appropriate based on the antimalware policy applied.

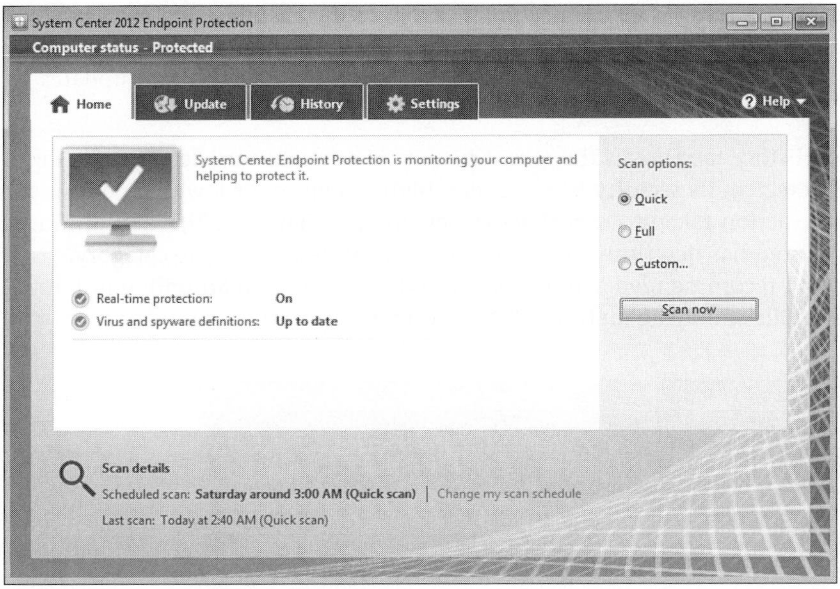

FIGURE 16.27   The Endpoint Protection client agent home screen.

FIGURE 16.28   The user is notified to clean the computer when a threat is detected.

The agent has four tabs visible in the main window:

▶ **Home:** This is the main window of the SCEP client. It provides a quick overview of how the client is performing by revealing whether the virus and spyware definitions are current and if real-time protection is on. It also lists scan details such as the date and type of the last scan, if a scheduled scan is enabled, and enables the end user to initiate a scan using the **Scan Now** button with three associated radio options: Quick, Full, or Custom. Selecting **Custom** allows the user to define what drives or folders to scan.

▶ **Update:** Similar to the Home tab, this tab reveals SCEP client virus and spyware definitions status; however, it goes into more granular detail by listing when the definitions were created, when they were last checked, the version of the virus definitions, and the version of the spyware definitions. There is also an **Update** button, allowing the end user to initiate a definition update status check. Clicking **Update** forces the client to poll its defined definition update sources for available definition updates and apply them if any are found.

▶ **History:** The History tab reveals the recent history of any malware detected, listing when it was detected, its security level (severe, high, medium, or low) where it was found, and the action taken to remediate the client (see Figure 16.29). In addition, any malware listed has descriptive text written about it describing the category, description, and recommended action that should be taken, and an online link to reveal more details about the malware. (This requires an Internet connection.)

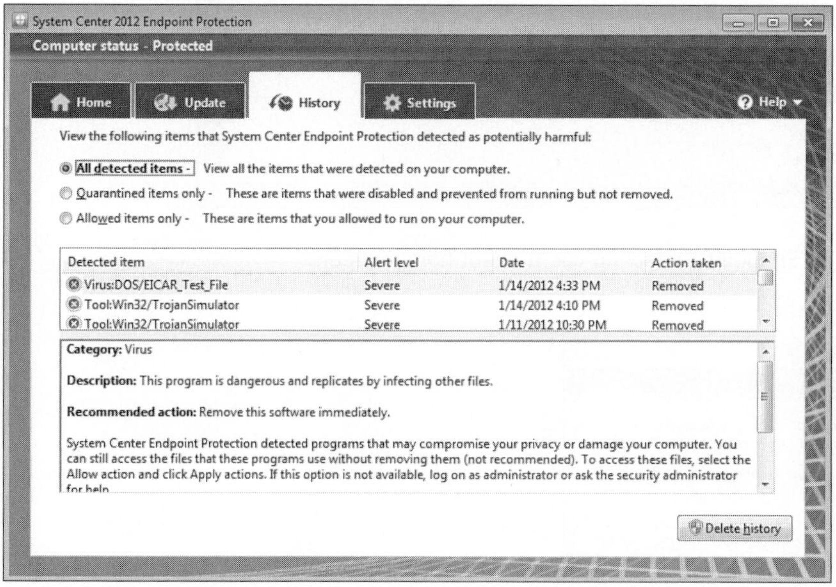

FIGURE 16.29   The History tab reveals malware activity and details.

▶ **Settings:** This tab allows the end user to review or change the malware policy settings applied to this computer if the malware policy is configured to allow the user to do so. Any options not configurable by the end user are grayed out and can be viewed only for information purposes.

There is also a **Help** button on the upper-right corner of the client agent window, which can provide online help and support for System Center Endpoint Protection. To the right of this button is a drop-down menu in the shape of a downward pointing arrow. This menu provides additional options such as offline help, the ability to submit a malicious sample, join the Customer Experience Improvement Program (CEIP), view the privacy statement, license agreement, check for software updates, or review detailed information about which malware policy was applied and when.

This last option is important as a troubleshooting step to determine if your client is using the correct policy because it lists the name of the policy and the date and time it was applied (see Figure 16.30). It also lists version details of the client agent, engine version, definition updates, spyware definitions, and network inspection system definition version.

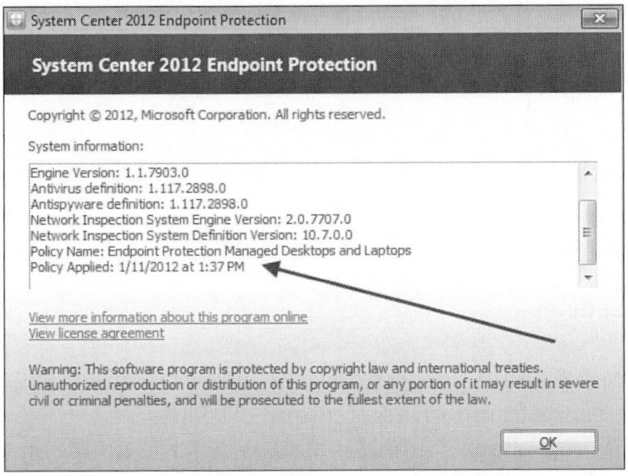

FIGURE 16.30   The Policy Name is listed in the About page.

The Endpoint Protection client logs to the EndpointProtectionAgent.log log file, found in %*windir*%\CCM\logs.

Installing the Endpoint Protection Client

The Endpoint Protection client is separate from the ConfigMgr client; however, it is prestaged on your clients when you deploy the ConfigMgr client. This means you do not have to create any separate applications or packages to install the Endpoint Protection client as was the case with Configuration Manager 2007 with Forefront Endpoint Protection 2010 integrated. The files necessary for installation are cached locally, and the SCEP client is installed only when the client agent settings are configured to enable the SCEP client.

Understanding Endpoint Protection Client Settings

There are six configurable options for the SCEP client settings, and they define how you install Endpoint Protection client. You can create multiple custom client settings, target them to different collections, and give those different priorities and functionality. These custom client settings always take priority over the default client agent settings. If a computer is in more than one collection targeted by custom client settings, the client settings with the highest priority wins. Figure 16.31 shows the default settings. Here are the settings that are configurable for the Endpoint Protection client:

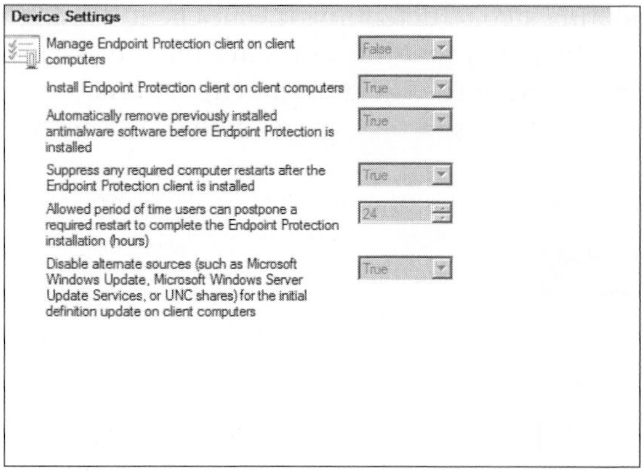

FIGURE 16.31   Endpoint Protection client settings.

▶ **Manage Endpoint Protection client on client computers:** This allows ConfigMgr to manage any Endpoint Protection client found on the computer that is a supported version. In other words, if your client computer already has the Endpoint Protection client, setting this to True has ConfigMgr manage that Endpoint Protection client as long as it is a supported version, which is the minimum version shipped with ConfigMgr.

▶ **Install Endpoint Protection client on client computers:** This setting controls installation of the Endpoint Protection client on client computers. Setting this to False and setting the settings in the first bullet to True allows you to script uninstallation of your own third-party antimalware software. Setting it to True forces installation of the Endpoint Protection client agent on the computers to which it is targeted.

▶ **Automatically remove previously installed antimalware software before Endpoint Protection is installed:** If configured as True, this uninstalls some McAfee, Symantec, and TrendMicro antimalware software; see the "Automatic Removal of Antimalware Software" section for additional details.

▶ **Suppress any required computer restarts after the Endpoint Protection client is installed:** In some cases, installing the Endpoint Protection client agent requires a restart, such as when removing certain third-party antimalware software or if there are missing files or required files are in use. In such scenarios, you would not want servers rebooting until their maintenance windows allow, so set this to True on servers to suppress restarts, and to False on client computers.

▶ **Allowed period of time users can postpone a required restart to complete the Endpoint Protection installation (hours):** This allows you to define how long the client computer can postpone any required restart occurring from installing the Endpoint Protection client.

▶ **Disable alternate sources (such as Microsoft Windows Updates, Microsoft Windows Server Update Services or UNC shares) for the initial definition update on client computers:** Setting this to True enables you to force the first update of endpoint protection definitions from ConfigMgr's distribution point framework rather than other sources. When the Endpoint Protection client is installed before receiving its first policy, it doesn't know where to get its definition updates from, so setting this option ensures that it polls only ConfigMgr for the definition updates.

Communication Between the Client and the Server

State messages are used via the ConfigMgr client agent and the site server to transmit information from the SCEP client pertaining to the last scan time, definition update version, whether a virus was detected, or if suspicious malware activity is detected. Here's how it works:

▶ There is a separate namespace in Windows Management Instrumentation (WMI) that the SCEP client accesses; this is `root\Microsoft\SecurityClient`.

▶ The Configuration Manager client agent monitors the `AntiMalwareHealthStatus` and `AntiMalwareInfectionStatus` classes for any changes; if found, a state message is sent. Here are the logs on the client system that provide additional information about what is submitted to the server:

  ▶ ExternalEventAgent.log

  ▶ StateMessage.log

▶ The state messages generated are found in WMI at `root\ccm\statemsg`; as they are processed regularly, any virus infection on a client can result in the server being alerted within 5 minutes.

Automatic Removal of Antimalware Software

The SCEP client installation lets you uninstall some third-party antivirus software. Setting the option **Automatically remove previously installed antimalware software before Endpoint Protection is installed** in the Endpoint Protection Client Settings screen to **True** directs the client to automatically uninstall the software listed here:

▶ All current Microsoft antimalware products except Windows InTune and Microsoft Security Essentials

▶ Symantec AntiVirus Corporate Edition version 10

▶ Symantec Endpoint Protection version 11

▶ Symantec Endpoint Protection Small Business Edition version 12

▶ McAfee VirusScan Enterprise version 8

▶ Trend Micro OfficeScan

16

Antivirus software not listed in this section must be identified and uninstalled with a custom uninstaller script or application prior to pushing out the SCEP client. Failure to do so leaves you with client computers running two antivirus solutions, introducing instability and/or loss of performance.

Removing the Endpoint Protection Client

Should you need to remove the Endpoint Protection client, you must target those systems where it is installed with a script that can uninstall it. Removing the Endpoint Protection client is not automatic, and disabling those specific client agent settings used to install it does not remove the client. Even if you remove the Configuration Manager client, the Endpoint Protection client agent will remain installed. To remove the Endpoint Protection client, you can uninstall it manually or use a script. Here is an example that performs a silent uninstall of the SCEP client; you could create a package/program to do this for you, which would include a script containing the following:

```
scepinstall.exe /u /s
```

Delivery of Definition Updates

When configuring custom antimalware policies for endpoint protection, you can configure definition update sources from a combination of five available options. The sources you choose is up to you, and you can choose just one or several. Determine the level of antimalware definition updates support you want for your clients and whether you want them to obtain definition updates from outside of your organization from places such as Microsoft Update. Here are the five sources:

▶ **Updates distributed from WSUS:** Select this option if you have WSUS installed and configured to obtain definition updates for endpoint protection, particularly if you are not using a SUP to deliver the definitions.

▶ **Updates distributed from Microsoft Update:** Selecting this source means the SCEP client can communicate with Microsoft Update to download definition and engine updates. This requires your client computers have an Internet connection.

▶ **Updates distributed from Microsoft Malware Protection Center:** These updates are typically malware definitions or other delta files and require an Internet connection on your client computers.

▶ **Updates distributed from Configuration Manager:** Selecting this option means that your SCEP client will receive its definition and engine updates from ConfigMgr's SUP, which means you have greater control of what the client computers get and when, and that you can use ConfigMgr's distribution points.

This option is preferred; it lets you use ADRs to download the updates on a recurring basis and automatically copy the new definition updates to all your distribution points prior to making the clients aware of the new definitions via client policy. It also gives you the capability to rollback definition versions (using a package/program type of solution) should any problems arise.

▶ **Updates from UNC file shares:** Choosing this option involves manual work, although it is scriptable. It requires copying endpoint protection definition updates to a network share accessible by your client computers. You want to do this several times per day or at least once daily to remain protected. You also need separate x86 and x64 folders in this UNC share to store the architecture specific files.

The advantage of using this method is the lack of a required Internet connection for your client computers because they need to access only a UNC share. The disadvantage is it may not always work (scripts sometimes fail) and the network share may not be available (computer rebooting or unavailable), in which case your client computers would not be updated with the latest signatures as quickly as they would with an automated solution.

Summary

Microsoft's decision to integrate System Center Endpoint Protection fully into System Center Configuration Manager was an appropriate one. By consolidating security tasks with client management and thereby reducing your costs and enhancing ability, Microsoft has extended the capabilities of SCEP to match the security constrains it needs to work with in these malware-prevalent times. The decision also removes confusion for organizations previously protecting their clients with multiple third-party software solutions because now they can simply enable the endpoint protection role within Configuration Manager, configure their client settings and custom antimalware policies, and secure their infrastructure easily and cost-effectively.

16

CHAPTER 17

Configuration Manager Queries

At this point in the book, your System Center 2012 Configuration Manager (ConfigMgr) infrastructure should be collecting considerable amounts of data from your ConfigMgr clients. Queries were mentioned briefly in Chapter 3, "Looking Inside Configuration Manager," as a means to retrieve information from the ConfigMgr database. You could use this information in a variety of ways, from something as simple as creating an ad-hoc list of clients with a specific operating system, to areas as complex as listing devices missing a certain type of software. However, queries are not just about hardware and software information. Information from component statuses and activity audits is also easily accessible by using queries.

ConfigMgr comes with a handful of predefined queries, but by the end of this chapter, you should be comfortable writing your own with the ConfigMgr query builder and with enough practice, writing queries by hand. This chapter provides information on objects, classes, and attributes, as well as descriptions of criterion types, operators, and joins to give you the insight to build your own queries.

Queries can be the basis of any well-constructed collection helping narrow the target of a deployment to the right set of devices. Although application intelligence reduces the necessity for intricate collections for deploying software in ConfigMgr, it is still vitally important to generate a target list of devices for other purposes, such as applying power management, maintenance windows, or endpoint protection settings.

Introducing the Queries Node

As introduced in Chapter 8, "The Configuration Manager Console," you manage and run queries using the Queries node of the Monitoring workspace, as shown in Figure 17.1.

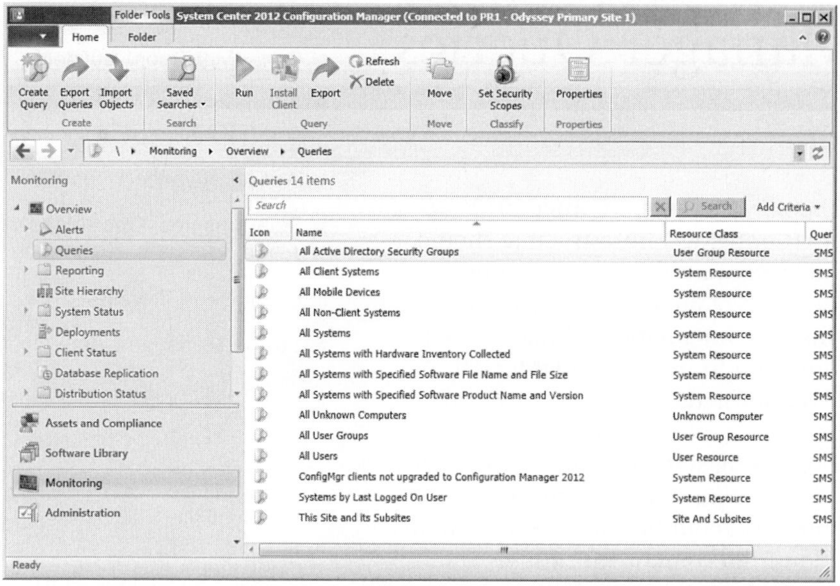

FIGURE 17.1   The Queries node of the Monitoring workspace.

When you select the query in the list pane, the ribbon bar displays the following set of options, as shown in Figure 17.2:

▶ **Create Query:** Creates new queries.

▶ **Export Queries:** Exports queries for use in other ConfigMgr environments.

▶ **Import Objects:** Imports queries.

▶ **Saved Searches:** Displays a drop-down list of previously saved searches.

▶ **Run:** Executes the selected query.

▶ **Install Client:** Initiates the Install Client Wizard targeting the objects of the selected query.

▶ **Refresh:** Refreshes the selected query.

▶ **Delete:** Deletes the selected query.

▶ **Move:** Moves the selected query to a different folder.

▶ **Set Security Scopes:** Associates the selected query to one or more security scopes.

▶ **Properties:** Displays the properties of the selected query.

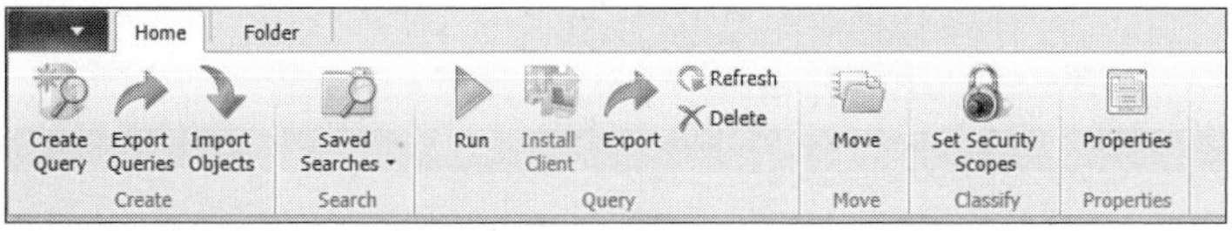

FIGURE 17.2   The Query ribbon bar.

Organizing the Query List Pane

After selecting the Queries node, the List pane displays the icon, name, resource class, and query ID of each query. You can add or remove columns to customize the List pane to fit the environment. For example, if your environment heavily utilizes comments, it might be beneficial to include this column in your list. Here are the available columns:

▶ **Icon:** This is self-explanatory.

▶ **Name:** This is the name assigned to the query.

▶ **Resource Class:** Indicates the type of object returned in the result set.

▶ **Query ID:** This is the unique ID assigned by the system to the query. Default queries begin with SMS, whereas custom queries begin with the site code.

▶ **Comments:** This is a free-form text field used to add a comment about the query, often used to help identity the query.

▶ **Expression:** This is the Windows Management Instrumentation (WMI) Query Language, known as WQL, statement inside of the query.

▶ **Limit to Collection ID:** If you specified a collection ID in the Collection Limiting section, the query retrieves only values that match the query and exist in the specified collection.

To select additional columns, right-click one of the column headers, as displayed in Figure 17.3, and select a column.

If you find adding and removing columns adds excessive white space between the column values, you can resize the columns to overlap data or fit it in. To resize columns, choose the separator bar between the column headers and drag it to the left or right. To resize the column to fit the contents automatically, you would right-click the column header and choose **Size Column to Fit**. Optionally, you can resize all columns to fit by choosing **Size All Columns to Fit**.

Although viewing all columns of interest is useful, it may be difficult to sort through the number of queries in the List pane. Clicking any of the column headers sorts the List pane results in the order of the arrow: up for ascending and down for descending. Sorting is also accessible via the menu available by right-clicking the column header area.

17

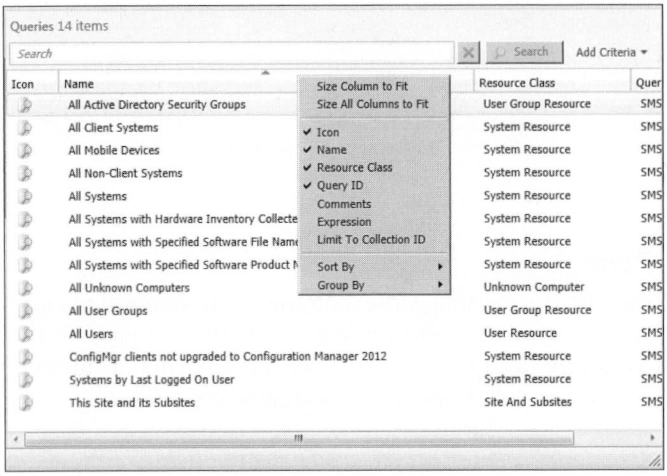

FIGURE 17.3   Managing column sizes in the console.

Another option to help sift through queries is grouping them by type. You can group queries by any column as long as the column has been selected for display. To group by a column, right-click in the column header area, choose **Group By**, and then select the column. Figure 17.4 shows how the List pane looks when grouping by the resource class. Grouping queries together provides the ability to collapse and expand groups.

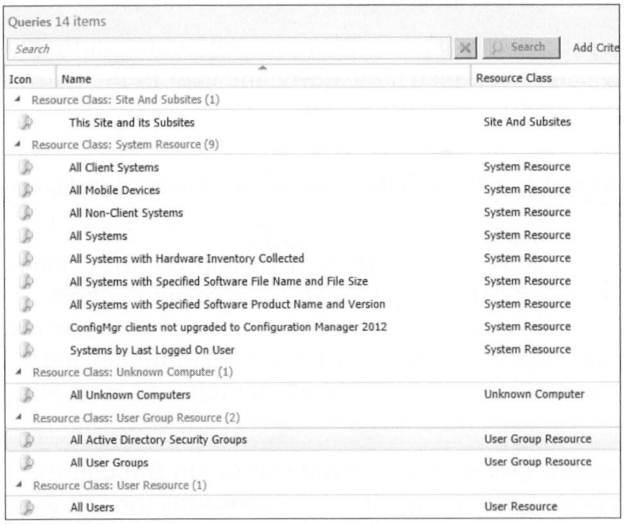

FIGURE 17.4   The List pane when grouping by the resource class.

> **TIP: GROUPING AVAILABILITY**
>
> Grouping is not just for managing queries; you can also use it to manage the set of results returned from a query using any of the available columns referenced in the query.

Query objects also benefit from the organizational use of folders and the search capabilities inherent in the ConfigMgr console. Having well-organized queries in structured folders (see Figure 17.5) not only makes searching faster, but also gives fellow administrators structure to look for items even if they do not know exactly what they are looking for! Take time to plan your folders to match the way your organization uses queries in ConfigMgr.

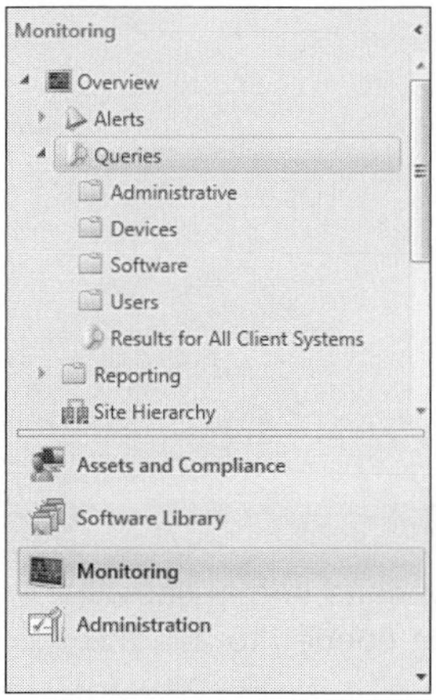

FIGURE 17.5   Structuring folders in the query node.

Viewing Queries and Query Results

To view a query, you must first run it. Either select the query and click the **Run** button in the toolbar, or right-click the query and choose **Run**. The easiest way to run a query is to double-click the query you are interested in.

If running a query results in a large number of returned objects, you can use the search bar to narrow the results. This makes finding information extremely fast because it does not require sorting the results or scrolling up and down to find the object in question.

Now that you have a result set from your query, you can perform the actions listed here and shown in Figure 17.6, against any of the objects in the set (provided the resource class is a system resource):

- ▶ Install Client
- ▶ Run the Resource Explorer
- ▶ Initiate Remote Control

▶ Run Remote Assistance

▶ Initiate the Remote Desktop Client

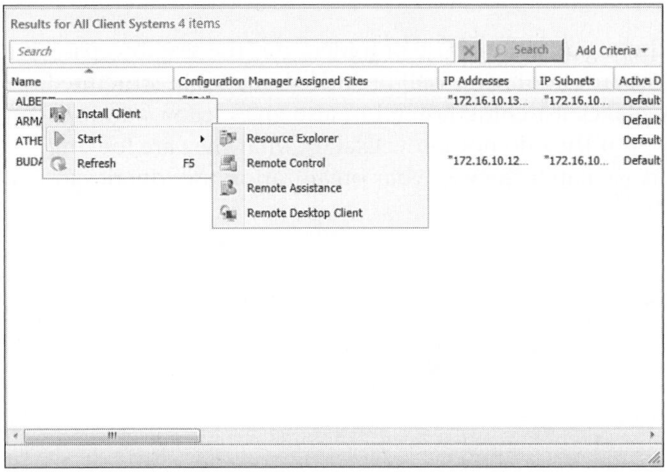

FIGURE 17.6   Available actions for system resource objects.

NOTE: DON'T FORGET TO ADD THE RESOURCE TYPE

Without the resource type attribute added to the results set, some options in this list will not be available. You should make it a standard practice when writing queries to add the resource type attribute.

In addition, without adding the Resource ID, although Resource Explorer may open, it will not contain data.

Creating Queries

ConfigMgr comes with just a handful of queries out-of-the-box that illustrates a small part of the rich amount of data available. Consider them a starting point; you should take time to review these queries to understand all the available query properties.

Using the query builder is a safe way to retrieve data from ConfigMgr. Because the class joins are built automatically behind the scenes, there is less concern of an improper query being resource intensive. (Although this is not entirely mitigated.) The next sections provide insight into WQL, the available object types to query, use of the query builder, and available operators.

WMI Query Language

ConfigMgr query expressions are written in WQL. Using WQL lets you gather information from the site database by accessing information through the WMI provider. If you are familiar with Structured Query Language (SQL) queries, the format of WQL queries should look familiar because WQL is a subset of SQL.

WQL is a Microsoft implementation of the CIM Query Language (CQL). CQL is a query language designed for the Common Information Model (CIM), a standard created by the Distributed Management Task Force (DMTF). That is quite a history of acronyms!

Here is an example of a WQL query that lists devices with more than 1,024MB of RAM:

```
select * from  SMS_R_System inner join SMS_G_System_X86_PC_MEMORY on
SMS_G_System_X86_PC_MEMORY.ResourceID = SMS_R_System.ResourceId where
SMS_G_System_X86_PC_MEMORY.TotalPhysicalMemory >= 1048576
```

MORE ABOUT WMI QUERY LANGUAGE

If you are familiar with SQL, you may notice this query looks similar to a SQL query. However, rather than querying tables, WQL queries classes, returning instances instead of rows. Another distinction is that WQL is strictly a retrieval language. You cannot use WQL to create, delete, or modify classes or instances.

Objects, Classes, and Attributes

Before starting to build your own queries, you need to understand some of the terminology behind the technology. Queries always consist of

- An object type

- One or more attribute classes

- One or more attributes

These are discussed in the following sections.

Object Type

An *object type* is a set of attributes representing a ConfigMgr database object. Such objects include applications, deployments, devices, and so on. Table 17.1 lists commonly used object types and their descriptions.

TABLE 17.1   Commonly Used Object Types

Object Type	Description
IP Network	A single attribute class containing data related to subnet addresses.
Package	A single attribute class that contains data in a ConfigMgr packages such as description, language, manufacturer, priority, programs, version, and so on.
Program	A single attribute class containing data relevant to programs such as command line, description, space requirements, run time, and so on.

17

Object Type	Description
Security Roles	A single attribute class that contains information specifically for security roles such as role name, created by, and users in the role.
Security Scopes	A single attribute class that contains data specifically related to security scopes such as scope name, creator, and category ID.
Site	A single attribute class holding data related to site information such as site code, server name, version, state, and so on.
Software Metering Rule	A single attribute class containing data specific to software metering rules such as file name, file version, date modified, and so on.
System Resource	The only multi-attribute class object type containing data from ConfigMgr devices, such as hardware, software, and discovery. This is the most often used object type when writing ConfigMgr queries.
Unknown Computer	A single attribute class containing unknown computer data such as CPU type, agent site, name, description, and so on.
User Group Resource	A single attribute class containing discovery data related to user groups such as domain, organizational unit, SID, group name, and so on.
User Resource	A single attribute class that contains the discovery data related to users such as name, SID, mail, user account control, and so on.

Attribute Class

An *attribute class* is a container object that groups related attributes together. Using the example in the "WMI Query Language" section, examine the `Memory` attribute class. The `Memory` attribute class contains attributes such as Available Virtual Memory, Total Page File Space (KB), Total Virtual Memory (KB), TotalPhysicalMemory, and so on. Because all these attributes are logically related to "memory," they are therefore grouped into this attribute class.

Most of the attribute classes exist as a part of the System Resource object type. Information in these attributes is provided by hardware inventory. If the available information is not adequate, you can extend the hardware inventory, providing the ability to add even more attribute classes to the System Resource object type. Extending hardware inventory is discussed in Appendix B, "Extending Hardware Inventory."

Attribute

An *attribute* is a property in an attribute class used for displaying or filtering data. For example, the TotalPhysicalMemory attribute of the `Memory` attribute class contains the total amount of RAM available, expressed in KB. You can use this attribute as a part of the result property to display data. Figure 17.7 illustrates the relationship of an object type to an attribute class and an attribute class to an attribute.

In the next query, the WHERE clause has been removed and the first line modified to display the device name and the TotalPhysicalMemory attribute as part of the result set:

```
select SMS_R_System.Name, SMS_G_System_X86_PC_MEMORY.TotalPhysicalMemory
from SMS_R_System inner join SMS_G_System_X86_PC_MEMORY on
SMS_G_System_X86_PC_MEMORY.ResourceID = SMS_R_System.ResourceId
```

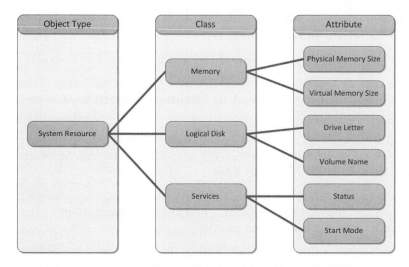

FIGURE 17.7   The relationship of an object type to an attribute class and an attribute class to an attribute.

This query returns all devices and their total physical memory. If it were desirable to return only a certain set of results, you could use attributes as a part of the criteria set to filter data based on an expression. The example in the "WMI Query Language" section uses the TotalPhysicalMemory attribute to specify the query to bring back only information from devices with more than 1024MB of RAM. The query is next modified to add criteria specifying the memory requirements:

```
select SMS_R_System.Name, SMS_G_System_X86_PC_MEMORY.TotalPhysicalMemory
from SMS_R_System inner join SMS_G_System_X86_PC_MEMORY on
SMS_G_System_X86_PC_MEMORY.ResourceID = SMS_R_System.ResourceId where
SMS_G_System_X86_PC_MEMORY.TotalPhysicalMemory >= 1048576
```

ConfigMgr Query Builder

Now create the query from the previous section. The ConfigMgr query builder has two modes of operation: design view and language view.

▶ The *design view* is where you are likely to spend most of your time as it simplifies the query building process.

▶ The *language view* provides enhanced query writing capability, discussed later in the "Writing Advanced Queries" section.

17

The easiest way to create a new query is with the Create Query Wizard. Perform the following steps to launch the wizard and create the query:

1. Click the **Queries** node, and choose the **Create Query** action to launch the wizard.

2. The first page is the General Query Settings page. Begin by filling in the Name of the query. For this example, use the name **Systems w/ Minimum 1024MB RAM**. Here are some other fields on this page:

   ▶ The Comment field is optional, but you should use it as a best practice to help identify the query and indicate its purpose. Fill in the comment with **Systems with at least 1024MB (1048576KB) of RAM**.

   ▶ The **Import Query Statement** allows you to browse through existing queries and use one as a starting point for building a query. As this query is built from scratch, do not use this feature at this time.

   ▶ **Collection Limiting** is another feature on this page. The feature limits results to objects that exist as members of a specified collection. You can specify the collection in the dialog as part of the query properties or have it prompt for a collection each time the query executes. Do not use collection limiting at this time.

3. Create a new query statement by clicking the **Edit Query Statement** button. The Create Query Wizard now displays the Query Statement Properties dialog box.

   To display device names and their associated total physical memory, add the attributes to the Results section. Click the **New** button to display the Result Properties dialog box. Click the **Select** button to bring up the Select Attribute dialog box and add the following paired values:

   ▶ Attribute class: `System Resource`

   Attribute: Name

   ▶ Attribute class: `Memory`

   Attribute: Total Physical Memory (KB)

   When completed, the General tab of the Query Statement Properties dialog box should look similar to Figure 17.8.

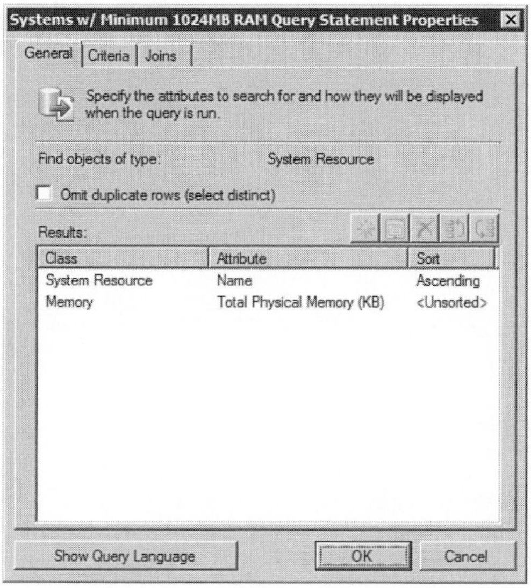

FIGURE 17.8   Attributes added to the General tab.

4. Now that you have defined the attributes you want to see in your query results, the next step is to specify criteria to display systems that match the requirements. In the Query Statement Properties dialog box, choose the **Criteria** tab. Click the **New** button to display the Criterion Properties dialog box.

Leave the default Criterion Type (discussed in the "Criterion Types, Operators, and Values" section) as **Simple** value. Click the **Select** button to display the Select Attribute dialog box, and add the **Memory** attribute class and the **Total Physical Memory (KB)** attribute.

Click **OK** to return to the Criterion Properties dialog box and set the Operator to **Is Greater Than or Equal To**. Specify **1048576** (1024MB expressed in KB) as the Value, as shown in Figure 17.9.

TIP: FILLING IN VALUES

If you are unsure of the kinds of values to use in the Value box, use the **Value** button. The Values dialog box returns a list of values that you can use.

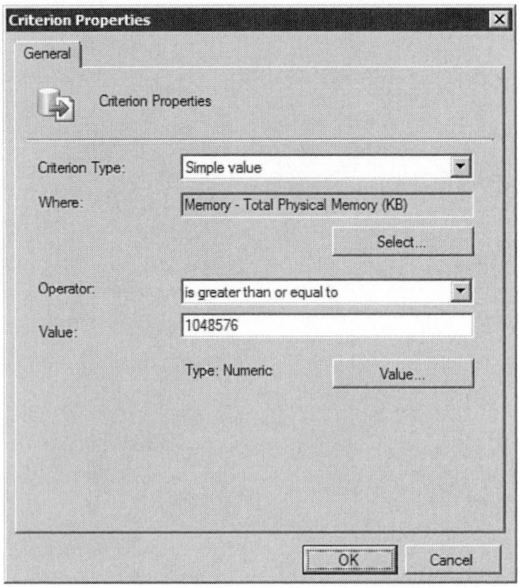

FIGURE 17.9   Criterion properties.

Click **OK** to close the Criterion Properties dialog box. Notice the Criteria is now filled with the criterion properties you just created (see Figure 17.10). Click **OK** to close the Query Statement Properties dialog box, returning you to the General Query Settings page.

5. Click **Next** to move to the Summary page, which displays the query properties for review, as shown in Figure 17.11. Clicking **Next** moves through the Progress page and brings up the Completion page with details. Click **Close** to complete the wizard.

TIP: USING TOOLS TO CREATE WMI QUERIES

At times, creating WMI queries through the wizard or by hand can be quite cumbersome. There are a number of tools available for free to help ease the process. Here are some popular ones:

▶ **WMI Code Creator:** https://www.microsoft.com/download/en/details.aspx?displaylang=en&id=8572

▶ **WMI Code Generator:** http://www.robvanderwoude.com/wmigen.php

▶ **Scriptomatic:** http://www.microsoft.com/download/en/details.aspx?displaylang=en&id=3284

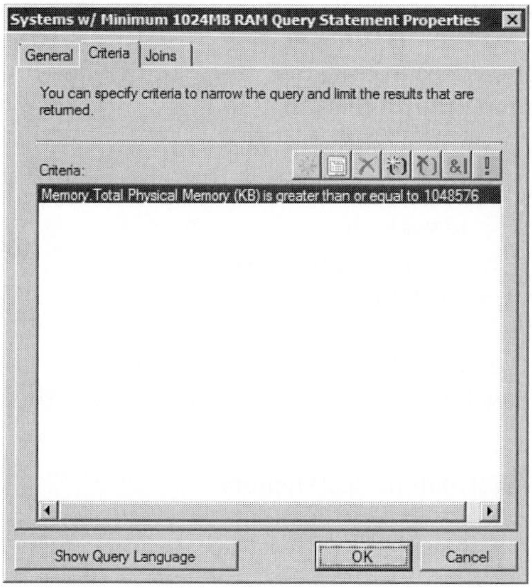

FIGURE 17.10   Memory expression in the Criteria tab.

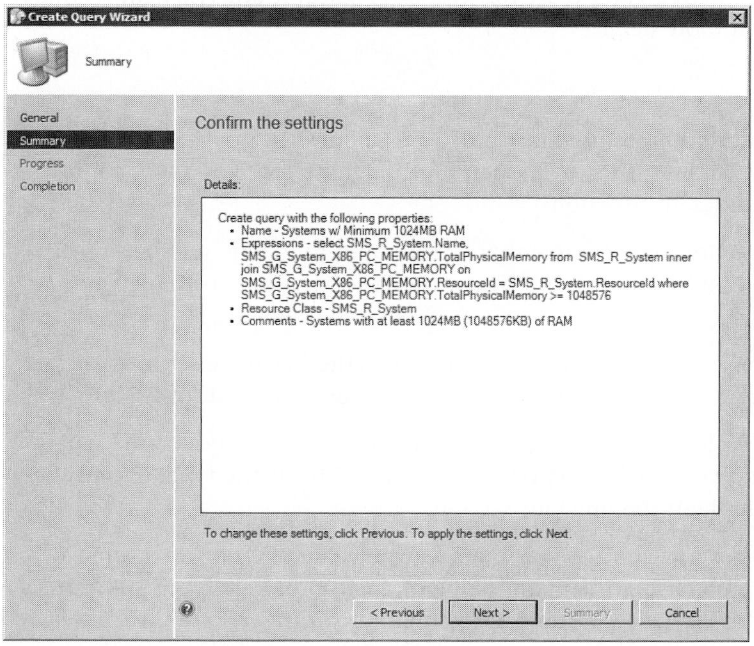

FIGURE 17.11   Query properties for review.

Criterion Types, Operators, and Values

The "ConfigMgr Query Builder" section briefly introduced types, operators, and values that are essential components of building the criteria that filters data. To illustrate this, here is the query discussed in that section:

```
select SMS_R_System.Name, SMS_G_System_X86_PC_MEMORY.TotalPhysicalMemory
from SMS_R_System inner join SMS_G_System_X86_PC_MEMORY on
SMS_G_System_X86_PC_MEMORY.ResourceID = SMS_R_System.ResourceId where
SMS_G_System_X86_PC_MEMORY.TotalPhysicalMemory >= 1048576
```

The criteria of the query follows after the word "where." This is known as a WHERE clause, made up of a property, an operator, and a value, closely matching the focus of this section:

▶ **Property:** SMS_G_System_X86_PC_MEMORY.TotalPhysicalMemory

▶ **Operator:** >= (is greater than or equal to)

▶ **Value:** 1048576

A WHERE clause limits the scope of data returned. If you recall, the WHERE clause illustrated here returns devices with greater than 1024MB of physical RAM. The next sections examine these elements in more detail.

Criterion Types

There are six different criterion types used in ConfigMgr queries, all serving the purpose of narrowing the amount of data returned by a query. Although all criterion types are used to limit data, each has a different function:

▶ **Null value:** This criterion type compares an attribute to null. One such use of this criterion type would be to search for devices where the AD Domain Name value is unknown.

To search for devices where the value is missing, the criteria can be set to Is NULL. Inversely, the criteria can also search for where the value is present (or Is Not NULL).

▶ **Simple value:** This criterion type compares an attribute to a constant value. This is the most basic and yet widely used type of criterion. This is the type used in the memory query example in the previous section.

▶ **Prompted value:** This criterion type prompts for the value to compare against at runtime. As an example, using the memory query, instead of specifying 1048576, the criterion type can be left as **<prompted value>**, providing the administrative user executing the query the ability to populate the value to something of their choosing. If 2048MB were more desirable, the administrative user would enter the value of **2097152** at runtime.

NOTE: PROMPTED VALUES ARE NOT SUPPORTED IN COLLECTIONS

Although the prompted value type exists in queries, you cannot use it in collections. Collections do not provide an interactive interface to prompt a user at runtime. All other criterion types are usable for query-based collections.

▶ **Attribute reference:** To compare two values from the ConfigMgr database, use the attribute reference criterion type. One example of such a use is to locate systems where the current processor clock speed is less than the maximum processor clock speed.

▶ **Subselected value:** In situations in which the queried attribute is multivalued and the operator to use is a type of NOT (not like, not equal to, and so on), a subselected value criterion type has to be used. Otherwise, a condition to match something such as all devices where Microsoft Visio 2010 is not installed would not work correctly, as every computer would have at least one entry in the Add/Remove Programs class that did not match the criteria. A query such as that would return every device, installed or not.

If you are not familiar with subselected queries, it can be a challenge to write one for the first time. Check the "Examples of Advanced Queries" section for a sample that should help.

CAUTION: BE CAREFUL WHEN RUNNING SUBSELECT QUERIES

It is not that using subselect queries is necessarily a bad thing. However, they are expensive to run. Because a subselect query is effective running two queries (one to return all matching objects and another to return subselect objects) if there is a high count to the number of objects, it can take a while for the query to complete. Of course, this is all subjective based on the performance of your server hardware.

▶ **List of values:** This criterion type compares the value to a list of constant values. A useful example of this is when searching for devices that match a certain chassis type. To find devices that match a desktop profile, you could use the values 3, 4, 6, and 7 as a starting point. Figure 17.12 shows the properties of the list of values criterion type when constructing such a query. Keep in mind that although you can add multiple values, you are restricted to using one operator type.

NOTE: INFORMATION ON CHASSIS TYPES

More information on chassis types can be discovered by researching the Win32_System Enclosure class. You can find other useful information in this class such as serial number, manufacturer, model, and so on. The MSDN article at http://msdn.microsoft.com/en-us/library/aa394474.aspx provides additional information.

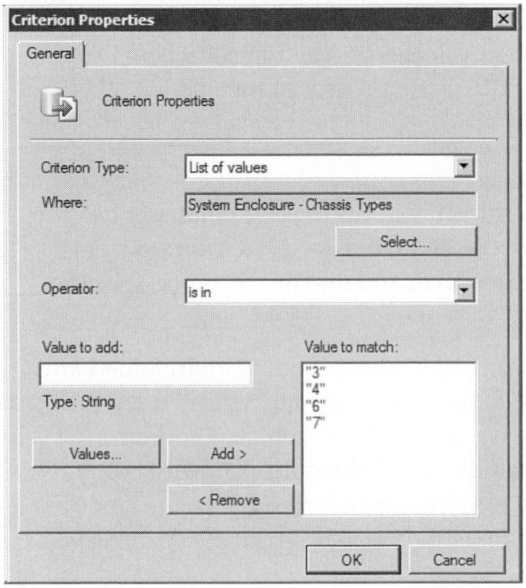

FIGURE 17.12   Using list of values to select certain chassis types.

Operators

Some operators indicate how to assess a value, whereas others are used to join expressions together. A relational operator indicates how to compare a value against a certain type of data. A logical operator, on the other hand, indicates how to join multiple expressions together.

Relational Operators

Depending on the criterion and data type, you will find that certain operators may not be available. Because the operators in ConfigMgr are relational in nature, the available operators depend on the data type of the specified attribute. For example, whenever a date value is utilized such as Workstation Status - Last Hardware Scan, additional operators become available specifically designed to query dates and parts of dates.

Here are the three types of relational operators:

▶ **Date and time operators:** Requires a value that matches the specified date/time operator. The operators match those found for the other criterion types (with the exception of the NULL value), pre-pended with one of the following: day, day of week, day of year, hour, millisecond, minute, month, quarter, second, week of year, and year.

▶ **Numerical operators:** Requires a numerical value; otherwise, the query fails. The numerical operator consists of the following: is equal to, is greater than, is greater than or equal to, is less than, is less than or equal to, and is not equal to.

▶ **String relational operators:** Requires a string to evaluate against the operator. Operators such as LIKE are available with strings.

Table 17.2 provides the available operators for each criterion type when using the string data type.

TABLE 17.2 Criterion Types and Operators

Criterion Type(s)	Operators
NULL value	Is NULL.
	Is not NULL.
Simple value, Prompted value, Attribute reference	Is equal to.
	Is greater than.
	Is greater than or equal to.
	Is less than.
	Is less than or equal to.
	Is like.
	Is not equal to.
	Is not like.
	Lowercase is equal to.
	Lowercase is greater than.
	Lowercase is greater than or equal to.
	Lowercase is less than.
	Lowercase is less than or equal to.
	Lowercase is like.
	Lowercase is not equal to.
	Lowercase is not like.
	Uppercase is equal to.
	Uppercase is greater than.
	Uppercase is greater than or equal to.
	Uppercase is less than.
	Uppercase is less than or equal to.
	Uppercase is like.
	Uppercase is not equal to.
	Uppercase is not like.
Subselected value, List of values	Is in.
	Is not in.
	Lowercase is in.
	Lowercase is not in.
	Uppercase is in.
	Uppercase is not in.

17

Logical Operators

Sometimes a query with a single expression will not have sufficient criteria to return the correct set of data. For example, suppose the criterion is more than simply looking for devices with greater than 1024MB of RAM. In addition to memory, you are interested in devices that also have more than 800MB of free disk space. With a logical operator, you can join the expressions together using an AND operator, causing both expressions to evaluate.

ConfigMgr has three types of logical operators to manage multiple expressions:

▶ **AND:** Finds all objects that match both expressions joined by AND. This is illustrated with the RAM and free space example in the "WMI Query Language" section.

▶ **OR:** Finds all objects that match either expression joined by OR. An example of an OR expression is to search for ConfigMgr client versions that match 5.00.7561.0000 or 4.00.6487.2157.

▶ **NOT:** Finds all objects that do not match the expression the NOT operator is applied to. For example, using NOT on an expression looking for ConfigMgr client version 5.00.7561.0000 would return any object with a different version of the client installed.

Operator Precedence Order

When you were in math class, your teacher may have talked about something called *order of operations*. This is a rule that defines which procedures go first. Just as in math, ConfigMgr query evaluations follow the same process. When writing queries that use logical operators, it is important to understand the order of operations that is followed to accurately predict the outcome of the query. And you thought you would never need to know what you learned in school!

Here is the order in which expressions are evaluated:

1. Any expressions inside parenthesis

2. Any expressions using NOT

3. Any expressions using AND

4. Any expressions using OR

To change the order of operations, you can use parentheses to force a certain expression to evaluate first. For example, if you have multiple AND statements, placing one of the AND statements inside of parentheses will cause it to evaluate first. Parentheses are also useful for breaking up complex expressions into something that is easier to understand.

Values

You can specify the value by entering it into the Value field. Clicking the Values button queries ConfigMgr for data from the specified attribute. The console displays a list of possible values, which is helpful to view a sampling of the content of data. If a value appears that is useful for the query, you can select it to insert into the Value field automatically. If the values returned are larger than 2,000 entries, the list of values is truncated. Keep in mind that there is no specifiable sort order for the list of values.

The Value field also accepts wildcards to help shape the query correctly. Wildcards work with operators that use the LIKE clause. Any other operators assumes the wildcard is a literal character. Table 17.3 details the available wildcards and their function.

TABLE 17.3   Available Wildcards and Their Functions

Wildcard	Function	Example
_ (underscore)	Matches any single character (can be used more than once)	_eek - geek, meek, peek, seek, week __eek - Greek, cheek, sleek _ea_ - beak, leaf, seal se__ - seal, seek
% (percent)	Matches any zero or more characters	%eek - Greek, geek, peek, sleek, eek g%eek - geek, Greek
[x] (bracketed character)	Matches any specified literal character once	[%]eek - %eek [?]eek - ?eek [_]eek - _eek [gps]eek - geek, peek, seek [gm]eek - geek, meek [w]eek - week
[x-x] (bracketed range)	Matches a range of specified characters once	[g-s]eek - geek, meek, peek, seek
[^x] (bracketed range with a carat)	Matches any single character not in the bracket once	[^m]eek - geek, peek, seek, week

You can mix and match wildcards together to create more definitive filters, providing ways to match widely and narrowly at the same time. Use the names Apollo, Ares, Artemis, Athena, Erebos, and Hermes, for example:

▶ **Apollo and Athena:** A%[ao]

▶ **Erebos and Hermes:** [EH]%s

▶ **Ares, Artemis, and Erebos:** _r%s

Writing Advanced Queries

Until now, the only type of query illustrated has been a simple value query to look for computers with more than 1024MB of RAM. However, the complexity in writing queries for ConfigMgr can grow to be quite challenging. Not only does ConfigMgr support a number of different criterion types, it also supports some hidden functions not readily exposed in the console.

Using the query builder is definitely a much simpler process than writing WQL queries by hand. However, the query builder is limited in the options it displays when in Design view. ConfigMgr supports the use of Extended WQL for query writing, which supports select clauses such as COUNT, DISTINCT, ORDER BY, DATEPART, and so on. Some of these options such as DISTINCT (area 1) and ORDER BY (area 2) are exposed (as shown in Figure 17.13), whereas other equally useful syntax must be manually entered, specifically the date and time functions.

FIGURE 17.13   Select distinct and order by exposed in the query builder.

Writing queries with certain criterion types such as a subselected value query is considered an advanced query as the process of writing it is not particularly straightforward. This type of query is extremely helpful when querying multivalued attributes such as Add/Remove Programs.

Next, look at a few of the restrictions of the implementation of Extended WQL as used in ConfigMgr to understand what is available with writing advanced queries.

Limitations of Extended WQL in ConfigMgr

Extended WQL has certain limitations in Configuration Manager (either inherently or because of the SMS Provider) to be aware of when writing queries. The following list explains these limitations:

▶ The use of COUNT does not display properly in query results and is therefore not useful for querying through the Configuration Manager console.

▶ COUNT and DISTINCT cannot be used together in a WQL query.

▶ Although supported, UPPER and LOWER is not helpful because WQL is entirely case-insensitive.

▶ The SMS Provider does not support querying against system properties. These properties are easily identifiable because they all begin with a double underscore like __CLASS, __NAMESPACE, __PATH, and so on.

▶ If the query is using the collection limiting option, the ORDER BY clause will not work.

▶ You cannot use date and time functions in the query following the SELECT clause. However, they can be used as a part of the WHERE clause, as shown in the next section.

Utilizing the Date and Time Functions in WQL Queries

There will be many occasions when applying a date filter to your query will be quite useful. For example, when creating queries, it is often helpful to know that the information retrieved is the most current available. Pulling changes to hardware inventory that occurred sometime in the last week is a likely scenario. ConfigMgr queries support the use of the following functions:

▶ **DateAdd()**: Returns a specified date value with a specified interval added to it.

```
DateAdd ( datepart, number, date )
```

  ▶ **Datepart:** Parameter that specifies the portion of the date to add the number to.

  ▶ **Number:** An integer value added to the specified datepart.

  ▶ **Date:** The initial date value to add the integer to.

Here's an example: 30 Days Ago from July 20, 2011

```
DateAdd(DD,-30,"7/20/2011")
```

▶ **DateDiff()**: Returns the difference between two date values in the increment of the datepart specified.

```
DateDiff (datepart, startdate, enddate)
```

  ▶ **DatePart:** Parameter that specifies the portion of the date to calculate the difference against.

  ▶ **Startdate:** Starting date to use in the calculation. Startdate is subtracted from enddate.

  ▶ **Enddate:** Ending date to use in the calculation.

Here's an example: Difference Between July 20, 2011 and Today in Days

```
DateDiff(DD,"7/20/2011",Getdate())
```

17

▶ **GetDate()**: Returns the current date value of the system executing the command.

Here's an example: 30 Days Ago from Today

```
DateAdd(DD,-30,GetDate())
```

Table 17.4 illustrates the components of datepart and their relative abbreviations.

TABLE 17.4   Components of DatePart

DatePart	Abbreviations
Year	year, yy
Month	month, mm
Day	day, dd
Hour	hour, hh
Minute	minute, mi
Second	second, ss

TIP: EXAMPLE DATE AND TIME QUERY

For an example of a query that uses the date and time function, refer to the query in the "Example: Querying for Devices with a Hardware Scan in the Last 15 Days" section.

The next section explores some different advanced queries. Understanding them can assist with broadening your query writing capability.

Examples of Advanced Queries

It is true that WMI queries are limited in functionality in contrast to SQL queries. However, combining all the query elements discussed in this chapter produces queries of certain complexity. Often times, these queries cannot be displayed in the ConfigMgr console because the graphical user interface (GUI) simply lacks the capability to show all the components.

The next sections provide examples of advanced queries; you should find these useful as a basis for constructing your own queries, using them as-is to tease out data for quick reporting, or applying a complex filter to isolate clients for targeting.

Example: Querying for Devices with a Hardware Scan in the Last 15 Days

The query in this section retrieves any device that has reported a hardware scan within the last 15 days. Look closely at the WHERE clause. The DateDiff function is used to calculate the difference between the last hardware scan date and the current date. If the calculated difference is less than or equal to 15 days, the device is included in the results:

```
select SMS_R_System.Name, SMS_G_System_WORKSTATION_STATUS.LastHardwareScan from
SMS_R_System inner join SMS_G_System_WORKSTATION_STATUS on
SMS_G_System_WORKSTATION_STATUS.ResourceId = SMS_R_System.ResourceId where
DateDiff(dd,SMS_G_System_WORKSTATION_STATUS.LastHardwareScan,GetDate()) <= 15
```

Although this example uses `DateDiff`, you can accomplish the same result with `DateAdd`, which can manipulate the current date (`GetDate`) into a date 15 days ago. Comparing the hardware scan date against the `DateAdd` manipulated date, you can bring back only devices that match the criteria, as illustrated here:

```
select SMS_R_System.Name, SMS_G_System_WORKSTATION_STATUS.LastHardwareScan from
SMS_R_System inner join SMS_G_System_WORKSTATION_STATUS on
SMS_G_System_WORKSTATION_STATUS.ResourceId = SMS_R_System.ResourceId where
SMS_G_System_WORKSTATION_STATUS.LastHardwareScan > DateAdd(DD,-15,GetDate())
```

Example: Querying for Newly Discovered Devices in the Last Day

To locate recently discovered devices, query against the record creation date. Calculating the creation date against the current date produces devices that are recently discovered. In this case, the value supplied of "1" (following the `DateDiff` function) looks for creation dates as recently as 1 day ago:

```
select SMS_R_System.Name, SMS_R_System.CreationDate from  SMS_R_System where
DateDiff(dd,SMS_R_System.CreationDate,GetDate()) <= 1
```

Example: Querying for Devices Without Microsoft Silverlight Installed

In this query, using the subselected criterion type, you can draw out devices that do not have Microsoft Silverlight installed. When writing a subselect query, a query is embedded inside another query.

The query in the WHERE clause creates a list of computers that match the criteria of having Microsoft Silverlight installed (displayed in Figure 17.14). The "outer query" uses an IS NOT IN operator to list any computers that are not in the initial query. Lastly, this query uses another criterion to qualify that the query should be limited to information where the resource is a ConfigMgr client:

```
select SMS_R_System.ResourceId, SMS_R_System.ResourceType, SMS_R_System.Name,
SMS_R_System.SMSUniqueIdentifier, SMS_R_System.ResourceDomainORWorkgroup,
SMS_R_System.Client from  SMS_R_System where SMS_R_System.ResourceId not in
(select distinct SMS_R_System.ResourceId from  SMS_R_System inner join
SMS_G_System_ADD_REMOVE_PROGRAMS on SMS_G_System_ADD_REMOVE_PROGRAMS.ResourceID =
SMS_R_System.ResourceId where SMS_G_System_ADD_REMOVE_PROGRAMS.DisplayName =
"Microsoft Silverlight") and SMS_R_System.Client = 1
```

Example: Querying for Computers and Logical Disks with a Prompted Value

This query displays the logical disk(s) of a specified computer. By using a prompted value, this query prompts the user to provide a computer name when it is executed. Because the

17

LIKE operator is in use for the prompted value, you can use a wildcard to mask part of the computer name and potentially return more than one computer:

```
select SMS_R_System.Name, SMS_G_System_LOGICAL_DISK.DeviceID,
SMS_G_System_LOGICAL_DISK.FileSystem, SMS_G_System_LOGICAL_DISK.Description,
SMS_G_System_LOGICAL_DISK.Size from  SMS_R_System inner join
SMS_G_System_LOGICAL_DISK on SMS_G_System_LOGICAL_DISK.ResourceID =
SMS_R_System.ResourceId where SMS_G_System_LOGICAL_DISK.Description =
"Local Fixed Disk" and SMS_R_System.Name like ##PRM:SMS_R_System.Name##
```

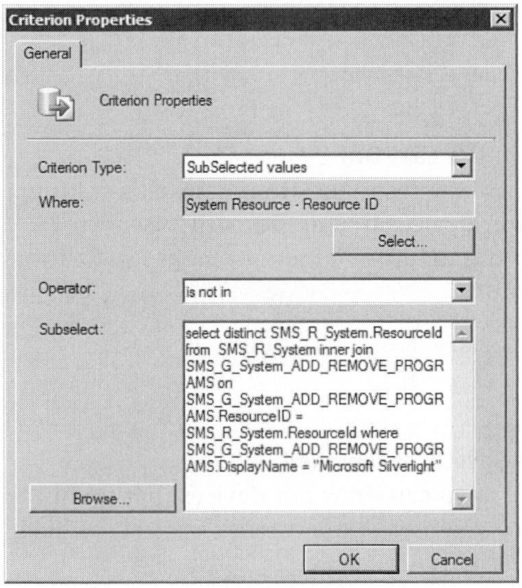

FIGURE 17.14   Subselect query looks for all clients with Microsoft Silverlight.

Example: Querying for Devices NOT in a Specified Collection

This query is designed to show devices that are not in a collection that you specify. The collection is referred to by the collection ID. In this example, the collection ID is PR10000A. When using this query in your environment, simply change the collection ID to one in your environment.

Similar to the earlier example with Microsoft Silverlight ("Example: Querying for Devices Without Microsoft Silverlight Installed"), this is a subselect query. This query statement, however, uses a class while not exposed in Query Builder's design mode can be pasted or typed into the query language window:

```
select sms_r_system.resourceid, sms_r_system.name
from sms_r_system
where resourceid not in
    (
    select sys.resourceid
    from SMS_CM_RES_COLL_PR10000A AS coll, sms_r_system as sys
    where sys.resourceid = coll.resourceid
    )
```

For additional information regarding this query, see http://marcusoh.blogspot.com/2007/08/sms-selecting-objects-not-in-collection.html.

Converting WQL to SQL

By now, you are probably writing queries you find useful enough that you want to move them into a SQL Server Reporting Services (SSRS) report to leverage all the formatting, sharing, and scheduling capabilities! Chapter 18, "Reporting," discusses SSRS in depth.

Now examine the query used previously in the "Example: Querying for Devices with a Hardware Scan in the Last 15 Days" section. To convert this query to SQL quickly, look at the ConfigMgr logs. Open smsprov.log and execute the query you want to convert. Look for a line that begins with Execute WQL. This entry displays the actual WQL query issued:

```
Execute WQL  =
select SMS_R_System.Name, SMS_G_System_WORKSTATION_STATUS.LastHardwareScan
from  SMS_R_System inner join SMS_G_System_WORKSTATION_STATUS on
SMS_G_System_WORKSTATION_STATUS.ResourceId = SMS_R_System.ResourceId
where DateDiff(dd,SMS_G_System_WORKSTATION_STATUS.LastHardwareScan,GetDate()) <= 15
```

As you can see, the query in the log matches the referenced query! The next line in the log, which begins with Execute SQL, contains the SQL query:

```
Execute SQL =
select  all SMS_R_System.Name0,___System_WORKSTATION_STATUS0.LastHWScan
from vSMS_R_System AS SMS_R_System INNER JOIN WorkstationStatus_DATA AS
___System_WORKSTATION_STATUS0 ON ___System_WORKSTATION_STATUS0.MachineID =
SMS_R_System.ItemKey
where DATEDIFF (day,___System_WORKSTATION_STATUS0.LastHWScan,GETDATE ()) <= 15
```

17

> **CAUTION: USE OF CONFIGMGR TABLES IS UNSUPPORTED**
>
> Though extracting the SQL query from smsprov.log is a useful trick, using ConfigMgr tables in a SQL query is not considered best practice. Microsoft may alter the database schema between versions to add functionality or improve performance. For this reason, Microsoft does not publish a database schema because it would imply that the schema is static. Wherever possible, use the provided ConfigMgr database views.

Relationships, Operations, and Joins

Until now, this chapter has not discussed relationships. The conversation has not been necessary because the ConfigMgr Query Builder dynamically manages these as you create the query. Earlier in the "ConfigMgr Query Builder" section, you used the General and Criteria tabs to build a query to find devices with greater than 1024MB of RAM. As illustrated in that same section, Figure 17.8 shows the Query Builder as having three tabs. The lower pane in Figure 17.15 shows the content of the Joins tab.

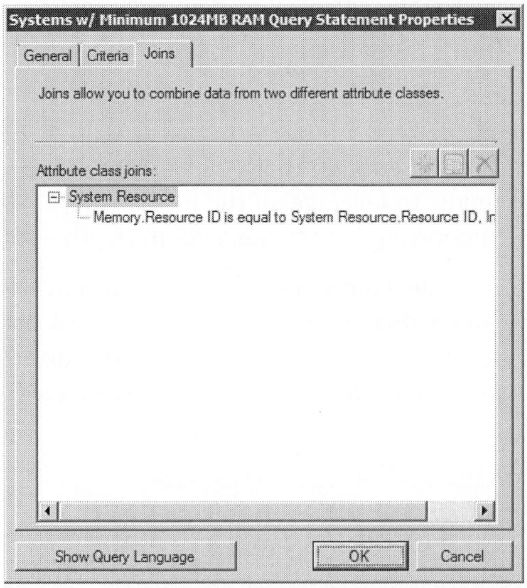

FIGURE 17.15   Content of the Joins tab.

In most scenarios, the Resource ID is used as the attribute for joining classes together. Notice that in Figure 17.16, both the join and base attributes are set to Resource ID. This is because Resource ID, a unique value that represents a ConfigMgr client resource, is in nearly every class.

The diagram in Figure 17.17 helps to illustrate how two classes such as `system resource` and `workstation memory` are joined together.

As discussed previously in the "Writing Advanced Queries" section, ConfigMgr uses Extended WQL. Through Extended WQL support, ConfigMgr can provide two kinds of join operations: inner and outer. Inner joins are limited to a single type of the same name: inner. Inner join types are the most common type of join used in WQL. (This is also the case with SQL.)

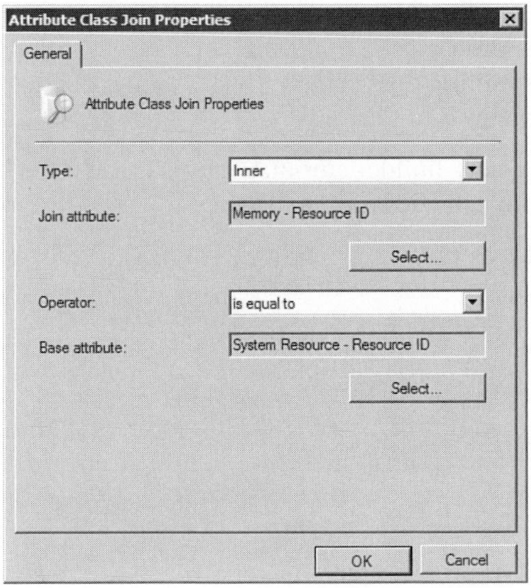

Attribute Class Join Properties
General
Attribute Class Join Properties
Type:
Inner
Join attribute:
Memory - Resource ID
Select...
Operator:
is equal to
Base attribute:
System Resource - Resource ID
Select...
OK
Cancel

FIGURE 17.16 Attribute Class Join Properties.

System Resource
Resource ID
Name
Memory
Resource ID
Total Physical Memory
Combined
Resource ID
Name
Total Physical Memory

FIGURE 17.17 Diagram of joins.

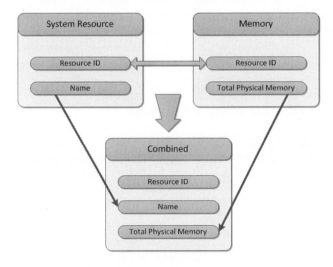

Outer joins, on the other hand, include full, left outer, and right outer. Queries are often optimized based on the join type selected. Depending on the join, it may mean the difference between pulling some select records versus pulling every record in the joined classes! Here is how data is brought together based on the join used:

- ▶ **Inner:** All joins created in the ConfigMgr Query Builder automatically use the inner join type when not specified. The inner join provides only matching results.

- ▶ **Full:** In contrast to the inner join, the full join type displays all the results for the base and the join attribute.

- ▶ **Left:** When using a left join type, all the results from the base attribute display. In addition, the matching results from the join attribute display.

- ▶ **Right:** The right outer join type is the exact opposite of the left outer join type. The matching results from the base attribute display along with all the results from the join attribute.

When then might you deviate from the default? As an example, say you want to retrieve a list of all your devices and the name and version number of internally developed software. The developer who wrote that software did not always populate the version number correctly. Running such a query with the default inner join type would result in bringing back only records where the device name, the software name, and the software version exist. Because you need to see the devices where the software is installed but the version value is potentially empty, you switch the join type to a left join to include all records.

To demonstrate, use a simple query that retrieves system enclosure information.

```
select SMS_R_System.Name, SMS_G_System_SYSTEM_ENCLOSURE.ChassisTypes
from  SMS_R_System inner join SMS_G_System_SYSTEM_ENCLOSURE on
SMS_G_System_SYSTEM_ENCLOSURE.ResourceID = SMS_R_System.ResourceId
```

Using the default join, only devices with a chassis type display. By switching the join type to left, all devices are displayed with a blank value for chassis type. The next query shows the join type modified to left. Note that the inner join has been replaced with left join.

```
select SMS_R_System.Name, SMS_G_System_SYSTEM_ENCLOSURE.ChassisTypes
from SMS_R_System left join SMS_G_System_SYSTEM_ENCLOSURE on
SMS_G_System_SYSTEM_ENCLOSURE.ResourceID = SMS_R_System.ResourceId
```

Querying Discovery Data

There are three different types of discovery data available for use in a query: system resource, user resource, and user group resource. Because some discovery data is captured through ConfigMgr discovery methods, this information is made available even before the device has a ConfigMgr client installed.

Each of these classes provides information discovered through the ConfigMgr discovery methods:

▶ **System Resource:** Use the `System Resource` class to draw out ConfigMgr information about the device such as the assigned, installed, or resident site, the client version, and so on. Other information such as the system name, IP address, subnets, and SID is also available. Finally, you can also query Active Directory (AD) information about the device such as the system organizational unit (OU) name, the system container name, the system group name, and so on.

▶ **User Resource:** Use the `User Resource` class to obtain information about user accounts from attributes such as the full user name, mail, unique user name, user account control (disabled, enabled, and so on), and such. In addition, AD information about the user account such as the distinguished name, user OU name, and user container name are available.

▶ **User Group Resource:** The `User Group Resource` class contains attributes related to AD user group properties such as the domain, organizational unit, unique user group name (the group id), group name, and so on.

With information available regarding AD accounts, you can use discovery data to build collections to support your ConfigMgr deployment. Collections can be created that group AD computer accounts together to install the ConfigMgr agent.

Querying Inventory Data

The `System Resource` class, discussed earlier in the "Objects, Classes, and Attributes" section, contains discovered attributes about an object. However, the `System Resource` class contains more than just discovered data.

All queries requiring data from hardware or software inventory need to utilize the `System Resource` class. In fact, most of the queries covered in this chapter use the `System Resource` class. That shows how prevalent this class is! Some popular hardware and software inventory classes are illustrated in Table 17.5.

TABLE 17.5   Useful Hardware and Software Inventory Classes

Class	Description
Add/Remove Programs	Based on `Win32Reg_AddRemovePrograms`. Now referred to as Programs and Features in newer operating systems (Windows Vista and above). Holds the same type of software information found in the Add/Remove Programs control panel applet. Systems running x64 holds data in the equivalent `Add/Remove Programs_(64)` class.
Computer System	Based on `Win32_ComputerSystem`. An eclectic class with information including hardware manufacturer and model. Also includes time zone data, domain role, and so on.

Class	Description
Disk Drives	Based on `Win32_DiskDrive`. Contains information about disk drives such as manufacturer, drive size, and count of partitions.
Logical Disk	Refers to `SMS_LogicalDisk`. Contains information related to logical disks such as drive letter, file system, size, and volume name.
Memory	Refers to `CCM_LogicalMemoryConfiguration`. Displays information for page file size, physical memory size, and virtual memory size.
Network Adapter Configuration	Based on `Win32_NetworkAdapterConfiguration`. Contains IP configuration such as the IP address, default gateway, subnet mask, and so on.
Operating System	Based on `Win32_OperatingSystem`. Contains details about the operating system such as the name, build number, version, last boot-up time, and so on.
Power Configuration	Refers to `CCM_PowerConfig`. Displays information such as peak and nonpeak power plan names, wakeup time, and so on.
Processor	Refers to `SMS_Processor`. Contains information about clock speed, number of cores, 64-bit capability, and so on.
Recently Used Applications	Refers to `CCM_RecentlyUsedApps`. Displays information about recent application usage including the last user, last used time, the application, and so on.
Server Feature	Based on `Win32_ServerFeature`. Displays installed server features.
Services	Based on `Win32_Service`. Displays information about services such as name, description, start mode, and status.
Shares	Based on `Win32_Share`. Displays configured shares of the operating system.
Software Files	Contains file information collected from Software Inventory.
Software Products	Contains information from file headers from Software Inventory.
Virtual Machine	Based on `Win32Reg_SMSGuestVirtualMachine`. Displays information related to the virtual machine host. Systems running x64 holds data in the `Virtual_Machine_(64)` class.
System Enclosure	Based on `Win32_SystemEnclosure`. Contains useful hardware information such as manufacturer, model, chassis type, and serial number.
Workstation Status	Refers to this class to query the last hardware inventory scan date.

This is just a small list of the rich amount of inventory data provided by ConfigMgr. Over time, as your environment changes, the inventoried classes change. ConfigMgr is flexible enough to evolve with these changes. Refer to Chapter 9, "Configuration Manager Client Management," on modifying hardware inventory classes.

If you find that a device does not contain the expected inventory class, the device may not be healthy. In these circumstances, the device may be incapable of running the inventory scan or sending the inventory to the site server, causing the expected information never to reach the site server.

Using Query Results

Queries are an excellent resource for administrators. They provide a means to view rich data in an ad-hoc manner from ConfigMgr. Such sources of data include discovery, inventory, advertisement, site status information, and so on. Queries can also be the basis of collections that dynamically update. You could also export queries to text files for use in other ways. The next sections discuss these topics.

Exporting Query Results to a Text File

Earlier versions of ConfigMgr included the ability to export query results to a text file. This option was available as a part of the MMC functionality, but Microsoft did not port it to System Center 2012 Configuration Manager. However, copy and paste still exists as a viable replacement for this functionality. Even though there is no option on the ribbon bar or the right-click context menu, highlighting the results and using CTRL+C stores it in memory. You can then paste these results into any text editor.

Importing and Exporting Queries Between Sites

Unlike previous versions, ConfigMgr 2012 no longer requires movement of queries between sites to share them because the queries are globally available in a hierarchy. However, this function remains available; it is still useful to export queries as a means to share them with other hierarchies or in community groups with other administrators.

To export a query object, perform the following steps:

1. Select the Queries node, and click the **Export Queries** button on the ribbon bar.

2. In the Export Objects Wizard, click **Next**.

3. Select the queries you want to export, as displayed in Figure 17.18, and click **Next**.

4. As shown in Figure 17.19, enter a valid path and filename for the export, and ensure it ends with a .mof extension. Click **Next**.

5. Confirm the settings and click **Next**. Click **Close** to exit the wizard.

17

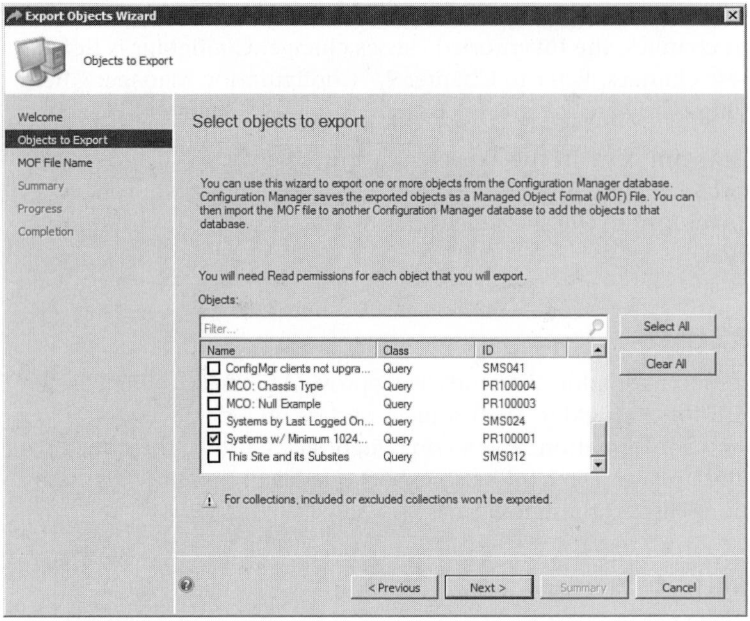

FIGURE 17.18   Select the queries to export.

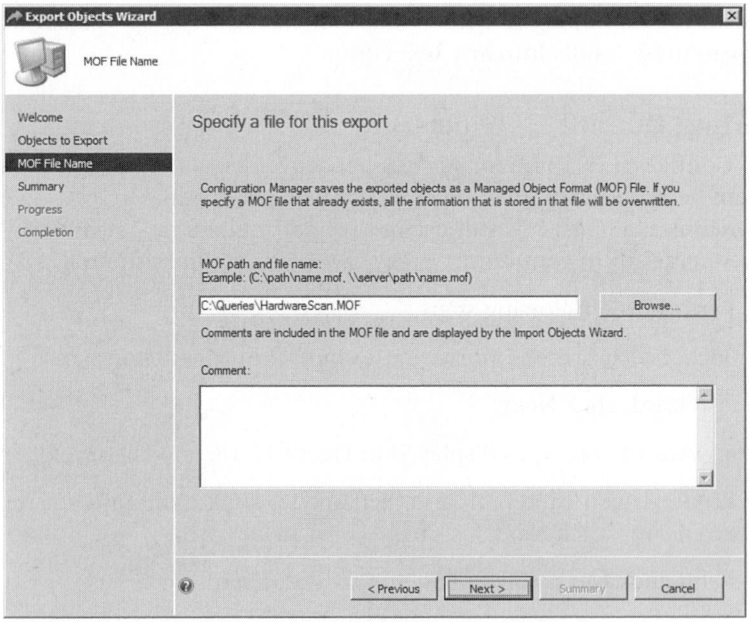

FIGURE 17.19   Provide a path and filename.

When completed, you can copy or move the file to a suitable location for importing into a different hierarchy. Before looking at the import steps, examine the file content of a sample export, which is based on the query built earlier in the section "Example: Querying for Devices with a Hardware Scan in the Last 15 Days." Here is the content of the file:

```
// ********************************************************************************
//
//          Created by SMS Export object wizard
//
//          Tuesday, August 09, 2011 created
//
//          File Name: C:\Queries\HardwareScan.MOF
//
// Comments :
//
//
// ********************************************************************************


// ***** Class : SMS_Query *****
[SecurityVerbs(-1)]
instance of SMS_Query
{
    Comments = "";
    Expression = "select SMS_R_System.Name,
SMS_G_System_WORKSTATION_STATUS.LastHardwareScan from  SMS_R_System inner join
SMS_G_System_WORKSTATION_STATUS on SMS_G_System_WORKSTATION_STATUS.ResourceId =
SMS_R_System.ResourceId where
DateDiff(dd,SMS_G_System_WORKSTATION_STATUS.LastHardwareScan,GetDate()) <= 15";
    LimitToCollectionID = "";
    LocalizedCategoryInstanceNames = {};
    Name = "Recent Hardware Scan (15 days)";
    QueryID = "";
    ResultAliasNames = {"SMS_R_System", "SMS_G_System_WORKSTATION_STATUS"};
    ResultColumnsNames = {"SMS_R_System.Name",
"SMS_G_System_WORKSTATION_STATUS.LastHardwareScan"};
    TargetClassName = "SMS_R_System";
};
// ***** End *****
```

The query itself remains intact in the expression line. Importing queries is just as easy as exporting queries. As an example, perform the following steps to import a query object:

1. Right-click the Queries node and choose **Import Objects**. This launches the Import Objects Wizard.

2. In the wizard, click **Next**.

17

3. Supply the path and name of the file to import. Click **Next**.

4. Review the name (or names) of the object(s) to import. Click **Next** and review the comments. Click **Next** when complete.

CAUTION: DUPLICATELY NAMED QUERIES ARE OVERWRITTEN

Review your existing objects carefully to ensure the query to import does not use an existing name. Any existing objects with a duplicate name are overwritten.

---

5. Confirm the settings on the Summary screen, and click **Next**. Click **Close** to exit the wizard.

Creating a Collection Based on Query Results

Before creating a collection that uses a query rule, examining the results in a query provides an opportunity to view attributes because a collection show only a default set of attributes. Because of this, you should create a query first, verify the results are as you expect, and then use it as the basis of your collection.

When you import a query into a collection, the additional attributes specified in your query are ignored and replaced with a default set. This process also occurs if you paste the WQL from a query to the collection rule directly. Looking at the previous memory query first examined in the "WMI Query Language" section, note the attributes requested in this select statement:

```
select SMS_R_System.Name, SMS_G_System_X86_PC_MEMORY.TotalPhysicalMemory
from SMS_R_System inner join SMS_G_System_X86_PC_MEMORY on
SMS_G_System_X86_PC_MEMORY.ResourceID = SMS_R_System.ResourceId
```

The following shows how the query is modified when imported or pasted into a collection:

```
select SMS_R_SYSTEM.ResourceID, SMS_R_SYSTEM.ResourceType, SMS_R_SYSTEM.Name,
SMS_R_SYSTEM.SMSUniqueIdentifier, SMS_R_SYSTEM.ResourceDomainORWorkgroup,
SMS_R_SYSTEM.Client from SMS_R_System inner join SMS_G_System_X86_PC_MEMORY on
SMS_G_System_X86_PC_MEMORY.ResourceID = SMS_R_System.ResourceId
```

Although the SMS_R_SYSTEM.Name still exists, the attributes for memory, SMS_G_System_X86_PC_MEMORY.TotalPhysicalMemory, are replaced with other values.

Status Message Queries

Status message queries are available to provide deeper insight into component-level activity and audit messages. Details such as user activity (changes to the hierarchy, sites, or client settings), deployed program messages, collection modifications, deployment, remote control, and even query activity is tracked and reported in status messages. You can find status message queries in the Monitoring workspace under the System Status parent node.

ConfigMgr comes stocked with more than 60 different status messages. If one of the standard status messages does not contain the information you want, you can create custom status messages. Currently, there is no documentation providing a translation of the status message IDs and their meaning. It is best that you build your queries from the existing queries as much as possible because the criteria may list the necessary message ID value, as shown in Figure 17.20, which shows the query titled **Deployments Created, Modified, or Deleted**.

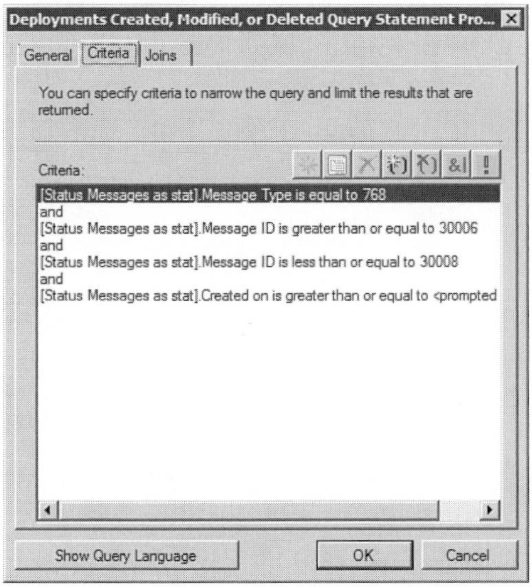

FIGURE 17.20   Status message criteria displaying message IDs and types.

Viewing Status Messages

Executing status message queries is a straightforward process, the only caveat being that they often prompt for information with a dialog with which you may not be familiar. Most times, status message queries filter by a date range so that the amount of information returned is not overwhelming and does not take a long time to execute.

For example, examine the query titled **Remote Control Activity Initiated by a Specific User**. It requests two pieces of information: property value and time. When looking for a property value, the value can be manually entered or selected from a drop-down list. If you are not familiar with the data or the format, it is often easier to go by the drop-down. When loaded, the drop-down list is filled with values.

NOTE: MANUALLY ENTER THE VALUE IF KNOWN

The disadvantage to using drop-down lists is time. As the option suggests, the option **Load Existing** queries the ConfigMgr database to retrieve a list of values.

Time values can be entered by using the Specify date and time option, which provides a calendar view as well as timeframe. If a specific date and time is unknown, use the Select date and time option, which provides some generic values to use as a date such as 1 hour ago, 12 hours ago, 2 weeks ago, 1 year ago, and so on. Viewing the query information after executing the query confirms what was entered if you use the values as expressed in Figure 17.21, including a date and time value of 1 year ago.

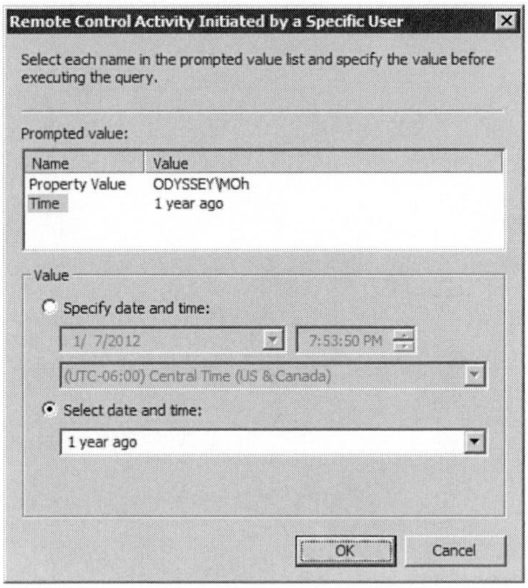

FIGURE 17.21   Using date and time in a status message query.

```
select stat.*, ins.*, att1.*, att1.AttributeTime from SMS_StatusMessage as stat left
join SMS_StatMsgInsStrings as ins on stat.RecordID = ins.RecordID left join
SMS_StatMsgAttributes as att1 on stat.RecordID = att1.RecordID inner join
SMS_StatMsgAttributes as att2 on stat.RecordID = att2.RecordID where
stat.MessageType = 768 and stat.MessageID >= 30069 and stat.MessageID <= 30087 and
att2.AttributeID = 403 and att2.AttributeValue = "ODYSSEY\\MOh" and
att2.AttributeTime >= '2011/01/08 01:47:23.000' order by att1.AttributeTime desc
```

Creating Status Message Queries

In the list of status message queries, there is a query titled **Clients That Received a Specific Deployed Program** and another titled **Clients That Rejected a Specific Deployed Program**. To view both statuses in the same list, you must create a custom status message query (or suffer through sifting through hundreds of records in the All Status Message query). To create a new status message query, perform the following steps:

1. Launch the Create Status Message Query Wizard. Give the query a name such as **Clients That Received and Rejected a Specific Deployed Program**.

2. To make it easier to create your new query, click the **Import Query Statement** button, and select the query titled **Clients That Received a Specific Deployed Program**, and click **OK**.

3. Click the **Edit Query Statement** button. Note that the contents of the selected query are imported.

4. Switch to the Criteria tab and highlight the line labeled **[Status Message as Stat]. Message ID is Equal to 10002**. Double-click the line, or select the properties icon to bring up the Criterion Properties dialog.

5. As shown in Figure 17.22, change the Criterion Type to **List of Values**, the operator to **Is In**, and add the following to the Value to match section: **10002, 10018, and 10019**.

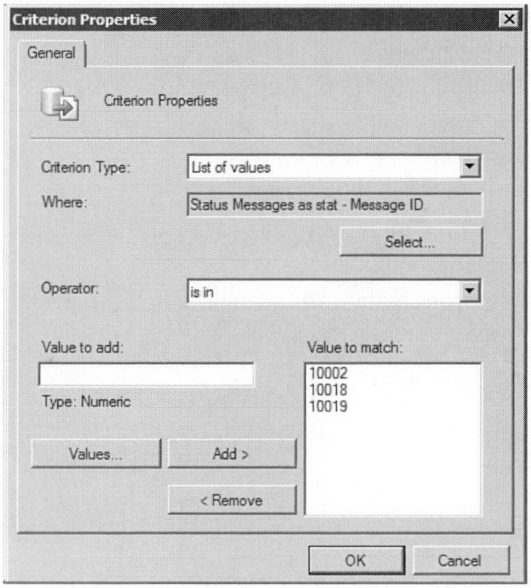

FIGURE 17.22   List of values criteria to display selected status message IDs.

6. Close all the dialog windows by clicking **OK** to commit the changes.

7. After returning to the Create Status Message Query Wizard, click **Next** to view the summary. Click **Next** again to create the query, and finally, click **Close** to end the wizard.

TIP: LEARNING ABOUT CRITERION PROPERTIES

For a refresher on criterion properties, read the "ConfigMgr Query Builder" section.

Most of the status message queries are named descriptively enough to identify its purpose. However, it is still helpful to point out some of the more useful queries. An additional benefit is understanding the various sources of data from which these queries can draw information. Table 17.6 lists some useful queries.

TABLE 17.6   Useful Status Message Queries

Status Message Query	Description
All Audit Status Messages for a Specific User	Shows the activity of a specific user.
Client Configuration Requests (CCRs) Processed Unsuccessfully	Failures related to processing client configuration requests (CCR) can be tracked through this status message query.
Collections Created, Modified, or Deleted	Displays audit messages related to collection modification displaying collections that have been modified or deleted and by whom.
Deployments Created, Modified, or Deleted	Displays audit messages related to creation, modification, and deletion of deployments.
Remote Control Activity Initiated by a Specific User	Shows the activity of any remote control sessions started by a specified user.
Server Component Configuration Changes	Useful to tracking changes made to any of the myriad ConfigMgr server components.
Server Components Experiencing Fatal Errors	Shows fatal errors displayed by any Configuration Manager server component.

Summary

Queries are an excellent means to gather data, test results for collections, and understand the requirements of creating reports. This chapter covered the use of the ConfigMgr query builder for constructing queries. It discussed how to use advanced functions to create complex queries for times when the query builder is inadequate, and the fundamentals about classes and operators to enable you to build your own queries. In addition, this chapter covered a method you can use to convert WQL to SQL, gave examples of advanced queries, and discussed creating status message queries.

Using reporting enables you to analyze the varied data collected by System Center 2012 Configuration Manager (ConfigMgr). The core product includes many predefined reports, which satisfy common reporting requests. You can also create custom reports. To use a mining analogy, the process of creating custom reports is similar to mining for gold. You know those gold nuggets are there; it is a matter of locating and extracting the nuggets from the ground. With custom reports, you must locate the data you need, construct a well-crafted query, and create the report based on that query.

This chapter discusses implementing reporting for System Center 2012 Configuration Manager. In addition, it focuses on how to implement reporting in a secure manner, and how to create custom reports when the need arises. The chapter also identifies and describes best practices such as backup and performance tuning and introduces the System Center data warehouse.

SQL Server Reporting Services Overview

SQL Server Reporting Services (SSRS) is part of SQL Server and was first released with SQL Server 2000. Technically, it is best understood as a Windows application because SSRS uses an application layer and stores its information in SQL Server databases running on Windows Server.

Microsoft first introduced SSRS integration for Configuration Manager with ConfigMgr 2007 Release 2 (R2) as a reporting option to augment the product's legacy (Active Server Pages [ASP]) reports. With the 2012 version of ConfigMgr, SSRS is now the only supported reporting solution because Microsoft has deprecated the legacy reporting feature.

SSRS offers many advantages as a reporting solution; here are several that this chapter covers in more depth:

▶ SSRS uses an industry standard reporting system.

▶ SSRS Report Definition Language (RDL) is stored in eXtensible Markup Language (XML) format. This lets you easily back up the RDL report files and migrate those files between reporting servers.

▶ Compared with legacy reporting, SSRS offers higher performance, availability, and scalability for reporting with ConfigMgr.

▶ The report building tools available with SSRS enable generating ad hoc reports.

▶ SSRS offers a number of performance enhancements such as report subscriptions and report caching.

▶ SSRS provides a number of interactive features for the report end user.

▶ SSRS enables users to export reports in a variety of popular formats, providing nine default formats.

▶ If you have struggled with reports timing out or exceeding row limits, SSRS offers adjustable report row limits and time out settings!

Implementing SSRS

The next sections discuss the design requirements and process necessary to implement SSRS properly. To use reporting for System Center 2012 Configuration Manager, you must first install SSRS.

SQL Server Version Selection

Implementing SSRS for System Center 2012 Configuration Manager requires Microsoft SQL Server 2008 SP1 (x64) or later. Although Microsoft supports SSRS 2008 R2 on the Windows Server 2003 x64 platform, the authors recommend the Windows Server 2008 x64 operating system.

> **TIP: USING THE WINDOWS SERVER 2008 PLATFORM**
>
> Although it is possible to install SSRS 2008 R2 on Windows Server 2003, given the age of that product and Microsoft's direction toward 64-bit computing, you should strongly consider using the Windows 2008 R2 environment.

Server Placement Options

Within the ConfigMgr hierarchy (discussed in Chapter 4, "Architecture Design Planning"), you can place the SSRS installation at the central administration site (CAS) or any other primary site in the hierarchy. SSRS installation at the CAS enables reporting on all global replicated data and activity initiated from the CAS. Installing SSRS at a primary site allows reporting global replicated data and activity initiated by that site. The primary site SSRS installation could be useful in distributed hierarchies where data, activities, and responsibilities are segmented by site.

You need to determine whether to install SSRS directly on the database server or on a separate, dedicated server. Here are advantages and disadvantages of each:

► **Installing SSRS directly on the database server**:

This is the simplest approach and does not require additional software licenses. As SSRS is a core part of SQL Server, the software required is already present on the database server. For best performance, scope your database server hardware with adequate memory, CPU, and available free hard disk space.

ConfigMgr now fully supports installing SSRS to a SQL Server named instance. Should you choose to install SSRS on the database server, the authors recommend installing SSRS as a separate, named instance on SQL Server.

Should you later decide you need to move your SSRS installation to another server, this is fairly easy to accomplish. For information on moving the report server databases to another computer, see http://technet.microsoft.com/en-us/library/ms156421.aspx.

► **Installing SSRS on a separate, dedicated server**:

For large ConfigMgr sites or those sites that might be concerned about potential performance impact on the ConfigMgr database server, choose a separate server for installation of SSRS.

Ideally, for best performance, you want this server located on the same subnet as the ConfigMgr database server. Using this configuration has the advantage of tuning SSRS separately, without potential impact on the ConfigMgr database server. The downside of this approach is the additional expense of the server and software.

ABOUT INSTALLING SSRS ON A SEPARATE SERVER

If you install SSRS on a separate dedicated server, you eliminate the load being placed on the ConfigMgr SQL Server for SSRS dedicated operations such as report subscriptions, rendering, and so on. The authors suggest this only for the largest sites, or for those that want to keep as much activity as possible off the database server hosting the ConfigMgr database. As reference, Microsoft suggests locating the reporting services point on a remote site system server as a best practice for performance reasons. For further information, see http://technet.microsoft.com/en-us/library/hh394138.aspx.

Regardless of where you install SSRS, the authors suggest identifying a baseline performance for the ConfigMgr database server. You should monitor performance of SQL Server after installing and configuring SSRS, and make adjustments as needed.

SSRS Installation

After determining placement of SSRS, the next step is to install the software itself. You must install SSRS in native mode for System Center 2012 Configuration Manager. For

information on the default configuration for a native mode installation, see http://msdn.
microsoft.com/en-us/library/ms143711.aspx.

NOTE: VERIFYING AN SSRS INSTALLATION

After installing SSRS, you should verify it is working correctly. The steps to determine
SSRS is installed correctly and functioning properly are documented at http://msdn.micro-
soft.com/en-us/library/ms143773.aspx.

After verifying your SSRS installation, you are ready to install the System Center 2012
Configuration Manager reporting services point role.

The following steps install the reporting services point on the site database server:

1. Using the System Center 2012 Configuration Manager console, open the
   Administration workspace. Select an available server to use as a site system, choose
   the **Create Roles Wizard**, select **Specify a FQDN for this site system for use on the
   Internet**, and type **amanda.odyssey.com**, as displayed in Figure 18.1.

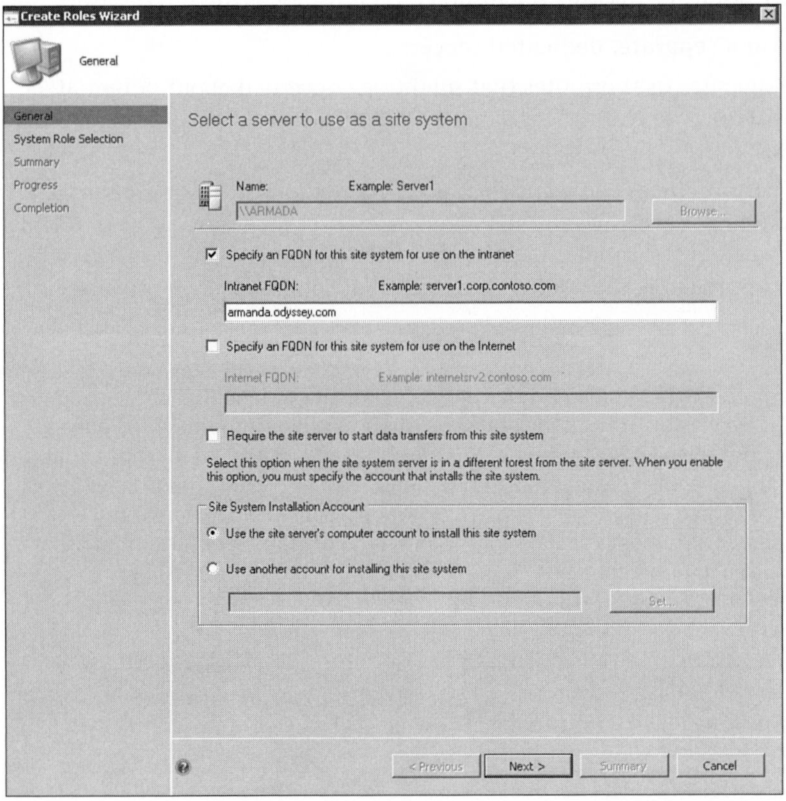

FIGURE 18.1   Specify the site system for the reporting services role.

2. Click **Next**, and then select **Reporting Services Point** as a system role, as shown in Figure 18.2.

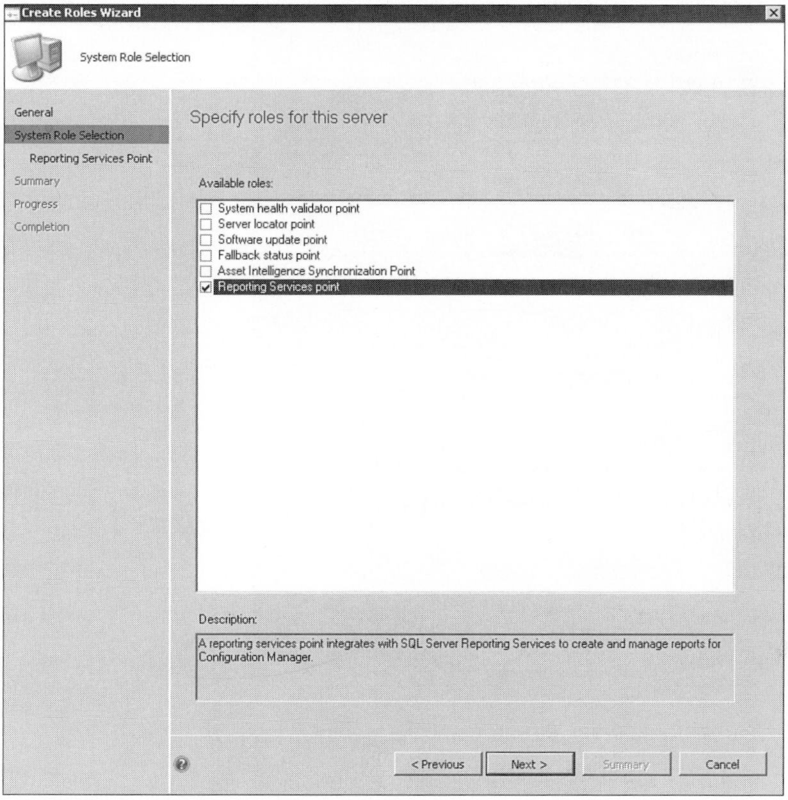

FIGURE 18.2   Specify the Reporting Services Point role in the wizard.

3. For the Specify Reporting Services settings screen displayed in Figure 18.3, verify that the site server and database names are correct.

In the folder settings section in the bottom part of Figure 18.4, the folder name corresponds to ConfigMgr_<*site code*>. Use an account that has administrative rights on the SSRS instance, and choose the option **Use as Windows credentials to connect to the data source**, as shown in Figure 18.4. Click **Next**.

TIP: SPECIFYING THE USE OF WINDOWS CREDENTIALS

To use Windows Authentication, you must select **Use as Windows credentials to connect to the data source**. Otherwise, the report server passes credentials to the database server as SQL authentication. If the database server cannot authenticate the credentials that you provide, the connection will fail.

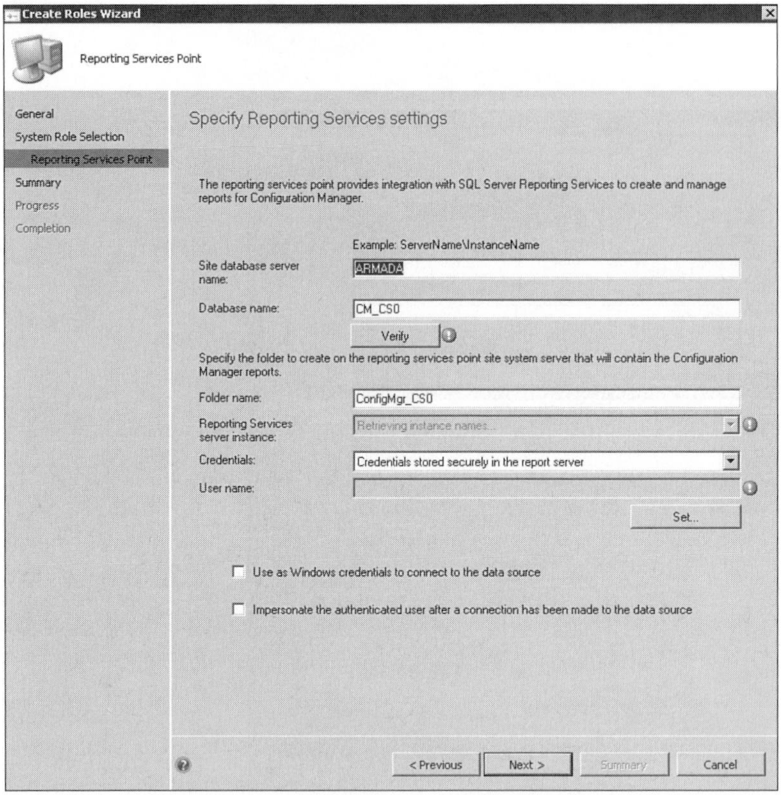

FIGURE 18.3   Verify the site database server and name.

4. Verify the settings are correct in the Summary dialog displayed, as shown in Figure 18.5, and click **Next**.

5. The Completion dialog, as shown in Figure 18.6, displays the results of the installation process.

SSRS Configuration

You now have SSRS installed, and ConfigMgr has the reporting services point role installed and enabled. It is important at this point to discuss SSRS role-based access control (RBAC) and implementing access control for your Reporting Services point role. There are several steps required to allow your end users access to Reporting Services for ConfigMgr; these are discussed in the next sections. SSRS security can be configured either from the ConfigMgr console as covered in the "Interacting with the Console" section or directly from SSRS Report Manager. Conceptually, you must understand that either technique interacts with the underlying RBAC security layer within SSRS.

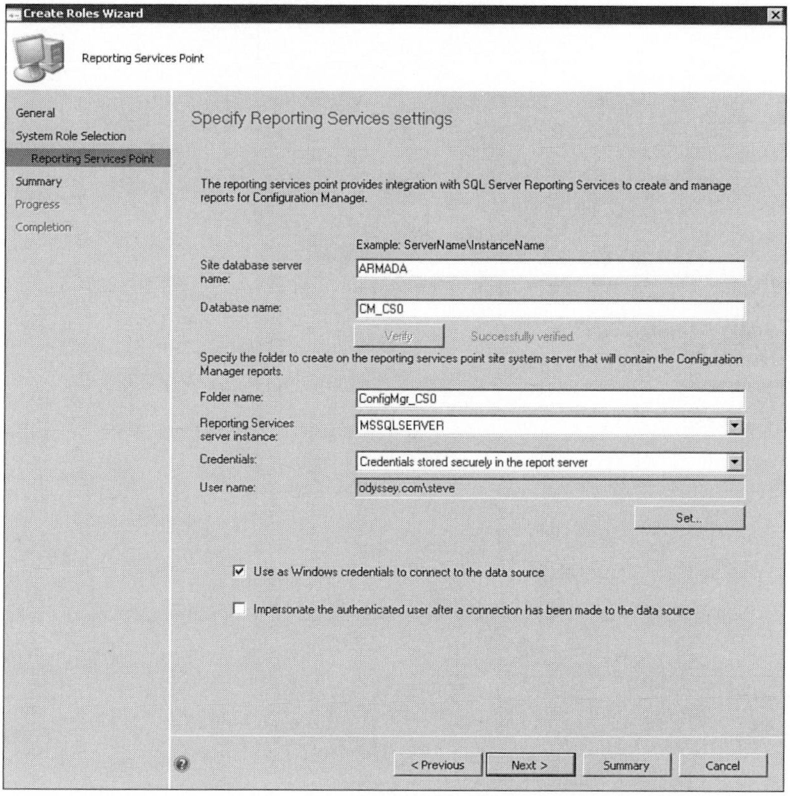

FIGURE 18.4   Site Server database name and credentials verified.

About RBAC

RBAC is conceptually similar to properly implemented NT File System (NTFS) security. Role assignments determine access to stored items and to the report server. ConfigMgr SSRS security must now be configured through the ConfigMgr console; System Center Configuration Manager can overwrite any SSRS permissions granted outside the console.

Here are the parts of a role assignment:

▶ **A securable item:** The item that needs controlled access. Examples of securable items include folders, reports, and resources.

▶ **A user or group account:** This is an account that can be authenticated by Windows security or another authentication mechanism.

▶ **Role definitions:** These define a set of tasks.

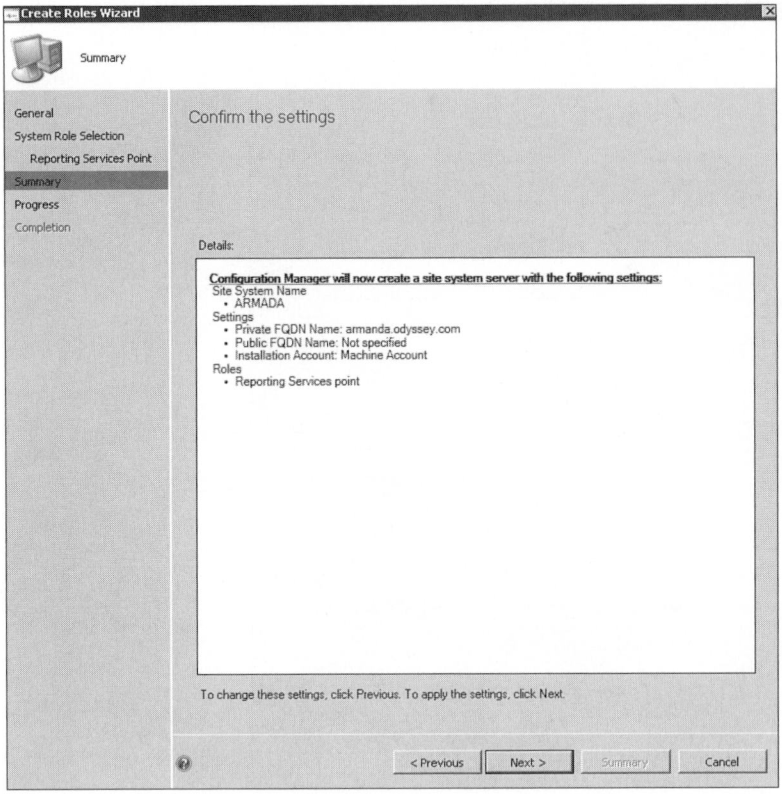

FIGURE 18.5   Confirming the settings.

The scope of a role will be system- or item-specific. Here's how they differ:

▶ A system-scoped role applies to the entire SSRS instance.

▶ An item-scoped role applies to specific folder(s) or report(s), depending on the role assignment.

Examples of predefined role definitions include System Administrator, Content Manager, and Publisher.

Table 18.1 provides a complete list of predefined roles in SSRS.

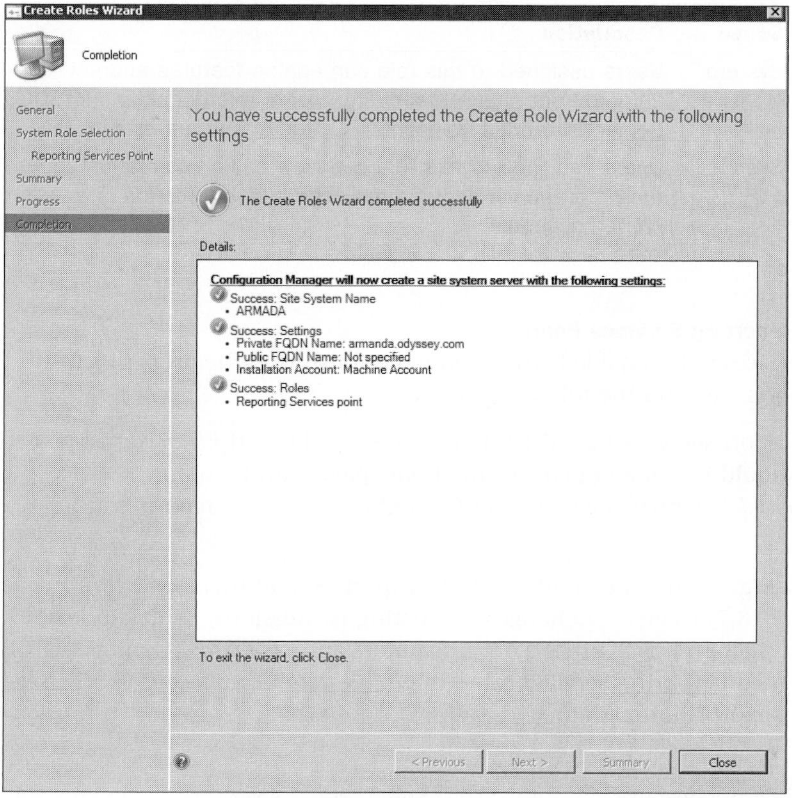

FIGURE 18.6   The completion screen in the Create Roles Wizard.

TABLE 18.1   Predefined Roles in SSRS

Predefined Role	Scope	Description
Content Manager	Item	Includes all item-level tasks. Users assigned to this role have full permission to manage report server content, including the ability to grant permissions to other users, and to define the folder structure for storing reports and other items.
Publisher	Item	Users assigned to this role can add items to a report server; this includes creating and managing folders that contain those items.
Browser	Item	Users assigned to this role can run reports, subscribe to reports, and navigate through the folder structure.
Report Builder	Item	Users assigned to this role can create and edit reports in Report Builder.
My Reports	Item	Users assigned to this role can manage a personal workspace for storing and using reports and other items.

18

Predefined Role	Scope	Description
System Administrator	System	Users assigned to this role can enable features and set defaults, set sitewide security, create role definitions in SQL Server Enterprise Management Studio, and manage jobs.
System User	System	Users assigned to this role can view basic information about the report server such as the schedule information in a shared schedule.

Accessing the SSRS Reporting Services Point

With the reporting services point enabled, you need to establish that the proper security groups can access reports. Perform the following steps:

1. Browse to your report server, where the home page should be http://<*reportserver*>/ Reports. There should be a folder beneath the home page with the name ConfigMgr_<*site code*>, which is where your ConfigMgr site server reports will be located.

2. Click the **ConfigMgr_<*site code*>** folder, select **Properties**, and then **Security** (on the left side of Figure 18.7) to view or change the existing permissions. By default, the Active Directory (AD) groups BUILTIN\Administrators and <*domain*>\ConfigMgr Full Admins are assigned Reporting Services roles; these roles are ConfigMgr Report Users and ConfigMgr Report Administrators.

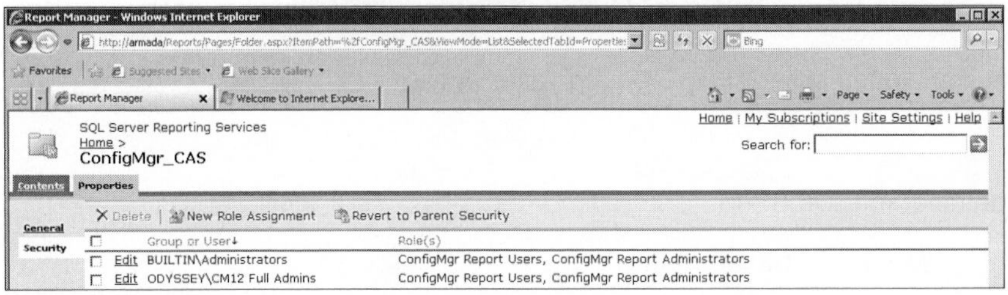

FIGURE 18.7   Default Reporting Services Role Permissions.

3. To allow a specific AD group, you have created to access the reports; click **New Role Assignment**, as shown in Figure 18.7.

   By default, installation grants all user accounts in ConfigMgr Configuration Manager Report Reader rights on the Reporting Services and Configuration Manager root folders. In addition, the installation grants all user accounts in ConfigMgr that have Site Modify rights, ConfigMgr Report Administrator rights on the Reporting Services, and Configuration Manager root folders.

   For more information, see http://technet.microsoft.com/en-us/library/gg712698. aspx.

For demonstration purposes, if you want to grant Authenticated Users access to SSRS, at the Group or User selection, enter *<domain>***ReportUsers**, check **ConfigMgr Report Users**, and then click **OK**. The example in Figure 18.8 allows all Authenticated Users access to ConfigMgr Reporting Services.

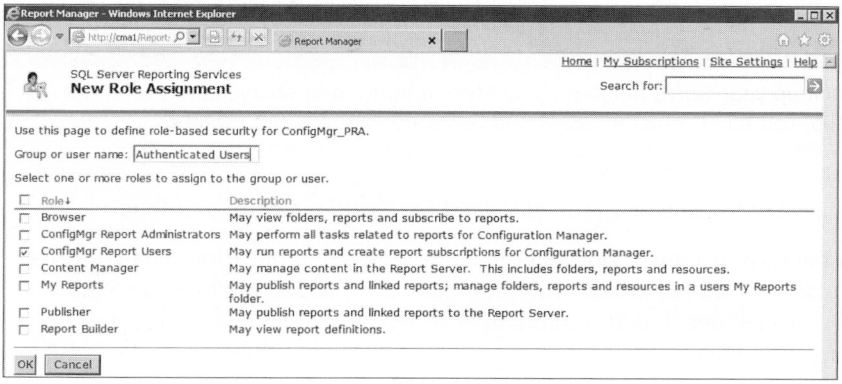

FIGURE 18.8   Reporting Services Role permissions.

Data Sources

Think of a *data source* as a connector between your report and the SQL Server database. The data source is essential for the report(s) to execute and return a result set. Data sources are discussed in the "Authoring Custom Reports" section. It is worth noting here that under the ConfigMgr site server reports folder there will be a data source named as a Globally Unique Identifier (GUID). Do not rename or delete this data source or your ConfigMgr reports will no longer function. Figure 18.9 shows a sample data source and GUID.

CAUTION: DO NOT DELETE THE GUID DATA SOURCE

If you delete the GUID data source, your ConfigMgr reports will no longer function.

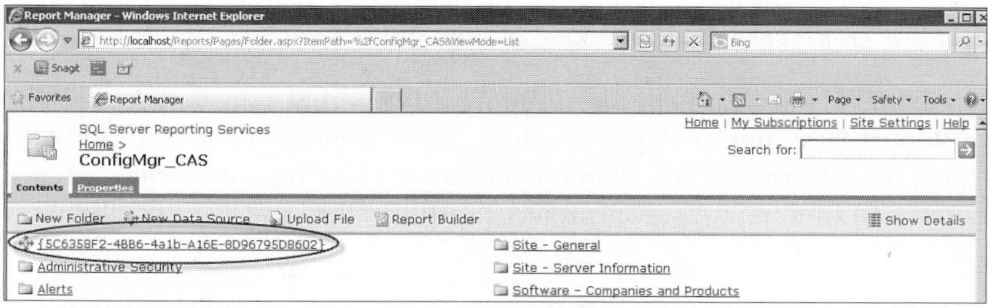

FIGURE 18.9   Reporting Services Data Source.

18

Backing Up SSRS

By now, you probably have the ConfigMgr backup task configured, scheduled, and running; Chapter 21, "Backup, Recovery, and Maintenance," provides information on backups. However, you may not be aware that this task is not backing up your SSRS databases and custom reports!

TIP: IMPORTANCE OF BACKING UP SSRS

If you do not back up your SSRS databases, custom reports, and encryption keys, if the report server fails, you must reinstall SSRS and re-create your custom reports.

Here is what is necessary to back up your SSRS database, configuration, and reports:

▶ **Schedule a backup of your report server databases.** All application data is stored in the Reportserver and Reportservertempdb databases, which are on your SSRS reporting server instance. Use the standard SQL Server backup task to schedule backups of these databases.

▶ **Back up the SSRS encryption keys and archive that file in a safe location.** Encryption keys contain the secure credentials and connection information used for report items such as data source names, subscriptions, and report caching. The encryption keys are essential for a restore of Reporting Services, or when migrating Reporting Services to a new server.

  Here are the two ways to back up the encryption keys:

  ▶ **Reporting Services Configuration Manager:** Connect to the proper SSRS instance; select **Encryption Keys** as shown on the left side in Figure 18.10.

    Next, select **Backup** on the upper right of the dialog; in the Backup Encryption Key dialog box, choose the file location and password, and then click **OK** (see Figure 18.11). Store your encryption keys in a safe location.

  ▶ **RsKeyMgmt.exe:** This utility runs as a command locally on the report server. Specify the following options, changing the file and password to suit your environment, as displayed in Figure 18.12. The syntax is `rskeymgmt -e -f <filename> -p<password>`.

    `RsKeyMgmt -e -f c:\SSRSEncryptionKkey20110814.snk -pCM2012`

▶ **Back up any custom report data files and report models that you may have created with Report Designer or Report Builder.** These include report definition (.rdl) files, report model (.smdl) files, shared data source (.rds) files, data view (.dv) files, data source (.ds) files, report server project (.rptproj) files, and report solution (.sln) files.

  Remember to back up any script (.rss) files that you created for administration or deployment tasks.

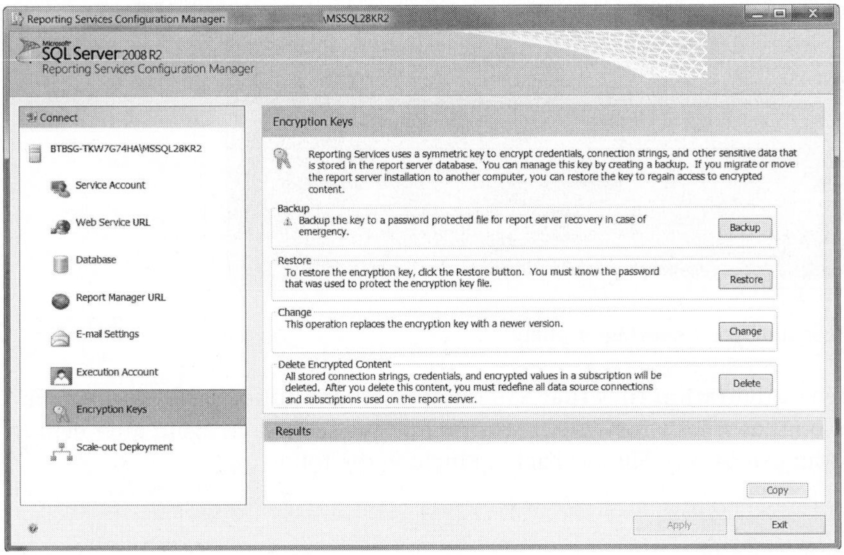

FIGURE 18.10   Reporting Services Configuration Manager Encryption Keys.

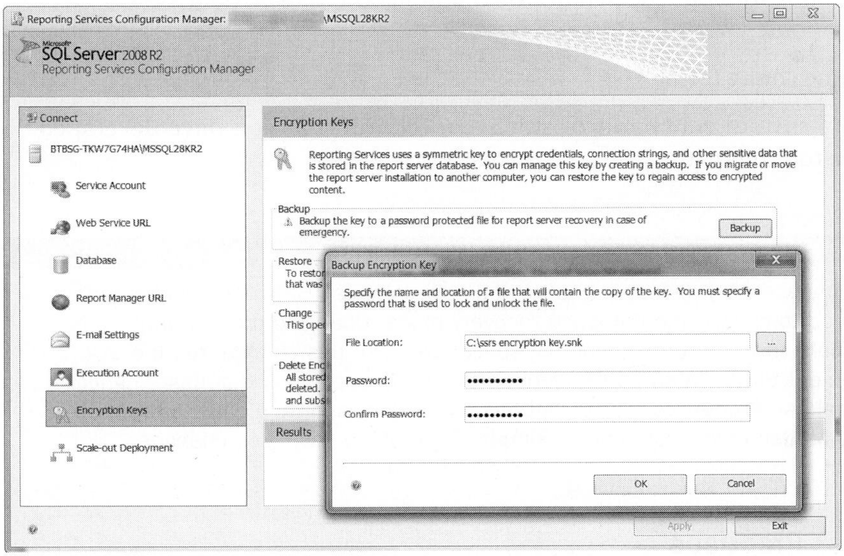

FIGURE 18.11   Reporting Services Configuration Manager Backup Key.

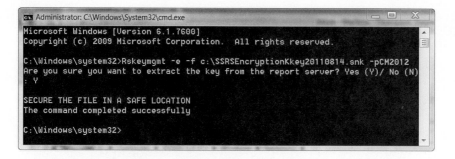

FIGURE 18.12   Executing the RskeyMgmt utility.

▶ **Back up the configuration files that SSRS uses to store application settings.** You should back up these files when you first configure the server and again after deploying any custom extensions. Files to back up include the following:

> ▶ Rsreportserver.config
>
> ▶ Rssvrpolicy.config
>
> ▶ Rsmgrpolicy.config
>
> ▶ Reportingservicesservice.exe.config
>
> ▶ Web.config for both the Report Server and Report Manager ASP.NET applications
>
> ▶ Machine.config for ASP.NET

▶ **Back up any custom views and/or stored procedures that you have developed for your custom reports.**

TIP: CONFIGURING SSRS DATABASE RECOVERY MODE

To avoid using unnecessary disk space, after you have installed SSRS and configured backups you need to change the database recovery mode. Changing the recovery mode from Full to Simple saves on transaction log space. To make this change, run the SQL Server Management Studio MMC application, select the ReportServer database, right-click and choose database **Properties**, select **Options** on the left, and then change the drop-down **Recovery Model:** mode from **Full** to **Simple**. Click **OK** to save your changes.

Reporting Best Practices

Here are some SSRS best practices:

▶ Create a SQL Server scheduled task to automate backup of the ReportServer and ReportServerTempdb databases.

▶ Create a script to automate backup of your key Reporting Service files.

▶ Be sure to save a copy of your SSRS encryption key to a safe and secure location.

▶ Save a copy of any custom SSRS reports, as you can easily re-create the stock, built-in reports.

▶ Script report backups using RS.EXE. This utility, available since SQL Server 2000, allows automated routine installation, deployment, report migrations between reporting servers, and other administrative tasks, and uses Visual Basic .NET code. For more information, see

   ▶ http://msdn.microsoft.com/en-us/library/ms162839.aspx

   ▶ http://msdn.microsoft.com/en-us/library/ms159720.aspx

▶ Consider using RSS Scripter, developed by a SQL Server MVP. This utility simplifies creation of VB scripts for RS.EXE. See http://www.sqldbatips.com/showarticle. asp?ID=62.

Interacting with Reports from the Console

You can find the reports under **Monitoring -> Overview -> Reporting -> Reports** in the ConfigMgr console, as shown in Figure 18.13.

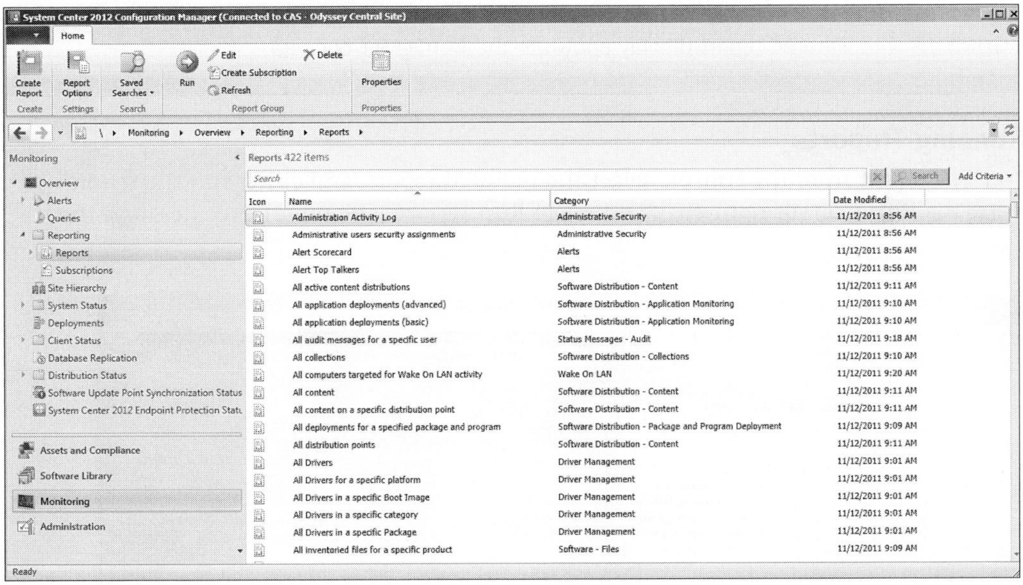

FIGURE 18.13   Reports in the ConfigMgr console.

Search Capability

The console has a rich search capability that allows you to locate a particular report or group of reports. For example, should you need to locate reports that pertain to hardware, enter **Hardware** on the search field, and click **Search** to return 59 items, as shown in Figure 18.14. From the console menu, you can refine the search criteria by using the

Add Criteria icon. The Search Settings icon allows the specification of the number of rows returned; the Save Current Search icon allows searches to be saved for subsequent use; and the Clear icon clears the current search criteria.

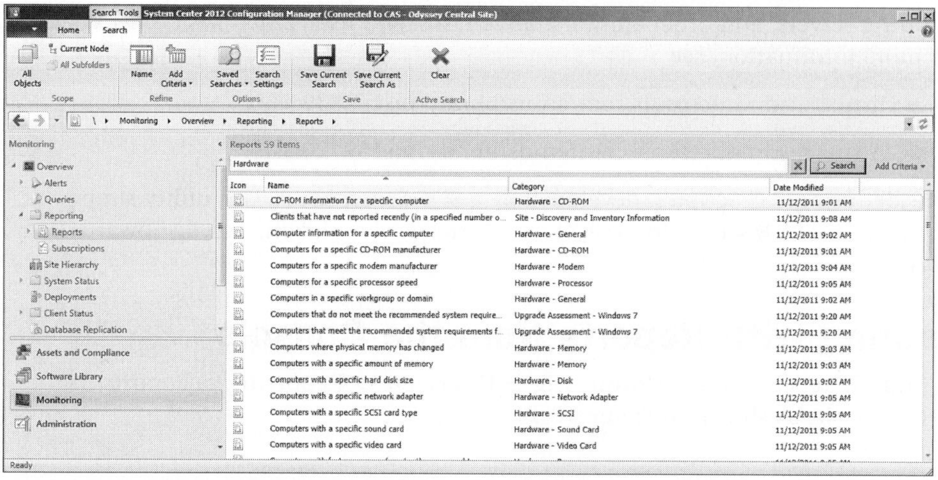

FIGURE 18.14   Filtered report display shown in the ConfigMgr console.

Running Reports

To run a report from the console select the required report, and either run the report using the **Run** icon, or right-click and select **Run report**. The report executes, and the

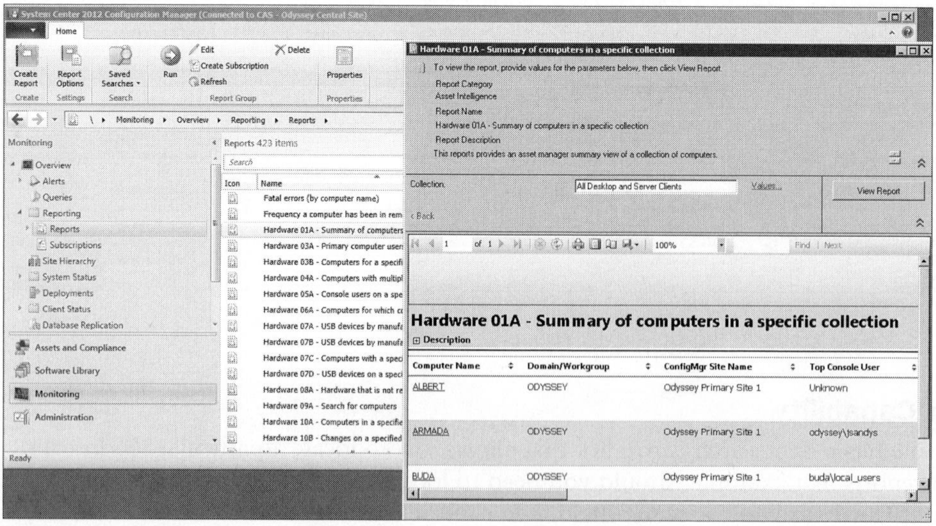

FIGURE 18.15   Report results run from the console.

results appear in a separate dialog. Figure 18.15 shows results for the Asset Intelligence > Hardware 01A - Summary of computers in a specific collection.

Creating Subscriptions

Report subscriptions enable reports to be scheduled to run at specific times, to be triggered by an event and post the report results to a file share, or sent to recipients via email. This topic is covered in more detail in the "Optimizing SSRS Performance" section.

TIP: ENABLING SUBSCRIPTIONS

You must enable subscriptions at the reporting server for the console settings discussed in this section to work.

From the ConfigMgr console, there are two ways to enable report subscriptions:

▶ From the menu, click the **Create Subscription** icon.

▶ Choose a report, right-click, and select **Create Subscription**.

This takes you to the Report Properties sheet, Subscriptions tab, as displayed in Figure 18.16. Click **Add** to add a new subscription, and the Create Subscription Wizard appears. Fill in the appropriate information, and choose **Render Format** to designate the report style, as shown in Figure 18.17. Click **Next**, and enter the appropriate schedule information. You can create and use that shared schedules, as shown in Figure 18.18. Click **Next**. If the report contains parameters, specify them as indicated in Figure 18.19. Review the Summary page, as shown in Figure 18.20, and then click **Next** to save the subscription.

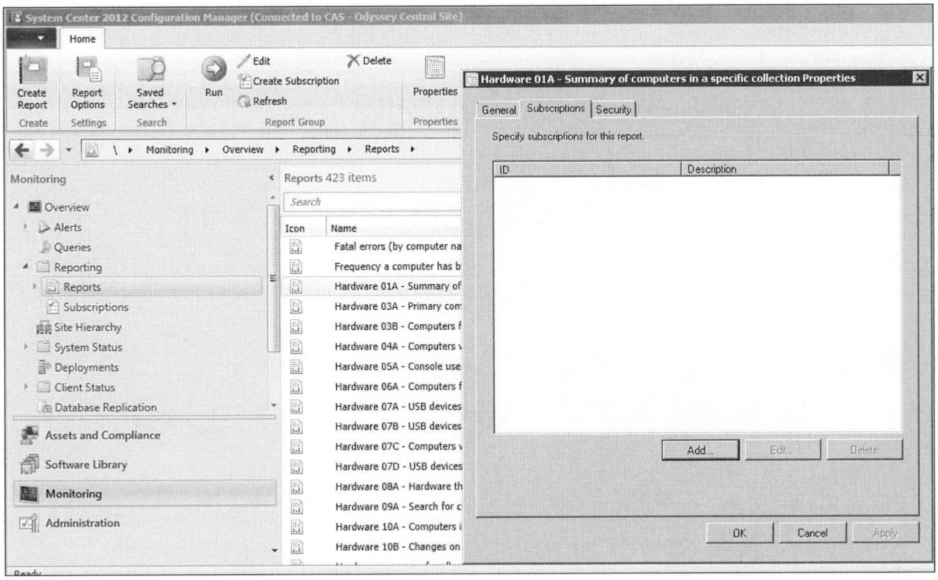

FIGURE 18.16   Creating a new subscription.

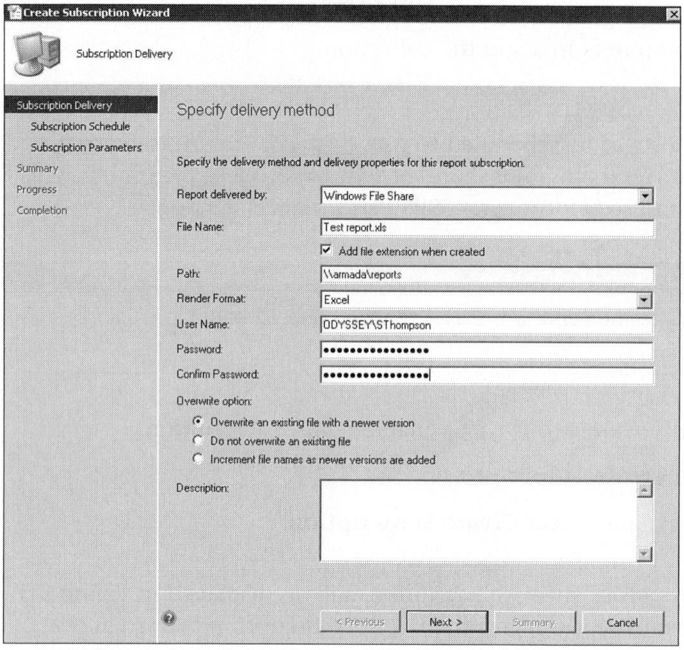

FIGURE 18.17   The Create Subscription Wizard.

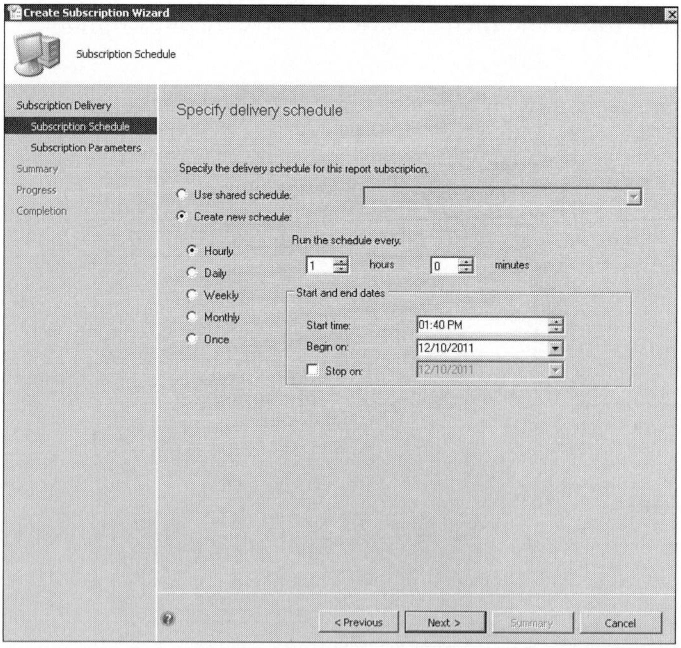

FIGURE 18.18   Scheduling in the Create Subscription Wizard.

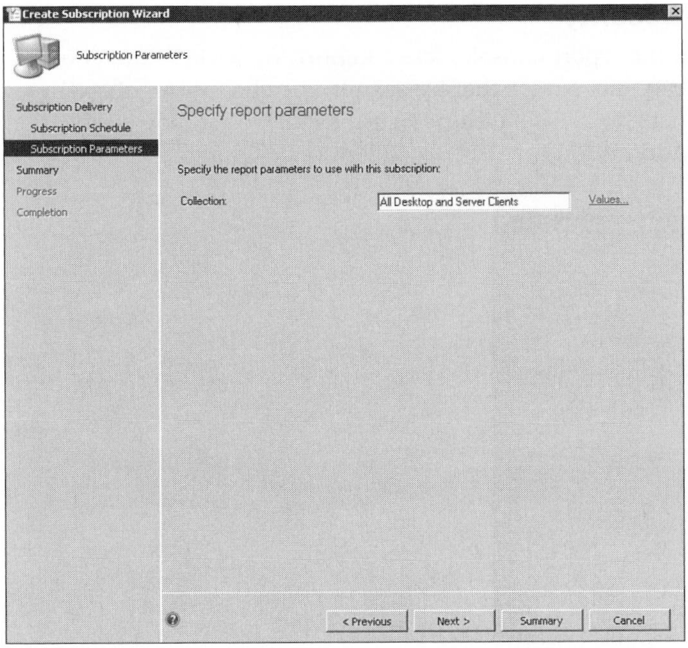

FIGURE 18.19   Specifying Report Parameters.

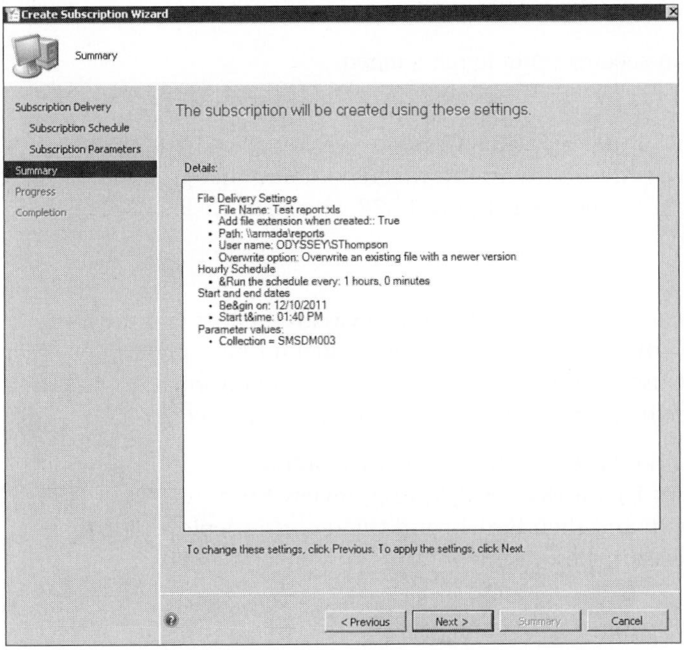

FIGURE 18.20   Summary page of the Create Subscription Wizard.

Managing SSRS Report Security

To manage report security from the report console, select **Report**, right-click, and choose **Properties**; then click the **Security** tab. Notice that by default, the check box **Inheriting rights from parent object** is enabled, as displayed in Figure 18.21. To modify, disable the check box, and then click the **Add** button for a set of role options to appear.

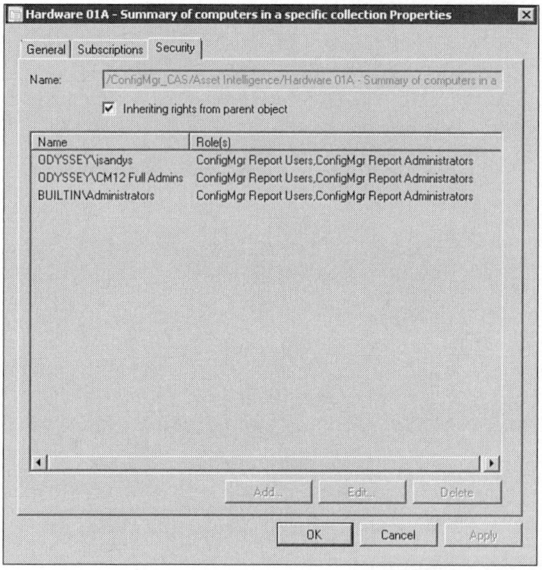

FIGURE 18.21   Assigning a group security rights to run a report.

Roles are covered in more detail in the "SSRS Roles" section. If you want to grant the group odyssey\authenticated users the ability to run this report, add that group in the user text box, select **Browser** role, as shown in Figure 18.22, and then click **OK**.

Creating a Report

To create a report from the console, choose the menu icon **Create Report** to launch the Create Report Wizard. You have the ability to use a report model if one is present, or use a SQL-based report. This example uses the SQL-based report. For more information on creating and using report models, see http://msdn.microsoft.com/en-us/library/ms345322.aspx.

Enter a name for your report, choose the Path icon, and select a folder location to which to save the report, as displayed in Figure 18.23. Click **Next**, review the Summary page, as shown in Figure 18.24, click **Next**, and then **Finish**, and the report is deployed to your report server, and Report Builder launches.

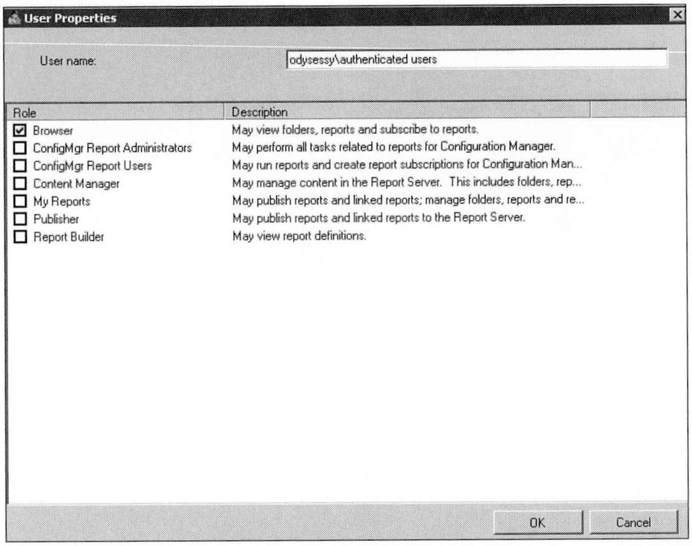

FIGURE 18.22   Assigning the Browser role.

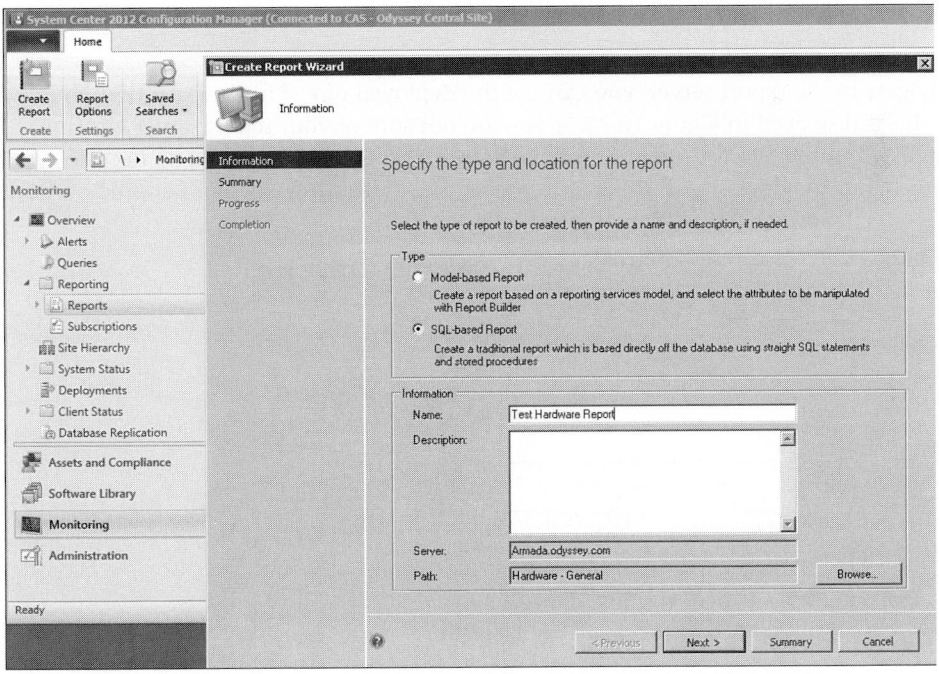

FIGURE 18.23   Specifying the type and location of the report.

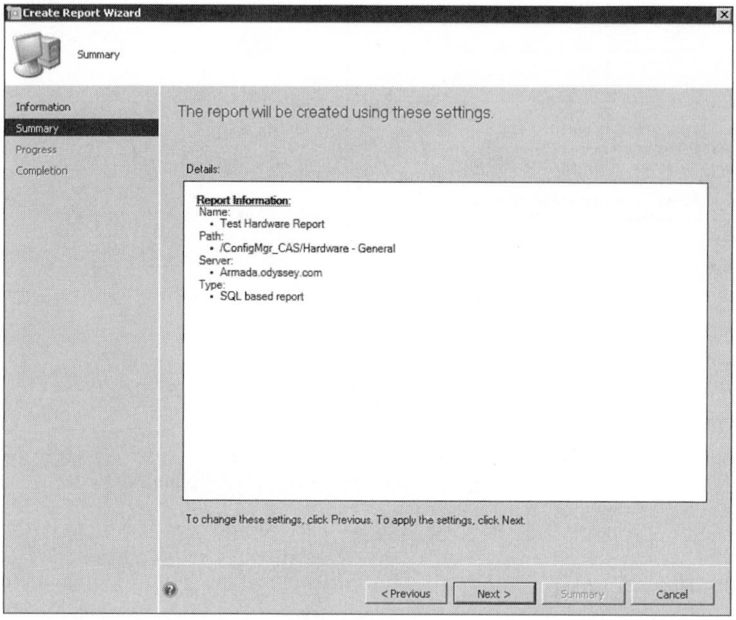

FIGURE 18.24   Summary screen of the Create Report Wizard.

If you navigate to the report server, you can see the deployed report in the path that you selected; this is displayed in Figure 18.25. If you are not sure of your report server location, this is discussed in the "SSRS Configuration" section earlier in this chapter. You need to author this report to add content; this is covered in the "Authoring Custom Reports" section.

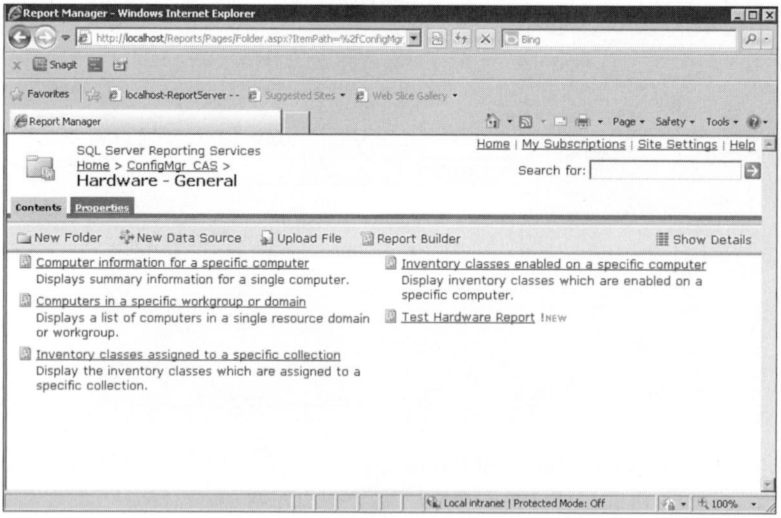

FIGURE 18.25   The deployed report.

Authoring Custom Reports

At some point, there will be a need to create or modify an existing report to provide information not part of one of the core reports. The next sections discuss selecting a development tool, creating and deploying a custom report, interactive reporting features, and advanced reporting techniques, and provide an example of building a more advanced report.

Development Tool Selection

There are two primary methods used to construct a custom report: Microsoft Report Builder and Microsoft Visual Studio. Here's some information:

▶ **Microsoft Report Builder:** Report Builder 1.0 first shipped with SQL Server 2005. Since then there have been two major upgrades, with Report Builder 3.0 emerging as the latest and the required version for SQL Server 2008 R2. Report Builder is available as a free download from an SSRS 2008 R2 installed reporting site, or at http://www.microsoft.com/download/en/details.aspx?displaylang=en&id=6116.

For creating reports, Report Builder 3.0 has several advantages for both the novice and the professional developer; it is easy to use, and there are a number of built-in wizards to facilitate the creation process. Report Builder 3.0 is demonstrated in the next section.

▶ **Microsoft Visual Studio:** There are really two parts to this development tool:

  ▶ The full Visual Studio Developer Edition

  ▶ BIDS (Business Intelligence Development Studio), which is included as an optional install with every SQL Server installation

Consider BIDS as a subset of Visual Studio, and because it is included with SQL Server, no additional licensing is required. Visual Studio is commonly used in team environments because you can use it with Team Foundation Services for source control and collaboration with multiple developers.

The primary advantage BIDS has when compared to Report Builder is its capability to maintain an entire custom reporting solution in one development environment. In addition, you can deploy the entire solution with several mouse clicks.

If you are new to report development, the authors recommend using Report Builder 3.0 as a starting point. As your development skills progress, you can also import custom reports created in Report Builder into a Visual Studio project.

Building a Custom Report

This section discusses how to create a custom report. Creating a report requires creating a data source and defining the data fields for your query. Some reports are best viewed using a chart, also discussed in this section.

18

First, you need a data source. A data source can be created as a shared data source, or created to be used by the report. The authors recommend creating a shared data source because the data source can be properly secured and be reused for multiple reports. Perform the following steps:

1. If this is your first custom report, here is how to create a shared data source. Navigate to your report server. The Home page should be http://<reportserver>/Reports_Instance. Navigate one level down to the Data Sources folder; if this folder does not exist, create a new folder named **Data Sources**. Click **New Data Source**, as shown in Figure 18.26.

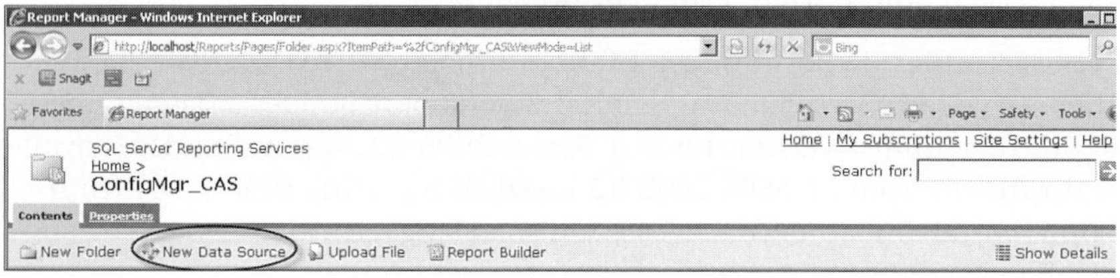

FIGURE 18.26   Creating a new data source.

2. Now, specify the settings for the data source. As displayed in Figure 18.27, provide a name; the connection string contains the necessary information to locate and communicate with the ConfigMgr database.

If the database is on the same server as the report server, the connection string should specify Data Source=**LOCALHOST**. If the ConfigMgr database is not local to the report server, specify the remote server name, which in this case Data Source=**AMANDA**. The Initial Catalog will specify the name of the database.

The Connect using section is displayed in Figure 18.27. Here are the options most typically used:

▶ **Credentials stored securely in the report server:** To use this option, you must create and enter an account and password; the account and password are encrypted and stored on the report server. This account should have minimal permissions on the database server. Choose the check box option **Use as Windows credentials when connecting to the data source**. This method is useful for custom or ad hoc report generation, as it allows a generic data source to be used instead of defining individual user or group permissions. (SQL Authentication is not recommended because this is a less secure means of connecting, primarily since the Kerberos security protocol cannot be used. The only time this method is recommended is when users need to connect from untrusted domains or are not authenticated by AD.) The article at http://msdn.microsoft.com/en-us/library/ms144284.aspx provides additional information on authentication modes.

▶ **Windows integrated security:** This allows the current user context to be authenticated at the database server.

After making your selection, click **Test Connection** to determine if you can make a connection to your database. If the connection is successful, click **OK** to save your new data source.

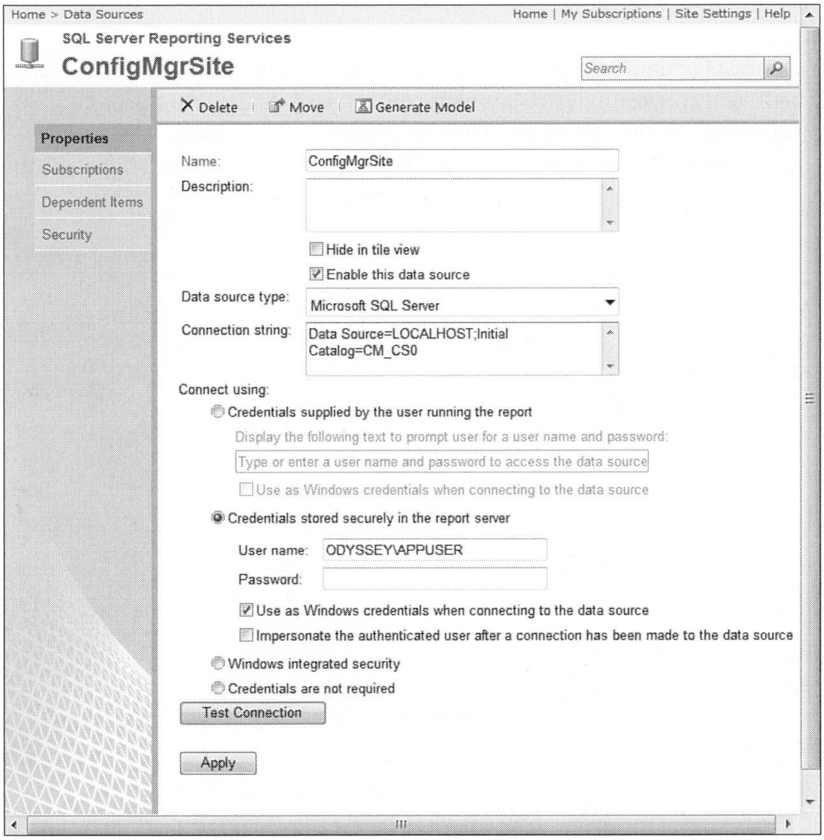

FIGURE 18.27   The Data Source Settings dialog.

With your data source defined, you now must determine the necessary data fields. For this example, you have been asked to create a new report based on a count of the number of computers by operating system, displaying the information using a pie chart. You must decide which data fields you need to report and construct the query. Review Chapter 17, "Configuration Manager Queries," if this is unfamiliar territory.

It is a recommended best practice to build and refine your query using SQL Server Management Studio. This allows you to rapidly view the query results and adjust the query as needed. Although Report Builder has an interface to create queries, the SQL Server Management Studio platform is more powerful.

The view to use for this query is v_GS_OPERATING_SYSTEM. However, when you run the Select DISTINCT query shown here to return only the unique operating system names, you will likely receive a number of variations of similar OS names.

```
SELECT DISTINCT Caption0 FROM v_GS_OPERATING_SYSTEM
ORDER BY Caption0
```

For one production ConfigMgr database that was sampled, more than 19 variations in the OS name were returned! You can resolve this by using the SQL CASE statement to consolidate the number of variations of the OS name. The next query consolidates, or normalizes the data, and you can extend it to handle future OS names. For that same production ConfigMgr database, this query produces just six variations in the OS name:

```
SELECT   CASE
   WHEN Caption0 LIKE '%XP%' THEN 'XP'
   WHEN Caption0 LIKE '%Windows 7%' THEN 'Windows 7'
   WHEN Caption0 LIKE '%Server 2008 R2%' THEN 'Server 2008 R2'
   WHEN Caption0 LIKE '%Server% 2008%'   THEN 'Server 2008'
   WHEN Caption0 LIKE '%Server 2003%'    THEN 'Server 2003'
   WHEN Caption0 LIKE '%Vista%'    THEN 'Vista'
   WHEN Caption0 LIKE '%Hyper-V%' THEN 'Server 2008 R2'
   ELSE 'Other' END 'OS Name',
   COUNT(sys.ResourceID) AS Total
FROM   v_GS_OPERATING_SYSTEM as os INNER JOIN v_GS_SYSTEM as sys
   ON os.ResourceID = sys.ResourceID
GROUP BY CASE
   WHEN Caption0 LIKE '%XP%' THEN 'XP'
   WHEN Caption0 LIKE '%Windows 7%' THEN 'Windows 7'
   WHEN Caption0 LIKE '%Server 2008 R2%' THEN 'Server 2008 R2'
   WHEN Caption0 LIKE '%Server% 2008%'   THEN 'Server 2008'
   WHEN Caption0 LIKE '%Server 2003%'    THEN 'Server 2003'
   WHEN Caption0 LIKE '%Vista%'    THEN 'Vista'
   WHEN Caption0 LIKE '%Hyper-V%' THEN 'Server 2008 R2'
   ELSE 'Other'
END
```

Table 18.2 shows sample results from this query.

TABLE 18.2   Sample Query Results

OS Name	Total
Server 2003	63
Server 2008	24
Vista	2993
Windows 7	523
Server 2008 R2	13
XP	6015

With your query defined, perform the following steps to create a chart.

1. Start Report Builder. If this is your first time running Report Builder, you must add the Reporting Services Web Service URL to the Report Builder Options.

   To add the URL, close the default New Report or Dataset Wizard, as shown in Figure 18.31. Now, click the Report Builder icon (Figure 18.28) and choose **Options** to open the Settings screen (refer to Figure 18.29). If you are uncertain of the web service URL, ask your SSRS administrator; or if you have access, open the Reporting Services Configuration Manager utility, and click the Web Service URL option to expose this information. After adding the URL, click **OK** to proceed.

2. To launch the Report Builder Wizard, click the Report Builder icon, click **New** from the list, and then the New Report or Dataset screen displays (refer to Figure 18.30). From here, choose **New Report**, and then select **Chart Wizard**.

3. Click **Next** on the Choose a Dataset page. On the Choose a connection to a data source page as displayed in Figure 18.31, click **Browse**, and locate the data source created earlier in this section. Click **OK** and then click **Test Connection** to validate that this data source is properly functioning. You should receive a response "Connection Created Successfully." If you do not, recheck the security credentials on the data source.

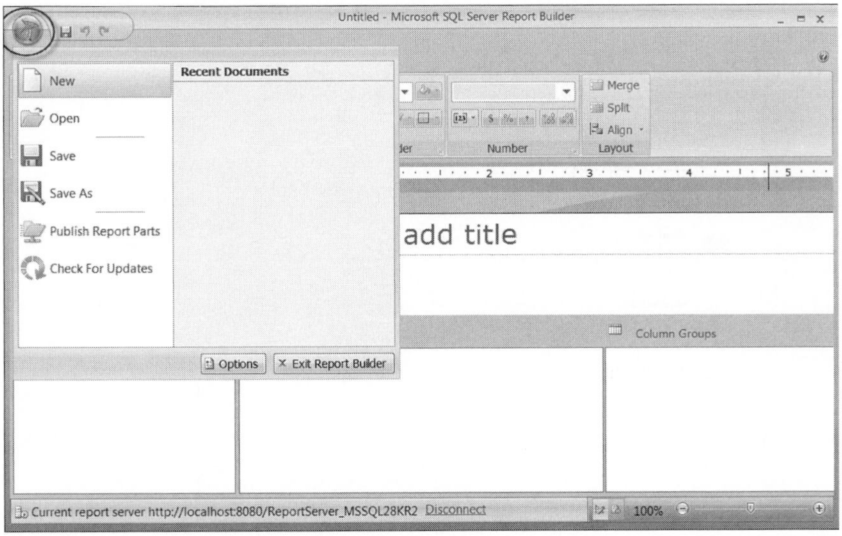

FIGURE 18.28   Select the Report Builder icon.

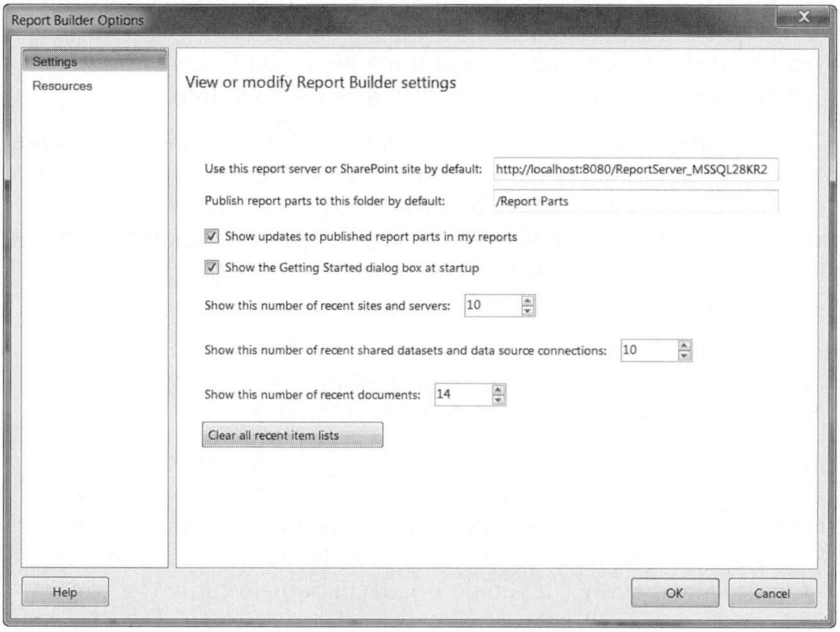

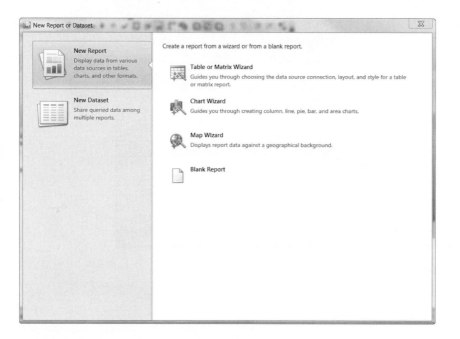

FIGURE 18.29   Report Builder Options dialog.

FIGURE 18.30   Report Builder Chart Wizard.

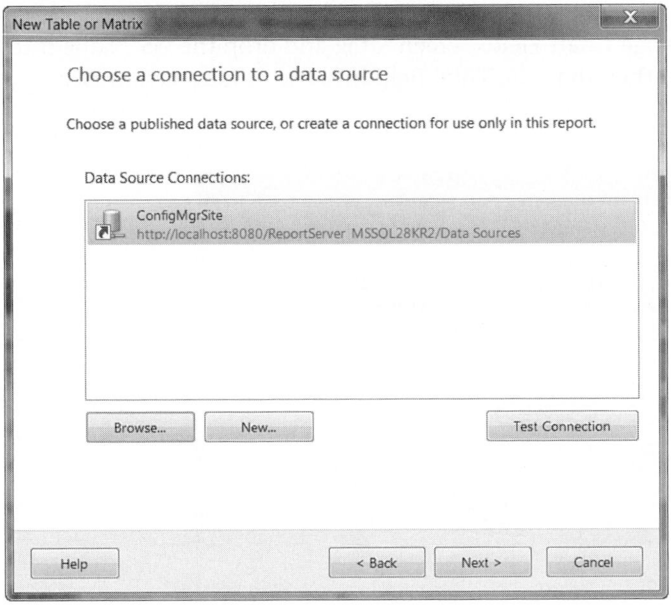

FIGURE 18.31   Report Builder Chart Wizard Select Data Source.

4. Click **Next** on the Design a query screen; then click **Edit as Text**. Now copy and paste the query provided earlier in this section, and then click the red exclamation mark to run. You should receive results similar to Figure 18.32.

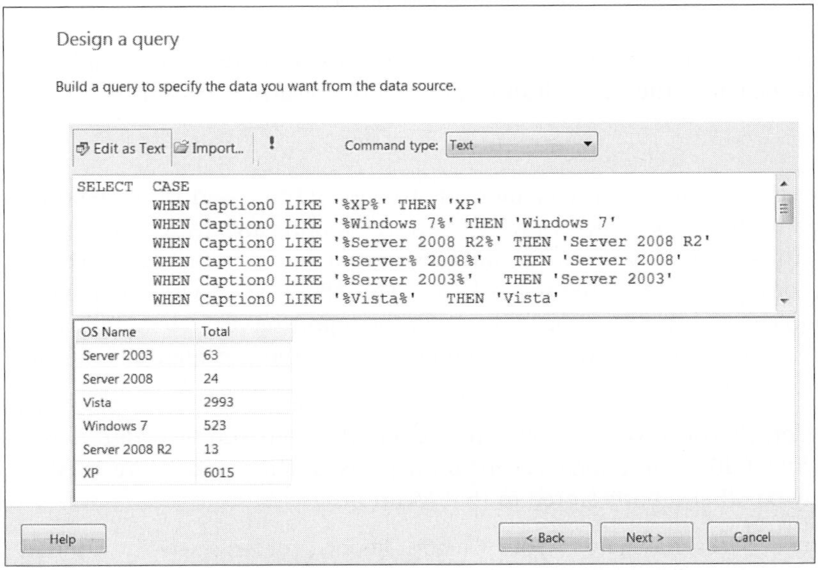

FIGURE 18.32   Report Builder Chart Wizard Query Design.

5. Click **Next** and you are presented with the Choose a Chart Type screen; select **Pie** and click **Next**. At the Arrange Chart Fields screen, drag and drop the OS_Name into the Categories section, and then drag the Total field into the Values section (see Figure 18.33).

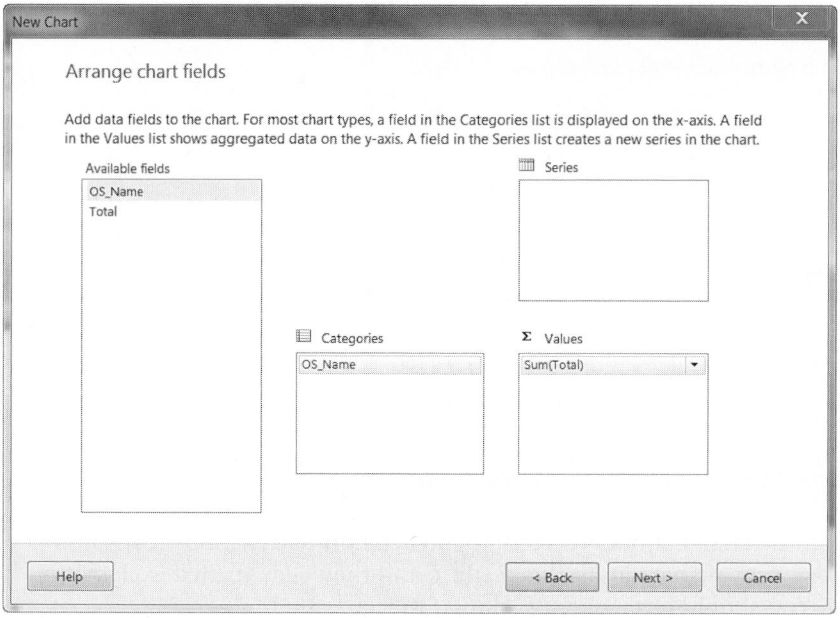

FIGURE 18.33   Report Builder Chart Wizard Arrange Chart Fields.

6. Click **Next**, choose the default Ocean style, and click **Finish**. Enter a title that is appropriate for the chart; then click **Run** to preview the results, shown in Figure 18.34.

When you are satisfied with the report, you are ready to deploy the report to the report server. As mentioned in the "Report Overview" section, the reports are created in XML format and stored with a file type of *.rdl. The authors recommend you first save a copy of your custom report locally or on a shared server UNC. (This allows you to maintain a copy of your custom reports, stored in a location other than the report server.) Then, upload the report from the saved location to the report server. Here are the two methods to place the report on the report server:

▶ In Report Builder, choose **Save As**, browse to the report server, and save your new report to a unique folder name such as Custom Reports, as shown in Figure 18.35. Note there may be other reports stored in that location.

▶ From Reporting Services, navigate to your Custom Reports folder; select the **Upload File** option, as shown in Figure 18.36, and then click **OK**.

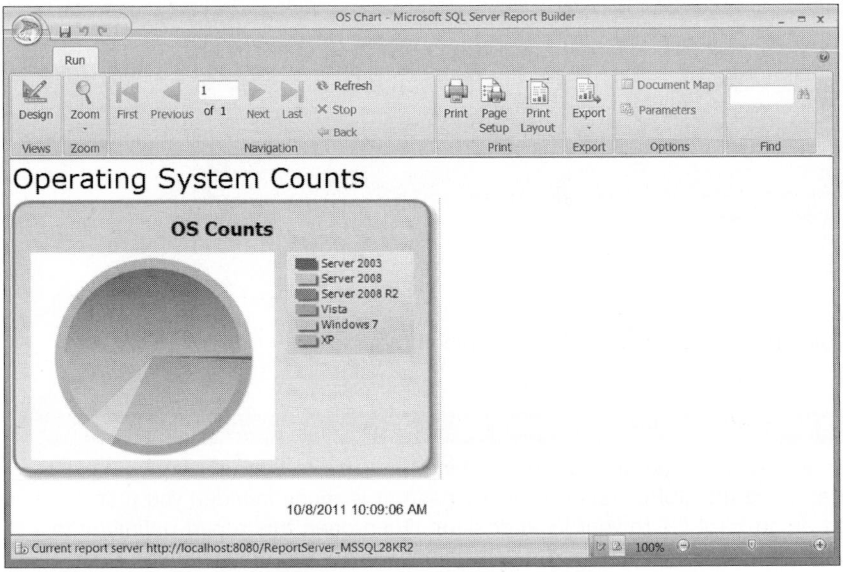

FIGURE 18.34   Report Builder Chart Wizard Complete.

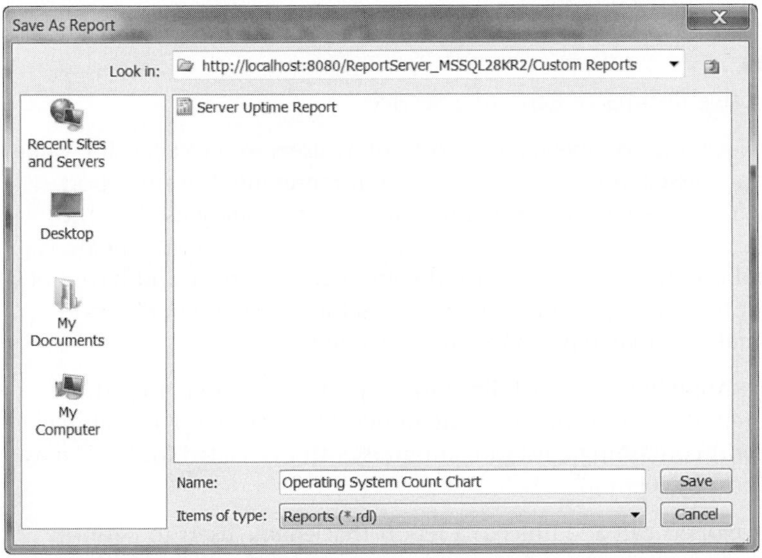

FIGURE 18.35   From Report Builder, Report Upload Method 1.

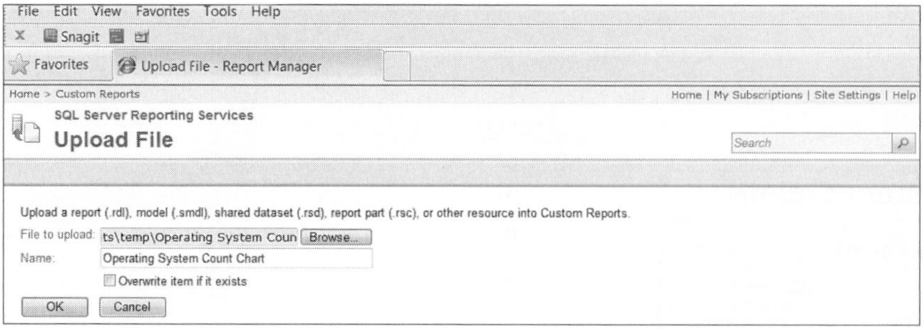

FIGURE 18.36   Using Reporting Services, Report Upload Method 2.

> **TIP: EXAMINE EXISTING CONFIGMGR REPORTS**
>
> Report Builder is an excellent tool to browse, examine, and use to learn more about existing SSRS reports. Using the SSRS Report Property page, it is recommended you first export the report as an *.rdl file to your local desktop. Then open this report definition to review the report construction. This is also a convenient way to add modifications to an existing report, and upload as a new, enhanced report.

See http://technet.microsoft.com/en-us/ff657833.aspx for additional information on Report Builder 3.0.

Interactive Features

Here are some key interactive features of Reporting Services:

▶ **Report parameters:** Adding parameters to reports allow users to select specific values when the report is processed, filtering the information represented in the report. This is accomplished by passing the selected parameter to the query used by the report. For example, a user could provide the name of a specific security update via a parameter list, and use that to display a list of computers that have and have not received a particular update. Report parameters are useful in helping both report authors and users make a single report more flexible and versatile.

▶ **Interactive sorting:** Applying sort capabilities to a report enable users to sort the data by any of the report columns in ascending or descending order. For example, a user viewing a report containing a list of computers with associated login ids may want to sort the report by login id.

▶ **Actions:** Report developers can add links to a report that enable users to perform actions; here are some examples:

  ▶ Embedding links in reports to link to external web content

  ▶ Using links that allow drilldown to other reports to provide additional detail

  ▶ Opening other reports using drill-through analysis

For example, a hardware report could be created that lists the number of computers by amount of installed memory. A report developer could add a drill-down capability to display a list of computers with less than 4MB of installed memory, as an example. The primary focus is allowing users additional navigational capability, which can provide the reporting results that they need. For more information on creating drilldown reports, see http://technet.microsoft.com/en-us/library/dd207042.aspx.

▶ **Document maps:** Users can use a document map to navigate a report easily. The document map displays as a side pane in the report, and users can use the hierarchy of links it contains to move around the various sections of the report.

▶ **Subreports:** Report developers can embed one report inside another as a subreport; this enables developers to display information from one report as a subregion directly within another report. For example, a developer might create a report that for each computer in ConfigMgr inventory list details for that computer such as available drives, network information, add/remove programs, and so on. You can use more than one subreport to accomplish your objectives.

Advanced Reporting Techniques

SSRS supports .NET, VBScript expressions, and Visual Basic (VB) 6.0 functions. As a report developer, you need to become familiar with the more common functions and expressions. Table 18.3 shows the left column as a VB function, followed by a description and an example as used in SSRS. Using the IIF function (also known as the Immediate If) as an example, the condition is evaluated for a True or False result. If True, it returns the portion immediately following the condition; if False, it returns the statement following the second comma. This is a useful function to know because you can use it for conditional line formatting or to control column visibility. See http://msdn.microsoft.com/en-us/library/ms157328.aspx for additional functions and examples.

TABLE 18.3   Common SSRS F and Expressions

Function	Description	SSRS Example
IIF(condition, True, False)	Immediate IF statement	=IIF(Fields!Number.Value>0, "True", "False")
FORMAT ( )	Returns a formatted string	=FORMAT(Fields!SomeDate.Value, "mm/dd/yy")
CSTR ( )	Converts any value to a string	=CSTR(Fields!SomeNumber.Value)
MID ( ) LEFT ( ) RIGHT ( )	Returns a specified number of characters	=LEFT(Fields!SomeText.Value, 5)
INSTR ( )	Return an integer for the first occurrence of a character in a string	=INSTR(Fields!SomeText.Value, ",")

Function	Description	SSRS Example
ISNOTHING( )	Tests for a NULL condition; returns True or False	=ISNOTHING(Fields!SomeText.Value)

Advanced Custom Report Example

After exploring Reporting Services features such as interactive reporting and functions, let's put that information to use. The example discussed in this section comes from a real-world scenario: You are responsible for using ConfigMgr to apply security updates to your servers. There is a group of servers with the security updates applied; however, rebooting is suppressed on those servers. Due to internal security compliance regulations, the administrators of the servers are supposed to reboot the servers within a 10-day period from the time the security updates are applied because the servers may be at risk until the reboot is complete. How can you determine if the administrators are complying with the compliance regulation, limit the report to only list servers, and allow it to be flexible enough to check for reboots within different time frames?

Using the concepts described in Chapter 16, "Endpoint Protection," start by creating and testing a query to locate the information you need. The primary views used for this query are v_GS_COMPUTER_SYSTEM, v_GS_OPERATING_SYSTEM, and v_GS_WORKSTATION_STATUS.

Start by examining the SELECT statement in the following query that will be used as the source for the report:

```
SELECT
  os.Caption0 as 'Operating System',
  cs.Name0 as 'Server Name',
  DateDiff(hour,os.LastBootUpTime0,ws.LastHWScan) as 'Uptime (in Hours)',
  os.LastBootUpTime0 as 'Last Reboot Date',
  ws.LastHWScan as 'Last Hardware Inventory'
FROM v_GS_COMPUTER_SYSTEM cs
  INNER JOIN v_GS_Operating_System os
    ON cs.ResourceID = os.ResourceID
 LEFT OUTER JOIN v_GS_WORKSTATION_STATUS ws
  ON ws.ResourceID = os.ResourceID
  WHERE  os.Caption0 LIKE '%server%'
  AND ws.LastHWScan <> 0 AND cs.Name0 IS NOT NULL
```

Here are some things you may want to note about this query:

▶ After the SELECT clause statement, the query presents a list of fields for use in the report.

▶ Notice the ability to "alias" the field name to be more descriptive; for example, Name0 displays as Server Name.

▶ A SQL function named `DateDiff` is used to calculate the number of hours since the last reboot.

▶ After the FROM clause, the JOIN statements are used to gather the related information from the various View statements.

▶ Alias names are used in each view for more concise field names.

▶ The WHERE clause is the query filter to limit the amount of information returned by the query result set.

To create the report, follow these steps:

1. Launch Report Builder as in the example in the "Building a Custom Report" section.

2. Start a New Report; choose the **Table or Matrix Wizard** option.

3. Click **Next** on the Shared Data Set Wizard, choose the shared Data Source Connection used in the example created in the beginning of the "Building a Custom Report" section (refer to Figure 18.18), and click **Next**.

4. On the Design a Query step, choose the **Edit as Text** option, copy/paste the query previously illustrated, and click **Execute** to determine results. You should see output similar to Figure 18.37.

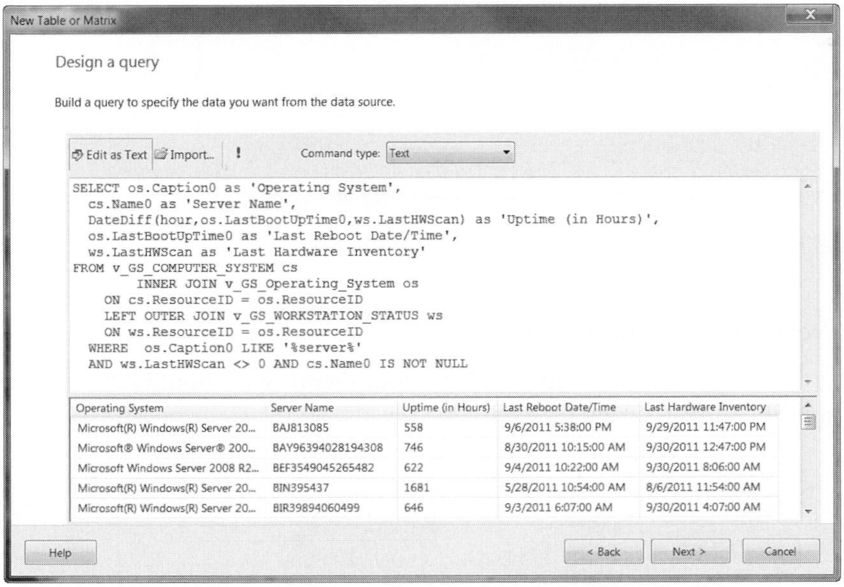

FIGURE 18.37   Server Uptime Query using Reporting Services.

5. Click **Next**. In the Arrange fields dialog, add the fields listed here and shown in Figure 18.38 to the Values box:

▶ Server_Name

▶ Sum(Uptime_in_Hours_)

▶ Last_Reboot_Data_Time

▶ Last_Hardware_Inventory

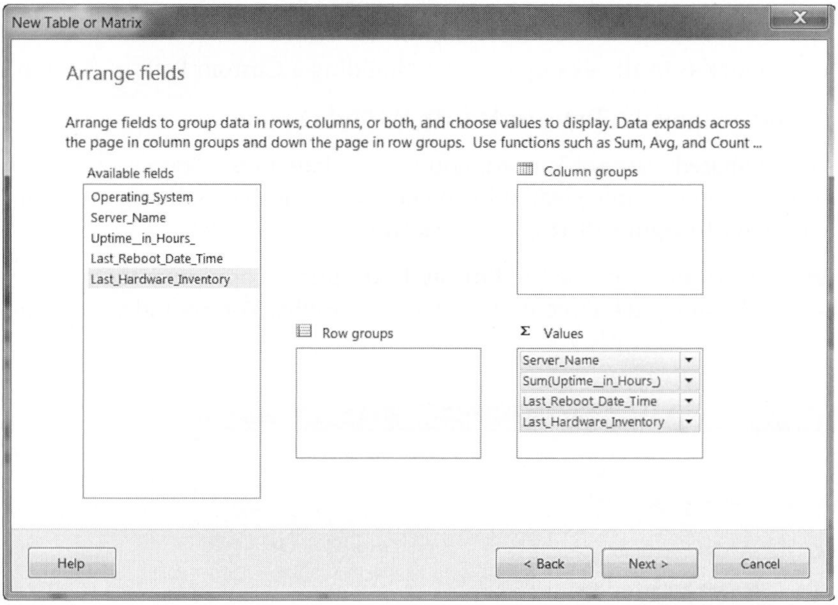

FIGURE 18.38   Defining Server Uptime Fields using Report Builder.

6. Click **Next**, **Next**, and then **Finish**.

7. After resizing the columns, and adding a title to your report, you should have a report that appears similar to Figure 18.39.

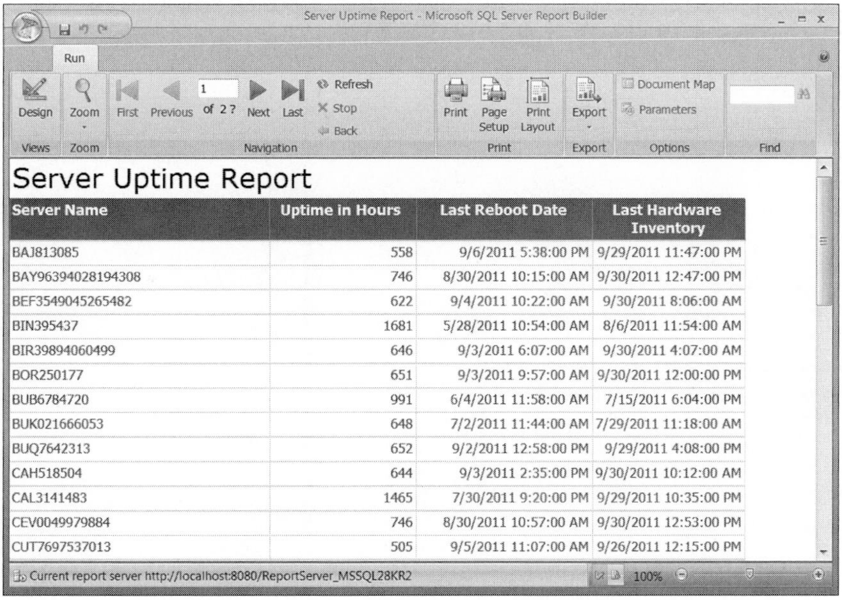

FIGURE 18.39   Server Uptime Display Report using Report Builder.

Now that you have a report that displays the basic information, perform the following steps to customize it further:

1. To add a report parameter to limit the amount of data returned and add interactive features such as column sort, toggle the report back to Design View, and add a new parameter by right-clicking **Parameter** (on left) and select **New parameter**. Now enter the information here to match what Figure 18.40 displays:

   ▶ **Name: LastRebootDate**

   ▶ **Prompt: Select Reboot Date**

   ▶ **Data Type:** Date/Time (dropdown)

   ▶ **Select Parameter Visibility:** Toggle (radio button)

18

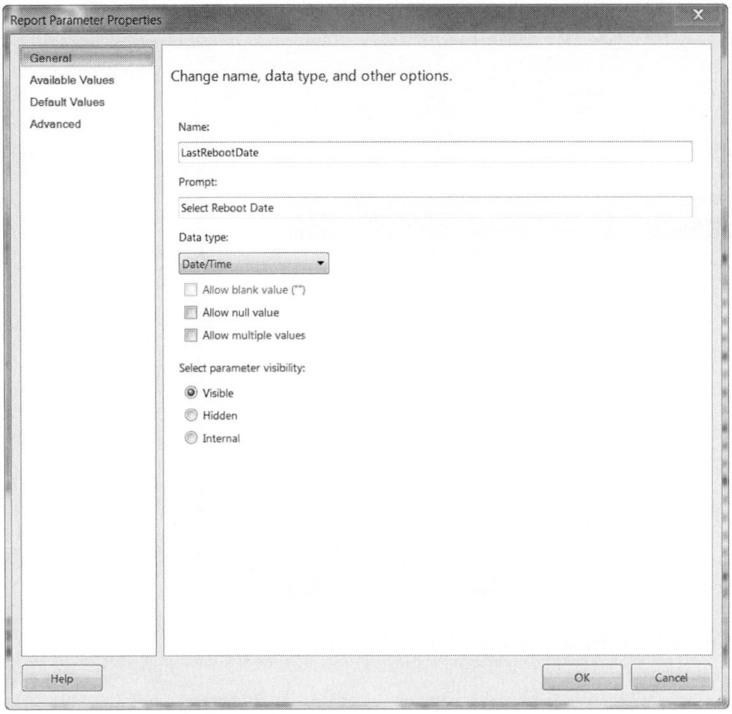

FIGURE 18.40   Add Parameter General Options using Report Builder.

2. For this report to show servers that have not been rebooted in the last 10 days, you must modify the Default Values of the Parameter Properties page.

   Click **Default Values**, **Specify Values**, and then the **Fx** button to the right of the Value row to build a custom function to launch the Expression Builder Wizard. A number of built-categories and items can assist in the function building process. Insert the following statement, which is a combination of two functions: Now() is the current date/time and DateAdd calculates the time interval specified.

   ```
   =DateAdd("d", -10, Now( ) )
   ```

   This creates a default date calculated based on 10 days from today. You can modify the value if wanted. The screen should look like Figure 18.41.

3. Click **OK** twice to save the report parameter.

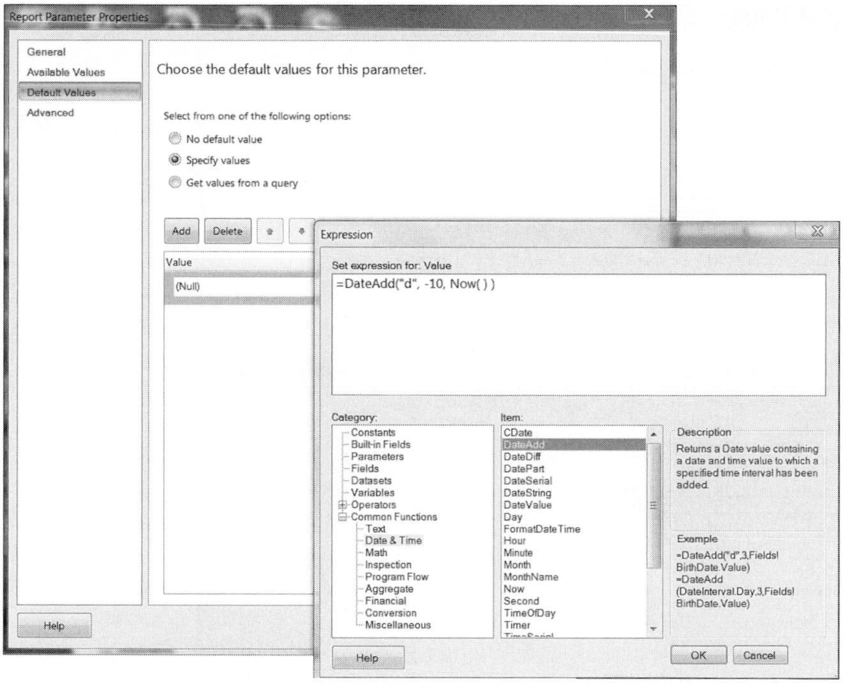

FIGURE 18.41   Using Report Builder, modify the Parameter Default Value.

The next step is integrating the report parameter with the report dataset. You want to return a list of servers with a last reboot date prior to the default date configured in the parameter. Perform these steps:

1. From the Report Designer, expand the Datasets node, right-click Dataset1, and then select **Dataset Properties**.

2. In the Query view, add the following statement after the WHERE clause:

```
AND os.LastBootUpTime0 < @LastRebootDate
```

This is displayed in Figure 18.42.

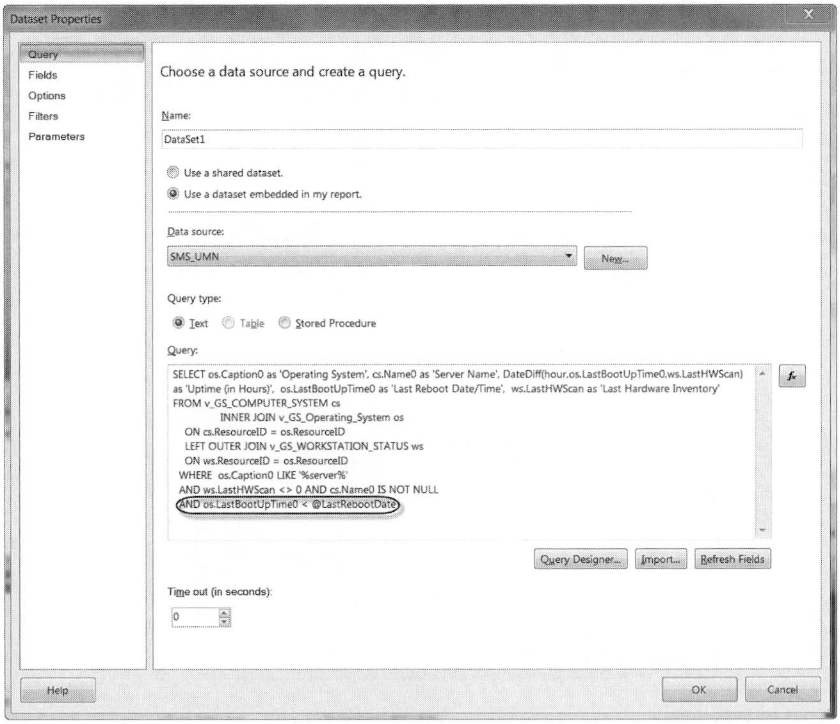

FIGURE 18.42   Add the Query Parameter in Report Builder.

3. You can add interactive column sort capability to allow users to determine quickly which servers have been running the longest without a reboot. Right-click the Uptime in Hours column; then select **Text Box Properties**. Choose **Interactive Sorting** on the left; then check **Enable interactive sorting on this text box**, and choose the **Uptime in Hours** field in the **Sort by:** drop-down selection. Figure 18.43 displays the options.

4. Click **OK** to save your changes. You can add sort capability to other columns as needed.

Save your report as **Server Uptime Report**. When the report runs, it is automatically populated with servers having a reboot date less than the dynamic default parameter. The user can select another date and interactively sort on Uptime in Hours, as displayed in Figure 18.44, or sort by Server Name. You can export this report as needed, or perhaps email it via SSRS subscription to be used for subsequent remediation.

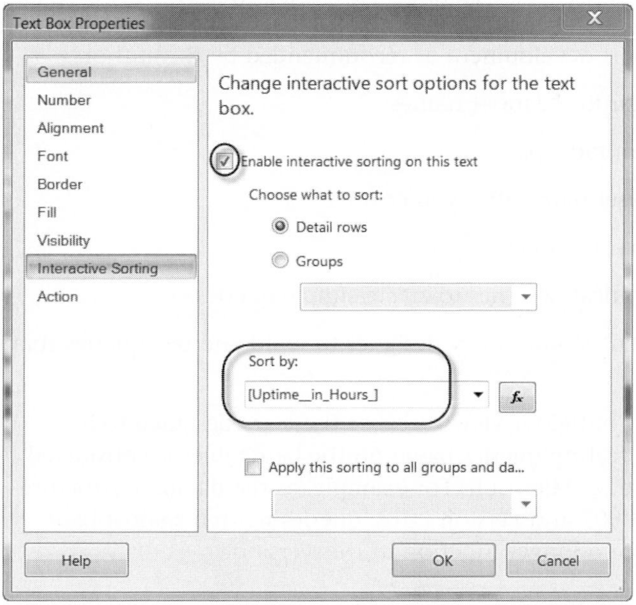

FIGURE 18.43   Defining Interactive Column Sort using Report Builder.

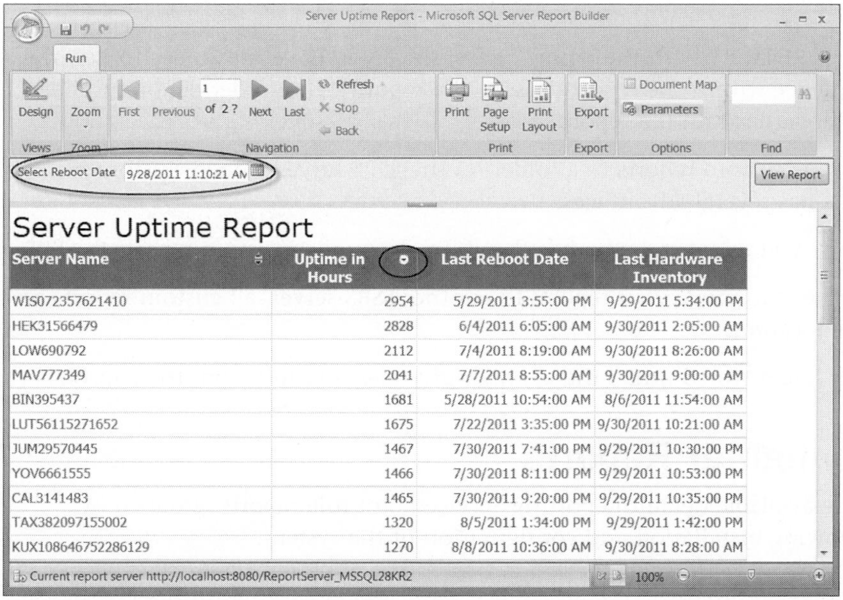

FIGURE 18.44   Testing Interactive Features using Report Builder.

Authoring Best Practices

Here are some best practices for report development as recommended by the authors.

- ▶ The following is suggested regarding dataset names:

    - ▶ Dataset names cannot contain spaces.

    - ▶ Avoid changing the dataset name after you create it!

    - ▶ Use something other than Dataset1.

- ▶ Use Report Builder T-SQL graphical designer to create simple queries.

- ▶ Use the SQL Server Management Studio query designer to build and test queries that are more complex.

- ▶ Create your queries based on ConfigMgr views because these are designed to function after product upgrades. Creating queries based on the base tables is considered problematic and not supported by Microsoft. For example, as the database structure changed between ConfigMgr 2007 and version 2012, queries written against base tables in ConfigMgr 2007 may no longer function in this version.

> **CAUTION: DO NOT QUERY THE BASE DATABASE TABLES**
>
> Microsoft does not publish the database schema because the structure could change at a future date. To avoid the impact of database changes, use database views.

- ▶ Avoid using ORDER BY with the report query; since you have the ability to define the sort sequence within the report dataset, the report will re-order data returned. This reduces overhead on the report server.

- ▶ Create and save custom reports to a folder on the SSRS server named Custom Reports. This has several advantages:

    - ▶ It allows you to control who has the ability to publish custom reports to SSRS.

    - ▶ If you need to move your reports to another SSRS server, all custom reports are in one location.

    - ▶ Report folder stored under the ConfigMgr folder is visible from the console.

Built-in ConfigMgr Reports

Table 18.4 lists the available default Reporting Service Point role reports, grouped by report folder, following installation and configuration of the system.

TABLE 18.4   Reports Provided with System Center 2012 Configuration Manager

Report Name	Description
Administrative Security	
Administration Activity Log	Shows the log of administrative changes made for administrative users, security roles, security scopes, and collections.
Administrative users security assignments	Shows administrative users, their associated security roles, and the security scopes associated with each security role for each user.
Objects secured by a single security scope	Shows objects secured by the selected security scope and assigned only to this security scope. Because this report does not display objects assigned to two or more security scopes, it might not display all the objects associated with the selected security scope.
Security for a specific or multiple Configuration Manager objects	Shows securable objects, the security scopes associated with the objects, and the administrative users with rights to the objects.
Security roles summary	Shows security roles and which ConfigMgr administrative users are associated with each security role.
Security scopes summary	Shows security scopes and the ConfigMgr administrative users and security groups associated with each security scope.
Alerts	
Alert Scorecard	Shows summary information for all closed alerts.
Alert Top Talkers	Shows summary information for alert activity.
Asset Intelligence	
Hardware 01A - Summary of computers in a specific collection	Provides an asset manager summary view of a collection of computers.
Hardware 03A - Primary computer users	Lists users and the count of computers on which they are the primary user.
Hardware 03B - Computers for a specific primary console user	Lists all computers for which a specified user is the primary console user.
Hardware 04A - Computers with multiple users (shared)	Lists computers that do not seem to have a primary user because no single user has a % console login time greater than 66%.
Hardware 05A - Console users on a specific computer	Displays all the console users on a specific computer.
Hardware 06A - Computers for which console users could not be determined	Helps administrators identify systems that need to have security logging turned on.
Hardware 07A - USB devices by manufacturer	Groups the USB devices by their manufacturer.

18

Report Name	Description
Hardware 07B - USB devices by manufacturer and description	Groups the USB devices by their manufacturer and description.
Hardware 07C - Computers with a specific USB device	Displays all computers with a given USB device.
Hardware 07D - USB devices on a specific computer	Lists all the USB devices on a specific computer.
Hardware 08A - Hardware that is not ready for a software upgrade	Shows hardware that does not meet the minimum hardware requirements.
Hardware 09A - Search for computers	Provides an asset manager summary of computers matching keyword filters on computer name, ConfigMgr site, domain, top console user, operating system, manufacturer, or model.
Hardware 10A - Computers in a specified collection that have changed during a specified timeframe	Displays list of computers in a specified collection where a hardware class has changed during a specified timeframe.
Hardware 10B - Changes on a specified computer within a specified timeframe	Displays the classes that changed on a specified computer within a specified timeframe. (Change Type: A=All, I=Insert, U=Update, D=Delete).
License 01A - Microsoft Volume License ledger for Microsoft license statements	Displays inventory of all Microsoft software titles available from the Microsoft Volume Licensing program. Channel Code: 0 = Full Packaged Product, 1 = Compliance Checked Product, 2 = OEM, and 3 = Volume, 6 = MSDN. Because of complex dependencies and limitations, Microsoft does not guarantee that the licensing information or the number of software installations is accurate. Do not rely solely on these reports to determine your license compliance.
License 01B - Microsoft Volume License ledger item by sales channel	Identifies sales channel for inventoried Microsoft Volume License software. Channel Code: 0 = Full Packaged Product, 1 = Compliance Checked Product, 2 = OEM, 3 = Volume, and 6 = MSDN. Any other value is undefined. The inventoried quantity shown represents the total installed instances discovered for each product. Accuracy of install quantities and license information may vary given complex dependencies and limitations.
License 01C - Computers with a specific Microsoft Volume License ledger item and sales channel	Identifies which computers have a specific item from the Microsoft Volume license ledger. Channel Code: 0 = Full Packaged Product, 1 = Compliance Checked Product, 2 = OEM, 3 = Volume, and 6 = MSDN. Any other value is undefined. Accuracy of install quantities and license information may vary given complex dependencies and limitations. Do not rely solely on these reports for determining your license compliance.

Report Name	Description
License 01D - Microsoft Volume License ledger products on a specific computer	This report identifies all Microsoft Volume license ledger items on a specific computer. Channel Code: 0=Full Packaged Product, 1=Compliance Checked Product, 2=OEM, 3=Volume, 6=MSDN. Any other value is undefined. Accuracy of install quantities and license information may vary given complex dependencies and limitations. Do not rely solely on these reports to determine your license compliance.
License 02A - Count of licenses nearing expiration by time ranges	The products listed are those with their licenses managed by the Software Licensing Service. Accuracy of install quantities and license information may vary given complex dependencies and limitations. Do not rely solely on these reports to determine your license compliance.
License 02B - Computers with licenses nearing expiration	Show the specific computers nearing expiration. License Status: 0 = Unlicensed, 1 = Licensed, 2 = Out of Box Grace, 3 = Out of Tolerance Grace/ Expiration Period, 4 = Non-Genuine Grace, 5 = Notification, and 6 = Extended Grace. Accuracy of install quantities and license information may vary given complex dependencies and limitations. Do not rely solely on these reports for determining your license compliance.
License 02C - License information on a specific computer	These products are those that have their licenses managed by the Software Licensing Service. License Status: 0 = Unlicensed, 1 = Licensed, 2 = Out of Box Grace, 3 = Out of Tolerance Grace/Expiration Period, 4 = Non-Genuine Grace, 5 = Notification, and 6 = Extended Grace. Accuracy of install quantities and license information may vary given complex dependencies and limitations. Do not rely solely on these reports to determine your license compliance.
License 03A - Count of licenses by license status	The products listed are those with their licenses managed by the Software Licensing Service. License Status: 0 = Unlicensed, 1 = Licensed, 2 = Out of Box Grace, 3 = Out of Tolerance Grace/Expiration Period, 4 = Non-Genuine Grace, 5 = Notification, and 6 = Extended Grace. Accuracy of install quantities and license information may vary given complex dependencies and limitations. Do not rely solely on these reports to determine your license compliance.

18

Report Name	Description
License 03B - Computers with a specific license status	The products listed here have their licenses managed by the Software Licensing Service. License Status: 0 = Unlicensed, 1 = Licensed, 2 = Out of Box Grace, 3 = Out of Tolerance Grace/Expiration Period, 4 = Non-Genuine Grace, 5 = Notification, and 6 = Extended Grace. Accuracy of install quantities and license information may vary given complex dependencies and limitations. Do not rely solely on these reports to determine license compliance.
License 04A - Count of products managed by software licensing	The products listed here are those with their licenses managed by the Software Licensing Service. Accuracy of install quantities and license information may vary given complex dependencies and limitations. Do not rely solely on these reports to determine your license compliance.
License 04B - Computers with a specific product managed by Software Licensing Service	The products listed here are those with their licenses managed by the Software Licensing Service. Accuracy of install quantities and license information may vary given complex dependencies and limitations. Do not rely solely on these reports to determine your license compliance.
License 05A - Computers providing Key Management Service	Lists computers acting as Key Management servers. Accuracy of install quantities and license information may vary given complex dependencies and limitations. Do not rely solely on these reports to determine your license compliance.
License 06A - Processor counts for per-processor licensed products	Provides the number of processors on computers using Microsoft products that support per-processor licensing. Accuracy of install quantities and license information may vary given complex dependencies and limitations. Do not rely solely on these reports to determine license compliance.
License 06B - Computers with a specific product that supports per-processor licensing	Provides a list of computers where a specific Microsoft product that supports per-processor licensing is installed. Accuracy of install quantities and license information may vary given complex dependencies and limitations. Do not rely solely on these reports to determine license compliance.
License 14A - Microsoft Volume Licensing reconciliation report	Provides reconciliation on software licenses purchased through the Microsoft Volume License Agreement and the actual inventory count. Accuracy of install quantities and license information may vary given complex dependencies and limitations. Do not rely solely on these reports to determine your license compliance.

Report Name	Description
License 14B - List of Microsoft software inventory not found in MVLS	Displays Microsoft software titles in use not found in the Microsoft Volume License Agreement. Accuracy of install quantities and license information may vary given complex dependencies and limitations. Do not rely solely on these reports to determine license compliance.
License 15A - General license reconciliation report	Provides reconciliation on general software licenses purchased and the actual inventory count. Accuracy of install quantities and license information may vary given complex dependencies and limitations. Do not rely solely on these reports to determine your license compliance.
License 15B - General license reconciliation report by computer	Lists computers that installed the licensed product with a specific version.
Software 01A - Summary of installed software in a specific collection	Provides a summary of installed software ordered by the number of instances found from inventory.
Software 02A - Product families for a specific collection	Lists the product families and the count of software in the family for a specific collection.
Software 02B - Product categories for a specific product family	Lists the product categories in a specific product family and the count of software within the category. This report is linked to "Software 2A - Product families for a specific collection."
Software 02C - Software in a specific product family and category	Lists all software in the specified product family and category. Linked to "Software 02B - Software categories for a specific product family."
Software 02D - Computers with specific software installed	Lists all computers with specific software installed. This report is linked to "Software 02C - Software in a specific product family and category."
Software 02E - Installed software on a specific computer	Lists all software installed on a specific computer.
Software 03A - Uncategorized software	Lists the software that either is categorized as unknown or has no categorization.
Software 04A - Software configured to automatically run on computers	Displays a list of software configured to run automatically on computers.
Software 04B - Computers with specific software configured to automatically run	Displays all computers with specific software configured to run automatically.
Software 04C - Software configured to automatically run on a specific computer	Displays installed software configured to run automatically on a specific computer.
Software 05A - Browser Helper Objects	Displays the Browser Helper Objects installed on computers in a specific collection.

18

Report Name	Description
Software 05B - Computers with a specific Browser Helper Object	Displays all the computers with a specific Browser Helper Object.
Software 05C - Browser Helper Objects on a specific computer	Displays all Browser Helper Objects on the specific computer.
Software 06A - Search for installed software	Provides a summary of installed software ordered by the number of instances based on search criteria for the product name, publisher, or version.
Software 06B - Software by product name	Provides a summary of installed software ordered by the number of instances based on selected Product Name.
Software 07A - Recently used executable programs by the count of computers	Displays executable programs used recently with a count of computers on which they have been used. You must enable the Software Metering client enabled for this site to view this report.
Software 07B - Computers that recently used a specified executable program	Displays the computers on which a specified executable program has recently been used when you enable the software metering client setting.
Software 07C - Recently used executable programs on a specified computer	Displays executables that have been used recently on a specified computer when you enable the software metering client setting.
Software 08A - Recently used executable programs by the count of users	Displays executable programs that have been used recently with a count of users that have most recently used them when you enable the software metering client setting.
Software 08B - Users that recently used a specified executable program	Displays the users that have most recently used a specified executable program when you enable the software metering client setting.
Software 08C - Recently used executable programs by a specified user	Displays executable programs that have been used recently by a specified user when you enable the software metering client setting.
Software 09A - Infrequently used software	Displays software titles not used during a specified period of time. You can specify a value that represents the number of days that have elapsed since the last use. (For example, if you enter 90 days, you see software not used in the past 90 days or more.) You can also leave the Days not used field empty to see all software titles never used.
Software 09B - Computers with infrequently used software installed	Displays computers with software installed not used for a specified period of time. The specified period is based on the value specified in the "Software 09A - Infrequently used software" report.

Report Name	Description
Software 10A - Software titles with specific multiple custom labels defined	Allows you to view software titles based on matching of all selected custom label criteria. You can select up to three custom labels to refine a software title search.
Software 10B - Computers with a specific custom-labeled software title installed	Shows all computers in this collection that have the specified custom-labeled software title installed.
Software 11A - Software titles with a specific custom label defined	Allows you to view software titles based on matching of at least one of the selected custom label criteria.
Software 12A - Software titles without a custom label	Displays all software titles that do not have a custom label defined.

Client Push

Client Push Installation Status Details	Provides a detailed status of the client push installation process for all sites. For additional client installation status information, see reports in the "Site - Client Information" category.
Client Push Installation Status Details for a Specified Site	Provides a detailed status of the client push installation process for a specified site. For additional client installation status information, see reports in the "Site - Client Information" category.
Client Push Installation Status Summary	Provides a summary view of the client push installation process for all sites. For additional client installation status information, see reports in the "Site - Client Information" category.
Client Push Installation Status Summary for a Specified Site	Provides a summary view of the client push installation process for a specified site. For additional client installation status information, see reports in the "Site - Client Information" category.

Client Status

Client Remediation Details	Provides client remediation details for a given collection.
Client Remediation Summary	Provides remediation summary for a given collection.
Client Status History	Provides a historical view of the overall client status in the environment.
Client Status Summary	Provides administrators with the current percentages of passed and active clients for a given collection.

18

Report Name	Description
Client Time to Request Policy	Shows the percentage of clients that have requested policy at least once in the last 30 days. Each day represents a percentage of total clients that requested policy since the first day in the cycle. This is useful for determining the time it would take to distribute a policy update to your client population. Client deployments or changes in client count can affect the accuracy of the report.
Clients with Failed Client Check Details	Displays details about clients that client check failed for a specified collection.
Inactive Clients Details	Provides a detailed list of inactive clients for a given collection.
Compliance and Settings Management	
Compliance history of a configuration baseline	Displays the history of the changes in compliance of a configuration baseline for specified date range.
Compliance history of a configuration item	Displays the history of the changes in compliance of a configuration item for the specified date range.
Details of compliant rules of configuration items in a configuration baseline for an asset	Displays information about the rules that were evaluated as compliant for a specified configuration item for a specified device or user.
Details of conflicting rules of configuration items in a configuration baseline for an asset	Displays information about rules in a configuration item that has been deployed to a specified user or device that conflict with other rules contained in the same, or another deployed configuration item.
Details of errors of configuration items in a configuration baseline for an asset	Displays information about errors generated by a specified configuration item for a specified device or user.
Details of noncompliant rules of configuration items in a configuration baseline for an asset	Displays information about rules that were evaluated as noncompliant for a specified configuration item, for a specified device or user.
Details of remediated rules of configuration items in a configuration baseline for an asset	Displays information about rules that were remediated by a specified configuration item for a specified device or user.
List of assets by compliance state for a configuration baseline	Lists the devices or users in a specified compliance state following the evaluation of a specified configuration baseline.
List of assets by compliance state for a configuration item in a configuration baseline	Lists the devices or users in a specified compliance state following the evaluation of a specified configuration item.
List of rules conflicting with a specified rule for an asset	Displays a list of rules conflicting with a specified rule for a configuration item deployed to a specified device.

Report Name	Description
List of unknown assets for a configuration baseline	Displays a list of devices or users that have not yet reported any compliance data for a specified configuration baseline.
Rules and errors summary of configuration items in a configuration baseline for an asset	Displays summary of compliance state of rules and any setting errors for a specified configuration item deployed to a specified device or user.
Summary compliance by configuration baseline	Displays a summary of the overall compliance of deployed configuration baselines in the hierarchy.
Summary compliance by configuration items for a configuration baseline	Displays a summary of the compliance of configuration items in a specified configuration baseline.
Summary compliance of a configuration baseline for a collection	Displays a summary of the overall compliance of a specified configuration baseline deployed to a specified collection.

Device Management

All mobile device clients	Displays all mobile devices clients. Mobile devices discovered by the Exchange Server connector are not included.
Certificate issues on mobile devices that are managed by the Configuration Manager client for Windows CE and that are not healthy	Contains detailed information about certificate issues on mobile devices managed by the ConfigMgr client for Windows CE.
Client deployment failure for mobile devices that are managed by the Configuration Manager client for Windows CE	Contains detailed information about deployment failure for mobile devices that are managed by the ConfigMgr client for Windows CE.
Client deployment status details for mobile devices that are managed by the Configuration Manager client for Windows CE	Contains summary information for the status of mobile devices managed by the Configuration Manager client for Windows CE.
Client deployment success for mobile devices that are managed by the Configuration Manager client for Windows CE	Contains detailed information about deployment success for mobile devices managed by the ConfigMgr client for Windows CE.
Communication issues on mobile devices that are managed by the Configuration Manager client for Windows CE and that are not healthy	Contains detailed information about communication issues on mobile devices managed by the ConfigMgr client for Windows CE.
Compliance status for the mobile devices that are managed by the Exchange Server connector	Displays a summary of the compliance status with the Default Exchange ActiveSync mailbox policy for the mobile devices managed by the Exchange Server connector.
Count of mobile devices by display configurations	Displays the number of mobile devices by display settings.

18

Report Name	Description
Count of mobile devices by operating system	Displays the number of mobile devices by operating system.
Count of mobile devices by program memory	Displays the number of mobile devices by program memory.
Count of mobile devices by storage memory configurations	Displays the number of mobile devices by storage memory configurations.
Health information for mobile devices that are managed by the Configuration Manager client for Windows CE	Contains detailed health information for mobile devices managed by the Configuration Manager client for Windows CE.
Health summary for mobile devices that are managed by the Configuration Manager client for Windows CE	Contains health summary information for mobile devices managed by the Configuration Manager client for Windows CE.
Inactive mobile devices that are managed by the Exchange Server connector	Displays the mobile devices managed by the Exchange Server connector and not connected to Exchange Server in a specified number of days.
Local client issues on mobile devices that are managed by the Configuration Manager client for Windows CE and that are not healthy	Contains detailed information about local client issues on mobile devices managed by the Configuration Manager client for Windows CE.
Mobile device client information	Displays information about the mobile devices with the Configuration Manager client installed. You can use this report to verify which mobile devices can successfully communicate with a management point.
Mobile device compliance details for the Exchange Server connector	Displays the mobile device compliance details for a Default Exchange ActiveSync mailbox policy configured using the Exchange Server connector.
Mobile devices by operating system	Displays the mobile devices by operating system.
Mobile devices that are unmanaged because they enrolled but failed to assign to a site	Displays the mobile devices that completed enrollment with ConfigMgr and have a certificate but failed to complete site assignment. This can occur when the mobile devices have not contacted a management point enabled for mobile devices, or there was a failure contacting the management point during site assignment.
Mobile devices with a specific amount of free program memory	Displays all mobile devices with the specified amount of free program memory.
Mobile devices with a specific amount of free removable storage memory	Displays all mobile devices with the specified amount of free removable memory.

Report Name	Description
Mobile devices with certificate renewal issues	Displays the enrolled mobile devices that failed to renew their certificate. If the certificate is not renewed before the expiry period, the mobile devices will be unmanaged.
Mobile devices with low free program memory (less than specified KB free)	Displays the mobile devices for which the program memory is lower than a specified size in KB.
Mobile devices with low free removable storage memory (less than specified KB free)	Displays the mobile devices for which the removable storage memory is lower than a specified size in KB.
Pending wipe request for mobile devices	Displays the wipe requests that are pending for mobile devices.
Recently enrolled and assigned mobile devices	Displays the mobile devices that recently enrolled with Configuration Manager and successfully assigned to a site.
Recently wiped mobile devices	Shows the list of mobile devices that were recently successfully wiped.
Settings summary for mobile devices that are managed by the Exchange Server connector	Displays the number of mobile devices that apply the settings for each Default Exchange ActiveSync mailbox policy managed by the Exchange Server connector.
Driver Management	
All drivers	Shows all drivers.
All drivers for a specific platform	Shows all drivers for a specific platform.
All drivers in a specific Boot Image	Shows all drivers in a specific boot image.
All drivers in a specific category	Shows all drivers in a specific category.
All drivers in a specific Package	Shows all drivers in a specific package.
Categories for a specific driver	Shows categories for a specific driver.
Computers that failed to install drivers for a specific collection	Shows computers that failed to install drivers for a specific collection.
Driver catalog matching report for a specific collection	Shows driver catalog matching report for a specific collection.
Driver catalog matching report for a specific computer	Shows driver catalog matching report for a specific computer.
Driver catalog matching report for a specific device on a specific computer	Shows driver catalog matching report for a specific device on a specific computer.
Driver catalog matching report for computers in a specific collection with a specific device	Shows driver catalog matching report for computers in a specific collection with a specific device.
Drivers that failed to install on a specific computer	Shows drivers that failed to install on a specific computer.
Supported platforms for a specific driver	Shows supported platforms for a specific driver.

18

Report Name	Description
Endpoint Protection	
Antimalware Activity Report	Shows an overview of antimalware activity.
Endpoint Protection - Hidden	
Antimalware Activity By Action	Shows antimalware activity broken down by cleaning action.
Computer Infection Status Summary	Shows a summary of remediation activity for a particular collection.
Computer Malware Details	Shows details about a particular computer and the list of malware found on it.
Computer Malware List	Shows a list of threats found on a particular computer.
Malware Details	Shows details about a particular threat and the computers it has been found on.
Top Malware by Computers	Shows the list of most frequently found malware.
Top Malware by Severity	Shows the list of the most severe malware
User Threat List	Shows the list of threats found under a particular user account.
Infected Computers	Shows a list of computers with a particular threat detected.
Top Users by Threats	Shows the list of users with the most number of detected threats.
User Threat List	Shows the list of threats found under a particular user account.
Hardware - CD-ROM	
CD-ROM information for a specific computer	Displays information about the CD-ROM drives on a single computer.
Computers for a specific CD-ROM manufacturer	Displays a list of computers that have a CD-ROM drive made by a specified manufacturer.
Count CD-ROM drives per manufacturer	Displays the number of CD-ROM drives inventoried per manufacturer.
History - CD-ROM history for a specific computer	Displays the inventory history for CD-ROM drives on a single computer.
Hardware - Disk	
Computers with a specific hard disk size	Displays a list of computers that have hard disks of a specified capacity. Use the Values button to see a list of all hard disk sizes currently reported by your computers.
Computers with low free disk space (less than specified % free)	Displays a list of computers and disks where the disks are low on space. Amount of free space to check for is specified as a percentage of disk capacity.

Report Name	Description
Computers with low free disk space (less than specified MB free)	Displays a list of computers and disks where the disks are low on space. The amount of free space to check for is specified in MB.
Count physical disk configurations	Displays the number of hard disks inventoried by disk capacity.
Disk information for a specific computer - Logical disks	Displays summary information about the logical disks on a single computer.
Disk information for a specific computer - Partitions	Displays summary information about the disk partitions on a single computer.
Disk information for a specific computer - Physical disks	Displays summary information about the physical disks on a single computer.
History - Logical disk space history for a specific computer	Displays the inventory history for logical disk drives on a single computer.
Hardware - General	
Computer information for a specific computer	Displays summary information for a single computer.
Computers in a specific workgroup or domain	Displays a list of computers in a single resource domain or workgroup.
Inventory classes assigned to a specific collection	Displays the inventory classes assigned to a specific collection.
Inventory classes enabled on a specific computer	Displays inventory classes enabled on a specific computer.
Hardware - Memory	
Computers where physical memory has changed	Displays a list of computers where the amount of RAM has changed since the last inventory cycle.
Computers with a specific amount of memory	Displays a list of computers with a specified amount of RAM (Total Physical Memory rounded to the nearest MB).
Computers with low memory (less than or equal to specified MB)	Displays a list of computers low on memory. Amount of memory to check for is specified in MB.
Count memory configurations	Displays the number of computers inventoried by amount of RAM.
Memory information for a specific computer	Displays summary information about the memory on a single computer.
Hardware - Modem	
Computers for a specific modem manufacturer	Displays a list of computers that have a modem made by a specified manufacturer.
Count modems by manufacturer	Displays the number of modems inventoried per manufacturer.
Modem information for a specific computer	Displays summary information about the modem on a single computer.

18

Report Name	Description
Hardware - Network Adapter	
Computers with a specific network adapter	Displays a list of computers that have a specified network adapter.
Count network adapters by type	Displays the number of inventoried network adapters cards of each type.
Network adapter information for a specific computer	Displays summary information about the network adapters on a single computer.
Hardware - Processor	
Computers for a specific processor speed	Displays a list of computers that have a processor of a specified speed.
Computers with fast processors (greater than or equal to a specified clock speed)	Displays a list of computers that have processors that run at or faster than a specified clock speed.
Computers with slow processors (less than or equal to a specified clock speed)	Displays a list of computers that have processors that run at or slower than a specified clock speed.
Count processor speeds	Displays the number of computers inventoried by processor speed.
Processor information for a specific computer	Displays summary information about the processors on a single computer.
Hardware - SCSI	
Computers with a specific SCSI card type	Displays a list of computers that have a specified SCSI card.
Count SCSI card types	Displays the number of inventoried SCSI cards by card type.
SCSI card information for a specific computer	Displays summary information about the SCSI cards on a single computer.
Hardware - Sound Card	
Computers with a specific sound card	Displays a list of computers that have a specified sound card.
Count sound cards	Displays the number of computers inventoried by sound card type.
Sound card information for a specific computer	Displays summary information about the sound cards on a single computer.
Hardware - Video Card	
Computers with a specific video card	Displays a list of computers that have a specified video card.
Count video cards by type	Displays a list of all video cards installed on computers with number of each type of video card.
Video card information for a specific computer	Displays summary information about the video cards on a single computer.

Report Name	Description
Migration	
Clients in Exclusion List	Shows clients excluded from migration.
Dependency on a Configuration Manager 2007 collection	Shows the objects that depend on a Configuration Manager 2007 collection.
Migration Job properties	Shows the contents of the migration job.
Migration jobs	Shows the list of migration jobs.
Objects that failed to migrate	Shows the list of objects that failed to migrate during the last attempt to migrate them.
Network Access Protection	
Comparison of software updates installed by software update deployments and NAP remediation	Provides a comparison summary of software updates installed by software update deployments and NAP remediation.
Frequency a computer has been in remediation within a specified period	Displays how often a computer has been remediated within a specified period.
List of computers that installed a specific software update through remediation during a specified period	Lists the computers that installed a specific software update through remediation during a specific time period (days).
List of computers that would be noncompliant based on selected software updates	Lists each computer that would be noncompliant based on selected software updates.
List of computers where NAP service could not be detected	Displays a list of computers where NAP service could not be detected.
List of NAP-eligible computers	Displays a list of computers where NAP agent is off or state is unknown.
List of Network Access Protection policies	Lists Network Access Protection policies with their effective dates.
List of noncompliant computers in remediation from last polling interval	Displays the list of noncompliant computers in remediation with their last known evaluation times.
List of non-compliant computers in remediation within a specified period	Displays the list of noncompliant computers in remediation within a specified time period.
List of remediation failures for specified time period	Lists the remediation failures for a specified number of days.
List of software updates installed through remediation	Lists the software updates installed through remediation for a selected period.
Summary of noncompliant computers in remediation from last polling interval	Shows a summary of noncompliant computers in remediation from last polling interval.
Summary of noncompliant computers in remediation within a specified period	Lists a summary of noncompliant computers in remediation within a specified time period.

18

Report Name	Description
Network	
Count IP addresses by subnet	Displays the number of IP addresses inventoried per IP subnet.
IP - All subnets by subnet mask	Displays a list of IP subnets and subnet masks.
IP - Computers in a specific subnet	Displays a list of computers and IP information for a single IP subnet.
IP - Information for a specific computer	Displays summary information about IP on a single computer.
IP - Information for a specific IP address	Displays summary information about a single IP address.
MAC - Computers for a specific MAC address	Displays the computer name and IP address corresponding to a single MAC address.
Operating System	
Computer operating system version history	Displays the inventory history for the operating system on a single computer.
Computers with a specific operating system	Displays computers with a specific operating system.
Computers with a specific operating system and service pack	Displays computers with a specific operating system and service pack.
Count operating system versions	Displays the number of computers inventoried by operating system.
Count operating systems and service packs	Displays the number of computers inventoried by operating system and service pack combinations.
Services - Computers running a specific service	Displays a list of computers running a specified service.
Services - Computers running Remote Access Server	Displays a list of computers running Remote Access Server.
Services - Services information for a specific computer	Displays summary information about the services on a single computer.
Windows Server computers	Displays a list of computers running Windows Server operating systems.
Out Of Band Management	
Computers with out of band management controllers	Displays a list of computers that have out-of-band management controllers.
Out of band management console activity	Displays a list of status messages identifying out-of-band management console activity.
Status of client out of band management provisioning	Displays a list of computers that have been provisioned for out-of-band management.
Power Management	
Power Management - Computer Activity	Displays a graph showing monitor, computer, and user activity for a specified collection over specified time period.

Report Name	Description
Power Management - Computer Activity by Computer	Displays a graph showing monitor, computer, and user activity for specified computer on specified date.
Power Management - Computer Activity Details	Displays a list of the sleep and wake capabilities of computers in the specified collection for a specified date and time.
Power Management - Computer Details	Displays detailed information about the power capabilities, power settings, and power plans applied to a specified computer.
Power Management - Computer Not Reporting Details	Displays a list of computers not reporting any power activity for a specified date and time.
Power Management - Computers Excluded	Displays a list of computers excluded from the power plan.
Power Management - Computers with Multiple Power Plans	Displays a list of computers with conflicting power settings.
Power Management - Energy Consumption	Displays the total monthly energy consumption (in kWh) for a specified collection over a specified time period.
Power Management - Energy Consumption by Day	Displays the total energy consumption (in kWh) for the last 31 days for a specified collection.
Power Management - Energy Cost	Displays the total monthly energy consumption cost for specified collection over specified time period.
Power Management - Energy Cost by Day	Displays the total energy consumption cost for a specified collection over the past 31 days.
Power Management - Environmental Impact	Displays a graph showing carbon dioxide (CO_2) emissions generated by a specified collection over a specified time period.
Power Management - Environmental Impact by Day	Displays graph showing CO_2 emissions generated by specified collection over the past 31 days.
Power Management - Insomnia Computer Details	Displays detailed information about computers that did not sleep or hibernate within a specified time period.
Power Management - Insomnia Report	Displays a list of common causes that prevented computers from sleeping or hibernating and the number of computers affected by each cause for a specified period of time.
Power Management - Power Capabilities	Displays the power management capabilities of computers in the specified collection.
Power Management - Power Settings	Displays an aggregated list of power settings used by computers in a specified collection.
Power Management - Power Settings Details	Displays further information about computers selected in the power settings report.

18

Report Name	Description
Site - Client Information	
Client Assignment Detailed Status Report	Contains detailed information on client assignment status.
Client Assignment Failure Details	Contains detailed information on client assignment failures.
Client Assignment Status Details	Contains overview information on client assignment status.
Client Assignment Success Details	Contains detailed information on successfully assigned clients.
Client Deployment Failure Report	Contains detailed information for clients that have failed to deploy.
Client Deployment Status Details	Contains summary information for the status of client installations.
Client Deployment Success Report	Contains detailed information for clients that have successfully deployed.
Clients incapable of HTTPS communication	Displays detailed information about each client in site that has run the HTTPS Communication Readiness Tool and reported to be incapable of communicating over HTTPS.
Computers assigned but not installed for a particular site	Displays a list of computers assigned to a particular site but that are not reporting to that site.
Computers with a specific Configuration Manager client version	Displays a list of computers running a single specified version of the ConfigMgr client software.
Count of clients and protocol used for communication	Displays summary information about the clients and the protocol used (HTTP/HTTPS) for communicating to site roles.
Count of clients assigned and installed for each site	Displays the number of computers assigned and installed for each site. Clients with a network location associated to multiple sites are counted as installed only if they are reporting to that site.
Count of clients capable of HTTPS communication	Displays detailed information about each client in site that have run the HTTPS Communication Readiness Tool and reported to be either capable or incapable of communicating over HTTPS.
Count of clients for each site	Displays the number of ConfigMgr clients installed by site code.
Count of Configuration Manager clients by client versions	Displays the number of computers discovered by ConfigMgr client version. (Client type: 1 = Computer; 3 = Mobile)
Problem details reported to the fallback status point for a specified collection	Displays detailed information for issues reported by clients in a specified collection if they have been assigned a fallback status point.

Report Name	Description
Problem details reported to the fallback status point for a specified site	Displays detailed information about issues reported by clients in a specified site if they have been assigned a fallback status point.
Summary of problems reported to the fallback status point	Displays information about all the issues reported by clients if they have been assigned a fallback status point.
Summary of problems reported to the fallback status point for a specific collection	Displays summary information for issues reported by clients in a specified collection if they have been assigned a fallback status point.

Site - Discovery and Inventory Information

Clients that have not reported recently (in a specified number of days)	Displays a list of clients that have not reported discovery data, hardware inventory, or software inventory in a specified number of days. An empty column indicates a client has not reported any data of that type. A column with an '*' means the client has reported data of that type within the specified period of time.
Computers discovered by a specific site	Displays a list of all computers discovered by a specific site and date of most recent discovery.
Computers discovered recently by discovery method	Displays a list of computers that have been discovered within the specified number of days and lists the agents that discovered them. A computer may appear more than once in the list if it has been discovered by multiple agents.
Computers not discovered recently (in a specified number of days)	Displays a list of computers that have not been discovered recently, and displays the number of days since they were discovered.
Computers not inventoried recently (in a specified number of days)	Displays a list of computers that have not been inventoried recently, and displays the last times they were inventoried.
Computers that might share the same Configuration Manager Unique Identifier	Displays a list of computers that have changed their names. A change in name is a possible symptom that a computer shares a Configuration Manager Unique Identifier with another computer.
Computers with duplicate MAC addresses	Displays computers that share MAC addresses between them.
Count computers in resource domains or workgroups	Displays the number of computers in each resource domain or workgroup.
Discovery information for a specific computer	Displays a list of the agents and sites that discovered a specific computer.
Inventory dates for a specific computer	Displays the date and time inventory was last run on a single computer.

18

Report Name	Description
Site - General	
Computers in a specific site	Displays a list of ConfigMgr client computers in a specific site.
Site status for the hierarchy	Displays the list of sites in the hierarchy with site version and site status information.
Site - Server Information	
Site system roles and site system servers for a specific site	Displays a list of system servers and their site system roles for a single site.
Software - Companies and Products	
All inventoried products for a specific software company	Displays a list of the inventoried software products and versions manufactured by a single specified company.
All software companies	Displays a list of all companies manufacturing inventoried software.
Computers with a specific product	Displays a list of the computers that a single specified product is inventoried on, as well as the versions of that product.
Computers with a specific product name and version	Displays a list of the computers that a single specified version of a product is inventoried on.
Computers with specific software registered in Add/Remove Programs	Displays a summary of all computers with specific software registered in Add/Remove Programs.
Count all inventoried products and versions	Displays list of the inventoried software products and versions, and the number of computers each is installed on.
Count inventoried products and versions for a specific product	Displays a list of the inventoried versions of a single specified product, and the number of computers each is installed on.
Count of all instances of software registered with Add/Remove Programs	Displays summary of all instances of software installed and registered with Add/Remove Programs on computers within specified collection.
Count of instances of specific software registered with Add/Remove Programs	Displays a count of instances for specific software packages installed and registered in Add/Remove Programs.
Products on a specific computer	Displays a summary of the inventoried software products and their manufacturers on a single specified computer.
Software registered in Add/Remove Programs on a specific computer	Displays a summary of the software installed on a specific computer that is registered in Add/Remove Programs.
Software - Files	
All inventoried files for a specific product	Displays a summary of the files inventoried associated with a single specified software product.

Report Name	Description
All inventoried files on a specific computer	Displays a summary of all the files inventoried on a single specified computer.
Compare software inventory on two computers	Shows the differences between the software inventory reported for two selected computers. Only the discrepancies are shown; if the same file appears on both computers, it will not be listed.
Computers with a specific file	Displays a list of the computers where a specified file name appears in the software inventory, as well as information about inventoried files. A computer may appear more than once in the list if it contains more than one copy of the file.
Count computers with a specific file name	Displays the number of computers that a single specified file is inventoried on.
Software Distribution - Application Monitoring	
All application deployments (advanced)	Displays summary information for all application deployments.
All application deployments (basic)	Displays summary information for all application deployments.
Application Compliance	Shows compliance information for selected application within selected collection. This is an application level report and may not reflect certain kinds of deployment specific errors, such as deployment conflicts. Total here represents the total number of machines and users where Microsoft has tried to detect the presence of the application and this value may be greater than the sum of the Success, Requirements Not Met, and Error.
Application Deployments per Asset	Shows applications deployed to the specified device or user.
Application Infrastructure Errors	Shows application infrastructure errors. These can include internal infrastructure errors as well as errors as a result of invalid requirement rules.
Application Usage Detailed Status	Displays the usage details of the installed applications.
Application Usage Summary Status	Displays the usage summary of the installed applications.
Software Distribution - Application Monitoring - Hidden	
Application deployment detailed status	Displays detailed status information for a deployment.
Application deployment statistics	Displays statistics about a selected deployment using live data.
Application deployment status	Displays the status details of a deployment.

18

Report Name	Description
Application Deployment Type Compliance	Shows compliance information for deployment types of selected application within selected collection.
Application Deployment Type Compliance Details	Shows asset details compliance information for selected application deployment type within selected collection.
Application Deployment Type Compliance Status	Shows compliance status information for selected application deployment type within selected collection.
Application Global Expression Details	Shows setting information for application global expressions.
Application Infrastructure Errors Details	Shows detailed information for application infrastructure errors. These can include internal infrastructure errors as well as errors as a result of invalid requirement rules.
Application requirements not met - Dependencies	Displays the dependencies for a given application deployment that have not successfully installed.
Application requirements not met - Details	Displays detailed information about applications that failed to install because their installation requirements were not met.
Results for Related Deployment Types	Shows the status of related dependency and supersedence deployment types for a particular machine and user. If user is not specified, this report shows results for deployment types targeted to the device.
Task Sequence Deployments Containing Application	Shows task sequence deployments that install a particular application.
Software Distribution - Collections	
All collections	Displays all the collections in the hierarchy.
All resources in a specific collection	Displays all the resources in a specific collection.
Maintenance windows available to a specified client	Lists all maintenance windows that are applicable to the specified client.
Software Distribution - Content	
All active content distributions	Displays all distributions points on which content is currently being installed or removed.
All content	Displays all applications and packages at a site.
All content on a specific distribution point	Displays all content currently installed on a specified distribution point.

Report Name	Description
All distribution points	Displays information about the distribution points for each site.
All status messages for a specific package on a specific distribution point	Shows all status messages for a specific package on a specific distribution point.
Application content distribution status	Contains information about the distribution status for application content.
Applications targeted to distribution point group	Contains information about applications that target a specific distribution point group.
Applications that are out of synchronization on a specified distribution point group	Lists the applications for which associated content files have not been updated with the latest version on a specific distribution point group.
Distribution point group	Shows information about a specified distribution point group.
Distribution status of specified package	Displays the distribution status for specified package content on each distribution point.
Packages targeted to distribution point group	Contains information about packages that target a specific distribution point group.
Packages that are out of synchronization on a specified distribution point group	Lists the packages for which associated content files have not been updated with the latest version on a specific distribution point group.

Software Distribution - Package and Program Deployment Status

All system resource package and program deployments with status	Displays all of the package and program deployments for the site along with a summary of the status of each deployment.
All system resources for a specified package and program deployment in a specified state	Displays a list of all resources in a specific state for a specific package and program deployment. For example, you can see which resources have successfully run a program being deployed. (Client type: 1 = Client; 3 = Device Client)
Chart - Hourly package and program deployment completion status	Displays the percentage of targeted computers that have successfully installed the package for every hour since the package and program deployment was created. Can use to track the average time for a package and program deployment.
Package and program deployment status messages for a specified client and deployment	Displays the status messages reported for a particular computer and package and program deployment.

18

Report Name	Description
Status of a specified package and program deployment	Displays the status summary of all resources targeted by a package and program deployment. The summary is in two parts. Acceptance status summarizes how many resources have received, rejected, or not yet received the package and program deployment. Delivery status summarizes the resources that have run or attempted to run the program being deployed.
All deployments for a specified package and program	Displays all the deployments of a specified package and program.
All package and program deployments	Displays all the package and program deployments at this site.
All package and program deployments to a specified collection	Displays all the package and program deployments to a specified collection.
All package and program deployments to a specified computer	Displays all the package and program deployments that apply to a specified computer.
All package and program deployments to a specified user	Displays all the package and program deployments to a specified user.

Software Metering

All software metering rules applied to this site	Displays a list of all software metering rules applied to this site.
Computers that have a metered program installed but have not run the program since a specified date	Shows all computers that have a specified metered software program installed as reported by software inventory, but have not run the program since the specified date. This report requires that software inventory be collected on the metered computers.
Computers that have run a specific metered software program	Displays a list of computers that have run programs matching the selected software metering rule within the specified month and year.
Concurrent usage for all metered software programs	Displays the maximum number of users who concurrently ran each metered software program during the specified month and year.
Concurrent usage trend analysis of a specific metered software program	Displays the maximum number of users who concurrently ran the selected metered software program during each month for the past year.
Install base for all metered software programs	Shows the number of computers with metered software programs installed as reported by software inventory. This report requires that software inventory be collected on the metered computers.
Software metering summarization progress	Shows the time at which the most recently summarized metering data was processed on the site server. Only metering data processed before these dates will be reflected in the software metering reports.

Report Name	Description
Time of day usage summary for a specific metered software program	Shows the average number of usages of a particular program for the past 90 days, broken down by hour and day.
Total usage for all metered software programs	Displays the number of users who ran programs matching each software metering rule locally or using Terminal Services within the specified month and year.
Total usage for all metered software programs on Windows Terminal Servers	Displays the number of users who ran programs matching each software metering rule using Terminal Services within the specified month and year.
Total usage trend analysis for a specific metered software program	Displays the number of users who ran programs matching the selected software metering rule locally or using Terminal Services during each month for the past year.
Total usage trend analysis for a specific metered software program on Windows Terminal Servers	Displays the number of users who ran programs matching the selected software metering rule using Terminal Services during each month for the past year.
Users that have run a specific metered software program	Displays a list of users who have run programs matching the selected software metering rule within the specified month and year.

Software Updates - A Compliance

Compliance 1 - Overall compliance	Returns the overall compliance data for a software update group.
Compliance 2 - Specific software update	Returns the compliance data for a specified software update.
Compliance 3 - Update group (per update)	Returns the compliance data for software updates defined in a software update group.
Compliance 4 - Updates by vendor month year	Returns the compliance data for software updates released by a vendor during a specific month and year. To limit the amount of information returned, specify the software update class and product.
Compliance 5 - Specific computer	Returns the software update compliance data for a specific computer. To limit the amount of information returned, you can specify the vendor and software update classification.
Compliance 6 - Specific software update states (secondary)	Returns the count and percentage of computers in each compliance state for the specified software update. For best results, start with the "Compliance 2 - Specific software update" report and then drill into this report to return the count of computers in each compliance state.

18

Report Name	Description
Compliance 7 - Computers in a specific compliance state for an update group (secondary)	Returns all computers in a collection that have a specific overall compliance state against a software update group. For best results, start with the "Compliance 1 - Overall Compliance" report to return the count of computers in each of the compliance states and then drill into this report to return the computers in the selected compliance state.
Compliance 8 - Computers in a specific compliance state for an update (secondary)	Returns all computers in a collection that have a specific compliance state for a software update. For best results, start with the "Compliance 2 - Specific software update" report. Next, drill into the "Compliance 6 - Specific software update states (secondary)" report to return the count of computers in each compliance state, and then drill into this report to return the computers in the selected compliance state.
Software Updates - B Deployment Management	
Management 1 - Deployments of an update group	Returns all deployments that contain all of the software updates defined in a specified software update group.
Management 2 - Updates required but not deployed	Returns all vendor-specific software updates that have been detected as required on clients but that have not been deployed to a specific collection. To limit the amount of information returned, you can specify the software update class.
Management 3 - Updates in a deployment	Returns the software updates contained in a specific deployment.
Management 4 - Deployments that target a collection	Returns all software update deployments that target a specific collection.
Management 5 - Deployments that target a computer	Returns all software update deployments that target a specific computer.
Management 6 - Deployments that contain a specific update	Returns all deployments that contain a specific software update and the associated target collection for the deployment.
Management 7 - Updates in a deployment missing content	Returns the software updates in a specified deployment that do not have all of the associated content retrieved, preventing clients from installing the update and achieving 100% compliance for the deployment.

Report Name	Description
Management 8 - Computers missing content (secondary)	Returns all computers requiring a specific software update contained in a specific deployment not provisioned on a distribution point. For best results, start with the "Management 7 - Updates in a deployment missing content" report to return all software updates in the deployment that have not been provisioned, and then drill into this report to return all computers requiring the software update.
Software Updates - C Deployment States	
States 1 - Enforcement states for a deployment	Returns enforcement states for a specific software update deployment, which is typically the second phase of a deployment assessment. For overall progress of software update installation, use this report with the "States 2 - Evaluation states for a deployment" report.
States 2 - Evaluation states for a deployment	Returns evaluation states for a specific software update deployment, which is typically the first phase of a deployment assessment. For overall progress of software update installation, use this report with the "States 1 - Enforcement states for a deployment" report.
States 3 - States for a deployment and computer	Returns the states for all software updates in the specified deployment for a specified computer.
States 4 - Computers in a specific state for a deployment (secondary)	Returns all computers in a specific state for a software update deployment. For best results, start with the "States 1 - Enforcement states for a deployment" or "States 2 - Evaluation states for a deployment" report to identify the states for the deployment, and then drill into this report to return all computers in the specific state.
States 5 - States for an update in a deployment (secondary)	Returns a summary of states for a specific software update targeted by a specific deployment. For best results, start with the "Management 3 - Updates in a deployment" report to return the software updates contained in a specific deployment, and then drill into this report to return the state for the selected software update.
States 6 - Computers in a specific enforcement state for an update (secondary)	Returns all computers in a specific enforcement state for a specific software update. For best results, start with the "Management 3 - Updates in a deployment" report to return the software updates contained in a specific deployment, drill into the "States 5 - States for an update in a deployment (secondary)" report to return the states for the selected software update, and then drill into this report to return all computers in the selected state.

18

Report Name	Description
States 7 - Error status messages for a computer (secondary)	Returns all status messages for a given update or deployment on a particular computer for a given status message ID.
Software Updates - D Scan	
Scan 1 - Last scan states by collection	Returns the count of computers for a specific collection in each compliance scan state returned by clients during the last compliance scan.
Scan 2 - Last scan states by site	Returns the count of computers assigned to a specific site in each compliance scan state returned by clients during the last compliance scan.
Scan 3 - Clients of a collection reporting a specific state (secondary)	Returns all computers for a specific collection and returned a specific compliance scan state during their last compliance scan.
Scan 4 - Clients of a site reporting a specific state (secondary)	Returns all computers assigned to a specific site and returned a specific compliance scan state during their last compliance scan.
Software Updates - E Troubleshooting	
Troubleshooting 1 - Scan errors	Returns the scan errors at the site and a count of computers that are experiencing each error.
Troubleshooting 2 - Deployment errors	Returns deployment errors at the site and a count of computers that are experiencing each error.
Troubleshooting 3 - Computers failing with a specific scan error (secondary)	Returns a list of the computers on which scan is failing because of a specific error.
Troubleshooting 4 - Computers failing with a specific deployment error (secondary)	Returns a list of the computers on which the deployment of update is failing because of a specific error.
State Migration	
State migration information for a specific source computer	Shows state migration information for a specific source computer.
State migration information for a specific state migration point	Shows state migration information for a specific state migration point.
State migration points for a specific site	Shows state migration points for a specific site.

Report Name	Description
Status Messages - Audit	
All audit messages for a specific user	Displays a summary of all audit status messages for a single user. Audit messages describe actions taken in the Configuration Manager Console that add, modify, or delete objects in ConfigMgr. NOTE: Clicking the Values button to select a user name might take a long time to return a list of values. If you know the name of the user, type it in using the *<domain>\<user name>* format.
Remote Control - All computers remote controlled by a specific user	Displays a summary of status messages indicating remote control of client computers by a single specified user.
Remote Control - All remote control information	Displays a summary of status messages indicating remote control of client computers.
Status Messages	
All messages for a specific message ID	Displays a list of messages with a single message ID.
Clients reporting errors in the last 12 hours for a specific site	Displays a list of computers and components reporting errors in the last 12 hours, and the number of errors reported.
Component messages for the last 12 hours	Displays a list of component messages for the last 12 hours for specific site code, computer, and component.
Component messages for the last hour (for a specific site computer and component)	Displays a list of the status messages created in the last hour by a specified component on a specified computer in a specified ConfigMgr site.
Count component messages for the last hour for a specific site	Displays the number of status messages by component and severity reported in the last hour at a single specified site.
Count errors in the last 12 hours	Displays the number of server component error status messages in the last 12 hours.
Fatal errors (by component)	Displays a list of computers reporting fatal errors by component.
Fatal errors (by computer name)	Displays a list of computers reporting fatal errors by computer name.
Last 1000 messages for a specific computer (Errors and Warnings)	Displays a summary of the last 1,000 error and warning component status messages for a single specified computer.
Last 1000 messages for a specific computer (Errors Warnings and Information)	Displays a summary of the last 1,000 error, warning, and informational component status messages for a single specified computer.
Last 1000 messages for a specific computer (Errors)	Displays a summary of the last 1,000 error server component status messages for a single specified computer.

18

Report Name	Description
Last 1000 messages for a specific server component	Displays a summary of the most recent 1,000 status messages for single specified server component.
Status Messages - Hidden	
Status Message Detail	Shows status message detail.
Task Sequence - Deployment Status	
All system resources for a task sequence deployment in a specific state	Displays a list of the destination computers for the specified task sequence deployment that is in specified deployment state.
All system resources for a task sequence deployment that is in a specific state and that is available to unknown computers	Displays a list of the destination computers for the specified task sequence deployment that is in the specified deployment state.
Count of system resources that have task sequence deployments assigned but not yet run	Displays the number of destination computers that have accepted task sequence deployments but have not run the task sequence.
History of a task sequence deployment on a computer	Displays the status of each step of the specified task sequence deployment on the specified destination computer. If no record is returned, the task sequence has not started on the computer.
List of computers that exceeded a specific length of time to run a task sequence deployment	Displays the list of destination computers that exceeded the specified length of time to run a task sequence. The length of time, in hours, is specified by this report.
Run time for a specific task sequence deployment on a specific destination computer	Displays the total amount of time that it took to successfully complete the specified task sequence on the specified destination computer.
Run time for each step of a task sequence deployment on a specific destination computer	Displays the time that it took to complete each step of the specified task sequence deployment on the specified destination computer.
Status of a specific task sequence deployment for a specific computer	Shows the status summary of a specific task sequence deployment on a specific computer.
Status of a task sequence deployment on an unknown destination computer	Displays the status of the specified task sequence deployment on the specified unknown destination computer.
Status summary of a specific task sequence deployment	Shows the status summary of all resources that have been targeted by a deployment.
Status summary of a specific task sequence deployment available to unknown computers	Shows the status summary of all resources that have been targeted by an deployment that is available to a collection containing unknown computers.

Report Name	Description
Task Sequence - Deployments	
All system resources currently in a specific group or phase of a specific task sequence deployment	Shows the list of computers currently running in a specific group/phase of the specified task sequence deployment.
All system resources where a task sequence deployment failed within a specific group or phase	Shows the list of computers that failed within a specific group/phase of the specified task sequence deployment.
All task sequence deployments	Displays details of all task sequence deployments initiated from this site.
All task sequence deployments available to unknown computers	Displays details of all task sequence deployments initiated from this site and that are deployed to collections that contain unknown computers.
Count of failures in each phase or group of a specific task sequence	Displays the number of failures in each phase or group of the specified task sequence.
Count of failures in each phase or group of a specific task sequence deployment	Displays the number of failures in each phase or group of the specified task sequence deployment.
Deployment status of all task sequence deployments	Displays the overall progress of all task sequence deployments.
Progress of a running task sequence	Displays the progress of the specified task sequence.
Progress of a running task sequence deployment	Displays the progress of the specified task sequence deployment.
Progress of all deployments for a specific task sequence	Displays the progress of all deployments for the specified task sequence.
Summary report for a task sequence deployment	Displays the summary information for the specified task sequence deployment.
Task Sequence - Progress	
Chart - Weekly progress of a task sequence	Displays the weekly progress of the task sequence starting from the day when first deployed.
Progress of a task sequence	Displays the progress of the specified task sequence.
Progress of all task sequences	Displays the progress of all task sequences.
Progress of task sequences for operating system deployments	Shows the progress of all task sequences that deploy operating systems.
Status of all unknown computers	Displays a list of the computers that were unknown at the time they ran a task sequence deployment and whether they are now known computers.
Task Sequence - References	
Content referenced by a specific task sequence	Displays content referenced by the specified task sequence.

18

Report Name	Description
Upgrade Assessment - Windows 7	
Computers that do not meet the recommended system requirements for Windows 7	Computers that do not meet the Windows 7 minimum hardware requirements for memory, processor speed, and free disk space.
Computers that meet the recommended system requirements for Windows 7	Computers that meet the Windows 7 minimum hardware requirements for memory, processor speed, and free disk space.
Hardware summary for all systems in a collection	Shows the operating system, memory, hard drive free space, and processor speed for each system in the specified collection, and whether each component meets the minimum requirements for upgrading to Windows 7.
	Note: Systems failing only the OS check may still run Windows 7, but a clean install of Windows 7 is required.
User - Device Affinity	
Historical User Device Affinity Associations By Resource	Shows all current and historical User Device Affinity assignments for all selected resources and totaled per resource.
Pending User Device Affinity Associations By Collection	Shows all pending User Device Affinity assignments based on usage data, for members of a collection.
User Device Affinity Associations Per Collection	Shows all User Device Associations for the selected collection, and groups the results by collection type (for example, user or device).
Users	
Computers for a specific user name	Displays a list of computers used by a single user.
Count users by domain	Displays the number of users in each domain.
Users in a specific domain	Displays a list of users and their computers in a single user domain.
Virtual Applications	
Computers with a specific virtual application	Summary of computers with the specified App-V application shortcut as created using the Application Virtualization Management Sequencer.
Computers with a specific virtual application package	Summary of computers that have the specified App-V application package.
Count of all instances of virtual application packages	Displays a count of detected App-V application packages.

Report Name	Description
Count of all instances of virtual applications	Displays a count of detected App-V applications.
Wake On LAN	
All computers targeted for Wake On LAN activity	All computers targeted for Wake On LAN activity.
All objects pending wake-up activity	Objects scheduled for wakeup.
All sites that are enabled for Wake On LAN	List of all sites in the hierarchy enabled for Wake On LAN.
Errors received while sending wake-up packets for a defined period	Errors received while sending wake-up packets to computers for a defined period.
History of Wake On LAN activity	Shows a history of the wakeup activity that has occurred since a certain period.

Troubleshooting SSRS

After it is installed and configured, SSRS is generally trouble-free. However, on occasion you will need to diagnose and correct issues that arise. There are two major areas to investigate issues within SSRS; those are the log files and event error logs, discussed in the next sections.

SSRS Logs

SSRS utilizes a number of log files; there are log files generated by interaction with ConfigMgr and those native to SSRS. This section lists the ones you should know about.

- ▶ **SQL Server 2008 R2 Report Server log files:** See http://msdn.microsoft.com/en-us/library/ms157403.aspx for a complete listing.

- ▶ **ReportServerService Trace Log:** This file is created daily and contains highly detailed information.

- ▶ **Report Server Execution Log:** This is a diagnostic log, which you can enable via reporting site settings.

- ▶ **Report Server HTTP Log:** This diagnostic log can be enabled by modifying the ReportServerService.exe configuration file.

- ▶ **Srsrpsetup.log:** This is the ConfigMgr SSRS reporting point installation wrapper log.

- ▶ **srsrpMSI:** srspMSI is the ConfigMgr SSRS MSI based installation log file for ConfigMgr SSRS.

- ▶ **Srsrp.log:** This log file contains ConfigMgr SSRS logging, with real-time reporting point information.

- ▶ **Windows Application Log:** The application log includes event logging and may provide clues about potential errors within SSRS.

18

Report Server Event Errors

Table 18.5 lists some errors you may receive from some common SSRS functions and expressions. For updates, see http://msdn.microsoft.com/en-us/library/ms165307.aspx.

TABLE 18.5   Common Errors in SSRS Functions and Expressions

Event ID	Type	Category	Source	Description
106	Error	Scheduling	Report Server	SQL Server Agent must be running when you define a scheduled operation (for example, report subscription, and delivery).
107	Error	Startup/ Shutdown	Report Server Scheduling and Delivery Processor	<Source> cannot connect to the report server database. For more information, see "Report Server Windows Service (MSSQLServer) 107," and "Troubleshooting Server and Database Connection Problems" at http://msdn.microsoft.com/en-us/library/aa337324.aspx and http://msdn.microsoft.com/en-us/library/ms156468.aspx, respectively.
108	Error	Extension	Report Server Report Manager	<Source> cannot load a delivery, data processing, or rendering extension. This is most likely the result of an incomplete deployment or removal of an extension. For additional information, see "Deploying a Data Processing Extension" at http://msdn.microsoft.com/en-us/library/ms155104.aspx and "Deploying a Delivery Extension" at http://msdn.microsoft.com/en-us/library/ms153647.aspx.
109	Information	Management	Report Server Report Manager	A configuration file has been modified. For more information, see the explanation at http://msdn.microsoft.com/en-us/library/ms155866.aspx.

Event ID	Type	Category	Source	Description
110	Warning	Management	Report Server Report Manager	A setting in one of the configuration files has been modified such that it is no longer valid. A default value will be used instead. For additional information, see http://msdn.microsoft.com/en-us/library/ms155866.aspx.
111	Error	Logging	Report Server Report Manager	*<Source>* cannot create the trace log. For more information, see http://msdn.microsoft.com/en-us/library/ms156500.aspx.
112	Warning	Security	Report Server	The report server has detected a possible denial of service attack. For additional information, see http://msdn.microsoft.com/en-us/library/bb522728.aspx.
113	Error	Logging	Report Server	The report server cannot create a performance counter.
114	Error	Startup/ Shutdown	Report Manager	Report Manager cannot connect to the Report Server service.
115	Warning	Scheduling	Scheduling and Delivery Processor	A scheduled task in the SQL Server Agent queue has been modified or deleted.
116	Error	Internal	Report Server Report Manager Scheduling and Delivery Processor	An internal error occurred.
117	Error	Startup/ Shutdown	Report Server	The report server database is an invalid version. For more information, see the article on "Troubleshooting Server and Database Connection Problems" at http://msdn.microsoft.com/en-us/library/ms156468.aspx.
118	Warning	Logging	Report Server Report Manager	The trace log is not at the expected location; a new trace log will be created in the default folder. For additional information, see the article at http://msdn.microsoft.com/en-us/library/ms156500.aspx.

18

Event ID	Type	Category	Source	Description
119	Error	Activation	Report Server Scheduling and Delivery Processor	<Source> has not been granted access to the contents of the report server database.
120	Error	Activation	Report Server	The symmetric key cannot be decrypted. Most likely, there has been a change to the account that the service uses. For more information, see http://msdn.microsoft.com/en-us/library/ms156274.aspx.
121	Error	Startup/Shutdown	Report Server	Remote Procedure Call (RPC) Service failed to start.
122	Warning	Delivery	Scheduling and Delivery Processor	Scheduling and Delivery Processor cannot connect to the SMTP server used for email delivery. For additional information about SMTP server connections, see http://msdn.microsoft.com/en-us/library/ms159155.aspx.
123	Warning	Logging	Report Server Report Manager	The report server failed to write to the trace log. See http://msdn.microsoft.com/en-us/library/ms156500.aspx for more information about the trace logs.
124	Information	Activation	Report Server	The Report Server service has been initialized. For additional information, see http://msdn.microsoft.com/en-us/library/ms157133.aspx.
125	Information	Activation	Report Server	The key used for encrypting data was successfully extracted. For more information about keys, see http://msdn.microsoft.com/en-us/library/ms156274.aspx.
126	Information	Activation	Report Server	The key used for encrypting data was successfully applied. http://msdn.microsoft.com/en-us/library/ms156274.aspx provides information about keys.

Event ID	Type	Category	Source	Description
127	Information	Activation	Report Server	Encrypted content was successfully removed from the report server database. For more information about deleting nonrecoverable encrypted data, see the article on "Configuring and Managing Encryption Keys" at http://msdn.microsoft.com/en-us/library/ms156274.aspx.
128	Error	Activation	Report Server	Reporting Services components from different editions cannot be used together.
129	Error	Management	Report Server Scheduling and Delivery Processor	An encrypted configuration file setting cannot be decrypted.
130	Error	Management	Report Server Scheduling and Delivery Processor	*<Source>* cannot find the configuration file. Configuration files are required by the report server.
131	Error	Security	Report Server Scheduling and Delivery Processor	An encrypted user data value could not be decrypted.
132	Error	Security	Report Server	A failure occurred during encryption of user data. The value cannot be saved.
133	Error	Management	Report Server Report Manager Scheduling and Delivery Processor	A configuration file failed to load. This error may occur if the XML is not valid.
134	Error	Management	Report Server	The report server failed to encrypt values for a setting in a configuration file.

Optimizing SSRS Performance

SSRS has several features that can enhance report performance and increase the usefulness of its reporting capabilities. These include subscriptions, report caching, report snapshots, and report timeout values, discussed in the following sections.

18

Subscriptions

Subscriptions enable you to deliver a report as a document to a server share on a scheduled basis. Enabling the report server email delivery extension gives you the ability to mail the contents of a report to an email alias, or deliver a copy of the report to a server share and a link to the report via email. Using subscriptions also requires that the report run in unattended mode, which means the credentials to run the report must be stored on the report server. See http://msdn.microsoft.com/en-us/library/bb283186.aspx for information regarding the process to create subscriptions.

Subscriptions serve a valuable purpose because you can schedule common report requests to be sent to users needing this information. You also have the additional advantage of scheduling complex or long-running reports to run during off hours when there is reduced SQL Server usage.

Report Caching

Report caching can shorten the time it takes for a user to retrieve a report, particularly if the report is large or accessed frequently. When a report is requested, a query is sent to the database, an intermediate form of the report is cached on the report server, and the final report is rendered to the end user. Report caching forces the intermediate version of the report to be cached on the report server and provides a more consistent user experience with a reduced load on the database. Report caching is defined on a per-report basis: From the report server, select **Manage Report** and **Cache Refresh Options** to create and manage cache plans. See http://msdn.microsoft.com/en-us/library/ms155927.aspx for more information on the configuration process.

Report Snapshots

A report snapshot is report output captured at a point in time that contains all report formatting information and full results. Report snapshots are run on a predetermined schedule, in essence allowing a report history to be created over time. Snapshots are rendered in a final viewing format such as HTML when an application or user requests them. This setting is configured on a per-report basis: Navigate to Report Manager, select **Report Properties**, and then select **Report History**. Refer to http://msdn.microsoft.com/en-us/library/ms156291.aspx for additional information.

Report Timeout Values

A common issue that surfaced with ConfigMgr legacy reporting was timeouts for long-running reports, or for reports that returned too many rows. Using SSRS instead of ASP reporting gives you the ability to configure report timeout values on a system level and tune timeout values on a per-report basis. To modify this setting on the system level, browse to **Report Manager**, and then **Site Settings**; by default, this value is set to 1800 seconds. You can override the report time-out parameter on a per-report basis by navigating to **Report Manager -> Report Properties** and selecting **Processing Options**; then modify the Report Timeout setting. For more information, reference http://msdn.microsoft.com/en-us/library/ms155782.aspx.

Performance Best Practices

A properly tuned report begins with a properly designed query. If you find that a report or reports run slowly, start by investigating the core query. There will be cases in which you cannot tune the report query to perform any faster. In that event, use report caching or report snapshots depending on the user requirements. Another excellent technique is implementing report subscriptions to run at times when the ConfigMgr database server is underutilized.

Reporting on Reporting Services

You can gain a lot of information from SSRS directly from the SSRS databases. Here are some questions about which you may have wondered:

- ▶ How many reports are run daily?

- ▶ Which reports are run most often, and by whom?

- ▶ Which reports have queries that run for a long time, or perhaps return large amounts of information?

- ▶ Which reports are NEVER run?

Some of the reports discovered by this process may make good candidates for report subscriptions, caching, or snapshots as described in the "Optimizing SSRS Performance" section.

Start by examining the data located in the report execution log on the reporting services database. This data is exposed by the reporting server views, with more information about the three views shown:

- ▶ **ExecutionLog:** Legacy view for backward compatibility.

- ▶ **ExecutionLog2:** Created for SQL Server 2008.

- ▶ **ExecutionLog3:** Created for SQL Server 2008 R2. Two fields were renamed in this log:

    - ▶ ReportAction to ItemAction

    - ▶ ReportPath to ItemPath

Here is a query you can use to select information from the execution log that returns all information included for that view. Table 18.6 displays a partial list of fields in the view.

```
SELECT * FROM ExecutionLog2
```

18

TABLE 18.6   Partial List of Fields in Execution Log

ReportPath	TimeStart	TimeEnd	TimeData Retrieval	Byte Count	Row Count
/Bridgepoint/OS Charts	9/18/11 3:37 PM	9/18/11 3:37 PM	170	1674	6
/Computer List by OS	9/18/11 3:15 PM	9/18/11 3:15 PM	2800	23864	523
/Computer List by OS	9/30/11 4:42 PM	9/30/11 4:42 PM	700	23864	523
/Computer list by OS Type	9/18/11 3:15 PM	9/18/11 3:15 PM	56	6009	9631
/Custom Report/Operating System Count Chart	9/24/11 3:03 PM	9/24/11 3:03 PM	33	23264	6
/Custom Report/Operating System Count Chart	9/24/11 3:07 PM	9/24/11 3:07 PM	30	23264	6

TIP: RETENTION PERIOD FOR EXECUTION LOG DATA

By default, execution log data is kept for only the last 60 days. To keep history longer than 60 days, you have two options:

► Increase the retention time of the execution log data beyond 60 days. To change the default retention period, run the following SQL statement on the report server, after changing the report server name to match your instance name:

```
USE ReportServer
GO
UPDATE ConfigurationInfo
SET Value = '365'
WHERE Name = 'ExecutionLogDaysKept'
```

► Create an SQL task or ETL (Extract, Transform, Load) job that runs to periodically copy records from the source table to an archival table and creating the reports based on the archival data.

Say you want to create a report based on information contained in the Execution Log, showing the top 10 most frequently executed reports.

In the following query, the first four lines after the comment are used to interactively test the query in SQL Server Management Studio as a batch statement prior to creating a report. The query joins the execution log to the catalog table to retrieve the name of the report and summarize information for active reports. Notice there is a date parameter filter that restricts the query to return information between the begin and end dates. You can find a high-level list of information captured by the report execution log at http://msdn. microsoft.com/en-us/library/ms159110.aspx.

```
/* The next 4 lines will be used only to test the query */
DECLARE @FromDate Date
DECLARE @ToDate Date
SET @FromDate = '2011-09-01'
SET @ToDate   = '2011-10-30'


/* Top 10 Most Frequent Reports - include only this portion for the report */
SELECT TOP 10
        COUNT(Name) AS ExecutionCount
    , Name AS ReportName
    , SUM(TimeDataRetrieval) AS TimeDataRetrievalSum
    , SUM(TimeProcessing) AS TimeProcessingSum
    , SUM(TimeRendering) AS TimeRenderingSum
    , SUM(ByteCount) AS ByteCountSum
    , SUM([RowCount]) AS RowCountSum
FROM
( SELECT c.Name, TimeDataRetrieval, TimeProcessing, TimeRendering, ByteCount,
[RowCount]
    FROM  Catalog c INNER JOIN ExecutionLog e
    ON c.ItemID = e.ReportID
     WHERE e.TimeStart BETWEEN @FromDate AND @ToDate AND Type = 2
) AS RS
GROUP BY Name
ORDER BY COUNT(Name) DESC, Name
```

To create your first report against the report server database, you must first create a new data source name. Use the same process as in the "Building a Custom Report" section; refer to Figure 18.14 in that section. For this new data source, use **ReportServer** for the name; the connection string uses the name of the reporting server name and instance (if applicable) and initial catalog name. Figure 18.45 shows a sample reporting server data source.

To create the report, follow these steps:

1. Launch Report Builder as shown in the example in the "Building a Custom Report" section.

2. Start a New Report; choose the **Table or Matrix Wizard** option.

3. Click **Next** on the Shared Data Set Wizard, choose the shared Data Source Connection created for the report server connection, as shown in Figure 18.46, and click **Next**.

4. On the Design a Query step, choose the **Edit as Text**, as shown in Figure 18.47; copy/paste the query illustrated in this section, included as online material for this book. See Appendix D, "Available Online," for information; do not include the first five lines.

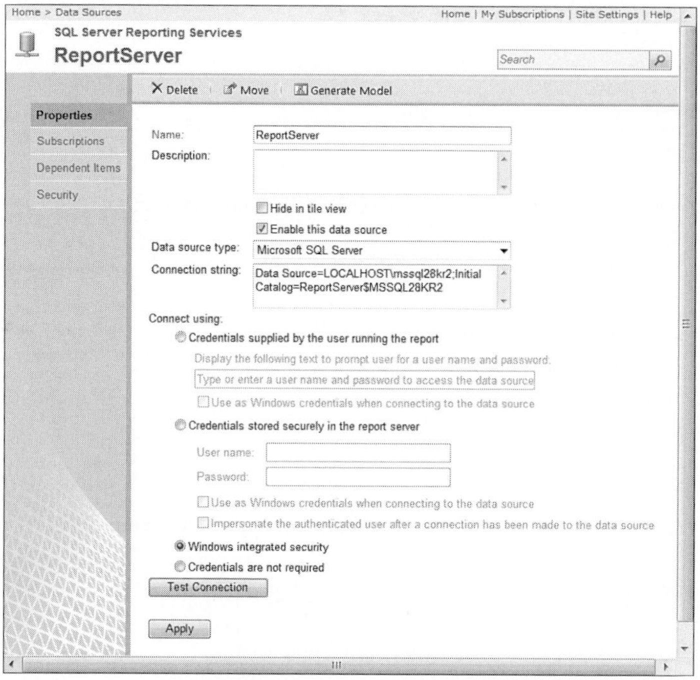

FIGURE 18.45   Report Server Data Source.

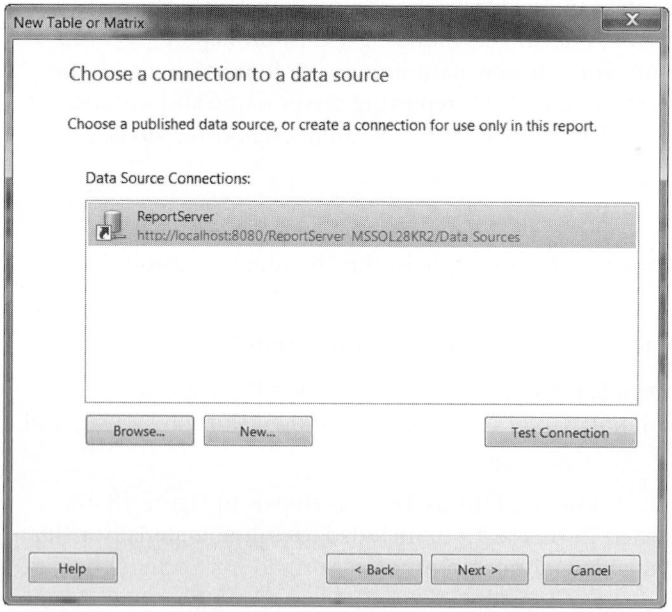

FIGURE 18.46   Choose the Report Server Data Source.

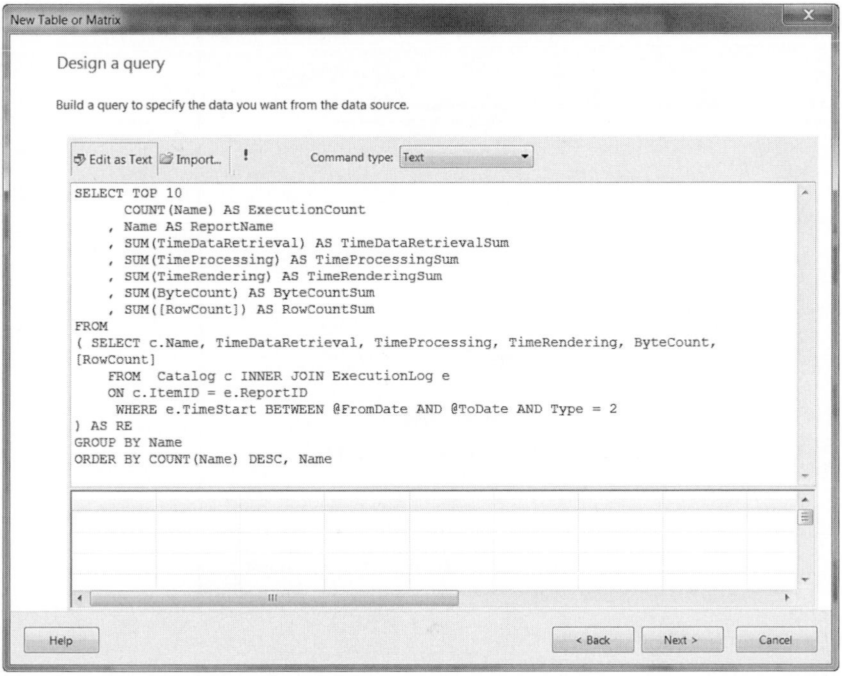

FIGURE 18.47   Design Report Query.

NOTE: REPORT BUILDER AUTOMATICALLY CREATES FILTERS

Report Builder automatically creates the date parameter filters for you; there is no need to include that information when you build your report.

5. Click **Next**. In the Arrange fields dialog, add the fields listed here and shown in Figure 18.48 to the Values box:

▶ Sum(ExecutionAccount)

▶ ReportName

▶ Sum(TimeDataRetrievalSum)

▶ Sum(TimeProcessingSum)

▶ Sum(TimeRenderingSum)

▶ Sum(ByteCountSum)

▶ Sum(RowCountSum)

6. Click **Next, Next,** and then **Finish**.

18

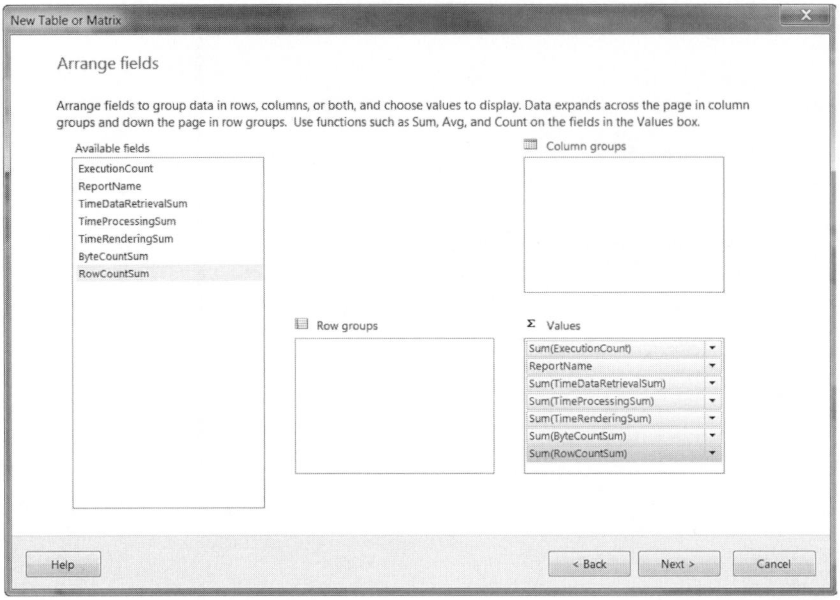

FIGURE 18.48   Arrange Report Fields.

7. After resizing the columns, and adding a title to your report, enter the From Date and To Date parameters. When you select **View report**, you should have a report that appears similar to Figure 18.49. When complete, save the report as **Top 10 Executed Reports** and publish to your report server.

As an added report enhancement, consider adding dynamic defaults in the Date parameter fields for the From and To Dates. For the From Date, set the default to be current date minus 60 days:

```
=DateAdd("d", -60, Now( ) )
```

For the To Date field, set the default to the current date:

```
= Now( )
```

For an example on creating parameter defaults, the "Advanced Custom Report Example" section includes an example with the Server Uptime Report.

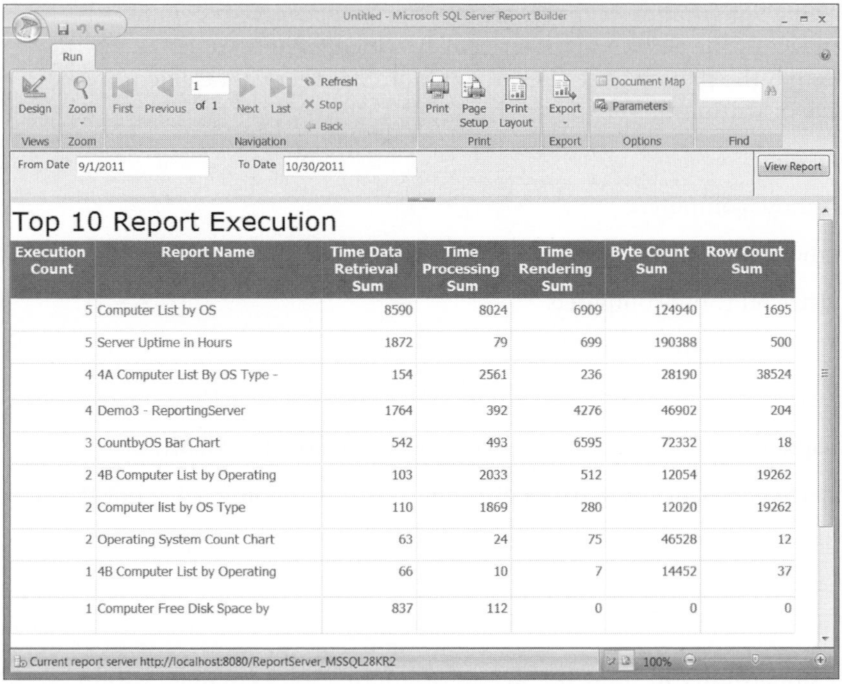

Execution Count	Report Name	Time Data Retrieval Sum	Time Processing Sum	Time Rendering Sum	Byte Count Sum	Row Count Sum
5	Computer List by OS	8590	8024	6909	124940	1695
5	Server Uptime in Hours	1872	79	699	190388	500
4	4A Computer List By OS Type -	154	2561	236	28190	38524
4	Demo3 - ReportingServer	1764	392	4276	46902	204
3	CountbyOS Bar Chart	542	493	6595	72332	18
2	4B Computer List by Operating	103	2033	512	12054	19262
2	Computer list by OS Type	110	1869	280	12020	19262
2	Operating System Count Chart	63	24	75	46528	12
1	4B Computer List by Operating	66	10	7	14452	37
1	Computer Free Disk Space by	837	112	0	0	0

FIGURE 18.49 Report Server Top 10 Execution.

System Center Data Warehouse

Microsoft's System Center Service Manager 2010 product incorporated a data warehouse to allow consolidation and reporting of System Center-related information. This includes incidents and change management created through Service Manager and related Operations Manager data, as well as configuration items based on Configuration Manager hardware and software inventory that is imported into Service Manager through a connector. The data warehouse uses a standard Microsoft SQL Server database, the Service Manager configuration management database (CMDB), to store the information and Analysis Server to present the data in a component known as a dimensional *cube*. A cube contains facts (nouns) and dimensions (adjectives). An Analysis Server cube enables business and technical people to analyze this information by providing the results they need to help make decisions.

With System Center 2012, Service Manager continues the capability to include data from System Center 2012 Configuration Manager into the data warehouse. This information, correlated with other System Center data such as Service Manager incidents and Operations Manager data, allows decision makers to examine specific events or trends in ways not previously possible.

A connector between Configuration Manager and Service Manager feeds data from Configuration Manager to the Service Manager CMDB, which is then presented via the data warehouse. Here is the planned list of Configuration Manager data elements to be included at the time of writing this chapter:

▶ Computers

▶ Hardware on those computers

▶ Software on those computers

▶ Software updates on those computers

▶ Correlate DCM error events to incidents

▶ Mobile devices

▶ Power data: Goes directly to data warehouse cube, not through CMDB

▶ Software update compliance data: Goes directly to data warehouse cube, not through the CMDB

Summary

SSRS gives you the opportunity to show the wealth of information contained within the ConfigMgr database using ConfigMgr reporting. It provides the security you need to manage the reports properly, allowing you to designate who can run and publish reports to the report server. Using SQL Server Management Studio, you can use the ConfigMgr views to build the query and evaluate the query results prior to creating the report. Report Builder and BIDS give developers the tools they need to produce professional and versatile reports. SSRS provides the additional functionality to tune reports for performance and for scheduled email delivery. Use the information contained in the reporting server database to understand which reports are candidates for performance enhancements, and how reports are run in your environment—and by whom.

CHAPTER 19

Operating System Deployment

Deploying a new operating system (OS) into any corporation, large or small, is a large undertaking with vast implications. The cost of not properly planning and executing your move to a new OS can be huge and includes things like extra work, upset users, and potential data loss. Understanding the technical complexity to deploy a new OS led to the operating system deployment (OSD) feature set introduced in Configuration Manager (ConfigMgr) 2007. OSD has been enhanced in ConfigMgr 2012 but the core functionality and look and feel remain the same.

This chapter covers OSD in depth including applicable scenarios, detailed use, guidance, best practices, and troubleshooting. Detailed, quick-start walkthroughs are discussed in the "Image Operations" section. This single chapter cannot and does not cover the complete range of information and knowledge required to deploy Windows fully in an enterprise environment, nor does it cover supplemental tools such as the Microsoft Deployment Toolkit (MDT). In addition, because the core of OSD has changed very little, most (if not all) information available on OSD in ConfigMgr 2007 is still applicable. Thus, some of the links or information presented in this chapter may specifically refer to ConfigMgr 2007.

NOTE: OPERATING SYSTEM COVERAGE

Although this chapter specifically covers Windows 7 deployments, nearly all concepts also apply to Windows XP; any differences will be mentioned and additional information or links to additional information provided. Nearly all deployment concepts applicable to Windows 7 are also applicable to Windows Vista, Windows Server 2008, and Windows 2008 R2; none of these other OS editions will be specifically called out in the text unless a significant difference in functionality exists from a ConfigMgr perspective. Similarly, Windows Server 2003 and Windows XP deployment concepts are nearly identical and thus Windows Server 2003 will not be mentioned. As Windows 2000 is not supported by ConfigMgr 2012 or Microsoft, it is not covered in this chapter.

Windows 8 also is not specifically discussed in this chapter for several reasons, including that it is a beta product (and subject to change) and that System Center 2012 Configuration Manager does not support it at RTM—if you try to deploy Windows 8 Beta with OSD in ConfigMgr, it will fail. It is also anticipated that Windows 8 will have many new setup and deployment-centric features, so much of this chapter may not even apply. Simply attempting to cover any Windows 8 information here would be a disservice to you and an exercise in futility.

What OSD Does

OSD is more than just a ConfigMgr feature; it is a methodology, even a mind-set for deploying Windows. At its core, OSD is about delivering a new instance of Windows to Windows-compatible devices, en masse. Although that sounds simple, it isn't always as easy as it sounds because of the philosophy and architecture of Windows—namely to support commodity hardware without restriction.

Mass delivery of Windows is nothing new. Organizations have been using third-party tools since the last century to capture an "image" of a single system and copy it to other systems. Windows is tolerant of this and starting with Windows Vista, Windows is even installed by the Windows setup routine using an "image."

What sets OSD apart? What makes it stand far above the crowd?

▶ OSD is about automating the entire process, from image creation and image maintenance to actual image deployment.

▶ OSD is not just about creating and deploying an image. OSD is an entire process that allows you to define actions before the image is applied to a system (such as partitioning and formatting the drive or even BIOS upgrades) and actions after the image is applied (such as software update installation or application deployment).

▶ OSD is dynamic, enabling different yet automatic deployment time behavior based on an unbounded set of criteria including things such as hardware type, location, and intended user or system roles.

▶ OSD is extensible to meet the needs of any organization. MDT and its subset feature User Driven Installation (UDI) are excellent examples of this extensibility from Microsoft, and OSD App Tree and OSD++ are excellent examples from a source other than Microsoft that are also widely used.

▶ OSD is integrated into ConfigMgr, which allows you to take advantage of the other powerful features of the product including software distribution, software updates, and reporting, all from a single management console in a seamless manner.

> **ABOUT MICROSOFT DEPLOYMENT TOOLKIT**
>
> MDT is a free and fully supported solution from Microsoft that is both a complete stand-alone solution for deploying Windows and an add-on to base functionality of OSD in ConfigMgr. As an add-on for OSD, MDT brings a great deal of commonly needed functionality and makes the deployment process dynamic and database-driven.
>
> Listing the complete capabilities MDT adds to OSD would be a large list; suffice it to say the functionality in MDT is often summarized as addressing issues and problems you never knew you had. Although the OSD toolset is clearly focused on providing flexibility, power, and tools that integrates with ConfigMgr enabling you to deploy Windows, MDT is focused on providing a complete, end-to-end solution for nearly every Windows deployment challenge and scenario. This essentially means MDT is a details-focused solution aimed at solving common challenges faced by most organizations when deploying Windows.
>
> MDT does add complexity to OSD in the form of additional moving parts such as configuration files, a separate workbench, and an optional database. These increase your learning curve and sometimes overwhelm those just beginning to learn OSD. MDT also hides some of the lower-level details of OSD, making it more difficult to troubleshoot. In addition, the database component is not necessarily enterprise-friendly in its default form because it is a single instance sitting at a single physical location.
>
> Just installing MDT does not force you to use it. Thus, it is highly recommended you at least review the capabilities of MDT and even install it to examine it fully.

What's New in OSD

Although on the surface OSD doesn't appear to be that different from its ConfigMgr 2007 predecessor, there are several improvements or additions to functionality. Here is a list summarizing these changes; complete discussions of each are incorporated into the appropriate or relevant sections of the chapter.

▶ **Offline Servicing:** This new capability lets you schedule ConfigMgr to apply updates to an OS image imported into ConfigMgr without actually deploying the image. This potentially removes the need to deploy updates during an image capture or deployment, greatly reducing the time and effort spent on them and ensuring that operating systems deployed by ConfigMgr are fully updated before brought online. This task is discussed in the "Image Maintenance" section.

▶ **Media Updates:** A small number of updates are incorporated into the media-based boot image capabilities of ConfigMgr. These allow for greater automation by exposing previously hidden features in the boot media creation user interface, including

  ▶ Specifying a prestart command (formerly known as a pre-execution hook). Prestart commands run first when a system is booted and allow you to provide custom actions such as displaying a user interface, querying ConfigMgr, or overriding predefined deployment behavior.

  ▶ Suppressing all start-up dialog boxes during deployment for a true unattended experience.

19

These improvements are discussed in the "Boot Images" section.

Hierarchy-wide media is an additional improvement. Previously, boot media created by ConfigMgr hard-coded the management point (MP) that it would contact for policies. This caused issues when the hierarchy contained multiple sites because the boot media would always "phone home" instead of contacting the nearest MP. The home MP might be located across a wide area network (WAN) link or not have the correct policies for the client being deployed.

Hierarchy-wide media dynamically finds the correct MP based upon site boundaries. You can override this by setting a variable in a prestart command. Using site-specific media is still an option, however.

▶ **USMT 4.0 Integration:** Although Service Pack (SP) 2 brought User State Migration Tool (USMT) 4.0 support to ConfigMgr 2007, its new features were never integrated into the interface. These are now fully exposed in the user interface. USMT 4.0 is discussed in the "State Migration" section.

▶ **Application Integration:** The awesome new application model (discussed in Chapter 12, "Creating and Managing Applications") is integrated into OSD. However, with the new application model and focus on user-centric deployment comes a shift in the philosophy of when to install applications: during OS deployment or after? The "User Device Affinity" section discusses this dilemma and its ramifications.

▶ **PXE Service Point Updates:** The PXE (Preboot eXecution Environment) service point is no longer a separate role in ConfigMgr; its complete functionality is now rolled into the distribution point (DP). A dedicated DP share is no longer required, which should eliminate the confusion its presence caused in ConfigMgr 2007. Windows Deployment Services (WDS) is still required for PXE functionality.

▶ **Deployment Alignments:** This is less of a new feature as it is a unification of terminology and user interface elements, resulting in a common administrative experience for software distribution, software updates, and OSD. Monitoring of each of the features is now combined in the Deployments node of the console under the Monitoring workspace. In addition, OS deployments are made available to users using the new Software Center, similar to both software distribution and software updates.

▶ **Centralized Management:** This is also not actually a feature but instead the result of changes in the ConfigMgr hierarchy implementation. Essentially, all OSD objects are global data (discussed in Chapter 5, "Network Design") and editable from the central administration site (CAS) or any primary site. This includes task sequences, which can now be deployed from the CAS or primary site. Computer associations can also be created and maintained at either the CAS or primary site, although both the specified source and destination systems must exist in the same primary site.

The first part of this chapter covers base OSD functionality and sets the stage for the remainder of the chapter. Using OSD also means implementing one site role—a distribution point—and can include the use of one other site role. Their installation and use is later covered in the "Site System Roles" section; this was not included at the beginning because their use is in OSD is mainly as supporting roles. Understanding the concepts of and base functionality of OSD is required before you can assess and implement these roles.

Deployment Scenarios

As a common point of reference, Microsoft has defined five Windows deployment scenarios. These scenarios cover the gamut of possibilities for deploying Windows in general to any organization; minor variations are possible, and implementation details may vary depending on the tools used or goals of the deployment. OSD handles four of these five scenarios:

▶ **Upgrade:** This scenario involves an in-place upgrade of the current OS to a new OS. It preserves user data as well as applications, and is thus (falsely) considered by some as the best choice when moving an organization to a new OS. The downfall is this scenario also preserves misconfigurations, unauthorized software, and any existing malware.

The Upgrade scenario is not supported by ConfigMgr—in neither OSD nor software distribution—making the choice easy. For OS deployments where a well-managed client infrastructure is important, that is, all environments, the refresh scenario is the preferred and highly recommended choice for upgrading the OS.

▶ **New Computer:** The name of this scenario is a little misleading because it can apply to new or old computers and applies to systems brand new out-of-the-box or those that are just being reloaded completely. The distinguishing factor in this scenario is that current user data and applications on a system, whether they exist or not, are ignored. This scenario is often referred to as *bare-metal* or *wipe-and-load* because it assumes that nothing on the system is currently valid, and it should be built from scratch or bare-metal.

This scenario is the easiest to deal with because you do not need to worry about user state; a user's state includes all the data, documents, and configuration of the system and applications that are unique to that user.

▶ **Refresh:** This scenario involves installing a fresh, new OS on an existing system while preserving applicable user data and reinstalling authorized applications, in effect refreshing just the OS. This reload can be the result of a variety of reasons:

   ▶ An upgrade such as Windows XP to Windows 7.

   ▶ The current OS installation is broken beyond repair.

   ▶ The OS installation does not meet current standards.

When a process is in place to rebuild systems quickly with OSD, organizations typically choose to re-image a system after the help desk spends a set amount of time troubleshooting without resolving an issue. This approach provides a way to decrease help desk costs spent on fixing operating systems.

19

NOTE: DON'T CONFUSE UPGRADE AND REFRESH

These two scenarios sound similar and even have a similar result; however, they are different. Upgrade is literally running setup.exe in the existing OS and allowing Windows setup to upgrade the OS in-place. Refresh involves wiping the disk (not necessarily format-ting it) and installing a clean version of Windows.

▶ **Replace:** The Replace scenario is similar to the Refresh scenario but involves swap-ping out or replacing the physical system. Because the user's state lives on the old system, this scenario adds the challenge of moving the user's state and can be both challenging and time-consuming. Rest assured, however, OSD is up to this task and provides you the necessary capabilities to accomplish this.

▶ **OEM:** This last scenario is similar to the New Computer scenario in that current user state is not involved. This scenario, however, is explicitly for new systems delivered from the Original Equipment Manufacturer (OEM) or vendor. It involves deliver-ing a seed image to the OEM for their use during the factory's system build process. Because the OEM cannot join a system to your domain or install applications from your internal network, the seed image, when booted, kicks off the rest of the process after the system is physically set up on your internal network to finish the deploy-ment process.

The advantage to this scenario is your OEM can drop-ship systems directly to your remote offices; the systems can easily be installed by non-IT resources and the deployment process finishes without any intervention. The disadvantage is that you will probably end up maintaining at least two sets of images: one for your in-house scenarios and one for the OEM scenario. Ensuring that the OEM has the latest image is also challenging and a possible disadvantage depending on how often you update your base image and how quickly they begin to use a new image.

Each vendor may also have varying states of support, procedures, and supplemental tools for this method. Contact them first before pursuing this option for their guid-ance and recommendations.

Table 19.1 summarizes the five scenarios.

TABLE 19.1   Deployment Scenarios

Name	Supported	User State	System Hardware
Upgrade	No	Preserved	Same
New Computer	Yes	Ignored or N/A	New
Refresh	Yes	Restored	Same
Replace	Yes	Restored	New
OEM	Yes	N/A	New

Tools Incorporated into OSD

Although completely integrated into ConfigMgr, OSD uses and takes advantage of multiple separate tools. Knowing how OSD uses these tools and each tool's function is beneficial and even critical when setting up a deployment and troubleshooting problems. Tools include Sysprep, the Windows Automated Installation Kit (WAIK), and USMT, covered in the next sections.

Sysprep

Sysprep, short for System Preparation, is one of the primary tools used for unattended setup of all flavors of Windows. When used for imaging, Sysprep removes the many unique identifiers specific to a particular installation of Windows and then configures the installation to run a brief, GUI-based, mini-setup when the system restarts. This mini-setup provides these benefits:

- ▶ Generates new and unique identifiers for the system

- ▶ Enables the input of a new Windows product key

- ▶ Reruns the plug-and-play hardware detection

- ▶ Reruns the driver installation process

For a complete and in-depth discussion of why Sysprep is the only supported method to make a Windows image generic, see Mark Russinovich's blog post at http://blogs.technet. com/b/markrussinovich/archive/2009/11/03/3291024.aspx.

Sysprep in OSD

OSD fully automates the mini-setup process with a configuration file. The name of the file varies based on the version of Windows used:

- ▶ Unattend.xml for Windows 7

- ▶ Sysprep.inf for Windows XP

OSD either builds the appropriate file or uses one supplied to it, inserting the information automatically into the Sysprep configuration file. This information includes the product key, organization name, networking information, and domain credentials.

Incorporating this functionality adds to OSD's flexibility by eliminating the need to maintain multiple Sysprep files supporting multiple deployment scenarios.

Version-Specific Flavors

Each version of Windows has its own specific version of Sysprep. For versions of Windows before Vista, you must make Sysprep available to the setup process separately by creating a package or placing the files in *%SystemRoot%*\sysprep. You can find these files in the deploy.cab compressed file located in the \Support folder on the installation media or download them from the Microsoft download site, http://www.microsoft.com/downloads.

19

Note that the deploy.cab contents are dependent on service pack level, so if you are sysprepping Windows XP SP 3, you should use the corresponding available download.

For Windows Vista and later, the Sysprep files come with the OS and are located in %*windir*%\System32\sysprep.

Windows Automated Installation Kit

WAIK installs as part of your ConfigMgr installation and is available as a separate download from Microsoft. Version 2.0 is installed with ConfigMgr 2012. This version of WAIK includes Windows Preinstallation Environment (WinPE) 3.1 boot images that are based on Windows 7 SP 1.

The WAIK is a set of tools designed to automate a Windows installation. ConfigMgr automatically uses some of the WAIK tools such as ImageX and the Deployment Image Servicing and Management (DISM) tool during the deployment process. WAIK also includes user guides on how to use these tools, reference documents on the various unattended setup files, and WinPE.

Using OSD fully automates and completely integrates the many details of using the tools in WAIK. You can, however, also manipulate images outside of OSD using WAIK tools.

ImageX

ImageX is a stand-alone tool that creates and deploys Windows Imaging Format (WIM) files from a Windows volume; because the tool is completely integrated into ConfigMgr, you do not need to install additional software. ImageX is also part of WAIK and can be installed and used separately by installing WAIK. Because of the tight integration, you can seamlessly use images created using ImageX outside of ConfigMgr in OSD; the opposite is also true.

ImageX can also "mount" previously created WIM files for read or read/write access. This allows you to access the files and folders stored in a WIM using a previously existing empty folder on the system. You can then add or modify files using Windows Explorer or any other tool, just as if they are part of the host system.

WIM files are the next generation of Microsoft's proprietary archive cabinet (.CAB) files. Using WIMs adds the ability to store metadata about the files and folders it contains; this capability allows you to restore a complete volume. Here are the advantages WIMs have over alternative, sector, or bit-based images created by third-party tools:

▶ **File system independent:** You can capture WIMs from or deploy them to either NTFS (NT File System)- or FAT (File Allocation Table)-based file systems.

▶ **Volume size independent:** WIMs do not store any information about the volume from which they are captured. You can deploy WIMs if enough room is available on the destination volume.

▶ **Processor architecture independent:** ImageX works identically on x86, x64, and Itanium processors. The WIMs created on each are the same format and interchangeable. This doesn't mean you can capture a 64-bit OS in a WIM and deploy it to a

32-bit system and expect it to run—just that the WIM file itself is processor architecture agnostic.

▶ **File-based compression:** Files are independently compressed inside the WIM; this often leads to better compression ratios than bit-based images.

▶ **Multiple images in one file:** Multiple distinct volume images can be contained in a single WIM file.

▶ **Single instancing of files:** Multiple identical files are stored only one time. This leads to huge space gains when a WIM contains multiple images.

▶ **Nondestructive image application:** Images can be applied to a volume without destroying existing files and data.

The WIM file has proven to be so useful and versatile that Microsoft chose to drop the previous method of installing Windows with a file copy and instead uses a WIM file! Installation media for Vista and beyond have a single WIM file containing the OS taking advantage of all the items listed in this section.

WinPE

WinPE is a mini-OS currently based on Windows 7. It includes support for networking, Windows Management Instrumentation (WMI), VBScript, batch files, and database access. Most things that run on a full-blown Windows 7 system also run in WinPE. The advantage of WinPE is that it is much smaller than the full-blown OS (typically approximately 150MB), loads from a read-only disk, and runs in a RAM disk. (A minimum of 512MB of memory is required for the version of WinPE included with and used by OSD in ConfigMgr 2012.) This makes WinPE suitable for booting from a CD/DVD, or over the network using PXE. OSD uses WinPE as a boot environment, ensuring the currently installed OS will not interfere with the deployment process.

Windows System Image Manager

Windows System Image Manager (WSIM) is part of the WAIK tools. WSIM is a GUI tool that builds unattended answer files for Windows 7. Instead of having to worry about the syntax of the answer file (particularly because the Windows 7 answer file is stored in XML), this tool graphically presents all available options and generates the unattend.xml file for you. This same file format is utilized for Sysprep equivalent files (sysprep.inf in Windows XP) used by the mini-setup to complete the setup of Windows 7 systems when Sysprep is used.

Deployment Image Servicing and Management

DISM is a command-line tool for manually servicing and managing Windows (Vista and above) and WinPE images. Servicing involves changing the content of the image and managing involves listing the content of the image file or combining two image files together. Servicing specifically includes adding updates and drivers to the image—both of which OSD uses DISM for.

19

These images can be either offline—not the currently booted OS—or can actually be online. Offline images also can be in one of two forms: in a WIM file or extracted to the disk. This makes managing many aspects of Windows seamless, no matter where the OS is or its current state.

User State Migration Tool

USMT is an extensive tool, deserving its own dedicated chapter if not an entire book! In short, USMT searches a system for all user data and settings, packaging them into a single archive file. You can then import this archive onto another system, restoring the user data and settings. USMT's default configuration captures all known Microsoft-centric settings and data, such as wallpaper, color scheme, Microsoft Office documents, favorites, and all files in the user's profile folders. You can customize these defaults based upon the requirements of your environment. The current version of USMT, 4.0, is part of WAIK and is the preferred version to use with OSD because it adds many capabilities. The "USMT Versions" section discusses the differences between the two current version of USMT and choosing between them.

Microsoft provides documentation on USMT 3.0 (required for migrating to Windows XP or Windows Vista) at http://technet.microsoft.com/en-us/library/cc722032.aspx and USMT 4.0 at http://technet.microsoft.com/en-us/library/dd560801(v=WS.10).aspx.

USMT Customization

The information USMT captures from a source system is highly customizable by modifying or creating a series of eXtensible Markup Language (XML) configuration files. These XML configuration files describe the files, folders, and registry entries that USMT captures; you can either specify exact filenames and registry locations, or perform wildcard searches to locate data or settings in these XML configuration files. USMT then uses these configuration files to capture all specified data and settings and put them into an archive for later use in restoring to a destination system.

The Tools in USMT

USMT actually consists of two tools:

- ▶ LoadState.exe
- ▶ ScanState.exe

As their names imply, ScanState.exe captures the data and settings, whereas LoadState. exe restores them. Although the use of these two tools is mostly hidden from OSD in ConfigMgr, it is worth noting.

OSD Phases

The phases of OSD line up with any good project management philosophy; you may have different names for them, but the principals remain the same. In addition, depending on your personal style or your organization's environment, the OSD process may be formal with much rigor and documentation, informal with handwritten notes and napkin doodles, or somewhere in between. The next sections discuss the phases you should use with OSD.

Planning

Like any complex endeavor, planning plays a key role in the success or failure of OSD. Planning for OSD involves defining the who, what, and when of Windows deployment for your organization—consider this the requirements gathering phase. The answers to these questions can guide how you go about technically implementing the process and making it work.

▶ **Who:** Who are you deploying Windows to or for? Is it your entire organization or just a subset? Who will be initiating the deployment to each of these systems? Will it be your end users, field technicians, you, or someone else?

▶ **What:** What OS are you deploying? What version and edition? Will different users or systems get different versions or editions? What applications do you want to deploy with the OS? Will this be different for different user or system roles? Are there other customizations that you need to make to the OS or applications? To which hardware models are you deploying the OS?

▶ **When:** When are you going to deploy? Is there a deadline that you must meet? Are you going to deploy during the day or after hours?

▶ **Other:** Do you care about user data? How do you handle updating Windows and other software in your organization? What other desktop standards exist in your organization that must be part of deploying Windows?

These questions and their answers can guide all your efforts; the answers are the blueprint for your Windows rollout. Depending upon your organization, you may not be able to answer all these questions yourself, and it may take a considerable amount of time to gain consensus from the key players. Knowing the answers ahead of time can save you work or rework down the line.

Preparation

When you understand the requirements for your deployment, you can set about gathering the needed resources, importing them into ConfigMgr, and performing any necessary ConfigMgr configuration or hierarchy modification to meet those requirements.

Necessary resources include OS source media, application source files, drivers, configuration scripts, test systems, and storage space. Many of these resources including the OS source files, drivers, and applications must be imported into ConfigMgr for use in OSD—the import of both OS source files and drivers is covered in the "Operating System Installers" and "Drivers" sections of this chapter. Applications and software distribution packages are covered in detail in Chapter 11, "Packages and Programs," Chapter 12, and Chapter 13, "Distributing and Deploying Applications."

Based upon the physical nature of your organization, you may need to add site systems. For example, smaller sites that normally would not require a site system for normal ConfigMgr operations such as inventory and software distribution may need to have one added to support PXE, the larger OS image files used by OSD, or the transient storage of user data. Alternatively, site systems may already exist at these locations and simply need these roles enabled—the "Site System Roles" section discusses the two supplementary OSD roles and installing them.

Creation

The core of the OSD process is putting all the requirements in place to deploy Windows. It involves stringing the various OSD building blocks (see the "OSD Building Blocks" section for complete details) into an ordered structure that meets your defined requirements.

This is often an iterative process, involving building a basic structure, testing, adding to the basic structure, testing again, and so on. As requirements change (or are revealed), the iterative process will continue even after you implement OSD into production.

Testing

This self-explanatory step is often over-looked and rarely given the time or attention that it deserves. So many different permutations and factors exist even in smaller and simpler environments that you can probably never test all of them; however, not properly and thoroughly testing as many as you can will result in poor results and lost data. In general, you should test against every scenario and model of hardware possible in your organization.

Much like a proper software development lifecycle, testing should account for most of your time when developing new task sequences. Although much of this time is watching progress bars, you will never actually know if your design work will result in the wanted outcome of a properly deployed Windows instance without it.

Productionization

Productionization is not a word in the dictionary, but it captures the essence of this last phase: rolling out your hard work into production and making Windows deployment an activity your desktop technicians and users no longer dread. If you have done your due diligence, properly gathered and accounted for all of the requirements, and tested everything possible, you are ready to put that work into motion.

OSD Building Blocks

There are many pieces in the ConfigMgr OSD feature that collectively come together to form a cohesive and comprehensive tool to deploy Windows in any environment. Knowing the ins and outs of these pieces, and how they fit together, is vital for using OSD to its fullest and best way possible for your organization's Windows deployment. The following sections describe each of these building blocks in detail in the order they appear in the console, as shown in Figure 19.1.

FIGURE 19.1   Operating systems node in the console.

Drivers

Using the Drivers node, you import drivers into the ConfigMgr drivers catalog. The deployment process uses this catalog to identify which drivers to copy to a system essentially injecting them into the OS deployed. Drivers injected into the process are not guaranteed to be used however. Windows setup still makes the ultimate decision of which drivers to actually install and use; however, for drivers to be available to the built-in driver tasks, they must be imported into ConfigMgr. The "Driver Management Section" has a complete discussion of using drivers during OSD.

Driver Categories

Categories are an optional classification tool used to track driver versions or separate and classify them in some other logical way that makes sense for your organization. Categories are used to filter which drivers are considered for installation during an OS deployment, but have no other specific function within ConfigMgr. Categories are assigned to drivers when you import them or by selecting one or more drivers displayed in the console and choosing **Categorize** from the ribbon bar or right-click context menu.

Drivers may have zero or more categories assigned to them. Adding drivers to multiple categories offers many advantages over simple hierarchical groups where drivers may be members of only a single group. This, combined with the new console filtering features, should be quite useful in environments with large driver repositories.

There are no default categories; the creation, definition, and use of all categories is completely up to you. Categories often are used to designate different hardware models or manufacturers. This enables you to limit the scope of drivers considered during the plug-and-play detection done by the task sequence, speeding up the process and reducing or eliminating the chance that a bad driver is installed and used. Note that using categories for device type is redundant because a class attribute already exists for each driver that defines the type of device for which the driver is applicable.

Another popular use for categories is for version control and testing of new drivers. Assigning a distinct version number using a category enables you to prevent the use of these newer drivers for production deployments until they are tested.

19

Consider also using console folders in addition to or instead of using categories because your drivers are then visually grouped together and easy to select en masse.

Importing Drivers

To import drivers into the ConfigMgr driver catalog, perform these steps:

1. Copy the driver files you want to import to a UNC accessible location; consider this location an initial import location. Do not delete or rearrange the files in this location after importing the drivers because ConfigMgr maintains a reference to this original location for each imported driver; deleting or rearranging these files or folders causes issues because ConfigMgr directly uses these original files when creating boot images that reference these drivers and creating driver packages. Also, do not confuse this location with the driver package source location (discussed in the "Driver Packages" section). These should be two distinct locations.

   ConfigMgr can import only raw driver files, not compressed files, or executables. You must extract the files from these packages to import them.

2. Navigate to **Software Library -> Operating Systems -> Drivers**. Choose **Import Driver** from the ribbon bar or right-click context menu to launch the Import New Driver Wizard, as shown in Figure 19.2.

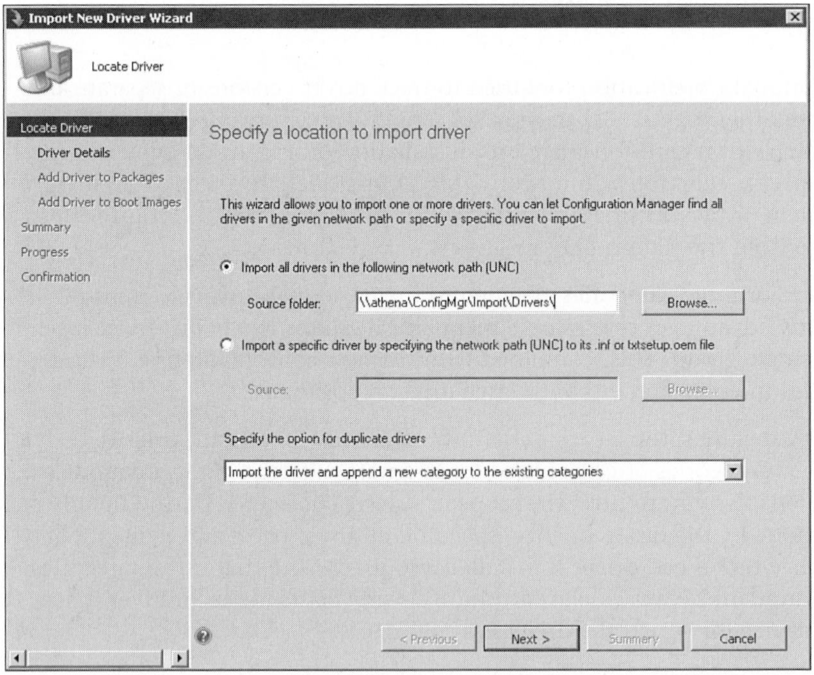

FIGURE 19.2   The Import New Driver Wizard.

3. On the Locate Driver page, select the location you copied the driver files to in step 1. If you have only a single driver to import, choose the second radio button and then enter or browse to the exact UNC location of the .inf or txtsetup.oem file. For multiple drivers, or to allow ConfigMgr to auto-locate all available drivers in a given path including all subfolders, use the first option, **Import all drivers in the following network path (UNC)**.

At the bottom of the Locate Driver page, choose your desired behavior to handle duplicate drivers:

▶ Import the driver and append a new category to the existing categories.

▶ Import the driver and keep the existing categories.

▶ Import the driver and overwrite the existing categories.

▶ Do not import the driver.

4. If you selected the first option on the Locate Driver page to import all drivers from a specific location, the Driver Details page shown in Figure 19.3 displays. All drivers found based on the location entered on the Locate Driver page are shown in a list box, where you can review the drivers and uncheck those that you do not want to import.

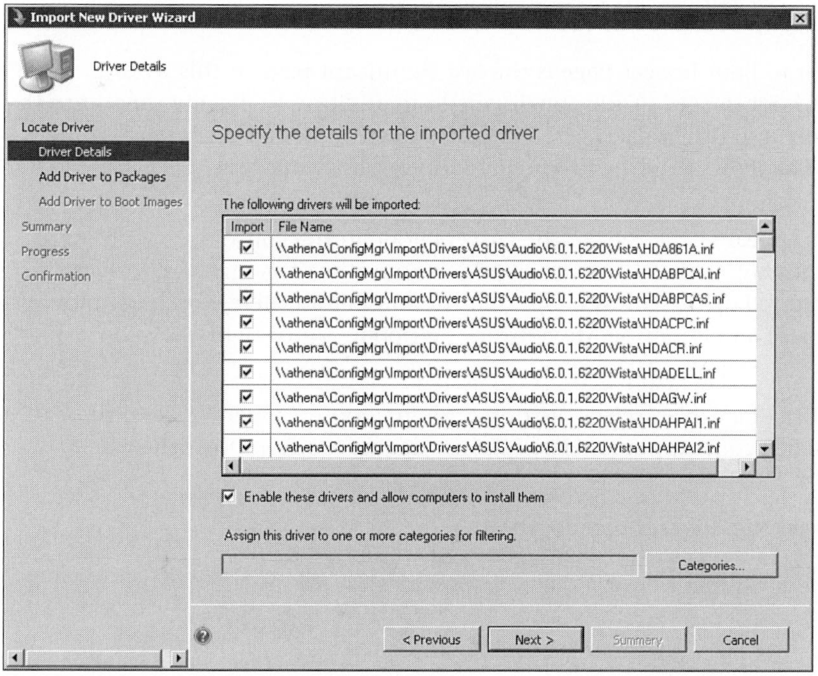

FIGURE 19.3   The Import New Driver Wizard.

If you selected to import only a specific driver on the Locate Driver page, a slightly different Driver Details page is shown with details about the specific driver chosen.

By default, all selected drivers are enabled after they are imported. To disable this behavior, uncheck the **Enable these drivers and allow computers to install them** check box or the **Enable this driver and allow computers to install it** check box depending on which Driver Details page is shown. Use the **Categories** button at the bottom of this page to create and assign one or more categories to the drivers imported. If importing more than one driver, all drivers imported will have the selected categories assigned. Driver categories are further discussed in the "Driver Categories" section.

5. On the Applicability page, which is displayed only when importing a single specific driver, modify those platforms for which the driver is applicable. In general, the authors do not recommend modifying the applicability for imported drivers because this information is directly pulled from the driver's .inf file as defined by the driver's vendor.

6. On the Add Driver to Packages page, create or select an existing package to which to add the drivers being imported. Drivers must exist in a driver package (discussed next in the "Driver Packages" section) to be accessible and usable during OSD. You may add drivers to packages later if you have not decided on your driver package structure at this time. Clicking the **New Package** button displays the Create Driver Package dialog, also described in the next section.

7. The Add Driver to Boot Images page is the last significant page in this wizard. Choose which boot images to add the drivers to in addition to placing them into the driver repository and driver packages. See the "Drivers in Boot Images" section for a discussion of exactly which driver to include in your boot images.

All imported drivers appear at the root of the Drivers node in the console. As with most other objects in ConfigMgr, you can create subfolders to further organize your drivers; however, newly imported drivers always appear at the root. From there, you must move them by selecting them and choosing **Move** from the ribbon bar or right-click context menu.

To view the properties of a driver, select the driver; then choose **Properties** from the ribbon bar or right-click context menu. Here is what you can do from the driver's Properties dialog box:

▶ View (or change) the driver source location.

▶ Enable or disable a driver for consideration during the plug-and-play detection step in OSD.

▶ Modify platform applicability.

▶ View which driver packages or boot images a driver is part of.

Driver Packages

Drivers imported into ConfigMgr must be stored in a driver package to be available during an OS deployment; driver packages, like all other package types in ConfigMgr, store the files associated with the drivers. You can create driver packages and add drivers to them during driver import as described in the "Importing Drivers" section, or you can use the Driver Packages node to create and manage the various driver packages for your deployments.

To create a new driver package, follow these steps:

1. Navigate to **Software Library** -> **Operating Systems** -> **Driver Packages**. Choose **Create Driver package** from the ribbon bar or the right-click context menu.

2. Fill in the following information on the Create Driver Package dialog:

    ▶ **Name:** The name for the driver package.

    ▶ **Comment:** Descriptive comments adding detail to the package's contents.

    ▶ **Path:** An accessible UNC path that stores the driver files for this package. As with other content types, each package should have its own distinct location. ConfigMgr creates the folders in the path entered if they do not exist.

This is not the path you imported the drivers from or will import them from, as described in the "Importing Drivers" section. This path is the source location used to populate the DP. Figure 19.4 shows a simple diagram depicting this process: Drivers are first copied from the driver import location to the driver package source specified by this path and then copied to the DP when the package is assigned to a DP, resulting in all drivers being located in three distinct locations. There is no shortcut to this process and deleting or manipulating the driver import location can create issues. Using the same path for both locations will bloat your driver packages and increase your download times, and may cause some confusion if you directly view the contents of the location.

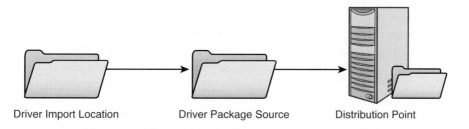

Driver Import Location   Driver Package Source   Distribution Point

FIGURE 19.4   Driver flow.

To add drivers to a package after they are imported, select or multiselect the drivers in the console, and choose **Driver Packages** from the Edit fly-out menu on the ribbon bar or right-click context menu. This displays the Add or Remove Drivers to Packages dialog where you can select existing packages to add the selected drivers to use the **New Package** button to create a new package, which displays the Create Driver Package dialog.

Operating System Images

This node lists all the OS images you have imported into ConfigMgr. OS images are those captured images in the form of a WIM file, used to mass-deploy Windows. The node also lists data images. Data images are also WIM files but do not contain an installed OS. They are simply a collection of files stored in the WIM that you would like to deploy to a system.

To import a new OS image, perform these steps:

1. Copy the WIM file to its permanent home in your source repository. Each WIM file does not need to be in a unique folder; ConfigMgr directly references the actual WIM file itself, making distinct folders for each WIM unnecessary.

2. In the console, navigate to **Software Library** -> **Operating Systems** -> **Operating Systems**, and choose **Add Operating System Image** from the ribbon bar, or right-click context menu to launch the Add Operating System Image Wizard.

3. The Add Operating System Image Wizard has two significant pages:

   ▶ **Data Source:** The exact UNC path to your WIM file containing the image you want to import

   ▶ **General:** Descriptive metadata for you to add a Name, Version, and Comment

Do not use a WIM file directly from a Windows DVD without first deploying and capturing it as a new image. If used directly, the default image.wim is installed to the D: drive instead of the typical C: drive. (This hopefully will be corrected in a future release of ConfigMgr.) To create a new OS image you can later import, see the "Image Creation" section.

Operating System Installers

Use this node to manage the actual Windows source files as copied from official Microsoft media (virtual or physical). The entire contents of the media are used to install the OS from scratch. Operating system installers are typically used only during automated image creation (described in the "Automatic Image Creation" section) but can also be used during mass deployments of an OS. They are not typically used for this purpose, as installing an OS from source files takes longer than deploying an image. In addition, raw source files straight from the media do not contain the latest security updates and are not customized for your organization. For a complete discussion of why you should use captured images, see the "Image Operations" section.

To import a new operating system installer, follow these steps:

1. Copy the entire contents of the Windows installation media to its own folder. This is typically within your software or source repository and must be accessible to the site's AD account and a UNC path. Creating a parent folder for all your OS source

folders is highly recommended for organizational purposes, with each separate OS edition and version in its own distinct subfolder.

2. Navigate to **Software Library** -> **Overview** -> **Operating System Installers**. All currently imported OS source files display on the right.

3. Choose **Add Operating System Installer** from the ribbon, or right-click the context menu to launch the Add Operating System Installer Wizard. Only two significant pages are in this wizard.

   ▶ **Data Source:** Enter the path to the source files folder created in step 1.

   ▶ **General:** On this page, enter metadata describing the OS being added including the Name, Version, and Comment. The name entered here displays in the console and so should be explicitly descriptive of the OS added; for example, Windows 7 Enterprise Service Pack 1 (x64).

Boot Images

From the perspective of a client system involved in OSD, WinPE is the core foundation of the entire process. It is required because the main operations of the deployment cannot actually occur from within a full install of Windows. Specifically, formatting the disk and applying an image file cannot happen while the target disk drive is in use and must be initiated from something that does not live on or run from that target disk.

WinPE is ideally suited for this task because it is small, easy to deliver, fast, and runs from a RAM disk without the need for persistent storage. WinPE also shares the core kernel and driver model with Windows itself, can run any valid native Windows executable, and provides much of the same automation enabling functionality including batch scripting and VBScript.

WinPE is contained in the boot images and delivered to a client system in one of three ways:

   ▶ PXE during a network boot

   ▶ Removable media such as a CD or DVD-ROM

   ▶ Download from a DP

The approach you choose does not matter to the OSD process, as long as WinPE is delivered to the target system. The next sections discuss these delivery methods.

PXE Booting

PXE booting is typically used for bare-metal or new hardware installations when the system does not have a ConfigMgr client agent installed or the currently installed OS cannot be started. PXE is a well-defined, industry standard used by ConfigMgr. ConfigMgr has almost no part in PXE booting a system; the majority of the work is performed by the target system's NIC and the network infrastructure.

19

NOTE: PXE BOOT DELIVERS ONLY BOOT IMAGES

The PXE boot process delivers only the initial boot image in ConfigMgr. All other content including the OS image, drivers, updates, applications, and such is delivered from a DP.

With the unification of the PXE role with the DP in ConfigMgr 2012, this distinction may be less important than it was in ConfigMgr 2007, but it is still an important and useful fact for troubleshooting the OSD process.

Here are the criteria required for using PXE boot:

▶ A DHCP server must be available for use.

▶ The network must allow the PXE broadcast packets to reach the PXE server. PXE and DHCP use BOOTP (Bootstrap Protocol), which is a broadcast-based protocol. Layer 3 network devices do not pass broadcast traffic by default; the PXE server must be on the same network segment as the client attempting to PXE boot, or you must configure your Layer 3 network devices to forward the broadcasts to the PXE server using IP helpers.

Most organizations already have BOOTP broadcasts forwarded on their Layer 3 devices to support DHCP; configuring them to forward BOOTP broadcasts to support PXE is a nearly identical process with the only difference being a different destination server.

Alternatively, you can configure DHCP options 66 and 67 in your DHCP scopes. These options instruct the NIC to look to a specific PXE server instead of using broadcasts to find one.

IP helpers are generally the preferred method because they do not rely on any intelligence or assumption of capabilities of the NIC in the target system.

▶ You must enable the boot images for PXE. This is a commonly forgotten step:

  ▶ Choose the boot image you want to make available using PXE, and choose **Properties** from the ribbon bar or right-click context menu.

  ▶ On the boot image's Properties dialog, select the Data Source tab.

  ▶ Select the **Deploy this boot image from the PXE service point** check box at the bottom of the page.

The boot image is now available to PXE boot systems on any PXE-enabled DP to which you assign the boot image.

NOTE: X86 OR X64 BOOT IMAGES FOR PXE

There are two basic types of boot images available: one for each major Windows architecture type. You should make both available on your PXE-enabled DPs. WDS requires a basic set of files for servicing PXE requests. This basic set of files is machine architecture-specific and independent of the OS architecture you are deploying. WDS extracts these files from the boot images you make available. To service both types of systems, both boot image architectures must be available to WDS to extract and use both sets of architecture-specific files. This has nothing to do with the OS architecture you are deploying; even if you are not deploying x64 editions of Windows and never actually use the x64 boot images, if the systems you are PXE booting have x64 hardware (which almost all do now), they require the x64 PXE files delivered from the PXE server.

Removable Media

You typically use removable media for bare-metal installation of new hardware where PXE booting is not feasible. This includes the following situations:

▶ The target system is across a WAN link. Although it is possible to PXE boot over a WAN link, performance can vary and may be unacceptable.

▶ The network infrastructure does not forward the PXE broadcasts, and DHCP options 66 and 67 cannot be configured.

▶ Another PXE server is already configured in the environment and cannot be supplanted or disturbed.

▶ Unavailable because the target system does not support it. (It has been a long time since network cards did not support network boot using PXE, but it is possible.)

▶ When you want to be absolutely certain that a system does not connect to the network prior to being fully loaded and fully patched to a designated baseline.

▶ The target system is in a protected subnet such as a DMZ (demilitarized zone, also referred to as a *perimeter network*) and cannot communicate back to the site system.

The main limitation of removable media is version control. Making changes to boot images hosted on a PXE server is trivial; making changes to boot images on multiple pieces of media no longer in your control or possession and in production use is often a logistical challenge.

You can create images for removable media by right-clicking any task sequence or the actual Task Sequences node in the navigation tree and choosing **Create Task Sequence Media** from the ribbon bar or right-click context menu. This launches the Task Sequence Media Wizard, allowing you to choose which type of media to create. You can burn the resulting image to a CD or DVD or place it on a bootable USB device. You can create three types of task sequence media:

▶ **Stand-alone media:** Creates a self-contained disk image that contains WinPE and all the packages and information specific to a task sequence—except for software updates.

Using stand-alone media allows you to run a task sequence on a target system without connectivity to a ConfigMgr site system.

When you create stand-alone media, the system prompts for a distribution point from which to copy packages. You can set task sequence variables specific to this media image, allowing you to customize the task sequence while knowing that it will not connect to the site server during installation.

The system also prompts you to choose a media size during the creation of the image: 650MB (CD), 4.6GB (DVD), or 8.5GB (DL-DVD). Depending on the size of packages included in the task sequence, there may be multiple disk images created; choosing the CD image size of 650MB guarantees multiple images. When you boot a system to stand-alone media, it acts as if the task sequence used to create the media were advertised to the system with a required deployment.

▶ **Bootable media:** Creates a burnable image of the chosen boot image. You can also initiate the task sequence in a bootable media image from within Windows using the autorun feature of the image.

A new option for ConfigMgr 2012 is to create bootable media that is not specific to a single site; this is called *dynamic media* and allows you to use the media at any site in the hierarchy. Dynamic media first contacts the MP specified during the creation of the media and then is redirected to a closer MP based on the boundaries of all sites in the hierarchy. Dynamic media is the default option.

Site-based media is the same as the bootable media created in ConfigMgr 2007 and can communicate only with the MP at the single site specified during the creation of the media. If your hierarchy contains only a single site, there is no functional difference between these two options.

You can also add prestart commands (as described in the "Boot Image Customization" section) and custom task sequence variables (as described in the "Variables" section) that are specific only to the boot media when creating bootable media.

NOTE: VERSION MISMATCH

If the bootable media used to boot a system does not contain the latest version of the boot image available, OSD downloads the latest version of the boot image from a DP and restarts the system into this latest version of the boot image, similar to the process described in the "Using a Distribution Point" section. This ensures the most current version of the boot image is always used.

▶ **Capture media:** Creates a CD that allows you to capture a reference system outside of a task sequence; the image is not bootable, and you must initiate it from within an installed OS using the Autoplay function or by manually running TSMBAutorun from the SMS\bin\i386 folder.

Capture media can be useful in a variety of circumstances, such as if you already have a perfect reference system or a perfect process for creating the reference system. Another use of the capture media would be importing an image from a competitive imaging system: you would first deploy the image to a suitable reference system and then recapture it into a WIM format using the image capture media.

Using capture media is covered in the "Manual Image Creation" section.

▶ **Prestaged media:** Creates a WIM file used by a custom task sequence to prestage the OS image on a computer, which saves time and network bandwidth when deploying new computers. The network bandwidth in question here is directly related to the WIM file itself, which can be several GB in size. By not downloading a large WIM file, you conserve network bandwidth and save deployment time.

When shipping computers from an original equipment manufacturer (OEM) to your organization, the computers arrive at your business with the OS image prestaged. You can then PXE boot them, and using another task sequence to deploy the OS, you modify the Format and Partition Disk step to check for the presence of a variable, called OEMmedia. If True, it skips this step (which is what you want because the WIM file is located on the hard disk already).

When you create prestaged media, the WIM image is first staged to the logged on user's temp folder, so be sure there is enough free space before starting this task. Otherwise, it will fail with an out of disk space message even though it is pointed to a drive or UNC with several GB of free space more than required.

Using a Distribution Pont

The final method to deliver WinPE is through ConfigMgr itself! If a system already has a ConfigMgr client agent installed and an OSD task sequence is deployed to the client and initiated, ConfigMgr downloads the boot image containing WinPE to a special pseudo-partition on the hard drive. This pseudo-partition is then set as the active partition. An automatic reboot is initiated, and the system is booted into the WinPE image contained in the active pseudo-partition. This method allows for tasks before the reboot into WinPE, including capturing user state or other data collection activities that can be used or restored during the deployment.

The "Task Sequence Targeting" section discusses deployments further.

Drivers in Boot Images

You may have to occasionally add drivers to boot images. Don't confuse this with adding drivers to the operating systems being deployed. Boot images require only minimal functionality for proper operation, including connectivity to the network and the ability to write to the system's hard drive. The drivers added to boot images in no way impact or affect the drivers used by the deployed OS.

In general, only drivers for network interface cards (NIC) and storage devices should be added to boot images and only if necessary. The WinPE images used in ConfigMgr 2012 are based on Windows 7 and thus include a large driver store sufficient for most hardware used, including Intel SATA devices. Like the entire OSD process, test your boot image on all applicable hardware in your organization and add only a NIC or storage driver if the boot image cannot establish a network connection or use the hard disk.

On rare occasions, other drivers may also be needed to support basic WinPE operations; such as pointing devices on slate systems. In general, never add a driver to WinPE unless you verify it is required for WinPE operation and your boot image does not contain a suitable driver that provides minimal functionality for the device. Adding extra drivers bloats the boot images and introduces the possibility of driver conflicts.

As described in the "Importing Drivers" section, you can add drivers directly to a boot image at the time you import them. Unless you are importing only a single driver that you know must be added to a boot image, it is generally recommended you not add drivers directly into boot images during the driver import process. Instead, after importing the drivers, select or multiselect those that you want to add to a boot image in the console, and choose **Boot Images** from the Edit fly-out menu on the ribbon bar or right-click context menu. This launches the Add or Remove Drivers to Boot Images dialog where you select boot images to which to add the selected drivers. An additional way to import drivers into a specific boot image is using its Properties dialog (shown in Figure 19.5) and selecting the starburst icon on the Drivers tab. From this tab, you can also remove drivers from a specific boot image using the red X icon.

TIP: USE CATEGORIES FOR BOOT IMAGE DRIVERS

Using a separate category (or set of categories) to organize drivers that you add to your boot images helps immensely should you ever recreate your boot images or create new ones.

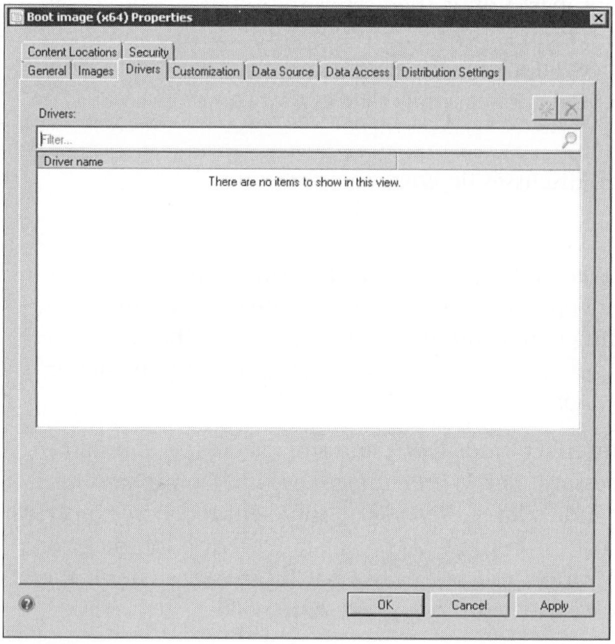

FIGURE 19.5   Boot Image drivers.

Boot Image Customization

Although you can create completely custom boot images from scratch, there is generally no need to do so; the built-in boot images are sufficiently customizable to meet nearly any need. The following customizations are available from the Customization tab of a boot image's Properties dialog box, as shown in Figure 19.6:

▶ **Enable prestart commands:** Prestart commands run before the OSD process even begins. Prestart commands are typically used to display information and prompt the interactive user for some type of input such as the system's location, wanted name, or role. There are no predefined prestart commands, and this type of customization is completely up to your needs and abilities. In general, you can use any valid Windows script (batch, VBScript or Jscript; PowerShell is not [yet] supported in WinPE).

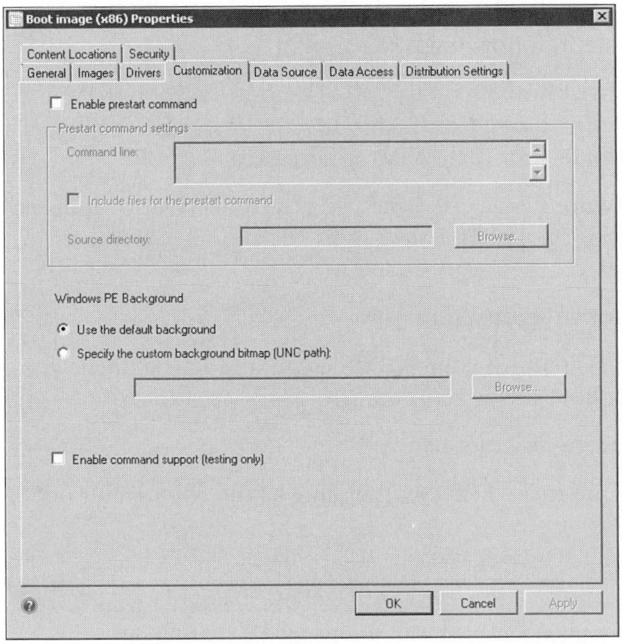

FIGURE 19.6   Boot Image customization.

Prestart commands often require additional files like scripts or executables that are not part of the default boot image. You can also add these files by specifying a folder containing them to this section in the Properties dialog, and they are added to the boot image when it is distributed to its assigned DPs. Even if you do not use a prestart command, using this section to add files to the boot image is helpful; such as diagnostic scripts that help during troubleshooting.

▶ **Windows PE Background:** In this section, specify an image to use as the background during OSD instead of the default one provided by Microsoft.

▶ **Enable command support:** Checking this check box enables you to launch a command prompt anytime during OSD. This is useful for troubleshooting issues during OSD and is discussed in the "Troubleshooting" section.

Although using these customizations should cover most needs, it is possible to create a completely new and custom WinPE boot image and import it into ConfigMgr. To do so, start with Microsoft's walk-through at http://technet.microsoft.com/en-us/library/cc766385.aspx and add whatever additional customizations are necessary. A common reason to create custom boot images is to add capabilities to the boot image such as supporting HTAs for displaying custom UI to the interactive user or the Microsoft Data Access Components (MSDAC) to query Active Directory or a database during the WinPE portions of OSD. Adding these packages is discussed at http://technet.microsoft.com/en-us/library/cc749470(v=WS.10).aspx.

To import a boot image after you create it, follow these steps:

1. Copy the WIM file to its permanent home in your source repository. Each WIM file does not need to be in a unique folder. ConfigMgr directly references the actual WIM file itself making distinct folders for each WIM unnecessary.

2. In the console, navigate to **Software Library** -> **Operating Systems** -> **Boot Images**, and choose **Add Boot Image** from the ribbon bar or right-click context menu to launch the Add Boot Image Wizard.

3. The Add Boot Image Wizard has two significant pages:

   ▶ **Data Source:** The exact UNC path to your WIM file containing the image you want to import and which boot image to import from the WIM file.

   ▶ **General:** Descriptive metadata for you to add a Name, Version, and Comment.

When imported, custom boot images are treated exactly the same as the two default boot images.

NOTE: DON'T USE BOOT IMAGES FROM THE WINDOWS INSTALLATION MEDIA

Do not use the boot images (boot.wim files) included with the Windows installation media—these are specially customized boot images that do not work properly with OSD.

Task Sequences

Task sequences are a core element for any OSD operation. They consist of a series of customizable tasks or sequentially performed steps. Many tasks types are built into ConfigMgr, and MDT adds a handful of useful tasks as well. In addition, you can create your own tasks using the ConfigMgr Software Development Kit (SDK) if you cannot find one that fits your needs.

The New Task Sequence Wizard, available from the context menu or ribbon bar of the Task Sequences node by selecting **Create Task Sequence**, quickly builds one of two default task sequence types or a custom task sequence:

▶ **Build and Capture:** This type of task sequence builds an OS image for you by performing the following steps:

- ▶ Installs Windows from an OS installer

- ▶ Installs software updates

- ▶ Installs software you want to include in the image

- ▶ Performs any other customizations you want to include in the image

- ▶ Prepares a system to be captured to an image by sysprepping it

- ▶ Captures an image of the system to a WIM file

▶ **Deploy an Image:** This type of task sequence deploys an OS image performing these steps:

- ▶ Optionally captures use state and data

- ▶ Prepares the hard drives

- ▶ Applies an OS image contained in a WIM file to the local hard disk

- ▶ Installs software updates

- ▶ Installs additional software

- ▶ Performs any other customizations

- ▶ Optionally restores user state and data

These two task sequence types take care of a majority of the scenarios in OSD (the "Image Operations" section includes walkthroughs); however, task sequences are flexible and not limited to what is produced by default. The task sequence editor allows easy customization of the task sequences; you can tailor task sequences to the specific OSD needs of an organization—and with a little imagination, software deployment.

The wizard also presents the option to build a custom task sequence; task sequences built using the custom option are initially blank and can be used for OSD task sequences built from scratch or non-OSD task sequences such as application deployment or software updates where a series of multiple actions are ordered and performed on the target system. Non-OSD task sequences were traditionally used in ConfigMgr 2007 in place of writing scripts, for inserting reboots into a set of tasks, or coordinating multiple tasks that must occur in a sequence at a given scheduled time. Using task sequences for non-OSD tasks, although discouraged in ConfigMgr 2012 because of the new application management capabilities specifically designed by the product team to provide all the capabilities that administrators use non-OSD task sequences for (and more of course), is still possible and has some benefits. Using task sequences in this manner is not explicitly covered in this chapter, but relatively straightforward.

Starting with the wizard-created deployment or Build and Capture task sequences is highly recommended because it properly inserts and orders a minimum set of tasks. Figure 19.7

19

shows the first dialog of the Create Task Sequence Wizard. Creating the two main types of task sequences is covered in the "Image Operations" section.

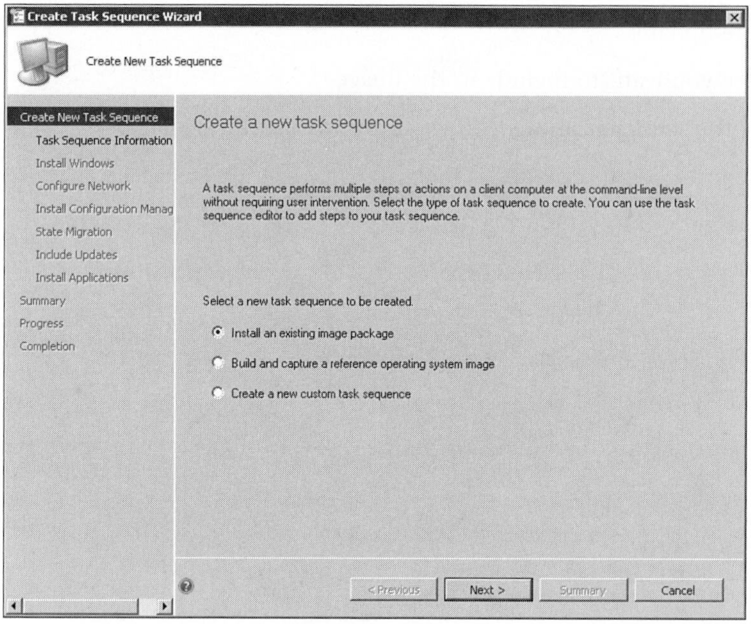

FIGURE 19.7   Create Task Sequence Wizard.

To edit a task sequence after creation, right-click it and choose **Edit** (choosing **Properties** from the context-menu results in the Properties dialog box of the task sequence and not the task sequence editor). Adding a task is a matter of choosing the **Add** drop-down menu, choosing a task category, and then selecting the task. Each task is customizable and has its own configurable parameters as discussed next.

Task Sequence Phases

Task sequences are not formally broken down into phases, but there are clearly different parts of the task sequence. Knowing what these different parts are responsible for is important to knowing how to organize your task sequence and how to troubleshoot it.

▶ **Startup:** This optional phase of the task sequence runs in a system's currently installed OS. This typically includes capturing the existing user data and saving it to an SMP or to the local hard disk using hard linking. Other possible tasks include upgrading the BIOS of the system, soliciting user input, or gathering other information about the system's current state or role.

This phase ends with a reboot into WinPE.

▶ **WinPE:** This phase executes completely in WinPE and prepares the system for Windows installation. It includes hard-drive preparation, unattended file creation and modification, and copying all files needed for Windows installation to the hard-drive including drivers and OS installation files.

This phase ends with a reboot to the OS installation files copied to the hard drive.

▶ **Windows Setup:** This phase runs Windows setup or mini-setup from the OS installation files copied to the hard drive—mini-setup is used if the OS installation files are from a sysprepped image, and full setup is run if they are from the installation media. Windows setup uses the information in the unattended file created and modified in the previous phase to ensure this phase is completely unattended. Applicable drivers are also installed by Windows setup, based upon what was copied to the hard disk in the WinPE phase and a plug-and-play scan of the existing hardware in the system.

This phase ends with a reboot into the newly installed Windows OS.

▶ **Post-Windows:** After Windows is installed, all other configurations that depend on the existence of a working installation of Windows are performed; thus, this phase executes in the newly installed Windows instance. This includes installing updates, applications, and performing any other customizations.

This phase ends when all tasks are finished in a normal deployment scenario. For Build and Capture task sequences, this phase ends when the preparation for imaging tasks begin.

▶ **Image Capture:** This final build and capture-only phase starts by preparing the ConfigMgr agent for imaging and sysprepping Windows; both of these tasks are performed in the newly installed Windows instance. Finally, the system is rebooted into WinPE, and the instance of Windows just installed is captured to a WIM file.

This phase ends when the image process completes. The system is rebooted after the image creation is complete; however, the system boots into the sysprepped version of the OS. Because no unattended setup file is available, the process stops to wait for user input at the beginning of mini-setup.

You can also execute commands before a task sequence even begins, using either a prestart command (discussed in the "Boot Image Customization" section) or by setting a program to run first (discussed in the next section) on the task sequence itself. Prestart commands execute in WinPE before the task sequence is executed and are a function of the boot image. Program dependencies execute in the current OS and only execute if the task sequence is initiated from the OS. Reasons for using one of these techniques include one or a combination of the following:

▶ Display a UI to the interactive to allow them to choose from a set of options.

▶ Configure the value of one or more task sequence variables used in the task sequence itself.

▶ Perform some other preparation of the system such as removing it from Active Directory, upgrading its BIOS, or checking the disk for errors.

Task Sequence Properties

A common mistake is to double-click a task sequence to edit the tasks it contains. (Don't confuse editing a task sequence, which involves creating, modifying, and deleting its tasks, with modifying its properties!). Double-clicking a task sequence, like nearly all double-clicks on objects in ConfigMgr, brings up the properties of that task sequence, which contains the following three pages:

▶ **General:** On this page, you set the Name and Description of the task sequence as well as defining a category. The title bar text of the progress dialog shown during the execution of the task sequence is also customized on this page.

▶ **Advanced:** This page contains several options:

> ▶ **Run another program first:** This option is valid only for task sequences started while in an existing OS. It runs the specified program from the specified package before executing the task sequence if the program has not previously run on the system. If the **Always run this program first** option is selected, the specified program is always run regardless of its previous run status or result.

> ▶ **Suppress task sequence notifications:** Does not notify the interactive user that the task sequence is available for deployment.

> ▶ **Disable task sequence on computers where it is deployed:** This disables the task sequence.

> ▶ **Maximum allowed run time (minutes):** The number of minutes specified for this option is used when calculating whether a task sequence should run in an available maintenance window. If a task sequence exceeds this time, it is not terminated; ConfigMgr simply ignores it.

> ▶ **Use a boot image:** Enables you to choose which boot image to use for this task sequence. For non-OSD task sequences, such as those used for deploying applications or a complex series of ordered tasks that may involve some advanced conditional logic available in a task sequence, you can choose to not use a boot image.

> ▶ **Run on any Platform or Run only on the specified platforms:** Enables you to limit which platforms a task sequence can run on. Note this setting is not honored if the task sequence is initiated from boot media or PXE. A common trick to allow constant task sequence availability from boot images or PXE but not the Software Center is to set this setting to an OS that is not in the environment or targeted by the deployment.

▶ **Security:** Identical to the security page for all other objects in ConfigMgr, this page displays which users have what permissions on this task sequence. You cannot edit permissions from this page.

Tasks

Tasks are the individual steps that perform each of the actions in a task sequence. Tasks and task sequences are similar to a macro-based programming language or a storyboard where you put together high-level steps and instructions using a graphical tool, without having to know or learn the syntax of the underlying language to take advantage of it fully. In addition, third parties can add tasks extending this pseudo-macro language, enhancing what you can do with task sequences.

There are six built-in categories of tasks:

▶ General

▶ Disks

▶ User State

▶ Images

▶ Drivers

▶ Settings

NOTE: MDT CATEGORY

MDT adds a seventh category to this list for its custom tasks; this category is appropriately named MDT.

Under each category is a set of tasks corresponding to that category. Each task is discussed briefly in the following sections. Some tasks must be combined with others and in a specific order for them to make sense—when required, it is noted in the discussion of that particular task.

You can disable each task independently using the Options tab; this allows you to disable tasks during troubleshooting.

General Category   Options under the General category (shown in Figure 19.8) include

▶ **Run Command Line:** This task allows you to run any valid command line that you want in your task sequence, including batch files and VBScripts. If the files referenced in the command line do not exist on the target computer, you can specify a package containing those files. Additional options include specifying a working directory for the command line, and a timeout to ensure that a command does not continue executing if it falls into an infinite loop or becomes otherwise hung.

The last option available allows you to specify the user account that runs the command. Without this option, the command uses the security credentials of Local System because all task sequences run in that context.

19

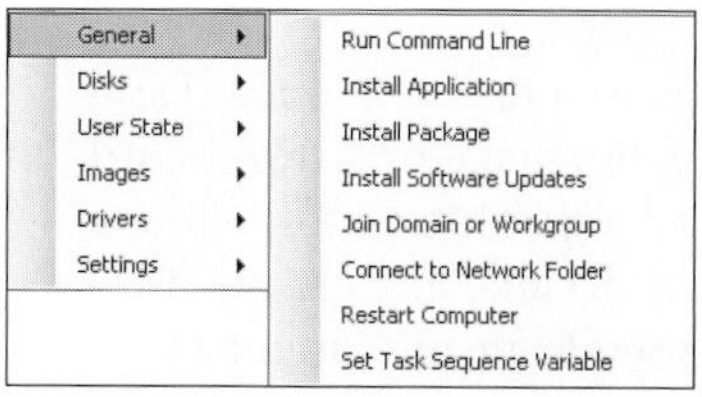

FIGURE 19.8   General tasks.

Because it is possible for multiple return codes to be considered as a successful execution of a given command line, there is an additional option on the Options tab, displayed in Figure 19.9, allowing you to configure numeric return values that should be considered a success. This field should contain integers separated by spaces. Only the first value listed can be negative. The typical success code of 0 is listed by default, along with 3010—denoting success with a reboot required.

NOTE: DOS COMMANDS

To use a DOS command such as md or copy, you must call the command as a parameter to the command interpreter cmd.exe—for example, `cmd.exe /c md MyNewDirectory`.

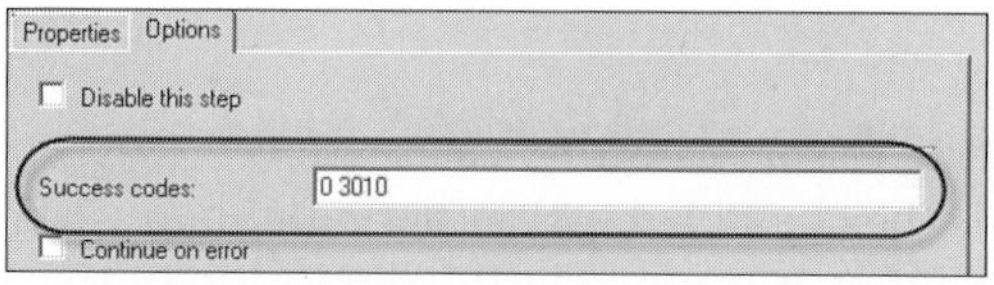

FIGURE 19.9   Run Command Line Success Codes.

▶ **Install Application:** This task installs a single application or multiple applications already defined in ConfigMgr, as described in Chapter 12.

The application must meet three distinct qualifications:

   ▶ It must run silently and not interact with the desktop.

   ▶ It must run with administrative privileges.

   ▶ It must not initiate a reboot; reboots can be handled with a task sequence if needed.

Any applications marked to run **Only when a user is logged on** or **Run with user rights** are not displayed and thus not selectable in this task.

When the Install Application step runs, the application checks the applicability of the requirement rules and detection method on the deployment types of the application. The application then installs the applicable deployment type. If a deployment type contains dependencies, the dependent deployment type is evaluated and installed as part of this step. Application dependencies are not supported for stand-alone media.

An advanced use of this task is to install multiple applications based on the value of a series of task sequence variables. You must name the variables with a single base name and then append a two-digit, sequential numeric suffix (such as Software01, Software02, Software03, and so on). Each variable should contain the name of application, nothing more, nothing less; this value is case-sensitive. A break in the sequence number stops evaluation of the variables; for example, if you have Software01, Software02, and Software04 and omit Software03, execution of programs stops at Software02.

Using a series of variables in this manner makes your task sequence dynamic by deferring the definition of which applications to install to the time it actually runs. The "Variables" section includes a complete discussion of defining and using task sequence variables.

Also, note that each application you intend to install using this task using a dynamic variable list must have the **Allow this application to be installed from the Install Application task sequence action instead of deploying manually** option set on the General tab of its Properties dialog box.

▶ **Install Package:** With this task, you can call any program from any package that you defined as part of software distribution. (Chapter 11 discusses defining packages for software deployment.) The program must meet the same three qualifications as those listed for applications in the previous bullet.

A caveat with program execution is that program dependencies are honored, but programs in the dependent chain are not automatically initiated. For example, if you configure ProgramA to run ProgramB with the Run another program first option, ProgramA does not automatically run ProgramB and fails to install unless ProgramB already ran on the system (presumably using another task). This occurs because the Run another program first option sets up a dependency chain that is checked before a program is run. In this example, ProgramA depends upon ProgramB. During software distribution, this setting automatically causes ConfigMgr to run ProgramB before ProgramA. However, this does not happen with OSD; the dependencies for ProgramA execution are not met, thus causing ProgramA to fail when it executes.

Similar to the Install Applications task described in this section, you can also specify a base task sequence variable name to install a list of packages. The format differs slightly though: each variable should contain a value matching the pattern `PackageID:Program Name`. Note the slight change from ConfigMgr 2007 where you used a three-digit suffix.

Also similar to applications, each program you intend to install with this task using a dynamic variable list must have the **Allow this program to be installed from the Install Package task sequence without being deployed** option set on the General tab of its Properties dialog box.

19

▶ **Install Software Updates:** This task allows you to incorporate software updates into an image, limiting the amount of time spent on updates after deploying the image. The task is also used to layer on updates not included in the image, allowing you to deploy fully patched systems. Updates used for this task are pulled directly from the ConfigMgr software updates facilities; these must be configured and performing properly and the ConfigMgr client installed on the target system prior to the task's execution. You cannot use this task to pull updates from any other source. There are two options for this task:

   ▶ **Install Mandatory Software Updates:** Installs all mandatory updates assigned to collection where the task sequence is advertised.

   ▶ **Install All Software Updates:** This installs all updates assigned to the collection where the task sequence is advertised.

NOTE: INSTALL UPDATES SECURITY EXPOSURE

The Install Software Updates task runs after Windows is installed and running on the target system. This means that any vulnerabilities not fixed by hotfixes or updates in the image deployed are subject to exploitation by the "bad guys." Here are some ways you can mitigate the risks:

▶ Building systems using OSD on a secured or locked-down network segment.

▶ Ensuring a quality host-based firewall (such as the built-in Windows firewall) is installed in the image and active as soon as the OS in the deployed image is booted. The Windows Firewall is enabled by default during WinPE portions of OSD and actively blocks all incoming traffic.

▶ Frequently rebuilding your base image to include the latest security updates (using a Build and Capture task sequence to automate the process).

▶ Using the built-in offline image maintenance capabilities to directly inject updates into images (see the "Offline Software Updates" section for details).

▶ Using the MDT Install Update Offline task. This task is similar to the built-in offline image maintenance capabilities but run during a Deployment task sequence. See http://blog.configmgrftw.com/?p=125 for an in-depth look at this task.

▶ **Join Domain or Workgroup:** This task allows you to join a workgroup or domain after Windows installation is completed later in a task sequence. Generally, this task is not used unless the domain join during Windows setup (which occurs during the Setup Windows and ConfigMgr task) fails to complete successfully. If you specify a domain name, you must also specify credentials capable of joining a system to the domain and an organizational unit (OU) to place the computer object.

CAUTION: DOMAIN USERS CAN JOIN ONLY 10 COMPUTERS TO A DOMAIN

By default, Domain Users can join only 10 computers to a domain (see Microsoft KB number 251335 for further details at http://support.microsoft.com/kb/251335). Because of the 10-computer join limitation, ensure that the account used in the Join Domain or

Workgroup task has been specifically delegated the ability to join systems to the domain. Failing to do so causes unexpected failures in the task sequence after it successfully runs 10 times.

▶ **Connect to Network Folder:** This task lets you map a drive letter to any shared folder using a UNC while specifying alternative credentials to make this connection. This drive letter is available in subsequent tasks to access resources available in that share. One common use for this task is to map a drive later used by another task to copy the task sequence logs to that shared folder, and then use it for troubleshooting or tracking purposes. An excellent discussion of this specific troubleshooting step is at http://blogs.msdn.com/steverac/archive/2008/07/15/capturing-logs-during-failed-task-sequence-execution.aspx.

▶ **Restart Computer:** This task restarts the host computer where the task sequence is currently running. After restart, the system can be set to boot either into the task sequence's specified boot image or into the just installed default OS. You can specify a message to display on the screen, providing feedback to anyone observing the task sequence's progress, along with a timeout in case no one is actually watching the task sequence.

CAUTION: YOU CANNOT BOOT INTO A PREVIOUSLY INSTALLED OS

After booting into WinPE during a task sequence, you cannot boot back into an OS instance that previously existed on the system using this task. Nothing prevents you from creating a task sequence that attempts this; however, this task will fail if a new OS has not been deployed during the task sequence.

▶ **Set Task Sequence Variable:** Setting task sequence variables allows you to configure available OSD-specific deployment options, configure variable application deployments with the Install Software task category, or execute future tasks in the task sequence conditionally.

Conditions can be applied to this step so that the variable is set only when specific conditions exist; you can then configure a future task to be performed based on this variable being set. The "Task Conditions and Grouping" section provides an example, and task sequence variables are covered in detail in the "Variables" section.

Disks Category A number of configurations are possible under the Disks option, shown in Figure 19.10:

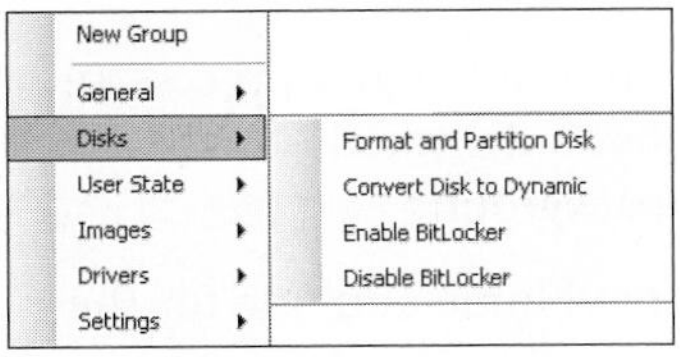

FIGURE 19.10 Disks tasks.

19

▶ **Format and Partition Disks:** This task allows you to configure the partitioning and formatting of all disks in the target system. If you plan to handle multiple physical disks, each must have its own instance of this task. Configuration options include specifying the physical disk number and the type of disk to create:

  ▶ A standard disk using a master boot record (MBR).

  ▶ A disk using a Globally Unique Identifier (GUID) partition table, known as a GPT. Note that GPT disks are not supported for boot disks except on Itanium systems.

In addition to specifying which disk to use and its partitions, you can create individual volumes:

  ▶ Each volume can be set to a percent of total space on the disk or hard-coded to a specific size.

  ▶ The format type can be specified (NTFS, FAT32, or none).

▶ The partition can be set to be a boot partition.

By default, a Quick format of the volume takes place; this is a change from ConfigMgr 2007 where a Quick format was not the default. A Full format can add unnecessary time to the task sequence when a quick format is normally sufficient.

The last option for this task allows you to store the drive letter used in a task sequence variable. This allows you to reference files on this volume or use the file system on this volume in future tasks by referencing this task sequence variable.

▶ **Convert Disk to Dynamic:** This task converts a specified disk to a dynamic disk. The only configuration option for this task is specifying the disk number to convert.

▶ **Enable BitLocker:** Only applicable to systems running Windows Vista or later, this task enables BitLocker on a specified disk. BitLocker encrypts the contents of an entire disk at a low-level. Here are additional configuration options:

  ▶ Where to store the startup key (Trusted Platform Module [TPM], USB drive, or both).

    Choosing USB startup key storage requires attaching a USB drive to the system during the execution of the task sequence.

  ▶ Where to store the recovery key (Active Directory or no storage).

  ▶ The final BitLocker configuration option chooses whether to wait for full encryption of the drive before the task sequence continues.

Depending on the current contents of the drive, this could be a lengthy process and greatly increase the running time of the task sequence. If you do not choose this option, drive encryption takes place dynamically in the background.

BitLocker requires two NTFS partitions: one for the system volume and one for the OS volume. The system volume partition must be at least 100MB in size with at least 64MB free and set as the active partition. Create these partitions in a Format and

Partition Disk task prior to executing the Enable BitLocker task in the task sequence if they do not already exist.

CAUTION: THE BITLOCKER PARTITION AND OS REFRESHES

The default and Windows-recommended method to partition a hard drive in preparation for Windows BitLocker is to include a 100MB system partition at the beginning of the drive, leaving the rest of the space for the partition holding the installed OS and protected by BitLocker encryption. If you manually install Windows 7, this partition scheme is automatic with Windows hiding the system partition.

Unfortunately, this partition is still visible to WinPE, meaning OSD sees this partition as the first partition on the disk and tries to use it when deploying the Windows image. With the partition being only 100MB, this operation will fail miserably.

The workaround is scripting a solution to detect the presence of this partition and adjusting the tasks accordingly, or using the easy solution of placing the boot partition at the end of the drive. This solution is even easier because the Windows team provided a BitLocker Drive Preparation tool (http://technet.microsoft.com/en-us/library/dd875534(v=WS.10).aspx) that shrinks the main partition of the drive and then adds a boot partition in the now-open space at the end. Using this tool also means not having to do anything special to your Format and Partition Disk task, and accounts for refresh scenarios that leave user data in place on the hard disk and therefore cannot format the disk.

Unfortunately, this does not address existing systems with the 100MB system partition at the beginning of the drive (you'll still have to script around those), but it prevents any of your deployed systems from causing a refresh to fail.

▶ **Disable BitLocker:** The exact opposite of enabling BitLocker, this task disables BitLocker on a specified drive. Decrypting the drive contents is dynamic and in the background; the task sequence does not wait for completion of this activity before continuing.

User State Category   A number of tasks are available under User State, displayed in Figure 19.11:

▶ **Request State Store:** The Request State Store task attempts to connect to a state migration point prior to capturing or restoring a user's state data.

If there are multiple state migration points in an environment, the task uses the first one listed on the site's management point with space available for the capture; for a site with multiple state migration points, each migration point is searched looking for the one with a computer association where the destination system is listed as a target.

You can specify the number of times to retry the connection and the delay between retries, and whether to capture or restore a user's state. An additional option allows using the Network Access account rather than the Computer account for connecting to the state migration point.

19

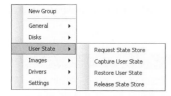

FIGURE 19.11   User State tasks.

This task creates a computer association if one does not already exist, as described in the "Computer Associations" section.

If the task is used to capture user state data, it creates an encryption key that stores the data securely; this key is stored with the computer association. If used to restore the user state data, this task retrieves the encryption key from the computer association.

The computer association also stores the exact path where the files are stored on the state migration point, and the times they were captured and restored. An additional option while creating a computer association is the ability to choose which user profiles to capture—either by using the User Accounts tab or by right-clicking an association after it is created and choosing **Specify User Accounts**. To recover captured user state data, see the discussion in the "Computer Associations" section in this chapter.

▶ **Capture User State:** This task initiates the use of USMT (described in the "User State Migration Tool" section) and captures the user state data using the USMT ScanState tool. A prerequisite for using this task is the existence of a software distribution package containing the files from an installation of USMT. In addition, you should place this task after a Request State Store task in your task sequence. Figure 19.12 shows the full Properties page for this task.

Additional options for this task include

  ▶ Use custom USMT configuration files

  ▶ Enable Verbose logging

  ▶ Skip files that use the Encrypting File System (EFS)

  ▶ Copy by using file system access

  ▶ Capture by using Volume Copy Shadow Services (VSS)

Select the Copy by using file system access has these additional options:

  ▶ Continue if some files cannot be captured

  ▶ Capture locally by using links instead of copying files

  ▶ Capture in off-line mode (Windows PE only)

Using each of these options is covered in detail in the "User State" section. Note the caveat next to some of the options, as shown in Figure 19.12, stating that USMT 4.0 is required.

You can customize the options passed to ScanState by setting the OSDMigrateAdditionalCaptureOptions task sequence variable.

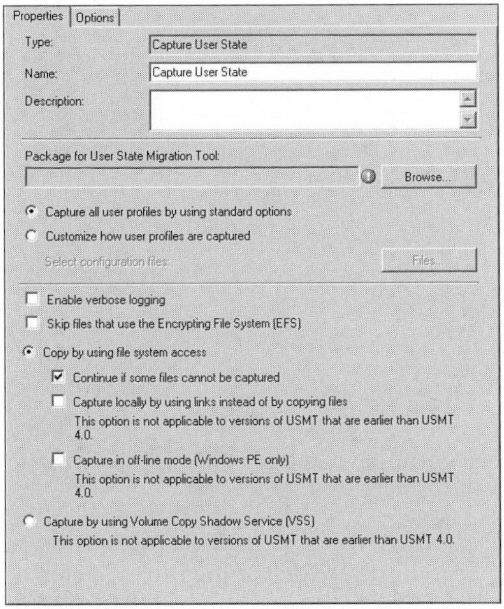

FIGURE 19.12   Capture User State Properties page.

▶ **Restore User State:** This is the mirror task for Capture User State and has similar options: a USMT package must exist, specification of non-default configuration files, continuation without raising an error when files cannot be restored, and verbose logging.

The one option that is different from the Capture User State task is the addition of a password for migrated local accounts. The password for these accounts cannot be migrated even though their data is, so you must supply a password to use them. You must use this task after a Request State Store task in a task sequence.

You can customize the options passed to USMT LoadState tool by setting the OSDMigrateAdditionalRestoreOptions task sequence variable.

▶ **Release State Store:** This task has no options and must be preceded by a Request State Store task and either a Capture User State or a Restore User State task.

    ▶ If used with a successful Capture User State task, this task tells the state migration point that the capture was completely successful and is ready to restore.

▶ If used with a successful Restore User State task, the task also communicates with the state migration point telling it that a successful restore took place. The state migration point then applies the configured retention settings on this data, allowing the storage space used by the data to be cleaned up.

Images Category   Tasks in the Images category focus on capturing and deploying images, OS configuration, Sysprep, and the ConfigMgr client agent. Figure 19.13 displays these tasks.

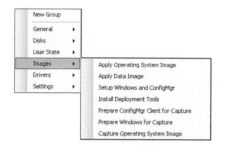

FIGURE 19.13   Image tasks.

▶ **Apply Operating System Image:** This is the central task in any OSD task sequence and performs one of two things:

  ▶ It applies an OS from a captured image to the target system. This is a destructive operation; OSD wipes the entire partition before delivering the image. A single folder is preserved from being wiped; the location of this folder is stored in the _SMSTSUserStatePath task sequence variable.

  ▶ It installs an OS on the target system using the original source files from an OS installer.

The options for this task are to specify a package containing unattended setup files and select a destination: Next available formatted partition, Specific disk and partition, Specific logical drive letter, or Logical drive letter stored in a variable.

If you specify an unattended files package for Windows XP and deploy an image, you should specify a sysprep.inf file. If you deploy an XP setup, use a unattend.txt file. Windows 7 uses the same XML file format regardless of the type of deployment. If you do not specify an unattended file, ConfigMgr uses an applicable default one.

If you need to create one (or more) of these unattended setup files, Microsoft provides several tools to facilitate this, depending on the OS being deployed:

  ▶ **Windows 7:** SIM for Windows 7 is part of the WAIK. A help file is also installed with the WAIK, Unattended Windows Setup Reference.chm, containing a comprehensive reference to the schema of the unattend.xml setup file.

▶ **Windows XP:** Setupmgr.exe for Windows XP is contained in the deploy.cab compressed file along with Sysprep. Also contained in deploy.cab is deploy. chm—a help file containing a complete reference to the valid schema and possible settings of the unattended setup files for Windows XP.

CAUTION: TASK SEQUENCE SIZE

Task sequences are limited to 10MB as measured by the size of the underlying XML that defines them—this is an increase from 4MB in ConfigMgr 2007. There is no corresponding absolute maximum number of task sequence steps, although in ConfigMgr 2007 the 4MB size often equated to approximately 450 tasks.

If you find yourself against this maximum size threshold, try moving some actions performed by your tasks into single, combined scripts or the unattended files.

▶ **Apply Data Image:** This task uses a pre-existing image imported into ConfigMgr as an OS image and applies it to a data partition. The same options for specifying a destination for the Apply Operating System Image task are available for the Apply Data Image task. Unlike the Apply Operating System Image task, this task is non-destructive and preserves all data on the specified destination.

▶ **Setup Windows and ConfigMgr:** This task must be included in task sequences as it actually initiates Windows setup (or mini-setup), reboots, and then installs the ConfigMgr agent allowing the rest of the task sequence to complete. There is no way to avoid installing the ConfigMgr client agent in a task sequence that deploys Windows.

The only prerequisite is the package containing the ConfigMgr client, which you must select for this task. Although you can create your own package for this, the best practice is to use the built-in Configuration Manager Client Agent package. Additional installation properties used to install the ConfigMgr client can also be specified. By default, any additional installation properties specified for client installation on the Installation Properties tab of the Client Push Installation Properties dialog are automatically copied to this task. See Chapter 9, "Configuration Manager Client Management," for more details about specifying client push properties.

▶ **Install Deployment Tools:** The main job of this task is to make the Sysprep files available to the task sequence. The task typically is used only in Build and Capture task sequences. Sysprep is included in the installation of Windows 7, so this task does not need a package specified when deploying Windows 7. If the OS version installed is XP, a package containing the Sysprep files from the corresponding deploy.cab file must be specified.

▶ **Prepare ConfigMgr Client for Capture:** This task is required before capturing an OS image from a target system. It prepares the ConfigMgr client agent to be part of an image by stripping it of any unique identifiers. There are no options for this task.

19

▶ **Prepare Windows for Capture:** This task runs the actual Sysprep on an installed OS, stripping it of any uniqueness and preparing it for capture in an image. There are only two options available for this task:

   ▶ Automatically build mass storage driver list.

   The build mass storage driver list option is equivalent to using the `bmsd` option with Sysprep and allows a deployed image to use any available mass-storage driver available. This option is not applicable to Windows 7 even though it is available.

   ▶ Do not reset activation flag.

   The Do not reset activation flag option is equivalent to the activate option of Sysprep and is only used only when you capture an image of an OS that has already been activated. This option is rarely used.

▶ **Capture Operating System Image:** This task captures an image of the installed OS on the target system to a WIM file using ImageX. Two parameters are required:

   ▶ The first parameter is a filename for the destination WIM file. This filename needs to be fully qualified to include the destination UNC and can be on any accessible folder share; for example, \\<servername>\Captures\ Win7SP1Ent-x64.wim.

   ▶ The second parameter is an account and its associated password with permissions to write to the specified location.

   Optional parameters are metadata to associate with the image including the creator, version, and description.

CAUTION: WIM CAPTURE

If you hard code the WIM filename and location, ensure you copy or move the WIM file from the folder where it was captured to prevent another execution of this task from over-writing it.

Drivers Category   There are two driver-specific tasks, as shown in Figure 19.14. Both tasks inject drivers into an image or OS during its deployment.

FIGURE 19.14   Driver tasks.

▶ **Auto Apply Drivers:** Using this task, you tell the task sequence to first run a plug-and-play check on the target system's hardware generating a list of plug-and-play IDs; this check emulates the plug-and-play check that Windows setup performs.

The task compares the list of IDs to the driver catalog maintained by OSD copying those best matched to the target system. For Windows 7, the drivers are directly added to the deployed image's driver store using DISM and its offline image management capabilities. For Windows XP, the unattended setup file is modified to reference the copied drivers for usage during the full Windows setup or mini-setup on Sysprepped images.

Options for this task include

  ▶ Copying the best matched drivers

  ▶ Copying all compatible drivers and choosing the categories of the drivers to consider for matching

  ▶ Bypass checking of a signature on drivers on operating systems that allow it— this option has no effect on 64-bit Windows editions because all drivers must be signed on these systems

▶ **Apply Driver Package:** Use this task to tell the task sequence to copy all the drivers in a particular driver package to a target system and either use DISM for Windows 7 to add them to the driver store or update the unattended setup files with those drivers for Windows XP. The Apply Driver Package task skips the plug-and-play pre-check performed by the Auto Apply Drivers task and forces ConfigMgr to copy the specified drivers.

Using this task, you can deploy mass-storage drivers such as SATA drivers to Windows XP. Windows 7 has no need to handle mass-storage drivers differently than regular drivers, so this option is a no-op if deploying Windows 7.

You would also use this task in cases where the plug-and-play pre-detection used by the Auto Apply Drivers task is not picking up the proper driver or the hardware is not yet attached to the system, as is the case for locally attached printers and scanners.

Options include choosing a particular package, choosing the specific mass-storage device driver to use from the package, and overriding the requirement to use signed drivers.

Settings Category   Settings tasks capture specific settings from a source system and restore them during an in-place migration or allows you to specify the specific settings during a side-by-side migration or new installation. These settings are not directly applied to the target system; they are merged into the unattended answer file in use for the application by Windows setup or mini-setup. Figure 19.15 shows available settings tasks.

FIGURE 19.15   Settings tasks.

▶ **Capture Network Settings:** This task, used for refresh scenarios, captures the network settings of a source system before wiping the system. These settings are automatically migrated to the system after deploying the OS and override any settings specified in an Apply Network Settings task. The two network settings that can be migrated are the domain and workgroup membership and the network adapter configuration. If neither option is selected, the task is benign.

▶ **Capture Windows Settings:** Similar to the Capture Network Settings task, this task captures specific Windows settings and migrates them during refresh scenario; these settings override any settings specified in an Apply Windows Settings task. The Windows settings that can be migrated are the computer name, username and organization name, and the time zone. If you do not select any options, this task does nothing.

▶ **Apply Network Settings:** This task sets network settings on a target system including joining a domain or workgroup and network adapter settings. If joining a domain, an account and password must be set that has privileges to join the domain. You can configure multiple network adapters individually; each can be set to use DHCP or a statically assigned Internet Protocol (IP) address. You can also specify static DNS and WINS settings and advanced filtering settings. Settings specified in this task are overridden by those captured using a Capture Network Settings task. Settings specified using this task are added to the unattended setup file in use, which is then used by Windows setup or mini-setup during the Setup Windows and ConfigMgr task.

For Build and Capture task sequences, joining a domain is not necessary and not recommended because systems joined to a domain often have configuration changes made to them by group policy, login scripts, or other tools that should not be in a generic, reference image.

CAUTION: ORGANIZATION UNITS AND DOMAIN FQDNS

Do not specify the default AD Computers container as the OU in the Apply Network Settings or Join Domain or Workgroup tasks. This container is not an OU and specifying it causes the domain join to fail. In addition, if you specify the FQDN of the AD domain you want the system to join you must also supply an OU; failure to do so also causes the domain join to fail. If you provide the NETBIOS (or short) name of the domain, you do not need to add the OU.

► **Apply Windows Settings:** This task sets specific Windows settings on the target system including username, organization name, product key, server licensing model, local administrator password, and time zone. Settings specified using this task are also added to the unattended setup file in use which is then used by Windows setup or mini-setup during the Setup Windows and ConfigMgr task. A product key is not required for Windows 7 because it automatically operates in an evaluation mode (called the *grace period*) for 120 days that does not require a product key. Settings specified in this task are overridden by those captured using a Capture Windows Settings task.

CAUTION: DO NOT DISABLE THE ADMINISTRATOR ACCOUNT IN WORKGROUPS

Do not set the local Administrator account to disabled when deploying an image to a system that will not be part of a domain; you will then have a system you cannot access because the only user account on the system is disabled.

Task Placement

Most tasks must be placed in relation to certain other tasks in a task sequence for them to properly function, specifically the Setup Windows and ConfigMgr task. While it is technically possible to place many tasks before or after this task, it doesn't usually make sense to do so. In addition, some tasks are only applicable when run in WinPE, the target instance of Windows being deployed, or the source instance of Windows in a refresh scenario. Table 19.2 lists these various placement requirements.

TABLE 19.2   Task Placement Requirements

Task Name	Before or After Setup Windows and ConfigMgr	WinPE, Deployed OS, or Source OS	Other
Run Command Line	Either	WinPE or Deployed OS	
Install Application	After	Deployed OS	
Install Package	After	Deployed OS	
Install Software updates	After	Deployed OS	
Join Domain or Workgroup	After	Deployed OS	
Connect to Network Folder	Either	WinPE or Deployed OS	
Restart Computer	Either	WinPE or Deployed OS	
Set Task Sequence Variable	Either	WinPE or Deployed OS	

Task Name	Before or After Setup Windows and ConfigMgr	WinPE, Deployed OS, or Source OS	Other
Format and Partition Disks	Before	WinPE	
Convert Disk to Dynamic	Either	WinPE or Deployed OS	
Enable BitLocker	After	Deployed OS	
Disable BitLocker	Before	Source OS	
Request State Store	Either	Any	
Capture User State	Before	WinPE or Source OS	The task must be preceded by a Request State Store task and followed by a Release State Store task if you want to store the state data on a state migration point.
Restore User State	After	Deployed OS	The task must be preceded by a Request State Store task and followed by a Release State Store task if you want to retrieve the state data from a state migration point.
Release State Store	Either	Any	This task must follow a Request State Store task. Typically a Capture User State or Restore User State task is inserted in between.
Apply Operating System Image	Before	WinPE	
Apply Data Image	Before	WinPE	
Setup Windows and ConfigMgr	N/A	WinPE	
Install Deployment Tools	After	Deployed OS	
Prepare ConfigMgr Client for Capture	After	Deployed OS	
Prepare Windows for Capture	After	Deployed OS	
Capture Operating System Image	After	WinPE	
Auto Apply Drivers	Before	WinPE	
Apply Driver Package	Before	WinPE	

Task Name	Before or After Setup Windows and ConfigMgr	WinPE, Deployed OS, or Source OS	Other
Capture Network Settings	Before	Source OS	
Capture Windows Settings	Before	Source OS	
Apply Network Settings	Before	WinPE	
Apply Windows Settings	Before	WinPE	

Variables

A major advantage that task sequences have over the traditional software delivery mechanism used in Systems Management Server (SMS) and now ConfigMgr is that they maintain state between steps. This state is embodied in a series of built-in variables and custom variables that survive reboots because they are stored in a locally persistent file, allowing you to pass data or configuration items from one step to the next. The task that the task sequence is currently executing is also part of the task sequence's state; in fact, every detail about a task sequence is stored as one or more task sequence variables. Variables are encrypted for security when initially transmitted between ConfigMgr and the target system and are securely stored on the target system. Here are the three types of variables available:

▶ **Action:** Specify parameters for specific tasks. Nearly all are directly editable using the task sequence editor.

▶ **Custom:** Simple name and value pairs that you can define as you see fit.

▶ **Built-in:** Mostly read-only, start with an underscore, are generated automatically by the task sequence, and generally describe the environment where the task sequence executes.

The full list of task sequence action and built-in variables is available at http://technet. microsoft.com/en-us/library/gg682064.aspx. Each UI field shown in a task in the task sequence editor has a corresponding task sequence variable. Setting these values in the UI defines the action's design time behavior. This is great if you want a completely static task sequence that always does the same thing. Setting task sequence variables based upon collection membership or using a script during the execution of the task sequence makes your task sequences dynamic, performing tasks differently or even performing different tasks based upon run-time conditions. Action variables and custom variables can be set in a number of ways:

▶ Using a Set Task Sequence Variable task

▶ Statically assigning them to a specific computer resource

19

▶ Statically assigning them to a collection

▶ Using the Microsoft.SMS.TSEnvironment COM object in a script or other COM
aware tool, development environment, or language. See http://msdn.microsoft.com/
en-us/library/cc145669.aspx for more information on using this COM object. A
small collection of useful sample starter scripts is available as online content for this
book and described in Appendix D, "Available Online."

You can also set a task sequence variable on a device collection or a computer resource in
the ConfigMgr console. For device collections, open the collection's Properties dialog and
navigate to the Collection variables page; for a computer resource, open the resource's
Properties dialog and navigate to the Variables page. Task sequences initiated on applicable resources will have all variables initially set.

If you leave the value of a collection or computer variable blank, the built-in task
sequence UI prompts the user for values for these empty variables. The article at http://
blog.configmgrftw.com/?p=44 provides a detailed description of this capability.

Here is the precedence for task sequence variables:

1. Task sequence variables set at run-time (using a Set Task Sequence Variable task or
   the Microsoft.SMS.TSEnvironment COM object)

2. Task sequence variables set on computer resources

3. Task sequence variables set on collections

4. Task sequence variables set at design-time in the GUI

You can use variables for these tasks:

▶ Conditionally execute tasks. (See an example of this in the "Conditions and
Groupings" section.)

▶ Perform string replacement in any text field in any task. (See the example later in
this section and Figure 19.16.)

▶ Provide task-specific parameter values. (See the example in this section and
Figure 19.16.)

▶ Perform string replacement in unattended files. (Ronni Pedersen's article at http://
myitforum.com/cs2/blogs/rpedersen/archive/2008/07/01/using-task-sequence-vari-
ables-to-customize-deployments.aspx provides a detailed example.)

For string replacement and parameter values, surround the name of the variable with %
symbols; for example for a variable named MyCustomVar, use %MyCustomVar%. The
task sequence engine replaces this with the value of the variable. For example, using the
following command as the command line for a Run Command Line task (as shown in

Figure 19.16) demonstrates adding an entry to the registry that you can later utilize to track the deployment version used when creating the system.

```
reg /add HKLM\Software\Odyssey\OSDBuild /v Version /t REG_STRING /d
➡%OSDBUILDVERSION%
```

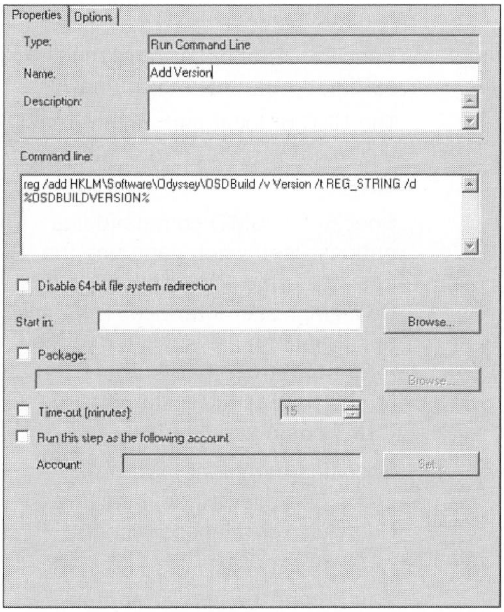

FIGURE 19.16   Task sequence variable replacement.

You can supply the actual value of OSDBUILDVERSION, and thus the version written to the registry, using any of the methods previously discussed in this section.

The "Task Conditions and Grouping" section gives an additional example of using custom variables. Some notable task sequence variables often set dynamically at run-time of the task sequence to customize the OS deployment outcome are listed in Table 19.3.

TABLE 19.3   Notable Task Sequence Variables

Variable	Tasks	Purpose
OSDDomainOUName	Apply Network Settings	Specifies the full path to the organizational unit (OU) that the computer joins (in RFC 1779 format). For example: LDAP://OU=MyOu,DC=MyDom, DC=MyCompany,DC=com

19

Variable	Tasks	Purpose
OSDDomainName	Apply Network Settings	Specifies the name of a Windows domain the destination computer joins.
OSDComputerName	Apply Windows Settings	Specifies the name of the computer.
OSDTimeZone	Apply Windows Set-tings	Specifies the default time zone setting that is used in the new OS.
OSDStateStorePath	Capture User State, Release State Store	The UNC or local path name of the folder where the user state is saved.
OSDMigrateAdditional CaptureOptions	Capture User State	Specifies (USMT) command line options used when capturing the user state, but not exposed in the ConfigMgr user interface. The additional options are specified in the form of a string that is appended to the automatically generated USMT command line.
SMSClientInstallProperties	Setup Windows and ConfigMgr	Specifies the client installation properties used when installing the Configuration Manager client.
SMSTSRebootDelay	N/A	Specifies how many seconds to wait before the computer restarts. The task sequence manager will display a notification dialog before reboot if this variable is not 0.
SMSTSAssignUsersMode	N/A	Used for enabling user device affinity (UDA).

Task Conditions and Grouping

You can apply conditions to the execution of any task allowing execution only when certain conditions exist or statements evaluate to true—for example, if the hardware model of the system is a Dell E6510. This makes task sequences flexible and allows you to build complex, multipurpose task sequences. Add conditions to a task by going to the Properties tab of a task and using the Add Condition drop-down button.

Each condition evaluates to either true or false; if all listed conditions evaluate to true, the task executes normally. The task is skipped if any condition evaluates to false.

Conditions can be combined using If statements forming a master conditional statement. Master statements are a collection of substatements; they evaluate to either true or false based upon the logical evaluation of their substatements. There are three types of master statements; each type of evaluation affects how the master statement is evaluated:

▶ All child statements must be true.

▶ Any child statement is true.

▶ No child statements are true.

You can chain If statements to form complex logical statements. If statements in this context closely resemble the traditional logical operators "and" and "or", and can be used in a similar way.

Conditions can be built based on the value of a task sequence variable, the OS version, a file's version or timestamp, a folder's timestamp, a value from the registry, a WMI Query, or installed software. One thing to be aware of is that conditions are evaluated at the point they are defined in the task sequence. What this means is that if you want to perform a task based on the state of the current OS after the initial reboot of the system into WinPE, you must set a conditional variable before the reboot and use that conditional variable to execute the desired task conditionally.

For example, perform the following steps to install Microsoft XML Notepad during a refresh scenario, using a task that executes only if the software was installed previously on the system:

1. Create a Set Task Variable task before the Restart in WinPE task. This is important to place before the first Restart in WinPE task so that it runs in the currently installed OS. This task is effectively a no-op in a replace or new computer scenario.

2. Set a variable, such as InstallXMLNotepad, to True.

3. Go to the Options tab of this task and add an Install Software condition; locate and select the installation MSI for the product when prompted, XMLNotepad.msi in this case. Figure 19.17 shows the result.

4. Highlight the Install XML Notepad task in the task tree on the left to edit it; select the Options tab for this task and add a new task sequence variable condition. Set this condition to check the value of InstallXMLNotepad equal to True.

You can collect tasks into a hierarchy of groups. This allows tasks to be aesthetically organized, and also gives the flexibility of conditionally executing tasks in a group and discontinuing the execution of a group of tasks if one fails, without affecting the entire task sequence. You can add separate execution conditions to each group in the exact same way that you add them to an individual task. ConfigMgr evaluates each task for its completion state; checking whether it completed successfully, and performs the following actions for an unsuccessful task:

▶ If a task does not complete successfully, the group containing the task is also set to unsuccessful, and ConfigMgr discontinues processing tasks in the group.

▶ If the task is not contained in a parent group, then the task sequence itself is set to unsuccessful and terminated.

19

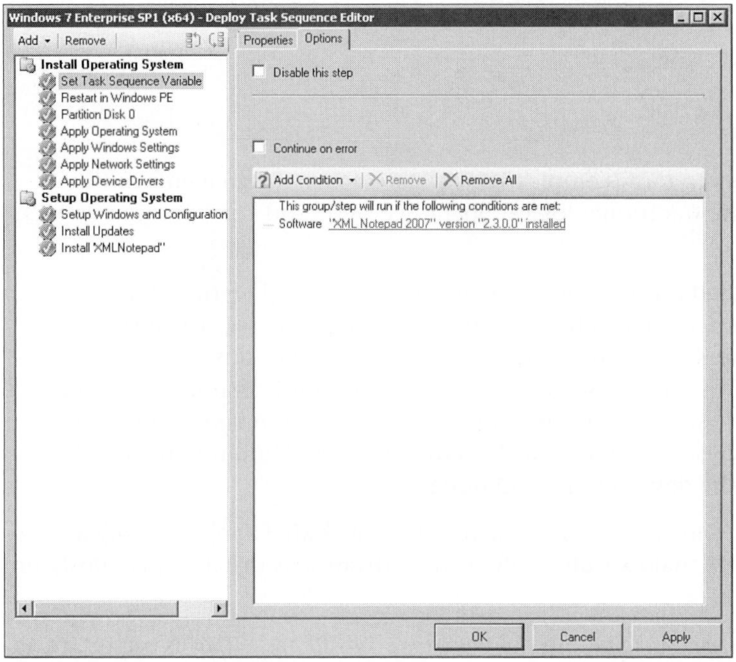

FIGURE 19.17   Checking for the Installation of XML Notepad.

You can override the default behavior using the Continue on Error option available on the Options tab of each task and group. If the Continue on Error option is set, ConfigMgr ignores the error state of the task or group and processing continues sequentially as if no error occurred. You can find an excellent example of grouping tasks together to control the flow of a task sequence and handling errors at http://blogs.msdn.com/steverac/archive/2008/07/15/capturing-logs-during-failed-task-sequence-execution.aspx.

Targeting and Execution

Like other deployable objects in ConfigMgr, task sequences must be deployed to a set of systems defined by a collection. Targeting a task sequence is similar to software distribution. Deployments can be either required or available. (This is the new terminology for ConfigMgr 2012; in ConfigMgr 2007, these were respectively referred to as mandatory or nonmandatory advertisements.) Required task sequences execute according to the defined schedule and require no human intervention.

> **CAUTION: REQUIRED TASK SEQUENCES**
>
> Poorly planned or executed required task sequences have wiped out production Exchange servers, CFO's laptops, and entire casinos, to name just a few known examples. Be careful when using required task sequences and ensure that you target the systems that you think you are targeting. There is no technical way to prevent administrator misconfiguration, whether accidental or willful.

You must define a network access account for task sequences to execute successfully. This is because part of the task sequence executes in an environment—WinPE—that has no identity on the network but requires access to network resources in the form of content on the DPs. Therefore, OSD uses the network access account as its identity for those tasks that require authentication across the network. The network access account requires no special permissions; it should be a normal user account and following the least-user privilege paradigm should not be any sort of administrator. Chapter 20 discusses the general use of the Network Access account, configured on a per-site basis. Follow these steps:

1. In the console, navigate to **Administration** -> **Site Configuration** -> **Sites**.

2. In the right pane, select the site where you want to configure the Network Access account.

3. Choose **Software Distribution** from the Configure Site Components fly-out menu on the ribbon bar or the right-click context-menu.

4. In the Software Distribution Component Properties dialog, select the Network Access Account tab. On this tab, select the **Specify the account that accesses network locations** option and use the **Set** button to configure the account.

To create a task sequence deployment, select the task sequence in the console, and choose **Deploy** from the ribbon bar or right-click content menu. This displays the Deploy Software Wizard with the following significant pages:

▶ **General:** On this page, choose the collection to target with this task sequence.

▶ **Deployment Settings:** Choose the purpose for the task sequence on this page: either Available or Required. Also, choose to make the task sequence available to boot media and PXE. Not choosing this option prevents the task sequence from being used for new computer scenarios.

▶ **Scheduling:** This page is for setting the available and expired times for the task sequence. For required deployments, you must also add an assignment schedule and choose the rerun behavior from these self-explanatory options:

    ▶ Never rerun deployed program

    ▶ Always rerun program

    ▶ Rerun if previous attempt failed

    ▶ Rerun if succeeded on previous attempt

Do not confuse the start time with the assignment schedule times. Deployment start times merely indicate when the deployment is visible to the targeted system, and assignment schedule times are when required deployments are actually set to run.

19

▶ **User Experience:** The following check box-based options exist on this page:

  ▶ Allow users to run independently of assignments—this option is always checked for available deployments

  ▶ Show Task Sequence progress

  ▶ Allow software installation outside the maintenance windows

  ▶ Allow system restart outside the maintenance window

  ▶ Allow task sequence to run for client on the Internet

▶ **Alerts:** This page is for setting up console-based alerts according to a threshold for successful or failed deployments. Only failed deployment alerts are available for available deployments.

▶ **Distribution Points:** On this page, specify if content is downloaded locally when needed by the running task sequence or if content is downloaded locally before starting the task sequence. In addition, the following two check boxes are provided to direct DP selection for content:

  ▶ When no local distribution point is available, use a remote distribution point

  ▶ Allow clients to use a fallback source location for content

Known Computers   As the name implies, known computers are those ConfigMgr has knowledge of. These are easy to target because they already exist as resources in ConfigMgr. You can add known resources to specific collections that have specific task sequences targeted at them. For example, you may have different task sequences for different Windows versions or editions or different departments in your organization. The requirements for each of these deployment types is separated into different task sequences that in turn are deployed to distinct collections. Placing the system into one of these collections deploys the corresponding task sequence to that system.

It is possible to pre-stage resources in ConfigMgr as long as you know the system's Media Access Control (MAC) address or SMBIOS GUID. Pre-staging computers is often used for new computer deployment scenarios. Pre-staging the systems allows you to place the computer resource in a specific collection so that it automatically receives a specific task sequence targeted at that collection. To pre-stage systems, follow these steps:

1. In the console, navigate to **Assets and Compliance -> Overview -> Devices**. Choose **Import Computer Information** from the ribbon bar or right-click context menu.

2. This launches the Import Computer Information Wizard, where you can add a single or multiple systems to the ConfigMgr database as a computer resource.

  ▶ To add a single computer, choose **Import single computer** from the first page of the wizard. The next page is the Single Computer page, as shown in Figure 19.18. Enter the desired computer name and either the MAC address or SMBIOS GUID of the new system; both are not required and using the MAC address is preferred because it is usually easier to obtain. If both are supplied, the SMBIOS GUID is tried first. You can obtain this information when PXE booting a system from the PXE boot screen or by checking smspxe.log. You can also get this information shipped to you by the computer manufacturer when it sends you the hardware. (Although ConfigMgr administrators often don't see the shipment manifest.)

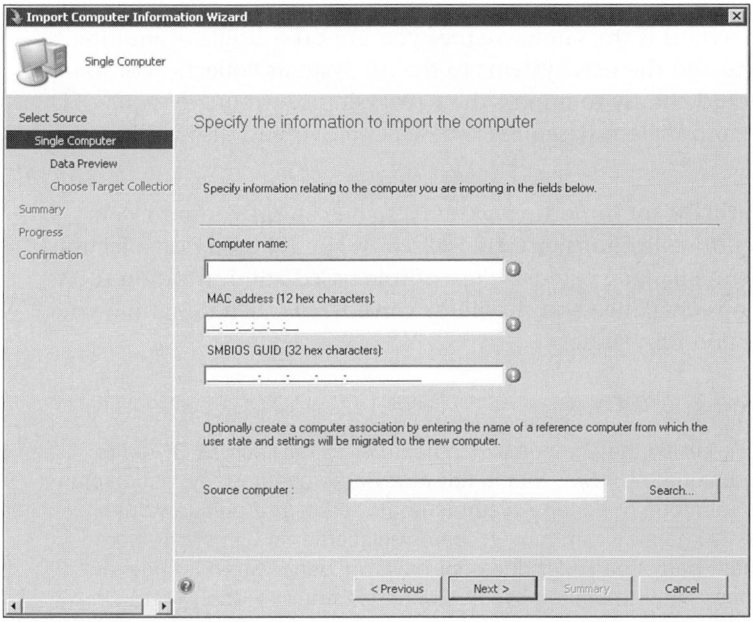

FIGURE 19.18   Importing a single computer using the Import Computer Information Wizard.

TIP: LOCATING THE SMSPXE.LOG

If the PXE deployment point is on a site server, the smspxe.log is located in %*ProgramFiles*%\SMS_CCM\Logs; otherwise, you can find it in %*windir*%\system32\ccm\logs.

You can also specify a source computer to import user and system state settings from; this creates a computer association with the specified computer as the source and the new system as the target. Do not confuse importing a computer using this wizard with creating a computer association. By specifying a source computer in this wizard, a computer association will also be created for you automatically; these are by no means the same thing though.

▶ Importing computers one at a time can be time-consuming; alternatively, you can import multiple computers at once using a file formatted with comma-separated values (CSV). Create this file with Microsoft Excel, Notepad, or any other text editor and save the file using plain text format. The file must contain the desired names of the systems and either their MAC addresses or SMBIOS GUIDs, comma-separated. Optionally, you can specify the source computer for user and system state migration.

To import multiple computers, choose the **Import computers** using a file option from the Import Computer Information Wizard. The wizard prompts you for the CSV file to use and allows you to map the data in the file to the correct columns.

The last page of the wizard is the same whether you import a single or multiple computers: Choose to add the new systems to the All Systems collection or to one you specify. You should choose to import the new systems into one of your OSD collections, so the appropriate task sequence-based deployments also apply to your new systems.

A major limitation at RTM for importing systems is you can only import new computer resources into collections directly limited by the All Systems collection. For larger environments making extensive use of role-based administration (RBA), this may pose a serious challenge and should be considered when designing your collection hierarchy and RBA strategy.

CAUTION: UNIQUE SMBIOS GUIDS

SMBIOS GUIDs are values set by the computer manufacturer at the factory. By definition, SMBIOS GUIDs are unique; however, this is not always the case. Many manufacturers of custom hardware solutions or generic systems do not configure unique values; this has also been known to happen with motherboard replacements by tier-one hardware vendors. For the most part, ConfigMgr does not have an issue with this; however, during PXE boot operations, the PXE booted system identifies itself to ConfigMgr using the SMBIOS GUID. With non-unique values, this becomes problematic. There is no supported solution to address this in ConfigMgr because the hardware vendors are not following their own accepted guidelines and standards for populating this value. For a complete discussion, see http://blogs.technet.com/b/system_center_configuration_manager_operating_system_deployment_support_blog/archive/2011/10/19/no-assigned-task-sequence-when-initiating-deployments-caused-by-duplicate-smbios-guids-system-uuids-in-system-center-configuration-manager-2007.aspx.

Unknown Computers   Prestaging all systems is a potentially labor-intensive task. An alternative to pre-staging systems not already in ConfigMgr is to use the two built-in unknown computer resources: one for x86 systems and one for x64. These resources do not represent a real computer but are used to target task sequence deployments for any system not yet known to ConfigMgr. Thus, any time a system not already managed by ConfigMgr begins the OSD process, one of these two objects is used to determine which task sequences are applicable. Unknown computer targeting is only applicable to new computer deployment scenarios in which the system is either PXE booted or booted from media directly into WinPE.

The All Unknown Computers collection is not a special collection in any way. It is often used because by default it contains the unknown computer objects. It is perfectly acceptable to add the unknown computer objects to other collections or remove them from the All Unknown Computers collection to manipulate task sequence deployment targeting; however, adding the unknown computer objects to multiple collections makes all task sequences deployed to those collections available to any unknown system starting a task sequence.

Each primary site has its own corresponding unknown computer objects. In practical terms, there is no real functional difference between the unknown objects of different sites: Unknown is unknown no matter which site the object lives in. If a system is unknown, it uses the unknown object of whichever site's management point it connects to during the initial start-up phase of the task sequence. With dynamic boot media, this could be variable based upon a client's location, making it possible to use different task sequences for unknown computers in different sites.

You must separately enable unknown computer support on each PXE-enabled DP and any boot media that you create. You may have reasons not to enable it for each and every one of these, though; this is perfectly valid.

Perform these steps to enable unknown computer support for your PXE-enabled DPs:

1. In the console, navigate to **Administration** -> **Site Configuration** -> **Servers and Site System Roles**, and select the site system hosting the DP.

2. In the Detail pane at the bottom, select **Distribution Point**, and then choose **Properties** from the ribbon bar or right-click context menu.

3. Select the PXE tab in the resulting Properties dialog, and check the **Enable unknown computer support** check box.

You can only enable boot media for unknown computer support at the time you create the media using the Create Task Sequence Media Wizard, as shown in Figure 19.19.

If a computer resource in ConfigMgr contains either the SMBIOS GUID or MAC address of a system, that system is known by ConfigMgr whether it has an active ConfigMgr client agent on it or not. This, by definition, means that the system is not unknown, and therefore task sequences targeted to the unknown computer resources are not applicable to it. To make a system unknown, simply delete the computer resource in ConfigMgr that contains that system's MAC address or SMBIOS GUID.

Sometimes it is difficult to locate which resource in the console references a system's MAC address or SMBIOS GUID. To locate the computer resource, use a query as discussed in Chapter 17, "Configuration Manager Queries."

Content Availability   For a task sequence to be successful, all the content it references and needs to execute must be available to the client while the task sequence runs. The first thing that the task sequence engine does when it executes a task sequence is verify that all content referenced in the task sequence is available on an accessible DP. Instead of manually having to find all the content in the task sequence and individually assigning each to a DP (as you had to in ConfigMgr 2007), the new Distribute Content Wizard in ConfigMgr 2012 determines all the content statically referenced in a given task sequence and assigns it to a DP. To launch this wizard, select any task sequence in the console and choose **Distribute Content** from the ribbon bar or right-click context menu. The only choice to make during the wizard is to choose a target DP or set of target DPs.

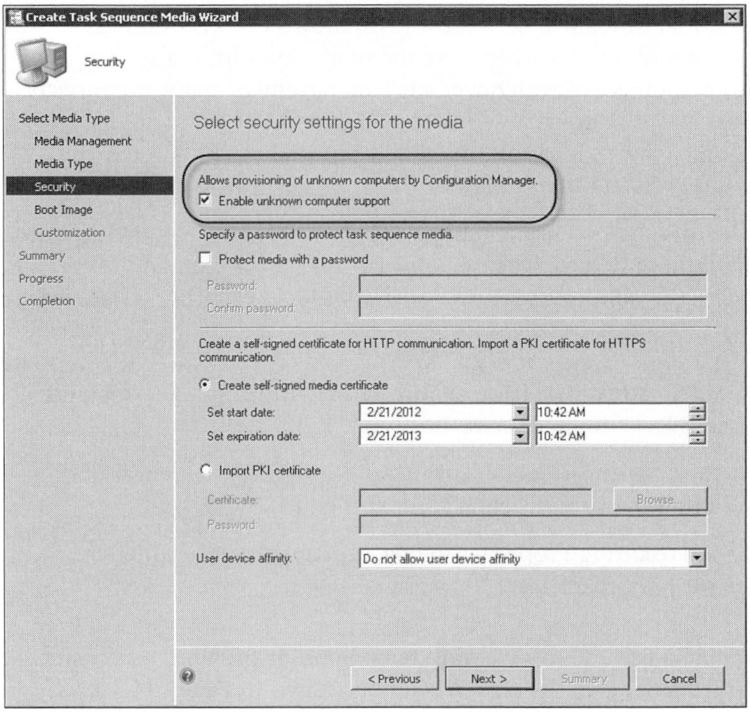

FIGURE 19.19   Enabling unknown computer support in the Create Task Sequence Media Wizard.

Execution Context

Execution context refers to a concept important to know when digging below the surface of OSD during troubleshooting, customization, or any advanced implementations.

Task sequences run as the Local System account of the system they run on. This includes the WinPE portions as well as the Windows portions and even non-OSD task sequences used for advanced application deployment or other tasks. This cannot be changed.

This means all tasks and commands run as Local System including application installation. If you specifically need to run a task as another user account, use the Run Command-Line task and its alternative credential capability.

Another ramification of using Local System is the system's Active Directory computer account is used to access network resources specifically referenced during the task sequence in custom scripts or command-line tasks. This does not include access to referenced ConfigMgr content or packages directly used by the task sequence that, as discussed in the "Targeting and Execution" section, use the Network Access account first and then fall back to this account if the Network Access account does not have access to the content.

Change Control and Portability

Nothing is specifically built in to assist in managing changes for task sequences, although there are several things you can do to avoid losing work:

▶ Always duplicate a task sequence for backup purposes after it is created, and any time you are about to edit. This is an easy and quick step you can perform by right-clicking any task sequence and clicking **Copy**. You can also set up a dedicated console folder to move your duplicates into to avoid clutter.

▶ Export the task sequence from the ConfigMgr console by right-clicking it and choosing **Export**; to export multiple task sequences simultaneously, use multiselect and then select **Export**. This exports the task sequence and optionally all its dependencies (including OS images, boot images, software packages, driver packages, and applications) to a zip file you can store externally. You can re-import exported task sequences by selecting the Task Sequences node and choosing **Import Task Sequence** from the ribbon bar or right-click context-menu. Note that passwords and Windows product keys are stripped from the exported files.

Exporting task sequences to zip files is also an approach for copying a task sequence to a ConfigMgr site in an alternative, unconnected hierarchy such as a test or quality assurance site or one at another organization. You simply copy the exported zip file to a location accessible by the destination site and import it. The first page of the Export Task Sequence Wizard is shown in Figure 19.20 and includes two options:

▶ **Export all task sequence dependencies:** This option exports a definition for all the referenced dependencies in the task sequence, so they can be created or re-created when the export file is imported. It does not include the actual content for the dependencies however. The original content locations must be available and accessible on the site where the task sequence is imported.

▶ **Export all content for the select task sequence dependencies:** This option includes both the definitions and content for all content referenced in the task sequence. Dependencies will be created when the task sequence is imported at the destination site using the exported files. The exported content is not actually included in the zip file; it is included in a like-named folder in the same folder specified for the zip export file.

19

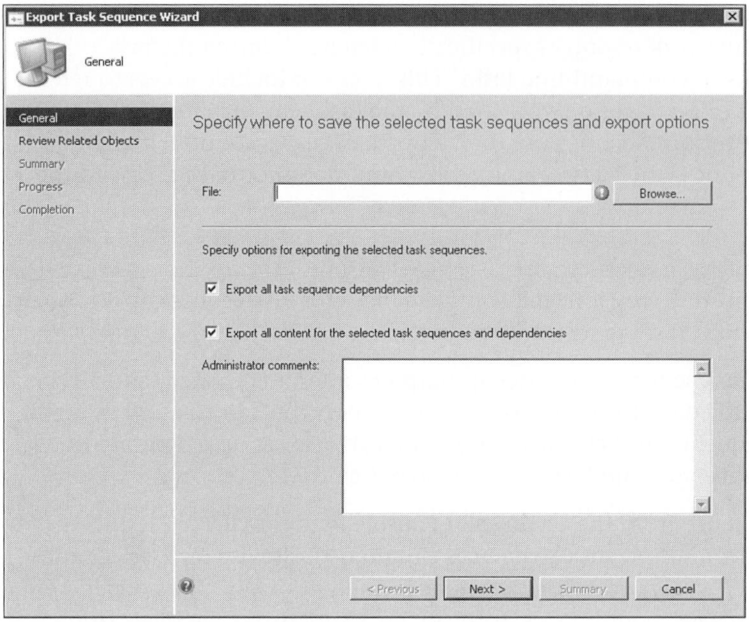

FIGURE 19.20   Export Task Sequence Wizard.

Content for dependencies from disabled tasks in the task sequence is not exported, although the task itself will be included in the exported task sequence. In addition, if your task sequence references the built-in Configuration Manager Client package in the Setup Windows and ConfigMgr task, this package will not be exported.

The second page of the Import Task Sequence Wizard is shown in Figure 19.21. This page displays all the content referenced in the task sequence and gives you one of three choices (listed under the Actions header in the dialog's list box) based upon the prior existence of the content at the site where you are importing the task sequence:

▶ **Create New:** Only available for dependencies that do not exist on the target site; this option creates the dependency from information in the zip file. If content was not exported, the original source location is referenced. If content was exported, its location is referenced.

▶ **Ignore duplicate:** This is the default option and does not import the dependency exported from the source site but instead links to the dependency that already exists on the target site.

▶ **Overwrite:** This option overwrites the existing dependency.

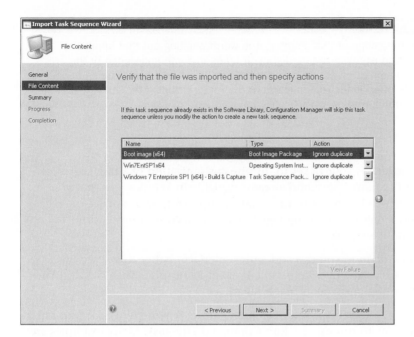

FIGURE 19.21   Import Task Sequence Wizard.

Customizing Task Sequences

The two default task sequence types, Build and Capture, and Deployment, are useful when beginning your use of OSD and task sequences. However, do not lock yourself into the tasks the Create Task Sequence Wizard places into these default task sequences. These two task sequences are just starting points for all but the most basic deployments. They are fully editable, allowing you to customize them as much or as little as you want. Ultimately, using these two task sequence types is not even required. You could start from a blank task sequence by choosing **Custom** in the New Task Sequence editor and start with a completely clean slate.

Interestingly enough, although task sequences are built for OSD, you can use them for software deployment or any other system configuration activity requiring multiple steps and possibly state maintenance during those steps. This gives rise to the scenario of allowing the activity to continue even after a reboot.

Many in-house or legacy applications require installing multiple packages or performing other configuration tasks in a specific sequence while also surviving a single or multiple intervening reboots. Repackaging these installations is often challenging if not impossible because of their nature. Task sequences are a perfect way to accomplish the many steps involved in these types of installations.

19

NOTE: APPLICATION REPACKAGING

Although well beyond the scope of this chapter, it is worth pointing out that application repackaging is not an exercise to take lightly. It takes in-depth knowledge of the application being installed as well as the application installation technology being used. Repacking applications often leads to issues down the road, including the inability to apply vendor-supplied updates.

Custom Commands

The Run Command Line task is your ticket to infinite customization of a task sequence. It provides the ability to run any command already available in Windows or that you include in a package. Refer to Figure 19.16 to see an example of how to update the registry. You can also import a registry file using regedit.exe, run a custom script, or install a device driver from a vendor-supplied .exe.

Using a Run Command Line task, you can add a user interface that enables users to provide input into your task sequence. An excellent example of this is the OSD App Tree, available at http://blog.configmgrftw.com?page_id=257.

The Microsoft Deployment Guys (http://blogs.technet.com/deploymentguys/default.aspx) present several useful scripts to run using a Run Command Line task. Many examples are geared toward use with MDT but are applicable to OSD with some minor tweaking in a few cases.

The possibilities are limited only by your resourcefulness and ability. With a little hard work and some examples, you can find or create a script or executable that automates anything and everything required by your deployment.

Site System Roles

There are two main supporting roles for OSD: distribution points (DP) and state migration points (SMP). These are discussed in the next sections.

Distribution Points

DPs are responsible for making all content used in ConfigMgr available to the clients. This also includes everything OSD needs to deploy Windows to a client system including

- ▶ Driver Packages
- ▶ Boot Images
- ▶ Operating System Installers
- ▶ Operating System Images
- ▶ Applications
- ▶ Software Distribution Packages
- ▶ Software Update Deployment Packages

With System Center 2012 Configuration Manager, the DP also handles all PXE and TFTP responsibilities for bare-metal booting of a target client system and delivery of the WinPE boot image. You probably already have a DP installed in your environment because ConfigMgr is limited without one. If you don't, Chapter 6, "Installing System Center 2012 Configuration Manager," includes a discussion of the DP role, its relevance to OSD, and how to install it.

PXE

For core OSD functionality, there is nothing additional to install or set up in ConfigMgr. To enable PXE boot capabilities for new computer scenarios in which existing data on the system is not a concern, follow this simple list of steps (because site configuration is global in nature, this can be done on any primary site in the hierarchy):

1. Navigate to **Administration -> Overview -> Distribution Points**.

2. Select the DP you want to enable PXE on from the list shown in right pane, and choose **Properties** from the ribbon bar or the right-click context menu.

NOTE: YOU CAN ENABLE ONLY SERVER-HOSTED DISTRIBUTION POINTS FOR PXE

You can only enable DPs hosted on Windows Server operating systems for PXE because this capability is actually provided by WDS, which is a server-only component. If you require or desire PXE-initiated OSD functionality at locations where you do not or cannot have a server OS, you should consider a third-party product offering client OS-hosted, peer to peer PXE capabilities such as Adaptiva's OneSite; see http://adaptiva.com/products_onesite.html for further information.

---

3. Select the PXE tab on the DP's Properties dialog box, as shown in Figure 19.22.

4. Check **Enable PXE support for clients** and acknowledge the resulting dialog box detailing the port requirements for PXE, displayed in Figure 19.22. Note the text under this check box: Windows Deployment Services will be installed if required. This is actually only true for Windows Server 2008 and 2008 R2; WDS is not automatically installed for Windows Server 2003 systems. For Windows Server 2003 systems, see http://technet.microsoft.com/en-us/library/cc766320(v=WS.10).aspx#BKMK_InstallingWDS for installation instructions. For Windows Server 2008 or 2008 R2, manually installing WDS is not necessary but possible using the Add Roles capabilities (http://technet.microsoft.com/en-us/library/cc771670(v=WS.10).aspx#BKMK_InstallingWDS contains explicit details of doing so). No configuration of WDS in the OS is needed or recommended as this is handled by ConfigMgr. Note that WDS is not supported on server core editions of Windows Server 2008 and 2008 R2.

5. The following options are also available after PXE is enabled:

   ▶ **Allow this distribution point to respond to incoming PXE requests:** This must be checked to actually activate the system's PXE capabilities.

19

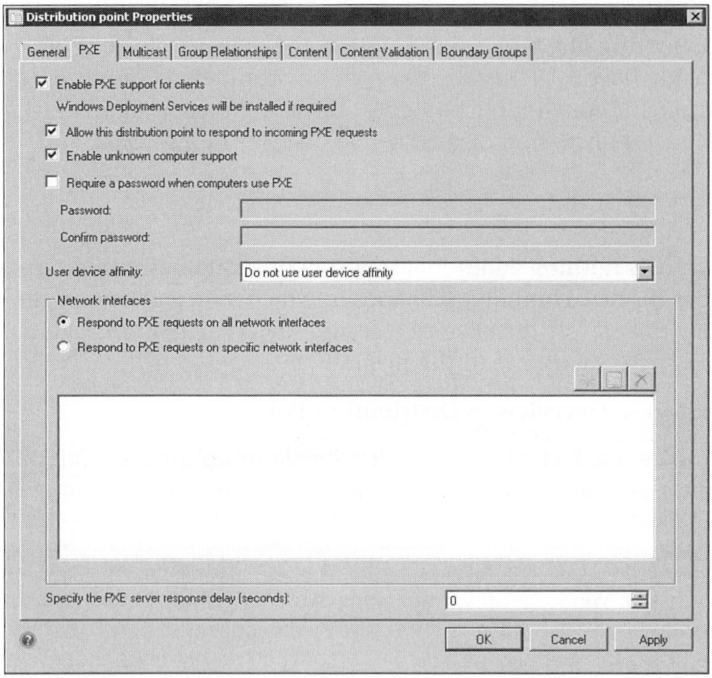

FIGURE 19.22   PXE tab.

▶ **Enable unknown computer support:** As described in the "Unknown Computers" section, this enables the DP to provide PXE boot capabilities to clients not known or prestaged in ConfigMgr. If you select this check box, Microsoft warns you about the potential for accidentally deploying Windows to systems where it should not be deployed. Heed this warning and plan your use of unknown computer support carefully. One way to mitigate this risk is to enable a password, as described in the next bullet.

▶ **Require a password when computers use PXE:** This self-describing option provides a level of security to prevent unauthorized or accidental imaging or reimaging of systems on the network. This is a shared password, so is not a perfect security mechanism, but it adds a level of user interactivity that can prevent deploying the corporate image to unauthorized users or the random user that accidentally PXE boots their system.

▶ **User device affinity:** This option disables the use of user device affinity, allows it with manual approval, or allows it with automatic approval for task sequences initiated using PXE from this DP. See the "User Device Affinity" section for further coverage of user device affinity.

▶ **Network interfaces:** If your DP happens to be multihomed, you can choose to allow PXE services on all or specify network interfaces in this section of the dialog.

▶ **Specify the PXE server response delay (seconds):** If you have multiple PXE servers responding to PXE requests in a subnet or through the use of IP helpers, you can set a precedence order using this delay; delaying the DP from responding to PXE requests allows other potential PXE servers to handle PXE requests first. If they choose not to reply to the system attempting to PXE boot, the DP responds to the system after the configured delay.

This is by no means a perfect prioritization system as the PXE booted system must be completely ignored by the first PXE responders for it to attempt to boot to later responders. For a ConfigMgr DP, if unknown computer support is enabled, it will never ignore a PXE request. Since the behavior of other PXE services in your environment may vary, testing is in order if you plan to coordinate the efforts of multiple PXE-enabled DPs or other PXE services.

MULTIPLE PXE PROVIDERS ON THE SAME NETWORK SUBNET

A question often fielded by ConfigMgr OSD implementers is how an organization can have multiple PXE providers on the same network subnet. Usually, the client organization already has a PXE server in place to support a legacy imaging product. The real answer to this question is that it depends on the network infrastructure, not on ConfigMgr.

PXE is a standards-based protocol based on DHCP and network broadcasts. The network card installed on a system controls the actual booting of a system; this is completely independent of ConfigMgr. Generally, the first PXE provider to respond to a PXE request is chosen by the network card that is booted. On a network level, it is best to segregate PXE providers on separate subnets to control the broadcasts.

You can also specify a specific PXE server using DHCP options 60, 66, and 67; however, these options are specific to a single network subnet and cannot be made more granular for PXE booting purposes. There are other options including a newer PXE specification, but this problem is completely outside the bounds of ConfigMgr and WDS.

Two excellent resources for detailed PXE information are at http://technet.microsoft.com/en-us/library/cc732351.aspx and http://support.microsoft.com/kb/244036. The second reference is a dated KB article referring to RIS, but the general PXE information is still valid.

Multicast

DPs also provide multicasting, which enables transporting a single stream of data over a network. Clients can then subscribe to this stream of data. The main advantage of multicasting over the traditional unicast model is using a single stream of data for multiple destination systems. Unicast communication requires a separate stream of data for every client system.

A downside for many multicast implementations for image deployment is you must manually coordinate the start of the data stream. All client systems you want to receive the stream must be waiting for the stream prior to its being sent. With WDS multicasting in Windows Server 2008, Microsoft implemented a catch-up feature. This enables clients that joined a stream midway through to continue to receive the entire stream.

19

WDS tracks when clients join the image stream and replays the stream until all clients subscribed to the stream have received the entire image.

Multicasting is used only for image deployment in OSD; it is not used for any type of package delivery including driver, application, or OS install. If you plan to use multicasting heavily, this may affect the decisions you make about what to put into the actual image. It may make more sense to make the image fatter to improve distribution times when using multicasting, which is often the case when organizations have rigid, time-based service-level agreements in place for deploying Windows to users. See http://blog.configmgrftw.com/?p=299 for a complete discussion of whether you should use multicasting.

To enable multicasting, follow these steps:

1. Navigate to **Administration -> Overview -> Distribution Points**.

2. Select the DP you want to enable PXE on from the list shown in the right pane, and choose **Properties** from the ribbon bar or the right-click context menu.

3. Select the Multicast tab on the DP's Properties dialog box, as shown in Figure 19.23.

4. Check **Enable multicast to simultaneously send data to multiple clients**. Note the text under this check box: Windows Deployment Services will be installed if required.

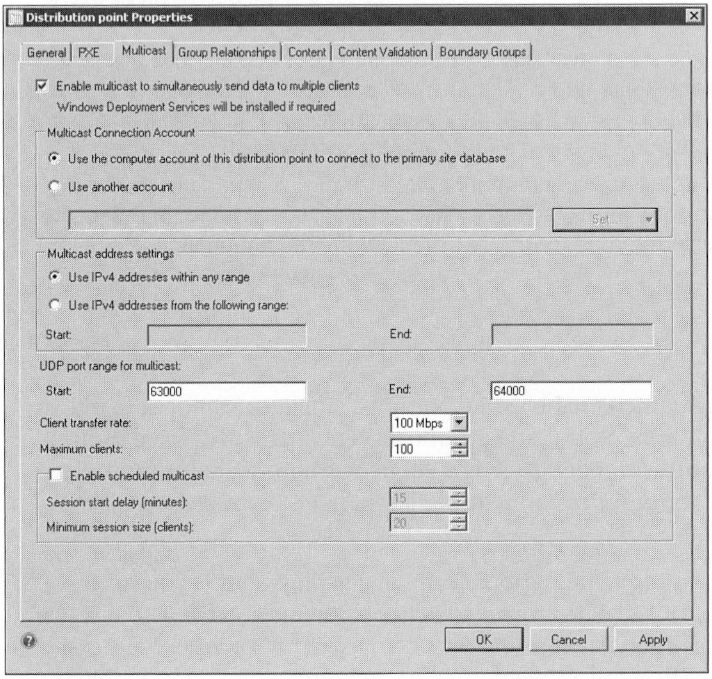

FIGURE 19.23   Multicast tab.

5. Here are the options also available on this tab once multicast is enabled:

▶ **Multicast Connection Account:** This account is used for communication back to the site database. By default, it is set to **Use the computer account of the distribution point to connect to the primary database** but you can choose another account.

▶ **Multicast address settings:** This allows you to specify a specific multicast address according to Request For Comment (RFC) 3171 (http://www.ietf.org/rfc/rfc3171.txt) or use the default of any available multicast address.

▶ **UDP port range for multicast:** Specify which User Datagram Protocol (UDP) ports to use for multicasting.

▶ **Client transfer rate:** This setting optimizes the performance of the multicast data stream for the selected network type.

▶ **Maximum clients:** This caps the number of clients that this distribution point serves using multicast. This number is cumulative across all multicast sessions.

▶ **Enable scheduled multicast:** Scheduled multicast configures a multicast session to wait for a specific number of clients to join a session or a number of minutes to wait before starting a session. This allows you to coordinate the client systems and ensure they are all online and available before the session starts. The use of the catch-up feature described in the "Utilizing Multicasting" section reduces the importance of this functionality, but it is still available.

State Migration Point

SMPs store user data as it is migrated from one instance of Windows to another. Typically, SMPs are used only for replace scenarios in which new physical hardware replaces the user's old system. Because the new system may not physically be online, the SMP provides a transient location on the network to store user data temporarily. From the SMP, the data is then copied to the user's new system. Actual user state data and settings are captured using the built-in functionality of USMT behind the scenes and is SMP-aware.

Another common scenario for using SMPs is a refresh scenario in which a third party, full-disk encryption product is in use or the current hard-drive must be reformatted. The typical path for the refresh scenario is to use the in-place hard-link capabilities of USMT 4.0. This greatly speeds the refresh of a system because the user's data never must be physically moved. However, with third-party, full-disk encryption products in the mix, the current data on the hard-drive is inaccessible during the initial WinPE phase of the build process, so the drive must be reformatted, which in turn wipes out the data stored locally by USMT. Thus, the only option is to move the user's data to a transient location like the SMP.

CAUTION: THIRD-PARTY FULL DISK ENCRYPTION

Unlike BitLocker, most third-party, disk-encryption products cannot be paused from within OSD and often require manual PIN or key entry. This is a challenge that Microsoft is not responsible for and cannot hope to address. If you find yourself using a third-party, full-disk encryption product, you can either use an SMP as stated in this section, treat the system as a bare-metal or new system, or contact the vendor for possible solutions they may have.

At its heart, the SMP is just a shared folder on a site system. Here are its advantages:

▶ ConfigMgr directly manages the SMP, so it is automatically locatable by the OSD process.

▶ Stored data is deleted automatically after a specified number of days.

▶ Data is securely and separately stored in case something goes wrong during the build process.

SMP Installation

To install an SMP, follow these steps; SMPs, like other client-centric roles, cannot be installed on the CAS because the CAS does not directly manage clients:

1. Navigate to **Administration** -> **Overview** -> **Site Configuration**. Select **Servers and Site System Roles**. All currently installed site systems display on the right.

2. To use an existing site server, right-click it and choose **Add Site System Roles** to launch the Add Site System Roles Wizard, as shown in Figure 19.24.

   If using a remote system that is not currently a site system, you must first make the system a site system by right-clicking the **Servers and Site System Roles** node in the navigation tree and selecting **Create Site System Server**.

3. On the System Role Selection page of the Add Site System Roles Wizard or the Create Site System Server Wizard, select **State migration point**. This adds two subpages to the wizard: State Migration Point and Boundary Groups.

4. The State Migration Point page (shown in Figure 19.25) has these choices:

   ▶ **Folder details:** This list box allows you to designate specific folders on the site system to use. You must specify a specific local path, the maximum number of clients to serve, and minimum amount of free space on the drive hosting the folder to consider the SMP healthy.

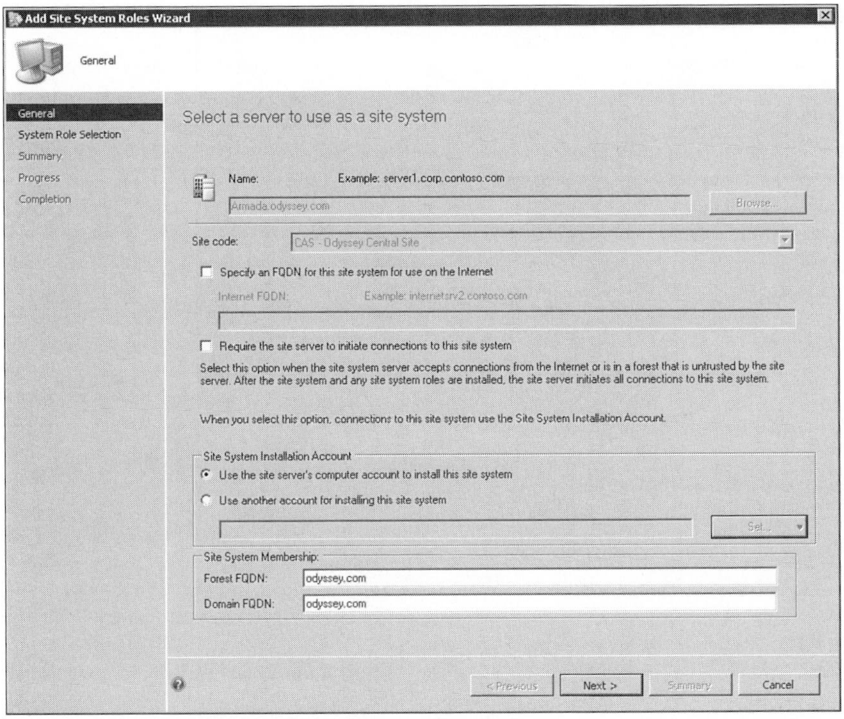

FIGURE 19.24   Add Site System Roles Wizard.

The paths specified are local paths relative to the system hosting the DP. If you specify multiple paths, each is tried in the order listed for state capture operations; paths over the maximum number of clients or below the minimum amount of free space available are skipped.

▶ **Deletion Policy:** In this section, you specify how long to save user state on a state migration point after it is restored.

▶ **Enable Restore-Only Mode:** This mode prevents this state migration point from accepting new user state, but allows retrieval of previously saved user state data. This is useful when retiring a server or preparing it for maintenance.

5. The Boundary Groups page (shown in Figure 19.26) presents these choices:

▶ **Boundary groups:** In this list box, you either select or create the boundary groups associated with this SMP. Selecting a boundary group here makes this SMP preferred for clients that fall within that boundary group. See the section on "SMP Selection" for details on how clients choose between multiple SMPs if they exist in an environment.

19

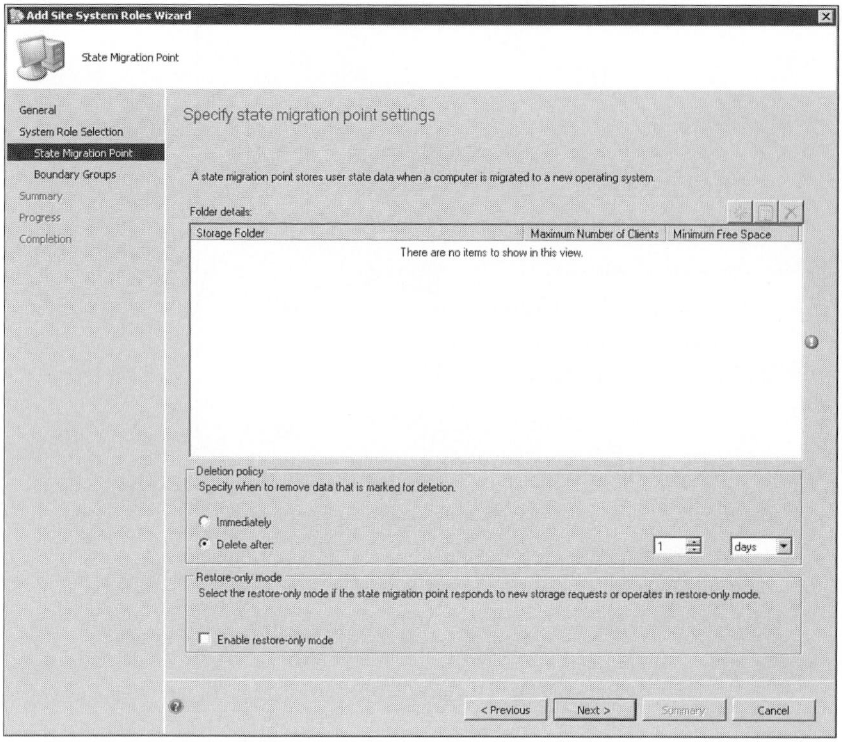

FIGURE 19.25   State Migration Point page.

▶ **Allow fallback source location:** If checked for an SMP, the SMP will service clients outside of its defined boundary groups if the client cannot find a preferred SMP.

TIP: BOUNDARIES AND SMPS

The relationship between boundaries and SMPs is identical to the relationship between boundaries and DPs.

After completing the wizard, ConfigMgr installs the SMP with the desired parameters. To change any of these settings after the SMP is installed, navigate to the Server and Site Systems node under **Overview -> Site Configuration** in the Administration workspace's navigation tree, select the site server from the list on the right, right-click **State Migration Point** in the Detail pane at the bottom, and select **Properties**.

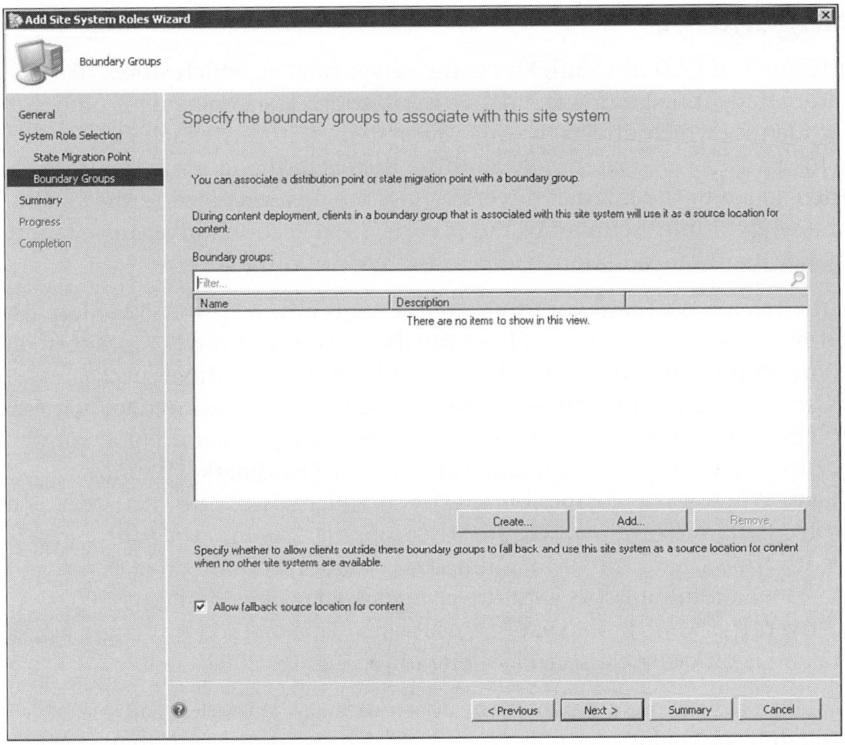

FIGURE 19.26   Boundary Groups page.

To verify correct installation and operation of the SMP, check smpMSI.log and smpmgr.log respectively in the server's log files folder for errors. Smpmgr.log has three lines similar to the following if the SMP is installed and functioning correctly:

```
Call to HttpSendRequestSync succeeded for port 80 with status code 200, text: OK
Health check operation succeeded
Completed availability check on local machine
```

SMP Selection
Similar to DPs, you can add multiple SMPs to a site or site hierarchy to provide redundancy and some load balancing. SMPs are chosen by clients systems wanting to capture user state in the same order as DPs:

1. SMPs defined in their boundary group and in their subnet

2. SMPs defined in their boundary group and in alternative subnets

3. All other SMPs

Within each of these groups, there is no defined order for the SMPs but some randomization does occur to create a pseudo load balancing.

Driver Management

One of the nicest features of OSD in ConfigMgr is the driver catalog, which stores all applicable drivers for all identified hardware in an organization. The deployment process uses this catalog to identify which drivers to copy to a system. Entries are made to the unattended setup file in use, which effectively adds the drivers to the internal Windows driver catalog. When added to the internal driver catalog, the drivers copied to the system are available for the setup or mini-setup plug-and-play device detection, driver installation processes, and any new hardware additions made to the system in the future.

Adding drivers to the catalog is a matter of following the steps in the "Drivers" section. As you must import drivers from a UNC path, it is worthwhile to create a driver repository on your network to store all the driver files. All drivers must be stored in a driver package as described in the "Driver Packages" section, regardless of the task type used to deploy them to a target system. This is a change from ConfigMgr 2007 where a popular driver deployment technique, called the Johan Method (named after Johan Arwidmark—Windows Deployment MVP and Windows deployment master), was widely used. This method, although unsupported by Microsoft, involved directly dropping files into the source location specified by a driver package without first importing them into ConfigMgr. It was an elegant solution to a handful of issues with driver management in ConfigMgr 2007— namely duplicate drivers that were problematic to deal with. This method no longer works in ConfigMgr 2012 and is officially classified as a bug in ConfigMgr 2007.

Just because you added a driver into a deployment does not mean Windows will use it. Windows goes through its own plug-and-play process to identify devices and then uses suitable drivers from its internal catalog; the internal catalog includes drivers you injected using one of the two task types. Insiders have described the Windows plug-and-play process as a black art. OSD attempts to replicate it as closely as possible, but there are many complicating factors, including parent-child relationships that hide child devices until the parent drivers are installed. Although the Auto Apply Drivers task generally works well, there are times where it will not identify and inject the proper driver. In these cases, add the problem driver to a driver package of its own and use a separate Apply Driver Package task to inject the driver for use by Windows.

Acquiring device devices is usually a straightforward process: Visit the hardware vendor's website and download those listed for the hardware models for which you are concerned. On occasion, however, you will find that the drivers are packaged in an installation program. In these cases, there are two options:

▶ Extract the driver files for the installation program. This is the best option but not always available because extracting them may be an undocumented or unsupported process.

▶ Create a software distribution package and install the drivers using a Software Install task. If you resort to this technique to install drivers, ensure you use the proper switches to install the drivers silently. You may also want to ensure the drivers installed in this fashion are installed only on specific hardware models. To achieve this, use a WMI Query conditional on the task (described in the "Task Conditions and Groupings" section), such as

```
SELECT * FROM Win32_ComputerSystem WHERE Model like "%760%"
```

Use the `root\cimv2` WMI namespace for this query and replace the text in the quotes with the appropriate model number. Note that the percent sign is a wildcard in the WMI Query Language (WQL) and represents zero or more of any character.

To determine the model attribute quickly on any system, run the following from a command prompt: `wmic computersystem get model`. Cliff Hobbs maintains a fairly up-to-date list of the results of this command from many different models for many different manufacturers, at http://www.faqshop.com/configmgr2007/admin/aosd/list%20wmic%20results.htm.

Drivers in the Image

Because you want your image to be as generic as possible and include only those items existing on every system in your organization, you want to minimize additional third-party drivers in the image itself. Minimizing drivers limits the size of the image; however, it is completely unavoidable to include some drivers—particularly those distributed with the OS and those required for the reference system itself. This is quite acceptable; do not worry too much about additional drivers; most are relatively small, and Windows does not use or load them if they are not for a currently installed device.

There might be times when you want to force certain drivers into every image; for example, when users use locally attached devices such as printers, scanners, card readers, or biometric devices not attached to the system during its deployment. In this case, make the same decision with these drivers as you do with software. Is the device going to connect to all (or nearly all) systems? If so, include it in the image. If not, it should be layered on after the image is deployed with an Apply Driver Package task.

Another common concern is that if you do not include a driver in the image, it will not be available to systems where you deploy the image. This particularly comes up as a concern for the built-in drivers. This is a false assumption. All drivers that come with Windows are still part of the image unless you go through a lot of pain and effort to remove them.

Drivers After the Image

Few, if any, organizations use the exact same desktop and laptop hardware for all their users. Although a desirable goal, it is unrealistic for most organizations because of many factors: the ever-changing model lineup delivered by hardware vendors, the diversity of user requirements, merges and acquisitions, hardware refresh cycles, and so on. This results in a wide range of hardware in your organization and many different drivers. As with software that is not ubiquitous throughout your organization, after deploying the image you must layer on various drivers by using one of the two driver task types, described previously in the "Drivers Category" section of this chapter:

19

▶ **Auto Apply Drivers:** Uses a plug-and-play detection during the task sequence to copy only the drivers for devices detected during the task sequence.

▶ **Apply Driver Package:** Copies all drivers in a given package to the system without any detection logic.

Driver management is an oft-discussed topic in the various Internet forums, including the main Microsoft Configuration Manager forums. Many different opinions exist on this topic and can be placed on a spectrum with "control freak" at one end and "chaos" at the other. Control freaks use only the Apply Driver Package tasks in combination with the WQL conditional presented in the "Drivers" section to ensure only specific drivers are deployed to systems in a controlled manner. Subscribers to the chaos methodology use only an Auto Apply Drivers task and let chaos reign with driver deployment.

Although neither methodology is necessarily wrong, the reality is that most OSD deployments fall somewhere in the middle depending on the drivers and systems you are deploying. As long as it works and enables you to deploy your systems successfully, the methodology you adopt cannot be wrong. An excellent blog post reinforcing some of the information presented here is available at http://blogs.technet.com/deploymentguys/archive/2008/02/15/driver-management-part-1-configuration-manager.aspx. The first part of an additional definitive blog post discussing driver management is available at http://blogs.technet.com/b/mniehaus/archive/2010/04/29/configmgr-2007-driver-management-the-novel-part-1.aspx (note this post is for ConfigMgr 2007 and that the Johan method mentioned in this post, as discussed above, no longer works).

User State

"Where's my data?" "Where's the spreadsheet I worked 20 hours on for the CEO?" "Where's the irreplaceable wallpaper of my darling grandson Johnny hitting the game winning homerun?" These are the last questions any helpdesk technician or system administrator wants to hear, especially right after an OS installation.

User data is the reason that we all exist, and we want to handle it with special care. Adding users' settings to their data gives us the users' state. A major goal in any system migration is to prevent users from losing any productive time because they do not have or cannot find their data. Although it is definitely a best practice to have users store their data in a central location, such as a server-based file share or a SharePoint site, this might not be possible for a variety of reasons because your organization might not enforce a centralized storage model. In addition, central data storage schemes tend to overlook things such as wallpaper, Outlook settings and configuration, and desktop shortcuts, letting these remain local to each system. When performing an OS deployment, you want to capture and restore the users' state to their new systems as seamlessly as possible.

OSD in ConfigMgr automatically uses USMT to identify, store, and restore user data according a set of XML configuration files built into USMT. The data can be stored locally, useful (but not required) for a refresh scenario in which the hardware is not replaced or stored on a state migration point for the replace scenario where new hardware is introduced.

The main benefits of local storage are that it minimizes network traffic and eliminates the need for server-based storage. This allows potentially quicker migrations and indefinite storage of the data archive.

CAUTION: LOCAL STATE STORAGE HAS ITS RISKS

Although more efficient and quicker, storing user state locally during a deployment has associated risks: specifically, the dependence on the local hard disk maintaining its integrity and not corrupting the data. This is typically an acceptable risk because that's where the data was initially but is still a risk to be accounted for.

In the case of a replace scenario, you must use the state migration point. (This is not entirely true; see the "User State Without SMP" section for further details.) This is essentially a secure file share for storing the USMT-produced archive. ConfigMgr encrypts and tags archives placed here for a specific destination system, using a computer association. If you did not create a computer association before running a Capture User State task in a task sequence, OSD creates it, specifying the same destination and source systems. ConfigMgr automatically purges the archives placed on a state migration point after the state is restored, based on the settings of the SMP.

The best part about state migration in ConfigMgr is it is simple and straightforward to set up. The only overhead truly incurred by state migration is storage space, and this is automatically maintained and cleaned. By default, the built-in wizard to create Image Deployment task sequences adds the steps to provision space on the state migration point, capturing user state data and transferring it to the SMP. It also adds the necessary tasks to retrieve the state from the SMP and apply it to the destination system.

This default behavior is perfect for a refresh scenario and works for a replace scenario with several small additions:

▶ Create a computer association to specify the source and destination systems by navigating to **Assets and Compliance -> User State Migration** and choosing **Create Computer Association** from the ribbon bar or right-click context-menu. If no association exists when storage is provisioned from the state migration point, a computer association is created with the same source and destination as the system being imaged—this is the desired configuration for refreshes. Alternatively, for a replace scenario, you must manually create a computer association before capturing the user state data; this computer association configures a pre-existing source system and a new or different destination system.

▶ You should also create a new task sequence to capture the user state data. You can create this abbreviated task sequence using the New Task Sequence Wizard, choosing to create either a custom task sequence or install an existing image package task sequence, and deleting everything except the three relevant capture state tasks.

19

Here are the four tasks associated with user state:

- ▶ Request State Store
- ▶ Release State Store
- ▶ Capture User State
- ▶ Restore User State

The Request State Store and Release State Store are always used, regardless of whether you capture or restore the user state. These tasks deal with the storage space on the state migration point where the user state data is stored.

The Release State Store task has no options, and the main option for the Request State Store task is determining whether user state is retrieved or stored. This task also either creates or retrieves the encryption key that protects the user state data; the encryption key is stored along with and is specific to a single computer association. As stated earlier in this section, this computer association is created automatically with the same source and destination system if the association does not already exist during a user state capture. If you perform a user state restoration and no computer association exists, the user state tasks are gracefully skipped.

The Capture User State and Restore User State tasks do exactly as their names imply. The two main configuration options for both of these tasks are a required package containing the USMT files and an optional package containing the custom USMT configuration files. Neither package requires any program files because they both just make the necessary files available for ConfigMgr to use. The "Creating the USMT Package(s)" section describes creating the USMT tools package.

USMT

USMT is the heart of maintaining user state both for refresh and replace scenarios. USMT intelligently captures user data according to a defined set of rules and bundles it up so that it can be easily stored or transferred. USMT comes with a default set of rules you can further customize based on the unique data and applications in your environment.

One of OSD's many virtues is that it seamlessly and transparently incorporates the full capabilities of USMT without any real heavy lifting. The default rule sets for USMT capture all data in a user's profile including documents, wallpaper, and other common customizations. By default, USMT searches the hard drive for known Microsoft file types such as those used by Microsoft Office and captures those as well. This actually may be sufficient for all user state migration needs in your organization, although only you can determine this and if you must to add customizations to USMT.

USMT Versions

The first actual decision to make when you choose to maintain user state is whether to use USMT version 3 or 4. Version 4 is of course newer and should be your first choice; however, there are multiple reasons why you may choose to use version 3, including

▶ You previously used version 3 and have custom configuration files for it.

▶ You are still deploying Windows XP; USMT 4 can be used only if the destination OS is Windows Vista or above. (The source OS does not matter.)

Based upon your deployment needs, you may use both versions, as they are by no means mutually exclusive. Remember, though, data captured with one version must also be restored by that same version.

For a complete discussion of what's new and different in USMT 4, check out http://technet.microsoft.com/en-us/library/dd560752(v=WS.10).aspx. Here are the most significant items as far as ConfigMgr OSD is concerned:

▶ **Hard-link migration:** Enables data to physically remain in place on a hard drive during a refresh scenario, greatly reducing the time and space required for capturing and restoring the data.

▶ **Offline migration:** Enables capturing the data in an installed instance of Windows without actually booting to that instance.

▶ **Volume shadow copy support:** Enables capturing data even in use or otherwise locked.

As described in the "User State Category" section, enabling each of these features is just ticking a check box on the Capture User State task.

This chapter could not possibly hope to cover enough information about customizing USMT to do any sort of justice. An excellent article more fully discussing what USMT migrates and how to customize its behavior is at http://blogs.technet.com/b/askds/archive/2011/05/11/does-usmt-migrate-lt-this-goo-gt.aspx.

Creating the USMT Package(s)

To use USMT in your task sequences, you must create a package containing the required files. This is a relatively simple task and follows the same procedures for creating packages as outlined in Chapter 11 with one omission: Programs are not necessary. The invocation of both ScanState and LoadState is fundamental to the use of USMT and thus running them is already part of the logic built into the Capture User State and Restore User State tasks.

USMT 4.0 is part of the WAIK, which is installed with ConfigMgr. Thus, to create a USMT 4.0 package, copy the files from *%ProgramFiles%*\Windows AIK\Tools\USMT to your source repository and reference this location when creating the USMT 4.0 package.

To obtain the source files for USMT 3.0, first download and install USMT 3.0. The download is freely available from Microsoft at http://www.microsoft.com/download/en/details.aspx?displaylang=en&id=10837. You can install it on any system available to you, including the site server if you so choose. The only real purpose of this installation, though, is to obtain the files it installs. After installation, copy the files from the installation folder to your source repository and use this location when creating the package. Copying the files to your source repository rather than directly referencing them is generally recommended because you can independently add updated XML configuration files to the source repository without affecting the original files. It also maintains a consistent package source location across your packages.

Computer Associations

Computer associations are records that track user data migrated between two instances of Windows using an SMP to store the data while it is in transition; they map the source system to a target system, both of which are identified by their MAC addresses. Computer associations are directly referenced (or created) by the User State tasks, as discussed in the "User State" section.

There are two types of migrations and thus two types of computer associations:

▶ In-place

▶ Side-by-side

Each association also records the date that state data was captured and restored, the location where state data is stored, and the encryption key for the state data.

For in-place migrations as part of a refresh deployment, a computer association is created automatically by ConfigMgr when the user state is first captured. Essentially, if ConfigMgr does not see an existing computer association specifying the current system as the source system, it assumes the data is meant to stay in-place and creates an in-place association that specifies the system as both the source and destination.

For side-by-side migrations as part of a replace scenario, you must create a side-by-side computer association manually before an applicable task sequence is run on a system; otherwise, an in-place association is automatically created. To create a new association, navigate to **Assets and Compliance -> User State Migration** and choose **Create Computer Association** from the ribbon bar or right-click context-menu. This displays the Computer Association Properties dialog box, as shown in Figure 19.27.

This dialog allows you to specify the source and destination computer. Use the User Accounts tab to specifically limit which profiles are captured or restored; the following profile-culling options are available and are equivalent of manually specifying the /ue option on ScanState or LoadState (described at http://blogs.technet.com/b/askds/archive/2009/11/30/understanding-usmt-4-0-behavior-with-uel-and-ue.aspx):

▶ Capture and restore all user accounts

▶ Capture all user accounts and restore specified accounts

▶ Capture and restore specified user accounts

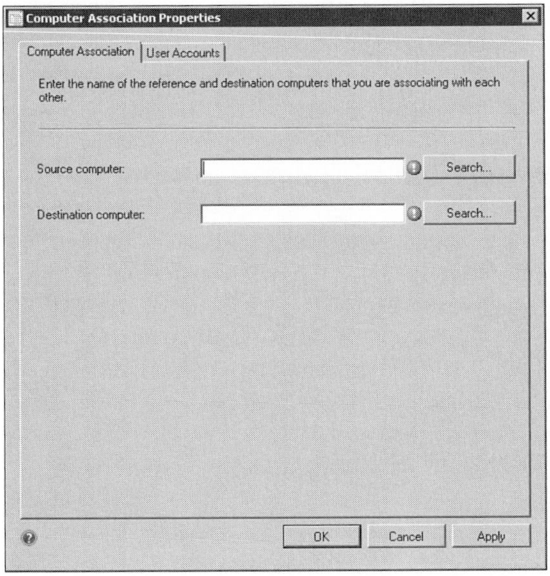

FIGURE 19.27   Computer Association Properties dialog.

To view existing computer associations, navigate to **Assets and Compliance -> User State Migration**. From here, you can delete or review any association. Note that you cannot change the source or destination computer for an association once it is created.

After creating an association, right-click it to view the following information:

- ▶ Source Computer Properties
- ▶ Destination Computer Properties
- ▶ User Accounts
- ▶ Recovery Information

This limitation manifests itself during replace deployment scenarios where you are transferring user state data to new hardware because the destination system must already exist in ConfigMgr. This occurs for security reasons. This doesn't mean the system itself must exist, just that you must pre-create a record for it in ConfigMgr. To pre-create a system, follow the steps outlined in the "Known Computers" section.

To recover previously captured user data manually, you must first extract the encryption key and the user state store location from the computer association. These display by selecting **View Recovery Information** from the context menu of an association (or the ribbon bar) used to capture data, as shown in Figure 19.28. You can then pass the key and the state location on a command line to USMT using the /decrypt option.

19

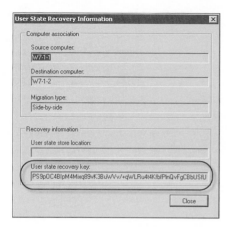

FIGURE 19.28   Computer Association Recovery Information.

Sample syntax would be

```
loadstate <state store path> /i <migapp.xml> /i <miguser.xml> /i <migsys.xml>
/decrypt /key: <encryption key>
```

User State Without SMP

For refresh scenarios, leaving data in place is preferred because it avoids the overhead of transferring any content across the network. There are two ways to do this, based on the new OS deployed to the system and the version of USMT used:

▶ **Hard-link:** Hard-link migration can be used only if using USMT 4.0 and the new OS is Windows 7 (initial OS does not matter). Hard-link migration takes advantage of advanced features of the NTFS file system that allow files to physically remain in-place and intact even after the drive is wiped (not formatted). When restored, pointers to the files are restored, so the files never physically have to be copied or moved anywhere.

   To use hard-linking, select the **Capture locally by using links instead of copying files** option in the Capture User State task (shown previously in Figure 19.12).

▶ **File copy:** If hard-linking is not selected, the traditional file copy method for storing user state is used. This method must be used if the OS you restore to is Windows XP or you use USMT 3.0. This file copy method literally copies all identified user state data to an alternative location on the hard-drive requiring extra disk space and extra time to complete the copy.

For either scenario, you must also set the OSDStateStorePath task sequence variable to a local path on the system. For hard linking, the recommended path is *%SystemDrive%* UserState. For file copy, the recommended path is the value of the built-in task sequence variable _SMSTSUserStatePath. Also, be sure you do not use a Format and Partition task during the task sequence because this wipes out the state store. If you build a task sequence using the Create New Task Sequence Wizard, all this is done for you.

Because hard-linking is much quicker than having to physically bundle and copy all the captured user state to another location on the drive and does not require the extra necessary free space to do so, it is the preferred method for maintaining user state in refresh scenario deployments.

Although using an SMP is preferred for replace scenarios because of its self-cleanup and automatic encryption of state data, it may not always be ideal for one or more of the following reasons (although other reasons to not use an SMP are also possible):

▶ Lack of a local site server or sufficient storage space on a local site server.

▶ Using a local NAS or USB drive is preferred.

▶ Transferring user state data twice (once from the source to the SMP and once from the SMP to the destination) is undesirable because of the extra time involved.

▶ The destination system in a replace scenario is not available or known at the time the computer association is created.

For all these scenarios, you can use a simple SMB file share instead of an SMP—of course, you will have to manually clean up the share, organize it, and maintain encryption keys. To do so, set the OSDStateStorePath task sequence variable to your custom location and only use the Capture User State and Restore User State tasks. For best results, set OSDStateStorePath to a path determined at run time. For example, you could use a Set Task Sequence task to set OSDStateStorePath to \\<servername> \<share>\%OSDComputerName%. This would cause USMT to create a subfolder in the share specified named for the current system when capturing data and store the captured user data there. You would then have to store this path somewhere (in an external file or database) or prompt the interactive user to choose a source computer to restore from when it is time to restore the data.

Another advanced approach is to prompt the interactive user for a destination computer and populate OSDStateStorePath with a path on the destination system, bypassing the use of an intermediary file share altogether.

Image Operations

It's all about the image. Well, not really, but the image is still a key component of deploying Windows and thus part of the critical path in any OSD project. The next sections provide a simple, step-by-step process for creating, maintaining, and deploying a Windows image.

Image Creation

As of RTM, you still have to recapture an installation of Windows to a custom image to avoid it from being deployed to the D: drive. This is a known "issue" and annoyance and (hopefully) slated to be fixed in a future version or service pack of ConfigMgr 2012. When it is fixed, you can directly use the core image that is included with the Windows installation media: image.wim. This in combination with the offline update installation capabilities of ConfigMgr 2012 (discussed in the "Offline Software Updates" section) should greatly simplify basic Windows deployment projects.

Even with the ability to directly deploy image.wim, there is still value in tailoring the image to include updates, applications, and customizations (for a complete discussion of this, see the "Image Maintenance" section later in this chapter). At a minimum, including the latest Windows updates is highly recommended.

Unless using the offline update functionality, you must have a reference system available to deploy Windows to during image creation. In general, the best choice for this reference system is a virtual machine. Since OSD is designed to be hardware agnostic, when you create an image, it should be as generic as possible. Virtual machines are the ultimate generic hardware and thus perfectly suited. In addition, virtual machines are easy to reproduce when needed, do not take any desk space, are relatively cheap, and remotely accessible at a (virtual) hardware level. Any of the major virtual machine software solutions (except Microsoft/Windows Virtual PC) is ideally suited for this task, including

▶ Microsoft Hyper-V

▶ VMware ESX or Workstation

▶ Oracle VirtualBox

Oracle VirtualBox is freely available for both corporate and personal use so is a popular choice by many. Along with VMware Workstation, many desktop administrators prefer it because they do not have to ask for server-hosted virtual machines. Windows 8 is planned to include Hyper-V and should become quickly popular for this task.

Automatic Image Creation

Automatic image creation is highly recommended. It involves creating a Build and Capture task sequence and some upfront work. When created, though, it is fully automated, repeatable, self-documenting, and resistant to human error, making all future image maintenance tasks relatively trivial.

Here are several possible negatives to automatic image creation:

▶ Task sequences run as Local System. On rare occasions, poorly written software installers do not deal well with the peculiarities of this account. There are workarounds including recapturing the software or using the alternate credentials functionality of the Run Command Line task. Other times, legacy applications require hands-on installation or configuration. This is difficult or impossible to perform during a task sequence, as the task sequence was not designed with user interactivity in mind. The solution is to automate the installation and configuration of this application with scripting or other automation techniques.

▶ Every detail must be automated. In general, this is good because it makes these details easily repeatable. This may be difficult for some to achieve though because they do not have the scripting or Windows automation background to accomplish this. In these cases, enlist the help of someone who does have the background or check the Internet. It may take a little discovery and trial and error to automate a particular task, but it is well worth the effort.

To begin your automatic image creation, first create a Build and Capture task sequence:

1. In the Software Library workspace, select **Overview** -> **Operating Systems** -> **Task Sequence**. Choose **Create Task Sequence** from the ribbon bar or right-click context menu to launch the Create Task Sequence Wizard.

2. Select **Build and capture a reference operating system image**.

3. The remaining significant pages in the wizard define how to build a reference system from scratch and then capture:

   ▶ **Task Sequence Information:** On this page, you define the Task sequence name and Description and set which boot image to use.

   ▶ **Install Windows:** Choose the OS Installer to use, enter a product key (not required if deploying Windows 7 and using a KMS), and enable or disable the local Administrator account; if enabled, you must also specify a password. For Build and Capture task sequences, you should also specify a password, so you can access the reference system to troubleshoot it if the deployment fails.

   ▶ **Configure Network:** Specify the workgroup or domain to join on this page along with the user account to use to join the domain. For Build and Capture task sequences, do not join a domain and simply supply a workgroup name such as BUILD.

   ▶ **Install Configuration Manager client:** Choose the built-in ConfigMgr client agent installation package and add any additional installation properties. For Build and Capture task sequences, adding the SMSMP= property is highly recommended because the system is not joined to the domain and therefore cannot locate the MP using AD.

   ▶ **Include Updates:** Choose whether to include updates in the reference system image. For updates to be considered, they must be deployed to the same collection targeted by this task sequence's deployment.

   ▶ **Install Applications:** Select applications to add to the reference image.

   ▶ **System Preparation:** For Windows 7 task sequences, this page has no options; for Windows XP task sequences, choose a previously created package containing the appropriate Sysprep files. This Sysprep package is a basic package created under the **Application Management** -> **Packages** node in the Software Library workspace. The source files for the package should contain the entire, extracted contents of the deploy.cab for the appropriate version of Windows being captured—no programs are needed.

▶ **Image Properties:** Enter some basic metadata that is added to the captured image on this page.

▶ **Capture Image:** On this page, enter the complete UNC path, including file-name of the WIM file to which to capture the reference image. Also, provide an account that has permissions to write to this path. This account requires no special permissions except Write permissions to the path specified. Using the Network Access account for this task is a popular choice as you should use a low-privilege account.

The information entered during the wizard populates the various tasks required for a Build and Capture task sequence. See the "Task Sequences" section for explicit descriptions of these tasks.

Complete the wizard to create your final Build and Capture task sequence. From there, deploy the task sequence to a collection containing your reference system. Deploying to the All Unknown Computers collection is often used for Build and Capture task sequences because it is similar to the new computer scenario. Just make sure that you disable this deployment after creating your reference image so that users do not accidentally choose it. In addition, if you use a system (or VM) that currently has a resource in ConfigMgr, you must first delete the resource from ConfigMgr to make it unknown again, as described in the "Unknown Computers" section.

You can now run your Build and Capture task sequence as often as necessary to update or refresh the reference image. After creating it, import the WIM file containing the reference image into ConfigMgr using the steps outlined in the "Operating System Images" section. To use this image, see the "Image Deployment" section.

Manual Image Creation

It is possible to create and capture an image manually. The downside is it is labor-inten-sive and prone to human error; the upside is that building the system does not require you to predefine and automate every little detail. It also sidesteps some issues involving poorly packaged drivers or applications that are difficult or impossible to install in a silent or automated fashion. Manually configuring a reference system is well beyond the scope of this chapter or book (and discouraged by the authors), and left to the expertise of the reader.

The best way to capture the system to an image is using an image capture CD and the following steps:

1. **Install Windows:** Manually install Windows, updates, and any desired applications and drivers, and apply every last tweak to a reference system. The system should also conform to the following rules:

   ▶ Not joined to a domain.

   ▶ Does not have the ConfigMgr client installed. This is not a strict requirement, but makes preparing the image easier.

► Has a blank local Administrator password.

► The system's security policy must not require strong passwords.

2. **Create the capture media:** Right-click the Task Sequences node under Operating System Deployment in the ConfigMgr console and choose **Create Task Sequence Media**. This launches the Task Sequence Media Wizard, which creates either a bootable USB drive or ISO image (which you can burn to CD or DVD) from a boot image.

3. **Run Capture:** Insert the capture media into the reference system, and from Windows autorun the media to initiate the capture wizard. This launches a wizard that copies WinPE to a hidden, bootable, file-based partition. It syspreps the system and then reboots into WinPE where it captures an image of the system.

   The wizard also prompts for a target location, filename, and credentials. Figure 19.29 shows the first screen of the wizard.

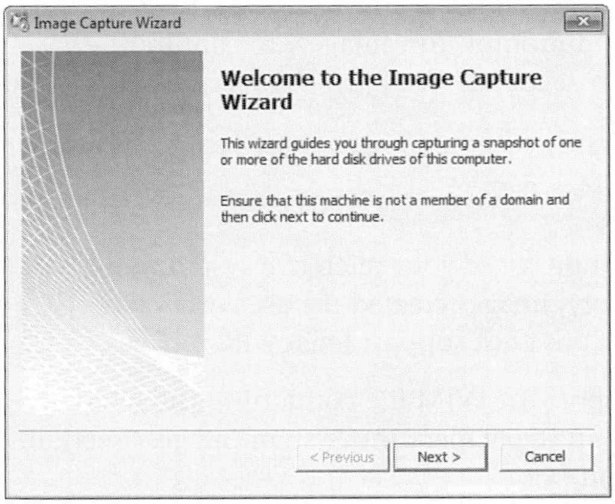

FIGURE 19.29   Capture Media Wizard.

The wizard checks for the existence of the proper sysprep folder and files on the target system. For Windows 7, this is not an issue because they are included with the OS; for Windows XP this means obtaining the proper set of sysprep files from the deploy.cab file and copying them into a new folder at the root of the C: drive named sysprep. Finally, the wizard prompts you for a UNC path to create the image at and credentials to access the UNC and then proceeds to capture the system.

It is also possible to boot into a custom version of WinPE and manually initiate ImageX. Follow these steps:

1. **Create a bootable WinPE Image:** See Microsoft's walkthrough at http://technet. microsoft.com/en-us/library/cc766385.aspx for complete details. Be sure to include ImageX in the image.

2. **Install Windows**: Install Windows according to the Install Windows step (step 1) in the previous procedure in this section.

3. **Sysprep Windows:** Run sysprep from the command line with the following options for Windows 7:

   ```
   sysprep /generalize /quiet /shutdown
   ```

   For Windows XP, run the following:

   ```
   sysprep /mini /quiet /reseal /shutdown
   ```

   You can also run the GUI version of sysprep by not specifying any command-line options and choose the options listed above in the resulting dialog box.

4. **Boot PE:** Boot the reference system into WinPE using the image you created.

5. **Map Network Drive:** From the PE command line, map a drive letter to the destination share (for example, `net use Z: \\<computername>\<sharename>`) and enter the proper credentials when prompted.

6. **Run ImageX:** From the same PE command prompt, run ImageX to capture the image using the following syntax: `imagex /capture [image_path] [image_file] ["name"] <"description">`. For example:

   ```
   imagex /capture c: z:\MyImage.wim "My Image Name"
   ```

Either method creates a WIM file containing an image of your reference system, fully compatible and usable by OSD. OSD also supports images created for use with WDS because they share the same WIM format. OSD does not support **legacy** RIS images.

After creation in the location you specified, import the WIM file containing the reference image into ConfigMgr using the steps outlined in the "Operating System Images" section. To use this, see the "Image Deployment" section.

Image Upkeep

Image upkeep involves either refreshing an image to include new items such as Windows and other software updates or completely new software applications, configurations, or customizations. Because your images should be hardware agnostic, you should never have to re-create or update them for new hardware or system models.

If you use Build and Capture task sequences to create your images, image upkeep is a matter of updating the task sequence as appropriate and rerunning it. For updates delivered using the built in software updates functionality of ConfigMgr, you won't even have to update the task sequence; simply re-run the task sequence. Using Build and Capture task sequences also ensures your image is built cleanly every time instead of working from a previous installation of Windows that may or may not be clean or could be in some unknown state.

If you choose to create your images manually, upkeep is somewhat more complicated and involves more manual work. If you haven't planned correctly, this may actually involve building your entire image from scratch again.

If you insist on manually creating and maintaining your images, an advanced technique is to use the restore point capabilities of your virtualization software. Using this technique, you create multiple save states including just before you prepare the system for imaging. This way, you can easily restore the state of the system to any point in time including just before it was sysprepped, make your desired changes including adding the latest Windows updates, and then sysprep and capture it—being sure to create another save state so that you can return to it in the future.

Returning to a save state before the sysprep is important, particularly with Windows 7 images.

▶ With Windows XP, many people simply redeployed their image, made their changes, sysprepped, and recaptured the system. Although this technically worked, it is discouraged for several reasons; the main reason not to do this is because re-sysprepping a system can and often does result in odd, unexplained behavior. This is well documented over the past decade; the best solution is to always use a clean system to install a fresh copy of Windows.

▶ With Windows 7, re-sysprepping is even more problematic because of the need to activate it. Windows 7 activation can be re-armed three times—sysprepping does not reset this counter and actually uses one of the possible re-arms. This means that you cannot re-sysprep a Windows 7 reference image more than three times. You could sysprep a Windows system without re-arming activation using the `-skiprearm` option, but this option does not reset the grace period for Windows activation, which can also be problematic.

This means you should not re-sysprep a system unless you like troubleshooting odd, one-off issues. And of course, always thoroughly test the new image to ensure you didn't break anything.

Offline Software Updates

Whether you use a Build and Capture task sequence to automatically build your images or manually build your images, a great new feature of ConfigMgr 2012 is the ability to install updates directly into an image contained in a WIM file. This functionality isn't actually new as it has existed in the stand-alone DISM tool from the beginning, but incorporating it directly into the ConfigMgr console makes it more accessible, enables it to leverage the software updates functionality of ConfigMgr itself, and makes it schedulable.

The only prerequisite for installing updates offline is that you have a properly installed and configured software update point and the desired updates are in a deployment package, as described in Chapter 14, "Software Update Management." Note that not all updates can actually be installed using this facility: only updates for Windows 7 itself can be installed. Specifically, only updates that are part of the Component-Based Servicing (CBS) model are available for installation offline—for more information on CBS, see http://blogs.technet.com/b/askperf/archive/2008/04/23/understanding-component-based-servicing.aspx.

To initiate offline updates, follow these steps:

1. Navigate to **Software Library -> Overview -> Operating Systems -> Operating System Images**. Select the image you want to update from the list of images on the right, and choose **Schedule Updates** from the ribbon bar or right-click context menu to launch the Update Operating System Image Wizard.

2. On the Choose Updates page, shown in Figure 19.30, select from the available updates. As mentioned above, only updates in a deployment package and that are CBS updates are available for selection. You can filter by architecture and by a simple filter box.

3. On the Set Schedule page, choose either to install updates as soon as possible or at a custom time.

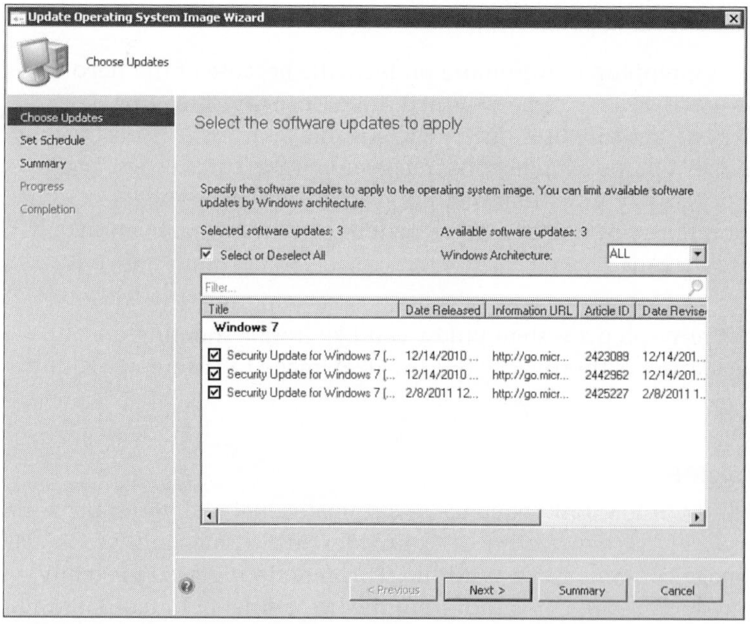

FIGURE 19.30   Choose Updates page of the Update Operating System Image Wizard.

Based on the schedule you set, ConfigMgr creates a copy of the image, mounts this image copy, automatically installs the updates you selected into the image, and moves the updated image back to its original location. In general, this process is not overly intensive but should still be scheduled after hours to avoid adversely affecting ConfigMgr's performance and avoid affecting active deployments. To allow for testing, it is best to create a full duplicate OS image package including a duplicate WIM to which to install the updates.

Image Deployment

After your image is created, it is time to deploy it using a Deployment task sequence. Deployment task sequences are typically much more involved than Build and Capture task sequences because they incorporate all the various tasks to deploy a complete end-user system.

To create a Deployment task sequence, you must first have an image to work with that is imported into ConfigMgr. If you also plan to migrate user data, you must also have a USMT package built and available, as described in the "Creating the USMT Package" section. Creating an Image Deployment task sequence is nearly identical to creating a Build and Capture task sequence, as outlined in the "Automatic Image Creation" section; to create one, follow these steps:

1. Navigate to Software Library -> **Overview** -> **Operating Systems** -> **Task Sequence**, and choose **Create Task Sequence** from the ribbon bar or right-click context menu to launch the Create Task Sequence Wizard.

2. Select **Install an existing image package**.

3. The remaining significant pages in the wizard define how to deploy a fully functional Windows system from a reference image.

   ▶ **Task Sequence Information:** On this page, you define the Task sequence name and Description and set which boot image to use.

   ▶ **Install Windows:** Choose the OS image to use, enter a product key (not required if deploying Windows 7 and using a KMS), and enable or disable the local administrator account. If enabled, you must also specify a password. By default, the task sequence is configured to Partition and format the target computer before installing the OS. If you are creating this task sequence for a refresh scenario and want to save user state locally, uncheck this check box.

   ▶ **Configure Network:** Specify the workgroup or domain to join on this page along with the user account to use to join the domain.

   ▶ **Install Configuration Manager client:** Choose the built-in ConfigMgr client agent installation package and add any additional installation properties. For deployments of workgroup systems, adding the SMSMP= property is highly recommended because the system is not joined to the domain and therefore cannot locate the MP or use AD.

   ▶ **State Migration:** Options specified on this page configure the task sequence for a refresh scenario by including an initial set of tasks to capture user state and optionally capture Windows settings and network settings, and a final set of tasks to restore user state. You must specify the USMT package to use here as well as whether to Save user settings on a State Migration Point or Save user settings locally. If you selected to format and partition the computer system on the Install Windows page, saving the user state locally option is not available for selection.

If you enable the capture of user state in the wizard, the resulting Capture User State task is configured to copy user state locally. As discussed in the "User State Without SMP" section, hard-linking is generally preferred, so you may want to update this task after the task sequence is configured so hard-linking is used instead.

If you plan to use this task sequence for a replace scenario on destination systems, the condition placed on the Capture Files and Settings group will prevent it from running because the task sequence is initiated in WinPE and not from a current OS. For a task sequence that captures only user state on the source system in a replace scenario, delete the Install Operating System and Setup Operating System groups.

▶ **Include Updates:** Choose whether to include updates in the reference system image. For updates to be considered, they must be in a deployment that targets the same collection also targeted by this task sequence's deployment.

▶ **Install Applications:** Select applications to add to the reference image.

Figure 19.31 shows a default task sequence generated by the Create New Task Sequence Wizard.

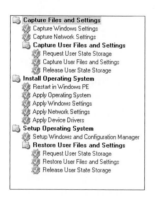

FIGURE 19.31   Default Image Deployment Task Sequence.

NOTE: X86 OR X64 FOR TASK SEQUENCE BOOT IMAGES

There are two basic types of boot images available: one for each major Windows architecture type. Which should you use? To deploy a Windows image using a Deployment task sequence, you can actually use either regardless of the architecture of Windows you are deploying. For a Build and Capture task sequence that directly references OS source files in the form of an OS Installer, the boot image used must match the architecture of the OS source files.

The primary point here is that using the x86 boot image for both x86 and x64 OS deployments is generally practiced by most organizations because it means not having to maintain both flavors of the boot image and eliminates any confusion over which boot image is being used or delivered to the client using PXE. You must still use the x64 boot image in x64 Build and Capture task sequences, but this limited use of the boot image makes it easier to manage.

The confusion arises when using unknown computer support in combination with available (nonrequired) task sequence deployments. In this case, ConfigMgr does not know which boot image to deliver to the client and chooses the boot image associated with the task sequence deployment with the highest assignment ID. This typically corresponds to the task sequence most recently deployed. This behavior is technically undefined, meaning it is not documented making it subject to change without notice.

User Device Affinity

As discussed in Chapter 13, user-centric is a main theme in ConfigMgr 2012. This means managing your users as well as the systems in your environment. This is most evident when deploying applications; no longer do you have to assign applications to systems that do not use applications. Instead, the users who request and actually use the applications are targeted, allowing the application to potentially follow users around to multiple systems or their new system without any additional work.

This last part is directly applicable to OSD. If you choose to deploy applications to users instead of systems in your organization, you can essentially forget about having to add any user-specific applications to your task sequences. This should greatly simplify your task sequences and the process of creating and testing them, because the only thing left after removing the user-specific applications is a static list of tasks and possibly some hardware-centric tasks.

If you choose to use the user-centric approach to deploy applications, assign the primary user to the system during the task sequence. Immediately following completion of the task sequence, the applications assigned to that user are deployed to the system without the user having to log onto the system—this is known as application pre-deploy. This partially violates the goal of having everything ready for the user at the completion of the task sequence, but it greatly reduces the complexity and enormity of managing software in your organization.

Another complication that may arise is as some (or all) software is deployed after the task sequence, it is possible the software installation overwrites some of the user's preferences previously restored during the task sequence using the user state capabilities of OSD and USMT. For Microsoft and well-behaved application installers this shouldn't be an issue, but only testing will reveal this issue in your deployment.

19

To enable user-centric application deployment in your task sequences, follow these steps:

1. For PXE initiated task sequences, you must enable the User device affinity option on the PXE tab of a DP's Properties dialog box (see Figure 19.22). A similar option is available for bootable media during its creation.

2. For non-PXE and nonbootable media initiated task sequences or to override the value set for PXE or in the bootable media, assign one of the following values to the SMSTSAssignUsersMode task sequence variable:

   ▶ **Auto:** Enables user assignment during the task sequence and automatically approves it.

   ▶ **Pending:** Enables user assignment during the task sequence but waits for administrator approval.

   ▶ **Disabled:** Does not allow user assignment during the task sequence.

   These two methods of setting the value enable scenarios in which users are involved initiating the deployment of a task sequence. For these user-initiated scenarios, setting the UDA assignment to pending may be preferred.

3. Assign the name of the primary user for the system to the SMSTSUdaUsers variable in domain\username format. To assign multiple users, add them to the same variable, in the same format, and separated by a comma; for example, to assign Niall and Greg from the Odyssey domain, set the variable to **odyssey\nbrady,odyssey\ gramsey**.

4. Ensure all applications that you want to pre-deploy based on UDA have deployments assigning them to the appropriate users. These deployments must be set to Required and must have the Deploy automatically according to schedule with or without user login option selected, as shown in Figure 19.32.

You can set the two variables listed here in any method that fits your needs as discussed in the "Variables" section. If configured correctly, the user-targeted applications will automatically begin pre-deploying within a minute of completion of the task sequence. Unfortunately, the only way to verify this is to check the system's log files or use ConfigMgr reporting. There is no notice of the beginning or completion of this process.

Deployment Challenges

Obstacles and barriers to successfully deploying Windows abound and are often unique to specific environments. Windows Vista added to these with multiple new features such as BitLocker and User Account Control (UAC). The Windows 7 base image size is also greatly increased over Windows XP, adding to overall deployment time and increasing the need for a well-connected environment for general deployment. The next sections discuss some of the more common deployment challenges.

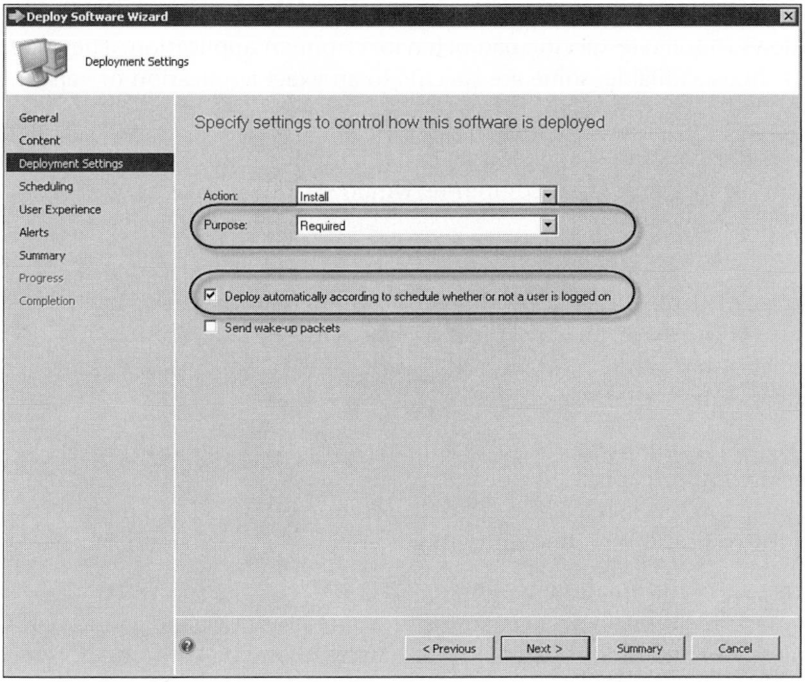

FIGURE 19.32   Pre-deploy Application Deployment options.

Application Compatibility

Application compatibility is the number-one challenge listed by the various think tanks (including Microsoft itself) when moving to Windows 7. Although this challenge is outside the scope of OSD, its importance cannot be stressed enough. You can perfectly plan and execute a Windows 7 deployment to your organization but if a single critical application, say the CEO's secretary's day-planner application does not run correctly under Windows 7, the success of your entire deployment (and possibly your job) are now in jeopardy.

Microsoft's Application Compatibility Toolkit (ACT) allows you to collect information about the various applications in your environment including a simple inventory as well as run-time diagnostics to identify potential issues—after running this tool, many organizations are quite surprised by not only the number of applications, but also the existence of various applications they have! ACT connects to Microsoft's application compatibility information repository to retrieve and present Microsoft-provided and peer-provided data on application compatibility. Using this data, you can proceed to perform your own application compatibility testing, which ACT can help you track. Finally, ACT is the gateway into remediation of applications when the vendor of the application cannot help for various reasons or you are stuck on using a specific incompatible version of an application.

ACT provides the ability to add fix-ups called *shims* that change the behavior of Windows itself or instruct Windows to tolerate specific bad behaviors from an application. There are thousands of different shims available; some are specific to an exact application or version and some are generic.

Microsoft provides an entire portal on application compatibility including in-depth information on ACT at http://technet.microsoft.com/en-us/windows/aa905066.aspx.

User Data

Maintaining user data when deploying a new OS is extremely important. Going back to the most important person in any organization, the CEO's secretary, if you somehow do not restore the wallpaper of her grandchildren or lose the data in her day planner, once again your deployment/job may be in jeopardy.

The only time user data is not important is with complete bare-metal scenarios. However, it is quite rare for users in your organization not to have a system with pre-existing data on it unless your organization has managed to centralize all user data using core file services or has forced the responsibility of maintaining user data on the users themselves.

In all other cases, users expect Information Technology (IT) to take care of their data. Thankfully, USMT does work almost like magic and is integrated into OSD in ConfigMgr, enabling you to seamlessly maintain user data without having to purchase a wand of your own.

Image Maintenance

An additional major challenge is image maintenance in general. Images are built from reference systems. Reference systems are systems used to build baseline images for deployment to the rest of the systems in your organization. Because hardware differences between a reference system and target deployment systems can cause issues, you must often use multiple reference systems to model your environment and thus create multiple images.

Enabling creation and deployment of this image is what OSD focuses on. However, OSD cannot automate the actual choice or definition of what goes into an image because this is not a technical decision.

A general definition of an image is a single file that stores all the files and information for a specific disk drive volume on a computer system. This file is portable and can be copied or deployed to a destination system. Deploying the image file creates an exact duplicate of the original source volume. This allows you to copy the content of a disk drive volume containing an OS, installed applications, and customizations to multiple other destination systems.

In effect, the image clones the source system and allows rapid deployment of an OS on a large scale. The process of copying the image to multiple machines is much quicker than a native Windows install and requires little manual intervention compared to a full Windows installation that includes applications and other miscellaneous configurations.

Each image is also specific to a specific OS version and edition. Thus if you want to deploy Windows 7 Professional x64, Windows 7 Professional x86, Windows 7 Enterprise x64, Windows XP Professional x32, and Windows Server 2008 R2 x64, you need five separate images.

A prerequisite to the imaging process is performing an inventory of all software and hardware in your organization. This helps you take into account all possible variations—you must know all the possibilities to create the best possible images.

A question often asked is whether to include applications in the image and which ones. Do you include Microsoft Office? Microsoft Silverlight? Antivirus? Questions like these abound and fuel the continuing debate between using a thick or thin image. The distinction between thick and thin images is somewhat subjective, so start with some simplistic definitions:

▶ **Thick image:** An image including the OS, OS updates and patches, miscellaneous components, drivers and applications

▶ **Thin image:** An image containing the OS with only a minimal set of updates and patches

Conventional wisdom is that a thin image is the better choice—why is this the case? A thin image is easier to maintain; it contains a minimal set of components and thus a smaller set of components that require updates. Like many theories, this sounds great, but reality gets in its way. If you automate creation of the image, updating it on a periodic basis, no matter how frequent, then creating a new image is as simple as added the latest updates (whatever they may be) and initiating the process. This is ultimately a subjective choice and depends upon your organization's goals and practices.

Here are several common or universal goals for deployment images that you should factor into your choice:

▶ **Hardware agnostic:** Few organizations can actually standardize on a single hardware system for all their workstations, so this goal should be obvious. What might not be as readily obvious is that it is achievable! The main obstacles to this goal are drivers and the Hardware Abstraction Layer (HAL) in Windows XP. Windows 7 changes the way mass-storage drivers are handled and automatically changes HALs as needed, so these concerns are no longer valid for the newer operating systems.

▶ **Universal:** Images should be a baseline for all your deployments; they should contain the greatest common denominator of all the desktop needs in an organization. If not everyone requires a specific application, component, driver, and so on, it should not go into the image—you want to layer it on after deploying the image. This simple but important goal greatly affects your success with OSD. Creating an optimal universal baseline relies on your knowledge of the hardware and software in use and the accuracy of your inventory. Being universal also implies a single base image is used on all hardware models. There are some limitations such as OS editions—Enterprise versus Professional or x86 versus x64—but fewer images means less work and less testing.

▶ **Deployment speed:** Although not as important as the previous goals in this section, deployment speed is still valid and becomes important if the network is not as fast as it should be or a WAN is involved. Applications and components included in an image only slightly increase the time it takes to deploy a system, as they are already installed and do not have to be pulled across the network separately. Applications and components layered on after the deployment might increase overall deployment time significantly because they are pulled over the network. Typically, installations include some files not even installed on the system, such as setup.exe or alternate language resource files (in the form of Dynamic Link Libraries or DLLs), which are installed only on systems supporting those languages. This can have a greater impact than first realized.

▶ **Ease of maintenance:** In traditional, image-only deployment systems, ease of maintenance is typically the most important factor. Creating and updating images is often an intensive and lengthy manual process. Images created for these systems are typically thinner, to avoid putting in any components that might need updating. This ultimately increases overall deployment time and can increase the complexity of the deployment. ConfigMgr automates creating images, greatly easing this burden and freeing you from making decisions about your images that are based solely on maintaining the images.

An additional consideration is whether you can install an application generically or have its internal unique identifiers stripped. Sysprep does this for Windows, and OSD properly prepares the ConfigMgr client, but you must also think about the applications in the image. Some centrally managed antivirus products have trouble when installed in an image; they customize themselves to the specific system they are installed on and do not behave well when copied to another system as part of an image. This is something to verify with the vendors of the products you plan to incorporate into the image and is an area you should test.

Ultimately, thin versus thick is a moot argument. Every deployment image will probably be somewhere in the middle, and what is right for one organization might not be right for another. Having a thin image, just for the sake of having a thin image, should not be a primary goal. Maintaining images, if it is automated and done correctly in line with the goals above, is a minor concern.

Hardware Considerations

Sometimes hardware differences between references systems cause problems. If you create the image properly, it can truly be hardware-agnostic. This task may be more difficult in Windows XP than Windows 7 because of HAL issues and mass storage drivers, but it is not impossible. To implement OSD successfully, you should derive a full inventory of all hardware used in the targeted environment. From this inventory, determine if any anomalies exist, if all the drivers are still available from the manufacturer, and if all the systems meet the minimum requirements for the OS you deploy.

As OSD includes the ability to inject drivers into the deployment process, you do not have to include all possible drivers from all systems in your organization, bloating your images with files not used on every system. Driver injection is discussed in the "Driver Management" section of this chapter.

When deploying Windows XP, different HAL types are potentially the biggest obstacle to creating a hardware agnostic image. Here are the six HAL types supported by XP:

- ▶ ACPI Multiprocessor PC

- ▶ ACPI Uniprocessor PC

- ▶ Advanced Configuration and Power Interface (ACPI) PC

- ▶ MPS Multiprocessor PC

- ▶ MPS Uniprocessor PC

- ▶ Standard PC

The non-ACPI HALs in this list are legacy types and normally needed only for old hardware. Based on your hardware inventory, you probably can rule out their use.

TIP: IDENTIFYING THE HAL

The Microsoft TechNet article "Identifying Hardware That Impacts Image-based Installations" (http://technet2.microsoft.com/windowsserver/en/library/942aaa8c-016f-4724-9a0f-04871abadd1a1033.mspx?mfr=true) describes how to identify what HAL a running system uses. Briefly, you must inspect the properties of the hal.dll file located in %*systemroot*%\ system32 and compare the file details to the chart in the article.

You can identify the exact HAL in a captured image by right-clicking the image in ConfigMgr and choosing **Properties**. In the resulting dialog box, choose the Images tab at the top; see Figure 19.33 for an example.

Eliminating legacy hardware typically leaves the following three ACPI HAL types three rules for imaging:

- ▶ **Images created with ACPI Uniprocessor PC HAL:** You can deploy these images to hardware requiring either ACPI Uniprocessor or ACPI Multiprocessor HALs.

- ▶ **Images created with ACPI Multiprocessor PC HAL:** You can deploy these images to hardware requiring either ACPI Uniprocessor or ACPI Multiprocessor HALs.

- ▶ **Images created using the Advanced Configuration and Power Interface (ACPI) PC HAL type:** You cannot use these images on systems requiring either of the other two HAL types. Fortunately, hardware requiring this HAL type is outdated and no longer common.

19

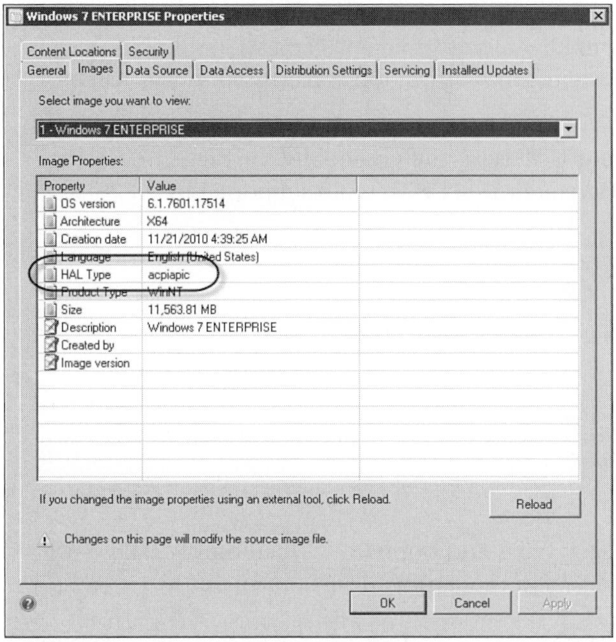

FIGURE 19.33   OS Image HAL Type.

This means you have to create only one image to support all your systems because they all require either ACPI Uniprocessor or ACPI Multiprocessor HALs. If through trial and error or through your hardware inventory you discover that another HAL type is in use, the only supported method of deploying images is to create multiple images, each containing a different HAL.

Mass storage drivers present a similar challenge; because they are essential to booting a system, they are referred to as *boot critical*. Windows XP does not include a huge variety of the modern boot critical drivers; this includes a lack of SATA drivers. You add boot-critical drivers to Windows XP in a different way than all other hardware drivers; you see this when manually installing a system requiring a boot-critical driver because you need to push F6 to install the driver during the blue screen pre-installation phase. OSD gracefully handles this situation with little overhead or extra work as discussed in the "Drivers Category" section.

Windows 7 includes the most popular SATA drivers out-of-the-box. If you do encounter a drive controller requiring a driver not included out-of-the-box, you can load the driver the same way as other hardware drivers—this is due to an architectural change made by Microsoft in the boot process and the handling of boot critical drivers starting in Windows Vista.

Although creating multiple images initially sounds like a bother, it should not be. If you have properly automated your image build process using a Build and Capture task sequence (discussed in the "Task Sequences" section), creating multiple images is as simple as running that sequence on a system supporting each type of HAL in your inventory. The task sequence is automated, so the images will be identical except for the HAL type that they contain. That's not to say that having multiple images of the same OS edition is a good thing, but in this case, there is no supported, practical alternative.

In addition, using the magic that is ImageX, these images can be merged into a single file using the /append option: imagex /append *<image_path> <image_file> <"image_name">* [*<"description">*]. Because of the single instancing of WIM images, the resulting WIM file contains only one copy of each file in common between the images (which will be every file except one, the hal.dll). The result is that the WIM file will be only slightly larger than maintaining separate WIM files for each version.

The only real pain point with this solution is finding a reference system for each type of HAL. Because most of these HALs are legacy and used only on aging or outdated hardware, chances are that you do not have any in your lab and will have to procure one from an active user.

Monitoring Task Sequence Deployments

How do you know what task sequences ran where? Did they complete successfully? Did you just accidentally image the CEO's secretary's system? These questions are similar to those that you ask about all of your deployments in ConfigMgr. The next sections discuss how to monitor your task sequence deployments.

Update Deployment Status

You can spot check individual task sequences in the console by selecting them under the **Operating Systems -> Task Sequences** node in the Software Library workspace and choosing the **Deployments** tab from the Detail pane at the bottom. Each task sequence listed in this view by default shows the deployment start times and an overall compliance percentage for all targeted systems. Multiselecting task sequences hides the Detail pane, so you cannot get a summarized pie chart from multiple updates in this view. Unfortunately, this view is devoid of any useable information and is thus essentially useless.

For those of you coming from ConfigMgr 2007, you may not know that the term *deployment* is now universally used for all types of activity in ConfigMgr 2012 that pushes something to a managed system or user including applications, software updates, and operating systems.

Following this terminology unification is also unification of reviewing and monitoring the deployments for all of these activities in the console, under **Monitoring -> Deployments**. Clicking the Deployments node lists all available deployments. Sort by the Feature Type column to isolate all Task Sequence deployments quickly; filter to narrow the results even more. Selecting a deployment here shows summarized information for the deployment in the Detail pane, including a pie chart showing completion statistics.

Double-clicking a deployment creates a sticky-node under the Deployment node in the navigation tree. Selecting this sticky node shows detailed information about the

19

deployment status of the deployment. The view pane shows five tabs, one for each deployment status:

▶ Success

▶ In Progress

▶ Error

▶ Requirements Not Met

▶ Unknown

Listed under each tab is the number of systems for that deployment status, and the actual systems with that status are listed in the **Asset Details** pane at the bottom.

The information displayed here is summarized from information in the actual database. Summarizations are automatically run on a periodic basis and can be forced by choosing the **Run Summarization** option from the ribbon bar. The time of the last summarization is displayed in the upper right of the view pane along with links to **Run Summarization** and **Refresh the view**.

Reporting

Reports are the final source for monitoring and reporting on actual update status, compliance, and installation results. Reports are advantageous because the consumer of the update status information does not require access to the ConfigMgr console to view the data. As described in Chapter 18, "Reporting," reports are flexible and do not require specific ConfigMgr administrator involvement.

Out-of-the-box, ConfigMgr contains 28 specific OSD reports. This should be sufficient for most organizations. The beauty of reporting services is that you or another user can create custom reports for your specific needs and organization.

Troubleshooting

Should one of your task sequences encounter an issue, you have to step into the world of OSD troubleshooting. Finding and correcting problems in OSD is similar to fixing issues elsewhere in ConfigMgr—check the logs. The trick, as always, is to find the correct log. You can find a complete list of all OSD logs as part of the log file listing in Appendix A, "Configuration Manager Log Files," and at http://technet.microsoft.com/en-us/library/ bb932135.aspx. OSD has expanded on this by including robust status messages and the OSD home page, which summarizes available information.

Command Line Support

A highly recommended troubleshooting step is to enable command line support in WinPE. When enabled, you can start a separate command line by pressing F8 while a target system is booted into WinPE. From this command line, you can launch Windows Notepad to view log files (such as smsts.log covered in the next section) or otherwise inspect the target system. A common use of this command line is to run `ipconfig /all` to verify that network drivers have been loaded with proper configuration of IP-related network information. To enable command-line support, edit the properties of your boot images by right-clicking them and selecting **Edit**. Go to the WinPE tab, and check the option to **Enable Command Support**, highlighted in Figure 19.34.

CAUTION: COMMAND SUPPORT SECURITY RISK

You cannot restrict access to the command line during a task sequence after it is enabled in a boot image. From the command line, internals of the OSD and Windows deployment process are accessible including certain passwords stored in clear text.

In general, enabling command support is considered an acceptable risk by most organizations as it is relatively hidden and obscure. Otherwise, there is no way to troubleshoot connectivity or other startup issues experienced in the OSD process. If you follow sound security practices, the accounts used and embedded in the process should be least privilege accounts that have the power to only do their specific tasks.

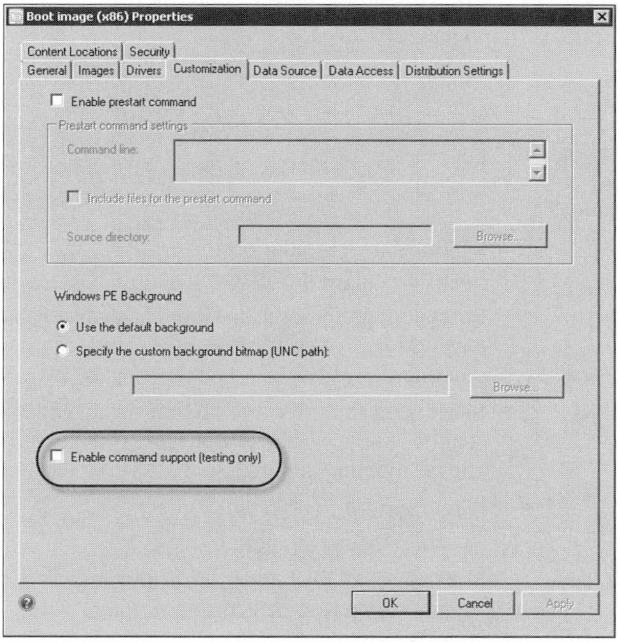

FIGURE 19.34   Enable Command Prompt Support Boot Image option.

NOTE: CMTRACE AUTOMATICALLY INCLUDED

Unlike ConfigMgr 2007, the ConfigMgr log viewing tool, now called CMTrace, is automatically included on all boot images.

The Smsts.log File

After checking deployment status, the next place to look when troubleshooting is the smsts.log on the target system. This client side log file lives in various places depending on the stage of the deployment, as listed in Table 19.4. The smsts.log file is a detailed log of every task sequence related action that takes place on a target system. It usually indicates exactly why a task sequence fails and reviewing it is the single most important step in troubleshooting a task sequence: when in doubt, check smsts.log.

You might also want to check http://blogs.technet.com/inside_osd/archive/2007/12/13/troubleshooting-tips.aspx for additional information. Steve Rachui of Microsoft discusses an excellent method for copying the OSD log files, including smsts.log, at http://blogs.msdn.com/steverac/archive/2008/07/15/capturing-logs-during-failed-task-sequence-execution.aspx. Note that although both of these previous links were written for ConfigMgr 2007, the information and techniques presented are still applicable.

One shortcoming of the smsts.log file is it has a maximum 2MB limit and is not verbose by default. Increasing this limit or enabling verbose logging involves multiple steps, described at http://blogs.technet.com/b/system_center_configuration_manager_operating_system_deployment_support_blog/archive/2011/10/12/how-to-change-logging-options-for-smsts-log-in-system-center-configuration-manager-2007.aspx.

TABLE 19.4   Smsts.log Locations

Deployment Finished	Status	ConfigMgr Client Installed?	Location
No	WinPE running	N/A	Windows temp folder on the WinPE RAM-disk: x:\windows\temp\smsts.log
No	Deployed OS running	Yes	Smstslog subfolder in the ConfigMgr client logging folder: usually *%windir%*\ccm\logs\smstslog
No	OS Setup running	No	SMSTSLog folder on the largest available volume: usually %*_SMSTSMDataPath*%\Logs\Smstslog\smsts.log
No	Deployed OS running	No	Windows temp subfolder: *%windir%*\temp\smstslog
Yes	WinPE running	N/A	SMSTSLog folder on largest available volume: usually %*_SMSTSMDataPath*%\Logs\Smstslog
Yes	Deployed OS running	Yes	ConfigMgr client logging folder: usually %windir%\ccm\logs
Yes	Deployed OS running	No	Windows temp folder: usually *%windir%*\Temp

ERROR CODES

There is no complete list of error codes that can be returned by a task sequence or the program and command lines it executes. This is because ConfigMgr and OSD use a variety of tools and Windows APIs to perform their work, and anything custom you add to a task sequence may have its own set of nonstandard error code. Here are several suggestions in diagnosing error codes:

▶ A good place to start is the ever-handy Trace32 log viewer. A built-in error lookup function in this tool available from the menu, **Tools** -> **Error Lookup**, attempts to look up an error number and return a friendly message. This message is often informative and can lead you down the path to finding the actual issue.

▶ You can also find a list of common OSD-relevant error codes and possible solutions available on TechNet, at http://technet.microsoft.com/en-us/library/bb735886. aspx.

▶ Another guide to helping decipher error codes is at http://blog.configmgrftw. com/?p=42.

One error that is commonly misinterpreted is 0x80004005. This error code is not "Access Denied," it is "Unspecified Error."

Windows Setup Log Files

As mentioned in the "Images Category" section, the Setup Windows and ConfigMgr task actually runs Windows setup, which is effectively a black box to the task sequence. If Windows setup has issues for whatever reason, these are not reflected in smsts.log. To troubleshoot these issues, reference the Windows setup log files as outlined at http://support.microsoft.com/kb/927521.

A related log file is %*windir*%\debug\Netsetup.log. This log file reflects domain join activity and should be reviewed if systems are not successfully joined to the specified domain during a task sequence.

Troubleshooting USMT

Troubleshooting USMT is a log examination exercise that first involves enabling verbose logging on the Capture User State and Restore User State tasks. A full discussion of the resulting log files is at http://technet.microsoft.com/en-us/library/ dd560780%28WS.10%29.aspx.

19

Summary

As is clearly seen by the size of this chapter, OSD is a huge topic that perhaps surprisingly is not even completely covered in this chapter. There are entire books dedicated to the subject that still do not cover every possible detail or nuance. Many organizations have dedicated deployment experts whose only job is deploying Windows and implementing OSD.

Although not dramatically changed from ConfigMgr 2007, OSD gives you the power and flexibility to deploy server and workstation images regardless of the hardware that you have in your organization. It enables you to prepare the hardware and layer on applications, drivers, and other customizations after deploying the image. Infinite customization allows it to fit your every need while also reducing the maintenance overhead involved with manually creating and maintaining multiple images.

PART V

Administering System Center 2012 Configuration Manager

IN THIS PART

Security and Delegation in Configuration Manager

Information is the most important asset belonging to most organizations today. Ensuring information integrity, confidentiality, and availability is a central value proposition for effective systems management. This chapter discusses the role of System Center 2012 Configuration Manager (ConfigMgr) in securing your environment. It presents the new role-based administration (RBA) model and considers the proper delegation of administrative roles to reduce the risk of accidental or intentional misuse of rights. A critical consideration is protecting your ConfigMgr infrastructure from being compromised and used against you. The chapter therefore takes an in-depth look at security for ConfigMgr servers, clients, and network communications. You should consider security requirements throughout the ConfigMgr deployment lifecycle.

Planning for Security and Delegation

ConfigMgr security is not a one-size-fits-all proposition. Choosing an appropriate security configuration and delegation of administrative rights requires a sound understanding of the technical issues involved. It is equally important to identify your most important information assets and understand your organization's business considerations around security. You should be aware of relevant policies and regulations as well as company standards for procedural and technical controls. Involve the security team early in your deployment planning. Not only can you avoid costly delays or poorly planned "bolt-on" security controls, you can likely gain a strong advocate for systems management as the security team becomes aware of the security and compliance solutions ConfigMgr can deliver.

The principal objectives of information security are to protect data confidentiality and integrity, and service availability. It is also essential to maintain a reliable audit trail of actions taken on the system. Here is how these objectives can be described:

▶ **Confidentiality:** Protecting company secrets as well as third party information in your company's custody is essential to avoid potential legal sanctions and financial losses.

▶ **Integrity:** Effective security must protect information and systems from unauthorized modification.

▶ **Availability:** An interruption of vital services might cause losses equal to or greater than a lapse in confidentiality or integrity.

▶ **Accountability:** To demonstrate you follow security policies and can take corrective action if a security breach occurs, you must maintain effective audit logs to track security sensitive operations on a per user basis. With increasing emphasis on regulatory compliance, the completeness and integrity of audit logs and records of user activity is an integral part of any security program.

A ConfigMgr security breach could compromise the confidentiality of data stored in the site database and on the managed systems. A poorly designed software package or malicious use of ConfigMgr tools can compromise service availability or data integrity in your environment. Some ConfigMgr services may have high availability requirements of their own. For example, users may depend on ConfigMgr to stream applications to their desktops. If you enforce Network Access Protection (NAP), clients might need to access ConfigMgr remediation services in order to access the network. You should consider potential scenarios and their business impact as you prioritize your security efforts.

A guiding principle in security is the concept of risk management. It is not possible for any organization to keep its assets completely secure. Here are some essential terms used in risk management:

▶ A *vulnerability* is a weakness that could result in compromise of the confidentiality, integrity, or availability of your information or systems.

▶ A *threat* is a potential danger to your information systems. Keep in mind that threats include both malicious and inadvertent actions. Good security helps protect against honest mistakes by users and deliberate breaches by hackers and malware creators.

▶ A *risk* is the likelihood of a threat being realized and the associated business impact. In some cases, you can quantify risk in monetary or other terms; however, it is often more practical to make a qualitative assessment. For example, you might determine that a particular risk is highly likely but has low business impact.

Effective risk management depends on understanding the risks to your systems and data, and making appropriate business decisions on how to deal with each set of risks. Here are some approaches for dealing with risk:

▶ **Risk avoidance:** You might decide the business value of undertaking a technology initiative simply does not justify the risk. For example, you determine the value to your company of Internet-based client management (IBCM) is not sufficient to justify exposing your ConfigMgr infrastructure to the Internet.

▶ **Risk mitigation:** You might decide to implement countermeasures to address potential threats to reduce risk. For example, you could choose to implement a public key infrastructure (PKI) and configure ConfigMgr clients for Hypertext Transfer Protocol Secure (HTTPS) to reduce the chances of a network-based attack on ConfigMgr communications.

▶ **Risk acceptance:** You might decide to accept certain risks if both the business value of the activity and cost of implementing additional controls to mitigate risk outweigh the potential losses posed by the risk. For example, you decide to accept the risk of using a system at a remote location as a distribution point (DP) that does not meet the normal security standards of your server infrastructure. You would choose to accept this risk if you determine the value of the services the DP provides is sufficient to justify the risk, and the cost of implementing a higher level of security is not justified by the risk mitigation it would provide.

Several ConfigMgr features can provide significant risk mitigation for your managed systems. The next section reviews these features.

ConfigMgr Security Solutions

System Center 2012 Configuration Manager can play a major role in supporting your security program. Previous chapters present a number of ConfigMgr features you can use to enhance the security of your environment. Here are some of these features:

▶ **Patch Management:** A large number of exploits take advantage of unpatched systems that remain vulnerable even after a fix is available from the software vendor. ConfigMgr facilitates patch management for Microsoft operating systems and applications through its software updates feature set. Chapter 14, "Software Update Management," discusses patch management.

▶ **Network Access Protection:** Keeping unpatched or otherwise inadequately protected systems from accessing your network and remediating those systems where possible provides a strong line of defense against threats that might use these systems to breach network security. Chapter 14 also includes a discussion of NAP.

▶ **Compliance Settings:** Misconfigured systems are another major category of vulnerabilities that can expose your network to attack. Microsoft provides a set of configurable baselines, which represent recommended best practices. The ConfigMgr compliance settings provide the capability to evaluate your systems against these

20

baselines. As the name suggests, the compliance settings feature also automates much of the reporting necessary to demonstrate regulatory compliance. Chapter 10, "Managing Compliance," discusses compliance.

▶ **Endpoint Protection:** ConfigMgr can provide centralized management of Windows firewall policies and System Center Endpoint Protection antimalware policies. Endpoint protection also allows you to manage System Center Endpoint Protection engine update and signature file distribution. Chapter 16, "Endpoint Protection," discusses endpoint protection.

Beyond these specific features, a well-managed environment is inherently more secure than a less managed environment. Central management of day-to-day IT functions such as software installation, operating system upgrades, and troubleshooting reduces the need for large numbers of privileged users and provides better auditing and control. Comprehensive inventory and reporting are essential to security planning. Much of this chapter focuses on potential misuse or compromise of the ConfigMgr infrastructure. You should keep in mind that the risks of not having effective configuration management are much greater.

The next section, "Role-Based Administration," describes how to assign the appropriate ConfigMgr administrative access.

Role-Based Administration

RBA is one of the most important enhancements in System Center 2012 Configuration Manager. It allows you to manage administrative rights efficiently so each user has only the access required for their job function. An administrator with full access to your ConfigMgr hierarchy has the ability to perform an almost unlimited range of actions within your managed environment. Here are some examples of what a person with the requisite permissions can do:

▶ Distribute and run any code of his choosing on any ConfigMgr client system, using either the privileged system account or the credentials of the logged-on user. This singular ability gives the administrator virtually unlimited control over the managed environment.

▶ Collect and view any file from client systems. This makes all data stored in the file systems of your client systems potentially accessible to the ConfigMgr administrator.

▶ Interact directly with client systems through remote tools or out of band (OOB) management. With OOB management, an administrator can reboot a client and interact with the system during boot sequence—potentially booting to an ISO image. This gives the administrator potential ways to view and control user activity or access the machines in an unauthorized manner.

Misuse of administrative rights can occur in three ways:

▶ An authorized ConfigMgr administrator can deliberately abuse his privileges.

▶ An attacker can gain access to the administrator's account. This is most often achieved though social engineering methods such as *spear phishing*—targeting the administrator with an email designed to install a key stroke logger or other malware on the administrator's system. Other methods such as hardware keystroke loggers, password cracking, or interception of network authentication traffic may also be used.

▶ An administrator may make an honest mistake. You need to understand that appropriate controls around system administration are as important for limiting accidental damage as they are for preventing malicious activity.

The ConfigMgr 2012 RBA security model is similar to that of other products in the System Center suite. A role is defined for each set of administrative tasks. Each user (ConfigMgr administrator) is assigned a role based on his or her job function. The role provides the minimum privilege required to carry out the user's responsibilities.

RBA replaces the class and instance security model used in previous versions of the product. The previous model required segregation of administrative access by sites. ConfigMgr provides a customized user experience to administrators, who see only objects and options relevant to their job function. This eliminates the need to create and distribute custom consoles as was commonly done in ConfigMgr 2007.

Managing Administrative Users

Before you can assign a user or group to a role, you must add them as an administrative user. Administrative users should not be confused with administrators; administrative users only have the rights provided by their specific roles. To add administrative users, perform the following steps:

1. Navigate to the Administration workspace, and right-click **Administrative Users** under the **Security** node; then select **Add User or Group**. Figure 20.1 shows the Add User or Group dialog.

2. Click **Browse**; then select a user or group from the Select User, Computer, or Group dialog. As a best practice, you should generally assign roles to Active Directory (AD) groups rather than individual users.

3. Click **Add**; then select one or more roles from the Add Security Role. Figure 20.2 shows the Add Security Role dialog with roles selected for key endpoint security functions.

4. Optionally, you can restrict the account to assigned security scopes or collections. The "Security Scopes" section of this chapter discusses these options.

20

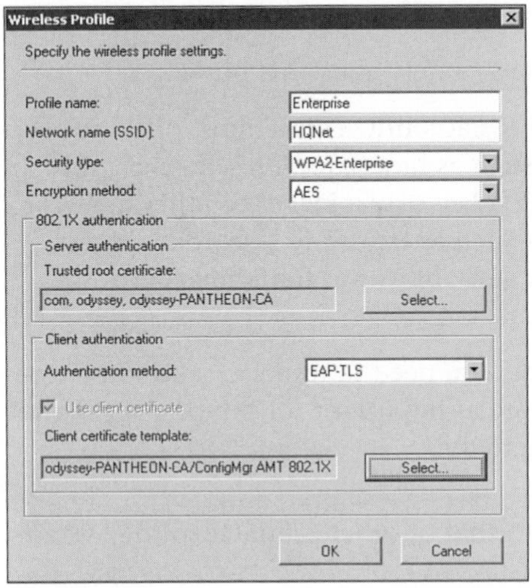

FIGURE 20.1   The Add User or Group dialog.

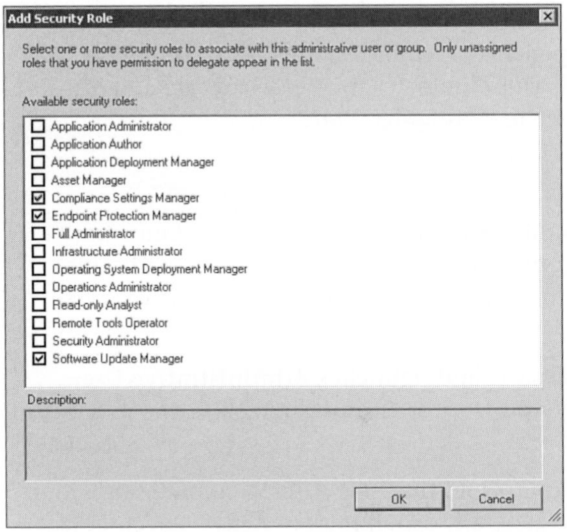

FIGURE 20.2   Associating Compliance Settings, Endpoint Protection, and Software Updates management roles with the new Endpoint Security user.

Security Roles

A *security role* consists of a set of related permissions that allow a user to perform specific tasks. System Center 2012 Configuration Manager provides several built-in roles addressing common administrative responsibilities. You can create additional roles and customize them to the particular needs of your organization. Security roles are hierarchy wide and replicate to all sites.

Built-In Roles

The built-in security roles represent typical sets of job responsibilities for Information Technology (IT) administrators needing access to ConfigMgr. If these roles meet your requirements, you can assign them to administrative users. Although you can view the properties of each in role, you cannot modify them. The "Custom Roles" section of this chapter describes how you can use these roles as templates to create custom roles. To access the built-in roles, navigate to **Administration -> Security** and select the **Security Roles** node. Table 20.1 presents the built-in security roles together with their descriptions.

TABLE 20.1   Built-In Roles

Role	Description
Application Administrator	Grants permissions to perform both the Application Deployment Manager role and the Application Author role. Administrative users associated with this role can also manage queries, view site settings, manage collections, and edit settings for user device affinity.
Application Author	Grants permissions to create, modify, and retire applications. Administrative users associated with this role can also manage applications, packages.
Application Deployment Manager	Grants permissions to deploy applications. Administrative users associated with this role can view a list of applications, and they can manage deployments for applications, alerts, templates and packages, and programs. They can also view collections and their members, status messages, queries, and conditional delivery rules.
Asset Manager	Grants permissions to manage the asset intelligence synchronization point, asset intelligence reporting classes, software inventory, hardware inventory, and metering rules.
Compliance Settings Manager	Grants permissions to define and monitor compliance settings. Administrative users associated with this role can create, modify, and delete configuration items and baselines. They can also deploy configuration baselines to collections, and initiate compliance evaluation, and initiate remediation for noncompliant computers.
Endpoint Protection Manager	Grants permissions to define and monitor security policies. Administrative users who are associated with this role can create, modify, and delete endpoint protection policies. They can also deploy endpoint protection policies to collections, create and modify alerts and monitor endpoint protection status.
Full Administrator	Grants all permissions in ConfigMgr. The administrative user who creates a new ConfigMgr installation is associated with this security role, all scopes, and all collections.
Infrastructure Administrator	Grants permissions to create, delete, and modify the ConfigMgr server infrastructure and to perform migration tasks.

20

Role	Description
Operating System Deployment Manager	Grants permissions to create operating system images and deploy them to computers. Administrative users associated with this role can manage operating system installation packages and images, task sequences, drivers, boot images, and state migration settings.
Operations Administrator	Grants permissions for all actions in ConfigMgr except for the permissions required to manage security, which includes managing administrative users, security roles, and security scopes.
Read-Only Analyst	Grants permissions to view all ConfigMgr objects.
Remote Tools Operator	Grants permissions to run and audit the remote administration tools that help users resolve computer issues. Administrative users associated with this role can run Remote Control, Remote Assistance, and Remote Desktop from the ConfigMgr console. In addition, they can run the out of band management console and AMT power control options.
Security Administrator	Grants permissions to add and remove administrative users and to associate administrative users with security roles, collections, and security scopes. Administrative users associated with this role can also create, modify, and delete security roles and their assigned security scopes and collections.
Software Update Manager	Grants permissions to define and deploy software updates. Administrative users associated with this role can manage software update groups, deployments, deployment templates, and enable software updates for NAP.

To mitigate the risks of someone with administrative access to ConfigMgr misusing her privileges, you should follow these principles as you develop your ConfigMgr administrative model and procedures:

▶ Employ separation of duties wherever possible to make it more difficult to abuse administrative access. When a person carries out improper activity on his own, the level of effort and risk of being caught is much lower than it would be if collusion with others were necessary. For example, a user with the Application Administrator role could introduce unauthorized or malicious code into an application and then target-specific systems for attack. The alternative of assigning the Application Author role and the Application Deployment Manager role to separate individuals helps to mitigate this risk. The extent to which you choose to separate responsibilities for related tasks depends on your security requirements and available resources.

▶ Grant the least privilege necessary for each administrator to carry out his responsibilities. Assigning overly broad privileges to users or administrators greatly increases the chances of compromising systems or data. Review permissions in the built-in roles and consider customizing the roles by removing those permissions not required in your administrative model.

The Full Administrator role provides unrestricted access to all ConfigMgr operations. If your organization separates security administration from operational duties, you might assign the Security Administrator and Operations Administrator roles to separate users; however, you must have at least one user with the Full Administrator role. The "Auditing ConfigMgr Administrative Actions" section explains how auditors or security personnel can keep an eye on all administrative users, including full administrators.

Custom Roles

You can create a custom role by copying an existing role and then editing the permission set of the copy. Here is the procedure to create a customized security role:

1. Navigate to **Administration** -> **Security**, and select the **Security Roles** node.

2. Right-click the role you want to customize, and choose **Copy**.

3. In the Copy Security Role dialog, enter the name and an optional description for the new role. Figure 20.3 shows the Copy Security Role dialog for the Service Desk Operator role. The Service Desk Operator role will be a copy of the Remote Tools Operator role with additional permissions to deploy specific diagnostic and maintenance software.

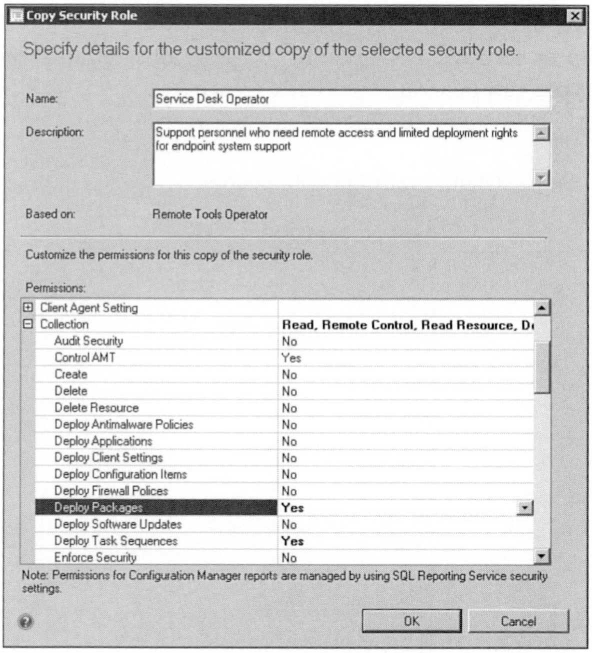

FIGURE 20.3   Copying and Configuring the new Service Desk role.

You can export a custom role and import it into a different hierarchy. For example, you might develop and test all custom roles in your lab environment, and import them in production. After creating a custom role, you can edit its permission set and other properties on the role's property sheet. Built-in roles and roles imported from other hierarchies are not editable.

Security Scopes

Security roles define the operations a user can perform on each class of securable objects. You can further limit an administrative user's access rights by specifying the securable objects users have for each role.

▶ To specify the set of devices and users an administrator can manage, assign specific device collections or user collections to the administrator. You can assign one or more collections to each user. You can also assign a different set of collections to a user for each role the user holds. By default, the All Systems and All Users collections are assigned to each administrative user.

▶ To specify other sets of objects an administrator can manage, assign specific security scopes to the administrator. A *security scope* is essentially a container that contains one or more types of securable objects. You can assign one or more security scope to each administrative user. You can also assign a different set of security scopes to a user for each role the user holds. The Default security scope is assigned to each administrator by default.

▶ Permissions on some types of objects apply to all type instances and cannot be restricted by collection membership or security scope. Table 20.2 lists all securable object types and indicates which types can be associated with security scopes.

TABLE 20.2   Securable Objects That Can Be Associated with Security Scopes

Object Type	Assignable to Scopes
Administrative User	No
Advertisement[1]	No
AI Software List	No
Alert	No
Antimalware Settings	Yes
Application	Yes
Authorization List	Yes
Boot Image Package	Yes
Boundary	No
Boundary Group	Yes
Client Settings	Yes
Client Settings Assignment[1]	No
Configuration Item	Yes
Configuration Item Assignment[1]	No

Object Type	Assignable to Scopes
Collection[2]	No
Device Enrollment Profile	No
Distribution Point	Yes
Distribution Point Group	Yes
Driver	No
Driver Package	Yes
Firewall Policy	No
Global Condition	Yes
Image Package	Yes
Inventory Report	No
Metered Product Rule	Yes
Migration Site Mapping	No
Migration Job	Yes
Mobile Device Setting Item	Yes
Mobile Device Setting Package	Yes
Operating System Install Package	Yes
Package	Yes
Query	Yes
Security Role	No
Secured Category	No
Site	Yes
Software Update	No
Software Updates Package	Yes
State Migration	No
Status Message	No
Subscription	Yes
Task Sequence Package	Yes
Template	No
User Machine Relationship	No

[1] *Advertisements, Client Settings Assignments, and Configuration Item Assignments are internal objects that represent relationships between other objects. Advertisements represent assignments of deployments to collections and should not be confused with advertisements used in earlier versions of the product.*

[2] *You can limit a user's view of collections in the actual user account definition as well, as described in the "Managing Administrative Users" section.*

20

There are two built-in security scopes: All and Default. Administrators assigned the All security scope can administer all objects related to their role. Built-in instances and newly created instances of securable objects are also assigned to the Default security scope. Here is the procedure to create additional security scopes:

1. Navigate to **Administration -> Security**, and right-click **Security Scopes**.

2. Choose **Create Security Scope**.

3. In the Create Security Scope dialog, enter the Security scope name and an optional description, and then click **OK**. Figure 20.4 shows the New Security Scope dialog for the Service Desk scope.

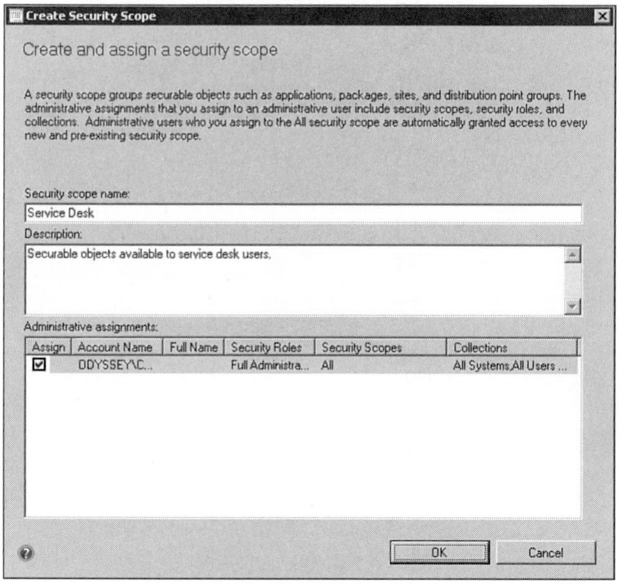

FIGURE 20.4   Creating the Service Desk Security scope.

After creating a new securable object, you can set its security scopes. Follow these steps:

1. Locate and right-click the object in the ConfigMgr console. You can use the standard CTRL and SHIFT options to multiselect objects for which you want to specify the same scopes.

2. Choose **Set Security Scopes**.

3. In the Create Security Scope dialog, select one or more scopes you would like to associate with the objects, and then click OK. Figure 20.5 shows the Set Security Scopes dialog.

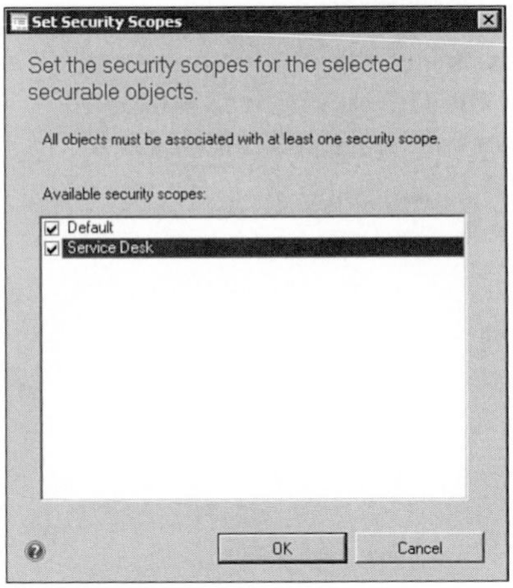

FIGURE 20.5   Associating the Service Desk Security Scope with an object.

In ConfigMgr 2007, it was common to create separate sites to restrict the scope of administrative access. Security scopes generally eliminate the requirement to use sites as a security boundary in System Center 2012 Configuration Manager. You may choose to remove the All Systems and All Users collections from all administrative users. This means users can only see and manage resources in collections to which you explicitly grant them access. Using this model minimizes the chances that a user can accidentally gain access to resources they do not need to see. Allowing access to All Systems and All Users collections simplifies administration by eliminating the requirement to grant access explicitly to individual collections. Keep in mind that when you create a collection, you can base the new collection on an existing collection. Users with access to the original collection inherit access on those collections based on it.

Associating Security Scopes and Collections with Individual Roles

An administrative user assigned more than one role may have the same security scopes and collections available for all roles, or have different security scopes and collections available for each role. For example, an endpoint security group might manage software updates and endpoint protection for both servers and desktops but compliance settings only on end user systems. To prevent this group from deploying compliance settings to servers, remove the All Systems collection and assign a collection consisting of desktops and laptops only. To prevent this group from deploying compliance settings designed for servers to user systems, remove the Default security scope, and add a security scope consisting of settings designed for the appropriate systems. Perform the following steps:

1. Navigate to **Administration -> Security**, and select **Administrative Users**.

2. Double-click the user you want to customize to open the Property page.

3. On the Security Scopes tab, select the radio button for **Associate assigned security roles with specific security scopes and collections**. Select the role you want to edit. Figure 20.6 shows the Security Scopes page for the Odyssey\CM12 Endpoint Security group with the Compliance Setting Manager role selected. Click **Edit** to open the Edit Security Scope dialog.

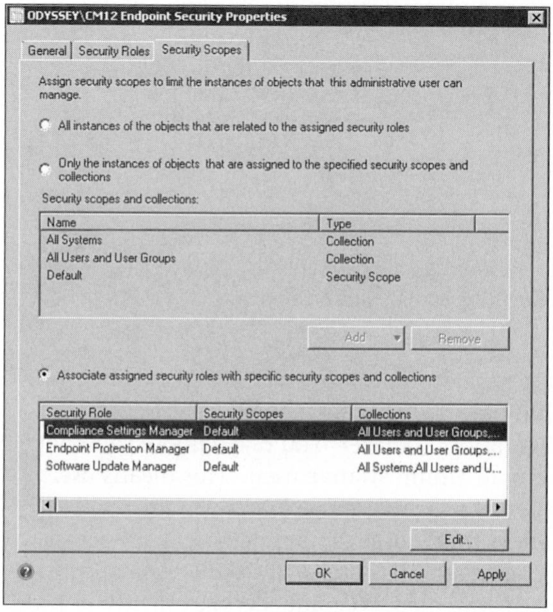

FIGURE 20.6   Associating roles with specific scopes and collections.

4. In the Edit Security Scope dialog, select the **All Systems** collection and the **Default** security scope, and click **Remove**. Click the **Add** button and choose **Collection**. Select **Device Collections** from the upper-left drop-down, and check the box for the appropriate collection; click **OK**. Click **Add** again and choose **Security Scope**, select the appropriate scope, and click **OK**. Figure 20.7 shows the edited list of security scopes, in this case for the Endpoint Security group.

Administrative Security Reports

ConfigMgr provides several reports related to security administration. To view these reports in the Odyssey environment, open http://armada/reports in a web browser, and click the **Administrative Security** folder. As an example, Figure 20.8 shows the rights for the Odyssey\CM12 Endpoint Security security group on Configuration Item objects. The report shows that the group only has rights on objects associated with the End User System Security scope. Chapter 18, "Reporting," provides detailed information about reports in ConfigMgr.

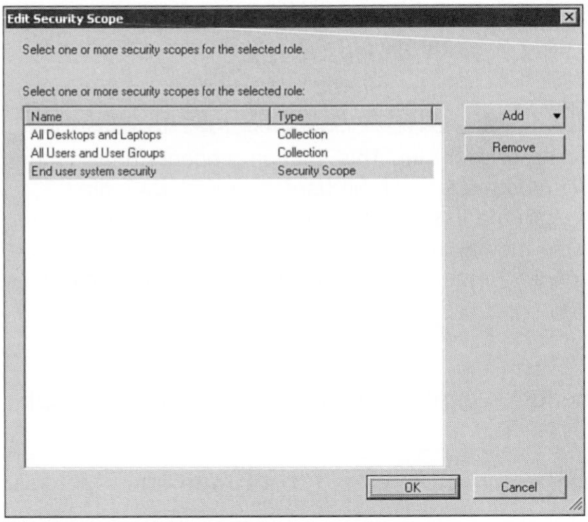

FIGURE 20.7   Security Scope and Collections for the Compliance Settings Manager role assigned to the Odyssey\CM12 Endpoint Security group.

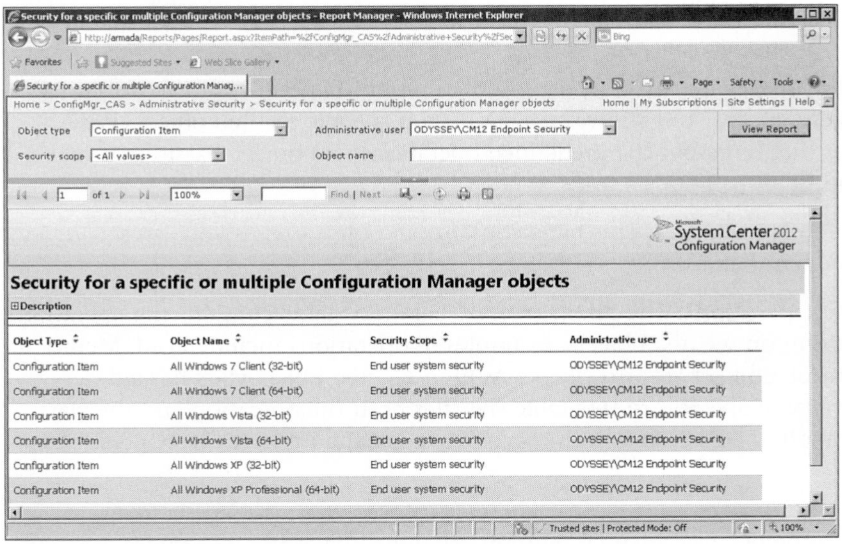

FIGURE 20.8   The Security for a Specific or Multiple Configuration Manager Objects report.

RBA Under the Hood

ConfigMgr stores data related to securable objects, administrative users, security roles, and other RBA constructs in the site database. Although you will not work directly with RBA data in the site database, looking at the inner workings of RBA can help you understand the concepts more fully. Chapter 3, "Looking Inside Configuration Manager," describes the site database and introduces the tools used to examine database objects.

> **CAUTION: DO NOT MODIFY THE SITE DATABASE DIRECTLY**
>
> The site database is critical to the functioning of your site. This section presents tools you can use to view the site database. This information can be useful for understanding how ConfigMgr works and for using ConfigMgr data in reporting. Do not attempt to create, delete, or modify any database objects, or to modify data stored in the database, unless asked to do so by Microsoft support personnel. Remember to test all modifications before applying them to your production environment.

Here are the database tables containing the RBA security objects you can manage through the ConfigMgr console:

▶ **RBAC_Admins:** This object contains the Active Directory identity and other metdata for each administrative user.

▶ **RBAC_Categories:** This contains the properties for each security scope and associated metadata.

▶ **RBAC_Roles:** This object contains the properties for each security role and associated metadata.

The "Security Roles" section of this chapter describes assigning permissions to a security role. These permissions consist of allowed operations on specific secured object classes. Here are the tables that represent the predefined operations and object classes that make up these permissions:

▶ **RBAC_SecuredObjectTypes:** This table contains all object classes you can secure through RBA permissions.

▶ **RBAC_ObjectOperations:** The RBAC_ObjectOperations table contains the operations you can perform on secured objects. Examples of operations include Read, Modify, Remote Control, and Set Security Scope. As each secured object class has a different set of available operations, this table specifies both the operation and the class to which it applies. Figure 20.9 shows several rows of the RBAC_ObjectOperations table.

The columns of this table reveal many important relationships of the RBA tables. Here are the RBAC_ObjectOperations columns:

▶ **ObjectTypeID:** This is the unique ID for the type of object and is defined in the RBAC_SecuredObjectTypes table. As an example, the ObjectTypeID of the Collection type is 1.

ObjectTypeID	BitNumber	OperationName	BitFlag	IsTypeWideOperation	IsReadOnly
4	0	Read	1	True	True
4	2	Delete	4	True	False
4	10	Create	1024	True	False
4	28	Run Report	268435456	True	True
4	29	Modify Report	536870912	True	False
6	0	Read	1	False	True
6	1	Modify	2	False	False
6	2	Delete	4	False	False
6	4	Set Security Scope	16	False	False
6	10	Create	1024	True	False
6	14	Meter Site	16384	False	False
6	16	Manage Status ...	65536	False	False
6	18	Modify CH Settings	262144	True	False

FIGURE 20.9   Some RBAC_ObjectOperations entries for object types StatusMessage and Site.

▶ **BitNumber:** This is the bit number used to represent the operation in GrantedOperations columns of various database tables and views, as illustrated in the example later in this section. This value is also used in the exported eXtended Markup Language (XML) files for security roles.

▶ **OperationName:** OperationName is the descriptive name for the operation.

▶ **BitFlag:** BitFlag is the computed value of a 1 in the position specified in the BitNumber column. For example, the third row shown in Figure 20.9 shows the Create operation has a BitNumber of 10 and a BitFlag of 1024, which is 2^10. BitFlag can be used in bitwise operations to construct and de-construct GrantedOperations values.

▶ **IsTypeWideOperation:** This specifies whether the operation can be applied to individual class instances or to all instances at once (type wide). Notice that all operations shown in Figure 20.9 with ObjectTypeID = 4 (the Status Message type) are type wide. Status Messages are therefore an example of a `TypeWide` class. Notice that there is no "set security scope" for this class. Since each operation on a `TypeWide` class applies to all objects of the class, assigning permissions for those operations is class wide and cannot be limited by security scopes. This means you cannot assign permissions on individual status messages. The figure shows several operations with ObjectTypeID = 6 (the Site type) and IsTypeWideOperation = False. The `Site` class is therefore not TypeWide and has a "set security scope" operation; you can therefore assign permissions on specific sites.

▶ **IsReadOnly:** This specifies whether the operation modifies the object.

Table 20.2 listed the securable object types and specified whether objects of each type can be associated with security scopes. Within the database, you can determine whether an object type can be associated with a security scope by examining the IsTypeWideClass column in the vRBAC_SecuredObjectTypes database view.

The tables discussed at this point are the building blocks of the RBA model. Here are some tables ConfigMgr uses to connect them into meaningful permissions assignments:

▶ **RBAC_RoleOperations:** This table specifies the permissions on each object type assigned to each role. Each row consists of only three columns:

▶ RoleID specifies the role with matching ID in the RBAC_Roles table.

▶ ObjectTypeID specifies the object type.

▶ GrantedOperations is composed of the bit values of each granted operation as defined in the RBAC_ObjectOperations.

▶ **RBAC_CategoryMemberships:** This defines the security scope assignments for each secured object. Each row of this table consists of only three columns:

▶ CategoryID specifies the scope with matching ID in the RBAC_Categories table.

▶ ObjectTypeID specifies the object type.

▶ ObjectKey specifies the object instance.

▶ ObjectKey corresponds to a key value in the primary table for the object type. You can see the primary tables for each object type by viewing the object definition language for the vRBAC_AllItemsID database view.

▶ **RBAC_ExtendedPermissions:** This table associates administrative users with roles and scopes. This is essentially the information displayed on the Security Roles and Security Scopes tabs of the administrative user property page. Each entry consists of four columns:

▶ AdminID and RoleID correspond to unique identifiers in the RBAC_Admins and RBAC_Roles tables.

▶ ScopeID and ScopeTypeID define the scopes and collections associated with the user.

▶ **RBAC_InstancePermissions:** This specifies the granted operations each administrative user has on each secured object. Each row of this table consists of an AdminID column that identifies the administrative user, the ObjectTypeID and ObjectKey columns described previously under RBAC_CategoryMemberships, and a GrantedOperations that functions identically to the same column of the RBAC_RoleOperations table.

Figure 20.10 provides a database diagram that illustrates how the RBAC_RoleOperations table associates data from the predefined object types and object operations with a role to construct the object type permissions for the role. The tables shown in the figure are used in the query results in this section.

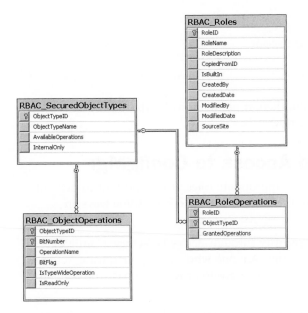

FIGURE 20.10 Database relationships used to specify role permissions.

As an example, here is one row of the RBAC_RoleOperations table:

```
RoleID          ObjectTypeID    GrantedOperations
CAS00004        44              268435457
```

RoleID CAS00004 matches this entry in the RBAC_Roles table:

```
RoleID          RoleName
CAS00004        Service Desk Operator
```

ObjectTypeID 44 matches the following entry in the RBAC_SecuredObjectTypes table:

```
ObjectTypeID    ObjectTypeName
44              SMS_InventoryReport
```

Converting GrantedOperations = 268435457 to binary yields 10000000000000000000000000001. The granted operations are therefore the operations on the Inventory Report object type with bit numbers 0 and 28 for in the RBAC_ObjectOperations table. The following query retrieves the granted operations:

```
SELECT [ObjectTypeID],[BitNumber],[OperationName],[BitFlag]
  FROM [CM_CAS].[dbo].[RBAC_ObjectOperations]
  WHERE [ObjectTypeID] = 44 and [BitNumber] in (0,28)
```

20

Here are the query results:

```
ObjectTypeID      BitNumber        OperationName     BitFlag
44                0                Read              1
44                28               Run Report        268435456
```

This example shows how the Read and Run Report permissions for the inventory reports are assigned to the Service Desk Operator role.

Preventing Unauthorized Access to ConfigMgr

In addition to assigning authorized users to appropriate roles, it is important to prevent unauthorized or inappropriate use of administrative access. Here are some ways an attacker could gain unauthorized ConfigMgr rights:

▶ An attacker could alter ConfigMgr security through Active Directory. ConfigMgr roles are assigned to AD users and groups. Anyone who gains the requisite Active Directory privileges could add themselves to a group or reset the password on a user account to get access to ConfigMgr.

▶ An attacker could alter ConfigMgr security by directly modifying the RBA objects in the site database.

▶ An attacker could steal the credentials or hijack the session of a legitimate administrator.

Protecting against these risks requires effective security at the Active Directory and database layers, and maintaining a strong auditing policy. The following sections address these issues.

Securing Access at the Active Directory Level

Here are some ways to protect groups and user accounts with privileged access to ConfigMgr:

▶ Restrict rights to manage administrative accounts and groups to a small group of senior administrators. You should remove any delegated rights to groups such as helpdesk personnel. Consider moving administrative accounts and groups to specific organizational units (OUs) to simplify security management.

▶ Set auditing to record any changes to these user accounts and groups. Auditing policies are defined in the Default Domain Controllers group policy under **Computer Configuration -> Policies -> Windows Settings -> Security Settings -> Local Policy -> Audit Policy**. Events specified through the audit policy are recorded in the local security event log of the domain controller on which the event occurs. Some specific auditing settings you might consider include

    ▶ **Audit account management:** Events in the account management category include such sensitive operations as setting the password on a user account or adding a member to a group. Auditing account management is discussed in http://technet.microsoft.com/en-us/library/cc737542.aspx.

> ► **Audit directory service access (Windows Server 2003) or Audit directory service changes (Windows Server 2008):** Events in the directory service access category include modifications to specific AD objects such as users or groups. When you enable the directory service access auditing category through group policy, you also need to turn on auditing of the specific objects. Directory services auditing is described at http://technet.microsoft.com/en-us/library/cc731607.aspx.

► Provide ongoing education for administrators on security best practices. Some of the highest profile security breaches have targeted administrators with phishing or other social engineering methods. A hacker who tricks an administrator into clicking the wrong link or attaching the wrong device to their system has a good chance of compromising the network. Administrators should use a nonprivileged account to log on to their local workstation and perform routine activities such as checking e-mail and accessing the Internet.

► Pay extra attention to securing administrative workstations and other systems where the console is installed. The security practices discussed in the "Securing Site Systems" section of this chapter apply to administrative workstations and to servers. It is especially important to disable password caching on administrative workstations and to locate these systems in areas that are physically secure and not easily accessible to shoulder surfing.

This section described some specific Active Directory security practices that are particularly relevant to ConfigMgr administrative access. Microsoft provides guidance on Active Directory security best practices at http://technet.microsoft.com/en-us/library/cc773365.aspx.

Securing Access at the Database Level

System Center 2012 Configuration Manager supports SQL Server in either mixed mode or Windows-only authentication; you should choose Windows-only authentication for all site database servers. Windows authentication provides much stronger account controls and authentication mechanisms than are available for accounts defined in SQL Server. Database logins should be granted to Active Directory users and groups, rather than local users and groups on the database server.

As with any administrative access, you should assign SQL Server access on a least privilege basis. It is particularly important to limit access to privileged server roles such as sysadmin and securityadmin. There is generally no reason to assign database roles for the site database directly to users, and you should avoid doing this. If possible, use a dedicated SQL Server that is not shared with other applications. This will reduce the number of users needing access to the server as well as the overall attack surface of the database server.

Microsoft provides guidance on security considerations for SQL Server at http://msdn.microsoft.com/en-us/library/ms144228.aspx. Microsoft also provides a SQL Server best practices analyzer available for download at http://www.microsoft.com/download/en/details.aspx?id=15289. SQL Server Reporting Services (SSRS) implements its own role-based access control model. Chapter 18 describes SSRS security.

Auditing ConfigMgr Administrative Actions

Ensure audit trails for all security sensitive actions are properly preserved and that regular audits of your IT environment review ConfigMgr activity. Any environment will include some group of individuals with authority to carry out those actions required to administer information systems. Although you cannot generally block the administrative group from all opportunities to misuse their authority, increasing the chance of detection acts as a strong deterrent and reduces the chance of repeated or ongoing breaches of security taking place. Auditing is an area in which separation of duties should be strictly enforced; you should not rely on the administrators responsible for normal operations as the sole source of data or reports used for auditing purposes.

ConfigMgr generates status messages of type *Audit* to provide an audit record of certain security sensitive operations. Audit messages are generated for remote control of client systems and OOB management console activity. The SMS Provider also generates audit messages when a user creates, modifies, or deletes a ConfigMgr object or changes the associated security scopes for an object. Audit messages for object modifications indicate the user making the change, the target object class and object ID, and details indicating when and how the change occurred. The specific attributes changed are not included. Figure 20.11 shows an audit status message.

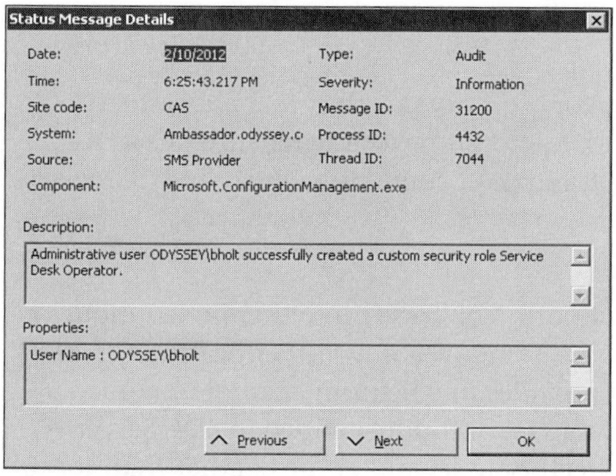

FIGURE 20.11   An audit status message for showing a new security role created.

Chapter 17, "Configuration Manager Queries," describes using how to run status message queries and create custom status message queries. Many of the built-in status message queries display audit messages. You can use these queries as provided and as examples to create your own queries. Here are the built-in status message queries you can use to audit administrative activity:

- ▶ All Audit Status Messages from a Specific Site
- ▶ All Audit Status Messages from a Specific User
- ▶ Boundaries Created, Modified, or Deleted

▶ Client Component Configuration Changes

▶ Collection Member Resources Manually Deleted

▶ Collections Created, Modified, or Deleted

▶ Deployments Created, Modified, or Deleted

▶ Packages Created, Modified, or Deleted

▶ Programs Created, Modified, or Deleted

▶ Queries Created, Modified, or Deleted

▶ Remote Control Activity Initiated at a Specific Site

▶ Remote Control Activity Initiated by a Specific User

▶ Remote Control Activity Initiated from a Specific System

▶ Remote Control Activity Targeted at a Specific System

▶ Security Roles / Scopes Created, Modified, or Deleted

▶ Server Component Configuration Changes

▶ Site Addresses Created, Modified, or Deleted

An important auditing consideration is the retention period for audit records. You may be required to retain audit data for a specified time to meet regulatory requirements. Chapter 21, "Backup, Recovery, and Maintenance," discusses audit message retention policy.

Chapter 18 describes the System Center 2012 Configuration Manager reporting features. ConfigMgr provides several reports based on audit messages. Table 20.3 lists reports you can use to audit sensitive actions.

TABLE 20.3   Reports Displaying Audit Messages

Report Folder	Report Name	Description
Status Messages - Audit	All audit messages for a specific user	Displays a summary of all audit status messages for a single user. Audit messages describe actions taken in the ConfigMgr console that add, modify, or delete objects in ConfigMgr.
Status Messages - Audit	Remote Control - All computers remote controlled by a specific user	Displays a summary of status messages indicating remote control of client computers by a single specified user.
Status Messages - Audit	Remote Control - All remote control information	Displays a summary of status messages indicating remote control of client computers.

20

Report Folder	Report Name	Description
Administrative Security	Administration Activity Log	This report shows the log of administrative changes made for administrative users, security roles, security scopes, and collections.
Out of band management	Out of band management console activity	Displays a list of status messages identifying out of band management console activity.

Figure 20.12 shows the Administration Activity Log report. This report can be filtered by user and activity type and makes a good starting point for reporting on auditable actions.

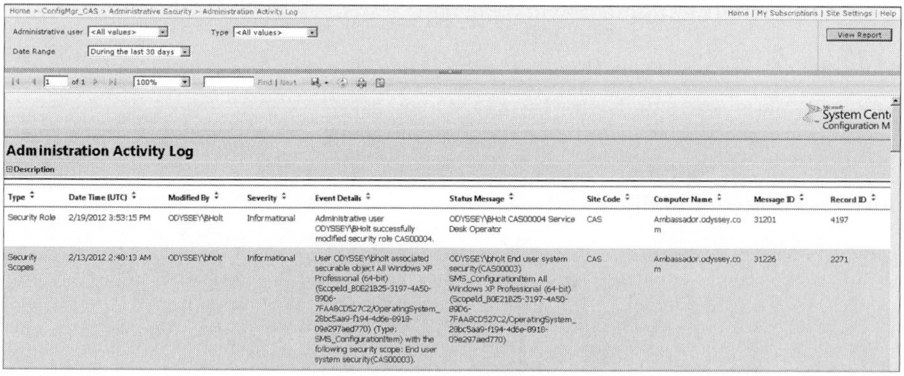

FIGURE 20.12   The Administration Activity Log report for all users and activity types.

Many organizations use a Security Information and Event Management (SIEM) solution to aggregate and correlate data from various security information and event sources. SIEM solutions monitor activity in real time and allow rapid detection and response to suspicious activity. If you have such a system available, it is desirable to connect all audit data feeds to the SIEM solution. Most SIEM solutions have facilities to extract event data from database sources. The site database stores status messages in the StatusMessages table in the site database. Audit messages can be distinguished by the condition [Type] = 768.

It is important to log and audit sensitive actions at every layer of the infrastructure. In addition to the auditing described in this section, auditing the following systems and services will help protect your ConfigMgr environment:

- ▶ Active Directory
- ▶ Site systems
- ▶ SQL Server activity
- ▶ Network infrastructure devices

Auditing for these environments is beyond the scope of this chapter. Microsoft provides extensive guidance on auditing AD, Windows, and SQL Server in the Learning Centers for each product.

Securing the ConfigMgr Infrastructure

Effective management and monitoring can greatly enhance the security of your environment. Potential compromise of a management application, however, is a threat you cannot afford to ignore. After all, why should an attacker go to the trouble of deploying and managing malware agents in your environment if he can just use the highly capable agents you have deployed for him? In recent years, many companies and government agencies have become victims of a class of attacks known as *advanced persistent threats* (APTs). APTs are created by sophisticated, well-financed hacker groups, often backed by nation states. Their targets include virtually every type of business, and their objectives are generally to steal valuable intellectual property and business secrets for military or economic advantage. These attackers often attempt to compromise domain controllers as a control point to reach systems across the enterprise. As companies use increasing vigilance to secure domain controllers, management systems become the next logical point of attack.

Critical infrastructure components that could be subject to attack include ConfigMgr site systems, accounts used by ConfigMgr, intersite and intrasite communications, and the file base and infrastructure services ConfigMgr depends on for its operations. Before considering each of these infrastructure components individually, look at how you should consider security when designing and planning your ConfigMgr infrastructure.

Building Security into Your Hierarchy

You should consider your organization's security requirements throughout the life cycle of your ConfigMgr implementation. During the design phase, keep the following considerations in mind:

▶ **Active Directory considerations:** Although it is possible for ConfigMgr sites and hierarchies to span more than one AD forest, this might compromise your AD security design. The forest is a security boundary in AD. Allowing administrators and systems in one forest to configure site systems or administer clients in a second forest could violate the autonomy of the forest in which the managed systems reside. The strongest protection for the integrity of your AD forests is to isolate each ConfigMgr hierarchy within a single forest. You should weigh this decision against the possible administrative advantages of using a single ConfigMgr hierarchy to manage multiple forests.

▶ **Configuration Manager site selection:** In general, the fewer sites you have, the easier it is to maintain site security. Additional sites increase the number of site servers, site databases and intersite communications links you need to administer and secure. In some cases, however, you might consider using dedicated sites for specific security needs, such as IBCM. Chapter 5, "Network Design," describes security considerations for IBCM.

20

▶ **Site system role assignment:** It is important to move client-facing roles, such as the management point and distribution point, off the site server. You can greatly reduce the risk of a network attack by restricting client access to only those server roles that require it. The site server and site database server are the most important roles in your site, and allowing clients to establish a network connection to these systems is a risk you should consider eliminating.

Separation of server roles generally reduces the requirement for services and open network ports on each system, thereby reducing the system attack surface. You need to weigh this advantage against the effort required to support and secure additional site systems. Installing Internet Information Services (IIS) on a server greatly increases the server's attack surface. For that reason, you should generally separate server roles requiring IIS from those that do not. You also need to separate the fallback status point (FSP) server role from all other system roles. The FSP must be configured to accept unauthenticated client data. Accepting unauthenticated client data presents a risk to which you should avoid exposing other site roles. Perhaps the most important security consideration for assigning system roles is to avoid using systems that host other applications as site systems, especially those with applications based on IIS or SQL Server. Poorly written or vulnerable web and database applications are favorite targets of attackers and could be exploited to gain control of a site system. Placing a distribution point on a server that provides file and print services is a much lower risk.

▶ **Server placement:** All site systems should be deployed in locations that are as secure as possible in terms of physical and network access. An attacker with physical access to a site system or administrative workstation could compromise your system. For example, the attacker could install a hardware device such as a keystroke logger or boot the system to an insecure operating system. Network traffic should be restricted to that necessary for ConfigMgr operations and basic server functions. If possible, place the site server and site database server in a secure management zone that is not easily accessible from systems with lower security requirements, such as user workstations. If administrators need to reach these systems from less secure network zones, they should use a virtual private network (VPN) to connect to systems in the higher security zone.

Securing Site Systems

Consider your ConfigMgr site server and site systems as among the most security-sensitive assets in your organization, on a par with domain controllers. All basic controls applicable to such systems should be applied to your site systems. The next sections discuss some of the types of controls you can use to protect site systems.

Physical Security and Hardware Selection

Choose the most secure possible location and hardware available for your site systems. Site servers and site database servers should be located in secure data centers. You need to balance security concerns with your other requirements as you consider the placement of client facing systems such as distribution points. Server-class hardware often provides functionality such as alarms that alert when detecting an open chassis or modifications to hardware. Newer hardware implements protection features such as processor-based data execution prevention (DEP). Choose hardware with the maximum reliability and redundancy for systems with high availability requirements.

System Software Security

Choose the most recent version of Microsoft Windows consistent with your system requirements, and stay current on all service packs and security patches. Evolving security awareness and technology is reflected in the design of modern operating systems, and each version of Windows has contained numerous security enhancements over its predecessor. Often the accumulation of small enhancements can make as much or more difference as the more highly publicized features. In addition to OS patches, you should keep system components such as the Basic Input Output System (BIOS) and firmware current and regularly update all drivers and applications installed on your systems.

A number of resources are available that provide current information on software and hardware vulnerabilities, threats, and countermeasures. The United States Computer Emergency Response Team (US-CERT) site, http://www.us-cert.gov/cas/alldocs.html, is a great place to start. US-SERT provides security bulletins, alerts, and a wide range of security-related information. Many software and security vendors provide additional vulnerability alerts and threat information services. Microsoft provides security bulletins related to Microsoft software and guides for securing Windows platforms and additional security information at http://www.microsoft.com/security/default.mspx.

Attack Surface Reduction and Server Hardening

A basic principle for securing any system is to reduce the number of potential vulnerabilities by eliminating unnecessary services, accounts, applications, network shares, open network ports, and so on. In addition to reducing the attack surface of your servers, you can "harden" the server by modifying default settings such as requiring the use of more secure network protocols and limiting access to certain graphical user interface (GUI) features. The key to reducing the attack surface without reducing required functionality is determining those features unnecessary on a particular system so you can turn them off. Microsoft provides a set of tools that greatly simplify attack surface reduction and server hardening for the Windows operating system and for ConfigMgr and SQL Server systems:

▶ **Windows Security Configuration Wizard (SCW):** The System Center 2012 Configuration Manager template for SCW is included as part of the Configuration Manager Toolkit, available at http://www.microsoft.com/en-us/download/details. aspx?id=29265. The authors highly recommend that you use this tool to configure all applicable site system roles.

▶ **SQL Server Surface Area Configuration for SQL Server 2008** or **Policy Based Management for SQL Server 2008 R2:** These tools assist you in turning off unnecessary SQL Server features.

▶ **ConfigMgr compliance settings:** Use the ConfigMgr compliance settings feature to ensure continuous compliance of system components such as IIS. Chapter 10 describes compliance settings.

20

Security Software

You should run antivirus software on all systems in your environment and update virus signatures regularly. Chapter 16 describes how you can use ConfigMgr to deploy and manage Microsoft endpoint protection software. Traditional antivirus software compares files and processes against a database of signatures used to recognize known malware. Signature-based malware detection is reasonably effective against widely deployed viruses, spyware, and other malware, and is an essential part of an antimalware strategy. Some antivirus programs also use behavior-based detection that responds to suspicious activity such as a program opening a network port. Additional enhancements include real-time feeds of threat intelligence information from the Internet. Even with these enhancements, traditional malware protection is only partially effective in detecting targeted threats, including APTs, for which signatures are unlikely to exist. Many organizations with high security requirements are incorporating application whitelisting programs into their malware protection strategy. Application whitelisting allows only specific processes to run on each system. Deploying application whitelisting technology requires that you provide methods to update all system components.

Software firewalls, including the Windows firewall, provide protection from network-based attacks. In high-security environments, you might choose to use specialized host intrusion prevention (HIP) software to provide an additional layer of protection by detecting and blocking a more extensive range of suspicious process activity, such as nonstandard memory access methods. File integrity monitoring (FIM) software protects critical files from alteration. You might consider using FIM to alert you if key ConfigMgr files such as the service executables, site control file, and client source files are altered.

Security programs are by their nature intrusive. They often consume significant amounts of system resources and sometimes block legitimate activity. You should test and adjust your security software settings in your proof of concept environment and monitor the impact of security software in your production environment. To improve system performance and availability, it is sometimes advisable to exclude certain directories from virus scanning. Exclusions are typically applied to files frequently accessed or generally locked during normal operations that are not common vectors for introducing malware into the environment, such as log files or the Windows paging file. Any scanning exclusions you create can introduce a potential weakness in your protection framework that could be exploited by malware. You should follow your organization's risk policy when considering any exclusions or exceptions in your controls framework. Microsoft recommends certain exclusions for all Windows systems as described in http://support.microsoft.com/kb/822158. Here are some additional virus scanning exclusions you might consider for ConfigMgr site systems:

▶ All files of type *.log.

▶ The Windows paging file, pagefile.sys.

▶ Any mapped network drives or Storage Area Network (SAN) storage mounted as drives. You can use antivirus software specifically designed for SAN environments to scan SAN storage.

▶ All files under the *<ConfigMgrInstallPath>*\Inboxes folder on ConfigMgr site servers, other than those in the clifiles.src sub folder.

▶ All files under the SMS_CCM\ServiceData folder on management points.

▶ The IIS Temporary Compressed Files and inetsrv folders on servers with IIS installed.

▶ The SQL Server database, backup, and log files on the site database server (*.mdf,*.ldf, *.ndf, *.bak, *.trn). If SQL Server is installed on a clustered SQL Server instance, you might also need to exclude the cluster folder and the quorum drive.

▶ The backup folder on the site server.

▶ The WSUS and MSSQL$WSUS folders on your SUP.

You should also consider any vendor-recommended exclusions for installed components such as backup software or host-based adapters (HBAs). Keep in mind, however, that vendors are typically more concerned with the functioning of their products than the security or your systems and might publish overly broad recommendations for excluding their software.

CAUTION: DO NOT DOWNLOAD FILES DIRECTLY TO EXCLUDED DIRECTORIES

With any exclusion, you should be sure to scan all downloaded files for malware before copying them to locations where they are excluded from scanning.

You should have a process to respond to events from security software such as malware detections and blocked activity. If you use System Center ConfigMgr Endpoint Protection, refer to Chapter 16 for information on alerts and notifications. If you find false positive detections, evaluate the impact on system functionality and modify security software settings as required. Chapter 3 introduces Process Monitor. If you suspect virus scanning is affecting system or application stability or performance, you can use Process Monitor to determine what files your virus scanner is opening. If you see files that are frequently scanned, you might consider them for exclusions. Some antivirus applications allow you to apply different on-access scanning exclusions based on the process accessing files. For example, a file modification by the Windows Module Installer (TrustedInstaller.exe) might be considered a low-risk event and not trigger a scan, while a file modification by Internet Explorer would be much more likely to introduce malware and warrant an immediate scan. Using this type of feature is safer than allowing all processes to read from or write to the excluded files without scanning. If your antivirus software supports it, designate the ConfigMgr processes as low risk and apply exclusions for specific site roles only to low risk processes. Here are some processes you might want to designate as low risk:

▶ ccmexec.exe (on management points)

▶ sitecomp.exe

▶ smsexec.exe

▶ smswriter.exe

▶ sqlservr.exe (on site database servers)

▶ sqlwriter.exe (on site database servers)

Securing Site System Local Administration

The built-in local Administrators group on any Windows system has complete and unrestricted access to the computer. Even without specific administrative rights within ConfigMgr, a member of the Administrators group on a ConfigMgr site system could potentially alter files, registry settings, or other items related to system configuration in ways that would affect ConfigMgr services. By default, the Domain Admins group for the local domain is part of the local Administrators group. Consider removing the Domain Admins group and replacing it with the appropriate AD group having direct responsibility for server administration of the site system. For non client-facing site systems, you might also consider removing the Domain Users group from the local Users group. The remaining built-in groups, such as Backup Operators and Power Users, should not contain any members unless required for your administrative processes. You should generally not create local users or groups on site systems other than those required by ConfigMgr. As with all Windows systems, rename the built-in Administrator account, set a strong password for that account, and use appropriate procedures to manage access to the account password. You should also disable the built-in Guest account. You can configure most of these settings locally or through group policy. Although Microsoft does not supply a tool to automate changes to the local Administrator account password across multiple systems, a number of third-party tools and scripts are available that supply this functionality.

> **CAUTION: ADMINISTRATION OF MACHINES DISJOINED FROM THE DOMAIN**
>
> The local Administrator account is often needed to log onto a machine that was removed from the domain. In this case, the account name reverts to its state before domain group policy was applied. You should always maintain accurate records of the local Administrator account name on each system independent of the group policy setting.

Just as auditing AD administration helps detect and deter misuse of domain level administrative privileges, auditing actions by administrators on site systems is an important part of your control framework. You can use group policy to enable the appropriate auditing. Here are some auditing categories you should consider enabling on site systems:

▶ **Audit account management:** Local user accounts and groups should rarely change, so auditing local account management on site systems will generate relatively little overhead.

▶ **Audit policy change:** As with account management, policy changes should rarely occur locally on servers. When changes do occur, you want to know about it.

▶ **Audit object access:** You should audit changes to files or registry setting that might affect ConfigMgr functioning. These might generate a considerable amount of audit events, so you need to set the audit policies carefully.

Auditing object access requires the policy to be set and auditing to be applied to specific objects. Here are some examples of objects you might want to audit on ConfigMgr site systems:

- ▶ Package source files
- ▶ Client source files
- ▶ The `HKEY_LOCAL_MACHINE\SOFTWARE\Microsoft\SMS\Security` registry key

As with any auditing, you should use caution and test your local audit settings thoroughly to avoid excessive auditing. Auditing large numbers of registry keys can have a severe performance impact.

Securing the Site Database

The site database server is the heart of your ConfigMgr site. Its security is at least as important as that of the site server. You should use a dedicated SQL Server for each primary site or locate the database on the site server. Microsoft continues to improve SQL Server security. You should use the latest version of SQL Server supported by ConfigMgr for site database servers and keep it updated with all service packs and security updates. At the time of writing this chapter, the recommended version is SQL Server 2008 R2 with Service Pack (SP) 1 and Cumulative Update (CU) 4. At secondary sites, be sure to apply the latest updates to your instance of SQL Server Express.

Configure SQL Server to use Windows authentication only and enable logging for at least failed logon attempts. Use a low privilege domain account for the SQL Server startup account, rather than running SQL Server under Local System. When you run SQL Server in a low privilege account context, you need to register the service principal name (SPN) for the server in AD manually. Clients use the SPN to locate SQL services. You can use the procedure described at http://technet.microsoft.com/en-us/library/hh427336.aspx#BKMK_ManageSPNforDBSrv to register the SPN.

Securing Additional Site Systems

Microsoft provides guidance for securing specific site system servers. You can access this guidance at http://technet.microsoft.com/en-us/library/gg682165.aspx#BKMK_Security_SiteServer. Here are the site systems for which Microsoft provides specific recommendations:

- ▶ Site servers
- ▶ Site database servers
- ▶ Site systems that run IIS
- ▶ Management points
- ▶ Fallback status point

20

ConfigMgr Cryptographic Controls

Cryptography is the science of using secrets to protect information. Cryptographic methods are an essential part of information security. ConfigMgr uses cryptography to support the following goals:

▶ **Confidentiality:** ConfigMgr uses encryption to prevent disclosure of sensitive data. Encryption converts data into a form that can only be read by parties with access to a secret key.

▶ **Authentication:** ConfigMgr uses digital certificates to authenticate the identity of systems during network communications and to sign sensitive files exchanged between systems. Chapter 4, "Architecture Design Planning," introduces the certificates used in ConfigMgr.

▶ **Integrity:** ConfigMgr uses hashing and digital signatures to protect the integrity of data such as the content used in software distribution. A hash is generated by applying a hashing algorithm to a file. The receiving system recreates the hash and compares it to the hash value provided by the sender. Any alteration of the file will also alter the hash and cause the comparison to fail.

Chapter 4 introduces ConfigMgr cryptographic controls from a planning perspective. Chapter 4 also provides an overview of public key infrastructure and its use in ConfigMgr. If you have a PKI, ConfigMgr will take advantage of it. If you do not have a PKI, ConfigMgr uses self-signed certificates in place of PKI certificates. A PKI can simplify administration by eliminating the need to revoke compromised certificates within ConfigMgr and to manage client approvals. Certain features require a PKI. Here are the features that require a PKI:

▶ HTTPS communications

▶ Support for clients on the Internet

▶ Mobile device management

▶ Out of band management

NOTE: ABOUT CRL CHECKING

Chapter 4 introduces certificate revocation list (CRL) checking. CRL checking increases security by preventing systems from accepting a certificate that is known to have been compromised and thus has been revoked. CRL checking requires planning to minimize performance and availability issues. You can find information about planning for CRL checking and other considerations for deploying AD certificate services at http://technet.microsoft.com/en-us/library/cc770357.aspx.

You should keep in mind that there are no "silver bullets" in security. Security researchers have recently discovered several flaws in cryptographic methods that have been Internet standards for many years. In addition, at least one major certificate vendor has had their root CA canceled. This does not detract from the importance of cryptographic controls in securing your data. It does underscore the importance of using multiple layers of security and keeping systems up to date on all security patches.

The next sections discuss the two principal scenarios in which ConfigMgr uses cryptographic controls: securing network communications and securing content distribution.

ConfigMgr Network Security

Network-based attacks are commonly used to steal data or carry out other malicious objectives. Here are some types of network attacks that could be launched ConfigMgr sites, site systems, and clients:

▶ **Misdirection attacks:** Where a client or site system is provided with the wrong name or Internet Protocol (IP) address for the partner with which it needs to communicate. To avoid misdirection attacks, you must secure service advertisement and name resolution services.

▶ **Spoofing attacks:** This is where a rogue system impersonates the actual system with which a client or site system needs to communicate. To defeat spoofing attacks, all communications must be properly authenticated.

▶ **Eavesdropping or sniffer-based attacks:** This occurs where an attacker intercepts network communications, gaining access to confidential information. Data encryption is the primary defense against breach of confidential communications.

▶ **Man in the middle (MITM) attacks:** These are attacks where an attacker steals, alters, or interrupts communications by routing data through an intermediate node under the attacker's control. You can often defeat MITM attacks by using mutual authentication. Digitally signing files can help you detect alterations due to MITM attacks.

▶ **Denial of service (DoS) attacks:** These occur when an attacker uses large amounts of data or malformed data packets to crash systems or clog communication links. A resilient network infrastructure and fault tolerant service delivery design is your best defenses against DoS attacks.

Microsoft provides several security features to protect the confidentiality, integrity, and availability of ConfigMgr communications. The next sections consider how you can use these features to secure communications between ConfigMgr clients and their site, and communications between ConfigMgr sites and site systems.

> **CAUTION: DON'T LET ATTACKERS USE ENCRYPTION TO BYPASS OTHER SECURITY CONTROLS**
>
> Cryptographic controls such as encryption and digital signatures are among the most important security mechanisms you can use to protect the confidentiality and integrity of data. Encryption can be something of a double-edged sword, as many other security controls do not work on encrypted data. For example, antivirus programs are typically unable to scan encrypted files. Similarly, network Intrusion Detection Systems (IDS) or Intrusion Prevention Systems (IPS) cannot inspect encrypted packets for attack signatures. You should consider procedures to make sure any files and packets that bypass one control are inspected by another, such as quarantining inbound encrypted files until they can be decrypted and scanned, or using a host-based IDS or IPS at each endpoint of an encrypted tunnel.

20

Client-to-Server Communications Security

Clients communicate with most site systems using either HTTP of HTTPS. Chapter 5 provides details on ConfigMgr network protocols. HTTPS communications require PKI certificates. A client configured to support HTTPS will select a site system using HTTPS if one is available. Here are the principal advantages of HTTPS:

▶ **HTTPS traffic is encrypted.** This prevents an attacker eavesdropping on client communications to gain access to sensitive data such as vulnerability data that could be used to attack the client.

▶ **ConfigMgr HTTPS implements mutual authentication.** Authentication protects the client from being re-directed to a rogue site system. With HTTP communication, the management point is authenticated using a self-signed certificate; however, other site systems are not authenticated. HTTP clients do not authenticate themselves to management points. This means either you accept the risk of untrusted clients joining your site or you accept the added effort of managing client approval.

▶ **Mutually authenticated HTTPS prevents an attacker from impersonating the client in order to carry out man in the middle attacks.** A MITM attack can be used to tamper with data as well as to access the data.

> **CAUTION: NOT ALL HTTPS COMMUNICATION IS MUTUALLY AUTHENTICATED**
>
> Do not assume that you are safe from MITM attacks when using HTTPS to access systems such as Internet web servers. Unlike ConfigMgr, most Internet sites using HTTPS do not implement mutual authentication.

For maximum security, always choose HTTPS communications between clients and servers. HTTPS is required for mobile device clients and Internet based clients.

Server-to-Server Communications Security

All communications between site systems within a site is authenticated using either a PKI certificate or a self-signed certificate. Intra-site server communication is not encrypted. You should consider the sensitivity of data exchanged between site systems and the risk of server-to-server communication being compromised. This risk will be higher for systems in less protected network zones, such as external facing DMZs. If your assessment indicates that server-to-server communications should be encrypted, consider implementing IPSec encryption between servers.

The site server should have the highest level of system, network, and physical security you can provide. There may be instances where you are not able to provide the same level of security for all site systems. In such instances, you should consider enabling the **Require the site server to initiate connections to this site system** setting on the less secure site systems. Chapter 6 describes this site system setting. This protects the site server by preventing less secure systems from initiating communication to the site server.

Site-to-Site and Communications Security

Sites share data using database replication and file-based replication. Chapter 5 discusses the data replicated by each mechanism. Database replication uses self-signed certificates to authenticate the replication connections and to sign and encrypt data. The certificate trust mechanism ensures that only ConfigMgr database servers can participate in database replication for the hierarchy. File-based replication implements data signing, but it does not provide encryption. If you want to encrypt file-based replication traffic, consider implementing IPSec communications between site servers.

The next sections describe how to provision server and client systems to use PKI certificates for HTTPS communications.

NOTE: ABOUT CERTIFICATE SERVICES

You may use any PKI implementation supporting x.509 version 3 certificates to provide the certificates described in these sections. The examples shown are based on a Microsoft enterprise certificate authority (CA). Chapter 4 describes ConfigMgr certificate requirements and presents the advantages of using a Microsoft enterprise CA.

Configuring Site Systems That Run IIS to Use PKI Web Server Certificates

Each site system running IIS requires a web server certificate to participate in HTTPS communications. To deploy these certificates efficiently, you should create an AD group consisting of the applicable site systems. In this example, the CM12 IIS Site Systems group is used for certificate provisioning. Before you can issue certificates to site systems, you must create a properly configured certificate template and configure your certificate authority to issue certificates based on the template.

Follow these steps to create the certificate template for IIS site systems and add it to your certificate authority:

1. On the server with certificate services installed, open the Certificate Authority console from the Administrative Tools program group. Navigate to the Certificate Templates node. Figure 20.13 shows the console tree expanded to the Certificate Templates node.

2. Right-click Certificate Templates and choose **Manage** to open the Certificate Templates console.

3. In the Certificate Templates console, right-click the Web Server template, and choose **Duplicate Template**. Ensure the Windows Server 2003 Enterprise option is selected, and click **OK**. (ConfigMgr cannot use Windows Server 2008 enterprise certificate templates.) Figure 20.14 shows the Certificate Templates console with the Duplicate Template dialog open.

20

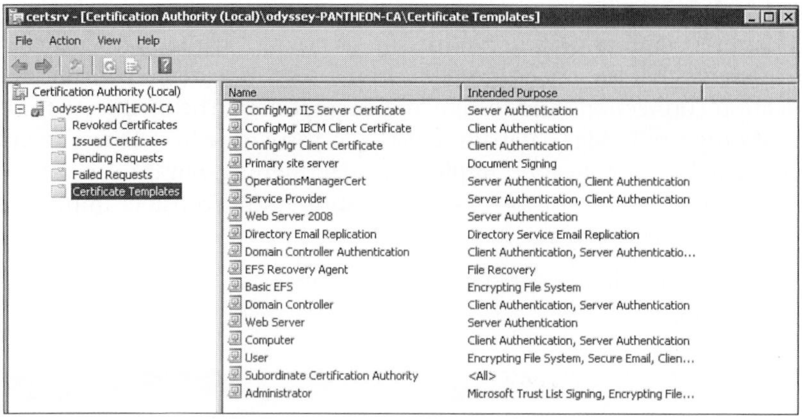

FIGURE 20.13   The Certificate Authority Console.

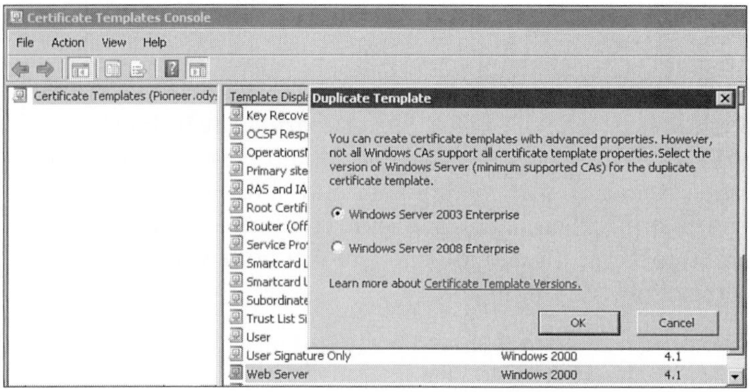

FIGURE 20.14   Duplicating the Web Server Certificate Template.

4. Configure these options on the New Templates property sheet:

   ▶ On the General tab, enter an appropriate template name and template display name.

   ▶ On the Subject Name tab, enable the **Supply in the request** option.

   ▶ On the Security tab, remove the Enroll permission from the Domain Admins, Enterprise Admins, and Authenticated Users groups. Add the group for your ConfigMgr IIS Site Systems group with Read and Enroll permissions. Figure 20.15 displays permissions for the IIS site server group.

5. Return to the Certificate Authority console by closing the New Templates property sheet in the Certificate Templates console. Right-click **Certificate Templates** and choose **New -> Certificate Template to Issue**. Choose the certificate template for your IIS site servers, and click **OK**. Figure 20.16 shows the Enable Certificate Templates dialog.

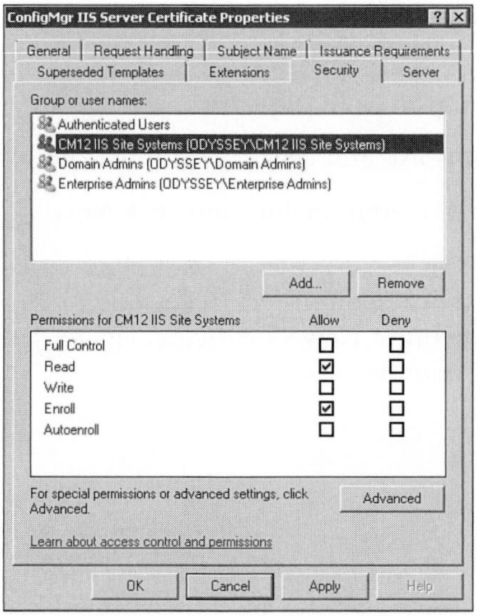

FIGURE 20.15   Setting Permissions on the Certificate Template.

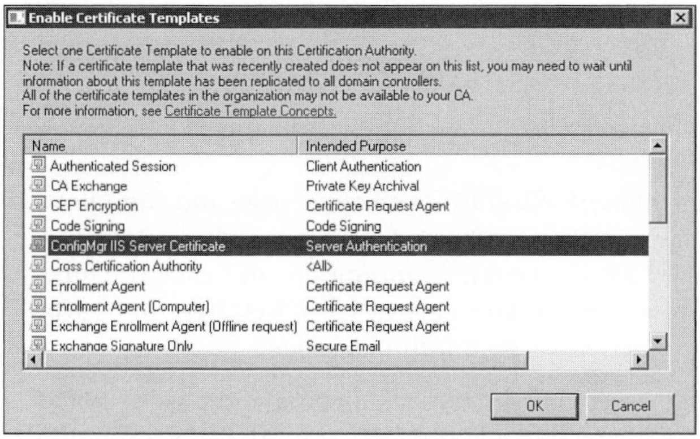

FIGURE 20.16   Enabling the Certificate Template.

When your certificate template is available, you can request and install the web server certificates on site systems running IIS. Perform these steps to request and install the certificate on a member server:

1. Restart each site system server you will configure for HTTPS communications. Restarting the system adds the new group membership to the computer account security identifier (SID). This provides the system with the Read and Enroll permissions configured for the group on the certificate template.

2. You can use the Certificate console to install the web server certificate in the local computer store. To run the console and point it to the correct store:

▶ Run mmc.exe and choose **Add/Remove Snap-in** from the **File** menu.

▶ Select Certificates from the available snap-ins list, and click the **Add** button.

▶ Select **Computer Account** in the Certificates snap-in dialog, and click **Next**; then click **OK**.

3. In the Certificates console, expand **Certificates (Local Computer)** -> **Personal**; then right-click **Certificates** and choose **All Tasks** -> **Request New Certificate**. Figure 20.17 displays the task menu for the Certificates console.

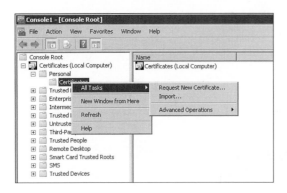

FIGURE 20.17   Initiating a certificate request.

4. Click **Next** on the Certificate Enrollment Wizard introductory page and the Select Certificate Enrollment Policy page. On the Certificate Enrollment page, select the certificate template you configured for site systems running IIS, and click the link **More information is required to enroll for this certificate. Click here to configure settings**. Figure 20.18 shows the Certificate Enrollment page.

5. On the Certificate Properties page, select the Subject tab and leave the value for subject name blank. Under Alternative name, choose **DNS** from the type drop-down list. Enter the site system FQDN as the value; click **Add** and then **OK**. Make sure that the FQDN you enter matches what you configured for the site system. If the site system accepts connections from both Internet and intranet clients and you have configured separate Internet and intranet FQDNs, you should enter both values on this page. Optionally, you may enter a friendly name on the General tab. Chapter 6 describes site system configuration. Figure 20.19 shows the Certificate Properties page for the web server certificate for charon.odyssey.com.

6. Select the appropriate certificate on the Request Certificates page, and click **Enroll**. When the certificate installation completes, click **Finish** to complete the Certificates Installation Results dialog box.

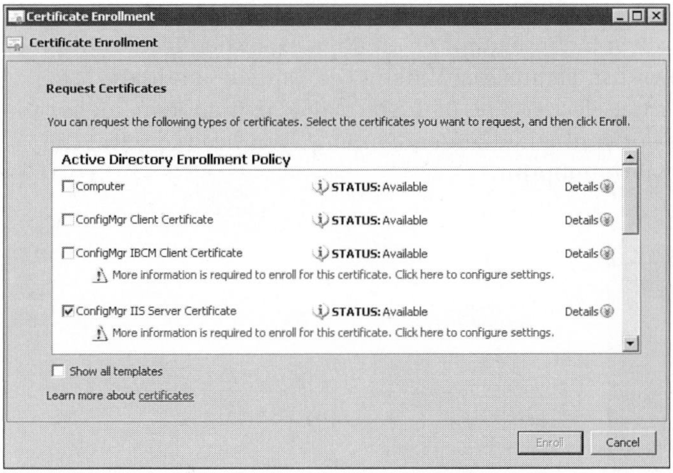

FIGURE 20.18   Selecting a certificate to enroll.

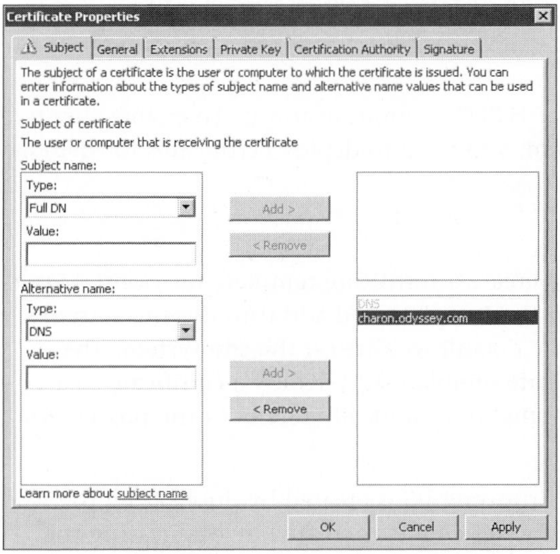

FIGURE 20.19   Specifying the server FQDN as an Alternative Name Certificate Property.

With the certificate installed in the site system's certificate store, the final task to enable HTTPS is to configure IIS to use the certificate. Here are the steps to bind the certificate to the default website on IIS:

1. On the site system running IIS, start Internet Information Services from the Administrative Tools program group.

2. Expand the Sites node, right-click **Default Web Site**, and select **Edit Bindings**.

20

3. In the Site Bindings dialog box, click **Add**. Select **https** from the Type drop-down list; then select the certificate you enrolled for ConfigMgr IIS authentication from the SSL certificate drop-down list. Figure 20.20 shows the Edit Site Bindings dialog box with the HTTPS certificate selected. The figure displays the friendly name for the SSL certificate. If you have not configured a friendly name, you need to select the certificate by its hexadecimal thumbprint.

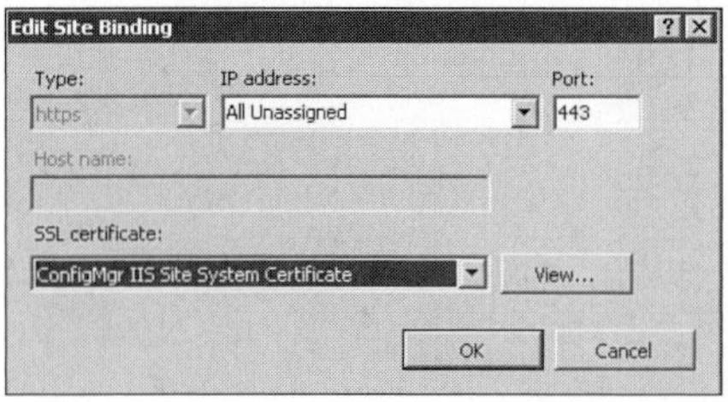

FIGURE 20.20   Configuring the SSL Certificate Binding.

4. Click **OK** to complete the Edit Site Binding dialog, and then click **Close** to exit the Site Bindings dialog.

You have now configured your site system for HTTPS communications. To enable clients to use HTTPS to communicate with the system, you need to deploy certificates to them as well, which is described in the next section.

Deploying Client Certificates

The previous section described the process to create a certificate template for ConfigMgr IIS site systems, request a certificate based on the template and add it to the site system's certificate store, and bind the certificate to the default website on the site system. The process to create the ConfigMgr client certificate template and deploy a certificate to an individual client system is similar. Here are some important differences in the process for provisioning client certificates:

▶ The certificate template for site systems running IIS is created by duplicating the web server certificate. The template for ConfigMgr clients is created by duplicating the Workstation Authentication template.

▶ The security settings for the certificate template for site systems running IIS included Read and Enroll permissions for a custom group containing the appropriate site systems. The security settings for the certificate template for the ConfigMgr client should include Read and Autoenroll permissions for the group containing the client systems that should use HTTPS. You may use the Domain Computers group for this purpose, or create a custom group if you want to limit access to the certificate template.

▶ Because the client will not be acting as a web server, binding the certificate to the default website is not applicable.

Manually requesting certificates for individual clients is appropriate for testing your certificate template. A more scalable process is to use AD group policy for client provisioning. Here is the process to provision workstation certificates using group policy:

NOTE: WORKING WITH GROUP POLICY

Some procedures described in this section assume familiarity with creating, editing, and linking group policy objects. The processes for working with group policy are fully documented online. For example, group policy management for Windows Server 2008 R2 is described at http://technet.microsoft.com/en-us/library/cc753298.aspx. Group policy management for other Windows server versions is similar and available in the Tech Center for your version of Windows server.

---

1. Create a new GPO and link it to the appropriate AD container(s) for the ConfigMgr client that will use HTTPS.

2. In the Group Policy Management Editor, expand **Computer Configuration -> Policies -> Windows Settings -> Security Settings -> Public Key Policies**. Figure 20.21 shows the specified node in the Group Policy Management Editor.

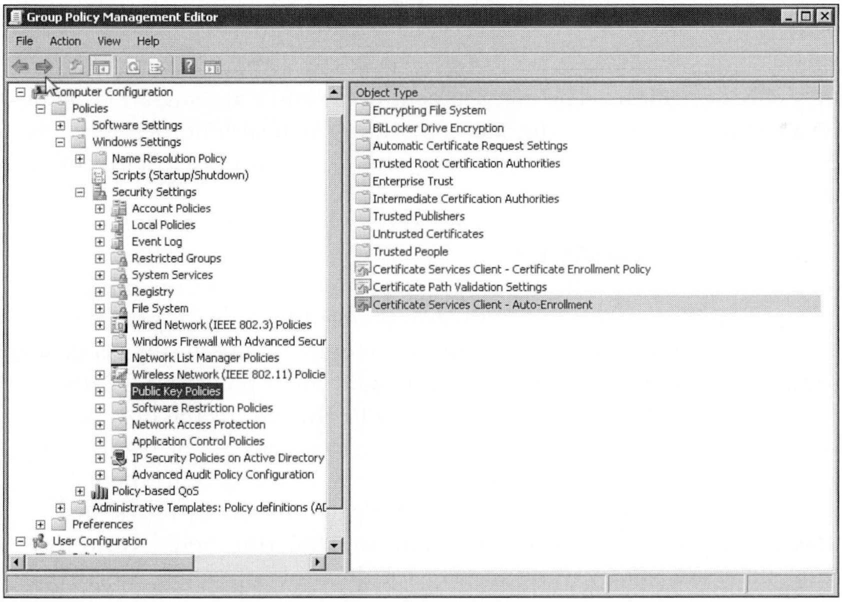

FIGURE 20.21   The Public Key Policies Node in the Group Policy Management Editor.

3. Right-click **Certificate Services Client – Auto-Enrollment** and choose **Properties**. Select **Enabled** from the drop-down list, and check the boxes for **Renew expired certificates, update pending certificates, and remove revoked certificates** and **Update certificates that use certificate templates**; then click **OK**. Figure 20.22

shows the Certificate Services Client – Auto-Enrollment Properties page with the appropriate options selected.

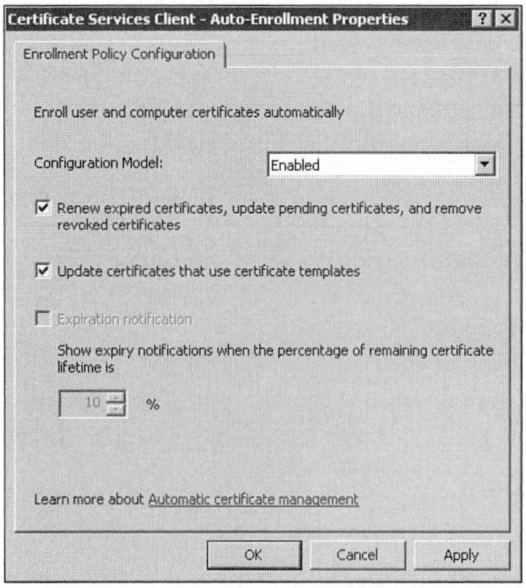

FIGURE 20.22   Setting Auto-Enrollment Properties.

Certificate provisioning through group policy is not available for workgroup clients. Some site systems require a client certificate. The management point and state migration point site systems require a client certificate for the site to monitor the health of these systems. The distribution point also requires a client certificate. The next section describes requirements for the DP certificate.

Deploying Distribution Point Client Certificates

Distribution points require a client certificate for HTTPS authentication to the management point to send status messages. Distribution points enabled for PXE support for clients also provide the client certificate to computers for temporary use during OS deployment. This allows task sequences to authenticate with management points for HTTPS communication. You must import the DP certificate as a file; this means the private key for the certificate must be exportable. Making the private key exportable creates an additional security risk because anyone with administrative access on the system where it is stored could potentially compromise the key. You can mitigate this risk by restricting administrative access and auditing administrative actions on DPs. You should avoid this risk on other systems such as clients by using a certificate that does not allow the private key to be exported.

NOTE: CERTIFICATES FOR BOOT IMAGES

Boot images may also include task sequences that require HTTPS authentication to management points. In this case, you must include a certificate in the boot image. The certificate requirements for boot images are the same as the requirements for distribution points, and you may use the same certificate template.

Creating the certificate template for DP client certificates is the same as the process for client certificates described in the previous section, with these exceptions:

▶ When duplicating the Workstation Authentication certificate template, check the **Allow private key to be exported** box on the Request Handling tab. Figure 20.23 shows the Request Handling tab with this option enabled.

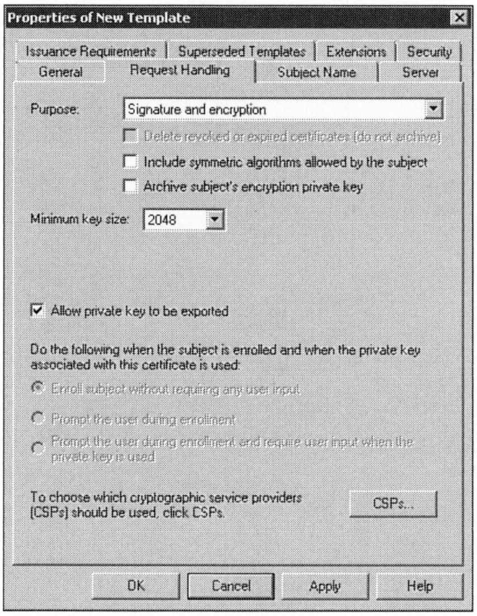

FIGURE 20.23   Configuring the template to allow private key export.

▶ Do not assign permissions to the Domain Computers group. Instead, use a group containing your distribution points. The required permissions are Read and Enroll; Autoenroll will not be used.

The process to request a certificate on a distribution point and install it in the local computer's private store is identical to the process described in the "Configuring Site Systems That Run IIS to Use PKI Web Server Certificates" section. The only difference is you choose the DP client certificate in place of the ConfigMgr IIS server certificate in the Certificate Enrollment dialog box.

The final task to configure a DP to use the client authentication certificate is to export the certificate from the computer's private store and import it into the distribution point properties in the ConfigMgr console. Follow these steps:

1. In the Certificates console Local Computer store, right-click the DP client certificate, select **All Tasks**, and then click **Open**. The "Configuring Site Systems That Run IIS to Use PKI Web Server Certificates" section of this chapter introduced the Certificates console.

2. On the Certificate Details tab, click the **Copy to File** button.

20

3. Click **Next** on the Certificates Export Wizard introductory page.

4. Choose **Yes, export the private key** on the Export Private Key page, and click **Next**. Figure 20.24 displays this option.

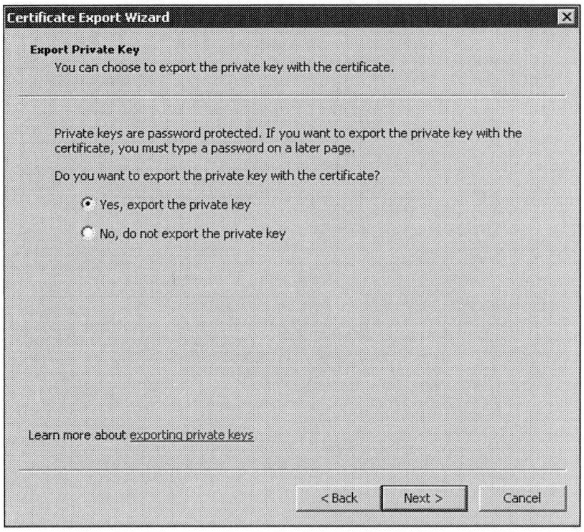

FIGURE 20.24   Configuring the Export Private Key option.

5. On the Export File Format page, ensure that the Personal Information Exchange - PKCS #12 (.PFX) option is selected, and click **Next**.

6. Enter and confirm a strong password on the password page, and click **Next**. Use an enterprise password management solution or other secure methods to store and control access to this password.

7. Specify the filename on the File to Export screen; then click **Next**. Be sure to choose a secure location for this file and keep all copies of the file secure.

You can now import the certificate file on the distribution point settings page during setup or from the distribution point properties page in the ConfigMgr console. Figure 20.25 displays the distribution point properties page.

The Mobile Device Enrollment Certificate Template

In-depth mobile device management requires a device client certificate on each mobile device. Chapter 15, "Mobile Device Management," describes in-depth device management. Chapter 15 also explains how to enroll certificates on mobile devices. This section explains how to create and issue the enrollment certificate template on the certification authority.

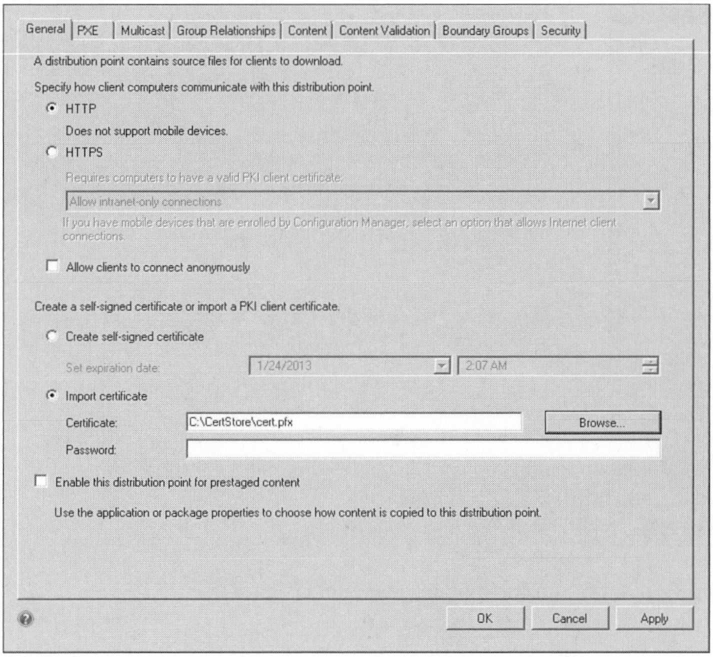

General | PXE | Multicast | Group Relationships | Content | Content Validation | Boundary Groups | Security |

A distribution point contains source files for clients to download.

Specify how client computers communicate with this distribution point.

(HTTP

Does not support mobile devices.

(HTTPS

Requires computers to have a valid PKI client certificate:

Allow intranet-only connections

If you have mobile devices that are enrolled by Configuration Manager, select an option that allows Internet client connections.

[ ] Allow clients to connect anonymously

Create a self-signed certificate or import a PKI client certificate.

(Create self-signed certificate

Set expiration date: 1/24/2013   2:07 AM

(Import certificate

Certificate: C:\CertStore\cert.pfx   Browse...

Password:

[ ] Enable this distribution point for prestaged content

Use the application or package properties to choose how content is copied to this distribution point.

OK   Cancel   Apply

FIGURE 20.25   Importing a PKI Certificate for the distribution point.

Mobile devices do not have AD accounts. The enrollment process for mobile devices therefore requires user authentication to create a security context for the enrollment request. Create an AD user group for users who will enroll mobile devices, and assign permissions on the certificate template to that user group. Perform the following steps to create and install the template:

1. Use the Certification Authority console to duplicate the Authenticated Session certificate template. The "Configuring Site Systems That Run IIS to Use PKI Web Server Certificates" section explains how to duplicate a certificate template.

2. On the Subject Name tab, verify that **Build from this Active Directory information** is selected. Select **Common name** from the Subject name format drop-down list, and clear the **User principal name (UPN)** check box. Figure 20.26 displays the correct settings on the Subject Name tab.

3. On the Security tab, add the security group you created for mobile device certificate enrollment, and assign Read and Enroll permissions to the group.

4. Use the Certification Authority console to add the ConfigMgr mobile device enrollment certificate template as a certificate template to issue. The "Configuring Site Systems That Run IIS to Use PKI Web Server Certificates" section describes the process for adding a certificate template to issue.

20

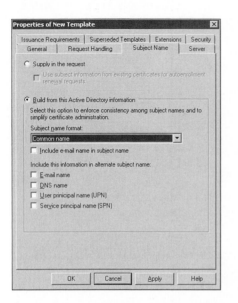

FIGURE 20.26   Configuring the Subject name for mobile device certificates.

Certificates for AMT

Chapter 4 introduces the ConfigMgr functionality enabled by Intel Active Management Technology (AMT). AMT management requires PKI certificates for the following functions:

▶ Before you can use AMT to manage a system, you must provision the management controller. This requires an AMT provisioning certificate.

▶ The management controller requires a web server certificate for secure communications with the ConfigMgr out of band management console. This seems counterintuitive at first; the ConfigMgr client installs the web server certificate. The reason for this is that the management controller runs a web application, and the OOB management console uses client protocols to access the management controller.

▶ If you use 802.1X for network access control (NAC), clients will use a client authentication certificate for 802.1X AMT-based computers to access the network. The 802.1X standard provides access control for wired and/or wireless networks at the port level, which is a stronger mechanism than NAC enforcement based on Dynamic Host Configuration Protocol (DHCP).

The provisioning process configures the AMT management components to communicate with ConfigMgr. Provisioning is the most challenging aspect of OOB management. The first step in the provisioning process is to establish an authenticated connection to the chipset management controller. A specially configured certificate, known as a provisioning certificate, is used to authenticate this initial connection. The AMT firmware includes a cryptographic hash, known as a thumbprint, of one or more trusted certificates. A trusted certificate must appear in the chain of authority used to sign the provisioning certificate for the management controller to accept the connection. By default, the AMT firmware will include thumbprints for specific public certificate providers such as Go Daddy, Comodo, Starfield, and Verisign; the exact list of providers depends on the AMT firmware version you have installed. If you will be provisioning systems with the standard AMT firmware, you need to purchase and install a provisioning certificate from one of these vendors. As an alternative, you may choose to have your system vendor customize the firmware with a certificate thumbprint from your CA. Adding a thumbprint for your enterprise CA simplifies provisioning. Removing the default thumbprints also eliminates the possibility of a compromised provisioning certificate signed by a public CA being used to carry out a rogue provisioning attack against your systems. Although rogue provisioning is possible, it would be difficult for an attacker to accomplish. You can also enter a certificate thumbprint manually through the AMT BIOS configuration screens on individual systems to test OOB functionality on a limited scale.

> **NOTE: ADDITIONAL PROVISIONING REQUIREMENTS**
>
> This section describes certificate requirements for AMT provisioning. The provisioning process has additional hardware, software, network, and service dependencies. Chapter 4 describes the prerequisites for OOB management.

Here are the steps to configure the provisioning certificate:

1. Create an AD security group containing the computer accounts of the out of band service point site system servers.

2. Use the Certification Authority console to duplicate the web server certificate template. The "Configuring Site Systems That Run IIS to Use PKI Web Server Certificates" section explains how to duplicate a certificate template.

3. On the Subject Name tab, select **Build from this Active Directory information**. Select **Common name** from the Subject name format drop-down list.

4. On the Extensions tab, select Application Policies and click **Edit**. In the Edit Application Policies Extension dialog, click the **Add** button, and then click the **New** button in the Add Application Policy dialog. In the New Application Policy dialog, enter **AMT Provisioning** in the Name field and enter **2.16.840.1.113741.1.2.3** in the Object identifier field. Figure 20.27 shows the New Application Policy dialog box with the appropriate values entered. Complete the dialogs by clicking **OK** on the New Application Policy, Add Application Policy, and Edit Application Policies Extension dialog boxes. The certificate template properties Extensions tab should now display Server Authentication and AMT Provisioning as application policies.

5. On the Security tab, add the security group you created for OOB service point systems, and assign Read and Enroll permissions to the group. Remove Enroll permissions from the Domain Admins and Enterprise Admins groups. Close the property page for your new ConfigMgr AMT provisioning certificate template, and close the Certificate Templates console.

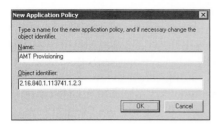

FIGURE 20.27   Configuring the AMT Provisioning Application Policy.

6. Use the Certification Authority console to add the ConfigMgr AMT provisioning certificate template as a certificate template to issue. The "Configuring Site Systems That Run IIS to Use PKI Web Server Certificates" section describes the process for adding a certificate template to issue.

Now that the ConfigMgr AMT provisioning certificate template is available from your CA, you can enroll the certificate in the Local Computer personal certificate store on your OOB service point site systems. The "Configuring Site Systems That Run IIS to Use PKI Web Server Certificates" section describes the process for installing certificates in the Local Computer personal certificate store.

When the ConfigMgr AMT provisioning certificate is available on the site system, you can use the Add Site System Roles Wizard to add the out of band service point role and configure OOB service point to use the provisioning certificate. Chapter 6 describes the Add Site System Roles Wizard. Figure 20.28 displays the AMT provisioning certificate configuration page.

During provisioning, each client system requests a web server certificate that will enable HTTPS connections to the management controller for OOB management. Here is how you can configure your CA to issue these certificates:

1. Create an empty AD universal security group to contain AMT managed computer accounts. ConfigMgr creates a special account for each system it provisions and adds it to this group. These accounts are created in a designated AD organizational unit.

2. Duplicate the Web Server template and configure your CA to issue your new certificate template. The process for creating and issuing this template is identical to the processes described in the "Configuring Site Systems That Run IIS to Use PKI Web Server Certificates" section with the following exceptions:

▶ On the Subject Name tab, select **Build from this Active Directory information**, select **Common name** from the Subject name format drop-down list, and clear the checkbox for **User principal name (UPN)** for the alternative subject name.

▶ Configure Read and Enroll permissions for the group you have configured for AMT computer accounts instead of the IIS site systems group.

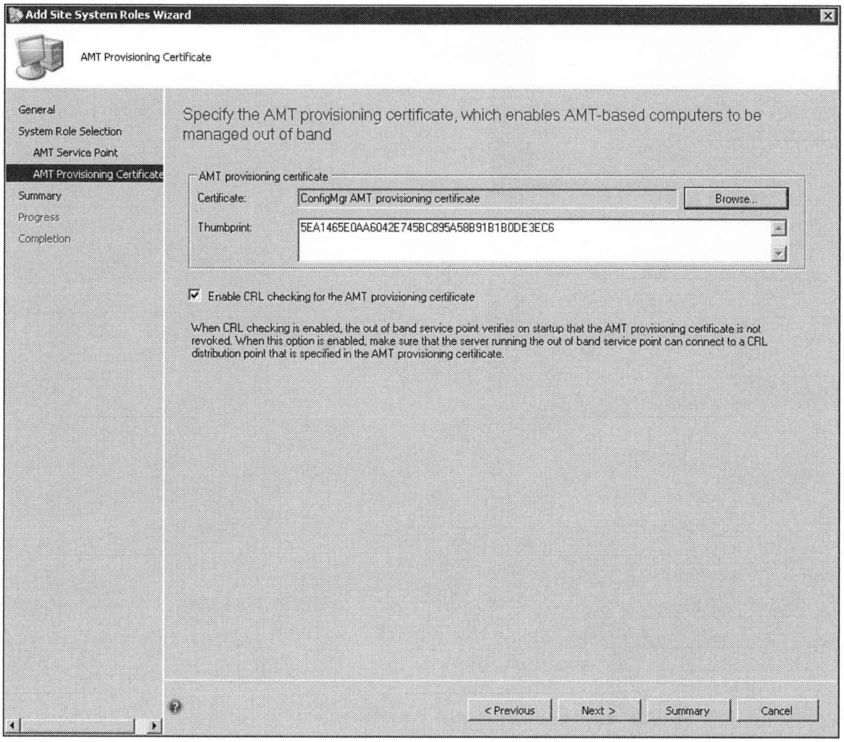

FIGURE 20.28   Configuring the OOB service point with the AMT Provisioning Certificate.

3. You can now configure the out of band management component properties for your sites. Chapter 6 describes how to configure site component properties. Figure 20.29 shows the General tab for the Out of Band Management Component Properties page. Among the options specified on this tab are the AMT web server certificate and the universal group and OU for AMT managed computers. The MEBx account is described in the "Accounts Used for Out of Band Management" section.

Chapter 14 describes the ConfigMgr network access protection feature used to protect networks from unauthorized systems or systems that do not meet minimum requirements for software updates. AMT capable computers offer a strong NAP authentication option based on the 802.1X port level access protocol for wired and wireless networks. The AMT-based system uses a workstation authentication certificate to authenticate to the protected network. Here is the procedure to configure AMT-based computers to use client certificates for 802.1X authenticated wired or wireless networks:

20

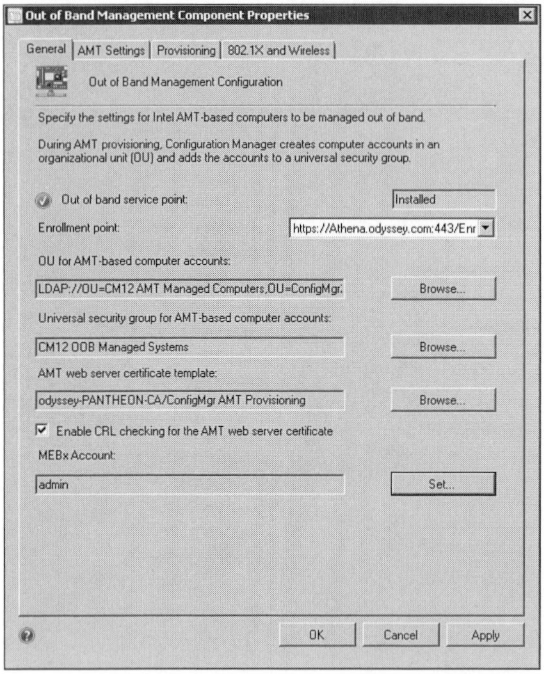

FIGURE 20.29   Out of Band Management Component Properties.

1. Duplicate the Workstation Authentication certificate template to create a ConfigMgr AMT 802.1X client authentication certificate template and configure your CA to issue the new certificate template. The "Configuring Site Systems That Run IIS to Use PKI Web Server Certificates" section described the processes for duplicating and issuing certificate templates. Configure the template with the following options.

▶ On the Subject Name tab, select **Build from this Active Directory information**, select **Common name** for the Subject name format drop-down list. Clear the **DNS name** check box for the alternative subject name, and select **User principal name (UPN)**.

▶ Configure Read and Enroll permissions for the group you have configured for AMT computer accounts and remove Enroll permission from all other groups.

2. On the 802.1X and Wireless tab of Out of Band Management Component Properties, click **Configure** to set up authentication to a wired network, or click the starburst icon to configure a wireless authentication profile. Select your enterprise CA as the trusted root and your ConfigMgr AMT 802.1X client authentication certificate template as the Client certificate template. Figure 20.30 displays the Wireless Profile configuration page.

Wireless Profile

Specify the wireless profile settings.

Profile name:	Enterprise
Network name (SSID):	HQNet
Security type:	WPA2-Enterprise
Encryption method:	AES

802.1X authentication

Server authentication

Trusted root certificate:

com, odyssey, odyssey-PANTHEON-CA   Select...

Client authentication

Authentication method: EAP-TLS

☑ Use client certificate

Client certificate template:

odyssey-PANTHEON-CA/ConfigMgr AMT 802.1X   Select...

OK   Cancel

FIGURE 20.30   Configuring a wireless profile.

If possible, configure your wireless networks to use the WPA-2 Enterprise security type and AES encryption method. These options provide the strongest security supported for wireless networks.

ConfigMgr Content Security

The integrity of the policy and content your clients receive is the paramount consideration when considering client-to-server communications. An attacker who could directly tamper with client policy could instruct the ConfigMgr agent to execute instructions of the attacker's choosing. Similarly, an attacker who could cause clients to use forged or altered software packages, OS images, or other content could gain control of client systems. ConfigMgr uses cryptographic controls to protect against such attacks. You should also use appropriate settings and procedures to ensure policy and content integrity.

Security in Policy and Software Distribution

To protect against policy tampering, the site server signs all client policy assignments using a self-signed certificate. The policy assignment tells the client which policies apply to it and contains a hash of each of those policies. After the client downloads the assigned policies, it generates a hash for each applicable policy and compares it with the hash in the signed policy assignment. The client will apply the policy only if the hash matches. In some cases, client policy may contain sensitive or confidential information. You may optionally encrypt policy to protect such information.

Each policy includes a hash for any packages referenced in the policy. When a client downloads a package, it validates the hash before installing the software. If you configure a deployment to run from a distribution point rather than using the Download and run option, the client does not have the ability to verify the hash before running content. The Run from distribution point option is therefore a less secure software distribution method.

The application catalog represents another potential point of attack against clients. Configure the application catalog website to use HTTPS rather than HTTP. The authors recommend separating the application catalog website and the application catalog web services role as a best practice, particularly if the website will accept connections from the Internet.

Another important consideration for software distribution is preventing users from leveraging deployments to gain elevated privileges. You should generally avoid using configuring both the **Allow users to view and interact with the program installation** and **Run with administrative rights** program options. With these options enabled, the user can influence the execution of a program running in an administrative context, generally Local System. In some cases, the user might break out of the user interface provided by the setup program and spawn another program, such as a command shell, which would provide unlimited access to the system.

ConfigMgr can only protect the content you provide. It is up to you to ensure the integrity of the source files. Download software only from trusted sources, and verify the files after download. Similarly, you should inspect any physical media used to receive files for a certificate of authenticity and tamper resistant packaging.

All source files should be scanned for malware and kept on a secure network share or storage system. Consider file integrity monitoring software to prevent alterations to source files.

Security for Operating System Deployment

ConfigMgr uses PKI certificates or self-signed certificates to authenticate both the clients and servers during OS deployment. Here are some points you should pay close attention to further secure OS deployment:

▶ Secure the reference computer by placing it in a secure network environment, blocking unauthorized access, and keeping patches and antivirus software current.

▶ Secure all boot images, OS images, drivers, and driver packages as you would secure package source files.

▶ Password protect all boot media, and keep media physically secure.

▶ User state migration can present privacy and confidentiality issues. Consider these issues as you determine the data and settings to migrate and how to protect user state data. If you decommission a user state migration point, you should manually delete all user content from the system.

▶ Enable encryption for all multicast packages to prevent tampering and exclude rogue computers from multicast sessions.

Securing ConfigMgr Accounts

ConfigMgr uses a variety of accounts as part of its operating framework. Many of these accounts are required in specific situations, such as accounts to support clients or site systems in untrusted domains. Other accounts are required to support only specific services, such as out of band management. You should use only the accounts required by your environment or to support specific ConfigMgr features you use. Follow best practices for configuring and managing accounts. Here are some principles for managing ConfigMgr accounts:

▶ Use strong passwords and change those passwords regularly.

▶ Enable the **Password never expires** and **User cannot change password** options for Windows and Active Directory accounts used by ConfigMgr.

▶ If you have an enterprise password management application, use it to secure ConfigMgr passwords. At a minimum, keep the passwords in a secure location protected by access controls and encryption, only allow administrators access to passwords on a need to know basis, and keep track of who knows those passwords. If a person with access to ConfigMgr passwords leaves the company or you suspect a password is compromised, change the affected passwords immediately.

▶ Keep track of which accounts are used where, and deprovision any accounts no longer needed.

▶ Configure each account with the minimum rights to accomplish its job.

▶ When you use AD accounts, allow time for newly created accounts to replicate throughout the domain before adding them to ConfigMgr.

▶ Do not grant these accounts the interactive logon right. Occasionally, you might need to grant the interactive logon right to one of these accounts temporarily, in order to log on with the account for troubleshooting purposes. The Task Sequence Run As account also needs interactive logon rights on systems where a task sequence configured to use this account runs.

Microsoft provides detailed descriptions of all ConfigMgr accounts in the online documentation. To help you sort out these accounts, the next sections present ConfigMgr accounts organized into functional groups. You can find additional details about ConfigMgr accounts at http://technet.microsoft.com/en-us/library/hh427337.aspx.

Accounts to Support ConfigMgr Infrastructure

ConfigMgr uses accounts to install components on site systems. Within the site server's AD forest or in domains trusting the site server's domain, use the site server machine account for these purposes rather than configuring separate accounts.

TIP: ASSIGNING RIGHTS TO MACHINE ACCOUNTS

Any time you use the site server machine account for ConfigMgr operations, ensure that the machine account has the required access rights for the task. In most cases, you can provide rights by adding accounts to groups. When you use Active Directory Users and Computers (ADUC) to add users to groups, only users, groups, and other objects such as contacts are available by default through the user interface. You can use ADUC to add machine accounts to groups by clicking the Object Types button in the Select Users, Computers, or Groups dialog box and checking the selection next to Computers. You can also specify machine accounts when using command-line tools or scripts by entering the computer name with a $ appended to the end.

Here are the accounts used for installation purposes:

▶ Site system installation accounts are used to install and configure site systems.

▶ Client push installation accounts are used to install and configure client systems if you use the client push installation method. Client push installation is less secure than other client installation methods and should be avoided if possible.

You can use either AD or local accounts for site system installation and client push. These accounts need to be in the local Administrators group on the target systems. Do not add these accounts to the Domain Admins group as this would provide excessive privileges to the accounts. Instead, create groups that include the appropriate accounts and use group policy or local computer management to add those groups to the local Administrators group. To limit the administrative scope of these accounts, consider using multiple accounts and granting each account access only on those systems on which you use it.

Database Connection Accounts

If you have site systems that do not reside in the same AD forest as the site database server or in a domain trusted by the site database server's domain, you must configure accounts these systems can use to connect to the database. Within the site database server's AD forest or in trusted domains, use the site system machine accounts for database connectivity. If you need database connection accounts, create these accounts as low privilege local accounts on the database server. You can specify a database connection account in the Add Site System Roles Wizard or on the site system role Properties page. Chapter 6, "Installing System Center 2012 Configuration Manager," describes site system role configuration. Chapter 7, "Migrating to System Center 2012 Configuration Manager," describes the configuration and use of the Source Site Database account. You will then add the connection accounts to predefined database roles to provide the access they require. Table 20.4 displays a list of these accounts and the database roles they require.

TABLE 20.4   Database Roles for Connection Accounts

Account Name	Database Role
Management Point Database Connection account	smsdbrole_MP
Enrollment Point Connection account	smsdbrole_EnrollSvr
Multicast Connection account	smsdbrole_MCS
Source Site Database account	db_datareader and smsschm_users on the source (ConfigMgr 2007) site database during migration
Reporting Services Point account	administrative rights on the SSRS instance

Accounts Used for OS Deployment and Software Distribution

ConfigMgr operating system deployment (OSD) requires accounts to carry out several specific task sequence actions. These accounts are specified in the task sequence properties. Chapter 19, "Operating System Deployment," discusses configuring task sequences.

Table 20.5 displays the task sequence accounts with information about their usage and required permissions.

TABLE 20.5   Accounts Used in Task Sequences

Account Name	Where Used	How Used	Required Permissions
Capture Operating System Image account	Task sequences with the Capture Operating System Image step	To access the folder where captured images are stored	Read/Write permissions on the network share where the captured image is to be stored
Task Sequence Editor Domain Joining account	Apply Network Settings task sequence OR Join Domain or Workgroup task sequence	To join newly imaged computers to the domain	Right to join computers to the target domain
Task Sequence Editor Network Folder Connection account	Connect to Network Folder task sequence	To connect to network shares	Access to content
Task Sequence Run As account	Run Command Line task sequence	To provide a context for running commands during a task sequence	Interactive logon rights and other rights required by the specific command

OSD accounts are generally AD domain accounts; however, you have the option to use local accounts for the Capture Operating System Image account and the Task Sequence Run As account.

In addition to the accounts listed in Table 20.5, both OSD and software distribution use the Network Access account to access network resources when the client computer account and/or current user does not have access. Generally, you need this account only for client computers in workgroups or untrusted domains or for use during operating system deployment before the computer has joined the domain. Grant the account Domain User permissions only.

For granular access to packages, you can specify one or more Package Access accounts on a per package basis. Package Access accounts can be any Windows user or group. You generally use existing groups as Package Access accounts rather than creating accounts for this purpose. The default Package Access accounts are Users with Read permission and Administrators with Full Control. In general, you change these defaults only to restrict packages to which you do not want all users to have access. Occasionally you might also need to grant Modify permission for package access accounts if a setup program needs to write back to the source folder.

Accounts Used for Out of Band Management

Because the management controller has low-level system access on managed clients, it is critically important that OOB management access should be as secure as possible. The

Intel Active Management Technology Management Engine uses three accounts that reside in the AMT BIOS extension (MEBx) firmware to provide OOB management functionality on client systems with supported OOB management controllers. These accounts are used for provisioning and remote administration. In addition, ConfigMgr uses a set of AD user accounts or groups to manage permissions for OOB management.

You can configure your site to use the three accounts that reside in the BIOS extensions through the Out of Band Management Properties sheet, located under **Site** -> *<site name>* -> **Configure Site Components** in the Administration workspace. Here are the three accounts:

▶ **MEBx account:** This account is used for initial authentication to the AMT firmware. The MEBx account is named admin, with the default password admin. If you or your computer manufacturer has configured the management controller with a different password, use the AMT Provisioning and Discovery account for provisioning instead of the MEBx account. ConfigMgr sets the MEBx account password during the provisioning process. You can specify the password on the OOB Properties General tab, or you can specify specific values for each computer in a comma-separated values (CSV) file and import them with the Import Computer for Out of Band Management Wizard. For instructions on running the Import Computer for Out of Band Management Wizard, see http://technet.microsoft.com/en-us/library/cc161950.aspx.

▶ **AMT Provisioning and Discovery account:** You can use this account to provision those computers provisioned previously using a different AMT management solution. Specify the account name and password on the OOB Properties Provisioning tab. You might need to specify more than one AMT Provisioning and Discovery account if you have computers provisioned with different usernames and passwords.

▶ **AMT Remote Admin account:** This account is used by the OOB service point to manage AMT network interface features. The AMT Remote Admin account is named admin, with the default password admin. During provisioning ConfigMgr resets the default password to a random strong value. If the password was previously changed locally, ConfigMgr sets the password to match the MEBx account password. If the password was reset through another AMT management solution, see http://technet.microsoft.com/en-us/library/cc161983.aspx for options for migrating to ConfigMgr.

You can delegate administrative access to OOB management by specifying up to eight AD users or groups as AMT user accounts on the OOB properties AMT Settings tab. Access control lists (ACLs) for AMT user accounts are stored in the management controller firmware. You can also use RBA to manage AMT access by assigning users to a security role with Collection -> Control AMT permission. The "Operating System Deployment" section of this chapter describes RBA.

The AMT Provisioning Removal account is a Windows account used to remove AMT provisioning information during site recovery or client reassignment. Configure this account on the OOB Properties Provisioning tab. You must also add the account as an AMT user account, and add it to the local Administrators group on the server with the out of band service point role. You cannot use this account if the AMT auditing log is enabled.

Accounts Used for Software Updates

ConfigMgr uses two accounts to authenticate to access content for software updates. Chapter 14 describes the software updates feature. Here are the accounts used with software updates:

▶ **Software Update Point Proxy Server account:** The SUP uses the Software Update Point Proxy Server account to authenticate to proxy server or firewall to synchronize with Microsoft Updates or an upstream WSUS server. You can use any account that can authenticate to your proxy server or firewall and access the site for WSUS synchronization for this account.

▶ **Software Update Point Connection account:** WSUS services use the Software Update Point Connection account to configure settings and request synchronization. This account is required only if the SUP role is assigned to a remote server or Network Load Balancing (NLB) cluster. This account must be a member of the local Administrators group on the SUP.

Accounts Used with Health State References

If you use ConfigMgr NAP and have system health validator points in a separate forest from the site server, ConfigMgr uses two accounts to manage health state references:

▶ **Health State Reference Publishing account:** ConfigMgr uses the Health State Reference Publishing account to publish health state references to AD. The Health State Reference Publishing account requires Read/Write permissions on the AD Systems Management container in the forest in which Health State References are stored.

▶ **Health State Reference Querying account:** The system health validator point uses the Health State Reference Querying account to read health state references from AD. The Health State Reference Querying account requires Read permission on the AD Systems Management container in the global catalog.

Chapter 14 describes configuration of these accounts. If the system health validator point(s) are in the same AD forest as the site server, these accounts are not required.

Accounts Used for Active Directory Discovery and Publishing

If possible, use the site server computer account to perform AD discovery and to publish site data to AD. For forests that do not trust the site server's forest, running the AD discovery methods or publishing to AD requires an account in the target forest. Here are the accounts ConfigMgr uses for AD discovery and publishing:

▶ **Active Directory Group Discovery account:** ConfigMgr uses this account to discover AD security groups and group memberships.

▶ **Active Directory System Discovery account:** ConfigMgr uses this account to discover computer objects.

▶ **Active Directory User Discovery account:** ConfigMgr uses this account to discover user accounts.

▶ **Active Directory Forest account:** ConfigMgr central and primary sites use this account to publish data to Active Directory. ConfigMgr also uses this account for AD network infrastructure discovery.

Each discovery account requires read access to the AD containers specified for discovery. The Active Directory Forest account also requires Full Control permissions to the System Management container to publish to AD.

Proxy Server Accounts

Here are the accounts ConfigMgr uses to connect to a proxy server or firewall when required for Internet connections:

▶ **Asset Intelligence Synchronization Point Proxy Server account:** The asset intelligence synchronization point uses this account for proxy authentication when connecting to System Center Online.

▶ **Exchange Server Connector Proxy Server account:** The Exchange server uses account for proxy authentication when connecting to the Internet.

Proxy server accounts should be configured with the minimum permissions required to authenticate to the proxy server.

Miscellaneous Accounts

Here are some additional accounts that ConfigMgr uses:

▶ **Endpoint Protection SMTP Server Connection account:** The site server uses this account to authenticate the mail server using simple mail transport protocol (SMTP) to send e-mail alerts for Endpoint Protection.

▶ **Exchange Server Connection account:** The site server uses this account to connect to the Exchange server for mobile device management. Chapter 15 explains how to configure this account and the permissions it requires.

▶ **Remote Tools Permitted Viewer accounts:** Any Windows users or group can be included in the permitted viewers list to allow remote control access to clients. Chapter 9, "Configuration Manager Client Management," describes how to configure permitted viewer accounts. Under most scenarios, it is better to use RBA to delegate remote control access rather than using permitted viewers.

▶ **Source Site account:** System Center 2012 ConfigMgr uses the Source Site account to connect to ConfigMgr 2007 sites during migration. This account required Read access on the source site and all objects to be migrated.

Summary

This chapter described the infrastructure security considerations for ConfigMgr and the appropriate delegation of administrative access. The chapter includes a detailed description of the new role-based administration model and a comprehensive overview of ConfigMgr cryptographic controls and security accounts. The chapter also provides general considerations for secure hierarchy design, audit support, and server configuration and placement. The next chapter describes ConfigMgr backup, recovery, and maintenance.

20

Backup, Recovery, and Maintenance

A critical piece of maintaining a healthy and functional system is to ensure its integrity through backup and recovery processes. All too often installations do not test backup and recovery procedures until an outage occurs, only to discover too late that the process was not set up properly. All production systems should have established backup and recovery procedures in place, and System Center 2012 Configuration Manager (ConfigMgr) is no exception. You must maintain data integrity and currency, and ConfigMgr provides a number of maintenance tasks to help assist with this.

Critical components in maintaining a healthy and functional environment are security, discussed in Chapter 20, "Security and Delegation in Configuration Manager," and ensuring its integrity through backup and recovery processes. This chapter discusses best practice approaches to backup, recover, and maintain your ConfigMgr environment.

Performing Site and SQL Server Backups

Out-of-the-box, System Center 2012 Configuration Manager includes a number of tasks to assist in maintaining your environment. One of these, the Backup Site Server maintenance task, can greatly simplify the process to back up your ConfigMgr environment. The next sections discuss backing up and restoring your ConfigMgr database and site.

Backing Up ConfigMgr

You can find site maintenance tasks, displayed in Figure 21.1, located in the ConfigMgr console on the Administration workspace. Navigate to **Overview -> Site Configuration -> Sites ->** *<site code>* **-** *<site name>* **-> Site Maintenance**.

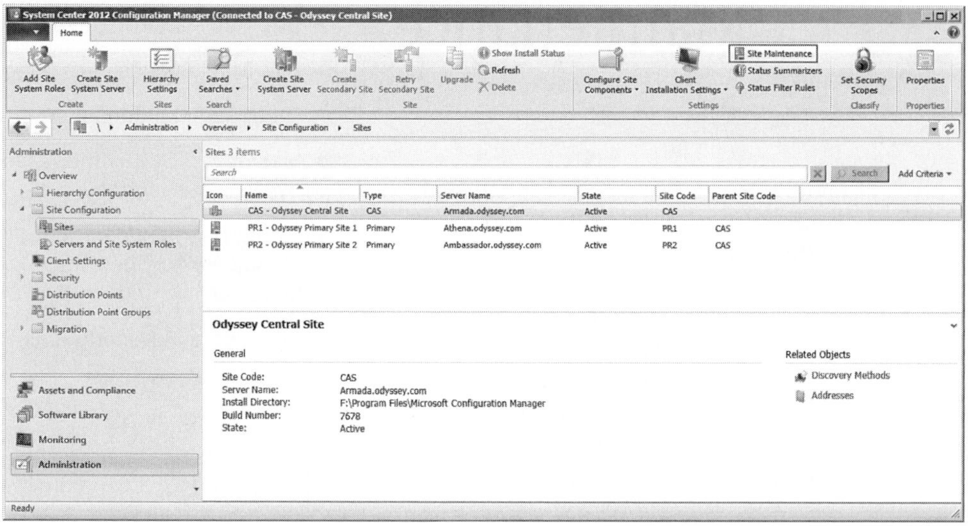

FIGURE 21.1   Location of site maintenance tasks in the ConfigMgr console.

> **TIP: INFORMATION ON SITE MAINTENANCE TASKS**
>
> The "Site Maintenance Tasks" section contains information regarding each of the site maintenance tasks available in System Center 2012 Configuration Manager.

The first task in the list shown in Figure 21.2, Backup Site Server, is not enabled by default. This task provides an automated method to back up the entire site including the site database, ConfigMgr files, registry keys, and system configuration information. Using the Backup Site Server task is the recommended approach for backups rather than using third-party vendor solutions because this is the only Microsoft-supported backup when you restore the ConfigMgr environment using the Configuration Manager Setup Wizard.

To enable the Backup Site Server task and configure it to back up your site, perform the following steps:

1. Select the Backup Site Server task, as shown in Figure 21.2. (In the Administration workspace, navigate to **Overview -> Site Configuration -> Sites ->** *<site code><site name>*.) Click **Site Maintenance** on the ribbon, highlight **Backup Site Server**, and choose **Edit** to open the Properties page.

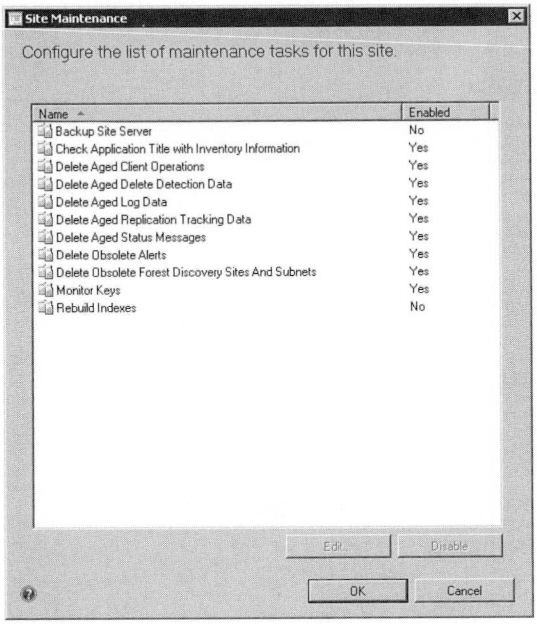

Site Maintenance

Configure the list of maintenance tasks for this site.

Name ▲	Enabled
Backup Site Server	No
Check Application Title with Inventory Information	Yes
Delete Aged Client Operations	Yes
Delete Aged Delete Detection Data	Yes
Delete Aged Log Data	Yes
Delete Aged Replication Tracking Data	Yes
Delete Aged Status Messages	Yes
Delete Obsolete Alerts	Yes
Delete Obsolete Forest Discovery Sites And Subnets	Yes
Monitor Keys	Yes
Rebuild Indexes	No

Edit...   Disable

OK   Cancel

FIGURE 21.2   Maintenance tasks on a central administration site (CAS).

2. The first option on the Backup Site Server Properties is to enable the task by selecting the check box on the top part of the Properties page, as shown in Figure 21.3.

After you enable the task, click the **Set Paths** button to define the path to which to back up the site and SQL information. The default configuration is to back up the information to a local drive on the site server, although the Set Paths option enables you to back up the information to a network path.

A commonly used configuration accepts the default backup timeframe to start between 2:00 AM and 5:00 AM daily and perform the system backup to the local drive on the site server, in this case G:\CM12Backup. Refer to Figure 21.3.

TIP: PROTECTING YOURSELF FURTHER WITH BACKUPS

The default approach to back up to a local drive is commonly used as a quick way to back up ConfigMgr information. However, this provides little benefit by itself because the backed-up information resides on the same machine that was backed up. You could augment this approach by scheduling a weekly backup that backs up the information stored on the local site server into an offsite rotation using a backup product such as System Center 2012 Data Protection Manager (DPM) or third-party backup solutions.

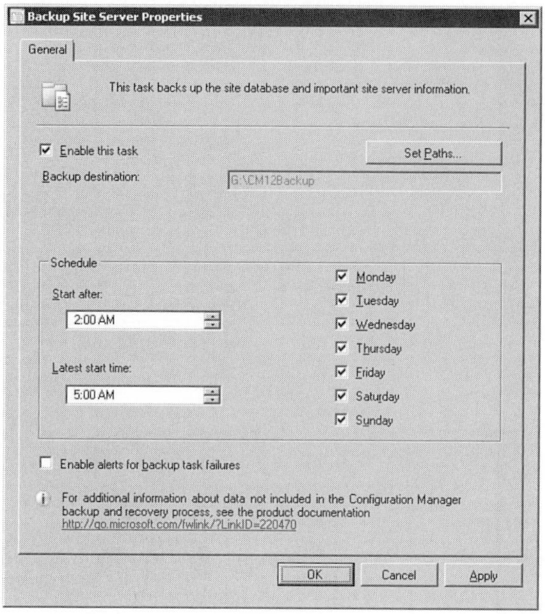

FIGURE 21.3   The Backup Site Server maintenance task.

A successful backup creates the following folders, displayed in Figure 21.4:

▶ *<site code>***Backup:** This contains BackupDocument.xml, ConfigMgrBackup.ini, and smsbkup.log.

▶ **SiteDBServer:** This folder, a subfolder of *<site code>*Backup, contains CM_*<site code>*. mdf and CM_*<site code>*_log.ldf.

▶ **SiteServer:** Also a subfolder of *<site code>*Backup, contains SMSbkSiteRegSMS.dat. A subfolder called SMSServer contains four additional folders (data, inboxes, Logs, and srvscct) and the install.map file.

TROUBLESHOOTING CONFIGMGR BACKUP ISSUES

ConfigMgr uses the Volume Shadow Copy service. Verify this service is not disabled, or your ConfigMgr backup will not run successfully.

To verify the health of the service, the command `vssadmin list writers` provides a list of all writers that are installed. SMS Writer should be in State: [1] Stable and Last error: No error.

A recommended backup approach uses a daily backup timeframe but sends the backup information to a Universal Naming Convention (UNC) path, specifying a location not on any of the ConfigMgr server systems. Data backups take place daily, with the backup retained for at least one month. Using this approach minimizes the risk that should the site server's drive fail, you would lose all information for ConfigMgr including the backup copy of the information. Performing this task on a daily basis minimizes the amount of information lost, in comparison to restoring from a backup that might have occurred a week earlier.

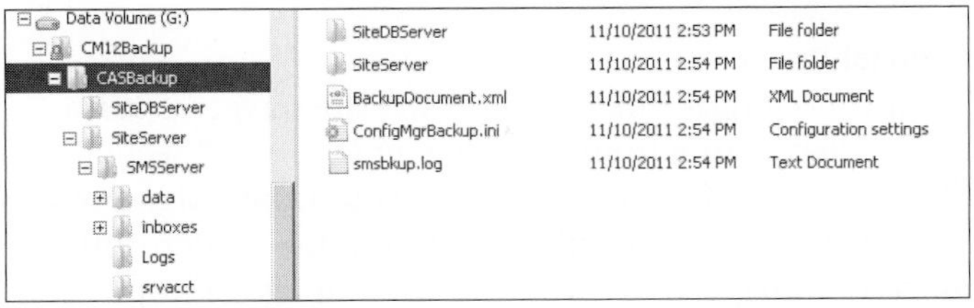

FIGURE 21.4   File structure created from a successful ConfigMgr backup.

You should also back up the files required to restore the operating system on the site server in the event of a full operating system (OS) crash. Using DPM or third-party products to provide a full backup of the OS is critical for system restores should the OS stop functioning. The authors recommend you perform monthly OS backups for all ConfigMgr site server systems.

CUSTOMIZING CONFIGMGR BACKUPS

Here are several ways to customize your ConfigMgr backup:

▶ **Afterbackup.bat:** The Backup Site Server maintenance task overwrites the output of the previous run so that only the most current set of backup files is available in the backup destination. By using a custom script in Afterbackup.bat, you could archive the backup snapshots to different locations. Afterbackup.bat, which must be placed in the *<ConfigMgrInstallPath>*\inboxes\smsbkup.box folder, is executed automatically after the Backup Site Server maintenance task runs. You could also use after-backup.bat to back up data not included in the ConfigMgr backup by default, such as application or package source files.

▶ **smsbkup.ctl:** *<ConfigMgrInstallPath>*\inboxes\smsbkup.box contains a file named smsbkup.ctl. You can use this file to customize ConfigMgr's backup behavior. The ASCII content is self-explanatory and consists of two different categories; these are sections where editing is allowed (E d i t i n g A l l o w e d), and sections where editing is prohibited (DO NOT MODIFY).

Restoring ConfigMgr Backups

With your ConfigMgr information backed up, now consider the process to restore it. Here are two common scenarios that might require recovering ConfigMgr:

▶ Site server OS crash

▶ ConfigMgr functional crash

The next sections discuss these scenarios.

Recovering from a Site Server OS Crash

Should a server OS crash, the first step is to restore the server from a backup. The "Backing Up ConfigMgr" section discusses the requirement to back up the OS on a regular basis. After installing the OS, you can continue through the steps required to restore from a ConfigMgr functional crash.

Recovering from a ConfigMgr Functional Crash

In the situation in which ConfigMgr is no longer functional (or the site server OS is no longer functional, as discussed in the "Recovering from a Site Server OS Crash" section), you can use the Configuration Manager setup program to recover your ConfigMgr environment. Start the setup program by navigating to **Start -> All Programs -> Microsoft System Center 2012 -> Configuration Manager -> Configuration Manager Setup**. Perform the following steps:

1. The first page of the wizard, as shown in Figure 21.5, describes what you should do before beginning this process. After verifying all prerequisites listed are met, press **Next** to continue.

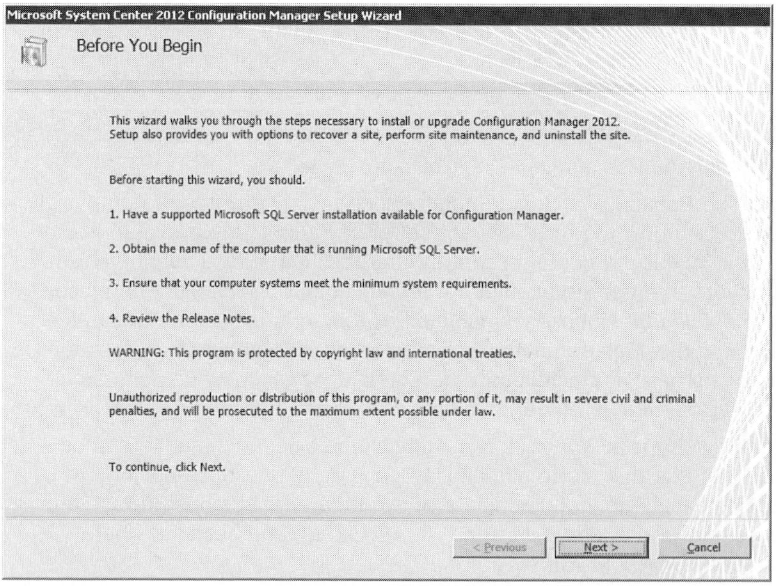

Microsoft System Center 2012 Configuration Manager Setup Wizard

Before You Begin

This wizard walks you through the steps necessary to install or upgrade Configuration Manager 2012. Setup also provides you with options to recover a site, perform site maintenance, and uninstall the site.

Before starting this wizard, you should:

1. Have a supported Microsoft SQL Server installation available for Configuration Manager.

2. Obtain the name of the computer that is running Microsoft SQL Server.

3. Ensure that your computer systems meet the minimum system requirements.

4. Review the Release Notes.

WARNING: This program is protected by copyright law and international treaties.

Unauthorized reproduction or distribution of this program, or any portion of it, may result in severe civil and criminal penalties, and will be prosecuted to the maximum extent possible under law.

To continue, click Next.

< Previous   Next >   Cancel

FIGURE 21.5   The System Center 2012 Configuration Manager Setup Wizard.

2. The Available Setup Options page, as displayed in Figure 21.6, contains all options you can initiate when running the setup routine:

   ▶ Install a Configuration Manager primary site

   ▶ Install a Configuration Manager central administration site

   ▶ Upgrade an existing Configuration Manager 2012 installation

▶ Recover a site

▶ Perform site maintenance or reset this site

▶ Uninstall a Configuration Manager site

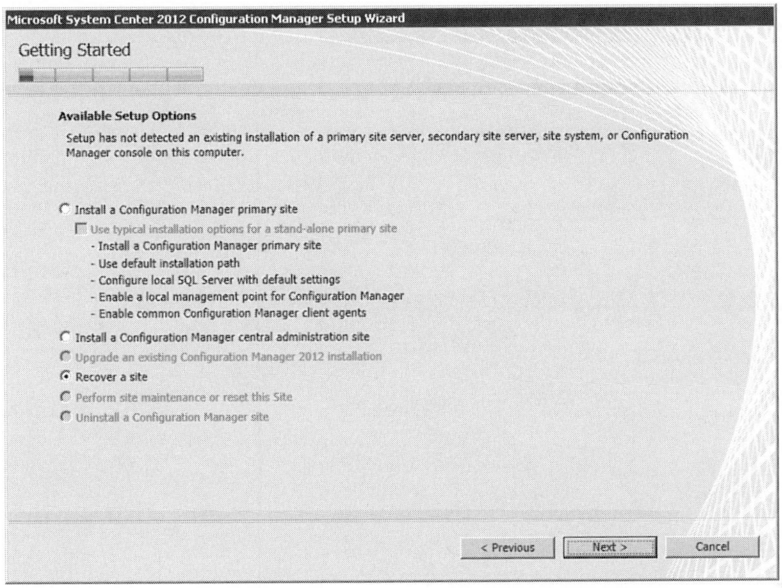

FIGURE 21.6   Available Setup Options in the System Center 2012 Configuration Manager
Setup Wizard.

Some of these selections are grayed out, depending on the state of the computer
where you started the setup program. Select **Recover a site** and press **Next**. (This
option is only available if you run setup from the original installation source. It does
not display if you initiate setup from the Start menu and an existing installation of
ConfigMgr is located.)

3. The next page, Site Server and Database Recovery Options (see Figure 21.7), lists the
possible recovery options. Select **Recover the site server from an existing backup**,
and click **Browse** to select the folder containing the ConfigMgr backup.

The bottom portion of Figure 21.7 allows you to choose to restore the database from
an existing backup:

▶ Select **Recover the site database using the backup set at the following
location**, and select the folder that contains the ConfigMgr backup.

▶ You could also restore the database manually by selecting **Use existing
manually recovered database**.

You could also skip the recovery of the database using **Skip database recovery actions**. (Use this option if the database server was unaffected.) This would be the case if the database were located on a remote server.

Press **Next** after making your selection.

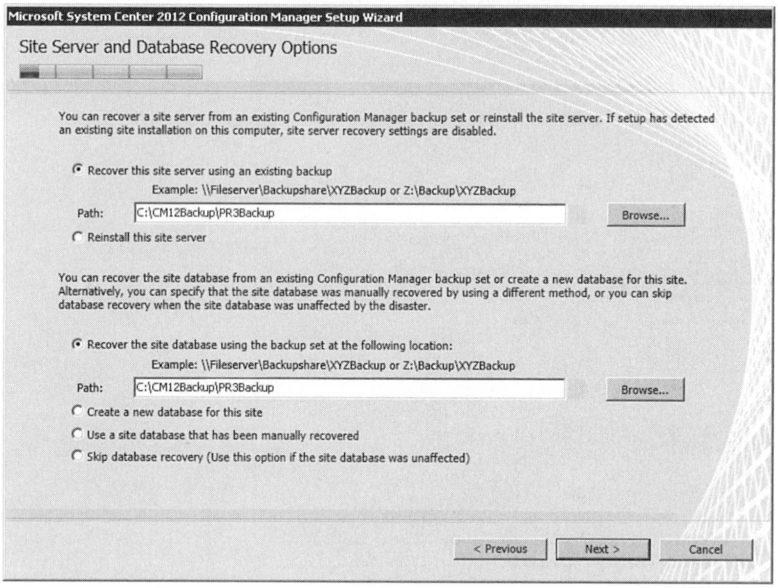

Microsoft System Center 2012 Configuration Manager Setup Wizard

Site Server and Database Recovery Options

You can recover a site server from an existing Configuration Manager backup set or reinstall the site server. If setup has detected an existing site installation on this computer, site server recovery settings are disabled.

   ⦿ Recover this site server using an existing backup

      Example: \\Fileserver\Backupshare\XYZBackup or Z:\Backup\XYZBackup

      Path: [C:\CM12Backup\PR3Backup]   [Browse...]

   ○ Reinstall this site server

You can recover the site database from an existing Configuration Manager backup set or create a new database for this site. Alternatively, you can specify that the site database was manually recovered by using a different method, or you can skip database recovery when the site database was unaffected by the disaster.

   ⦿ Recover the site database using the backup set at the following location:

      Example: \\Fileserver\Backupshare\XYZBackup or Z:\Backup\XYZBackup

      Path: [C:\CM12Backup\PR3Backup]   [Browse...]

   ○ Create a new database for this site

   ○ Use a site database that has been manually recovered

   ○ Skip database recovery (Use this option if the site database was unaffected)

[< Previous]   [Next >]   [Cancel]

FIGURE 21.7   Site Server and Database Recovery Options.

4. If the site you restore is a standalone primary site, you do not need to specify anything on the Site Recovery Information page shown in Figure 21.8. You can specify a reference site if the site is a CAS or joined to a hierarchy. Reference sites are used to restore global data information that was replicated to other sites (see Chapter 5, "Network Design"). Press **Next** to continue.

5. You can read, print, and accept the End User License Agreement (EULA) on the Microsoft Software License Terms page. Press **Next** to continue.

6. You can either download or use already downloaded ConfigMgr prerequisites on the Updated Prerequisite Components page, displayed in Figure 21.9. Choose **Use previously downloaded updates from the following location** if you previously downloaded the installation files (setupDL.exe, as discussed in Chapter 6, "Installing System Center 2012 Configuration Manager"), or **Download and use the latest updates. Updates will be saved to the following location.** (Downloading requires an Internet connection.) Make your selection and press **Next**.

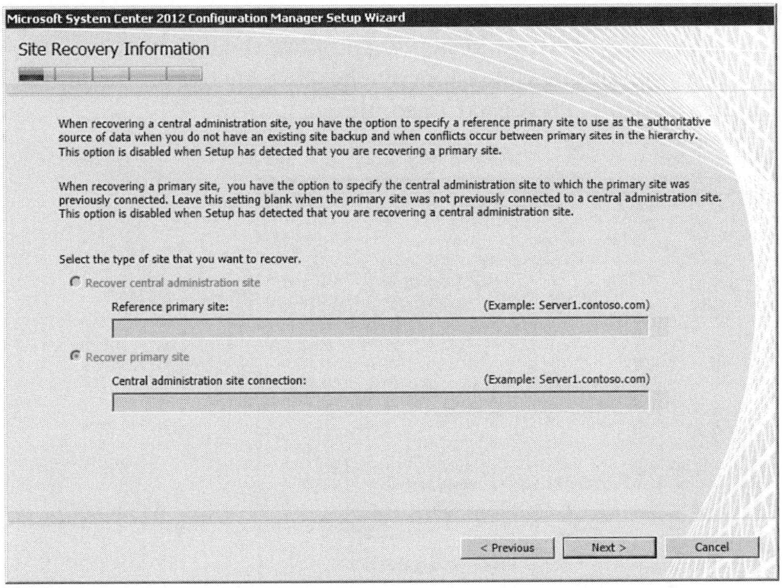

FIGURE 21.8   Site Recovery Information.

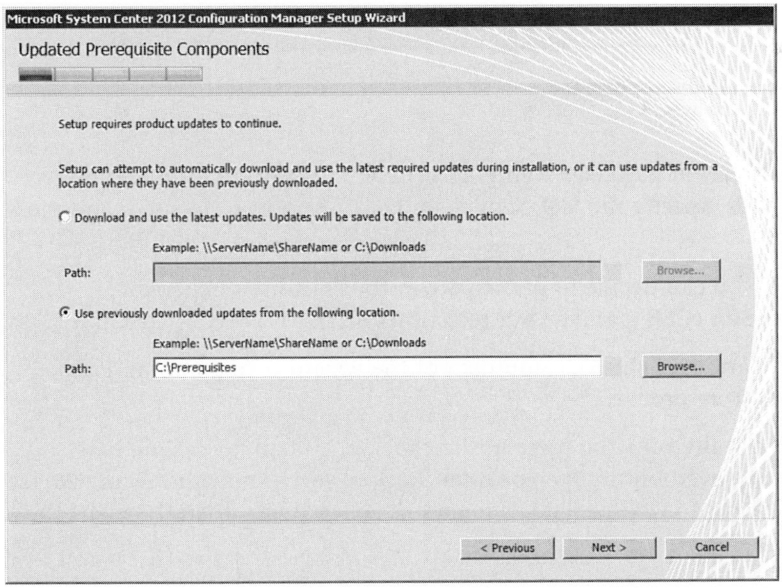

FIGURE 21.9   Specifying whether to use updated prerequisite components.

7. The Site and Installation Settings page, displayed in Figure 21.10, contains information taken from the backup files specified in step 4. You have the option to install the ConfigMgr console as well during the restore by checking the option **Install the Configuration Manager console**. Press **Next** to continue.

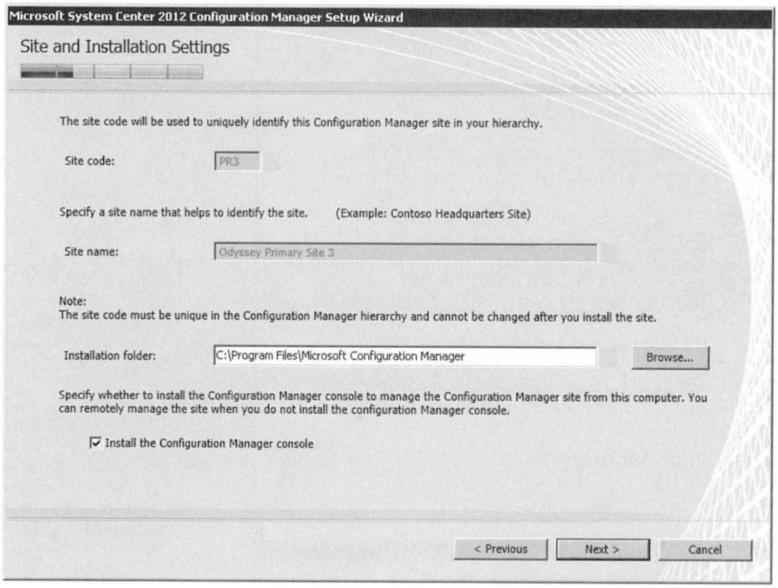

FIGURE 21.10   Site and Installation Settings.

8. The Database Information page (see Figure 21.11) contains information also taken from the backup files. Specify the SQL Service Broker (SSB) port to be used, and press **Next** to continue.

9. On the next page, you can decide to participate in the Customer Experience Improvement Program (CEIP). Make your selection and select **Next** to continue.

10. The Settings Summary page shows a summary of the wizard configuration. Press **Next** to start the restore process.

11. The wizard automatically runs the prerequisite checker, and any deficiencies in prerequisites are displayed on the Prerequisite Check page, as shown in Figure 21.12. All activities are logged to C:\ConfigMgrPrereq.log. Select **Begin Install** to start the recovery process.

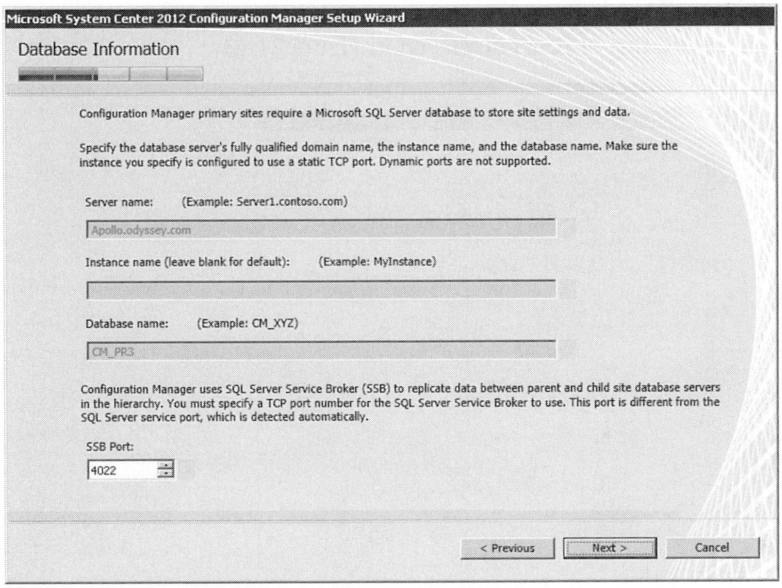

FIGURE 21.11   Specifying Database Information.

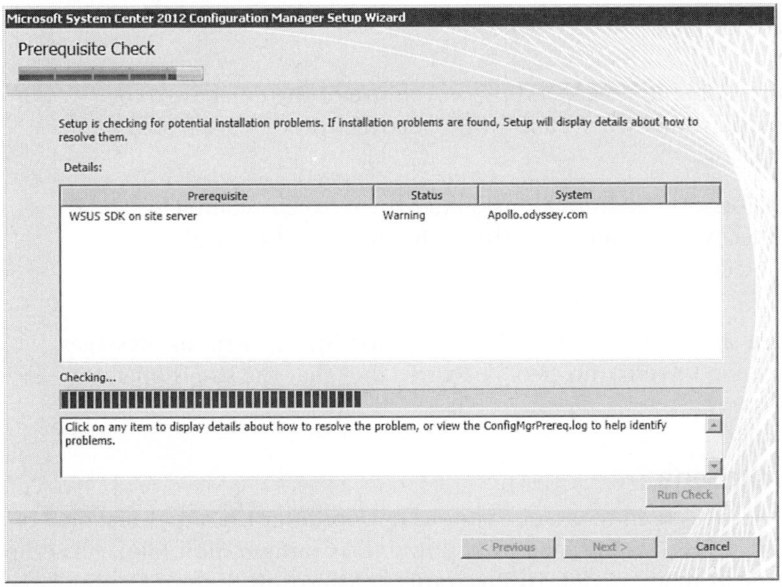

FIGURE 21.12   Results from the Prerequisite Check.

12. After the prerequisite check completes, the actual recovery process begins. You can monitor its progress on the Install page, displayed in Figure 21.13.

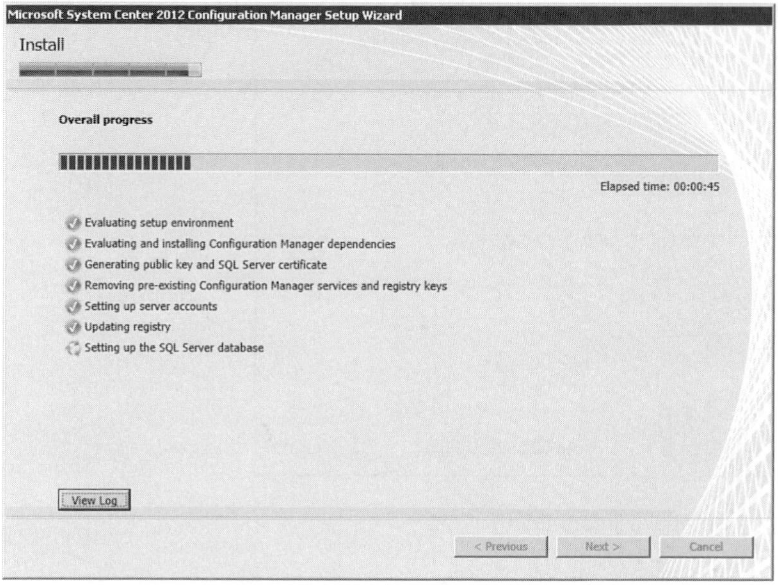

FIGURE 21.13   Installation status.

The restore can take some time, depending on the size of the database to be restored and server performance. Details of the recovery process are stored in C:\ConfigMgrSetup.log.

13. You might need to perform additional tasks after the restore is complete. These tasks, on the Post-recovery actions page shown in Figure 21.14, are saved to C:\ConfigMgrPostRecoveryActions.html.

After restoring a site, you should examine the Configuration Manager status messages, site status, and the event log to verify no errors occurred and that the site is operating normally again.

Site Maintenance Options

The Site Maintenance wizard is used to change various options after the site is installed or to re-apply default permissions. It is initiated by running the Configuration Manager setup program, located in the Start menu under **All Programs -> Microsoft System Center 2012 -> Configuration Manager -> Configuration Manager Setup**.

There are four different options available, displayed in Figure 21.15, and described in the next sections.

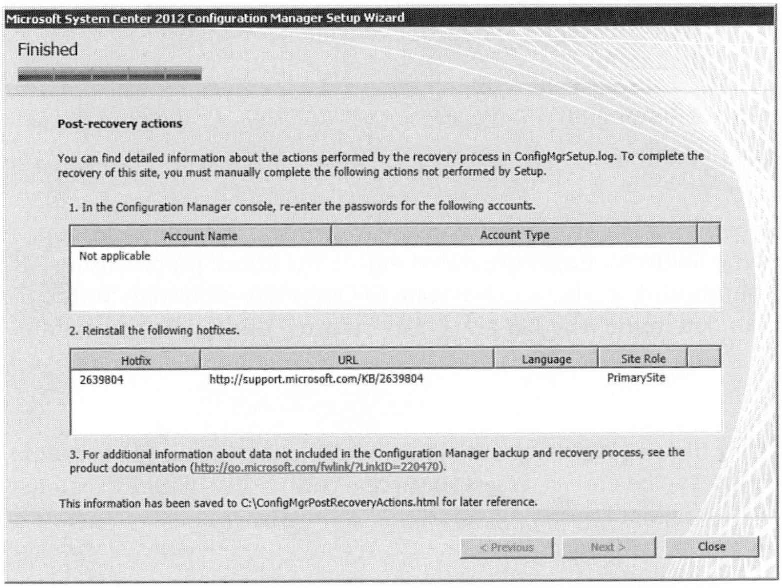

FIGURE 21.14   Post recovery actions.

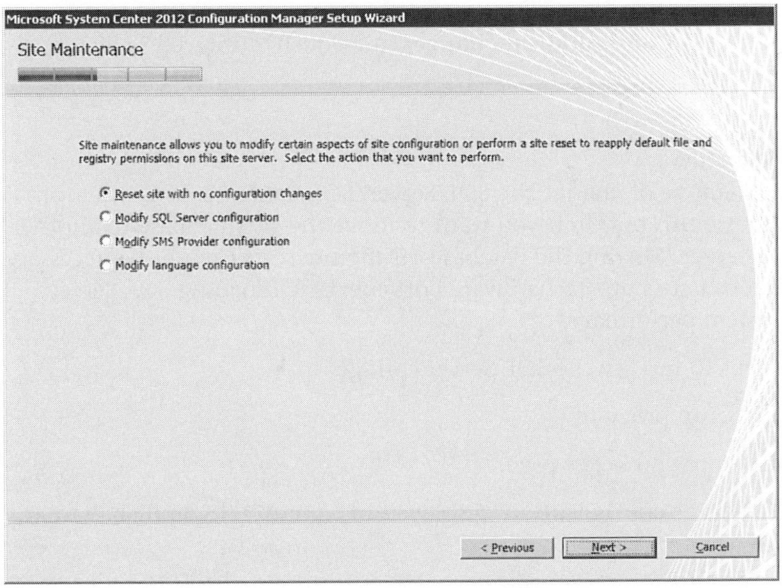

FIGURE 21.15   Site maintenance options.

▶ Reset site with no configuration changes

▶ Modify SQL Server configuration

▶ Modify SMS Provider configuration

▶ Modify language configuration

You can monitor the process for each of these options by watching C:\ConfigMgrSetup. log. You can also review the Status Messages generated during the entire process using **All Status Messages** in the Monitoring workspace. Navigate to **Overview -> System Status -> Status Message Queries** to determine whether any errors occurred during the site maintenance process.

Performing a Site Reset

A site reset reapplies default file and registry permissions. It also ensures that the accounts used by ConfigMgr components are correct, resets the access control lists used by remote site systems, and restores ConfigMgr registry keys and the ConfigMgr folder structure. It also re-installs each Configuration Manager component.

Perform the following steps to perform a site reset:

1. Run the ConfigMgr Setup program.

2. Click **Next** on the Before you begin page.

3. Select **Reset site with no Configuration changes**, previously displayed in Figure 21.15, and click **Next**.

Modify SQL Server Configuration

You can use this option to move or change the SQL Server, SQL database, SQL instance, or SSB port. You can also use this option if you want to move the site database to another server or back to the site server. Moving the database off the site server might be necessary if you run into performance issues due to hardware bottlenecks. Offloading SQL Server could increase overall system performance.

Perform the following steps to modify the SQL Server configuration:

1. Run the ConfigMgr Setup program.

2. Click **Next** on the Before you begin page.

3. Select **Modify SQL Server configuration**, displayed in Figure 21.15, and click **Next**.

Modify SMS Provider Configuration

This option enables you to add an additional SMS Provider on another server or to remove an existing one. The latter option is only available if there are at least two provider servers detected. A typical reason to add an additional SMS Provider is scalability. This is usually needed only in large environments in which many administrator consoles are necessary or automation tools connect to the site.

Perform the following steps to modify the SMS Provider configuration:

1. Run the ConfigMgr Setup program.

2. Click **Next** on the Before you begin page.

3. Select **Modify SMS Provider configuration**, previously displayed in Figure 21.15, and click **Next**.

Modify Language Configuration

Use this option if you want to add or remove additional languages for a Configuration Manager site. This might be necessary if a company merges with a foreign one. Additional languages can be used to provide a localized experience for the admin console and clients.

Perform the following steps to modify the language configuration:

1. Run the ConfigMgr Setup program.

2. Click **Next** on the Before you begin page.

3. Select **Modify language configuration** (refer to Figure 21.15).

4. Select **Download required files** on the Prerequisite Downloads page if you want to download the latest prerequisites components (Internet connection required) or **Use previously downloaded files** if they are already downloaded, and click **Next**.

5. Select the server language(s) you want to install or uninstall on the Server Language Selection page, and click **Next**.

6. Select the client language(s) you want to install or uninstall on the Client Language Selection page. You can also check the option **Enable all languages for mobile device clients**. Click **Next**.

7. The **Settings Summary** page contains a summary of all actions to perform. Clicking **Next** begins the actual installation or removal process of languages.

Using Backup and Restore to Migrate to New Environments

You can utilize the steps used to back up and restore the site as discussed in the "Restoring ConfigMgr Backups" section to move an existing environment to new hardware or build out a new environment. The next sections discuss each of these scenarios.

Moving ConfigMgr to New Hardware

A frequently asked question is how to move an existing ConfigMgr environment to new physical hardware. This could become necessary if the original hardware for ConfigMgr was not assessed adequately or the scope of your ConfigMgr environment has significantly increased.

Microsoft does not support changing the name of the server on which Configuration Manager is installed. The only way to alter the name is by performing a full reinstall. If renaming the server is not a requirement, you can perform the backup, re-install, and restore process. Here are the high-level steps required to perform this type of migration:

1. Backup the existing ConfigMgr server. When the backup completes, shut down the ConfigMgr server.

2. Install a new server with the same name and configuration as discussed in Chapter 6, "Installing System Center 2012 Configuration Manager."

3. Restore ConfigMgr as discussed in the "Restoring ConfigMgr Backups" section.

Building a New ConfigMgr Environment

It may become necessary to build out a new ConfigMgr environment to replace an existing one. This could occur if a ConfigMgr server cannot retain the same name and needs to be moved to new hardware (see the "Moving ConfigMgr to New Hardware" section). A new environment might also be required when significant issues are in an existing ConfigMgr environment to the point where replacing it is the most reasonable solution.

Here are the high-level steps required to perform this type of migration:

1. Install the new ConfigMgr server, as discussed in Chapter 6, using a different site code than that used by the original ConfigMgr site.

2. Set the ConfigMgr server environment to the settings you require, including Active Directory System Discovery. Set the site boundaries to overlap with the original ConfigMgr environment.

3. When all systems are listed in the All Systems collection, right-click the collection, and select **Install Client** to the collection to deploy the client.

4. You can export objects (collections, applications, packages, baselines, and so on) from the old site and import them on the new site if needed.

SQL Replication

Prior to System Center 2012 Configuration Manager, replication of data between sites occurred using a file-based replication model. This mechanism has changed to SQL replication, as introduced in Chapter 3, "Looking Inside Configuration Manager." You need to monitor the status of SQL replication and generate alerts when there are replication issues; the following sections discuss these activities.

Monitoring SQL Replication

The status of the SQL replication between sites is essential for a System Center 2012 Configuration Manager environment and can be monitored using the ConfigMgr console. This is important because a consistent state of global data and replicated site data within the entire hierarchy is required for a healthy infrastructure. It ensures that the same information of global data is available on each primary site, a subset of global data is on each secondary site, and that site data is replicated to the CAS (for additional information, see Chapter 3).

To monitor SQL replication, select the Monitoring workspace, and open the **Database Replication** node, as displayed in Figure 21.16.

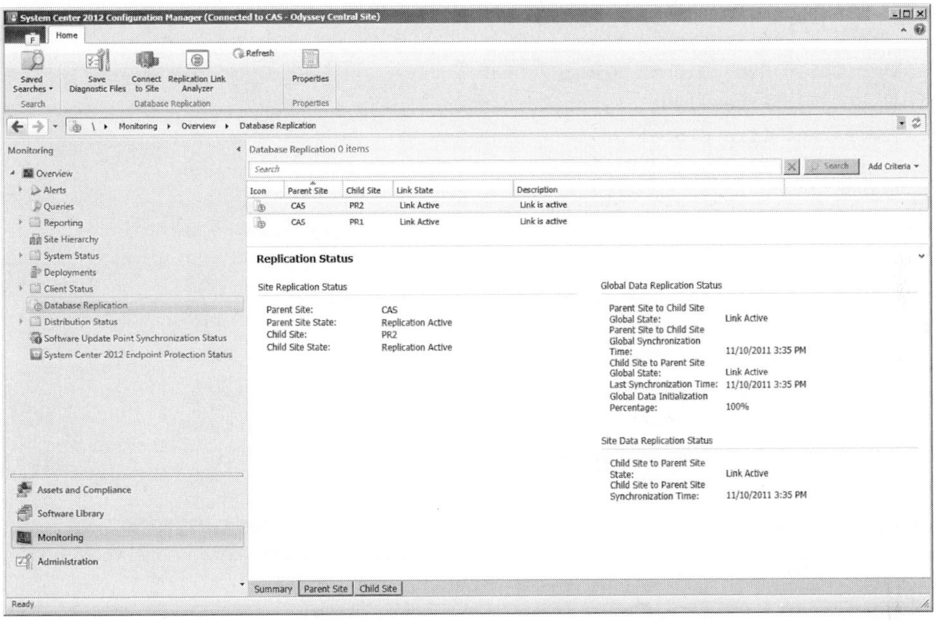

FIGURE 21.16   Database Replication.

By highlighting a set of replication partners, you can obtain a detailed status summary of several replication types:

- ▶ **Site Replication Status:** This lists the sites involved and their replication state.

- ▶ **Global Data Replication Status:** This status lists the status for Parent-to-Child and Child-to-Parent replication with the timestamp of the last synchronization time and the Global Data Initialization Percentage.

- ▶ **Site Data Replication Status:** This lists the status for Child-to-Parent replication with the timestamp of the last synchronization time.

You can navigate to the Parent Site or Child Site tab to get details for each site. This includes the computer account, database file disk free space, database file location, firewall ports, machine certificate, SQL Server certificate, SQL Server port, SQL Server role, and SQL Server service broker port.

To save this information, right-click one of the Database Replication items, and select **Save Diagnostics File**.

Here is a sample SQL Replication diagnostics file:

```
Summary
CAS <-> PR1
Parent Site = CAS
Parent Site State = Replication Active
Child Site = PR1
Child Site State = Replication Active
Parent Site to Child Site Global State = Link Active
Parent Site to Child Site Global Synchronization Time = 11/10/2011 9:52:34 PM
Child Site to Parent Site Global State = Link Active
Last Synchronization Time = 11/10/2011 9:48:17 PM
Child Site to Parent Site State = Link Active
Child Site to Parent Site Synchronization Time = 11/10/2011 9:47:17 PM


Parent Site (CAS)Parent Site Configuration
State,Monitored Item,Current Configuration,Description
Success,"Machine certificate","cn=Armada.odyssey.com
Expires: 2111-10-11","Certificate is still valid for Armada.odyssey.com."
Success,"SQL Server certificate","cn=SSB Transport Security Certificate
Expires: 2029-01-01","Service Broker certificate is still valid for
Armada.odyssey.com."
Success,"SQL Server port","1433","Port 1433 still valid for Armada.odyssey.com."
Success,"SQL Server service broker port","4022","Service Broker Armada.odyssey.com
Port 4022 still valid."
Success,"Database file location","E:\Program Files\Microsoft SQL
Server\MSSQL10.MSSQLSERVER\MSSQL\DATA\CM_CAS.mdf
E:\Program Files\Microsoft SQL
Server\MSSQL10.MSSQLSERVER\MSSQL\DATA\CM_CAS_log.LDF","Configuration Manager Data-
base file location is still valid."
Success,"Database file disk free space","E:\ 9GB","Configuration Manager Database
File Disk still has enough free space."
Success,"Computer account","ODYSSEY\Armada$","Configuration Manager Site Server
Account Armada.odyssey.com still valid."
Success,"SQL Server role","smsdbrole_MP, smsdbrole_MCS, smsdbrole_DMP,
smsdbrole_siteprovider, smsdbrole_siteserver, smsdbrole_AMTSP, smsdbrole_AIUS,
smsdbrole_AITool, smsdbrole_extract, smsdbrole_WebPortal, smsdbrole_EnrollSvr,
smsdbrole_DViewAccess, smsschm_users","All Configuration Manager SQL Roles still
valid."
Success,"Firewall ports","1433, 4022","Configuration Manager SQL Server ports 1433,
4022 still active on Firewall exception."


Child Site (PR1)Child Site Configuration
State,Monitored Item,Current Configuration,Description
Success,"Machine certificate","cn=Athena.odyssey.com
```

```
Expires: 2111-10-11","Certificate is still valid for Athena.odyssey.com."
Success,"SQL Server certificate","cn=SSB Transport Security Certificate
Expires: 2029-01-01","Service Broker certificate is still valid for Athena.odyssey.
com."
Success,"SQL Server port","1433","Port 1433 still valid for Athena.odyssey.com."
Success,"SQL Server service broker port","4022","Service Broker Athena.odyssey.com
Port 4022 still valid."
Success,"Database file location","E:\Program Files\Microsoft SQL
Server\MSSQL10.MSSQLSERVER\MSSQL\DATA\CM_PR1.mdf
E:\Program Files\Microsoft SQL
Server\MSSQL10.MSSQLSERVER\MSSQL\DATA\CM_PR1_log.LDF","Configuration Manager Data-
base file location is still valid."
Success,"Database file disk free space","E:\ 9GB","Configuration Manager Database
File Disk still has enough free space."
Success,"Computer account","ODYSSEY\Athena$","Configuration Manager Site Server
Account Athena.odyssey.com still valid."
Success,"SQL Server role","smsdbrole_MP, smsdbrole_MCS, smsdbrole_DMP,
smsdbrole_siteprovider, smsdbrole_siteserver, smsdbrole_AMTSP, smsdbrole_AIUS,
smsdbrole_AITool, smsdbrole_extract, smsdbrole_WebPortal, smsdbrole_EnrollSvr,
smsdbrole_DViewAccess, smsschm_users","All Configuration Manager SQL Roles still
valid."
Success,"Firewall ports","1433, 4022","Configuration Manager SQL Server ports 1433,
4022 still active on Firewall exception."
```

Replication Link Analyzer

Start this tool by clicking **Replication Link Analyzer** on the ribbon on the **Monitoring ->
Database Replication** workspace in the console. This icon is not available on standalone
primary sites. The Replication Link Analyzer can help you to detect, analyze, and remediate SQL replication-related problems in a ConfigMgr hierarchy.

Here are the items checked when you run the tool:

▶ SMS_Executive service state

▶ SMS_Replication_Configuration_Monitor state

▶ Dynamic SQL ports configuration

▶ Site activity

▶ Version of SQL Server

▶ Network connectivity

▶ ConfigMgr and temp database free space

▶ SQL service broker configuration

▶ SQL service broker certificates

▶ Status of the ConfigMgrDRSQueue, ConfigMgrDRSSiteQueue, and ConfigMgrRCMQueue

▶ Time sync

▶ Transmission state

▶ Key conflicts

▶ Existence of degraded links

▶ Existence of failed links

The results are stored in two output files:

▶ *%userprofile%*\Desktop\ReplicationAnalysis.xml

▶ *%userprofile%*\Desktop\ReplicationLinkAnalysis.log

Alerts for SQL Replication

Alerts in ConfigMgr provide a near real-time view about problems that occur in a Configuration Manager site or hierarchy. There are two pre-created alerts for SQL replication:

▶ Replication link down between parent site and *<child site>* (only available in a hierarchy)

▶ Database Replication component failed to run on site *<site code>*

Figure 21.17 displays these alerts.

Alerts appear in the Monitoring workspace on the Overview page in the Alerts node and can have four different states:

▶ **Never triggered:** This alert has not yet been triggered.

▶ **Active:** Indicates an active alert.

▶ **Canceled:** The state changes automatically to Canceled if the condition triggering the alert is no longer present.

▶ **Postponed:** This indicates an administrator postponed the alert. Postponed alerts are removed from the Recent Alerts section on the Overview view in the Monitoring workspace of the console.

Icon	Alert State	Name	Type	Severity
▷	Never Triggered	Database Replication component failed to run on site CAS	Database Replication component failed to run	Critical
▷	Never Triggered	Database Replication component failed to run on site PR1	Database Replication component failed to run	Critical
▷	Never Triggered	Database Replication component failed to run on site PR2	Database Replication component failed to run	Critical
▷	Never Triggered	Replication link down between parent site and PR1	Site to site connectivity	Critical
▷	Never Triggered	Replication link down between parent site and PR2	Site to site connectivity	Critical

FIGURE 21.17   Default database replication alerts.

Site Maintenance

In addition to having a solid backup and recovery procedure in place, you also want to maintain the data in your site and site database. There are many concepts to consider when performing site maintenance, including site maintenance tasks, data discovery record (DDR) retention, and dealing with obsolete database records. These are discussed in the following sections.

Site Maintenance Tasks

Site maintenance tasks are a vital part of maintaining your site. After installing and performing other initial configurations, it is imperative you understand and configure these tasks to best suit your particular ConfigMgr hierarchy.

Before making any changes to site maintenance tasks, here are several points about the tasks in general:

▶ Site maintenance tasks are set at each individual site and not automatically transferred to any other sites in your ConfigMgr hierarchy.

▶ Some of the site maintenance tasks can cause unnecessary and conflicting processing on the ConfigMgr site. These pitfalls are noted with each task.

▶ Several of the tasks perform maintenance on the database, such as deleting old data or summarizing current data. Balance the amount of data manipulated at one time by scheduling the tasks to run more frequently and at different points of time.

There are different maintenance tasks available depending on the site type. These tasks are discussed in Tables 21.1, 21.2, and 21.3.

TABLE 21.1   Maintenance Tasks Available on a CAS

Task	Enabled by Default	Configuration Defaults	Description
Backup Site Server	No	Daily between 02:00 AM and 5:00 AM	Backing up the ConfigMgr site server is one of the most important tasks. After installation, determine the appropriate schedule and configure this task. See the "Backing Up ConfigMgr" section for more information on what is stored and the section "Restoring ConfigMgr Backups" for performing a restore if necessary.

Task	Enabled by Default	Configuration Defaults	Description
Rebuild Indexes	No	Every Sunday between 12:00 AM and 5:00 AM	Database indexes speed the execution of searches in the SQL database, and most tables in the ConfigMgr database have at least one index. This task evaluates those indexes and rebuilds them if more than 50% of the data is unique to keep your ConfigMgr site running at peak efficiency. The task drops indexes if the data in the table drops to less than 50% uniqueness. This task is also discussed in the "Database Maintenance" section.
Monitor Keys	Yes	Every Sunday between 12:00 AM and 5:00 AM	Primary keys in the ConfigMgr database maintain relationships between the various SQL tables. This site maintenance task checks the keys to ensure that the associations are valid. The task is discussed further in the "Database Maintenance" section.
Deleted Aged Status Messages	Yes	Every day between 12:00 AM and 5:00 AM	This is potentially one of the largest tasks the site server runs. The number of status messages generated by the myriad of site and client components can be high; this task is designed to keep that number in check. This task might run for a long time due to the number of status messages that can be deleted. The authors recommend you run this task more frequently to reduce the number of status messages deleted in each pass and shorten the length of each individual run. The task is discussed further in the "Maintaining Status Data" section.
Delete Obsolete Alerts	Yes	Delete data older than 30 days, every day between 12:00 AM and 5:00 AM	This task deletes alerts where the linked object has already been deleted. For example, the compliance rate alert will be deleted via this task if the associated baseline deployment was deleted.
Delete Aged Log Data	Yes	Delete data older than 30 days, every day between 12:00 AM and 5:00 AM	This task cleans up SQL replication logs and object lock requests.

21

Task	Enabled by Default	Configuration Defaults	Description
Delete Aged Replication Tracking Data	Yes	Delete data older than 7 days, every day between 12:00 AM and 5:00 AM	This task deletes records older than the selected range in the maintenance task from DRSSentMessages and DRSReceivedMessages tables at each site. These tables can grow large as the messages for both ConfigurationData and SCF Replication groups are kept in these tables and only used for debugging purposes.
Delete Obsolete Forest Discovery Sites and Subnets	Yes	Delete data older than 30 days, every Saturday between 12:00 AM and 5:00 AM	This deletes sites and subnets not discovered via Active Directory Forest Discovery for the configured period of time.
Check Application Title with Inventory Information	Yes	Delete data older than 7 days, every Saturday between 12:00 AM and 5:00 AM	This task matches installed software with asset intelligence catalog data by calculating the software properties hash based on Product Name, Publisher, and Product Version from the Inventory table.
Delete Aged Client Operations	Yes	Delete data older than 7 days, every day between 12:00 AM and 05:00 AM	This task deletes one-time policies created for endpoint protection scanning for clients. When a device or device collection gets the "Scan now" action, a one-time policy is created if it did not already exist. This maintenance task cleans out aged one-time policies for endpoint protection scans.
Delete Aged Delete Detection Data	Yes	Delete data older than 5 days, every day between 12:00 AM and 05:00 AM	This deletes aged data from the database created by extraction views. Those views are disabled by default and can be enabled using only the software development kit (SDK).

TABLE 21.2   Maintenance Tasks Available on a Primary Site

Task	Enabled by Default	Configuration Defaults	Description
Backup Site Server	No	Daily between 02:00 AM and 5:00 AM	Backing up the ConfigMgr site server is one of the most important tasks. After installation, determine the appropriate schedule and configure this task. See the "Backing Up ConfigMgr" section for more information on what is stored and "Restoring ConfigMgr Backups" for performing a restore if necessary.
Check Application Title with Inventory Information	Yes	Every Saturday between 12:00 AM and 5:00 AM	This task is to match installed software with asset intelligence catalog data by calculating the software properties hash based on Product Name, Publisher, and Product Version from the Inventory table.
Clear Install Flag	No	Clear install flag for clients not discovered for 21 days, every Sunday between 12:00AM and 5:00 AM	The clear install flag is designed to help clear out stale records from the ConfigMgr database. When a client is installed, a flag is set in the database—marking the computer as installed and current. The task clears that flag if a heartbeat DDR is not received in the configured amount of time. If the Client Rediscovery period is set lower than the heartbeat discovery cycle, you can cause clients to reinstall if the client push installation method is also set. This can lead to unnecessary churn on the clients (as they reinstall over a presumably healthy client) and the site server (DDRs, Management Information Files [MIFs], and so on).
Delete Aged Application Request Data	Yes	Delete data older than 30 days, every Saturday between 12:00 AM and 5:00 AM	Deletes application requests that are cancelled/denied and older than the specified time.
Delete Aged Client Operations	Yes	Delete data older than 7 days, every day between 12:00 AM and 5:00 AM	This task deletes one-time policies created for endpoint protection scanning for clients. When a device or device collection gets the "Scan now" action, a one-time policy is created if it did not already exist. This maintenance task cleans out aged one-time policies for endpoint protection scans.

Task	Enabled by Default	Configuration Defaults	Description
Delete Aged Collected Files	Yes	Delete data older than 90 days, every Saturday between 12:00 AM and 5:00 AM	Deletes collected files older than the specified time.
Delete Aged Computer Association Data	Yes	Delete data older than 30 days, every Saturday between 12:00 AM and 5:00 AM	Computer associations are used in operating system deployments that transfer user data. These associations are marked as ready for deletion after the user state restore has completed. This task removes those old associations.
Delete Aged Delete Detection Data	Yes	Delete data older than 5 days, every day between 12:00 AM and 5:00 AM	This deletes aged data from the database created by extraction views. Those views are disabled by default and can only be enabled using the SDK.
Delete Aged Device Wipe Record	Yes	Delete data older than 180 days, every Saturday between 12:00 AM and 5:00 AM	Deletes wipe records for Exchange devices that are older than the configured amount of days.
Delete Aged Devices Managed by the Exchange Server Connector	Yes	Every Saturday between 12:00 AM and 5:00 AM	This deletes mobile devices managed by the Exchange connector that have not connected to Exchange for a period of time longer than the maximum limit set in the Exchange connector properties.
Delete Aged Discovery Data	Yes	Delete data older than 90 days, every Saturday between 12:00 AM and 5:00 AM	When discovery data has reached a specified age, this task removes it from the ConfigMgr database. The task deletes any system that has not been discovered in the specified threshold. A common thought on this is that it refers to a system that has not been discovered by Heartbeat Discovery; however, that is incorrect. If any discovery method (network, active directory) has discovered the system within the threshold, the system will not be deleted. For example, you can have a system that has been gone from the site for a while but still remains in the collections because Active Directory Discovery found it in Active Directory (AD). This can happen in environments where AD is not well maintained.

Task	Enabled by Default	Configuration Defaults	Description
Delete Aged Endpoint Protection Health Status History Data	Yes	Delete data older than 365 days, every Saturday between 12:00 AM and 5:00 AM	This task deletes the history of summarized endpoint protection health status history data per collection that is older than the configured value.
Delete Aged Devices Managed by the Exchange Server Connector	Yes	Delete data older than 180 days, every Saturday between 12:00 AM and 5:00 AM	This will remove all obsolete records that are in the Exchange partnership properties table that have LastSuccessSyncTimeUTC earlier than X days ago. X is configurable on the Exchange connector. It will also decommission the system records that correspond to the obsolete partnership entries if they are solely Exchange-managed.
Delete Aged Enrolled Devices	Yes	Delete data older than 90 days, every Saturday between 12:00 AM and 5:00 AM	This task deletes mobile device records for enrolled mobile devices that have not contacted the management point for a configured period of time.
Delete Aged Inventory History	Yes	Delete data older than 90 days, every Saturday between 12:00 AM and 5:00 AM	The Delete Aged inventory History task removes data from the ConfigMgr database after the specified number of days. After a client inventory agent is enabled, clients perform the specified actions and report it back to the ConfigMgr database. This task examines that data and determines if it is older than the number of days specified in the days. Data removed by this task includes data from the hardware and software inventory client agents.
Delete Aged Log Data	Yes	Delete data older than 30 days, every day between 12:00 AM and 5:00 AM	This task cleans up SQL replication logs and object lock requests.
Delete Aged Replication Tracking Data	Yes	Delete data older than 7 days, every day between 12:00 AM and 5:00 AM	This task deletes records older than the selected range in the maintenance task from DRSSentMessages and DRSReceivedMessages tables at each site. These tables can grow large as the messages for both ConfigurationData and SCF Replication groups are kept in these tables and only used for debugging purposes.

21

Task	Enabled by Default	Configuration Defaults	Description
Delete Aged Software Metering Data	Yes	Delete data older than 5 days, every day between 12:00 AM and 5:00 AM	When both the Software Metering client agent and a software metering rule are enabled on a ConfigMgr site server, clients begin to gather and report that data on the specified schedule. This task removes the data from the site server when it reaches a certain age.
Delete Aged Software Metering Summary Data	Yes	Delete data older than 270 days, every Sunday between 12:00 AM and 5:00 AM	The Summarize tasks take software metering data and summarize it in the ConfigMgr database. This task removes summarized data over a certain age, keeping only the most current dataset.
Delete Aged Status Messages	Yes	Every day between 12:00 AM and 5:00 AM	This is potentially one of the largest tasks run by the site server. The number of status messages generated by the myriad of site and client components can be high; this task is designed to keep that number in check. This task might run for a long time due to the number of status messages that could be deleted. The authors recommend you run this task more frequently to reduce the number of status messages deleted in each pass, and shorten the length of each individual run. The task is discussed further in the "Maintaining Status Data" section.
Delete Aged Threat Data	Yes	Delete data older than 30 days, every Saturday between 12:00 AM and 5:00 AM	This task deletes malware incidents that happened earlier than a configured number of days.
Delete Aged User Device Affinity Data	Yes	Delete data older than 90 days, every Saturday between 12:00 AM and 5:00 AM	This task deletes inactive UDA (user device affinity) records from the database older than a configured number of days.

Task	Enabled by Default	Configuration Defaults	Description
Delete Inactive Client Discovery Data	No	Delete data older than 90 days, every Saturday between 12:00 AM and 5:00 AM	Clients can be marked inactive when the Client Status Tool marks it as such or when a client is marked obsolete. This task removes the discovery data associated with clients marked inactive; this commonly happens when a client does not heartbeat within the required time frame.
			This is a discovery method that acts specifically on heartbeat data. If heartbeat data has not been received, the system is marked as inactive and is a candidate for deletion.
			Similar to the Clear Install Flag task, this task is closely tied to Heartbeat Discovery. The authors recommend that the Delete data older than (days) option be set higher than your ConfigMgr heartbeat discovery cycle.
			Because clients are marked inactive via other mechanisms, this particular task can be set to a fairly low number of days without risking data loss. If a client is marked inactive, it was already marked as such by the Client Status Tool, or via normal obsolete client processing.
Delete Obsolete Alerts	Yes	Delete data older than 30 days, every day between 12:00 AM and 5:00 AM	This task deletes alerts where the linked object has already been deleted. For example, the compliance rate alert will be deleted via this task if the associated baseline deployment was deleted.
Delete Obsolete Client Discovery Data	No	Delete data older than 7 days, every Saturday between 12:00 AM and 5:00 AM	When a client is marked obsolete, this task removes that client's discovery data from the ConfigMgr database. A client is marked obsolete if superseded in the ConfigMgr database by another record. See the "Obsolete Clients" section for details. Obsolete records are not deleted until this task runs but there is no impact on software deployment, and so on.

21

Task	Enabled by Default	Configuration Defaults	Description
Delete Obsolete Forest Discovery Sites and Subnets	Yes	Delete data older than 30 days, every Saturday between 12:00 AM and 5:00 AM	Deletes sites and subnets not discovered via Active Directory Forest Discovery for the configured period of time.
Delete Unused Application Revisions	Yes	Delete data older than 60 days, every day between 12:00 AM and 5:00 AM	Removes any application revisions that have not been used for the specified period of time.
Evaluate Collection Members	Yes	Every 5 minutes	Defines the interval used to dynamically add new members to collections. See Chapter 13, "Distributing and Deploying Applications," for details.
Evaluate Provisioned AMT Computer Certificates	Yes	Pending days to expiration: 42, every Saturday between 12:00 AM and 5:00 AM	The task checks the validity period of the certificate issued to Intel Active Management Technology (AMT)-based computers and automatically requests a new certificate before it expires. Requesting a certificate renewal 42 days (default) before it expires allows plenty of time if there are issues, such as the issuing certification authority is not available, or there are connectivity issues.
Monitor Keys	Yes	Every Sunday between 12:00 AM and 5:00 AM	Primary keys in the ConfigMgr database maintain relationships between the various SQL tables. This site maintenance task checks the keys to ensure that the associations are valid. The task is discussed further in the "Database Maintenance" section.
Rebuild Indexes	No	Every Sunday between 12:00 AM and 5:00 AM	Database indexes speed the execution of searches in the SQL database, and most tables in the ConfigMgr database have at least one index. This task evaluates those indexes, and rebuilds them if more than 50% of the data is unique to keep your ConfigMgr site running at peak efficiency. The task drops indexes if the data in the table drops to less than 50% uniqueness. This task is also discussed in the "Database Maintenance" section.

Task	Enabled by Default	Configuration Defaults	Description
Summarize Installed Software Data	Yes	Every day, between 12:00 AM and 5:00 AM	This task is for displaying data in the Asset Intelligence dashboard. It summarizes the asset intelligence inventory data on the scheduled intervals for updating the dashboard.
Summarize Software Metering File Usage Data	Yes	Every day between 12:00 AM and 5:00 AM	When this task runs, it combines multiple entries in the ConfigMgr database down to a single record. This saves space in the ConfigMgr database and ultimately helps performance.
Summarize Software Metering Monthly Usage Data	Yes	Every day between 12:00 AM and 5:00 AM	When this task runs, it combines multiple entries in the ConfigMgr database down to a single record. This saves space in the ConfigMgr database and ultimately helps performance.
Update Application Catalog Tables	Yes	This task updates the Application Catalog tables on a dynamic interval. It can also be configured to run on a fixed interval of X minutes (default = 1380min). It can also be run on demand by checking **Run This Synchronization Task as Soon As Possible**	This task periodically rebuilds the application catalog website metadata cache tables. When applications or packages are created or updated, the metadata cache tables in the database are updated automatically, but if those updates were skipped (e.g., SQL was too busy) or if application deployments were deleted, this task will update the cache tables with the latest information. The application catalog website metadata cache tables allow the catalog to quickly query all the applications published to the catalog, especially in large environments with over 100,000 users and 100's–1,000's of published applications.

TABLE 21.3   Maintenance Tasks Available on a Secondary Site

Task	Enabled by Default	Configuration Defaults	Description
Rebuild Indexes	No	Every Sunday between 12:00 AM and 5:00 AM	Database indexes speed the execution of searches in the SQL database, and most tables in the ConfigMgr database have at least one index. This task evaluates those indexes and rebuilds them if more than 50% of the data is unique to keep your ConfigMgr site running at peak efficiency. The task drops indexes if the data in the table drops to less than 50% uniqueness. This task is also discussed in the "Database Maintenance" section.
Delete Aged Log Data	Yes	Delete data older than 30 days, every day between 12:00 AM and 5:00 AM	This task cleans up SQL replication logs and object lock requests.
Delete Aged Replication Tracking Data	Yes	Delete data older than 7 days, every day between 12:00 AM and 5:00 AM	This task deletes records older than the selected range in the maintenance task from DRSSentMessages and DRSReceivedMessages tables at each site. These tables can grow large as the messages for both ConfigurationData and SCF Replication groups are kept in these tables and used only for debugging purposes.

MONITORING THE EFFECTS OF MAINTENANCE TASKS

You can use the status message query **All Status Messages from a Specific Component at a Specific Site** to query for the activities of SMS_Database_Notification_Monitor or examine the smsdbmon.log file. These messages provide details regarding the outcome of each task.

DDR Retention

After installing a ConfigMgr site, you add clients and resources to the site. These objects are added using a discovery method. (The only required discovery method is Heartbeat Discovery.) Various discovery methods can be used that search Active Directory or the network for resources. Those resources include computers, Active Directory objects, site systems, routers, hubs, printers, and Internet Protocol (IP)-addressable devices. Chapter 9, "Configuration Manager Client Management," covers discovery in detail, and Chapter 5 provides information on network discovery.

As ConfigMgr discovers resources, it creates files with a .DDR—or in cases of initial client registration, a registration discovery record or .RDR—extension that is added to the ConfigMgr database. These data discovery records refer to the .ddr file format and the actual file used by ConfigMgr to report discovery data to a Configuration Manager site database. You could use those records to target installations for client deployment. DDRs are the main method to tell ConfigMgr site crucial details about clients. Without DDRs, no clients would be in the database for you to manage!

DDRs are generated based upon the type of discovery method used and based on a polling schedule that indicates when ConfigMgr performs the actions required to execute the discovery, such as querying Active Directory for systems in the container specified within the discovery method.

Heartbeat Discovery is unique because the ConfigMgr server does not poll these systems; the discovery configuration specifies only how frequently the clients send their heartbeats DDRs to the ConfigMgr site. The specific information contained in each record can vary depending on the particular resource.

As previously mentioned in this section, Chapter 9 covers discovery in detail, but as a reminder, here are the different discoveries available in System Center 2012 Configuration Manager:

▶ Active Directory Forest Discovery

▶ Active Directory Group Discovery

▶ Active Directory System Discovery

▶ Active Directory User Discovery

▶ Heartbeat Discovery

▶ Network Discovery

Data collected can include things such as the NetBIOS name of the computer, the IP address, the MAC (Media Access Control) address, and the IP subnet of the discovered computer or device.

You can configure each type of discovery method on its own custom schedule. When ConfigMgr runs discoveries, it generates resource DDRs to keep discovery data current in the database and inform ConfigMgr that the resource is still valid for the site.

DDRs are not intended for use as extended inventory; they contain basic information that gives the ConfigMgr site enough information to place the client in the database and determine if it were reported previously.

Here is a sample of a heartbeat DDR file created for the Athena server. It was captured from \auth\ddm.box. Note the NetBIOS name information for the Athena server, IP address information, AD site, ConfigMgr site, and domain information:

```
    FV°    jⱽ  <System>
BEGIN_PROPERTY
<8><SMS Unique Identifier><19><64><GUID:7436AF46-4A64-462E-BD4E-0F9AD15FEDEB>
END_PROPERTY
BEGIN_PROPERTY
<0><Client Version><19><32><5.00.7678.0000>
END_PROPERTY
BEGIN_PROPERTY
<0><Client Type><8><8><1>
END_PROPERTY
BEGIN_PROPERTY
<0><Unknown><8><8><>
END_PROPERTY
BEGIN_PROPERTY
<0><Client><8><8><1>
END_PROPERTY
BEGIN_PROPERTY
<8><NetBIOS Name><19><64><ATHENA>
END_PROPERTY
BEGIN_PROPERTY
<0><Resource Domain OR Workgroup><19><255><ODYSSEY>
END_PROPERTY
BEGIN_PROPERTY
<0><AD Site Name><19><128><Default-First-Site-Name>
END_PROPERTY
BEGIN_PROPERTY
<0><Is Assigned To User><10><1><1>
END_PROPERTY
BEGIN_PROPERTY
<0><Is Machine Changes Persisted><10><1><1>
END_PROPERTY
BEGIN_PROPERTY
<0><Is Virtual Machine><10><1><1>
END_PROPERTY
BEGIN_PROPERTY
<0><Virtual Machine Host Name><19><128><HOST8>
END_PROPERTY
BEGIN_PROPERTY
<17><IP Addresses><19><64>
BEGIN_ARRAY_VALUES
<172.16.10.143><fe80::f58c:9c5:a72d:8a72>
END_ARRAY_VALUES
END_PROPERTY
BEGIN_PROPERTY
<25><MAC Addresses><19><18>
BEGIN_ARRAY_VALUES
```

21

```
<00:15:5D:0A:81:06>
END_ARRAY_VALUES
END_PROPERTY
BEGIN_PROPERTY
<17><IP Subnets><19><64>
BEGIN_ARRAY_VALUES
<172.16.10.0>
END_ARRAY_VALUES
END_PROPERTY
BEGIN_PROPERTY
<25><Resource Names><19><256>
BEGIN_ARRAY_VALUES
<Athena.odyssey.com>
END_ARRAY_VALUES
END_PROPERTY
BEGIN_PROPERTY
<17><SMS Assigned Sites><19><128>
BEGIN_ARRAY_VALUES
<PR1>
END_ARRAY_VALUES
END_PROPERTY
BEGIN_PROPERTY
<0><Operating System Name and Version><19><128><Microsoft Windows NT Server 6.1>
END_PROPERTY
BEGIN_PROPERTY
<0><Previous SMS UUID><19><64><GUID:7436AF46-4A64-462E-BD4E-0F9AD15FEDEB>
END_PROPERTY
BEGIN_PROPERTY
<0><SMS UUID Change Date><12><19><12/14/2011 21:00:18>
END_PROPERTY
BEGIN_PROPERTY
<0><Hardware ID><19><64><2:C8205C67CDB053057CF8B252EBC95AE2D369BB43>
END_PROPERTY
BEGIN_PROPERTY
<0><SMBIOS GUID><19><38><F0028AE6-62D4-47AA-A94D-F3A93E87681D>
END_PROPERTY
BEGIN_PROPERTY
<17><SMS Installed Sites><19><128>
BEGIN_ARRAY_VALUES
<PR1>
END_ARRAY_VALUES
END_PROPERTY
AGENTINFO<Heartbeat Discovery><PR1><12/14/2011 15:25:39>
FEOF
  FV
```

21

TIP: CAPTURING HEARTBEAT DISCOVERIES ON THE CLIENT SIDE

If you want to preserve the data collected in the data discovery or inventory record for troubleshooting purposes, create an empty file named **archive_reports.sms** on the agent system in the inventory\temp folder. You can verify this location by checking the registry entry setting located at HKEY_LOCAL_MACHINE\Software\Microsoft\SMS\Mobile Client\Inventory\Temp.

After this file is created, the discovery and other inventory records are stored in XML format in the inventory\temp folder as they are processed.

The same heartbeat discovery record just listed is saved on the client as the following xml file if archive_reports.sms was used:

```
<?xml version='1.0' encoding='UTF-16'?>
<Report>
<ReportHeader>
<Identification>
<Machine>
<ClientInstalled>1</ClientInstalled>
<ClientType>1</ClientType>
<ClientID>GUID:7436AF46-4A64-462E-BD4E-0F9AD15FEDEB</ClientID>
<ClientVersion>5.00.7678.0000</ClientVersion>
<NetBIOSName>ATHENA</NetBIOSName>
<CodePage>437</CodePage>
<SystemDefaultLCID>1033</SystemDefaultLCID>
</Machine>
</Identification>
<ReportDetails>
<ReportContent>Inventory\x0020Data</ReportContent>
<ReportType>Full</ReportType>
<Date>20111214152539.000000-360</Date>
<Version>4.0</Version>
<Format>1.1</Format>
</ReportDetails>
<InventoryAction ActionType="Predefined">
<InventoryActionID>{00000000-0000-0000-0000-000000000003}</InventoryActionID>
<Description>Discovery</Description>
<InventoryActionLastUpdateTime>20111104151100.000000+000</InventoryActionLastUpdate-
Time>
</InventoryAction>
</ReportHeader>
<ReportBody>
<Instance ParentClass="CCM_NetworkAdapterConfiguration"
Class="CCM_NetworkAdapterConfiguration" Namespace="\\ATHENA\root\ccm\invagt"
Content="New">
<CCM_NetworkAdapterConfiguration>
```

```
<IPSubnet>172.16.10.0</IPSubnet>
</CCM_NetworkAdapterConfiguration>
</Instance>
<Instance ParentClass="SMS_Authority" Class="SMS_Authority"
Namespace="\\ATHENA\ROOT\ccm" Content="New">
<SMS_Authority><Name>SMS:PR1</Name></SMS_Authority>
</Instance>
Instance ParentClass="CCM_ClientIdentificationInformation"
Class="CCM_ClientIdentificationInformation" Namespace="\\ATHENA\ROOT\ccm"
Content="New">
<CCM_ClientIdentificationInformation>
<HardwareID1>2:C8205C67CDB053057CF8B252EBC95AE2D369BB43</HardwareID1>
</CCM_ClientIdentificationInformation>
</Instance>
<Instance ParentClass="CCM_ComputerSystem" Class="CCM_ComputerSystem"
Namespace="\\ATHENA\root\ccm\invagt" Content="New">
<CCM_ComputerSystem>
<Domain>ODYSSEY</Domain></CCM_ComputerSystem>
</Instance>
<Instance ParentClass="CCM_DesktopMachine"
Class="CCM_DesktopMachine" Namespace="\\ATHENA\root\ccmvdi" Content="New">
<CCM_DesktopMachine><HostIdentifier>HOST8</HostIdentifier>
<IsAssignedToUser>1</IsAssignedToUser>
<IsMachineChangesPersisted>1</IsMachineChangesPersisted>
<IsVirtual>1</IsVirtual>
</CCM_DesktopMachine>
</Instance><Instance ParentClass="CCM_ExtNetworkAdapterConfiguration"
Class="CCM_ExtNetworkAdapterConfiguration" Namespace="\\ATHENA\root\ccm\invagt"
Content="New">
<CCM_ExtNetworkAdapterConfiguration>
<FQDN>Athena.odyssey.com</FQDN></CCM_ExtNetworkAdapterConfiguration>
</Instance>
<Instance ParentClass="Win32_NetworkAdapterConfiguration"
Class="Win32_NetworkAdapterConfiguration" Namespace="\\ATHENA\root\cimv2"
Content="New">
<Win32_NetworkAdapterConfiguration>
<Index>7</Index>
<IPAddress>172.16.10.143</IPAddress>
<IPAddress>fe80::f58c:9c5:a72d:8a72</IPAddress>
<MACAddress>00:15:5D:0A:81:06</MACAddress>
</Win32_NetworkAdapterConfiguration>
</Instance>
<Instance ParentClass="CCM_Client" Class="CCM_Client" Namespace="\\ATHENA\ROOT\ccm"
Content="New">
<CCM_Client>
<ClientIdChangeDate>12/14/2011\x002021:00:18</ClientIdChangeDate>
```

```
<PreviousClientId>GUID:7436AF46-4A64-462E-BD4E-0F9AD15FEDEB</PreviousClientId>
</CCM_Client>
</Instance>
<Instance ParentClass="CCM_ADSiteInfo" Class="CCM_ADSiteInfo"
Namespace="\\ATHENA\root\ccm\invagt" Content="New">
<CCM_ADSiteInfo>
<ADSiteName>Default-First-Site-Name</ADSiteName>
</CCM_ADSiteInfo>
</Instance>
<Instance ParentClass="Win32_ComputerSystem" Class="Win32_ComputerSystem"
Namespace="\\ATHENA\root\cimv2" Content="New">
<Win32_ComputerSystem>
<Name>ATHENA</Name>
</Win32_ComputerSystem>
</Instance>
<Instance ParentClass="Win32_ComputerSystemProduct"
Class="Win32_ComputerSystemProduct" Namespace="\\ATHENA\root\cimv2" Content="New">
<Win32_ComputerSystemProduct>
<IdentifyingNumber>6859-1412-2813-3236-4354-1422-44</IdentifyingNumber>
<Name>Virtual\x0020Machine</Name>
<UUID>F0028AE6-62D4-47AA-A94D-F3A93E87681D</UUID>
<Version>7.0</Version>
</Win32_ComputerSystemProduct>
</Instance>
<Instance ParentClass="CCM_DiscoveryData"
Class="CCM_DiscoveryData" Namespace="\\ATHENA\root\ccm\invagt" Content="New">
<CCM_DiscoveryData>
<PlatformID>Microsoft\x0020Windows\x0020NT\x0020Server\x00206.1</PlatformID>
</CCM_DiscoveryData>
</Instance>
</ReportBody>
</Report>
```

The next listing shows a sample of an Active Directory System Discovery DDR file created for the Athena server. (Note the sample includes the NetBIOS name, domain of ODYSSEY, Active Directory site name, IP address, the discovery method used, and other fields that would be relevant to discovery on a Windows-based server.)

```
  ‰  FV°   EᴶÜ  <System>
BEGIN_PROPERTY
<8><NetBIOS Name><19><32><ATHENA>
END_PROPERTY
BEGIN_PROPERTY
<1><Operating System Name and Version><19><32><Microsoft Windows NT Server 6.1>
END_PROPERTY
BEGIN_PROPERTY
```

```
<0><Resource Domain OR Workgroup><19><32><ODYSSEY>
END_PROPERTY
BEGIN_PROPERTY
<0><AD Site Name><19><32><ConfigMgr-2012-Lab>
END_PROPERTY
BEGIN_PROPERTY
<16><IP Addresses><19><64>
BEGIN_ARRAY_VALUES
<10.0.0.21>
END_ARRAY_VALUES
END_PROPERTY
BEGIN_PROPERTY
<16><IP Subnets><19><64>
BEGIN_ARRAY_VALUES
<10.0.0.0>
END_ARRAY_VALUES
END_PROPERTY
BEGIN_PROPERTY
<24><Resource Names><19><256>
BEGIN_ARRAY_VALUES
<ATHENA.odyssey.com>
END_ARRAY_VALUES
END_PROPERTY
BEGIN_PROPERTY
<0><Primary Group ID><8><4><515>
END_PROPERTY
BEGIN_PROPERTY
<0><User Account Control><8><4><4096>
END_PROPERTY
BEGIN_PROPERTY
<8><SID><19><64><S-1-5-21-4138751091-3288835667-1361212631-1117>
END_PROPERTY
BEGIN_PROPERTY
<0><Object GUID><19><64><CB321A3C-669E-4260-B388-BF1A4316CA95>
END_PROPERTY
AGENTINFO<SMS_AD_SYSTEM_DISCOVERY_AGENT><PR1><08/14/2011 08:27:42>
FEOF
  FV
```

Obsolete Records

Obsolete records occur when a newer record for same client is inserted in the database and ConfigMgr cannot match it with an existing one. The new record supersedes the former one and becomes the client's current record. The old one is then marked as obsolete.

How a Record Can Be Marked Obsolete

ConfigMgr tries to merge records for the same client using either Windows authentication of the computer account or a PKI certificate from a trusted source. An obsolete record is created only if this process fails.

Consider the following scenario that might generate an obsolete record:

1. Machine XYZ is not joined to an AD domain or using PKI certificates, is a current ConfigMgr client, and is healthy.

2. Machine XYZ has a resource ID (a unique id) of 1234 and a hardware ID (another unique ID) of ABCD. (In reality, the hardware ID is a long string of fixed length but is short and simple for the purpose of this example.)

3. Machine XYZ is reimaged from Windows XP to Windows 7. A new client is installed during the imaging process.

4. Machine XYZ sends a heartbeat DDR to its ConfigMgr site.

5. ConfigMgr processes the DDR and notices that this machine has the same hardware configuration as an already existing record with the hardware ID ABCD.

6. ConfigMgr creates a new resource ID of 1235 for the client and marks the old resource ID of 1234 as obsolete.

7. ConfigMgr now updates information only from that machine in accordance with resource ID of 1235—unless of course it is reimaged again!

ConfigMgr's default configuration is to resolve client records for duplicate hardware IDs automatically. This setting is configured using the **Hierarchy Settings** button on the Administration workspace ribbon; navigate to **Overview -> Site Configuration -> Sites**. Handling of conflicting records is configured on the Client Approval and Conflicting Records tab. There is also the option to resolve conflicting records manually. If this setting is used, you can choose what happens when a conflicting record is detected. Any conflicting records are shown in the Monitoring workspace at **Overview -> System Status -> Conflicting Records**.

Right-clicking a record listed here presents several options:

▶ **Create:** Creates a new client record for the selected system. The former record becomes obsolete.

▶ **Merge:** Merges data into the old record. This is a good option if you know the system is the same and want to retain historical data for that system.

▶ **Block:** Blocks the selected client record. This prevents the client from receiving policies.

Here's how ConfigMgr cleans out obsolete discovery data from the site database:

▶ Obsolete discovery data stays in the database until the Delete Obsolete Client Discovery Data site maintenance task runs.

▶ If the Delete Obsolete Client Discovery Data task is not enabled, the data persists until the client is marked inactive and the Delete Inactive Client Discovery Data task runs. An obsolete client is, by its nature, inactive, so these records would be removed in any case when the Delete Inactive Client Discovery Data task runs.

▶ If the Delete Inactive Client Discovery Data task is also disabled, the data remains.

These tasks are available in the ConfigMgr console in the Administration workspace; navigate to **Overview -> Site Configuration -> Sites -> <*site code*><*site name*> -> Site Maintenance**.

TIP: SETTING THE RETENTION PERIOD FOR A DELETE SITE MAINTENANCE TASK

When configuring a Delete Site Maintenance task, you must set the retention period of the task to a period that is higher than the discovery frequency. Removing discovery data that is not aged sufficiently causes unnecessary churn on the ConfigMgr site. A good rule of thumb is to set this to twice the heartbeat discovery interval or 7 days; whichever is longer.

For example, the Delete Obsolete Client Discovery Data task deletes the obsolete client database records related to the DDR records, discussed in the "DDR Retention" section. Obsolete client records are generally marked as such because they are replaced by a newer record that discovered the same client. The new client record becomes the current client record, and the previous discovery record is now obsolete. This task is not enabled by default. To remove obsolete records, enable the task and give it an interval greater than the heartbeat discovery schedule (which defaults to once a week), as shown in Figure 21.18, which specifies deleting data older than 7 days and running each Saturday morning.

DELETE OBSOLETE CLIENT DISCOVERY DATA TASK THRESHOLDS

Because a client is marked as obsolete when a new record is processed for the same client, it is fairly safe to run the Delete Obsolete Client Discovery Data task with a rather low threshold. Nondiscovery data from obsolete clients is removed by the various other site maintenance tasks.

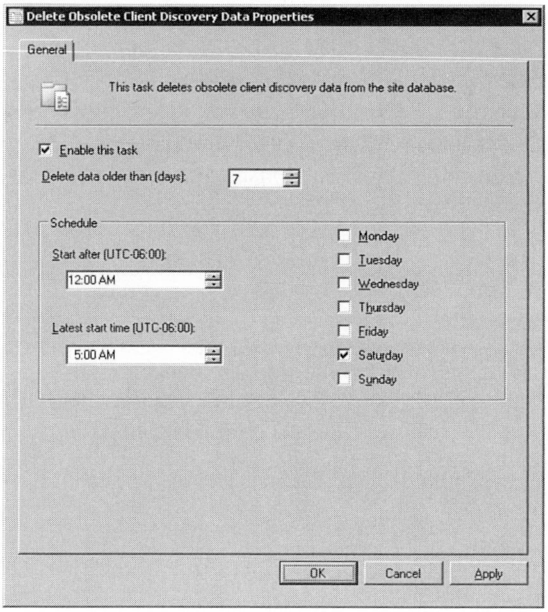

FIGURE 21.18   Enabling the Delete Obsolete Client Discovery Data task.

Database Maintenance

When maintaining the ConfigMgr site database, it is vital to back up the database, as previously discussed in the "Backing Up ConfigMgr" section. An effective backup strategy is crucial to providing a functional database environment for ConfigMgr; however, additional tasks also need to occur to maintain your ConfigMgr database effectively.

Database maintenance is performed using two tasks defined during site installation. These tasks are available in the ConfigMgr console in the Administration workspace. Navigate to **Overview -> Site Configuration -> Sites -> *<site code><site name>* -> Site Maintenance**. The two tasks of note for database maintenance are the Monitor Keys and Rebuild Indexes tasks:

▶ **Monitor Keys:** This task is enabled by default and runs Sunday mornings between 12:00 AM and 5:00 AM. ConfigMgr works like other database applications in that it uses primary keys to identify unique records in a table quickly. A primary key is a column (or multiple columns) that uniquely identifies one row from any other row in a database. The ConfigMgr Monitor Keys task monitors the integrity of these keys within the ConfigMgr database. Because ConfigMgr runs this task, the responsibility of the ConfigMgr administrator is to ensure this task is occurring and completing successfully when it executes.

▶ **Rebuild Indexes:** By default, the task is not enabled. If enabled, this task runs every Sunday between 12:00 AM and 5:00 AM. ConfigMgr, similar to other database applications, uses indexes to speed up data retrieval. As the data in the ConfigMgr database constantly changes, this task improves performance by creating indexes on database columns that are at least 50% unique. The task also drops indexes on columns that are less than 50% unique and rebuilds all the existing indexes to maximize the performance when accessing these columns. The authors recommend you enable this task to achieve best performance.

TIP: RUNNING REBUILD INDEXES WITH A LARGE AMOUNT OF DATABASE DATA

If your ConfigMgr site database holds a large amount of data, the Rebuild Indexes task can take a considerable amount of time to run. This task is different from most tasks in that running it more frequently does not guarantee a shorter execution time but ensures your ConfigMgr site uses the database in the most efficient manner.

Making the Status Message System Work for You

Status messages provide one of the primary means to look at the health of your ConfigMgr infrastructure and identify any problems that might occur. Nearly all ConfigMgr components generate status messages to report various milestones (Table 21.4 lists some examples of milestones) and events. ConfigMgr clients send status messages to their management point or fallback status point, site systems send status messages to the site server, and child sites replicate messages to the CAS. Status messages—as part of site data—are stored on the originating site and replicated to the CAS using SQL replication.

TABLE 21.4   Milestone Examples

Message ID	Severity	Component	Description
3015	Warning	SMS_CLIENT_CONFIG_MANAGER	Client Configuration Manager cannot find machine "PANTHEON" on the network. The operating system reported error 53: The network path was not found.
5460	Information	SMS_MP_CONTROL_MANAGER	MP Control Manager verified that Management Point is responding to HTTP requests.
11171	Information	Task Sequence Manager	The task sequence manager successfully completed execution of the task sequence.
7403	Error	SMS_SRS_REPORTING_POINT	The report server service is not running on reporting services point "Armada.odyssey.com"; start the service to enable reporting.

You can adjust the number of status messages generated by configuring the Status Reporting component, which can be found in the Administration workspace. Navigate to **Overview -> Site Configuration -> Sites -> <*site code*><*site name*> -> Configure Site Components -> Status Reporting** to open its Properties window, displayed in Figure 21.19.

Here are the possible options:

▶ All Milestones and All Details

▶ All Milestones

▶ Error and Warning Milestones

▶ Error Milestones

Enabling the **Log** selection also writes status messages to the event log.

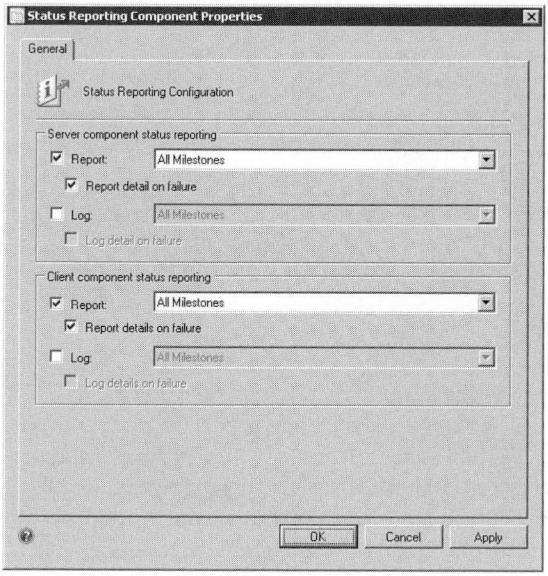

FIGURE 21.19   Status Reporting configuration.

Maintaining Status Data

ConfigMgr retains two different types of status data, which are specified in the ConfigMgr console, in the Administration workspace. Navigate to **Overview -> Site Configuration -> Sites -> <*site code*><*site name*> -> Status Filter Rules**, as displayed in Figure 21.20.

▶ **Audit messages:** Audit messages retention is configured within the **Write audit messages to the site database and specify the period after which the user can**

delete the messages rule. This status filter rule has a default setting of 180 days before the user can delete messages.

▶ **All other messages:** Other message data retention is configured within the **Write all other messages to the site database and specify the period after which the user can delete the messages** rule. This status filter rule has a default setting of 30 days before the user can delete messages.

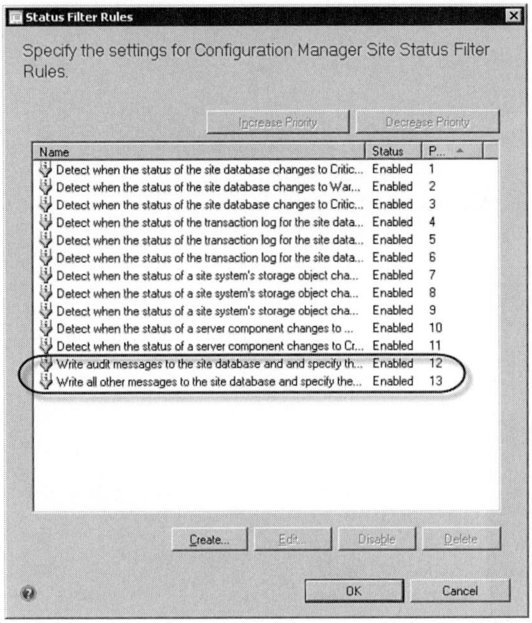

FIGURE 21.20   Status Filter Rules properties.

These messages are removed from the ConfigMgr database through the Delete Aged Status Messages task. (In the ConfigMgr console, navigate to the Administration workspace and select **Overview -> Site Configuration -> Sites -> <site code><site name> -> Site Maintenance.**) This task runs daily between midnight and 5:00 AM. The task deletes status messages older than 7 days.

For example, in a default configuration all audit messages are retained 180 days, and all other messages are retained 30 days. If you decrease the All other messages setting from 30 days down to 14 days and rerun this task, it will not have what might be the expected results, which is to delete messages older than 14 days (other than audit messages).

This is because when status messages are written to the database, the date they are scheduled to be deleted is written based on the setting on the status filter rule at that point in time. The date is calculated based upon the settings that existed for the appropriate message retention task. When the retention period is changed, the new messages remain for the time defined when they are written.

The authors recommend you retain the status messages as long as is required to diagnose the status of your ConfigMgr system. If you need to minimize the amount of space used by status messages, you can decrease the retention periods within the two rules listed in this section—although making this change is not suggested, unless it is necessary to decrease the amount of data retained.

Status Filter Rules

Status filter rules can be a critical method of tuning performance and eliminating unneeded information.

Rules are set in a top-down ranking, meaning that rules listed at the top of the list are processed first, followed by those listed next. This assumes that a higher-level listing does not stop processing of lower-priority rules. Think of status filter rules as a series of gates that each status message must pass through. Each gate has a set of criteria against which each message is checked.

▶ If the message does not match the criteria, it passes through the gate to the next rule.

▶ If it matches, a set of actions can be taken, including either allowing the message to continue on its path, or stopping all further activity for the message.

ConfigMgr comes with a number of status filter rules predefined and enabled by default. These status filter rules provide actions that occur when various conditions are met, as shown in Table 21.5.

TABLE 21.5   Status Filter Rules in System Center 2012 Configuration Manager

Status Filter Rule Name	Default Condition	Default Action
Detect when the status of the site database changes to Critical because it could not be accessed.	Source: Site Server Component: SMS_SITE_SYSTEM_STATUS_SUMMARIZER Message ID: 4703	Report to the event log.
Detect when the status of the site database changes to Warning due to low free space.	Source: Site Server Component: SMS_SITE_SYSTEM_STATUS_SUMMARIZER Message ID: 4713	Report to the event log.
Detect when the status of the site database changes to Critical due to low free space.	Source: Site Server Component: SMS_SITE_SYSTEM_STATUS_SUMMARIZER Message ID: 4714	Report to the event log.

Status Filter Rule Name	Default Condition	Default Action
Detect when the status of the transaction log for the site database changes to Critical because it could not be accessed.	Source: Site Server Component: SMS_ SITE_SYSTEM_STATUS_ SUMMARIZER Message ID: 4706	Report to the event log.
Detect when the status of the transaction log for the site database changes to Warning due to low free space.	Source: Site Server Component: SMS_ SITE_SYSTEM_STATUS_ SUMMARIZER Message ID: 4716	Report to the event log.
Detect when the status of the transaction log for the site database changes to Critical due to low free space.	Source: Site Server Component: SMS_ SITE_SYSTEM_STATUS_ SUMMARIZER Message ID: 4717	Report to the event log.
Detect when the status of a site system's storage object changes to Critical because it could not be accessed.	Source: Site Server Component: SMS_ SITE_SYSTEM_STATUS_ SUMMARIZER Message ID: 4700	Report to the event log.
Detect when the status of a site system's storage object changes to Warning due to low free space.	Source: Site Server Component: SMS_ SITE_SYSTEM_STATUS_ SUMMARIZER Message ID: 4710	Report to the event log.
Detect when the status of a site system's storage object changes to Critical due to low free space.	Source: Site Server Component: SMS_ SITE_SYSTEM_STATUS_ SUMMARIZER Message ID: 4711	Report to the event log.
Detect when the status of a server component changes to Warning.	Source: Site Server Component: SMS_ COMPONENT_STATUS_ SUMMARIZER Message ID: 4610	Report to the event log.
Detect when the status of a server component changes to Critical.	Source: Site Server Component: SMS_ COMPONENT_STATUS_ SUMMARIZER Message ID: 4609	Report to the event log.

Status Filter Rule Name	Default Condition	Default Action
Write audit messages to the site database and specify the period after which the user can delete the messages.	Message type: Audit	Write to the Configuration Manager database. Allow the user to delete messages after how many days: 180.
Write all other messages to the site database and specify the period after which the user can delete the messages.		Write to the Configuration Manager database. Allow the user to delete messages after how many days: 30.

Using the ConfigMgr console, you can create new status filter rules or update existing ones. Utilize these status filter rules to change how these configurations function, or to add matching and actions for additional configurations not predefined within ConfigMgr.

You can configure status filter rules in the Administration workspace by navigating to **Overview -> Site Configuration -> Sites -> <site code><site name> -> Status Filter Rules**.

REAL WORLD: SUPPRESSING STATUS MESSAGES

Most of the space in the ConfigMgr database is consumed by status messages that are also automatically replicated to the CAS. Some of them are less important, and you might want to keep them from being generated; this is particularly true for informational status messages.

Example: The SMS_AD_System_Discovery_Agent creates at least three different status messages every time it runs:

- ▶ MessageID: 500, Description: This component started.
- ▶ MessageID: 5202, Description: Active Directory System Discovery Agent read the AD Containers and found 2 valid AD Container entries in the site control file.
- ▶ MessageID: 502, Description: This component stopped.

This agent is running once every 5 minutes by default. That makes three status messages every 5 minutes, or 36 per hour, or 864 per day.

You can decrease the amount of status messages by preventing MessageIDs 500 and 502 from being written to the database. This reduces the amount of messages from 864 to 288 per day.

In the Administration workspace, navigate to **Overview** -> **Site Operations** -> **Sites** -> **Status Filter Rules**. Create a new Status Filter Rule, enter an appropriate name (such as **Suppress MsgID 500**), select the Message ID, set it to 500, and enable the option **Do not process lower-priority status filter rules**. Increase the priority of this new status filter rule so that it will be higher than the default ones.

Repeat this process to create a second status filter rule for Message ID 502.

Status Summarizers

In addition to individual status messages, each ConfigMgr site maintains status summary data by default. As with individual status messages, you can decide whether to replicate status summary data to the parent site and the data priority to assign to the replication.

There are four different status summarizers to configure in ConfigMgr, as shown in Figure 21.21:

▶ Application Deployment Summarizer

▶ Application Statistics Summarizer

▶ Component Status Summarizer

▶ Site System Status Summarizer

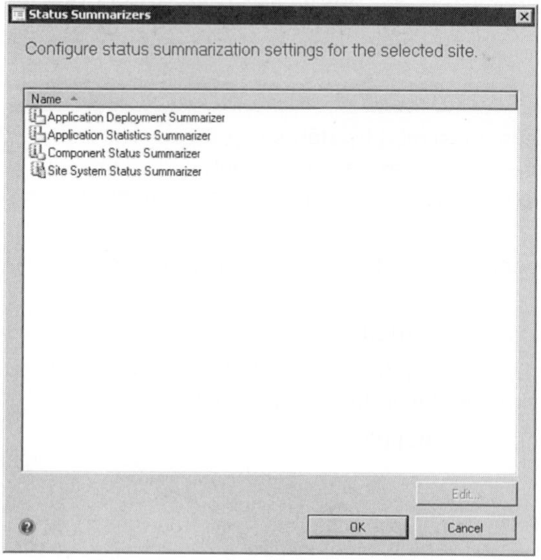

FIGURE 21.21   Status summarizers.

Perform the following steps to configure status summarizers:

1. In the Administration workspace, navigate to **Overview -> Site Configurations -> Sites -> <site code><site name> -> Status Summarizers**.

2. Select and click on the summarizer you want to configure.

3. Select **Edit**.

Table 21.6 lists the defaults of each task.

TABLE 21.6   Status Configuration Settings

Task	Defaults	Thresholds
Application Deployment Summarizer	Summarization Interval: 30 days or less: Every 60 Minutes Between 31 days and 90 days: Every 24 Hours Greater than 90 days: Every 7 Days	n/a
Application Statistics Summarizer	Summarization Interval: 30 days or less: Every 240 Minutes Between 31 days and 90 days: Every 24 Hours Greater than 90 days: Every 7 Days	n/a
Component Status Summarizer	Enable status summarization Replicate to parent site Replication priority: Normal Threshold period: Since 12:00:00 AM	Informational status messages: Warning threshold: 2000, Critical threshold: 5000 Warning status messages: Warning threshold: 10, Critical threshold: 50 Error status message: Warning threshold: 1, Critical threshold: 5
Site System Status Summarizer	Enable status summarization Replicate to parent site Replication priority: Normal Status summarization schedule: every 1 hour	Default thresholds: Warning: 10485760 KB, Critical 5242880 KB Specific thresholds: Database / Transaction Log: Warning threshold: 10485760, Critical threshold: 5242880

You can see the results of status summarization tasks in the Monitoring workspace of the console. Navigate to **Overview -> System Status -> Deployments and Overview -> System Status -> Site Status and Component Status**.

You can adjust the threshold for each ConfigMgr thread separately. Adjust the settings according to the size of your site and amount of activity. This is an ongoing task, which should be performed on a regular basis. You must find the balance between setting the thresholds too low and too high. Low thresholds on one hand might result in a component or site system status all set to yellow (warnings) or red (errors) even if no serious errors occurred. High thresholds on the other hand will result in a green status, and you might miss important events.

Monitoring Configuration Manager with Operations Manager

Chapter 1, "Configuration Management Basics," introduces Microsoft System Center, which includes Configuration Manager, Operations Manager, Service Manager, Data Protection Manager, Virtual Machine Manager, Orchestrator, and Advisor. An important part of a server maintenance strategy should include effective monitoring of what occurs on the servers and applications in your organization.

System Center 2012 Operations Manager (OpsMgr) provides proactive server and application monitoring and displays the information into a centralized console. OpsMgr provides a way to identify issues before they affect the environment, enabling a quicker resolution for issues when they are identified.

ConfigMgr provides its own method of status reporting through status messages (discussed in the "Making the Status Message System Work for You" section) and alerts (discussed in Chapter 8, "The Configuration Manager Console"), so at first glance it would appear that using OpsMgr to monitor ConfigMgr would be redundant. Status messages provide a great level of details related to the internals of what is occurring within ConfigMgr; however, this is not designed to provide proactive monitoring or to alert when critical events occur. Status messages are designed to provide only information that determines what occurs within ConfigMgr.

Operations Manager provides the ability to monitor the physical hardware, operating system, and core functionality such as SQL, DNS, DHCP, and Active Directory; and it provides the ability to monitor applications such as Configuration Manager. OpsMgr's functionality is available through management packs (free with the product) that are available from Microsoft's System Center Marketplace on PinPoint at http://system-center.pinpoint.microsoft.com/en-US/applications/search/operations-manager-d11?q=. For information on the ConfigMgr management pack, search for **System Center 2012 Configuration Manager**.

The ConfigMgr management pack provides the health state for all ConfigMgr servers and services and provides performance and availability reports for ConfigMgr. It also provides alerting for critical ConfigMgr status messages and tracks processing rates and metrics such as the processor, memory, and disk system usage. The management pack includes product knowledge to assist with resolving alerts identified for the ConfigMgr environment.

For more information on System Center Operations Manager, the authors of this book recommend the Microsoft website for Operations Manager (http://www.microsoft.com/en-us/server-cloud/system-center/operations-manager.aspx) and/or *System Center 2012 Operations Manager Unleashed* (Sams, 2012), available at http://www.amazon.com/dp/0672335913.

Services and Descriptions

Configuration Manager uses a variety of services, which run either on the agent or on the various site servers. Knowing what services ConfigMgr uses and the functions they provide can assist with debugging issues that occur in the ConfigMgr environment. This can be critical when identifying issues that might occur after performing a ConfigMgr recovery. Table 21.7 provides a list of these services and their descriptions.

TABLE 21.7   Services Used in System Center 2012 Configuration Manager

Service Name	Description
CCMSetup.exe	Runs on the client agent systems. Temporary service used to install the SMS Agent Host service on client systems.
SMS Agent Host	Runs on the client agent systems and management points. Provides change and configuration services for computer management systems. Set to Automatic.
SMS_EXECUTIVE	Runs on the ConfigMgr server systems. Provides the primary service, which executes the ConfigMgr functions. Set to Automatic.
SMS_SITE_BACKUP	Runs on the ConfigMgr server systems. This service executes the backup task functionality. Set to Manual; activates when the backup task executes.
SMS_SITE_COMPONENT_MANAGER	Runs on the ConfigMgr server systems. Installs and removes server components at a ConfigMgr site and installs any necessary server components. Set to Automatic.
SMS_SITE_SQL_BACKUP	Runs on the ConfigMgr server systems. Performs the SQL backup for the Backup ConfigMgr Site Server task. Set to Automatic.
SMS_SITE_VSS_WRITER	Runs on the ConfigMgr server systems. Creates the backup snapshot for the Backup ConfigMgr Site Server task. Set to Automatic.
SMS_SERVER_BOOTSTRAP_<servername>	Runs on the ConfigMgr server systems. Installs secondary sites or site system roles that are created from the ConfigMgr console. Set to Automatic. This service is automatically deleted after the bootstrap operation is finished.
AI_Update_Service_Point	Runs on the ConfigMgr server systems. Connects to the System Center online services and updates the asset intelligence database tables. Set to Automatic.

Summary

This chapter focused on the steps required to back up, recover, and maintain your ConfigMgr environment. It discussed DDR retention, obsolete records, and database records. It also discussed ConfigMgr Status Messages and using OpsMgr to monitor ConfigMgr. The chapter finished with listing the maintenance services used within ConfigMgr.

This chapter completes the last part of the book, which focuses on how to administer System Center 2012 Configuration Manager. Hopefully, this has been a useful guide to ConfigMgr and provided you with an in-depth level of understanding of the product.

PART VI

Appendixes

IN THIS PART

Configuration Manager Log Files

Since the early days of System Management Server (SMS), the application has used numerous log files for tracking and troubleshooting purposes. This appendix discusses how to enable logging as well as listing the log files used by specific Configuration Manager (ConfigMgr) 2012 components. Little has actually changed in logging from ConfigMgr 2007, and even System Management Server (SMS) 2003 for that matter. Therefore, if you are familiar with logging in either of these previous versions of the product, the contents of this appendix should be familiar. Each version does introduce a new set of log files to support each of the additional features though, and these are covered in this appendix.

To assist with identifying changes from ConfigMgr 2007, the authors have incorporated the following conventions for this appendix:

▶ Log files with an asterisk are new in this version.

▶ Log files with two asterisks are renamed from ConfigMgr 2007.

REAL WORLD: WINDOWS EVENT LOGS

ConfigMgr uses the Windows Application Event log to record both client and server side activity; however, the events recorded in this facility are usually generic and do not provide much help when troubleshooting an issue or insight into how ConfigMgr works. In the real world, the Windows Event logs are all but ignored by most administrators when it comes to ConfigMgr.

Related Documentation

Microsoft-related articles on log files are available in a number of places, including the following:

▶ General information is available at http://technet.microsoft.com/en-us/library/hh427342.aspx.

▶ Information regarding the SMSTS.log file is located at http://blogs.technet.com/carlossantiago/archive/2009/01/19/how-can-i-increase-the-size-of-the-smsts-log-file.aspx.

Viewing Log Files

All ConfigMgr log files are simple text files, as are other supporting log files mentioned in this appendix. Thus, you can view them using a variety of tools, including Windows Notepad if you want. However, Microsoft has traditionally supplied an enhanced log file viewer in an accompanying toolkit for SMS and ConfigMgr called SMSTrace or Trace32. For ConfigMgr 2012, this tool has been updated and renamed CMTrace and is included with the default installation of every central administration server (CAS) or primary site server in *<ConfigMgrInstallPath>*\tools. As the log file format has slightly changed, using the older Trace32 can give varying levels of success depending upon exactly what log file you view and therefore not recommended by the authors.

Here are some advantages of using CMTrace instead of Notepad or other text-viewing tools:

▶ ConfigMgr log files, although in plain text, are in a special tagged format. This tagged format decreases the readability of the log files when viewed by a normal text processing application. However, when viewed with CMTrace, these tags help the utility divide the log file into columns that enhance readability.

▶ CMTrace dynamically refreshes the view of the log file, ensuring that you see new lines as they are added to the log file without having to close and reopen the log file.

▶ CMTrace automatically highlights log lines that contain the word **warning** in yellow and the word **error** in red.

▶ CMTrace includes complete search, highlighting, and filtering capabilities.

▶ CMTrace has an Error Lookup feature (available from the Edit menu) that looks up any error code you give and translates the error code to an error message.

Enabling Logging

Some logs are initially enabled, whereas others are not.

▶ To disable or enable site server component logging, use the Configuration Manager (ConfigMgr) Service Manager, discussed in the "Using ConfigMgr Service Manager" section of this appendix. The site server components are located on the machine with the SMS_Executive service installed, in the registry under HKEY_LOCAL_MACHINE\ Software\Microsoft\SMS\tracing, where you can view the configuration by each component. However, Microsoft prefers you use ConfigMgr Service Manager rather than making modifications directly to the registry.

▶ Client-based files are enabled by default and can be disabled through the registry on the client under HKLM\Software\Microsoft\CCM\Logging.

Those logs, enabled by default, may include only high-level information to try to reduce overhead. Enabling more detailed logging produces low-level information that might be useful for troubleshooting problems. Microsoft recommends you avoid this in production sites because it can lead to excessive logging, which may make it difficult to find relevant information in the log files. In general, to avoid the overhead associated with extra and verbose logging, you should disable this additional logging after completing troubleshooting. However, if you feel this overhead is tolerable and having the extra logging available for future troubleshooting endeavors is beneficial, leaving extra and verbose logging enabled is certainly plausible.

Debug and Verbose Logging

The level of logging enabled determines whether all the files listed on the client and Management Point (MP) actually exist. To enable debug or verbose logging after installing Configuration Manager for the client or MP, run the registry editor (Start -> Run, and type **regedit.exe**) and then make the following registry changes:

▶ For debug logging, stop the SMS Agent Host service; then create the HKLM\Software\ Microsoft\CCM\Logging\DebugLogging key.

Restart the SMS Agent Host service (this is also described in Microsoft TechNet knowledgebase article 833417 at http://support.microsoft.com/kb/833417).

▶ For verbose logging, change the value of Loglevel to 0 at HKLM\Software\Microsoft\ CCM\Logging\@Global\Loglevel. (You might need to right-click the @Global key and change permissions to allow the current user to change the data in this key.) The @Global key globally affects all logging values, or you can set them on individual CCM threads.

A reboot is not required for either of these changes.

Using ConfigMgr Service Manager

To toggle logging off or on for individual server components, perform the following steps:

1. In the ConfigMgr console, navigate to the Monitoring workspace, and select **Overview -> System Status** or **Overview -> Component Status**. From the ribbon bar, expand the Start fly-out menu, and click **Configuration Manager Service Manager**.

2. Navigate to those components for which you want to change the logging settings.

3. In the right pane, select one or more components.

4. Right-click and select **Logging**.

5. In the ConfigMgr Component Logging dialog box, check or uncheck the **Logging enabled** option, as appropriate.

6. Click **OK**.

To expand the log file size, run ConfigMgr Service Manager, and in step 6 select the log size in MB.

Admin Console Logs

The following log files for the Admin User Interface (UI) are located in *%ProgramFiles%* Microsoft Configuration Manager\AdminConsole\AdminUILog on the system running the console:

▶ **ResourceExplorer.log:** Records errors, warnings, and information about running the Resource Explorer.

▶ **SmsAdminUI.log:** Records Configuration Manager console activity.

Sometimes you might want to see a little more detail in the ConfigMgr console log files. Here's how to enable debug logging on the ConfigMgr 2012 console:

1. From an administrator command prompt, use Windows Notepad to open the config file for the console, located at *%ProgramFiles%*Microsoft Configuration Manager\ AdminConsole\bin\Microsoft.ConfigurationManagement.exe.config.

2. Search for **switchValue="Error"** and change to **switchValue="Verbose"**. Save your changes.

3. Restart the console for debug logging to take effect.

NAL Logging

NAL logging shows network connection processing as the server runs. When enabled, it adds entries to any server-side log that has to negotiate a network connection, such as the Distribution Manager. NAL logging produces a sizeable amount of error messages in the logs that may be misleading; the system is trying to work through all the different connectivity options and determine the best one—so the "errors" are not necessarily indicative of fatal issues.

To turn on NAL logging with all verbosity levels for the client, make the following registry changes. You may need to add the Logging subkey.

▶ `HKLM\SOFTWARE\Microsoft\NAL\Logging\Verbosity(DWORD)value=00000007`

▶ `HKLM\SOFTWARE\Microsoft\NAL\Logging\Log To(DWORD)value=00000003`

Role-Based Administration

Two log files encompass the details for role-based administration. These are both server-side log files and located in *<ConfigMgrInstallPath>*\Logs on the primary site server:

▶ **Hman.log:** Records information about site configuration changes, and the publishing of site information to Active Directory Domain Services.

▶ **SMSProv.log:** Records Windows Management Instrumentation (WMI) provider access to the site database.

SQL Logging

To enable logging for the SQL component, edit the registry, and go to `HKLM\Software\Microsoft\SMS\Tracing`. Change `SQLEnabled` to `1`; restarting the SMS_EXECUTIVE service is not required. SQL Logging dumps every SQL call for any component that interacts with the database on the server side to its associated log file. This logging tends to be rather verbose.

Client Logs

Multiple types of log files may exist on a client, depending on what you are troubleshooting and the type of client device you are examining. These are covered in the following sections.

Client Installation Logs

Client installation logs should give you the exact clues to troubleshooting why a client is not installing correctly. These three log files are located in *%windir%*\ccmsetup\.

▶ **ccmsetup.log:** Records information about the ccmsetup bootstrap process including downloading and installing client prerequisite components as well as actual client installation using the client.msi Windows Installer.

▶ **client.msi.log:** The verbose log file output from the client.msi Windows Installer.

▶ **CcmRepair.log:** Records setup tasks performed by client.msi and used to troubleshoot client installation or removal problems.

Often, Windows Installer packages fail for an unknown reason and return an error code of 1603. This generic Windows Installer error message simply means **Fatal Error During Installation**. To determine the exact cause of this error, you must examine the actual log of the Windows Installer package—in this case, client.msi.log. Finding exact errors in an MSI log is more of an art than a science, though; here is a simple two-step process you can follow that can help:

1. Open client.msi.log and search for **return value 3**. This almost always takes you to the location in the log file representing the time when the fatal error occurred and Windows installer gave up trying.

2. Search the log file above **return value 3** for a more detailed error message or code. This is a detailed process and takes some familiarity with searching through MSI log files, but with some experience is not too difficult.

Here are several additional notes on reviewing MSI log files:

▶ Searching for key words like **error** is usually fruitless as this word appears in many contexts during the installation of an MSI.

▶ The messages and error code at the very end of the log file are useless—they only reflect the successful or unsuccessful completion of the installation and a generic message. If you are looking at the log file, you already know you have an issue and need information that is more detailed.

▶ Ignore all lines near the end of the log file that begin with **Property(S)**. These lines are simple dumps of all internal properties used by the MSI during installation and are interesting during MSI development but not during most troubleshooting exercises.

Client Operations Logs

Client log files are used to track various problems occurring on the ConfigMgr client. The location of these files varies when the client is also a management point.

▶ If the client is a MP and the MP is created prior to the client being installed, the client log files are located in the %SystemDrive%\SMS_CCM\Logs folder.

▶ If the client is not a MP or the client was installed prior to the MP role being added, the client log files are located at %windir%\ccm\logs.

Client log files are a great place to begin troubleshooting efforts. Files include the following:

▶ **CAS.log:** Content Access service for the local machine's package cache.

▶ **Ccm32BitLauncher.log*:** Records actions for starting applications on the client marked as "run as 32bit."

▶ **CcmEval.log*:** Records Configuration Manager client status evaluation activities and details for components that are required by the Configuration Manager client.

▶ **CcmEvalTask.log***: Records the Configuration Manager client status evaluation activities that are initiated by the evaluation scheduled task.

▶ **CcmExec.log**: Tracks the client's activities and SMS Agent Host service information.

▶ **Ccmperf.log**: Records activities related to the maintenance and capture of data related to client performance counters.

▶ **CcmRestart.log***: Records activities related to the maintenance and capture of data related to client performance counters.

▶ **CCMSDKProvider.log***: Records activities related to the maintenance and capture of data related to client performance counters.

▶ **CCMVDIProvider.log**: Indicates whether a client system is physical or virtual.

▶ **CertificateMaintenance.log**: Records activities for the client SDK interfaces.

▶ **CIDownloader.log***: Records details about configuration item definition downloads.

▶ **CITaskMgr.log***: Records tasks that are initiated for each application and deployment type, such as content download or install or uninstall actions.

▶ **ClientAuth.log**: Records the signing and authentication activity for the client.

▶ **ClientIDManagerStartup.log**: Used for maintenance of the resource's Globally Unique Identifier (GUID).

▶ **ClientLocation.log**: Tracks site assignments.

▶ **CMHttpsReadiness.log***: Records the results of running the Configuration Manager HTTPS Readiness Assessment Tool. This tool checks whether computers have a public key infrastructure (PKI) client authentication certificate that can be used for ConfigMgr.

▶ **ContentTransferManager.log**: Records scheduling information for the Background Intelligent Transfer Service (BITS) or the Server Message Block (SMB) to download or to access ConfigMgr packages.

▶ **DataTransferService.log**: Records all BITS communication for policy or package access.

▶ **EndpointProtectionAgent.log***: Records information about the installation of the Endpoint Protection client and the application of antimalware policy to that client.

▶ **Execmgr.log**: Records deployment information for classic packages and programs as they are executed on the client.

▶ **ExpressionSolver.log***: Records details about enhanced detection methods that are used when verbose or debug logging is enabled.

▶ **ExternalEventAgent.log**: Records information about external events.

▶ **FileBITS.log**: Used to record SMB package access tasks.

▶ **FileSystemFile.log**: Records the activity of the WMI Provider for software inventory and file collection.

▶ **FSPStateMessage.log:** Records the activity for state messages that are sent to the fall-back status point by the client.

▶ **InternetProxy.log:** Records the network proxy configuration and usage activity for the client.

▶ **InventoryAgent.log:** Creates data discovery records (DDRs) as well as hardware and software inventory records.

▶ **LocationCache.log*:** Records the activity for location cache usage and maintenance for the client.

▶ **LocationServices.log:** Locates MPs and distribution points.

▶ **MaintenanceCoordinator.log*:** Records the activity for general maintenance task activity for the client.

▶ **Mifprovider.log:** Management Information Format (MIF) File WMI provider.

▶ **PolicyAgent.log:** Requests policies by using the Data Transfer service.

▶ **PolicyAgentProvider.log:** Records any policy changes.

▶ **PolicyEvaluator.log:** Records any new policy settings.

▶ **PolicySdk.log*:** Records activities for policy system SDK interfaces.

▶ **SCClient_*<domain>*@*<username>*_1.log*:** Records the activity in Software Center for the specified user on the client computer.

▶ **SCClient_*<domain>*@*<username>*_2.log*:** Records the historical activity in Software Center for the specified user on the client computer.

▶ **Scheduler.log:** Records schedule tasks for all client operations.

▶ **SCNotify_*<domain>*@*<username>*_1.log*:** Records the activity for notifying users about software for the specified user.

▶ **SCClient_*<domain>*@*<username>*_2.log*:** Records the historical activity in Software Center for the specified user on the client computer.

▶ **setuppolicyevaluator.log*:** Records configuration and inventory policy creation in WMI.

▶ **Smscliui.log:** Records usage of the Systems Management tool in Control Panel on the client.

▶ **SrcUpdateMgr.log:** Records activity for installed Windows Installer applications that are updated with current distribution point source locations.

▶ **StatusAgent.log:** Logs status messages created by the client components.

▶ **UpdateTrustedSites.log:** Records sites added to the client trusted sites list for use with the application catalog.

▶ **UserAffinity.log*:** Records details about user device affinity.

- ▶ **VirtualApp.log:** Records information specific to the evaluation of App-V deployment types.

- ▶ **XMLStore.log:** Records information about accessing internal XML client data.

The following client log files do not exist until you enable debug logging as described in the "Debug and Verbose Logging" section:

- ▶ CcmPerf.log

- ▶ ClientAuth.log

- ▶ FileBITS.log

- ▶ XMLStore.log

Mobile Device Management Client Logs

See http://technet.microsoft.com/en-us/library/bb680409.aspx for the locations of log files on managed mobile devices and those computers used to deploy the mobile device client; these settings are configurable. The default setting on the client is *%temp%*\DMClient\ logs. On Window Mobile Smartphone 2003, this location is redirected to \Storage\ temp\DMClientLogs. The following log files exist on supported mobile devices with the ConfigMgr agent installed:

- ▶ **DmCertEnroll.log:** Records certificate enrollment data on mobile device clients.

- ▶ **DMCertResp.htm (in \temp):** Records the HTML response from the certificate server when the mobile device Enroller program requests a client authentication certificate on mobile device clients.

- ▶ **DmClientSetup.log:** Records client setup data on mobile device clients.

- ▶ **DmClientXfer.log:** Records client transfer data for Windows Mobile Device Center and ActiveSync deployments.

- ▶ **DmCommonInstaller.log:** Records the client transfer file installation for setting up mobile device client transfer files on client computers.

- ▶ **DmInstaller.log:** Records whether DMInstaller correctly calls DmClientSetup, and whether DmClientSetup exits with success or failure on mobile device clients.

- ▶ **DmSvc.log:** Records mobile device management service data on mobile device clients.

Windows Update Agent Logs

The Windows Update Agent (WUA) is actually a component of Windows and not ConfigMgr. However, as discussed in Chapter 14, "Software Update Management," the WUA is still heavily utilized for the software update process on managed systems. To this end, the WUA's log file is important. It is always located in *%windir%* on every managed client and is named WindowsUpdate.log. Specifically, this log records details about when the WUA connects to the WSUS server and retrieves the software updates for compliance assessment and whether there are updates to the agent components.

To enable extended or verbose logging for the WUA so that extra detail is added to the WindowsUpdate.log log file, add this registry key:

```
HKEY_LOCAL_MACHINE\SOFTWARE\Microsoft\Windows\CurrentVersion\WindowsUpdate\Trace
```

You must also add two values. Here is the first value:

- ▶ **Value name:** Flags
- ▶ **Value type:** REG_DWORD
- ▶ **Value data:** 00000007

Here is the second value:

- ▶ **Value name:** Level
- ▶ **Value type:** REG_DWORD
- ▶ **Value data:** 00000004

For a detailed look at reading the WindowsUpdate.log file, see http://support.microsoft.com/kb/902093.

Server Logs

ConfigMgr server logs are usually key to deciphering what's going on as a whole across your organization. Depending on the complexity of your hierarchy, these log files may be spread around on the various site systems you may have depending upon exactly which system is performing the activity in question. Make sure you first know exactly which site system to look at before digging through log files on a system that is not running the role or performing the activity that you are troubleshooting.

Server Setup Logs

This section lists setup-specific log files for the ConfigMgr site server installation. Setup logs for individual components are included in the section documenting log files for that component.

Nearly all site installation information appears in the logs on the root of the system drive, making the log files a primary source when you are troubleshooting installation issues. Setup logs include the following:

- ▶ **%SystemRoot%\ConfigMgrPrereq.log:** Shows the results of the prerequisite checker, created in the root of the system drive.

▶ **%SystemRoot%\ConfigMgrSetup.log:** Installation log, updated with results from running the ConfigMgr setup program and upgrades.

▶ **%SystemRoot%\SMS_BOOTSTRAP.log:** Installation log for secondary site servers when the installation is initiated from the parent site.

▶ **%SystemRoot%\ExtAdSch.log:** Created from the ExtADsch utility to extend the Active Directory Schema.

▶ **msxml6_x64MSI.log:** MSXML 6 installation information. This log file is actually located in *<ConfigMgrInstallPath>*\Logs.

Site Server Common Logs

All server log files are located in the *<ConfigMgrInstallPath>*\Logs folder on the server where the role is installed. Log files for particular components are listed in those respective sections. Some of these log files will not appear on a CAS as a CAS does not manage clients. The common server log files are as follows:

▶ **Adctrl.log*:** Records enrollment processing activity.

▶ **Ccm.log:** Logs information regarding client ConfigMgr tasks, which is responsible for client agent push operations.

▶ **CertMgr.log*:** Records the certificate activities for intrasite communications.

▶ **chmgr.log*:** Records activities of the client health manager.

▶ **Cidm.log:** Records changes to the client settings by the Client Install Data Manager (CIDM).

▶ **Colleval.log:** Logs when collections are created, changed, and replicated to child sites as well as deleted by the Collection Evaluator.

▶ **Compmon.log:** Maintains registry setting for discovery components.

▶ **Compsumm.log:** Records Component Status Summarizer tasks.

▶ **ComRegSetup.log:** Records the initial installation of COM registration results for a site server.

▶ **Despool.log:** Records incoming site-to-site communication transfers, including received data, decompression of the data and data moves.

▶ **Distmgr.log:** Records content creation, compression, delta replication, and information updates.

▶ **Fspmgr.log:** Records activities of the fallback status point site system role.

▶ **Fspmsi.log:** Records detailed Windows Installer information for the installation of the fallback status point site system role.

▶ **Hman.log:** Records site configuration changes as well as publishes site information in Active Directory Domain Services.

▶ **Inboxast.log:** Records files moved from the MP to the corresponding SMS\INBOXES folder.

▶ **Inboxmgr.log:** Records file maintenance. This log confirms inboxes were successfully created on the site server and the MP.

▶ **Inboxmon.log:** Monitors the file count in various inboxes.

▶ **Ntsvrdis.log:** ConfigMgr server discovery information. Server discovery is a "hidden" discovery method that has no user-configurable properties. It runs by default on the site server every 24 hours and its only role is to "discover" any system configured as a site system and create a DDR for it.

▶ **Objreplmgr.log:** Records the processing of object change notifications for configuration item replication.

▶ **Offermgr.log:** Records new and changes to existing deployments.

▶ **Offersum.log:** Records summarization of deployment status messages.

▶ **OfflineServicingMgr.log*:** Records the activities of applying updates to operating system image files.

▶ **Outboxmon.log:** Records the processing of outbox files and performance counter updates.

▶ **PerfSetup.log:** Records the results of the installation of performance counters.

▶ **PkgXferMgr.log*:** Records the actions of the SMS Executive component that is responsible for sending content from a primary site to a remote distribution point.

▶ **Policypv.log:** Records updates to the client policies to reflect changes to client settings or deployments.

▶ **Rcmctrl.log*:** Records the activities of database replication between sites in the hierarchy.

▶ **Replmgr.log:** Records replication of files between the site server components and the Scheduler component.

▶ **Ruleengine.log*:** Records details about Auto Deployment Rules around the identification, content download, and update group and deployment creation.

▶ **Schedule.log*:** Records the activities for standard sender content scheduling jobs.

▶ **Sender.log:** Records file-sending activity to other sites and remote DPs.

▶ **Sitecomp.log:** Records maintenance of installed site components. This log verifies successful installation of the ConfigMgr components (or reinstallation in the case of a site reset).

▶ **Sitectrl.log:** Records site setting changes to the site control file, now stored in the database rather than the file system as was sitectrl.ct0 in previous versions of ConfigMgr.

► **Sitestat.log:** Records the monitoring process of all site systems.

► **SMSAWEBSVCSetup.log:** Records the installation activities of the application catalog web service.

► **Smsdbmon.log:** Records responses to database changes related to software updates.

► **SMSENROLLSRVSetup.log:** Records the installation activities of the enrollment web service.

► **SMSENROLLWEBSetup.log:** Records the installation activities of the enrollment website.

► **Smsexec.log:** Records the processing of all site server component threads.

► **SMSFSPSetup.log**:** Records messages generated by the installation of a fallback status point.

► **SMSPORTALWEBSetup.log*:** Records the installation activities of the application catalog web site.

► **Smsprov.log:** Records WMI provider access to the site database.

► **Smstsvc.log*:** Records information about the installation, use, and removal of a Windows service that is used to test network connectivity and permissions between servers, using the computer account of the server initiating the connection.

► **Srvacct.log:** Records the maintenance of accounts when the site uses standard security.

► **Statesys.log:** Processes and summarizes state messages.

► **Statmgr.log:** Writes all status messages to the database.

Backup Log Files

Here are the files related to backup activity:

► **ConfigMgrSetup.log:** Records information about setup and recovery tasks when Configuration Manager recovers a site from backup.

► **Smsbkup.log:** Used with the site backup task, located in the site backup folder.

► **Smssqlbkup.log:** Records the backup process for the site database.

► **Smswriter.log:** Manages volume snapshots for backups.

Content Management

These log files record all activity corresponding to content management on site systems:

► **PrestageContent.log*:** Records the details about the use of the ExtractContent.exe tool on a remote prestaged distribution point. This tool extracts content that has been exported to a file.

▶ **SMSdpmon.log*:** Records details about the distribution point health monitoring scheduled task that is configured on a distribution point.

▶ **smsdpprov.log*:** Records details about the extraction of compressed files received from a primary site. This log is generated by the WMI provider of the remote distribution point. This log file exists only on a distribution point server that is not co-located with the site server.

Discovery

Here are the logs that detail site system discovery activities:

▶ **Adsgdis.log:** Active Directory Security Group Discovery log.

▶ **Adsysdis.log:** Active Directory System Discovery log. Active Directory System Discovery is a primary discovery method used to create DDRs for computers.

▶ **Adusrdis.log:** Active Directory User Discovery log file showing when the discovery method runs as well as its results.

▶ **ADForestDisc.log*:** Records Active Directory Forest Discovery actions.

▶ **Ddm.log:** Saves data discovery record information to the Configuration Manager database by the Discovery Data Manager and processes PDR (processed DDR) information. DDRs include information from all discovery types including the hidden registration discovery.

▶ **Netdisc.log:** Shows activity regarding network discovery.

A single client side log file, located in *%windir%*\ccm\logs on the client, records discovery information; this is InventoryAgent.log, which records data discovery records as well as hardware and software inventory records.

Inventory

The following logs describe site system inventory activities:

▶ **Dataldr.log:** Processes MIF files for hardware inventory in the Configuration Manager database.

▶ **Invproc.log:** Records processing of delta MIF files for the Dataloader component from client inventory files.

▶ **Sinvproc.log:** Records client software inventory data processing to the site database in Microsoft SQL Server.

MP Log Files

You can find the MP log files at *%ProgramFiles%*\SMS_CCM\Logs\ on the MP if the MP was created prior to the client being installed. Otherwise, they are at *%windir%*\ccm\logs. These files include the following:

▶ **CcmIsapi.log*:** Records client messaging activity on the endpoint.

▶ **MP_ClientREG.log:** Used at client registration during the initial installation to verify it is an approved system.

▶ **MP_Ddr.log:** Records the conversion of XML.ddr records from clients as well as copies them to the site server.

▶ **MP_DriverManager.log:** Provides information about the MP when it responds to a request from the Auto Apply Driver task sequence action. The log is generated on the MP.

▶ **MP_Framework.log:** Records the activities of the core MP and client framework components.

▶ **MP_GetAuth.log:** Records the status of the site MPs including IIS access errors specific to MP authorization.

▶ **MP_GetPolicy.log:** Records policy information that can help diagnose problems accessing Windows Management Instrumentation (WMI).

▶ **MP_Hinv.log:** Records eXtensible Markup Language (XML) hardware inventory record conversion after submitted by clients to the MP.

▶ **MP_Location.log:** Only useful if you have verbose/debug logging enabled; the same is true for several other MP_ logs. Records location manager tasks and is useful for troubleshooting problems accessing Internet Information Services (IIS) and WMI. For OSD, provides information about the MP when it responds to request state store or release state store requests from the state migration point. The log is generated on the MP.

▶ **MP_OOBMgr.log*:** Records the MP activities related to receiving OTP from a client.

▶ **MP_Policy.log:** Records MP to database communication, including all new and updated policy assignments and activity and client policy requests.

▶ **MP_Relay.log:** Records all file copy operations for files submitted by the clients including hardware inventory, software inventory, software metering, client discovery, and status message files.

▶ **MP_Retry.log:** Records the hardware inventory retry processes; useful for validating corrupt hardware inventory files.

▶ **MP_Sinv.log:** Records XML software inventory record conversion after they are submitted by clients to the MP.

▶ **MP_SinvCollFile.log:** Records details about file collection.

▶ **MP_Status.log:** Records XML.svf status message conversion after submitted by clients to the MP.

▶ **Mpcontrol.log:** Records the registration of the MP with Windows Internet Naming Services (WINS) and records the availability of the MP every 10 minutes.

- **Mpfdm.log:** MP component that moves client files to the corresponding SMS\ INBOXES folder.

- **MPMSI.log:** MP .msi installation log.

- **MPSetup.log:** Records the MP installation wrapper process and provides information about MP installation. Resides on the site server.

Here are MP log files that are largely void of any useful content unless verbose logging is enabled as described in the "Debug and Verbose Logging" section:

- MP_ClientREG.log

- MP_Policy.log

- MP_Relay.log

Migration

The migctrl.log* records information for migration actions involving migration jobs, shared distribution points, and distribution point upgrades.

WSUS Server Log Files

You can find the following WSUS log files running on the software update point site system role in *%ProgramFiles%*\Update Services\LogFiles\:

- **Change.log:** Captures data about the WSUS server database information that has changed.

- **SoftwareDistribution.log:** Provides information about the software updates that are synchronized from the configured update source to the WSUS server database.

Functionality Logs

The following sections contain log files specific to distinct sets of functionality in ConfigMgr. Based upon the functions and features you use, these log files may or may not exist and will be located on the site system hosting the role that implements the corresponding functionality.

Application Management

A number of logs are available related to application management, discussed in the following two sections.

Application Management Site Server Log Files

Here are the logs that describe site server application management activities:

- **awebsctl.log*:** Records the monitoring activities for the Application Catalog web service point site system role.

▶ **awebsvcMSI.log*:** Records detailed installation information for the Application Catalog web service point site system role.

▶ **Colleval.log:** Logs when collections are created, changed, and replicated to child sites as well as deleted by the Collection Evaluator.

▶ **portlctl.log*:** Records the monitoring activities for the Application Catalog website point site system role.

▶ **portlwebMSI.log*:** Records the MSI installation activity for the Application Catalog website role.

▶ **PrestageContent.log*:** Records the details about the use of the ExtractContent.exe tool on a remote prestaged distribution point. This tool extracts content that has been exported to a file.

▶ **ServicePortalWebService.log*:** Records the activity of the Application Catalog web service.

▶ **ServicePortalWebSite.log*:** Records the activity of the Application Catalog website.

Application Management Client Log Files

These logs detail client Application Management activities:

▶ **AppDiscovery.log*:** Records details about state application discovery.

▶ **AppEnforce.log*:** Records details about enforcement of applications including their uninstallation and installation.

▶ **AppIntentEval.log*:** Records details about the current and intended state of applications, their applicability, whether requirements were met, deployment types, and dependencies.

▶ **AppProvider.log*:** Records details about attempted installs and uninstalls of application deployment types. It also contains details about the detection method evaluation.

▶ **CCMSDKProvider.log*:** Records activities related to the maintenance and capture of data related to client performance counters.

▶ **ConfigMgrSoftwareCatalog.log*:** Records the activity of the Application Catalog, which includes its use of Silverlight.

▶ **SoftwareCatalogUpdateEndpoint.log*:** Records the activities for managing the URL for the Application Catalog shown in Software Center.

▶ **SoftwareCenterSystemTasks.log*:** Records the activities for Software Center prerequisite component validation.

Asset Intelligence

If enabled, a number of logs are available related to Asset Intelligence, as discussed in the following two sections.

Asset Intelligence Site Server Log Files

Here are the logs that detail site server Asset Intelligence activities:

- ▶ **aikbmgr.log:** Records details about the processing of XML files from the inbox for updating the Asset Intelligence catalog.

- ▶ **AIUpdateSvc.log:** Records the interaction of the Asset Intelligence synchronization point with SCO (System Center Online), the online web service.

- ▶ **AIUSMSI.log:** Records details about the installation of Asset Intelligence synchronization point site system role.

- ▶ **AIUSSetup.log:** Records details about the installation of Asset Intelligence synchronization point site system role.

- ▶ **MVLSImport.log*:** Records details about the processing of imported licensing files.

Asset Intelligence Client Log Files

A single client-side Asset Intelligence log file exists in %*windir*%\ccm\logs: AssetAdvisor. log. This log records the activities of Asset Intelligence inventory actions on the client.

Compliance Management Log Files

A number of logs are available related to compliance management, discussed in the following two sections. Because compliance management is foundational for many of the main features in ConfigMgr, such as application deployment global conditions and software update compliance evaluation, these log files are also applicable to these features and used for troubleshooting them.

Compliance Management Site Server Log Files

There are no log files specific to compliance management on site servers.

Compliance Management Client Log Files

The following files are located with the ConfigMgr client computer log files (%*windir*%CCM\Logs). For those client computers that are also MPs, the client log files are located in the %*SystemDrive*%\SMS_CCM\Logs folder.

- ▶ **Ciagent.log:** Provides information about downloading, storing, and accessing assigned configuration baselines.

- ▶ **CITaskMgr.log*:** Records tasks that are initiated for each application and deployment type, such as content download or install or uninstall actions.

- ▶ **Dcmagent.log:** Provides high-level information about the evaluation of assigned configuration baselines and desired configuration management processes.

▶ **DCMReporting.log*:** Records information about reporting policy platform results into state messages for configuration items.

▶ **DcmWmiProvider.log:** Records information about reading configuration item synclets from WMI.

▶ **EventLogForwarder.log:** Used for writing events to the event log when Compliance Management flags a configuration item as out of compliance. These events are potentially available for Operations Manager (OpsMgr) to generate an alert to flag a problem condition.

▶ **SmsClrHost.log:** Client log file that includes details about ConfigMgr's use of the .NET Framework (required for Compliance Management).

Endpoint Protection Log Files

If enabled, a number of logs are available related to Endpoint Protection, as discussed in the following two sections.

Endpoint Protection Client Log Files

The Endpoint Protection client logs to the EndpointProtectionAgent.log log file, found in *%windir%*\CCM\logs.

Endpoint Protection Site Server Log Files

On the site server, the following log files are found in *<ConfigMgrInstallPath>*\Logs:

▶ **EPCtrlMgr.log*:** Records details about the synchronization of malware threat information from the Endpoint Protection role server into the Configuration Manager database.

▶ **EPMgr.log*:** Monitors the status of the Endpoint Protection site system role.

▶ **EPSetup.log*:** Provides information about the installation of the Endpoint Protection site system role.

▶ **Notictrl.log*:** Records Endpoint Protection email notification activity.

Metering

If enabled, a number of logs are available related to software metering, as discussed in the following two sections.

Metering Site Server Log Files

Swmproc.log processes metering files and maintains settings for site server software metering activities.

Metering Client Log Files

The following logs detail client Software Metering activities:

- ▶ **Mtrmgr.log:** Tracks software-metering processes.

- ▶ **SWMTRReportGen.log:** Generates a usage data report that is collected by the metering agent. (This data is logged in Mtrmgr.log.)

Mobile Device Management Log Files

If you have enabled mobile device management in your site hierarchy, the following mobile device management log files will be present and divided between three different types, covered in the following sections.

Enrollment

The following device enrollment logs exist on the site server in *<ConfigMgrInstallPath>*\ Logs unless otherwise noted:

- ▶ **DMPRP.log:** Records communication between MPs that are enabled for mobile devices and the MP endpoints. This log file is located in the *%ProgramFiles%*\CCM\ Logs folder of the MP that the mobile device client uses.

- ▶ **Dmpmsi.log:** Records the Windows Installer data for the configuration of a MP that is enabled for mobile devices.

- ▶ **DMPSetup.log:** Records the configuration of the MP when it is enabled for mobile devices.

- ▶ **EnrollsrvMSI.log:** Records the Windows Installer data for the configuration of an enrollment point.

- ▶ **Enrollmentweb.log:** Records communication between mobile devices and the enrollment proxy point.

- ▶ **EnrollwebMSI.log:** Records the Windows Installer data for the configuration of an enrollment proxy point.

- ▶ **Enrollmentservice.log:** Records communication between an enrollment proxy point and an enrollment point.

- ▶ **SMS_DM.log:** Records communication between mobile devices and the MP that is enabled for mobile devices.

Exchange Server Connector

A single log exists for the Exchange connector and is located in *<ConfigMgrInstallPath>*\ Logs: easdisc.log*. This log file records the activities and the status of the Exchange Server connector.

Legacy

The following site server log files are typically stored in the *<ConfigMgrInstallPath>*\Logs folder of the mobile device management point (DMP) computer:

▶ **DmClientHealth.log:** Records the GUIDs of all mobile device clients communicating with the DMP.

▶ **DmClientRegistration.log:** Records registration requests from and responses to the mobile device client in native mode.

▶ **DmpDatastore.log:** Records all the site database connections and queries made by the DMP.

▶ **DmpDiscovery.log*:** Records all the discovery data from the mobile device legacy clients on the MP that is enabled for mobile devices.

▶ **DmpHardware.log:** Records hardware inventory data from mobile device clients on the DMP.

▶ **DmpIsapi.log:** Records mobile device communication data from device clients on the DMP.

▶ **DmpMSI.log:** Records MSI data for DMP setup.

▶ **DmpSetup.log:** Records the mobile device management setup process.

▶ **DmpSoftware.log:** Records mobile device software distribution data from mobile device clients on the DMP.

▶ **DmpStatus.log:** Records mobile device status messages data from mobile device clients on the DMP.

▶ **FspIsapi.log:** Records fallback status point communication data from mobile device clients and client computers on the fallback status point.

Network Access Protection Log Files

If enabled and configured, there are a number of logs are available related to Network Access Protection (NAP), as discussed in the following two sections.

Network Access Protection Site Server Log Files

System health validator (SHV) point log files are located in *%systemdrive%*\SMSSHV\SMS_SHV\Logs. The SHV log files include the following:

▶ **Ccmperf.log:** Contains information about initializing the SHV point performance counters.

▶ **SmsSHV.log:** The main log file for the SHV point; logs basic operations of the System Health Validator service, including the initialization progress.

▶ **SmsSHVADCacheClient.log:** Contains information about retrieving ConfigMgr health state references from AD.

▶ **SmsSHVCacheStore.log:** Information about the cache store used to hold the ConfigMgr NAP health state references retrieved from AD, such as reading from the store and purging entries from the local cache store file. The cache store is not configurable.

▶ **SmsSHVQuarValidator.log:** Records client statement of health information and processing operations. To obtain full information, change the registry key `LogLevel` from `1` to `0` at `HKLM\SOFTWARE\Microsoft\SMSSHV\Logging\@GLOBAL`.

▶ **SmsSHVRegistrySettings.log:** Records any dynamic changes to the SHV component configuration while the service is running.

▶ **SMSSHVSetup.log:** Records the success or failure (with failure reason) of installing the System Health Validator point. This log is located at *<ConfigMgrInstallPath>* Logs\.

Network Access Protection Client Log Files

The default location for client log files related to NAP is *%windir%*\CCM\Logs. For those client computers that are also MPs, the log files are found in *%ProgramFiles%*\SMS_CCM\ Logs. The log files include the following:

▶ **Ccmcca.log:** Logs the processing of compliance evaluation based on Configuration Manager NAP policy processing, and contains the processing of remediation for each software update required for compliance.

▶ **CIAgent.log:** Tracks the process of remediation and compliance. (The software updates the log file Updateshandler.log, which provides more informative details on installing the software updates required for compliance.)

▶ **Locationservices.log:** Used by other ConfigMgr features (such as information about the client's assigned site), but also contains information specific to NAP when the client is in remediation. This log records the names of the required remediation servers (MP, software update point, and distribution points that host content required for compliance), which are also sent in the client statement of health.

▶ **SDMAgent.log:** Shared with the Configuration Manager Compliance Management feature and contains the tracking process of remediation and compliance. (The software updates the log file Updateshandler.log, which provides more informative details about installing the software updates required for compliance.)

▶ **SMSSha.log:** The main log file for the ConfigMgr NAP client; this contains a merged statement of health information from the location services (LS) and configuration compliance agent (CCA) ConfigMgr components.

SMSSha.log also contains information about the interactions between the ConfigMgr System Health Agent and the operating system NAP agent, and also between the ConfigMgr System Health Agent and both the configuration compliance agent and the location services. It provides information about whether the NAP agent successfully initialized, the statement of health data, and the statement of health response.

OSD Log Files

The following OSD log files are located at *<ConfigMgrInstallPath>*\SMS_CCM\logs\ unless otherwise noted:

▶ **CCMSetup.log:** Provides information about client-based operating system actions. Located at *%windir%*\ccmsetup.

▶ **Client.msi.log:** Setup log file for the client. Located at *%windir%*\ccmsetup.

▶ **CreateTSMedia.log:** Information about task sequence media when it is created. The log is generated on the computer running the Configuration Manager administrator console. Located at *<ConfigMgrInstallPath>*\%temp%.

▶ **Dism.log*:** Records driver installation actions or update apply actions for offline servicing.

▶ **DriverCatalog.log:** Provides information about device drivers that have been imported into the driver catalog. This file is found at *<ConfigMgrInstallPath>*\logs.

▶ **MP_ClientIDManager.log:** This log file provides information about the ConfigMgr MP when it responds to ConfigMgr client ID requests from boot media or the Preboot Execution Environment (PXE). This log is generated on the ConfigMgr MP.

▶ **MP_DriverMGR.log:** Provides information about the ConfigMgr MP when it responds to a request from the Auto Apply Driver task sequence action. The log is generated on the ConfigMgr MP.

▶ **MP_Location.log:** Provides information about the ConfigMgr MP when it responds to request state store or release state store requests from the state migration point. This log is generated on the ConfigMgr MP.

▶ **OfflineServicingMgr.log*:** Records details of offline servicing schedules and update apply actions on operating system .WIM files.

▶ **Setupact.log:** This log file provides information about Windows Sysprep and setup logs. It is located at *%windir%*.

▶ **Setupapi.log:** Provides information about Windows Sysprep and setup logs. It is located in *%windir%*.

▶ **Setuperr.log:** Provides information about Windows Sysprep and setup logs. It is located in *%windir%*.

▶ **SmpIsapi.log:** Provides information about the state migration point ConfigMgr client request responses.

▶ **Smpmgr.log:** Provides information about the results of state migration point health checks and configuration changes. The log file is found at *<ConfigMgrInstallPath>*\sms\logs\.

▶ **SmpMSI.log:** Provides information about the state migration point and is generated when the state migration point site server has been created. The log file is found at *<ConfigMgrInstallPath>*\sms\logs\.

▶ **smpperf.log*:** Records the state migration point performance counter updates. The log file is located at *<ConfigMgrInstallPath>*\logs\.

▶ **Smspxe.log:** Provides information about the ConfigMgr PXE service point.

▶ **SMSSMPSetup.log:** Provides information about the state migration point and is generated when the state migration point site server has been created. The log file is found at *<ConfigMgrInstallPath>*\sms\logs\.

▶ **Smsts.log:** The SMSTS.log is used for operating system deployment and task sequence log events. SMSTS.log describes all task sequencer transactions and is used to help troubleshoot OSD issues. Depending on the deployment scenario, it may exist in one of the following locations:

   ▶ **%temp%\SMSTSLOG:** Used if the task sequence completes when running in the full operating system without an agent installed in the computer.

   ▶ **<CCMInstallDir>\logs:** Used if the task sequence completes in the full operating system with a ConfigMgr client installed on the computer.

   <CCMInstallDir> is typically %windir%\ccm\logs, although it is *<ConfigMgrInstallPath>*\SMS_CCM for the site server.

   ▶ **<largest fixed partition>\SMSTSLOG:** Used if the task sequence completes when running.

Unlike all other ConfigMgr components, you cannot configure its size in the registry. To increase the size of SMSTS.log, create a file named SMSTS.INI in the Windows folder (%windir%), with the following contents:

```
[Logging]
        LogMaxSize=<maximum log file size in bytes>
        LogMaxHistory=<number of history files to maintain>
```

If you are booting up from media or using PXE, edit your boot image for the smsts.ini file to be in the Windows folder.

▶ **TaskSequenceProvider.log:** Provides information about task sequences when they are imported, exported, or edited. The log file is found at *<ConfigMgrInstallPath>*\logs\.

▶ **USMT Log loadstate.log:** USMT Log loadstate.log provides information about the User State Migration Tool (USMT) regarding the restore of user state data. It is located at %windir%\ccm\logs.

▶ **USMT Log scanstate.log:** Provides information about the USMT regarding the capture of user state data. It is located at %windir%\ccm\logs.

The following logs are specific to multicast functionality in OSD and are located in *<ConfigMgrInstallPath>*\sms\logs:

▶ **McsExec.log:** McsExec.log provides information about multicast packages, namespace management, session creation, and health checking for multicast.

▶ **McsISAPI.log:** Provides information about the multicast service point Configuration Manager client request responses.

▶ **McsMgr.log:** Provides information about multicast availability and changes to multicast configuration.

▶ **McsMSI.log:** Provides information about the .msi setup for the multicast service point. It is generated when the multicast service point site server has been created.

▶ **McsPerf.log:** MCSPerf.log provides information about the multicast performance counter updates.

▶ **McsPrv.log:** This file provides information about the interaction between multicast components and the Windows Deployment Service (WDS) components, such as the creation, reading, and distribution of namespaces.

▶ **McsSetup.log:** Provides information about the multicast service point role setup. The log file is generated when the multicast service point site server has been created. It confirms the environment has been successfully set up and runs the .msi file.

Out of Band Management Log Files

Out of Band (OOB) Management log files are found in the following locations:

▶ On the OOB service point site system server

▶ On any computer running the OOB Management console from the ConfigMgr console

▶ On client computers running the Configuration Manager client that are managed out of band

Out of Band Service Point Log Files

The following logs are located at *<ConfigMgrInstallPath>*\Logs on the site system server selected to host the OOB service point role:

▶ **ADctrl.log:** Records details about managing Active Directory accounts that are used by out of band management.

▶ **ADService.log*:** Records account creation and security group details in Active Directory.

▶ **AMTSPSetup.log:** Shows the success or failure (with failure reason) of installing the OOB service point.

▶ **Amtopmgr.log:** Shows the activities of the OOB service point relating to the discovery of management controllers, provisioning, and power control commands.

▶ **Amtproxymgr.log:** Shows the activities of the site server relating to provisioning, which include the following:

   ▶ Publishing provisioned computers to Active Directory Domain Services

   ▶ Registering the service principal name of provisioned computers in Active Directory Domain Services

   ▶ Requesting the web server certificate from the issuing Certificate Authority (CA)

It also shows the activities of sending instruction files to the OOB service point, which include the following:

   ▶ Discovery of management controllers

   ▶ Provisioning

   ▶ Power control commands

Finally, it shows the activities related to OOB Management site replication:

   ▶ **EnrollsrvMSI.log:** Records the Windows Installer data for the configuration of an enrollment point.

   ▶ **Enrollmentweb.log:** Records the Windows Installer data for the configuration of an enrollment proxy point.

Out of Band Management Console Log File

Oobconsole.log shows the activities related to running the OOB Management console. It is located at *<ConfigMgrInstallPath>*\AdminConsole\AdminUILog\ on any computer running the OOB Management console from the ConfigMgr console.

Out of Band Management Client Log File

Oobmgmt.log shows OOB Management activities performed on workstation computers, including the provisioning state of the management controller. It is found at *%windir%*\CCM\Logs on workstation computers running the ConfigMgr client that are managed out of band.

Power Management

The following logs detail client power management activities.

Power Management Site Server Log Files

There are no log files specific to power management on site servers.

Power Management Client Log Files

These logs are client side and located in *%windir%*\ccm\logs on the client:

▶ **Pwrmgmt.log:** Records details about power management activities on the client computer, which include monitoring and the enforcement of settings by the Power Management Client Agent.

▶ **PwrProvider.log:** Records the activities of the power management provider (PWRInvProvider) hosted in the Windows Management Instrumentation (WMI) service. On all supported versions of Windows, the provider enumerates the current settings on computers during hardware inventory and applies power plan settings.

Remote Control

The following logs detail client remote control activities.

Remote Control Site Server Log Files

There are no log files specific to remote control on site servers.

Remote Control Client Log Files

Two client side log files exist in *%windir%*\ccm\logs on the client:

▶ **RemoteControl.log**:** Records the activities of remote control.

▶ **CmRcService.log*:** Records information for the remote control service.

Reporting

The following logs detail reporting activities.

Reporting Site Server Log Files

The following logs detail site server Reporting Point activities; these logs are found in *<ConfigMgrInstallPath>*\Logs:

▶ **srsrp.log:** Records information about the activity and status of the reporting services point.

▶ **srsrpMSI.log:** Records detailed results of the reporting point installation process from the MSI output.

▶ **srsrpsetup.log**:** Records the reporting point installation.

Reporting Client Log Files

There are no log files specific to reporting on clients.

Software Updates Log Files

Log files for software updates are maintained on both the site server and client. The next two sections discuss these files.

Software Updates Site Server Log Files

By default, these files are found in *<ConfigMgrInstallPath>*\Logs:

▶ **Smsdbmon.log:** Provides information about when software update configuration items are inserted, updated, or deleted from the site server database, and creates notification files for software updates components.

▶ **SUPSetup:** Provides information about the software update point installation. When the software update point installation completes, "Installation was successful" is written to this log file.

▶ **WCM.log:** Information about the software update point configuration and connecting to the Windows Server Update Services (WSUS) server for subscribed update categories, classifications, and languages.

▶ **WSUSCtrl.log:** Provides information about the configuration, database connectivity, and health of the WSUS server for the site.

▶ **Wsyncmgr.log:** Information about the software updates synchronization process.

Software Updates Client Computer Log Files

The following files are located with the ConfigMgr client computer log files (%*windir*%\ CCM\Logs). For those client computers that are also MPs, the client log files are located in the %*SystemDrive*%\SMS_CCM\Logs folder.

▶ **CIAgent.log:** Provides information about processing configuration items, including software updates.

▶ **LocationServices.log:** Provides information about the location of the WSUS server when a scan is initiated on the client.

▶ **PolicyEvaluator:** Provides information about the process for evaluating policies on client computers, including policies from software updates.

▶ **RebootCoordinator.log:** Information about the process for coordinating system restarts on client computers after software update installations.

▶ **ScanAgent.log:** Provides information about the scan requests for software updates, what tool is requested for the scan, the WSUS location, and so on.

▶ **SdmAgent.log:** Provides information about the process for verifying and decompressing packages containing configuration item information for software updates.

▶ **ServiceWindowManager.log:** Provides information about the process for evaluating configured maintenance windows.

▶ **SmscliUI.log:** Information about the Configuration Manager Control Panel user interactions. This includes initiating a software updates scan cycle from the Configuration Manager Properties dialog box, opening the Program Download Monitor, and so on.

▶ **StateMessage.log:** Provides information about when Software Updates state messages are created and sent to the MP.

▶ **UpdatesDeployment.log:** Provides information about the deployment on the client. Deployment information includes software update activation, evaluation, and enforcement. Verbose logging shows additional information about the interaction with the client user interface.

▶ **UpdatesHandler.log:** Provides information about software update compliance scanning and about the download and installation of software updates on the client.

▶ **UpdatesStore.log:** Provides information regarding the compliance status for the software updates that were assessed during the compliance scan cycle.

▶ **WUAHandler.log:** Information about when the Windows Update Agent on the client searches for software updates.

Software Updates Admin Console Log Files

There is a single log file, **PatchDownloader.log**, which records details about the process of downloading software updates from the update source to the download destination on the site server. This log file is found on the system running the console that initiated the update download in the *<ConfigMgrInstallPath>*\sms\logs folder.

Wake On LAN Log Files

If used, the log files described in the next sections are available to review and troubleshoot Wake On LAN (WOL) issues.

Wake On LAN Site Server Log Files

The site server log files related to WOL are located in the folder *<ConfigMgrInstallPath>*\Logs on the site server.

▶ **WolCmgr.log:** Contains information about which clients need to be sent wake-up packets, the number of wake-up packets sent, and the number of wake-up packets retried.

▶ **Wolmgr.log:** Contains information about wake-up procedures, such as when to wake up deployments or deployments that are configured for WOL.

Wake On LAN Client Log Files

There are no client-side log files for WOL.

Software and Application Installation Logs

A common task is troubleshooting actual installations of software and applications delivered using ConfigMgr. This task is technically outside the scope of ConfigMgr, which just runs the command-line you give it. What happens after that is up to the command-line but still well within the circle of responsibility of most ConfigMgr admins.

Just as with ConfigMgr, getting a log file for the installation can greatly help in figuring out what's broken or what went wrong. For Windows Installer (MSI)-based installations, generating a log file is quite easy: Add /l*v C: \Windows\Temp\mymsi.log to the msiexec command line specified in the deployment type or program, where C: \Windows\Temp\ mymsi.log is any filename and file path you choose. This causes Windows Installer to generate a detailed and verbose log file of the installation on the client. As discussed in the "Client Installation Logs" section, digging through verbose Windows Installer logs is more of an art than a science. Using the technique outlined in that section should greatly help in this endeavor.

In addition, you can enable Windows Installer logging on a global basis on a client system by updating this value in the registry:

HKEY_LOCAL_MACHINE\Software\Policies\Microsoft\Windows\Installer

You must also add two values. Here is the first value:

- ▶ **Value name:** Logging
- ▶ **Value type:** REG_SZ
- ▶ **Value data:** voicewarmup

Here is the second value:

- ▶ **Value name:** Debug
- ▶ **Value type:** REG_DWORD
- ▶ **Value data:** 00000007

This creates a log file in the *%Temp%* location on the system (usually C: \Windows\ Temp) with a random name prefixed with MSI and a .log filename extension.

> **NOTE: VOICEWARMUP**
>
> The preceding voicewarmup registry value is an unusual coincidence and not intended to be a single word; instead, it is the combination of letters each representing a different Windows Installer logging mode. This is fully described at http://support.microsoft.com/ kb/223300.

For other executable—exe—installer types, there is no one-way-fits-all to enable logging. Often, running the executable at the command-line with a /? or -? shows all options available for that executable including logging options; append these to the exe installer's command line. Consulting the vendor's documentation that created the exe installer is also a good way to figure out what options are available. Be aware that there is no guarantee that there is any logging (or options). At that point, you can try manually executing the installer and looking for a log file in the same folder or *%temp%*. Your last resort is contacting the vendor of the installation.

Log File Mining

Anyone who has dealt with ConfigMgr knows that the log files are invaluable for troubleshooting issues and day-to-day monitoring. One of ConfigMgr's strengths is that nearly everything, in detail, is in a log file—somewhere.

The problem that often crops up is knowing which log file to look in; although the main purpose of each log file is documented here in this appendix and on TechNet, it's often difficult to narrow down exactly which log file to dig through. Log files also roll (by default) every 2MB: For some log files, this is a lot; for others, like ccm.log, this might last only a couple of hours or minutes especially during a large client push.

Wouldn't it be nice to have a single, searchable repository for all your log files? Not only combining one or two log files on a single system (which CMTrace can actually do), but also a true repository that does the following:

▶ Automatically collects log files from all of your site systems

▶ Doesn't roll-over

▶ Is easily accessible using a web interface

▶ Does not require permissions on site servers themselves

▶ Uses a single repository for Windows event logs and other logging sources for correlation

Enter Splunk, which is a free tool (up to 500MB a day of logs) that can suck in and index all the specified log files on a system. It does more than just text log files, but for ConfigMgr, that's all to really be concerned with. Splunk then provides a web-based search page for all the indexed data so you can search for all occurrences of a string. Splunk also creates fields based on name=value pairs, has an event definition mechanism, and provides data tagging.

Splunk enables you to forward the data from one system to another. The obvious application here is to forward all the collected logs from all the site servers to a central Splunk server, perhaps your primary site server. You could forward everything from your primary and secondary site servers also giving you a single, central, searchable repository for all your logs from all of your sites.

Splunk includes much more than just searching through log files though and incorporates many advanced data analysis tools, including

▶ Data indexing for fast searches

▶ Advanced query and search syntax

▶ Interactive search results with drilldown and timeline capabilities

▶ A customizable knowledge base

▶ Monitors and alerts

▶ Ad-hoc reports to identify trends

▶ Real-time dashboards

There is an Enterprise version of Splunk that costs money (some of the features noted in the list are only in the Enterprise version), so it may be worth looking into if you have a large installation or require some extra security. The standard free version should suffice for most single site installations.

Extending Hardware Inventory

In Configuration Manager (ConfigMgr) 2007, you could extend hardware inventory by modifying two files: Configuration.mof, which contained the classes for reporting and told the client how to report, and SMS_Def.mof, which included the to-be-inventoried classes with their attributes telling the client what to report. Configuration.mof was responsible for defining the data classes to be inventoried, and for registering and defining the Windows Management Instrumentation (WMI) providers that add functionality to hardware inventory. An example would be reading the registry, which is more than simply using WMI.

This procedure is similar in System Center 2012 Configuration Manager, except the information that was in the SMS_Def.mof file is now configured from the console, making SMS_Def.mof obsolete. This allows you to select different WMI classes and attributes to be inventoried using custom client settings. Chapter 3, "Looking Inside Configuration Manager," provides information about WMI and how ConfigMgr interacts with it.

INVENTORY

Before deciding to extend hardware inventory, verify that it is necessary. The newly introduced deployment types for applications can handle many scenarios for which you would have extended hardware inventory in ConfigMgr 2007. Be careful when extending hardware inventory, ensure you understand how it works, and test every modification you want to implement first on a stand-alone client as described in the next section. Not being careful could lead to WMI corruption on every client receiving the modifications.

How to Extend Hardware Inventory

Extending hardware inventory consists of executing these tasks:

▶ Creating a new version of Configuration.mof for your tests and checking and testing the modifications using the Mofcomp.exe and WBEMTest.exe tools.

▶ Replacing the current Configuration.mof, found in *<ConfigMgrInstallPath>* under the inboxes\clifiles.src\hinv folder, with this new Configuration.mof.

▶ Checking whether your Configuration.mof changes were accepted by inspecting the dataldr.log file residing on the site server, and whether the changes were executed on your clients by checking the inventoryagent.log file on the client.

▶ Selecting the classes with their attributes to be inventoried by modifying the hardware inventory settings, using the default settings at the hierarchy level.

▶ Enabling which classes and attributes should be inventoried using custom client settings.

USING COMMUNITY TOOLS TO EXTEND HARDWARE INVENTORY

Many community-written tools and guidelines exist to address challenges associated with extending hardware inventory. Although the majority of those resources still focus on ConfigMgr 2007, the information is still valid, with minimal modifications for System Center 2012 Configuration Manager.

Sherry Kissinger, a Configuration Manager MVP, provides extensive examples of how to extend hardware inventory. Sherry provides several "MOF Snippets" that can help solve your hardware inventory challenges. A snippet contains only the changes you need to make to your Configuration.mof and SMS_Def.mof (now in the console). Most of those snippets are ready for use, whereas some require some external scripting to populate the data in WMI. Other snippets need slight modifications to reflect settings specific to your environment.

Sherry blogs at http://myitforum.com/cs2/blogs/skissinger/default.aspx. Another useful resource is the Inventory section of the ConfigMgr Wiki, also hosted by myITforum, located at http://www.myitforum.com/myitwiki/SCCMINV.ashx. You may also want to consider SCCM Expert's Start to Finish Guide to MOF Editing, available for purchase at http://smsexpert.com/mof_guide.aspx.

The RegKeytoMof tool can assist with using the hardware inventory feature to inventory a specific registry key. Written by Mark Cochrane, RegKeytoMof allows you to browse for a registry key and presents the corresponding sections to add to Configuration.mof and the information to import in the hardware inventoried classes. RegKeytoMof is available at http://myitforum.com/cs2/files/folders/proddocs/entry152945.aspx.

These types of tools do not absolve you from understanding what occurs and how the custom MOF files work before using them in a production environment. Test all your MOF edits in an offline environment, and when in doubt consult one of the experts using the Microsoft forums at http://social.technet.microsoft.com/Forums/en-us/category/systemcenter2012configurationmanager.

After Configuration.mof is modified and the classes are added using the client agent settings, the new hardware is shown in the Resource Explorer and can be reported on using Configuration Manager reporting, discussed in Chapter 18, "Reporting."

Example of Extending Inventory

The following example uses one of Sherry Kissinger's MOF snippets to inventory whether Auto Admin Logon is enabled on ConfigMgr clients. Test the customizations on a test system; ensure you have a stand-alone system, preferably a VM, available to perform your tests. Perform the following steps:

CAUTION: PRECAUTIONS WHEN MODIFYING YOUR MOF FILES

Be sure to open your MOF files with Windows Notepad or another script editor. Verify no special characters are in the document. As an additional precaution, consider modifying your Configuration.mof file offline and checking the file using `mofcomp.exe` with the `-check` switch, which checks the syntax. This utility is located in the *%windir%*\ System32\wbem folder. You can also use this utility to import the MOF file into the local WMI repository, and `WBEMTest.exe` to verify the changes end up in the expected location.

---

1. Download the MOF snippets from http://myitforum.com/cs2/blogs/skissinger/ default.aspx and copy the 1-AutoAdminLogin folder to the top site server in your hierarchy (either a stand-alone primary site or the central administration site [CAS]). The modifications implemented on the top site server are replicated to the child servers.

2. On that site server, copy Configuration.mof from the *<ConfigMgrInstallPath>*\ inboxes\clifiles.src\hinv folder to a location of your choice.

3. Add the content of the AddtoConfigurationMof.txt file to your own Configuration. mof file between the Added extensions Start and Added extensions End sections. Here is that content:

```
//   <:[-<>>>>>>>>>>>>>>>>>>>>>>>>>>>BEGIN>>-AutoAdminLogon-
<<BEGIN<<<<<<<<<<<<<<<<<<<<<<<<<>-]:>
//'''*._.*'''*-
//   Data Class - for ConfigMgr, put this section in configuration.mof
//'''*._.*'''*-
//Contributed by Sherry Kissinger
  [DYNPROPS]
  class AutoAdminLogon
{
 [key] string   Keyname="";
       string   DefaultDomainName;
       string   DefaultUserName;
       string   DefaultPassword;
```

```
        string  AutoAdminLogon;
        uint32  AutoLogonCount;
};
[DYNPROPS]
instance of AutoAdminLogon
{
  KeyName = "AutoAdminLogon";
   [PropertyContext("local|HKEY_LOCAL_MACHINE\\Software\\Microsoft\\
Windows NT\\CurrentVersion\\Winlogon|DefaultDomainName"), Dynamic,
Provider("RegPropProv")] DefaultDomainName;
   [PropertyContext("local|HKEY_LOCAL_MACHINE\\Software\\Microsoft\\
Windows NT\\CurrentVersion\\Winlogon|DefaultUserName"), Dynamic,
Provider("RegPropProv")] DefaultUserName;
   [PropertyContext("local|HKEY_LOCAL_MACHINE\\Software\\Microsoft\\
Windows NT\\CurrentVersion\\Winlogon|DefaultPassword"), Dynamic,
Provider("RegPropProv")] DefaultPassword;
   [PropertyContext("local|HKEY_LOCAL_MACHINE\\Software\\Microsoft\\
Windows NT\\CurrentVersion\\Winlogon|AutoAdminLogon"), Dynamic,
Provider("RegPropProv")] AutoAdminLogon;
   [PropertyContext("local|HKEY_LOCAL_MACHINE\\Software\\Microsoft\\
Windows NT\\CurrentVersion\\Winlogon|AutoLogonCount"), Dynamic,
Provider("RegPropProv")] AutoLogonCount;
};
//   <:[-<>>>>>>>>>>>>>>>>>>>>>>>>>>>END>>-AutoAdminLogon-
<<END<<<<<<<<<<<<<<<<<<<<<<<<>-]:>
```

Adding this section to the Configuration.mof file creates the AutoAdminLogon data class in WMI under the `root\CIMV2` namespace, which contains the data classes and instances. This namespace is used because the `root\CIMV2` namespace is selected in the Configuration.mof just before the Added extensions section; thus, this namespace is used to fill the values of the AutoAdminLogon class unless declared otherwise. Data classes can also reside in other classes, though.

Within `root\CIMV2`, the data class information is directly available or a pointer shows where the data can be retrieved. The `AutoAdminLogon` data class will be created on the machines receiving Configuration.mof; these are all machines in the ConfigMgr hierarchy.

The `AutoAdminLogon` data class will be extended with the following instances:

▶ `Keyname` as string and as key value

▶ `DefaultDomainName` as string

▶ `DefaultUserName` as string

▶ `DefaultPassword` as string

▶ `AutoAdminLogon` as string

▶ `AutoLogonCount` as 32-bit integer

Once the data class and instances are defined, properties are populated; the Keyname property is filled with the AutoAdminLogon value, and the DefaultDomainName property is filled with the value of the DefaultDomainName Registry key under HKEY_LOCAL_MACHINE\Software\Microsoft\Windows NT\CurrentVersion\WinLogon, using the WMI Registry provider. The other properties are filled with other values coming from the registry.

TIP: DOCUMENT YOUR EDITS

Document your edits and add the edits in a well-formatted manner; this way when you add or troubleshoot the extensions later, things will be easily readable in the MOF file.

---

4. Use Mofcomp.exe with the -check option to check the syntax of the Configuration. mof file, the outcome of Mofcomp.exe -check is displayed in Figure B.1 and below.

FIGURE B.1   Mofcomp check output.

```
C:\Users\KSurksum\Downloads>mofcomp -check configuration.mof
Microsoft (R) MOF Compiler Version 6.1.7600.16385
Copyright (c) Microsoft Corp. 1997-2006. All rights reserved.
Parsing MOF file: configuration.mof
MOF file has been successfully parsed
Syntax check complete.
WARNING: File configuration.mof does not contain #PRAGMA AUTORECOVER.
If the WMI repository is rebuilt in the future, the contents
of this MOF file will not be included in the new WMI repository.
```

> To include this MOF file when the WMI Repository is automatically
> reconstructed, place the #PRAGMA AUTORECOVER statement on the first line of
> the MOF file.
> Done!

5. Copy your custom Configuration.mof to the test machine, and use Mofcomp.exe with the argument `Configuration.mof` to import the contents of Configuration.mof into WMI of the test machine.

6. Using WBEMTest, query WMI to check if the `AutoAdminLogon` class was created.

   Open WBEMTest.exe and click **Connect**. In the NameSpace field, type **root\cimv2** because that is where you added the `AutoAdminLogon` class, and click **Connect**. When connected, click **Enum Classes** to open the Superclass Info box. Select **Recursive** and click **OK** to open the Query Result box. Browse the query result box to see if the `AutoAdminLogon` class is available; it should be situated above `CCM_LogicalMemoryConfiguration`, as shown in Figure B.2.

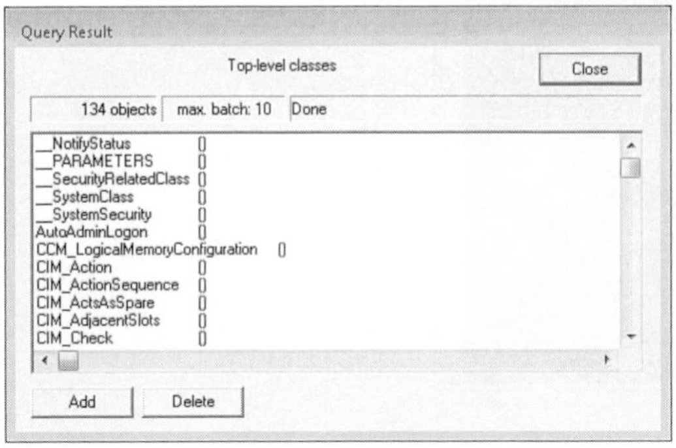

FIGURE B.2   WBEMTest Query Result.

As discussed in step 3, data classes don't necessarily have to reside in `root\cimv2`; they can reside in other locations within WMI although `root\cimv2` is most commonly used. For additional information about WMI and locations where data can reside, see Chapter 3.

7. After verifying the syntax of your custom Configuration.mof and testing the file on a stand-alone test system, copy your Configuration.mof over the already existing one in the <*ConfigMgrInstallPath*>\inboxes\clifiles.src\hinv folder. Next, open dataldr.log in the log files folder under <*ConfigMgrInstallPath*> using CMTrace or Notepad to determine whether ConfigMgr is accepting the change. You should see the following text:

```
A configuration.mof change has been detected
Compiling MOF files and converting to policy
```

Confirm the modification was added successfully by checking for

```
Running MOFCOMP on F:\Program Files\Microsoft Configuration Manager\inboxes\
clifiles.src\hinv\configuration.mof
MOF backed up to F:\Program Files\Microsoft Configuration Manager\data\
hinvarchive\configuration.mof.bak
Successfully updated configuration.mof in the database.
End of cimv2\sms\inv_config-to-policy conversion; returning 0x0
```

8. After modifications to Configuration.mof are successfully translated to a policy, verify the new configuration is being applied to your clients. You can ensure the client has received its new policy by manually initiating a machine policy refresh on the client.

To initiate a machine policy refresh manually, go to the Configuration Manager Control Panel applet and select the **Actions** tab. Select the **Machine Policy Retrieval & Evaluation Cycle** action, and then select **Run Now**. On the client, open the PolicyEvaluator.log file in *%windir%*\CMM\Logs and check whether the client has received a new policy.

9. Using WBEMTest, query WMI to check whether the `AutoAdminLogon` class was created, using the same procedure as in step 6.

10. After verifying the `AutoAdminLogon` class is created on the client, you can select it by modifying the default client settings in the Administration workspace.

Open the ConfigMgr console and browse to the Administration workspace. Select the **Client Settings** node, and open **Default Client Settings**. Under Default Client Settings, open the **Hardware Inventory** section, and select **Set Classes**. There are two options in the Hardware Inventory Classes box:

▶ Import the provided AddtoSmsDefMof.txt file that you will rename to AddtoSmsDefMof.mof and check using Mofcomp.exe.

▶ Browse to the classes using the Add Hardware Inventory Class tool. Here are the contents of that file:

```
//   <:[-<>>>>>>>>>>>>>>>>>>>>>>>>>>>>BEGIN>>-AutoAdminLogon-
<<BEGIN<<<<<<<<<<<<<<<<<<<<<<<<<<>-]:>
//''''*._.*''''*-
//  Reporting Class - for ConfigMgr, put this section in sms_def.mof
//''''*._.*''''*-
[SMS_Report(TRUE), SMS_Group_Name("AutoAdminLogon"),
SMS_Class_ID("SMSExpert|AutoAdminLogon|1.0")]
class AutoAdminLogon : SMS_Class_Template
{
  [SMS_Report(TRUE),key] string KeyName;
  [SMS_Report(TRUE)]      string DefaultDomainName;
  [SMS_Report(TRUE)]      string DefaultUserName;
  [SMS_Report(TRUE)]      string DefaultPassword;
```

```
    [SMS_Report(TRUE)]        string AutoAdminLogon;
    [SMS_Report(TRUE)]        uint32 AutoLogonCount;
};
//   <:[-<>>>>>>>>>>>>>>>>>>>>>>>>>>>END>>-AutoAdminLogon-
<<END<<<<<<<<<<<<<<<<<<<<<<<<<>-]:>
```

When hardware inventory commences, it checks the root\CIMV2\SMS namespace
on the local machine for the reporting classes, which contain entries corresponding
with the data classes in root\CIMV2. Notice that the data classes and corresponding
reporting classes share the same name. The AddtoSMSDefMof.mof file starts with the
SMS_Report (TRUE) part, which tells hardware inventory the block of code containing the AutoAdminLogon reporting class should be reported to ConfigMgr. The
SMS_Report (TRUE) value is actually the property you can now control using custom
client settings, allowing you to indicate whether ConfigMgr should report on devices
in a certain collection only. Each field also contains a SMS_Report (TRUE) section,
enabling you to specify if reporting should be allowed for that property field; you
can also use custom client settings to identify which ones will be allowed.

SMS_Group_Name specifies the name of the group you will see in the Resource
Explorer; SMS_Class_ID with value AutoAdminLogon is the unique identifier for the
class, SMSExpert (which stands for the class group) and 1.0 are identifiers only and
can contain any value. Class AutoAdminlogon is the declaration, where the name of
the class must be identical to the corresponding data class, which you either created
using an addition to Configuration.mof or already existed.

To import the AddtoSmsDefMof.mof file, select the **Import** button in the Hardware
Inventory Classes screen, browse to the AddtoSmsDefMof.mof file from the MOF
snippet, and click **Open**. This opens the Import Summary screen, providing you with
options to import the hardware inventory classes and settings, only the classes, or
only the settings. Select the option to import only the inventory classes, as you will
be enabling the classes with custom client settings later. If the AddtoSmsDefMof.mof
file is accepted, a green check mark appears, and you can select **Import** to use the
MOF file.

In the Hardware Inventory Classes screen, you can now see AutoAdminLogon
added and not enabled by default. By clicking the + sign, you can expand the
AutoAdminLogon class to see its attributes, which in this case are KeyName,
AutoAdminLogon, AutoLogonCount, DefaultDomainName, DefaultPassword, and
DefaultUserName.

You can also add the AutoAdminLogon class by browsing for it, for example, when an
AddtoSmsDefMof.mof file is not available because you are creating your own custom
hardware inventory extension. In this case, click the **Add** button in the Hardware
Inventory Classes screen to open the Add Hardware Inventory Class screen.

When the computer running the ConfigMgr console has a ConfigMgr client
installed (make sure it received policy, so the WMI extensions are added!), you can
select **Connect** and keep the default settings to connect to the local machine; or
provide the details of a remote computer with the necessary credentials to connect

to that computer, as shown in Figure B.3. Clicking **Connect** connects to WMI on the local or remote computer.

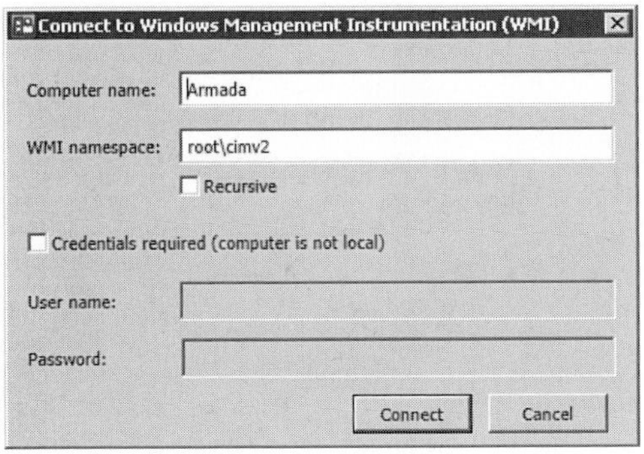

FIGURE B.3   Connecting to WMI.

After clicking **Connect**, you return to the Add Hardware Inventory Class screen. Notice the Inventory classes are now loaded, as displayed in Figure B.4. The Inventory classes should now include `AutoAdminLogon` if the policy was received and the WMI extensions were added. Select **AutoAdminLogon** to verify the check box is checked. Optionally, you can select **Edit** to modify the properties so its value represents a unit that can be Megabytes, Kilobytes, Decimal String, Seconds, Hex String, or Date String; the default is None.

The units are not modified in this example, so click **OK**. Notice the `AutoAdminLogon` class is added and selected. Deselect the `AutoAdminLogon` class on the Default Settings level because you can enable these with custom client settings later. Click **OK** to close the Hardware Inventory Classes dialog, and click **OK** to close the Default Settings box.

11. With the AutoAdminLogon classes imported, you can enable them using custom client settings that will be applied to one of your collections. In the Client Settings node of the Administration workspace, select **Create Custom Client Settings** from the ribbon bar to open the Create Custom Client Device Settings page. Provide a Name to identify the setting, and select the **Hardware Inventory** check box. You can find more information about default and custom client settings in Chapter 9, "Configuration Manager Client Management."

Select **Hardware Inventory** under General on the left side of the page to open the Hardware Inventory settings, and click **Set Classes** to open the Hardware Inventory Classes page. Select the **AutoAdminLogon** class, and click **OK** to save the custom client setting. With your custom client setting still selected, select **Deploy** from the ribbon bar and select the collection where you want to deploy your custom client setting. Click **OK** to finish.

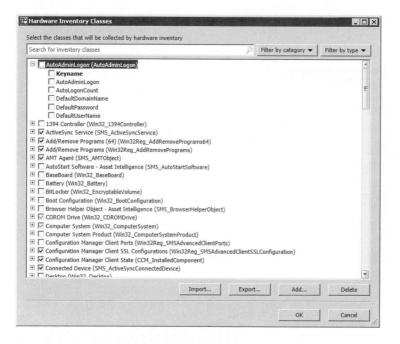

FIGURE B.4   Hardware Inventory Classes.

12. With the `AutoAdminLogon` class enabled in a custom client setting and that custom client setting deployed to a collection, you can trigger hardware inventory on a client belonging to that collection:

▶ Initiate a Machine Policy Retrieval & Evaluation Cycle from the Configuration Manager Control Panel applet, and check the PolicyEvaluator.log file to determine whether the new policy was retrieved from the management point.

▶ When the policy is successfully retrieved, initiate a hardware inventory cycle. From the Actions tab in the Configuration Manager Control Panel applet, select **Hardware Inventory Cycle**, and click **Run Now**.

▶ Check the inventoryagent.log file in the *%windir%*\CCM\Logs folder to see whether the hardware inventory was successful. Search the file for the **AutoAdminLogon** text to verify the requested new classes were inventoried, and check the lines that follow in the log file to determine if there were problems during inventory. Here is an example:

```
Collection: Namespace = root\cimv2; Query = SELECT __CLASS, __PATH,
__RELPATH, Keyname, AutoAdminLogon, AutoLogonCount, DefaultDomainName,
DefaultPassword, DefaultUserName FROM AutoAdminLogon; Timeout = 600 secs.
```

13. **Knowing the hardware inventory was successful on the client, now determine whether its site server is processing the inventoried data.** It may take a short time for all the data to be replicated to the CAS in a multi-site environment, where the client is a member of a primary site below the CAS. On the primary site server hosting the site the client is member of, open the dataldr.log file and locate the `Processing Inventory for Machine:` *<your machine name>* line to determine if the inventoried data has been processed. Here is an example of information after that line:

```
Begin transaction: Machine=ALBERT(GUID:E13C8E9C-A680-4CF9-
A280-449D0FD48C08)  $$<SMS_INVENTORY_DATA_LOADER><02-
20-2012 18:10:54.046+360><thread=5108 (0x13F4)>
Commit transaction: Machine=ALBERT(GUID:E13C8E9C-A680-4CF9-
A280-449D0FD48C08)  $$<SMS_INVENTORY_DATA_LOADER><02-
20-2012 18:10:55.182+360><thread=5108 (0x13F4)>
Done: Machine=ALBERT(GUID:E13C8E9C-A680-4CF9-A280-
449D0FD48C08) code=0 (13 stored procs in XHRDXGTGN.MIF)
$$<SMS_INVENTORY_DATA_LOADER><02-20-2012
18:10:55.182+360><thread=5108 (0x13F4)>
```

14. **Now, check whether the necessary database tables were created by opening SQL Server Management Studio.** Connect to the server hosting the ConfigMgr database, and open the database. Under Views, you should see a table called dbo.v.GS_AUTOADMINLOGON. Select this table, and right-click to choose **Select Top 1000 rows** to query the table. If there is any information in the table, it is reflected in the query results, as shown in Figure B.5.

15. **Because inventory has occurred, check if the data is available in the Resource Explorer initiated from the ConfigMgr console on the primary site server of the client.** Open the ConfigMgr console, and select the **Assets and Compliance** workspace; select the collection you just targeted with your custom client settings, and select the device on which you just ran the hardware inventory. With the device selected, use **Start -> Resource Explorer** to open the Resource Explorer for that device, as shown in Figure B.6. You now see that AutoAdminLogon is added to the Resource Explorer.

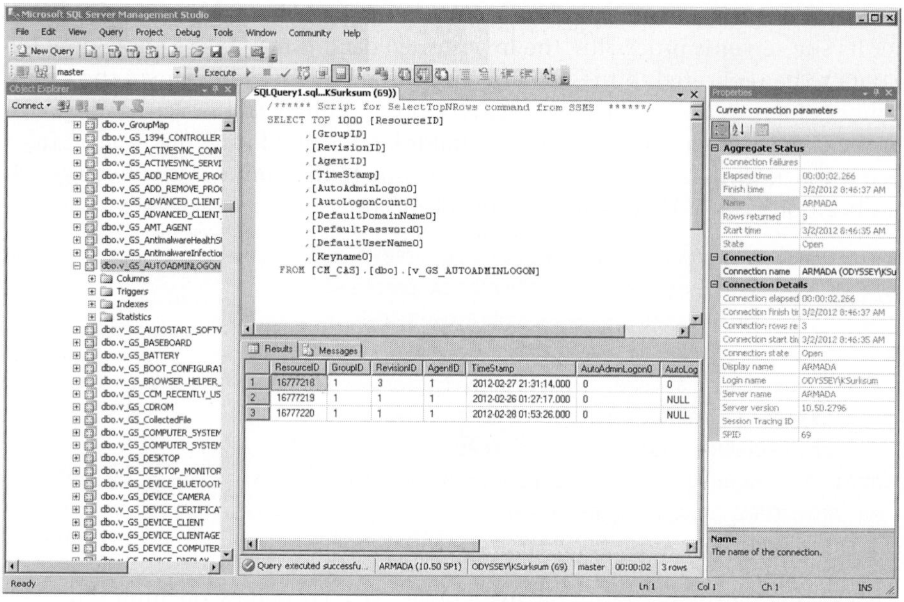

FIGURE B.5   SQL Management Studio showing top 1,000 rows.

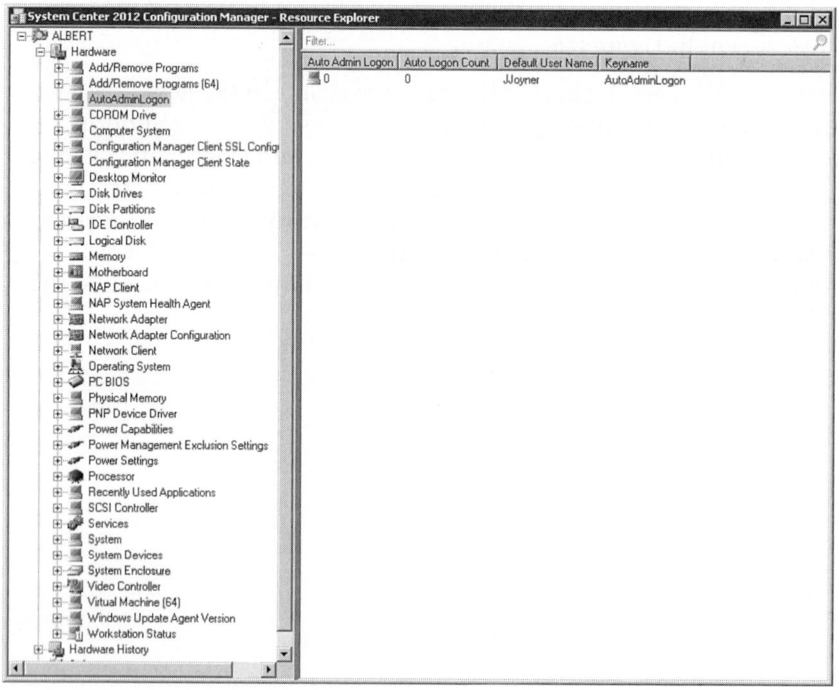

FIGURE B.6   Resource Explorer.

Creating a Device Collection

After verifying that the AutoAdminLogon information shows correctly within the Resource Explorer, you can use this information, say to create a device collection. You could then create custom device settings and deploy them to this collection.

To create the device collection, perform these steps in the ConfigMgr console:

1. In the Assets and Compliance workspace, navigate to **Device Collections**.

2. In the ribbon bar, click **Create**, and click **Create Device Collection** to open the Create Device Collection Wizard.

3. Provide a Name, Description, and Limiting collection on the General page, and click **Next** when finished:

   ▶ **Name:** AutoAdminLogon

   ▶ **Description:** Device Collection containing devices having Automatic Logon enabled

   ▶ **Limiting Collection:** All Systems

4. On the Membership rules page, click **Add Rule** to open up the Query Rule Properties screen, and select **Query rule**. Provide a name for the query such as **AutoAdminLogon**, and click **Edit Query Statement** to open the Query Statement Properties page.

5. In the Query Statement Properties page, select the **Criteria** tab, and click the starburst (asterisk) icon to open the Criterion Properties page. Click **Select** to open the Select Attribute screen, and select **AutoAdminLogon** from the drop-down list next to Attribute Class. Select **AutoAdminLogon** from the Attribute drop-down list, and click **OK** to return to the Criterion Properties screen.

6. Click **Value** in the Criterion Properties screen to select a value from the list. Select **1** if already inventoried and available in the list; if not, provide **1** as a value. Click **OK** to close the Criterion Properties page.

7. Click **OK** in the Query Statement Properties screen to return to the Query Rule properties page, as shown in Figure B.7.

8. Click **OK** in the Query Rule Properties page to return to the Membership Rules section of the Create Device Collection Wizard. Optionally, select if you want to use incremental updates for the collection, and when a full update of the collection should be scheduled. Click **Next** to continue.

9. Verify the settings on the Summary page, and click **Next**. Complete the Create Device Collection Wizard by clicking **Close** when it creates the device collection successfully.

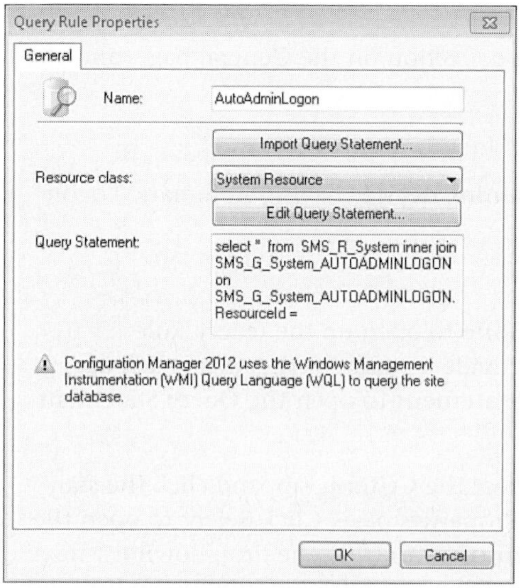

Query Rule Properties

General

Name: AutoAdminLogon

Import Query Statement...

Resource class: System Resource ▾

Edit Query Statement...

Query Statement: select * from SMS_R_System inner join SMS_G_System_AUTOADMINLOGON on SMS_G_System_AUTOADMINLOGON.ResourceId =

⚠ Configuration Manager 2012 uses the Windows Management Instrumentation (WMI) Query Language (WQL) to query the site database.

OK   Cancel

FIGURE B.7   Query Rule Properties.

You have now seen how to extend hardware inventory, using an example to determine those machines with automatic administrator logon enabled. That information was used to create a device collection. Now you can deploy a specific package or application to that collection, or decide to give the members of the collection different client device settings, as described in Chapter 9. The key message of this appendix is to test everything you do before actually implementing these types of changes in your ConfigMgr production environment.

APPENDIX C

Reference URLs

This appendix includes a number of reference URLs associated with System Center 2012 Configuration Manager (ConfigMgr). URLs do change; although the authors have made every effort to verify the references here as working links, there is no guarantee they will remain current. It is quite possible some will change or be "dead" by the time you read this book. Sometimes the Wayback Machine (http://www.archive.org/index.php) can rescue you from dead or broken links. This site is an Internet archive, and it will take you back to an archived version of a site—sometimes.

These links are also available "live" at Pearson's InformIT website, at http://www.informit.com/title/9780672334375, under the Downloads tab. Look for Appendix C, "Reference URLs."

General Resources

A number of websites provide excellent resources for Configuration Manager. This section lists some of the more general resources available.

▶ http://www.myITforum.com is a community of worldwide Information Technology (IT) professionals and a website established in 1999 by Rod Trent. myITforum includes topics on System Center and Information Technology.

The list of blogs and other ConfigMgr-related articles at myITforum.com is enormous. This appendix includes some specific links and pertinent information, but it does not include everything.

▶ A great source of information for all things System Center-related, including Configuration Manager, is System Center Central (http://www.systemcentercentral. com).

▶ If you are not already receiving email notifications of new articles in the Microsoft Knowledge Base from kbalertz, you can sign up at http://kbalertz.com/. You just need to create an account and select those technologies you want to be alerted about.

▶ The System Center Virtual User Group is dedicated to providing educational resources and collaboration between System Center users worldwide. Bi-monthly meetings present topics from industry experts, including Microsoft engineers. These Live Meeting sessions are recorded for your convenience. To join the user group, go to http://www.linkedin.com/groupRegistration?gid=101906.

▶ FAQShop.com, published by ConfigMgr MVP Cliff Hobbs at http://www.faqshop. com/, provides hints, tips, and answers to frequently asked questions (FAQs) related to Microsoft's various systems management technologies including System Center. Cliff is completely redeveloping FAQShop, which will include System Center 2012 Configuration Manager content.

▶ With the release of System Center 2012, Microsoft is bundling the different components as a single product. http://www.microsoft.com/en-us/server-cloud/system-center/datacenter-management-capabilities.aspx provides an overview of the System Center components and capabilities.

▶ The Microsoft System Center website is at http://www.microsoft.com/en-us/server-cloud/system-center/.

▶ Microsoft's jumping off point for System Center technical resources starts at http://technet.microsoft.com/en-us/systemcenter/.

▶ Microsoft has published a whitepaper on performance tuning guidelines for Windows Server 2008 R2 at http://msdn.microsoft.com/en-us/windows/hardware/gg463392.

▶ Here are links to previous versions of performance tuning guidelines:

  ▶ You can download the Windows Server 2008 version from http://msdn. microsoft.com/en-us/windows/hardware/gg463394.aspx.

  ▶ The Windows Server 2003 version is available at http://download.microsoft. com/download/2/8/0/2800a518-7ac6-4aac-bd85-74d2c52e1ec6/tuning.doc.

▶ Michael Pearson has an excellent article discussing SQL Server Reporting Services (SSRS) recovery planning, available online from the SQL Server Central community (SQLServerCentral.com) at http://www.sqlservercentral.com/columnists/mpearson/recoveryplanningforsqlreportingservices.asp. You must register with SQLServerCentral to view the full article.

▶ http://technet.microsoft.com/en-us/library/ms156421.aspx discusses moving the SSRS databases to another computer.

▶ For information on SQL Server best practices, see http://technet.microsoft.com/ en-us/sqlserver/bb671430.aspx.

The SQL Server 2008 R2 Best Practice Analyzer is available for download at http:// www.microsoft.com/downloads/details.aspx?FamilyID=0FD439D7-4BFF-4DF7- A52F-9A1BE8725591&amp;displaylang=e&displaylang=en.

▶ Use the SQL Server Profiler to view SQL requests sent to a SQL Server database. See http://msdn.microsoft.com/en-us/library/ms187929.aspx for information.

▶ To test Simple Mail Transfer Protocol (SMTP) using Telnet from a command prompt, follow the steps at http://technet.microsoft.com/en-us/library/ aa995718%28EXCHG.65%29.aspx.

▶ Somewhat dated, although still useful, is an IDC whitepaper sponsored by Microsoft that quantifies how businesses can reduce costs by managing the Windows desktop. This whitepaper is available for download at http://download.microsoft.com/ download/a/4/4/a4474b0c-57d8-41a2-afe6-32037fa93ea6/IDC_windesktop_IO_white- paper.pdf.

▶ Read about proactive desktop management in Greg Shield's article in Redmond Magazine on best practices for desktop management, at http://redmondmag.com/ columns/article.asp?editorialsid=2635.

▶ According to the SANS Institute, the threat landscape is increasingly dynamic, making efficient and proactive update management more important than ever. http://www.sans.org/top20/ provides information.

▶ See a Microsoft-sponsored IDC whitepaper on the relationship between IT labor costs and best practices for managing the Windows desktop at http://download.microsoft. com/download/a/4/4/a4474b0c-57d8-41a2-afe6-32037fa93ea6/IDC_windesktop_IO_ whitepaper.pdf.

▶ For information about Active Directory in Windows Server 2008 R2, see http://www. microsoft.com/windowsserver2008/en/us/active-directory.aspx.

▶ Information regarding the Active Directory schema is at http://msdn.microsoft.com/ en-us/library/ms675085(VS.85).aspx.

▶ Information on LDIFDE is located at http://technet.microsoft.com/en-us/library/ cc731033(v=WS.10).aspx.

▶ http://support.microsoft.com/kb/555636 describes the process of exporting and importing objects using LDIFDE.

▶ Interested in learning more about the Microsoft Operations Framework (MOF)? Information about version 4.0 is at http://technet.microsoft.com/library/cc506049. aspx.

▶ Information on the MOF Deliver Phase is at http://technet.microsoft.com/en-us/ library/cc506047.aspx.

► You can read about the MOF Envision SMF at http://technet.microsoft.com/en-us/library/cc531013.aspx.

► For information on MOF 4.0 and the Manage layer, see http://technet.microsoft.com/en-us/library/cc506048.aspx.

► Information on the IO (Infrastructure Optimization) model is available at http://www.microsoft.com/technet/infrastructure.

► If you want to learn about Service Modeling Language (SML), see http://www.w3.org/TR/sml/. For additional technical information on SML from Microsoft, visit http://technet.microsoft.com/en-us/library/bb725986.aspx.

► Information on the IO (Infrastructure Optimization) model is available at http://www.microsoft.com/technet/infrastructure.

► Virtual labs for System Center components including Configuration Manager, Virtual Machine Manager, Application Virtualization, and more are located at http://technet.microsoft.com/en-us/bb539977.aspx.

► The Windows Server technical library is located at http://technet.microsoft.com/en-us/library/bb625087.aspx.

► Microsoft's TechNet Magazine is available online at http://technet.microsoft.com/en-us/magazine/default.aspx.

► Microsoft's Sysinternals website is at http://technet.microsoft.com/en-us/sysinternals/default.aspx.

► Download the Microsoft Security Compliance Manager (SCM) solution accelerator at http://www.microsoft.com/download/en/details.aspx?displaylang=en&id=16776.

► Silect Software (http://www.silect.com) offers CP Studio. CP Studio, like SCM, enables authoring of configuration baselines and configuration items outside the ConfigMgr console.

► XML Notepad 2007 is an intuitive tool for browsing and editing XML documents. Read about it at http://msdn2.microsoft.com/en-us/library/aa905339.aspx, and download the tool from http://www.microsoft.com/downloads/details.aspx?familyid=72d6aa49-787d-4118-ba5f-4f30fe913628&displaylang=en.

► Windows IT Pro is an online publication including articles about System Center and other topics. See http://www.windowsitpro.com/ for information.

► Microsoft provides an entire portal on application compatibility at http://technet.microsoft.com/en-us/windows/aa905066.aspx.

► Want to create drilldown SSRS reports? See http://technet.microsoft.com/en-us/library/dd207042.aspx.

► http://msdn.microsoft.com/en-us/library/ms157403.aspx provides a complete listing of SQL Server 2008 R2 Report Server log files.

▶ Trying to understand licensing?

  ▶ General licensing information is at http://www.microsoft.com/licensing/
    default.mspx.

  ▶ http://www.microsoft.com/calsuites/en/us/products/default.aspx discusses
    Server CALs (Client Access Licenses) and the suites they may be included on.
    The most current list of Microsoft CAL suite technologies can be found at
    http://download.microsoft.com/download/3/D/4/3D42BDC2-6725-4B29-B75A-
    A5B04179958B/Licensing_Core_CAL_and_Enterprise_Suite.docx.

  ▶ System Center volume licensing is discussed at http://www.microsoft.com/
    licensing/about-licensing/SystemCenter2012.aspx.

Microsoft's Configuration Manager Resources

The following list includes some general Microsoft resources available for System Center
2012 Configuration Manager:

▶ Microsoft's Configuration Manager website is located at http://www.microsoft.com/
  en-us/server-cloud/system-center/configuration-manager-2012.aspx.

▶ For an overview of System Center 2012 Configuration Manager's capabilities, see
  http://www.microsoft.com/en-us/server-cloud/system-center/configuration-manager-
  2012-capabilities.aspx.

▶ Find Microsoft's Configuration Manager TechNet main library page at http://technet.
  microsoft.com/library/gg682129.

▶ What's new in Configuration Manager? See http://technet.microsoft.com/en-us/
  library/gg699359.aspx and Meged Ezzat's posting at http://blogs.technet.com/b/
  meamcs/archive/2011/08/10/what-s-new-in-configuration-manager-2012-sccm-2012.
  aspx.

▶ The documentation library with links to the different technical guides is at
  http://technet.microsoft.com/en-us/library/gg682041.

▶ For a list of technical publications for Configuration Manager, see http://technet.
  microsoft.com/en-us/library/hh531521.aspx.

▶ Information on supported configurations for Configuration Manager is available at
  http://technet.microsoft.com/en-us/library/gg682077.aspx.

▶ Microsoft has created a survival guide for Configuration Manager at http://social.
  technet.microsoft.com/wiki/contents/articles/7075.system-center-2012-configuration-
  manager-survival-guide.aspx (you can also access the survival guide at http://www.
  configmgrsurvivalguide.com). This is a pointer to information on the Internet
  regarding System Center 2012 Configuration Manager.

▶ Documentation on planning for software updates and Windows Server Update
  Services (WSUS) is at http://technet.microsoft.com/en-us/library/gg712696.
  aspx#BKMK_SUMCapacity, and http://technet.microsoft.com/en-us/library/

dd939928(WS.10).aspx documents WSUS 3.0 system requirements. You may also want to view http://technet.microsoft.com/en-us/library/hh237372.aspx, which lists prerequisites for software updates.

▶ Steve Rachui has written a series of blog posts on the software updates process as viewed through the log files. See

    ▶ http://blogs.msdn.com/b/steverac/archive/2011/04/10/software-updates-internals-mms-2011-session-part-i.aspx.

    ▶ http://blogs.msdn.com/b/steverac/archive/2011/04/16/software-updates-internals-mms-2011-session-part-ii.aspx.

    ▶ http://blogs.msdn.com/b/steverac/archive/2011/04/30/software-updates-internals-mms-2011-session-part-iii.aspx.

▶ Microsoft recommends installing the reporting services point on a remote site system server for improved performance. See http://technet.microsoft.com/en-us/library/hh394138.aspx.

▶ SSRS should be installed in native mode for System Center 2012 Configuration Manager; this is discussed at http://msdn.microsoft.com/en-us/library/ms143711.aspx.

▶ You can script report backups using RS.exe. Documentation is available at http://msdn.microsoft.com/en-us/library/ms162839.aspx and http://msdn.microsoft.com/en-us/library/ms159720.aspx.

▶ You should always verify your reporting services installation before installing the reporting services point. http://msdn.microsoft.com/en-us/library/ms143773.aspx discusses the steps to take.

▶ Configuring reporting in ConfigMgr is discussed at http://technet.microsoft.com/en-us/library/gg712698.aspx.

▶ Hardware sizing information for site systems can be found at http://technet.microsoft.com/en-us/library/hh846235.aspx.

▶ Ports used by Configuration Manager are discussed at http://technet.microsoft.com/en-us/library/bb632618.aspx. Information on configuring ports for Network Access Protection (NAP) is located at http://technet.microsoft.com/en-us/library/bb694170.aspx.

▶ See http://technet.microsoft.com/en-us/library/gg712701.aspx#Support_Internet_Clients to plan for implementing Internet-based client management.

▶ Configuring a service principal name (SPN) for SQL Server site database servers is discussed at http://technet.microsoft.com/en-us/library/bb735885.aspx.

▶ Guidance for securing specific site system servers is at http://technet.microsoft.com/en-us/library/gg682165.aspx#BKMK_Security_SiteServer.

▶ Best practices for collections are at http://technet.microsoft.com/en-us/library/gg699372.aspx.

▶ Tips on installing and configuring distribution points are at http://technet.microsoft. com/en-us/library/gg682115.aspx#BKMK_InstallDistributionPoint. You may also want to view http://technet.microsoft.com/en-us/library/hh272770.aspx, which discusses installing and configuring site system roles.

▶ Read about operating system deployment (OSD) and multicast at http://blog. configmgrftw.com/?p=299.

▶ http://technet.microsoft.com/en-us/library/bb932135.aspx is a list of log files for OSD.

▶ http://blogs.technet.com/b/inside_osd/archive/2007/12/13/troubleshooting-tips.aspx discusses OSD troubleshooting tips.

▶ Microsoft provides guidance on upgrading from Configuration Manager 2007 to System Center 2012 Configuration Manager at http://technet.microsoft.com/ en-us/library/gg682006.aspx. Related is http://technet.microsoft.com/en-us/library/ gg712336.aspx, which discusses security and privacy for migration to ConfigMgr 2012. The article at http://technet.microsoft.com/en-us/library/gg712275.aspx discusses planning for content deployment during your migration.

▶ Troubleshooting your ConfigMgr migration? See http://technet.microsoft.com/en-us/ library/gg712297.aspx.

▶ Prerequisites for deploying the ConfigMgr client are discussed at http://technet. microsoft.com/en-us/library/gg682042.aspx.

▶ Need help with troubleshooting client push installation? Check out http://blogs. technet.com/b/sudheesn/archive/2010/05/31/troubleshooting-sccm-part-i-client-push-installation.aspx.

▶ A step-by-step guide on using software metering is available at http://blogs.msdn. com/b/minfangl/archive/2011/04/29/step-by-step-on-how-to-use-software-metering. aspx.

▶ http://technet.microsoft.com/en-us/library/hh427342.aspx is a technical reference for ConfigMgr log files.

▶ See http://technet.microsoft.com/en-us/library/bb680409.aspx for the locations of log files on managed mobile devices.

▶ Task sequence variables are documented at http://technet.microsoft.com/en-us/ library/gg682064.aspx.

▶ For a TechNet webcast on how Microsoft IT (MSIT) is deploying System Center 2012 Configuration Manager, see https://msevents.microsoft.com/CUI/EventDetail. aspx?culture=en-US&EventID=1032498175&CountryCode=US.

▶ Microsoft's IT showcase for Configuration Manager is available at http://technet. microsoft.com/en-us/library/bb687796.aspx. It includes MSIT's early adopter experiences, best experiences, and lessons learned from their deployments of System Center Configuration Manager.

▶ To configure SQL Server site database replication, check out http://technet.micro-soft.com/en-us/library/bb693697.aspx. http://technet.microsoft.com/en-us/library/bb693954.aspx discusses disabling database replication.

▶ A TechNet virtual lab introducing System Center 2012 Configuration Manager is available at https://msevents.microsoft.com/CUI/EventDetail.aspx?EventID=1032499 898&culture=en-us.

▶ Here are some videos on System Center 2012 Configuration Manager:

   ▶ Wally Mead presents a ConfigMgr 2012 administration overview at the Belgian System Center Day 2011 on November 3, 2011; this was organized by the Belgian System Center User Group (http://scug.be/). See http://technet. microsoft.com/en-us/edge/Video/hh536213.

   ▶ Kenny Buntinx presents a deployment and infrastructure technical overview at the June 15, 2011 "Best of MMS" event, available at http://technet.microsoft. com/en-us/edge/video/configuration-manager-2012-deployment-and-infrastructure-technical-overview.

▶ The different database roles used in Configuration Manager are discussed at http://technet.microsoft.com/en-us/library/bb632943.aspx. Although referring to ConfigMgr 2007 when this appendix was written, the information is still applicable.

▶ Information on managing mobile devices in Configuration Manager is at http://technet.microsoft.com/en-us/library/gg682022.aspx.

▶ To identify the Windows groups and accounts used in Configuration Manager and any requirements, see http://technet.microsoft.com/en-us/library/hh427337.aspx.

▶ Configuration packs can be found at the System Center Marketplace; see http://systemcenter.pinpoint.microsoft.com/en-US/applications/search/configuration-manager-d10?sort=released&q=partnername%3aMicrosoft+System+Center.

▶ Information on Windows Management Instrumentation (WMI) is available at http://msdn.microsoft.com/en-us/library/aa394582.aspx.

▶ http://msdn.microsoft.com/en-us/library/aa394564(VS.85).aspx discusses WMI logging.

▶ For a discussion of User Account Control and WMI, see http://msdn.microsoft.com/en-us/library/aa826699(VS.85).aspx.

▶ Command-line tools to manage WMI can be downloaded at http://msdn.microsoft.com/en-us/library/aa827351(VS.85).aspx.

▶ See http://blogs.technet.com/b/askperf/archive/2008/07/11/wmi-troubleshooting-the-repository-on-vista-server-2008.aspx and http://blogs.technet.com/b/configmgrteam/archive/2009/05/08/wmi-troubleshooting-tips.aspx for information on WMI troubleshooting.

▶ John Kelbey of Microsoft has a TechNet Magazine article on gathering WMI data using WMIC at http://technet.microsoft.com/en-us/magazine/2006.09.wmidata.aspx.

▶ CIM is the Component Information Model that WMI is based on. To learn more about CIM, there is a tutorial at http://www.wbemsolutions.com/tutorials/CIM/index.html. The full CIM specification can be found at http://dmtf.org/standards/cim.

▶ For information regarding WMI Query Language (WQL), see http://msdn.microsoft.com/en-us/library/aa394606.aspx.

▶ Steve Rachui discusses state messaging in depth at http://blogs.msdn.com/b/steverac/archive/2011/01/07/sccm-state-messaging-in-depth.aspx.

▶ Information regarding Windows Network Load Balancing (NLB) is available in the Network Load Balancing Deployment guide at http://technet.microsoft.com/en-us/library/cc754833(WS.10).aspx.

▶ http://technet.microsoft.com/en-us/library/cc732906(WS.10).aspx provides information on requesting an Internet Server certificate.

▶ The best way to add a certificate to a certificate store en masse is to use group policy; http://technet.microsoft.com/en-us/library/cc770315(WS.10).aspx provides a step-by-step example.

▶ PKI certificate requirements for ConfigMgr are also discussed at http://technet.microsoft.com/en-us/library/gg699362.aspx.

▶ http://technet.microsoft.com/en-us/library/cc732597(WS.10).aspx provides information about acquiring a code signing certificate.

▶ Package Conversion Manager (PCM) allows you to convert ConfigMgr 2007 packages into ConfigMgr 2012 applications. See http://technet.microsoft.com/en-us/library/hh531583.aspx for information.

▶ Prerequisites for System Center Endpoint Protection are documented at http://technet.microsoft.com/en-us/library/hh508780.aspx.

▶ The ConfigMgr 2012 SDK, in prerelease when this appendix was written, is discussed at http://msdn.microsoft.com/en-us/library/hh948960.aspx and can be downloaded from http://www.microsoft.com/download/en/details.aspx?id=29559.

▶ For a complete discussion of what's new and different in USMT 4, check out http://technet.microsoft.com/en-us/library/dd560752(v=WS.10).aspx.

▶ Microsoft provides solution accelerators, which are guidelines and tools to leverage the full functionality of Microsoft usage within your organization. These are available for download at no cost at http://technet.microsoft.com/en-us/solutionaccelerators/dd229342.

▶ http://msdn.microsoft.com/en-us/library/ms345322.aspx is a tutorial on creating model-based reports in Report Designer.

Other Configuration Manager Resources

Microsoft of course is not the only organization to discuss Configuration Manager. A number of websites provide excellent resources for ConfigMgr. Here are several you may want to investigate:

▶ Looking for training?

  ▶ Microsoft provides course 10747A, "Administering System Center 2012 Configuration Manager." Information on this five-day class is available at http://www.microsoft.com/learning/en/us/course.aspx?ID=10747A.

  ▶ A great ConfigMgr trainer who teaches the ConfigMgr MOC is Michael Head. His current course schedule is located at http://www.HeadSmartGroup.com/.

  ▶ Infront Consulting Group offers System Center training; curriculum and syllabi are available at http://www.infrontconsulting.com/training.php. http://www. infrontconsulting.com/docs/InfrontSCCMBootcamp.pdf describes their four-day Configuration Manager 2012 Administration boot camp.

  ▶ Microsoft Virtual Academy provides an overview course at http://www. microsoftvirtualacademy.com/tracks/overview-and-infrastructure-changes-in-sccm-2012.

▶ http://www.windows-noob.com/forums/index.php?/forum/92-configuration-manager-2012/ is a forum on System Center 2012 Configuration Manager.

▶ Curious about the new content library store? See Kent Agerlund's blog post at http://blog.coretech.dk/kea/understanding-the-new-content-library-store-in-5-minutes/.

▶ TechNet Magazine provides a look at Configuration Manager 2012's user-centric approach at http://technet.microsoft.com/en-us/magazine/gg675930.aspx.

▶ Niall Brady, a ConfigMgr MVP and contributor to this book, publishes guides for ConfigMgr 2012 at http://www.windows-noob.com/forums/index.php?/topic/4045-system-center-2012-configuration-manager-guides/.

▶ Michael Niehaus writes about ConfigMgr driver management at http://blogs.technet.com/b/mniehaus/archive/2010/04/29/configmgr-2007-driver-management-the-novel-part-1.aspx.

▶ For information on converting WQL to SQL, Brian Leary has a nice article at http://www.myitforum.com/articles/8/view.asp?id=9908. Written for web reporting with ConfigMgr 2007, the information is still applicable.

▶ Marcus Oh writes about retrieving objects into a collection that do not exist in another collection at http://marcusoh.blogspot.com/2007/08/sms-selecting-objects-not-in-collection.html.

▶ Beginning with Configuration Manager 2007 R2, ConfigMgr has the ability to define a task sequence variable on a collection of individual resource about a value. Read about it at http://blog.configmgrftw.com/?p=44.

▶ Ronni Pederson writes about using task sequence variables to customize deployments at http://myitforum.com/cs2/blogs/rpedersen/archive/2008/07/01/using-task-sequence-variables-to-customize-deployments.aspx.

▶ When a user with write permissions browses to a distribution point share on a Windows 7 system, he can accidentally modify the source for any package by simply viewing the contents. Win7 creates a thumbs.db that contains thumbnails of images in the folder. For additional information, see Greg Ramsey's post at http://gregramsey.wordpress.com/2012/02/13/interesting-issue-with-thumbs-db/.

▶ For general guidance on software deployment, see http://www.itninja.com/software.

▶ Flexera's AdminStudio (http://www.flexerasoftware.com/products/adminstudio-suite.htm) is a popular software packaging suite.

▶ Adaptiva Software (http://www.adaptiva.com) extends Microsoft's technologies to enhance PC power management. 1E (http://www.1e.com) also has a number of products to assist with sustainability and energy efficiency.

▶ Adaptiva's OneSite product is a ConfigMgr 2012 add-on that enables you to manage a large distributed network as if it were a single network. http://adaptiva.com/products_onesite.html provides details.

▶ Athena MDM from Odyssey Software (now part of Symantec) is a mobile device management product, http://www.odysseysoftware.com/products/athena-for-configuration-manager.aspx#sccm provides details.

▶ Quest Software is offering its QMX (Quest Management Xtensions) for System Center Configuration Manager. For information, see http://www.quest.com/management-xtensions-device-management-cm/.

Blogs

Here are some blogs the authors have used. Some are more active than others, and new blogs seem to spring up overnight!

▶ http://bink.nu is managed by Steven Bink, former MVP for Windows Server Technologies. According to the blog, it "watches Microsoft like a hawk."

▶ Garth Jones, a ConfigMgr MVP, posts articles at http://www.myitforum.com/contrib/default.asp?cid=116. He also is affiliated with the SMS User Group in Canada; those blogs are at http://smsug.ca/blogs/.

▶ ConfigMgr MVP Kaido Jarvernet blogs at http://depsharee.blogspot.com/. Check his blog (along with coauthor Greg Ramsey's) for PowerShell automation tips.

▶ http://sms-hints-tricks.blogspot.com/ is by Matthew Hudson, ConfigMgr MVP.

▶ Don Hite blogs at http://myitforum.com/cs2/blogs/dhite/.

▶ Ronni Pederson's blog is at http://ronnipedersen.com/. Older articles are at http://myitforum.com/cs2/blogs/rpedersen/.

▶ Ron Crumbaker, ConfigMgr MVP, blogs at http://myitforum.com/cs2/blogs/rcrumbaker/.

▶ Kim Oppalfens blogs at http://blogcastrepository.com/blogs/kim_oppalfenss_systems_management_ideas/default.aspx.

▶ Sherry Kissinger, ConfigMgr MVP, blogs at http://myitforum.com/cs2/blogs/skissinger/.

▶ Roger Zander blogs at http://myitforum.com/cs2/blogs/rzander/default.aspx.

▶ Rod Trent's blog is at http://myitforum.com/cs2/blogs/rtrent/default.aspx.

▶ http://systemscentre.blogspot.com/ is maintained by Steve Beaumont.

▶ Anthony Clendenen has a myITforum blog at http://myitforum.com/cs2/blogs/socal/default.aspx.

▶ By Carlos Santiago, a Premier Field Engineer at Microsoft: http://blogs.technet.com/carlossantiago.

▶ The OSD Support Team blog is at http://blogs.technet.com/b/system_center_configuration_manager_operating_system_deployment_support_blog/.

▶ The Microsoft "Deployment Guys" have a blog at http://blogs.technet.com/deploymentguys/default.aspx.

▶ Check out the blog at http://blog.configmgrftw.com/.

▶ http://blogs.msdn.com/shitanshu/—blog by Shitasnhu Verma of Microsoft.

▶ Paul Thomsen blogs at http://myitforum.com/cs2/blogs/pthomsen/.

▶ Scott Moss's blog is at http://myitforum.com/cs2/blogs/smoss/.

▶ Andrius Kozeniauskas maintains a blog at http://andrius.kozeniauskas.com/blog/category/microsoft/sccmsms2003/.

▶ http://blogs.technet.com/b/configmgrteam/ is the official blog of the Microsoft System Center Configuration Manager product group.

▶ Kevin Sullivan's Management blog is at https://blogs.technet.com/kevinsul_blog/. (Kevin is a Technology Specialist at Microsoft focusing on management products.)

▶ www.systemcenterguide.com is a System Center blog by Duncan McAlynn.

▶ See http://blogs.msdn.com/b/shitanshu/ for information about Configuration Manager in Microsoft IT.

Here are our own blogs:

- ▶ Kerrie Meyler, MVP and lead author for *System Center 2012 Configuration Manager Unleashed*, maintains a blog at www.networkworld.com/community/meyler.

- ▶ A blog by ConfigMgr MVP and coauthor Jason Sandys is at http://blog.configmgrftw. com/.

- ▶ Greg Ramsey, ConfigMgr MVP and a coauthor for this book, blogs at http://gregramsey.wordpress.com/.

- ▶ http://marcusoh.blogspot.com/ is a blog by Marcus Oh, MVP and a coauthor for this book.

- ▶ Steve Rachui is a CSS guru on ConfigMgr and our technical reviewer. Check out his blog at http://blogs.msdn.com/steverac/.

- ▶ Kenneth van Surksum, MVP and contributor to this book, blogs at http://www.techlog.org.

- ▶ http://www.msfaq.se/ is Stefan Schörling's blog on Microsoft System Management. Stefan is a ConfigMgr MVP and contributor to this book.

- ▶ Niall Brady, ConfigMgr MVP and contributor to this book, blogs at http://www.niall-brady.com/. Former postings are at http://myitforum.com/cs2/blogs/nbrady/.

- ▶ Sam Erskine, contributor to this book, blogs at http://myitforum.com/cs2/blogs/serskine/.

- ▶ Torsten Meringer, ConfigMgr MVP and contributor to this book, manages the German ConfigMgr blog at http://www.mssccmfaq.de.

- ▶ http://myitforum.com/cs2/blogs/sthompson is the blog for Steve Thompson, ConfigMgr MVP and a contributor to this book.

Microsoft System Center

With the release of System Center 2012, Microsoft is bundling the different components as a single product. http://www.microsoft.com/en-us/server-cloud/system-center/datacenter-management-capabilities.aspx provides an overview of the capacities and components.

Public Forums

If you need an answer to a question, first check the Microsoft public forums. A list of available TechNet forums is maintained at http://social.technet.microsoft.com/forums/en-US/categories/. It is best to see if the question has already been posted before you ask it!

The link to all the System Center 2012 Configuration Manager forums is http://social.technet.microsoft.com/Forums/en-US/category/systemcenter2012configurationmanager. Here are the specific forums (English):

▶ Configuration Manager 2012: General (http://social.technet.microsoft.com/forums/en-US/configmgrgeneral/threads)

▶ Configuration Manager 2012: Site and client and site deployment (http://social.technet.microsoft.com/Forums/en-US/configmanagerdeployment/threads)

▶ Configuration Manager 2012: Application management (http://social.technet.microsoft.com/Forums/en-US/configmanagerapps/threads)

▶ Configuration Manager 2012: Security and compliance (http://social.technet.microsoft.com/Forums/en-US/configmanagersecurity/threads)

▶ Configuration Manager: Operating System Deployment (http://social.technet.microsoft.com/forums/en-US/configmgrosd/threads)

▶ Configuration Manager: SDK (http://social.technet.microsoft.com/forums/en-US/configmgrsdk/threads)

▶ Configuration Manager 2012: Migration (http://social.technet.microsoft.com/Forums/en-US/configmanagermigration/threads)

▶ myITforum also has a discussion list for Configuration Manager along with a number of other discussion lists; see http://myitforum.com/myitforumwp/support/email-lists/.

Utilities

Here are some utilities, both Microsoft and third party:

▶ The WMI Diagnosis Utility (WMIDiag) is available at the Microsoft download site, http://www.microsoft.com/downloads/details.aspx?familyid=d7ba3cd6-18d1-4d05-b11e-4c64192ae97d&displaylang=en.

▶ The WMI Administrative Tools are downloadable at http://www.microsoft.com/download/en/details.aspx?id=24045.

▶ The Windows PowerShell Scriptomatic tool, created by Ed Wilson, allows you to browse WMI namespaces and automatically generate PowerShell code to connect to WMI objects. You can download the tool from http://www.microsoft.com/download/en/details.aspx?displaylang=en&id=24121.

▶ Use Process Monitor to capture detailed process activity on Windows systems. For information and a download link, see at http://technet.microsoft.com/en-us/sysinternals/bb896645.aspx.

▶ NetDiag is a diagnostic tool that helps isolate networking and connectivity problems. For information, see http://technet.microsoft.com/library/Cc938980.

▶ Netperf is a benchmark that can be used to measure performance of many types of networking. It provides tests for both unidirectional throughput and end-to-end latency. For more information and to download the tool, see http://www.netperf. org/netperf/.

▶ You can download and install add-ons and extensions for System Center 2012 Configuration Manager at http://www.microsoft.com/download/en/details. aspx?id=29265. This includes the ConfigMgr toolkit and PCM.

▶ Troubleshoot port status issues using PortQry and PortQryUI, downloadable from http://www.microsoft.com/downloads/details.aspx?familyid=89811747-C74B-4638-A2D5-AC828BDC6983&displaylang=en and http://www.microsoft.com/downloads/details.aspx?FamilyID=8355E537-1EA6-4569-AABB-F248F4BD91D0&displaylang=en, respectively.

▶ System Center Update Publisher (SCUP) enables third-party vendors and IT administrators to import, manage, and develop software update definitions that can be deployed with ConfigMgr. You can download SCUP from http://www.microsoft. com/download/en/details.aspx?id=11940.

▶ At times creating WMI queries can be quite cumbersome. There are a number of tools available for free to help ease the process. Here are some popular ones:

  ▶ **WMI Code Creator:** https://www.microsoft.com/download/en/details. aspx?displaylang=en&id=8572

  ▶ **WMI Code Generator:** http://www.robvanderwoude.com/wmigen.php

  ▶ **Scriptomatic:** http://www.microsoft.com/download/en/details. aspx?displaylang=en&id=3284

▶ RSS Scripter, developed by SQL Server MVP Jasper Smith, simplifies creation of VB scripts for RS.EXE. Information is available at http://www.sqldbatips.com/showarticle.asp?ID=62.

▶ You can download Microsoft Report Builder from a SSRS 2008 R2 installed reporting site or at http://www.microsoft.com/download/en/details. aspx?displaylang=en&id=6116. http://technet.microsoft.com/en-us/ff657833.aspx provides information on Report Builder 3.0.

APPENDIX D

Available Online

Online content is available to provide add-on value to readers of *System Center 2012 Configuration Manager Unleashed*. This material, organized by chapter, can be downloaded from http://www.informit.com/store/product. aspx?isbn=9780672334375. This content is not available elsewhere. Note that the authors and publisher do not guarantee or provide technical support for the material.

SQL Profiler Template

Chapter 3, "Looking Inside Configuration Manager," discusses replication configuration monitor activity. ReplicationActivity.tdf is the SQL Profiler template used to capture these events from the site database.

Top 10 Most Executed Reports Query

Chapter 18, "Reporting," steps through the process to create a report showing the top 10 most executed reports. Top 10 most frequent reports.sql is the query used to create this report.

OSD Starter Scripts

Chapter 19, "Operating System Deployment," provides a thorough discussion of implementing and using OSD. Here are Visual Basic scripts that could be useful:

▶ **CompName.vbs:** Automatically generates a computer name based on the system's vendor, serial number, and chassis type, and then sets the OSDComputer task sequence variable

- **DumpVariables.vbs:** Dumps all task sequences variables
- **GenAppList.vbs:** Creates a series of task sequence variables for use with the multiple install functionality of the Install Package task
- **GetProcs.vbs:** Sets a task sequence variable to the number of processors in the system
- **Pause.vbs:** Pauses the task sequence until the file go.txt is created on the X: drive
- **RestoreExtraState:** Copies the OSDStateStorePath TempSave subfolder to c:\temp
- **SelectImage.vbs:** Changes the image index used by the Apply Image task based upon the number of processor in the system
- **SetComputerName:** Sets the computer name based on the BIOS asset tag
- **SetDriverCategory.vbs:** Changes the driver categories used by an Auto Apply Drivers task

Live Links

Reference URLs (see Appendix C, "Reference URLs") are provided as live links. These include more than 200 (clickable) hypertext links and references to materials and sites related to Configuration Manager.

A disclaimer and unpleasant fact regarding live links: URLs change! Companies are subject to mergers and acquisitions, pages move and change on websites, and so on. Although these links were accurate as of Spring 2012, it is possible some will change or be "dead" by the time you read this book. Sometimes the Wayback Machine (http://www.archive.org/index.php) can rescue you from dead or broken links. This site is an Internet archive, and it will take you back to an archived version of a site—sometimes.

Index

Symbols

7-Zip, 537, 571

64-bit site system requirements, 62

106-134 report server event errors, 946-958

802.1X authentication, 195

0x80004005 error code, 1061

[] (brackets), 851

% (percent sign), 851

/? property (CCMSetup), 435

" " (smart quotes), 610

_ (underscore), 851

A

About Configuration Manager command, 379

accepting risk, 1067-1123

access control entries (ACEs), 510

access control lists (ACLs), 99-100, 510

accessing SQL Server Management Studio, 134

access rules for mobile devices, 762-764

accountability, 1066-1123

accounts

    Active Directory Forest account, 1122

    Active Directory Group Discovery account, 1121

    Active Directory System Discovery account, 1121

    Active Directory User Discovery account, 1122

    AMT Provisioning and Discovery accounts, 1120

    AMT Remote Admin accounts, 1120

    Asset Intelligence Synchronization Point Proxy Server account, 1122

    Endpoint Protection SMTP Server Connection account, 1122

    Enrollment Point Connection account, 1118

    Exchange Server Connection account, 1122

    Exchange Server Connector Proxy Server account, 1122

    Health State Reference Publishing account, 1121

    Health State Reference Querying account, 1121

    machine accounts, assigning rights to, 1117

    Management Point database Connection Account, 1118

    MEBx accounts, 1120

    Multicast Connection account, 1118

    Remote Tools Permitted Viewer accounts, 1122

    Reporting Services Point account, 1118

    security

        accounts to support ConfigMgr infrastructure, 1117-1118

C

H

I

J

M

How can we make this index more useful? Email us at indexes@samspublishing.com

O

How can we make this index more useful? Email us at indexes@samspublishing.com

P

Q

R

How can we make this index more useful? Email us at indexes@samspublishing.com

S

How can we make this index more useful? Email us at indexes@samspublishing.com

service triangle, 14

ServiceWindowManager.log, 1206

SetComputerName, 1242

SetDriverCategory.vbs, 1242

SetSecurityDescriptor method, 110

Set Security Scopes option (Queries node), 834

Set Task Sequence Variable task, 993

Settings category tasks, 1001-1003

settings management reports, 920-921

Settings page (Create Configuration Item Wizard), 501

Setupact.log, 1201

Setupapi.log, 1201

Setuperr.log, 1201

Setupmgr.exe, 999

setuppolicyevaluator.log, 1186

Setup Windows and ConfigMgr task, 999

Shared Data Set Wizard, 953-956

shared distribution points, 366-367

Shares class, 862

Shield, Greg, 1227

showing. See viewing

Show Install Status page (Create Secondary Site Wizard), 294

"Show Me" behavior, 395-396

SHV (System Health Validator) points, 47, 169, 742-744, 1199

Silect Software CP Studio, 525, 1228

Silverlight, querying for, 855

Simple Object Access Protocol (SOAP), 92

simple schedules, 459

simple value criterion type, 846

simulating deployment, 667

single-instance store, 636

Sinvproc.log, 1192

site codes, choosing, 168

Sitecomp.log, 1190

Site Component Manager status messages, 251-252

Site Component Status node, 295

Site Configuration node (console), 384

Sitectrl.log, 1190

site database servers, 46

Site Hierarchy node (console), 386

site installations

CAS (Central Administration Site), 271-278

hierarchy, 270-271

installation validation

console, 294-296

log files, 296

primary sites

checklist of activities, 279

child primary sites, 286-287

stand-alone primary sites, 282-285

supported site roles, 278-281

secondary sites, 288-294

stand-alone sites, 271

troubleshooting, 315-316

unified installer, 270

uninstallation process

full hierarchy, 314-316

primary sites, 309-312

secondary sites, 312-314

Site Maintenance wizard, 1136-1139

language configuration, modifying, 1139

site resets, 1138

SMS Provider configuration, modifying, 1138

SQL Server configuration, modifying, 1138

site mode, 321

How can we make this index more useful? Email us at indexes@samspublishing.com

T

U

X-Y-Z

Your purchase of *System Center 2012 Configuration Manager Unleashed* includes access to a free online edition for 45 days through the **Safari Books Online** subscription service. Nearly every Sams book is available online through **Safari Books Online**, along with thousands of books and videos from publishers such as Addison-Wesley Professional, Cisco Press, Exam Cram, IBM Press, O'Reilly Media, Prentice Hall, Que, and VMware Press.

Safari Books Online is a digital library providing searchable, on-demand access to thousands of technology, digital media, and professional development books and videos from leading publishers. With one monthly or yearly subscription price, you get unlimited access to learning tools and information on topics including mobile app and software development, tips and tricks on using your favorite gadgets, networking, project management, graphic design, and much more.